AUSTRALIA IN THE WAR OF 1939-1945

SERIES ONE
ARMY

VOLUME III
TOBRUK AND EL ALAMEIN

AUSTRALIA IN THE WAR OF 1939-1945

SERIES 1 (ARMY)
    I. To Benghazi. *By Gavin Long.*
    II. Greece, Crete and Syria. *By Gavin Long.*
    III. Tobruk and El Alamein. *By Barton Maughan.*
    IV. The Japanese Thrust. *By Lionel Wigmore.*
    V. South-West Pacific Area—First Year. *By Dudley McCarthy.*
    VI. The New Guinea Offensives. *By David Dexter.*
    VII. The Final Campaigns. *By Gavin Long.*

SERIES 2 (NAVY)
    I. Royal Australian Navy, 1939-42. *By G. Hermon Gill.*
    II. Royal Australian Navy, 1942-45. *By G. Hermon Gill.**

SERIES 3 (AIR)
    I. Royal Australian Air Force, 1939-42. *By Douglas Gillison.*
    II. Air War Against Japan, 1943-45. *By George Odgers.*
    III. Air War Against Germany and Italy, 1939-43. *By John Herington.*
    IV. Air Power Over Europe, 1944-45. *By John Herington.*

SERIES 4 (CIVIL)
    I. The Government and the People, 1939-41. *By Paul Hasluck.*
    II. The Government and the People, 1942-45. *By Paul Hasluck.**
    III. War Economy, 1939-42. *By S. J. Butlin.*
    IV. War Economy, 1942-45. *By S. J. Butlin.**
    V. The Role of Science and Industry. *By D. P. Mellor.*

SERIES 5 (MEDICAL)
    I. Clinical Problems of War. *By Allan S. Walker.*
    II. Middle East and Far East. *By Allan S. Walker.*
    III. The Island Campaigns. *By Allan S. Walker.*
    IV. Medical Services of the R.A.N. and R.A.A.F. *By Allan S. Walker and others.*

* Not yet published.

The writers of these volumes have been given full access to official documents, but they and the general editor are alone responsible for the statements and opinions which the volumes contain.

TOBRUK AND EL ALAMEIN

by

BARTON MAUGHAN

The Naval & Military Press Ltd

Published by
The Naval & Military Press Ltd
5 Riverside, Brambleside, Bellbrook
Industrial Estate, Uckfield, East Sussex,
TN22 1QQ England
Tel: +44 (0) 1825 749494
Fax: +44 (0) 1825 765701
www.naval-military-press.com
www.military-genealogy.com

In reprinting in facsimile from the original, any imperfections are inevitably reproduced and the quality may fall short of modern type and cartographic standards.

*"Poor souls! to have never known the immortal will
That never owns defeat, the heroic deed
Whose doing is its only glory still."*
                                                    (C. J. Brennan)

CONTENTS

	Page
Preface	xv
List of Events	xix

Chapter		Page
1	THE "MINIMUM POSSIBLE FORCE" GUARDS CYRENAICA	1
2	DEFENCE BASED ON MOBILITY	24
3	THE "BENGHAZI HANDICAP"	52
4	AT BAY—THE EASTER BATTLE	111
5	STRIKING BACK	159
6	ASSAULT WITHSTOOD	195
7	MIDSUMMER IN THE FORTRESS	236
8	LAST COUNTER-ATTACK AND A CONTROVERSIAL RELIEF	305
9	PARTING SHOTS AND FAREWELL SALUTES . .	384
10	ED DUDA	418
11	IN PALESTINE, SYRIA AND THE LEBANON . .	514
12	AT EL ALAMEIN UNDER AUCHINLECK . . .	542
13	ALAM EL HALFA AND "BULIMBA"	603
14	LAUNCHING THE BATTLE	639
15	THE DOG FIGHT	677
	APPENDIXES:	
	1 Prisoners of the Germans and Italians . . .	755
	2 The Haifa-Beirut-Tripoli Railway	823
	3 Abbreviations	830
	INDEX	833

ILLUSTRATIONS

	Page
Benghazi Harbour	76
Headquarters 26th Brigade area, 4th April 1941	76
Tobruk port and town, April 1941	77
Major-General L. J. Morshead and his senior commanders at Tobruk	108
Headquarters 2/24th Battalion at Tobruk, April 1941	108
Rommel in the Western Desert	109
Looking across to the Derna Road from Post S17	109
Aerial view of Post R39	156
Lieut-Colonel J. W. Crawford, commanding the 2/17th Battalion, with a knocked-out German tank	156
German dive-bombing attack on the 2/24th Battalion	156
Headquarters 2/23rd Battalion, in the Salient	156
A rubble-littered street in Tobruk	157
A bomb-damaged ship in the harbour	157
The 2/17th Battalion "bush artillery" firing an Italian 75-mm field gun	157
A gun position of the 3rd Australian Light Anti-Aircraft Regiment	157
Tobruk Truth printing press	284
A soldier reading *Tobruk Truth*	284
"Aldershot" ovens at Tobruk	284
Drawing water from a well in Tobruk	284
Loading stores at a 9th Divisional A.A.S.C. supply depot	285
A camouflaged headquarters at Tobruk	285
The "Garden of Eden"	285
Post R25, manned by the 2/13th Battalion	285
Men of 2/13th Battalion in Post R8, during a truce	300
Bombs bursting among shipping, August 1941	300
Underground headquarters of the 9th Division at Tobruk	301
The Figtree	301
Sandbagged sangars near the El Adem Road	332
Shells from "Bardia Bill" falling near anti-aircraft positions	332
An Australian infantry section on the move at Tobruk	333
Night air raid, September 1941	333
Brigadier J. J. Murray, commanding the 20th Brigade, with his battalion commanders	364

	Page
Men of the 9th Divisional A.A.S.C. manning Post Z84	364
Brigadier A. H. L. Godfrey, commanding the 24th Brigade, with his battalion commanders	365
Camouflaged hangars at El Gubbi, September 1941	365
Major-General Morshead with Major-General R. MacK. Scobie	396
The Australian memorial at the Tobruk War Cemetery	396
Australian and Polish soldiers at Tobruk	397
Australian troops on a destroyer bound for Alexandria, after the relief	397
Salum bay and township	492
Men of the 19th New Zealand Battalion and 4th Royal Tank Regiment at Ed Duda	492
Looking towards Tripoli (Syria) and Chekka village	493
On the Turkish-Syrian border	493
In Syria at the time when the 9th Division was relieving the 7th Division	524
The Nahr el Kelb in Syria, showing bridges under construction by the Australians	524
Crusader tanks of the 9th Divisional Cavalry Regiment on their way to the El Alamein front	525
Dispersed British vehicles at El Alamein, July 1942	525
The railway cutting at Tel el Eisa	556
Tel el Eisa railway station	556
German trucks destroyed near the Tel el Eisa cutting, July 1942	557
Ruin Ridge, November 1942	557
Mr Winston Churchill and General Morshead	588
A 2/2nd Machine Gun Battalion position at El Alamein	588
Interrogating a German officer captured at El Alamein	589
General Sir Claude Auchinleck and Lieut-General W. H. C. Ramsden	589
Bombs bursting near the 9th Divisional Cavalry Regiment headquarters at El Alamein	604
A Bofors gun crew of the 4th Light Anti-Aircraft Regiment at El Alamein	604
General Sir Harold Alexander meets Australian officers at 20th Brigade headquarters	604
Lieut-General B. L. Montgomery with General Morshead and other Australian officers during a visit to the 9th Division	604
Preparing barbed-wire defences at El Alamein	605
Brigadier Godfrey inspecting a Russian anti-tank gun	605
German leaflets dropped over Australian positions at El Alamein	605
Laying armoured signal cable, October 1942	605

	Page
A roadside security sign in the Australian sector	620
An Australian salvage notice near El Alamein	620
Brigadiers D. A. Whitehead and A. H. Ramsay	621
Brigadier R. W. Tovell, commanding the 26th Brigade, with his battalion commanders	621
A tank with a false truck body attached, as part of the British deception arrangements at El Alamein	652
A dummy light anti-aircraft gun position	652
Australian positions near the sea, El Alamein, September 1942	653
A church service at El Alamein, September 1942	653
El Alamein, 9.40 p.m. 23rd October 1942	684
British bombers over the battle area, El Alamein	685
Enemy night raid on Alexandria, October 1942	685
"Scorpions", manned by Australian engineers, at El Alamein	716
Captured enemy anti-tank guns at El Daba, November 1942	716
A German tank destroyed at El Alamein	717
Feeding captured Italians	717
Positions of the 24th Brigade, west of Tel el Eisa, under enemy shell fire	732
A Sherman tank	732
Abandoned German positions at Ring Contour 25	732
Transport moving in the wake of Rommel's retreating army, 13th November 1942	732
Scene of a decisive tank battle near the Blockhouse, west of Tel el Eisa	733
German 88-mm gun and tractor destroyed by fire from the 2/7th Field Regiment	733
The ceremonial parade of the 9th Division at Gaza, 22nd December 1942	733
General Sir Harold Alexander taking the salute at the parade	733
Stowing kits on to a lighter for trans-shipment to the *Queen Mary*	748
Troops of the 9th Division aboard the *Nieuw Amsterdam*, homeward bound	748
Prisoners of war in transit by cattle truck from Italy to Germany	749
Stalag 383, Hohenfels	749
"Anzac Avenue", Stalag 383	780
A play presented at Oflag VIIB, Eichstatt	780
Men from Stalag 383 halt during their forced march southwards	781
Recovered prisoners of war at a transit centre at Brussels	781

MAPS

	Page
The Eastern Mediterranean	5
The Western Desert	13
Dispositions, Tobruk, afternoon 5th May 1941	220
Dawn at El Alamein, 24th October 1942	668
Prisoner-of-war camps in Europe	758

SKETCH MAPS AND DIAGRAMS

The Mediterranean and Middle East	2
The 20th Brigade dispositions, 11th March 1941	16
The Jebel Achdar	25
General Morshead's proposed defence line	31
The 2/13th Battalion's dispositions, 4th April	69
The German thrust into Cyrenaica	83
Tobruk defence lines	126
An outer perimeter post	131
The Egyptian frontier area	135
The German attack, 13th-14th April	147
The 2/48th Battalion raid on Carrier Hill	175
The 2/23rd Battalion raid, 22nd April 1941	176
Dispositions of the 2/24th Battalion, 30th April	192
Panoramic view Bianca-Medauuar, looking south-west	197
The garrison counter-attacks, 1st May	218
The Salient, morning 2nd May	228
The 18th Brigade attack, 3rd-4th May	231
The 2/12th Battalion sally, White Knoll area, 15th May	247
The 2/23rd Battalion attacks on Posts S6 and S7	258
Panoramic view of the Water Tower-Post S7 area	263
Dispositions, 20th Brigade, 11th-12th June	273
Operation BATTLEAXE	282
Advancing the left flank of the Salient, 29th June-3rd July	290
Shortening the Salient, May-July 1941	291
Tobruk outposts, eastern sector	302
The 2/28th Battalion attacks on S6 and S7, 2nd-3rd August	320

The 2/43rd Battalion attack on R7, 2nd-3rd August	324
"Summer Night's Dream", 14th September 1941	361
The 2/32nd Battalion attack on Dalby Square, 13th-14th September	371
The 2/28th Battalion attack on White Cairn, 13th-14th September	372
Diagram showing battalion reliefs, October 1941	396
The Wadi Sehel	402
A 2/1st Pioneer Battalion patrol, 29th June	403
The 2/28th Battalion raid, 17th-18th July	403
A 2/32nd Battalion patrol, 24th-25th July	404
A 2/43rd Battalion patrol, 22nd-23rd July	404
Patrols of the 2/10th Battalion, 19th-20th July	405
A 2/12th Battalion patrol, 10th July	405
A 2/15th Battalion patrol, 31st August	406
A 2/43rd Battalion patrol, 10th May	407
A 2/23rd Battalion patrol, 9th-10th July	409
The Tobruk break-out, 21st November 1941	439
Dispositions 18th November 1941	442
The capture of Sidi Rezegh airfield, 19th November	443
Situation 20th November 1941	445
Enemy dispositions in the Sidi Rezegh area	446
Defeat at Sidi Rezegh, 22nd November	449
The German frontier foray, 24th-25th November	454
Westward advance of the New Zealand Division, 21st-26th November	456
Movements of armoured formations, 27th November	465
Attacks on Ed Duda and Point 175, 29th November	474
The 2/13th Battalion, Ed Duda area	476
Enemy and Allied movements, 30th November-1st December	484
Turkey, Syria and the Lebanon	517
Syrian-Turkish frontier area	520
The Tripoli area of Syria	522
El Alamein	543
Dispositions, 24th and 26th Brigades, 1st July 1942	546
Situation, noon 5th July	553
Movements 10th-12th July	560

	Page
The attack on Ruweisat Ridge, 14th-15th July	568
The 2/23rd Battalion attack on the double Point 24 feature, 16th July	570
The 24th Brigade attacks, 17th July	572
Dispositions, 24th Brigade, 18th July	575
The 26th Brigade attack, 22nd-23rd July	580
The 2/28th Battalion attack, 22nd-23rd July	587
Plan of attack, Miteiriya Ridge, 26th-27th July	589
Australian dispositions, noon 7th August 1942	618
The Battle of Alam el Halfa, 30th-31st August 1942	628
Operation BULIMBA, 1st September 1942	631
The XXX Corps' objectives, 23rd-24th October	657
Situation, 23rd October 1942	664
Dispositions, XXX Corps, dawn 24th October	674
Australian dispositions, dawn 25th October	681
Dawn, 26th October	691
Dawn, 29th October	704
The 26th Brigade attack, 30th-31st October	712
Australian dispositions, dawn 1st November 1942	725
Operation SUPERCHARGE, 2nd November 1942	730
The 2nd, 8th and 22nd Armoured Brigades, 2nd-4th November	733
Australian dispositions, dawn 3rd November 1942	735
Dawn, 5th November 1942	739
Movements of prisoners of war in Europe, 1944-45	809
The Beirut-Tripoli railway	825

PREFACE

THIS volume of the series *Australia in the War of 1939-1945* chronicles the participation of Australian military forces in the North African campaigns from March 1941 to December 1942. In the opening campaign the British forces retreated from Cyrenaica and came close to outright defeat; when the story ends, they had driven the Axis forces from Cyrenaica and were pursuing them along the Tripolitanian coast. The book tells how Australian soldiers and their leaders contributed to that achievement. Australian sailors and airmen also played a part, but their contribution, having been recorded in other volumes, is mentioned only when it impinges on the military story.

In summary, it is the story of the 9th Australian Division from its formation until its departure from the Middle East, and of other Australian formations and units while they fought with or near it in that theatre. The operations of British forces and other national forces under British command taking part in the same campaigns are also recounted, being described in greater or less detail according to their relevance to Australian operations. Thus the doings of some British units and of individual officers and men belonging to them who served under Australian command or cooperated with Australian units, particularly in the retreat from Cyrenaica and the siege of Tobruk, are in some instances related in more detail than in the British official history.

Disparagement of war histories is fashionable, as though to praise men who nobly fought were to advocate a warlike national philosophy. It is in adversity, however, that man's nobility most shines forth, whether in peace or war. The greatness of the Australian soldier, which superbly exemplifies the quality of our people, is the unsullied theme of the military volumes of the official war history, all of which have been written in the tradition that Dr C. E. W. Bean established and Gavin Long, the general editor of this series, worthily carried on. The object is to relate not only what governments arranged and generals ordered and what results they achieved but also how these were accomplished by the soldiers themselves. Their trials, their triumphs, their disasters. Their comradeship, transcending war's engendered hates. Of necessity we watch mainly those at the front of the stage, failing often to notice others moving shadowily behind them, such the signallers, the runners, the stretcher bearers, the cooks, the truck drivers, all doing their simple but essential work, sometimes across fire-swept ground. The tragedies, the extinction of full-blooded lives, these are the strongest arguments for peace.

I saw many and knew some of these men and have enjoyed chronicling their deeds, because my experiences with them transformed my own attitude to the men and women whose daily toil sustains my country, as their toil in war protected and honoured it. I was with the 20th Brigade, later transferred to the 9th Division, when it sailed to the Middle East but not when it moved to Cyrenaica nor during the retreat to Tobruk and early days of the siege. Rejoining it from Mersa Matruh after the failure of Operation BATTLEAXE I served with it thenceforth in various minor roles, mainly with the 2/13th Battalion, throughout most of the subsequent operations described.

The story has been compiled primarily from official records and war diaries, including some British ones. These were supplemented by narratives and enemy appreciations from the Historical Section of the United Kingdom Cabinet Office and the unexcelled campaign narratives of the War History Branch of the New Zealand Department of Internal Affairs, and in particular by Mr W. E. Murphy's narrative of the second Libyan campaign, from which the main thread of the operational narrative in the Ed Duda chapter was drawn. Numerous other sources have been acknowledged in the footnotes.

Those for whom this book has been written have waited too long for it. The late Chester Wilmot was first chosen to be the author but had not started work on it before his tragic death. I began the task in 1955, and with less talent have striven to produce a volume he would not have thought inadequate. There was nothing then to distract me, but unexpected problems soon arose. Some people could doubtless have better surmounted difficulties such as subsequently confronted me; but the completion, if tardy, has not been reached without effort. Nor without help generously given. Particularly should I mention the extensive leave granted me by my employer, The Zinc Corporation, Limited.

I owe an immense debt to the dedicated people of the Official War History staff whose devotion to their task has sometimes been given in disregard of prospects of advancement in other directions: A. E. Field who wrote the appendixes dealing with the Haifa-Beirut railway and prisoners of war and the description of the 9th Division's Gaza parade and whose notes on operations and narratives of non-operational phases I used extensively; Jim Brill, who gave me not only diligent help but friendship in a strange city; Geoff McKeown whose painstaking research provided a solid factual basis to the maps and to many battle descriptions; Hugh Groser for his expert cartography; Mary Gilchrist, who saw the volume into the press; Ann Ellis, who typed most of the numerous drafts; and last but not least, A. J. (Bill) Sweeting who took charge of the Official War History staff after Gavin Long retired and whose scholarly judgment has saved the volume from several faults.

Many of high and low rank have helped by corresponding with me or the general editor and his staff or granting interviews, and I am specially indebted to Sir Claude Auchinleck and the late Sir Leslie Morshead for the time they spared. The book also owes much to Sir Victor Windeyer's suggestions and constructive criticism made against the background of his deep learning and extensive reading of military history; and to the well-informed criticism of Brigadier H. B. Latham (Historical Section, United Kingdom Cabinet Office) and of Mr Ronald Walker, the New Zealand historian, both of whom enabled some errors to be avoided.

I owe most to Gavin Long. His unobtrusive teaching and guidance, his unfathomable patience, his faith in me albeit misplaced. I cannot speak of his help without repeating what has been said again and again in their prefaces by other writers of the official histories, all sustained (but none more than I) by his encouragement, his scholarship, his wisdom and his strong loyalty.

It is time to say my last thanks to all these people. There are others I should name, and there is one I cannot, who gave me constant help.

B.M.

Broken Hill,
1st January 1965.

LIST OF EVENTS
FROM MARCH 1941 TO DECEMBER 1942

Events described in this volume are printed in italics

1941	31 Mar	*Enemy counter-attack in North Africa*
	3 Apr	*British evacuate Benghazi*
	6 Apr	Germans invade Greece and Yugoslavia
	7 Apr	*British and Australian troops evacuate Derna. Generals O'Connor and Neame captured by Germans*
	11 Apr	*Siege of Tobruk begins*
	14 Apr	*General Morshead appointed commander of Tobruk fortress*
	22 Apr	Embarkation of troops from Greece begins
	20 May	Germans invade Crete
	27 May	German battleship *Bismarck* sunk 400 miles west of Brest
	8 Jun	Allied invasion of Syria begins
	15-17 Jun	*Operation Battleaxe*
	22 Jun	Germany invades Russia
	12 Jul	Armistice in Syria
	29 Aug	Mr Fadden becomes Prime Minister of Australia
	7 Oct	Mr Curtin becomes Prime Minister of Australia
	18 Nov	*British offensive in Western Desert (Operation Crusader) begins*
	30 Nov	*Germans capture Sidi Rezegh*
	7-8 Dec	Japanese attack Malaya and Pearl Harbour
	10 Dec	*Prince of Wales* and *Repulse* sunk off Malaya
	26 Dec	British garrison at Hong Kong surrenders to Japanese
1942	23 Jan	Japanese capture Rabaul
	19 Feb	First Japanese air raid on Darwin
	8 Mar	Japanese occupy Lae and Salamaua
	17 Mar	General MacArthur arrives in Australia
	26 Mar	General Blamey becomes Commander-in-Chief, Australian Military Forces
	5-8 May	Battle of the Coral Sea
	20 May	Allied forces withdraw from Burma

31 May-1 Jun	Japanese midget submarines attack Sydney Harbour
4-6 Jun	Battle of Midway Island
21 Jun	*Axis forces capture Tobruk*
25 Jun	*General Auchinleck assumes command of the Eighth Army*
	9th Australian Division ordered to move to Egypt
21 Jul	Japanese land in Gona area, Papua
7 Aug	Americans land in the Solomons
13 Aug	*General Montgomery takes command of the Eighth Army*
15 Aug	*General Alexander succeeds General Auchinleck as Commander-in-Chief Middle East*
25-26 Aug	Japanese land at Milne Bay
30-31 Aug	*Battle of Alam el Halfa*
1 Sep	*Operation Bulimba*
23-24 Oct	*Battle of El Alamein begins*
2 Nov	Kokoda recaptured
7-8 Nov	Allied landings in French North Africa
9 Dec	Australians capture Gona

CHAPTER 1

THE "MINIMUM POSSIBLE FORCE" GUARDS CYRENAICA

IN February 1941 Greece was at war with Italy, but not with Germany. The British Commonwealth was at war with both Axis powers. Of the other nations of the world, though few were unconcerned and some had aligned themselves closely with one or other belligerent group—as Russia had, for example, by the Soviet-German Non-Aggression Pact—none was committed to fight. When it came to fighting, Britain's only allies outside the Commonwealth were the handful of governments-in-exile of already vanquished nations and the homeless people who still gave them allegiance. And although by day and by night the naval and air forces of both sides were carrying on the struggle on all seven seas and under them, and in all skies within their reach, British Commonwealth ground forces were in action in one theatre only, the Middle East.

The Mediterranean, though one sea, comprises two distinct basins linked by a sea passage through the Sicilian Narrows. In 1940 and 1941 the Axis powers were well disposed to dominate both basins by deploying their preponderant air power across the Narrows from Italian airfields in Sicily and North Africa. Isolated Malta, alone still challenging Axis supremacy there, could surely be neutralised and, if need be, overcome. For complete mastery of the Mediterranean, however, more was needed: first, control of its three gateways—the western gateway at Gibraltar and the two gateways to the eastern basins, the Suez Canal and the Dardanelles —and then domination or neutralisation of the whole littoral to sufficient depth to protect the seaways from sustained air attack. This in turn would necessitate gaining control of the territories on the southern and eastern shores of the Mediterranean then held by British forces. Of utmost strategic importance on the North African coast was Tunisia, which afforded the shortest sea-route between Europe and Africa across the central Mediterranean; yet in the peace terms imposed on France Hitler had been content to leave this territory under French control.

Even while the German High Command had been pressing forward with preparations to invade England, Hitler had considered the possibility of German participation in land operations in North Africa. An offer of collaboration by German forces had been made to Italy, but the Italians had not immediately accepted.

When later the German High Command had turned with misgiving from the project of invading England, the Chief of the German Naval Staff, Admiral Raeder, had lost no opportunity to impress upon Hitler the importance of the Mediterranean theatre. The seizure of Gibraltar with Spanish collaboration, an advance through Syria with the acquiescence of Vichy France, and a thrust by the Italian forces in North Africa into western Egypt had then been proposed by Hitler as first steps towards bringing the Mediterranean completely under Axis control. Later, when Italy's attack on Greece, mounted without consultation with her ally, complicated German plans, and by its first failures threatened to weaken the Axis position in the eastern Mediterranean, Hitler determined to occupy the Greek peninsula with German forces.

But no sooner had the German leader outlined a pattern for action in the Mediterranean theatre than he was induced to change it. Early in December 1940 Franco made it known to the German High Command that Britain would have to be reduced to the point of collapse before Spain would actively participate in war against her. Having no wish to add to the number of his enemies, Hitler ordered the discontinuance of preparations to seize Gibraltar. About the same time, General Sir Archibald Wavell's desert army began an advance which soon threatened the Italian

forces in Africa with total destruction. Finally Hitler took the most fateful decision of an evil career when, on 18th December, he issued a directive which set his armed forces that most formidable task: the overthrow of Russia. "The Army," stated the directive, "will have to employ for this purpose all available troops, with the limitation that the occupied territories must be secured against surprise."

The intention to subordinate military effort to this single, paramount aim was clearly stated. Mediterranean operations, except to the extent that they involved the security of the southern flank of Germany's eastward thrust towards Russia, now fell into a place of secondary importance in Hitler's thought and strategy. The conquest of eastern Europe would be completed, the northern Mediterranean seaboard firmly held. But henceforward German policy for operations across the Mediterranean, whether in Africa or in Asia, was to be marked by opportunism and inconstancy. The High Command adhered to no fixed purpose, but with each change of fortune changed its policy. If Axis forces in Africa were advancing— if the Suez Canal and the Middle Eastern oilfields seemed prizes within easy reach—aims became more ambitious, plans bolder. If their advance was checked, or if military power in Africa seemed for the moment to be in the balance, interest waned; limited objectives were set. If disaster threatened, the greatest efforts were made to retrieve the situation.

Of just such an opportunist character was the German decision taken early in 1941 to revive the shelved plans for sending a German force to Africa[1] and yet to assign to the force only the very limited tasks of securing the defence of Tripolitania and possibly later taking part in a short advance to Benghazi.

The British War Cabinet, on 7th February 1941, immediately after the capture of Benghazi, directed General Wavell that his "major effort" should go into lending all possible aid to Greece, that he should press on with plans for occupying the Italian Dodecanese, and that he should hold the western flank of the Egyptian base at the frontier of Cyrenaica and Tripoli. Immediately Wavell had to regroup the forces under his command. In addition to the tasks laid down by the War Cabinet's directive, he was committed to operations in Eritrea and East Africa, the early conclusion of which would set free forces greatly and urgently needed for use elsewhere.

The forces Wavell had available were:

In the Western Desert—
    7th Armoured Division
    6th Australian Division

In Egypt—
    2nd Armoured Division
    6th British Division (in process of formation)
    New Zealand Division
    Polish Brigade Group

In Palestine—
    7th and 9th Australian Divisions (less one brigade and other units still in transit from England, and one battalion still in Australia)

In Eritrea—
    4th and 5th Indian Divisions (engaged in front of Keren)

In East Africa—
    1st South African Division
    11th African Division
    12th African Division (about to begin operations against Kismayu)

Of the two armoured divisions, the 7th had been fighting continuously for eight months and was mechanically incapable of further action, while the 2nd was not at full strength: it had only two cruiser regiments and two light-tank regiments. Moreover, when the latter division had arrived in Egypt its commander, Major-General Tilly,[2] had told Wavell that his cruiser tanks were in appalling mechanical condition. The engines had already done a considerable mileage, the tracks were practically worn out. It had been intended to fit fresh tracks specially made in Australia when the division arrived in the Middle East, but these proved "practically useless" and the old tracks were retained. Writing afterwards, Wavell said

---
[1] See Gavin Long, *To Benghazi* (1952), pp. 277-9, in this series.
[2] Maj-Gen J. C. Tilly, DSO, MC. GOC 2 Armd Div 1940-41. Regular soldier; b. 27 Jan 1888. Died 16 Jan 1941.

that it was hoped that the old tracks "would give less trouble in the desert than they had at home".[3] Yet there were no tank transporters in the Middle East in those days. Even if these tanks were to be shipped to Tobruk or, still farther, to Benghazi (in the event, they were shipped to Tobruk), there would remain great distances over rough ground to be traversed on their outworn tracks to reach a front where they would be required to operate over very broken country. To hope for a reasonable performance was to be unreasonably optimistic.

Of the infantry, the divisions engaged in East Africa and Eritrea were committed to other tasks. If, however, operations there proved as successful as hoped, one Indian division might become available in about two months and possibly one South African division—provided that the Government of South Africa would agree to its employment so far afield. The African divisions of native troops, however, were not suitable for employment in the operations required by the War Cabinet's directive.

Thus the infantry available in the near future consisted of one New Zealand division, three Australian divisions, one British division and the Polish Brigade; but of the five divisions only three were completely equipped. Field guns and other supporting arms were scarce. The artillery regiments of the British division and of one Australian division had not yet received their guns.

Wavell decided to split his only available armoured formation, sending part—the better part—to Greece and retaining the rest for Cyrenaica. To the Grecian expedition and the assault on the Dodecanese he allotted all his available infantry except one division and more than half of the armoured division; the remaining infantry division and the rest of the 2nd Armoured Division would have to suffice for holding the western frontier of Cyrenaica. But would it suffice? To every available formation under his command he had allotted an operational role. Patently there was a danger that compliance with the War Cabinet's wishes might involve his having forces committed to combat simultaneously in Greece, Cyrenaica, East Africa and the Dodecanese; unless this could be avoided he would be left with no general reserve.

In effect, Wavell had decided that "the minimum possible force" then necessary to secure his western flank was an armoured force of the strength of one very weak armoured brigade operating with one battalion and a half of motorised infantry and one division of static infantry, and with artillery support on about the normal scale for an infantry division. He had plans for some early strengthening of this force, but not to any substantial extent.

Even before it had been split between two theatres, the 2nd Armoured Division with its outworn cruisers had had but two-thirds of the normal number of tanks of an armoured division. To augment the tank strength of what now remained Wavell decided to provide an additional tank battalion and to equip it with captured Italian medium tanks. He also

---

[3] Wavell, despatch, *Operations in the Middle East from 7th February, 1941 to 15th July, 1941*, para 7.

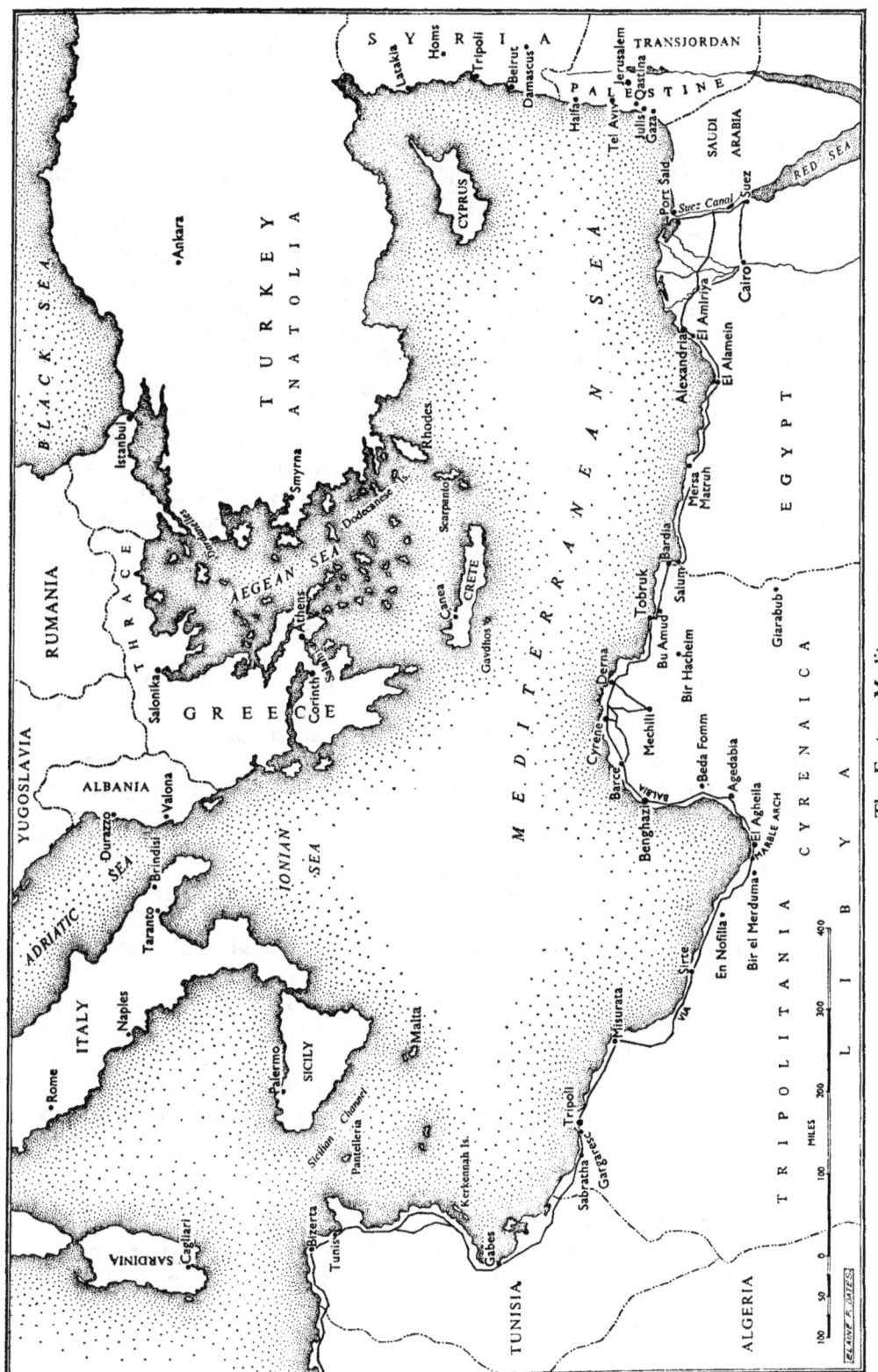

The Eastern Mediterranean

planned to make available the 3rd Indian Motor Brigade (of three motor battalions) as soon as its training had been completed. But no other reinforcements were contemplated in the near future.

Wavell "estimated that it would be at least two months after the landing of German forces at Tripoli before they could undertake a serious offensive against Cyrenaica, and that, therefore, there was not likely to be any serious threat to our positions there before May at the earliest". He calculated that it would be safe to garrison Cyrenaica with comparatively unequipped and untrained troops so long as they could be made ready for battle by May, when, he hoped, reinforcements of at least one Indian division would also be available from the Sudan.[4]

Wavell originally intended that the battle-tried 6th Australian Division, already in Cyrenaica, should be the western-frontier force's infantry division and that the Australian contingent for Greece should comprise the 7th and 9th Divisions. Lieut-General Sir Thomas Blamey (G.O.C. A.I.F. Middle East) insisted, however, that the 6th Division should be one of the two to go to Greece, for he was determined that the contingent for so hazardous an expedition should be formed of his best-trained troops. Wavell was therefore obliged to relieve the 6th Division with one of the other Australian divisions, a change in his plans which involved relying on a raw and partially-equipped formation to provide the infantry component of the frontier force.

To enable the best-trained Australian units to be sent to Greece General Blamey carried out an extensive reorganisation and regrouping of the A.I.F. in the Middle East. The formation that constituted the 9th Division before this reorganisation and the formation that emerged from it as the 9th Division, assigned to the task of garrisoning Cyrenaica, were very differently composed. Of its original three brigades, but one remained with it; of the battalions now comprising its infantry, not one had originally been raised for the 9th Division.

Since its fortunes over a period of almost two years will be the principal concern of this volume, it will be worth while to review the division's origins and to see of what units it was now composed and what degree of training they had achieved.

The decision to form a fourth A.I.F. division, to be known as the 9th Australian Division, was made by the Australian War Cabinet on 23rd September 1940. But many of the units of which it was to be constituted had already been formed: most of them were originally raised for either the 7th or the 8th Division. Already three complete A.I.F. infantry divisions with normal complement of supporting arms and two additional infantry brigades without supporting arms, had been raised. These were the 6th Division in Egypt and Palestine, the 7th and 8th in Australia, and in England the 18th Brigade (the headquarters and battalions of which had originally belonged to the 6th Division before that division was reduced in size from twelve to nine battalions) and the 25th Brigade, which had

---

[4] Wavell, despatch, para 10.

been formed in England mainly by a reorganisation of troops who had arrived there in the same convoy as the 18th Brigade. Two additional field regiments and two medium regiments had also been formed in Australia as corps troops for the I Australian Corps.

It was decided that the two brigades in England would form the nucleus of the new (9th) division and that its commander would be Major-General H. D. Wynter, then commanding the force in England. To provide the artillery for an additional division three field regiments would be required. These were to be found by utilising the two corps field regiments and by converting one of the corps medium regiments to field artillery. To complete the division, an additional infantry brigade, an anti-tank regiment and engineer, medical, and supplies and services units would be raised in Australia. It was intended that the new division should be assembled in the Middle East, together with the 6th and 7th Divisions.

When General Blamey was advised of these decisions, he criticised the policy of combining the two brigades in England—composed of some of the first-enlisted and best-trained troops in the A.I.F.—with units yet to be raised whose training would take a considerable time to complete. He insisted that the new division should be made up from units already formed. It was therefore decided to take the 24th Brigade, the 2/3rd Anti-Tank Regiment and the field companies from the 8th Division to bring the 9th Division up to strength, and to use new units to be raised to replace the transferred units in the 8th Division which, bound for Singapore, had less prospect of early operational employment. Thus the infantry of the 9th Division was to comprise the 18th and 25th Infantry Brigades, then with Major-General Wynter in England, and the 24th Brigade then in Australia.

Wynter was appointed to command the division on 23rd October 1940. He sailed from England on 16th November for the Middle East, where the division was to be assembled; in the same convoy was one of his brigades, the 18th. At Capetown he left the convoy and flew to Cairo, arriving on 18th December. Immediately he commenced consultations to settle arrangements for the assembly of the division and the reception of the various units as they reached the Middle East. On 24th December he opened divisional headquarters at Julis in Palestine. Colonel C. E. M. Lloyd, who had already been appointed his chief staff officer (G.S.O.1), joined the headquarters on the same day.

Two field regiments and a field company in Palestine were the only units of the division already in the Middle East but about one-third of its strength, including the 18th Brigade, was then at sea and due to arrive at the end of the month. On 3rd January 1941 two more convoys set sail: from England came the 25th Brigade and some other units; out of Fremantle sailed the 24th Brigade (less one battalion) and most of the divisional troops raised in Australia. The 24th Brigade began to arrive in the Suez Canal area at the end of January. The 25th Brigade did not arrive until the second week in March, by which time it had been transferred to the 7th Division.

General Wynter was never to exercise command of the 9th Division as an effective formation. In mid-January 1941, Brigadier L. J. Morshead's 18th Brigade was detached for duty in the desert (and to prepare for operations against Giarabub) and the divisional engineers were sent to Cyrenaica where, together with the 2/4th Field Company, they were employed on maintenance and construction work, initially in the area from Tobruk to Derna. Before either of his other two brigades had arrived in the Middle East, Wynter fell seriously ill. It soon became clear that he would not be fit for operational employment in the foreseeable future and would have to be relieved of his command. Brigadier Morshead was appointed to succeed him, yielding command of the 18th Brigade to Lieut-Colonel G. F. Wootten. It was fitting that Wynter's mantle should fall on Morshead, who had loyally served under Wynter although the latter had superseded him to command the force in England.[6]

Morshead was informed of his appointment on 29th January. After handing over his brigade to Brigadier Wootten at Ikingi Maryut and reporting to General Blamey at corps headquarters in Cyrenaica, he arrived at divisional headquarters at Julis on 5th February and assumed command.[7] While Morshead had been reporting to Blamey, the 24th Brigade and other divisional units from Australia had been disembarking in the canal zone and moving to camps in Palestine. For the first three weeks after his appointment, Morshead was mainly concerned with arrangements for their training.

It was on 18th February that Wavell gave Blamey the outline of the plan to send a force to Greece, and it was probably also at this meeting that Blamey advised Wavell that the 9th Division, not the 6th, should be assigned to Cyrenaica Command.

On 19th February, Mr Anthony Eden, the British Secretary of State for Foreign Affairs, and General Sir John Dill, Chief of the Imperial General Staff, arrived in Cairo to take charge of negotiations with the Greek Government. On 23rd February the Greek leaders accepted the British offer to send an expeditionary force. The planned regrouping of Wavell's forces, which had already been put in train, now proceeded swiftly. On 24th February, Blamey's I Australian Corps headquarters left

---

[6] Blamey first requested that Major-General J. Northcott should be sent from Australia to take over the command, but the Chief of the General Staff, Lieut-General V. A. H. Sturdee, advised that Northcott, then Deputy Chief of the General Staff, could not be spared, since he was required to form the 1st Armoured Division in Australia. Blamey also pointed out that although no restriction existed on his authority to make appointments, divisional commanders had so far been appointed by War Cabinet. He contended that this procedure was undesirable except for formations in Australia. Mr Spender, the Minister for the Army, agreed that Blamey should make the appointment. On 27th January Blamey informed Sturdee that Morshead would command the 9th Division and Wootten the 18th Brigade.

[7] At the time of Morshead's appointment, the 9th Division included the following units (most of them, however, not at this time under command):
 Artillery: 2/3rd, 2/7th, 2/12th Field Regiments; 2/1st Anti-Tank Regiment.
 Engineers: 2/3rd, 2/7th, 2/13th Field Companies; 2/4th Field Park Company.
 Infantry: 18th Brigade (2/9th, 2/10th, 2/12th Battalions); 24th Brigade (2/25th, 2/28th, 2/43rd Battalions); 25th Brigade (2/31st, 2/32nd, 2/33rd Battalions).
 Medical: 2/3rd, 2/8th, 2/11th Field Ambulances; 2/4th Field Hygiene Section.
 Under command, but not at this time belonging to the division, were—2/2nd Machine Gun Battalion, 2/8th Field Regiment and 2/3rd Anti-Tank Regiment.

Cyrenaica, handing over operational command there to Cyrenaica Command. On the same day, a battalion of the Support Group of the 2nd Armoured Division—the 1st Battalion, Tower Hamlets Rifles—arrived in Tobruk; on the next, the Support Group of the 7th Armoured Division left for Egypt. On 26th February, Lieut-General Sir Philip Neame arrived at Cyrenaica Command headquarters at Barce to take over the command (on the 27th) from Lieut-General Sir Maitland Wilson, who had been appointed commander of the expedition to Greece.

General Neame was a British regular officer who had had a varied and successful career marked by gallantry in the first world war, during which, after serving in the front line with distinction and being awarded the Victoria Cross, he held a number of staff appointments, finally becoming senior staff officer of a division. When the second war was about to break out, Neame was at first chosen to be Chief of the General Staff to the British Expeditionary Force but eventually went to France as Deputy Chief of Staff. In February 1940 he was transferred to the Middle East to command the 4th Indian Division and in August of that year was appointed General Officer Commanding-in-Chief, Palestine and Transjordan. He experienced some disappointment at not receiving command of the Western Desert Force in Wavell's first campaign; he had a claim for consideration on the ground of seniority.[8] Thus it was natural that this professionally eminent commander with a gallant record should now be chosen for appointment to the Cyrenaican command.

On 26th February, the day on which Neame arrived in Cyrenaica, Blamey gave directions for the reorganisation of the A.I.F. in the Middle East. The detailed orders were issued at Headquarters British Troops in Egypt at a staff conference called by the I Australian Corps, just arrived from Cyrenaica. The 18th and 25th Brigades, the original nucleus of the 9th Division, were to be transferred to the 7th Division, the 20th and 26th Brigades from the 7th to the 9th Division. The infantry of the 9th Division would now comprise the 20th, 24th and 26th Brigades, the artillery, the 2/7th, 2/8th and 2/12th Field Regiments and the 2/3rd Anti-Tank Regiment. The regrouping was to be effective forthwith "as a temporary expedient only". The 9th Division, less its field artillery which was not yet equipped or fully trained, was to be prepared to move to Cyrenaica immediately to relieve the 6th Division. The 20th Brigade, which would go first, was warned to be prepared to move within 24 hours. It was intended that this brigade, which had been formed two months earlier than the others and had been longer in the Middle East, should take over in the forward zone while the remaining brigades would be employed on garrison duties in the Derna-Tobruk area and undergo further training.

The division was one infantry battalion short of full strength. Only two of the three battalions of the 24th Brigade had arrived: the third, the 2/25th, had remained on garrison duty at Darwin when the brigade had sailed from Australia and was not due to arrive until the end of April.

---

[8] Sir Philip Neame, *Playing with Strife* (1947), p. 262.

Thus General Morshead found himself in command of an infantry division composed of brigades selected by the test that they were the least trained or most recently enlisted, and now destined for garrison duty on a frontier where the enemy was in contact. That the division might become heavily engaged in two or three months was not merely possible, but likely. Morshead's urgent task was to move his division to Cyrenaica, see to its training and equipment, and build it into a team before the enemy could interfere. There was much to do to fit the division for war.

Morshead laboured under a number of disadvantages. The foundations for a divisional *esprit de corps* were lacking. They would have to be laid. He had a most competent assistant in Lloyd, his senior staff officer, but as yet only a skeleton staff. In the case of only one of the brigades (Brigadier E. C. P. Plant's 24th) had there been any personal contact between Morshead and the brigade commander or between Morshead's headquarters and the brigadier's staff, and then only for a period of less than a month. Within a week Plant departed to take charge of the newly-constituted Rear Echelon Headquarters of the A.I.F. in the Middle East. Two of Morshead's brigades, Brigadier Murray's[9] 20th Brigade and Brigadier Tovell's[1] 26th Brigade, had just been divorced from their parent formation, the 7th Division, to which they felt they belonged. Their pride had been hurt. Just as a soldier who had enlisted early in the war would distinguish himself from one who joined later by his lower "army number", so men cherished the honour of belonging to a low-numbered unit, units the honour of belonging to a low-numbered division. The 18th Brigade, for example, retained their 6th Division colour patches until the end of the war. To be transferred from the 7th to the 9th Division seemed to the 20th and 26th Brigades like demotion. It was moreover unfortunate that the brigade commanders and heads of other arms and services in the division should have been told that the regrouping would be effective as a temporary expedient only, as they were in the notes circulated by Lloyd summarising the conference on 26th February at which the new organisation was laid down. A belief in the permanency of the arrangements was needed to foster in the transferred units a sense of belonging to the division, solid achievement to foster their pride in so belonging.

The 20th Brigade, formed in May 1940, had been in Palestine three months, the 26th Brigade, formed in July 1940, about two months, and the 24th Brigade, also formed in July, less than one month. Not one unit had been issued with its full complement of arms; but although "mock-up" weapons had been used for much of the training, each unit had fired automatic weapons in range practice. Individual training of the men was well advanced and there had been some sub-unit training, but battalions

---

[9] Maj-Gen J. J. Murray, DSO, MC, VD, NX365. (1st AIF: Maj 53 and 55 Bns.) Comd 20 Bde 1940-41; GOC 4 Div 1942-44, Rear Ech First Aust Army 1944, NT Force 1945. Salesman; of Mosman, NSW; b. Sydney, 26 Apr 1892. Died 9 Sep 1951.
[1] Brig Hon R. W. Tovell, CBE, DSO, ED, VX46983. (1st AIF: 46 Bn, 4 Pnr Bn; BM 4 Bde.) Comd 26 Bde 1940-42; DA&QMG II Corps 1942-43; comd Southern Rft Base Sub-Area 1943, Moresby Base Sub-Area 1944; DAG LHQ 1944-45. Chartered accountant; of Brighton, Vic; b. Brighton, 9 Mar 1890.

and regiments had not yet been exercised as units. Hence the training of the brigades as battle groups had not even begun. The state of training may be inferred from statements of two of the brigadiers at a conference called by Major-General J. D. Lavarack (who was then their divisional commander) on 14th January. "I shall be ready," said Murray, "to go on with battalion training during the week after next," and Tovell commented: "We will have completed platoon training by 14th February, when company training will be commenced." In short, the soldiers had been trained to fight but the officers and staffs had yet not been trained in battle management.

The responsibility, laid on Morshead, of swiftly moulding these raw units into a division fit for the vital role of frontier defence was not light; but he was qualified to bear it. He was not a professional soldier, yet had been soldiering all his life, in peace, and in war. As a young man he had made soldiering his consuming hobby when, before the first world war, he began his civilian career as a schoolmaster. He was a captain at the Gallipoli landing, saw heavy fighting on the first day and the six months that followed, was wounded and invalided to Australia, but not out of the army. He was soon appointed to raise a new battalion, the 33rd, which he trained, took to France and commanded with distinction until the armistice. Dr Bean has described him in those days as a battalion commander marked beyond most others as a fighting leader

in whom the traditions of the British Army had been bottled from his childhood like tight-corked champagne; the nearest approach to a martinet among all the young Australian colonels, but able to distinguish the valuable from the worthless in the old army practice . . . he had turned out a battalion which anyone acquainted with the whole force recognised, even before Messines, as one of the very best.[2]

Between the wars Morshead combined success in business—he became the Sydney manager of the Orient Line—with continued interest in soldiering. He commanded a militia brigade for seven years; once he devoted part of a business vacation to visiting army training schools and attending manoeuvres in England. When war again broke out in 1939, he was chosen—at 50 years of age—to be a brigade commander of the 6th Division. There could have been few generals in 1941 able to match his experience of front-line warfare and in the exercise of command.

Morshead was every inch a general. His slight build and seemingly mild facial expression masked a strong personality, the impact of which, even on a slight acquaintance, was quickly felt. The precise, incisive speech and flint-like, piercing scrutiny acutely conveyed impressions of authority, resoluteness and ruthlessness. If battles, as Montgomery was later to declare, were contests of wills, Morshead was not likely to be found wanting. He believed that

battles and campaigns are won by leadership—leadership not only of senior but of junior commanders—by discipline, by that knowledge begotten of experience—

---

[2] C. E. W. Bean, *Official History of Australia in the War of 1914-1918*, Vol V (1937), p. 301.

knowing what to do and how to do it—and by hard work. And above all that, by courage, which we call "guts", gallantry, and devotion to duty.³

Unsparing, unforgiving, outspoken in criticism, he was yet quick to commend and praise when he thought men had fought as they should; such men he respected, admired and honoured. "Ming the Merciless" was the unduly harsh nickname by which he first came to be known in the 9th Division; softened later to just "Ming", as a bond of mutual affection and esteem grew up between the general and his men.

Morshead's task would have been harder, particularly in the early days, when his headquarters were short staffed, if he had not had the competent assistance of Lloyd as chief of his headquarters staff. Lloyd was well described by Chester Wilmot:[4]

> Big and bluff, Lloyd has a manner that is a strange mixture of bluntness and friendliness. His initial bluntness springs from a dislike of humbug and a desire to come straight to the point; but those who stand up to him and have something to say find him most approachable. He is no respecter of persons and is essentially a realist who sees a job to be done and goes about it in the most direct way.⁵

Lloyd was a regular soldier, commissioned in 1918, but his interests extended beyond soldiering as he proved by later taking a degree in law at Sydney University. Possessed of organising ability and always willing to accept responsibility, he was well qualified to carry out the primary function of a chief staff officer: to ensure that the commander's intentions are carried out and that he is not troubled with inessential problems.

The 20th Brigade (2/13th, 2/15th and 2/17th Battalions) was the first to move to Cyrenaica. On 27th February, the day after the brigade's transfer to the 9th Division had been announced, the first road convoy bearing Brigadier Murray's headquarters set out from Kilo 89. The first train left at 7 p.m. on the same day with the 2/13th Battalion on board. Within two days the whole brigade was moving westwards, mainly by train, across the Suez Canal and to Mersa Matruh where the desert railway terminated. On 2nd March, a bleak day of cold and rain, brigade headquarters and the 2/13th Battalion both reached Mersa Matruh, closely followed by the 2/15th and 2/17th. There for the first time the men saw the transformation war can cause. The little Mediterranean port was ringed by a wired perimeter and anti-tank ditch, dug defences and minefields; its buildings bore the scars of bombing; many were empty shells.

On 3rd March, the brigade moved in four convoys, with brigade headquarters in the van, to Buq Buq; on the 4th to Tobruk. Next day the troops were permitted to explore the fortress, littered as it was with the debris of war; but a searing sandstorm blew up, blotting out the sun

---

³ Address by General Morshead to the 26th Brigade Group on 12th August 1945.
⁴ R. W. W. (Chester) Wilmot. War correspondent for ABC 1940-42, for BBC 1944-45. Author and broadcaster; of Melbourne; b. Brighton, Vic, 21 Jun 1911. Killed in aircraft accident 10 Jan 1954. Author of *Tobruk* (1944), the first authoritative published account of the siege, and *The Struggle for Europe* (1952). He was chosen in 1946 as the author of the present volume, and was killed while returning to England after visiting Australia to confer with the General Editor.
⁵ Wilmot, *Tobruk*, p. 113.

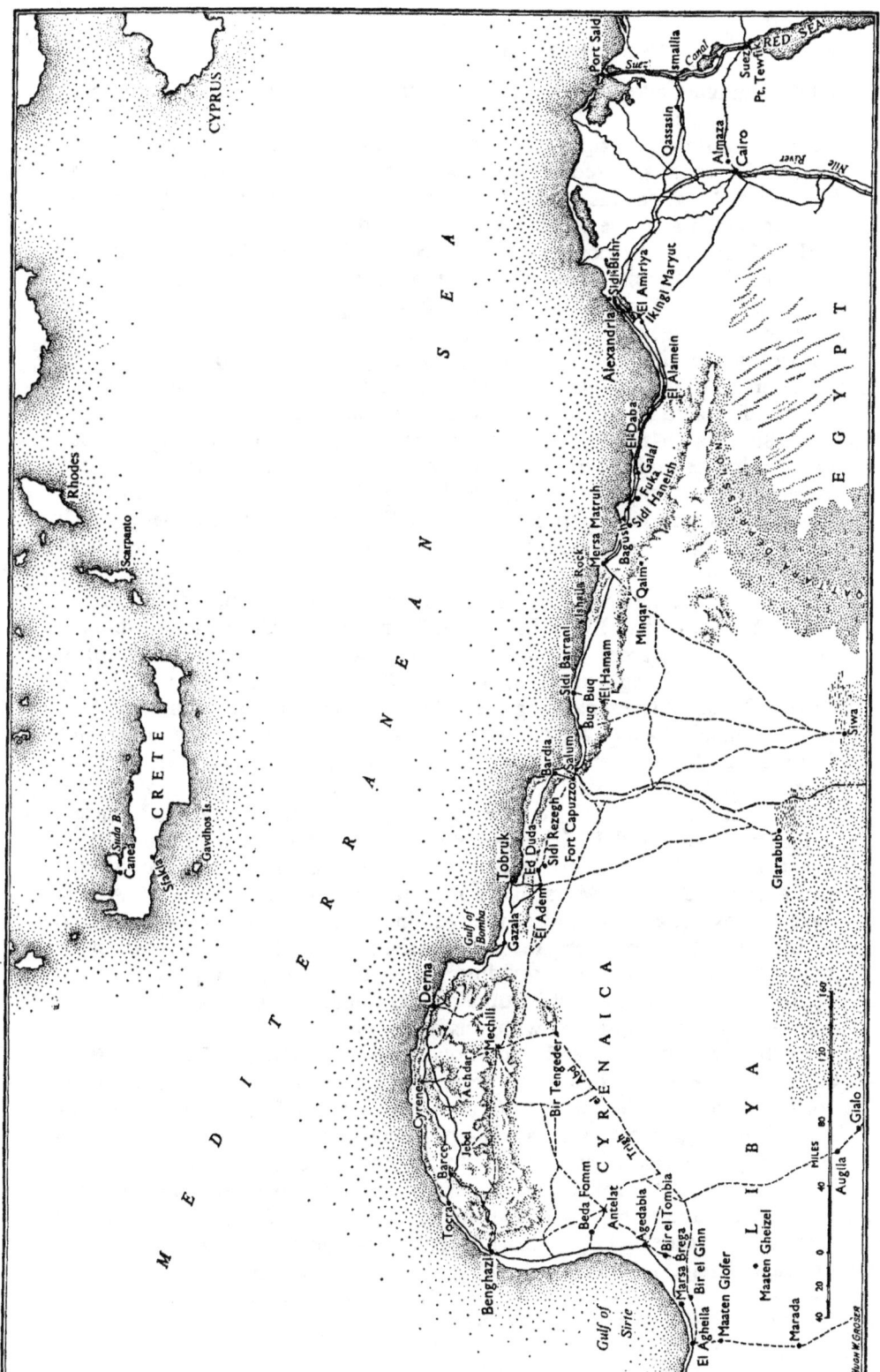

The Western Desert

and discouraging all except the most determined ramblers. The opportunity would come later.

On 6th March the brigade moved out to west of Derna. In the morning the 9th Division suffered its first war casualties. The convoy bearing the 2/13th Battalion was attacked for half an hour by five Heinkel aircraft: two were killed and one wounded, and some damage was done to vehicles. In the afternoon, the convoys descended by the magnificent Italian-built road, the Via Balbia, from the high escarpment to the small port of Derna, a town of white houses and flowering shrubs, but climbed the escarpment again by a zigzagging pass to the west of the town, and there camped for the night. Next day the brigade continued on to Tocra, leaving the desert to pass through a land of wooded hills and green plains. Italian settlers still toiled in the fields, as if the war had never been.

On 8th March the brigade, in the final stages of its journey, passed the outskirts of Benghazi along an avenue of Australian gum-trees, then drove south out into the desert to the Agedabia area. The 2/13th was detached and sent to the coast near Beda Fomm, less one company which was left at Barce as a security guard for the headquarters of Cyrenaica Command.

Divisional headquarters arrived at Tobruk on the same day. On 7th March, Morshead and Lloyd had flown from Cairo to Cyrenaica Command headquarters at Barce. Morshead was to take over responsibility forthwith for the fighting troops in western Cyrenaica from Major-General Sir Iven Mackay (commanding the 6th Australian Division), upon whom their command had devolved when Blamey's headquarters had left for Cairo on 24th February. On arrival at Barce, Morshead learned from Neame that his responsibility for the forward troops would be of limited duration. It was intended that on or about 19th March the headquarters of the 2nd Armoured Division should take over command in the frontier area from the 9th Division and that, while the 20th Brigade would stay in the forward zone, Morshead's headquarters should move to Ain el Gazala to exercise command of the remainder of his division and supervise its training. Thus one brigade of Morshead's division would assume a major operational role by providing the main infantry component of the frontier force but would not be under his command. Morshead told Neame that he was "not impressed with this arrangement".[6]

On 8th March Morshead and Lloyd arrived at the 6th Division headquarters to take over command from Mackay, who flew to Cairo on the 9th to prepare for the move to Greece. And on the 9th Brigadier Murray arrived at Brigadier S. G. Savige's headquarters to arrange for the 20th Brigade (which had arrived the night before) to relieve the 17th Brigade.

At the time of the relief the frontier force comprised Savige's experienced infantry brigade group and the lighter elements of one inexperienced armoured brigade. Savige's brigade held positions near the small haven of Marsa Brega, in dunes and rolling ground surrounded by marshes. The

---

[6] Liaison letter No. 1, 9 Aust Div, 26 Mar 1941.

area was naturally strong in defence but vulnerable to encirclement from the south. The protection of the southern flank was the responsibility of the 3rd Armoured Brigade (Brigadier Rimington[7]) and had been left to a shadow force consisting of the 3rd Hussars (with an effective strength of 32 aged, light tanks) and an infantry support group of two motorised companies of the 1st Free French Motor Battalion. Forward reconnaissance to the frontier at El Agheila and to the south was being carried out by the 1st King's Dragoon Guards (Lieut-Colonel McCorquodale[8]), an armoured-car regiment recently converted to a reconnaissance role. To the rear a squadron of the 6th Royal Tank Regiment was being equipped with captured Italian M13 tanks at Beda Fomm, while the 1/Tower Hamlets Rifles, a motor battalion (which with the two Free French motorised companies constituted the half-strength Support Group of the 2nd Armoured Division[9]) was guarding prisoners of war at Benghazi. The 1/Northumberland Fusiliers, a machine-gun battalion, was similarly employed. The Tower Hamlets was a highly mobile unit but not suited to holding ground in prolonged defence, since it could place only about 250 men on the ground.

The main tank strength of the one armoured brigade was at El Adem, south of Tobruk, some 400 miles distant from Marsa Brega by the desert route (500 miles by the well-built coast road). Here were the 5th Royal Tank Regiment, with its outworn cruisers, and the 6th Royal Tank Regiment (less the squadron at Beda Fomm) reorganising before moving to Beda Fomm where it was to equip itself with the captured Italian tanks.

In artillery—the only arm that could stop tanks—the force again was at half strength. Instead of six or seven field regiments—normal complement of a corps of two divisions—the frontier force had three; instead of two or three anti-tank regiments, it had only one battery. The 1st Royal Horse Artillery arrived on 10th March. The other two field regiments (104th Royal Horse Artillery and 51st Field Regiment) and the anti-tank battery ("J" Battery, 3rd Royal Horse Artillery) did not come forward until the last week of March. The 51st was equipped with first-world-war 18-pounder guns and 4.5-inch howitzers, a number of which were in workshops.[1]

The relief of Savige's brigade by Murray's was completed before midnight on 9th March. Immediately after dusk, Lieut-Colonel Marlan's[2] 2/15th Battalion and Lieut-Colonel Crawford's[3] 2/17th Battalion moved up to the Marsa Brega area. The 2/15th Battalion relieved the forward companies of the 2/5th and 2/7th Battalions half a mile north-east of

---

[7] Brig R. G. W. Rimington; comd 3 Armd Bde 1941. Regular soldier; b. 12 Nov 1891.
[8] Col D. McCorquodale, OBE; CO 1 KDG 1940-42. Regular soldier; b. 4 Apr 1902.
[9] Normal strength of the Support Group was two motor battalions, one field, one anti-tank and one light anti-aircraft regiment.
[1] At the beginning of March this unit had handed over its 25-pounder equipment to the 2/2nd Field Regiment, destined for Greece, receiving the 18-pounders and howitzers in exchange. It complained bitterly of the condition of the weapons taken over.
[2] Col R. F. Marlan, QX6175. (1st AIF: Capt 20 Bn.) CO 2/15 Bn 1940-41. Regular soldier; of St Leonards, NSW; b. Armidale, NSW, 19 Jun 1896. Died 1957.
[3] Brig J. W. Crawford, DSO, ED, NX378. CO 2/17 Bn 1940-42; comd 11 Bde 1942-43. Solicitor; of Turramurra, NSW; b. Sydney, 8 Jul 1899. Killed in aircraft accident 7 Mar 1943.

Marsa Brega while, some ten miles farther back, the 2/17th relieved the main body of the 2/7th Battalion. Lieut-Colonel Burrows'[4] 2/13th Battalion (less the company at Barce), as brigade reserve, remained in the Beda Fomm area near the coast some 13 miles south-west of the town and was ordered to provide detachments to guard important road centres.

On 11th March 9th Division headquarters arrived at Bir el Tombia to relieve 6th Division headquarters, and command passed to the 9th Division on the 12th. But when the relief was completed Morshead had in Cyrenaica only one of his infantry brigades; the other two were still in Palestine.

A small but important unit did not share in the general relief of the 6th Division: the 16th Anti-Tank Company remained to give support to the foremost troops. The company had left Tobruk at the end of February for the frontier region, where it had been placed under the command of the 3rd Armoured Brigade. The 2/1st Pioneer Battalion was another unit to remain: its headquarters were at Derna with companies engaged in engineering and repair work throughout Cyrenaica, at Benghazi, Tmimi, the Wadi Cuff and Tobruk. Also in western Cyrenaica, now engaged in engineering work from the Barce plain, north-east of Benghazi, to the frontier zone, were the 9th Division's engineers and the 2/4th Field Company.

11th March 1941

To hold so important a frontier, though but temporarily, with only one untried infantry brigade and a few light tanks, and to plan further to hold it for a prolonged period with little more while the main force of the 9th Division completed its training, were bold decisions, typical of Wavell's strategy and military direction. They were based on a reasoned, and indeed reasonable, appreciation. "My estimate at that time," Wavell told Churchill a month later, "was that Italians in Tripolitania could be disregarded and that the Germans were unlikely to accept the risk of sending large bodies of armoured troops to Africa in view of the inefficiency of the Italian Navy."[5]

---

[4] Brig F. A. Burrows, DSO, MM, ED, NX383. (1st AIF: Lt 7 Bn.) CO 2/13 Bn 1940-41; comd 1 Bde 1942-45. Business manager; of Lindfield, NSW; b. Corowa, NSW, 10 Nov 1897.
[5] W. S. Churchill, *The Second World War*, Vol III (1950), p. 179.

In the field of Intelligence, as in every other respect, Wavell was short of the means to provide a fully effective service. In obtaining information of enemy activity in Tripolitania he was handicapped in two respects: first, because the provision of Intelligence from this area had been regarded as a French responsibility until the collapse of France, for which reason the British had not established their own network of clandestine agents before hostilities opened, and second, because the increasing superiority of the German Air Force in this region severely hampered, and to a degree prevented, British reconnaissance from the air. Yet, however much Wavell and his staff may have been assailed by doubts and uncertainties, and even though they may have momentarily erred, in retrospect what is remarkable is the accuracy of their assessments of enemy strengths and the almost exact correspondence of Wavell's appreciations with the actual intentions of the German High Command. There was occasionally a time lag in obtaining information, but not a great lag; there were at times wrong estimates but not gross miscalculations of enemy strength. The real and great lack was not Intelligence but the means to counter the risks Intelligence revealed.

In one important instance, however, the time lag may have vitally affected the whole course of the war in the Middle East. On the day on which Greece accepted the British offer of an expeditionary force (23rd February), Headquarters Cyrenaica Command stated in an operational instruction addressed to General Mackay:

> At present there are no indications that the enemy intends to advance from Tripolitania. His principal effort will probably continue to be made in the air.

On the very next day, 24th February, Lieutenant Williams'[6] and Lieutenant Howard's[7] troops of the King's Dragoon Guards and Lieutenant T. Rowley's troop of anti-tank guns of the 16th Australian Anti-Tank Company were ambushed near Agheila by a German patrol of tanks, armoured cars and motor-cycle combinations. Three prisoners, including Rowley, were taken by the Germans.[8] This was the first contact on the ground between British and German forces in Africa. The Germans could not have timed it better.

Other evidence of the arrival of German and Italian reinforcements quickly accumulated and on 2nd March, while Morshead's headquarters and Murray's brigade were travelling post-haste to Cyrenaica to take over the defence of the frontier from the 6th Division, Wavell told the Chiefs of Staff that the latest information indicated that two Italian infantry divisions, two Italian motorised artillery regiments and German armoured troops estimated at a maximum of one armoured brigade group had recently arrived in Tripolitania. Wavell's comment was:

> Tripoli to Agheila is 471 miles and to Benghazi 646 miles. There is only one road, and water is inadequate over 410 miles of the distance; these factors, together

---

[6] Brig E. T. Williams, CB, CBE, DSO. 1 KDG; GSO1(Int) Eighth Army 1942-43; BGS(Int) 21 Army Gp 1944-45. Warden of Rhodes House, Oxford, since 1952. University lecturer; b. 20 Nov 1912.
[7] Capt H. R. Howard; 1 KDG. Regular soldier; b. 16 Apr 1920.
[8] Long, *To Benghazi*, pp. 285-6.

with lack of transport, limit the present enemy threat. He can probably maintain up to one infantry division and armoured brigade along the coast road in about three weeks, and possibly at the same time employ a second armoured brigade, if he has one available, across the desert via Hon and Marada against our flank.[9]

In fact Wavell was now acknowledging the possibility that he might be faced with a German armoured force twice as strong as any he himself could field. He tended, however, to underrate the danger. He gave his appreciation thus:

> He may test us at Agheila by offensive patrolling, and if he finds us weak push on to Agedabia in order to move up his advanced landing grounds. I do not think that with this force he will attempt to recover Benghazi.

Wavell added that eventually two German divisions might be employed in a large-scale attack but, because of shipping risks, difficulty of communications, and the approach of the hot weather, he thought it unlikely that such an attack would develop before the end of summer. He did not yet know who was the commander of the German force in Africa; but within a week he learned that his opponent was General Rommel, a fairly junior commander with, however, an impressive record as a tactician in both infantry and armoured warfare.

It is idle to conjecture whether Churchill, Eden, Dill and Wavell would have still offered to lend aid to Greece if they had known earlier of German intentions to send a strong armoured force to Africa, or to consider how they might then have deployed their forces. The important fact is that when the new hazards became apparent they did not change their plans. The Australian Government was not informed of the danger that now appeared to threaten one of its divisions. The oversight is easy to understand, though less easy to justify. Churchill and Wavell, and Blamey even more so, were preoccupied with the seemingly greater risks looming up in the path of the British expedition to Greece. Moreover Blamey had not at this stage adopted the practice of proffering independent advice to his Government.[10]

What enemy forces had in fact arrived in Tripolitania? And what were the German and Italian plans for the coming months? The considerations that led to the German High Command's decision to intervene in Africa and the steps taken early in 1941 to do so have been related earlier in this series.[1] Early in January, a formation to be known as the *5th Light Motorised Division* was improvised for employment in Africa by detaching units from the *3rd Armoured Division*: lacking medium or heavy tanks, it was similar to the support group of a British armoured division. Later the division's establishment was revised and strengthened, the most important addition being two battalions of medium and light tanks. For a brief period in early February, as the British westward advance in Africa continued unchecked, the Germans hesitated to proceed, fearing that their forces might arrive in Africa too late; but on 3rd February, while

---

[9] Churchill, Vol III, p. 175.
[10] See Gavin Long, *Greece, Crete and Syria* (1953), p. 20, in this series.
[1] Long, *To Benghazi*, pp. 278-80.

apparently not committing himself irrevocably to the dispatch of the whole force, Hitler directed that the move should commence; and even while the hesitancy persisted, and while the *5th Light Division* was still in process of formation, he decided that, if this formation were sent, a complete German armoured division would later be added to the force. He so informed Mussolini on 5th February. On 6th February the Commander-in-Chief of the Army, Field Marshal von Brauchitsch, instructed General Rommel to take command of the expeditionary force. His first task would be to make an immediate reconnaissance in Libya. Rommel saw Hitler on the same day and was informed that Hitler's chief adjutant, Colonel Schmundt, would accompany him on his reconnaissance.

Swift action was taken to get the German force moving. On 8th February the unloading party of the *5th Light Division* sailed from Italy; on the 10th, the first transport echelon sailed; other convoys followed in the next few days. Meanwhile the British advance had come to a halt on the Cyrenaican frontier. Anxiety lest the German division might be attacked before its assembly at Tripoli could be completed was soon allayed.

This German decision to intervene in Africa was no translation from realms of fantasy into action of Hitler's summer dream of assaulting the Middle East simultaneously from the north (through the Caucasus and Syria) and the west (through Cyrenaica). The ambition to conquer Russia had caused that grandiose project to be shelved. The intervention was made simply to stave off the danger of imminent conquest of Tripolitania by Wavell's desert force; though doubtless, when the German High Command decided to retain a foothold in Africa, it envisaged the destruction of British power in the Middle East as the eventual, if distant, outcome.

The Italian forces then in Tripolitania consisted on paper of four infantry divisions and an armoured division. But the infantry divisions comprised little more than their infantry battalions (six to a division), almost all their supporting arms having been lost in the campaign just ended, and the armoured division, *132nd (Ariete) Division,* though it had some 80 tanks, lacked anti-tank weapons, partly because of shipping losses. A fifth infantry division—*102nd (Trento) Motorised Division*—was in the process of arriving at Tripoli.

The composition of the German force to be transferred to Africa was laid down in orders issued by the Army Command on 10th February. Its fighting component was to be the *5th Light Division,* which had now become an armoured formation, but weaker than a normal German armoured division. Moreover, the German command, preoccupied with the problem of finding equipment for the coming invasion of Russia, and assuming that the division would have the comparatively passive role of constructing and holding a defensive position, had made a one-third reduction in its allocation of motor transport. Nevertheless by British standards this was a formidable formation, far stronger than the depleted 2nd Armoured Division it would oppose. It consisted of a headquarters, a tank regiment, a machine-gun regiment, a reconnaissance battalion, an artillery regiment, two anti-tank battalions, an anti-aircraft battery, an air reconnaissance unit, and supply, maintenance and other services. The tank regiment comprised two battalions, and had some 150 tanks, more than half of which were medium tanks armed with either 50-mm or 75-mm guns. The machine-gun regiment had two fully motorised battalions, each with its own engineers. One of the anti-tank or tank-hunting (*Panzer-Jäger*) battalions was armed with the 50-mm anti-tank gun, the other with the versatile 88-mm anti-aircraft gun, to be used in a ground-to-ground role, certainly the most effective tank destroyer used in the fighting in Africa. Again, the eight-wheeled armoured cars of the reconnaissance battalion outmatched, as the British were soon to discover, the Marmon-Harringtons of the King's Dragoon Guards in both hitting power and cross-country performance. Field artillery was the only major armament in which the German formation was not stronger than the British force opposing it. Moreover the German combatant units drawn from the *3rd Armoured Division* had had operational experience in Poland and France.

It was laid down that Marshal Gariboldi, who had just replaced Graziani as Italian commander in Libya, was to be Commander-in-Chief, North Africa. Rommel, though empowered to offer "advice" to the Italian commander, was to be subject to his tactical direction, but responsible to the German authorities in other respects. It was stipulated, however, that German formations were to be employed only in self-contained units of at least divisional strength under German command. On paper Rommel's responsibilities were similar to those of the commander of a Dominion contingent under Wavell. Rommel, however, was not one to measure and define his authority by referring to the wording of a staff instruction.

Rommel's character was the one decisive factor in the enemy situation that Wavell failed to appreciate correctly. Although in his fiftieth year, Rommel's vitality still burned with a scorching flame. A professional soldier who had known no other profession, nor any other interests except his home life, he had chosen the army for a career at the completion of his schooling and thereafter devoted himself to his profession with complete absorption. In the first world war, as an infantry officer, his career was distinguished by exceptional initiative and endurance. After the war he was one of the professional officers selected for retention in service when the Treaty of Versailles reduced Germany's army to a strength of 100,000 effectives and 4,000 officers. Between the wars he became an instructor at an infantry school, the commander of a mountain battalion, an instructor at a war academy, an adviser to the Hitler Youth Organisation, the commandant of another war academy, and finally the commander of Hitler's bodyguard. It is said that Hitler chose him for this appointment after reading *Infantry Attacks,* a manual on infantry tactics of which Rommel was the author and which was based on his lectures at the infantry school. Rommel held this position when the war broke out and during the campaign in Poland. Later Hitler gave him command of the *7th Armoured Division,* which he led with success in the campaign in France, adding to his reputation not only by excelling in the "lightning war" principles of mobile operations but also by his habit of personal command and leadership in the forefront of the battle.

The British Intelligence service knew the outline of his military career. When, about 8th March, it was learnt that he was the commander of the German *Africa Corps,* enough was known to conclude that here was an audacious, indeed impetuous, and able commander and a good tactician, with a flair for flank attacks. These were not unusual characteristics for a man selected to command a detached force. But the exceptional drive, the bent for taking risks, the flair for seizing opportunities and exploiting success were yet to be revealed; and if these qualities were not fully appreciated, another could scarcely have been foreseen: a penchant for acting independently of higher formation that would impel him to exceed his own personal authority, transgress the explicit orders of the German High Command and overstep the limits it laid down for the employment of his forces. So Wavell, while correctly judging what the German command intended, misjudged what their subordinate might do.

The belief current on the British side during the war that the German troops destined for Africa had received special adaptive training is not supported by the evidence.[2] There were some unfruitful experiments to devise ways of improving the wading capacity of vehicles through sand, but the only problem that appears to have received much study was the loading, unloading and transportation of armoured fighting vehicles. The first vehicles intended for Africa were not fitted with diesel engines (which desert experience later proved to be the most practical) because it was feared they might overheat; motor vehicles had twin-tyres, which caused considerable trouble because stones lodged between them. The first tanks were not equipped with oil filters. The importance of fresh food was overlooked. These and other mistakes were speedily corrected; much other improvement of equipment was undertaken in the light of experience; but the Germans did not arrive in Africa with perfected equipment. Nor had they received any special training or acclimatisation for desert conditions. On the other hand their well-tested and robust equipment was not likely to need much adaptation, nor was it likely that troops well trained in an established battle-drill and already tempered by practical experience in war should have any difficulty in accustoming themselves to a new terrain.

Rommel arrived in Rome on 11th February to consult with the German military attaché, General von Rintelen, and the Italian authorities. There he announced that the first line of defence would be at Sirte—some 150 miles west of the British advanced positions at El Agheila—and the main line at Misurata, midway between Sirte and Tripoli. Doubtless Rommel was echoing Brauchitsch's instructions.

---

[2] See Wilmot, *Tobruk,* p. 66. "On a sandy peninsula in the Baltic, he [Rommel] had found terrain which approximated that in Libya and there had worked out tactical and maintenance problems. The troops had lived and worked in over-heated barracks and artificial sandstorms, and on strictly rationed water and limited food."

On 12th February Rommel flew to Tripoli. "I had already decided," he wrote afterwards, "in view of the tenseness of the situation and the sluggishness of the Italian command, to depart from my instructions to confine myself to a reconnaissance, and to take command at the front into my own hands as soon as possible, at the latest after the arrival of the first German troops."[3] The first battle units of the German force—the reconnaissance battalion and one of the anti-tank battalions—arrived there on the 14th, only two days later. Rommel immediately ordered them forward to Sirte. On the same day, he told the German Army command that it was his intention to hold Sirte, to carry out reconnaissance raids immediately to acquaint the British with the arrival of the German force and to conduct an offensive defence with air cooperation. On 16th February, the first detachments of the *X Air Corps* arrived. It had a strength in serviceable aircraft of 60 dive bombers and 20 twin-engined fighters and in addition could call on German long-range aircraft based on Sicily. Its task was to move the airfields up as close to the front as possible and to attack both air and ground forces of the British in the forward area. On 19th February the High Command directed that the German military force in Africa should be known as the *Africa Corps*.

By the end of the month, the advanced force of the *5th Light Division* was well forward of Sirte in the En Nofilia area, with forward reconnaissance units at Arco dei Fileni, later known to the British as Marble Arch. There in the middle of the desert Air Marshal Balbo had erected a huge florid archway supporting two giant statues of the legendary Phileni brothers, to commemorate in one monument both his own construction of the Via Balbia, the magnificent coast highway spanning Italian North Africa from Tunisia to Egypt, and the patriotism in ancient times of the Phileni, whose self-sacrifice in agreeing to be buried alive, according to the legend, enabled a frontier dispute between Carthage and Cyrene to be peaceably settled. *"Dulce et decorum est pro patria mori."* What sentiment more fitting for a Fascist to extol! Arco dei Fileni was some 40 miles from the frontier at El Agheila. Spaced at intervals along 200 miles of coast road behind the advanced forces were the *Bologna* and *Pavia Divisions* (infantry), the *Ariete Division* (armoured), and the *Brescia Division* (infantry). Another division (*Savona*) and other garrison troops were in Tripoli.

Rommel had now acquainted himself thoroughly with his problem. On 1st March he issued an appreciation. It is clear that he was still thinking only in terms of resisting a resumed offensive by the British, but it is interesting to note his appreciation of the ground and how clearly he perceived the dominant tactical importance of the salt lakes west of El Agheila. The line from Marada (a desert oasis 75 miles south of El Agheila) to the salt lakes south-west of El Agheila was, he said, the ideal defence position against any attack from the east. In the north the only ground requiring to be held was a strip of land on either side of the road, which could be defended by a reinforced battalion. If a battalion

---

[3] *The Rommel Papers*, edited by B. H. Liddell Hart (1953), p. 101.

were placed in Marada, the enemy would have to use tanks to make an attack. If he attempted to thrust across the difficult terrain south of the salt lakes, he could easily be halted by a formation of the strength of the *5th Light Division* with good support from the air. "Since I cannot count on the arrival of reinforcements for several weeks," he wrote, "it appears to me to be essential (*a*) to occupy the coastal strip west of El Agheila at the most favourable point and to defend it resolutely, employing mines and mobile forces; (*b*) to occupy the area south of the salt lakes in order to interfere with enemy ground reconnaissance and, in close cooperation with the air force, to halt the advance of larger enemy forces. As yet it seems too early to occupy Marada, since the forces there are still insufficient." He added that the ultimate aim should be to occupy the El Agheila salt lakes—Marada line with about two static divisions and strong artillery and to assemble the mobile troops—"e.g. *5 Light Division, 15 Panzer Division, Ariete* and motorised divisions"—behind them for offensive defence.

On 1st March General Leclerc's Free French forces, operating from Chad Territory, took Kufra oasis. On 3rd March Rommel moved forward the advanced force of the *5th Light Division* and began the construction of a defence line in the pass 17 miles west of El Agheila, between the salt lakes and the sea; to prevent this position from being bypassed, other defences were constructed to the south. By 9th March, the day on which Murray's brigade relieved Savige's brigade at Marsa Brega, Rommel felt that the immediate threat to Tripolitania had been eliminated; on that day he suggested to the German Army Command (O.K.H.) that it might be possible to pass to the offensive before the hot weather started. He suggested three objectives: first, the reoccupation of Cyrenaica; second, northern Egypt; third, the Suez Canal. He proposed 8th May as the starting date and detailed the reinforcements he would need.

On 11th March the *5th Light Division's* armoured regiment, equipped with its tanks, completed its disembarkation at Tripoli. On the 13th Rommel moved his headquarters forward to Sirte, and on the same day ordered the occupation of Marada (on the inland flank of the El Agheila position), which reconnaissance had shown to be unoccupied. Two days later he dispatched a force south into the Fezzan, partly to allay Italian fears engendered by Leclerc's capture of Kufra oasis, but mainly to test the performance of German motorised equipment in long marches across the desert.

Meanwhile Wavell's "minimum possible force" guarded the frontier.

CHAPTER 2

DEFENCE BASED ON MOBILITY

FOR two years and a half, from the summer of 1940 to the winter of 1942, the British and Axis armies in Africa fought each other across a strip, about 600 miles long, of comparatively passable land bordered on one side by the Mediterranean, hemmed in on the other by hardly traversable sand seas and partially closed at both extremities: by salt lakes near El Agheila, and by the morass of the Qattara Depression south and west of El Alamein. On the inland flank were important oases —Gialo, Giarabub and Siwa—and Kufra deep in the desert—which attracted and supported subsidiary operations, but the crucial battles were fought within 50 miles of the sea, some much closer. Problems of supply compelled the armies to hug the coast for most of the time, their occasional sweeps inland being no more prolonged than their tactical purposes necessitated. Apart from the railway to Mersa Matruh, later extended to Tobruk, a single main road along the coast, which linked Egypt with Tripolitania and Tunisia, served as the primary supply line to both armies.

The armies and their supply columns trundling back and forth across this arid coast land had by no means an unobstructed passage. Salt lakes, sand dunes, cliff-faced wadis[1] and escarpments constricted movement in many places. In much of the desert over which the 9th Australian Division fought, a long, steep escarpment was the dominant feature. In western Egypt the main escarpment emerged from the desert near the Qattara Depression and ran westward parallel to the coast, becoming gradually steeper, until it turned north into the sea near Salum. Here, at the pass of Halfaya, the main coast road tortuously climbed up from the maritime plain to the plateau. "Bottleneck" is a good metaphor to describe this western outlet of Egypt.

Across the Libyan border the northern scarped edge of the plateau ran from Bardia through the Tobruk perimeter to Gazala, the southern edge from near Fort Capuzzo through Sidi Rezegh, Ed Duda and El Adem to the Rigel and Raml Ridges (overlooking what was to become the battlefield of Knightsbridge): farther west the ridges became less distinct and the southern edge gradually converged on the northern. The part of the northern escarpment enclosed by the Tobruk perimeter divided above the harbour so as to form two escarpment lines that parted and rejoined within the perimeter. The southern perimeter posts of the fortress were south of the escarpments and looked out across the plateau.

West of Gazala, about midway between Tripoli and Alexandria, lay the "hump" of Cyrenaica, where the "Green Mountain", the Jebel Achdar, rose from the desert, gathering winter rain to water its slopes. Girdled by the walls of two escarpments, the mountain rose precipitously in three

---

[1] Wadi, a valley or re-entrant.

terraces: from the sea in the north, where the bottom escarpment fronted the shore, and from a maritime plain in the west towards Benghazi. From the south (or inland) side the ascent was less abrupt; but the Jebel's shoulders here were rough and scarred, and dissected by many gorges. Hence the southern slopes formed a flank more easily ascended than traversed.

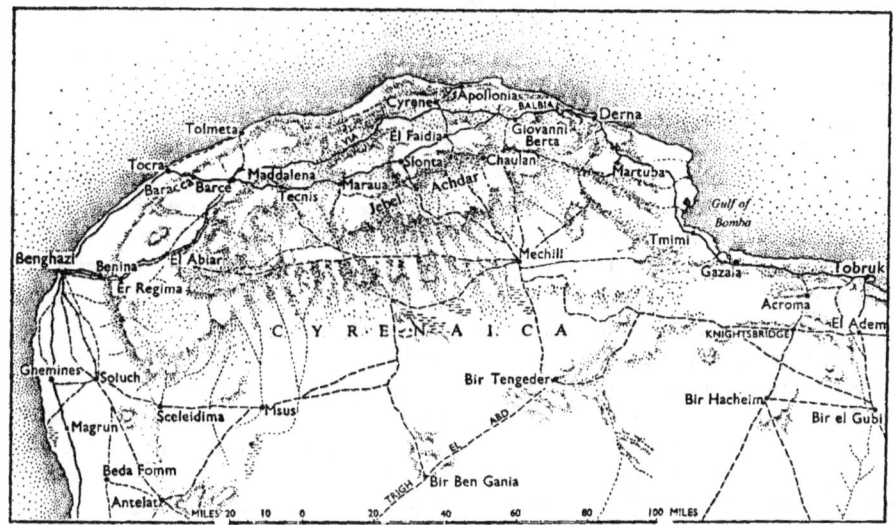

The Jebel Achdar

South from Benghazi the Jebel Achdar's rain-giving influence was lost: the maritime plain rapidly became arid. The escarpment, a wall of limestone, hemmed the plain in, running parallel to the coast for about 60 miles and gradually diminishing. There was a cleft in the escarpment at Esc Sceleidima, where it was ascended by the track and telegraph line leading to Msus. Beyond Antelat it became lost in the desert.

Along the shores of the Gulf of Sirte, from north of Agedabia to west of El Agheila, sand dunes and chains of salt lakes and marshes fringed the coast whilst the country inland was a desolate waste. Some of the salt lakes were very large, particularly those west and south of El Agheila—where Rommel had noted that they formed an ideal defensive position—and at Marsa Brega, now held by the 20th Brigade.

Several tracks, but no formed roads, traversed the Cyrenaican hinterland south of the "hump". From El Agheila the Trigh el Abd, an age-old caravan route led across the desert to the oasis of Bir Tengeder whence one track branched off northwards to Mechili whilst the main track continued northeast to link with the caravan routes coming out of Egypt. From Mechili other tracks led north (to Giovanni Berta and to Derna) and east (to the Gulf of Bomba and to El Adem).

The lie of the land had certain tactical consequences not all of which appear to have been sufficiently taken into account. The hill country of Cyrenaica was very favourable to the defence; but although a force ensconced there could threaten the flank of an army crossing the desert to the south, its own supply line would be very vulnerable. There were only two ports within the protection afforded by the Jebel Achdar's ramparts—the tiny harbours of Derna and Apollonia; these did not have the capacity to sustain a large force. So an army on the Jebel had to be sustained by road from either Benghazi or Tobruk and could only maintain itself on the mountain massif if it dominated the approaches to its supply port and line of communications. Thus it could be compelled to give battle in the desert. It must either defeat the armour of a hostile force in open warfare or block it at some defile, if a suitable one could be found.

The defile at El Agheila, which could not be outflanked except by a long march through difficult terrain, was the only place on the western approaches to Cyrenaica where overland movement was substantially constricted, so that to defend Cyrenaica from the west it was necessary either to hold the hostile force on the El Agheila line or to win a battle of manoeuvre in open country. In such a battle, infantry would be of little account: the armour would determine the issue.

When the British forces halted on the western frontier of Cyrenaica at the conclusion of Wavell's first campaign, a plan to defend the captured territory against attack from the west was made, which rested on the concept of engaging the enemy at the southern outlet of the Benghazi plain. General Wilson, writing after the war, described it thus:

> The escarpment follows the coast from east of Benghazi southwards . . . and loses itself gradually as it nears Antelat where there is easy rolling desert offering excellent scope for a tank battle: nearer the frontier the country is too flat and marshy while to the south difficulties with deep sand are encountered. I recommended that the defence of Benghazi should be from a flank pivoted on the end of the escarpment and that for this the line of supply to Msus and thence south of the Green Mountain should be maintained.[2]

Later the plan was modified, at General Blamey's suggestion, by advancing the line to Marsa Brega. Wilson's scheme of defence was evolved when the superiority of the British armour over any the Italians could field was incontestable. Its hypothesis was that the armour could invite and win a battle in the open country between Antelat and Agedabia: both El Agheila and Marsa Brega were regarded as only outpost lines. But the concept of pivoting the defence on the Antelat escarpment lingered on in later plans developed after the situation had vastly changed. On 23rd February, the day before first contact was made with German ground forces, Cyrenaica Command headquarters instructed General Mackay (then in command of the force on the frontier) that the role of the forward troops in the unlikely event of the enemy's adopting the offensive would be to delay him until reinforcements could be brought up, and that, in accordance with this policy, the 3rd Armoured Brigade would assemble at Antelat while the remainder of the 6th Division

---

[2] Lord Wilson, *Eight Years Overseas 1939-1947* (1950), pp. 63-4.

(that is, other than the brigade at Marsa Brega) would be brought up east of the Antelat-Sceleidima escarpment; from this area both formations would attack the enemy in flank or rear should he continue his advance.[3] The instruction was not changed when the arrival of German forces was confirmed, nor when their strength was ascertained.

When General Morshead succeeded to General Mackay's responsibility, he lost no time in acquainting himself both with the units committed to his command and with the territory to be defended. He visited, in turn, the forward infantry, the armour in the forward area and the army-cooperation squadron operating from the airfield at Agedabia (No. 6 Squadron, R.A.F.). He viewed the situation he found with some apprehension. The aircraft of the cooperation squadron reported a constant increase of enemy vehicles near the frontier while other aircraft, investigating at longer range, disclosed considerable shipping activity in Tripoli Harbour, also ships moving to the small ports east from Tripoli. German aircraft were becoming increasingly aggressive; Morshead's own headquarters were compelled by bombing attacks to execute a short move. The armoured cars of the King's Dragoon Guards were being persistently bombed and machine-gunned. Their patrols continued to report increased ground activity near the frontier, though on 13th March a patrol reported that Marada oasis appeared to be unoccupied. On the same day, Lieutenant MacDonald[4] of the 2/15th Battalion, with a sergeant and eight men, and an escort of two armoured cars from the King's Dragoon Guards, travelled about 45 miles into the desert and patrolled the south-western approaches to El Agheila. Although they met no enemy they saw trails left by reconnoitring tanks. Australian engineer patrols of the 2/3rd Field Company led by Lieutenant Bamgarten[5] which were reconnoitring for water to the south-west deep into the desert, even beyond Marada, brought back similar reports. On the 14th, the King's Dragoon Guards captured a lone German airman in the desert who contended that he had parachuted from a plane that crashed into the sea. From him it was learnt that the enemy had laid a deep minefield astride the coast road about 15 miles west of El Agheila.

Morshead knew that in the estimation of Wavell's headquarters it was probable that a complete German armoured brigade had arrived in Tripolitania, including a regiment of tanks (at least 150 tanks, probably 240), and that it was thought new arrivals might possibly bring the German formation up to the strength of a complete armoured division.[6] Moreover the appreciation of Middle East headquarters was that the enemy was likely to initiate an early offensive reconnaissance against El Agheila and seize it, if he found the opposition weak, as an advanced base for future operations. Morshead's own strength near the frontier was a light-tank

---

[3] Cyrenaica Command Operation Instructions Nos. 2 and 3.
[4] Brig A. L. MacDonald, OBE, QX6229. 2/15 Bn; BM 14 Bde. CO 3 Bn RAR, Korea, 1953-54. Regular soldier; of Brisbane; b. Rockhampton, Qld, 30 Jan 1919.
[5] Maj A. E. Bamgarten, NX3539. 2/3 Fd Coy; OC 2 Fd Coy 1943-45. Mining engineer; of Carcoar, NSW; b. Tumbarumba, NSW, 23 Dec 1907.
[6] GHQ ME Intelligence Summary 10 Mar 1941 reproduced in 9 Div Intelligence Summary 19 Mar 1941.

regiment, an armoured car regiment, and an infantry brigade, with another tank battalion in process of equipping itself with captured Italian tanks of doubtful value. This force, observed Lloyd, his chief staff officer, in a report written a week later, was "completely without hitting power". It lacked the strength even to fight for information by aggressive reconnaissance. In weapons of passive defence (excepting field artillery) it was no better provided: there were only 15 anti-tank guns (nine 2-pounders and six Bredas) and 19 light anti-aircraft guns (16 Bofors and 3 Bredas) in the whole frontier region. Moreover the vital defile west of El Agheila had not been secured nor were any ground troops holding El Agheila itself. Major Lindsay[7] of the King's Dragoon Guards took an armoured car patrol up to the fort at El Agheila each morning at first light but retired at dusk.

There was much else to concern Morshead. Not only was the frontier force too small; in every branch there were deficiencies of equipment. Every unit, every service was short of motor transport and the deficiencies were becoming progressively worse because the few vehicles possessed were overworked and spare parts were lacking to maintain them. "Two lorries sent to Tobruk . . . several days ago to get essential spares came back with a speedometer cable only," wrote Lloyd, on 26th March. Because of enemy bombing, Benghazi had not been used as a supply port since 18th February: all supplies had now to be brought up by road from Tobruk, a distance of over 400 miles from the forward area. In second-line transport the division had been provided with only one echelon of a divisional supply column:[8] this, it was thought, should suffice for the daily requirements of an estimated force of one brigade (with divisional troops). However, the task involved a turn-around of 150 miles a day, half of it made in the dark hours and half in the daylight when attack from the air was likely—and no day passed without a strafe along the Benghazi-Agedabia road, called "bomb alley" by the Australians. The strain was telling, not only on the vehicles, but on the men.

Just as serious was the lack of equipment for the signals sections. Colonel C. H. Simpson, the Chief Signals Officer of I Australian Corps, had told Lloyd in Cairo that the situation in the forward area could be dealt with by the signal sections of the infantry brigades and a small detachment for divisional headquarters. On arrival it was found that in the provision of signals equipment (as in the case of motor spares) the requirements of the force for Greece had been given absolute priority. "We arrived," Lloyd reported, "with a detachment of No. 1 Company consisting of one officer and 12 other ranks possessing three W/T sets, six telephones, three fullerphones,[9] two switchboards and one mile of cable. These stores were obtained mainly by theft." The battalions had also left Palestine without signals equipment. But the personnel of signals

---

[7] Lt-Col M. J. Lindsay, DSO; 1 KDG. Regular soldier; b. 20 Jul 1908.

[8] An echelon was designed to bring forward a division's daily requirement of supplies from the depots (normally adjoining railhead or roadhead) on every second day, two echelons keeping the division continuously supplied.

[9] Conversations on ordinary telephones can frequently be intercepted through induction by a close enemy using special equipment: fullerphones are secure against this.

sections did not lack initiative; each battalion section had "acquired" much essential equipment. In a note written in Tobruk about two months later, one commanding officer remarked: "There has never been a phone issued to the battalion, yet we have over 20 miles of wire and 16 sets of phones working (all Italian), found, repaired and installed by my own personnel."[1]

The methods of unauthorised acquisition were various. At Tobruk, near Derna, and north of Agedabia, large quantities of abandoned Italian equipment littered the countryside, much of it collected into temporary dumps pending removal to depots, some of it lying where the original owners left it. As the units of the division paused at these places on their westward journey to the frontier, "scrounging" parties scoured the country and the dumps, searching for, and appropriating to themselves, not only personal perquisites but essential fighting equipment. The diarist of the 2/17th Battalion wrote of his unit's halt near Agedabia on 9th March, where it was waiting until the fall of darkness would permit its forward move to Marsa Brega: "The day is spent by the battalion fossicking in the area of the dumps. . . . Valuable equipment is secured here to assist the battalion, which is alarmingly ill-equipped—three motor-cycles, some hundreds of camouflage sheets, several Breda and Fiat guns, ammunition, tools and many odds and ends." A less commendable method of drawing stores is revealed in the diary kept by a member of a unit responsible for repairing vehicles and equipment close to the front. The setting is Benghazi:

> The R.A.O.C. were on the job sorting out the spares that were of value to the army and had a huge stock neatly labelled and stacked in bins ready for removal to the base. Here was a God sent opportunity for the boys and did they avail themselves of it. It was a common thing for one to keep the Tommy in charge in conversation or otherwise keep him occupied while several others raided the store. . . . It was all in a good cause and the unit was much better fitted up than most others.

Lloyd meanwhile was doing his best to remedy the deficiencies in the proper manner, but without immediate success. He made strong representations to A.I.F. headquarters at Alexandria. He could draw little consolation from their reply that the shortage of motor spares would be relieved "by shipment on water from Australia", nor from the action taken to provide signallers. The personnel of the divisional headquarters signals section were sent to Cyrenaica, but without signals equipment or motor transport or even cooking gear. Their war equipment reached Mersa Matruh by ship on or about 26th March! In the meantime, the best that could be done was to billet them in the rear, near Gazala. In the infantry the deficiency of mortars and anti-tank weapons was serious. Some shortages were made good with captured weapons but to what extent cannot be determined.

Although the plans of Cyrenaica Command prescribed only delaying actions at Marsa Brega as a prelude to giving battle on the plains before Antelat, Morshead believed that the El Agheila defile was the key to the defence. When he visited the 2/17th Battalion on 16th March, he expressed

---

[1] War diary, 2/23 Bn, Mar-Apr 1941.

the opinion (as the diarist of that unit noted) that the forward infantry were too far from the enemy. He was also very worried that means were not available to prevent encirclement of his battalions, nor to move them if threatened with encirclement. In the meantime he had been ordered to hand over command in the forward area to the 2nd Armoured Division, but to leave Murray's brigade at Marsa Brega and Beda Fomm under the armoured division's command. He committed his thoughts to paper. In a memorandum written on 17th March and addressed to General Neame (but never delivered, for reasons which will appear) he reviewed the current situation and defence policy, and requested that the 20th Brigade should be relieved. The brigade's armament, he pointed out, was far from complete. Against a mobile armoured enemy it would be practically immobile. If a German armoured formation advanced, the brigade's presence in the forward area would only embarrass the 2nd Armoured Division by restricting its mobility and liberty of action. He submitted that it should be moved to the Benghazi-Barce area to execute work on defences already contemplated there. In addition he made pertinent comments on the defensive policy of Cyrenaica Command:

> The capture and retention of the defile on the Tripolitanian frontier . . . I consider to be the basis of the successful defence of the present forward area. . . . I understand that administrative considerations precluded the occupation of this defile in the first instance but I am of opinion that it may not be too late now to consider its execution. . . .
> Cyrenaica Command Operation Instruction No. 3 . . . contemplates a defensive battle in the area between Agheila and the general line Ghemines-Soluch. I am of opinion that having regard to the force available the area in question is unsuitable for a defensive battle. The instruction proceeds . . . to direct troops in the forward area to delay and harass the enemy without becoming seriously committed. For the reasons set out above 20 Aust Inf Bde cannot avoid being seriously committed if retained in the forward area.

On the very day that Morshead wrote this memorandum he was unexpectedly summoned to meet General Dill and General Wavell, who had flown to Neame's headquarters and with him were motoring down the coast road towards the frontier. As soon as Dill and Wavell met Morshead at the pre-arranged point near Beda Fomm, Wavell asked him for his appreciation. This he gave in the terms of the memorandum he had just composed, urging that the frontier defence should be based on the line of salt lakes from El Agheila to Maaten Gheizel and requesting that his unmotorised infantry should be withdrawn. Dill commented that he understood that the Marsa Brega position was well suited to the defence. Morshead replied that there were no more features in the surrounding country than on a billiard table. Wavell, turning to Neame, asked him to relieve the 20th Brigade in accordance with Morshead's request. Neame said that it could be arranged in about a week. "In a week," Morshead replied, "it cannot wait a week. Not a day can be lost."[2] Back in Cairo next day, Dill telegraphed similar views to London. The outstanding

---
[2] British records agree that Wavell gave this instruction. The detail of the conversation is based on statements of Morshead to the author in March 1955.

fact, he said, was that between El Agheila and Benghazi the desert was so open and so suitable for armoured vehicles that, other things being equal, the stronger fleet would win; there were no infantry holding positions.

Wavell reported to the Chiefs of Staff (on 20th March) that an attack on a limited scale on the frontier seemed to be in preparation. He said that, if the advanced troops were driven from their present positions, it would be of no use to hold positions south of Benghazi. For administrative reasons, only a limited enemy advance was likely.[3]

Preparations were meanwhile well advanced for the assault on Giarabub, a desert oasis south of Salum where an Italian garrison, bypassed by the earlier British offensive, still held out, receiving supplies by air. The 18th Australian Brigade (Brigadier Wootten) was poised to deliver the final blow. On his return from Cyrenaica Wavell authorised the attack to proceed. On 21st March Giarabub was captured:[4] the last offensive action the British would take in the desert for many days.

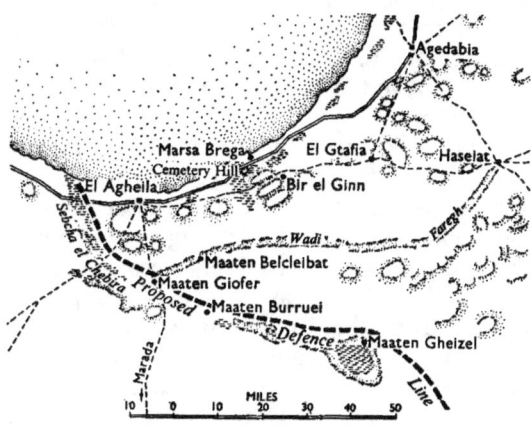

Morshead's proposed defence line

General Wavell's departing instructions to General Neame had been to the effect that if the enemy attacked he was to fight a delaying action to the escarpment east of Benghazi without permitting his forces to become committed; he was even to evacuate Benghazi if the situation demanded, provided that he held on to the high ground on the escarpment to the east for as long as possible.[5]

Major-General M. D. Gambier-Parry, who had in February been recalled from command of the British troops in Crete to take charge of the 2nd Armoured Division, had already arrived in the forward area. At midday on 20th March he took over responsibility for the frontier troops from Morshead, who then moved his headquarters to the vicinity of El Abiar, an inland village on the plateau above Benghazi at the southern end of the Barce plain. The relief Morshead had requested was then arranged. The Support Group of the 2nd Armoured Division was to relieve the 20th Brigade. The 1st and 104th Regiments, Royal Horse Artillery, were allocated to the forward area while the 51st Field Regiment was allotted to the 9th Division. To conceal the change of dispositions from the enemy and safeguard the troops from air attack, the relief was to take place at night. Wireless silence, already imposed, would be continued.

[3] Churchill, Vol III, p. 178.
[4] Long, *To Benghazi*, pp. 287-303.
[5] Wavell despatch, para 24; Neame, p. 268.

The 1/Tower Hamlets Rifles was brought forward from Benghazi and on the harshly-cold moonless night of 22nd March the three Australian infantry battalions were taken back in draughty trucks to the plateau east of Benghazi. The convoy to lift the 2/13th Battalion overshot the meeting point, attracted enemy attention, was heavily attacked from the air, and got back to the battalion only just before dawn, which necessitated a dangerous but uneventful journey back by day. Simultaneously the 51st Field Regiment began moving up from Gazala to join the 9th Division and on 24th March the 104th R.H.A. (less one battery already at Marsa Brega) moved forward from Tecnis to join the Support Group in the forward zone.

Meanwhile other movements were taking place to build up both divisions. The 9th Division's engineers, who had been employed directly under Cyrenaica Command since mid-January, were placed under Morshead's command and began rejoining the division: the 2/7th Field Company from the Agedabia area and the 2/13th from Maddalena. The 2/3rd Field Company remained temporarily in the forward zone. The 2/4th—from the 7th Division—was to move back to Mersa Matruh to join the 18th Brigade.[6] The headquarters and two battalions (2/24th and 2/48th) of the 26th Brigade, less one company of the 2/48th detached for garrison duty at Derna, were meanwhile encamped at Ain el Gazala, while the third battalion (2/23rd) had remained at Tobruk. The 24th Brigade (two battalions only) arrived at Mersa Matruh from Palestine on 24th March. Brigadier A. H. L. Godfrey, who had succeeded Brigadier Plant to its command, joined it there. On the 26th it arrived in Tobruk. On that day Brigadier Tovell's headquarters, the 2/24th Battalion (Major Tasker,[7] temporarily in command), and two companies of the 2/23rd Battalion (under Captain Spier[8]) left Ain el Gazala to join the division in the forward area. Another company of the 2/23rd went to Derna, while the remaining company and the 2/48th Battalion were engaged in guarding (and evacuating) prisoners of war at the cages at El Adem and Tobruk. Meanwhile the 5th Royal Tank Regiment, the only battalion of the armoured brigade equipped with cruiser tanks, was dispatched from El Adem to the front, some 400 road-miles distant. "The latter of course should have been forward all the time," wrote Lloyd on 26th March, "and may possibly not get up on time."[9]

As the 5th Royal Tank Regiment moved up, its worn-out cruisers broke down at an alarming rate. The light tanks were in scarcely better shape. A technical officer reported that it was hardly worth while putting new engines into most of them, because the gear boxes and transmissions were so badly worn. The 3rd Hussars had now about 30 light tanks

---

[6] The 2/4th Field Company left Barce on 26th March and arrived at Mersa Matruh on the 29th. Later it was to accompany the 18th Brigade to Tobruk, where it came under command of the 9th Division during the siege.
[7] Lt-Col H. McK. Tasker, MBE, VX47925. 2/24 Bn; CO 47 Bn 1942-43; comd Milne Bay Sub-Area 1943; BBCAU 1945. Schoolmaster; of Hawthorn, Vic; b. Seymour, Vic, 29 Sep 1900. Died Sep 1958.
[8] Maj P. E. Spier, ED, VX48398; 2/23 Bn. Architect; of Heidelberg, Vic; b. Charters Towers, Qld, 2 Feb 1909.
[9] Liaison letter No. 1, 9 Aust Div.

but it was planned to withdraw some from this unit to equip one squadron of the 6th Royal Tank Regiment. The aim was to equip these two units as follows:

> 3rd Hussars—2 squadrons of light tanks, one squadron of Italian M13's.
> 6th Royal Tank Regiment—1 squadron of light tanks, 2 squadrons of M13's.

In the meantime one squadron was withdrawn from the 3rd Hussars to exchange its light tanks for M13's, and as each squadron of the 6th Royal Tank Regiment received its equipment of Italian tanks it was placed under command of the 3rd Hussars. The process of equipment with captured tanks was not completed when the crisis arose and this dubious, improvised organisation was still in force.

By contrast, the Marmon Harrington armoured cars of the King's Dragoon Guards, driven by their 30 horse-power Ford V8 engines, were mechanically reliable, though their springing was not equal to the strain of cross-desert running. But they were weakly armed and armoured. Their only weapons, for a crew of four, were one Bren light machine-gun and one Boyes anti-tank rifle (.55-inch) and one Vickers medium machine-gun mounted for anti-aircraft defence: their only protection, 6-mm armour. Such light protection left them almost defenceless against either low strafing aircraft or enemy armoured cars. Writing on 19th March of the German reconnaissance cars, the diarist of the King's Dragoon Guards commented:

> These 8-wheeled armoured cars are faster, more heavily armed with a 37-mm gun and more heavily armoured than our armoured cars. Their cross-country performance is immeasurably superior to ours over rough-going.

The weakness of the British on the ground was matched in the air. This reflected a grave shortage of aircraft throughout the whole Middle East command. There was no ideal solution to the problem of aircraft distribution. In a global war it may be beyond human power to avoid seeing problems with a local perspective. The Middle East commanders-in-chief believed that their requirements had not been sufficiently regarded. While they were not in a position to assess their theatre's needs against needs elsewhere, it may be questioned whether those who made the decisions were not unduly biased in favour of calls to meet the deficiencies closer to them.

The consequences of the provision made, whether right or wrong, were both an appalling shortage and an inferiority in quality. Gladiators and Blenheim fighters were matched against Italian CR.42's, Hurricanes against Me-110's. Headquarters Cyrenaica (Group Captain L. O. Brown) had only 30 aircraft: a squadron of Hurricanes at Bu Amud for the defence of Tobruk (No. 73 Squadron R.A.F.), a squadron of Hurricanes (only four) and obsolescent Lysanders at Barce and Agedabia for army co-operation, and a bomber squadron at Maraua. The airfield at Agedabia, which alone was in close reach of the forward troops, could not safely be used at night, a fact soon discovered and exploited by the enemy, who flew many sorties at first and last light. The Germans alone had

90 Messerschmitt fighters and more than 80 bombers in Africa, with other aircraft in Sicily on call. The Italian Air Force was by no means negligible. On 22nd March Group Captain Brown, perturbed at the ground situation, issued warning orders to prepare for a rearward move.

The General Headquarters Middle East were of opinion that the enemy was likely to attempt a limited advance in the second week of April. General Neame felt that he had been given an impossible task. On 20th March he set out what, in his opinion, were the minimum reinforcements required ("within six weeks, or less if possible") to enable him to discharge his responsibilities. He asked for two motor transport companies, additional signallers, a squadron of infantry tanks, a regiment of cruiser (medium) tanks, another motor battalion, additional artillery (field, anti-tank and anti-aircraft) and more air support, "also, if and when available a fully equipped and mobile division to replace 9 Aust Div who should garrison Tobruk and train there until fully equipped". Major-General Arthur Smith, Wavell's chief of staff, replied next day that before the end of the month or in early April a regiment and two batteries of field guns and the 3rd Indian Motor Brigade with two equipped battalions would be provided, to be followed by additional transport, but that no further reinforcements would be available in the immediate future. In reply Neame pointed out that the scheme of defence depended entirely on mobile operations by the 2nd Armoured Division which was not a mobile formation because it lacked transport, maintenance facilities and spare parts. Any large moves would involve a rapid wastage of tanks.

Neame was meanwhile doing everything possible to make the armour as mobile as possible. Since transport was short, a chain of dumps was being built up, from which it was hoped that the armour could be supplied at short range. Supplies were already available at Benghazi and Magrun and dumps were being established at Martuba, Tecnis, Msus and Mechili. This task was given first priority in the allotment of motor transport.

On 20th March, when the 2nd Armoured Division took over the forward area from the 9th Division, Neame issued a statement of policy for the defence of Cyrenaica based on the altered dispositions. It was not to be expected, he said, that the enemy would advance in force before the first week in April. If an advance were made, there were two possible routes the enemy armour might take: north, by the coast, to Benghazi; or eastwards across the desert south of the Jebel Achdar. The former was the more likely but the desert route could not be entirely ruled out; in any event, an advance by the desert would have to be accompanied by an advance through Benghazi and Derna to obtain use of the coast road for supply. The first task of the 2nd Armoured Division was to hold the Marsa Brega line and deny the area between there and the frontier to the enemy for as long as possible by active patrolling. If the enemy advanced in force, he would be delayed as much as possible; the 3rd Armoured Brigade would manoeuvre on his eastern flank "with the object of shepherding him into the plain between the sea and the escarpment running north from Antelat" and, if he continued towards Benghazi, would keep him to the plain. The 9th Division would then deny the enemy access from the plain to the escarpment east and north of Benghazi "from inclusive Wadi Gattara to the sea at Tocra", while the 2nd Armoured Division would prevent supplies from reaching him by road, block him if he attempted to move out of the plain to approach Barce or Derna in rear of the 9th Division, and protect the 9th Division's left flank. Thus if the enemy could not be held at Marsa Brega, it was intended to allow him access, if need be, to Benghazi and the surrounding plain; but the escarpment was to be held so that he would be contained in the *cul-de-sac* formed by the convergence of the escarpment on the coast to the northeast of Benghazi. The armour meanwhile, pivoted on Antelat, would harry his flank and rear.

This was an evolution of Wilson's scheme, but with the emphasis on evading rather than seeking an armoured engagement. The concept of "shepherding" the enemy armour had a wishful ring. Its postulate was ability to deploy armour in sufficient strength to compel a hostile force to conform: the paramount fact, in the situation as known, was that such strength was lacking. If the armour could not block the enemy at Marsa Brega, it could hardly prevent him from bypassing the Antelat position by the Trigh el Abd route, provided that he could muster the supply facilities to use it.

Whether, as Morshead proposed, the defile at El Agheila could have been effectively defended was not put to the test. Wavell wrote later that he had given orders for it to be occupied (to whom, or when the orders were given is not stated); but he added that it proved impossible to carry out the maintenance of the force there.[1] It was true that Neame's whole force could not be maintained at El Agheila. Nor could less than the whole have done much to block a determined German thrust. But the problem was not whether a decisive engagement with the entire force committed should be sought there or elsewhere; it was whether the attempt to establish an effective if only temporary block should be undertaken at El Agheila or Marsa Brega. El Agheila fort is 25 miles south-west of Marsa Brega; the defile through the salt lakes (so narrow that only a small part of the force could have been stationed there) another 15 miles: 40 miles in total. The distance from Tobruk, the supply port, was some 450 miles by the coast road. Was this extension of the supply route critical? There were other factors: wastage through greater exposure to air attack; the difficulty, if the 2nd Armoured Division's supply line were to be thus extended, of building up dumps in rear against a possible withdrawal; a greater danger that the escape route might be closed. In the outcome no force of consequence was placed at El Agheila. The armour was tied to supply dumps farther back. The enemy came through the front gate of Cyrenaica while the frontier watch-dog was chained at Marsa Brega.

Nevertheless Neame and Gambier-Parry took steps to establish a permanent outpost at El Agheila. The force operating forward from Marsa Brega consisted of the 1st King's Dragoon Guards (stationed two

---

[1] Wavell despatch, para 23.

miles east of Marsa Brega with a squadron to the south at Bir el Ginn), with under command, three guns of the 2/3rd Australian Light Anti-Aircraft Regiment, three guns of the 37th Light Anti-Aircraft Regiment and two guns of the 16th Australian Infantry Anti-Tank Company (Lieutenant Simpson[2]). They kept a northern patrol in the El Agheila area and a southern patrol near Maaten Giofer, each comprising one armoured car and one gun of the anti-tank company. Larger patrols were from time to time organised for specific tasks. On 20th March Gambier-Parry arranged for a platoon of the 1/Tower Hamlets Rifles (then ensconced in the Marsa Brega position) to guard El Agheila fort by night. Lieutenant Cope,[3] whose platoon had been selected, reconnoitred the area and recommended that the patrol should be stationed south of the fort, to keep watch on the Giofer track and prevent the enemy's approach from that direction. Cope took his platoon out to this position on the 21st. A plan was then worked out to establish an ambush on ground west of the fort, close to the defile through the salt lake; two troops of the King's Dragoon Guards were to cooperate with Cope for the operation, which was set down for 24th March. Accordingly on 22nd March Major Lindsay's "C" Squadron of the Dragoons relieved Cope's platoon, which, however, left one section to guard the southern approach.

On 23rd March Lieutenant Weaver[4] of the 1st King's Dragoon Guards patrolling near Giofer with two armoured cars and an anti-tank gun of the 16th Anti-Tank Company manned by Corporal Kennedy's[5] section surprised at breakfast a small German force which was on the way to Marada oasis. Two or three armoured cars, two or three tanks, four field guns and from fifteen to twenty motor vehicles were seen. The British patrol was at first not sure whether this force was friend or enemy, but when Kennedy fired a round over their heads, the reaction dispelled the uncertainty. The anti-tank gunners then opened up, firing at about 1,000 yards' range, and knocked out two vehicles in about a minute while Weaver's two armoured cars parted and attacked the enemy at speed from either side. The Germans mounted their vehicles and made off. The Australian gunners, continuing to engage, knocked out a third vehicle at an extreme range of about 2,500 yards although the sights of their 2-pounder gun were calibrated to only 1,800 yards. Some enemy armoured cars later turned and stalked the British patrol; but Weaver succeeded in evading them and remained in the area until the afternoon.

The Axis forces also had designs on El Agheila but were planning a larger operation than the British. The German staff now knew that "green" formations had replaced the British forces that had routed Graziani's army. From the recent imposition of wireless silence and other

---
[2] Capt A. M. Simpson, NX3863. 2/1 Bn, 16 A-Tk Coy. Journalist; of Sydney; b. Glasgow, Scotland, 1 Mar 1910. Killed in action 20 Nov 1942.
[3] Maj J. F. Cope, MC; Tower Hamlets Rifles. B. Hackbridge, England, 12 Dec 1911.
[4] Lt M. H. Weaver; 1 KDG. Barrister and politician. Killed in action Oct 1941.
[5] Sgt M. J. Kennedy, MM, NX1551. 2/2 Bn, 16 A-Tk Coy, 2/1 A-Tk Regt, NG Air Warning Wireless Coy. Farm hand; of Gloucester, NSW; b. Barrington, NSW, 31 Jan 1919.

signs they had surmised that the British were withdrawing part of their force from the forward area. On 18th March Rommel left Africa by air to report to the German High Command; but before leaving he ordered that plans should be made for an operation to seize the eastern outlet of the El Agheila defile on 24th March. On the 19th he saw Hitler, General Brauchitsch and the Chief of the General Staff, General Halder, at Hitler's headquarters. He told Hitler that the British were thinking defensively and concentrating their armour near Benghazi, intending to hold the Jebel Achdar area. He asked for reinforcements, contending that it would not be possible to bypass the hump of Cyrenaica by attacking along the chord of the arc in the direction of Tobruk without first defeating the British in the Jebel Achdar. Hitler and Brauchitsch replied that the *15th Armoured Division,* due to be dispatched in May, was the only reinforcement Rommel could expect. When it arrived he was to make a reconnaissance in force to Marsa Brega, attack the British around Agedabia and possibly take Benghazi; but he was to adopt a cautious policy in the meantime. The German High Command had its eyes on other commitments: Greece and Crete. And Russia. Rommel later recorded that he "pointed out that we could not just take Benghazi, but would have to occupy the whole of Cyrenaica, as the Benghazi area could not be held by itself".

Restless and impetuous though he was, there is no evidence that when Rommel flew back to Africa with instructions to bide his time, he contemplated undertaking instead an immediate general offensive or that he even thought he was strong enough to do more than exploit a local disparity of strength. In fact he was using dummy tanks to create an illusion in his opponents' minds of a strength that he lacked. (Neame was doing likewise.) It is hardly likely that Rommel assumed that an enemy which, during his absence in Europe, had attacked and taken Giarabub, would not stand and fight. The German *Africa Corps'* estimate of the British battle order in the Marsa Brega-Agedabia area was of a force not materially differing in strength from the German component of Rommel's force. The estimate, though inaccurate in detail,[6] was in summation a reasonably close approximation to its actual strength, though the British formations had weaknesses not ascertainable until they were engaged.

But Rommel was not one to stand idly by while waiting for the *15th Armoured Division* to arrive. His planning had heretofore been complicated by two divergent aims: attacking the British position near Marsa Brega, and preparing an operation to relieve the Giarabub garrison. The fall of Giarabub had left him free to concentrate on the frontier operations. The *5th Armoured Regiment's* tanks had arrived: 90 medium and 45 light tanks, all in the forward area. Enough petrol was held for an advance of about 400 miles. On his return to Africa on 23rd March, Rommel immediately ordered the attack on El Agheila to proceed on the following day. Its capture would both provide him with a forward

---

[6] The infantry strength was overestimated, the artillery underestimated. The tank strength was assessed as one armoured battalion.

base for a later general offensive and alleviate his immediate water-supply problems. The task was assigned to the *3rd Reconnaissance Unit*, supported by artillery and machine-gun detachments and a company of tanks.

The 24th March, it will be remembered, was the day on which the British command had planned that Cope's platoon should occupy an ambush position west of El Agheila. On the 23rd, the R.A.F. discovered that the enemy had brought into use a new landing ground in the forward area, at Bir el Merduma. The pilots also reported having seen a large enemy force moving eastward near El Agheila, including armoured cars, 20 medium tanks (reported as Italian) and artillery. That night Lieutenant Williams' troop of "C" Squadron 1st King's Dragoon Guards and Cope's platoon, with one of Simpson's anti-tank guns, spent the night 1,000 yards west of the fort. The plan was that Cope should report the fort clear of the enemy at 6 a.m. and then push a section forward. Meanwhile Lieutenant Whetherly's[7] troop (of "A" Squadron, King's Dragoon Guards, which was to relieve "C" Squadron that day) would patrol to the intersection of tracks 12 miles to the south and report it clear. When Cope's report was received, Williams' patrol was to move up to the ground secured by Cope's section. A troop of "B/O" Battery of the 1st Royal Horse Artillery was to give support.

Accompanied by Williams' patrol, Cope approached El Agheila fort at first light in a truck, dismounted and went forward towards the fort on foot. Suddenly he saw that it was occupied by the enemy. "He shot two and ran for his life, reaching his truck to get away in a hail of bullets," wrote "C" Squadron's diarist later. Guns from the fort then opened fire on Williams, who had just observed tanks approaching from the south. Williams withdrew his car behind a mound and brought the anti-tank gun into action. An enemy armoured car topped the rise: both cars and the gun opened fire simultaneously. The enemy car was hit and put out of action; but the Australian gunner was killed and the corporal wounded.

Williams withdrew his patrol to squadron headquarters, obtained another anti-tank gun, and moved out to a position covering the squadron. Whetherly had meanwhile reported 10 enemy tanks and 20 motor vehicles just east of the fort. Soon afterwards the Italian flag was hoisted there. And that evening the King's Dragoon Guards' squadrons retired to the Marsa Brega area. The gateway between Tripolitania and Cyrenaica was in Rommel's possession. "This rather altered arrangements," commented the diarist of the 1st R.H.A.

In the occupation of this most important position, the only losses suffered by the enemy were those inflicted by Cope himself, the armoured car, and the anti-tank gunners, and damage caused to two tanks that ran on to mines.

The enemy exploited no farther forward for several days; but the landing ground at El Agheila was brought into immediate use. The Marsa

---

[7] Maj R. E. Whetherly, MC; 1 KDG. B. London, 23 Jul 1916. Killed in action 27 Nov 1943.

Brega position, which had now become the British foremost line of defence, had several weaknesses. It was overlooked by a feature known as Cemetery Hill, which was beyond the salt lakes that gave frontal protection to the line. Rolling sand dunes near the shore provided a covered approach to its right flank while the left flank could be encircled not only immediately to the south of the salt lakes but also by a wider turning movement in the desert south of the Wadi Faregh, where the going was good for vehicles. The front, which was eight miles wide, was to be held by one battalion and one company of motorised infantry. The minefield in front was now primed and the armoured cars of the King's Dragoon Guards came in behind it. The armoured brigade guarded the left flank at the edge of the salt lakes while, farther south, a squadron of the Dragoon Guards established a standing patrol at Maaten Gheizel to watch for a deep turning movement from Marada.

For a few days there was no contact with the enemy. There were frequent "khamsins"—dust-charged windstorms that swept off the Sahara, blotted out both sky and sun, and sometimes reduced visibility to a few feet. A khamsin raged on the 26th, on the 27th the wind blew harder; on the 28th it subsided. The first ground contact with the enemy after the loss of the frontier occurred on the 29th at Maaten Belcleibat, on the Wadi Faregh outlet from El Agheila, where Lieutenant C. F. S. Taylor's troop of the Dragoon Guards encountered two German eight-wheeled armoured cars. The stronger German vehicles gave pursuit and in the running fight one of Taylor's cars was knocked out. Enemy tanks were also seen that day at El Agheila and the German Air Force's strafing and bombing were severe. A dive-bombing attack near Soluch completely destroyed a petrol train—a serious loss.

While at El Agheila, Marsa Brega and Beda Fomm the khamsin had reduced both desert armies to immobility, events of some importance had taken place in Europe. On 25th March, the Government of Yugoslavia had signed the Tripartite Pact; but on the 27th that government was overthrown and another, favourable to the Allies, installed under the youthful King Peter. The German Government at once ordered a simultaneous invasion of Yugoslavia and Greece. On the same day, in Eritrea, General W. Platt's forces captured the key Italian port of Keren, and in Abyssinia, General A. G. Cunningham's army occupied Harar—except for Addis Ababa the largest town in Abyssinia—so bringing closer the day when Indian divisions could be transferred from that front to the desert. The reoccupation of British Somaliland had been completed three days before. On the 28th, Vice-Admiral Sir Andrew Cunningham's battle fleet, with Royal Air Force support from Greece, intercepted an Italian fleet near Cape Matapan, sinking four cruisers and three destroyers and damaging other ships. The victory had a powerful moral effect, which probably contributed to the later failure of the Italian Navy to intervene effectively with surface vessels in the evacuations from Greece and Crete.

Wavell's written instructions confirming his oral orders to Neame were dispatched from Cairo by air on the 20th but did not reach Neame until the 26th. Their underlying concept was that Neame should strive to keep his force intact rather than treat any ground as vital. "The safeguarding of your forces from a serious reverse," he wrote in the first paragraph, "and the infliction of losses and ultimate defeat on the enemy, are of much greater importance than the retention of ground. The reoccupation of Benghazi by the enemy, though it would have considerable propaganda and prestige value, would be of little military importance, and it is certainly not worth while risking defeat to retain it." He directed Neame to consider whether the position held on the frontier might be improved by advancing to the defile formed by the salt marshes west of El Agheila. Whatever the decision, Neame was to retain there only mobile covering forces, which must be able to manoeuvre rapidly in retreat if necessary. If a withdrawal became necessary, a small mobile force of infantry and guns should withdraw down the road to Benghazi, delaying the enemy and inflicting loss on him without becoming seriously engaged, while the armoured troops were to manoeuvre on his flank, taking up a position near Antelat so as to be able to keep on his flank whichever way he went. Neame was to consider whether a defensive position could be found immediately south of Benghazi; if not, he was to hold the defiles through which the railway and two roads leading east from Benghazi mounted the escarpment to the first plateau and the Barce plain.

The salient feature of these instructions was that the first phase of the defence should be an action of manoeuvre, harassment and quick disengagement, a role in which the 2nd Armoured Division with its obsolescent tanks was still ill-starred. Wavell afterwards wrote that he did not become aware of the dangerously poor mechanical state of these tanks till a few days before the enemy attack, which is comprehensible in the light of the many responsibilities he was shouldering.[8] Nevertheless he had been forewarned when the tanks had first arrived in Egypt.

When Churchill learnt that the Germans had taken El Agheila, he asked Wavell for an appreciation of the situation. Churchill's telegram expressed concern at the "rapid German advance to El Agheila".

> It is their habit to push on whenever they are not resisted. I presume you are only waiting for the tortoise to stick his head out far enough before chopping it off. It seems extremely important to give them an early taste of our quality.[9]

Wavell replied on the 27th that there was no evidence yet that there were many Germans at El Agheila. The force was probably mainly Italian with a small stiffening of Germans. Wavell admitted to having taken a considerable risk to provide the maximum force for Greece, with the result that he was weak in Cyrenaica; moreover no reinforcements of armoured troops, which were his chief need, were available. The next month or two would be anxious; but the enemy had a difficult problem. He was sure that their numbers had been exaggerated.

---

[8] Wavell despatch, para 23.
[9] Churchill, Vol III, p. 178.

Meanwhile, on the plateau east of Benghazi, the 9th Australian Division was making ready to defend the escarpment and its passes and to deny the enemy access from the plain, should he choose to advance that way. From Benghazi two roads led up the first escarpment, climbing through passes at Er Regima and near Tocra to the intermediate plateau. Two roads also mounted the second escarpment through passes near Barce and near Maddalena. Both roads proceeded to traverse most of the tableland by winding but approximately parallel routes, then converged, and from the junction one trunk road led on to Giovanni Berta. Thence the main coast road proceeded to the port of Derna, descending the escarpment to the harbour and mounting it again just beyond by two steep and tortuous passes. From the top of the eastern pass it led south-east to Ain el Gazala and to Tobruk. But the Derna passes could be bypassed by a rough track that went out from Giovanni Berta into the desert and rejoined the main road near Martuba.

On 24th March Morshead's headquarters issued written orders defining the division's task as being to hold the escarpment from the sea at Tocra to the Wadi Gattara and setting out the method by which this was to be done. The escarpment was to be defended and the passes blocked. The right sector was given to the 26th Brigade with the task of blocking the road pass near Tocra; the left sector to the 20th Brigade with the main task of blocking the road and railway at the Er Regima pass. Each brigade was to be given one composite battery of the 51st Field Regiment, comprising six 18-pounders and six 4.5-inch howitzers, and nine 47-mm Italian anti-tank guns "to be transported and fought portee". The 2/13th Field Company (less one section) was allotted to the 26th Brigade, the 2/7th (less one section) to the 20th.

On the 26th, Brigadier Murray made an aerial reconnaissance of the escarpment with his three battalion commanders, after which he allotted defence sectors to his battalions: to the 2/17th the right flank north from Er Regima, which consisted of about 20 miles of steep escarpment, ascended here and there by rough foot-tracks; to the 2/13th (which was still without one company, on security duty at Benghazi), the Er Regima pass and, on the left flank, the Wadi Gattara; to the 2/15th Battalion a defensive position near El Abiar, where an inland track led into the rear of the area occupied by divisional headquarters. Next day the three battalions took up these positions.

On the 28th Brigadier Tovell's headquarters, the 2/24th Battalion and two companies of the 2/23rd Battalion arrived from Gazala. Tovell's headquarters went to a position near Baracca, west of Barce, and the 2/24th Battalion to the Tocra area. The two companies of the 2/23rd were directed to Barce, where Captain Spier was installed as Town Major. As soon as the 2/24th arrived Lieutenant Serle[1] and the Intelligence section of the 2/24th Battalion reconnoitred the escarpment from Tocra to Tolmeta and established that it was not feasible for vehicles to ascend

---

[1] Maj R. P. Serle, VX48826; 2/24 Bn. Insurance clerk; of Hawthorn, Vic; b. Hawthorn, 18 Nov 1914.

the escarpment except by three passes: one at Tolmeta, one at Tocra, and a central one between these two. The battalion was therefore disposed with three companies forward, one covering each pass, and the fourth company stationed in reserve near battalion headquarters, just behind the Tocra pass. While the 2/24th was getting ready to block the northern passes, the engineers were putting down a field of about 700 mines in the Er Regima pass and laying charges beneath the road and railway.

The escarpment line, east of Benghazi, which had a total length of 62 miles, was thus held by three battalions, with a fourth battalion disposed on the southern flank; there were no reserves at all within close call.

On 26th March, Neame's headquarters issued a most secret instruction to Morshead informing him what positions were to be occupied if it should become necessary to withdraw from the lower escarpment. In that event the intermediate plateau was to be yielded but the defence was to be conducted from the tableland above to a plan aimed at blocking the enemy advance at two defiles. Of the two roads leading eastward from Barce and across the tableland one was to be denied to the enemy by holding the scarp and pass east of Barce; the other (northern) route, however, which was the main road, was to be blocked, not at the escarpment line but some 55 miles farther east, at the Wadi Cuff—the "valley of caves"—at a point where the road was carved into a steep hillside and crossed the watershed through a steep and wooded defile. This plan involved holding two defensive positions which, as the instruction pointed out, were tactically disconnected; it suffered from the "textbook" defect that the line of communications ran parallel to the front. The instruction also provided that if a further withdrawal became necessary, the 9th Division would fight the enemy on the general line of the Wadi Derna.

Cyrenaica Command also ordered the creation of a "military desert" in front of the line to be held by the 9th Division. At Benghazi, Magrun, Agedabia, and Msus and in the surrounding country, all military stores, wells and installations were to be prepared for demolition. Both English and Australian engineers were busily engaged on the work.

Morshead's forward units were now 100 miles from the armoured division. His complete lack of motorised troops for reconnaissance was a continual worry, and he asked to be given the 6th Division's cavalry regiment—a request that could not be granted. Moreover his only troop-carrying transport was being employed away from his control on the establishment of dumps at Msus and Tecnis. On the 27th he made representations to General Neame about these deficiencies. Neame informed him that two motor battalions of the 7th Armoured Division's Support Group were soon to arrive in Cyrenaica and that the first to come would be allotted to the 9th Division.

Morshead also pressed Neame to arrange for the early evacuation of all civilians, both Arabs and Italian colonists, from the region the 9th Division was preparing for defence. There were political difficulties in agreeing to this. After consultation with his senior political officer, Neame adopted a compromise solution of declaring certain limited areas to be prohibited zones.

On 28th March, Morshead and Lloyd inspected the left (southern) flank of the division's area and, finding the approaches open, decided to place the 1/Royal Northumberland Fusiliers (less one company with the 2nd Armoured Division) and the 24th Anti-Tank Company immediately at Bir es Sultan, astride the track leading in from the south. On the 29th it became clear that the enemy knew something of the new positions held, for the 2/13th Battalion was attacked by aircraft; five bombs were dropped on the battalion. Also on the 29th the cutting and stealing of signal wires by Arabs seriously interfered with the battalion's communications. Morshead saw the Mukhtar of the adjoining native village next day and charged him with the responsibility to have the pilfering stopped. It is doubtful whether the motive had been sabotage. The leaders of the Senussi sect, to which most Libyan Arabs belonged, were openly allied to Britain. They had raised a Libyan force of several battalions which, fighting under its own flag, was serving with the British. Libyan units were being employed at Giarabub, Tobruk and elsewhere.[2]

The division's two most serious and embarrassing shortages—of signals equipment and of motor transport—had not been in any way relieved. The headquarters signals section was still at Gazala. So serious was the deficiency of signals equipment that to a large extent use had to be made of the civilian telephone lines, which passed through the civilian-manned exchange at Benghazi. As for motor transport, the shortage made it impossible for Morshead to employ more than five of his eight battalions and even restricted the movement of those. The 2/48th Battalion was waiting at Gazala until vehicles could be found to move it up to the 26th Brigade's defence-sector. Because the division had been issued with first-line transport for only five battalions, the 24th Brigade was grounded at Tobruk.[3]

The behaviour of a garrison force towards the civilian population is commonly a matter of concern for force commanders and of worry for their staffs dealing with civil affairs, who have to endure the criticism, complaints and ill-will resulting from each instance of misbehaviour. It is only too easy to identify the character of whole units and formations with that of a few offenders and to project anger on their commanders and officers.

On 31st March Neame wrote Morshead a long letter about the conduct of Australian soldiers in towns. Alleged disorderly conduct by Australians

---

[2] See J. P. Evans-Pritchard, *The Sanusi of Cyrenaica* (1949), p. 227.
[3] First-line transport is that which "belongs" to a forward unit and is used for its internal needs. Food, ammunition, petrol and other supplies are brought to the unit's area from the rear by second-line transport, whence they are distributed within the battalion by its first-line transport. Other uses of first-line transport are:
    (a) to carry the unit's food, stores, field kitchens, etc;
    (b) to move heavier weapons, operational equipment and ammunition;
    (c) to transport key personnel and provide a means of intercommunication.
An ordinary (unmotorised) infantry unit is not provided with first-line transport for lifting the fighting personnel. It makes and breaks contact with the enemy on foot.

was a long-standing grievance of Cyrenaica Command, which had been nurtured since the beginning of the occupation. After the capture of Derna, General R. N. O'Connor had written to General Mackay charging Australian soldiers with looting and the commission of serious civil offences. The allegations were discussed earlier in this series, where it was pointed out that although some looting by small parties had occurred the town had already been looted on three separate occasions before the Australians reached it and on the other hand had been effectively policed immediately after their entry.[4] In subsequent months Cyrenaica Command made further allegations of misconduct by Australian troops to Mackay's headquarters and, in turn, to Morshead's, of which Neame's letter was the culmination. The discipline of Australian troops being a matter of internal administration, Australian commanders were responsible for its enforcement to the General Officer Commanding-in-Chief of the A.I.F. not to the local British commander.[5]

The only reasonably effective way of controlling soldiers in towns when not in formed bodies is to employ military police; but Morshead had none. When Neame wrote his letter, the division's provost company was in Tobruk. Transport to bring it forward had been requested but not provided. In the course of the letter, Neame said:

I now have to bring to your notice the fact that since I was forced to withdraw the Tower Hamlets picquets at Benghazi for urgent operational reasons, parties of Australians have entered Benghazi presumably without leave, at least I hope so, and cases of Australian drunkenness have again occurred there.

Since 20 Inf Bde of 9 Aus Div was moved to Regima area, numerous disgraceful incidents have occurred in Barce, drunkenness, resisting military police, shooting in the streets, breaking into officers' messes and threatening and shooting at officers' mess servants, even a drunken Australian soldier has come into my own headquarters and disturbed my staff. This state of affairs reached a climax yesterday Sunday 30th March, when the streets were hardly safe or fit to move in; officers of my Staff were involved in endeavouring to support the action of the military police. . . .

As I have told you in a previous letter on this subject, I consider it disgraceful that I and my Staff should have our attention and time absorbed by these disciplinary questions at a time when we have to consider fighting the Germans and Italians. . . .

I am at a loss for words to express my contempt for those who call themselves soldiers who behave thus. They have not learnt the elements of soldiering among the most important of which are discipline, obedience of orders, and soberness. And their officers are equally to blame, as they show themselves incapable of commanding their men if they cannot enforce these things.

I did not mention it the other day, but I must tell you now that the C.I.G.S. and C. in C. when visiting me here were accosted in the street by a drunken Australian soldier. I myself have had the same experience in Barce. . . .

Your Division will never be a useful instrument of war unless and until you can enforce discipline. . . . And all the preparations of the Higher Command may be rendered useless by the acts of an undisciplined mob behind the front.

I must hold you responsible for the discipline of all Australian troops in this Command, as I have no jurisdiction in the matter.

Unless an improvement can be rapidly achieved, I shall be forced to report the whole case to G.H.Q. for transmission to the Commander A.I.F.

---

[4] Long, *To Benghazi*, pp. 254-5.
[5] See General Blamey's charter, Long, *To Benghazi*, p. 100.

These were strong words to use to Morshead. Angered though he was by the threat that an adverse report would be made to Blamey and by the manner in which Neame presumed to lecture him on the importance of military discipline, Morshead's main objection to the letter was that Neame, by the tone in which he wrote and the use of such phrases as "Australian drunkenness" and "undisciplined mob" had displayed a palpably anti-Australian attitude and had gone beyond the justifiable censuring of specific cases of misbehaviour to impugn generally, in immoderate, contemptuous words, the quality, and military virtue of the officers and men whom Morshead commanded. "Why don't British M.P's arrest these men? We must have identification and charges," Morshead wrote in his diary, to which he confided his thoughts as follows:

> Without in any way condoning any offences I cannot help feeling that it is the same old story of giving a dog a bad name. And we rather sense the cold shoulder in Barce. . . .
> Take the case of the Australian pte who entered the officers' mess at Barce. He was accompanied by two British ptes. What has happened to them?

That day Morshead had asked to see Neame's senior administrative officer on another matter. Neame himself came and Morshead took the opportunity to protest. He told Neame that he objected to his anti-Australian attitude, that the same attitude had permeated to Neame's staff, and that he was forwarding the letter to General Blamey and considering forwarding it to Australia, if not to Wavell.[6]

Nevertheless Morshead caused a message to be sent immediately to all formations and units under his command placing all towns, villages and native camps out of bounds. Next day he called his senior commanders to a conference on discipline, after which a staff instruction was issued repeating earlier orders, providing a system of passes for men required to proceed to Benghazi or Barce on duty and stressing the need to restore discipline by firmness and adequate punishment.

If some censure was on this occasion deserved, it was a lapse from a high standard previously set and afterwards maintained. The formations and units then in Cyrenaica had come there with a record of good behaviour in towns and on leave.

Neame, writing after the war in his autobiography, was able to make a different assessment of the 9th Division, its commander, its officers and its men, which one may willingly suppose was as sincere as it was generous. After mentioning that the division was only half-trained and half-equipped, he added:

> Let me say at once that the 9th Australian Division fought magnificently, and was splendidly led by Morshead and his Brigadiers; and well served by its staff. I could have had no better fighting troops under me in the fighting near Benghazi.[7]

General Rommel meanwhile was less concerned with what was happening in the 9th Division's area than with what the 2nd Armoured Division

---
[6] Based on statements of Morshead to the author in 1955, and in line with diary statements of his intentions.
[7] Neame, p. 269.

was doing immediately in front of El Agheila, at Marsa Brega. "It was with some misgivings," he wrote later, "that we watched their activities, because if they had once been allowed time to build up, wire and mine these naturally strong positions, they would then have possessed the counterpart of our position at Mugtaa,[8] which was difficult either to assault or to outflank from the south. . . . I was therefore faced with the choice of either waiting for the rest of my troops to arrive at the end of May—which would have given the British time to construct such strong defences that it would have been very difficult for our attack to achieve the desired result—or of going ahead with our existing small forces to attack and take the Marsa Brega position in its present undeveloped state. I decided for the latter."[9] Again, the problem of water-supply was a second but important reason for attacking. "An operation against Marsa Brega," he wrote, "would give us access to plentiful water-bearing land." In the meantime the German Army command suggested an operation to capture Gialo oasis. This was planned as an airborne operation by a reinforced machine-gun platoon.

Preparations for an attack on Marsa Brega were put in hand. The *8th Machine Gun Battalion* was brought forward to El Agheila so that the *3rd Reconnaissance Unit* would be freed for preliminary reconnaissance. On 28th March the *5th Light Division* (with the *I/75th Artillery Regiment*) reached the area round En Nofilia, and on the 30th Rommel gave orders to its commander, General Streich, to take Marsa Brega on the next day. German reconnaissance had established that the salt marsh (on either side of the main road) near the British position was not passable but that there was a track through high dunes about six miles south of the road by which the defended area might be cut off. The plan was to advance in two columns. On the right, a small column consisting of the *2nd Machine Gun Battalion* and an anti-tank battalion was to advance by the track while the main force, consisting of the *5th Armoured Regiment*, the *8th Machine Gun Battalion* and the *3rd Reconnaissance Unit*, with artillery and anti-tank support, would advance along both sides of the main road. Two days later an attack on Gialo was to take place.[1]

On perusing Wavell's tardily-received instructions for the conduct of the defence, Neame concluded that they required no change in his own orders. In general, the written instruction was but an elaboration of the instructions Wavell had given to him orally. One elaboration was a direction that a small force of infantry and guns should hinder and delay any enemy advance by the coast to Benghazi. If this became necessary, Neame would be hard put to it to find an infantry force of sufficient strength to be effective; the entire Support Group, even if intact, would be small for the task. On 30th March Cyrenaica Command issued an

---
[8] At the defile west of El Agheila.
[9] *The Rommel Papers*, p. 107.
[1] It was later deferred because of unavailability of aircraft and subsequently cancelled as unnecessary.

operation instruction defining the roles of formations and laying down code words for the evacuation of Benghazi and the demolition of stores and installations there. The instruction was concerned with what to do if the enemy advanced but stated that there were no signs that, having taken El Agheila, he was preparing to advance farther, nor was there conclusive evidence that he intended to take the offensive on a large scale in the near future or would be in a position to do so. An Intelligence summary issued by G.H.Q. had been separately circulated in which the German force in Libya had been estimated as a divisional headquarters, a reconnaissance unit, a lorried infantry brigade, a machine-gun battalion and possibly two tank battalions. Neame was careful to impress on his commanders and forward units that, while they were to execute a withdrawal rather than become committed, they were not to withdraw unless forced to do so: orders taxing forward commanders with perhaps too fine a discrimination.

Cyrenaica Command had received several reinforcements since the fall of Agheila. The largest was the 3rd Indian Motor Brigade, now at El Adem and patrolling deeply—to Mechili (where the dumps were guarded by a company of Senussi), Bir Tengeder, and Ben Gania along the Trigh el Abd. The brigade had three motor battalions, which were equipped with a full complement of vehicles but armed only with light weapons. Wavell warned Neame of the danger of exposing them to combat with armoured troops. "A" Squadron of the Long Range Desert Group was another reinforcement. It had left Cairo on the 24th and arrived at Barce on the 30th, where its role was to watch for enemy movement eastwards, on the desert flank towards Gialo and Giarabub. Neame ordered it to establish its headquarters at Marada. Accordingly the commander, Major Mitford,[2] sent out a patrol on the next day (31st) to make a complete circuit of the oasis as a preliminary reconnaissance.

Meanwhile, as Rommel had observed, the position at Marsa Brega was being strengthened. On 26th March a company of the 1/Royal Northumberland Fusiliers (machine-gun battalion) was brought forward from Benghazi and placed under the command of the 1/Tower Hamlets Rifles (a platoon being placed in support of each forward company). On the 28th the 1st Company of the French Motor Battalion was moved forward to the left flank of the Tower Hamlets, where it replaced "A" Squadron of the King's Dragoon Guards, who were now freed for their normal operational role of reconnaissance. On the 29th "J" Battery of the 3rd Royal Horse Artillery arrived, providing some solid, if rather scanty, close gun-defence against tanks at Marsa Brega.

The 5th Royal Tank Regiment had arrived in the forward area; but owing to severe losses from mechanical breakdown on the way, there remained of its full complement of 52 cruisers, only some two dozen, all of which had covered at least 15,000 miles (some 20,000) and reached the end of their life expectancy. The process of equipping squadrons of the other two tank units with captured tanks was still proceeding.

---

[2] Col E. C. Mitford, MC. Royal Tank Regiment; LRDG. Regular soldier; b. 20 Nov 1908.

The Italian M13's were proving most unsatisfactory; the engines boiled every 10 or 12 miles, which restricted their daily radius of movement to 48 miles. The division's total strength in serviceable and semi-serviceable tanks of all kinds was 68. Moreover, as now constituted and equipped, it was a completely unexercised formation. This was particularly serious with respect to its intercommunications, for almost all of its original signallers had been given to the portion of the division sent to Greece.

By 30th March the newly-arrived units had settled down. On the right, the Support Group (Brigadier Latham[3]) held the eight miles of front within the Marsa Brega salt marshes with the Tower Hamlets (less one company) and the 1st Company of the French Motor Battalion, and with the 104th R.H.A. under command. An infantry outpost (one company of the Tower Hamlets with two sections of machine-guns) was sited on Cemetery Hill, to the front, covering an artillery observation post. One company ("D") of the Tower Hamlets was preparing a position in rear, about a mile north of Agedabia. On the left flank, the ground for about five miles south of the road was inaccessible to tanks. Beyond this, the 3rd Armoured Brigade (Brigadier Rimington) was echeloned to the north-east. Foremost were the 3rd Hussars (26 British light tanks and Italian M13's) organised into four squadrons (two manned by 3rd Hussars and two by 6th Royal Tanks personnel) with whom was Lieutenant Weir's[4] platoon of the 16th Australian Anti-Tank Company. Behind was the 5th Royal Tank Regiment. With each regiment was a battery of the 1st R.H.A. and two light anti-aircraft guns. The 6th Royal Tank Regiment was to the rear at Beda Fomm with one squadron of 6th Royal Tank Regiment personnel already manning M13 tanks and one squadron of 3rd Hussars personnel in the act of taking over their complement.

In front of the armour, patrols of armoured cars from the King's Dragoon Guards kept watch. "A" Squadron (from behind the infantry positions at Marsa Brega) sent forward two patrols daily to the El Agheila area. Another squadron guarded the left flank at the Wadi Faregh, keeping a patrol farther out at Maaten Gheizel at the end of the chain of salt lakes.

Major-General Gambier-Parry's orders to the armoured division were to the effect that if attacked in force it should withdraw on the axis Agedabia-Antelat-Msus.[5] In brief, a firm attempt to bar entry into Cyrenaica was not to be made, but the armoured brigade and the Support Group were to conform in a delaying withdrawal to a position behind Agedabia; separate withdrawal axes were prescribed for each formation and intermediate lines of resistance laid down, each with its allotted code name.

On the morning of 31st March, the northern El Agheila patrol of

---

[3] Brig H. B. Latham. (1914-18: Maj RA, Mesopotamia 1914-18, France 1918.) CO Support Group, 2 Armd Div 1940-41. Regular soldier; of London; b. Toorak, Vic, 29 Aug 1892.

[4] Capt J. H. Weir, NX333. 2/3 Bn, 16 A-Tk Coy. Regular soldier; of Mildura, Vic; b. Pyramid Hill, Vic, 20 May 1912. Killed in aircraft accident 19 Dec 1943.

[5] War diary, 104 RHA.

the King's Dragoon Guards was under command of Lieutenant Budden,[6] the southern of Lieutenant Whetherly. The latter patrol was to be accompanied by Major Pritchett's[7] squadron of the 5th Royal Tank Regiment with its four cruiser tanks—all that remained to the squadron after the rigours of the march from El Adem. At Marsa Brega, the Support Group's program for the day was one of offensive patrolling forward of the marsh, with both infantry and carrier patrols.

Pritchett and Whetherly intended to set an ambush near Maaten Giofer for some enemy tanks seen on the previous day. At first light, near the road north of Giofer, they suddenly encountered a group of German tanks. There was a brisk engagement, in which one of Pritchett's cruisers suffered damage; but more German tanks, going down this road, threatened to encircle the British patrol, and it was seen that they were followed by many lorries and several guns. Pritchett and Whetherly withdrew—with the German tanks in pursuit; there was another short engagement near the salt marsh east of El Agheila; then the German tanks turned south along the marsh, leaving the British patrol to return unmolested. Budden, however, remained out near El Agheila, among the dunes, whence he reported to headquarters the eastward movement of a huge German force rolling past him towards Marsa Brega.

It was at 7.45 a.m. that the infantry near Marsa Brega first saw the enemy. The outpost at Cemetery Hill observed, about 5,000 yards to the south-west, 5 enemy tanks and 2 trucks, from which 20 to 30 men dismounted. Budden's reports, and others from the pilots of scouting aircraft—who had seen 200 tanks and armoured cars, with swastika markings, moving east about seven miles from the British positions—left no doubt that the German advance in force, predicted by Neame's headquarters for the first week in April, had already begun.

At 9 o'clock, outposts of the 1/Tower Hamlets Rifles (Lieut-Colonel E. A. Shipton) saw this force cautiously drawing near. After much obvious reconnoitring, groups of tanks, armoured cars and lorries were seen to deploy; some were observed at a mosque to the front, others farther north and again a small group about six miles to the south. About 9.30 a.m. the enemy began to advance and the British infantry patrols came in, but the carrier scout platoon stayed out in front, keeping watch. About 10 o'clock the enemy brought up a gun, covered by four tanks, to a ridge some four miles to the west, pressed forward and drove the scout platoon back to the outpost at Cemetery Hill; the company there was then withdrawn with the exception of the machine-gunners and one platoon of riflemen. The carrier platoon remained to give them support. The gunners of the 339th Battery, directed by the observation post at Cemetery Hill, went into action: they were to have a busy day.

Half an hour later, enemy infantry preceded by two motor-cycle combinations and ten tanks began to close on Cemetery Hill from the south. The outpost called on the gunners for defensive fire, which the 104th

---

[6] Lt-Col T. R. Budden; 1 KDG. Regular soldier; b. 26 Apr 1914.
[7] Maj T. K. D. Pritchett; 5 RTR. Regular soldier; b. 3 Aug 1905.

R.H.A. put down, and the infantrymen and machine-gunners came back behind the forward defences to a position on a ridge astride the road. The scout platoon, however, remained with its carriers behind the hill and later confounded the enemy by engaging his approaching tanks at a range of 300 yards. It was not until 11.30 a.m. that the Germans occupied Cemetery Hill; by that time they had worked round the flank of the position. The scout platoon then withdrew. At midday, as the enemy showed signs of renewing the advance, the Tower Hamlets closed the road-block. Eight-wheeled armoured cars then approached and fired on the forward infantry, but were engaged and driven off by a troop of the 104th R.H.A. whose observation post was under heavy enemy fire.

The main column of Rommel's thrust seemed to have been brought to a halt; the British armour waited unmolested on the left flank, while to the far south, on the Wadi Faregh, "C" Squadron of the King's Dragoon Guards reported no enemy seen. (Rommel's southern column had been delayed by "bad going"; they were not seen all day and arrived too late to affect the battle.) The Support Group at Marsa Brega were confident. The battery commander with the Tower Hamlets reported to his commanding officer that the infantry were quite happy and intended to stay where they were.

At 1 o'clock, hard upon an attack by German dive bombers, a force of tanks and lorries, with tanks in the van, appeared on Cemetery Hill. They were engaged by the 25-pounders of the 339th Battery and the anti-tank guns of "J" Battery (3rd R.H.A.) and forced to withdraw. Latham decided to give pursuit with a small force, including a troop of field guns, but the German tanks reappeared before this could be organised. This time they came on with more determination, but failed to surmount a sand ridge close in front of the British positions. The gunners, on Latham's orders, engaged them with all guns and once more forced them back. The tanks executed a confused withdrawal, some being hit and others bogged. Meanwhile the afternoon reconnaissance of the R.A.F. had confirmed that the enemy was thrusting with his main forces.

Twice repulsed, the enemy made no move forward for two hours. Then two dive-bombing attacks were launched against Marsa Brega (in the second of which the defence shot down two planes) and at 5 p.m. enemy guns began shelling the British defences.[8] At 5.30 parties of infantry were seen to be working through the sand dunes along the foreshore, which afforded good cover, while German tanks advanced to give support. Latham requested Gambier-Parry to commit some tanks against the Germans' southern flank but Gambier-Parry replied that there would be "insufficient time to get them into action from their present position before dark".

<blockquote>When the German assault had come to a halt, Rommel had personally reconnoitred the battlefield and decided to put in an attack north of the coast road. The task was allotted to the *8th Machine Gun Battalion.*</blockquote>

---

[8] Timings given are Egyptian summer time, advanced by one hour from normal Egyptian time.

At 6 o'clock the full force of the German attack came in on "A" Company of the Tower Hamlets, holding the right flank. The assault was held; but a second thrust, in which light tanks supported the German infantry, drove a wedge in the company's front. The whole of the Support Group's position was now endangered. A counter-attack made with the carrier platoon (in which eight carriers were lost) temporarily threw the enemy into confusion and restored the position sufficiently to enable the company to be extricated (not, however, without loss); but the penetration could not be sealed off. At 7 p.m. German armoured cars and tanks entered Marsa Brega village. As darkness fell the Support Group withdrew about eight miles. The enemy did not follow up.

Fifty-five infantrymen (including two officers), a few machine-gunners[9] and engineers, an anti-aircraft gun and a considerable amount of transport were lost, in addition to the carriers already mentioned. The Support Group, under instructions to withdraw rather than become heavily committed, had done more than its orders required; but the enemy now held Marsa Brega. The way to Benghazi and to Tobruk had been prised open.

The Support Group drew farther back during the night to a position 20 miles in front of Agedabia, "in which area", Latham told his gunners, "we shall fight tomorrow". The 3rd Armoured Brigade conformed. The first phase of the defence had been conducted in accordance with Neame's plan. For the next phase the plan was to shepherd the enemy into the Benghazi plain and (as Wavell's instruction required) to oppose his northward advance with a small force, while the armour pivoted on Antelat.

---

[9] No. 1 Section of 11 Platoon, "Y" Company 1/RNF, kept its guns firing until all its ammunition was used. The section leader, Cpl Harman, was killed and three gunners wounded. Cpl Harrison's section (12 Platoon) also ran out of ammunition and was overrun. Cpl Harrison, mortally wounded, spent the last minutes of his life burying the locks and spare parts of his guns. These were recovered two years later and one lock was placed in the regimental museum.

CHAPTER 3

THE "BENGHAZI HANDICAP"

MANY a retreating army has yearned for the night to blind its enemy to its withdrawal. Night had enfolded the 2nd Armoured Division as it stole away from Marsa Brega, planning to confront the enemy on the morning of 1st April with a new line of resistance in the desert farther east; but daylight had returned before the last units moved. The enemy, however, did not pursue.

The Support Group took up a position in sand dunes to cover the main road near the Kilo 840 stone,[1] about 30 miles from Marsa Brega. A marsh on the right flank afforded some protection against encirclement. The 2nd Armoured Division came into position on the left, the 3rd Hussars, with "B/O" Battery of the 1st Royal Horse Artillery in support, doing "protection rear" during the withdrawal. A desert track to the east of the coast road was covered by the 5th Royal Tank Regiment, which now had only 23 tanks. At El Gtafia this track bifurcated; one arm ran northwards to the west of a line of scarps and low hills to Agedabia, the other—the Trigh el Abd—branched east into the desert, thence north-east—the inland caravan route to Egypt. The 5th Royal Tanks came in to El Gtafia, then moved to a position astride the Agedabia track four miles to the north, while about six miles south-east of El Gtafia the armoured cars of the King's Dragoon Guards watched for an encircling move on the desert flank.

General Neame came forward to see General Gambier-Parry at his headquarters at Maaten el Baghlia, and later ordered the 2nd Armoured Division to withdraw towards Benghazi. The withdrawal axis for the main body was through Agedabia to Antelat and then to Er Regima by the route at the foot of the escarpment; but after Agedabia the Support Group was to follow the main coast road. Thus, north of Agedabia, the Support Group and the armour were to diverge. If the enemy advanced to Benghazi, the armour's task would be to harass his right flank and protect the left flank of the 9th Australian Division.

Gambier-Parry began to withdraw his foremost units at once. Early in the afternoon, the 5th Royal Tanks came back to a position astride the track at Bir el Tombia, where Brigadier Rimington had established his headquarters. The 3rd Hussars acted as rearguard. In the evening the 1st King's Dragoon Guards moved 15 miles north-east to a position overlooking the track coming into Agedabia from Haseiat on the desert flank, and "B" Squadron of the 6th Royal Tank Regiment, with its 13 light tanks, which had remained in contact with the Support Group north-west of Gtafia, was now ordered to rejoin the 3rd Hussars. This it endeavoured to do that night, but could not find them. Meanwhile Neame had ordered the Benghazi garrison to complete the preparation of demolitions and be ready to evacuate at 24 hours' notice.

---
[1] That is, 840 kilometres from Tripoli.

It is not easy to recapture the atmosphere of those early days of the war when the British, almost unaided, were pitted against an overwhelmingly powerful alliance. Had not the German Army coursed through Poland, seized Denmark and Norway, subjugated the Netherlands, conquered France and forced the best of the British Army to flee from Dunkirk in little ships without its equipment, and now almost immediately on its first appearance in Africa, taken El Agheila and Marsa Brega? If the British soldiers believed themselves the equal of the enemy, yet the day of meeting him on equal terms seemed indefinitely remote.

Some elements of the Cyrenaican force were undoubtedly prey to the myth that the Germans could not be stopped and might appear anywhere at any moment unexpectedly. How rumours can start in such an atmosphere, notwithstanding all efforts of the higher command to stem them, is well illustrated by an encounter that occurred on this first day of April near Msus, the all-important but ill-protected supply point for the armour in the Antelat pivot plan. Portion of "A" Squadron of the Long Range Desert Group had set out from Barce on 31st March to investigate whether Marada oasis had been occupied by the enemy (with a view to later establishing a base there).[2] Next day the remainder of the squadron left Barce for Augila via Tecnis and Msus. The following account of its experiences on 1st April is from a British narrative:

> Going was rough which made progress slow, and at 1700 hrs the squadron was no further than Bir el Melezz, ten miles east of Msus. At this point a party of six trucks, with four or five men in each, was sighted through the mirage. They were approaching in line, but when the squadron turned to meet them they went about at great speed and scattered in an easterly direction. Capt [P. J. D.] McCraith was wounded in the arm by the explosion of a thermos bomb under his truck. . . . The squadron halted for the night 25 miles east of Msus. . . . On 2 April the squadron moved into Msus where they found a French Motor Company. . . . Maj Mitford warned them of the party he had seen the night before, and also informed the Cyrenaican Command, who appeared to think that the trucks in question were our own, which was unlikely.

One of two long-range patrols sent out by the 3rd Indian Motor Brigade then at El Adem also had an encounter near Msus on 1st April.

> Pushing on to Msus the next day, 1st April, they came in along the southern track from Bir Belamed. In the afternoon some vehicles were sighted in the distance. Dorman[3] at once thought they were Acworth's[4] patrol and turned to meet them. . . . On closer approach, however, first the vehicles and then the men in them appeared strange and the obvious deduction then was that they were Free French. It must be remembered that neither patrol had any news of the start of the Axis offensive nor of the presence of the Africa Corps in Libya.[5]
>
> Both parties continued to approach each other suspiciously, until it became obvious that the strangers were hostile. As they were in superior numbers (the enemy column included a field gun), Dorman wisely went about rapidly and ordered full speed ahead. Then followed a most exciting, stern chase for thirty miles until darkness

---

[2] This group, after encircling Marada oasis, eventually made its way back to Giarabub on one truck, having to abandon its other vehicles because of lack of petrol. (The petrol gave out 15 miles from Giarabub.) It reached Giarabub on 10th April.
[3] Capt E. A. J. R. Dorman; 2 Royal Lancers. Regular soldier; b. 18 Oct 1915.
[4] Capt G. W. Acworth; 2 Royal Lancers. Regular soldier; b. 31 Jul 1916.
[5] Both patrols would surely have known, however, that the Germans were on the Libya-Tripolitania frontier and had taken El Agheila.

fell, enabling the patrol to make good its escape. The only apparent casualty on either side was one enemy vehicle overturned.

. . . Dorman pressed on through the night to report his encounter as early as possible to R.H.Q., which he reached at midday on the 2nd. Even at this stage, however, Cyrenaica Command at Derna were sceptical about the Germans being east of Msus. But few can have any doubt now that Dorman's patrol encountered a German reconnaissance patrol feeling forward in preparation for Rommel's outflanking move. . . . Indeed, the air reported a whole German tank battalion at Msus on the 3rd.[6] [An erroneous report.]

When Dorman's patrol reported in, Lieut-Colonel Munro[7] of the 2/3rd Australian Anti-Tank Regiment, who was the senior officer with the 3rd Indian Motor Brigade during the temporary absence of Brigadier Vaughan,[8] sent a squadron of the 18th Cavalry to the area in an endeavour to make contact with the German force; but for three days after its departure no more was heard from this detachment.

At first light on 2nd April, carrier scout platoons of the Tower Hamlets Rifles checked enemy armoured units probing forward about three miles in front of the battalion. The force deployed, German infantry dismounted from trucks and assembled in attack order. At 10.30 a.m. an attack was launched with infantry and 40 tanks.[9] On orders from Support Group headquarters the battalion withdrew,[1] but eight German tanks got in behind "B" Company, cutting its withdrawal route. Endeavouring to get back by another route, the company became bogged on treacherous salt pans and was overrun. Meanwhile the scout platoon of another company engaged the enemy tanks, enabling the rest of the battalion to make good its withdrawal; but the scout platoon was lost.

The Support Group then withdrew some 30 miles to a position north of Agedabia, where the infantry again deployed. The 3rd Armoured Brigade conformed and moved to a position east of Agedabia with the 3rd Hussars on the right and the 5th Royal Tanks on the left. "B" Squadron of the 6th Royal Tanks doing protection rear for the 3rd Hussars saw enemy armoured vehicles following for the first three miles or so, but as the withdrawal continued, the enemy lost contact. Just before 1 p.m., however, the 5th Royal Tanks observed that an enemy force of some 40 to 50 vehicles was following them. Meanwhile the Dragoon Guards on the open desert flank reported enemy armoured cars pushing north towards Antelat.

The British tendency to withdraw, which could not be disguised, had been reported to the German commander both by his air force and by ground patrols. Nothing was more likely to induce Rommel to resume the advance; but General Gariboldi, his nominal superior, opposed action

---

[6] E. W. D. Vaughan, *A History of the 2nd Royal Lancers (Gardner's Horse) from 1922-1947* (1951), pp. 73-4.
[7] Lt-Col E. E. Munro, ED, NX496. (1st AIF: Lt 3 Pnr Bn.) CO 2/3 A-Tk Regt 1940-41, No. 3 Reception Camp UK 1945. Civil servant; of Manly, NSW; b. Sydney, 13 Feb 1892.
[8] Brig E. W. D. Vaughan, CB, DSO, MC. Comd 3 Indian Motor Bde. Regular soldier; b. 12 Mar 1894.
[9] 50 tanks according to some reports.
[1] The battalion may have received orders before the attack was mounted that it should withdraw at this hour; the armour had previously been ordered to withdraw at 10.30 a.m.

on a large scale until more German forces had arrived. Hence the orders to the *5th Light Division* for 2nd April, after an inactive day on the 1st, had been for only a limited reconnaissance towards El Gtafia and Agedabia. This was to be undertaken by the *3rd Reconnaissance Unit*. But when the British forces withdrew farther after first contact on the morning of the 2nd, Rommel took the bit in his teeth and ordered a general advance of the division to Agedabia and the little port of Ez Zuetina, farther north. "It was a chance I could not resist," Rommel wrote afterwards, "and I gave orders for Agedabia to be attacked and taken, in spite of the fact that our instructions were not to undertake any such operation before the end of May."[2]

Even after it had become clear that the Axis forces had resumed their advance, General Neame sought to keep the withdrawal under his personal control. "Do not commit the 3rd Armoured Brigade to counter-attack," he signalled Gambier-Parry just before midday, "without reference to me." Neame's message directed that the Support Group was to block the road to Benghazi as long as possible but without risking being overrun; if the enemy continued to advance towards Benghazi, the armoured brigade would continue to withdraw, keeping below and west of the escarpment as far north as the pass at Esc Sceleidima, or even farther north if routes could be found by which it could retire at any time up the escarpment. In essentials this direction accorded with Wavell's instructions of 19th March, but involved withdrawal of the division in two groups not within supporting distance of each other, one near the coast and one near the escarpment.

Gambier-Parry's acknowledgment, which took almost two hours to transmit, arrived in mid-afternoon. He said that he understood that the armoured brigade should not be committed at the present stage but pointed out that an opportunity to counter-attack later from the escarpment might be fleeting. Gambier-Parry "urged seriously" that whether the armour should be committed was a matter for his discretion. He also advised Neame that he might have to evacuate Agedabia that night. In that event he thought it preferable to avoid a course of action that involved splitting his force and so risking defeat in detail, even though keeping the Support Group and armoured brigade together might result in uncovering the coast road to Benghazi. He said that the strength of the armoured brigade was now down to 22 cruisers and 25 light tanks and that he anticipated further losses through mechanical failure at a rate of approximately one tank per ten miles.

At 4 p.m. the armoured units of the 2nd Armoured Division were still moving back towards the new line of resistance north and east of Agedabia. The speed of withdrawal of the 5th Royal Tanks had been reduced by the need to conform with that of "A/E" Battery of the 1st R.H.A., which could only cover seven miles in each hour. The 6th Royal Tanks (less "A" and "B" Squadrons but with "B" Squadron of the 3rd Hussars), which had been standing by at Beda Fomm since the German advance

---

[2] *The Rommel Papers*, p. 109.

began and was equipped with about 40 Italian M13 tanks, was now ordered to move to Antelat.

At 4.30 p.m. the 5th Royal Tanks (Lieut-Colonel Drew[3]) met two of its petrol lorries and halted to refuel. Just then radio contact was established with brigade headquarters, who began passing orders to the regiment. Meanwhile nine tanks doing protection rear observed 30 to 40 enemy vehicles approaching from the south-west. Brigade had just reported that the 3rd Hussars were involved with the enemy and needed assistance. Drew sent four tanks to their aid. The nine tanks now took up hull-down positions behind a ridge. About the same time, farther west, the enemy prepared to advance with tanks on the delaying position taken up by the Tower Hamlets. The British artillery engaged, forcing the enemy to deploy, whereupon the infantry withdrew, this time with little loss. Some enemy tanks turned in towards them and a few broke through the gun area of the 104th R.H.A., but they did not follow up the British withdrawal.

At 5.30 p.m. the enemy force in front of the 5th Royal Tanks, which included between 40 and 60 tanks and some field guns, advanced from the direction of the setting sun. Though thought to be Italian, they were in fact the *II/5th Armoured Battalion*. The British regiment, with only 14 of its 18 tanks and without artillery support, gave battle. A brisk engagement followed in which the Germans lost three tanks and the British five, with one more damaged. Colonel Drew ordered his rear squadron to withdraw to the next ridge. This was accomplished. The enemy failed to follow up, missing an opportunity to cripple in one blow almost the entire British medium-tank force.

After this action Gambier-Parry ordered the whole of the 2nd Armoured Division to withdraw to Antelat. The coast road to Benghazi was thus uncovered but Cyrenaica Command headquarters was not informed of this.

At 7 p.m. the 5th Royal Tanks resumed their slow withdrawal, continuing until 2 a.m., when a halt for sleep was taken by the roadside. Battle casualties and mechanical failures had together reduced the battalion to a strength of 12 tanks. In the early evening, most of the remainder of the armoured division had reached Antelat where they spent a peaceful night. On the desert flank the King's Dragoon Guards, making a wide detour to the east, executed a trying march across rough country in pitch darkness. They arrived at Antelat about 9 a.m. next morning.

The situation at nightfall on 2nd April was serious, but in hand. Indeed, except that the coast road was now unblocked, the execution of the withdrawal had conformed well to the plan. Some battle losses had been suffered but were not substantial. On the other hand the tank strength had continued to dwindle as a result of mechanical failures.

In the 9th Australian Division, the only reliable news of the German advance was the scanty information in official situation reports, which had been enlarged upon and distorted by rumour. Exactly what had happened, nobody knew; but none doubted that the division would soon face the enemy. The test might be severe and on unequal terms: the men may have

---

[3] Brig H. D. Drew, OBE, MC. CO 5 RTR. Regular soldier; b. 14 Apr 1895.

been apprehensive but they were ready and anxious to try conclusions. They were as yet unshocked by battle. And were they not volunteers?

The 26th Brigade, which had been assigned the task of defending the lower escarpment from Tolmeta to Tocra (on the right-hand sector of the division's front), had had only one battalion available, the 2/24th, when the German advance had begun. Transport had now been provided to move up most of the 2/48th Battalion from Ain el Gazala. The battalion (less one company, which remained at Derna) embussed at dawn on 2nd April and arrived at Baracca at 5.30 p.m. Next morning it occupied a front of 10 miles to the south of the Tocra pass, with forward outposts on the escarpment. Positions were taken up for the most part in dense scrub adjoining the cultivated fields of an Italian settlement.

Wavell had watched the development of the German advance with anxiety. Reporting it to London, he told the Chiefs of Staff that the mechanical condition of the armoured brigade was causing Neame much concern and that he had directed Neame to keep his armoured units in being, even if this involved a withdrawal from Benghazi. The mere mention of withdrawal was enough to anger the British Prime Minister. He replied on 2nd April, in a message through which there ran a vein of irony, that a rebuff to the Germans would be of far-reaching importance for prestige. He continued:

> It would be all right to give up ground for the purposes of manoeuvre, but any serious withdrawal from Benghazi would appear most melancholy. I cannot understand how the enemy can have developed any considerable force at the end of this long, waterless coast-road, and I cannot feel that there is at this moment a persistent weight behind this attack in Cyrenaica. If this blob which has come forward against you could be cut off you might have a prolonged easement. Of course, if they succeed in wandering onwards they will gradually destroy the effect of your victories. Have you got a man like O'Connor or Creagh dealing with this frontier problem?

These were acid words, but it was typical of Wavell that, rather than be discouraged, he distilled the good sense of the message from its corrosive medium. As his colleague of those days, Admiral Cunningham, afterwards wrote of him:

> He was cool and imperturbable when things went wrong, and steadfastly refused to be riled by the prodding messages to which he, like myself, was at times subjected from the authorities at home, and which were, it must be confessed, singularly unhelpful and irritating at times of stress.

Wavell flew up to the front to see the situation for himself. He arrived at Cyrenaica Command headquarters at Barce just after Neame had received the message in which Gambier-Parry sought permission to uncover the road to Benghazi in order to avoid splitting the armoured division. Neame was disposed to accede; but Wavell intervened, insisting that the coast road be blocked. It will be recalled that his previous instructions had provided that a small mixed force should delay any advance by this route. Now that Gambier-Parry's force was too small to split, Wavell ordered the whole division to withdraw by this route. Perhaps he thought that if (as Gambier-Parry stated) the armoured division was likely to lose one tank out of its small force in each ten miles of movement, little advantage was to be gained by expending it in long withdrawals out of contact; that, if something positive were not done to oppose the enemy, the Germans might indeed, in Churchill's phrase, "succeed in wandering onwards".

Wavell's next action was to send for General O'Connor and inform G.H.Q. that O'Connor would immediately take over the Cyrenaican command from General Neame. One cannot be sure exactly when Wavell received Churchill's message, but the coincidence between Churchill's suggestions and Wavell's decisions is remarkable.

Just before 9 p.m. orders were sent to Gambier-Parry from headquarters Cyrenaica Command to the effect that the task of the division was to impose the maximum delay on any advance by the enemy along the main coast road. The whole armoured division was to operate together, withdrawing by bounds to Magrun. Beyond Magrun the Support Group accompanied by a squadron of tanks and a squadron of armoured cars would continue northwards by the coast route, while the remainder of the division was to withdraw east up the escarpment at Esc Sceleidima, thus covering the left flank of the 9th Australian Division.

Neame had no tactical headquarters close to the forward formations. With his main headquarters located more than 100 miles from the scene of the day's fighting, he could have exercised effective control only if detailed and timely reports of the situation had reached him promptly and his signals network had operated efficiently. Neither condition pertained. Gambier-Parry did not receive Neame's signalled orders till 2.25 a.m.

Gambier-Parry replied that to attempt to block the road to Benghazi was beyond the capability of his force. He was committed by force of circumstances to withdraw by Esc Sceleidima to El Abiar, where he would reorganise, "an essential preliminary to further action". The Tower Hamlets, which had already been committed three times, was now reduced to half its strength. He described the depleted state of the 3rd Armoured Brigade and said that its headquarters were out of touch with the 5th Royal Tanks and had "only just got hold of" the 6th Royal Tanks.

Gambier-Parry's signal left no alternative to Wavell and Neame but to accept his proposal. What they were not told, however, was that the Benghazi road had already been unblocked. Yet it was fortunate that the coast route was not taken as Wavell desired, for the supply dump at Magrun had been destroyed on the preceding day by the 2/3rd Australian Field Company. The circumstances leading to this action were later investigated by Brigadier Kisch,[4] the Chief Engineer of Cyrenaica Command, who reported on 4th April that he was satisfied that the decision had been correctly taken.

At 7.30 a.m. Neame ordered that the demolition program in Benghazi and elsewhere should be put in hand immediately and that the city should be evacuated. The main burden of the demolitions at Benghazi fell on

---
[4] Brig F. H. Kisch, CB, CBE, DSO. CE Cyrenaica Comd and Eighth Army 1941-43. B. Darjeeling, India, 23 Oct 1888. Killed in action 19 Apr 1943.

the 295th Company, R.E., a section of the 2/3rd Field Company, some men of the 2/7th Field Company and two companies of the Royal Northumberland Fusiliers. The 2/3rd had already carried out a demolition program in the area south and east of the escarpment, as far south as the line Magrun-Soluch-Sidi Brahim. At the Er Regima pass the 2/7th, with the assistance of a section of the 2/3rd, fired demolitions in the railway cutting. When, as expected, these exploded the adjacent minefield by sympathetic detonation, the engineers re-mined the pass with 600 anti-tank mines. The 2/13th Field Company was engaged on similar tasks in the 26th Brigade area.

About 10 a.m. on 3rd April Cyrenaica Command issued instructions authorising Gambier-Parry to take the action he had proposed and laying down that his tasks were now to deny the enemy access to the escarpment from the Esc Sceleidima pass to the Wadi Gattara inclusive and to cover the left flank of the 9th Australian Division. Early in the morning Generals Wavell and Neame visited the 9th Division and informed General Morshead that General O'Connor would soon arrive to take over command from General Neame.[5]

O'Connor, bringing with him Brigadier J. F. B. Combe, who had commanded the 11th Hussars in the first desert offensive, had left Cairo at 7.45 a.m. by air. When he arrived at El Adem, O'Connor warned the 3rd Indian Motor Brigade to be prepared to send two of its regiments to Mechili as flank protection for the British forces.

No forward move appears to have been made by the Axis forces on the morning of 3rd April. On 2nd April Gariboldi had sent Rommel a message:

> From information I have received I deduce that your advance continues. This is contrary to my orders. I ask you to wait for me before continuing the advance.

This may have influenced Rommel's temporary pause. But air reports of continued British withdrawal were soon to stir him to action.

The relative inactivity of the Axis forces and their failure to keep contact on 3rd April provided the 2nd Armoured Division with a needed opportunity to reorganise. By the end of the day, however, it had become much more disorganised as a result, not of enemy action, but of failures in the mechanism of communications and command.

At 5.30 a.m., the 3rd Armoured Brigade was ordered to move to just south of the pass at Esc Sceleidima with a view to ascending the escarpment at this point, for beyond Esc Sceleidima the scarp becomes rugged and can nowhere be easily ascended until the pass at Er Regima is reached. The first unit to move (at first light) was the 6th Royal Tanks; but it set off from Antelat in a south-westerly direction, not towards Esc Sceleidima. This was in accordance with orders received about 1 a.m.; the latest instruction had not reached the regiment. Three hours later, having seen neither friend nor foe, they came to the conclusion that something was amiss and returned to Antelat, found that place abandoned

---
[5] Liaison letter, 9 Aust Div, 27 Apr 1941.

and pushed on towards Esc Sceleidima, making but five miles in the hour because their Italian tanks were continually overheating.

From 8 a.m. onwards the rest of the armoured division withdrew to Esc Sceleidima, the Support Group preceding the armoured brigade while "A" Squadron of the King's Dragoon Guards pushed out armoured car patrols to the south. Shallow wadis, which had to be crossed, broke up the traffic flow of armoured units moving close to the escarpment. "Columns crossed and re-crossed," wrote a diarist, "and tanks, armoured cars, anti-aircraft and field guns and other vehicles were all mixed up together."[7] The historian of the King's Dragoon Guards wrote:

> There is a series of wide tracks running from Antelat to Sceleidima, parallel with and west of the escarpment, and it was on joining these tracks that the Regiment saw a huge cavalcade of vehicles all streaming north, and creating an immense sand cloud as it went. The whole desert was alive with vehicles. . . . The Luftwaffe seemed to take no great interest . . . although a few Stuka attacks had left their trail. . . .[8]

The division arrived at Esc Sceleidima shortly before midday, whereupon commanders were called by Gambier-Parry to a conference. Orders were given that the division should deny the escarpment north from Esc Sceleidima to the enemy; the Support Group was to defend from the Wadi Gattara (on the left flank of the 2/13th Battalion) to Sidi Brahim, the armoured brigade from Sidi Brahim south to Esc Sceleidima. Just as this conference was breaking up, and after the armoured brigade and Support Group representatives had left, a report was received from the R.A.F. that an enemy reconnaissance column was approaching Msus from Antelat: other columns were said to be advancing north from Agedabia, both by the coast road to Benghazi and by the inland route to Antelat by which the division had just travelled. Divisional headquarters reported this to Cyrenaica Command, who, however, inferred from the message as received that the enemy were already in Msus. In fact the King's Dragoon Guards were patrolling in the Antelat area and the 6th Royal Tank Regiment, returning from its fruitless journey, was laboriously coming along from Antelat to Msus. Soon afterwards the 5th Royal Tanks were ordered to engage and destroy eight enemy tanks approaching Esc Sceleidima from the south. These proved to be the 6th Royal Tanks.

The 2nd Armoured Division then issued new orders that the Support Group (less the company of French marines) and the 6th Royal Tanks should hold the escarpment while the armoured brigade (less the 6th Royal Tanks) and the French marines should proceed to Msus to deal with the enemy column. Some units heard of the earlier orders, some of the later. Subordinate formations issued orders and counter-orders with bewildering rapidity.

Portions of the Support Group began moving north in conformity with the divisional orders, which had reached Latham in good time, but had not yet reached Rimington. Other units (including the 1st R.H.A.),

---

[7] War diary, 1 RHA.
[8] D. McCorquodale, B. L. B. Hutchings, A. D. Woozley, *History of the King's Dragoon Guards 1938-1945*, p. 71.

unable to obtain any orders, followed the general movement. Part of the Tower Hamlets (with their supporting artillery and anti-tank gunners) laboriously took up positions on the escarpment in the area from Sidi Brahim to about one mile farther south. Not until about 4 p.m. did the altered orders reach the 3rd Armoured Brigade, which then issued warning orders to the 5th Royal Tanks and 3rd Hussars but was unable to contact the 1st R.H.A. and other units intended to form the column for Msus. Most of these had in fact begun to move independently northwards below the escarpment. Meanwhile the 6th Royal Tanks, which was to join the Support Group, having been given neither the location of the Support Group headquarters nor its wireless frequency, had elected to remain at Esc Sceleidima.

While the 3rd Armoured Brigade was waiting at Esc Sceleidima and striving to assemble the units allotted to it, the headquarters of the 2nd Armoured Division was reporting to Cyrenaica Command headquarters that it was impossible to establish troops along the escarpment between Esc Sceleidima and the Wadi Gattara since there was no route by which supplies could be brought up to them from the rear. Accordingly Command headquarters (at which Wavell was still present and O'Connor had now arrived) authorised a general withdrawal of the division through Er Regima.

The report that an enemy force was advancing towards Msus appears to have been erroneous. Headquarters had discounted similar reports on earlier days and indeed had just passed an order to the Long Range Desert Group to make its base at Msus; but confusion concerning the whereabouts of all units had now become so great that to sift truth from rumour had become impossible. There is evidence that the body reported by the air force as an enemy force moving towards Msus may have been the recovery section of the armoured brigade; it is also possible that the R.A.F. had mistaken one of its own columns, which was the last British unit reported passing through Msus.

The garrison at Msus was a company of the French Motorised Brigade and some Senussi soldiers. It was subject to the directions of an English liaison officer, Captain Hore-Ruthven,[9] whose orders were to ensure at all costs that the dump there did not fall into the hands of the enemy. On receiving the report that the enemy column was approaching, Hore-Ruthven ordered the destruction of the dump so laboriously built up as a first-priority task in the previous fortnight. He then withdrew the garrison. Other reports of unidentified vehicles from patrols of the Long Range Desert Group and King's Dragoon Guards operating near by supported the belief that the enemy was close. Meanwhile Command headquarters had sought confirmation from the R.A.F., which now reported that there were 40 to 50 enemy vehicles, probably tanks, at Msus. Such was the state of affairs when at 5 p.m. Wavell departed to return to Cairo. Wavell

---

[9] Capt Hon A. H. P. Hore-Ruthven; The Rifle Bde. Regular soldier; b. 31 Aug 1913. Died of wounds Dec 1942. Only child of Lord Gowrie, VC, then Governor-General of Australia, and author of *The Happy Warrior* (poems).

left Neame in command but arranged that O'Connor should remain to assist and advise Neame.

When the 2nd Armoured Division received the air reconnaissance report that the enemy was at Msus in strength, Gambier-Parry ordered the armoured brigade to follow the rest of the division to Er Regima.[1] Most of the division's wheeled vehicles were already on the move north, travelling at the foot of the escarpment. Gambier-Parry's headquarters had crossed the Wadi Gattara in the late afternoon. Shortly afterwards an aircraft dropped a message from Cyrenaica Command headquarters on the northward moving column. Timed 10 a.m., it stated, "You must get east of escarpment before you reach Wadi Gattara to avoid own minefield," and added instructions about a guide. This was interpreted as meaning that the Er Regima pass had been closed.

As the message passed up the moving column, it became distorted; to some units it was reported that the minefield through the pass had been primed and the demolitions blown. The mass of vehicles travelling northwards in the gathering dusk now reversed and moved southwards, turned up the rugged Wadi Gattara and sought in the darkness to find a way up the escarpment on to the plateau. Here most of the wheeled portion of the division became blocked in a conglomerate mass, scarcely diminishing as small groups laboriously filtered through the bottleneck throughout the night.

The rumour about the closing of the pass had not reached some of the foremost elements of the Support Group in the van of the withdrawal. These retired in some confusion during the night through the 2/13th Australian Infantry Battalion holding the pass; other vehicles retired through the 26th Brigade at Tocra.

On hearing that the Er Regima pass had been closed, Rimington, still at Esc Sceleidima, cancelled the orders to his brigade to move by this route. His communications with Gambier-Parry having broken down, he decided to remain at Esc Sceleidima and to hold the pass there until they were restored. He directed that the 3rd Hussars were to guard the eastern entrance to the pass and the 5th and 6th Royal Tanks the western end. Soon enemy were reported approaching from the east and the four light tanks of "A" Squadron 6th Royal Tanks with the 3rd Hussars were ordered to engage them. The "enemy", however, proved to be a returning patrol of the King's Dragoon Guards.

Rimington's orders cancelling the northward move do not appear to have reached the 3rd Hussars, for at approximately 8 p.m. they began moving towards Er Regima, believing themselves the vanguard of the brigade. After a few miles, however, on making their first halt, they contacted brigade headquarters and were ordered back. Rimington, having failed to re-establish contact with divisional headquarters, had meanwhile decided on his own initiative to collect together all the forces near Esc

---

[1] "A/E" Battery of the 1st RHA (which regiment, having lost wireless contact with brigade headquarters, was moving independently on the basis of intercepted orders) was just moving out to Msus when unfortunately it heard this order, turned round and began moving north. But for this, the falseness of the reports concerning Msus might have been soon discovered.

Sceleidima, advance at first light on Msus next morning, and, if the reported enemy occupation proved correct, engage the enemy force. During the night he was joined at Sceleidima by the headquarters and most of what remained of the Tower Hamlets Rifles (which was unable to establish satisfactory communications with the Support Group headquarters) and by the two squadrons of the King's Dragoon Guards that had been patrolling that day south and west of Esc Sceleidima. Earlier in the evening the regimental headquarters and the remaining squadron of the King's Dragoon Guards had begun to withdraw to Er Regima but had returned to Esc Sceleidima on hearing that Er Regima pass was blocked. They intended to proceed independently to El Abiar on the morrow, leaving the other two squadrons to accompany Rimington to Msus.

Soon after Wavell departed, Cyrenaica Command decided, having regard to the supposed enemy occupation of Msus, to close down the headquarters at Barce and move back to Maraua. At 6 p.m. a staff conference was called at headquarters, to which Colonel Lloyd was summoned as the 9th Division's representative. On arriving there about one hour later, Lloyd found an atmosphere of uncertainty. Communications with the 2nd Armoured Division had broken down. Nobody knew where it was; it was feared that it had been overwhelmed. The number of enemy vehicles supposed to be in Msus had now risen to 100, though a liaison officer of the armoured division's artillery averred to Lloyd that the force at Msus was the 3rd Armoured Brigade.

After some discussion it was decided to execute a general withdrawal to a line running from the Wadi Derna to Mechili, thus yielding almost the entire Jebel Achdar massif to the enemy. The 3rd Indian Motor Brigade (still at El Adem) was to occupy Mechili, into which the 2nd Armoured Division (or so much of it as remained) would withdraw "with all possible speed" to provide field and anti-tank guns, which the Indian brigade lacked. (One squadron of the motor brigade—Major Rajendrasinhji's[2] "B" Squadron of the 2nd Royal Lancers—was already there, having moved out that morning to provide protection to some engineers preparing demolitions.) The 9th Australian Division was to establish two battalions forthwith on the second escarpment east of Barce, using all available transport. These were to be placed at the head of the two passes through which the two roads that traverse Cyrenaica mount the second escarpment from the intermediate plateau. The 1/King's Royal Rifle Corps, a motor battalion from the 7th Armoured Division's Support Group, which had arrived at Barce in the early afternoon—pursuant to Wavell's promise of reinforcements—was placed under Morshead's command to protect his division's left flank by taking up positions astride the tracks coming in from the south.

The securing of the second escarpment was to be the first stage in a general withdrawal. The 9th Division's confirmatory orders, issued at 2 a.m. on the 4th, stated that its intention was to move to the Derna area by stages. Such were the orders that concluded a day's operations

---

[2] General Maharaj Shri Rajendrasinhji, DSO; 2 Royal Lancers. Chief of Staff, Indian Army 1953-55. Regular soldier; b. 15 Jun 1899. Died 1 Jan 1964.

during which it is doubtful whether the Axis ground forces had fired a single shot.

Morshead directed that the required moves to the second escarpment were to take place forthwith. The 26th Brigade was ordered to move the 2/48th Battalion (which only that day had occupied the position west of Baracca, on the lower escarpment) to the northern pass at Maddalena; the 20th Brigade to move the 2/15th Battalion (then in reserve) to the southern pass, due east of Barce.

The 1/Royal Northumberland Fusiliers had been placed under Morshead's command that afternoon and, with the 24th Anti-Tank Company, had been detailed to hold the left flank near El Abiar, thus freeing the 2/15th Battalion for the new role now allotted to it.

The moves could not be made immediately because the division had no troop-carrying transport; but during the night transport columns were organised by taking first-line vehicles from units. By first light next morning the two battalions were able to move. The 1/King's Royal Rifle Corps on the other hand, being fully mobile, began moving during the night and was in position next morning by 9 a.m.

Of Morshead's five battalions, four were now holding pass-heads—two on each escarpment. The fifth battalion, the 2/17th, which had been deployed on the escarpment north of Er Regima, with one company at a distance of 17 miles by a track not passable to vehicles, had been assembling throughout the night in an area near El Abiar. Here it was to await second-line transport, its own first-line vehicles having been used to move the 2/15th Battalion. It was to be the first unit to withdraw behind the new line.

Great difficulty was experienced in finding transport for the 2/17th Battalion. Major Barham[3] of the divisional staff, just arrived from Cairo, set off in the early hours of the morning for Barce, whence the divisional transport had been operating while employed by force headquarters in stocking up supply dumps. Barham found that the transport company was being used to evacuate the 4th Australian General Hospital. He followed Cyrenaica Command headquarters to its new report centre at Maraua, where he eventually managed to obtain 20 Italian lorries manned by Royal Army Service Corps drivers.[4] Other transport was collected next day by Major Dodds[5] at a report centre at Barce. But not until mid-afternoon of the 4th was it possible to begin moving the units who had lent their first-line transport to other units.

Although no sizable portion of the British force had been committed before his departure, Wavell had appreciated that the situation was critical. On reaching Cairo he informed Churchill that the 7th Australian Division, which was about to embark for Greece, would have to remain, that it

---

[3] Brig R. J. Barham, DSO, OBE, WX1560. HQ 9 Div 1941 and 1942; CO 2/15 Bn 1942-43; GSO1 9 Div 1943-44; Col GS (Ops) Adv LHQ 1944-45. Regular soldier; of Parramatta, NSW; b. Berry, NSW, 18 Jan 1908.
[4] The 14th RASC.
[5] Lt-Col N. G. Dodds, QX6060. 2/9 Bn; DAQMG 9 Div. Insurance manager; of Brisbane; b. Brisbane, 18 Nov 1910. Died 1 Mar 1942.

must move to the Western Desert, and that the 6th British Division, earmarked for the projected assault on Rhodes, must instead be held in reserve. Meanwhile the British Prime Minister had just telegraphed to Mr Eden, then in Athens, recalling that Wavell had previously given "many cogent arguments for believing his western flank secure".

> Far more important than the loss of ground (he continued) is the idea that we cannot face the Germans and that their appearance is enough to drive us back many scores of miles. This may react most evilly throughout Balkans and Turkey. Pray go back to Cairo and go into all this. Sooner or later we shall have to fight the Huns. By all means make the best plan of manoeuvre, but anyhow fight.

In the early afternoon of the 3rd Rommel went out to the advanced forces of the *Ariete Division* on the track from Agedabia to the Trigh el Abd, satisfied himself that the going was reasonable, returned, and, at 2.45 p.m.[6] ordered an advanced detachment of the *Ariete Division* to reconnoitre the Trigh el Abd route as far as Ben Gania and also to reconnoitre the track to Msus. At 4.45 p.m., after reports had been received that Magrun had been abandoned, the *3rd Reconnaissance Unit* was ordered to advance by the coast road to that place and to reconnoitre forward. In the evening Rommel drove north to the advanced columns of the *3rd Reconnaissance Unit* near Magrun. Finding that no contact had been made with British troops, learning also that it had been reported that Benghazi had been evacuated, he ordered the German forces to press on to the city during the night. This they did, entering the town about an hour before dawn.

On his return south to his headquarters, Rommel met Gariboldi, who had just arrived. Gariboldi asked that in future the *Africa Corps* should report the situation to him and that Rommel should make no forward move except on his orders. "General Gariboldi wanted to get authority from Rome first," Rommel wrote afterwards, "but that way days could go by unused."[7] Rommel contended that as a German general he had to give orders to suit the situation confronting him at the moment. He demanded complete freedom of action. The outcome of the conflict was hardly in doubt but according to both the war diary of the German *Africa Corps* and Rommel's own account the matter was clinched for Rommel by the arrival during the conference of a message from the German High Command promising him complete freedom of action.

Undoubtedly Gariboldi was so informed. There must be some doubt, however, whether in fact this was true and whether the war diary records supporting the assertion are genuine; for a directive issued by the German High Command on this very day, over Field Marshal Keitel's signature, stated that Hitler had "reached the following decisions on 2nd April":

1. For the time being the main task of the German Africa Corps is still to defend positions reached and to hold down as great a part as possible of the British forces in North Africa.

---

[6] Egyptian summer time—not used by German forces.
[7] *The Rommel Papers*, p. 111.

The resultant offensive operations with limited objectives may not be expanded further than weak forces permit before the arrival of the 15th Panzer Division. Above all an endangering of the open right flank, which would necessarily arise in the case of a pivot movement in a northerly direction on Benghazi, must be avoided.

2. Even after the arrival of the 15th Panzer Division, an extensive operation with Tobruk as the objective cannot be undertaken for the time being.

The commitments in other theatres of operations of the bulk of Fliegerkorps X and of Italian forces which cannot be further motorised at present will not permit an extension of objectives before the autumn of 1941.

A change in these plans could be considered only if the bulk of British armoured forces were withdrawn from Cyrenaica. New measures are being kept in reserve for this eventuality.

3. Cooperation with Italy will remain limited for the time being to the subordination, if necessary, of an additional motorised division (102nd) to the German Africa Corps, in addition to those forces already under Africa Corps command.

New coordination is being held in reserve for a large scale offensive later.

4. The German general at Comando Supremo is requested to obtain Italian High Command agreement to these principles.

Is it not possible, indeed likely, that the message received by Rommel during the conference with Gariboldi was in fact that conveying these decisions?

That evening Rommel wrote to his wife:

The "brass" at Tripoli, Rome and possibly Berlin will gasp. I took the risk against all orders and instructions because I saw an opportunity. No doubt it will all be pronounced good later and I am sure that anybody in my position would have done the same thing. The first objective set down for the end of May has been reached. The British are in flight.[8]

It is a tribute to the efficiency with which the engineers of the 2nd Armoured Division and the 2/3rd Australian Field Company had carried out their program of demolitions that the Germans were unable to keep their armour sufficiently supplied to maintain the momentum of their advance. On the afternoon of 3rd April the *5th Light Division* reported that it would require four days for refuelling. Rommel thereupon ordered that the division should be grounded for 24 hours, with the exception of the reconnaissance group on the coast road and one protective detachment, and that all vehicles should be unloaded and used to bring forward the supplies and ammunition needed. Thus the British forces were to be vouchsafed at least one more day of freedom from major assault by the German armour.

At 6 a.m. on 4th April, most of the force Rimington had taken under his command at Esc Sceleidima, including two squadrons of the King's Dragoon Guards and what was left of the three tank regiments, commenced the advance on Msus; the remainder made its way direct to El Abiar. About 8.30 a.m. two squadrons of Dragoon Guards leading Rimington's force entered Msus, but found no sign of the reported enemy. However they did find a "most excellent" ration dump undestroyed, which met an urgent need of food. Soon afterwards enemy aircraft bombed them and signalled their presence by dropping a flare. The rest of the armoured

---

[8] Translation by the Historical Branch, United Kingdom Cabinet Office.

brigade followed, moving very slowly and continuing to shed tanks because of mechanical failures and overheating caused by shortages of water for radiators.[9] The 6th Royal Tanks did not arrive until early afternoon. Ironically Rimington was rewarded for his initiative and bold action by the discovery that though the reported enemy occupation was false yet the fuel dumps had been destroyed. Although some 250 gallons of petrol were actually found at Msus and used mainly to refuel some of the wheeled vehicles, the tanks were now precariously short of fuel. Colonel Fanshawe,[10] the brigade second-in-command, was sent north to organise more supplies.

At 8 a.m. Cyrenaica Command issued an order which stated that it was apparent the main enemy column was making for Benghazi, and prescribed that the task of the 2nd Armoured Division was to protect the flank of the 9th Division by moving to Mechili by the El Abiar-Mechili track. Later O'Connor set out from headquarters to contact Gambier-Parry while Neame reconnoitred the Wadi Cuff, which appeared to be a good delaying position.

By mid-morning the elements of the Support Group that were not with the 3rd Armoured Brigade had finished moving through the defiles at the Wadi Gattara and Er Regima and were now dispersed between Er Regima and El Abiar. Stragglers coming up the pass at Er Regima reported that the enemy was in Benghazi and that the Italian flag was flying above the town. Both Gambier-Parry's and Latham's headquarters were now established at El Abiar not far from Morshead's. By early afternoon the 1st and 104th R.H.A., "J" Battery (less one troop) of the 3rd R.H.A. and one company of the French Motor Battalion were concentrated there. The 9th Division lacked transport for quick moves. And against a thrusting enemy Morshead was dependent for the protection of his flank and for early warning if the enemy came on in strength or broke through, on a formation of which the dwindling combatant units were to a large extent out of communication and short of fuel.

At midday O'Connor called an orders conference at Gambier-Parry's headquarters. Morshead attended. Although Gambier-Parry was still uncertain of the exact condition and location of the 3rd Armoured Brigade, Morshead's impression was that the headquarters of the armoured division were not unduly alarmed at the situation. According to Morshead's report, Gambier-Parry expressed the view that, having taken Benghazi, the enemy had secured his final objective for the present. General O'Connor was apparently of the same opinion, for his orders were that the 9th Division should halt its withdrawal. The division was to continue holding the Tocra-Er Regima line on the first escarpment with the 2/24th and 2/13th Battalions "until forced to withdraw by enemy action", but was not to become committed.[1] The 2/17th Battalion, however, would not return to the first escarpment but would take up a position on the second escarpment east of Barce.

---
[9] The diarist of one squadron mentions that troops were ordered to urinate into radiators.
[10] Col G. H. Fanshawe, OBE; 3 Armd Bde. Regular soldier; b. 16 Jan 1899.
[1] Liaison letter No. 2, 9 Aust Div, 27 Apr 1941.

An army that had failed to maintain contact with its enemy was in no position to assess what that enemy would do. Not only had ground contact been lost; air reconnaissance was also temporarily unavailable. The supporting air force, with but a handful of aircraft, had been making a maximum effort but was hampered by being constantly on the move,[2] and No. 3 Squadron R.A.A.F., on which the army depended for tactical reconnaissance, had spent the latter part of the night and most of the morning moving back from Got es Sultan to Maraua.

At the conclusion of the conference, O'Connor returned to Cyrenaica Command headquarters and confirmed with Neame the orders he had given. Morshead went immediately to the headquarters of the 20th Brigade, near the 2/17th Battalion, to convey the new orders to Brigadier Murray, only to discover that Murray was himself on the way to divisional headquarters. Morshead was relieved to find that the 2/17th Battalion was at last ready to move, a transport column having just arrived. The battalion was ordered to occupy a position behind the 2/15th, on the Barce pass. Morshead now returned to his own headquarters at El Abiar. When he arrived there, he learnt that reports were being received of an impending attack on the 2/13th Battalion at Er Regima.

The escarpment east of Benghazi is a wall of hard, shaly rock rising some 400 feet above the maritime plain. In some parts covered with a shallow layer of dun-coloured earth, for the most part bare rock, devoid of vegetation save for a low, stunted shrub known as camel-thorn, its slopes and re-entrants offered little cover or concealment to the men assigned to hold it. Unable in many places to dig down into the hard ground in the time and with the equipment available, the Australians had erected sangars of stones for section posts. These offered some protection from machine-gun and rifle fire, but not from artillery.

In several places the escarpment face was broken by wadis. Of these the one at Er Regima, through which ascended the road and narrow-gauge railway to Barce, offered the easiest ascent. Near the top of the escarpment there was an anti-tank ditch which, however, had been constructed by the Italians to check an enemy approaching from the east. In rear was a second anti-tank ditch, also facing east.

Lieut-Colonel Burrows had only three companies of the 2/13th Battalion available for the defence, since Major Chilton's[3] "C" Company, which had been detached on the battalion's arrival in Cyrenaica, was still at Barce on internal security duties. The front was too extended to be defended for its entire length. Burrows had two companies forward: "D" Company (Captain Handley[4]) on the right, astride the pass, "B" Company (Captain Hill[5]) on the left, covering likely avenues of encirclement, including some ground passable to tanks; between them was an

---
[2] No. 3 Squadron RAAF, on 3rd April, patrolled in turn from Benina airfield (which was abandoned at 9 a.m. that day), Esc Sceleidima and Got es Sultan.
[3] Lt-Col H. H. M. Chilton, OBE, ED, NX12218. 2/13 Bn; CO 13/33 Bn 1942-43, 12/50 Bn 1943-45, 28 Bn 1945. Fruit merchant; of Turramurra, NSW; b. Turramurra, 28 Sep 1909.
[4] Maj E. A. Handley, MC, NX12222; 2/13 Bn. Salesman; of Ingleburn, NSW; b. Kogarah, NSW, 8 Aug 1917.
[5] Maj A. J. Hill, MBE, ED, NX380. 2/13 Bn; GSO3 9 Div 1942-43; BM 20 Bde 1943-45. Schoolmaster; of Randwick, NSW; b. Sydney, 2 Jul 1916.

undefended gap. Captain Fraser's[6] "A" Company was in reserve. Burrows had prepared alternative positions for the reserve to occupy according to the point of enemy attack. He had under command four 4.5-inch howitzers of the 51st Field Regiment and a machine-gun company of the Royal Northumberland Fusiliers; an additional battery of 25-pounders had been promised. Although he had been under orders to withdraw as soon as transport could be made available he had kept the whole battalion in battle positions. He was as yet unaware of the decision just made that his battalion, and the 2/24th in the north, should continue to hold their ground.

The 4th of April was a tense day for the men guarding the pass. On the preceding morning, they had waved their hats in farewell to the Hurricanes of No. 3 Squadron as they took off for the last time from Benina airfield on the plain just below the pass; all that day they had heard explosions, as demolitions at Benghazi and elsewhere had been fired; then they had watched the transport of units from the plains and the desert go past, for a while densely packed, then thinning out and hurrying away. But for some time all traffic had ceased. The Germans were thought to be in Benghazi, about 15 miles across the plain. Smoke still drifted above the distant white city, from which a road ran out to the foot of the escarpment. All eyes were on that road.

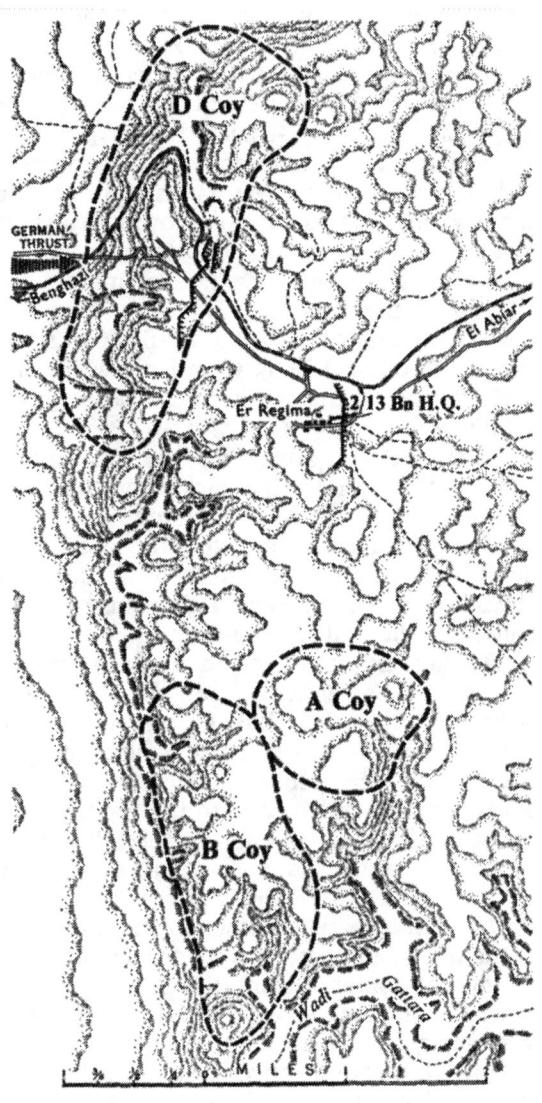

---

[6] Capt T. K. Fraser, NX12385; 2/13 Bn. Warehouseman; of Macquarie Fields, NSW; b. Roseville, NSW, 1 Aug 1912.

In the early afternoon, a column of vehicles came out from Benghazi towards the pass. The Australians moved into battle positions. As the column approached the Benina airfield, the vehicles fanned out: tanks and armoured cars could be discerned and behind them 30 to 40 troop-carrying lorries. It was judged that the force was about 3,000 strong.

Sixteen tanks came to the fore in line abreast, in two waves, and moved up towards the pass, with trucks following. As the tanks reached the point where the road crossed the railway line, howitzers of the 51st Field Regiment and two salvaged Italian mortars manned by the Australians engaged them. Some direct hits were scored, one mortar putting a light tank out of action. The tanks and armoured cars withdrew, but the infantry dismounted, and deployed to assault. The prepared demolitions in the pass were fired. Unfortunately they detonated before the enemy had reached the mined area; yet more unfortunately the concussion set off part of the minefield by sympathetic detonation and caused some of the 2/13th's sangars on the left flank to fall away. A third misfortune was that the 20th Anti-Tank Company, which had been under orders to move back to the second escarpment as soon as the pass was blown, then withdrew with its guns.

As the German advance began, one light tank came up the pass ahead of the infantry and a few moved out on either side. An Arab, or possibly an enemy scout in Arab clothing, was now seen to be signalling on the left flank by flashing a petrol tin in the sun. Hither four armoured cars made their way to the mouth of an unguarded and unmined wadi. They attempted to get in behind the Australians guarding the pass, but were halted by the Italian anti-tank ditch.

The first assault came in at the pass itself against 18 Platoon, commanded by Sergeant Simmons,[7] a born leader; 16 Platoon was on the right, 17 on the left, but not within supporting distance. To the right of Simmons' platoon, the road wound tortuously down the pass to cross the railway line, which, making a more gradual descent, came in from a wider sweep still farther to the right. Behind Simmons' positions ran the anti-tank ditch. On a knoll to the left, Simmons could see the men of the mortar platoon, under Sergeant McLaughlin,[8] firing at an unorthodox rate; one of the weapons was almost shaken to pieces, requiring one man to steady the barrel, another to lie across the base-plate.[9]

Simmons' platoon was better equipped than most. Yet their British equipment comprised but 30 rifles, one Boyes anti-tank rifle and one light machine-gun among 32 men. (These were supplemented by two Italian machine-guns, unofficially acquired.) The Australians waited until the enemy were within range, then gave them all the fire these weapons could provide. The enemy took cover. Down the road behind Simmons' platoon came four 18-pounder guns of the 51st Field Regiment, one of which

---

[7] Sgt R. E. Simmons, NX13887; 2/13 Bn. Clerk; of Asquith, NSW; b. Asquith, 10 Jun 1918. Died 28 Jan 1958.
[8] Sgt R. B. McLaughlin, NX14956; 2/13 Bn. Garage assistant; of Taree, NSW; b. Taree, 6 Apr 1919. Killed in action 29 Oct 1942.
[9] Of this crew, one man was killed, three wounded, of whom one died and two were taken prisoner.

swung into action at lightning speed, fired, and knocked out the leading tank of three light tanks coming up the pass. Another tank then engaged the gun and put it out of action; three other guns soon suffered the same fate but a second tank was knocked out. Two of the "characters" of 18 Platoon were "Little Bill" Andrews[1] and "Big Bill" Andrews.[2] Simmons sent "Little Bill" Andrews back to company headquarters to inform Handley of the strength of the opposition. "Big Bill" Andrews meanwhile was effectively engaging the enemy tanks with the Boyes rifle. The enemy was beginning to work round Lance-Corporal Weissmann's[3] section on the left flank.

In the meantime the other two platoons, in their sangars on the escarpment, had come under heavy fire from machine-guns, tanks and field guns (75-mm) and from mortars. The two remaining tanks, after the 18-pounders had been silenced, came up to the top of the pass and cruised up the anti-tank ditch. Although the enemy fire tore through the sangars, the Australians replied with their rifles, their few Bren guns, and their Boyes anti-tank rifles. The men clung to their positions but, gradually encircled, were forced bit by bit to yield. Lieutenant Wilson's[4] platoon on the right flank was outflanked by tanks which came into the rear of their positions. While well-aimed and courageously sustained fire forced the leading tank to close down its observation slits, the platoon moved round the side of a feature and gradually returned along a wadi.

Lieutenant Burrell's[5] platoon, on the left flank, was soon in difficulties because some of the sangars of its section posts had been shattered by the detonation of the minefield. Burrell contested each enemy advance, but unable to prevent infiltrations was forced to withdraw gradually to the anti-tank ditch.

To hold a front of some seven miles with three companies of lightly-armed men against attack from a well-equipped force 3,000 strong might well dismay the most confident commander. Colonel Burrows had just the qualities needed. Aged 43 years, a sales executive in civilian life, he had served in the ranks with distinction in the first world war at Gallipoli and in France, where he was commissioned in 1918, and had retained his interest and enthusiasm for soldiering between the wars by service in the militia. At the outbreak of war, he was the commanding officer of the 36th (New South Wales) Battalion, from which he was appointed to form the 2/13th Battalion. Thick-set, of rather pugilistic features, with an erect carriage and alert, roving eyes, he enforced discipline with a caustic tongue and often a resonant command, a characteristic that earned him his nickname, "the Bull". His attributes as a battalion

---

[1] Pte W. Andrews, NX22041; 2/13 Bn. PMG messenger; of Sydney; b. Paddington, NSW, 1 Jul 1922. (Correct name W. B. S. Dryvynsyde.)
[2] Pte R. C. S. Andrews, NX18324; 2/13 Bn. Dairy farmer; of Singleton, NSW; b. Singleton, 18 Apr 1918.
[3] L-Cpl F. B. Weissmann, NX45393; 2/13 Bn. Engineer; of Newcastle, NSW; b. Lewisham, NSW, 19 Sep 1913.
[4] Capt K. C. Wilson, NX15031. 2/13 Bn; staff and training appointments 1943-45. Station manager; of Merriwa, NSW; b. Ganmain, NSW, 11 Jan 1913.
[5] Maj J. R. Burrell, MC, NX15678. 2/13 Bn; BM 29 Bde 1945. Audit clerk; of Cremorne, NSW; b. Sydney, 21 Aug 1914.

commander included aggressiveness and, as events were to prove, a cool head in trouble.

Burrows had been informed at midday that the transport being collected at Barce to move the battalion back would not arrive until at least 7 p.m. He was expecting his missing company to arrive at any moment from Barce, but in the meantime Captain Fraser's company, which was not centrally disposed, was his only reserve. When Burrows reported the impending German assault to Murray, he was informed that, in order to enable the troops in rear to be cleared, he was to hold his position at all costs until after dark; then the battalion would be withdrawn according to the original plan. Morshead had in the meantime directed that the recently-cancelled plan of withdrawal should now be adhered to, since the intention of the latest conference had been to delay the withdrawal only so long as this did not involve becoming committed.

Handley had given Burrows by phone a running commentary on the approach of the enemy. When Burrows heard that the Germans were beginning to infiltrate through Handley's company, he sent the carrier platoon to a position on the right flank at the head of the wadi north of the railway line and used his small transport reserve to bring one platoon (Lieutenant Peterson's[6]) of Fraser's company to the fort near battalion headquarters. The rest of Fraser's company set off on foot in the same direction while more transport was being mustered to fetch them; and Fraser went ahead to report to Burrows.

When Peterson's platoon reached the fort, Burrows already knew that Wilson's platoon had been encircled. Therefore he sent Peterson to the head of the wadi to block and reinforce the carrier platoon. This would safeguard the fort against infiltration from the left as well as protecting the rear of "D" Company.

Some transport which had been lent to the 2/15th Battalion for its move, but had returned without having been employed for this purpose, was now used to bring up the remaining two platoons of "A" Company and Captain Fraser was ordered to take them to the area already held by Peterson's platoon. The two platoons, however, missed the way and went into position immediately behind "D" Company, where they soon became involved with the enemy thrusting in that area.

Communications between Burrows and Fraser soon broke down. It was evident that both Fraser's and Handley's companies were becoming disorganised. Burrows therefore sent Major Turner[7] forward to coordinate the action of all the troops that had become involved.

When the two platoons of Fraser's company had taken up their positions, one of the enemy tanks came within range. A man from Lieutenant Watch's[8] platoon, firing from the anti-tank ditch, knocked it out with his Boyes rifle. The crew jumped out. Firing his Bren gun from the hip

---

[6] Capt H. A. Peterson, MBE, NX12414; 2/13 Bn. Bank clerk; of Canberra; b. Burwood, NSW, 22 Aug 1918.
[7] Lt-Col R. W. N. Turner, NX12213. 2/13 Bn (CO 1942). Barrister; of Roseville, NSW; b. Paddington, NSW, 8 Jul 1909. Died of wounds 27 Oct 1942.
[8] Lt-Col J. R. Watch, NX12394. 2/13 and 47 Bns. Employment registrar; of Killara, NSW; b. Sydney, 4 Jul 1916.

Private Eland[9] dashed forward, mortally wounded one of the crew and captured the rest—three Germans. Meanwhile Burrell's platoon, completing its withdrawal, had linked up with Watch's platoon.

Burrows now ordered Captain Hill's company, which had not been engaged, to come in to the fort from the left flank in order to cover the withdrawal of the forward troops. No. 10 Platoon was to be brought in by transport; the rest on foot, north-eastwards across country, on a compass bearing.

In the meantime Simmons' platoon was being encircled round its left flank, where there was dead ground behind a knoll. Simmons had sent a runner to Handley suggesting that the platoon be withdrawn behind the anti-tank ditch. Handley replied that he was to "work on his own initiative". By the time that this message reached Simmons, his platoon's position had become precarious, casualties had been incurred and he had been compelled to withdraw behind Weissmann's section. On receiving Handley's message Simmons decided to withdraw the whole platoon at once behind the anti-tank ditch, sending back Private Easter[1] to inform Handley of his intention. Easter came under heavy fire as he ran back after crossing the ditch, but succeeded in reaching Handley's headquarters.

Simmons now strove to withdraw his men, but as they went back towards the anti-tank ditch they were caught by fire in enfilade from the left, where the Germans had occupied some old Italian sangars. Casualties began to come fast. Private Thompson[2] and Private Morrice[3] were killed; others were wounded. The platoon fought back, Simmons shouting encouragement, but were overrun by Germans emerging on their left at the end of the anti-tank ditch. Only five men got away. These reached the anti-tank ditch and escaped along it to join Burrell's platoon.

Enemy were also closing in on Burrell's and Watch's platoons. Watch sent Corporal Leach[4] and his section forward of the ditch to silence a harassing machine-gun post; but as they emerged, an enemy party came in behind them, calling *"Hände Hoch!"* This party was quickly engaged, but another party of enemy came down the ditch from the other side. Watch's entire platoon had now perforce to withdraw down the ditch at the double towards the fort; the three German prisoners showed a tendency to linger until Private "Scout" Love,[5] at Sergeant Robinson's[6] command of "Stir 'em along Scout", prodded the rearmost with his bayonet.

On the right some hundreds of enemy had moved up out of the wadi head that Burrows had intended to be held by the whole of "A" Company.

---

[9] Pte S. Eland, NX20837; 2/13 Bn. Butcher; of South Strathfield, NSW; b. Low Fell, England, 15 Sep 1917. Killed in action 4 Apr 1941.
[1] WO2 R. K. Easter, DCM, NX18260; 2/13 Bn. Stockman; of Widden, NSW; b. Paddington, NSW, 14 Dec 1916.
[2] Pte H. Thompson, NX17822; 2/13 Bn. Farm worker; of Bathurst, NSW; b. Macksville, NSW, 14 Oct 1907. Killed in action 4 Apr 1941.
[3] Pte A. O. Morrice, NX23275; 2/13 Bn. Salesman; of Bellambi, NSW; b. Dubbo, NSW, 12 Mar 1917. Killed in action 4 Apr 1941.
[4] Sgt G. L. Leach, NX18768; 2/13 Bn. Upholsterer; of Dolls Point, NSW; b. Melbourne, 23 May 1913.
[5] Pte P. L. Love, NX17277. 2/13 and 2/28 Bns. Stockman; of "west of the Darling River", NSW; b. Bristol, England, 28 Jan 1918.
[6] WO2 D. S. Robinson, NX56791; 2/13 Bn. Clerk; of Chatswood, NSW; b. Cremorne, NSW, 25 Jul 1908.

Here Peterson's platoon and the carrier platoon, which had taken up positions between the railway station and the fort, were hard pressed. Behind them some guns of the 51st Field Regiment came into action, with, however, only 17 rounds remaining of the small amount of ammunition allotted to them. They fired their rounds and departed.

It was becoming dark. Captain Fraser received a message from Lieutenant Watch, heavily involved with "D" Company, asking for help. Fraser decided to make a blind but bold assault on the enemy party. But, just as his men were moving off, an enemy group—more than a company strong—emerged from the wadi on the right and completely surrounded Fraser, Peterson and many of their men. Corporal Kinder's[7] section, following behind, then encountered this body head-on. Peterson, with his runner, Private Spooner,[8] escaped to rejoin the Australians and immediately organised a bayonet charge, those men with automatics firing from the hip, with terrible effect; the enemy were "falling around us like ninepins", as one Australian prisoner of the German party later wrote. In the mêlée Captain Fraser escaped and with Sergeant Robbins[9] rejoined Peterson, who was continuing to advance, moving sections forward alternately in bounds. But this gallant action served only to take the platoon deeper into the midst of the enemy. Peterson took up a position in rear of the anti-tank ditch; the enemy, less than 50 yards away, began using a knocked-out tank as a strongpost.

Meanwhile in the gathering dark the area around the fort had come under heavy fire: red and white tracers cut trails of light across the ground, while shells fired from the plain below burst with a red glow. The English howitzers replied tirelessly (their flashes illuminating more Germans coming over the escarpment) until, their last rounds expended, they fell silent and departed. At headquarters a report was received from "D" Company stating that it had been compelled to withdraw. Burrows, whose promised reinforcements had not arrived, then decided to retire behind the second anti-tank ditch in rear of Er Regima village and to establish his headquarters down the road, where it would meet the transport as it came forward.

The leading section of Hill's company, which had now reached the fort, was sent to clear the ditch in front of the railway station, where a party of enemy threatened to cut the route of retirement. Corporal Boreham[1] took the section forward and drove out the enemy. As the remaining sections of this platoon arrived, Major Turner sent them across to consolidate the battalion's hold on the area Boreham had cleared. The rest of Hill's company were met by Captain Walsoe[2] where they struck the road at the ditch-crossing east of Er Regima fort, and there began

---

[7] Sgt A. G. Kinder, NX12808; 2/13 Bn. Clerk; of Enfield, NSW; b. Flemington, NSW, 21 Sep 1917.
[8] Pte A. D. Spooner, NX15043; 2/13 Bn. Insurance agent; of Artarmon, NSW; b. Failford, NSW, 18 Aug 1914.
[9] Sgt L. S. Robbins, NX16213; 2/13 Bn. Motor mechanic; of Epping, NSW; b. Newcastle, NSW, 24 Mar 1912.
[1] Sgt F. J. Boreham, NX15012; 2/13 Bn. Schoolteacher; of Gosford, NSW; b. London, 1 May 1910.
[2] Maj O. M. Walsoe, MC, NX70221. 2/13 Bn 1940-43; BM 4 Bde 1943-44; MA to Dir of Inf War Office 1944-46. Salesman; of Sydney; b. Hamburg, Germany, 31 Mar 1908.

to take up a blocking position through which the rest of the battalion might be extricated. Meanwhile, about 9 p.m. Burrows himself went to the anti-tank ditch, collected the forward sections as they were falling back, and ordered them into position astride the road 400 yards in front of the ditch to allow time for Hill's company to organise the defensive position behind.

Two companies of the Royal Northumberland Fusiliers, with the 24th Anti-Tank Company under command, arrived almost an hour later; but the officer commanding the machine-gunners informed Burrows that, as a daylight reconnaissance had not been made to lay down fixed lines of fire, the guns could not be effectively employed. Burrows sent one company back to block the road behind the battalion in case the unit should be overrun. The remainder were held with the battalion, one platoon being placed in rear to cover the withdrawal.[3]

"B" Company got into position without more trouble and by 10 p.m. the rest of the troops had withdrawn behind it. The enemy had apparently paused to reorganise. But there was still no sign of the troop-carrying transport Burrows had been expecting since 7 p.m. Could it have become lost? Had it been ambushed?

At 10.15 p.m. the anxious Burrows ordered all troops except those holding the covering position to move off down the road. About half an hour later an English transport company with Cypriot drivers met them. The battalion was withdrawn without further engagement. The dejected men were packed tight into too few trucks. Some travelled on running boards, a few on a gun tractor. The convoy carried them back across the plain and through the town of Barce, whose shops and dumps were ablaze, to a point some 10 miles past the town, where the men were dispersed in scrub cover for some rest as the next day began to break.

Peterson's platoon and some others, including Captain Fraser, were not in this convoy. They had waited by the anti-tank ditch for over two hours, had repelled with grenades an enemy party calling on them to surrender, and about 10.30 p.m. had managed to extricate themselves; but they were too late to make contact with the battalion before it withdrew. They moved on into the hills that night. In succeeding days Fraser and Peterson and their men continued moving eastwards, never catching up, however, with the retreating forces. Eventually this party of 2 officers and 23 men, helped continually by Senussi Arabs, reached Gazala in a body, having lost but a few of their number. Here they split up. Most were captured between 29th April and 4th May, some on the verge of the Tobruk perimeter. One man, Private Jenkins,[4] succeeded in rejoining his unit in Tobruk; he came into the perimeter along the coast with two English soldiers on the night of 10th May, almost six weeks later.

---

[3] The promised 25-pounders had not arrived. Burrows had expected two batteries. In fact only one troop—the Rocket Troop of the 1st RHA—was sent, but was unable to arrive before dark, and therefore returned without going into action.
[4] Pte P. H. Jenkins, NX17368; 2/13 Bn. Station hand; of Cubbacoo Siding, NSW; b. Huelgoat, France, 28 Feb 1919.

The 2/13th Battalion suffered 98 casualties including three officers in this engagement. Five men were killed. The 51st Field Regiment suffered one man killed and 5 (including an officer) injured. One officer was missing.

The thrust towards Er Regima was the only important action undertaken by the German forces that day. While the *5th Light Division* remained grounded, the 2nd Armoured Division had another day of misfortune. Efforts were made to take fuel to the 3rd Armoured Brigade near Msus. Colonel Fanshawe set off with a petrol column, met another on the way and took it too, only to be attacked by 18 German fighters and bombers and to lose the entire convoy of 21 vehicles carrying 1,600 gallons of petrol. During the afternoon, the brigade moved some distance to the north-east in the direction of Bir el Melezz. Orders were later received from 2nd Armoured Division headquarters (based apparently on a report of dubious accuracy that there was a strong enemy column between Bir el Melezz and Mechili) cancelling the brigade's move by the Mechili track; instead the brigade was to strike north to the El Abiar-Maraua track.

The 5th Royal Tanks, now having only nine cruisers, halted for the night 15 miles north-west of Bir el Melezz. To the south-west the 6th Royal Tanks (who had not received the order cancelling the move to Mechili) were reorganising by scrapping the less serviceable of their Italian tanks and keeping the nine most serviceable to form a headquarters and two small troops, while the 3rd Hussars, with two squadrons of the 6th Royal Tanks (now possessing only four light tanks) under command, were undergoing a similar process 14 miles north-east of Msus. Farther south in the desert, "A" Squadron of the Long Range Desert Group had moved south to the Trigh el Abd and along it to Bir Ben Gania; they reported that no enemy were to be seen. In the evening a single German reconnaissance aircraft flew over this column.

It was on this day, 4th April, that the 3rd Indian Motor Brigade commanded by Brigadier Vaughan moved to Mechili. Mechili's only building was the old Italian fort, a stone and mud structure useless for modern war. Old trenches surrounded it but were silted with sand. The importance of Mechili was that it contained good supplies of water, which would be invaluable to the enemy if he attempted to operate a force across the desert south of the Jebel Achdar.

Vaughan's brigade consisted of three lightly-armed but fully-mechanised Indian cavalry regiments—the 2nd Royal Lancers (Gardner's Horse), the 11th (Prince Albert Victor's Own) Cavalry and the 18th (King Edward VII's Own) Cavalry. Brigadier Vaughan had been making a reconnaissance of the Barce escarpment on 3rd April when Neame and O'Connor decided to send his brigade to Mechili. Vaughan ordered the brigade (less the 18th Cavalry Regiment, which was to remain at El Adem to guard the airfield) to come forward immediately by night to Tmimi, where he would meet it next day.

(Australian War Memorial)
The harbour at Benghazi with the Outer Mole in the right background.

(Capt J. S. Cumpston)
The valley in which 26th Brigade headquarters was established on 4th April 1941. Barce is situated on the plain in the left background. The 2/48th Battalion and a company of the 2/23rd held positions on high ground in the left middle distance. The 1/Royal Northumberland Fusiliers occupied the high ground to the right.

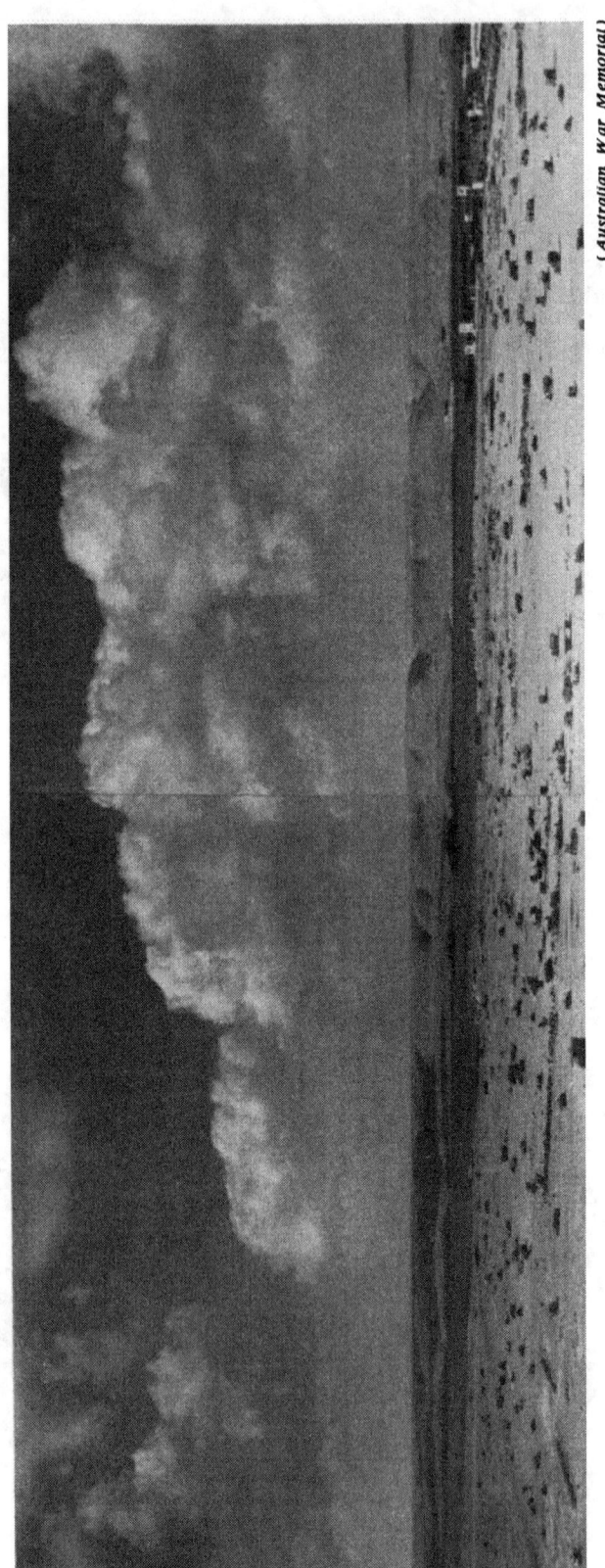

Tobruk port and town looking south-west, April 1941.

(Australian War Memorial)

The 2/3rd Anti-Tank Regiment (Lieut-Colonel Munro), less two batteries,[5] had been stationed at El Adem with Vaughan's brigade. Before the decision to withdraw from the Er Regima-Esc Sceleidima escarpment was made, Neame had decided to bring the regiment forward and place it under Morshead's command. In the afternoon of 3rd April the regiment had begun moving towards Derna; a bivouac was made for the night near Gazala. When Munro arrived at Barce for orders, he was informed that his regiment was now to accompany the Indian brigade to Mechili. Munro met Brigadier Vaughan that evening and arranged to meet the brigade next morning with his regiment at Tmimi.

Air reconnaissance reports had indicated an enemy force in Mechili so Vaughan decided to move from Tmimi in fighting formation. Munro allotted one battery to the command of the 11th Cavalry for the move, one to the command of the 2nd Lancers. One of the battery commanders, Major Nehl,[6] afterwards wrote of this move:

> And so the brigade group was ready to move and at the allotted time the signal code was hauled up above the Brigade Major's vehicle and the group moved off as one vehicle; the sight of a thousand vehicles of all types moving in formation across a fairly level plain was a sight that one could never forget. Down through the years before the war whilst training in the Militia I had worked out exercises and manoeuvres on sand tables and blackboards, but never did I imagine that such a huge force could be controlled as perfectly as was the 3rd Indian Motor Brigade and its attached troops on that morning.[7]

The brigade left Tmimi airfield at 10 a.m., arriving at Mechili at 3.30 p.m. Here they met Rajendrasinhji's squadron, also the patrol of the 18th Cavalry Munro had sent out to investigate movement near Msus. Because of wireless breakdowns no messages had been received from either of these squadrons since their departure. They now reported that no enemy had been seen. Another squadron of the 18th Cavalry (commanded by Captain Barlow[8]) had been sent to the track junction at Gadd el Ahmar, where the track from Mechili to El Adem joins the Trigh el Abd. (Thereafter it sent in a patrol each day to Mechili for supplies.) In the evening, "M" Battery of the 3rd R.H.A. (an anti-tank regiment which had arrived at Derna from Egypt only that morning) came in to Mechili to join the force.

Mechili fort was in a flat, sandy depression sunk in desert that was rough and broken except to the west. An irregular perimeter to conform with the ground, enclosing about 1,200 yards from east to west, and 800 yards from north to south was established around the fort. To the south of the perimeter was a primitive landing ground. The eastern portion of the perimeter was held by the 11th Cavalry in whose area were sited the guns of the 10th Battery. The 2nd Lancers held the western sector, with the guns of the 11th Battery in the north-west.

---

[5] One of these was at Tobruk, the other at Mersa Matruh.
[6] Maj W. B. Nehl, ED, NX70408; 2/3 A-Tk Regt. Moulder; of Newcastle, NSW; b. Newcastle, 7 Feb 1905.
[7] 2/3rd Anti-Tk Regt Association's News Bulletin, 1 Apr 1956.
[8] Brig J. M. Barlow, DSO, MC; 18 (King Edward VII's Own) Cavalry. Regular soldier; b. 18 Apr 1905.

As soon as Neame learnt of the enemy assault in force against the 2/13th Battalion, he authorised a withdrawal from the lower escarpment. The new orders were issued at 8.30 p.m. The 9th Division was to withdraw to the Barce escarpment, which it was to hold until forced to withdraw by the enemy. The 2nd Armoured Division, other than the units which had accompanied the 3rd Armoured Brigade to Msus, was to retire to Tecnis, some distance farther east. The portion of the 2nd Armoured Division with the 3rd Armoured Brigade (now in the Bir el Melezz region) was to move north to Charruba. These orders were in fact confirmatory of moves which, as we have seen, had already begun to take place in both the 9th Division and the 2nd Armoured Division.

While the 2/13th Battalion had been delaying the German vanguard at Er Regima, all units and sub-units of both divisions located on the plain between the two escarpments had been withdrawn behind the second escarpment. To avoid congesting the 2/13th Battalion's axis of withdrawal, Brigadier Latham sent part of the Support Group (including his headquarters and the 1st R.H.A.) back by a country track to near Ghedir esc Sciomar, where they deployed just before dawn. Nevertheless, the diarist of the 2/17th Battalion commented:

> The road is choked with military vehicles of all kinds which hurry ceaselessly along through the night. The dust is almost unbearable and the sense of general confusion on the road terrific.

One of the last units to receive the withdrawal orders was the 2/24th Battalion, which had been holding the northern passes on the lower escarpment while the 2/13th held that at Er Regima. There were three passes on this flank, but only one was now blocked by the 2/24th. Early on the morning of the 4th, "A" Company had been withdrawn from the most northerly and "C" Company from the central pass, leaving only the main pass at Tocra guarded by Captain Andersen's[9] "B" Company. "A" and "C" Companies concentrated at Baracca, where the 370th Battery (51st Field Regiment) came in to support them. Here they waited until, at 5 p.m., an English transport company arrived to "move the battalion to another area". Major Tasker, however, had received no orders to withdraw and requested the transport officer to stand by. The latter refused because he was due to report again at El Abiar at 9 p.m.: probably his was the convoy required to move the 2/13th Battalion. So the column moved off with vehicles empty. Shortly afterwards two armoured vehicles were seen to be approaching Tocra pass. The pass demolitions were then blown and the battalion, except for rearguards, was concentrated at Baracca.

The withdrawal orders reached the battalion just before 11 p.m. The rearguards were then withdrawn and the battalion assembled to await the arrival of the additional transport needed to move it complete with stores. Major Gehrmann[1] of the 2/13th Field Company pressed Tasker

---

[9] Capt L. E. Andersen, VX48255; 2/24 Bn. Silk merchant; of Glen Iris, Vic; b. Adelaide, 4 Nov 1903.
[1] Lt-Col A. S. Gehrmann, DSO, ED, QX6024. OC 2/13 Fd Coy; CRE 9 Div 1942-44; comd 1 Water Transport Trg Centre 1944-45. Engineer; of Brisbane; b. Brisbane, 6 Feb 1914.

to withdraw at once to permit time for the blowing of the bridge between Baracca and Barce. Eventually, at 3.15 a.m., with less than three hours of darkness remaining, Tasker complied. He ordered the destruction of blankets and surplus gear, crowded the men on to the few vehicles available and moved off, whereupon Gehrmann's sappers carried out some very effective demolitions. At Barce the battalion met 20 trucks sent to meet them by Tovell's headquarters; the journey was continued in greater comfort. Tasker's destination was the Wadi Cuff; but before dawn he halted the convoy to bivouac beside the road.

Meanwhile Morshead had organised the defence of the second escarpment. The 2/48th Battalion less one of its own companies still in Derna, but with Captain Spier's and Captain Rattray's[2] companies of the 2/23rd under command and Major Ingledew's battery of the 51st Field Regiment in support, had moved back during the night and taken up a position guarding the pass at Maddalena by which the northern road from the Barce plain mounts the escarpment, and also a smaller track to the northwest. The southern pass, to the east of Barce, was held by the 2/15th Battalion; about three miles behind, the 2/17th deployed into a defensive position at first light on the 5th. To give depth to the defence, it was planned that the 2/24th and 2/13th Battalions should move, after their men had been rested, into positions behind the 2/48th and 2/15th; the 2/24th Battalion to the Wadi Cuff (where demolitions were being prepared to destroy a road the 2/1st Pioneer Battalion had just laboriously constructed to replace the demolished Italian road); the 2/13th to a position astride the southern road near Slonta, south of the Wadi Cuff. The 104th R.H.A., which had so far been with the Support Group, had just been placed under Morshead's command. Having now two field regiments, Morshead allotted one to each brigade: the 104th to the 26th Brigade, and the 51st to the 20th. The 1/King's Royal Rifle Corps again came under Morshead's command; its task would be to watch and safeguard his left flank.

On the evening of 4th April Neame and O'Connor had received information from Middle East Command that reinforcements were being dispatched: these included portion of the 11th Hussars, with 32 armoured cars, the 1st Royal Tanks with 33 tanks, the 18th Australian Infantry Brigade, and the 107th Royal Horse Artillery.

On the morning of the 5th Neame left command headquarters to visit the forward formations while O'Connor went to the Wadi Cuff to superintend the occupation of the position there. Before his departure O'Connor sent Wavell a message commending General Neame's conduct of operations and recommending that Brigadier W. H. E. Gott, who had commanded the 7th Armoured Division's Support Group in the first offensive, should be sent forward to command a Support Group now being formed from 7th Armoured Division units.

---

[2] Maj R. Rattray, MC, VX38937; 2/23 Bn. Fisherman; of Port Franklin, Vic; b. Bendigo, Vic, 1 May 1907.

Meanwhile Neame had met Morshead on the track between D'Annunzio and Tecnis about 11 a.m. Neame told Morshead, who had been left under the impression that O'Connor was in command, that O'Connor had declined the command because he thought the proposal to replace Neame at the onset of operations was unfair. Neame, Morshead was informed, would continue as commander while O'Connor would perform liaison work with subordinate formations. Morshead asked for an assurance that any orders given by General O'Connor would carry the authority of the commander-in-chief.[3]

At this meeting Neame endorsed Morshead's plan to move the 2/24th and 2/13th to the Wadi Cuff-Slonta position. Orders to this effect were accordingly given. The 2/24th went into position at 2 p.m., the 2/13th three hours later. O'Connor met the 2/24th as they were about to occupy the position originally selected for them near the western entrance to the gorge and directed them instead to another blocking the eastern exit.

Nothing of moment occurred in the morning. In the afternoon the 3rd Armoured Brigade, still dangerously short of fuel, travelled north and reached the El Abiar-Charruba track (whereupon the Tower Hamlets rejoined the Support Group) while Gambier-Parry's headquarters moved to a position farther east. The two squadrons of the King's Dragoon Guards that had been operating near Msus followed the armoured brigade northwards. Meanwhile Gambier-Parry sent a message to the Mechili garrison asking for the dispatch from there of "M" Battery of the 3rd R.H.A. to give his headquarters anti-tank protection while moving to Mechili. The German Air Force heavily attacked the armoured division this day and destroyed a subsidiary supply dump between Maraua and Msus, adding to its supply difficulties.

Command headquarters' main problem was to ascertain what action the enemy was taking. The R.A.F. reported much enemy movement on the coastal plain and on the two tracks leading across the Jebel Achdar from Benghazi. Some confusing reports in the early afternoon and information that the armoured brigade was in a still more weakened state and short of fuel caused Morshead great concern. He left his headquarters to visit the 2/13th Battalion, then moving into the Slonta area—an idyllic place in a pine forest—and commended them for their stand at Er Regima. When he returned he called in at the forward command post of Cyrenaica Command at Maraua and learned that the latest reports from the air were of a large enemy column moving eastwards from Msus.

Early on the morning of 4th April, the day on which Rommel had grounded the main force of the *5th Light Division,* a detachment of the *Brescia Division* was sent forward to Benghazi to relieve the *3rd Reconnaissance Unit* there, while other advanced units of the main Axis force began moving across the desert south of the Jebel Achdar. It is evident from the orders given that morning that Rommel, after his brush with Gariboldi, had determined to attempt the recapture of the whole of

---

[3] Liaison letter No. 2, 9 Aust Div.

Cyrenaica by striking with his main force across the desert towards the British rear. The Fabris unit, a motor-cycle company with motorised artillery which had set out the previous day along the Trigh el Abd, was ordered to press on to Ben Gania—and thence to Mechili—as advanced guard of the *Ariete Division,* which was to follow as soon as possible by the same route. Another, stronger force was to follow by the same route as far as Ben Gania, but then to cut through to the coast at Tmimi with Tobruk as its ultimate destination. This force, which was to be the advanced guard of the main body of the *5th Light Division,* was placed under the command of Lieut-Colonel von Schwerin, who was already on the Trigh el Abd with an Italian battalion and a small German force originally intended to capture Gialo oasis. The headquarters of the *5th Light Division* with a machine-gun battalion, an anti-tank company and a squadron of tanks was ordered to follow behind the Schwerin Group.

At midday Rommel drove to Benghazi. There he gave orders to the *3rd Reconnaissance Unit* to make for Mechili by the route through Er Regima as soon as its relief by the *Brescia* detachment had been completed. It set off early in the afternoon but encountered opposition, as we have seen, at the Er Regima pass. Later it reported that it had been unable to break the British resistance until next morning and that its tank squadron had suffered such severe casualties in the minefield that it was unable to proceed.

The Italian General Staff had advised Rommel against using the route from Agedabia to the Trigh el Abd; but Rommel preferred to base his decision on his own observation of the day before. By nightfall, the *5th Light Division* was convinced that the Italians were right; it had suffered severe vehicle casualties, outrun its supplies, and covered only about two-fifths of the distance to Ben Gania. The Schwerin Group with the advantage of a day's start was close to Ben Gania but had also outrun supplies and was immobilised. Rommel himself flew above the advancing columns. He thought he could identify the foremost about 12 miles east of Ben Gania (but this was probably Mitford's squadron of the Long Range Desert Group).

In the early morning of the 5th, Rommel ordered his headquarters protection unit on the road to Ben Gania. Two more detachments of the *Ariete Division* were ordered to follow the Fabris unit. At midday, after having made a further reconnaissance of the columns on the march, he ordered a strong force of tanks, including the *5th Armoured Regiment,* less one squadron, and part of the *Ariete Division* (40 Italian tanks), with supporting field and anti-tank artillery, to advance on Msus by the southern route from Antelat while the *2nd Machine Gun Battalion* simultaneously approached from the west by the road from Soluch through Esc Sceleidima. The whole force was placed under the command of Colonel Olbrich. The departure of these columns was reported, as mentioned, to Neame and O'Connor by the R.A.F.

On hearing that enemy columns had passed Msus and were advancing east, skirting the Jebel Achdar, Neame decided to withdraw immediately to the line of the Wadi Derna. He realised that the 3rd Armoured Brigade was in no state to intervene effectively (only nine cruiser tanks remained) and that his entire force was therefore in imminent peril of encirclement. Morshead received oral orders to this effect while at Cyrenaica Command, returned immediately to his own headquarters, and there, since line communication was unreliable, dictated orders to liaison officers requiring an immediate move to be made that night to the Wadi Derna region. As the liaison officers were about to set out, Brigadier A. F. Harding telephoned from Cyrenaica Command to inform Morshead that there was considerable doubt of the accuracy of the air reports and that it was thought from reports of the 1/K.R.R.C. (which had recently reverted to the command of the armoured division) that the movement seen was our own armoured brigade. Morshead was instructed to hold his present positions, but to be prepared to withdraw at any moment.

Later Harding telephoned a second time and ordered the withdrawal to proceed. Liaison officers set out to units, food and petrol dumps were fired and very soon unit columns were setting out along the roads. Just at this moment, Command headquarters telephoned once more to order that the move be stopped and the positions on the Barce escarpment be reoccupied. With some difficulty the columns were halted and turned round on the narrow roads. Major Barham, who had been on the move almost continuously for 48 hours, was met on the road by Lloyd and sent to stop the destruction of supply and petrol dumps near Tecnis. Fortunately Barham met Burrows and Crawford on the way just as their battalions were moving out, and told them of the withdrawal's cancellation before the orders reached them by the normal channel of command. Such frequent changes in orders sapped confidence.

It was the 1/K.R.R.C. that had contradicted the false rumour concerning enemy occupation of Msus. This battalion—later described by Morshead as "well disciplined, well commanded, well trained; a first-class unit"—was patrolling in the area south of Tecnis and Maraua. They had heard with amazement that the enemy were supposed to be in that region and were quick to report that the information was false. The 9th Division's withdrawal had then been temporarily deferred. Not satisfied with this, they sent their forward company commander, Lieutenant Hornsby,[4] to Cyrenaica Command headquarters, and it was on the basis of his unequivocal reports that the 9th Division's withdrawal, which had again been set in motion, was finally reversed. Meanwhile "A" and "C" Squadrons of the King's Dragoon Guards, who had been patrolling in the Msus region but had found difficulty in maintaining wireless communication, had come north with the 3rd Armoured Brigade and rejoined their regimental headquarters 20 miles south of Maraua. They too confirmed that no enemy had been seen near Msus.

The enemy had not in fact reached Msus that evening but at the end of the day the *2nd Machine Gun Battalion,* advancing from the west, was not far away. It planned to link up early next morning in Msus with

---

[4] Capt D. F. Hornsby; 1/KRRC. Regular soldier; b. 26 Feb 1920.

Olbrich's main tank force coming up from the south. Meanwhile Rommel had also received erroneous reports from air reconnaissance. In the afternoon of the 5th he had flown to Ben Gania, where he was informed that reconnaissance aircraft had seen no British at Mechili. Rommel signalled Schwerin's force (which, as mentioned, had been directed to make for Tmimi on the coast): "Mechili clear of enemy. Make for it. Drive fast. Rommel."[5] He now planned to dispatch a force to Mechili by air, but later air reconnaissance reports that a British force was there caused him to cancel the project.

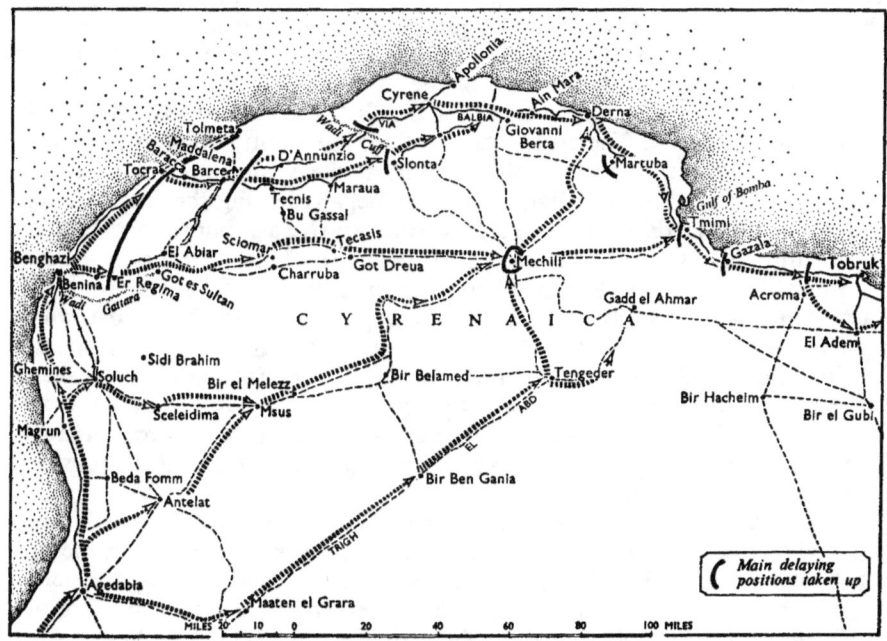

The German thrust into Cyrenaica

By the end of the day, Schwerin's advanced party had reached Tengeder, with units of the *Africa Corps* strung out at wide intervals along the Trigh el Abd. That night Rommel and his staff drove forward along this track with headlights blazing. A bombing attack by British aircraft was the condign reward for this rashness; afterwards the journey was continued with lights extinguished.

At Mechili on the morning of the 5th Brigadier Vaughan and Lieut-Colonel Munro, while on reconnaissance, came under fire from an enemy party on some high ground outside the defence line. The Indians quickly dispersed the enemy, whose presence at Mechili does not appear to be recorded in German documents unless they were members of a small party whom Rommel had sent to mine the tracks to the east.

[5] *The Rommel Papers*, p. 113.

The day was spent in improving defences. In the afternoon a German Storch aircraft flew over (in which was Lieutenant Schulz, Rommel's A.D.C., making a reconnaissance). The message from the 2nd Armoured Division asking for Major R. A. Eden's "M" Battery to be sent forward was received but its authenticity doubted. Vaughan asked that the message be repeated, mentioning Eden's nickname for identification. A reply was not received that day. One 25-pounder gun of the 104th R.H.A. arrived —the fort's only artillery. In the evening patrols reported dust in the direction of Tengeder; the brigade's field squadron, which had been at Tengeder, came in and reported having had a brush with an enemy party. During the night there were many reports of activity outside the perimeter.

Towards dawn on the 6th several Very lights were fired from the direction of the landing field south of the fort. Just on daylight two aircraft landed there. Vaughan sent a troop of the 2nd Lancers to investigate, but the aircraft made off. The troop then noticed an enemy column approaching from the south. Other patrols sent out at the same time returned with prisoners. After 9 a.m. two light field guns began shelling the fort. Another gun soon afterwards opened fire from the north-east but was driven off by a patrol of the 11th (Prince Albert Victor's Own) Cavalry.

About 11 a.m. two lorries filled with infantry made a charge at the eastern sector held by the P.A.V.O., coming straight up the road towards an anti-tank gun of the 11th Battery, 2/3rd Anti-Tank Regiment manned by Bombardier Rayner[6] and a crew of four. Fire from the Australians' gun stopped both trucks and enemy troops jumped out to take cover. Major Glover[7] and Lieutenant Mulgrue[8] went out in a breakdown truck, and a German officer and 20 Italian soldiers surrendered. Their equipment included a 47-mm gun.

Mitford's squadron of the Long Range Desert Group, which had spent the night some miles to the south-west of Mechili, now arrived on the outskirts of the fort. Mitford came in with a party to fetch petrol and reported to Vaughan, who arranged that he should operate from outside the perimeter. Mitford split his force into two parties. One of these, which Mitford himself commanded, soon captured the Italian officer in charge of the two guns shelling the fort, which then stopped firing. Meanwhile confirmation of the orders to "M" Battery had been received. Since the enemy had not yet closed in on the west, the battery set forth to meet the armoured division, escorted by a troop of the Lancers and taking with it the solitary 25-pounder of the 104th R.H.A.

The two aircraft which took off from Mechili airfield after having evaded the patrol of the 2nd Lancers flew south for about 15 miles to the head of Schwerin's column, with which Rommel's column had caught up during the night. Here they put down their passengers—a party which had been laying mines near Mechili. From the officer-in-charge Rommel

---

[6] Bdr V. A. Rayner, MM, NX33858; 2/3 A-Tk Regt. Farmer; of Mudgee, NSW; b. Mudgee, 3 Jan 1913.
[7] Lt-Col H. J. H. Glover, DSO, NX35070. (1st AIF: Maj 3 Div Arty.) 2/3 A-Tk Regt (CO 1941-42). Grazier; of Brewarrina, NSW; b. Goulburn, NSW, 11 Nov 1895. Died 1946.
[8] Lt G. E. Mulgrue, NX70284; 2/3 A-Tk Regt. Writer and broadcaster; of Perth, WA; b. Geraldton, WA, 11 Jun 1911.

received a first-hand report of the presence of a substantial British force. His reaction was characteristic. "There was now no time to lose," he wrote afterwards, "otherwise the bird would be flown. As we were still 12 miles from Mechili, I instructed Lieutenant Behrend to push forward at top speed to the Mechili-Derna track and close it at a suitable point. Lieut-Colonel Ponath, of whose force[9] there were unfortunately only 15 vehicles with us, was dispatched to Derna, where he was to close the Via Balbia (the main road) in both directions." Ponath noted the incident laconically in his own diary.[1] "Rommel bellows and chases us forward out of touch with the battalion across stony desert. Only 10 vehicles with us. With these against the rear of the enemy at Derna."

Rommel now directed that all forces should be concentrated against Mechili. When a message to this effect was received at *Africa Corps* headquarters, the operations officer, who had deduced from the presence of shipping in Tobruk Harbour that the British intended to evacuate by sea, noted in the war diary: "Tobruk would, however, have been a desirable target, in order to block the coast road and prevent embarkation; screening operations only at Mechili."

Rommel planned to attack Mechili at 3 p.m. that day.

The 6th of April was a day of important events and decisions. The invasion of Greece in the morning by German troops marked the beginning of a new campaign, while the appearance of Rommel's forces before Mechili caused the British command to abandon the entire Cyrenaican peninsula. That evening Wavell and the other commanders-in-chief in Cairo decided that an attempt would be made to hold Tobruk.

At first light on 6th April the King's Dragoon Guards sent a patrol back to Msus to investigate the accuracy of the reports that had caused so many changes of orders. The patrol found a large enemy force moving east from Msus and stayed in the vicinity, reporting direct to regimental headquarters, until discovered and forced to withdraw. But communications through the 2nd Armoured Division had been for days in a state of chronic breakdown. Neither the King's Dragoon Guards' reports, nor those of the R.A.F., who had been bombing enemy columns on the Trigh el Abd during the night, could have reached Neame before he set off that morning to visit Morshead and Gambier-Parry. Neame was in a confident frame of mind when he arrived at Morshead's headquarters at Tecnis. He told Morshead that the previous day's reports had been misleading and that it was now his intention to undertake a protracted defence of the Barce escarpment, combined with offensive patrols on to the Barce plain, and he instructed that the 2/24th and 2/13th Battalions should be brought forward from the Wadi Cuff-Slonta positions, where they had been preparing a second line of defence. Neame then left Morshead's headquarters to go in search of Gambier-Parry.

Morshead immediately dictated orders to his liaison officers in accordance with these instructions. Just when this had been completed, and not

---

[9] The *8th Machine Gun Battalion*.
[1] Later captured at Tobruk.

more than half an hour after Neame's departure, O'Connor telephoned from command headquarters that the enemy had shelled Mechili that morning and was advancing across the desert in strength: the 9th Division was therefore to be prepared to move back to the Wadi Derna. Morshead urged that the division should go back forthwith to the Gazala area, where the withdrawal routes could be less easily blocked, but O'Connor was reluctant to agree in Neame's absence. O'Connor was in an awkward situation. The command arrangements actually operating were the converse of those Neame had outlined to Morshead: O'Connor was at the command centre, Neame performing liaison duties—with unsatisfactory results.

Meanwhile the 2nd Armoured Division was in an unhappy state. Rimington had gone from his headquarters in search of Gambier-Parry. An order was issued to units to treat any vehicles to the west as enemy. A troop of the 5th Royal Tanks heard the order and, scouting to the south-west, fired on the 6th Royal Tanks' only remaining squadron where it had halted the night before, having experienced trouble from overheating of engines in the heavy uphill going. The regiment's commanding officer, Lieut-Colonel Harland,[2] had gone forward to brigade headquarters and was still there. About 10 a.m. brigade headquarters were told that enemy columns were approaching from the direction of Msus and that the armoured brigade was to withdraw east. Harland then sent one of his officers to bring up the squadron of the 6th, while the 5th Tanks waited to cover their withdrawal. But the squadron did not appear, and about 11.30 a.m. the 5th Tanks moved off. Eventually the officer returned and reported to Harland that the squadron was not to be found.

It is not easy to make sense of the accounts of 2nd Armoured Division's movements for the rest of 6th April. Reports emanating from the various command levels are irreconcilable. What is certain is that in the late morning the whole of the armoured division was moving eastwards in the direction of Mechili but in the early afternoon both the Support Group and the armoured brigade turned north towards Maraua and Derna while the divisional headquarters continued the journey alone.

About 10.45 a.m. Cyrenaica Command received a report from Mechili that a light German thrust of less than battalion strength had been repulsed. This information was passed to the 2nd Armoured Division, which issued orders for all its units to move to Mechili forthwith. Divisional headquarters itself then set off for Mechili. So neither Rimington, nor Neame —freshly planning in his mind a prolonged defence—succeeded in seeing Gambier-Parry that morning. Divisional headquarters' orders were passed to the 3rd Armoured Brigade by the Support Group. By 11.30 a.m. the 5th Royal Tank Regiment was withdrawing east in conformation.

When O'Connor received the reports of the enemy advance on Mechili, he went to the Derna landing ground to obtain first-hand information from the pilots who had been out that morning, a prudent course after recent experiences. He learnt of three enemy columns moving eastwards, one

---

[2] Lt-Col L. S. Harland, DSO, MC. CO 6 RTR. Regular soldier; b. 5 Jul 1894.

from Msus, one from Agedabia and one in the far south towards Gialo. Within a short time another report from Acroma, near Tobruk, indicated that at least some enemy bodies had gone far beyond Mechili. An enemy patrol had attacked a Royal Air Force post at Acroma. A squadron of the 18th Cavalry, then at El Adem, had come to the assistance of the R.A.F., driven off the patrol, and captured 18 Italian prisoners, who had stated that more troops were on the way.

O'Connor returned to his headquarters and sent out orders in the early afternoon (according to the Cyrenaica Command war diary) to the 2nd Armoured Division that it was to move immediately to Mechili with the Support Group, and that the 3rd Armoured Brigade should move in the same direction more slowly; he then informed Middle East headquarters that this might involve withdrawing the 9th Division to the Derna line.

About 1 p.m. the Support Group headquarters, with the 1st R.H.A. and the Tower Hamlets Rifles, had halted near Tecasis when orders were received by radio to withdraw by the main coast road instead of by Mechili, because enemy forces were near. Brigadier Latham and his staff were convinced that the voice giving the orders was that of Gambier-Parry's senior staff officer, Colonel G. E. Younghusband. Younghusband was captured at Mechili. His immediate subordinate (General Staff Officer, Grade 2) who was not captured stated in a report written soon afterwards that the headquarters of the armoured division ordered the 3rd Armoured Brigade to follow it to Mechili but Cyrenaica Command ordered the Support Group to withdraw north to Maraua. Whatever the explanation the fact is that the Support Group set off for Maraua, and the armoured brigade headquarters took the instructions to withdraw by that route as applying also to itself, for it passed orders to its tank units to retire to the El Abiar-Maraua track "as enemy columns were thought to be close to the south-west".[3] But Gambier-Parry and his headquarters continued to expect the brigade to follow them to Mechili; so did the Germans. The operations officer of the *Africa Corps* noted in the war diary that there were indications that the tanks which had been at Msus would "put in an appearance at Mechili on the morning of the 7th". Meanwhile O'Connor had ordered the 3rd Indian Brigade to send out a petrol convoy from Mechili to meet the 2nd Armoured Division.

On the way north Latham encountered Neame, who instructed that the Support Group was to take over the outpost line from the 1/K.R.R.C. Meanwhile Brigadier Rimington, who had spent much of the day unsuccessfully trying to see Gambier-Parry, had received orders from O'Connor that the armoured brigade was to proceed to Mechili by the Got Dreua track.

O'Connor had again discussed the situation with Morshead and, though reluctant to permit any move in daylight, had now agreed with Morshead's suggestion that the 9th Division be withdrawn immediately to the Gazala area. Since the armoured division was not available for flank support, it

---

[3] War diary, 5 RTR.

was decided to send ahead the 2/13th Battalion to Martuba and the 2/48th Battalion to Tmimi to hold these two key points on the withdrawal route. The rest of the division would withdraw through them, while the 1/K.R.R.C., once more transferred to Morshead's command, would provide rearguards for the engineers carrying out the demolition of bridges and defiles and the destruction of supply dumps.

With widely dispersed units, poor communications and a paucity of vehicles, it was no easy matter to organise the movement of all units of the division at short notice, carry out all the demolitions, and yet ensure that no unit was left without transport or cut off. To muster sufficient transport required much improvisation. Urgency precluded arranging a time-table; in the circumstances some mixing of units was inevitable. The division was to withdraw by the two parallel roads across the Cyrenaican massif. These converge about six miles west of Giovanni Berta; from the junction a single road proceeds to Giovanni Berta, where it turns north to Derna. But Morshead feared that the two tortuous passes by which the main road descended to Derna and climbed the escarpment again beyond the town might prove a dangerous bottleneck. Brigadier Kisch, who happened to be at 9th Division headquarters when authority to withdraw was received, suggested to Morshead that the division should proceed from Giovanni Berta to Martuba by the inland track which had been improved during the British advance earlier in the year. Morshead decided to send the division by this route.

The withdrawal orders were sent out to units at approximately 4 p.m. and by 5 p.m. the first columns were on the road. Just as the orders reached the forward units, the enemy made his first attempt to probe the defence on the Barce escarpment. At 4.15 p.m., at the pass east of Barce, Captain Peek's[4] company of the 2/15th Battalion shot up an enemy reconnaissance patrol attempting to drive up the pass; every member of the party was killed. About 5 p.m., at the northern pass lorried infantry escorted by a light tank and armoured cars drove across the right flank of the 2/48th Battalion, just after the commanding officer, Lieut-Colonel Windeyer,[5] had given out orders to withdraw. The enemy dismounted and opened fire. It appeared that the disengagement might become a difficult rearguard action; but good firing by the machine-gunners of the Royal Northumberland Fusiliers deterred the enemy from pressing the assault home and enabled the infantry to withdraw without casualties. The Fusiliers were less fortunate: one man was killed and two wounded. The author of a narrative of the 2/48th Battalion's experiences commented:

> The troops started out tired and unshaven and unwashed. They seemed to be abandoning an ideal position for a stand and running away once more—contrary to everyone's wish to "have a go" at the enemy. They piled into overcrowded vehicles amid rifles, Bren guns and gear and equipment where no position offered comfort yet no move was possible. The sleep they needed was unattainable. Some

---

[4] Maj A. E. de L. Peek, QX6220. 2/15 and 31/51 Bns. Dairy farmer; of Sexton, Qld; b. Sydney, 14 Apr 1907.

[5] Maj-Gen Rt Hon Sir Victor Windeyer, KBE, CB, DSO, ED, NX396. 2/13 Bn; HQ 7 Div; CO 2/48 Bn 1940-42; comd 20 Bde 1942-45; admin comd 9 Div 1945-46. Barrister-at-law; of Sydney; b. Hunter's Hill, NSW, 28 Jul 1900.

strange conveyances were used, too. A number of men travelled a great part of the journey on an Italian table-top lorry which was hitched behind a truck and towed along.

About 5 p.m. command headquarters heard from the Mechili garrison that the enemy force surrounding them was growing larger. An attack was expected next day; Vaughan asked for assistance.

The investment of Mechili was not yet in fact sufficiently close to prevent parties from operating outside the defence perimeter and P.A.V.O. patrols brought in several prisoners during the day. The road was closed to the east, but not to the west. A patrol from the squadron at Gadd el Ahmar, which had come in for replenishments, found the way blocked when it attempted to return. On the other hand, in response to Cyrenaica Command's request, a petrol convoy was successfully dispatched, under escort of a troop of the 2nd Lancers, on the route by which the 2nd Armoured Division was expected.

Towards the end of the day a German officer came in with a flag of truce to demand the garrison's surrender. He was brought before Brigadier Vaughan without being blindfolded; but the brigadier sent him back blindfolded by a different route with, of course, a categorical refusal.[6]

For Rommel, 6th April had been a frustrating day. His main forces had made disappointing progress and could not be mustered at Mechili in sufficient strength to attack. Some units were halted for want of fuel, others by mechanical difficulties caused by the excessive heat; others again had received no rations for four days. Many were lost or out of touch. But the Fabris unit reached Mechili in the evening and was placed in position to the east. Rommel planned to attack at 7 a.m. next day.

After receiving General O'Connor's orders, Brigadier Rimington returned at once to his brigade at the old fort south-east of Tecnis and called a conference of his commanders, at which "owing to the present shortage of petrol and the difficult nature of the country"[7] it was decided to move back into Derna via Maraua and then to proceed to Mechili by a track that left the main road four miles east of Derna. Rimington had some reason for lack of confidence in the command; some reason to doubt whether any of his tanks would reach Mechili if he took the more direct route. But if his decision to act independently had the virtue of husbanding what was left of the armour, it had the vices of delaying the arrival of reinforcements at Mechili and deranging the withdrawal plan for the rest of the force. It meant that his brigade's axis of withdrawal would merge with, and then cross, the withdrawal route Morshead had chosen (without Rimington's knowledge) for the 9th Division.

The armoured brigade began to move soon after 5 p.m. Rimington and Fanshawe went forward to arrange fuel replenishments and sent an

---
[6] There is a reference in a contemporary war diary to the failure to blindfold this emissary. On the other hand some Australian members of the garrison insist that every emissary brought in was first blindfolded.
[7] War diary, 5 RTR.

officer to command headquarters to report the decision, which caused some consternation there. Soon afterwards Morshead arrived, having seen his columns on the road. Neame, recently returned, told Morshead that "3rd Armoured Brigade was in fact moving on Maraua and urgently needed petrol".[8] This was likely to disorganise the Australian withdrawal, but there was nothing Morshead could do.

When about 5 p.m. Lieut-Colonel Burrows received orders to take his battalion immediately to Martuba, he left at once with his adjutant, Captain Kelly,[9] to reconnoitre the area and ordered the battalion to follow; it was on the road 20 minutes later. "What we were *not* told," he wrote afterwards, "was that the enemy might be there before us." Burrows and Kelly arrived at Martuba about 8.30 p.m., having travelled by the better road through Derna, where they had "found everybody in panic. They just dropped everything and cleared for their lives, with motor vehicles going everywhere."[1] Burrows learnt that an enemy column had cut the inland track from Giovanni Berta to Martuba where it was intersected by the track coming up from Mechili and the south. Another enemy group was leaguering three miles south of Martuba. He went to Cyrenaica Command headquarters to report these developments.

The 2/13th reached Martuba soon afterwards and deployed defensively in the dark. The ground was hard and open and the men, dispirited and exhausted, built themselves shelters of stones. The German party that had cut the road had apparently moved on, for the battalion had not encountered it; but the other party to the south of Martuba remained.

In the absence of traffic control, units travelling on the overloaded southern road became intermingled when vehicles from the side tracks joined the main traffic stream. Most unit convoys, except the first away, became split up. At the junction of the two roads and at the refuelling points at Maraua and Giovanni Berta confusion grew worse. At Giovanni Berta most of the Australian vehicles left the bitumen road to take the desert track. The heavy pounding by hundreds upon hundreds of wheels broke down the road surface to an uneven stony bottom, over which, head to tail, and at times three vehicles abreast, the long line of transport crawled through a pall of dust at a speed of about six miles an hour, halting repeatedly as one vehicle after another broke down or was compelled to pause by overheating.

The Support Group came into the southern road from Tecasis; the 3rd Armoured Brigade and King's Dragoon Guards came in from the El Abiar-Maraua track (the 5th Royal Tanks with a strength of only seven cruisers, the 3rd Hussars with only six light tanks) and halted awhile off the road as Australian units passed. Meanwhile the unfortunate squadron of the 6th Royal Tanks, who had not seen the officer sent by Harland that morning, and whose wireless link had broken down, was slowly

---

[8] 9 Australian Division Report on Operations in Cyrenaica, March-October 1941, including the Defence of Tobruch.
[9] Lt-Col J. L. A. Kelly, DSO, NX12214. 2/13 Bn; CO 31/51 Bn 1944-45. Regular soldier; of Bondi, NSW; b. Cowra, NSW, 10 Mar 1907.
[1] Letter dated 8 May 1941 to the President of the 2/13th Battalion Comforts Fund.

climbing up to the abandoned plateau, nursing its few remaining tanks, and travelling too slowly to reach the main road that night.

The last Australian battalion to move was the 2/24th. The staff of Morshead's headquarters experienced great difficulty in mustering transport to lift it. Major Dodds went for help to the 2/17th, where Lieut-Colonel Crawford told him that he had already made five lorries available to move other forward units. Nevertheless Crawford unloaded his blankets and reserve rations to provide six trucks. Eventually, at 9.30 p.m., Dodds arrived at the 2/24th with 14 vehicles (most of the rest had been provided by the engineers). Major Tasker managed to get his men aboard these and a few unit vehicles. He set off about 9.45 p.m. Near Cyrene, about 11 p.m., Major Barham met the battalion with two more trucks. The convoy became irretrievably broken up after passing the road junction west of Giovanni Berta, where the two withdrawal axes merged; further separation occurred at Giovanni Berta. The battalion arrived at its destination, Tmimi, in small separate groups about two hours after sunrise next morning.

Although the crossroads at the intersection of the Giovanni Berta-Martuba and Mechili-Derna tracks had earlier been blocked by an enemy column, later traffic passed along the east-west desert track without interference. The enemy column was undoubtedly Ponath's group. It would appear that Ponath did not linger at the crossroads because his orders were to close the main coast road at Derna and his forces were too small to close both routes; his group proceeded on towards Derna, near which, according to his diary, a disturbed night was spent in some caves, known as the "Rocknest", close to where the main road issued on to the plateau after climbing the escarpment east of Derna. An ambush was established on the north-south track, probably more with the object of protecting the resting column at the Rocknest than of collecting prisoners.

The 9th Division's provost section, which had at last arrived in the forward area, was ordered to establish traffic points at Giovanni Berta and on the inland track. The traffic control at these crossroads, however, appears to have operated very strangely. Afterwards the belief was almost universally held in the 9th Division that the Germans had captured an English provost at this point, donned his uniform and then misdirected the traffic towards the German ambush; but there is no reliable evidence that this occurred. (Similar unfounded stories circulated through France after the first German offensive.) Major Fell,[2] on liaison duties for divisional headquarters, took the inland road from Maraua just before 9 p.m. and found the traffic control very bad and all units thoroughly mixed up. His diary records his arrival at the crossroads:

> Eventually got to Derna X roads. Saw traffic in front take left turn—no police on turn. Got out and looked at sign board—straight ahead to Martuba so feeling a bit bothered got in and went straight on. . . . No other traffic. Passed one police half asleep but found oasis Martuba.

---

[2] Maj L. A. Fell, VX47818; 2/24 Bn. Grazier; of Metung, Vic; b. Ulverston, England, 16 Mar 1899.

Morshead bade farewell to Neame and O'Connor at Maraua about 8 p.m. and, travelling by the main coast road, passed through Derna just as the Germans were arriving. Neame, O'Connor and Combe departed soon afterwards, taking the inland track. At the Derna-Mechili crossroads, following a line of vehicles in front, their car turned left. The column—possibly the very one seen by Major Fell—ran into the German ambush. The generals were captured.[3]

Later during the night a small group of trucks in charge of Lieutenant L. K. Shave came down the same road, bearing members of the Intelligence, operations and cipher sections of the 9th Division. They came to a halt behind other vehicles. The occupants at the back of the cipher section van, which contained ciphers and other secret documents, found themselves facing a German with a sub-machine-gun, who ordered them from the vehicle. Shave, in the front seat, heard the guttural voice, got out of the truck on the opposite side, went round to the back of the vehicle and shot the German soldier, saying "Take that you . . .". The men returned and the trucks drove off without interference.

Major Risson[4] and Lieutenant Moulds[5] with a section of the 2/7th Field Company and some vehicles of the 2/3rd Field Company were travelling along the inland track in the early hours of the morning. At the crossroads, where the traffic was still undirected, they also turned left and took the track to Derna. After travelling about six miles, they came up to a deserted convoy, which included staff cars (probably those in which Neame's party had been travelling). They attempted to bypass it, but were halted by fire from in front. Risson decided to wait until dawn to see whether the rescue of any men taken prisoner could be attempted. About 6.45 a.m., before it was fully light, the Australians came under heavy fire; several vehicles were lost and many men wounded. The party managed to get away in four trucks and proceeded to Martuba, where the 2/13th Battalion's medical officer treated their wounded.

About 5 a.m. Corporal Dunn[6] of the 2/7th Field Company had arrived with his subsection at the halted tail of Risson's convoy. Firing opened up just after his arrival. Dunn organised a getaway of about 30 men in the rearmost trucks. The party got back to the crossroads, where Dunn arranged with an officer to prevent other traffic from using the northern track and then went on towards Martuba. Dunn soon came across the 2/15th Battalion, to which he reported the enemy ambush.

That several groups had chosen the wrong road in the darkness is not surprising. No maps had been issued to unit commanders; there were none available. One commanding officer guided his battalion using a rough map in a press cutting his wife had sent to him from Australia.

---

[3] There is evidence that the capture was made by one officer and three men. See Wilmot, *Tobruk*, p. 78.

[4] Maj-Gen R. J. H. Risson, CB, CBE, DSO, ED, QX6062. OC 2/3 Fd Coy; CRE 7 Div 1941-42, 9 Div 1942-43; CE II Corps 1943-44, I Corps 1944-45. Civil engineer; of Brisbane; b. Grantham, Qld, 20 Apr 1901.

[5] Maj W. J. Moulds, MBE, QX6233; 2/3 Fd Coy (OC 1943). Architect; of Brisbane; b. Oakey, Qld, 14 Jul 1909.

[6] Cpl E. Dunn, QX7533; 2/7 Fd Coy. Labourer; of Mareeba, Qld; b. London, 7 Dec 1901.

When command headquarters heard of the cutting of the inland track by the enemy, orders were sent to the traffic control points at Giovanni Berta to divert all traffic by the main road through Derna. Most unit convoys had already been split up before this was put into effect. The result was that parts of units proceeded by the one route, parts by the other. Most of the 2/48th Battalion, going to Tmimi, travelled by the inland track, but the tail of their column, including parts of "B" and "C" Companies, was directed through Derna. The 2/15th Battalion suffered similarly, the head of the column, including battalion headquarters, the headquarters company and part of "B" Echelon proceeding by the inland track, the rest following through Derna. The battalion headquarters' convoy of the 2/15th halted by the roadside between the Derna crossroads and Martuba just after dawn to wait for the rest of the battalion and re-form the convoy. The commanding officer, Lieut-Colonel Marlan, who had stayed at the old position until the last of his companies had departed, was to join them there about half an hour later.

While all this traffic was moving eastwards, important demolition work was being done behind the withdrawing units by both British and Australian engineers, under the efficient direction of Brigadier Kisch, and with the reliable protection of the 1/K.R.R.C. None had worked more continuously in the last few days than the engineers, many of whom had had practically no sleep since 3rd April. It was at first arranged that the Australian engineers should fire all demolitions, but when it later became apparent that they would be unable to complete the task, Kisch arranged for much of the rearward demolition to be undertaken by the 295th and 552nd Companies, R.E., under the direction of Lieut-Colonel Boddington.[7] Water points, pumping plants, and abandoned tanks and armoured cars were destroyed, dumps demolished, bridges blown, roads cratered; all carefully timed to avoid cutting off portions of the retiring force. Firing parties (including Lieut-Colonel Mann,[8] Morshead's chief engineer officer, with some of his staff, and Major Gehrmann with some of his staff) took over each demolition in turn from others who had prepared them.

Lieutenant Roach's[9] section of the 2/3rd Field Company had prepared extensive demolitions in the ammunition dump at Ain Mara, west of Derna, the largest in Libya. They handed them over to Boddington soon after 11 p.m. Later in the night, Roach and his men ran into the German ambush and were captured, with the exception of one man, Sapper Ryan.[1] Sergeant Greasley[2] of Lieutenant Faine's[3] section of the 2/7th Field Company blew the pass east of Barce and the bridge. Notwithstanding that

---

[7] Col N. Boddington, OBE; Royal Engineers. Regular soldier; b. 11 Aug 1900.
[8] Brig J. Mann, DSO, VX250. (1st AIF: Lt 2 Fd Coy Engrs 1918.) CRE 9 Div 1940-41 and 1941-42; DCE Western Desert Force Apr-Oct 1941; CE First Army 1942-44, NGF 1944, II Corps 1944-45; Comd 1 Aust CE (Wks) 1945. Regular soldier; b. Melbourne, 8 Jul 1897.
[9] Maj W. G. Roach, NX9536; 2/3 Fd Coy. Regular soldier; of Maroubra, NSW; b. Sydney, 6 Aug 1914.
[1] Spr C. Ryan, SX842; 2/3 and 2/15 Fd Coys. Fruiterer; of Benalla, Vic; b. Glenmaggie, Vic, 24 Nov 1911. Another, Spr K. R. Ogilvie (of Glenelg, SA), escaped, and reached Tobruk on 9th April.
[2] WO2 C. A. Greasley, MM, QX8767; 2/7 Fd Coy. Truck driver; of Ipswich, Qld; b. Ipswich, 3 May 1912.
[3] Capt C. R. Faine, QX6441; 2/7 Fd Coy. Factory manager; of Brisbane; b. Brisbane, 9 Jul 1915.

the enemy had earlier approached, he and his men reconnoitred the damage done, re-mined the foot of the pass and then the pass itself. Later, four sappers of this section were also ambushed.

Meanwhile Gehrmann's company was busy on the northern route. At midnight the Tocra pass was blown, two large craters being formed across the road. Extensive demolitions were then effected in the Wadi Cuff. At 2 a.m. more demolitions were carried out at Cyrene and Apollonia (from which the Australians evacuated an English engineer unit that had not heard of the withdrawal order). Between 4 a.m. and 4.30 a.m. further demolitions were effected along the road in rear of Apollonia. In the forenoon the work of destruction continued: at 9.30 a.m. a bridge west of Giovanni Berta; between 10 and 10.30 a.m., after the last troops of the 2nd Armoured Division had passed through, dumps of mines and explosives near Giovanni Berta;[4] between 11.30 and midday, the ammunition dump at Ain Mara and a bridge near by.

With the exception of some water points near Maraua, nothing in the demolition program was missed. Germans who later advanced by this route reported that at every turn obstacles and mines were encountered.

Cyrenaica Command headquarters arrived at Tmimi soon after midnight on 6th April but moved on again to Gazala when it was learned that the enemy was in the vicinity. About 4 a.m. Morshead arrived at the Tmimi roadhouse to find Brigadier Harding there, very worried because Neame and O'Connor had not arrived. As time passed, Morshead and Harding concluded that the two generals must have been intercepted and were probably captured, and that they must themselves determine the immediate action to be taken. They decided to organise the next line of resistance at Gazala, where the escarpment defining the northern edge of the Libyan plateau rises from the desert and to order the force at Mechili to withdraw immediately to El Adem; but the message conveying that order appears to have been addressed only to the 2nd Armoured Division and 3rd Armoured Brigade and does not appear to have been received by the Mechili garrison. Harding's and Morshead's headquarters and the reconnaissance wing of the R.A.F. were withdrawn to Gazala.

At dawn on 7th April, the road that descends the pass into Derna and climbs the tortuous second pass east of the town was chock-full of crawling vehicles. For some hours all traffic had been diverted this way from the inland desert track. A long line of vehicles, in many places three or four abreast, stretched from Giovanni Berta to Derna, thence south-east into the desert. "A" Company of the 1/K.R.R.C. was blocking the track coming into Giovanni Berta from Mechili and the south, the Tower Hamlets guarding the western pass-head at Derna. The 3rd Armoured Brigade was extended over a great distance, the foremost elements near Derna, the rearmost (including most of the tanks) almost as far west as Slonta.

During the night trek Brigadier Rimington's command vehicle had fallen down a steep bank. About 4 a.m. he woke Lieut-Colonel Drew,

---
[4] At Giovanni Berta, a Lysander dropped a message asking the location of 9th Division headquarters. Mann lined up a lot of stragglers to spell the word "Tmimi".

whose 5th Royal Tanks had halted for a rest on the southern road near Slonta, to inform him that because of the accident he might arrive late at a conference beyond Derna arranged for next day. Rimington and Fanshawe later tried to bypass the traffic stream by taking the desert route to Derna, drove into the German ambush and were captured: Rimington was mortally wounded. Thus, with the exception of Gambier-Parry, almost every senior British commander in the desert had fallen into Ponath's trap. Gambier-Parry had arrived meanwhile at Mechili, the garrison of which was now encircled.

Many units of the 2nd Armoured Division had halted during the night to rest. They included the headquarters of the Support Group, which had leaguered off the inland track near Giovanni Berta, the King's Dragoon Guards, bottled up in the traffic queue approaching Derna, and the 1st R.H.A. which had made a brief halt at 5 a.m. five miles west of Derna. Near them, breakfasting, was a company of the 1/K.R.R.C., another company of which was passing through Derna. A third company and the headquarters group were moving out across the desert by the main road from Derna to Mechili: ahead of them were the 51st Field Regiment, most of the Northumberland Fusiliers, most of the 2/15th Battalion and, farther ahead, close to Tmimi, split-off portions of the 26th Brigade, diverted from the main body at the Giovanni Berta turn-off. On the southern inland track, the 2/17th Battalion was travelling eastwards towards the Mechili-Derna crossroads, near which it later passed Lieut-Colonel Marlan and his staff at breakfast and, soon afterwards, the 2/15th Battalion headquarters. The 2/13th Battalion was still at Martuba. Farther to the east the leading elements of the 2/48th Battalion were approaching Tmimi, followed by leading elements of the 2/24th.

Major Batten[5] had preceded the 2/48th to Tmimi and was ready to direct it into position. Meanwhile Morshead had sent Major White[6] of his operations staff there to intercept the foremost groups arriving. White had collected a mixed group of engineers and elements of the 2/48th Battalion to man the buildings there and armed them with anti-tank rifles.

Major Loughrey's[7] company of the 2/48th, returning from protective duties at Derna, reached Tmimi before the rest of the battalion. Batten directed it into position about 1,000 yards south of the road. The company's foremost truck (in which were travelling Warrant-Officer Stewart[8] and four men), breasting a small rise, ran into three vehicles in a slight depression. They were enemy reconnaissance cars, one of which opened fire. In the skirmish Stewart was wounded, two enemy were killed, and two wounded, Private Searle[9] firing most effectively. By a strange chance,

---

[5] Maj R. L. Batten, SX8894; 2/48 Bn. Department manager; of Prospect, SA; b. Prospect, 5 Jun 1904. Died of wounds 23 Nov 1943.
[6] Brig T. W. White, MVO, VX20316. GSO2 9 Div 1940-41; CO 2/1 Bn 1942; various staff appts 1942-45. Regular soldier; b. Brisbane, 28 Nov 1902.
[7] Lt-Col J. Loughrey, ED, VX40200. 2/48 and 2/24 Bns; CO 2/28 Bn 1942-43, LTD Vic L of C Area 1943-45. Solicitor; of Toorak, Vic; b. Leongatha, Vic, 2 Jul 1909.
[8] WO2 D. P. S. Stewart, SX8033; 2/48 Bn. Clerk; of Gladstone, SA; b. Gladstone, 4 Nov 1918.
[9] Pte H. S. Searle, SX8143; 2/48 Bn. Motor mechanic; of Alberton, SA; b. Stirling West, SA, 22 Mar 1919. Killed in action 26 Oct 1942.

a British cruiser tank was passing through Tmimi in the column of withdrawing vehicles at this very moment.[1]

It was directed to the scene of the skirmish, whereupon the other two enemy vehicles made off while Searle bailed up with his rifle the occupants of the one that had fired on the Australians. Six prisoners (two of whom later died of their wounds) and two light machine-guns, as well as the truck, were captured.

Brigadier Tovell soon arrived at Tmimi with his headquarters, which he established in the roadhouse now vacated by Cyrenaica Command; the main body of the 2/48th with Lieut-Colonel Windeyer in command followed. A quick-spoken, dynamic Irish lieut-colonel arrived soon afterwards and approached Windeyer. "Can you tell me the object of the exercise?", he asked. It was Windeyer's first meeting with Lieut-Colonel Martin,[2] commanding the 1/Royal Northumberland Fusiliers, which had been delayed by the congestion near Derna, but was to support the infantry at Tmimi.

Meanwhile orders had been sent to the 2/13th Battalion to withdraw from Martuba to Tmimi and take up a defensive position on the right of the 2/48th Battalion, while the 2/24th, 2/15th and 2/17th, as their columns passed through Tmimi, were told to proceed to Gazala, where the next line of resistance was being organised by the 20th Brigade.

Lieut-Colonel Marlan caught up with the 2/15th Battalion headquarters group, halted by the inland track, just before 8 a.m. and was surprised to find that the rifle companies, which had left before him, had not arrived. He also learnt from Major Barton[3] that there were enemy in the vicinity. Marlan decided to wait for his rifle companies, expressing the view that the battalion would then be better able to fight its way clear if intercepted. About 9 a.m., fearing that the other companies might have travelled by the coast road, he sent his Intelligence officer, Lieutenant Gemmell-Smith,[4] to see if traffic was still using the Derna Road. Marlan himself made a reconnaissance and saw that his headquarters could safely make its way to the east but he continued to wait for his rifle companies. Soon afterwards a mixed German force, including three or four armoured cars, bore down on the halted column and began shelling it. The Australians brought into action the few weapons they had, mainly rifles. Four anti-aircraft guns of the 8th Light Anti-Aircraft Battery mounted on Italian lorries engaged the armoured cars. Two guns were hit and burnt; the other two fired until they exhausted their ammunition.[5] Eventually the German vehicles completely encircled Marlan's men. Judging that escape was impossible, Marlan capitulated.[6]

---

[1] The fortuitous appearance of this tank at this moment is mysterious. The 5th Royal Tanks had halted for three hours at 3 a.m. on the road between Giovanni Berta and Slonta, far to the west.

[2] Brig E. O. Martin, DSO. CO 1/RNF. Regular soldier; b. 28 Jan 1900.

[3] Lt-Col C. N. Barton, OBE, ED, QX6198; 2/15 Bn. Civil engineer; of Brisbane; b. Bowen, Qld, 5 Jul 1907.

[4] Maj G. A. Gemmell-Smith, QX8571. 2/15 Bn and staff appts. Sugar chemist; of Edmonton, Qld; b. Fiji, 11 Feb 1916.

[5] L-Sgt A. Adams, of Brunswick, Vic, fought his gun after his vehicle had been hit several times and was on fire. He continued firing until all ammunition was expended.

[6] The group comprised 2/15th Bn (8 officers, 175 ORs) and 8th Lt AA Bty (1 officer, 22 ORs).

It is surprising that with their superior air power the Germans had not managed to inflict greater damage on the columns of the retreating forces packed tight along the roads. For this, much credit must go to No. 3 Squadron R.A.A.F. and No. 73 Squadron R.A.F., who had kept their Hurricanes almost continuously in the air in the last few days. On this morning, however, the German Air Force struck in considerable strength at the Derna defiles, inflicting much damage and seriously delaying the withdrawal.

About 10 a.m. the 1st R.H.A., having moved through Derna and ascended the eastern pass beyond the town, arrived at the Derna airfield. There a halt was called to reassemble the regiment so that it could proceed properly organised. Near the landing ground "B" Company of the 1/K.R.R.C. had also halted to gather its scattered sub-units into proper order. Just as the Chestnut and Rocket Troops of the 1st R.H.A. were forming up to move on, an enemy column consisting of three vans, an armoured car and one gun appeared from the south; it began to machine-gun and shell the road, catching some elements of the Tower Hamlets in the open. Both R.H.A. troops were in action in a flash, engaging the vehicles over open sights; one vehicle received a direct hit. An Australian anti-tank gun and a Bofors anti-aircraft gun came into action alongside. The enemy column made off rapidly, but no British armoured cars or tanks were at hand to give chase. The 1st R.H.A. moved on, leaving Captain Loder-Symonds[7] with "B/O" Battery to keep the road open. Latham's headquarters and a company of the French Motor Battalion passed through and the 104th R.H.A., whose 339th Battery had a brush with an enemy column, joined the main coast road from the Mechili track. Then the King's Dragoon Guards (less one squadron still west of Derna) arrived at the airfield, and a squadron was detached for local protection while the rest of the regiment continued to march. While one troop of this squadron was detailed to protect Loder-Symonds' guns another was sent southwards in an attempt to outflank the enemy column, but was halted by shell fire.

Lieut-Colonel de Salis,[8] commanding the rearguard companies of the 1/K.R.R.C., had come forward on hearing the firing. He ordered Captain Mason's[9] company into a covering position west of the main road, instructing them to remain there as long as possible but to withdraw if the position became untenable. The riflemen were attacked by enemy infantry almost as soon as they were in position and for more than two hours they kept the enemy at bay. Unfortunately "B/O" Battery and the Australian anti-tank gun had moved on just before the action commenced.

Meanwhile the 5th Royal Tanks, reduced to seven cruisers, were beginning to climb the escarpment. The steep ascent was too much for three of the tanks; after being stripped they were left for the demolition parties to destroy. One caused great difficulty, completely blocking the road for some time. Only four tanks now remained. Their commander, Lieut-

---
[7] Brig R. G. Loder-Symonds, DSO, MC; 1 RHA. Regular soldier; b. 1 Mar 1913.
[8] Lt-Col S. C. F. de Salis, DSO; 1/KRRC. Regular soldier; b. 5 Aug 1898.
[9] Maj G. H. Mason; 1/KRRC. Regular soldier; b. 17 Jun 1908.

Colonel Drew, with Lieut-Colonel Petherick[1] of the 3rd Hussars (whose last tank was abandoned in Derna), had gone forward in search of Rimington. As the two officers approached the airfield, they were fired on from a small fort and could see the armoured cars of the King's Dragoon Guards engaging an enemy force. Drew spoke to the commander of a platoon of the Tower Hamlets Rifles holding a ruined building near the road and then returned to the pass to organise assistance from the rearguard parties.

"A" Company of the 1/K.R.R.C. (which was supported by a section of "J" Battery of the 3rd R.H.A.) had been withdrawn from its position covering the approaches to Giovanni Berta at 10 a.m. and was in Derna. By 2.30 p.m. the last of the armoured division had passed through the town, where the demolitions had meanwhile been completed by Lieutenant Barlow[2] of the 2/1st Pioneers. During the next half-hour the engineers fired two craters in the western pass and four in the eastern, and destroyed the abandoned tanks. The rearguards then withdrew up the pass. At the top they were met by Colonel Drew, who took the rearguard commanders to reconnoitre the enemy road-block. More enemy vehicles were seen to be approaching on a broad front from the south. A staff officer of the 3rd Armoured Brigade unfortunately chose this moment to authorise the withdrawal of the armoured cars and this order was wrongly passed to one of the platoons of Mason's company of the 1/K.R.R.C. without Mason's knowledge. Soon afterwards another of Mason's platoons was cut off; then the remaining platoon and his headquarters were surrounded. Mason refused a demand for his surrender and succeeded in withdrawing his men into a neighbouring wadi. Here they played hide-and-seek with the enemy for two hours.[3]

On his second reconnaissance Drew therefore found the enemy in complete possession of the aerodrome area. He had a small but effective mixed force, which included "A" Company of the 1/K.R.R.C., one rifle company and other elements of the Tower Hamlets, a section of anti-tank guns of "J" Battery, 3rd R.H.A. and four tanks. Drew ordered the three motorised platoons of the 1/K.R.R.C. to a position covering the road, with the tanks on their left, while their scout platoon was sent to reconnoitre to the east. The riflemen went into position with skill and great dash, while the Tower Hamlets company took up a position in reserve behind them. But the K.R.R.C. scout platoon became heavily engaged and could not be extricated.

Although the Germans had gained control of the airfield zone, they had been slow to exploit by seizing the pass. Now they made a move to do so. About 4 p.m. a force of five armoured cars, five lorries of infantry and two anti-tank guns, supported by two gun-howitzers, attacked round the right flank, south of the road. A section of three 2-pounder guns did some fine

---

[1] Lt-Col W. G. Petherick; 3 Hussars. Regular soldier; b. 25 Aug 1898.
[2] Capt L. Barlow, NX59151; 2/1 Pnr Bn. Construction foreman; of Ryde, NSW; b. Ryde, 7 Oct 1912.
[3] Later in the evening they were joined by other stragglers. They laid up in the pass that night and the whole of the next day. Moving off at 9 p.m. on the 8th, they managed to escape and reached Salum on 10th April.

shooting, setting all the vehicles afire. One blew up. Soon afterwards three armoured cars came round the left flank. The British gunners quickly changed position and set these afire too. The enemy was driven back south of the road, but his machine-guns still covered it at fairly close range. The diarist of the company of the 1/K.R.R.C. later remarked drily that the enemy "had almost unconsciously thrown us on the defensive".

By 4.30 p.m. the firing had ceased and the gun-howitzers had retired. Drew now planned to bypass the enemy by a fighting move in force at 5.15 p.m. under cover of the four remaining tanks of his regiment, nearly all that remained of the 2nd Armoured Division's tank force.[4] At 5.20 the cruisers advanced line-ahead up the east side of the landing ground, engaging the enemy machine-gun posts. Behind them came some 50 vehicles, the 1/K.R.R.C. leading. Among them were the Australian demolition firing parties: Lieut-Colonel Mann with Captain Smith[5] and Lieutenant Overall[6] (his adjutant and Intelligence officer respectively), and Major Gehrmann with Lieutenants Young[7] and Moodie;[8] also Lieutenant Barlow and some pioneers who had had charge of the demolitions in Derna.[9] The charging column created a cloud of dust, which impeded the German firing. The tanks fought magnificently until all were knocked out. Many vehicles were hit, but others always stopped to load up with stranded men until they could take no more. Unable to penetrate by the way planned, the column, after a hurried conference, made a circular movement to the left near the sea; but there it was halted by a deep wadi. At this point Gehrmann, Young and Moodie, with six other vehicles, made a dash south across broken country to reach the open road; the exhaust silencers were smashed, and the roar of the fleeing vehicles' engines dramatically announced their progress across the desert. Mann's party took a different route; their car became stuck in the bottom of a deep wadi. They abandoned it, and set off on foot.[1] The rest of the column, though much diminished in size by casualties,[2] reached the main road about an hour and a half later, then journeyed without further incident to Tobruk, which they reached late at night.

By coincidence Rimington's decision to route the 3rd Armoured Brigade through Derna had brought the 5th Royal Tanks to the place where they were most needed and could be most effectively employed that day. It was

---

[4] Three qualifications should be made to this statement. Gambier-Parry had taken one cruiser to Mechili and, two were withdrawing independently farther east. "C" Squadron of the 6th RTR, left behind near Tecnis, still had one M13.

[5] Lt-Col J. W. Smith, NX351. RAE 9 Div 1940-41; engineer staff appts 1942-45. Civil engineer; of Hunter's Hill, NSW; b. Adelaide, 15 Feb 1901.

[6] Lt-Col J. W. Overall, CBE, MC, NX35058. 2/13 Fd Coy; 1 Para Bn (CO 1944-45). Chairman National Capital Development Commission since 1958. Architect; of Sydney; b. Sydney, 15 Jul 1913.

[7] Lt-Col G. E. Young, QX6045. 2/13 Fd Coy; OC 24 Fd Pk Coy; CRE 2 Aust CRE 1944-45. Mechanical and electrical engineer; of Brisbane; b. Chillagoe, Qld, 31 Jul 1912.

[8] Maj R. O. K. T. Moodie, QX6522. 2/13 Fd Coy (OC 1942-44); SORE 2 VIII British Corps 1944-45; OC 2/11 Fd Coy 1945. Mining engineer; of Sydney; b. Sydney, 1 Sep 1916.

[9] A graphic picture of Barlow is given by D. V. Duff in *May the Winds Blow* (1948), pp. 314-15.

[1] They were to reach Tobruk.

[2] At Derna the Tower Hamlets lost practically all that remained of their "C" Company, and some two-thirds of their headquarters group. Lt-Col Boddington's firing party turned back along the coast on foot. His party was later ambushed, and he was captured.

a fitting end for a regiment that had acquitted itself well throughout notwithstanding that its equipment, its supplies and its communications continually broke down. It had lost 38 tanks in Cyrenaica. Of these one was destroyed by running over a thermos bomb, nine in action with the enemy. The rest were lost simply because they had reached the end of their useful life. At what great risk and cost had these tanks been shipped across the seas from England to the Middle East! Churchill's courage, energy and determination in sending munitions to Wavell had been frustrated because others failed to ensure that the equipment sent was at least battle-worthy.

The units of Drew's force were not the last to leave Derna. A group of the armoured division's "B" Echelon had allowed themselves to fall behind and from Giovanni Berta onwards were everywhere confronted by the engineers' demolitions. Working strenuously they gradually cleared their way through to reach Derna by 8 p.m., where, after an interchange of fire, they laid up for the night.[3] They managed to get away at 4 a.m. next morning—the 8th. But one small group of the armoured division—"C" Squadron of the 6th Royal Tanks—was still west of Derna. Having failed to reach the southern road the previous night, they found next morning that troops wearing the bluish-grey uniform of Axis forces were passing by their southern flank. By evening they still had not reached the road. Later in the night their last tank broke down.[4]

While the rearguards near Derna had been seriously embroiled, the 9th Division farther east had been having a comparatively peaceful time. After leaving Martuba, Burrows' battalion came back to a position on the right of Windeyer's battalion near Tmimi, on the edge of a small escarpment by the sea. When the first company to arrive went out to their allotted area they found that there were five German armoured cars on a ridge some 2,000 yards away. These were engaged by some men of the 2/48th with Boyes rifles; some appeared to have been disabled. Two cruiser tanks arrived from somewhere and moved forward. The Germans did not attempt to try conclusions with them. Meanwhile Burrows, carrying a Tommy-gun, and his pockets bulging with grenades, stood by the road and intercepted groups of supporting arms as they came back, deploying them to thicken the defence. Anti-tank gunners of "J" Battery of the 3rd R.H.A. willingly

---

[3] There was an unfortunate disposition in some units to decry the work of others in general and Australians in particular. An English unit's diarist, reporting this, refers in a derogatory manner to the quality of the demolitions and to the fact that they were executed by Australian engineers. No body of men did more commendable work in the withdrawal than the corps of British and Australian engineers, working with admirable cooperation under Brigadier Kisch. Demolitions never have more than a delaying effect, and inevitably the effect of some is less than intended. Australian unit diaries expressed satisfaction with the result of most that they fired; but although the demolitions which hindered the way of this "B" Echelon group had been fired by Australians, almost all had in fact been laid by British engineers.

[4] During the early morning of the 8th this squadron moved close to an Italian armoured column, necessitating a further detour. It was not until 5 p.m. on the 8th, two days after the withdrawal had commenced, that they emerged on to the southern road about a mile west of Maraua. Soon afterwards they heard on the B.B.C. news that the enemy had taken Derna. With two lorries, a 30-cwt truck, a water-truck and 80 gallons of petrol taken from broken-down light tanks left by the withdrawing forces, they went south into the desert. After two harrowing days of travel, they met a patrol of the 11th Hussars near El Adem on the 10th, who escorted them to that place. Just as this ill-used, unhappy group was crossing the El Adem aerodrome on the way into Tobruk, at 11 p.m. that night, a series of enormous explosions occurred; among the men, with nerves at breaking-point, panic ensued. The commander, who had great difficulty in reassembling his unit, decided to take them direct to Mersa Matruh.

lent their aid. The 51st Field Regiment came in behind, and the 104th R.H.A. later paused to lend support. The enemy kept his distance.

At Gazala, about 25 miles in rear, the 20th Brigade had organised a defence perimeter on the escarpment south of the road with the 2/17th and 2/24th Battalions and the rifle companies of the 2/15th Battalion. Enemy armoured cars approached during the afternoon of the 8th, but did not come within firing distance.

Early that afternoon Morshead drove back into Tobruk, where to his surprise he found that, as well as the 24th Brigade (Brigadier Godfrey), the 18th Brigade (Brigadier Wootten) was in the fortress. The two brigades were manning the perimeter defences under Wootten's competent direction. After a discussion with Harding, who had moved command headquarters to Tobruk earlier in the afternoon, Morshead decided to withdraw closer to Tobruk that night. He returned to Gazala and ordered a general withdrawal of the division to the Acroma area, about 20 miles west of the Tobruk perimeter.

About 5 p.m. the 26th Brigade group withdrew from Tmimi to Acroma, rearguard duty being performed by a company of the Northumberland Fusiliers supported by a troop of the 51st Field Regiment. Two hours later, after the 26th Brigade had passed through, the 20th Brigade withdrew from Gazala. This withdrawal, coming after a period of 48 hours with no rest, was most exasperating to the men and was in many cases ill-executed. The diarist of the 2/15th Battalion noted that difficulty and delay were caused by the weariness of the drivers, who fell asleep at every halt.

Near Acroma, the division took up position with the 26th Brigade (2/13th and 2/48th Battalions under command) on the right and the 20th Brigade (2/15th, 2/17th and 2/24th Battalions under command) on the left, with left flank refused. Morshead's headquarters had meanwhile moved just inside the Tobruk perimeter. The area occupied by the 26th Brigade was near a white house, known as a landmark to all soldiers of both armies who came that way. One of its walls had been decorated two months earlier by Sapper Dawes[5] with a huge painted sign extolling the virtues of an Australian beer. Within a few days Rommel was to make it his headquarters. There Windeyer's battalion took up a position covering the road. The 2/13th Battalion had been instructed to take over the area from north of the road to the sea, but Burrows judged it impracticable to do so in the dark. About midnight the 20th Brigade came in on the left of 26th Brigade. Meanwhile what remained of the Support Group had moved into Tobruk, with the exception of a company of the French Motor Battalion, which went to El Adem to strengthen the force there.[6] The 1/K.R.R.C. also leaguered in Tobruk.

When Gambier-Parry arrived at Mechili late at night on 6th April, he immediately called a conference at which it was announced that he would

---

[5] Spr L. J. Dawes, SX538; 2/3 Fd Coy. Painter; of Broken Hill, NSW; b. Port Augusta, SA, 27 Mar 1911.
[6] In the withdrawal the Tower Hamlets Rifles had lost 16 officers and about 350 men, 42 carriers out of 44 and nearly 150 vehicles.

take command of the garrison force. Vaughan had informed Gambier-Parry that the enemy did not yet appear to be in sufficient strength to threaten the garrison and that he judged the enemy demands for surrender to be bluff designed to obtain quick access to the water-supplies of Mechili. Gambier-Parry had brought with him Major Eden's battery of the 3rd R.H.A. and their escort, whom the garrison had sent out to meet him, but he had brought no other combatant units. He told the conference that the rest of his division should reach Mechili by the following night but he disclosed that most of its tanks had been jettisoned. He decided to await their arrival; he could hardly have adopted any other course. In the desert not far away Rommel, meanwhile, had reconsidered his plan to assault next morning and decided to wait until his main force arrived.

The British garrison had observed an enemy force going into leaguer east of Mechili on the afternoon of the 6th and Lieut-Colonel Munro had arranged with Brigadier Vaughan to raid it at dawn on the 7th with the guns of his 10th Battery escorted by a troop of Indian cavalry. Major Glover was put in charge. The raid was not a success but at least established that the enemy was German and very much alert. One of the two guns was lost, one man—Gunner Humphries[7]—was killed and one wounded. Later, about 11 a.m., a battery of enemy guns opened up from a ridge to the north-east. Warrant-Officer Cowell[8] went out in a truck with a Vickers gun attempting to capture these guns, but was unable to get sufficiently close under cover. The shelling continued, causing some damage to vehicles but few casualties. Soon afterwards an emissary brought a second demand for surrender, which was rudely repulsed.

No word was received that morning from Cyrenaica Command, itself on the move, but in the early afternoon communications were re-established and a message was received which stated that the 104th R.H.A. had been dispatched to Mechili on the preceding day and ordered that the garrison should withdraw if it was in danger of encirclement.

Late in the afternoon Italians in lorries made a half-hearted thrust towards the sector held by the 2nd Lancers, who were supported by the Australian 11th Battery; the Italians were easily repulsed. One gun scored a direct hit on an enemy lorry; more prisoners were taken and a second 47-mm gun captured. Munro now had two of these anti-tank guns and he decided to organise them into a section. He took one to the perimeter to test its sights and chose as target a group of enemy seen to be moving into position. This proved to be an enemy battery which, in retaliation, shelled the camp for half an hour. Meanwhile "A" Squadron of the 18th Cavalry Regiment (Captain Barlow) had come into the perimeter from Gadd el Ahmar, having had a skirmish with enemy armoured cars on the way.[9]

Late in the evening Rommel sent another emissary to demand surrender, offering on this last occasion "the full honours of war"; but the reply was

---

[7] Gnr H. S. Humphries, NX40629; 2/3 A-Tk Regt. Ganger; of Wee Waa, NSW; b. Wee Waa, 21 Apr 1916. Killed in action 7 Apr 1941.
[8] WO1 C. M. Cowell, NX57824. (1st AIF: 8 Bn.) 2/3 A-Tk Regt. Fireman; of Coledale, NSW; b. Lindenow, Vic, 29 Jan 1895.
[9] Variously reported as at 7.30 a.m. and "early in the afternoon".

no less brusque than before. As soon as the emissary had returned to his own lines, about 14 guns began shelling the garrison. Machine-gun fire was also brought to bear and continued for more than an hour, though not with damaging effect. Just before dusk enemy armoured cars forced the withdrawal of a standing patrol of the 2nd Lancers in the south-western sector near the landing ground, but the enemy later drew back and the position was reoccupied.

Rommel had first intended to attack on the 6th but had still not done so by the evening of the 7th. He spent most of the day waiting for Olbrich's force, which was coming along the track from Msus; towards evening he set out to search for it in his Storch. The defenders saw the small aeroplane circling above the perimeter before it made off west but did not guess that it bore the German commander. Rommel found Olbrich's column still some 30 miles from Mechili; but he now felt himself strong enough to attack without it. Various groups, including a mixed unit of the *Ariete Division,* had reached Mechili during the day and been put into position, and the main body of *5th Light Division's* advanced force (the Streich Group), which had originally been instructed to advance on Tobruk, arrived as darkness fell. He ordered his forces to assault at daylight next morning.

Gambier-Parry, on the other hand, had waited in vain for the reinforcements he expected. At dusk on the 7th he sent a message to Cyrenaica Command asking where they were. It was after 10 p.m. when he received the disconcerting reply: the 104th R.H.A. was not coming to Mechili; the location of the 3rd Armoured Brigade was uncertain. Gambier-Parry sent at once for Brigadier Vaughan, informed him that Cyrenaica Command had ordered a withdrawal and directed that Vaughan's brigade was to break forth at first light next morning and move to El Adem, providing protection on the way to the 2nd Armoured Division's headquarters.

Vaughan gave out his plan at a conference about midnight. The move was to be executed in box formation. Captain Barlow's squadron of the 18th Cavalry, together with the single cruiser tank of 2nd Armoured Division headquarters, were to form the advanced guard. The headquarters of both the brigade and the division were to follow and, behind them, the engineers and other services, protected on the flanks by the P.A.V.O. with the headquarters and one squadron on the left, and the other squadron on the right. Behind them, as the main guard, were to come the 2nd Royal Lancers, less two squadrons; the latter, under Major Rajendrasinhji, were to form the rearguard. Munro was ordered to provide two troops of anti-tank guns with the advanced guard and brigade headquarters, one troop with each flank guard, and two troops for the 2nd Lancers. Major Eden's battery of the 3rd R.H.A. was to protect 2nd Armoured Division headquarters. Munro assigned the three troops of the 10th Battery to the advanced guard and two flank guards. To find the additional troop for the advanced guard he withdrew Lieutenant Browning's[1] troop from the 2nd

---

[1] Maj H. G. M. Browning, NX34842; 2/3 A-Tk Regt. Accountant; of Belmore, NSW; b. at sea, 25 Sep 1912.

Royal Lancers.² Major Nehl was placed in command of the advanced guard guns, Major Anderson³ of the two rearguard troops.

The break-out plan required the advanced guard to charge the guns to the east of the perimeter before it was light enough for them to fire by sight. This was timed to start at 6.15 a.m. The whole force was to debouch to the east, where the enemy was in greatest strength; any other course would necessitate taking a circuitous route through more difficult terrain and running the risk of later interception, which appeared to outweigh the advantage of light initial opposition.

It was a strenuous night for the men; few slept at all. In the early morning the noise of preparations seemed sure to warn the enemy of what was afoot. A gusty wind blew up, as though the desert itself shared the restlessness.

If the original plan had been adhered to, if it had been boldly executed, a great measure of success might have been achieved. But the operation miscarried badly. The cruiser tank did not arrive on time at the starting point. Vaughan, expecting it at any moment, held up the departure of Barlow's squadron for 15 precious minutes, during which the darkness lifted inexorably from the desert. It was light when they set off; yet they appeared to achieve surprise. They passed the guns, turned, and charged straight at them, all 24 vehicles in line. As they reached the gun-line the squadron divided—one troop to the left, one to the right—and halted; the men jumped down, attacked with the bayonet, threw the entire battery of 12 guns and their supporting infantry into confusion, then returned to their vehicles and drove off. They had lost 17 men, of whom two were known to have been killed.

Perhaps a great part of the garrison might have made good its escape if it had followed hard and fast in the wake of Barlow's squadron. But the 2nd Armoured Division headquarters, which was to have followed after Vaughan's, had not appeared at the starting point; the others held back waiting for them. Just as the enemy was recovering from Barlow's assault, the tardy cruiser tank⁴ set off; the P.A.V.O. flank guards now moved out, widening the gap, and were followed by Brigadier Vaughan and his headquarters. Munro, his acting adjutant, Lieutenant Sharp,⁵ and his orderly, Gunner Weirs,⁶ followed Vaughan. The solitary tank then charged straight for the guns and engaged them valiantly until it met with its inevitable destruction, not long delayed: the entire crew was killed. But it was now the zero hour for Rommel's attack. As Vaughan's group set out, guns to the east, south-east and south opened a rapid bombard-

---

² In *A History of the 2nd Royal Lancers*, p. 109, Major Rajendrasinhji refers to the absence of this troop next morning: "I found Lakhan Singh's troop completely isolated and the anti-tank gunners that were there the previous evening had gone." Rajendrasinhji's orders, as his own account shows, included the information that only one troop of guns was to remain.

³ Maj E. Anderson, NX12583; 2/3 A-Tk Regt. Secretary; of Dulwich Hill, NSW; b. Sydney, 15 Dec 1902.

⁴ Without seeking the cause of its late arrival, one may comment that there is no reason to suppose that this obsolescent last-surviving tank of the 2nd Armoured Division had not been giving the usual mechanical trouble.

⁵ Capt F. Sharp, MC, NX60017. (1st AIF: 12 LH Regt, 12 FA Bde.) 2/3 A-Tk Regt. Hotel keeper; of Newcastle, NSW; b. Hamilton, NSW, 6 Apr 1895.

⁶ Gnr P. A. Weirs, NX46958; 2/3 A-Tk Regt. Labourer; of Singleton, NSW; b. Singleton, 24 Mar 1920.

ment, machine-guns raked the break-out route, and German tanks approached from the south and east. Greatly helped by the cruiser tank's action and by clouds of dust put up by their own movement, Vaughan's headquarters and a good part of the P.A.V.O. broke through the enemy cordon. But the enemy continued to close and the troops heading the main body halted as they approached the fire-beaten zone and saw enemy tanks ahead. They pulled back.

The wind that had earlier stirred the desert became intense as the sun rose up, and swirling dust clouds made it impossible for the men within the perimeter to see what was happening or for their commanders, awaiting their turn, to gauge when they should sally forth.

Major Anderson had placed one of the two troops of Australian anti-tank guns (Lieutenant Browne's)[7] under the command of Captain Dorman of "A" Squadron, 2nd Royal Lancers. The guns of "G" Troop (Lieutenant Gill),[8] with Rajendrasinhji's rearguard, were to remain in action in dug gun-positions until the rearguard's movement began. Only then were the portees[9] to be brought to the guns. German tanks now approached the perimeter from the south-east, paused near a re-entrant that crossed their path and there formed up in line; then one tank pushed on towards the perimeter. This was just opposite Bombardier Rayner's anti-tank gun of "G" Troop, manned by Lance-Bombardier Ledingham[1] (gunlayer), Gunner Howe[2] (loader), Gunner Galvin[3] (ammunition number) and Gunner Gros[4] (driver). Writing since the war, Rayner has described the action:

> Then suddenly I saw our convoy coming back in at a fairly smart pace, and next thing about half a dozen enemy tanks lined up a few hundred yards away. One tank which appeared to be much larger than the rest moved away to the right, turned and came straight at us. . . . We fired shell after shell at this tank and still it came on. We fired at it side on—must have been only fifty yards away—followed it around, and I can remember the last order I gave. All thoughts of army drill were forgotten. I just gave the order: give him another one, the last one in the tail.

At this moment, a shell from one of the German tanks blew the gun to pieces, wounded Rayner (badly in the legs) and Galvin, and so seriously wounded Howe that he died later where he lay.

Other German tanks had followed the leading tank. These were now engaged by another Australian gun, in charge of Sergeant Kelly,[5] a former international Rugby Union player. Since the tanks were not within the

---

[7] Maj D. S. Browne, NX70314; 2/3 A-Tk Regt. Clerk; of Hamilton, NSW; b. West Maitland, NSW, 10 Mar 1915.
[8] Lt W. G. Gill, NX12572; 2/3 A-Tk Regt. Clerk; of Strathfield, NSW; b. Casino, NSW, 12 Jan 1911.
[9] The portee was a specially-constructed vehicle from which the gun could be fired.
[1] L-Bdr L. G. Ledingham, NX51287; 2/3 A-Tk Regt. Station hand; of Moree, NSW; b. Moree, 18 Nov 1920.
[2] Gnr E. Howe, NX40662; 2/3 A-Tk Regt. Labourer; of Llangothlin, NSW; b. Guyra, NSW, 27 Oct 1919. Killed in action 8 Apr 1941.
[3] Gnr C. J. Galvin, NX40919; 2/3 A-Tk Regt. Labourer; of Tambar Springs, NSW; b. Gunnedah, NSW, 12 Mar 1920.
[4] Gnr A. F. Gros, NX4082; 2/3 A-Tk Regt. Miner; of Quirindi, NSW; b. Quipolly, NSW, 31 May 1917.
[5] Sgt R. L. F. Kelly, NX59997; 2/3 A-Tk Regt. Bank clerk; of Strathfield, NSW; b. Murwillumbah, NSW, 25 Nov 1909. Died of illness 25 Dec 1943.

section's zone of fire, Kelly had first to move his gun to fire in their direction. As the tanks crossed the re-entrant, Kelly engaged them. His crew comprised Bombardier McIntosh[6] (layer), Gunner Coppock[7] (loader) and Gunner Campbell[8] (ammunition). McIntosh has written an account of their experiences:

> As the first one came up the bank we had our first success with a shell right into the belly. We lined up three tanks almost side by side as they attempted to come up the bank. We kept firing as they came to the wadi hitting some going down the bank, some coming up. I have no idea what damage we did or how many we stopped or disabled but we did notice that some of those we stopped moved off again up the wadi away from us.

During the action Sergeant Kelly was wounded by a burst of machine-gun fire and became paralysed. McIntosh took charge.

> The tanks were closing in rapidly and one at about 50 to 60 yards away stopped. I was directing Ted Coppock to fire at it when I saw the barrel of a gun swing round on us and evidently it fired before we did because, when I regained my senses, Ted Coppock had been blown right from his seat back on top of me.

The shell had killed Coppock, wounded Campbell and given McIntosh concussion. Of the eight men forming these two gun crews with the rear-guard only one man had not been disabled by fire.[9] No tanks approached the troop's other two guns dug in to the west of where the break-in occurred.

Within 45 minutes of the commencement of the German attack the heavy tanks had reached the old Italian stone and mud fort, near the centre of the perimeter, where the headquarters of the 2nd Royal Lancers had been established. Meanwhile Vaughan and his party, accompanied by Munro, had successfully broken through the enemy ring. About two miles out Vaughan halted on a small hill to observe the progress of the sortie; but could see no forces following. He spoke to Gambier-Parry from an armoured command vehicle, and asked him why this was so. Gambier-Parry replied that the fire had become too heavy to take the soft-skinned

---

[6] Bdr R. H. McIntosh, MM, NX51281; 2/3 A-Tk Regt. Grazier; of Moree, NSW; b. Mosman, NSW, 20 Feb 1918.

[7] Gnr C. G. A. Coppock, NX51322; 2/3 A-Tk Regt. Grazier; of Moree, NSW; b. Moree, 1 Mar 1911. Killed in action 8 Apr 1941.

[8] Gnr M. J. A. Campbell, NX27204; 2/3 A-Tk Regt. Share farmer; of Ulamambri, NSW; b. Wellington, NSW, 11 Jan 1916.

[9] An oddly different account of the action of the Australian guns is given by Brigadier Vaughan in the extracts from his report printed in *A History of the 2nd Royal Lancers* (p. 101). After referring to the coolness, steadiness and discipline of the Lancers in the engagement, he comments: "They had no weapons capable of making any impression on the German Tanks, and the Australian A/T. Gunners did not function to any noticeable extent. I am told that an Indian officer of (C) Squadron manned an abandoned Bofors gun, and though he had never handled the weapon before, knocked out a German Tank. . . . Men of (C) Squadron were with difficulty restrained from attacking tanks with the bayonet when their ammunition was finished."

The charge that the Australian gunners did not function to any noticeable extent is echoed by the author of Chapter IV (p. 88), who gives the name of the Indian officer who is said to have manned the gun. The survivors of the Australian gun crews will never believe that an Indian officer fired one of their guns; but it is possible that the officer may have manned Kelly's gun just after McIntosh's gun crew had been knocked out and while they were still dazed. This is not irreconcilable with the following extracts from McIntosh's account: "The shell had completely destroyed our gun. . . . When I regained my senses there was a German standing over us and right beside us was a tank. . . . Seeing that tank with the two dead men has always remained very closely in my mind just as clearly as I can remember wondering how it got there with the dead crew, and how it missed running over us."

vehicles through. Vaughan suggested that an endeavour should be made to break out to the south and told Gambier-Parry that he would return. As Vaughan went back to his truck, he told Munro the gist of the conversation, and added: "I am going to get my rearguard out." Munro followed the brigadier back, but his car broke down; he then transferred to his adjutant's truck, in which both succeeded in running the gauntlet back to the fort. On reaching Mechili, Munro found the blown-out guns of the 11th Battery with two or three disabled light tanks near by. He discovered Anderson at regimental headquarters of the 2nd Royal Lancers, with their commanding officer and second-in-command. The three officers were sheltering in a donga, which the heavy tanks were striving to break into. Later this party of officers (including Munro) retired to a near-by depression, where they were captured. Meanwhile the force Vaughan and Munro had left outside the perimeter proceeded to El Adem, which was reached in due course.[1]

When the main force failed to debouch, Gambier-Parry ordered the 2nd Lancers to remain in position to cover the withdrawal of divisional headquarters, which would now be made to the west. When Vaughan returned to Mechili, he found Gambier-Parry's vehicles west of the fort and facing west. Vaughan suggested that they break out eastwards by the original route. The vehicles were turned round and the column set off, Vaughan accompanying Gambier-Parry in his armoured command vehicle. Almost immediately they were subjected to heavy machine-gun fire. Gambier-Parry, who had to think of the men behind him in open trucks, put up a white handkerchief out of the roof of his command vehicle, and the following vehicles of his headquarters were quick to follow suit. Not so "M" Battery of the 3rd R.H.A. escorting them. " 'M' Battery had to avoid the surrendering as best they could," noted their diarist.

Dorman's squadron (with whom were Browne's troop) and Rajendrasinhji's squadron, having been detailed as rearguard under Rajendrasinhji's command for the latest move, were following "M" Battery. Rajendrasinhji was fortunate to run across Eden just at that moment. They decided to break out westwards and passed the order on to Dorman. The plan was simple: to charge on as broad a front as possible and at full speed. Its execution showed what determination can do. Few, if any, vehicles that made the dash were hit, though in each squadron some did not venture. An enemy force in some strength, with field guns, barred the way; but Eden's columns drove straight through their positions. The gun crews were observed with their hands up. A long wadi led away from the centre of the axis of their advance. Most of the vehicles, including Browne's troop, kept to the right of it, but part of Dorman's group, including Dorman himself, went to the south, only to find that the wadi continued west interminably. The party could not get back north—only one truck later reached Tobruk.

The rest proceeded some 20 miles to the west, turning north in the early afternoon, to a lonely wadi, where Major Eden decided to lie in

---

[1] From El Adem they were soon sent back to Egypt to re-form.

concealment until dark. His force now comprised his own battery,[2] Browne's troop, some 90 sappers of the 4th Field Squadron, and some 60 men of the Lancers under Rajendrasinhji. In the late afternoon an enemy scouting force approached but did not find them.

At 9 p.m. the force moved off slowly over most difficult ground, choosing a wide circular route; south-east for 50 miles, then east for 100 miles, then north, close to an enemy encampment. It halted for a rest about an hour before dawn. As the next day (9th April) broke, Eden's column was just on the point of resuming its march when the sentry noticed some shapes looming up through the morning mist. The column made straight for the enemy party, a mixed German and Italian supply group about 30 strong,[3] who surrendered, were searched and disarmed. The column proceeded with its prisoners, some of whom had to be abandoned when their trucks failed. Later a lone German scout car was captured. About 5 p.m. some armoured cars were seen and engaged. Eden's battery and Browne's troop had each fired one round when Eden ordered the fire to cease. The supposed enemy was the 11th Hussars; they led Eden's force back to El Adem, which was reached at 2 a.m. next morning. At 10 a.m. on the 10th Browne and his men, escorting four German and Italian prisoners, arrived in Tobruk.

Because of the sand-storm, Gambier-Parry's act of surrender was seen only by the troops nearest to him. The others, waiting for orders to move, learnt only gradually, as the word spread around, that there had been a capitulation. Fighting at Mechili ceased about 8 a.m. on the 8th. Some 3,000 prisoners were taken by the Germans, including 102 Australians. Scarcely less serious, was the loss of vehicles and of the dumps of undestroyed supplies—which had been built up on a scale sufficient to maintain the armoured division for 30 days.[4]

After the conclusion of his desert campaigns, Rommel, summarising the rules of desert warfare, had this to say about encircled garrisons:

> The encirclement of the enemy and his subsequent destruction in the pocket can seldom be the direct aim of an operation; more often it is only indirect, for any fully-motorised force whose organisational structure remains intact will normally and in suitable country be able to break out at will through an improvised ring. Thanks to his motorisation, the commander of the encircled force is in a position to concentrate his weight unexpectedly against any likely point in the ring and burst through it. This fact was repeatedly demonstrated in the desert.

The experiences of Barlow's squadron, of Vaughan's headquarters and of Eden's and Rajendrasinhji's forces support Rommel's conclusion. It is a fitting comment on his own tactics, which achieved undeserved success.

Around the White House near Acroma, on the morning of the 8th, the Australian infantry stood wearily to arms at first light in a strong khamsin and peered through the swirls of ochre dust, half expecting the

---
[2] Portion of "M" Battery, which had lost contact, turned up later in the day.
[3] Reported in Rajendrasinhji's account as 300 strong: probably a printer's error. *A History of the 2nd Royal Lancers*, p. 113.
[4] A German report states that the dumps were so well concealed that they were not discovered for several days.

(Australian War Memorial)

Major-General L. J. Morshead and his senior commanders at Tobruk. *Left to right*: standing, Brigadier J. N. Slater, Colonel R. C. Keller, Brigadiers G. F. Wootten and A. H. L. Godfrey; seated, Brigadiers L. F. Thompson and R. W. Tovell, General Morshead and Brigadier J. J. Murray.

(Capt J. S. Cumpston)

Headquarters 2/24th Battalion at Tobruk, 13th April 1941. Major C. G. Weir (extreme left) and Lieutenant J. T. Brock (at telephone).

(Luce)

Rommel in the Western Desert

(K. Gillam collection)

Looking across to the Derna Road from Post S17 near the head of the Wadi Sehel.

shapes of an enemy force to loom up. Some units that had not attempted to take up their assigned positions in the dark moved across to them as soon as daylight broke; others improved their dispositions. The British artillery came into action behind, the 1st R.H.A. facing south, the 51st Field Regiment west. An occasional vehicle carrying stragglers came along the road, but no enemy.

Late in the morning Morshead visited Cyrenaica Command headquarters and found that General Wavell had just arrived from Cairo by air, bringing with him Major-General Lavarack. Wavell was already in conference with Lavarack, the chief staff officers of Cyrenaica Command and the local naval and air force commanders. Morshead, the senior military commander of the field force, had not been invited but was at once shown in. He reported that his division had had few casualties and was in good order, deployed defensively near Acroma. Wavell announced that General Lavarack had been appointed Commander-in-Chief of Cyrenaica Command and proceeded to give directions for the future conduct of the campaign: Tobruk was to be held, if possible, for two months.

Nine days had elapsed since the *Africa Corps* had attacked at Marsa Brega. In so short a time had the force to which Wavell had committed his western flank's defence been driven from the field and entrapped; so soon had the prestige the British had won by victories against the Italians been lost in retreat before a predominantly German force. Nor were British losses in trained men, equipment, vehicles and stores of little consequence.

A wrong presumption that Germany was unlikely to risk any sizable force in Africa; an unwillingness to recast plans when it was learnt that a formidable expedition had been dispatched; a disinclination to retract the undertakings given to Greece, so eagerly, if not rashly, pressed upon her; too little regard for the consequences of equipment shortages and mechanical deficiencies; a fatal tendency showing up to employ infantry and armour apart and separately; a failure to maintain control when telegraphic communications failed; hesitancies at Mechili, born of inexperience: all these had contributed, in great degree or small, to the catastrophe. Tested by results the main decisions had been proved wrong; the prime cause was too much daring. "War is an option of difficulties"[5] had been Wavell's pithy comment upon reading a staff paper pointing out some he was incurring. Disdaining a cautious role appropriate to slender resources, disliking a comfortable "safety first" policy while Greece fought alone, inspirited by the British Prime Minister's distant exhortations, goaded a bit beyond prudence, perhaps, by his irony, Wavell and the other commanders-in-chief had called on men who did their faithful best to attempt too much with too little. That a large share of the responsibility was his, Wavell never sought to deny. He had given the British Government the advice it wanted. But it may be questioned whether any other would have been acceptable in London.

---

[5] Quoting General James Wolfe (1727-1759). Sir Francis de Guingand, *Operation Victory* (1947), p. 55.

Rommel, not a more modest man than Wavell, later wrote with some appreciation of his own part in the denouement. He was astray in imagining that his deceptive measures had led the British to believe his force to be stronger than it was. Their estimate was nearly right. But his assessment that "it was principally our speed that we had to thank for this victory"[6] may be accepted. His own vigour, his urgent passion to clutch the dangled trophies of war had more than anything else encompassed the British collapse.

A sure tactical instinct had told Rommel it was the time to strike; but the charge was later brought against him that by striking when he did he had frustrated German higher strategy. His unauthorised advance, it was said, had caused a premature withdrawal of British forces from Greece.[7] That was not literally correct. Had Rommel bided his orders, however, both the 7th Australian Division and the Polish Independent Brigade Group would have been sent to Greece—the departure of the former, due to embark on 6th April, was cancelled only on the 4th. A later and perhaps stronger and perhaps better prepared German advance might have found Wavell with perilously few forces to oppose it.

To Wavell it was never given to operate with any but the scantiest resources. His decision to hold the western front so lightly should not be condemned by the verdict that later events proved him wrong but rather judged in the light of the situation at the decisive moment and on the evidence then available. Nor must it be forgotten that although the Germans intervened sooner and in greater strength, and were opposed less effectively, than Wavell had expected, although defeat was suffered, prestige lost, territory yielded, yet the German advance was soon stopped; and Tobruk was held.

---

[6] *The Rommel Papers*, p. 120.
[7] *The Rommel Papers*, p. 119.

CHAPTER 4

AT BAY—THE EASTER BATTLE

ON 21st January 1941 a small group of officers watched the assault on Tobruk by the 6th Australian Division. One was Brigadier Morshead, just arrived in the Middle East from Britain; another was Lieut-Colonel T. P. Cook, who had been appointed to take charge of the base sub-area to be established there; a third was Lieut-Commander D. V. Duff, who was later to be Naval Officer-in-Charge at Derna during the "Benghazi Handicap" and still later in command of the schooners and other small craft running supplies to Tobruk during the siege.

Brigadier Morshead spent several days, after Tobruk's fall, inspecting the defences of the fortress. Thus he acquired a knowledge of their quality. Later, when the 9th Division's withdrawal from the Jebel country of Cyrenaica had become inevitable, it was invaluable to Morshead, foreseeing that the division would have to stand at Tobruk, to know what its defences had to offer.

Lieut-Colonel Cook's task of course involved his remaining in Tobruk. The base sub-area staff (which had been recruited mainly from the A.I.F. staging camp at Amiriya) moved into the town as soon as the harbour was captured. On 29th January Brigadier Godfrey, who had been appointed area commander,[1] established his headquarters in the town area and delegated the task of establishing the base to Cook. Within a fortnight, Godfrey was recalled to Palestine and Cook succeeded him as area commander.

The speed with which the fortress was organised into a working base and provisioned during the next month was remarkable. The stocks of food and other supplies then built up were soon to stand the fortress in good stead. In the first fortnight two excellent water-pumping stations, one in the Wadi Sehel just outside the perimeter, the other in the Wadi Auda, which, though mined by the Italians, had not been demolished, were repaired, the electrical power system was put in working order and the bulk petrol storage system repaired: most of this work was done by the 2/4th Field Company. In addition, in the first fortnight of February, 8,000 of the 25,000 prisoners taken at Tobruk were removed. Much other work was done.

Soon after his appointment as area commander, Colonel Cook became very concerned at the number of rumours circulating through the fortress—some of them harmful to morale. The way to counter falsehood, he decided, was to publish the truth. Sergeant Williams[2] of the Australian Army Service Corps was commissioned to publish a daily news sheet, under the title *Tobruk Truth* or "The Dinkum Oil". Though unpretentious, it served its purpose well, publishing news culled from B.B.C. broadcasts together with items of local interest; like most daily newspapers it was "printed"

---

[1] He had entered Tobruk as a battalion commander, marching with his men in the assault.
[2] Capt W. H. Williams, VX27459. 7 Div AASC 1940-42; and public relations appts. Journalist; of Edithvale, Vic; b. Melbourne, 23 Oct 1911.

(in fact, roneoed on a captured Italian duplicator) in the very early hours of the morning so that it could be sent to the depots for issue with the daily rations. It was a going concern when the siege began and continued throughout the siege; when later the duplicator was wrecked by bomb-blast, other means of continuing publication were quickly found. To cater for its wider public, it increased its circulation to 800 copies a day; every unit and detachment received a copy. Sergeant Williams did almost all the work lone-handed.

On 8th March, Colonel Cook issued an "appreciation" on the problem of defending Tobruk. Points in his plan were:

to organise the defenders into three components—a mobile striking force, a mobile reserve, and the rest of the garrison; to withdraw "all troops who are outside the inner perimeter closer to the town"; and "to place control posts at all roads through the inner perimeter and reconstruct the Italian road blocks".

Tobruk Fortress Operations Order No. 1, embodying this plan, was issued two days later.

On 17th March and succeeding days the 26th Brigade arrived in Tobruk, to be followed on 26th March by the 24th Brigade with two battalions, the 2/28th and 2/43rd. On 25th March, the 24th Brigade, which Brigadier Godfrey now commanded, took over duties from the 26th Brigade as the latter moved out to join Morshead's division on the escarpment above Benghazi.

Godfrey, with his operations staff officer, Major Ogle,[3] made a detailed reconnaissance of the defences, after which he suggested to Cook (on 31st March) that the defence plan should be modified by the occupation of part of the perimeter defences. In the next few days the situation in Cyrenaica deteriorated. By 6th April the perimeter defences in the west had been occupied in a wide arc from the Derna Road to Post R19. All available troops were used: Australian Army Service Corps men, unemployed because of the shortage of vehicles, took over prisoner-of-war guard duties, freeing a company of the 2/23rd Battalion.

In the story of the defence of Tobruk, a place of honour will always be reserved for the "Bush Artillery"—those captured Italian guns in great variety of size, vintage, and reliability, that infantrymen without gunner training manned and fired in a manner as spirited as the fire orders employed were unorthodox. The bush artillery was born before the siege began.

When General Neame issued his "Policy for Defence of Cyrenaica" on 20th March, he included a paragraph providing for the organisation of the Tobruk defences which contained the sentence: "Italian field guns will be placed in position for anti-tank duties." Colonel Cook found that most Italian guns at Tobruk were not usable because of corrosion through exposure to the weather or damage before capture. He brought a large number of Italian 40-mm anti-tank guns from Bardia (in contravention of instructions issued by Neame's headquarters) and gave the workshops

---

[3] Lt-Col R. W. G. Ogle, DSO, ED, NX12305. 2/17 Bn; BM 24 Bde 1940-41; CO 2/15 Bn 1941-42; staff appointments 1943-45. Electrical and mechanical engineer; of Wollongong, NSW; b. Waratah, NSW, 21 Nov 1904.

the task of reconditioning them and the few usable field guns left in Tobruk. Cook next organised a school to train the infantry in their use. It was run by the Nottinghamshire Sherwood Rangers, who were manning the coastal defence guns.[4] The object, as Cook later said, was "to run half-day classes in how to load, aim and fire an Italian gun with the least risk to the firer and the maximum to the enemy . . . they did learn something from this, using lanyards of telephone wire 100 feet long, chocking wheels to gain elevation". Brigadier Godfrey cooperated enthusiastically. As the reconditioned guns left the workshops, he allotted them to units and saw to it that they were well manned and sited. The 2/28th Battalion war diary has an interesting entry on 7th April:

> Personnel of No. 6 Platoon[5] did a good job on previous night which was pulling into position of five Italian 75-mm field pieces together with ammunition for the same. This brought total to 8 all manned by 4 Platoon.[6]

On 7th April the 18th Brigade (Brigadier Wootten) arrived, some parties coming by road, but the main body by sea. Brigadier Wootten was appointed commander of the force in Tobruk, Lieut-Colonel J. E. G. Martin taking over acting command of the brigade. Wootten decided that, with the larger number of troops, the whole perimeter should be occupied, the 24th Brigade, with its two battalions and attached troops in the western sector, the 18th Brigade in the eastern sector, with two battalions on the perimeter and one in reserve. These positions were being taken up when, on the morning of the 8th, General Wavell and General Lavarack flew in.

Wavell had foreseen, after he had returned to Cairo from Neame's headquarters on the evening of 3rd April, that the abandonment of Cyrenaica could not be long delayed. He knew the time for deciding whether an attempt should be made to hold Tobruk was imminent. Having advised the Chiefs of Staff that the plans for operations in Greece and the Dodecanese would have to be modified, he lost no time in sending to the desert front all reinforcements he could muster. An improvised tank force comprising the 1st Royal Tank Regiment with 11 cruiser and 15 light tanks, the 107th R.H.A., the 14th Light Anti-Aircraft Regiment, the 11th Hussars (less one squadron), the 3rd Royal Horse Artillery (whose "J" Battery was already with the 2nd Armoured Division) and the 4th Royal Horse Artillery were ordered on the 4th to move next day to the desert. The 7th Australian Division (Major-General Lavarack) was at this time preparing to move from Palestine to Greece; General Lavarack and a nucleus staff had already received orders to proceed to Alexandria, arriving on 5th April for embarkation on the 6th. Passing through Cairo on 4th April, Lavarack received a message directing him to report to General Headquarters. There, in the evening, Wavell received him. Lavarack later reported the gist of the conversation:

> General Wavell consulted me on the question of sending my 18th Infantry Brigade to Tobruk together with 2/4th Australian Field Company, 2/5th Australian Field

---

[4] It was never fully converted to an artillery regiment and later became an armoured regiment.
[5] The drivers of the battalion's first-line vehicles.
[6] Bren gun carrier platoon.

Ambulance and a British Army field regiment in an endeavour to forestall the danger to 9th Australian Division's flank and rear. This consultation was probably more formal than real, as something had to be done in any case to assist 9th Australian Division and the troops named were the only ones available. I agreed. I was also informed that the move of my division to Greece would probably be cancelled and the division employed in an endeavour to stabilise the situation in the Western Desert.[7]

After the conference, at 6 p.m., orders were given by telephone to the commander of the 18th Brigade to move his brigade to Tobruk next morning, in part by road, but mainly by ship. General Wavell telegraphed these intentions to General Sturdee, Chief of the Australian General Staff, in a message the text of which was repeated to General Blamey, then in Greece. In this, after indicating the current situation of the 9th Australian Division in Libya, Wavell said:

> 18th Australian Infantry Brigade has been ordered to proceed at short notice to Tobruk. Remainder 7th Australian Division is in Palestine and I hope to send it to Greece but may be compelled to send it to Cyrenaica. . . . Am keeping Blamey in touch situation and much regret necessity to alter plans. Have explained situation personally to Lavarack and C.I.G.S. approves change of plan.

One may surmise that Wavell chose to make the decision without seeking General Blamey's prior consent and to announce it in the way he did because he intended to leave no opening for disagreement with the arrangements.[8] Although Wavell told Sturdee that he was "keeping Blamey in touch", it would appear that this very message was the first intimation to Blamey of any question of diverting to the desert some of the forces previously allocated to Greece, including one of his own divisions.

The Australian Government was very disturbed. Mr Spender, the Minister for the Army, cabled General Blamey seeking his comments on General Wavell's communication and his assessment of its effect on the Greek expeditionary force. He told Blamey that the Government was "greatly concerned and unwilling".

General Blamey's reaction was such as Wavell might have feared. He cabled Wavell on the 5th (and repeated the cable to Australia) suggesting that full advantage should be taken of the desert and of British amphibious power to increase the enemy's maintenance difficulties in North Africa and that the retention of Libya was not vital to the defence of Egypt, however much its loss might affect British prestige; with all of which Wavell would probably have fully agreed. Blamey added that the Imperial forces in Greece would shortly be in grave peril if not built up to adequate strength. But Blamey, it should be observed, while stressing the danger to the Grecian expedition, did not seek to limit Wavell's freedom to dispose the Australian formations as he thought best. In the field in Greece, Blamey was in no position to assess the complete situation. This incident points the difficulties that may arise if the commander of a Dominion expeditionary force of which the component formations are engaged on two

---

[7] In an undated report written in 1943 or earlier for Chester Wilmot.
[8] See Long, *To Benghazi*, pp. 77-9.

or more fronts exercises field command on one of them, and raises the question whether such a commander should not always be so placed as to be in close touch with the theatre commander directing all the operations in which (except for minor detachments) the Dominion formations are engaged.

Replying to Blamey, Wavell said that he fully sympathised with his views about the 7th Division and much regretted the necessity of moving the 18th Brigade to Tobruk; but Blamey would realise the importance of a secure base in Egypt on which the successful maintenance of the forces in Greece depended. Wavell said that the situation in Cyrenaica was now slightly better and that he still hoped to send the other brigades of the 7th Division to Greece and later, when he could make other troops available, the 18th Brigade also.

If the situation was "slightly better" on the 5th, it was incomparably worse on the 6th when Wavell learnt in turn of the German advance into Greece, the outflanking move against Mechili and the withdrawal of the 9th Division to Gazala. While the news of events in the desert was being telegraphed to Cairo on the afternoon of the 6th, a conference was being held at General Headquarters to decide future policy in relation to Tobruk. As well as the commanders-in-chief of the three Services in the Middle East, Mr Anthony Eden and Sir John Dill were present. General de Guingand has described the conference:

> The atmosphere was certainly tense. The subject was Tobruk. I noticed Eden's fingers drumming on the table; he looked nervous. . . . After the problem had been discussed from each service point of view, Wavell was asked to give his views. I admired him tremendously at that moment. He had a very heavy load to carry but he looked calm and collected, and said that in his view we must hold Tobruk, and that he considered that this was possible. One could feel the sense of relief that this decision produced.[9]

So the conference decided that an attempt would be made to stabilise the desert front at Tobruk. It was thought that this might involve holding the Tobruk defences for the next two months, after which, it was hoped, sufficient armoured forces would be available to launch a counter-offensive.

General Wavell determined that the rest of the 7th Australian Division should be sent to Mersa Matruh instead of to Greece and that the bulk of the 6th British Division should also be diverted to the Western Desert from the Nile Delta, where it had been training for a projected operation against Rhodes. He also decided that General Lavarack should succeed General Neame as commander-in-chief in Cyrenaica. In the immediate future the main burden of the attempt to stabilise the front at Tobruk would have to be borne by the four Australian brigades already with Cyrenaica Force and, for the time being, the remainder of the 7th Australian Division would constitute the main force available for the defence of Egypt. It was therefore natural that consideration should have been given to placing the force under an Australian commander. In Lavarack,

---

[9] De Guingand, p. 73.

Wavell had chosen for the appointment a senior professional soldier who had not only had extensive operational experience in the first world war but also had served for four years between the wars as Chief of the Australian General Staff.

No time was lost in acting upon these decisions. That evening the 22nd Guards Brigade with supporting field and anti-tank artillery set out from Cairo for the frontier area. General Lavarack was summoned to Wavell's headquarters.

Meanwhile Wavell had learnt of the capture of Generals Neame and O'Connor and Brigadier Combe. General de Guingand has written that Wavell was greatly affected. He received Lavarack at midday on the 7th, proposed to him that he should take over the Cyrenaican command, and sought his concurrence in the cancellation of the embarkation of the rest of the 7th Division (the 18th Brigade had arrived in Tobruk that morning). Lavarack agreed to both arrangements. Wavell decided to fly with Lavarack to Tobruk next day to install him in his new command. The 7th Division was warned to move immediately from Palestine to Amiriya, for forward movement to Mersa Matruh.

Wavell reported the current situation to the Chiefs of Staff and General Sturdee (and to General Dill and General Blamey in Greece) indicating his intention to fly to Tobruk on the morrow with Lavarack "who will probably take over command of all forces in Cyrenaica". His current intentions and his contemporary estimate of the enemy are both revealed in the two messages sent by him on this day to London and Melbourne. In the first, he announced that it was hoped to stabilise the front at Tobruk and that he estimated that the German force in Cyrenaica might consist of all or part of one armoured and two motorised divisions. In the second, his perhaps unduly sanguine comment was that, although the situation in Cyrenaica remained obscure, the general impression of the enemy was rather more of a series of raids by light forces than large-scale attacks.

Meanwhile Mr Churchill, ceaselessly striving to imbue the British forces with his own spirit of aggression and defiance was exhorting his commander-in-chief in the Middle East to stop the retreat and fight back. "You should surely be able to hold Tobruk," he told Wavell in a message sent on the same day, "with its permanent Italian defences, at least until the enemy brings up strong artillery forces. It seems difficult to believe he can do this for some weeks." He pointed to the risk the enemy would run in masking Tobruk and advancing upon Egypt, and added: "Tobruk therefore seems to be a place to be held to the death without thought of retirement."

When General Wavell and General Lavarack landed at the Tobruk airfield at 10 a.m. on the 8th, the khamsin which that morning had heralded the German attack on Mechili was blowing fiercely; almost an hour elapsed after their landing before their reception party found them amidst the swirling sand and dust. As soon as they arrived at command headquarters, Wavell held a conference with Brigadier Harding and other senior staff of Cyrenaica Command, at which Captain Poland,[1] the Senior Naval Officer, Inshore Squadron, and Group Captain Brown, the Royal Air Force commander, were present, and at which, as we saw, General Morshead soon afterwards arrived. Wavell heard Harding's and Morshead's reports, briefly studied a map of Tobruk and announced that Lavarack would take over command of all British forces in Cyrenaica. There were no forces between Tobruk and Cairo, he said, but a stand was to be made at Tobruk; it might have to be held for about two months while other forces were assembled. He then wrote out in pencil on three sheets of note-paper the following instruction to General Lavarack:

1. You will take over command of all troops in Cyrenaica. Certain reinforcements have already been notified as being sent you. You will be informed of any others which it is decided to send.

2. Your main task will be to hold the enemy's advance at Tobruk, in order to give time for the assembly of reinforcements, especially of armoured troops, for the defence of Egypt.

3. To gain time for the assembly of the required reinforcements, it may be necessary to hold Tobruk for about two months.

4. Should you consider after reviewing the situation and in the light of the strength deployed by the enemy that it is not possible to maintain your position at Tobruk for this length of time, you will report your views when a decision will be taken by G.H.Q.

5. You will in any case prepare a plan for withdrawal from Tobruk, by land and by sea, should withdrawal become necessary.

6. Your defence will be as mobile as possible and you will take any opportunity of hindering the enemy's concentration by offensive action.

In the afternoon, Wavell set off to fly back to Cairo and Lavarack farewelled him at the airfield. But after a false start the aircraft had to return for repairs. It was dusk before it took off again. Within a short time it developed engine trouble and was forced to make a night landing in the desert some distance out from Salum; the machine was wrecked. For six anxious hours General Headquarters, Cairo, feared that, following on the capture of Generals Neame, O'Connor and Gambier-Parry, there had occurred, to cap all, an even greater misfortune, the loss of their commander-in-chief. But a patrol found Wavell's party in the desert that night and brought them into Salum. Early next morning Wavell flew on in a Lysander[2] to Cairo.

There, on the 9th, Wavell sent a cable to London and Melbourne describing the situation in Tobruk and western Egypt. He added:

I have put Lavarack, G.O.C. 7th Australian Division, in command in Cyrenaica for the present. Am considering re-organisation of command placing whole western desert defences from Tobruk to Maaten Bagush under one command. Although the first enemy effort seems to be exhausting itself I do not feel we shall have long respite and am still very anxious. Tobruk is not a good defensive position. Long line of communication behind is hardly protected at all and is unorganised.

From this message it is apparent that General Wavell still tended to underestimate the extent to which General Rommel could surmount his

---

[1] Vice-Adm Sir Albert Poland, KBE, CB, DSO, DSC; RN. Comd HMS's *Black Swan* 1939-40, *Liverpool* 1940-41, *Jervis* and Capt (D) 14 Flotilla 1942-43; Cmdre (D) Eastern Fleet 1944-46. B. 18 Jun 1895.
[2] A small army-cooperation aircraft.

administrative and supply difficulties and hoped not only to halt the enemy's advance at Tobruk but to keep the land route to Egypt open as a supply line, a plan to which (as General Auchinleck was to observe some nine months later) the configuration of the coast did not lend itself. That intention, however, had been less clearly expressed in his unpremeditated orders to General Lavarack. It also appears that, in appointing Lavarack to the Cyrenaican command "for the present", Wavell was deferring until later, when the situation had become less fluid, a decision on the final form of organisation for the desert command and the choice of the commander. General Wavell wrote to General Blamey on the same day and told him of his visit to Tobruk. The trouble in Cyrenaica, he explained, had been mainly caused by mechanical failures in the 3rd Armoured Brigade. He commended the part played by the 9th Australian Division, and continued:

> I am very sorry to have had to use part of the 7th Division without reference to you, but the need was urgent and I had the support of the C.I.G.S. and Eden, who was acting as the P.M's Emissary out here. . . . I know you did not altogether approve of the decisions taken, but in the circumstances I think they were perhaps inevitable; anyway in the circumstances that arose I felt bound to take the decision I did and am fully responsible for it.

As a postscript to the typewritten letter, doubtless written, as he said, in great haste, he added the following sentence in his own handwriting:

> As you probably know, Neame and O'Connor disappeared during the retreat. I have put Lavarack in command at Tobruk and enclose a copy of the instructions I gave him yesterday.

Wavell's decision to send one additional brigade (the 18th) from the 7th Division to Tobruk indicated that he had decided that the size of the force with which he would attempt to hold Tobruk would be approximately four infantry brigade groups plus a small tank force—all the tanks he could muster. Subsequent experience indicated that a force of this size was just adequate for the task but gave no safety margin. In later months the garrison was strengthened in various minor respects but its size was not materially increased.

General Wavell's concept had been to use the garrison force to establish a stronghold at Tobruk while utilising the mobile forces, mainly the 3rd Indian Motor Brigade and the reinforcements from the 7th Armoured Division sent forward to strengthen the Support Group, to harass the enemy in the desert. Brigadier Gott had just arrived in the Tobruk area to take command of these, an appointment which, as we saw, General O'Connor had suggested to General Wavell. But the prospective strength of the mobile force, parts of which had been battered in the Marsa Brega-Agedabia phase, had been critically reduced by further losses sustained around Derna, followed by the capture that very morning of most of the 3rd Indian Motor Brigade at Mechili. The 1/Tower Hamlets could muster only one strong company.

General Lavarack's urgent tasks were to acquaint himself with the considerable but unintegrated forces committed to him, to give them an ordered system of organisation and command, to reconnoitre the terrain and defences and to report in due course, as Wavell's instruction to him required, whether it would be practicable with the forces available to attempt to hold Tobruk for two months.

In detail the composition and location of the forces placed under Lavarack's command on the 8th were as follows. At Acroma, west of Tobruk, were the 20th and 26th Brigades with the 1st R.H.A., the 51st Field Regiment and the 1/Royal Northumberland Fusiliers in support. In Tobruk were the 18th and 24th Brigades with the 104th R.H.A., what was left of the Support Group and the 3rd Armoured Brigade, anti-tank and anti-aircraft artillery units, and the newly arrived 1st Royal Tank Regiment. The 107th R.H.A. was due to arrive by sea on the morrow. In addition there were the normal complement of troops of the various Services, three Libyan refugee battalions and three Indian pioneer companies. On this day the 11th Hussars were moving up to El Adem from the frontier and the 3rd R.H.A. and other minor units destined for the Support Group arrived in Tobruk by road.

The 18th (Indian) Cavalry Regiment was at El Adem, where it was joined that day by Captain Barlow's squadron, followed, in the next 24 hours, by other elements of the 3rd Indian Motor Brigade, Major Eden's anti-tank battery and most of the 2/3rd Australian Anti-Tank Regiment—all having broken out of Mechili.

General Lavarack decided to divide his combatant forces into three groups. The first group, being the main force, was to be responsible for the defence of Tobruk fortress. General Morshead would command it and would be appointed fortress commander. Its main components would be the 9th Division with its eight infantry battalions, the 2/1st Pioneer Battalion, and other attached troops, the four British artillery regiments, the 1/Royal Northumberland Fusiliers (medium machine-guns) and the 1/King's Dragoon Guards (as a reconnaissance regiment). The second group would be the mobile force, under Brigadier Gott's command—a reorganised Support Group strengthened by some units just arrived in the forward zone of which the most important were the 11th Hussars (less one squadron) and the 4th R.H.A. (less one battery): it was to operate outside the perimeter. The third group, which would constitute Cyrenaica Command's force reserve, would comprise the 18th Brigade with a battery of anti-tank guns ("J" Battery, 3rd R.H.A.) and an improvised armoured force containing all the available tanks.

The adoption of this organisation involved freeing the 18th Brigade from its task of occupying part of the Tobruk perimeter and using the whole of the 9th Division for the perimeter defence. Lavarack visited Morshead on the afternoon of the 8th to inform him of these intentions. He instructed Morshead that the rest of the division was to be withdrawn within the perimeter and arranged with him to reconnoitre the perimeter defences next day.

What remained of the 2nd Armoured Division was split up amongst the three main groups. The only tanks the division had brought back into Tobruk were one light tank of the brigade headquarters recovery section and two cruisers (presumably those two which, separated from the main body, had come to the 9th Division's assistance at Tmimi). But the 1st Royal Tank Regiment had just arrived with 11 cruisers and 15 light tanks, and there were in the Tobruk workshops 18 serviceable light tanks and some 26 medium undergoing repair. Lieut-Colonel Drew took charge of all armoured units on the 8th and organised them into a formation to be known as the 3rd Armoured Brigade, in which initially there were two tank units: the 1st Royal Tanks, and a composite unit of 3rd Hussars and 5th Royal Tanks personnel. The composite unit was immediately equipped, out of the workshops, with 4 cruisers and 18 light tanks.

Units from the 2nd and 7th Armoured Divisions' Support Groups were variously allocated. The 1/King's Dragoon Guards were, as mentioned, allotted to the 9th Division. The French motor infantry were directed to Salum. The 1/King's Royal Rifle Corps (less Mason's company, which had been cut off at Derna) was sent to rejoin Gott's force together with a composite motorised company organised from what remained of the 1/Tower Hamlets Rifles. On the other hand, the 18th Cavalry Regiment (whose carriers were used to equip the 1/K.R.R.C.) was to be brought into Tobruk and placed under command of the 9th Division. The role of Gott's force was defined. It was to harass the enemy south of the main coast road.

The 9th Division had come to Cyrenaica without its artillery[3] and therefore the headquarters had no staff to control the four regiments allotted to it.[4] The task of forming a command organisation was given to Brigadier Thompson,[5] who had recently arrived from Palestine to take up the appointment of senior artillery officer with Cyrenaica Command. One of the most urgent tasks was to allot the anti-tank artillery, which comprised the 3rd R.H.A., the 2/3rd Australian Anti-Tank Regiment (less the two rearguard troops lost at Mechili, and one battery at Mersa Matruh), and the four Australian brigade anti-tank companies. Of the three batteries of the 3rd R.H.A. immediately available, one ("M" Battery) was allotted to the fortress command, one, "D" Battery—made up to strength at the expense of "J" Battery—to Gott's force, and one ("J" Battery) to the reserve.

Meanwhile the anti-aircraft artillery, destined to play a leading role in the defence of Tobruk, was being strengthened as guns came back from Cyrenaica and outlying airfields and others arrived by sea. Its main strength, when the investment began, consisted of 16 heavy (3.7-inch) guns.

While Lavarack's force, with its four brigade groups, its few tanks and its light harassing detachment, was being organised at Tobruk, other

---

[3] What happened to the 9th Division's artillery is recounted in Chapter 6.
[4] Lt-Col E. J. Todhunter of the 104th RHA had originally been appointed to be CRA of the British artillery allotted to the 9th Division while in Cyrenaica, but his staff was not sent forward from Tobruk. He temporarily joined HQ 2nd Armoured Division and was captured at Mechili.
[5] Brig L. F. Thompson, CBE, MC; RA. Regular soldier; b. 13 Sep 1892.

forces were moving towards the frontier. The 22nd Guards Brigade was already in Mersa Matruh, whence one of its battalions with a squadron of light tanks of the 7th Hussars was moving forward to Salum. A second brigade of the 6th British Division was moving towards Mersa Matruh. To provide some further insurance, arrangements were being made to ship the 4th Indian Division from the Sudan to Egypt; the first brigade was due to arrive on the 11th.

To the west of Tobruk, on the morning of 8th April, the exhausted troops of the 9th Division were improving their positions astride the main coast road at Acroma and keeping the best watch they could, through thick dust, for the enemy's approach. News of the most recent reverse— the fall of Mechili—reached them in the morning. During the day battalions were sorted out, exchanged positions and reverted to their normal brigade commands. The 26th Brigade held the right from the road to the sea, while the 20th Brigade watched and guarded the open desert flank. For the first time for two days, a hot evening meal was served. Between the Australian infantry and the British troops supporting them mutual regard and trust had already developed. "We still have the 1/Northumberland Fusiliers with us (and our fellows swear by them)," wrote the diarist of the 2/48th, adding that the defences were now well organised and that everyone was "praying for the Hun to 'have a go'."

The enemy ground forces took no offensive action that day, although in the early afternoon a few German armoured cars reconnoitred on the fringe of the 2/17th Battalion. Some stragglers escaping from Derna reported that the British prisoners captured there, including the two generals, were being held in a wadi near the town and very lightly guarded. Morshead arranged with Brigadier Murray to send out a patrol that night to attempt their rescue. Major Allan[6] was appointed to command it and the 1/King's Dragoon Guards were instructed to provide four armoured cars as protection. Their commanding officer, Lieut-Colonel McCorquodale, protested to Morshead that the task was a misuse of armoured cars because of their vulnerability at night when confined to roads. Morshead had his way, but the patrol left late, was delayed by demolitions made the previous day near Gazala and, being then unable to reach Derna in the night hours, returned with its task unaccomplished.

On 9th April, General Lavarack, in company with General Morshead, Brigadier Harding and Brigadier Wootten, made an extensive reconnaissance of the fortress area—a very good reconnaissance, Morshead later called it. Wavell had suggested to Lavarack that the outer perimeter of the fortress, which was some 28 miles in length (the total length of the "Red Line" defensive works was 30 miles and a quarter), was too extended to hold with the forces available and that the defence should be based on the "inner perimeter". Wavell may have derived the notion that there was an inner perimeter at Tobruk from reading Colonel Cook's appreciation, but Lavarack soon discovered that no real inner defence

---

[6] Col H. T. Allan, OBE, MC, ED, NX12229. (1st AIF: Capt 17 Bn.) 2/17 Bn; BM 20 Bde 1941; Base and Sub-Area Comds 1943-45. Gold miner; of Wau, NG; b. Hunter's Hill, NSW, 5 Jan 1895.

perimeter existed. There were a few rudimentary weapon-pits and ineffective tank traps behind the "outer" perimeter, but no connected or useful system of defence. Lavarack had quickly concluded that there was no practicable alternative to holding the developed perimeter defences, protected as they were in great part by wire, anti-tank mines and ditches. The purpose of his reconnaissance was therefore to determine brigade sectors, to site a second line of defence, and to establish a "last-ditch" line surrounding the harbour area; also to decide on a location for the reserve brigade.

Lavarack desired to bring the 9th Division within the perimeter immediately. Morshead, on the other hand, was anxious to spare his men the fatigue of an intermediate move before arrangements could be made for them to occupy their allotted sectors. But, after a quiet morning, an enemy column approached the Acroma positions in the early afternoon and reports from the air force, which came in soon after Lavarack's reconnaissance had been completed, indicated that about 300 vehicles were approaching Tobruk from the west while other columns of vehicles were setting out eastwards from Mechili. The withdrawal of the two brigade groups from exposed positions outside the perimeter had become urgent. Morshead ordered them to retire from Acroma that night. The fortress had meanwhile received two important reinforcements by sea—the 107th R.H.A. (bringing the fortress's field artillery up to four regiments) and portion of the 4th Royal Tank Regiment, with four infantry (heavy) tanks.

The enemy column that had approached Acroma in the early afternoon halted just out of range of the British guns. German armoured cars nosed forward as though to determine the limits of the ground held. There were signs that an attack was being prepared. Towards sundown an enemy gun to the west opened up and lightly shelled the 26th Brigade —for many of the men their first experience of battle-fire—while enemy vehicles appeared over the skyline. The 51st Field Regiment replied at once; soon afterwards the 1st R.H.A., having turned their guns through an arc of 125 degrees, joined in the bombardment. The enemy vehicles hastily retreated, the 51st pushed forward a troop to engage them, and the enemy replied with mortars. Firing continued till after dark. As soon as the enemy had ceased firing, the 1st R.H.A. moved back to Tobruk and took up a position in the Pilastrino area, facing south. One by one the other units at Acroma followed during the night; the 2/48th Battalion, which stole away at 4 a.m., was the last to move.

The impetuous Rommel's purposeful organisation of the German and Italian forces had been marked by an extreme degree of improvisation. New groupings and new commands were set up almost every day. Each of the major formations—the German *5th Light Division* and the Italian *Ariete* and *Brescia Divisions*—was split into a number of independently operating groups. The *5th Light Division* had been organised in three main columns, the Schwerin Group (from which the Ponath and Behrend detachments had been sent to Derna), the Streich Group, and the Olbrich Group. The former two had been directed on Mechili by the Trigh el Abd route; the latter had been sent by the northerly route through Msus, and had not reached Mechili in time to take part in the assault. The *Ariete Division,* broken up into numerous groups, had taken the Trigh el Abd route, while the main body of the *Brescia Division,* under the direction of Major-General Kirchheim, had pushed east by the two roads across the Jebel Achdar in the wake of the withdrawing 9th Australian Division. The *3rd Reconnaissance Unit,* which had encountered the 2/13th Battalion at Er Regima, appears also to have travelled by this route. Meanwhile the first units of the *Trento Division* had reached Agedabia.

After the capture of Mechili on the 8th, General Rommel ordered the Italian formations in that region to garrison the fort while the Streich Group (the main body of the *5th Light Division*) was detailed to protect it from attack from the north and west. Meanwhile the other two German groups (Schwerin and Olbrich) were directed to Derna, where the *3rd Reconnaissance Unit* and the *Brescia Division* were also arriving on the 8th. Rommel himself drove thither in the evening.

General Kirchheim had been wounded, but Major-General Prittwitz, the commander of the *15th Armoured Division,* who was on a reconnaissance tour of Africa, had just arrived at Rommel's headquarters. Although that division was not due to reach Africa until May, arrangements were being made to fly in some of its lighter units immediately. Rommel at once pressed Prittwitz into service in place of Kirchheim, appointing him to command the northern group of German forces now converging on Derna. These consisted in the main of a reconnaissance unit, one machine-gun battalion and a half, a battalion of field artillery and an anti-tank battalion.

On the 9th Rommel directed the pursuit to be resumed with the object of encircling the British at Tobruk. He ordered a deployment around Tobruk: Prittwitz Group to the east and south-east of Tobruk, Streich Group to the south-west, *Brescia Division* to the west. Early that day, the Ponath detachment, in the van of the Prittwitz Group, arrived 50 miles east of Derna. When this was reported to Rommel, he directed the Prittwitz Group to advance into the area south of Tobruk and ordered the *Brescia Division* to approach the British force west of Tobruk, stir up as much dust as possible, and subject the British formations to fire from artillery and other heavy weapons so as to contain the force there until the Prittwitz and Streich Groups could attack from the south-east.

The German commander then returned to the Mechili area to spur on the Streich Group and the *Ariete Division* (some units of which were still more or less immobilised on the track to Mechili) and hasten their arrival. "It was now of great importance," Rommel wrote afterwards, "to appear in strength before Tobruk and get our attack started as early as possible, for we wanted our blow to fall before the enemy had recovered his morale after our advance through Cyrenaica, and had been able to organise his defence of Tobruk."

On the morning of 10th April, Rommel issued a statement of his intentions.

> I am convinced that the enemy is giving way before us. We must pursue him with all our forces. Our objective, which is to be made known to all troops, is the Suez Canal. In order to prevent the enemy breaking out from Tobruk, encirclement is to go forward with all available means.

That morning, leaving Mechili in the early hours, he drove back to the Tobruk front. On the main coast road west of Tobruk he encountered the Prittwitz Group. Finding that it had not yet commenced the ordered encircling movement to the south, he instructed General Prittwitz to launch an immediate attack with part of his force astride the main coast road and directed the *3rd Reconnaissance Unit* to move around the right flank on El Adem. Prittwitz ordered Lieut-Colonel Ponath's *8th Machine Gun Battalion* to lead the *Brescia Division* in the frontal attack and Ponath's column set off along the road towards Tobruk at 9 a.m., but without its supporting artillery, which had not arrived. Soon its forward company reconnoitring the route encountered fire from British armoured cars.

The German forces, reaching the neighbourhood of Tobruk so unexpectedly soon, were to suffer from the disadvantage that they knew nothing of the defences and fieldworks there. Not for several days were their Italian allies able to provide them with a map. Groups which in the meantime reconnoitred towards the port or skirted the Tobruk defences brushed up against anti-tank obstacles and wire in unexpected places and found them hotly defended.

Having arranged with General Morshead on 9th April that the 9th Division would hold the perimeter defences, General Lavarack sent General Wavell a message telling him of this arrangement and of the decision to keep the 18th Brigade and the armour in reserve. He also told Wavell that he had decided to hold the original Italian perimeter in order to take advantage of the existing wire and obstacles until an inner and shorter perimeter had been constructed. The time factor made it essential, he said, to make use of the existing defences; but to hold them with his present force would leave him with insufficient reserve in depth. He was therefore strongly of the opinion that the rest of the 7th Division should be sent up to Tobruk without delay.

General Wavell did not reply immediately. He was on the point of going to Greece to review operations on that front with General Wilson and General Blamey. Probably one reason for Wavell's visit was that he wished to explain personally to Blamey why he had diverted the 7th Australian Division from Greece to the desert, an action with which Blamey appeared to have been very displeased. The officer who first conveyed the decision to Blamey is said to have reported his reaction thus: "When the General read that telegram, he blew up."[7] Before Wavell left for Greece, he told the Chiefs of Staff in London that he had decided to hold Tobruk, to place a mobile force on the Egyptian frontier and

---

[7] R. J. Collins, *Lord Wavell* (1948), p. 372.

to build up the defences of Mersa Matruh: the distribution of his force so as to gain time and yet not risk defeat in detail would be a difficult calculation; it would be a race against time. That message reached London just as another exhortation from Mr Churchill urging that Tobruk be held was about to be dispatched: it was not transmitted.

General Lavarack sent for Brigadier Gott on the morning of 10th April to settle with him the policy for the future employment of the mobile forces. The main question to determine was what the Support Group should do in the likely event that enemy forces in strength should threaten to embroil it in its present position at El Adem. Lavarack decided that if this happened the mobile force should operate from the frontier rather than risk being bottled up in Tobruk. He instructed Gott that if it was pressed by the enemy, it was to retire towards the Egyptian frontier. For the aim, expressed in Wavell's orders, of holding the enemy's advance at Tobruk Lavarack had substituted an intention to hold Tobruk against an encircling force, encirclement being regarded as almost inevitable.

The 10th April, for many men of the 9th Division their first day in Tobruk, began quietly. Mobile patrols going out at first light from the 18th Cavalry Regiment and the 1/King's Dragoon Guards had nothing to report. A patrol of the 18th Cavalry mounted the escarpment overlooking the Derna Road along which the enemy's first approach was expected but saw nothing. As the sun rose, a searing wind-storm blew up, concealing the landscape beneath a stream of dust and sand, which reduced visibility to a few feet: "the filthiest day ever," one unit diarist called it. Units moved out to take up their allotted positions along the perimeter but the men could not see the terrain; as they shovelled sand from trenches, the wind relentlessly replenished them. The khamsin caused intense anxiety to the artillery officers striving to keep the approaches to the perimeter under observation while the posts were being occupied, and to the infantry commanding officers endeavouring to acquaint themselves with the areas they were to defend. Reports that the enemy was approaching under cover of the dust heightened the tension.

The perimeter on which Lavarack had decided to base the forward defence ran in a wide but not perfect arc some 28 miles in length. The chord of the arc was a bare 17 miles—that was the distance, as the crow flies, separating the two headlands in the east and west at which the perimeter touched the coast. The average radius—or average distance of the perimeter from Tobruk town—was about 9 miles. The bay provided a deep and well-sheltered natural harbour, the best in Italian North Africa, but now fouled by several sunken ships. The coast, except near the harbour, was broken by a succession of narrow inlets between high headlands. There was a plain about three miles wide west of the town. It was bounded on the south by an escarpment, at the top of which was a ledge of land leading to a second escarpment. Southwards from the top of the second escarpment the country flattened out towards the perimeter, except in the south-west where it swept up towards a dominant point on the skyline, Ras el Medauuar, which was surmounted by a blockhouse. In the east the plain narrowed to nothing as the two escarpments converged on the coast near the perimeter boundary.

The 28 miles of perimeter were to be taken over on this day by the three brigades of the 9th Division—from right to left, the 26th, 20th and 24th Brigades—using six battalions to man the perimeter line. One regiment of field guns was allotted to each brigade sector and, pending the development of a communications network to enable the artillery to be coordinated from fortress headquarters, the regiments were placed under the command of the infantry brigades. In the southern sector (20th Brigade) the 107th R.H.A. was superimposed on the 1st R.H.A.

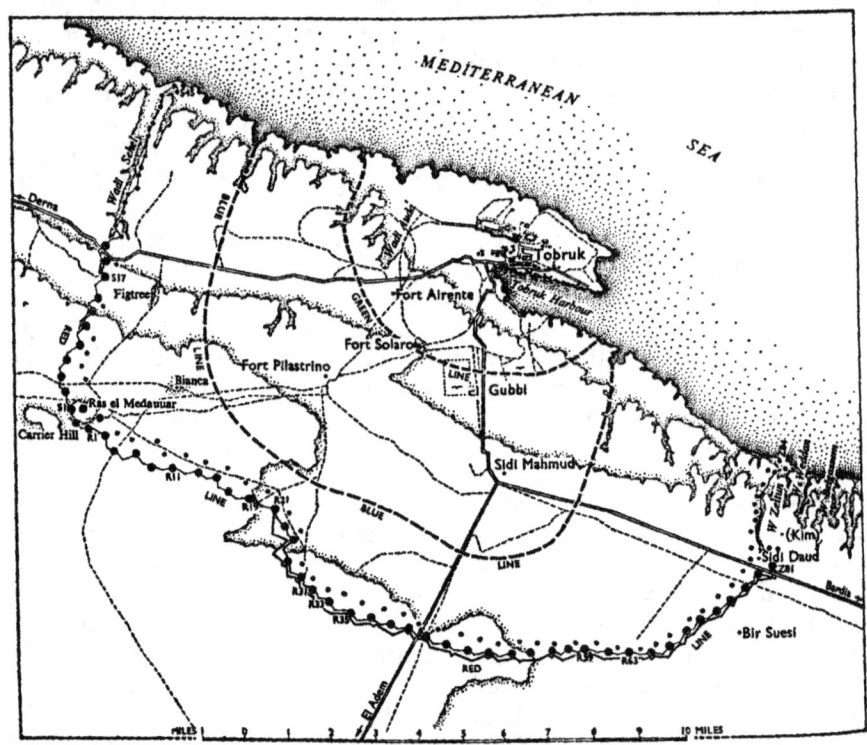

Tobruk defence lines

The 2/24th Battalion plus one company of the 2/23rd Battalion was ordered to occupy the right-hand sector, from the coast to the escarpment, a distance of six miles. It would thus be placed astride the main coast road coming in from Derna and the west by which the division had just entered the perimeter, and along which the Axis forces could be expected to follow. There the defences were sighted near the crest of the slopes of a huge gorge, the Wadi Sehel, which cut right across the plain from the sea to the coast road and, continuing, cleft the escarpment to the south of the road. To the left of the 2/24th, the key western sector, which included Ras el Medauuar, the highest point on the perimeter, was allotted to the 2/48th Battalion. On its left again the 2/17th Battalion was to guard the southern approaches to Fort Pilastrino, in which area were sited the old Italian headquarters, now taken over by Morshead's headquarters. Next would be the 2/13th Battalion, astride the El Adem Road, then the 2/28th Battalion, and, to complete the arc, the 2/43rd Battalion occupying the eastern sector from the main east-west road to the coast.

Before these positions were occupied, and while battalion commanding officers were reconnoitring the areas allotted to them, reports were received that the enemy was approaching. Soon after 9 a.m. Lieutenant Bamgarten of the 2/3rd Field Company demolished the bridge over the wadi at the western gateway of the perimeter just as the first troops of Ponath's column, which had been pursuing a look-out patrol of the King's Dragoon Guards, came down the road towards it. The German column consisted of about two companies of infantry, with machine-guns, some light field guns and seven light tanks.

About 500 yards behind the wire where the Derna Road entered the perimeter was dug in one of the bush artillery guns of the 2/28th manned by Corporal Tracey-Patte.[8] "C" and "E" Troops of the 51st Field Regiment, whose guns were also sited close to the perimeter behind the roadblock, engaged the German vehicles as they came into sight through the screening dust-storm, causing them to withdraw and deploy, and Tracey-Patte's gun joined in. Captain Jackman[9] of the 1/Royal Northumberland Fusiliers, reconnoitring the area at this moment, saw the enemy approaching and called up two platoons of machine-gunners, who engaged the enemy at a range of two miles as they deployed. Some of the vehicles moved south of the road, mounted the escarpment by a track and turned in towards Tobruk above the escarpment, only to bump into the perimeter defences at Post S17, where they were engaged by another bush gun manned by a crew commanded by Sergeant Rule.[1]

As Prittwitz's main column set off down the main road, attempting by the speed of its thrust to take the defenders by surprise, three armoured cars had ascended to the plateau in search of a way into Tobruk by a route which would bypass whatever blockage might have been set up across the direct route. These made for the high ground at Ras el Medauuar, where Lieut-Colonel Lloyd,[2] commanding the 2/28th Battalion, had set up his headquarters in a location where he would be likely to be the first to see any approaching enemy, if not to engage them. That honour, however, appears to have fallen to two of his bush guns, under the spirited command of his transport officer, Lieutenant Lovegrove.[3] One gun, the blast of which was alarming and damaged

---

[8] Sgt J. J. Tracey-Patte, WX4479; 2/28 Bn. Timberman (mining); of Reedy, WA; b. London, 4 Jul 1908.
[9] Maj J. J. B. Jackman, VC; 1/RNF. Regular soldier; b. 19 Mar 1916.
[1] Capt E. D. Rule, WX7303; 2/28 Bn. Salesman; of Mount Hawthorn, WA; b. Perth, WA, 18 Mar 1919.
[2] Brig J. E. Lloyd, CBE, DSO, MC, ED, WX3346. (1st AIF: 23 and 24 Bns. Indian Army 1918-22.) CO 2/28 Bn 1940-42; comd 16 Bde 1942-43, 2 Aust PW Reception Gp 1945. Secretary; of Perth, WA; b. Melbourne, 13 Apr 1894. Died 24 Dec 1965.
[3] Capt E. A. Lovegrove, MC, NX3431; 2/28 Bn. Salesman; of Claremont, WA; b. Yarloop, WA, 29 Nov 1907.

the gunpit, "proved more menacing to the Don Company personnel in the vicinity than to the German armoured cars",[4] but the other, commanded by Corporal Warren,[5] assisted by the expert advice of an amused senior British artillery officer who happened to be there, was quickly firing so close to the mark that the armoured cars made off.

The Germans did not try to assault across the wadi near the Derna Road but took up positions on the far side and, reinforced by the forward elements of the *Brescia Division,* brought machine-guns, mortars and light artillery into action. Desultory firing continued throughout the day. Growing more intense in the early afternoon, it interfered with the 2/24th Battalion's occupation of the sector and eventually forced the two troops of field guns to withdraw. Two gunners and one infantryman were killed; more than 30 men (including 19 gunners) were wounded. The enemy also suffered casualties. Major-General Prittwitz himself was killed.

During the morning Brigadier Gott's Support Group reported from near El Adem that 40 armoured fighting vehicles were moving north-east from about 10 miles south of the perimeter. Meanwhile, the German *3rd Reconnaissance Unit,* feeling its way round the British flank, had a brush with a patrol of the 18th Cavalry Regiment. Pushing on, they came up against the perimeter wire in the western sector, where the defences were still held by the 2/28th Battalion. Several local engagements were fought. Lieut-Colonel Crellin's[6] bush artillery had their first operational shoot, landing some shells amidst the leading enemy vehicles. Guns of the 1st R.H.A. quickly engaged the enemy columns, causing them to disperse. Soon afterwards a British truck was halted by enemy fire as it attempted to leave the perimeter in the southern sector by the El Adem Road. For more than an hour there was no further indication of the enemy's presence but just before 1 p.m. five enemy tanks were seen in the south-eastern sector from an observation post of the 107th R.H.A.

In the early afternoon the 20th Brigade occupied the perimeter in the southern sector. Soon afterwards men of the 2/13th Battalion discerned a party of enemy infantry about 400 yards to their right front and engaged them with small-arms fire. The enemy went to ground and made off under cover. But in the section of the western sector where the perimeter defences climbed the second (or higher) escarpment, the enemy stayed close and dug in machine-guns opposite the perimeter defences. As the afternoon wore on reports accumulated that the enemy was augmenting his strength in that sector, while other enemy groups, including one of 10 tanks,[7] were seen moving round to the south-east.

Meanwhile, the pilots of scouting aircraft reported that three columns, each of 200 vehicles, were approaching El Adem from the direction of Mechili. About 5 p.m. one of these groups encountered Gott's force some 12 miles south-west of the perimeter. Approximately 150 enemy vehicles

---
[4] P. Masel, *The Second 28th* (1961), p. 20.
[5] Lt R. Warren, WX8405; 2/28 Bn. Clerk; of Perth, WA; b. Lake Darlot, WA, 29 Aug 1914.
[6] Col W. W. Crellin, VX14029. (1st AIF: 14 Bn.) CO 2/43 Bn 1940-41; and training appts. Regular soldier; b. Malvern, Vic, 1 Jun 1897.
[7] According to *The Rommel Papers* (p. 123) the tank regiment of the *5th Light Division* had arrived with 20 tanks and "were immediately sent in to attack Tobruk from the south-east".

assembled there and were attacked by the Royal Air Force. Towards nightfall they were shelled by a battery of the 4th R.H.A. and forced to disperse. Three German officers were captured.

During the afternoon Gott had reorganised his force. An independent column under Lieut-Colonel J. C. ("Jock") Campbell was detached to operate against any enemy advancing along the roads leading to the frontier: a precursor of the "Jock" columns that were to set the pattern for much of the desert fighting in the next 18 months.

Firing continued in the western sector for the rest of the afternoon and evening. A company of the 2/48th Battalion relieved portion of the 2/28th Battalion on the perimeter south-west of Medauuar. But even after dark enemy activity continued to be heard to the west in front of part of the perimeter still held by the 2/28th Battalion to the north of Medauuar; after 9 p.m. enemy troops, estimated to number between 600 and 1,000, seemed to be assembling on what appeared to be a start-line for an attack on the battalion's front; but none developed. The men of the 2/28th stood to arms until the early hours of the 11th, when the rest of the 2/48th Battalion, after an exhausting night march, arrived to take over the sector from them. The 2/28th then moved across to the south-east and arrived in its new sector just as the next day was breaking.

In the evening of 10th April Lavarack had placed the 1st Royal Tank Regiment under Morshead's direct command, stipulating, however, that his own approval should be obtained before it was committed. A liaison officer from the General Headquarters had arrived at Lavarack's headquarters during the day; his mission had been to inform Lavarack that it was Wavell's intention to merge Cyrenaica Command into a Western Desert Command and to confirm that his policy was to conduct an active defence at Tobruk and the frontier for two months, after which he would attack. That night the liaison officer returned to Cairo bearing Lavarack's reply. Lavarack urged that if Tobruk were to be used as a base for offensive defence with frequent sorties, a garrison of two complete divisions would be required. He requested that this submission should be placed before Wavell for decision and suggested that the rest of the 7th Division should be used to build up the garrison strength to two divisions.

The khamsin that had raged in the early morning of 10th April was subsiding in the afternoon. Next day, Good Friday—a week since the Australians had first encountered the Germans on the escarpment above Benghazi—dawned bright and calm and clear. The men of the 9th Division surveyed the land they had come to live in and defend. From the perimeter defences they looked out across ground that was soon to become the no-man's land between two static defence lines. Except at the perimeter's eastern and western extremities, where the wire descended the escarpments to link with the cliff walls of the Wadi Sehel and Wadi Zeitun (these wadis were deep chasms eroded out of solid rock), the perimeter defences traversed a plateau some 400 to 500 feet above sea-level. Beyond them the terrain was ridged to the west and south-west, but almost flat to the south and south-east, where the ground stretched towards an inland escarpment visible from points of vantage within the perimeter but not from ground-level at the wire. It was arid, desert country—mottled in parts with a sparse, dwarf shrub-growth (colloquially known as "camel-thorn"), in parts quite bare—and treeless except for a few solitary fig-trees near desert wells, which stood out in their barren environment as remarkable landmarks.

Each day's first light etched the desert scene in clear outline but as the summer day warmed, a mirage would subtly transform it. The change was scarcely apparent at a casual glance: the colour, the broad masses, were unaltered. But a more intent examination would fail to reveal the detailed configuration of remembered features, which tantalisingly shimmered in eddies of sun-scorched air, as though seen through a watery glaze. That occurred every day unless cloud or dust had blotted out the sun. The mirages soon imposed a degree of regularity on siege artillery programs, for only in the early mornings or late evenings could guns be ranged onto targets by observation, or the effectiveness of their fire be gauged. As each new day dawned, the guns of both sides saluted it; as it departed before the oncoming night, they saluted again.

At the eastern and western extremities, the defences in the two comparatively short lengths of perimeter between the road and the sea to the north of it were for the most part sited just below the lips of the wadi walls, which were in general effective obstacles to tanks; there the layout of the defences varied to take advantage of the favourable terrain. But the wide arc of perimeter south of the coast road ran through terrain that did not aid defence, neither hindering frontal assault nor providing concealment to obstacles and weapon-pits. The Italians had surrounded almost the entire perimeter with an excellent "box" wire obstacle; where this had not been completed, concertina wire had been employed. Outside the wire a deep anti-tank ditch, designed to link with the wadis near the coast, had been partly excavated—hewn in solid rock—but not completed. In the apex of each "dog-leg" in the perimeter wire, was sited a perimeter post. These frontal posts were spaced at intervals of about 750 yards; about 500 yards behind them, covering the gaps between each two, was a second row of posts. The perimeter posts were numbered consecutively, the odd-numbered being on the perimeter wire, the even-numbered behind.

The perimeter wire was purely frontal, not extending round the posts. Much of it had fallen into disrepair; some had been removed. The anti-tank ditch had been completed for only about one-fifth of the perimeter south of the coast road. Most of the uncompleted parts were covered by a comparatively ineffective belt of concertina wire. A thin line of anti-tank and anti-personnel mines had been laid in front of the wire, but many of these had been removed since the Italian occupation.

A typical frontier post contained three concrete circular weapon-pits sited at ground level and interconnected by concreted subterranean passages, which led also to bomb-proof subterranean living and storage quarters. But the protection thus afforded was in large part illusory, for while a post might shelter many, few could fight from its three weapon-pits.

If these few were intimidated or subdued—a role for which tanks were admirably suited—the rest of the garrison, trapped below, was at the attackers' mercy. On the other hand, the siting of the posts was excellent. If there were too few weapon-pits, their field of fire was good. And the perimeter wire was well placed, zigzagging in dog-legs out from one post and in to the next. A forward post could in most cases perfectly enfilade by fire both arms of the perimeter fence leading out from it; which fire would form a beaten zone forward of the next post.

Behind the thin line of perimeter posts, no well-planned arrangement of defences in depth existed. Numerous unsubstantial sangars and shallow weapon-pits were scattered aimlessly about. The so-called "inner perimeter" had consisted of nothing more than a few ineffective anti-tank ditches and breastworks on the main axes of approach.

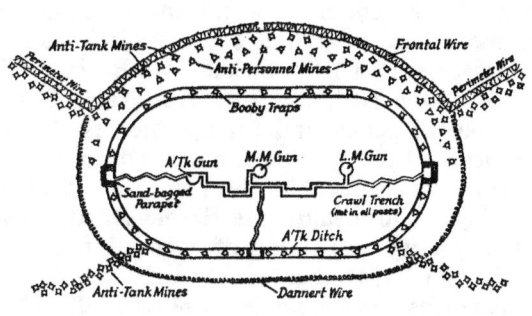

From the first day of occupation the garrison set about strengthening the defences. This was most arduous work because in most places rock was encountered beneath the surface soil at a depth of less than a foot. The destruction of the two road bridges by which the main coast road traversed the anti-tank obstacle at the western and eastern entrances to the perimeter, and the creation of effective road-blocks on all other roads leading into Tobruk, were the first measures taken. Priority was then given to mining the cross-country approaches to the perimeter in sectors where the anti-tank ditch was not effective, and repairing or restoring the perimeter wire. In the first few days most of the combatant troops were engaged in improving their own local defences; but the burden of the main works fell upon the field engineers, who were allowed no rest after their labours during the withdrawal. The 2/3rd and 2/13th Field Companies began mining the gaps in the anti-tank ditch and restoring the perimeter wire on the night of the 10th.

Notwithstanding the enemy activity opposite the western sector during the night of the 10th, a patrol of the 18th Cavalry, which early next morning went out in four open 15-cwt trucks onto the escarpment overlooking the Derna Road, reported that no enemy could be seen. Farther out, however, in the desert south of the coast road, a column of Gott's force shelled an enemy column about 12 miles west of the Tobruk perimeter.

It was apparent that enemy columns were leaving the coast road some distance to the west of the perimeter, mounting the escarpment and moving into the desert to the south, just skirting the defences. In mid-morning about 50 vehicles appeared near the western sector on the right of the 20th

Brigade's front; they were shelled by the garrison's artillery and dispersed. Lieut-Colonel Crawford sent out a platoon with an artillery observation officer to continue harrying them. On another occasion a patrol of seven enemy tanks was seen, but soon withdrew. Meanwhile the Support Group had reported that about 40 tanks were approaching the El Adem sector of the perimeter from about 10 miles to the south, in which region about 300 vehicles had assembled. At 11.30 a.m. these split into two columns, one of which began moving east along the Trigh Capuzzo.

By noon it was apparent that the enemy was astride the El Adem Road opposite the southern sector in considerable force and was continuing to move east to complete the encirclement. At 12.20, 10 enemy tanks approached Post R59, on the 24th Brigade's front, and came within 1,000 yards of the post; the 24th Anti-Tank Company engaged them, putting five out of action and forcing the rest to withdraw. Towards 1 o'clock between 20 and 30 trucks appeared outside Post R63. Guns of the 104th R.H.A. forced them to disperse. But other vehicles continued to appear, moving round towards the Bardia Road; they were engaged by the 104th as they went. A platoon of enemy infantry, which had dismounted from their vehicles, then attacked R63 on foot. They were repulsed, but two Australians were wounded, one mortally. A similar fray took place near the boundary of the 2/28th and 2/43rd Battalions. Meanwhile the enemy had cut the Bardia Road. The siege had begun.

At 1.30 p.m. Gott ordered his mobile forces to withdraw to the frontier, communicating this decision to Lavarack by means of an agreed code word. The group's supply vehicles, which happened to be within the Tobruk perimeter when the road was cut, were compelled to remain there.[8] To Morshead's annoyance, Gott took with him to the frontier the seven antitank guns of "D" Battery of the 3rd R.H.A. In doing so, however, he was acting in conformity with Lavarack's instructions.

By 1 p.m. 50 vehicles had crossed the Bardia Road. Soon another column of about 40 vehicles came up and, under fire from the British guns, discharged troops astride the road about two miles east of the perimeter, who then moved forward to within half a mile of the defences and there began to dig in. More vehicles followed. Later the 2/43rd Battalion reported that a force of about the strength of one battalion, with supporting arms, armoured cars and a few light tanks had taken up a position between the main road and the coast in mid-afternoon.

Meanwhile, about 3 p.m., enemy infantry had begun advancing towards the perimeter in front of the 2/13th Battalion. The Australians and the British machine-gunners supporting them at first held their fire, but when the enemy were within 400 yards, opened up with all arms. The enemy went to ground. Soon afterwards six enemy lorries drove down the El Adem Road towards the perimeter. The 1st and 104th R.H.A. brought down concentrations which forced their withdrawal. A group of seven tanks then appeared in front of Post R31 and began to advance towards the perimeter, but were hotly engaged by the guns of "B/O" Battery.

---

[8] Also two armoured cars of the 11th Hussars, which attached themselves to the 3rd Hussars.

About a quarter of an hour later, at 4.15 p.m., artillery observers reported that deployed infantry were advancing towards the 2/17th Battalion positions near R33 from about a mile to the south. Major Goschen[9] of the 1st R.H.A. engaged them with 25 rounds of gunfire, which put a stop to the infantry advance. But 20 tanks passed through the barrage and made straight for the perimeter in front of Captain Balfe's[10] company. Captain Balfe later described the action:

> About 70 tanks came right up to the anti-tank ditch and opened fire on our forward posts. They advanced in three waves of about twenty and one of ten. Some of them were big German Mark IV's, mounting a 75-mm gun. Others were Italian M13's and there were a lot of Italian light tanks too. The ditch here wasn't any real obstacle to them, the minefield had only been hastily re-armed and we hadn't one anti-tank gun forward. We fired on them with anti-tank rifles, Brens and rifles and they didn't attempt to come through, but blazed away at us and then sheered off east towards the 2/13th's front.[1]

About this time, communication between Lieut-Colonel Crawford's headquarters and Captain Balfe was cut. Crawford, watching the action through binoculars from his command post, saw three tanks that appeared to him to move quickly down the escarpment in rear of Post R32 (Balfe's headquarters) and reported to Brigadier Murray that a penetration of the perimeter by tanks had occurred. When this was reported to fortress headquarters, the 1st Royal Tank Regiment—with its two squadrons, one of cruisers, and one of light tanks—was placed under Murray's command. Murray directed them to Crawford for orders. But when the light tanks reached Crawford's headquarters, he had ascertained that no penetration had occurred. Crawford sent them, and the cruisers which followed later, in the direction in which the German tanks had last been observed.

The German soldiers, who had been taught by their experiences in Europe to believe that boldness and a disregard of risks alone would suffice to carry them to their objectives, were soon to shed their illusions before Tobruk. Encouraged by seeing their tanks firing at point-blank range into the Australian positions without coming to harm, the German infantry came forward again—about 700 men in all—advancing in a mass, shoulder to shoulder. Although the British gunfire fell right among them, still they came on. The Australians in the perimeter posts saw them and waited. "The infantry are still holding their fire," reported an artillery observation officer, as the enemy closed on Balfe's company.

> When the infantry were about 500 yards out (Balfe said later) we opened up, but in the posts that could reach them we had only two Brens, two anti-tank rifles and a couple of dozen ordinary rifles. The Jerries went to ground at first, but gradually moved forward in bounds under cover of their machine-guns. It was nearly dusk by this time and they managed to reach the anti-tank ditch. From there they mortared near-by posts heavily. We hadn't any mortars with which to reply and our artillery couldn't shell the ditch without risk of hitting our own posts.[2]

---

[9] Maj G. W. Goschen, DSO, MC. 4 and 1 RHA. Regular soldier; b. Addington, Surrey, England, 9 Jun 1911. Lost in sinking of *Chakdina* 5 Dec 1941.
[10] Lt-Col J. W. Balfe, MC. NX12329. 2/17 Bn; CO 2/32 Bn 1942; staff appts 1944-45. Company secretary; of Sydney; b. Charters Towers, Qld, 18 Jul 1912.
[1] Wilmot, *Tobruk*, p. 94.
[2] Wilmot, *Tobruk*, p. 95.

Meanwhile the 1st Royal Tank Regiment, with its 11 cruiser tanks, was moving up towards the El Adem road-block. The enemy tanks, after they had left the 2/17th Battalion front, had moved along the 2/13th Battalion's perimeter, shelling the forward posts as they went. Near the El Adem Road, men of the 2/13th's mortar platoon, who were manning two Italian 47-mm anti-tank guns, knocked out one Italian medium tank and hit several others. An Italian light tank disabled by small-arms fire was knocked out by one of the anti-tank guns and its crew captured.

At the El Adem Road the enemy tanks encountered a minefield the engineers had laid on the preceding night and were turning away from the perimeter just as the tanks of the 1st Royal Tank Regiment arrived. There was a skirmish at long range between the British tanks and the last wave of 10 enemy tanks. Three light and one medium Italian tanks were knocked out by the British tanks and a German medium tank was destroyed by gunfire; two British medium tanks were lost.[3] The enemy force then withdrew.

Meanwhile a detachment of mortars under Sergeant O'Dea[4] had succeeded in bringing down fire on the anti-tank ditch in front of Balfe's company. Later, strong fighting patrols from the 2/17th's reserve company found that the enemy had departed.

After darkness fell, several enemy tanks probed along the anti-tank ditch in front of the 2/13th Battalion, looking for a crossing. After they had withdrawn, a standing patrol in front of the battalion's wire reported the approach of a strong enemy party. The patrol engaged the enemy with such good effect that they fled. Other patrols failed to make contact. The intercepted party's task had apparently been to make a breach in the anti-tank ditch and wire, for it abandoned demolition charges, Bangalore torpedoes, tools and a pack radio transmitter.

The day's events had revealed that the enemy was both ignorant and optimistic. It seemed that he had hoped to find some approaches to Tobruk unguarded and to exploit through the gaps towards the harbour area; it was obvious that he was closing all routes of exit, and hoped to capture the entire garrison.

Wavell's orders and messages had required the development of two main lines of resistance: one at Tobruk, the other at Mersa Matruh, where his counter-offensive force was to be assembled. Between them a mobile force was to be placed on the frontier; but Wavell had not prescribed a "do or die" defence of the crucial Salum-Halfaya bottleneck.

As Rommel's forces were closing the ring round Tobruk, the jejune preparations to meet his advance at the frontier envisaged a delaying withdrawal rather than a determined attempt to stop it there. A weak company of the French Motor Battalion was guarding the Halfaya pass-head. On the morning of the 10th the 3/Coldstream Guards with a squadron of the 7th Hussars and a battery of the 8th Field Regiment came

---
[3] Of the tank crews, one man was killed and two wounded.
[4] Lt L. H. O'Dea, NX14998. 2/17 and 2/15 Bns. Hairdresser and tobacconist; of Concord, NSW; b. Warialda, NSW, 30 Apr 1918.

forward from Mersa Matruh. In the late afternoon they took up a position west of the frontier wire near Capuzzo, astride the north-west approaches of Salum, while Lieut-Colonel Campbell's detached column (one company of the 1/K.R.R.C. with a troop of field guns and a section of anti-tank guns in support) was ordered to operate in the Musaid area, with the task of delaying any enemy advancing along the Trigh Capuzzo or the Bardia Road. That evening a battery of the 2/3rd Anti-Tank Regiment arrived at Salum; it was followed later by Lieutenant Shanahan's[5] troop of the 2/2nd Anti-Tank Regiment, which left Mersa Matruh the same night for Salum, providing anti-tank protection to a column of the 1/Durham Light Infantry coming up to the frontier.

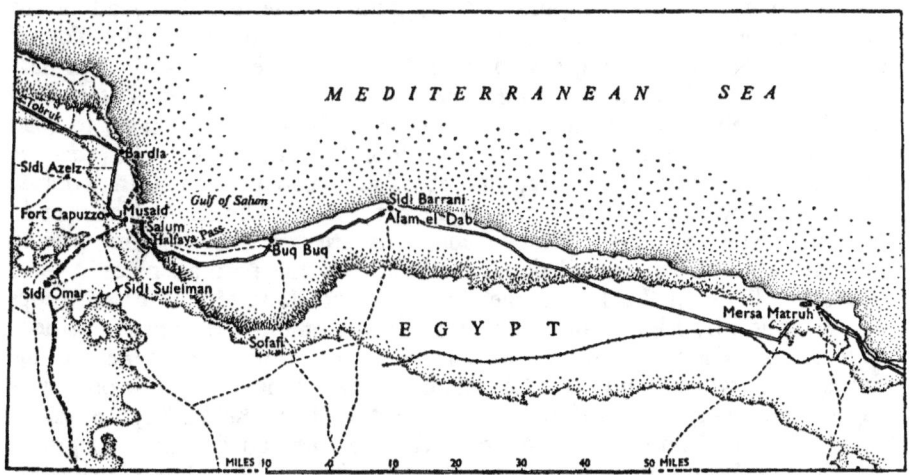

The Egyptian frontier area

Of the batteries of the 2/3rd Anti-Tank Regiment, the 10th and 11th Batteries had fought at Mechili and were now in Tobruk, except some sections lost at Mechili, the 9th Battery had reached Tobruk just before the Axis ring closed round it, and the 12th Battery, the last to move, had set off to make Tobruk by road but had been stopped at Salum because the road had been cut. Commanded by Major Argent,[6] it had left Palestine on 5th April, drawn weapons and other equipment while at Amiriya on the 7th, departed for "Cyrenaica" on the night of the 9th, reached Mersa Matruh at 1.30 a.m. next morning and six hours later had set off for Salum. Having passed through Sidi Barrani in the early afternoon of the 10th the battery arrived at the Salum staging camp at 6.30 p.m. that evening. Major Argent at once sought out the town major who instructed him to report to Brigadier Erskine[7] (commanding the 22nd Guards Brigade) at the barracks above the Salum Pass.

---

[5] Capt M. S. Shanahan, QX6191; 2/2 A-Tk Regt. Apprentice panel beater; of Brisbane; b. London, 20 Jun 1920.
[6] Col J. N. L. Argent, OBE, ED, NX12179; 2/3 A-Tk Regt (CO 1944-46). Building contractor; of Westmead, NSW; b. Sydney, 26 Apr 1905.
[7] Maj-Gen I. D. Erskine, CB, CBE, DSO. CO 2 Bn Scots Guards 1940; comd 22 Guards Bde 1941; staff and training appts 1942-45. Regular soldier; b. 17 Mar 1908.

The battery had almost "to fight its way up the pass" against a stream of eastward-hurrying vehicles, a number with wounded aboard. Major Argent found Brigadier Erskine in conference with Brigadier Gott, who told him that the enemy had cut the road to Tobruk.[8] Argent then placed himself under their orders, which were cheerful enough: that the Salum and Halfaya Passes were to be held "at all costs" for 36 hours, until units of the Guards Brigade took over the local defence.

Gott, as we saw, had conferred with Lavarack in Tobruk that morning. His forward columns were operating at that time south-west of Tobruk, in which region three enemy columns of 200 vehicles were proceeding eastwards along the Trigh Capuzzo. At nightfall, however, the head of the Axis force was still not as far east as the western fringe of the Tobruk perimeter. To have attempted to pass Argent's battery into Tobruk next day would have been unjustifiably hazardous. By one day the battery thus failed to rejoin its regiment and its division. There was no haste to send the battery on by other means; four months later it was still on the frontier. Gott needed it there, but Morshead also needed it in Tobruk. This was only one of many examples of the Middle East Command's tendency, which General Blamey trenchantly criticised, to allow improvised arrangements to persist and detachments to become permanencies.[9]

At first light on the 11th Argent's battery headquarters and two troops (commanded by Lieutenants Rennison[1] and Kinnane[2]) occupied positions in the Fort Capuzzo-Salum Barracks area, covering approaches to the Salum Pass, while Lieutenant Cheetham's[3] troop took up a position covering the company of the French Motor Battalion at the Halfaya Pass.

The forward elements of the two enemy columns on the Trigh Capuzzo, which had begun moving eastwards at 11.30 a.m., had a brush soon afterwards with the Support Group's right-hand column. About midday, as we noted, another enemy force of tanks and mobile troops operating closer to Tobruk cut the Bardia Road about 8 miles east of the perimeter. By 1 p.m. the enemy columns advancing towards the frontier were almost due south of Tobruk and had crossed the Tobruk-El Adem road, whereupon (at 1.30 p.m.) Gott (as he informed Lavarack) ordered the Support Group's columns operating outside Tobruk to come back to the frontier. General Headquarters, Middle East, then assumed command of them.

The column of the 1/Durham Light Infantry (Lieut-Colonel E. A. Arderne), with which was Lieutenant Shanahan's anti-tank troop, reached the Halfaya Pass in the late morning. In the afternoon Colonel Arderne took command of the area above the passes. A defensive position based

---

[8] "Silver John" (J. N. L. Argent), *Target Tank* (1957), p. 122. The history of the 2/3rd Australian Anti-Tank Regiment.

[9] The 12th Anti-Tank Battery was one of a number of detachments listed by General Blamey in a letter to G.H.Q. Middle East dated 17th June in which he requested their return to their parent formations.

[1] Maj A. C. Rennison, NX12581; 2/3 A-Tk Regt. Clerk; of Dulwich Hill, NSW; b. North Sydney, 1 Mar 1916.

[2] Lt J. Kinnane, NX34880; 2/3 A-Tk Regt. Nurseryman; of Canberra; b. Narromine, NSW, 2 Dec 1910.

[3] Capt R. T. Cheetham, NX12584; 2/3 A-Tk Regt. Clerk; of Bellevue Hill, NSW; b. Adelong, NSW, 10 Aug 1905.

on the Halfaya Pass was then organised, with one company of the Durham Light Infantry (and Lieutenant Kinnane's troop in support) at the top of the pass. Fort Capuzzo, Fort Salum and the Salum Passes were not to be defended. The 12th Anti-Tank Battery's positions in the Fort Capuzzo-Salum area were abandoned about 5 p.m. and the guns were then sited defensively in the coast sector two miles in rear of brigade headquarters, where the battery was joined by Lieutenant Shanahan's troop. About 10 p.m. the withdrawn desert columns reached the top of the pass. Later "C" Troop of the 2/2nd Anti-Tank Regiment relieved Shanahan's troop. On the succeeding two nights, Australian anti-tank guns accompanied British patrols probing forward.

When Major-General Prittwitz was killed Colonel Schwerin took over command of his group. General Rommel was at the Tobruk front on the whole of the 11th directing operations by personal order in the field. On his orders the Schwerin Group had closed the perimeter to the east blocking the coast road. In the early afternoon, when it was reported that Gott's force was withdrawing towards the Egyptian frontier Rommel ordered the *3rd Reconnaissance Unit*, with reinforcements, to proceed along the main road to Bardia, which it was ordered to reach that night. He also directed that a special force be formed from units of the *15th Armoured Division*, just arrived by air in the forward area, to join in the pursuit to the frontier by the inland track through El Adem.[4] This force was ordered to be ready to depart by dawn on the 12th with Salum as its objective. The group comprised a motor-cycle battalion, an anti-tank battalion, and two batteries of anti-aircraft artillery (one light and one heavy). It was to be commanded by Lieut-Colonel Knabe.

The German component of the tank force that had attacked the 2/17th Battalion was the regimental headquarters and the *II Battalion* of the *5th Armoured Regiment*, with 25 tanks. The regimental commander, Colonel Olbrich, concluded his report on this operation with the comment: "Reports given to the regiment had led it to believe that the enemy would retire immediately on the approach of German tanks."[5] The *Brescia Division* still held the Derna Road sector. The Fabris and Montemurro detachments had arrived—these probably provided the Italian tanks for the afternoon's attack; but other German and Italian units had yet to arrive from Mechili.

During the 11th, further reorganisation had been proceeding within the fortress. Morshead's headquarters issued an operation order, of which one most important paragraph laid down that each brigade on the perimeter should hold one battalion in reserve. So extensive was each brigade's front that to hold its sector of the perimeter defences with but two forward battalions posed difficult problems for the brigade and battalion commanders, particularly in the case of the 26th Brigade. Some small alleviation was afforded by organising the dismounted troops in the 3rd Armoured Brigade into infantry units. The 5th Royal Tank Regiment provided two squadrons for this purpose and the 6th Royal Tanks and the 1/King's Dragoon Guards one squadron each.

Of no less importance, another paragraph of this operation order decreed that active infantry patrolling should be carried out in all sectors with the utmost vigour, so inaugurating that aggressive patrolling policy pursued relentlessly throughout the siege. The garrison at once asserted

---

[4] Some of the more lightly-equipped units of this division were flown direct to El Adem.
[5] A copy was captured by the Tobruk garrison.

its mastery over no-man's land during the night hours and never lost it, keeping the besiegers' front-line infantry continually on the defensive.

Meanwhile the engineers with the three forward brigades were busy on all fronts, strengthening the perimeter defences. The 2/3rd Field Company laid more than 5,000 mines that night on the 24th Brigade front; by morning the front of the entire sector was protected by anti-tank obstacles. The feat was recorded in some verses written by Sapper Bingham[6]:

> "Dooley"[7] scratched his tousled locks and racked his puzzled brain . . .
> Then called his long lieutenant in, to ease his mental strain.
> He said "Now listen, Ray, we must strengthen all our lines
> So tonight you take 9 Section and lay Five Thousand Mines;
> And when you get them finished, report straight back to me
> In the meantime I'll have more work from the acting C.R.E."[8]

When General Headquarters Middle East heard that the Bardia Road had been cut, Lieut-General Arthur Smith, Wavell's Chief of Staff (Wavell was in Greece on this day) telegraphed Lavarack:

> Am sure you will realise that enemy force astride Tobruk-Bardia road impedes reinforcement of Tobruk. Desirable if practicable it should be removed.

Another message followed suggesting that the medium and light tanks in Tobruk might be more profitably employed with Gott's force on the frontier and that, if Lavarack agreed, they might be sent there, escorting at the same time Gott's supply transport cut off in Tobruk. General Smith added that he realised that the man on the spot was the best judge of what was practicable.

Lavarack replied to both messages next day (12th April). He said that he fully realised the importance of reopening the road and would seize any opportunity of doing so. As for the medium tanks, the large area of the perimeter made it necessary that the defence of Tobruk should be mobile. The armoured force within Tobruk was probably less than the minimum that would be considered necessary for its defence and was subject to attrition. Two tanks had been lost in the action on the previous day.

That day General Wavell visited General Blamey at his headquarters in Greece. Wavell may have gone to this meeting with some apprehension but at its conclusion he telegraphed General Smith that Blamey had been "most helpful in every way and very sensible". Wavell said that he had discussed with Blamey Lavarack's request for further reinforcement of Tobruk with the remainder of the 7th Division. Blamey thought that four brigades should suffice for an active defence of Tobruk and that it would be better to strengthen the defence with infantry tanks rather than more men, keeping the rest of the 7th Division outside; if, however, Lavarack felt unhappy without further infantry reinforcement Blamey

---

[6] WO2 F. P. Bingham, MM, TX813; 2/3 Fd Coy. Fitter; of Gormanston, Tas; b. Hobart, 10 Jul 1914. Died of wounds accidentally received 3 Aug 1945.
[7] Capt D. O. Muller, acting OC 2/3rd Field Company.
[8] Since Colonel Mann's failure to get back from Derna, Major Risson, OC 2/3rd Field Company, had been acting as CRE.

suggested that he be given another brigade provided that it could be passed safely in and out; Blamey had also stressed that the defence should be based on mobility and counter-attack, the "outer line" being held for observation only.

The enemy's probing thrusts at the perimeter defences during 11th April, his haste to block the garrison's road communications with Egypt, the approach of more columns from the south-west indicated by air reconnaissance reports in the evening, the noise after dark of continued movement outside the perimeter in the south-eastern sector, and the discovery of an enemy party with engineer stores in the anti-tank ditch all seemed to point to the imminence of an assault on the fortress and to the likelihood that it would be made at first light on the 12th near the boundary of the 20th and 24th Brigades. Reports of the enemy's activity continued to reach headquarters during the night, and General Lavarack decided that it would be prudent to move his reserve nearer to that sector. The 18th Brigade was in the Wadi Auda, near the sea west of the town. Just after 11 p.m. Lavarack ordered Brigadier Wootten to move the brigade to the junction of the El Adem and Bardia Roads in time to be ready to repel a dawn attack. The brigade embussed at 3 a.m. and was in position by first light. When the tank demonstration had been made against the 2/17th Battalion, a troop of the 3rd R.H.A. had been sent to the threatened sector but arrived too late to be used. The importance of disposing the garrison's anti-tank guns closer to the perimeter was then appreciated and during the night both batteries of the 3rd R.H.A. were also moved forward.

Intent and tense, the whole garrison stood to arms as the darkness lifted next morning; but the expected attack did not develop. At dawn a gusty wind was blowing. As vision improved, the men in the 2/17th Battalion could see enemy dug in about a quarter of a mile from the perimeter in front of Balfe's company. Seven anti-tank guns of the 3rd R.H.A. arrived; the gunners began to dig them in near the perimeter. Enemy snipers fired at them intermittently. As the morning progressed, machine-gun and mortar fire was brought down on the battalion front and movement outside the posts became extremely dangerous. A party of men under Corporal Benson[9] nevertheless went out from Post R35 to repair a gap in the wire and, lying on their backs under the fence, effected the repairs under fire while Private McKee[1] covered them with his Bren gun, engaging the interfering enemy machine-guns and eventually silencing them all.

In mid-morning the 18th Brigade was withdrawn. Its forward movement, though abortive, had been a useful rehearsal and, as rehearsals do, had indicated that there was much scope for improvement in the counter-attack arrangements. In particular, Lavarack came to the conclusion that the time needed to move reserve units from the Wadi Auda to a threatened

---

[9] Cpl F. A. Benson, NX14372. 2/17 Bn; 9 Div HQ. Bank clerk; of Ashfield, NSW; b. Goulburn, NSW, 3 Jan 1920. Killed in action 4 Sep 1943.
[1] Pte E. McKee, NX17846; 2/17 Bn. Boiler attendant; of Paddington, NSW; b. Moree, NSW, 26 Aug 1920.

sector was too great. Accordingly he ordered Wootten to dispose his battalions in three areas: one battalion at Fort Airente, one at Fort Pilastrino and one south-east of the junction of the Bardia and El Adem Roads; in fine, one battalion astride each road giving access to the port.

It had seemed that the Axis air forces had enjoyed complete mastery of the skies since the German offensive began. The British infantry never saw a plane but presumed it enemy; they were seldom wrong. Yet the Royal Air Force, hampered both by a scarcity of aircraft and by the necessity to abandon one airfield after another during the retreat, had been striking at the enemy columns with all the force it could muster—actions which unfortunately the Allied ground troops could seldom witness. Diaries of German soldiers kept at that time did not suggest that their *Luftwaffe* ruled the skies but rather testified to the effectiveness of R.A.F. efforts. On 12th April the R.A.F. bombed and strafed a column moving round to the south of the perimeter from the Derna Road, and later bombed another of 100 vehicles on the coast road to the east. An entry in the German *Africa Corps'* war diary on 14th April paid tribute to the effectiveness of the R.A.F's work; it stated that the British had enjoyed absolute air superiority since the siege began.

Since the 9th Division's arrival in Cyrenaica enemy bombing and strafing attacks of varying severity had been experienced on every day of reasonable flying weather. The very rapidity of the enemy's advance had nevertheless prevented his giving maximum close support from the air to his ground forces; but from the 12th onward, the Tobruk defenders had to endure an increasing weight of air attack. No. 73 (Fighter) Squadron R.A.F. (Squadron Leader Wykeham-Barnes[2]) and No. 6 Squadron R.A.F. were meanwhile operating from the small Tobruk airfield at the south of the port but had only 12 Hurricanes. No replacements could be expected. Great calls, to which the response was unfailing, were made on the pilots but they were a dwindling company, operating as they often did against enemy aircraft in superior numbers.

Since 7th April there had been a considerable amount of shipping at Tobruk. The ships were there because of the steps taken to reinforce the fortress but, as we now know, the German command believed that they were standing by to evacuate the garrison. In the early afternoon of 12th April 15 dive bombers, with a fighter screen, pressed home an attack on ships in the harbour. The British anti-aircraft artillery put up a strong barrage and shot down three; the ships escaped damage. Later, an enemy aircraft crash-landed in the 2/43rd Battalion area, and the two aircrew were taken prisoner.

During the morning of 12th April, a few tanks had approached the wire in front of the 2/17th Battalion, apparently looking for gaps in the anti-tank ditch. Farther out dust clouds rising from hollows betrayed the movement of vehicles. The 1st R.H.A. heavily shelled one concentration

---

[2] AVM P. G. Wykeham, CB, DSO, OBE, DFC, AFC, 33211 RAF. 80, 274 and 257 Sqns RAF; comd 73 Sqn RAF 1941, 257 Sqn RAF 1942, 23 Sqn RAF 1942-43, RAF fighter sectors and wings 1943-45. Regular air force offr; b. Sandhurst, England, 13 Sep 1915. Changed name from Wykeham-Barnes by deed poll, 1955.

for an hour and a half, three Blenheim aircraft bombed another; when the shelling stopped, many ambulances appeared and began picking up casualties. Other R.A.F. aircraft strafed a concentration farther east, on the 24th Brigade front. An intense, hot wind then blew up and swept clouds of thick dust across the front. Under its cover, enemy infantry began to advance towards Posts R33 and R35. From Post R32 Major Loder-Symonds brought down fire upon them from both troops of "B/O" Battery, and put most of the enemy to ground about 500 yards from the wire; but after about an hour they resumed their advance. The battery shelled first their flanks and then their centre, breaking up most of the attack. Many took shelter in the anti-tank ditch but one group prepared to attack R33, and engaged in a fire fight with a section of reinforcements who had arrived in Tobruk on the preceding day. Stimulated by the good spirits of their leader Lance-Corporal Dunbar,[3] the section fought back with a will and broke the attack.

Lieut-Colonel Crawford had meanwhile asked for air support. From the higher ground farther west, held by the 2/48th Battalion, about 125 vehicles could be indistinctly seen through the dust and haze to the south of Crawford's sector. Lavarack asked the R.A.F. to bomb this concentration. At 4 p.m. the defenders were elated to see six bombers of the R.A.F. come over and drop their bombs on about 60 tanks and other vehicles then, in the improving visibility, clearly perceptible near the El Adem Road. The enemy infantry then retired to about 1,500 yards from the perimeter. The honours of the day had gone to the defenders, but their satisfaction was somewhat marred by news received in the evening that the enemy had occupied Bardia.

The wind ceased as the sun set, and the moon rose early, bestowing the boon of good observation on the anxious defenders. About 10 p.m. Captain Balfe saw two groups of vehicles crossing his front—29 lorries filled with troops and 12 vehicles apparently towing guns. From the artillery observation post at R32, from which Loder-Symonds had departed after directing his guns' fire all that long summer's day, Balfe himself directed a moonlight shoot by the British guns on the vehicles. More than 400 rounds were fired. Such was the mutual confidence and esteem that in only two days had sprung up between these Australian infantry and the British gunners supporting them.

Wavell returned from Greece on 12th April and at once turned his attention to organising the defence of Egypt against Rommel's threat. In outline the plan was still to build up a substantial force in the area of Mersa Matruh while screening the frontier area with only light forces. At Mersa Matruh were the 7th Division (less the 18th Brigade in Tobruk), the 16th Brigade and part of the 22nd Guards Brigade. A brigade of the 4th Indian Division, from the Sudan, was to form the nucleus of the defence of the Hagamush Nullah while the Polish Brigade (like the 7th

---

[3] Lt A. E. Dunbar, MM, NX16216; 2/17 Bn. Milk carter; of Manly, NSW; b. Glen Innes, NSW, 18 Sep 1915.

Division, withdrawn from the expedition to Greece) was to hold the approaches to Alexandria.

In the Salum area, early on the morning of the 12th, a company of the 1/Durham Light Infantry relieved the 3/Coldstream Guards, which was then sent back to Mersa Matruh. The role given out that day to Gott's mobile forces was to operate for as long as possible above the Halfaya-Sofafi escarpment, then delay the enemy as long as possible on the coast east of the escarpment, then withdraw to the line Buq Buq-Sofafi. They were still organised into three columns. Lieut-Colonel Campbell's column, which was to be called "Paul", was to operate in the Musaid area with a screen of armoured cars of the 11th Hussars; a second column, including most of the 1/K.R.R.C. was stationed on the left flank, near Sofafi; the third, with the 1/Tower Hamlets Rifles (one strong motor company), was in reserve at Buq Buq. Thus dispersed to cover several points, no part of the force could punch with any weight. This was true not only of the frontier components but of all forces west of the Nile.

Late on the night of the 12th, the 5th Battery (Major Wilson[4]) of the 2/2nd Anti-Tank Regiment came under the command of Support Group headquarters about four miles east of Salum, having escorted a convoy of nineteen ammunition lorries sent forward from Mersa Matruh.

General Lavarack's command outside Tobruk had lapsed by force of circumstances. The very situation in which the forces available to defend the desert flank found themselves, strung out and passively waiting, as they were, at widely separate points along the invader's path to the canal zone, importuned the appointment of a commander to take charge of all of them, to reconsider their deployment, especially as between Mersa Matruh and the frontier, and to inject purpose and vigour into the conduct of the defence. Wavell ordered that next day, the 13th, commencing from midnight, Major-General J. F. Evetts, then commanding the British Troops in Egypt and the 6th (British) Division (with headquarters at Maaten Bagush), should take over their command "pending the arrival of H.Q. Cyrcom" from Tobruk.

During the morning of the 12th, Lavarack's headquarters received a message setting out the projected reorganisation of command in the Western Desert and stating that the arrangements were to take effect as from one minute after midnight on 14th April. A "Western Desert Force Headquarters" was to be reconstituted, the message said, from Headquarters of Cyrenaica Command. Pending its reconstitution General Evetts would command all the forces in the Western Desert except those at Tobruk. Tobruk was to be organised without delay as "Tobruk Fortress" under Morshead's command. "Major-General Lavarack and Headquarters Cyrenaica Command," continued the message, "will move to Maaten Bagush under arrangements to be made by [General Headquarters] and on arrival HQ Western Desert Force will assume command of all forces in Western Desert including Tobruk fortress in relief of General Evetts,

---

[4] Brig C. H. Wilson, ED, QX6177. 2/2 A-Tk Regt, 2/6 Fd Regt; CO 11 Fd Regt 1942-44, 57 AA Regt 1944, 13 Fd Regt 1944-45. Solicitor; of Brisbane; b. Townsville, Qld, 4 Jul 1904.

who will revert to the command of British Troops in Egypt" (i.e. the troops east of the eastern boundary of Western Desert Force, which was given). The message was ambiguous. What was the subject of the verb "will assume"? Was Lavarack to assume command on arrival at H.Q. Western Desert Force, or was H.Q. Western Desert Force to assume command on the arrival of Lavarack and Cyrenaica Command headquarters? Military command is exercised not by headquarters but by commanders. Perhaps the writer of the message had deliberately avoided mentioning General Lavarack by name as taking over command from General Evetts or assuming command of Western Desert Force but, if an implication that he might not do so was intended, so obliquely was it conveyed that it was missed by the recipients. Lavarack and others read the message to mean that he had been nominated to command the Western Desert Force about to be constituted, and he received congratulations from his staff and from Morshead.

Another message followed, from General Smith, which informed General Lavarack that General Wavell had discussed the defence of Tobruk with General Blamey, and told Lavarack of their views substantially in the terms of Wavell's earlier message to Smith; namely, that four brigades should suffice for an active defence, that Wavell and Blamey preferred to keep the rest of the 7th Division in reserve and to strengthen the defence with infantry tanks and that they suggested that the "outer line" should be used mainly for observation, the defence to be based on mobility and counter-attacks. "I am therefore arranging to send 8 more 'I' tanks[5] to you," General Smith continued, "and hope your cruisers can operate outside under Gott." Lavarack replied that the only chance of a successful defence lay in covering the existing obstacle while holding mobile reserves ready to counter-attack any penetrating force. A force of 12 infantry tanks in Tobruk would make it possible to dispense with some, if not all, of the cruisers but it was doubtful whether they could break out of the perimeter at present without serious loss. Unless the situation changed it would be necessary to evacuate them by sea.

Rommel's two forward columns, the *3rd Reconnaissance Unit* (in the lead) and the Knabe Group (a motor-cycle battalion with anti-tank and anti-aircraft artillery), had continued their eastward advance with unexpected speed. In the early morning of 12th April, the *3rd Reconnaissance Unit* had entered Bardia, which it reported unoccupied. *Africa Corps* headquarters received air reconnaissance reports to the effect that the British forces were very weak on the frontier and there were none behind them until far beyond Mersa Matruh. The policy prescribed by Rommel was therefore to push east with advanced columns as fast as possible to defeat in detail any British reserves being hurried forward before more substantial forces could be brought from Abyssinia or Greece; his main force would follow when the supply position could be made secure. For that it was necessary to capture Tobruk at the earliest possible moment.

On the 12th, the German commander at last received maps of the

---

[5] There were then four at Tobruk.

Tobruk defences. According to Rommel's A.D.C. only two had been sent: one Rommel kept for himself, the other he gave to General Streich, commanding the *5th Light Division*.[6] These were enough, however, to enable an accurate assault plan to be made and by 13th April the Axis forces were ready to strike. The Schwerin Group was in the eastern sector, opposite the 24th Brigade. The *5th Light Division,* which was to be the assault force, was disposed in the south on either side of the El Adem Road, opposite the 20th Brigade. On its left were the *Ariete Division* and farther left a regiment of the *Trento Division* around a high feature west of Ras el Medauuar, known to the Australians as "Carrier Hill". The *Brescia Division,* still astride the Derna Road, completed the circuit. The plan required that the *5th Light Division* should make a breach in the perimeter defences on the evening of the 13th and penetrate to the junction of the Bardia and El Adem Roads while the *Brescia Division* staged a demonstration in the west to pin down the forces there. In the early hours of the next morning the main force would thrust through this bridgehead to launch at dawn an attack towards the harbour.

Meanwhile the eastward thrust was being pressed towards Capuzzo. At 3 p.m. on the 13th Knabe's most forward column skirmished with some of Colonel Campbell's armoured cars, who took some German prisoners; from these they learnt that there was a battalion in the vicinity. At dawn, the company of Durham Light Infantry on the escarpment at Salum was withdrawn and demolitions in the pass were fired behind them. Knabe's force soon cleared the demolitions. By noon another of Knabe's columns, harassed by the Jock column, was deploying to assault Capuzzo. Capuzzo was captured at 2 p.m., the small British force withdrawing under fire after having oiled the wells. The Germans continued the advance in several columns. There were skirmishes along the frontier wire, where most of the enemy were turned back by Campbell's troops, but the Salum barracks were occupied at 4 p.m. Half an hour later a German attempt to continue the advance from the barracks was halted.

General Evetts then directed the 3/Coldstream Guards to return to the frontier zone to reinforce Gott's force and at 6 p.m. ordered General Gott to destroy the enemy in Musaid and Capuzzo in order to "restore the offensive spirit". If Gott's puny force had tried conclusions with its adversaries the ensuing destruction might have been not of the enemy but of itself—the Marmon-Harringtons of the 11th Hussars were no match for the well-armed German eight-wheelers—but the movement forward of the Coldstreams (they reached Sidi Barrani that night) would at least temporarily restore to something closer to parity the strength of opposing forces near the frontier. The British frontier columns' most urgent need, however, which had been reflected in General Smith's messages to General Lavarack, was cruiser tanks.

While on this Easter Sunday (13th April) light German forces were making their first penetrations of the Egyptian frontier, the main Axis

---

[6] H. W. Schmidt, *With Rommel in the Desert* (1950), p. 38.

force before Tobruk was making its last preparations to storm the fortress. For two days the R.A.F. had been reporting the convergence of enemy columns from Derna and Mechili on Tobruk, with numerous tanks among them, and this day Lavarack's headquarters were receiving up-to-the-minute reports of the progress of the German advance near Salum from the gunboat *Aphis,* standing off shore. In the afternoon, General Headquarters informed Lavarack that the eight infantry tanks and four medium (60-pounder) guns—the garrison had no medium artillery—were being dispatched in two or three days' time. But reports coming in from the perimeter indicated that a major attack might develop before these would arrive.

In the morning motor-cyclists, followed by a staff car, were seen out in front of the 2/17th Battalion and it appeared as if a headquarters were being set up. The anti-tank gunners engaged the staff car at extreme range and the artillery shelled the area with good effect. Soon afterwards a Heinkel aircraft made a low-level reconnaissance of this part of the perimeter. Later, enemy aircraft scattered leaflets over the fortress. These read:

> The General Officer Commanding the German forces in Libya hereby requests that the British troops occupying Tobruk surrender their arms. Single soldiers waving white handkerchiefs are not fired on. Strong German forces have already surrounded Tobruk and it is useless to try and escape. Remember Mekili. Our dive-bombers and Stukas are awaiting your ships which are lying in Tobruk.

Morshead, in a report written a few days later, commented that because of the prevailing dust and of the need to ration water for essential purposes, no white handkerchiefs were available.

Until mid-afternoon, however, the enemy appeared to be less active than usual. In both the western and the eastern sectors, single British-type trucks drove up to the perimeter. The one in the eastern sector made off when fired upon but in the western sector the 2/48th Battalion captured the vehicle, in the back of which were found two motor-cycles and an Australian and an Indian uniform. The 2/48th later took several prisoners by surprising other vehicles approaching the wire.

The Germans were not attempting to disguise their intentions. Armoured cars next probed the southern perimeter and lorries brought up troops to an assembly area some 4,000 yards out from the perimeter wire, where they dismounted and remained bunched, making no attempt at concealment until the British artillery caused them to scatter. Then very small detachments were brought forward to about 1,500 yards from the perimeter wire and there set up machine-guns, which brought fire to bear on the perimeter posts, opening up whenever movement occurred. Enemy aircraft simultaneously cruised over the perimeter, as though plotting the defences. There could be no doubt that the enemy was paying special attention to the sector held by the 2/17th Battalion. Colonel Crawford had read the signs correctly. Crawford, a solicitor by profession, was a man of suave manner which would not have suggested, if one had met him in civil life, that he would have made soldiering his hobby. Devoted pursuit of military efficiency from school days onwards had brought him at the early age of

34 to command of the Sydney University Regiment, an appointment in which he had been succeeded in 1937 by Colonel Windeyer.[7] At 4 p.m. he moved his reserve company up behind Captain Balfe's company (holding Posts R30 to R35) through which he expected the thrust to be made.

The German plan required the preliminary operation to breach the anti-tank ditch to be carried out by Lieut-Colonel Ponath's *8th Machine Gun Battalion*. This had been timed to start at 5 p.m. At that hour, heavy artillery concentrations were brought down on Balfe's company.[8] Half an hour later, heavy small-arms fire was directed across the same area, and enemy infantry with a few tanks were seen to be advancing about 500 yards from the wire; but the guns of the 1st and 107th R.H.A. fired into their ranks with such good effect that they did not press on. After darkness fell, two or three enemy tanks cruised singly along the anti-tank ditch, possibly looking for the gap that should have been made. The imminence of a major attack was confirmed by the air force's evening reconnaissance, which reported that there was a concentration of 300 vehicles astride the El Adem Road.

Such was the situation at Tobruk when a message was received from General Wavell, addressed to General Morshead on the eve of his assumption of command. The defence of Egypt, Wavell told Morshead, now depended largely on holding the enemy on the Tobruk front and inflicting loss on him while forces were organised in rear. "I am glad," he continued, "that I have at this crisis such stout-hearted and magnificent troops in Tobruk. Am very heartened by what I have heard of their fighting spirit and conduct during these operations. I know I can count on you to hold Tobruk to the end. My best wishes to you all." Although the message ended on a perhaps unduly sombre note, it was promulgated to all ranks next day, by which time the men of the garrison were confident not only that they could hold Tobruk but that the "end" would not be of the enemy's choosing.

Wavell also reported the new organisation of command in the Western Desert to London. He said that if there were time to put the organisation into effect, he would be back to something like the situation of the previous autumn "with additional excrescence of Tobruk". "I can see no hope," he said, "of being able to relieve Tobruk for at least several months."

One event that day had brought gladness to Morshead's headquarters. Lieut-Colonel Mann, Morshead's chief engineer officer, with his adjutant, Captain Smith, came into the perimeter at the Wadi Sehel, having travelled by foot from Derna, 100 miles distant. Lieutenant Overall, Mann's Intelligence officer, who had travelled ahead of Mann to seek assistance, had come into the perimeter on the preceding day. Preparations had already been made to rescue them with the help of the Royal Navy. Mann attributed their safe arrival to Smith's genius for finding water in the desert and the skilled guiding of a young Senussi through enemy positions on the perimeter.

---

[7] Two other future battalion commanders in the 9th Division—R. W. N. Turner and C. H. Grace —were officers of the S.U.R. in 1939.
[8] According to *The Rommel Papers*, p. 124, by the *18th Anti-Aircraft Battalion*.

There was a program of deep patrolling for the night of 13th April around the whole perimeter. One of these patrols, a platoon from the 2/43rd Battalion led by Lieutenant Sunter,[9] had the task of locating enemy positions near the coast opposite the eastern sector and assaulting them. The patrol, wearing soft hats and sandshoes to guard against noise, intended to surprise the enemy in the Wadi Belgassem, some 2,000 yards distant from the perimeter, but were themselves surprised and caught by mortar fire and crossfire from machine-guns. Five men were lost and five badly wounded.

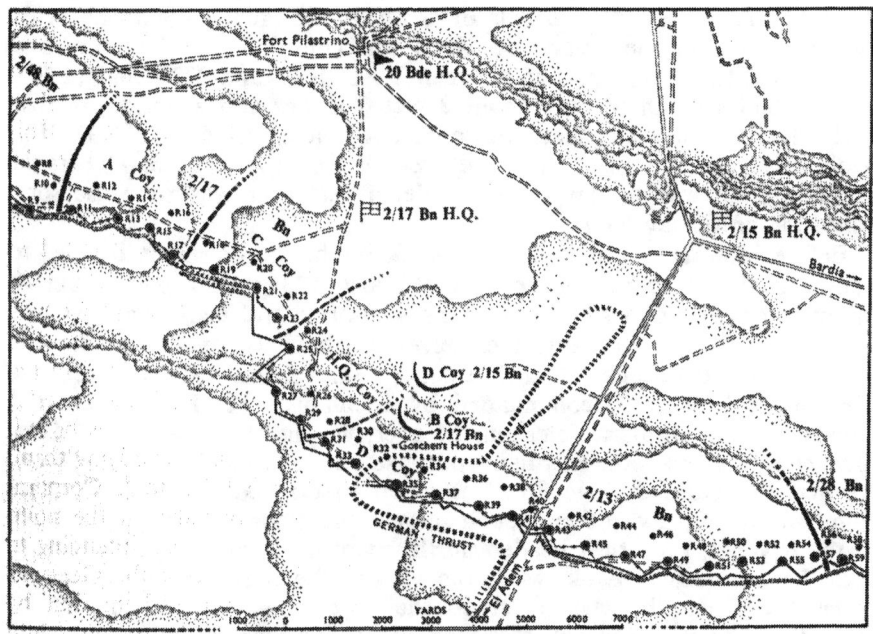

The German attack of 13th-14th April

On the 2/17th Battalion's front, Lieut-Colonel Crawford sent out two patrols under Lieutenant Pitman[10] and Lieutenant Geikie[1] to locate the positions the enemy had taken up near Post R33 during the afternoon. "No prisoners yet," the battalion diarist noted at 9 p.m. But Pitman and Geikie each brought back a prisoner, from the German *8th Machine Gun Battalion,* and also reported movement by groups of enemy right along the front of Captain Balfe's company. Crawford warned the commander of his reserve company, Captain Wilson,[2] to be ready to make a strong

---

[9] Maj J. S. Sunter, SX8976. 2/43 Bn; and staff appts. Clerk; of Adelaide; b. Adelaide, 12 Jul 1915.
[10] Maj C. G. Pitman, NX70231; 2/17 Bn. Builder; of Strathfield, NSW; b. Melbourne, 9 Dec 1916.
[1] Capt W. B. A. Geikie, NX12372; 2/17 Bn. Solicitor; of Darling Point, NSW; b. Picton, NSW, 28 Nov 1912.
[2] Capt C. H. Wilson, NX12212; 2/17 Bn. Journalist; of Dover Heights, NSW; b. Paddington, NSW, 3 Dec 1913.

counter-attack at dawn from behind Post R32 (500 yards behind the perimeter wire).

By the vigilance and aggressiveness of the defence, and by counter-patrolling, the enemy had been prevented from making much close reconnaissance. The point at which the German command decided to effect the penetration was not the best it might have chosen, if it had been permitted to learn more. The plan was laid down from maps which left much unshown. The anti-tank ditch was not continuous on the 2/17th's front. There was no ditch from R11 to R21; but although that portion of the front gave direct access to the vital Pilastrino ridge, it lay far to the west of the El Adem Road—the axis of advance chosen by Rommel.[3] In the sector chosen for the breach the ditch was continuous and for the most part about 12 feet deep, but between Posts R27 and R29 and at Post R33, it had a depth of only about 2 feet 6 inches and a bottom of solid rock. The German engineers chose to effect a crossing near R33. This again was some two miles and a half west of the El Adem Road where the break-through was to have been made, a fact that was to cause some confusion and delay later.

Before blowing a gap in the anti-tank ditch, the Germans decided to neutralise the neighbouring strongpoint, Post R33. At 11 p.m. about 30 infantrymen with two small field guns, a mortar and eight machine-guns broke through the wire, dug themselves in about 100 yards to the east of the post and brought all their weapons into action against it. But the garrison of Post R33, commanded by Lieutenant Mackell,[4] a cheerful personality and an alert, determined leader, was not to be easily subdued. Mackell had guessed the Germans' purpose and set about dislodging them. At first he returned their fire, but when that failed he took Corporal Edmondson[5] and five other men to attack the enemy party at the point of the bayonet. First they headed north, away from the post, intending to take the Germans in flank, while the men in the post kept the Germans under fire. Soon the enemy turned their weapons upon them, but by sprinting in bounds Mackell managed to get his men without harm into position for an assault. Mackell later said:

> We'd arranged with them that, as we got up for the final charge, we'd shout and they would stop firing and start shouting, too. The plan worked. We charged and yelled, but for a moment or two the Germans turned everything onto us. It's amazing that we weren't all hit. As we ran we threw our grenades and when they burst the German fire stopped. But already Jack Edmondson had been seriously wounded by a burst from a machine-gun that had got him in the stomach, and he'd also been hit in the neck. Still he ran on, and before the Germans could open up again we were into them.

They left their guns and scattered. In their panic some actually ran slap into the barbed wire behind them and another party that was coming through the gap

---

[3] Compare Schmidt in *With Rommel in the Desert*, p. 41: "Certainly the defences had been stronger than we expected. Later we learned that close to the scene of the attack there was a sector almost entirely bare of tank traps."

[4] Lt-Col F. A. Mackell, OBE, MC, NX12231. 2/17 Bn 1940-42; staff appts 1943-45. Commercial traveller; of Merrylands, NSW; b. Merrylands, 26 Nov 1917.

[5] Cpl J. H. Edmondson, VC, NX15705; 2/17 Bn. Farmer; of Liverpool, NSW; b. Wagga Wagga, NSW, 8 Oct 1914. Died of wounds 14 Apr 1941.

turned and fled. We went for them with the bayonet. In spite of his wounds Edmondson was magnificent. As the Germans scattered, he chased them and killed at least two. By this time I was in difficulties wrestling with one German on the ground while another was coming straight for me with a pistol. I called out—"Jack"—and from about fifteen yards away Edmondson ran to help me and bayoneted both Germans. He then went on and bayoneted at least one more.[6]

Meanwhile the other patrol members continued the attack with the bayonet. Mackell was soon on his feet, grabbed his rifle, broke his bayonet on one German and clubbed another with the butt. Edmondson continued fighting till he could no longer stand. The seven Australians accounted for at least twelve Germans and took one prisoner; the rest fled, leaving their weapons. Sadly the men helped Edmondson back to the post. He died there in the early morning.[7]

Mines lifted by the Germans had been neatly stacked on either side of the intended gap, but the ditch—shallow though it was—was still unbreached. At half an hour past midnight a German tank approached, inspected it at this point and retired. Almost two hours elapsed before the enemy came back. Then (at 2.30 a.m.) about 200 infantry broke through the wire near R33 and fanned out for several hundred yards inside. Balfe called for artillery fire by Very light signal. The 1st and 107th R.H.A. put down a heavy bombardment and the infantry in the posts joined in with their small arms. Ambulances began moving about outside the wire, but the enemy remained inside the perimeter.

The resolute action of the mere handful of men in Post R33 led by Mackell had deranged the enemy's plans by causing him to commit to the holding of the bridgehead a substantial part of the forces intended to follow up the assault. The commander of the *5th Armoured Regiment,* in a report on the operation, commented later that when the tanks assaulted only two and a half sections of the *8th Machine Gun Battalion* went forward, instead of 300 men.

When Brigadier Murray had heard of the first assault on Mackell's post, he had warned the 2/15th Battalion to hold a company ready to help the 2/17th Battalion if required. Lieut-Colonel Crawford now asked Murray for assistance and Captain Peek's company of the 2/15th was sent to Crawford, who arranged for it to go into position in rear of Balfe's company.

The enemy plan was simple. The *5th Armoured Regiment,* with 38 tanks, was to make a deep northerly penetration from the break-in point, followed by the *8th Machine Gun Battalion.* After penetrating for two miles, the leading tank battalion was to make for Tobruk while the other would "pursue the retreating enemy" westwards.

Towards 4 a.m. enemy tanks were seen in the moonlight assembling not far from the wire near the El Adem Road and were shelled, but without observed effect. About 4.45 a.m. they approached the perimeter at R41 near the El Adem Road. A contemporary German report stated

---
[6] Wilmot, *Tobruk,* p. 98, where the author mentions that Mackell only consented to describe the action after much persuasion.
[7] For this action Cpl Edmondson was awarded the Victoria Cross—the first to be awarded to an Australian in the war of 1939-45.

that the officer detailed to guide the *5th Armoured Regiment* to the gap lost his way and led it to a point too far to the east and that the regiment had to drive back west along the ditch, thus forfeiting surprise and losing the benefit of the preliminary German bombardment. At 4.50 a.m. some 40 tanks were reported moving west from R41 along the perimeter just outside the wire. One light tank was stopped by fire from a 2/13th Battalion post.

Enemy guns began to bombard the garrison defences. The fire was largely air-burst shells from 88-mm guns, possibly the first instance in Africa of the employment of this versatile anti-aircraft weapon as field artillery. The tanks continued to skirt the perimeter and the Chestnut Troop of the 1st R.H.A. engaged them. At 5.20 a.m. the first tanks turned and entered the perimeter through the gap near Mackell's post and made straight for Balfe's headquarters. There were 15 in the first wave, some of them towing anti-aircraft and anti-tank guns.

Instructions for the conduct of the defence in a tank attack had been issued at Morshead's direction. The infantry were told to avoid attracting the tanks' attention but to engage the following infantry when the tanks had passed. The tanks passed by the front perimeter posts and assembled almost on top of Balfe's headquarters in R32; 15 to 20 men followed each tank or rode on it, but dropped behind once they were within the perimeter. The British artillery defensive fire had been falling just in front of the wire; the range was now shortened and fire was brought down right on Balfe's headquarters, with excellent effect. The enemy machine-gun crews who had been riding on the tanks were mostly killed or wounded; the tanks moved on without them, while the accompanying infantry scattered and moved back towards the wire and, for the most part disorganised, were engaged from the posts. But one strong group established itself in some sangars and a ruined house behind Balfe's headquarters, which rightly belonged to Major Goschen of the 1st R.H.A. by virtue of prior occupation.

The tanks moved back eastwards on the Tobruk side of the wire until they were within a mile of the El Adem Road. Then they turned northeast, moved for a short time parallel to the road, and, facing northwards, halted to await the dawn about a mile and a half from "A/E" Battery of the 1st R.H.A. Tracers from their machine-guns told the R.H.A. where the tanks were. The gunners allowed them no peace. On the perimeter, in the meantime, the forward posts kept the perimeter gaps under steady fire, blocking the follow-up of unarmoured reinforcements, while the weapons in the second-line posts, covering the ground between, prevented the enemy from recovering the cohesion lost when the first artillery concentrations had fallen among them. How effectively the Australians used their weapons was discovered later; numerous enemy dead were found in hollows in the ground between the posts, many of them shot through the head.

As dawn came, the fire fight increased in intensity. Near Balfe's headquarters, three German anti-tank guns and a small field-piece were brought into action, firing behind the post. Balfe's men engaged the crews with rifle fire; the enemy in reply turned their guns onto the post; but the Australians continued to snipe the gun crews until all were killed (Lieutenant Geikie shot four by aimed fire). Next the Germans brought up to the gap a 75-mm field-piece and some huge, long-barrelled guns—these were the 88-mm guns not yet known to the Australians; but the infantry in the posts dealt with their crews in the same manner. As the light increased, the location of enemy machine-guns within the perimeter was revealed. They were engaged and one by one subdued.

When Lavarack learned that a substantial tank penetration had occurred, he went to Morshead's headquarters so that he could, if necessary, commit the force reserve without delay or take any other major decision that an unfavourable development of the battle might require. Earlier the cruiser tanks had been ordered to cover the approaches to Pilastrino, the infantry tanks the approaches to the El Adem-Bardia Road junction. As soon as the location of the intruding force was established, Morshead ordered the two cruiser squadrons of the 1st R.T.R. to engage the enemy tanks at first light.

As visibility improved after first light, the British cruisers began passing across the El Adem Road and the enemy tanks could be seen in a huddle one and a half miles to the south of the guns of "A/E" Battery, which brought down concentrated fire upon them. The German tanks spread out and began to work forward in groups towards the gap between the battery's two troops, the lighter tanks firing their guns as they went, the heavier stopping as they fired their 75's.

In the meantime one troop of "M" Battery 3rd R.H.A. was fighting a spirited action with its five guns on portee in the open. The troop worked round to the rear of the tanks, came up on the right flank and engaged them in a running fight, using mosquito tactics and accounting for several, but leaving two of their own guns and their portees destroyed.[8]

Fired at on all sides, the tanks, which had at first advanced well dispersed, tended to bunch, but continued to fight their way forward by bounds. One group would stop to fire their guns, while another moved on through them. Like a monster gathering in its haunches at each bound, the whole body of tanks thus advanced implacably and relentlessly on the guns of the Chestnut Troop of the 1st R.H.A. The British gunners had no armour-piercing shell but their fire was effective. The foremost tanks came within 600 yards of the gun positions. At that range the 25-pounders were deadly and the gunners firing over open sights, did not relent when casualties mounted fast. In no time, five tanks were burning and one 22-ton Mark IV tank—probably the tank battalion commander's —had its turret blown clean off. Two veered to the right to work their way round the flank only to be engaged and checked by some anti-tank guns of the 2/3rd. The *II/5th Armoured Battalion,* which had been leading the German advance, halted, turned its tanks round and retreated,

---

[8] There appears to be some overlapping of reports of tank destruction which is not surprising when it is realised that guns of the 1st, 3rd, 104th and 107th RHA and 2/3rd A-Tk Regt all engaged the tanks. Seventeen were knocked out during the penetration.

but ran straight into the *1/5th Armoured Battalion*, which was following up. There was confusion and several collisions.

The battle had reached its crisis. The penetration had not yet been contained, but the assault had been turned. To "A/E" Battery must go the main credit. For 45 minutes they had contested the seemingly relentless enemy advance, standing to their guns and proving themselves more steadfast than their enemy; the German tank crews were first to quail. The battery had one gun knocked out. In the Chestnut Troop 5 men were killed, and 3 were wounded, including both the officers at the guns. "E" Troop's casualties were 6 killed or badly wounded, of whom only one survived.

The German tanks next turned eastwards, but ran into the fire from a section of guns of the 2/3rd Anti-Tank Regiment commanded by Sergeant Knight[9] while "B/O" Battery also engaged them hotly with 25-pounders. Two guns of the 2/3rd under Sergeant Hinds[1] caught them in enfilade while the R.H.A. engaged them frontally. Both anti-tank guns opened fire simultaneously. A medium German tank was stopped. One of the anti-tank guns was put out of action and the gunner, Scholfield,[2] killed. Hinds continued firing the other. When the tanks had passed on and the smoke and dust had cleared, there were four enemy tanks knocked out in front of Hinds' gun.[3] The Rocket Troop, in a close duel, had three guns knocked out, two tractors destroyed and many men killed. The cruisers of the 1st Royal Tanks, which had meanwhile taken up position to the east of the El Adem Road, intending to attack at sunrise with the sun behind them, then opened fire at a range of about one mile and began to close in. But there was no sun that morning, only a thick layer of cloud at 4,000 feet.

Over the whole area of the break-in, and above, the battle was now being fought with great intensity and with weapons of every calibre from rapid light automatics to field guns. Drifting smoke and dust, billowing up, showed where the ground fighting was severest. Near the perimeter gap a counter-attack was being made on the enemy in Goschen's house while beside the El Adem Road the German tanks were being engaged simultaneously by the guns of "B/O" Battery, the 2/3rd's anti-tank guns and the cruiser tanks. In the air above, Tobruk's Hurricanes were fighting an unequal battle with German and Italian fighters, while anti-aircraft guns hosed their fire at the weaving aircraft. On the harbour side, the anti-aircraft gunners could hear with their instruments the approach of about 50 enemy bombers. In spectacular dog-fights above the battlefield the Hurricanes brought down four enemy planes. One Hurricane was engaged by the anti-aircraft gunners; while the pilot was frantically trying

---

[9] WO2 A. H. Knight, MM, NX56272; 2/3 A-Tk Regt. Storekeeper; of Lithgow, NSW; b. Lake Cargelligo, NSW, 4 Nov 1903.

[1] Sgt D. Hinds, NX58477; 2/3 A-Tk Regt. Labourer; of Dulwich Hill, NSW; b. Sydney, 30 Nov 1919. Killed in action 21 May 1941.

[2] Gnr J. W. Scholfield, NX32909; 2/3 A-Tk Regt. Wharf casual; of Glebe, NSW; b. Sydney, 19 Dec 1914. Killed in action 14 Apr 1941.

[3] Here again it is possible that other guns shared in the destruction of these four tanks.

to signal their mistake, he was surprised by an enemy aircraft and shot down.

On the perimeter the German infantry, whose task was to broaden the gap in the perimeter and secure the flanks, were for the most part scattered in hollows in the ground, making use of the cover they offered. The Australians near the gap meanwhile waged a continuous fight to recover mastery of the bridgehead. The enemy pockets close to the gap were soon subdued but groups who had penetrated in rear of the perimeter posts continued to give trouble. About the time when, some two miles within the perimeter, the two German tank battalions had been in disordered collision under the fire of "A/E" Battery's guns, Crawford had sent two platoons to clear up the area behind Balfe's company. Two sections, led by Sergeant McElroy,[4] approached Goschen's house under covering fire from other sections. The Germans in the house, feigning to be Australians, answered a call from Sergeant Brady,[5] but shot the Australian as he approached. McElroy's men then charged from dead ground 50 yards in front, hurling grenades as they went. Some Germans rushed out surrendering; others did not and were dispatched with the bayonet. Eighteen were captured, eighteen killed; a few escaped.

Engaged on all sides the German tanks had decided to extricate themselves; the sooner the better, it seemed. They turned and made for the gap by which they had come, harassed still by the unrelenting fire of "B/O" Battery and the 425th Battery. Now they encountered the mobile anti-tank guns of Lieutenant Hatch's[6] troop of "J" Battery, 3rd R.H.A., which in turn found itself surrounded by enemy infantry gathering near the tanks. But the Englishmen fought their guns, knocking out tank after tank. Next the tanks came within range of some guns of the 9th Battery, 2/3rd Anti-Tank Regiment. Meanwhile the British cruisers were following behind the German tanks, and two infantry tanks, which had closed in on the gap, joined in the fray. The German tanks did not delay their going forth.

No less than eight tanks were knocked out there with hits from both anti-tank and field guns. Bombardier McNally's[7] and Bombardier Cousins'[8] guns of the 9th Battery had a hand in this destruction. Two members of one English anti-tank gun crew were killed and one badly wounded by German machine-gun fire. The wounded man, Gunner R. Atkins, took over the gun and fired it single-handed until enemy machine-gun fire ignited his ammunition, wounding him a second time and badly disabling him. Bombardier G. T. Rudd dragged him to safety under fire.

As the tanks, much reduced in strength, approached the gap, they caught several bodies of Australians defenceless in the open while engaged in mopping-up operations, and began to force some to surrender. When

---

[4] Lt R. McL. McElroy, MM, NX23052; 2/17 Bn. Bank clerk; of Neutral Bay, NSW; b. Picton, NSW, 20 Mar 1920. Killed in action 27 Oct 1942.
[5] Sgt H. M. Brady, NX14388; 2/17 Bn. Clerk; of Sydney; b. Sydney, 16 Jun 1916. Killed in action 14 Apr 1941.
[6] Maj C. G. Hatch; 3 RHA. Engineer-estimator; b. Ilford, England, 31 Aug 1915.
[7] Lt J. S. McNally, NX57120; 2/3 A-Tk Regt. Commercial artist; of Roseville, NSW; b. Sydney, 31 Jul 1915.
[8] Sgt H. S. Cousins, NX60126; 2/3 A-Tk Regt. Upholsterer; of Marrickville, NSW; b. Marrickville, 26 Dec 1920.

this was seen from the posts, Bren gun fire was directed at the tanks. This forced them to close up while the Australians flung themselves to earth, and compelled the German infantry who had clambered on the backs of the tanks for the return journey to jump off and take cover.

There was much confusion as the tanks made their exit—tanks and infantry pushing through the gap together. One of the tank commanders[9] ruefully commented in his diary (which was afterwards captured) that their own anti-tank and 88-mm guns were almost deserted, with the crews lying silent behind them: the Italian artillery was also deserted, he said. Captain Balfe later described the scene:

> The crossing was badly churned up and the tanks raised clouds of dust as they went. In addition, there was the smoke of two tanks blazing just outside the wire. Into this cloud of dust and smoke we fired anti-tank weapons, Brens, rifles, and mortars, and the gunners sent hundreds of shells. We shot up a lot of infantry as they tried to get past, and many, who took refuge in the anti-tank ditch, were later captured. It was all I could do to stop the troops following them outside the wire. The Germans were a rabble, but the crews of three tanks did keep their heads. They stopped at the anti-tank ditch and hitched on behind them the big guns, whose crews had been killed. They dragged these about 1,000 yards, but by then we had directed our artillery on to them. They unhitched the guns and went for their lives.[1]

By 7.30 a.m. the German tanks were in full retreat. Forty Ju-87 (Stuka) dive bombers then dropped out of the cloud above the harbour to bomb the town area in an attack timed to synchronise with the intended arrival there of the leading German tank battalion. The dive bombers attacked an anti-aircraft gun site, without causing serious damage; but near the gun site two men were killed and nine wounded. The Hurricanes shot down two more planes; the anti-aircraft gunners destroyed four.

Behind Goschen's house about 100 enemy had established themselves on a reverse slope; they continued to prove troublesome after the house had been cleared. Assisted by the containing action of Peek's company of the 2/15th, which was deployed behind, Wilson personally led a platoon from his over-worked company against this enemy group. It achieved complete success: a few Germans were killed, 75 were captured, the rest fled.

The battle was over by 8.30 a.m., but sporadic fighting continued until mid-morning in operations to clear the anti-tank ditch, to prevent the abandoned German infantry from escaping, and to locate and subdue the enemy pockets. Near "A" Company of the 2/15th Battalion, where the main battle between the field guns and the tanks had occurred, the company sergeant-major, Sergeant Robinson,[2] noticed about 8.45 a.m. that, under cover from German infantry in a tank trap 700 yards from the company area, the crews of some damaged German tanks were trying to get their tanks moving. Lieutenant Yates[3] with his platoon—30 strong—was sent out to deal with the infantry pocket, Robinson acting as guide.

---
[9] Lt Schorm, *II/5th Armoured Battalion*.
[1] Quoted in Wilmot, *Tobruk*, p. 106.
[2] Lt K. E. Robinson, QX754. 2/15 and 2/25 Bns. Fruitgrower; of Imbil, Qld; b. Maryborough, Qld, 17 Sep 1909.
[3] Capt R. A. Yates, MC, QX6256; 2/15 Bn. Oil company representative; of Ascot, Qld; b. Toowoomba, Qld, 21 Oct 1912.

Yates managed to invest the position closely but was unable to subdue the enemy. Sergeant Keys[4] was then sent to his assistance with two carriers taking with him two 2-inch mortars and four men from "A" Company as mortar crews. While the mortars fired on the enemy from behind a knoll, the two carriers moved to either end of the anti-tank ditch and fired into the enemy positions. Three enemy were killed, 87 captured (7 badly wounded), and numerous weapons of many varieties were taken.

The German commander's first major operation against the fortress had ended in complete defeat. A second attack, timed to start at 6 p.m., was cancelled. The assault troops must have suffered heavy casualties in the evening attack when the British artillery fire broke up the first attempt to establish a bridgehead, for numerous ambulances were seen when the firing ceased; other casualties must have been incurred outside the perimeter that night and next day. Inside, 150 enemy dead were counted on the battlefield and 250 prisoners were taken. The garrison's casualties were 26 killed and 64 wounded. Seventeen enemy tanks (out of 38 that went into the battle) were destroyed, two British cruisers knocked out.

General Rommel had watched the operation from close to the wire, but his signals vehicle was observed and came under artillery fire. The German commander drove off to the *Ariete Division* to spur them to carry out their role of exploiting the German division's penetration. When he returned to his headquarters, it was to learn that the *5th Armoured Regiment* had come back. General Streich and Colonel Olbrich (the commander of the armour) reported to Rommel and had to endure the lash of his tongue. "I was furious," he wrote later, "particularly at the way that the tanks had left the infantry in the lurch, and ordered them forward again immediately to open up the breach in the enemy line and get the infantry out."[5] When Rommel later (on 22nd July) removed General Streich from his command, he gave as one reason that Streich had declined to take the responsibility for carrying out an order to return to the *8th Machine Gun Battalion's* assistance.

Believing that the *8th Machine Gun Battalion* was still holding out, Rommel decided to attempt its rescue next day by a penetration through the western sector. He ordered the *Ariete Division* to move into position there in the evening. He records in his account of the campaign that, while doing so, they broke up in panic on coming under fire from the guns of the fortress: but the incident went unnoticed in Australian and British diaries.

Two comments in his published papers reveal Rommel's opinion on why the operation failed:

> The division's command had not mastered the art of concentrating its strength at one point, forcing a break-through, rolling up and securing the flanks on either side, and then penetrating like lightning, before the enemy has had time to react, deep into his rear. . . . Had the *5th Light Division* been in a position to secure its

---

[4] Capt J. T. Keys, QX5874. 2/15 and 57/60 Bns. Carpenter; of Toowoomba, Qld; b. Bombala, NSW, 6 Jun 1902.
[5] *The Rommel Papers*, p. 125.

two flanks and thus allow the artillery and the *Ariete* to follow through the breach, Tobruk would probably have fallen on the 14th or 15th April 1941.[6]

These were the tactics Rommel employed with complete success when his forces stormed and took Tobruk in the succeeding year, but not many will accept the judgment in the second sentence. The prime causes of failure were the Germans' and Rommel's over-confidence and their underestimation of the strength of the defence. A battle plan based on the false assumption, drawn from European experience, that opposition would collapse when the tanks broke through the perimeter went agley when that did not occur. Both senior and junior commanders lost their nerve, the force its cohesion. Colonel Olbrich wrote in his report on the operations:

> The information distributed before the action told us that the enemy was about to withdraw, his artillery was weak and his morale had become very low. . . . The regiment had not the slightest idea of the well-designed and constructed defences nor of a single battery position nor of the awful number of anti-tank guns. Nor was it known that he had heavy tanks.

The whole responsibility for the miscalculation was Rommel's, who recorded that the *5th Light Division*, which was to mount the attack, was pessimistic about the plan. To form a bridgehead, roll up the flanks, hold the gap open and provide at the same time 300 men to accompany the tank penetration was a prescription that one machine-gun battalion and a company of engineers might have accomplished against cowards but not against a spirited defence.

The failure of the assault forces to reinforce the bridgehead promptly and strongly rather than the British counter-measures caused the debacle. On the British side the prompt dispatch of the tanks to meet the threat, their advantageous placing for a counter-attack on the flank, and the speed with which local counter-attacks were mounted by the battalion, company and platoon commanders were meritorious. But the victory belonged in the main to the gunners who had fought it out with the German tanks, to the Bren gunners and machine-gunners in the posts who had not been intimidated or subdued and to the patrolmen whose bayonet charges had dislodged the enemy infantry before they could consolidate. One may accept the summing up by the diarist of "B/O" Battery:

> The two outstanding features of the battle were:
> (i) "A/E" Battery's tank shoot, which finally stopped the tanks.
> (ii) The infantry in "D" Company remaining in their positions completely unperturbed by the tanks and then attacking the ensuing infantry, together with an excellent counter-attack by "B" Company.

General Lavarack issued an order of the day congratulating all ranks of the garrison on their stern and determined resistance. But the sweets of victory had been soured for Lavarack himself. He had received at 2.30 p.m. a personal message from Wavell which told him that arrangements had now been made for Cyrenaica Command to be merged into Western Desert Force and that on return to Egypt he would therefore resume com-

---

[6] *The Rommel Papers*, pp. 123-4, 126.

(R.A.F.)

A post-war photograph of Post R39 in the southern sector. The perimeter defences between R33 and R35 (then held by the 2/17th Battalion) were breached by the Germans in the Easter attack on Tobruk.

(Australian War Memorial)

Lieut-Colonel J. W. Crawford (centre), commanding the 2/17th Battalion, beside a German tank knocked out during the Easter attacks.

The German dive-bombing attack on the 2/24th Battalion's positions before the enemy assault on 30th April-1st May 1941, as seen from a carrier of the 2/48th Battalion. In the foreground is the barrel of a Boyes anti-tank rifle mounted on the carrier.

(Australian War Memorial)

Headquarters of the 2/23rd Battalion, at the head of the Wadi Giaida, in the Salient sector.

(Australian War Memorial)
A rubble-littered street in Tobruk port.

(Australian War Memorial)
A bomb-damaged ship in Tobruk Harbour.

(*Australian War Memorial*)
The "bush artillery" of the 2/17th Battalion in action with a captured Italian 75-mm field gun.

(*Australian War Memorial*)
A gun position of the 8th Battery, 3rd Australian Light Anti-Aircraft Regiment, alongside the remains of a Stuka dive bomber at Tobruk.

mand of the 7th Division, less the 18th Brigade. Wavell concluded his message:

> Most grateful your invaluable services in stabilising situation in Cyrenaica.

To Lavarack, the able soldier and patriot who in peace had reached the summit of professional eminence, it must have seemed that the fates were in conspiracy to thwart his desire to exercise high military command in war. Chief of the Australian General Staff in 1939, he had been overseas when war had been declared. He had returned to Australia to learn that General E. K. Squires would replace him in that office and General Blamey would command the A.I.F. Later he had accepted a reduction of rank from lieut-general to major-general to enable him to take command of an A.I.F. division but had then been appointed to the command of not the senior division but the second to be formed. Now he had been ordered in the very hour of success to step down from an operational command of utmost responsibility.

Later, after Blamey had suggested to Lavarack that the reason for his non-appointment to the Western Desert Force command might have been his several requests for a force of two divisions to defend Tobruk, Lavarack wrote to Wavell to ask him to correct that misapprehension. Wavell replied (on 13th May 1941) that the changes in command did not reflect on Lavarack in any way whatever. He pointed out that when Tobruk had been cut off, a reorganisation of command had become necessary: the headquarters of the Western Desert Force had to be outside Tobruk, and there was sufficient staff for only one headquarters. He continued:

> While I was considering this reorganisation I visited Greece and saw General Blamey and asked him whether he recommended leaving you in command at Tobruk. He thought you would probably be better outside. I then considered you as the Commander of Western Desert Force, but decided instead to recommend Beresford-Peirse to War Office since the enemy attack might come very shortly and he had dealt with the same problem last year and knew the ground and the problem.
> I can assure you that your recommendation of two divisions for the defence of Tobruk did not affect my decision; to the best of my recollection my opinion was that two divisions would be a suitable garrison if they were readily available. But I did not consider at that time that they could be spared. . . .
> I was very pleased with the way you handled the force at Tobruk and Gott's force while in command.

Once Tobruk had become isolated, it was clearly right to organise its defence under one headquarters and one commander. Since Morshead's division formed the main component of the defence force, Blamey's decision that Morshead rather than Lavarack should be given the command was both sound and proper.

There was probably a further reason not mentioned by Wavell for not appointing General Lavarack to the Western Desert Force command. It was not usual to appoint Dominion generals to senior commands of other than Dominion formations. The Middle East command structure was a segment of the British Army into which Dominion components under Dominion command were fitted. The idea of a mixed Commonwealth force with senior commanders freely interchangeable among the high posts on a basis of experience and capability was not conceived.

Seldom are military decisions the product of only one man's thought. But Lavarack must be given credit for several decisions for which the responsibility was his while he was in command of Cyrenaica Force at Tobruk: undertaking to defend Tobruk with the allotted force rather than recommending its withdrawal; basing the defence on the existing perimeter; organising it in depth, including the decision to construct a second line of defence (the Blue Line) with switch-lines; holding one brigade in rear as a mobile counter-attack force; and refusing to be drawn from the main task of holding Tobruk into expending his force in enterprises to open the coast road and dispatch the cruiser tanks to the frontier.

General Lavarack yielded command at Tobruk to General Morshead at 6 p.m. on 14th April and returned that night to Egypt with the headquarters of Cyrenaica Command. General Evetts continued to command the forces on the frontier and at Mersa Matruh until General Beresford-Peirse arrived.

CHAPTER 5

STRIKING BACK

GENERAL Wavell's message to General Morshead, which had sombrely told him that the defence of Egypt depended largely on holding the enemy at Tobruk, epitomised Morshead's grave responsibility: a much heavier responsibility than a divisional commander normally bears. Usually the commander of a division in the field can refer in critical moments to his corps or army commander; likewise a corps or army commander usually shares the burden of decision on grave issues with his superiors. But Morshead, because of the very isolation his task imposed, had to bear his responsibilities alone. If a crisis arose, the decision would be his alone to take.

He had already made clear the spirit in which he would conduct the defence. On the evening before the withdrawal into Tobruk, he had called his brigadiers together. "There'll be no Dunkirk here," he had said. "If we should have to get out, we shall fight our way out. There is to be no surrender and no retreat." So each unit, as it had moved into its allotted position within the perimeter had been told (and had heard with relief) that this time it would hold its ground and give the enemy no quarter.

The men under Morshead's command numbered about 35,700, but not all of them were combatant troops. Apart from the Royal Navy and the Royal Air Force, the strength of the fighting units was approximately 24,000, of whom 14,270 were Australian and approximately 9,000 British. In the base area were some 5,700 British Commonwealth troops (including 547 Australian, 3,583 British and 1,579 Indian troops), 3,000 Libyan refugees organised into labour battalions and 2,780 prisoners of war. One of Morshead's first concerns was to reduce the number of useless mouths by cutting down the personnel in the base area to what was necessary to support and service the fighting units. The reduction took place gradually, beginning with prisoners of war and surplus non-combatant people and extending to the return to Egypt of all men of the depleted 2nd Armoured Division (other than its artillery) not required to man the few tanks and armoured cars in Tobruk. To look forward momentarily: by 18th June the total strength in the base area had been reduced by one half to less than 5,700, of which some 4,400 were British Commonwealth base troops and most of the remainder Libyan refugee personnel. By 31st July the base area strength, excluding prisoners of war, was 1,397.

Morshead's defence policy was based on four principles: that no ground should be yielded; that the garrison should dominate no-man's land; that no effort should be spared in improving defence works and constructing new obstacles; and that the defence should be organised in the greatest depth possible, with the maximum of reserves. He insisted that no-man's land should be patrolled in breadth and depth each night, with no exceptions. Distrusting the Italian strongpoints because they provided so few fire-bays and enabled men to shelter without fighting, he ordered the immediate construction of additional weapon-pits, with intercommunication trenches. He pushed forward the construction of an inner second line of defence (the Blue Line). When, on General Lavarack's departure, the 18th Brigade group came under his command, he ordered the 2/4th Field Company supporting it to start work on the Blue Line defences next day. He was continually inspecting one or other unit or formation in the fortress; often, on leaving it, he would deliver an admonition for failure to carry out his policy with the energy and thoroughness he demanded.

Apart from Colonel Lloyd, his able, thoroughly trained and quick-thinking chief staff officer—who was always at his best when the situation was most difficult—Morshead depended on his four Australian infantry brigadiers and two British artillery commanders for the execution of his policy. They served him well. All four brigade commanders had served with distinction as infantry officers in the first world war. The senior was Wootten of the 18th Brigade. A veteran of Gallipoli, Wootten had begun his career as a professional soldier, graduated at Duntroon, served both in operations and on the staff during the first world war with unusual distinction, and after the war had completed a brilliant course at Camberley. He left the army in 1923 to study law and practised between the wars as a solicitor, but returned to active service as C.O. of the 2/2nd Battalion when the Second A.I.F. was formed. Becoming corpulent in middle age, he exhibited nevertheless an active mind and naturally well balanced judgment, and carried the burdens of command with ease. Already, as brigadier, he had one successful operation to his credit—the capture of Giarabub. Brigadier Murray, who commanded the 20th Brigade, was a different personality. A genial temperament endeared him alike to his commanders and his staff; his outstanding characteristic was his straightforward, unqualified loyalty to all who worked with him. Where Wootten was solid, Murray was imaginative; he abounded with suggestions which Morshead, however, sometimes regarded as ill-conceived. Brigadier Tovell, commanding the 26th Brigade, had been a brigade major when the first war ended. He was a hard-working commander, with a sense of humour, who took a friendly interest in his officers and men and was generally liked, but lacked the streak of ruthlessness common to most successful commanders. A chartered accountant in civilian life, he had made soldiering his hobby between the wars. Brigadier Godfrey, the most recently appointed of the brigadiers, who commanded the 24th Brigade, was also a first war veteran and keen peace-time civilian soldier. Godfrey believed in his soldierly mission and imparted his enthusiasm to his men. As a battalion commander in the 6th Division in the attacks on Bardia and Tobruk, he had won a reputation for moving with the troops in the front of the fighting.

Morshead's field and anti-aircraft artillery commanders, both British regular soldiers, were able, technically proficient and zealous. They represented the very best of the British military tradition. Brigadier Thompson, who commanded the field and anti-tank artillery, at once displayed his capability by the excellence of his dispositions and arrangements, which assured that the guns of the fortress were used to maximum efficiency. Foreseeing from the beginning that the field artillery would be the garrison's main defence against the tank, he insisted that the guns should be sited to carry out an anti-tank role to best effect. Gunpits were made large and shallow, sacrificing some protection to enable quick traverse and assure an unobstructed field of fire in all directions.

The forty-eight 25-pounder guns of the Royal Horse Artillery regiments and the twelve 18-pounders[1] and twelve 4.5-inch howitzers of the 51st Field Regiment were organised into three groups, with zones of primary responsibility corresponding to the three brigade sectors. In the central (or southern) sector held by the 20th Brigade, whence artillery support could be given not only to the front but also to the more vulnerable zones of the brigades on either flank, the 107th R.H.A. was superimposed on the 1st R.H.A. to form a tactical group of 32 guns. The 51st Field Regiment was in direct support of the 26th Brigade in the west, the 104th R.H.A. of the 24th Brigade in the east. The guns were mainly deployed at the escarpment below Pilastrino and near Sidi Mahmud. This organisation and deployment had the advantage of giving the greatest possible protection to the commanding Pilastrino ridge. Also it enabled the fire of the maximum number of guns to be concentrated on any part of the front while permitting some to be moved to any threatened sector without unduly weakening the front as a whole.

Brigadier Slater,[2] who commanded the 24 heavy and 60 light guns (of which 4 heavy and 43 light guns were captured Italian equipment) of the garrison's anti-aircraft defences, proved himself to be an officer of exceptional determination, energy and originality, qualities he was soon required to exercise to the full in protecting the port against the air strikes the R.A.F. could do so little to oppose.

For the time being the supply situation was good but ahead lay the prospect of a long siege. Two months had been specified as the minimum period before a relief could be effected; it was clear that the fortress would have to depend for provisions on the navy. The naval officer-in-charge, Captain Smith,[3] brought to his task an ability and a devotion typifying the highest traditions of the Royal Navy. Such was his enthusiasm that during the siege, as Admiral Cunningham has told, he declined the offer of a command of a ship to remain in charge at Tobruk.[4] The Naval Inshore Squadron, which Admiral Cunningham had constituted during General Wavell's first offensive to act in support of the army and to control the ports of the North African coast, was now based on Tobruk and operated a variety of small ships—gunboats, minesweepers, armed boarding vessels,

---

[1] These obsolescent guns were not replaced until the 51st was relieved by the Polish artillery regiment in August.
[2] Maj-Gen J. N. Slater, CBE, MC. Comd 4 AA Bde BEF, France, 1940; comd anti-aircraft defences Tobruk 1941. Regular soldier; b. 25 Nov 1894.
[3] Capt F. M. Smith, DSO, RD; RNR. Naval Officer-in-Charge Tobruk 1941-42. Killed in action 20 Jun 1942.
[4] Viscount Cunningham, *A Sailor's Odyssey* (1951), p. 415.

sloops, trawlers, whalers and others. Henceforward their main but by no means only task would be the formidable one of bringing to Tobruk across sea-ways dominated by a hostile air force all the munitions and supplies necessary for its garrison's survival.

The victory of 14th April brought congratulations to the fortress commander and the garrison from the British Prime Minister. Mr Churchill asked General Wavell to convey the War Cabinet's congratulations to all engaged in the fight. He went on to say that the War Cabinet regarded it as vital that Tobruk should be regarded as a sally-port. "Can you not find good troops who are without transport to help hold the perimeter," he asked, "thus freeing at least one, if not two, Australian brigade groups to act as general fortress reserve and potential striking force?" Wavell, hard pressed to find sufficient forces to guard his western flank, ignored the question but conveyed the British Prime Minister's congratulations to Morshead in a message in which he suggested that the enemy's discomfiture might provide an opportunity for a counter-stroke. Morshead had Churchill's congratulations promulgated to all ranks.

General Rommel, as we saw in the last chapter, had intended to renew the assault on the garrison on the 15th by attacking in the west. He had ordered the *Ariete Division* into position south of Ras el Medauuar on the 14th, but under British artillery fire they had streamed back from the ground to be occupied.

The hill Ras el Medauuar Rommel was planning to take stood in the centre of the front of the 2/48th Battalion commanded by Lieut-Colonel Windeyer. Windeyer was a Sydney barrister, lecturer, and author of works on legal history and practice, who combined eminence in his chosen profession with intense interest in soldiering. His deliberative speech and contemplative manner, unusual in a military leader, masked a competent and determined personality. As already mentioned he was a product of the Sydney University Regiment in which he had risen by 1937 to command. He gained his first appointment to the A.I.F. in May 1940 by stepping back a rank but was soon seconded from his battalion to join the original staff of the 7th Division. Two months later he had been promoted to command the 2/48th, which was being raised in South Australia. It was not usual at that time for an infantry C.O. to be brought in from another State, but Windeyer quickly won the South Australians' confidence, and later their affection. General Rommel was soon to rue the consequences of his vigorous and imaginative defence.

Soon after dawn on the 15th, an enemy party appeared in the west just in front of the 2/48th and only about 150 yards from the wire. They were driven back by Bren gun fire. Throughout the morning group after group of infantry, each group seeming larger than the last, approached the perimeter; each as it came into view through the dancing mirage, was in turn halted by the guns of the 51st Field Regiment. All appeared to be Italian. By midday the front was quiet.

The Australians had noticed that many of the enemy had sought refuge from the gunfire in a wadi on the escarpment some three-quarters of a mile from the perimeter. Windeyer sent out a patrol from his reserve company to mop them up. It was commanded by Lieutenant Jenkins,[5] who took 22 men out towards the wadi while the gunners harassed the Italians to compel them to keep their heads down. About 1,000 yards from the wire Jenkins' patrol surprised an enemy party, threw grenades into their midst, charged with the bayonet and captured an Italian officer and 74 men.

No sooner had Jenkins' patrol returned than an attack threatened against the 2/24th Battalion (commanded by Major Tasker) and the right flank of Windeyer's battalion. About 5.30 p.m. Italian infantry numbering about 1,000 advanced on the wire against the left company of the 2/24th and the right platoon of the 2/48th. Some of the enemy penetrated the wire on the front of the 2/24th Battalion and one post was overrun. Brigadier Tovell arranged with Lieut-Colonel Evans[6] to send his "A" Company of the 2/23rd Battalion to counter-attack. Meanwhile the 2/24th was regaining control of the situation by keeping those who had penetrated pinned to the ground by automatic fire. The company of the 2/23rd on arrival counter-attacked the few still holding out. By 6.15 p.m. there were no enemy inside the wire, except those who had been captured; these numbered 113 and included two officers. It was estimated (in the divisional Intelligence summary) that about 250 men had been killed; perhaps an over-estimate, but the execution done by both shell fire and automatics on bunched groups of enemy in the open had been very great.

As darkness fell the enemy was again massing and bringing up guns, this time farther to the left, on the 20th Brigade front. An attack was expected but did not develop. It seemed that Rommel still hoped to take Tobruk by a quick assault. "My plan now," he wrote later in his memoirs, "was to take the hill, Ras el Medauuar, using elements of the *Ariete* and *Trento* and several German companies attacking under strong artillery support."

While on this moonlight night of 15th April the Tobruk garrison was making ready to repel the expected German thrust against the 20th Brigade, four British destroyers which had left Malta at 6 p.m. were steaming at speed towards the Kerkennah Islands. On the morning of the 16th, two hours after midnight, they intercepted an Italian convoy of five merchant vessels, escorted by three destroyers, bound for Africa. The entire convoy and its escort were sunk. An important part of its cargo had been much of the transport and heavy equipment required for the German *15th Armoured Division*, some of the lighter elements of which, it will be recalled, had already arrived and been sent to the Salum front. Since Wavell's ability to defend the British base in the Middle East depended on his assembling reinforcements before his adversary could muster strength to strike, the Royal Navy's effective intervention was invaluable.

---
[5] Lt W. C. Jenkins, SX7686; 2/48 Bn. Storeman; of Croydon, SA; b. Croydon, 4 May 1913. Killed in action 16 May 1941.
[6] Brig Sir Bernard Evans, DSO, ED, VX47819. CO 2/23 Bn 1940-42; comd 24 Bde 1942-43; CI LHQ Tactical School 1943-45. Lord Mayor of Melbourne 1959-61. Architect; of Melbourne; b. Manchester, England, 13 May 1905.

If the British command was apprehensive of a further German advance at the frontier, General Rommel soon became no less apprehensive of the possibility of British counter-action; not without reason, for his frontier force, though more than a match for any Jock column, was weaker than the British, except in armoured cars. The Knabe Group comprised a reconnaissance battalion (*3rd Reconnaissance Unit*), a motor-cycle battalion, a battalion of anti-tank artillery and a light anti-aircraft battery; it was reinforced by a mixed Italian detachment (*Montemurro Unit*) brought across from Bardia.

Providentially the Germans did not attempt to force the Halfaya position after Salum fell. Knabe's "further task"—advance to Mersa Matruh —was cancelled and on the 14th—the day on which the tank attack on Tobruk was launched—the force went over to the defensive. The result of the attack did not encourage General Rommel or Colonel Herff—who assumed the frontier command that day—to take new risks. When the Royal Navy's Inshore Squadron bombarded Bardia, the town was evacuated, much to Rommel's annoyance, who ordered its reoccupation "without fail" when he visited the front a few days later. So well did British patrols evince the offensive spirit that General Evetts had enjoined, so many losses did they inflict on the garrison at Salum, that it was mostly withdrawn, only a small permanent patrol remaining.

Early on the morning of the 16th a message from General Headquarters at Cairo was received at Morshead's headquarters to the effect that the enemy was planning a large-scale attack by air and land against Tobruk that day. This prediction seemed to be confirmed by markings found on a map captured from the enemy during the attack on the preceding afternoon, and also by the enemy's subsequent concentration of force against the 20th Brigade. Morshead ordered a general stand-to of the whole garrison, including the base troops. Throughout that long day they stood to arms; but as the forenoon dragged on to afternoon, the enemy remained strangely quiet.

Each brigade sent out patrols beyond the wire to see if anything was afoot. In the east a patrol from the 2/43rd Battalion led by Corporal Joy[7] shot up two enemy parties, which then made off. In the southern sector, a patrol from the 2/13th Battalion sent out in the morning to investigate across the whole front of the battalion was chased home by enemy tanks, but not before it had captured a prisoner. A 2/17th Battalion patrol in the early afternoon attacked and routed the occupants of an enemy post, but machine-gun fire brought down from the flanks, which forced the patrol to withdraw, left no doubt that the enemy was now well entrenched in that sector.

Neither in the south nor in the east did an attack appear to be imminent. It was in the west that signs of trouble brewing were first observed. There the morning, though quiet, had not been uneventful. Patrols were sent out from the 2/24th and 2/48th Battalions to collect war material aban-

---

[7] Lt F. N. Joy, MM, SX5093; 2/43 Bn. Labourer; of Streaky Bay, SA; b. Streaky Bay, 26 Jan 1913.

doned by the enemy in their flight on the previous evening. One, under Lieutenant Wardle,[8] attacked a party of Italians in a wadi. After one enemy had been killed, the rest numbering 97, surrendered, and were shepherded inside the wire. Patrols from the 2/24th meanwhile had been equally active; one took 6 officers and 57 men prisoner, another captured a Breda machine-gun and 8 prisoners. It was good hunting. Colonel Windeyer sent out more patrols from the 2/48th, including one in the late evening of three carriers which that morning had been made available to him from the 2/23rd Battalion. The carriers discovered an enemy battalion approaching from Acroma and were just in time to warn a patrol from "B" Company, who were making straight for them. Both patrols returned and gave warning of the enemy's approach.

The enemy battalion deployed for attack in front of "B" Company, but heavy shelling from the 51st Field Regiment made them scatter in disorder. The guns then lifted and put down a heavy curtain of fire behind them, while "B" Company kept them under small-arms fire. As the enemy went to ground, 12 tanks were revealed in rear; these were also shelled and chose to scatter. Lieutenant Isaksson[9] was then sent out with a section of Bren gun carriers to work round the enemy's flank, an operation which, with the assistance of a platoon of "B" Company, was accomplished with remarkable success. The complete force was captured and the men of the 2/48th on the perimeter were presented with (to quote the battalion's diarist)

the ludicrous sight of a battalion of infantry being herded like so many sheep through a gap in the wire into our hands.

A crew member of one of the carriers afterwards described the action.

As we drove out they put up a few shots (said Private Daniels[1]), but we kept our Brens and anti-tank rifles spraying them. When we got near they stopped firing. One carrier went round each flank and one ran straight through the middle of them. We fired over their heads; they dropped their rifles and machine-guns, waved white handkerchiefs, and put up their hands. As we drove through they began marching towards our wire, leaving all their gear on the ground.[2]

As the Italians moved in towards the perimeter, four of the tanks came forward. A "few spiteful rounds", which appeared to the Australians to come from the enemy tanks, were then fired into the Italian infantry. The Australian carriers were also engaged. But retaliatory gunfire from the British artillery quickly put an end to the enemy's shooting; his fire had, however, caused several casualties among the Italians and wounded two Australians of the 2/48th Battalion, one mortally. These were the only garrison casualties in the action. The 2/48th Battalion's "bag" for the day was 803 prisoners, including one German officer and 25 Italian officers. In the next divisional Intelligence summary the following entry appeared in the section dealing with identification of enemy units:

1 Bn 62 Regt—Trento Div—Completely captured.

[8] Capt A. Wardle, SX1291; 2/48 Bn. Schoolteacher; of Adelaide; b. Darwin, 11 Sep 1902. Died 4 May 1954.
[9] Maj O. H. Isaksson, MC, SX9461; 2/48 Bn. Salesman; of Adelaide; b. Exeter, SA, 29 Jun 1917
[1] Sgt R. G. Daniels, MM, SX7863; 2/48 Bn. Fibrous plasterer; of Rosewater Gardens, SA; b. Exeter, SA, 7 Mar 1918.
[2] Wilmot, *Tobruk*, p. 118.

Interrogation of the prisoners revealed that they were underfed and very thirsty. The object of their operation had been to seize a road junction behind Ras el Medauuar. They were to be supported, they said, by a group of tanks of the *5th Armoured Regiment*: but the coordination was apparently faulty despite the attachment of a German liaison officer to the Italian unit, for the prisoners complained that the German tanks did not arrive according to plan. Most of those captured were confused about their objectives.

The Italians may have been in error in believing that they would be supported by the *5th Armoured Regiment,* for the only tanks engaged in the operation appear to have been their own. General Rommel reports that he launched the armoured battalion of the *Ariete* (6 medium and 12 light tanks) against Hill 187 in conjunction with an attack by the Italian infantry. He accompanied the attack on its left flank. The Italians drove to the highest point of 187 and halted.[3] There they were shelled and retired in confusion to a wadi. Meanwhile one of Rommel's staff officers reported that the Italian infantry attack had broken up into a wild rout to the west. On returning the same officer had fired on a British "scout car" herding a company of Italians, intending to give the Italians a chance of escape, and had later shot up some British Bren gun carriers with three anti-tank guns placed at his disposal by Rommel.

Many Italian prisoners did not conceal their dislike of their German allies. Perhaps they were the more inclined to make it known because they believed that the German tanks had failed to participate in the operation except to fire at them when the battle was lost. One senior Italian officer collaborated in the composition of a leaflet in Italian to be scattered from aircraft over the enemy lines. The leaflet, which was dispersed next day, read as follows:

> Soldiers of Italy!
> Old companions in arms, a return to peaceful and happy times can be quickly brought about. Throughout all Africa your comrades have ceased fire, in Abyssinia the war is over. The Duke of Aosta's emissary has come to our Headquarters for armistice preliminaries. Yesterday thousands of your comrades were captured at Tobruk; greater sacrifices on your part would be useless. All captured Italian soldiers have been accorded friendly treatment.
> End it all: still greater losses can be avoided.

When General Wavell was informed of the day's operations, he sent General Morshead a personal message:

> Well done indeed. Keep at it. Will support boldest action.

Wavell followed up his congratulations with a further message on the 17th stating that the recent events indicated the need for a counter-stroke in force from Tobruk. Such an operation, if successful, would place the German forces at Salum in a dangerous position and might cause the entire enemy plan to collapse. The opportunity for a counter-stroke might not return. He asked Morshead to submit proposals. But Morshead declined

---

[3] The only feature on the map corresponding to this description is within the perimeter. If this is the feature referred to, Rommel was in error in believing that the Italians reached it.

to be drawn; his main present anxiety was to find sufficient forces to maintain adequate reserves while manning a system of defences more than 30 miles in length. In one respect the strength of Morshead's reserves had just been substantially increased. The additional tanks promised by Major-General Arthur Smith had arrived on the 16th by sea: 12 infantry tanks, with a squadron of the 7th Royal Tank Regiment to man them.

Heavy shelling on the western sector throughout the night of 16th-17th April suggested that another attack might be developing. Once more the garrison made ready to rebuff the attackers. To augment his reserves Morshead ordered the 2/1st Pioneer Battalion, which had been employed on the construction of second-line field works, to resume an infantry role. But he did not repeat the stand-to order. There was a growing confidence in the garrison's ability to repel whatever assault the enemy might make.

It was again in the western sector, and against the 2/48th Battalion, that the next enemy thrust was made. At 10 a.m. (17th April), enemy were observed massing on the right of Ras el Medauuar; much motor transport was seen including some vehicles which, through the mirage, looked like tanks.

The enemy shelled first the left flank of the battalion, then the right flank, then the high ground in the centre, where the main artillery observation post was situated; the post had to be evacuated. Well-concealed machine-guns and mortars raked the entire area of the centre company with fire, the heaviest the unit had experienced. Meanwhile enemy troops dismounted from the vehicles and, soon after midday, came forward to attack along the whole front of Captain Tucker's[4] company in the centre. The attacking force appeared to comprise two companies in line abreast with two following; behind them again were some 15 to 20 vehicles, armed with machine-guns and carrying troops. Tanks appeared and rumbled forward through the advancing infantry. They crossed the minefield, which did not operate, presumably having been disarmed by the enemy during the night. Some tanks were held up at the perimeter but at 1 p.m. six managed to break through the wire near Post R2. Coming round the back of Ras el Medauuar, they surprised the crew of an anti-tank gun, who when fired upon made off in a 15-cwt truck.

After the Easter battle the garrison had adopted a firm policy for the conduct of the forward infantry in tank attacks: the infantry were to keep under cover in their posts till the tanks passed, then deal with the following enemy infantry. Tucker's company employed these tactics; but the enemy infantry assault petered out under the British field-gun fire. Meanwhile the tanks—mainly Italian light tanks—circled the old fort at Ras el Medauuar as though their intention was to subdue the defenders while their infantry who should have been following were coming forward; but when the tanks came under the anti-tank gun fire of Sergeant Bettsworth and later of Bombardier Lane of "J" Battery, 3rd R.H.A., they pushed on into the reserve company area. Brigadier Tovell then asked divisional

---

[4] Lt-Col F. A. G. Tucker, DSO, ED, SX10310. 2/48 Bn; CO 2/23 Bn 1943-46. Schoolmaster; of Fullarton, SA; b. Fullarton, 2 Nov 1911.

headquarters for armoured assistance and seven cruiser tanks were sent forward. Before these arrived some of the Italian tanks had been put out of action by anti-tank rifle and gun fire; the cruisers on arrival dispatched others. In all five Italian tanks (including one medium tank) were captured; only one of those that penetrated the perimeter escaped; four others were abandoned in enemy territory.

Meanwhile the enemy infantry and some less adventurous tanks clung to the ground where their advance had been halted by the defenders' artillery fire, as though not daring to risk an assault nor willing to withdraw. They remained just outside the wire, whence the artillery was unable to dislodge them before nightfall. Colonel Windeyer proposed that a counter-attack be made but this was not acceded to. The commanding officer of the 51st Field Regiment, Lieut-Colonel J. S. Douglas, was wounded in the action. Two prisoners captured from one of the tanks disclosed that the enemy intention had been to take "B" Company's area (Ras el Medauuar) at all costs, but not an inch of ground had been yielded.

In the evening there was another alarm on the south side of the perimeter, where 12 tanks were reported. The cruisers manned by the 1st Royal Tank Regiment responded quickly to their second call of the day. Three enemy tanks were knocked out without loss in a running fight across the perimeter wire.

After dark a patrol under Warrant-Officer Noble[5] went out from the 2/48th to investigate a truck abandoned by the enemy after it had been stopped by fire from an anti-tank rifle. Behind the truck they found an anti-tank gun on a trailer and brought it in: an important capture, for it proved to be a new type of weapon and was subsequently flown to England.

Engineers of the 2/13th Field Company went out after dark in front of the 2/48th Battalion and attempted to investigate whether the minefield in front of the wire had been interfered with by the enemy, but were prevented by heavy enemy mortar fire. They laid a new minefield in the wire in and around the gaps made by the passage of the enemy tanks. The afternoon's demonstration of the unreliability of the existing minefields had provided a useful warning. New mines were laid and many mines in the existing fields later converted to hair-trigger detonation.

General Rommel stated in his account of the operations of the 17th that the Italian armour, which was led by a German staff officer, had advanced in front of the infantry contrary to orders. Later these tanks were mistaken by Rommel for British tanks and engaged by his order with anti-tank gun fire. He contended that two were hit. Apparently the Italian armoured division had suffered wastage on a comparable scale to the 2nd British Armoured Division, for according to Rommel the *Ariete Division* had on this day 10 tanks left out of 100 with which they had begun the offensive, notwithstanding that, until the last two days, they had seen little action.

Rommel was beginning to feel the stress of his extended line of com-

---

[5] WO2 E. A. Noble, SX3480; 2/48 Bn. Miner; of Adelaide; b. Teatree Gully, SA, 29 May 1914.

munications. His force had been issued with transport only on the scale laid down for operations in Europe, but had to transport its main supplies from Tripoli, some 900 miles from Tobruk, until the port of Benghazi could be put into working order. British air attacks on supply columns, carried out on an ever-increasing scale, were causing mounting losses. Ammunition had not at first been a problem, for little had been expended in the initial advance; but if operations were to be continued on the recent scale replenishment would be difficult.

The supply problem was not the only factor indicative of the need to adopt a conservative policy; another was the resilience of the Tobruk defence. As Rommel wrote later:

> It was now finally clear that there was no hope of doing anything against the enemy defences with the forces we had, largely because of the poor state of training and useless equipment of the Italian troops. I decided to break off the attack until the arrival of more troops.[6]

It must indeed have already been clear that the brunt of any future thrust would have to be borne by German troops, of which there were, at the time, only about 32,000 in Africa. Not only were they burdened with a maintenance problem of unusual severity; there was both a frontier to be held and a siege to be maintained. It is not surprising that Rommel decided to await the arrival of the remainder of the *15th Armoured Division,* which had been delayed as a result of the British destroyer action on the 16th and was now due to arrive about the middle of May. In the meantime, moreover, the Italian Supreme Command had made representations to the German High Command that, before the advance into Egypt was continued, a halt should be called to provide time for reinforcement, reorganisation and the building up of supplies. The German High Command had replied that Hitler was in agreement with the Italian views: the most important requirement was that the supply lines should be secured against British attacks; in particular it was essential to capture Tobruk. That interchange of views had not yet been communicated to Rommel.

By comparison with the last few eventful days, but not by any other standard, 18th April was quiet. At dawn enemy tanks and other armed vehicles were still just outside the wire in front of the 2/48th whence they opened fire on any movement within range. Their purpose was apparently to cover the withdrawal of their own infantry. The latter had spent an uneasy night close to the perimeter where they had been forced to ground the previous evening, but were now retiring to about a mile distant. During the morning, however, new concentrations of enemy infantry were seen gathering to the west of Ras el Medauuar; these made half-hearted attempts to push in on the right flank and centre of the 2/48th Battalion. Artillery fire from the 51st Field Regiment quickly checked them and threw the assault parties into confusion. The enemy then brought up mortars and field guns with which he subjected the area to heavy shelling; an artillery observation officer and six members of a party of

---
[6] *The Rommel Papers,* p. 128.

Australian stretcher bearers were either killed or mortally wounded by the fire.

Another attack was thought to be imminent. Morshead directed that a counter-attack should be prepared, to be mounted by a company of one of the battalions of the fortress reserve, the 2/12th, supported by Bren gun carriers and tanks of the 3rd and 5th Hussars; but reconnaissance showed that the tanks and carriers would have to file across the wire and minefields through narrow gaps exposed to intense shelling at short range. The operation was therefore cancelled. No enemy attack developed.

The next two days—19th and 20th April—produced no alarms. It was apparent that the first rounds in the battle for Tobruk had been won by the defenders. The enemy had not abandoned his intention to take Tobruk by storm, but he had at least been compelled to pause.

The diminution in the scale and strength of enemy ground operations had enabled specialist and other reserve troops to be released from emergency defensive roles for other tasks. Work on the Blue Line, the second line of defence, was again pushed forward. The mining of the line was completed on the 19th though many positions had yet to be dug. The engineers were also busy preparing demolitions for all plants and wells within the perimeter against the possibility of an enemy break-through.

Meanwhile Morshead was reorganising his forces to augment his reserves. The 18th Cavalry Regiment was placed under Brigadier Tovell's command and relieved the 2/24th Battalion in the sector near the coast, where the defensive positions were set into the eastern walls of the Wadi Sehel. The sector astride the Derna Road, from the head of the Wadi Sehel to the top of the escarpment south of the road was taken over by the 2/23rd Battalion. The 2/24th Battalion moved into reserve. Simultaneously Morshead directed that an infantry company be organised from members of the Australian Army Service Corps and that arrangements should be made for it to take over the perimeter near the coast in the eastern sector, on the edge of the Wadi Zeitun which, like the Wadi Sehel, provided a formidable natural defensive system. This would free the 2/43rd Battalion for reserve duties in the 24th Brigade.

When these arrangements had been made, each of the three forward brigades would have one complete infantry battalion in reserve, while the divisional reserve would still comprise three infantry battalions and one pioneer battalion; of the eleven infantry battalions only five would be on the perimeter. Defence in depth was the fundamental principle of Morshead's holding policy. He told his brigadiers that if they represented to him that they lacked confidence in their ability to hold the perimeter with the forces allotted to them for that purpose, his reply would be to require them to keep in reserve even more of their strength.

A complete reorganisation of the garrison's armour was also effected. The squadron of the 7th Royal Tank Regiment, which had arrived on the 16th, took over the four infantry tanks already in Tobruk from the 4th Royal Tank Regiment, the personnel of which were then sent out by sea. The tanks were now organised into three homogeneous units. The 3rd

Hussars took the light tanks; the 1st Royal Tank Regiment took over the cruisers (of which about 15 were operational) and organised them into two squadrons; the squadron of the 7th R.T.R., which had been kept under direct operational control of armoured brigade headquarters, was given the 16 infantry (heavy) tanks. Colonel Birks,[7] who arrived in Tobruk on the 18th, took over command of the brigade from Lieut-Colonel Drew. Morshead quickly formed a high opinion of Birks' ability.

Most heartening to Morshead was the sure evidence both from prisoners' statements and from captured diaries that the enemy morale was very low. This was true of the Germans no less than of the Italians. Many prisoners taken were very hungry; some spoke, perhaps with exaggeration, of being without rations for days. One German diary captured at this time contained the following entry:

> They already have a lot of dead and wounded in the 3rd Company. It is very distressing. In their camp faces are very pale and all eyes are downcast. Their nerves are taut to breaking point.

On the other hand the spirit of the defenders, stimulated by repeated successes, could not have been better. Morshead, though never lavish with praise, knew the value of well-earned commendation for sustaining morale; he wrote to Lieut-Colonel Windeyer on the 19th:

> My compliments to you and your battalion on the splendid show which you have put up all the week. That you have stood so firm and been so resolute has been of the utmost importance and does you all the greatest credit.

A feature of those early days of the siege was the bold action of the artillery observation officers. No day went past but that one or other, or several, did not issue forth from the perimeter with no greater escort than two or three Bren gun carriers, sometimes with no escort at all, to shoot up enemy concentrations and gun positions.

There had been little activity at the frontier. The Support Group had been reorganised into four columns—Beam, Nire, Paul and Unor—later to become the 7th Support Group (Support Group of the 7th Armoured Division). They were not armoured columns but merely roving batteries of field guns protected by about a company of motor infantry and one or two anti-tank guns. The strategy of their employment was to keep as many enemy forces as possible tied down to tasks of local defence.

The lack of tanks confronted the British command with a difficult problem in deciding what forces to commit on the frontier and how much to hold behind the prepared defences at Mersa Matruh (where Lieut-Colonel R. F. Monaghan, commanding officer of the 2/2nd Anti-Tank Regiment, was in charge of the plans for anti-tank defence). The static front was held with two battalions forward: the 3/Coldstream Guards on the right, the 1/Durham Light Infantry on the left, with left flank resting on the top of the Halfaya Pass. When the 3/Coldstream Guards first took over part of the front, the anti-tank guns of both the 5th Battery of the 2/2nd

---

[7] Maj-Gen H. L. Birks, CB, DSO. GSO1 7 Armd Div 1939-40; 4 Armd Bde 1940-41; comd 11 Armd Bde 1941; GOC 10 Armd Div 1942; MG RAC 1944. Regular soldier; b. 7 May 1897.

Anti-Tank Regiment and the 12th Battery of the 2/3rd were under Major Argent's command. He disposed them across the front of both battalions, except for two guns sited for defence in depth. Next day, however, the 5th Battery (Major Wilson) was withdrawn and except for one troop and one section came under the direct command of Headquarters 22nd Guards Brigade. Wilson's battery was then re-deployed for defence in depth, its guns being sited in seven different localities from near Salum to Sidi Barrani. Those of Argent's battery were redisposed with the forward battalions. "K" Troop and two guns of "J" Troop were placed across the front of the Coldstream Guards, the other two guns of "J" Troop near the Halfaya Pass turn-off. On the left of the line, but with no dishonour, were the four guns of "L" Troop: three at the top of the pass, one a third of the way down. Each day one gun was pushed out forward of the pass-head, coming back at night for close defence.

On 19th April General Rommel paid a visit to the frontier, saw for himself the tactical importance of the Salum-Sofafi escarpment and noted that the British hold on the pass and escarpment was precarious. He found the impulse to exploit such patent weakness irrepressible, forthwith reinforced the advanced force with a battery of medium artillery and issued an order to the *Trento Division* to move forward from the region of Acroma to Bardia on the 23rd.

Meanwhile the British Intelligence service had discovered that elements of the *15th Armoured Division* were on the frontier. The units identified were the light units of the division that had preceded the main body to Africa and had later been incorporated in Colonel Knabe's force; that the rest would soon follow, if not already present, had to be assumed. Wavell regarded the prospect with some alarm, all the more so when it was discovered that the *15th* was to be a complete armoured division and not, as had been previously thought, a "colonial" or light division with a reduced scale of armament like the *5th Light Division*, the first sent to Africa. Wavell believed that a complete division contained about 400 tanks and in 1939 and 1940 this had been so. In France in 1940, however, the 400-tank division had proved impossible to control in battle and the Germans abandoned their light tanks and drastically reduced the establishment of their armoured divisions. On the 20th, in two messages to London setting out the situation in general outline and in detail, he appealed to the Chief of the General Staff to lend his personal assistance in meeting the threat. The future outlook, he said, would be one of anxiety for some time, because of his weakness in tanks, especially cruiser tanks. He had only one weak mixed tank unit in Tobruk and one squadron of cruisers at Mersa Matruh while his opponent probably had 150 tanks, of which half were medium, in the fighting line in Cyrenaica. The best he could hope for by the end of the month was two weak tank regiments, one of cruisers and one of infantry tanks, each less a squadron. Even by the end of May only two regiments were in sight, with no reserves to replace casualties, whereas there were now in Egypt "an excellent personnel for six tank regiments". The provision of cruiser tanks in addition to infantry tanks was vital, since infantry tanks lacked speed and the radius of action required for desert operations.

The gravity of the situation emphasised by these messages stirred the British Prime Minister to quick action. They reached him at a weekend retreat on the morning of Sunday, 20th April.

On reading these alarming messages (he wrote afterwards) I resolved not to be governed any longer by the Admiralty reluctance, but to send a convoy through the Mediterranean direct to Alexandria carrying all the tanks which General Wavell needed.[8]

A convoy containing large armoured reinforcements was on the point of departure for the Middle East by the Cape. Churchill decided that the fast, tank-carrying ships in the convoy should turn off at Gibraltar and make straight for Alexandria through the Mediterranean, thus saving 40 days. At once he sent General Sir Hastings Ismay,[9] his chief staff officer, to London with a message calling the Chiefs of Staff to a conference at noon next day (Monday, 21st April) to arrange the details. The fate of the war in the Middle East, Churchill stated in the message, might turn on a few hundred armoured vehicles.

They must if possible be carried there at all costs. . . . General Wavell's telegram shows that machines, not men, are needed. The risk of losing the vehicles, or part of them, must be accepted. Even if half got through, the situation would be restored. The five MT ships carry 250 tanks, all but fourteen of which are "I" tanks. Every endeavour should be made to increase the numbers of cruiser tanks in this consignment. . . . The Admiralty and Air Ministry will consider and prepare *this day* a plan for carrying this vital convoy through the Mediterranean. Of course we must accept the risk, and no guarantee can be expected. . . . Speed is vital. Every day's delay must be avoided. Let me have a time-table of what is possible, observing that at 16 knots the distance is only about eight days—say, ten—from the date of sailing, viz., April 23. This would give General Wavell effective support during the first week in May.[1]

At the conference on the morrow, the First Sea Lord, Admiral of the Fleet Sir Dudley Pound, lent his support to the proposal to send the tanks through the Mediterranean. Churchill wanted to add two more ships to the convoy to carry 100 additional cruiser tanks, but met with opposition from the Chief of the General Staff, General Sir John Dill, who was concerned over the shortage for home defence. Eventually it was decided to add one additional ship containing 67 of the latest cruiser tanks, making a total to be transported through the Mediterranean of 295 tanks. The operation was called "Tiger".[2]

While the Chiefs of Staff were debating these measures in London, the overburdened General Wavell was in Greece, where resistance to the German advance was on the point of collapse. It was on the same day that Wavell decided to re-embark as much of the British force as could be got away.

---

[8] Churchill, Vol III, p. 218.
[9] General Rt Hon Lord Ismay, GCB, CH, DSO. Chief Staff Officer to Minister for Defence 1940-46. Regular soldier; b. 21 Jun 1887.
[1] Churchill, Vol III, pp. 218-19.
[2] One ship carrying 57 tanks was sunk en route, but 135 infantry, 82 cruiser and 21 light tanks were landed safely.

General Rommel had meanwhile received the memorandum of the German High Command advocating the early reduction of Tobruk. On 20th April he directed that preparations be put in hand for a large-scale attack, using all available formations simultaneously along the whole front; but in reporting to the high command, he stated that an attack on the scale required, in view of the strength of the fortifications, could not take place until the arrival of the main body of the *15th Armoured Division*. He deprecated suggestions that Italian reinforcements should be sent for this purpose. They had proved themselves unreliable; better use could be made of the available shipping. His most urgent need was reinforcement in the air to counter British sea and air attacks on Axis supplies.

General Morshead had taken advantage of the enemy's recent quietness to plan an offensive counter-stroke. Three raids designed to unsettle the besiegers and if possible capture a substantial number of them were to be mounted simultaneously. The most important was to be carried out by the 2/48th Battalion. Ras el Medauuar, that high point more than 600 feet above sea-level towards which the boundary wire in the 2/48th Battalion's sector swept upwards from west and north, was a commanding feature but was very vulnerable. At a distance of not much more than 1,000 yards from the perimeter, there was a small hill, known as Carrier Hill (because there was a derelict carrier on its slopes), from which most of the western plateau within the perimeter, except the portion lying behind Ras el Medauuar, could be observed; it provided a constant threat to the defenders for, small though it was, and more the sky-line crest of a long feature stretching some way back than the isolated hillock it appeared, still there was sufficient dead ground there to conceal an assault force close to the defences. For that reason Lieut-Colonel Windeyer had made sure that it was regularly and vigorously patrolled, hoping thus to prevent its occupation. But on the 20th a carrier patrol scouting in that direction was seen to turn about very quickly when about 2,000 yards out. It reported on its return that a substantial infantry force was dug in behind the hill, with about 40 vehicles and 4 tanks. A battery of 75-mm guns was also known to be there.

Morshead decided to raid the locality with the object of capturing its garrison and destroying the guns. Two other large-scale raids were to be mounted simultaneously on either flank; on the right by the 2/23rd Battalion, with the object of capturing enemy located in wadis close to where the Derna Road entered the perimeter, and on the left by the 2/17th in the southern sector, where the plan was to attack an enemy field artillery battery and destroy the guns.

Reconnaissances and final preparations were made on the 21st. The raid on Carrier Hill was to be undertaken by "C" Company (Captain Forbes[3]) of the 2/48th, Windeyer's reserve company, with five carriers of the 2/48th, three infantry tanks of the 7th Royal Tank Regiment, and four 2-pounder anti-tank guns of "M" Battery of the 3rd R.H.A. There

---
[3] Maj W. Forbes, DSO, ED, SX10312; 2/48 Bn. Schoolteacher; of Plympton, SA; b. Wallsend-on-Tyne, England, 18 Sep 1911.

were, of course, arrangements for support from the ever-reliable field artillery. A forward observation officer from the 51st Field Regiment was to accompany the raiders; but there was to be no artillery preparation lest the enemy might be forewarned. The plan included protection by fighter aircraft and the use of a low-flying Lysander to drown the noise of the approaching carriers and tanks.

At 6.40 a.m. on the 22nd the raiders set off. Captain Forbes, a strong, spare, red-headed schoolteacher from Adelaide, God-fearing but fearless of the King's enemies, led the attack in person, at first in a carrier and then on foot. The operation went according to plan, except that the tanks moved too fast for the infantry and lost contact. The tanks moved out, the carriers and then the infantry followed and the anti-tank guns brought up the rear. The enemy put down a heavy artillery barrage when he saw the raiders debouch, but the force moved out under perfect control; every man got through the wire. An hour later the tanks and the carriers had reached the far side of Carrier Hill. The following infantry heard them engaging the enemy to the east. The carriers,

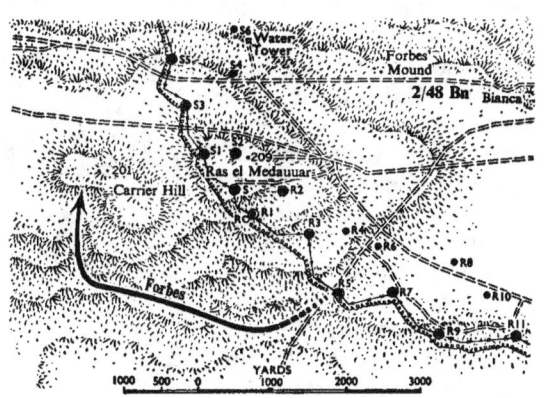

under Sergeant Batty,[5] rejoined the infantry as they were coming up to the rising ground on the hill's south side, and described the enemy positions to Captain Forbes. Ordering the carriers to approach the enemy battery from the rear Forbes took two of his platoons, commanded by Lieutenant Jenkins and Lieutenant Kimber,[6] out to the left in a wide arc to outflank the battery from the south-west while Lieutenant Wardle's platoon swung out to the right to come in on the other flank. The two parties closed in on either side in line abreast.

When the Australian infantry suddenly appeared on each side from dead ground, the Italian battery, which had been endeavouring to engage the tanks, was taken completely by surprise. The leading infantry charged it with the bayonet while others engaged in a fire fight with the Italian garrison. Batty's carriers circled the position at a range of less than 50 yards, directing intense and accurate fire at the enemy gun crews.

For a short time the Italians stood to their positions and engaged the Australians with infantry weapons at short range but could not halt them, and the sight of the assaulting infantry coming forward with fixed bayonets

---

[5] Sgt L. W. C. Batty, DCM, SX7605; 2/48 Bn. Engine driver; of Mount Gambier, SA; b. Bordertown, SA, 15 May 1916.
[6] Capt D. G. Kimber, SX10330; 2/48 Bn. Insurance clerk; of Brighton, SA; b. Monreith, SA, 9 Jan 1917.

soon proved too much for the Italians. Generally they surrendered though isolated pockets continued to resist. Sergeant Batty's carrier was engaging one of these when it received a direct hit from an anti-tank shell. Batty was wounded. His gunner, Private Daniels, engaged the enemy from the ground until he too was wounded. The driver, Private Spavin,[7] then took over and kept the enemy at bay until help arrived.

An hour later the entire Italian garrison had been rounded up and were on their way to Tobruk. The Italian prisoners numbered 368, of whom 16 were officers. These included the major part of the *Fabris Battalion,* which had been in the van of the advance on Mechili. The booty included four 20-mm anti-tank guns, machine-guns, motor transport, motor cycles — and gun-sights, much needed by the bush artillery. Unfortunately the guns from which the sights were taken were not destroyed, though grenades were exploded inside the barrels. Maps and instructions were captured which indicated that the enemy intended to make renewed efforts to subdue the fortress. The only material loss by the attackers was an anti-tank gun and portee which ran onto an enemy minefield. The 2/48th Battalion, whose casualties were two killed and seven wounded, one mortally, had good reason to be satisfied.

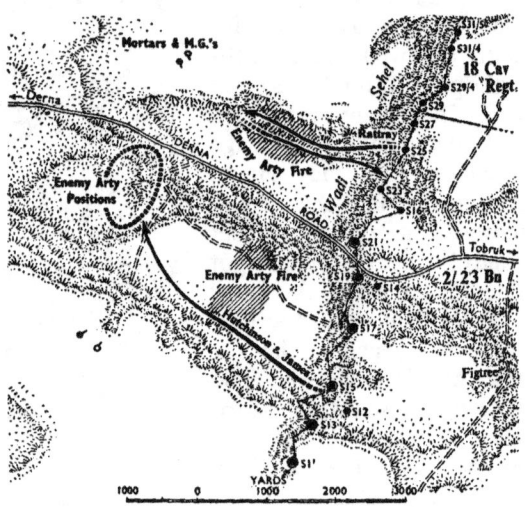

Scarcely less success attended the raid executed simultaneously by the 2/23rd Battalion (Lieut-Colonel Evans). It was also of company strength and was commanded by Captain Rattray. Rattray divided his company into two forces, intending that they should advance by approximately parallel routes and if possible link up after taking their first objectives. Captain Barlow, of Mechili fame, was to take out two troops of the 18th Indian Cavalry about three miles to protect Rattray's right flank.

Rattray personally led the party on the right. Protected on the open flank by a platoon from "A" Company, it advanced along a wadi that led westward from the perimeter. The enemy held strong positions at the head of the wadi from which intense machine-gun fire was brought to bear on the advancing Australians. Rattray was forced to take cover in a side wadi. The enemy heavily shelled and mortared it. Rattray then decided to leave the wadi and attack across the open plateau, boldly

---

[7] Pte J. L. Spavin, MM, SX7272; 2/48 Bn. Labourer; of Yongala, SA; b. Jamestown, SA, 16 Jan 1915. Killed in action 10 Jul 1942.

risking the exposure involved. As the Australians appeared over the skyline, the Italians turned their guns upon them; but spirited attacks with bayonet and grenade, one by two sections at the head of the main wadi, the other by one section at the head of the side wadi, carried the raiders right into the Italian sangars, where the occupants received them waving white handkerchiefs. Rattray's party next strove to advance southwards to converge from a flank on the enemy opposed to the left party, but intense fire from both flanks on the bare, flat ground made a further advance impracticable. Rattray returned with 40 prisoners.

Meanwhile Lieutenant Hutchinson,[8] commanding the left-hand party, was having a hard fight. Advancing south of the Derna Road the party assaulted an anti-tank/anti-aircraft battery, behind which were two batteries of field guns. The enemy held his fire until the leading platoon, commanded by Lieutenant James,[9] was within 500 yards. Then all weapons —field guns, anti-aircraft guns, machine-guns and mortars—brought down a concentrated fire. James and his men were on an open slope. Hutchinson, seeing the danger, led his reserve of two sections round the flank, while four carriers, who were protecting that flank, joined in the assault. The infantry advanced in bounds to within throwing distance of the enemy sangars, hurled in grenades, then charged with the bayonet. The Italian defenders ran out with their hands up and were dispatched to the perimeter, a move executed by them with a good turn of speed.

Although the anti-aircraft battery had been captured, Hutchinson's men were being subjected to heavy fire at point-blank range from field guns behind the battery position and from the infantry protecting the guns. The fighting strength of Hutchinson's force had been almost halved, but he pushed on up the wadi towards the guns, hoping to link up with Rattray's party on the way. The carriers, more exposed, came bravely with them. Fifty yards from the battery, Hutchinson put his patrol to ground and taking one man, Lance-Corporal Crummey,[1] with him, charged the nearest gun. The crew fled; but Crummey was shot as he was throwing a grenade. It exploded, killing Crummey and wounding Hutchinson so badly in the leg that he could not move. Meanwhile the carriers were coming under heavy fire. Two were hit and set afire; two others broke down. But with exemplary discipline the crews dismounted with their weapons to give covering fire as the infantry withdrew. Other carriers took wounded back to the perimeter. One returned for more.

Four hours after Hutchinson's party sallied forth that morning, those who were left returned to the perimeter. Eighty per cent had become casualties: 24, including Hutchinson and James, did not return, 22 of those who did had been wounded.[2] But much had been accomplished. A prisoner captured later in that area said that of his company of 100

---

[8] Maj J. A. Hutchinson, DSO, VX45182; 2/23 Bn. Clerk; of Melbourne; b. Weymouth, England, 28 Jul 1918.
[9] Lt R. W. James, VX38852; 2/23 Bn. Schoolteacher; of Hawthorn, Vic; b. Colac, Vic, 25 May 1912. Killed in action 22 Apr 1941.
[1] L-Cpl W. Crummey, VX42173; 2/23 Bn. Lithographic printer; of Northcote, Vic; b. Abbotsford, Vic, 6 Jun 1920. Killed in action 22 Apr 1941.
[2] Though believed to have been killed, Lt Hutchinson survived and was taken prisoner.

men only 10 had remained after the raid. In mid-morning a carrier patrol was sent out from the 18th Cavalry to see how the besieging force had reacted to the raids; it patrolled westwards for seven miles along the coast and found no sign of the enemy. Rattray's and Hutchinson's patrols captured 87 men (including 2 officers), 3 anti-aircraft guns, 5 machine-guns and 4 mortars.

The third sortie on the 22nd, by the 20th Brigade in the southern sector, was unsuccessful. The plan was to attack and destroy a battery of enemy field guns with a mixed force of an infantry company (from the 2/17th Battalion), a squadron of cruiser tanks, two troops of light tanks and a company of the 2/1st Pioneers, supported by a battery of the 1st R.H.A. The force set off before dawn, but when daylight came found itself under heavy fire from three sides. It was compelled to withdraw. One light tank was knocked out by a well-concealed anti-tank gun. With the help of gunfire, skilfully directed by Major Goschen, the withdrawal was executed with little loss.

Next day the men in Tobruk heard the German radio's account of their exploits. "Yesterday morning," said the announcer, "the British force besieged in Tobruk made a desperate attack, which was repulsed with terrific loss of men and material, while our own force is still complete." The Axis forces surrounding Tobruk probably derived no less amusement than the defenders from this announcement. Rommel, at least, was in no doubt concerning who had suffered the losses. He saw for himself, as appears from the following account written by his A.D.C.:

> A report had come in that the Australians in the sector facing the Italians had been feverishly active during the night. Rommel wanted a precise picture of the situation, and so went to see in person. As we approached the sector, we thought it completely calm and were ready to conclude that the reports of enemy activity overnight had been, as so often before, exaggerated by our Allies. Even the enemy artillery in Tobruk seemed quiet. But the puzzle was soon solved: we found not a single Italian in the whole sector, barring a few isolated artillery batteries in rear, entirely unprotected by infantry. We peered cautiously over a rise and were met by the sight of hundreds of discarded sun-helmets gaily decorated with multi-coloured cock's feathers—Bersaglieri helmets. Otherwise, not a thing. It dawned on us that the Australians must have "collected" the entire battalion of our Allies during the night.
> Rommel hurriedly ordered up a scratch assortment of troops from Acroma to act as a stop-gap in the denuded sector. Then he issued a sharp order, afterwards much discussed and disputed in high Italian circles, to the effect that he would, in future, expect the immediate execution of officers showing cowardice in the face of the enemy.[3]

Rommel, as appears from his own account, at first feared a British thrust towards his rear. He alerted the *15th Armoured Division,* part of which had now arrived in the operational area, and ordered it to occupy a position on the coast road 18 miles west of Tobruk, with a detachment east of Acroma. To replace the *Fabris Battalion* opposite Medauuar, he detached a battalion from the *Trento Division,* which had been under orders to move to the frontier. Rommel was anxious to regain the initiative

---
[3] Schmidt, pp. 47-8.

there and now ordered the rest of that division to proceed. As soon as possible after their arrival an attack was to be mounted in the Salum area. The object was, by inflicting a severe defeat on the British frontier force, to set free some of the German forces there for the intended assault on Tobruk. Colonel von Herff, who had succeeded Colonel Knabe as commander in that region, was to have charge of the operation.

At the frontier the 22nd Guards Brigade group was now entrenched in the Halfaya position and the four columns of Brigadier Gott's mobile force of about one battalion group with supporting arms were operating from Halfaya, Sofafi, Buq Buq and Sidi Barrani. The more forward columns, while not seeking close battle, were exploiting their mobility to harass the enemy whenever they could catch him unawares. On the 23rd, a strong raid on German transport between Capuzzo and Sidi Azeiz executed by armoured cars of the 11th Hussars with support from other arms caused Herff to believe that an attempt was being made either to cut the main coast road behind the enemy forward troops or to take them in rear: so he informed Rommel. A further message to Rommel's headquarters next morning, in which Herff reported that the previous evening's "attack on Capuzzo" had been repulsed and that Sidi Azeiz was still in German hands inevitably gave Rommel an exaggerated idea of the magnitude of the British operation.

Characteristically Rommel's reaction was to order his own planned offensive to be carried out as soon as practicable, but it is clear that he shared Herff's apprehensions. He reported to the German Army Command on the 24th that the situation was becoming more serious every day at Bardia and Tobruk. If Bardia and Salum were lost or cut off, the struggle for Tobruk would have to be abandoned. The only solution to the problem was to send in German reinforcements and replenishments by air, to reinforce the air force, and to use U-boats between Salum and Tobruk. This communication must have given considerable concern to the German Army Command, who had already become apprehensive of the situation in Africa. On the preceding day, the 23rd, General Halder had noted in his diary that he had a feeling that things in Africa were in a mess; air transport could not keep up with Rommel's senseless demands. The army command decided to send to Africa a senior general—General von Paulus —with instructions to ascertain and examine Rommel's intentions, report on the situation, and consider what action should be taken should Salum be lost. He was also to explain to Rommel and impress upon him the limitations on the resources that could be sent to him. Paulus had been chief of staff to the *Sixth German Army,* which had fought against the B.E.F. during the German offensive in western Europe.

It is a part of generalship to preach the virtues of offensive action; it is the prerogative of the private soldier, when called upon to practise the virtues, to receive such excellent exhortations with scepticism. But it would be hard to find a more convincing demonstration of the advantages a weak force may sometimes win for itself by a display of aggression than the German reaction to Gott's and Morshead's raids. At a time when

Wavell, dangerously inferior in armoured strength, was scraping the barrel to find forces for blocking the way into Egypt, when the security of the Tobruk fortress itself rested on never so slender a margin, when the British frontier forces, lacking armour, were powerless to inflict severe injury on their adversaries, when in truth Rommel had no cause (if he had but known all the facts) to fear what the British might attempt, a few raids with limited local aims had instilled unease, apprehension, and anxiety for the immediate future into all levels of the German staff, from the frontier of Egypt to the headquarters of the High Command in Germany.

In the week following the raids on the 22nd, while the main preoccupation of the British command in the Middle East was the evacuation of the force in Greece, the garrison of Tobruk concerned itself with strengthening its defences against a renewed onslaught, which documents captured in the most recent raid confirmed to be in course of preparation. It was anticipated that the assault would be made as soon as the *15th Armoured Division* had arrived at the front. A substantial portion of the division was known to have disembarked between 12th and 15th April. It was believed, as Wavell told the British Chiefs of Staff, that its transfer to Africa would have been completed by 21st April, except for losses sustained in crossing the Mediterranean. Wavell now estimated that the Axis commander would be able to bring into the battle by the middle of June two German divisions (the *15th Armoured* and the *5th Light*) and the Italian *Ariete* and *Trento Divisions*. The Tiger convoy with Wavell's tank reinforcements was due in Alexandria in mid-May. Thus each side's armoured reinforcements were likely to reach the front about the same time. But Wavell was careful to point out to the Chiefs of Staff that the enemy might well improve on that estimate of his capabilities. Moreover Morshead was warned that another German armoured division might be expected to appear before Tobruk about 1st May,[4] a prediction which, if made more out of caution than in accordance with expectations, was nevertheless to prove extraordinarily accurate. Morshead in turn, having been so warned, planned to be ready to meet an assault several days earlier.

It was in armour principally that Morshead was outmatched. With few tanks and few anti-tank guns, minefields would inevitably constitute the main defence against an armoured penetration. The Easter battle had revealed serious weaknesses in the anti-tank defence. The anti-tank ditch was the only effective obstacle to tanks, but even where it was effective it could be breached; minefields forward of the perimeter could be lifted in preliminary operations. What was needed was anti-tank defence in depth to check the impetus of an assault after the first penetration.

Two measures were immediately put in hand. Minefields outside the perimeter were lifted and re-laid in the wire in front of the posts; more important a system of inner minefields was planned to a design which would confine the forward and lateral movement of an armoured penetra-

---

[4] Liaison letter No. 2, 9 Aust Div, 27 April 1941.

tion in any sector, boxing the tanks in between the perimeter (the Red Line of defences) and the second line of defence (the Blue Line). Since it was adjudged that the vulnerable but dominant Ras el Medauuar sector would be the point of assault (though in fact Rommel's intention so far had been to attack along the whole front) priority was given to laying the first inner minefield behind Ras el Medauuar. The 2/7th Field Company began laying the field on the 20th. Morshead directed that the work should be pushed ahead with all speed both on this minefield and on the Blue Line defences behind it; the work was to be completed in readiness to meet an enemy attack on the sector by the 27th. Confirmation, though not needed, of the wisdom of this policy was provided on the 25th when the enemy made two obvious attempts to explode the minefield near the El Adem Road in front of the 2/13th Battalion, one by a bombing attack from the air, one by shelling from tanks; the Chestnut Troop of the 1st R.H.A. engaged the tanks with customary accuracy, forcing them to withdraw.

Morshead's other great weakness was in the air. Although Rommel was calling for air reinforcements, the Tobruk defenders were aware only of a growing strength and intensity of air attack, which was directed primarily at shipping in the harbour; though dive-bombing and machine-gunning attacks on the combatant troops were also becoming more frequent. In a raid on the harbour on the 21st by a force of 24 bombers escorted by 21 fighters, the quay was hit, two ships were sunk and two were put out of action. It was little consolation for such severe losses that the few Hurricanes of Nos. 73 and 274 Squadrons intervened with great success and shot down four enemy aircraft. Morshead called a conference next day to devise counter-measures, attended by his commander of anti-aircraft artillery, Brigadier Slater, and by the two senior R.A.F. commanders. Slater, who had been intensely studying the problem, proposed to change the method of fighting the heavy anti-aircraft guns from predictor laying on individual machines to an umbrella barrage. This was agreed to. It was also decided to form the nucleus of an observation corps, with three observation posts in a wireless network, to combat dive-bombing attacks on the forward troops.

On the next day, the 23rd, air activity was almost continuous and more ships were hit. Three of the garrison's dwindling force of aircraft were shot down, and two were damaged. But Slater had the satisfaction of knowing that his umbrella barrage plan had greatly increased the effectiveness of the defence. Of 13 aircraft that raided the harbour and landing ground, 6 were brought down.

The comparative peace on the land front in the past few days was broken by an Axis assault on the western defences at dawn on 24th April. It followed what was becoming a set pattern. At the end of the morning stand-to, as soon as it was light, the fiercest artillery barrage the defenders had yet known rained down upon the forward posts in the western sector between Ras el Medauuar and the Derna Road. About 7 a.m. large bodies of infantry were observed about 1,000 yards from the wire advancing as usual in the close formation that some Axis commanders at this stage of the war seemed to favour for its very boldness, but which British teaching forbade because of the target wantonly offered to field artillery. The British field gunners and machine-gunners and—as the attackers closed in—the Australian infantry in the perimeter posts, firing their light automatics, made the most of the opportunity presented.

The enemy made two main thrusts. One, on the right, came in upon Captain Spier's company of the 2/23rd Battalion holding ground above the Derna Road on its southern side. About 600 men were involved. When the first British artillery concentrations fell, the enemy fanned out, went to ground and began moving forward in waves and bounds. The artillery replied with sweep and search fire. Some enemy doubled forward to escape it, worked around the left flank where there was some cover and made for home. The rest were pinned to the ground. Fire from the forward posts quickly checked each attempt at forward movement. By 8 a.m. the enemy advance had been completely thwarted. Soon the 2/23rd mortar platoon under Sergeant Lazer[5] came into action to engage enemy pockets; those that remained began to withdraw in small groups. Spier sent out two patrols, and each returned with a few prisoners. The last glimpse of the enemy was of a group of stragglers observed retreating hurriedly over the sky-line at 9.45 a.m.

The thrust on the left, which came in over the northern shoulder of Ras el Medauuar, was made across more exposed ground. There, during the night, "C" Company of the 2/48th had moved up from the reserve position to relieve "B" Company on the perimeter. Under cover of darkness and a dawn artillery bombardment about a battalion of enemy infantry appeared before the wire opposite Posts S1 and S3, which were occupied by a platoon under Lieutenant Kimber. About a company established itself in the perimeter wire between the two posts.[6] Kimber's posts were brought under fire but returned it with all weapons while from behind the artillery joined in the deadly work. A fire fight on such terms was all the defenders could have wished for. After about 20 minutes there was a fluttering of white flags, which appeared to have become standard battle equipment of the Italian infantry at Tobruk. Kimber, who had had previous experience of mustering on the battlefield, lost no time in sending out one of his sections. They brought in 107 prisoners, including two officers and several Germans; in addition the Italians left some 40 dead on the battlefield.

As though to show their Italian allies how it should be done, some 30 or 40 Germans made a further thrust about midday to the south of Ras el Medauuar between Posts R3 and R5, this time against Major Loughrey's company. Fire from the posts forced them to ground about 300 yards from the wire. A patrol was sent out and in a brief running fight as the enemy withdrew several Germans were killed, and seven,

---

[5] Lt B. L. B. Lazer, VX33517; 2/23 Bn. Professional golfer; of Oakleigh, Vic; b. Windsor, Vic, 24 Dec 1919.

[6] The two posts were more than 600 yards apart.

including an officer, were captured. This brought the total "bag" for the day to 5 officers (of whom two were German) and 125 other ranks.

Not only did these operations, small though they were, and with limited aims, provide one more success to sustain the garrison's high confidence: they also provided useful information to British Intelligence of enemy build-up in the Tobruk area. From the prisoners it was established that a battalion of the *Trento Division* had replaced the *Fabris* unit in the west and that the *19th* and *20th Regiments* of the *Brescia Division* (less one battalion still at Tripoli) were on the west side of Tobruk. More ominous, an infantry regiment, an artillery battery and a company of engineers of the German *15th Armoured Division* were identified and found to be already in the Tobruk area.

Although the enemy's operations on the 24th were repulsed, they caused renewed anxiety that he might be concentrating against the Medauuar sector. Early on the morning of the 25th Lieut-Colonel Windeyer sent a carrier patrol to the Carrier Hill area to see if the cover of this feature was being used to conceal hostile preparations, but the patrol reported that the area had not been reoccupied after the raid on the 22nd.

Morshead was concerned lest recent successes should lead to complacency. He warned his commanders that continued vigilance was vital and stressed that work on the defences must be pushed forward. A long instruction on defensive arrangements and defects was issued from his headquarters on the 25th. "It must be impressed on all," it stated, "that future attacks are certain to be carried out with extensive artillery preparation and air attack." On no account must there be any pause in the task of improving the defences. Every day and night, if possible, must be utilised, and every available man. Units on the Red, Blue, and Green Lines were to develop them to their utmost capacity.

It was laborious work. In most places, rock was encountered under a shallow sub-soil; compressors were few and explosives scarce; for the infantry it was a labour of hacking out rock with pick and shovel. For this reason, although the main positions constructed by the engineers with mechanical aids and explosives were satisfactory, communication trenches dug by the infantry were often so shallow that commanders regarded them with dismay.

On 25th April the defenders scored another success in the struggle to dominate the western approaches to the perimeter. A series of daylight patrol actions by the 2/23rd Battalion dislodged the enemy from outposts near the Derna Road. The object of Lieut-Colonel Evans' patrolling policy was to keep the enemy at a distance of about 3,500 yards from the perimeter, for he feared that a closer investment would gravely prejudice his battalion's security. The terrain in front of the sector it held was rugged—deep wadis cut across the coastal plain on the right of the road while two irregular escarpments rose in tiers above it on the left—and would afford ample cover to an enemy in possession of it to concentrate forces for an attack.

From various reports, including observations made by the 18th Indian

Cavalry patrols, Evans had been led to believe that on his front the enemy had established two forward posts, containing anti-aircraft guns. One was about 2,000 yards from the perimeter—at the head of a wadi that led in towards the perimeter north of the coast road; the other was on a high feature about 1,000 yards farther north. These were on his right flank across the Wadi Sehel. To the left (south) of the road, enemy had also been observed working forward and apparently laying telephone lines. About noon, taking advantage of the midday mirage, a reconnaissance patrol from "B" Company was sent out to locate the posts north of the road and find whether they were occupied. The more northerly of the reported posts was found to be deserted, but on reaching the other—at the head of the wadi—the patrol surprised a platoon of Germans digging defences. In a short encounter one German was killed and one Australian wounded. The Australian patrol scattered and withdrew.

Evans then ordered an immediate attack on the post by a fighting patrol from "B" Company while simultaneously "A" Company on their left was to search the ground south of the road with patrols along the line of each escarpment. At 3.45 p.m. Lieutenant Gardiner,[7] in command of "B" Company's fighting patrol, crossed the perimeter wire with 22 infantrymen and a section of mortars and began climbing the wadi. It took the mortarmen 45 minutes to manhandle their weapon and ammunition to within range of the post. By the time Gardiner arrived the enemy was withdrawing and had laid down a screen of artillery and machine-gun fire right across the front. Meanwhile two patrols from "A" Company were going out along the two escarpments south of the main road. The patrol along the southerly or higher escarpment captured an enemy officer and a sergeant; the one along the lower escarpment brought in 30 of the enemy, some ammunition and some medical equipment, and located in a wadi about a dozen enemy vehicles loaded with ammunition. That night and the next Evans sent out patrols to the trucks: they destroyed eleven on the first night and brought in the twelfth on the next. The 18th Cavalry also sent out a deep patrol on the night of the 25th, which captured 33 Italians, including an officer, in a wadi near the coast more than 4,500 yards out from the perimeter.

While the garrison's hold on its ground was becoming stronger every day, one aspect of the defence arrangements was not improving and was causing Morshead much disquiet. On the 24th he sent a signal to Western Desert Force headquarters pointing to the increase in enemy air activity. He stated that, if it continued unchecked, the use of the harbour would be restricted, and asked for information of the R.A.F's counter-offensive plan. As No. 204 Fighter Wing lost aircraft through combat or otherwise, the losses were no longer being replaced; the loss of three aircraft on the 23rd forced the issue and provoked an unpleasant decision. On 25th April, the R.A.F. Command decided to withdraw the fighter wing with its two remaining Hurricanes from Tobruk. Only two Lysanders of the

---

[7] Lt G. Gardiner, VX38674; 2/23 Bn. Farmer and wrestler; of Auckland, NZ; b. Bay of Plenty, NZ, 3 Aug 1903. Died of wounds 18 May 1941.

army-cooperation squadron were to remain. Morshead caused a message to be sent to R.A.F. Command pointing out that without fighter support it would be impossible to direct artillery shoots from the air with the Lysanders; the garrison's artillery would thus be rendered vulnerable to enemy counter-battery action. To General Beresford-Peirse he signalled that he viewed the change in policy with the gravest concern. It would affect morale more quickly than anything else and give the enemy aircraft greater freedom to operate against both the troops and the port. He most strongly urged that despite the risks at least one squadron should be stationed in Tobruk. Beresford-Peirse replied that the decision, taken by both Commanders-in-Chief, though deplorable from Morshead's point of view, was a hard necessity, occasioned by the shortage of aircraft. For all fighter duties, including Tobruk, only 13 Hurricanes were available. To put them into Tobruk would merely be to lose them. Until the fighter strength increased, the Tobruk airfield could not be maintained. Despite this uncompromising reply, however, one flight of Hurricanes was allowed to remain for the time being for reconnaissance.

The 26th April was a very quiet day because a khamsin blew up, reducing visibility along the front to about 300 yards. Meanwhile the engineers were working feverishly to complete their tasks in readiness for the expected attack, which divisional headquarters thought the enemy might launch by the 27th. In the western sector two sections of the 2/13th Field Company were laying "hair-trigger" anti-personnel mines in both the perimeter wire and the post wire while the remainder toiled to complete the inner B1 minefield behind Ras el Medauuar.

The morning of the 27th brought a revival of the khamsin, but the wind abated as the day progressed. The improvement in visibility brought a severe attack by 24 dive bombers on the heavy anti-aircraft guns near the harbour. One aircraft was shot down but four guns were temporarily put out of action. The anti-aircraft artillery suffered almost 50 casualties. Six men were killed; two died later of wounds.

Brigadier Slater investigated the action. He found that first an attack had been made by numerous high-level bombers (Ju-88's) with fighter escort to draw the fire of the heavy anti-aircraft guns. Then 50 dive bombers attacked the guns, at least 12 to each site.[8] In some cases their approach was not seen, for they came out of the sun. At two of the gun sites attacked, "porcupine" formation was adopted—all guns pointing outwards and firing at over 65 degrees elevation—and the guns continued firing throughout the attack. At these two sites the damage was not great; one man was killed, one wounded. At the other two sites the personnel took cover after the first bomb had fallen; at one of them the approach of the dive bombers had not been seen. At these sites there were 46 casualties, including 5 killed, 4 guns were put out of action for 48 hours and other serious damage was done. It was a hard, bitter teaching of the lesson that the greatest safety for the gun crews lay in fighting their guns. To remain exposed, to quell the instinct to take cover from dive-bombing

---

[8] Later, further inquiries indicated that probably the number was considerably greater.

or machine-gunning attacks, required high courage and iron nerves. In the last 20 days of April the harbour guns engaged 386 dive bombers in 21 actions. Frequent exposure to such great strain inevitably took its toll. Yet, though the nerve of some inevitably succumbed, the anti-aircraft regiments won the battle of morale. They continued fighting with all guns.

But it was not enough to draw the lesson that the guns must never fail to fight back. If each site were to use its guns for its own protection, this form of attack, Slater apprehended, could nullify the harbour barrage, and that, just at the time when fighter protection was being withdrawn; for on the afternoon that this raid had taken place all fighter aircraft in Tobruk except those required for reconnaissance had left the El Gubbi aerodrome to fly back to Egypt. There was only one possible answer to the problem: to deprive the enemy of the foreknowledge that enabled him to plan such attacks, to deceive him by camouflage, concealment, the construction of dummy positions and frequent changes of the defensive layout. Slater immediately took counter-measures for this purpose. A camouflage officer was appointed to the anti-aircraft brigade. Work was started at once on the construction of alternative gun-sites. Dummy sites were erected close to real sites and much ingenuity and effort applied to making them realistic. As well as the dummy guns, these sites were provided with dummy men, vehicles, tracks and dumps. During air raids explosives were fired to simulate gun-flashes and stir up dust in them as in real sites. At the same time existing sites, which the raid on the 27th had shown to be inadequately protected, were counter-sunk and strengthened. These measures were to prove effective; in future raids enemy dive-bomber pilots attacking the guns divided their attentions impartially between the real and dummy sites: never again were casualties inflicted on a comparable scale.

The respite from major operations at Tobruk was like a spell of fair weather between storms. There were signs, however, that it would not hold; air reports showed that the enemy was gathering strength around the fortress. But it was on the frontier that the first turbulence occurred. From interrogations of British prisoners captured in the raids in the Capuzzo area on 23rd and 24th April, the German *Africa Corps* headquarters inferred that the purpose of the raids had been to break the Axis grip on Tobruk by an encircling attack on Capuzzo. Rommel, as we saw, had ordered the Herff Group to take the offensive on the frontier as soon as the battalion from the *Trento Division* arrived. In the early afternoon of the 25th a German force attacked Brigadier Gott's covering forces around Capuzzo. The British withdrew towards Halfaya, held by the 1/Durham Light Infantry at the top of the pass and the 3/Coldstream Guards at its foot, with the 2/Scots Guards in reserve.

On the 25th Lieutenant Thomas[9] of the 2/2nd Anti-Tank Regiment, with four guns of that regiment, took charge of the anti-tank defence on the Coldstream Guards front. Lieutenant Scanlon's[1] troop (2/3rd Anti-

---

[9] Maj V. C. Thomas, MC, QX6359. 2/2 A-Tk Regt; staff appts 1943-45. Clerk; of Brisbane; b. Nambour, Qld, 12 Sep 1917.
[1] Lt J. O. Scanlon, NX35065; 2/3 A-Tk Regt. Clerk; of Fivedock, NSW; b. Drummoyne, NSW, 12 Apr 1918.

Tank Regiment), part of Lieutenant Cheetham's troop (2/3rd) and a section of "B" Troop (2/2nd) were with the Durham Light Infantry; "K" Troop (Lieutenant Rennison) was with Beam column. Although the forward infantry were to stand their ground if attacked, the over-all plan was to withdraw them if hard pressed, for which eventuality code words were ready.

The pass was bombed and machine-gunned on the evening of the 25th and on the 26th Herff's force launched an attack against it. The ensconced infantry held to their positions, but their front was narrow and lacked flank protection. Enemy infiltrating along the escarpment threatened to outflank them. The anti-tank gunners of the 12th Battery took part in the battle in an infantry-gun role, using high-explosive shell. Sergeant Templeman's[2] gun registered a direct hit on an enemy field gun as it was coming into action.

After dark the withdrawal plan was put into effect and the code words issued. The 2/Scots Guards established a delaying line from Buq Buq to Alam el Dab, two miles west of Sidi Barrani, through which the forward battalions withdrew. The 12th Battery guns covered the withdrawals of the battalions they were supporting. The two companies of the 1/Durham Light Infantry, covered by Lieutenant Scanlon's troop, left the Halfaya position at 10.30 p.m., and the rearguard at Salum, with which was Lieutenant Cheetham's troop (less one section), departed at 40 minutes past midnight.

The various troops and sections of Major Argent's battery continued to cover their battalions until Buq Buq was reached, where they were detached and joined the 2/Scots Guards. Some went to the mobile delaying force at Buq Buq called "Rushforce"—comprising a company of the Scots Guards, a battery of the 8th Field Regiment and six guns of Argent's battery—others to the left flank at Alam el Dab, and two went to the Support Group headquarters, about two miles east of Sidi Barrani. The guns of Major Wilson's battery were disposed with the 2/Coldstream Guards, the 1/Durham Light Infantry and the French Motor Company.

On the 27th the Axis forces advanced their forward mobile units to the line Sidi Omar—Sidi Suleiman—and north to Musaid. Here they halted to form a defensive line; approaches to Halfaya were blocked while patrols were pushed out into the coastal plain. The Mediterranean Fleet, though preoccupied with the evacuation of Greece, found time to detail the gunboat H.M.S. *Aphis* to engage the advancing German forces from seaward, but bad weather prevented her intervention.

Possession of the Halfaya Pass and the escarpment around the bottleneck greatly strengthened Rommel's eastern flank and gave him freedom to concentrate his forces on Tobruk. The advanced units of the *15th Armoured Division* were withdrawn, with the exception of most of the *15th Motor Cycle Battalion* and two tanks. The *3rd Reconnaissance Unit* was also left on the frontier as a mobile reserve. None the less the defence

---

[2] Sgt B. A. Templeman, NX58486; 2/3 A-Tk Regt. Salesman; of Homebush, NSW; b. Paddington, NSW, 8 May 1919. Died of wounds 28 Jul 1942.

of the main frontier positions was left to two Italian units: in the Salum-Capuzzo area, a mixed unit of the *Ariete Division* (the *Montemurro Unit*) with an infantry company from the recently arrived battalion of the *Trento Division* and an Italian battery of medium artillery (105-mm); at Bardia the rest of the *Trento Division*.

The last days of April saw the Axis forces in Africa gathering around Tobruk in readiness for a major onslaught, and across the Mediterranean the collapse of resistance by the Greek and British forces in Greece. The evacuation of the British Expeditionary Force with the loss of all its heavy equipment marked the end of another successful German campaign. The last large-scale evacuations took place on the 29th. Most of the re-embarked forces were trans-shipped to Crete, the supply and defence of which from the dwindling resources of the Middle East now became for the three British Commanders-in-Chief an urgent but intractable problem.

That the enemy would before long make another attempt to reduce Tobruk was not doubted at Morshead's headquarters; that the assault would be made through the western sector defences seemed likely, but by no means certain. The no less important question, when the attack was likely to be launched, was one, however, to which no answer could yet be formulated. The defenders looked for signs, but saw few. Most of the enemy forces were beyond the garrison's range of vision. What was needed was a continual and comprehensive air coverage; the R.A.F. could not provide it. There were no aircraft available for photographic reconnaissance. Morshead had to make do with such information as could be gleaned from quick tactical reconnaissance flights and the restricted observations of his own ground patrols, most of them night patrols; and as often as not, daylight reconnaissance could reveal little more than the driving dust raised by the recurring khamsins. On the 27th, for example, little could be seen until evening, though a carrier patrol from the 2/48th was sent out at dawn before visibility became bad. It found no indications of unusual activity but surprised the enemy in bed, and inflicted several casualties without loss to itself. By the evening the dust-storm had subsided. Next morning the air reconnaissance at dawn revealed that some increase had occurred in the amount of motor transport in the southern sector and that weapon-pits and trenches were being dug along the western and south-western sectors; but still there was no indication of preparations for an attack.

However the day brought an intensification of enemy activity. At 6 a.m. the harbour area was heavily raided. A bomb almost destroyed "Admiralty House", the naval headquarters. "A good drop of slum clearance" commented Captain Smith, the naval officer-in-charge, in reporting the damage to headquarters. Air raids continued throughout the day. And large numbers of vehicles were observed during the forenoon and early afternoon moving up from south to west, towards the road leading to Acroma from which all previous attacks on the western sector had come.

In the past week great progress had been made in strengthening the defences in depth and developing the Blue Line, particularly in the western sector. The engineers had continued working round the clock laying the tactical minefields. The 26th Brigade (Brigadier Tovell) holding the western sector had a frontage of about twelve miles to defend. For three miles from the coast, where the Wadi Sehel led up from the sea in a great gash gouged almost 200 feet deep out of the rock-table, the wadi's perpendicular cliffs and slopes gave great strength to the defence; but for the remaining nine miles of the brigade front the configuration of the land provided little hindrance to military movement. The arduously-constructed but thinly-manned defence works alone barred the way. Along the Wadi Sehel the 18th Cavalry Regiment manned the perimeter defences. On their left, from near the head of the wadi, across the Derna Road (the main coast road) up 50 feet to the top of the first escarpment, thence southwards to the second one mile distant, up 25 feet and out onto the plateau, the front was held by the 2/23rd Battalion. From the left flank of the 2/23rd Battalion the perimeter swung out from south to east in a wide arc around the forward slopes of Ras el Medauuar. For 18 days the 2/48th Battalion had held the five miles of exposed front on this vital but vulnerable sector against frequent if not always determined assault; in that time it had captured much equipment and taken 1,375 prisoners; its own casualties for the period were 15 killed and 20 wounded. It was due for a rest and was now to be relieved by the 2/24th Battalion (Lieut-Colonel Spowers[3]), from which it would take over the role of brigade reserve and of manning the newly constructed Blue Line. Spowers was a leading Melbourne businessman who had been twice decorated as a subaltern in a British regiment in the first war and had seen some years of service in the militia between the wars. An athlete in his younger and not-so-young days he was now 48 but won the regard of his young officers and men by reason of his fitness and stamina as well as by his commanding presence.

The main relief by the 2/24th was to take place at night but the reserve companies changed over on the afternoon of the 28th. While this was in progress, the enemy air force concluded a day of frequent raids (directed mainly against gun positions and the perimeter defences) with a heavy attack on the 2/48th's sector during which the whole area was strafed and more than 150 bombs were dropped; one scored a direct hit on the weapon-pit of S11, leaving it unusable and a potential danger in the defence. Simultaneously the area was shelled. It was thought this activity might presage an attack, but none occurred to complicate the relief, which proceeded after dark without misadventure. There was unusual shelling that night of the Blue Line positions, just before the 2/24th vacated them to move forward, and of the cross-roads on the track leading up to the front, as though the enemy had discovered that the relief was taking place.

Next day (29th April) the 2/48th settled into the Blue Line—it was the first time since the battalion had left Maddalena, on the escarpment north

---

[3] Col A. Spowers, CMG, DSO, MC, VX14840. (1914-18: Capt 6 Bn E Lancs Regt.) CO 2/24 Bn 1940-42. Company director; of Melbourne; b. Melbourne, 9 Jul 1892.

of Benghazi, that there had been any troops between it and the enemy—
while Colonel Spowers toured the positions his battalion had taken over,
viewing with some concern in the light of his first-world-war experience
the shallow, rock-bottomed pits and trenches that constituted the ancillary
defences dug outside the deeply-sunk, concrete Italian perimeter posts.
At his bidding the company commanders, with new-broom enthusiasm,
soon had their men working with a will in deepening trenches and
strengthening sangars; and every available sandbag was collected and filled
with rubble to build up fire-steps in the Italian posts. The forward companies were commanded by (from right to left) Captain Budge,[4] Major
Fell and Captain Bird.[5] Captain Gebhardt[6] commanded the reserve company on Forbes' Mound (named after Captain Forbes of the 2/48th),
just behind the inner minefield.

One of Morshead's brigades, the 24th, was still without one of its
three battalions, owing to the late arrival of the 2/25th from Australia,
which was due to arrive in Palestine in a few days time. General Wavell
and General Blamey decided that the completion of the 9th Division could
not wait upon this battalion's arrival, reconditioning, equipment, and final
training for war. The 2/32nd Battalion, which had been formed in England
in 1940 mainly from personnel who had gone there with the 18th Brigade
when invasion threatened, was therefore directed to Tobruk. The battalion began embarking at Mersa Matruh in the *Chakla* on the 28th, but
because of bad weather embarkation was suspended after only one company had been taken on. With this diminished complement the *Chakla*
set forth, arriving in Tobruk Harbour next morning just after 8 a.m. The
company was immediately organised into a composite force with the 2/3rd
and 2/4th Field Companies and put into a reserve defensive position covering the route from the eastern sector to the harbour.

The morning tactical air reconnaissance on the 29th revealed a continuation of the westward movement of transport across the front of the
20th and 26th Brigades. The tempo of enemy air activity, high on the
previous day, was stepped up still further as the day progressed. Field
gun positions, forward infantry posts and infantry in reserve areas were
bombed and strafed. In one attack three men were killed and eight wounded
in the 2/10th Battalion. The 20th Brigade's sector was shelled all morning.
Soon after midday a dive-bombing and machine-gunning attack was made
on the 2/24th Battalion during which an enemy aircraft swept back and
forth over a stone hut with tarpaulin roof in the right company's area.
It happened that Captain Budge, the company commander, was conferring
with other officers in the hut; one was killed, and four wounded, including
Budge himself and Captain Oakley.[7] Captain Canty[8] took over command

---

[4] Maj W. F. R. Budge, ED, VX48105. 2/24 Bn; "Z" Special Unit. Schoolteacher; of Ringwood, Vic; b. Ballarat, Vic, 3 Dec 1906.
[5] Maj A. C. B. Bird, ED, VX47496; 2/24 Bn. Joinery works manager; of North Balwyn, Vic; b. Richmond, Vic, 2 Jan 1906.
[6] Maj P. Gebhardt, VX14044; 2/24 Bn. Pastoralist; of Toorak, Vic; b. Port Wakefield, SA, 30 Sep 1911.
[7] Maj A. W. Oakley, VX48762; 2/24 Bn. Manufacturer's agent; of Ormond, Vic; b. Richmond, Vic, 28 Apr 1906.
[8] Capt L. G. Canty, VX48356; 2/24 Bn. Postal official; of Box Hill, Vic; b. Dunolly, Vic, 4 Sep 1912.

of the company. Another raid followed in the same area, the target apparently being the perimeter wire and minefields; some damage was caused to the defence works but this time there were no casualties. At 2 p.m. 30 bombers attacked the gun positions of "E" Troop of the 1st R.H.A. at the junction of the El Adem and Bardia Roads; the gun crews suffered four severe casualties, of whom only one survived. About 4.30 p.m. the harbour was heavily raided and the *Chakla* sunk.[9] About 5 p.m. 30 bombers executed another raid on the 2/24th Battalion, but no damage was reported. An hour later an enemy patrol of armoured cars and infantry reconnoitred towards Ras el Medauuar; they were fired upon and quickly retired. In the late evening about 30 aircraft (one report[1] put the number as high as 63) using the last of the daylight dive-bombed the rear areas of the 20th Brigade; more than 30 men were wounded, including 3 officers when the brigade headquarters officers' mess was hit. The day ended with an artillery bombardment of the reserve positions of the 26th Brigade. But the night was quiet. In the port three lighters arrived, unloaded six infantry tanks and took back with them some of the German tanks captured in the Easter battle for examination by the equipment experts in England.

At first light on 30th April, Major Fell, standing near his headquarters on the forward slopes of Ras el Medauuar, had his attention drawn by Lieutenant Meighan[2] to clouds of dust in the west in the direction of Acroma, stirred up, it could be perceived, by moving vehicles. More than 100 were seen. Soon afterwards, farther north, about 20 armoured vehicles were observed moving in along the top of the escarpment, until shells from the defending artillery began to fall among them, whereupon they withdrew. The aircraft that made the morning tactical reconnaissance returned to report an increase in motor transport around the fortress and at Acroma. About 9 a.m. enemy infantry could be seen in the distance from the slopes of Medauuar. They dismounted from trucks coming from the direction of Acroma and advanced in line in low ground south of the Acroma Road to within 4,000 yards of the perimeter; there they sat down. Major Fell judged that some of the enemy were within range and asked the artillery to engage them. The artillery were at first sceptical but later fired a few rounds. The infantry heard the whistling passage overhead of the shells; but where their fall could be seen, they were short of the enemy. An inconstant wind got up as the sun climbed higher. Curtains of dust closed and parted, giving momentary, hazy views of enemy territory where continuous movement of men and tanks could be indistinctly perceived all day. It was noticed that the infantry were slowly coming closer, close enough for the defenders to see that they were Italians. Behind them, beyond the ridges, a great volume of dust rose up, more it seemed than the slight wind alone would have raised.

---

[9] Morshead, in consequence of this sinking, sent a personal message to General Wavell urging that until adequate fighter protection and increased anti-aircraft artillery could be provided, personnel ships should arrive and depart at night and only small vessels should be employed for the carriage of stores. This became the policy in future.

[1] War diary, 2/15 Bn.

[2] Lt R. D. Meighan, VX48559; 2/24 Bn. Clerk; of Fairfield, Vic; b. Melbourne, 17 Feb 1919.

Commanders and artillery officers in the western sector had become accustomed to reading the signs of an enemy assault. What they saw suggested the possibility of another attack from the west, probably against Medauuar. The 2/24th was ready to meet it as previous assaults had been met; moreover shell-proofing of the artillery observation post on top of Ras el Medauuar, which overlooked all approaches, had just been completed by Captain Young and sappers of the 2/13th Field Company. Yet the morning and afternoon passed quietly on the battalion's front with the exception of some light shelling on Ras el Medauuar by 105-mm guns and of a repetition of the almost regular dive-bombing attacks on the forward troops, chiefly in the western sector. The other westward-facing battalion, the 2/23rd, was meanwhile planning, with care and great attention to detail, a strong company raid to be mounted next day; its object was to destroy enemy batteries, located in a re-entrant between the two escarpments, 3,000 yards west of the battalion's front wire.

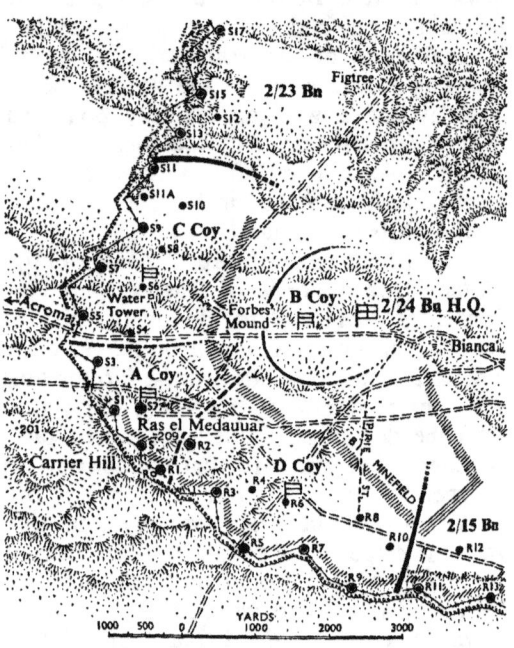

30th April 1941

The setting of the dust-dimmed sun on that last day of April signalled the end of a month in which the forces of Morshead's command had retreated to a firm base, turned at bay, and thereafter not only repulsed every enemy assault, but achieved success in most of their own. The quality of the troops had been abundantly demonstrated; if only the odds could be kept about equal in the score of relative armaments, there was reason to be confident that the garrison would continue to hold. The staff, too, for all but few of whom this campaign had been their first experience of real warfare, were quickly assimilating its lessons and growing in competence and confidence. As each report reached the headquarters, whether of ground or air observations, whether of enemy concentrations or of an actual assault, no undue alarm was caused; it was coolly and unhurriedly assessed. Such reports were continually being received. The divisional operations log for the last four hours of 30th April provides a good example of how they were handled in the operations room at divisional headquarters at Pilastrino. Although the last hour or two of daylight each day, when the mirage cleared and dust-raising winds subsided, was always attended by an increase of shelling, the gunfire heard in the west that evening of 30th April had seemed more intense than normal. At 7.15 p.m. a drumming of anti-aircraft guns and crunching of bombs in the same area indicated that an air raid was in progress. At 7.20 p.m. a telephone message from the 26th Brigade was received at divisional headquarters, and recorded in the operations log, reporting that the 2/24th Battalion was being dive-bombed; also that there were about 100 infantry one mile and a half out from the battalion's wire and a number of vehicles about two miles out. The duty officer passed the information to General Morshead and Colonel Lloyd. Fifteen minutes later the 26th Brigade reported a further heavy dive-bombing attack on the 2/24th Battalion, mainly on Major Fell's company: 40 aircraft had taken part, one had crashed. The message stated that this, in conjunction with the move up of a small party of infantry followed by dispersed vehicles, some of which were possibly tanks, might indicate that a half-hearted attack would be made at dusk. Lloyd was informed of this by the duty officer; but before his tour of duty ended at 8 p.m., the duty officer recorded only one other message, which was about a dive-bombing attack on a minesweeper.

At 8 p.m. a heavy bombardment out towards the western perimeter was heard over the whole fortress area; it seemed to be falling on the 26th Brigade. Simultaneously a solitary, long-range gun began slowly shelling the landing ground a few hundred yards from divisional headquarters. One of the few places in Tobruk where the hostile rumble of this gunfire might not have been heard was the headquarters operations room itself; it was a subterranean chamber excavated in solid rock, one of several located at the end of a tunnel burrowed deep into the face of the second escarpment. The first message received there by the officer who took over duty at 8 p.m. came, however, not from the 26th but the 24th Brigade, at the other extremity of the perimeter. Just after 8.20 p.m. Brigadier Godfrey reported that a minor attack by about 40 men was being made on the defences at the fringe of the Wadi Zeitun near the coast in the eastern sector; they had come from the next adjoining wadi and were being engaged with infantry weapons by men of the Australian Army Service Corps who were employed as infantry to hold that part of the perimeter. Nothing further of interest was reported to the operations room until 8.50 p.m., when a message was received from the 26th Brigade that the barrage was slackening slightly and that there had been no reports of any enemy infantry through the wire or of enemy tanks. This information was passed on to Colonel Lloyd. Five minutes later the 26th Brigade reported that a few heavy-calibre shells were falling on the 2/24th Battalion; this time the message was passed to the commander of the fortress artillery.

Forty minutes passed before, at 9.30 p.m., the next communication from the 26th Brigade was received. The brigade reported that the artillery fire had now died out; a considerable number of green and white flares had been seen along the perimeter;³ there was no further information available because Major Fell's and Captain Canty's companies, on whose front the flares had been seen, were out of communication. Fifteen minutes later (9.45 p.m.) the operations room received a reassuring message from the headquarters of the fortress artillery: they had been in touch at 9.30 p.m. with the artillery observation post in Fell's area at Ras el Medauuar; it had reported "everything O.K."; the two observation posts farther to the right sited on each of the escarpments in the 2/23rd Battalion area had reported some gun flashes, mortar fire and machine-gun fire away from the wire, but no infantry or vehicles had been seen.

The front now seemed to have relapsed into the quietness of a normal night, like the peace after a brief storm. Nothing further was reported to the operations room for an hour and a half. Then at 11.20 p.m. came a message from the 26th Brigade. The duty officer entered it briefly in the log as follows:

Penetration 2/24 Battalion area possible but situation not certain.

---

³ The flares did not conform to any signals code being used by the defenders.

CHAPTER 6

ASSAULT WITHSTOOD

WHEN General Morshead was wakened as usual at dawn on 1st May, he learnt from Colonel Lloyd that the enemy had penetrated the perimeter in the centre and on the right of the 2/24th Battalion front, around Ras el Medauuar. But Lloyd could tell Morshead little else. Some enemy infantry had established themselves inside the wire, some tanks were moving about outside, some German prisoners had been taken; patrols from the 2/24th and 2/23rd Battalions were trying to clarify the situation. The width and depth of the penetration were uncertain, though it did not appear to have been effected in great strength. Morshead, who was never given to hasty, ill-considered action, decided that better information must be obtained before counter-measures were considered.

How the situation had appeared to the divisional staff in the operations room during the first few hours of the operation can be imagined from the narrative at the end of the last chapter. This in turn reflected in outline, if it did not exactly mirror, the picture in the minds of the brigadier and his staff at the 26th Brigade headquarters, from whom the reports to divisional headquarters had come. The commander of the 2/24th Battalion was forming a different picture which, if less sketchy, still incompletely represented the magnitude of the developing onslaught.

The knowledge gained by the commanders at the various levels was derived in part from what they personally saw or heard, but mainly from what was reported to them; but no reports had come through during the night from the closely invested front, except on the right flank. The modern commander, who unlike his predecessors in history can rarely observe the course of the battle, is most dependent on good communications; but the communications network operating in Tobruk was incomplete, unreliable and vulnerable. An acute shortage of equipment was the chief cause. Most units had still received little of the battle equipment laid down in war equipment tables. One battalion had arrived in Tobruk with only a few signal flags; other units had more or less illicitly made up some deficiencies from captured material in western Cyrenaica, but again much of this had been left and lost because there had been insufficient transport to move it or time to take it up in the precipitate withdrawals.

Owing to lack of equipment radio telephony had not yet been introduced as a normal method of infantry intercommunication at Tobruk. A line-telephone network, following the normal lines of command, was laid down from fortress headquarters right out to the perimeter as well as throughout the base area. The headquarters of battalions had lines to the headquarters of companies, companies to some posts on the perimeter: usually to those in which platoon commanders were located. The cable and switchboards were mainly Italian. These were supplemented by a wireless telegraphy network which for security reasons would not be operationally used except in an emergency; its use was limited also by a grave inadequacy of battery-charging facilities resulting from a complete lack of piston ring replacements for charging sets. Moreover there were not enough battalion wireless sets to provide a service within battalions.[1] As soon as secure communications to brigade commands had been established at the inception of the siege, a separate artillery cable and wireless network had been set up. The artillery line, partly because it rightly had priority for the best equipment, became the most reliable channel of communication to the perimeter at those points where artillery forward observation officers were stationed.

The inadequacy of wireless telegraphy as an alternative to telephones for military operational use, particularly when the delays and textual corruptions resulting from enciphering are added to normal delays of transmission, is known only too well to anybody who has been thrown back upon its employment in battle; yet the line communication in the forward area of Tobruk, which even in quiet times was subject to random breaks and failures, was very susceptible to interruption in operations, because the cables were almost invariably laid above ground and not enough was available for laying duplicate lines on alternative routes.

The alternatives to laying lines on the surface were to carry them above ground or to bury them. Poles were used in the rear areas. So far from directing their erection in the forward areas the operational staff ordered the removal of most of those left by the Italians, because they provided the enemy with useful aiming marks. Moreover, as between laying cable on the surface and burying it, a deliberate choice was made in favour of surface lines, for the sake of ease and speed of maintenance. To locate a break in a buried cable had proved impossible at night, and extremely difficult in such featureless country even in daylight, because shifting sands would obscure the route. Test-points along a buried line were also liable to be lost in drift-sand. Because of the distances involved, the number of test-points required would have been great on many lines and the time required to test from them intolerably long. Moreover in many areas the rocky surface precluded burying unless engineers were to be taken from other urgent work to excavate the routes. For these reasons all lines to the forward posts were laid on the surface and liable to be cut by an artillery barrage or deliberately by assaulting infantry.

A road ran past Colonel Spowers' headquarters westwards, crossing the perimeter guarded by his foremost troops more than two miles distant, and continued on, above and not far from the edge of the second escarpment, which it followed, to Acroma. Astride the road, past Forbes' Mound and about 1,000 yards from Spowers' headquarters, was "B" Company, his reserve. South-west from Forbes' Mound, the country rose up, in a bare expanse of brown dust littered with war debris, to an apex at Ras el Medauuar, on top of which the grey-white concrete observation post

---

[1] Sets Nos. 18 and 108.

sat like a helmet.[2] In front the perimeter ran out on either side. The front-row perimeter posts, which were from 500 to 700 yards apart and not interconnected, were surrounded by small anti-tank ditches but at too small a radius to prevent domination and bombardment of the weapon-pits by tanks standing close-in. The general tank ditch had not been extended to this sector; the Italians had laid a belt of mined concertina wire beyond the zigzag perimeter apron fence, which was an inadequate substitute.

Panoramic view Bianca-Medauuar, looking south-west

What had happened on the perimeter that night when the duty officers at divisional headquarters had been recording the messages quoted in the last chapter? Throughout the anxious daylight hours of 30th April, Spowers had been in constant touch with his forward companies, almost each report telling of a glimpse of enemy movement seen through the dust screen. When visibility began to improve in the late afternoon, Spowers, with his Intelligence officer, Lieutenant Serle, visited the headquarters of Captain Canty, whose company was on the right, above the escarpment, and saw enemy infantry and vehicles massing to the west. Soon after 5 p.m. Canty reported that a platoon of enemy infantry was moving towards him, followed by some motor-cycles. They did not advance far. At 5.30 p.m. an air raid was made on the right of Canty's company against Captain Spier's company of the 2/23rd Battalion, killing one man and wounding four others. At 5.45 p.m. enemy shells began falling on the western sector. At 5.55 p.m. Fell, from his lookout on Ras el Medauuar, reported that a platoon of enemy infantry and four vehicles were advancing along the Acroma Road. Ten minutes later, he reported that they were 150 strong and now 3,000 yards from the wire; the shelling had stopped. Meanwhile Canty reported that he could see between 30 and 40 vehicles loaded with troops but could not see the infantry mentioned by Fell. Soon after 6 p.m. Fell reported that the enemy appeared to be advancing in two waves, the first of about two companies, the second about one company; there was no sign of tanks. About 6.30 p.m. another company of infantry was observed in vehicles farther to the right, slowly advancing

---

[2] It stood about 8 feet above ground.

towards Canty's positions. At 6.45 p.m. it was reported from Fell's company that vehicles could be seen moving in rear of the infantry. This was confirmed by Captain Bird's company on the left, who reported that the vehicles had disappeared behind Carrier Hill; it could not be discerned whether they were tanks.

Meanwhile the infantry advance appeared to be slackening at a distance of 1,800 to 2,000 yards from the wire. The enemy troops were well dispersed; the absurd bunching so pronounced in previous assaults had been avoided. Post R1, on the southern shoulder of Medauuar, was receiving a heavy pasting from artillery or mortars. By 7 p.m. it could be seen that tanks were moving behind the infantry. Dust raised by the shelling of both sides made it impossible to gauge the number, but later 16 were counted. At 7.15 p.m., as the sun passed below the horizon like a fire suddenly extinguished, four enemy reconnaissance planes flew out of the west. Several squadrons followed, the atmosphere reverberating with their engine-roar: the sky above Medauuar was filled with dive bombers. The first wave of more than 20 dive-bombed and machine-gunned the perimeter on the south side of Medauuar. Others came in their wake. At 7.30 p.m. more than 30 aircraft dive-bombed the perimeter on the north side; one failed to recover from its dive and was seen to crash in flames. Fell reported that the bombs had been falling in and near the wire: no casualties had been caused. Spowers was reporting all these events to Tovell's headquarters. Yet the impression conveyed by the officer who passed the information on to divisional headquarters was such that his appreciation was summarised in the log by the duty officer there in the words "may indicate a half-hearted attack at dusk".

At 7.45 p.m. as the towers of dust raised by the bombing began to clear, more infantry were seen in the dying light to be gathering about 3,000 yards in front of Fell's company. The telephone line to Fell had gone dead, but there was still communication to the companies on either flank. Spowers ordered the whole battalion to stand to arms.

At 8 p.m. a heavy artillery barrage was brought down on 4,500 yards of the perimeter on either side of Ras el Medauuar, enveloping the front in a pall of dust as the light continued to fade. At first it fell on the wire. At 8.15 red and green flares were seen outside the wire, the barrage lifted and concentrations were brought down with great accuracy upon the perimeter posts themselves. Automatic fire was heard and streams of tracer bullets were seen drifting in towards the wire. On the right Canty reported that enemy infantry, apparently not in great strength, had approached posts S5 and S7; they had been promptly engaged by fire from the posts; no tanks had been seen. There was mortar fire on S7. On the left of the battalion front, posts on the left of Bird's company were also mortared. What was happening in Fell's company in the centre no one could tell, but not much small-arms fire was heard from that direction. Linesmen went out to restore the line.

About 8.30 p.m. the enemy fired a white flare, there was a pause in the artillery fire and then the perimeter wire was blown with bangalore torpedoes between Canty's and Fell's companies, in the region where the road from Acroma crossed the perimeter. Canty reported, however, that the fire was not intense and few infantry could be seen. Lieutenant Shelton,[3] commanding the carrier platoon, obtained Spowers' permission to move his platoon up in line with the reserve company behind the inner minefield and bring his anti-tank rifles into action; but the twilight ebbed to total darkness before that could be done. Spowers then ordered the carriers, his only uncommitted reserve, to stand by at instant call near battalion headquarters. The line to Fell's company being still silent, linesmen were sent out with messages on foot.

At 8.40 p.m. there was a new burst of activity. In Bird's company shelling recommenced on Post R5, where the track leading south-west crossed the perimeter; the telephone line to the post was dead. In Canty's company, green and white flares were fired in front of the perimeter posts on either side of the east-west road and from Post S4 small-arms fire was reported astride the road about 1,000 yards behind the perimeter. The 51st Field Regiment were meanwhile maintaining a steady fire on defensive tasks. Spowers was striving to get in touch by wireless with Major Fell, from whose area there had been no word since the barrage had opened 50 minutes earlier. At 8.55 p.m. Captain Canty reported that firing was still intense in front of his posts on the north side of the road; fire could also be heard on other parts of the front.

At 9 p.m. a white enemy flare was seen just south of Ras el Medauuar, whereupon the enemy bombardment suddenly ceased, but the automatic fire of infantry weapons was still heard; it persisted along most of the battalion front. Spowers now found that the line to Canty's company had also gone dead; linesmen were sent out to repair it. Spowers turned his thoughts to closing the gap reported to have been made near the east-west road; at his request the 2/13th Field Company agreed to prepare wire for use when opportunity offered but stated that no mines were available. Ten minutes after the enemy artillery barrage had ceased, the 51st Field Regiment asked Tovell whether they too should cease firing and were told to do so. At 9.25 p.m. the regiment informed brigade headquarters that at 9.15 p.m. they had made contact with their observation officer at Fell's company on Ras el Medauuar who had reported that there had been no attack there and that all was well. That report does not appear to have reached Spowers, who discovered soon after 9.30 p.m. that his lines to brigade headquarters and to the brigade reserve battalion (the 2/48th) were both dead. The wireless link to brigade was opened and the slow process of passing enciphered messages began.

After the artillery bombardment ended, the front lapsed into comparative quietness but not complete peace for an hour and a half, like an eruption which, its main fury spent, continues to sputter menacingly. From time to time enemy signal flares were seen outside the wire; machine-guns opened fire and were again silent, first in one part of the front,

---

[3] Lt J. T. Shelton, VX47976; 2/24 Bn. Grazier; of Avenel, Vic; b. Avenel, 24 Jan 1905. Killed in action 1 May 1941.

then another; spasmodically a few artillery or mortar shells rained down among the forward posts or near battalion headquarters. On the left, Bird reported that he had re-established communication with Post R5 which was intact and had suffered no casualties; but from Fell in the centre and Canty on the right there was still no word. The lack of information was disturbing.

At 10.14 p.m. Spowers received a report from the commander of his reserve company, Captain Gebhardt, whose forward platoons were astride the east-west road about a mile and a half from where the penetration of the perimeter had been made. His right platoon, Gebhardt said, had been fired on from the north-west at a range of 500 yards; the report indicated that the fire was coming from near the inner minefield about half a mile north of the road. Spowers ordered Gebhardt to send out a patrol to ascertain what troops were firing on them and directed the carrier platoon to provide two Bren guns each to battalion headquarters and Gebhardt's company for local protection. Just after this the linesmen repairing the line to Fell's company tapped in and reported that they were pinned to the ground by fire just behind the inner minefield. About 10.30 p.m. it was found that the line to Bird's company had also been cut, which left Spowers with no line communication to front or rear, except to his reserve company just forward of battalion headquarters. More linesmen went out to repair the new break. The signalmen toiled, while Spowers anxiously waited for news of the reserve company's patrol near the inner minefield, and for word to reach him from his forward companies.

Such was the state of indeterminacy at Spowers' headquarters about 10.30 p.m. In the ensuing hour and a half nothing occurred to resolve it. Occasionally the enemy struck out fitfully with swift spiteful jabs of fire, then fell silent. There had been only one improvement in Spowers' unsatisfactory communications: the lines to brigade headquarters and the 2/48th Battalion were again operating. At 11 p.m. a message reached the 26th Brigade headquarters through the 51st Field Regiment from the artillery observation post on the right of Canty's company to the effect that Canty was out of contact with Spowers and wished Spowers to be informed that his company was safe and well. An earlier enciphered wireless message from Spowers conveying the information that fire was being brought down on his reserve company by troops near the inner minefield was not delivered to the command post at Tovell's headquarters until just after 11 p.m. Almost immediately afterwards line communication with Spowers' headquarters was restored. Spowers reported to Tovell's headquarters that the enemy appeared to be through the wire; he had not been able to get through to his forward companies for two hours and a half but thought they were all right; there appeared to be a party of Italians north of "B" Company; the whole position was obscure.[4]

When this information reached divisional headquarters, General Morshead had retired. Colonel Lloyd warned the other brigades and sought a detailed report from Tovell. Apparently regarding the situation with

---

[4] Summary based on contemporary battalion telephone log.

less equanimity than some of the staff interpreting Spowers' reports, he then told Brigadier Wootten (commanding the division's reserve brigade) that the enemy appeared to be holding a bridgehead in front of Ras el Medauuar between Posts S3 and R3[5] from which to launch an attack in the morning. Wootten ordered his battalions to stand to arms.

Just before midnight Spowers at last received word from Gebhardt that the reconnaissance patrol had located the "Italian" party. Spowers ordered Gebhardt to "collect them if possible" by means of a fighting patrol at least a platoon strong.

In the eastern (24th Brigade) sector, the raid of 40 enemy from the Wadi Weddan, which Brigadier Godfrey had reported to divisional headquarters at 8.20 p.m., came in near the head of the Wadi Zeitun, on the coast side of the main road and near the boundary of the 2/43rd Battalion and the Army Service Corps company. Two days earlier the enemy had been seen occupying positions astride the road about 2,000 yards out and to a depth, in rear, of about two miles; throughout the day there had been sporadic shelling by Italian field guns. Thus the intrusion could not be lightly regarded; but when small-arms fire was brought down on the raiding party in front of Post Z80 the raiders went to ground; later they withdrew. About 10 p.m. the approach of an enemy party, possibly the same force, was heard a little farther north. The area was raked with small-arms fire by the 2/43rd Battalion and artillery fire by the 104th R.H.A.; no assault developed. The front of the 24th Brigade thereafter remained dormant for the rest of the night.

At midnight 30th April-1st May, Major White, on duty in the operations room of Morshead's headquarters, asked Tovell's headquarters if it was yet known whether the enemy had penetrated. He was told all that was known: the wire had been gapped between Posts S3 and S5, Post R5 had come under heavy fire, and machine-gun fire had been brought down on Spowers' reserve company from 500 yards to the north-west.

Colonel Lloyd now gave thought to strengthening the anti-tank defence in the penetration area, the inadequacy of which was the perimeter strongpoints' principal weakness. The infantry tank-attack weapons that were provided later in the war in such variety had not yet been developed; not even the rudimentary Molotov cocktails had been delivered to Spowers' perimeter posts. The field artillery, though wisely sited for anti-tank defence as its crucial role, was nevertheless located too far in rear for effective, close anti-tank support at the perimeter. The latter, of course, was provided by the anti-tank artillery. If the anti-tank gunners' hearts were stout, however, their guns were few. There were, on Spowers' front of about five miles of perimeter, with its two rows of perimeter posts (23 in all), eight static and two mobile anti-tank guns.[6] Two more static guns were in rear of the inner minefield.[7] Colonel Lloyd arranged for Captain

---

[5] This indicated a span of more than 2,000 yards of the perimeter.
[6] Eight manned by "J" Battery (Maj L. H. Lewin) of the 3rd R.H.A., two by the 26th Anti-Tank Company.
[7] One, with the reserve company, manned by the 26th Anti-Tank Company, the other, providing rear protection for battalion headquarters, by "J" Battery.

Norman's[8] 24th Anti-Tank Company, then stationed near fortress headquarters but which had been in the Medauuar sector before, to return there and informed Spowers that they were to reach his headquarters in time to be put into position before first light. Lloyd also ordered the 3rd Armoured Brigade to move up the tanks during the night behind the Medauuar sector to an area about 1,000 yards in rear of Spowers' headquarters, where they would be astride the tracks leading in from there to the Pilastrino ridge, on which most of the field guns were sited and below which Morshead's headquarters were located.

At 12.30 a.m., the divisional duty officer, at Lloyd's direction, asked the 26th Brigade headquarters what action was being taken to determine the situation and to counter-attack if necessary. He recorded in his log that he was informed that the 2/24th Battalion had sent out patrols, the 2/48th Battalion was ready to move if a counter-attack was necessary, and the 2/23rd Battalion was standing by. His brief note may have adequately summarised what he was told, but was an incorrect summary of the actual state of affairs. As for the readiness of the 2/48th Battalion for a move, Windeyer, commenting some years later, stated[9] that he recollected a telephone call from Tovell (but could not say at what time it was made) in which Tovell had said:

"Jiggy"[1] is going to have a go at them and you have to be ready to go in to mop up.

Windeyer commented[2] on this instruction:

My understanding was that I might have to provide a party to aid some operation which Spowers had in mind. But I was told I would get details later if I had to do anything. I cannot remember taking any action except that I think the adjutant Scott[3] put one company on some notice.

Windeyer's recollection receives some confirmation from a later entry in the divisional log in which reference is made to the "mopping-up company" of the 2/48th.

Meanwhile Spowers was renewing his efforts to find out the situation of his forward companies. At 12.32 a.m. an attempt was made through the 51st Field Regiment to obtain a report from the artillery observation officers with Canty's company. The first one contacted was stationed farther north than the region from which enemy activity had been reported; he knew nothing of the situation. Before word was received from the other, a disturbing report from the field regiment was received at both Tovell's and Spowers' headquarters to the effect that the officer sent to relieve their observation officer with Fell had been unable to get through; on the way he had been fired at from a wooden hut near Ras el Medauuar, apparently occupied by the enemy. There was, it should seem, at some

---

[8] Brig C. H. B. Norman, DSO, MC, WX3421. OC 24 A-Tk Coy 1940-41; 2/28 Bn (CO 1943-45). Administrator of Norfolk Island 1953-58. Grazier; of Perth, WA; b. Sydney, 20 Feb 1904.
[9] In an interview with the author on 7 Apr 1955.
[1] Lt-Col Spowers.
[2] In 1955.
[3] Brig T. H. Scott, DSO, ED, SX10309. 2/48 Bn 1940-42; CO 2/32 Bn 1942-45. Purchasing officer; of Glenelg, SA; b. Broken Hill, NSW, 16 Sep 1907.

point along the line of communications between the frontal wire and divisional headquarters an inclination, not easily accountable, to regard the evidence slowly but ineluctably accumulating as less ominous than it was. It is possible that a practice in the 2/24th Battalion of using the term "Ities" (slang for Italians) as a generic term signifying enemy may have contributed to that result. The incident just described is recorded in the 51st Field Regiment's war diary as follows:

> Captain A. D. Clapham and line party went out to try and re-establish OP at Pt 209.[4] About 1,000 yards away from it he heard German voices and was met by small-arms fire and unable to reach it.

Yet the 2/24th log records the message received from the regiment about this as follows:

> Mudy [51st Field Regiment] reported Italians in wooden hut right of 209. . . . Officer of artillery was challenged and shot at by Italians from wooden hut.

The commander of the field regiment, Lieut-Colonel A. G. Matthew, in a report written after the operation commented on the incident as follows:

> This information was passed on to Inf Bde H.Q. and H.Q. R.A. but in the absence of confirmation was rather suspect by them.

Spowers now attempted to enlist the aid of the battalions on his flanks to contact his forward companies. A message was sent through brigade headquarters to Lieut-Colonel Evans asking him to make contact with Canty's posts. A similar message intended for the 2/15th Battalion was sent requesting that contact be made with Bird's company but an error appears to have been made in the code name used for the addressee (2/17th Battalion in the message as recorded). The actual message does not appear to have reached the 2/15th, but in due course they were told of the required action and took it, sending out a patrol to R9, on the left flank of Bird's company. A little later Spowers sent out Lieutenant Serle with two linesmen and two regimental police to contact Captain Bird.

At 1.15 a.m. brigade headquarters suggested to Spowers that a patrol of some size, at least a platoon, should be sent out from the reserve company to make contact with Fell's company; but Spowers pointed out that one platoon was already absent from the reserve company; to send out another, he maintained, would seriously weaken the defence in depth of the battalion position. This sound contention was accepted.

Scarcely had that discussion concluded when the 51st Field Regiment delivered to Spowers a message from Lieutenant Rosel,[5] who was commanding the right-hand platoon of Canty's company. Canty's headquarters, Rosel's message stated, were in urgent need of help, the enemy being very close; Rosel had sent one of his sections to their assistance. Spowers ordered Shelton to take three of his Bren gun carriers up to Canty's company. At 1.27 a.m. an N.C.O. of the signals section reported in to battalion

---
[4] Ras el Medauuar.
[5] Capt J. S. Rosel, MC, VX48603; 2/24 Bn. Bank clerk; of Hawthorn, Vic; b. Natimuk, Vic, 26 Jan 1917.

headquarters, having just arrived from Canty's company, which he had left at 9 p.m.; he had been repairing breaks in the line ever since, but had not met any enemy. At 1.30 a.m. Spowers reported Rosel's message to Brigadier Tovell and informed Tovell that he was sending a section of carriers to Canty's aid; he was also sending two men out to contact the forward companies. At 1.45 a.m. Brigadier Tovell reported to Morshead's headquarters that Spowers was still out of touch with his companies. Tovell was of opinion that there had been infiltration on the whole front of Spowers' battalion, but that it was not serious.[6] He might use a company of the 2/48th Battalion for mopping up later. Colonel Lloyd arranged with Colonel Birks, commanding all tanks in Tobruk, that two light tanks should go up to Tovell's headquarters for redirection to the mopping-up company of the 2/48th and to assist it if required.

A thick ground mist had meanwhile settled in the hollows to add to Spowers' difficulties. As a result Lieutenant Serle lost his way to Bird's company, returned, and set out again at 2 a.m. About this time, three carriers left for Canty's company, but they too lost their way. It was learnt through the artillery, however, that Post S6, a second-row post in Canty's company only about 700 yards north of the Acroma Road, was on the fringe of the enemy penetration but intact, and would try to make contact with Fell's company. Lieut-Colonel Evans then offered to send a patrol to contact Fell through Spowers' right-hand company. Spowers gladly accepted and asked that assistance be given to Canty if required. Later it was learnt from the 51st Field Regiment that the patrol had made contact with Rosel.

About 2.30 a.m. Spowers heard from Gebhardt's company that his patrol was on its way back. It was believed to have prisoners, but owing to mist the visibility was practically nil. Another 45 minutes elapsed before the report of the patrol was received; the enemy party had been put to flight, three prisoners, an anti-tank weapon and a sub-machine-gun had been captured, and four more enemy had been left wounded on the minefield. The enemy had been German. The company also reported that enemy could be heard digging in on their right flank. Meanwhile Norman's anti-tank company had arrived. One gun had been put into position near battalion headquarters; five had been sent to the reserve company to cover the inner minefield, but only four could be put into position because of the proximity of the enemy. Captain Clapham of the 51st Field Regiment also arrived at battalion headquarters to act as a forward observation officer.

In the next two hours, Spowers received from within his battalion only one report of his forward companies. That was at 3.40 a.m., when a linesman and a runner, who had left Captain Bird's company soon after his telephone line had failed early in the night but had later become lost in the mist, reported that all had then been well there. They said they had observed fire coming from Post R2 and had seen, in the light of a

---

[6] As recorded in the divisional operations log.

flare, a small party of "Italians" digging in close to the post. At 4.15 a.m. the Germans captured by Gebhardt's patrol arrived at Spowers' headquarters and were dispatched to fortress headquarters for interrogation. Meanwhile (unknown to Spowers) the 2/23rd Battalion's reserve company (Captain Malloch's[7]) had engaged about 40 Germans who approached from their left rear; 31 had been captured. About this time Tovell's headquarters made a detailed report of the current situation to Morshead's headquarters; this was followed soon afterwards by a report from Brigadier Murray in the southern sector that tanks were moving about outside the wire forward of Post R32, which was near the point at which the tanks had penetrated the perimeter in the Easter battle. It was also learnt from Murray's headquarters that contact had been made with Post R9, on the left flank of Bird's company, where not a shot had been fired.

At 4.40 a.m. the 51st Field Regiment reported that on the 2/24th Battalion's right flank a party of Germans had slipped through the neighbouring company, moving eastward. At 4.50 a.m. Spowers told Tovell's headquarters that he proposed sending six carriers up to Major Fell's company at first light. But he was advised "to wait and see what he was up against".[8] Tovell was becoming increasingly anxious. At 5 a.m. he told Colonel Evans that it seemed that Canty's company was surrounded. Evans, who had previously planned to employ Malloch's company that morning in a raid on enemy artillery positions, offered to use it for a counter-attack against the enemy in Canty's area. Tovell agreed and Evans issued orders accordingly.

About 5 a.m. an engagement in front of "C" Company of the 2/13th Battalion on the El Adem Road sector was reported. The enemy force, which was German, was first observed by a deep patrol of section strength led by Corporal Hewitt;[9] they were moving noisily down the El Adem Road towards the perimeter; Hewitt estimated that they were about 50 strong. Hewitt realised that they would run into "C" Company's standing patrol outside the wire, so stationed his patrol to cut off their retreat. His prediction was fully realised. Caught in the standing patrol's hot fire the enemy beat a hasty retreat, only to be engaged by Hewitt's men. The enemy dropped their stores, including wire-cutting tools and explosives, and fled. Six prisoners were taken, all of them wounded.

At 5.15 a.m. Spowers asked Gebhardt to send out a small patrol of three or four men to contact Fell's company. At 5.25 a.m. Lieutenant Serle returned from Bird's company, which he had reached on his second attempt. He reported that all was quiet in the area, though the telephone to the right-hand platoon (Lieutenant Mair[1]) in Post R4 was not working.

---

[7] Lt-Col G. I. Malloch, MC, VX48694; 2/23 Bn. Importer; of Toorak, Vic; b. Adelaide, 29 May 1905.
[8] Operations log, 26th Brigade.
[9] Sgt G. V. Hewitt, NX14887; 2/13 Bn. Jackeroo; of Glen Innes, NSW; b. Glen Innes, 23 Feb 1914. Killed in action 25 Jun 1941.
[1] Lt J. L. Mair, VX38646. 2/24 Bn; RAE (Water Tpt). Clerk; of Albury, NSW; b. Melbourne, 2 Sep 1919.

Spowers told Bird to contact Mair's platoon and the platoon of Fell's company on Mair's right and warned Bird that an enemy tank attack at first light was likely. He issued a similar warning to the commander of the anti-tank artillery in the sector.

The enemy artillery, which had long been silent, opened a bombardment at 5.45 a.m.; it seemed to be directed mainly against the perimeter defences on the left of the battalion's area. As it began, Malloch's company (less one platoon) began moving out towards the left flank of Evans' battalion, whence its counter-attack was to be launched.

It was then just on first light; but as though in conspiracy with the enemy, thick mist drifted across the front to prolong the defenders' ignorance of what the night's alarms portended. Gebhardt's company reported that the enemy had been digging in on their left flank; he was waiting until it was light enough to deal with them. Spowers ordered Shelton to investigate with a section of carriers. At 6.30 a.m., in heavy mist, the section moved out and found that weapon-pits had been dug on the left of Gebhardt's company but were unoccupied. Shelton told Spowers that he had been fired on from the north side of the Acroma Road by a large body of troops that he thought might be Malloch's company. He offered to try to contact Fell's company. Spowers agreed.

With a crew of three, Shelton left almost immediately, driving his own carrier. The mist partly cleared and watchers at Spowers' headquarters could see Shelton's carrier moving up past the wooden hut by the Acroma Road towards Fell's headquarters. Shelton reported at 6.42 a.m. that the hut was occupied by the enemy (by "Italians", according to the battalion action log). At 7.10 a.m. he reported again that he could see only for a distance of 200 yards, and had been fired on by a large body of troops, but would try to contact Fell's company. From battalion headquarters it had seemed that Shelton had almost reached Fell's headquarters on Ras el Medauuar, when mist rolled up again to blot the carrier from view.

Gebhardt's company reported that they could see no sign of the enemy on either flank, and Spowers reported to Tovell's headquarters that the situation seemed to have clarified; Canty's company appeared to be all right, also the "centre" and left flank. The shelling had ceased but occasional bursts of sub-machine-gun fire could still be heard. He was awaiting the return of Shelton's carrier from Fell's company. A note in the 26th Brigade log made at 7.20 a.m. indicates that it was then thought that Evans' battalion together with Canty's company would be able to clear the enemy from Fell's area.

But the hard light of day was soon to dispel that remarkably sustained optimism. Just afterwards the sun broke through and the mist cleared; Shelton's carrier could be seen burning on the Acroma Road. He had run into fire from enemy tanks standing to the south-east of Ras el Medauuar and had been killed instantly; but his foot had jammed on the accelerator, and the man at his side, leaning across his body, had managed to drive the carrier back to the Acroma Road. There it was hit again and the petrol tank set alight. Later a carrier under the command of

Sergeant Catherall,[2] endeavouring without success to get through to "C" Company with a load of ammunition, picked up the members of Shelton's crew. As the fog dispersed, heavy firing broke out along the perimeter in the Medauuar sector; dive bombers swept down with blaring sirens and other aircraft strafed the front. Some 10 minutes later the patrol sent out by Gebhardt returned and reported that they had been unable to reach Fell's company. They said that there were six enemy tanks on the east side of Ras el Medauuar.

Just at that time Malloch's two platoons from the 2/23rd reported back to their headquarters; they had passed right through Canty's area and had had a brush with the enemy. Canty's posts, though surrounded during the night, had regained control of their ground and Malloch felt confident that it could be held.

Had Malloch's men pushed a little farther south, however, they would have told a different story. Some 15 minutes after their return, about a battalion of enemy infantry were perceived by artillery observers advancing eastwards from the area near the hut north of Ras el Medauuar, which was approximately on the boundary of Canty's and Fell's companies. Gunfire from the 51st Field Regiment effectively broke up the advance. Meanwhile at 7 a.m. five tanks had approached the 2/13th Battalion's wire where Corporal Hewitt's patrol had intercepted the enemy engineer party. They came as if to attack and searched for a gap. The 1st R.H.A. engaged and the tanks soon withdrew.

Five minutes after the return of the patrol from Gebhardt's company 30 enemy tanks were seen on the slope of Ras el Medauuar, some towing anti-tank guns. At 8 a.m. they began to come over the sky-line south of that high point, moving eastwards. Behind them more followed. In all, about 40 took part in this thrust—there were about 80 inside the wire. The British gunners were at first reluctant to engage them, fearing that their fire might harm Australian infantry in the same area. But the tanks came on, and soon encountered the fire of every artillery piece the defenders could bring to bear. Captain Norman's 24th Anti-Tank Company engaged them in flank. Corporal Aston's[3] gun knocked out one German Mark III and two other tanks, but was then beset by 11 or 12. Two of the crew (Lance-Corporal Luck[4] and Private Bridges[5]) were seriously wounded but the others kept the gun firing until it was smashed by a direct hit. Norman's company lost three guns in the action. From behind Forbes' Mound a gun of the 26th Anti-Tank Company commanded by Corporal Edmonds[6] also engaged the German tanks, scoring several hits and stopping two; even after pieces had been torn off his gun's recoil-

---
[2] Capt J. McP. Catherall, VX32634; 2/24 Bn. Salesman and clerk; of Hawthorn, Vic; b. Balwyn, Vic, 18 Aug 1917.
[3] Cpl F. C. Aston, MM, WX7959; 24 A-Tk Coy. Optical mechanic; of Petersham, NSW; b. Urunga, NSW, 21 Aug 1916.
[4] L-Cpl H. J. Luck, WX7020; 24 A-Tk Coy. Jockey and reinsman; of Victoria Park, WA; b. London, 22 Jun 1915.
[5] Sgt E. L. R. Bridges, WX6892. 24 A-Tk Coy, 2/3 A-Tk Regt, 2/28 Bn, 20 Malaria Control Unit. Cleaner; of Perth, WA; b. London, 15 Nov 1913.
[6] Cpl F. E. Edmonds, VX18744; 26 A-Tk Coy. Boiler attendant; of Yallourn, Vic; b. Swindon, England, 22 Apr 1913. Died of wounds 2 May 1941.

spring cover and breech-block by fire from the tanks, Edmonds kept firing his gun, until he fell mortally wounded. Private Bilston[7] and Private Donaldson,[8] coming to his aid, then brought him in under fire to a neighbouring infantry post.

The German tank column, shedding one or two tanks damaged by gunfire, moved forward irresistibly until it ran straight onto the B1 minefield in front of Gebhardt's company. Within a few minutes 17 tanks had struck mines and come to a halt. There was a clearly marked gap in the field, where it was traversed by a well-worn track used by garrison vehicles. It had not been closed, but the German tanks did not attempt to nose their way through.

About a battalion of German infantry followed the tanks but, as they reached the perimeter defences, came under intense fire from the guns of the 51st Field Regiment firing at extreme range; the infantry advance was broken up. Some Germans opened fire on the posts but most appeared willing to leave the task of subduing them to the armour. About 15 minutes later more infantry were driven up in lorries about 2,000 yards out from the perimeter opposite Canty's company. There they left their vehicles and advanced between Posts S8 and S9. They too were subjected to gunfire by the 51st Field Regiment.

While the 51st was concentrating its fire on the infantry on the right, the 1st and 107th R.H.A. were engaging the tanks. Behind the first column of 40, which had become bogged down in the B1 minefield, a second containing 30 more was now moving among the perimeter posts east of Ras el Medauuar. One or two flame-throwers were towed by tanks, but they proved very vulnerable to fire. Each post was attacked in turn. As the head of the column reached a post, two or three tanks remained to stand over it while the rest moved on. Smoke was laid down continuously to cover the column's operations but seems to have impeded observation more from the east than from the north. The column was hotly engaged by the four anti-tank guns of "B" Troop (Lieutenant Hatch and Sergeant Carley) of "J" Battery of the 3rd R.H.A. Bombardier Lane's gun was overrun by seven tanks but four of these were later knocked out by another gun and their crews, as they emerged, were shot up by Gunner Deane with his Bren. Bombardier Rudd succeeded in scoring hits against six tanks in all and in keeping his gun in action though attacked on all sides.

Three British cruiser tanks of "B" Squadron advanced towards the German tanks in the area R6-R8, fired a few rounds and then withdrew behind a ridge. The enemy put down smoke. The German tanks soon afterwards withdrew, probably to marry up with the leading tank column, which had meanwhile withdrawn from the B1 minefield.

Part of the latter column had turned south as though to link up with the column moving along the perimeter; their route took them past a

---

[7] S-Sgt R. Bilston, VX29091. 26 A-Tk Coy, 2/24 Bn. Machine attendant; of Yallourn, Vic; b. Mirfield, England, 24 Nov 1915.

[8] Cpl G. A. Donaldson, VX23269. 26 A-Tk Coy, 2/48 Bn. Bus driver; of Williamstown, Vic; b. Williamstown, 26 Feb 1915.

gun of the 26th Anti-Tank Company commanded by Corporal Biggs,[9] who staunchly engaged them. They did not proceed, however, but turned back by the way they had come to rally near Ras el Medauuar. Meanwhile, near the El Adem Road, the enemy was laying a smoke screen in the region where Corporal Hewitt's patrol had ambushed the German demolition party.

Nobody knew what had happened to Spowers' infantry on the perimeter who had been out of touch throughout the night and through whose defences the German tanks had broken in such alarming numbers, nor was their story to become known until long after the siege of Tobruk had ended. What had in fact occurred was that after the barrage had ceased at 8.30 p.m. and the wire had been blown, at least two penetrations had been made close to Medauuar, one to the north of it, near S5, the other near R1. No infantry attack was made on the dominant Ras el Medauuar posts before daylight. Although the defences in the assault areas were subjected to heavy fire, the intruders preferred not to close, but penetrated between the posts and established themselves, in the one case, as we have seen, near Gebhardt's company, in the other near the hut just south of Point 187. The main bridgehead was between S3 and S7, made, as we now know, with the intention of taking Medauuar in rear. The enemy made use of the hours of darkness to lift the minefields in front of the perimeter, and to some extent within it, and to pull away the wire with tanks using grappling irons. When daylight came the post defenders were therefore exposed to the full force of the enemy assault with little more than small arms to defend themselves; there was no hope for the few men still holding out in the stone sangars hastily rebuilt after the night's bombardment. Some of the anti-tank gun positions of the 3rd R.H.A. (being outside the posts) had already been overrun as had most of 7 Platoon, who had occupied sangars. An account written later by Major Fell, whose company was responsible for the Ras el Medauuar area and a front of about 2,500 yards, conveys a vivid picture of what happened after dawn. His headquarters were in Post S2.

> By 0730 hrs the ground mist had cleared and I could see two German tanks surrounding S1. S1 was bombarded from a range of 100 to 200 yards by these tanks, and eventually I saw Walker[1] and his men being brought out of the pit. These tanks then moved on S2 and when within 200 yards they concentrated on the sangars and pits, blowing away the sandbags and destroying the sangars. Each tank had two or three infantrymen, riding in or on the tank. These men, under cover of the tank fire, eventually dropped grenades into the weapon-pit. We then surrendered and were taken out by the tank crews. . . . At this time there were no Italian infantry in sight and only a small number of Germans—mostly riding on tanks. . . . We lay behind Hill 209 about an hour. . . . We were then taken through the wire under tank escort. A large gap had been made in the wire due west of Hill 209 (Ras el Medauuar). . . . We were then moved to German Divisional HQ. . . . The German Divisional Staff were convinced that the fall of Tobruk would happen within a few hours. Later in the morning we were marched to . . . Acroma.

---

[9] Cpl J. W. Biggs, VX25008. (1st AIF: MG Corps.) 26 A-Tk Coy. Plumber; of Yarram, Vic; b. Yarram, 5 Jun 1897.
[1] Lt L. C. Walker, VX48625; 2/24 Bn. Farmer; of Loch, Vic; b. Dandenong, Vic, 11 Feb 1913.

General Rommel, who had visited Kirchheim's headquarters about an hour later, saw these men setting off on their march to Acroma. He wrote of them:

> Shortly afterwards a batch of some fifty or sixty Australian prisoners was marched off close behind us—immensely big and powerful men, who without question represented an *élite* formation of the British Empire, a fact that was also evident in battle. Enemy resistance was as stubborn as ever and violent actions were being fought at many points.[2]

The confused and violent battle soon enveloped more than four miles of the perimeter on either side of Ras el Medauuar. The main ordeal fell on the infantry in the perimeter posts and the few anti-tank gunners still unsubdued. There was no overhead cover above the fire-bays and communication trenches of the posts. Fire directed from the tanks standing over them damaged the automatic weapons and drove most of the defenders below ground. But although the posts were neutralised many of their garrisons fought back for some time.

The post weapons, additional to the personal weapons (rifles and grenades) normally carried by infantrymen, usually consisted of about two light or medium machine-guns with, in some cases, a light mortar or a so-called anti-tank rifle. After S1 and S2 were taken other posts had similar experiences. Some surrendered after their gun emplacements had been blasted in; in others the garrison held off the enemy until their ammunition was exhausted. In turn Posts S3, R, R1, R2 and R3 were captured but Post R4, where Lieutenant Mair had his headquarters, held out until after midday. Farther north, S5 in the centre of the main penetration was overrun at first light but S6 (Lieutenant Kelly[3]), where Captain Canty had established his headquarters, was not surrendered until 9 a.m., when 17 out of the garrison of 26 had become casualties. S4 (Corporal Deering[4]) resisted until after 11 a.m.

Post S7, which was on the northern edge of the main enemy bridgehead, was reported by the Germans during the battle as one of the most obstinate points of resistance, inflicting on units attacking it 50 per cent casualties—in some instances more. It was manned by eleven men under Corporal Thomson,[5] who were armed with two Bren guns and a rifle. They were surrounded during the night when the penetration was made, and next day held the enemy off until their ammunition was exhausted. Grenades thrown into the underground shelters enforced their surrender about 11 a.m.

As the German armour moved on, officers of the British artillery continually moved about the battlefield directing fire upon both tanks and infantry concentrations—Captain Clapham of the 51st Field Regiment in his 8-cwt truck, Captains May and Goschen of the 1st R.H.A. and Captain G. J. S. Slinn of the 107th, to name some that are recalled—while others

---
[2] *The Rommel Papers*, p. 132.
[3] Lt M. J. Kelly, VX48564; 2/24 Bn. Law student; of Kew, Vic; b. Warburton, Vic, 7 Oct 1919.
[4] Cpl R. T. Deering, VX28869; 2/24 Bn. Baker; of Camberwell, Vic; b. Camberwell, 13 Aug 1914.
[5] Cpl A. Thomson, VX31033; 2/24 Bn. Process worker; of Toorak, Vic; b. Edinburgh, Scotland, 11 Oct 1908.

no less staunch continued to observe and to direct the guns from near the edge of the turmoil area, like Captain Hay who remained all day at Post R14 and who directed the fire of the "B/O" Battery against the first tank assault. The Axis air force dominated the skies above the battlefield and was continually active that day—in one attack on "B" Troop of the 1st R.H.A. five men were killed and four wounded, two mortally.

The burden of decision now pressed heavily on Morshead. In the threatened sector he had one battalion uncommitted, the 2/48th Battalion, in reserve on the Blue Line, where its primary function was to provide the extreme need of defence in depth behind the thinly-held perimeter. If the battalion was to hold the second line firm, it could not be used to counter-attack at the break-through point. The effective infantry strength of Morshead's fortress reserve was four battalions—the 18th Brigade of three infantry battalions, and the 2/1st Pioneer Battalion partly committed to providing a second line of defence in Brigadier Murray's sector. Morshead's tank strength was 35 infantry and cruiser tanks in varying states of mechanical fitness: in the 1st Royal Tanks were 17 cruisers, organised into a headquarters (3 tanks), and 2 squadrons—one of 5 tanks, one of 9; the 7th Royal Tanks had 18 infantry tanks in 2 squadrons. There were also the light tanks of the 3rd Hussars, which were, however, too lightly armoured for effective employment in other than reconnaissance roles. The space-time factor required two hours to move a reserve battalion into the battle area.

On the first irruption of the enemy tanks, the cruisers of the 1st Royal Tanks had been ordered to move to the area just to the east of the southern end of the B1 minefield for possible participation in a counter-attack, while one of the infantry-tank squadrons, with two troops of the 3rd Hussars attached, had been ordered forward to engage the enemy tanks advancing from Ras el Medauuar; but the latter were recalled without making contact when the enemy turned back from the B1 minefield (though the light-tank troops were pushed out on either flank for observation). In fact, the very minefields which had stopped the enemy were an obstacle to the deployment of the garrison's tanks.

Morshead was not prepared to commit his reserves until he had more information. He was not yet convinced that the first enemy thrusts were more than a diversionary demonstration designed to draw off his reserves before the main assault was made elsewhere.[6] The dawn tactical reconnaissance from the air had been delayed by morning fog. When the first reports were received, they were indeed alarming: 200 enemy tanks were said to be approaching from the direction of Acroma in the west. Morshead, however, doubted their accuracy and called for another reconnaissance. If the first reconnaissance had over-estimated the enemy tank strength, the second under-estimated it, for only 40 tanks were then reported. More had already been sighted within the perimeter. Morshead summoned Wootten to his headquarters: together they assessed the reports of the developing onslaught.

---

[6] Statement based on interview with Sir Leslie Morshead in 1954.

The German tanks that had retired from the B1 minefield to reassemble behind Ras el Medauuar, re-formed and thrust south-eastwards, followed by troop transporters, to continue the process of rolling up the perimeter posts. Two or three tanks peeled off at each post to shoot in the weapon-pits. Then stick grenades were thrown right into the posts. Although numbers of troop-carrying vehicles were sighted, the enemy infantry in the main failed to follow behind their tanks in this thrust to take full advantage of their dominance. A passage from *The Rommel Papers* may explain why:

> With British artillery fire sweeping the whole area, the Italians crept under their vehicles and resisted all their officers' attempts to get them out again.[7]

The head of the column of tanks pushed on through Lieutenant Mair's platoon area (Posts R2, 3 and 4), past Posts R5 and 6 to the east of Post R7, and there formed a semi-circle facing eastwards. Other tanks began breaking down the perimeter wire by dragging cable stretched between two tanks across it. Some infantry advanced on Post R5 under cover of a small ditch. Corporal Gazzard[8] stood up above his weapon-pit to engage them, a living symbol of utmost valour, until swift death ended his moment of uncoveted heroic distinction. Posts R5 (Sergeant Poidevin[9]), R6 (Captain Bird) and R7 (Corporal Jones[1]) held out.

Meanwhile about 300 enemy infantry who had followed the first tank thrust into the perimeter were being mercilessly harassed both by the artillery and by the machine-guns of a detachment of the Royal Northumberland Fusiliers stationed at Point 171. Many dispersed and sought cover in the area to the west of Bianca, a white mound that lay astride the northernmost of the two tracks leading into Pilastrino. Other infantry of the attacking force were digging in near the breach in the perimeter north of Ras el Medauuar, and farther north above the escarpment.

About 11.30 a.m. the now stationary spearhead of the enemy tank force, comprising about 25 tanks, was attacked by the cruiser tanks of "C" Squadron, 1st R.T.R., with "B" Squadron in support—10 cruiser tanks in all. Several hits were scored on the intruding tanks at a range of from 700 to 800 yards. Then one medium and two light German tanks were seen to catch fire. The enemy put down smoke, which halted the engagement; but one of the British squadron commander's tanks was destroyed and two of the cruisers were hit as they turned right along the edge of the minefield to withdraw. The guns of the 1st and 107th R.H.A. then concentrated on the German armour, which apparently decided that to remain longer in such an exposed position was unwise. The tanks withdrew behind Ras el Medauuar.

Like so many battles it was a confused fight, of which no coherent picture could be obtained at the time. Tanks and gunfire had cut all tele-

---

[7] *The Rommel Papers*, p. 132.
[8] Cpl L. H. Gazzard, VX27439; 2/24 Bn. Schoolteacher; of Bostock's Creek, Vic; b. Lismore, Vic, 21 Sep 1914. Killed in action 1 May 1941.
[9] Sgt G. G. Poidevin, VX29686; 2/24 Bn. Labourer; of Corowa, NSW; b. Corowa, 30 Mar 1917.
[1] Cpl K. S. Jones, VX29657; 2/24 Bn. Labourer; of Corowa, Vic; b. Finley, NSW, 23 Nov 1918.

phone lines in the penetration area. Smoke from shells and bombs and burning vehicles, smoke screens deliberately laid and dust churned up by tanks and trucks were daubed across a blurred landscape indeterminately shimmering under the spell of a mirage through which the black forms of moving tanks could be but vaguely apprehended. As the day advanced, a hot wind got up and lifted more dust.

By the end of the morning the attackers firmly held both the high ground immediately surrounding the Ras el Medauuar feature and about 2,000 yards of the perimeter on either side. They were astride the east-west track that passed out of the perimeter west of Point 187 and the south-west track leading out past Point 179; they controlled the track leading from Point 187 to Point 179, and had established themselves firmly from the junction of tracks near Point 187 northwards to the Water Tower at Point 178. Seven tanks had been pushed out about 600 yards along the track which from there led down the two escarpments to the coast and were in a position to shoot up anything that came up over the escarpment towards the penetration area. Axis infantry had dug themselves in outside the perimeter along the second escarpment and thence northwards to the west of the perimeter to safeguard against a flanking counter-attack.

Soon after midday the attackers exerted pressure on both flanks to extend the width of their breach. On the northern flank a small group of tanks outside the perimeter thrust past Post S7 until, near S13 and S15, they were bombarded by the 51st Field Regiment just before 1 p.m. and forced to withdraw. Infantry in trucks followed the tanks, dismounted and attacked the posts from S7 northwards, but with little success against staunch defence. Lieutenant Christie,[2] with headquarters in Post S8 and a forward section in the neighbouring S9, though surrounded, hung on. So did Lieutenant Rosel whose platoon, on the extreme right of the battalion front, held the three posts north of S9 (Posts S10, S11 and S11A). Rosel had taken charge of the company after Captain Canty's surrender had been enforced earlier in the morning. When Rosel found his ammunition stocks dwindling he sent to the neighbouring 2/23rd Battalion for replenishment. About 2.30 p.m. a party led by Corporal Jackson[3] was sent out and delivered several thousand rounds of small-arms ammunition to Rosel in S10. Rosel wrote a message reporting the situation and gave it to Corporal Jackson to take back. His report vividly describes the state of the battle there:

To   D Company 2/23rd Battalion
From   14 Platoon 2/24th Battalion

Received ammunition. No idea how 15 Platoon and Company Headquarters are faring. 13 Platoon lost forward section Post S7. Enemy have occupied this post in strength. Also have light gun on ridge above this post making holding of this platoon area untenable. Enemy also have mortar in position on ridge. Propose

---

[2] Capt J. S. Christie, VX48605; 2/24 Bn. Farmer; of Katunga, Vic; b. Numurkah, Vic, 23 Feb 1913. Died of wounds 13 Jul 1942.
[3] WO1 J. W. Jackson, VX29824; 2/23 Bn. Manufacturer; of Upway, Vic; b. Elsternwick, Vic, 11 Aug 1918.

withdraw men from 8 and 9 and place them in 10 and 11A with my men. I have no communications with anyone outside. There appear to be some two hundred enemy across the wadi from S11. Came up in transport and are digging themselves in. Post S8 have 5 German prisoners, one being badly wounded. Wire in front of my position worthless. In 10 I have 1 Breda, plenty of ammunition, 1 Bren, 4,000 rounds. In 11A 2 Brens with total of 2,000 rounds. Post 11—this includes your section—1 Bren with 3,000, 1 Breda 3,000, 1 Iti mortar with 300 bombs, only 50 ballistite rounds, 1 Anti-Tank Rifle, 220 rounds. Another 2 days rations still on hand. Could you possibly contact ISKO [2/24 Battalion headquarters] and hand on this information. Hope you can understand this. Viva la battalion. The position tonight is going to be very serious and if some reinforcements could be produced we would stand a fair chance. ISKO might know how our Company HQ and 15 Platoon stand. Here's hoping.
Thanks for your assistance

    J. Rosel   1540 hrs   1 May

Keeping one of your Brens.

The main weight of the attack next fell on the defenders' left flank where the Axis command was renewing the eastward thrust along the perimeter to broaden the gap. Post R5 was surrounded, its weapon-pits blown in and its surrender enforced about 1 p.m. Groups of infantry were pushed through a gap between R5 and R6 and, accompanied by tanks, advanced eastwards. The 1st and 107th R.H.A. engaged and compelled the infantry to scatter; but the tanks pushed on. Posts R6 (Captain Bird) and R7 (Corporal Jones) remained in Australian hands. Reports were received about 1.30 p.m. that the tanks had been attacking R8 and R9. Two squadrons of cruisers of the 1st Royal Tanks were sent forward to observe, but not engage closely. The German tanks, however, had then withdrawn to a hull-down position about a mile to the west though enemy infantry were endeavouring, in the face of heavy fire, to infiltrate between R5 and R6. About 3.15 p.m., a number of enemy tanks made another eastward attack along the perimeter and were soon reported to be massing between R8 and R10. The British tank force was ordered to engage them. A composite force of 7 cruiser tanks (1st Royal Tanks) and 5 infantry tanks (7th Royal Tanks) was organised, while the remaining cruisers (of "C" Squadron) were sent to the top of the Pilastrino pass to guard the approaches to fortress headquarters.

The renewed pressure by ground forces was accompanied by heavy dive-bombing attacks on the garrison artillery. At 1 p.m. guns of the 51st Field Regiment were the target. At 1.30 p.m. both troops of "B/O" Battery (1st R.H.A.) were bombed and seven men killed or mortally wounded. At 2 p.m. "E" Troop of the same regiment, at the junction of the El Adem and Bardia Roads, was bombed, with a loss of three lives and serious injury to a fourth man.

In the early afternoon Morshead had decided to mount an infantry counter-attack with tank support with the object of recovering the breach in the Medauuar sector. It was to be made in mid-afternoon and the task was assigned to the 2/48th Battalion. It is not certain when Colonel Windeyer was first warned of this nor is there a record of what he was told; but his first impression was that he was to assist Colonel Spowers' battalion in a counter-attack and at 2 p.m. he telephoned Spowers to see if it would be possible to arrange a joint meeting with the tank commanders to plan the operation.

At 2.30 p.m. Lieut-Colonel Verrier's[4] 2/10th Battalion was warned that it would be required to relieve Windeyer's battalion to release the latter, and at 3 p.m. Tovell ordered Windeyer to visit Spowers' headquarters and there discuss with the tank commander a proposal to counter-attack for the perimeter posts lost on Spowers' front. When Windeyer reached Spowers' headquarters, however, he learned that some 20 minutes earlier Spowers had received a message cancelling the counter-attack because of the engagement of the armour against the eastward-thrusting German tanks.

The mixed British tank force of seven cruisers and five infantry tanks (Matildas) was now moving forward under orders to drive back the German tanks. The armoured brigade's infantry-tank force (7th Royal Tanks) had been divided into two squadrons (Dyne I and Dyne II) each of nine tanks, but the afternoon's operational tasks appear to have been assigned to only one of these (Dyne I), which by that time had been reduced to five tanks, one having been damaged in a dive-bombing attack, and three immobilised by mechanical breakdown. Small as this mixed tank force of cruisers and Matildas was, after a squadron had been detached to guard the approach to the Pilastrino pass, its striking power was further attenuated by a decision of the commander to leave all the cruisers except the headquarters tanks in reserve at R14 because some of them were reporting mechanical trouble. The decision was probably also influenced by the fact that the action in battle of the cruisers and the infantry tanks could not be closely coordinated because there was no radio-telephonic communication between them.

The plan was simple. The striking force, now reduced to five Matildas and the three cruisers of regimental headquarters, was to advance along the perimeter between the front and inner row of perimeter posts straight towards the enemy. Posts R11 and 12 were reached about 4 p.m. and it was found that the Australians were still in occupation: they had not been closely engaged. The Matildas then led the advance to Posts R8 and 9, about 1,000 yards distant, from which region the German tanks had withdrawn towards Medauuar a short time before. Here again the Australian garrisons were still hanging on, though many of the men were badly wounded. Leaving two of his infantry tanks at R8 (Lieutenant Gray[5]), the tank commander then advanced to R6 with six tanks, three Matildas and three cruisers, the Matildas leading. Gray accompanied them, to report to Captain Bird. Again it was found that the Australian garrison was holding out. Four German light tanks could then be seen inside the perimeter wire at Post R5 while one German medium tank was visible

---

[4] Col A. D. Verrier, DCM, ED, SX1445. (1st AIF: 50 Bn.) CO 2/10 Bn 1939-41; training appts 1941-43; Inspector Military Prisons and Detention Barracks LHQ 1943-45. Public servant; of Unley, SA; b. Goodwood, SA, 11 Feb 1896.

[5] Lt R. J. Gray, VX46535; 2/24 Bn. Horticulturist; of Red Cliffs, Vic; b. Hornsby, NSW, 17 Aug 1914.

at R4. A staff car drove up to the light tanks; four men—evidently the tank commanders—dismounted and entered the tanks. A British cruiser tank advanced towards the German medium at R4. Fourteen German medium tanks came up from the rear and opened fire at 1,000 yards' range. The Matildas moved round to the west of R6 and advanced to meet them. The British commander's cruiser was hit at R6, the crew climbed on to the outside of the adjutant's tank and the two cruisers still mobile returned to R8 where orders were given to the two Matildas left there to join the three already engaged. But the forward tanks now returned, one having been damaged and all its crew except the driver killed. Another force of German tanks engaged from the flank. The five British infantry tanks then fought a rearguard action, greatly outnumbered but effectively supported by the British gunners. Only one cruiser and two Matildas got back to R14. Two Matilda tanks and two cruisers had been lost; one Matilda had been damaged, but was later recovered.

While the British tanks had been moving forward to meet the German thrust, Captain Provan's[6] company of the 2/1st Pioneer Battalion, which had been attached to the 2/15th Battalion, had been sent forward to Posts R8, 9 and 10, which had been reported abandoned earlier in the afternoon. He reached the area about 6 p.m. As Provan was coming forward Sergeant Thurman[7] withdrew the garrison of Post R8 (of whom 8 out of 12 had been wounded) to R10, and the garrison of R9 came back to R11. When Provan arrived, Post R9 was reoccupied and Posts R9, 10 and 11 were reinforced but R8 was left unmanned. The wounded of the 2/24th were evacuated. Provan's company then began to prepare a switch line east of the minefield, which was to become the new front line.

Disengaging from the battle with the withdrawing British tanks, the German tanks turned to give support to their infantry closing in, as night fell, on Posts R6 and 7. Both posts had been under heavy fire throughout the afternoon. R7 managed to hold out but R6, where the automatic weapons had been smashed and the garrison of 14 men under Captain Bird had suffered more than 50 per cent casualties, succumbed at 7.30 p.m. R7 was then completely isolated in an overrun area, cut off from water, food and ammunition. Corporal Jones, the post commander, has described the experiences of the garrison in a report written for the historian of the 2/24th:

> That night the slightest move would bring a flare over our position and the area would be lit like day. We passed a night of merry hell as the pounding went on.

Next morning, Jones made "a hurried neck-jerking survey" just after daybreak and saw infantry assembling for an attack. Powerless to hit back, he surrendered his men. After they had been taken back, General Rommel spoke to them. "For you the war is over," he said, "and I wish you good luck."

---

[6] Capt W. R. Provan, QX6283; 2/1 Pnr Bn. Master builder; of Brisbane; b. Cairns, Qld, 17 May 1897. Died 7 Apr 1963.

[7] Maj E. B. Thurman, MM, VX31583. 2/24 Bn, 2/3 Docks Coy, HQ 3 Docks Gp. Railways fireman; of Bendigo and Melbourne, Vic; b. Brunswick, Vic, 30 Mar 1913.

The pressure on the northern flank during the afternoon had been less severe than in the south, where the main tank thrust had been made. The enemy appeared to be in command of the perimeter area from Ras el Medauuar for about a mile north to the top of the higher escarpment, where Posts S6 and S7 were reported to be in enemy hands. When Colonel Evans had received Corporal Jackson's report of his patrol to S10 to deliver ammunition to Lieutenant Rosel, he had sought Tovell's permission to mount a counter-attack. At 5 p.m. Tovell granted permission to stage a limited operation after dark to restore the position below the escarpment. Evans' battalion was not to push on up the escarpment, because this would conflict with operations planned for Windeyer's battalion.

Meanwhile at 4 p.m. Morshead had set off for Tovell's headquarters to issue orders for a counter-attack in the centre of the area of penetration. At 4.20 p.m. he stated his requirements to Brigadier Tovell: the 2/48th Battalion was to counter-attack to restore the perimeter defence line but was first to be relieved in its defensive positions on the Blue Line by the 2/10th Battalion, which was then located at the junction of the Bardia and El Adem Roads. Brigadier Murray was given command of the eastern flank of the breach and the 2/9th Battalion (near Pilastrino) was placed under his orders. The attack was to be mounted before night fell.

When Windeyer arrived back at the 2/48th Battalion headquarters after visiting Spowers, he was informed that his battalion was to mount a counter-attack at dusk that evening and that written orders were on their way. The orders were received soon afterwards, at 4.45 p.m. Windeyer was dismayed. He requested Tovell by telephone to postpone the operation until the next morning, pointing out that the battalion was distributed in defensive positions over a wide front from which they must first be relieved before being assembled to attack. Tovell told him that Morshead would speak to him. Writing later, Windeyer described the conversation.

> The G.O.C. said "Listen Windeyer, it is important that this be done and done today." I said it was impossible. He asked why. I said the troops were spread over miles and could never be assembled and got to the start-line in time. He said he would send vehicles to move them. So I said, that being so, we would do our best. I asked for tank support.

Morshead informed Windeyer that the tanks were to engage enemy on the southern flank at 5 p.m. but would thereafter be available to protect the battalion's left flank. Morshead also told Windeyer to put down one company in position south of the Acroma Road, facing south.

Windeyer's orders were to retake that part of the perimeter which the Axis forces had seized, from S7 to the road running through R5, a span of about 4,500 yards. The reserve company of Spowers' battalion was attached for the operation. Setting these objectives involved the capture of some 12 heavily fortified posts on a most extended front, a task that one battalion could scarcely achieve in an improvised operation except against a demoralised or unresisting foe.

After complying with the fortress commander's direction to establish a company in a firm position south of the Acroma Road, Windeyer would have available for his formidable task only four infantry companies, including the reserve company of the 2/24th Battalion. There was barely time to assemble the troops for the attack. The need was for a simple plan that could be conveyed by brief orders and executed without reconnaissance and detailed planning. In substance Windeyer's plan was that his companies which, before being relieved by the 2/24th, had held the part of the perimeter to be retaken, should attack in the areas they had held. The Acroma Road was to be the axis of the attack on the right. Captain Woods'[8] company, with Gebhardt's company of the 2/24th Battalion taking up a position on its left, facing south, was to advance on the right of the Acroma Road to take Posts S7 to S3 (including the original enemy bridgehead), attacking first for the Water Tower area above the southern escarpment. Loughrey's company was to attack south of the road and retake the posts from the left shoulder of Medauuar to the road running southwest. Of the other two companies, Windeyer kept one as a reserve attacking force, to follow behind Woods' company with a view to reinforcing the final assault on

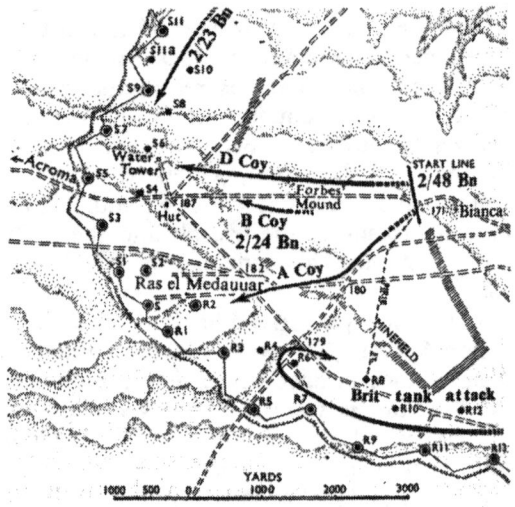

The counter-attack, 1st May

Medauuar; the other was sent to Forbes' Mound to occupy the old reserve company positions and face south, thus fulfilling Morshead's instruction. Little information of enemy dispositions was available except some afforded by the 2/23rd Battalion, though it could be taken for granted that the enemy would hold the fortified perimeter posts in strength. The artillery plan allowed for concentrations in front of the perimeter during the 20 minutes preceding the attack; shelling of the perimeter posts while the assault troops would be approaching them from the start-line; and finally shelling in areas the Axis forces might use as forming-up places for counter-attack. The start-time was fixed for 7.15 p.m.

There was no time for reconnaissance; there was barely sufficient to complete the relief and to move to the pre-attack assembly area near Bianca. As happens not seldom in battle crises, the hastily summoned transport did not arrive on time. Vehicles of the 2/10th Battalion had

---

[8] Capt H. A. Woods, SX10311; 2/48 Bn. Letterpress machinist; of Malvern, SA; b. Ororoo, SA, 31 Aug 1910. Died of wounds 2 May 1941.

to be commandeered. When at last the battalion was embussed and under way, low-flying enemy aircraft attacked the convoy, vehicles dispersed, one truck was destroyed, troops debussed; more time was lost.

The battalion arrived, in a dust-storm, late at its start-line, hastily dismounted, and moved off to attack into the glare of a fiery setting sun. The men ran into heavy shell fire almost at once, but pressed on, leaving casualties behind. The main thrust was on the right; Loughrey's company on the left, following a different axis, moved off on its own along a track known as Pirie Street towards Medauuar. The artillery program had begun at the appointed time, but the infantry were at least 20 minutes behind schedule and thus lost irretrievably the benefit of close artillery support.

On the right Captain Woods' company moved out along a valley north of the Acroma Road, which was defiladed from most of the enemy posts. Captain Tucker's company followed 600 yards in rear. Woods intended to capture the right posts first and then exploit southwards towards Medauuar. As his company came within range of the second line of perimeter posts, they were pinned to the ground by heavy machine-gun fire from the area of the Water Tower and water points. It was becoming dark.

Windeyer had noticed that Woods' company was tending to veer to the right, so he ordered Tucker to attack the enemy in the Water Tower area and close the gap. While Tucker's company was coming up, Woods' was striving to get forward. He sent his rear platoon, under Lieutenant Robbins,[9] to find a way round under cover of a ridge following the Acroma Road, but Robbins came under fire from S10, which was believed to be still held by Australian troops. (In fact, although S10 was still holding out, it had been closely invested by Italian infantry.) Lieutenant Isaksson's carrier platoon, going forward with the object of locating enemy machine-guns by drawing their fire, was checked by anti-tank guns and by fire from damaged tanks immobilised in the minefield.

On the left of the attack, Major Loughrey's company had set off under heavy shell fire towards the minefield. Knowing that the plan included tank support on the left flank, the men were pleased to obtain glimpses through the dust of six tanks moving westwards towards them. The tanks followed, and came up within 30 yards on the left, when it was seen that they carried German flags. With the exception of one burst, the tanks did not fire, but filed past the company's left forward platoon, commanded by Lieutenant Morphett.[1] Perhaps, owing to poor visibility, they were uncertain of the nationality of the infantry. When Loughrey's men had got to within 200 yards of Point 209, however, the tanks wheeled round and opened fire from in front. The infantry went to ground. Sergeant Farrell's[2] platoon, which was bringing up the rear, engaged with Boyes

---
[9] Capt P. Robbins, SX10325; 2/48 Bn. Salesman; of Malvern, SA; b. Adelaide, 5 Apr 1920. Killed in action 31 Oct 1942.
[1] Maj H. C. Morphett, MC, SX9990; 2/48 Bn. Oil company representative; of Burra, SA; b. Sydney, 31 Mar 1906.
[2] Lt G. J. Farrell, SX8276; 2/48 Bn. Diesel engineer; of Croydon, Vic; b. Melbourne, 14 Mar 1914. (Correct name G. J. Jackson.)

anti-tank rifle but with no effect. Loughrey sent a runner back to Windeyer with a message that the company was held up by enemy tanks. There was no cover from the fire of the German tanks, no effective weapon to combat them, no British armour. The company found itself in a hopeless, demoralising situation. The forward platoons came back while Farrell's men continued to engage; then the whole company withdrew.

Meanwhile, on the right, when Robbins' attempt to get forward had failed, Woods had sent a runner back to Windeyer to tell him that the company was held up. On the way back the runner gave a report of the situation to Captain Tucker, who then moved up his company behind Woods. In due course the runner reached Windeyer. Windeyer reported to Tovell that the battalion's counter-attack was not making progress. Tovell in turn reported the situation to Morshead and recommended that the attack be discontinued for the time being but resumed at first light. Morshead, however, urged that the attack should be continued. Any postponement, he said, would greatly assist the enemy.

Tucker's company was now coming in behind Woods' company, and "B" Company of the 2/24th, relieved by Captain Forbes' company of the 2/48th, was advancing along the Acroma Road. Woods was making a valiant effort to move his men forward by short bounds, keeping ahead himself and calling each platoon forward in turn. Lieutenant Larkins'[3] turn came first, but his platoon ran into fire as it moved forward. Larkins was wounded, two men of his headquarters were killed, other men were hit, and the platoon became inert. Next it was the turn of 17 Platoon under Sergeant Tonkin,[4] who had assumed command that morning; but Tonkin was killed as the platoon attempted to get forward, and one of the sections was badly cut up and disorganised.

Tucker, his company now in position close behind Woods' company, came forward and conferred with Woods. They decided to press on, Tucker lending Woods one of his platoons (under Lieutenant Bryant[5]) to compensate for the loss of part of Larkins' platoon. Then Sergeant Legg,[6] in charge of the remaining two sections of 18 Platoon, took another forward bound, which met with greater success. They were followed by 17 Platoon, now in charge of Corporal Evans,[7] with Robbins' platoon and Tucker's company not far in rear.

Woods then decided to rush the enemy machine-gun nest in a bayonet charge. With his company sergeant-major, Noble, and two runners, he crawled forward to locate it. Robbins moved his platoon up. Woods got within earshot of the enemy, but in the dark was still unable to locate the positions. The Germans called on the Australians to surrender and one of Woods' men hurled back abuse. The enemy replied with heavy

---

[3] Maj G. D. Larkins, SX10332; 2/48 Bn. Clerk; of St Peters, SA; b. Adelaide, 22 Oct 1920.
[4] Sgt L. K. Tonkin, SX6911; 2/48 Bn. Farmer; of Minlaton, SA; b. Minlaton, 16 Nov 1915. Killed in action 1 May 1941.
[5] Lt-Col D. Bryant, MBE, MC, SX10329; 2/48 Bn. Clerk; of Seacliff, SA; b. Kapunda, SA, 24 Feb 1918.
[6] Lt F. H. Legg. SX9652; 2/48 Bn; war correspondent for ABC 1943-45. Journalist and broadcaster; of Adelaide; b. Deal, England, 26 Jun 1906. Accidentally killed 30 Mar 1966.
[7] Sgt L. R. Evans, SX7979; 2/48 Bn. Stockman; of Keyneton, SA; b. Keyneton, 8 Oct 1919. Killed in action 22 Jul 1942.

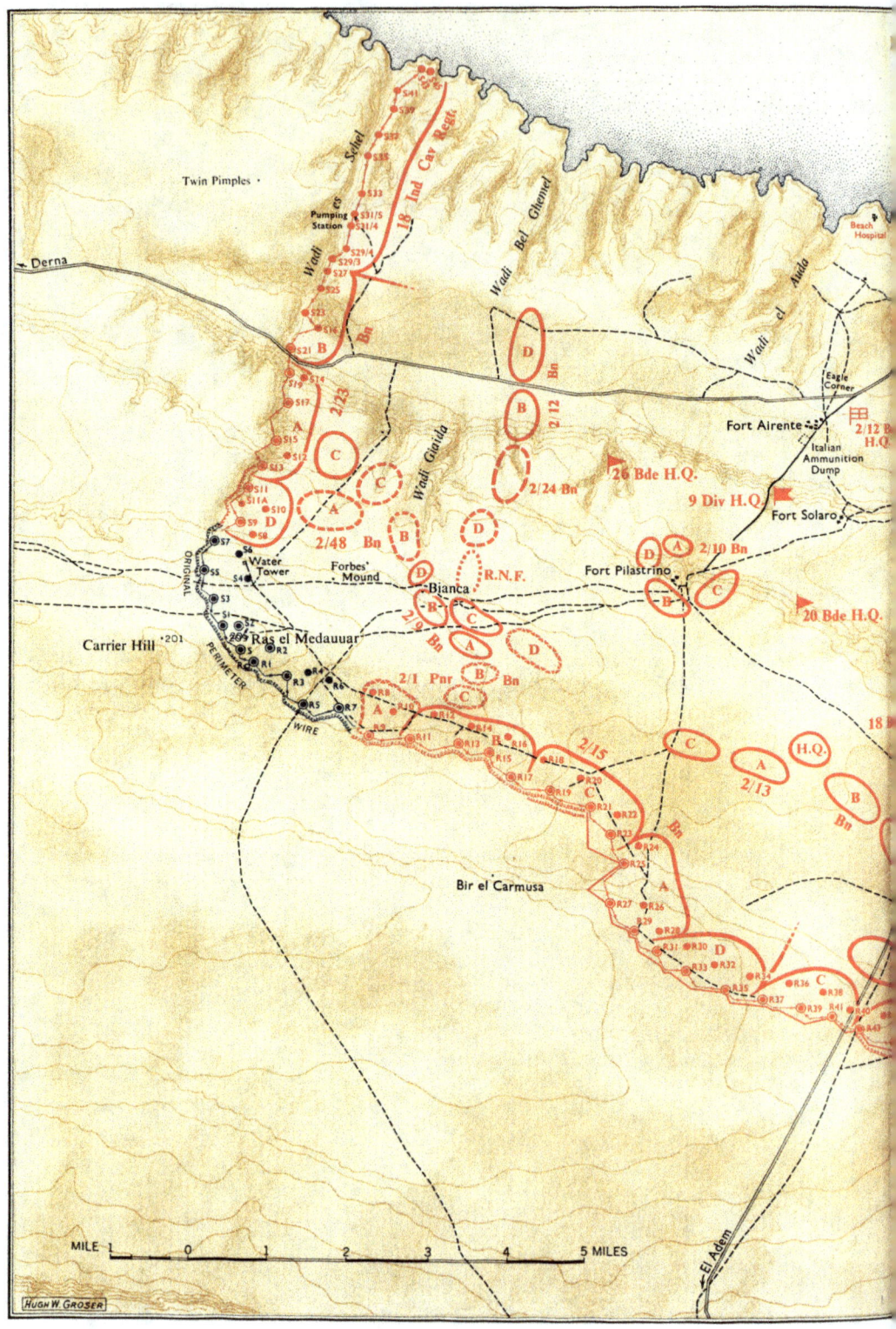

Dispositions, after

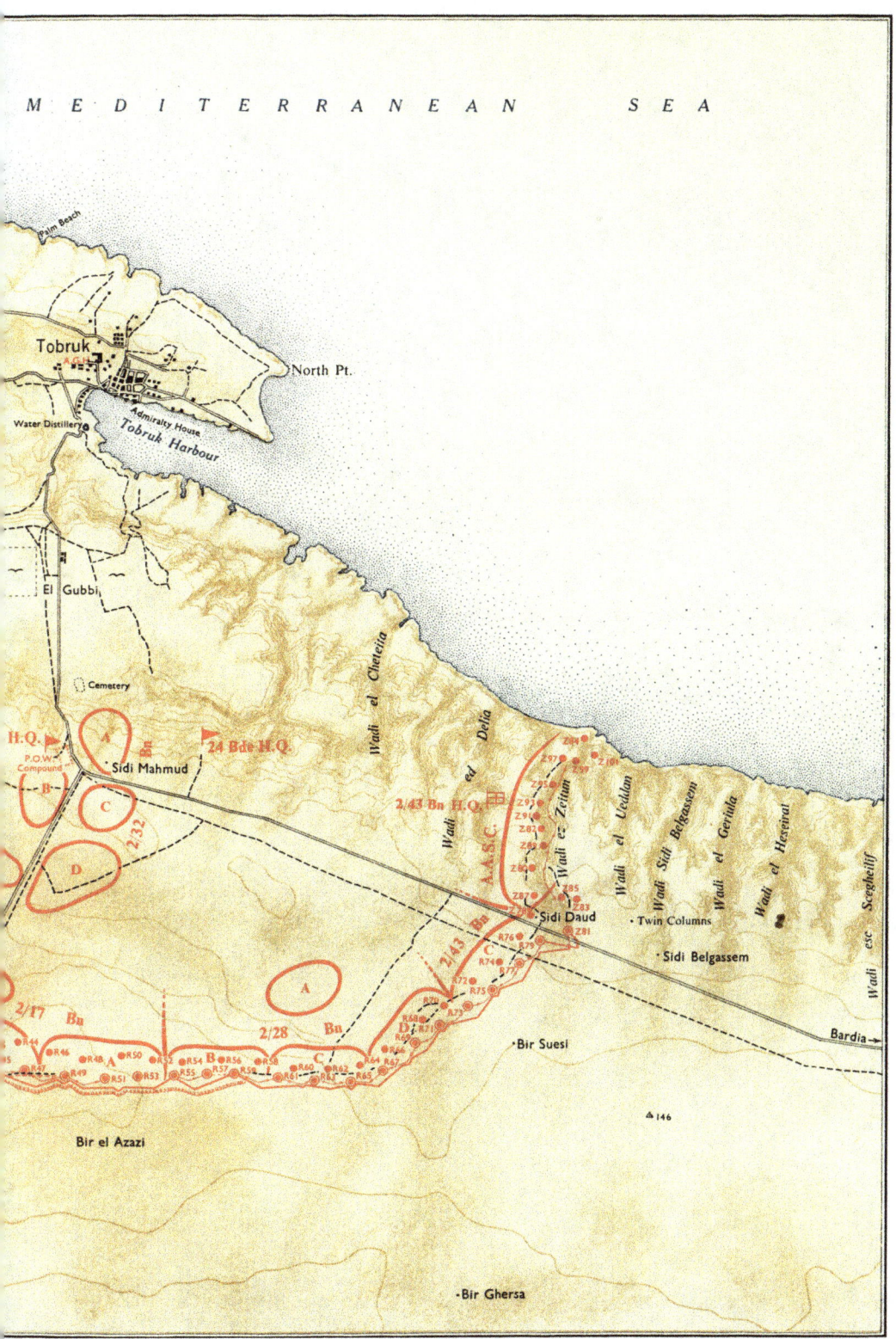
noon 5th May 1941

fire. Woods and one of his runners, Private Carvosso,[8] were severely wounded. Woods sent Carvosso back. Noble came to Woods' assistance but Woods told him to go back to Robbins with a message that in Woods' opinion the company could not be got forward: Robbins was authorised to withdraw the company if Tucker agreed. Robbins and Tucker conferred and decided (about 9.30 p.m.) to withdraw. Then Robbins and Noble went forward again and, while the enemy, about 100 yards away, were calling upon them to surrender, rescued Woods. But Woods was mortally wounded. "B" Company of the 2/24th Battalion, which had attacked along the Acroma Road, had been pinned down by machine-gun fire after advancing 600 yards.

More success was achieved by Captain Malloch's company of the 2/23rd in operations below the escarpment on the right of Woods' company. Moving southwards with carriers on the flank at the time when Woods' company was struggling to get forward, Malloch's men first made contact with S11 and S10 and engaged near-by enemy machine-gun nests. Moving on to S8 they found the post garrison's fighting strength reduced to five. Next they found S9 to be surrounded. Attacking in the face of mortar and machine-gun fire, Lieutenant Bowden's[9] platoon overran the investing troops, killing many and capturing 36 Italian prisoners in the anti-tank ditch round the post. They found that Lieutenant Christie and five men were still holding out in the post. Five men of Bowden's platoon were wounded.

Windeyer reported the failure of his attack to Tovell and then spoke to Lloyd, who told him to assemble his battalion in rear of Bianca. Morshead had been forewarned of likely failure by reports through artillery channels from the forward observation officers and had already reached a decision that the perimeter line should be re-formed in the area of the breach. When Windeyer's report was received, Morshead summoned Brigadier Tovell and Colonel Verrier to headquarters to make plans for a switch line to hold the gap between S8 and Bianca and thence to link up with the switch line already being formed by Brigadier Murray on the eastern side of the penetration. On the right the 2/23rd Battalion was to hold the original perimeter as far south as S8; the 2/48th Battalion was to link S8 with the right of the reserve company position of the 2/24th and the Blue Line; and the 2/10th Battalion was to link up between the left of the 2/24th and the new 20th Brigade switch line. "B" Company of the 2/24th had returned to its original position after the counter-attack, there relieving Forbes' company which rejoined the 2/48th.

In about 24 hours of operations Rommel's forces had seized and obtained a firm hold on an arc of the perimeter of Tobruk spanning three miles and a half, including its highest point; they had captured or killed about

---

[8] Pte R. W. Carvosso, SX7888; 2/48 Bn. Junior clerk; of Glenelg, SA; b. Glenelg, 26 Sep 1921.
[9] Lt J. N. Bowden, VX45357; 2/23 Bn. Farmer; of Won Won, Vic; b. Sale, Vic, 22 Dec 1907. Killed in action 17 May 1941.

one-half of one of the garrison's battalions; of the garrison's small tank force they had destroyed four tanks; they had sliced off a part of the front but had failed to carve right through the defence. How did this achievement compare with Axis plans?

At the end of April General Rommel had at his command a force of all arms which, both in striking power and in the effectiveness of its command organisation, had no match in Africa. It must have galled him to contemplate that the Middle East and the Suez Canal were prizes only just beyond his reach. His armour could not strike into the heart of the Middle East so long as Tobruk held out; his supply line would be too attenuated. Tobruk was therefore denying him the most rewarding use of his strongest arm. Even if the supply problem could be temporarily solved, where were the infantry necessary to consolidate his hold on any territory a strong armoured thrust might overrun? If his infantry were released from the investment of Tobruk, the garrison could sally forth and cut his supply route. Rommel had therefore chosen the logical course, to use his armour first to subdue Tobruk. His plan was to breach the defences at their highest, most dominating point (Ras el Medauuar), to secure a firm lodgement inside the perimeter at Bianca and thence to mount a full-scale attack aimed at the harbour.

General Paulus, whom the German Army High Command had sent to Africa to report on Rommel's operations, arrived at Rommel's headquarters on 27th April to find that Rommel was on the point of ordering an attack on Tobruk. Paulus declined to assent to the plan without detailed reconnaissance, consultation with the commanders and further consideration, but two days later gave his assent.

General Rommel's order for the operation thus described his intention:

The Africa Korps will force a decision in the battle round Tobruk during the night 30 April-1 May by an attack from the west.

The attack was to be made on a two-divisional front; two German divisional groups were to make the first assault, each to be followed by two Italian divisional groups. The first objective (to be attained at 8 p.m. on 30th April) was a penetration of the perimeter on both sides of Ras el Medauuar. Early next morning the attack was to be continued through Bianca and Pilastrino (the fortress headquarters and an artillery area) and was to be aimed at the town and harbour.

Rommel's battle groups were composed of improvised combinations of units, sub-units and bits of sub-units, the precise strength of which defies accurate assessment. The front-line divisions were the Kirchheim Group of the *5th Light Division* on the right and the *15th Armoured Division* on the left. The *Ariete Division* was to follow the Kirchheim Group, the *Brescia Division* to come in on the left of the *15th Armoured Division*. Because of differences of opinion with General Streich, commander of the *5th Light Division*, Rommel had sent for Major-General Kirchheim, then at Tripoli recovering from a wound, to take charge of the division's battle group.

The Kirchheim Group might be described as an armoured brigade group. Its close combat units were the *5th Armoured Regiment*, comprising 81 tanks (9 Mark I, 26 Mark II, 36 Mark III and 8 Mark IV plus 2 large commander's tanks), organised for the operation into a composite battalion of four companies;[1] the *2nd Machine Gun Battalion* almost up to strength (1,400); the *8th Machine Gun Battalion* (one and a half companies—its strength having been reduced from almost full strength to 300 in the attack on 14th April); and two companies of an engineer battalion. Field, anti-tank and anti-aircraft artillery were on a scale appropriate for a brigade group. The *15th Armoured Division* comprised only advanced elements of that division, the most important close combat units being two battalions and a half of lorried infantry, one battalion of engineers, one company of special duty engineers, and one company of the *8th Armoured Regiment* (strength unascertainable—probably not more than 10 tanks).[2] There were normal supporting arms for a brigade, including an artillery regiment. The exact strength of the groups from the *Ariete* and *Brescia Divisions* which were employed is uncertain, but appears to have approximated about one weak infantry brigade group in each case.

This formidable force was directed at the centre of the 2/24th Battalion which, with three companies forward and one sited in depth, was holding an arc of the perimeter five miles in extent. (By the end of the battle the assault had overrun the centre company and the two inner platoons of each of the flanking companies, but had failed to dislodge the reserve company.) The plan was to penetrate with the assault divisions on either side of Medauuar, then capture Medauuar from the rear. The Italian divisions were then to roll up the flanks of the perimeter, while the German divisions were to seize the Bianca (or Giaida) area (or, if that was strongly held an area to the south-west) and to develop the seized area for defence against counter-attack. The importance attached in the plan to the Bianca defensive position, which was non-existent, was probably due to Rommel's having seen the Italian plans of the Tobruk defences received about a fortnight earlier, which showed a system of earthworks and artillery positions there.[3]

The operation commenced with dive-bombing and artillery preparations, after which, at 8 p.m., engineer troops made narrow penetrations. On the left a gap was made just north of S3; possibly a further gap near S7.[4] Tanks (probably of the *8th Armoured Regiment*) were employed to drag away the wire with grappling irons. Some placed themselves across the fixed lines of small-arms fire coming from the perimeter posts. So sheltered, the infantry passed beside the tanks into the perimeter. Just one hour and a half after the attack began the capture of Ras el Medauuar was signalled by a white light. In fact, the old fort used for artillery observation had been taken but the adjacent perimeter posts had not been molested. Sub-

---

[1] Battle report of Abteilung Hohmann, 2 May 1941.
[2] Six tanks observed within the perimeter during the night of 30 April were probably from this company.
[3] See *The Rommel Papers*, pp. 128-9.
[4] The Germans reported themselves to be much farther north.

sequently about six tanks were established on the Tobruk side of Medauuar. The Kirchheim Group on the right next cleared a small gap in the perimeter near R1 and dispatched part of the *2nd Machine Gun Battalion* to Point 182 near the crossroads about 1,200 yards in from Medauuar, while the *15th Armoured Division* dispatched an assault detachment from the *104th Lorried Infantry Regiment* with orders to proceed to Bianca. This detachment was probably the one that was intercepted by Gebhardt's patrol and which later dug in about 500 yards from "B" Company of the 2/24th Battalion. The *Brescia Division,* which was to attack on the left of the *15th Armoured* (i.e. on the 2/23rd front) was shelled in its assembly area, moved north and eventually came into the perimeter through the gap cleared by the Germans.

The failure to clear the defenders from the perimeter posts (or perhaps the failure of the defenders to surrender voluntarily[5]) enforced a change of plan. When the *5th Armoured Regiment* reported to Kirchheim's headquarters for orders at 5.30 a.m. (the crews having slept beneath their tanks since 10.30 p.m.), it was ordered to support an attack on Medauuar ("which was occupied by the enemy") by part of the *2nd Machine Gun Battalion* and the company of the special duties *200th Engineer Battalion.* The morning fog delayed operations. One company (about 20 tanks) split into two; one group operating with an engineer battalion rolled up the right flank to R5, while the other first cooperated with the *2nd Machine Gun Battalion* to subdue the perimeter posts at Medauuar, and then widened the flank to the left. Another company was detailed to lead the advance to Bianca, with battalion headquarters following and the other two companies in rear. This company ran on to the B1 minefield where 12 of its tanks (9 medium, 3 light) were immobilised, but not destroyed, by mines. Meanwhile the tanks were coming under British artillery fire. Rommel, who had come forward to Kirchheim's headquarters, then ordered the tank battalion to attack with the engineers south-eastwards along the perimeter. The *Ariete Division* was to be brought in to take over the positions taken. However these operations made less progress than Rommel had hoped because British artillery fire hampered cooperation between ground troops and tanks.

About midday the *2nd Machine Gun Battalion* reported that it had captured Point 180, and the *15th Division* that it was constructing a defensive position east of Point 187—S4 (the position that Woods' company was later to encounter, in the 2/48th Battalion's counter-attack); the rest of the battalion attacking Bianca was withdrawing to this line. By 1 p.m. a heavy sand storm had blown up and the tank battalion drew together to replenish ammunition from trucks brought up under cover of the dust. This had been completed by 3.15 p.m.

While the tank battalion was replenishing, Paulus was conferring with Rommel. Paulus advised that there was no prospect of continuing the attack with success. Rommel agreed and ordered that the advance should

---

[5] The Germans who captured the garrison of S2 expressed surprise that they had not come out and surrendered after the Stuka attacks. (Letter of Major Fell to author.)

be discontinued for that day and the next, and switched operations to widening the bridgehead to S7 in the north and R14 in the east. The S7 area was effectively consolidated but little progress was made to the east. R6, as we have seen, did not succumb till night fell nor R7 till next morning. During the remainder of the day the tank battalion was engaged more in manoeuvring to meet the garrison's counter-measures than in extending the bridgehead. From 3.45 p.m. it occupied positions ready to meet a British tank force of 22 tanks which appeared to be threatening to attack the *2nd Machine Gun Battalion's* positions. The *5th Company* attempted to cut off the British tanks. It was claimed that four British tanks, three of them Mark II's (Matildas), were put out of action, while four of the company's tanks were hit.

About 5.30 p.m. portion of the *Ariete Division* arrived. The attack eastwards was resumed in a combined operation until R8 was reached, when strong British fire came down as daylight faded. At 7 p.m., the *5th Company* reported that two British infantry companies (in fact, Loughrey's company of the 2/48th) were advancing towards the point of break-through. At 7.15 p.m. the tank battalion and two companies of Italian infantry moved up to meet the attack but on arrival a section of tanks returning from a reconnaissance reported that the attackers were moving back. Counter-attacks were also withstood in the left sector. The tank battalion then leaguered near Posts R5, 6 and 3 but was later ordered to Carrier Hill, which it reached at 2 a.m., to replenish half an hour later.

At the end of the day's operations the battalion had but 35 of the 81 tanks still ready for action (3 Mark I, 12 Mark II, 12 Mark III, 6 Mark IV and the 2 commander's tanks). But it appears that only 12 were irrecoverable.[6]

Of the three objectives of the Axis assault on Tobruk—the breaching of the outer defence ring at Medauuar, the securing of a firm lodgement within the perimeter at Bianca and the enforcement of a capitulation by seizing the harbour—only the first had been attained. That, though tactically advantageous, was the least important. It was a success achieved by tanks against infantry stripped of anti-tank defence; but comparative weakness in infantry had lost Rommel the second objective and the prospect of the ultimate prize.

It has been said that if Rommel had resumed his attack on the second day, he might have captured Tobruk, but the outcome would have been doubtful if the original plan had been followed. The German tanks had so far fought beyond effective anti-tank range of the British field artillery. With tank strength now reduced to approximately that of the force that had failed to run the gauntlet in the Easter battle, Rommel would have had to deploy the tanks within close range of the main concentration of the garrison's field guns. If, avoiding a direct onslaught on the gun positions, a portion of the tank force had broken through to the coast, it is not

---

[6] The only casualties to tank crews were 2 officers and 12 other ranks wounded; 1 missing.

to be supposed that the anti-aircraft guns and the guns of H.M.S. *Gnat* would have offered no opposition. In fact a khamsin hid the fortress in a pall of dust that day; further large-scale tank attack was not practicable. On the other hand, a continued use of tanks against the infantry on the outer perimeter would have presented Morshead with an extremely grave problem.

Morshead held the fortress but lost part of the perimeter. Both results flowed from his policy of defending in depth at the cost of weakness at the outer ring. There were mistakes before the battle, but once it was joined it was well, if not perfectly, fought. Before the battle the evidence of a possible impending assault on Medauuar was not interpreted as sufficiently strong to warrant moving a counter-attack force to the area. Effective interference with the first breaching of the perimeter or intervention to close the gaps and re-establish the wire and minefields as soon as the penetrations had been made would have required the employment of units free of other commitments and ready for the task. But the only reserve units close enough were committed to defensive tasks.

The enemy having made his first moves and the defenders being unprepared for effective counter-moves before dawn, the defence could have done little to prevent the attack from following the course it took. The small anti-tank gun screen of two-pounders, firing projectiles that could maim and halt tanks but seldom kill them, could be quickly brushed aside. The infantry, without weapons that could harm the tanks, which could fire into their weapon-pits, could then be subdued post by post. The process could continue so long as the tanks could survive the shells of the British field guns firing at a range too great for pin-point accuracy. With greater energy and initiative on the left flank, however, R7 probably would not have been lost, R6 might possibly have been saved.

A counter-attack mounted earlier than the 2/48th counter-attack (that is, in broad daylight) would have courted disaster from intervention by the German tanks. By that time a deliberate counter-attack was required, but the 2/48th operation was mounted in haste and without reconnaissance. Morshead set the 2/48th Battalion a task that would have taxed a brigade; Windeyer perforce gave his forward companies tasks that battalions might have failed to accomplish. If, by attacking in greater strength on a narrower front, greater immediate success had been achieved, it is doubtful whether next day the gains could have been held. The counter-attack did not, as used to be supposed, stay the enemy offensive, but the enemy decision to discontinue the assault, reached six hours earlier, might possibly have been reversed if the garrison had not thus displayed that its spirit and power of retaliation had survived the ordeal.

Returning from Morshead's headquarters in the early hours of the 2nd May, Lieut-Colonel Verrier found his vehicle's progress slowed down more and more by dust until it became impossible to pick the way forward in the dark. He continued on foot but did not reach his battalion until it was standing to arms at 4 a.m. The battalion's new task of linking S8 with Bianca, for which he brought orders, had to be executed at first light.

The diarist of the 2/10th noted that at 6 a.m. all companies were moving to their new positions: no reconnaissance had been made; all movement was by map and compass. The advance was executed with three companies forward less one platoon sent to an artillery battery on the previous day. The diarist also recorded that the move was completed by 6.30 a.m., but did not indicate the precise positions taken up. The diarists of both the 18th Brigade and 9th Division headquarters recorded the new positions as linking up with the 2/24th Battalion's reserve company position behind the B1 minefield, but it soon became evident that this was not so. Verrier's left flank was on Bianca, about 1,500 yards behind the positions held by "B" Company of the 2/24th. Windeyer pointed out to Verrier that the 2/24th company's flanks were exposed, whereupon Verrier told Spowers, who was under his command, to withdraw behind the new line. The move was executed by the main body in good order, though one or two outlying sections came back individually, and a group of men under Lieutenant Macfarlane[7] was pinned down for some time and mostly killed. Macfarlane eventually came in carrying Lance-Corporal Alleyne,[8] who was badly wounded. At Forbes' Mound he encountered a German motor-cyclist armed with a sub-machine-gun, who let him pass unharmed. For a time the 2/24th company went into position at the stone wall near Bianca with the 2/10th, but were later withdrawn. Meanwhile the 2/48th Battalion moved into its old positions vacated by the 2/10th.

It is fair to say that Morshead would not have approved of this deliberate withdrawal from a prepared defensive position within the perimeter, for from the time that a part of the perimeter was lost the desire to take it back dominated his operational plans. It is not hard to understand why the new line had not incorporated the 2/24th reserve position. What happened resulted from fatigue and the individual decisions of leaders of men moving forward who chose what appeared to them to be the best holding positions. There is no doubt that Morshead had intended to incorporate the reserve company position of the western sector in the new front line, but this intention may not have been understood by the company commanders. Later Verrier ordered an advance of 700 yards forward of the positions first taken up. The historian of the 2/10th Battalion later explained the reason for the forward move thus. At dawn "companies found themselves in position mostly on reverse slopes so it was necessary to move forward to better positions. 'B', 'C' and 'D' Companies advanced to a slight ridge some 700 yards forward." Before the 2/10th moved forward Verrier had advised Brigadier Tovell that he thought the 2/24th Battalion had reached the limits of endurance and that, since they were under his command, he proposed to replace them. Therefore he chose the line that seemed to him most feasible to hold with his own battalion. Holding

---

[7] Maj A. Macfarlane, VX15247; 2/24 Bn. Horticulturist; of Mildura, Vic; b. Wallasey, England, 13 Sep 1918.
[8] Sgt F. O. Alleyne, VX46811; 2/24 Bn. Transport driver; of Carnegie, Vic; b. Echuca, Vic, 4 Oct 1906. Killed in action 31 Oct 1942.

a forward slope overlooked by Ras el Medauuar may have been adjudged impracticable, but considerations of great consequence were involved. The virtual abandonment of the B1 minefield increased the immediate danger in view of the possibility that the enemy would resume his assault with tanks, but the main disadvantage was the long-term consideration that the line taken up ran in an arc with a big radius and was thus undesirably long.

Verrier's battalion linked up on its left flank with positions occupied astride the roads south and south-east of Bianca by "C" Company of the 2/1st Pioneer Battalion (Lieut-Colonel Brown[9]). A machine-gun platoon of the Royal Northumberland Fusiliers with two Bren guns from the battalion's headquarters company was later stationed at Bianca as a stop against enemy infiltrating between the 2/10th and the pioneers. The machine-gunners' commanding officer protested, pointing out that the conformation of the ground did not lend itself to Vickers gun employment and unavailingly advocated that he should instead be permitted to shoot the enemy up in rear by enfilade fire from R12. It was probably not realised at divisional headquarters that the infantry did not form a continuous front forward of this feature, as the reported dispositions indicated, and that the Fusiliers' position was in fact a forward outpost in the centre of the enemy's line of thrust.

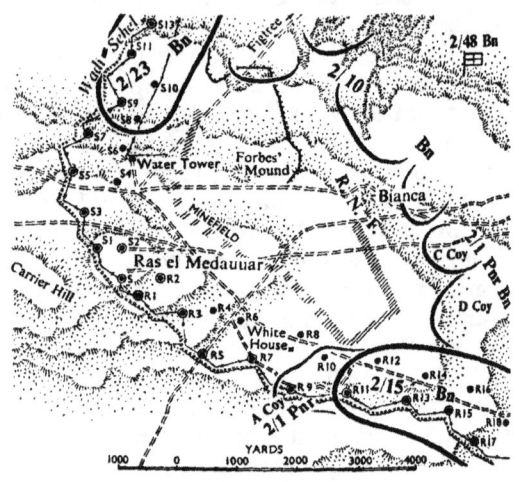

Morning, 2nd May

Before first light "D" Company of the 2/1st Pioneer Battalion had moved forward to take up a line running north from R14 to the left flank of "C" Company, thus completing the new front line. The decision to link with R14 rather than with R12 on the old inter-brigade boundary had the result that the posts from R10 to R12 formed a narrow salient with open flanks. In the opinion of Captain Sheehan[1] of the 26th Anti-Tank Company, who had received his instructions from Brigadier Murray, a line should have been occupied 1,500 yards farther forward. Sheehan discussed the position with the company commander. It was then proposed to advance the infantry line and meanwhile Lieutenant Summerton's[2]

---

[9] Lt-Col A. Brown, DSO, OBE, MC, NX393. (1st AIF: Maj 28 Bn.) 2/1 Pnr Bn (CO 1941-42, 1943); CO 36 Bn 1942. Stock and station agent; of Coonabarabran, NSW; b. Hunter's Hill, NSW, 22 Jul 1894. Died 6 Mar 1960.

[1] Maj W. J. Sheehan, VX44981. 2/24 Bn (OC 26 A-Tk Coy 1940-41). Railway porter; of Dandenong, Vic; b. Ascot Vale, Vic, 20 Apr 1909.

[2] Lt-Col J. Summerton, OBE, VX48010. 2/24 Bn and 26 A-Tk Coy; HQ 9 Div; BM 7 Bde 1944-45. Clerk; of Yallourn, Vic; b. Kew, Vic, 23 Jan 1914.

platoon went forward to place its guns in position. About an hour later, however, the enemy came forward and overran the gun positions, capturing the entire platoon except Summerton and seven men.

The day's operations developed into an artillery duel while the infantry of both sides consolidated their positions, but the enemy staged some local thrusts, which were broken up by gunfire. Forward observation officers of the 1st and 104th R.H.A. continuously roamed the battlefield in carriers, shooting up opportunity targets. A raging dust-storm blanketed the battle area.

At 6.45 a.m., after the surrender of Post R7, the enemy appeared to be assembling a mixed force of infantry and 30 tanks for a renewed thrust against R8 (in fact no longer held) but they were dispersed by concentrated gunfire. About 2 p.m. a flame-thrower was brought up to attack Post R9 under cover of two light tanks and an armoured car. The post's garrison met the challenge and set the flame-thrower afire with a hit from its Boyes rifle. The light tanks and armoured car were then engaged with rifles and withdrew. In the early afternoon enemy infantry also began to close in on the 2/1st Pioneers in the new salient. Just before 5 p.m. Sergeant Christsen[3] took out a carrier patrol to come to their assistance. The patrol ran into heavy fire, and one man was killed and one wounded. One carrier broke down but Christsen, under heavy fire, linked it to his own carrier and towed it back. At 5 p.m. guns began bombarding the 2/10th Battalion's positions. Fifteen minutes later about 600 German infantry advanced upon the left company of the 2/10th Battalion in the direction of Bianca. This attack and a second thrust half an hour later aimed between the 2/10th's right and left centre companies were both broken up with help from the artillery and the machine-guns of the Fusiliers on Bianca. Tanks in rear approaching the minefield were shelled.

Towards 5.30 p.m. the dust cleared, revealing about 100 vehicles and tanks on the forward slopes of Medauuar. The 51st Field Regiment brought forward a section of guns and the enemy vehicles were driven back to dead ground in some confusion. In the succeeding two hours before dusk the enemy endeavoured to assemble a strong, mixed force of tanks and infantry for an attack on the left flank but the force was scattered and broken by continual fire. Finally a night attack was made on R10 just before 11 p.m. but was held off by artillery concentrations. A daring but unsuccessful operation was attempted at 6 p.m. by the tank-hunting platoon of the 2/1st Pioneer Battalion of which Lieutenant Osborn[4] had taken charge when the platoon's commander, Lieutenant MacAdam,[5] had failed to return from a reconnaissance earlier in the afternoon. The mission was to destroy an enemy post reported to be west of Bianca, but the objective was found to be a strongly held position. After executing a difficult advance and withdrawal 600 yards under fire, Lieutenant Osborn

---

[3] WO2 J. W. Christsen, DCM, QX6940; 2/15 Bn. Builder's labourer; of Woolloongabba, Qld; b. Bundaberg, Qld, 17 Oct 1909. Killed in action 31 Oct 1942.
[4] Maj G. S. Osborn, MVO, ED, NX12484; 2/1 Pnr Bn. Bank clerk; of Raymond Terrace and Sydney, NSW; b. West Maitland, NSW, 13 Jan 1918.
[5] Lt J. A. MacAdam, NX65156; 2/1 Pnr Bn. Regular soldier; of King's Cross, NSW; b. Bangalore, India, 20 May 1906.

returned alone to rescue a missing member of his patrol and, finding him dead, brought his body in.

The diarist of the 1st R.H.A. recorded that each gun of the regiment fired about 900 rounds that day. For the 3rd R.H.A. the day brought good news. Three gun detachments, overrun and missing in the previous day's operations, found their way back, bringing their breech blocks with them.

As the enemy had failed to resume the offensive, Morshead began planning to use his reserves in a counter-attack directed at retaking the lost territory. Brigadier Wootten, who knew his commander's mind, had spent the day with the 20th Brigade acquainting himself with the situation in the battle area.

Orders for the operation were given at a conference at divisional headquarters on the morning of 3rd May. Wootten was given a choice of three possible methods of counter-attack. He chose a method involving a night attack from the flanks with artillery support, hoping thus to get in behind the forward enemy positions in the Salient. The attack was to be made by two battalions attacking from right and left along the perimeter and rolling up the enemy's flanks to the apex at Ras el Medauuar. The 2/12th Battalion (Lieut-Colonel Field[6]), on the right, was to attack through to Medauuar, the 2/9th (Lieut-Colonel Martin), on the left, up to the left shoulder of that feature, stopping at R1. The 2/10th Battalion was to push forward from its positions in the centre, send out fighting patrols to give support on the left flank of the 2/12th Battalion's attack, and assist in mopping up. Some of the artillery had been redisposed during the night in preparation for the attack. Approximately three artillery regiments were to support the operation. A timed artillery program was worked out. Barrages were to move to the first objectives at the rate of 100 yards in three minutes, then fire on the second objective for 90 minutes, followed by timed concentrations of less duration on subsequent objectives. An anti-tank regiment, 2 platoons of machine-guns, 12 light tanks and 7 infantry tanks were to be available for consolidation. The start-time was fixed at 7.33 p.m.

Battalion commanders issued preliminary orders to their company commanders in the early afternoon. The next few hours were spent by company commanders in reconnaissance and detailed planning. Brigadier Wootten held a final coordinating conference in mid-afternoon at which it was decided to defer the start-time to 8.45 p.m. to deny the enemy observation of the infantry approach. Final orders were issued to company commanders just after 5 p.m.

The 3rd of May was a quiet day by comparison with the two immediately preceding. At 9.30 a.m. two companies of enemy infantry advancing on R10, the isolated rear perimeter post on the extreme left

---

[6] Brig J. Field, CBE, DSO, ED, TX2002. CO 2/12 Bn 1939-42; Comd 7 Bde 1942-45 (Admin Comd 3 Div Mar-Jul 1944). Mechanical engineer and university lecturer; of Hobart; b. Castlemaine, Vic, 10 Apr 1899.

flank, were dispersed by artillery fire from "B/O" Battery and beat a hurried withdrawal through the wire. This was followed by a further attack of about one-company strength which was similarly dispersed. At 10 a.m. a considerable enemy force formed up in front of Bianca but was successfully engaged by the artillery, the machine-guns of the Royal Northumberland Fusiliers and the mortars of the 2/10th Battalion. Throughout the morning enemy were observed lifting mines on the B1 minefield and subjected to harassing fire. The positions of the Fusiliers covering Bianca were subjected to much interference from enemy machine-gunners located near a white house forward of the extreme left flank. During the afternoon the enemy could be seen reinforcing the area with anti-tank guns. From this region the perimeter posts on the left flank, from R14 forward, were then kept under continuous fire.

Wootten's counter-attack was made in almost pitch darkness with little aid from a low moon which was in its first quarter and obscured by a slightly overcast sky. Field's battalion on the right started on time, but Martin's battalion was late in coming forward, necessitating half an hour's postponement of its attack.

From its assembly area in a wadi on the left of the Fig Tree Road (where it had received some casualties from intermittent shelling), Field's battalion moved, without drawing any fire, to the start-line on the right of the Fig Tree Road behind the 2/10th Battalion's forward positions. The attack was made on a frontage of 500 yards with two companies up, "C" and

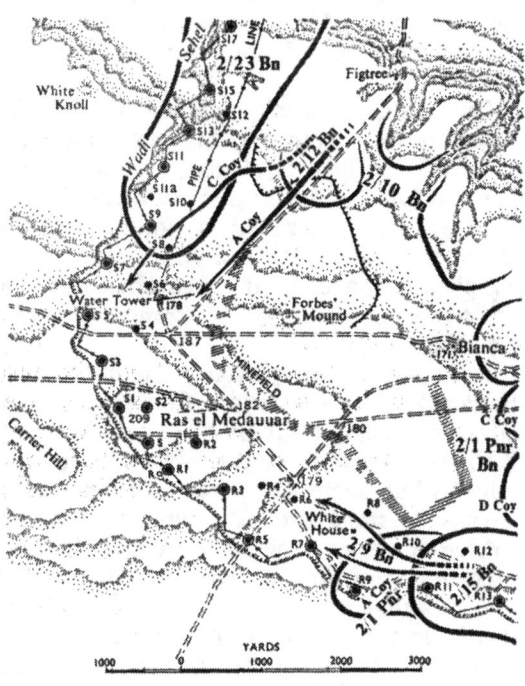

18th Brigade attack, 3rd-4th May

"A" Companies in front ("C" on the right), "D" and "B" Companies ("D" on the right) followed 100 yards in rear. "C" Company was to take the first three posts encountered (S7, 6 and 5); "D" was then to come round and take the next two.

After passing through the 2/10th Battalion positions the forward companies ran into cross-fire from each flank fired from machine-guns situated, on the right, outside the perimeter, and on the left, deep within the Salient. This put the troops to ground, and the noise and darkness combined to render coordinated movement forward extremely difficult. On the right some groups were able to infiltrate outside the perimeter along the anti-tank ditch past S7, and on the left other groups got forward to the vicinity of S6 by following a pipe-line ditch. Many of the men simply got lost. For four hours and a half efforts were made to re-establish organisation and infiltrate the troops forward while the ground continued to be lacerated by machine-gun and mortar fire from nests mainly outside the zone covered by the artillery program. At 12.30 a.m. the commander of "C" Company informed Field that he would be able to mount an assault on S6 and S7 if 15 minutes of artillery fire could be arranged. Field at first tried to arrange an artillery program on the unneutralised machine-gun positions on the flanks but found that to do so would require lengthy calculations, which ruled it out as an immediate possibility. Eventually a repetition of the original program was arranged for 15 minutes from 1.15 a.m. The enemy fire was not neutralised, however, and the attack could not be pressed home. Field reported the failure to Wootten.

On the left of Field's battalion, Captain Lines'[7] company of the 2/10th Battalion was given the task of mopping up enemy posts established forward of a line of diggings running south-west of the Water Tower. The two forward platoons were stopped by heavy cross-fire, but Lieutenant Bidstrup[8] later succeeded in working his way to the left and got through to the tank ditch. There a position was taken up, from which a German patrol of seven men was ambushed and captured. Lines' company later assisted in reorganising "A" Company of the 2/12th Battalion and getting out their wounded.

A patrol of two platoons from the reserve company of the 2/10th Battalion under Lieutenant Cook[9] was given the task of mopping up an advanced enemy position 800 yards west of Bianca. The patrol set off at 9.10 p.m. after its objective had been bombarded with mortars for 10 minutes but, some 400 yards from its start-line, ran into machine-gun fire from at least six guns. Lieutenant Cook immediately ordered his platoon to charge the machine-gun nest with the bayonet. As the men drew close, grenades were thrown into the enemy position, which was then stormed and captured without loss. On the left Lieutenant Beames'[1] platoon was caught in a cross-fire as it advanced. Beames and other members of the patrol were wounded and the platoon was pinned down. At Cook's behest Lance-Corporal Taylor[2] made three searches in an endeavour to find Beames' party. During one of these he located an enemy machine-gun post and charged it single-handed with his Tommy-gun, slaying all six

---

[7] Capt E. H. D. Lines, SX1439; 2/10 Bn. Civil servant; of Adelaide; b. Adelaide, 14 Aug 1910.
[8] Capt M. L. Bidstrup, MC, SX4500. 2/10, 39 and 2/2 Bns. Chemical works manager; of Wallaroo, SA; b. Adelaide, 6 Oct 1911.
[9] Lt-Col F. W. Cook, DSO, MC, SX1225; 2/10 Bn. Laboratory assistant; of Firle, SA; b. Southampton, England, 12 May 1918.
[1] Maj W. B. Beames, SX515; 2/10 Bn. Cost accountant; of Broken Hill, NSW; b. Adelaide, 26 Mar 1914.
[2] Lt A. J. Taylor, DCM, QX2687; 2/10 Bn. Hide grader; of Gladstone, Qld; b. Brisbane, 5 Jul 1916.

members of the gun crew. Another troublesome post was assaulted by a section led by Corporal Fricker.[3] The enemy in the post were annihilated, with the exception of two taken prisoner. An anti-tank gun, a machine-gun, a mortar and two motor-cycles were collected and brought in. Private Jones[4] was wounded in this action. He was subsequently taken prisoner, but escaped from his captors during some shelling of their positions and got back to the battalion some 36 hours later.

The platoon tried to hang on to its ground but constant fire caused casualties to mount. After an hour and a half a controlled withdrawal was executed. The patrol lost 4 men killed and 3 missing, and 9 men were wounded in addition to Lieutenant Beames.

Although, on the left of the attack, the 2/9th Battalion was late in arriving, it proved possible to defer the artillery program for half an hour. Even so, the battalion did not arrive at the start-line until just as the guns started up. The men hurried forward without properly forming up. The battalion was to attack in two phases with two companies up for each phase, "A" and "D" ("A" on the right), followed by "C" and "B" ("C" on the right). The first phase included the capture of the four posts, R8, 7, 6 and 5 and the White House near R8. In the second phase Posts R4, 3, 2 and 1 were to be taken. The area to be attacked was found to be garrisoned mainly by Italians.

Concentrations of gunfire falling on the start-line as the men set off caused some confusion and intermingling between the forward and rear companies. Enfilade machine-gun fire from both flanks did not improve matters. Enemy machine-guns were also firing down the road on fixed lines, but the lines of fire were obligingly illuminated with tracers. Captain Fleming's[5] company on the right experienced difficulties from insufficient knowledge of the ground. The leading platoon commanders positioned themselves by reference to the road leading to R6, but the lie of the road in use differed from that shown on the map. Lieutenant W. H. Noyes' platoon's objective was Post R8. He searched for it in vain on the left of the road he was following; it was in fact on the right. The platoon pushed on, encountered an enemy position behind a mound of stones, threw in grenades and charged in with the bayonet. They killed a large number and drove out the rest of the garrison, which Noyes reported to be about 80 strong. This position was to the north of R7.

On the left, Captain F. E. C. Loxton's company, somewhat disorganised, closed in on Post R7 through heavy artillery and machine-gun fire. Some of the men managed to get into the anti-tank ditch surrounding the post. The enemy garrison then set two blankets alight, creating a most unwelcome illumination.

Meanwhile three Italian light tanks came down the road towards Noyes'

---

[3] Lt D. C. Fricker, SX1783; 2/10 Bn. Bank clerk; of Balaklava, SA; b. Largs Bay, SA, 23 Feb 1918.
[4] Pte M. E. Jones, SX3158; 2/10 Bn. Labourer; of Kalangadoo, SA; b. Port MacDonnell, SA. 23 Nov 1918.
[5] Lt-Col E. W. Fleming, DSO, ED, QX6064. 2/9 and 49 Bns; CO 2/9 Bn 1945-46. Advertising copywriter; of Wynnum Central, Qld; b. Nambour, Qld, 7 Oct 1908.

platoon. Noyes and Sergeant Hobson[6] sneaked up to the tanks, lifted the turret lids and dropped hand grenades inside. The tanks burst into flames but this drew the enemy's fire. Noyes led his dwindling platoon on, striking some more enemy in shallow ditches near R6. These were also cleaned up. With the remnants of his platoon, now numbering but six men, Noyes turned back to find the rest of the company. Coming back on the north of the road he stumbled upon his original objective, R8, only to find that the post had not been occupied.

Soon afterwards most of Captain B. M. Lovett's company arrived at R8 and decided to carry on where Noyes left off. The company, however, veered to the left and encountered Post R7. The post was assaulted, most of the garrison were slain and two prisoners were taken. Four 47-mm guns and a heavy Breda machine-gun were found in the post. Almost immediately, however, the Australians were counter-attacked by a medium tank and three armoured cars, probably attracted by the burning blankets. The Australians fell back.

There is no doubt that Noyes' and Lovett's men had inflicted severe casualties. A German diary subsequently captured referred to the state of utter confusion to which the Italian garrison in the area had been reduced by the assault. The diarist, possibly with some exaggeration, wrote that, of 150 men in this locality, 100 had been killed or wounded. But by this time the battalion, fragmented into small groups, had become disorganised. With the exception of a garrison in R8 there was a general withdrawal to the area of R14, where the battalion began to reorganise for a further attack directed at Posts R5 and R6. It was planned to mount the second attack at 4.15 a.m.

Meanwhile, just after 3 a.m., Morshead had asked Wootten to report the situation on both flanks in half an hour in order to enable a decision on future action to be reached before the approach of daylight. Wootten duly did so before 3.40 a.m. Morshead then ordered the attack to be broken off. The assault battalions were withdrawn into reserve before daylight.

In a report on this operation, Wootten made the sound comment that "in view of the enemy's defensive strength and dispositions it appears that any further large-scale infantry operations will require the support of many more guns and tanks."

Even if on that night many more guns and tanks had been available, it is doubtful whether much greater success would have been achieved. Formation commanders were setting units, and therefore unit commanders were setting their men, tasks well beyond their powers. For a formation that had developed a detailed battle-drill for night operations and rehearsed it up to the last minute, such a night attack in depth on fortified posts through a succession of objectives would have been a formidable proposition under a quarter moon, even with full knowledge of the enemy's dispositions and time to work out a plan of assault on each locality.

---

[6] Lt R. W. Hobson, DCM, QX1399. 2/9 Bn, 2/4 Pnr Bn. Company manager; of Cunnamulla, Qld; b. Cunnamulla, 4 Jan 1910.

To require a system of developed defences to be penetrated and overrun to a depth of two or three miles in a night attack was asking a great deal of the battalions. To mount the operation at short notice with unrehearsed troops hastened into the attack and with but the sketchiest knowledge of how the enemy was disposed was to invite confusion in the execution of a very doubtful enterprise.

Nevertheless the operation had achieved positive results. Wootten's brigade incurred 155 casualties (10 killed, 121 wounded and 24 missing), but inflicted equally heavy losses and 23 prisoners were in the bag. Next morning enemy ambulances came up to the posts and throughout the day were seen to be collecting the wounded and removing the dead. In the 24 hours to the evening of 4th May, the German *15th Armoured Division* incurred 53 casualties (10 killed, 40 wounded, 3 missing) and the *Ariete Division* 150 (26 killed, 65 wounded, and 59 missing). The *15th Armoured Division* had held the northern sector attacked by the 2/12th Battalion, the *Ariete* the eastern sector where the 2/9th attacked. It must be remembered that, although outmatched in artillery performance, the Germans were better armed and equipped than the Australians. The achievement was not to be measured in casualties. The real achievement was the fact that the aggressive conduct of the defence compelled Rommel to hold his salient in strength with some of his best troops, which augmented the inhibiting effect of the Tobruk fortress on his power to strike at the frontier of Egypt.[7]

Congratulations on the garrison's successful resistance reached General Morshead from all sides, including messages from Mr Menzies and General Blamey. Morshead would have appreciated General Wavell's signal

> Your magnificent defence is upsetting the enemy's plans for the attack on Egypt and giving us time to build up force for counter offensive. You could not be doing better service. Well done. . . .

but the men manning the perimeter defences, the guns and the tanks may have drawn more encouragement from Churchill's purposeful rhetoric:

> To General Morshead from Prime Minister of England. The whole Empire is watching your steadfast and spirited defence of this important outpost of Egypt with gratitude and admiration.

---

[7] Fortress casualties from 29th April to 4th May were:

	Killed		Wounded		Missing		Total
	Offrs	OR's	Offrs	OR's	Offrs	OR's	
	7	52	16	339	13	370	797

In the operations from 30th April to the evening of 3rd May the Axis forces had lost:

	Killed		Wounded		Missing		Total
	Offrs	OR's	Offrs	OR's	Offrs	OR's	
German	7	108	19	340	1	127	602
Italian	2	50	10	205	1	84	352
Total	9	158	29	545	2	211	954

CHAPTER 7

MIDSUMMER IN THE FORTRESS

THE failure of the 18th Brigade's counter-attack marked the end of a phase. No longer was it possible to regard the ground given up as a temporary loss to be recovered at first opportunity. The aim of re-establishing the perimeter on the original line, if not discarded, was at least deferred. The immediate emphasis changed to a policy of improving the new line opposite the Salient and of recovering organisation by reverting as far as possible to normal brigade groupings through a succession of reliefs. There had been a degree of improvisation in the dispositions made to block further penetration after the perimeter had been breached.

The regrouping was to begin on the night of 4th-5th May. In the Salient sector Lieut-Colonel Windeyer's 2/48th Battalion was ordered to take over the right of the new defence line from the two right-hand companies of Lieut-Colonel Verrier's 2/10th Battalion, while Lieut-Colonel Martin's 2/9th Battalion, coming under command of Brigadier Murray's brigade, was to take over defences in the centre of the Salient, near Bianca, from the left company of the 2/10th Battalion and the right company of Lieut-Colonel Brown's 2/1st Pioneer Battalion.

On the afternoon of 4th May, Martin made preliminary moves in conjunction with Brown's battalion, bringing forward part of his own battalion to close a gap on Brown's right flank. Simultaneously Brown's right-hand company, under Captain Graham,[1] moved forward for about a quarter of a mile, dislodging an enemy machine-gun post in the process. Three members of a covering party provided by the 2/1st Pioneers for the forward move of the 2/9th were killed. Private Rundle[2] saw Privates Cheney[3] and Goodfellow[4] fall. From a position of comparative safety he went to their assistance, found Goodfellow dead, but decided to carry in the mortally wounded Cheney; on this compassionate errand Rundle was shot down and killed. Heavy machine-gun fire caused some of the ground taken up by the 2/9th to be relinquished.

The planned reliefs took place on the night of the 4th May. Graham's company of the 2/1st Pioneers was relieved by the left company of Martin's battalion, then side-stepped to the left and pushed forward through the neighbouring company of the Pioneer battalion which held the switch-line running north from R14, and took up a position in front of the old switch-line and to the right of the previously isolated forward perimeter posts west of R14. The 2/10th Battalion was withdrawn, after its relief, into reserve at Pilastrino.

---

[1] Lt-Col G. J. Graham, MM, NX394. (1914-18: 10 Royal Fusiliers; later Indian Army.) 2/1 Pnr Bn (CO 1943-44). Company director; of Sydney; b. London, 14 Jul 1897.
[2] Pte H. R. Rundle, NX28066; 2/1 Pnr Bn. Labourer; of Nimbin, NSW; b. Kearsley, NSW, 6 Apr 1918. Killed in action 4 May 1941.
[3] Pte L. Cheney, NX28413; 2/1 Pnr Bn. Carpenter; of Tarcutta, NSW; b. Wagga Wagga, NSW, 10 Jan 1908. Killed in action 4 May 1941.
[4] Pte J. T. R. Goodfellow, NX28444; 2/1 Pnr Bn. Builder's labourer; of Canberra; b. Adelaide, 12 Jul 1903. Killed in action 4 May 1941.

Later in the night the main body of the 2/32nd Battalion, of which one company was already in the fortress, arrived at Tobruk from Mersa Matruh in the destroyers *Decoy* and *Defender*. This brought Morshead's infantry strength up to four complete brigades. The new battalion was temporarily placed under Brigadier Wootten's command and immediately put into a defensive position near the junction of the El Adem and Bardia Roads.

On the morning of 5th May Colonel Martin, surveying the positions he had taken over during the night, found his battalion holding a general north-south line running through the important track junctions (not all printed on the map) behind and east of Bianca. Appreciating the need of denying to the enemy that dominant point of vantage and observation, Martin at once decided to push his line forward. The move was executed in the early afternoon under intense machine-gun fire and shelling. Ten men were killed and 22 wounded (one mortally) and 2 men were reported missing; but though costly in life the realignment added greatly to the security of the defence at its weakest point and moreover enabled an excellent, if vulnerable, observation post for the artillery, later known as Nixon's[5] Post, to be established.

The enemy made a last attempt to extend the breach of the perimeter on the morning of 6th May. About 7.30 a.m. a strong German fighting patrol closed in on Post S9 in the area held by Captain Malloch's company of the 2/23rd Battalion. The attack was driven off with the help of artillery fire and supporting fire from Post S8 but one man in the post was killed and another wounded. More enemy, estimated to be in excess of one company, were then observed about 300 yards from the wire; but after enduring fire for two hours the enemy withdrew at 9.30 a.m.

Henceforward the positions in the Salient were steadily improved by digging, wiring and mining, and were edged forward when opportunity offered. As each side developed its positions and pushed them out towards the other, the strain on the men holding the front, particularly in the Salient, became intense, sapping vigour and draining away enthusiasm. The hard work of constructing the defences had all to be done at night in conjunction with a vigorous program of night patrolling and vigilant manning of the forward defences. By day the scorching sun withheld sleep after the night's exertions. The rations were good and well-balanced but for long, unbroken periods, were "hard" and monotonous and in the forward posts had to be eaten "hard", except at night, when a hot meal cooked in the "B" Echelons was brought forward in hot boxes. Many men tended to go off their food. The water, of which the daily ration was only half a gallon per man, was brackish and unpalatable.

Morshead insisted that the defence should never be inactive. The mastery of no-man's land by all brigades was positively required and was unrelentingly maintained throughout the siege by patrols and excursions beyond the wire and aggressive employment of the artillery. As soon as the front was stabilised after the thrusts and counter-thrusts of the first few days

---

[5] Named after Lt A. F. Nixon-Smith of the 2/9th Battalion.

of May, the patrolling policy was intensified along the whole length of the perimeter from the Wadi Sehel (held by the 18th Indian Cavalry Regiment) in the west to the Wadi Zeitun in the east.

In the early hours of 10th May Lieutenant Brown[6] of the 2/23rd Battalion led out a fighting patrol of platoon strength from S13 and proceeded westward along the escarpment south of the coast road to attack an enemy position about 2,500 yards from the perimeter. As the patrol was approaching its objective it surprised a large Italian working company and shot down a great number. The remainder surrendered and 31 prisoners were brought in. In the 2/48th Battalion area patrols to the old headquarters area of the 2/24th Battalion and Forbes' Mound were boldly executed. One day a fighting patrol commanded by Lieutenant Bryant skilfully extricated a small daylight patrol which had attracted enemy attention while recovering equipment from the old headquarters. A night fighting patrol under Lieutenant Kimber to Forbes' Mound ambushed a German patrol; Kimber was wounded but all the enemy were killed. Meanwhile patrols from the 2/15th Battalion holding the perimeter adjoining the left of the Salient were, night by night, deeply and vigorously probing the enemy's right flank.

In Brigadier Godfrey's sector on the east of the perimeter Lieutenant Pratt[7] and Captain Sudholz[8] of the 2/43rd Battalion and Lieutenant Masel[9] of the 2/28th executed in daylight several Bren gun carrier patrols deep into enemy-held territory near the Bardia Road, shooting up working parties and taking prisoners. Carriers with the Army Service Corps detachment manning the perimeter along the Wadi Zeitun also patrolled adventurously. These successes encouraged Brigadier Godfrey and Lieut-Colonel Crellin, commanding the 2/43rd Battalion, to plan a more ambitious foray. Captain Jeanes'[1] company was assigned the task of destroying the enemy at the head of the Wadi Belgassem, on its western edge, about a mile and a half beyond the perimeter. From the prisoners captured by the carrier patrols the Intelligence staff had been able to ascertain that a *Bersaglieri* regiment occupied, with at least two battalions, a defensive line that extended south from the head of the wadi through Sidi Belgassem and across the Bardia Road. (Later it was established that a third battalion was present.) One troop of infantry tanks and two of cruisers were to neutralise the enemy positions covering the approaches and to protect the open flanks; three armoured cars were to provide communication between the tanks and infantry; two carrier detachments (one provided by the A.A.S.C.)—7 carriers in all—a platoon of machine-guns, a detach-

---

[6] Maj W. F. Brown, VX48589; 2/23 Bn. Grocer's assistant; of Numurkah, Vic; b. Wangaratta, Vic, 9 Jun 1916.

[7] Lt L. J. Pratt, SX9465; 2/43 Bn. Clerk; of Walkerville, SA; b. Waikerie, SA, 1 May 1919. Killed in action 13 May 1941.

[8] Capt R. F. Sudholz, SX8975; 2/43 Bn. Garage proprietor; of Willunga, SA; b. Adelaide, 30 Jan 1908. Died of wounds 8 Aug 1942.

[9] Brig P. Masel, OBE, WX3392; 2/28 Bn. Business manager; of Nedlands, WA; b. Perth, WA, 25 May 1908. Author of *The Second 28th* (1961).

[1] Lt-Col M. R. Jeanes, DSO, MC, ED, SX9364. 2/43 Bn (CO 1945). Inspector of food and drugs; of Largs Bay, SA; b. Adelaide 21 Dec 1911.

ment of 3-inch mortars and a battery of field guns were to give close-support fire-power.

The assault was made at first light on 13th May but the coordinating arrangements broke down and confusion set in. Furthermore the noise of the tracked vehicles had alerted the enemy. The carrier appointed to guide the infantry tanks towards the objective from the right flank missed the way in a fog and brought them across close to where the infantry were waiting to advance. The tanks opened fire indiscriminately and the thoroughly roused enemy replied with all weapons, pinning down the infantry. Jeanes at first strove vainly to redirect the tanks but, failing to do so, instructed the three accompanying carriers to attack if necessary without them. While this was taking place a neighbouring enemy unit by mischance fired a light signal corresponding with that arranged for the withdrawal of the force, and most of the infantry went back before Jeanes could stop them. Meanwhile the infantry tanks, at last discovering the error, boldly turned east and advanced frontally towards the enemy positions. One tank veered to the north and, advancing through heavy machine-gun and anti-tank fire, succeeded in knocking out two anti-tank guns, but the other two ran head-on into the fire of the anti-tank guns in the main position and were disabled. The cruiser tanks were also engaged but moved out of range. Jeanes attempted to get an attack going with the carriers and the few remaining infantry whose withdrawal he had been able to check. Pratt led his three carriers at the strongpoint, but two were knocked out and Pratt was killed. As his handful of infantry were again pinned down, Jeanes ordered a withdrawal. The A.A.S.C. carriers, accompanied by the armoured cars, came across to help, engaged the enemy positions and laid a smoke-screen enabling the infantry to withdraw and the crews of three immobilised carriers to be rescued. Then the cruiser tanks moved forward. They saw the two damaged infantry tanks surrounded by enemy infantry but were soon driven back by renewed anti-tank gunfire. This operation unfortunately tended to undermine the confidence of the tank commanders and their crews not only in the ability of their tanks to withstand punishment but also in the reliability of the infantry.

The "bush artillery" became very active in Godfrey's sector. If the doubtful parentage and mixed breeding of the bush guns disentitled them to join the aristocratic ranks of the Royal Horse Artillery, their growing skill and improved performance were nevertheless earning them a standing of respectability. When Godfrey's brigade was given responsibility for the eastern sector, his two battalions brought with them the captured guns with which they had been equipped before the siege began, and both battalions found means of adding to their batteries. The diarist of the 2/28th Battalion noted on 1st May that the unit now had 11 guns manned as anti-tank weapons and that they had already accounted for 9 enemy vehicles. By 5th May the 2/43rd Battalion possessed nine guns of calibres ranging from 75-mm to 149-mm. (Some other units followed suit but being late starters failed to collect such formidable arrays.) Both battalions' guns were very active. On the evening of 8th May, for example, Crellin's artillery fired 150 shells into the Wadi Geriula.

As the siege progressed, the bush artillery developed into a useful harassing arm linked into the artillery network and not curtailed by ammunition shortage as the British field pieces were for long periods: the garrison's reserves of captured Italian ammunition were almost inexhaustible. The reason why these guns had not already been commandeered by the ordnance department was that they were defective in one or most respects, such as lack of sights; but in time some defects were made good from "scrounging" or by using parts taken from enemy guns by night patrols. They were originally manned by "all hands and the cook", but in course of time many of the crews were more selectively chosen and were usually commanded by officers having some training in the handling of medium-range weapons, such as anti-tank guns and mortars. Their incorporation into the garrison's artillery plan involved taking most of them from their original owners and having them manned by whatever infantry unit for the time being held the sector where they were sited. Chester Wilmot in *Tobruk* tells a story, probably true, of a bush-gun crew who combined pleasure with profit by charging passers-by "2 piastres a pop" for the privilege of firing their gun at the enemy. The business was closed down on the protest of a neighbouring infantry commander whose headquarters became the delivery point for returns.

While the landward pressure on the fortress diminished as the new front stabilised, the attack from the air on the port and the ships whose cargoes sustained the garrison was waged with growing intensity. During May 734 Axis aircraft were over Tobruk. The hospital ship *Karapara*, flying a huge Red Cross flag 40 feet square at its forepeak, and bearing other Red Cross markings plainly visible, was circled by Messerschmitt aircraft as she approached Tobruk on 4th May. An hour and a half later 12 bombers escorted by fighters attacked her in waves of three. Although she was not sunk, the enemy achieved his purpose. In view of this and two earlier attacks on hospital ships in Tobruk waters, it was decided that all sick and wounded would henceforth be evacuated by destroyer. The minesweeper *Stoke* was sunk on 6th May by three direct hits in a raid by 40 aircraft; of its intrepid crew, numbering 55, 11 were killed and 34 wounded. H.M.S. *Ladybird*, a floating battery for the army, escaped several near misses in the harbour, and scored several hits on aircraft in reply, but was sunk by bombs on 12th May, her guns still firing and her White Ensign flying as she grounded on the bottom, ending her career afloat by shooting down a bomber after she had been struck. Her commander, Lieut-Commander J. F. Blackburn, signalled Morshead before abandoning ship:

> One wicket down for Yorkshire. Nine more to go yet. Play up Australia. We will catch them on a sticky wicket.

Morshead replied:

> Great innings by *Ladybird* and we are all extremely sorry that it has ended. We will beat them on any wicket.

The decision at the end of April to withdraw combatant aircraft from Tobruk was followed by an order from Western Desert Force headquarters that the army-cooperation squadron personnel should be returned. Morshead protested without avail in a message sent on 7th May. He submitted that execution of the order would prejudice the security of the fortress unless, before No. 6 Squadron was withdrawn, it was replaced by an army-cooperation unit equipped to provide tactical and artillery reconnaissance under his orders; he had no effective air reconnaissance at all and it was urgently necessary that he should be provided with air observation for his artillery and the means to photograph enemy positions of which ground observation was impossible. General Beresford-Peirse replied with sympathy, expressing hopes of better things to come, but indicated that nothing could be provided from the current scanty resources of aircraft.

Morshead wrote in similar vein to General Blamey a few days later:

> I am anxious to push the Boche out of our territory but it is a first essential that we know his dispositions. Tac/Rs by Hurricanes do not give sufficient details, they generally consist merely of the whereabouts of MT and AFVs and an estimate of their numbers often so inaccurate as to be seriously misleading. I have repeatedly asked for air photographs but have not yet had a single one, this over a period of two months. Until I can get photographs of this area I do not feel disposed to launch a big attack. When we do attack we shall put everything we possibly can into it including all our I tanks which at present number 12 effectives, the biggest tally we have had since 1 May. If only we had a Bn of I tanks we'd clean the whole show up inside and outside the perimeter.
>
> Col Birks who has been in charge of the tanks here is returning to M.E. tonight and he is to tell GHQ of the position.
>
> You are, of course, aware of the air position as it affects us. I sincerely hope that it will very soon improve. Now we have to rely on Tac/Rs from Bagush: a very serious handicap.
>
> The men are in good fettle and as eager as ever. They are a grand lot. Health is good considering the conditions—a dust storm practically every other day and ½ gal of water a day. The artillery also is doing a wonderful job: they are splendid fellows and each Bde swears by the regiment supporting them. And the A/Tk and A/A gunners are excellent, too.
>
> Lloyd continues to do extremely well. He is sound, hardworking, calm and gets on well with everybody. The Bde Comdrs are all on their toes, Murray particularly. As soon as I possibly can I shall relieve Tovell by Wootten and follow that up with other reliefs.

The inter-brigade relief predicted in this letter took place on the night of 13th May, when Wootten's brigade relieved Tovell's brigade in the Salient. The 2/12th Battalion replaced the 2/23rd from the Derna Road to the Salient. In the Salient the 2/10th Battalion took over from the 2/48th on the right, the 2/9th, reverting to command of its parent formation, remained in position in the centre, and the 2/13th Battalion, placed temporarily under Wootten's command, relieved the 2/1st Pioneer Battalion (on the night 11th-12th May) on the left.

Brigadier Wootten's assumption of responsibility for the western sector marked the opening of a counter-offensive in the Salient, which was to continue throughout the summer months until about the end of the first week in August. From the time the relief took place, and through a succession of later reliefs, the defence line was, little by little, pushed forward and much of the ground previously lost recovered, but at great cost in battle strain, wounds, and loss of life. Some of the lost perimeter posts were to be retaken, only to be lost again. But the enemy was made to fight repeatedly to retain the ground wrested from the garrison.

Morshead's attitude was reflected in his first instruction to Wootten before the relief: he was to site his headquarters farther forward than the existing headquarters site in the western sector. (A suitable more forward site could not immediately be found but, as we shall see, the instruction was carried out in due course.) Wootten in turn sent out a memorandum to his commanding officers on the conduct of the defence, which included points concerning patrolling, concealment, deception, enticing the enemy to expend ammunition and other tactical advice. The opening paragraph gave the theme:

> The responsibility will immediately fall upon each line unit therefore: not only to maintain intact the line and territory which it takes over; but also to put in hand *at once* a policy of aggression against the enemy; to exert and maintain a superiority of morale over him; to systematically wipe out his forward posts and to occupy with its own troops the same ground, and thus incessantly to exert pressure upon the enemy and relentlessly drive him back bit by bit on battalion fronts, under arrangements made within battalions. It is to be made perfectly clear to all ranks that we are not simply there to hold a line; but that we are there definitely with the purpose and intention of regaining ground previously lost, and of inflicting loss on the enemy by every means in our power.

The new phase opened with a fierce fire-fight in the front of Lieut-Colonel Burrows' 2/13th Battalion at dawn on the morning after it had taken over on the left of the Salient. The enemy no doubt had heard the relief. Each side strove for mastery in a duel repeated for several mornings until, on 15th May, the battalion's diarist was able to record that the forward companies had gained control of the front. From the time that his battalion came to the Salient, Burrows, an aggressive commander with a fighter's instinct for coming to close grips with his enemy, constantly and ardently advocated a policy of advancing and shortening the line. On 14th May he pushed forward part of his left forward company and dug them into a new position 350 yards forward. This was but a foretaste.

Wootten took command of the western sector on the night of 13th May. Next morning he received an order from Morshead's headquarters requiring him immediately to stage a demonstration to give the enemy the impression that a full-scale attack was being carried out. The order advised that British forces were advancing in the Salum area. The object of Wootten's operations would be to prevent the enemy from moving his forces from Tobruk. Operation BREVITY had begun.

Operation BREVITY was General Wavell's conception. For once the Middle East Command surprised the British Prime Minister by proposing to attack without being first goaded thereto by his own remonstrations. Mr Churchill later dramatically described the purpose of this operation as being "to claw down Rommel before the dreaded 15th Panzer Division arrived in full strength over the long road from Tripoli, and before Benghazi was effectively opened as a short cut for enemy supply";[2] but Wavell was more modest in describing his aims. He hoped, by concentrating all available tanks, to gain a local success on the frontier and would then consider action to drive the enemy west of Tobruk.

The Tiger convoy with its precious cargo of tanks was due in Alexandria about 12th May; several weeks would be required to clear them through the workshops and equip the formations to use them. But Wavell had perceived opportunities for offensive action before the newly-arrived tanks would be ready. The fact that Rommel had been forced to divide his forces between Tobruk and the frontier while undertaking the added commitment of garrisoning Bardia appeared to offer an opportunity to achieve temporary superiority at Salum, to strike there while the enemy force was divided and, if an immediate defeat could be inflicted at the frontier, to advance quickly to Tobruk whence a combined operation could be mounted with the fortress garrison. That final development was perhaps more a hope in Wavell's mind than an expectation. Rommel later wrote of Wavell:[3]

> What distinguished him from other British army commanders was his great and well-balanced strategic courage, which permitted him to concentrate his forces regardless of his opponent's possible moves.[4]

But for maximum success to be achieved Wavell's audacity would require to be matched by fine judgment on the part of his armoured force commander in exploiting with economy, speed, audacity and ingenuity a slender and only temporary local superiority. Whether Brigadier Gott was such a man was yet to be discovered.

Wavell's aggressive impulse was born as great disaster befell his command and while further dangers loomed. April 28th marked the end of efforts to extricate the main force of the British expedition to Greece. On the same day the British Prime Minister telegraphed Wavell, on the basis of reports from Intelligence sources, that it seemed clear that a heavy airborne attack by German troops and bombers would soon be made on Crete. "It ought to be a fine opportunity for killing the parachute troops. The island must be stubbornly defended," Churchill declared. Wavell had also been requested from London to advise what troops could be brought to the aid of General Dentz, the Vichy commander in Syria, in the event that the Germans launched an airborne attack against Syria. Wavell replied on 28th April that he had only a cavalry brigade group available. Meanwhile, in Iraq, the pro-Axis Rashid Ali had seized power. It had been agreed with the Chiefs of Staff that any operations requiring intervention in Iraq should be the responsibility of India. An Indian brigade group was moved into Basra in mid-April, in ostensible exercise of treaty rights for the passage of military forces through Iraq and on the pretext

---
[2] Churchill, Vol III, p. 299.
[3] Referring specifically to operation BATTLEAXE.
[4] *The Rommel Papers*, p. 146.

that the force was en route to Palestine. Rashid Ali requested that the troops move on quickly and, when the request was refused, moved two Iraqi divisions stationed in Baghdad on to the neighbouring plateau to pose a threat to the British Air Force training base at Habbaniya. Wavell had consistently opposed the imposition of a further commitment in Iraq upon his overstrained resources but now learnt that he would be required to send assistance from Palestine. On 30th April Wavell flew to Crete, there to meet Generals Wilson and Freyberg. He surprised the generals by immediately assigning to each of them new responsibilities: to the one, the defence of Crete, to the other, control of operations against Iraq.

Back in Cairo on 1st May Wavell sent a note to General Beresford-Peirse stating that it was his intention "to take the offensive in the Western Desert as soon as our resources permit". There was no reason, he said, to accept that the enemy would be in greatly superior strength at any time. Tobruk must operate to hold an equal force of enemy and be prepared to take full part in the counter-stroke when it took place. He asked Beresford-Peirse to have the whole problem examined in detail and to consider with other questions "the best line of offence to drive the enemy out of Egypt and eventually beyond Tobruk". Perhaps Wavell may have also found a few spare moments to give thought to the problem of finishing off the East African campaign as the summer rains set in and of extricating some of the forces employed there for future use in the Western Desert. The Emperor Haile Selassie was to be reinstalled as Emperor of Abyssinia on 5th May.

On 2nd May the Defence Committee in London decided that the responsibility for Iraq should revert to the Middle East Command. Wavell was asked if he had strong objections. He had; but on 5th May the command passed to him. Mr Churchill wrote later—

> General Auchinleck continued to offer reinforcements up to five infantry brigades and ancillary troops by June 10 if shipping could be provided. We were gratified by his forward mood—General Wavell only obeyed under protest.

On 6th May, Churchill minuted for the Chiefs of Staff Committee:

> I am deeply disturbed at General Wavell's attitude. He seems to have been taken as much by surprise on his eastern as he was on his western flank, and in spite of the enormous number of men at his disposal and the great convoys reaching him, he seems to be hard up for battalions and companies. He gives me the impression of being tired out.[5]

The impressions of General Auchinleck as forward and energetic, and of General Wavell as tired, were to persist.

Meanwhile Wavell developed his plan to seize the initiative on the Egyptian frontier. The nature of the forward British defence on the frontier was the same, though the formations and units had changed. It rested on a screen of four mobile columns, three above the escarpment on the open desert flank, and one on the coast, the inland and coast forces each being under a separate headquarters. Both headquarters were in the Buq

---

[5] Churchill, Vol III, pp. 228-9.

Buq area after 7th May, when the 7th Armoured Division Support Group headquarters, in charge of the inland columns, came there from Sidi Barrani. Attached to each force was a troop of Major Argent's 12th Battery, 2/3rd Anti-Tank Regiment, with the third troop providing a section of guns with each force headquarters.

On 6th May the German High Command, on the recommendation of General Paulus, ordered General Rommel to prepare a defensive line from Gazala to Gadd el Ahmar on which to fall back if the Salum-Bardia front had to be abandoned. The message was intercepted by the British Intelligence and encouraged Wavell to move quickly. Preliminary British moves on 8th and 9th May in the Sidi Suleiman, Point 206 (south of Capuzzo) and Halfaya areas alerted the enemy and an intercepted weather report, transmitted by the British to all units in a form known from experience to precede a British operation, confirmed the apprehensions of the German command, which made dispositions to meet the threat. The *33rd Reconnaissance Unit,* a battalion of the *Trento Division,* Hohmann's *II Battalion* of the *5th Armoured Regiment* and a motor-cycle battalion were sent from Tobruk to join the Herff Group at Salum, and on 11th May an extensive sweep of mobile forces and armour aimed at Deir el Hamra was made across the plateau south of Salum, dislodging British outposts. On the 12th the German screening columns edged forward both above and below the escarpment to an area north-east of Sofafi. (Near Qaret el Reteim a gun of Sergeant Gillam's[6] troop of the 12th Anti-Tank Battery engaged German armoured cars and scored a direct hit.) The German columns drew back to the Salum area on the night of the 13th.

General Beresford-Peirse's instructions to Morshead for participation by the fortress were sent under cover of a letter written on 8th May but were not delivered to Morshead until 13th May. They reached him just as a major relief within the fortress was being effected. The chance that aggressive action by the fortress might affect the enemy's dispositions favourably for the prospects of a frontier operation was not great in view of the disclosure of the real intention and the taking up of pre-battle dispositions before Morshead could act. Nevertheless Morshead did the best he could at such short notice and planned operations with real, if limited, objectives while seeking at the same time to aggrandise them in the enemy's eyes to the appearance of a full-scale attack. The deceptive measures for this purpose were to be simulated radio and wireless deception and transport moves on a scale for major operations.

A general increase in activity in the western sector was immediately put in hand. Major Arnold[7] of the 2/10th Battalion took out a patrol about 3 p.m. on the 14th to the old 2/24th Battalion headquarters area and brought in two vehicles, one of which the patrol loaded with equip-

---

[6] Lt W. J. F. Gillam, NX51414; 2/3 A-Tk Regt. Clerk; of Manly, NSW; b. Burwood, NSW, 21 Feb 1919.
[7] Lt-Col A. S. W. Arnold, OBE, ED, SX1468. 2/10 Bn; CO 2/12 Bn 1942-43. Public servant; of Kensington Gardens, SA; b. Tumby Bay, SA, 18 Apr 1906.

ment. In the El Adem sector Lieutenant Maclarn[8] of the 2/17th and Lieutenant D. C. M. Salt of the Chestnut Troop went out with six carriers to shoot up a hull-down tank south of R39 and three tanks farther east. The tanks battened down and gave chase, but Maclarn's and Salt's carriers came safely in at Post R43. The tanks shelled that area and then returned to the sally port at R39 and there began to do likewise but did not tarry long under the concentrated fire of the Chestnut Troop and "C" Troop, 426th Battery. During the night the tempo of artillery activity increased and all units probed deeper with patrols. Major Bruer[9] arranged two patrols from the 2/10th Battalion. Earlier patrol exploits at the old 2/24th Battalion headquarters had suggested that the ground to the 2/10th's immediate front was unoccupied, and this the patrols confirmed.

On the morning of 15th May Bruer recommended to Brigadier Wootten that the battalion should advance its line provided that the 2/9th Battalion would conform by moving forward on his left. Bruer put in hand preliminary arrangements in anticipation of approval. Bruer's report satisfied Wootten that a forward movement was practicable. He called a conference of commanding officers and directed that the front should be advanced that night and that patrolling of the areas to be occupied should be carried out during the day. Meanwhile the divisional signals in conjunction with the 3rd Armoured Brigade set in train an increase of wireless and radio-telephone traffic, using sets specially brought forward to the western sector.

The active program for 15th May began with tank sorties from the perimeter in the early morning followed by artillery registration in the western sector combined with smoke-screens, then observed shooting in the Salient by guns with a liberal ammunition allotment and a general increase in carrier and other offensive patrolling. In the early afternoon large-scale transport movement was organised in the western sector and to points under enemy observation behind the Derna Road perimeter entrance, also to Pilastrino. Vehicles were directed to use the dustiest routes. The movement continued till sundown. Dust billowed up in full view of the investing forces. When the darkness closed in, the wireless and radio traffic was augmented, the weight and tempo of the artillery concentrations were increased and Very lights and other ruses were adopted to simulate a night attack.

To heighten this impression of an impending attack Wootten's brigade had planned to execute a number of limited operations that day. A foray of infantry and cruiser tanks in two thrusts along the first and second escarpments south of the Derna Road was the first to be set in train. The operation had been jointly planned by Lieut-Colonel Drew (then in command of the armoured brigade) and Lieut-Colonel Field. Two infantry platoons were to move out 800 yards from the perimeter under cover of darkness; there they were to get into position ready to move forward

---

[8] Maj L. C. Maclarn, MC, NX12228; 2/17 Bn. Chain store manager; of Sydney; b. Wellington, NZ, 5 Jul 1911.
[9] Lt-Col L. G. Bruer, SX1432. (1st AIF: Lt 16 Bn.) 2/10 Bn (CO 1941). Architect; of Walkerville, SA; b. Walkerville, 22 Feb 1895.

along the escarpments at 9 a.m., when artillery concentrations were to be laid down. Cruiser tanks would then come out from the perimeter and assist the infantry as they moved forward.

At 4 a.m. Lieutenant Thomas[10] and 24 men armed with grenades, rifles, three Bren guns and a Tommy-gun moved out from S19 in bright moonlight, gapped the wire and took up position in a small re-entrant northeast of White Knoll on the first escarpment. Another patrol of platoon strength commanded by Lieutenant Haupt[1] went out from Post S15 at 6 a.m. moving out some 800 yards towards the foot of the second escarpment below White Knoll, and there waited for the tanks to appear. During the night the 18th Indian Cavalry Regiment had been patrolling aggressively from the Wadi Sehel.

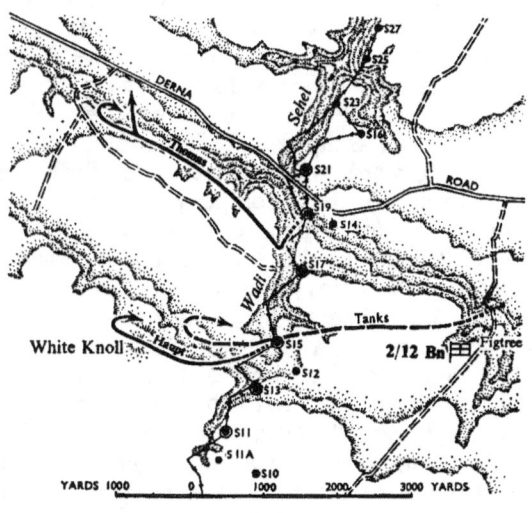

Meanwhile, in the 20th Brigade sector, six carriers, one of them bearing Captain Armitage of the 1st R.H.A., had sallied forth at 6 a.m. near the El Adem Road to lure the enemy tanks in that sector into the fire of the garrison's 25-pounders. The tanks responded to the ruse and were shelled by guns specially sited near the wire.

The cruiser tanks allotted to Field's excursions were true to form in mechanical unreliability; one developed a track defect, leaving only two to participate. These encountered artillery fire as they were approaching the perimeter and moved out of sight into a wadi until the firing ceased. Consequently they were half an hour late in debouching. Lieutenant Thomas rightly set off at 9 a.m., on time, and moved away from the perimeter along the escarpment overlooking the Derna Road. After about half a mile the patrol came under fire from a 20-mm Breda machine-gun. With fire and movement the Australians executed a good assault on the enemy post, killed two of the enemy gun crew and wounded two; the Italians retreated rapidly, assisting their wounded. Other enemy in neighbouring positions, discarding jackets and leaving behind greatcoats and equipment, beat a rapid retreat to the north-west, where about 150 startled Italians jumped out of their trenches and stood up to see what was happening. This was the site of Brown's successful fighting patrol

---

[10] Maj K. B. Thomas, OBE, MC, TX885; 2/12 Bn. 2 Bn RAR Korea 1953. Regular soldier; of Ulverstone, Tas; b. Launceston, Tas, 5 Jul 1914.

[1] Maj F. K. Haupt, TX882; 2/12 Bn. Regular soldier; of Launceston, Tas; b. Hamley Bridge, SA, 14 Jun 1913.

a few nights before. Thomas proceeded to a distance of about 500 yards from the position, which was found to be extensively developed and appeared to be arranging a reception. Thomas could not expect the tanks, who had not even been invited to this party, to put in an appearance, so he then withdrew his patrol by bounds under covering fire provided by alternating sections, silencing a sniper post on the way. The patrol was shelled and mortared as it returned. One man was wounded.

On the second escarpment to the south Lieutenant Haupt waited half an hour for the tanks. Thus for the advantage of their support, he lost the benefit of the timed artillery concentrations. His objective was a feature aptly called White Knoll, which was known to be occupied by the enemy. White Knoll was an outcrop near the top edge of the second escarpment and stood almost a mile out from the perimeter across the wadi on the fringe of which the perimeter defences were laid out. While the tanks were coming up, enemy were observed going back from the knoll. Haupt set off at 9.35 a.m. with two tanks giving close support. The tanks briefly bombarded the knoll with 2-pounder and Besa guns and then withdrew. Haupt pressed on, found the knoll unoccupied, and sent a section forward, which came under fire. The patrol then attacked into what appeared to be a company position disposed in depth. Some of the enemy in the forward posts broke. Greatly assisted by the initiative and dash of Private Croker,[2] the patrol's forward movement was sustained notwithstanding heavy mortar fire, and the enemy began to fall back; but the action had to be broken off when the ammunition carried was almost expended. A fighting withdrawal was executed. Six men of the patrol were wounded, most of them severely.

Owing to the late arrival of the tanks these two patrol actions had not been fought simultaneously. The enemy probably did not suffer as great immediate apprehension as had been hoped, but the action, in conjunction with the extensive artillery program conducted simultaneously in the Medauuar sector, must have caused uneasiness. Morshead did not have the satisfaction of knowing that a message from the *Brescia Division* on this sector reached German *Africa Corps* headquarters at the same time as the first reports of British successes on the frontier: it reported an attack in battalion strength just south of the coast road.

During the next night both sides took offensive action in the western sector. From the 18th Cavalry positions on the right of the perimeter to the left of the Salient and the adjacent enemy hinterland, violent clashes occurred. In the early afternoon small patrols of two or three men had probed the ground forward of the 2/10th and 2/9th Battalions. Two men from the 2/10th found Forbes' Mound unoccupied. As night fell gunfire beat down on the enemy Salient positions. Then the two battalions pushed their lines forward on the right of the Salient. The move began at 9 p.m. Just at this time the northernmost perimeter posts of the neighbouring 2/12th Battalion—S8, S9 and S10—were brought under heavy enemy machine-gun fire and an anti-tank gun began blasting

---

[2] Cpl M. O. Croker, QX3563; 2/12 Bn. Labourer; of Malanda, Qld; b. Malanda, 28 Jan 1918.

at S10 from the overlooking escarpment near Post S7 (which the enemy had captured on 1st May).

The move forward of the 2/10th Battalion was not without its moments of anxiety. On the right Captain Martin's[3] company had difficulty in positioning themselves by reference to a wrecked plane, a landmark in the area, which for a time could not be found. The right and centre companies got forward without casualties; the fact that later in the night the enemy directed fire over their heads on to their old positions suggests that their advance had not been detected. The left company (under Captain Cooper[4]) going to the Forbes' Mound area was less fortunate and became involved in a fire fight, suffering several casualties, including two men killed. Corporal Laud[5] ambushed two Germans but one escaped to inform the enemy of what was afoot. The 2/9th Battalion, simultaneously moving its line forward on the right of Bianca, had some difficulty in linking up on the right flank with Cooper's company. The new front took in the old 2/24th Battalion headquarters and Nixon's Post.

Meanwhile at 9 p.m. a fighting patrol of 68 men (including three engineers) commanded by Major Peek had gone out in a south-westerly direction from the 2/15th Battalion. Its mission was to destroy transport in the enemy rear areas south of Carrier Hill and Ras el Medauuar about 2,000 yards out from the original perimeter. The assault component of the patrol comprised two platoons commanded by Lieutenant Harland[6] and Warrant-Officer Scoggins.[7] A second patrol of comparable strength was provided as a reserve to help in extrication, if necessary. The enemy transport had apparently been brought back to safer ground during the preceding day's artillery bombardment, for the patrol could not discover a single vehicle. But Harland's men found other objects worthy of unfriendly attention. A field gun was discovered and Harland sent in a section to assault it. The enemy had meanwhile been alerted and moved to cut off the patrol, but Peek had lost contact with Scoggins' platoon on the way out and could do nothing to counter the move. Machine-guns opened up in all directions. A general mêlée developed in the course of which sections of the patrol in separate fights damaged the field gun and killed its crew, assaulted three machine-gun posts, driving out or killing the occupants, and destroyed a tank. One section became scattered and was lost but all except one man found his way back. Only three men had been wounded and the patrol had covered about twelve miles. "The boldest patrol since the occupation of the fortress," commented the diarist of the 1st R.H.A.

At 2 a.m. on 16th May a strong German attack was made from the southern shoulder of the Salient on Post R8 on the left flank of the 2/13th

---
[3] Maj G. G. F. Martin, SX1440; 2/10 Bn. Salesman; of Adelaide; b. Adelaide, 22 Feb 1906. Killed in action 28 Aug 1942.
[4] Lt-Col G. D. T. Cooper, MBE, SX1435. 2/10 Bn; CO 2/27 Bn 1942-43; and training appts. Mechanical engineer; of Leabrook, SA; b. Adelaide, 2 Apr 1912.
[5] WO1 H. Laud, SX487; 2/10 Bn. Labourer; of Sydney; b. Beverley, England, 6 Apr 1910.
[6] Maj M. Harland, QX6242. 2/15 Bn and air liaison appts. Bank clerk; of Brisbane; b. Labasa, Fiji, 21 Apr 1912.
[7] Capt D. W. R. Scoggins, QX6518. 2/15 Bn, "Z" Special Unit. Regular soldier; of Diamond Creek, Vic; b. St Kilda, Vic, 19 Feb 1914.

Battalion. The enemy brought up two tanks to dishearten the defenders; but the Australians got the upper hand without incurring casualties and the Germans, identified as engineers, retired leaving six men killed and three wounded. Meanwhile, from the corresponding positions on the northern shoulder of the Salient, Captain Vincent's[8] company of the 2/12th Battalion, holding Posts S8, S9 and S10, was calling on the artillery to bring gunfire down on to Post S7, whence the anti-tank gun was continuing its bombardment of Post S10. The artillery obliged with five rounds of gunfire, but the enemy responded with an intense bombardment of the entire battalion sector.

About 2.30 a.m. an enemy attack or raid was made north of the Derna Road on the 18th Cavalry Regiment but the Indians allowed no penetration of their lines. Simultaneously at least a company of Italians, led by two storming parties and accompanied by groups of special wire-cutting engineers, assaulted Posts S15, S13 and S11 south of the road. Flame-throwers were brought up. The Italians pressed home their attack and managed to penetrate the wire near S15 but suffered appalling casualties in the wadi in front of S15, into which Lieutenant Haupt's platoon pumped mortar bombs and threw grenades. By 3.30 a.m. the company commander reported the situation to be under control.

But a more serious situation had arisen on the left of Field's battalion, where a strong attack was made by Germans on Vincent's company in Posts S8, S9 and S10, masked by the Italian attack on the posts from S11 to the north. Machine-guns firing tracers on fixed lines that intersected above the posts guided in the attackers, who brought up five tanks and a flame-thrower to assist their assault parties. For about 15 minutes an intense mortar bombardment was brought down on the posts while the irrepressible anti-tank gun continued firing down into Post S10 from the ridge near S7. The enemy moved in. An intense clamour of automatic weapons proclaimed close fighting in which some men would surely die. The 51st Field Regiment put down defensive fire. Bursts of lurid flame shot forth. Later the firing died down and dark shadows moving through the area could be dimly perceived from the neighbouring posts. All signal lines to Vincent's company had been cut and no word came to dispel fears as to their fate. Field ordered the commander of the adjoining company to make ready for a counter-attack.

Simultaneously, in the Salient, an enemy attack was made on Forbes' Mound after a bombardment by artillery and mortars on the positions just vacated by the 2/10th Battalion in the forward move. Cooper's company beat off the attack but one man was killed. About the same time four enemy tanks approached the 2/9th Battalion. The two leading tanks ran into the wire and were stopped, but the other two tanks towed them off. Later five tanks were reported to be probing farther west.

When dawn came enemy still lingered outside the wire of Field's battalion between the first and second escarpments south of the Derna Road.

---

[8] Maj T. H. Vincent, ED, TX2024. 2/4 and 2/12 Bns. Clerk; of New Town, Tas; b. Zeehan, Tas, 11 Feb 1909.

Patrols went out over a battleground strewn with dead and rounded up 21 broken-spirited Italians. Seven light machine-guns, two medium machine-guns and two flame-throwers were also brought in.[9] But there was still no news from Field's four northernmost perimeter posts, S8, S9, S10 and S11. Field had decided not to send out a patrol in the dark for fear that his own men might clash with each other, but had ordered that a fighting patrol should investigate at first light. This task was given to Lieutenant Rose.[1]

Setting out with his platoon at 6 a.m. Rose came first to S11 and the neighbouring section Post S11A and found that the garrisons were still intact. Proceeding up to S10 the patrol was suddenly caught in the open by flanking machine-gun fire. Rose, badly wounded, came back to report that the enemy appeared to hold S10, in which Captain Vincent had had his headquarters.

As the morning wore on, there was no news from Vincent's other two posts, S8 and S9. Field began to plan a counter-attack with artillery support to be mounted just after midday. To enable Field to release men from perimeter defence to participate in the attack Wootten had earlier ordered the 2/24th Battalion to provide a relief garrison for Post S13. Meanwhile a German and six Italians had been captured. The German, from the *33rd Engineer Battalion,* was dispatched to divisional headquarters, where under interrogation he gave a false account of the capture of S10 early in the night, before the moon rose: he stated that the garrison had surrendered without a fight and without suffering casualties.[2] General Morshead was deeply angered when he read this report and sent a personal memorandum to his brigade commanders:

> Today we lost posts R8, R9 and R10 [sic], the occupants having been taken prisoners in the circumstances set out in the attached document. This is the second time that portion of our garrison has vanished. As far as can be ascertained the number of casualties was negligible, the posts having been just mopped up—rather a new experience for the A.I.F.
>
> So long as posts are not defensively prepared and improved but are just sleeping or funk holes we shall lose more prisoners . . . positions outside the post must be dug at once and manned in preference to the concrete post itself. . . .

Some of the positions taken up during the night on the fronts of the 2/10th and 2/9th Battalions were found next morning to be exposed and unsuitable for holding. This was so particularly at the junction of the two battalions. The shallow rock-bottomed positions dug by Lieutenant Syme's[3] platoon on the left of the 2/10th were so dominated by fire from higher enemy positions that they became untenable. Two men were killed; Syme and four others were wounded. Private Hackett[4] gamely made a dash

---

[9] Such battle trophies were not mere museum-pieces to the Tobruk garrison. More automatic weapons were urgently needed to increase the fire-power of the perimeter posts.
[1] Capt G. H. Rose, QX3668; 2/12 Bn. Salesman; of Cairns, Qld; b. Brisbane, 23 Nov 1906.
[2] When the post was recaptured, severely wounded members of the original garrison were rescued, who reported that others had been killed and buried by the Germans. The post had been overrun because it proved impossible without observation or tracer to counter fixed-line fire into the weapon-pits coming from higher ground near Post S7.
[3] Capt D. M. Syme, SX4856; 2/10 Bn. Clerk; of Adelaide; b. Adelaide, 13 Sep 1916.
[4] L-Sgt C. G. Hackett, MM, SX2448; 2/10 Bn. Labourer; of Port Elliot, SA; b. Ororoo, SA, 20 Mar 1920. Killed in action 1 Jul 1945.

across 500 yards of fire-raked open ground to inform Captain Cooper of the situation. New positions were chosen in rear and, pivoting on Forbes' Mound, the company line was swung back about 8.30 a.m. into a favourably situated re-entrant under cover of smoke and an artillery bombardment. In the 2/9th Battalion, on the other hand, it was found possible to advance the line 150 yards forward of the positions taken up on the left of the old 2/24th Battalion headquarters. This was put in hand later next night.

At 11 a.m. Morshead went to Wootten's headquarters to discuss the recapture of Posts S8, S9 and S10. It was thought that an attack in battalion strength would probably be required. The 2/23rd Battalion, commanded by Lieut-Colonel Evans, was selected. Evans, an architect in civil life, was a leader who combined great drive with strong sympathies and loyalties towards the men he led. He had served in the militia continuously ever since he was a youth and had been commanding a militia battalion when, at the age of 35, he was chosen to form the 2/23rd Battalion. He was then the A.I.F's youngest battalion commander. Evans was summoned to attend a conference with Wootten and Morshead at 3 p.m. When the message reached him he was reconnoitring with his sub-unit commanders in the eastern sector, where it had been intended that the 26th Brigade should relieve the 24th Brigade in the next stage of the relief program. Morshead ordered the postponement of the relief and placed Evans' battalion under Wootten's command. Morshead and Wootten decided that Field's planned fighting patrol action against S10 would be allowed to proceed: it might succeed and would at least test the enemy's strength.

No word came back through the morning from Posts S8, S9 and S10. At 12.15 a.m., hard upon an artillery bombardment laid down by the 51st Field Regiment, Lieutenant Steddy[5] led a strong fighting patrol across fire-swept ground to attack S10. The post was retaken and the German garrison of one officer and 26 men captured, together with all weapons. Two Australian wounded, who had been held as prisoners but well cared for, were released. Meanwhile to the south, under the hot noonday sun, Posts S8 and S9 lay deceptively quiet, seemingly without menace.

At 3 p.m. Wootten gave Evans preliminary orders to attack S8 and S9. Morshead and Lloyd attended the conference. Evans was not only to recapture these two posts, but then to push on and capture Posts S7 and S6, on the escarpment overlooking S9 and S8. Three troops of infantry tanks, a troop of anti-tank guns and a company of machine-guns were to be placed under his command; he was to have the support of 39 field guns and a company of engineers. A commanders' reconnaissance was conducted in the afternoon, when Evans made an outline plan and pointed out routes and objectives on the ground. The final orders conference was held at 8.30 p.m. at Wootten's headquarters, where detailed written orders were distributed.

---

[5] Lt E. M. C. Steddy, QX6234; 2/12 Bn. Grazier; of Ascot, Qld; b. Townsville, Qld, 17 Sep 1914. Killed in action 1 Jan 1943.

The 2/23rd Battalion, which was then on the coastal plain at Airente, was to move out to its forward assembly area half an hour after midnight. The leading companies had already been embussed and Evans was about to close his headquarters when he received a message that Post S8 had been retaken by the 2/12th. Evans decided to discuss the new situation with Wootten on the way forward.

This blood-letting flare-up at the edge of the Tobruk perimeter had been ignited and kindled by impulses transmitted from the control centres of the two forces clashing on the Egyptian frontier. The lifting of the siege of Tobruk was the principal aim of operation BREVITY; even if only temporarily achieved, this would be an adequate reward for snatching a quick victory, of which there was no promise but some hope. General Beresford-Peirse had written to Morshead (in the letter received on 13th May):

> You will see herewith an outline of how I am proposing to start an offensive. If the enemy are in as bad a plight for "Q"[6] reinforcement as they are believed by "I" to be it might have far-reaching consequences. Anyway a diversion by you will assist to make Rommel scratch his head and perhaps withdraw.
> If we achieve even temporary opening of Tobruk you can relieve yourself of many "bouches inutiles" and give us much material that is badly wanted to organise the offensive force—particularly MT. . . . We are taking a considerable gamble if we launch the offensive with very few suitable troops but the possible political and psychological, as well as tactical, results justify it.
> Meanwhile the formation of a proper offensive force is progressing.

Although Wavell had informed Churchill on 13th May, perhaps with unwarranted optimism, that he would consider "immediate combined action by Gott's force and Tobruk garrison to drive enemy west of Tobruk" if the operation succeeded, Beresford-Peirse seemed to have his eye rather on the proximate arrival of the Tiger convoy and the "proper" offensive force that would then be his. The forces to do battle in BREVITY were indeed puny by comparison.

The plan and conduct of operation BREVITY foreshadowed in miniature the pattern of several later armoured engagements fought in the desert war. The cruiser tanks had twice the range and thrice the speed of the infantry tanks. Combining their action in operations therefore posed problems. Ought the cruisers to be harnessed to such slow partners? Should they not be set free to exploit their greater speed and range in faster action? The heavy tanks had moreover inherited unfortunate names: as if "Matilda" were not enough, these poor lumbering "heavies" were officially regarded as "infantry tanks". The term seems to have exerted its own influence, dictating that such slow coaches should be used mainly to support the plodding infantry—a role for which, as Rommel shrewdly remarked, the armour-piercing projectiles of their guns were ill-suited. The assignment of the infantry tanks to these pedestrian tasks, furthermore, would relieve the cruiser tanks of such embarrassing obligations and set their squadrons free to seek conclusions with similarly freed

---

[6] Supply.

enemy tanks in battles of manoeuvre. So the solution found to the difficult problems of fighting cruiser tanks in combination with infantry tanks, and armoured formations in combination with infantry formations, was to employ them in different directions.

The British plan envisaged a three-pronged attack—an infantry attack by the 2/Rifle Brigade below the escarpment to capture the bottom of the Halfaya Pass and subsequently Salum, an attack in the centre by the 22nd Guards Brigade and the 4th Royal Tank Regiment with 24 infantry tanks to take the top of the pass, secure Capuzzo and exploit northwards, and an advance on the open left flank to Sidi Azeiz by the 7th Armoured Brigade, comprising the 2nd Royal Tank Regiment (29 cruiser tanks) and three Support Group columns (Roze, Beam and Nire), destroying any enemy encountered on the way. Each Support Group column had with it a troop of the 12th Anti-Tank Battery, Major Argent himself being with Roze Column. Headquarters anti-tank defence on the coast was taken over by a troop of the 5th Battery, 2/2nd Anti-Tank Regiment. The operation began at dawn on 15th May.

Local surprise was achieved although the German command had been expecting an attack. The centre group struck first and captured the top of Halfaya Pass.[9] The Scots Guards were then signalled to begin the attack at the bottom of the pass, but encountered stiffer resistance, which was not overcome until about 5 p.m. Meanwhile the centre force had sent a detachment (Nire Column, with which was Lieutenant Scanlon's troop) with two infantry tanks to Salum, which was taken with 123 prisoners, while a battalion of the Durham Light Infantry with nine or ten tanks set off for Capuzzo. Capuzzo was captured but most of the tanks were temporarily disabled. Even with reinforcements brought up from Halfaya only six tanks in fighting state could be spared to guard the infantry at Capuzzo.

The German Command was gravely perturbed, the more so because early reports greatly over-stated the strength of the British forces. Mobile formations on the Tobruk front were redisposed to forestall a possible move to relieve the fortress. The *I Battalion* of the *8th Armoured Regiment* was ordered to Ed Duda, a detachment of Italian tanks to El Adem.

The German frontier force, called (after its commander) the Herff Group, reported that its front line was just north of Capuzzo and that it intended to hold from Sidi Azeiz to the north-west and thence eastwards to the coast south of Bardia. In other words it was for the time being acting defensively. Nevertheless at 2.45 p.m., while Gott's force of cruiser tanks was away to the flank on the conventional but unrealistically vague mission of destroying enemy, but was in fact sagely keeping beyond close range of the German forces masking Sidi Azeiz, a counter-attack on Capuzzo by Hohmann's *II Battalion* of the *5th Armoured Regiment* (reported four hours earlier as having only twelve runners) drove out the Durham Light Infantry, captured part of that battalion and regained the fort. The disabled British infantry tanks were left on the battlefield. Some

---

[9] Lt A. C. Rennison's troop of the 2/3rd Anti-Tank Regiment was with this column.

of these were recovered during the night, some destroyed, but some were later recovered by the enemy.

When night fell the field commanders of the opposing forces were both in cautious mood. Herff reported to Rommel that the British group at Sidi Azeiz appeared to have 40 or 50 armoured fighting vehicles and was expected to continue the offensive towards Tobruk in the morning, detaching elements to contain Herff's forces. Herff proposed to withdraw 10 kilometres west of Azeiz where his force would be in a harassing position from which a counter-attack could be launched later, when greater strength was assembled. Gott reported to Beresford-Peirse that the Guards Brigade group was in an exposed position at the top of the escarpment. If a tank attack seemed likely he proposed a withdrawal on to Halfaya.

Herff's report was made at 10 p.m. At 10.30 p.m. Rommel's headquarters instructed Herff to counter-attack via Sidi Azeiz and the south (presumably Capuzzo). The tank battalion at Ed Duda was told to move by night to Herff's group, to be ready for counter-attack at dawn. Soon the German groups were moving to concentrate. Another mixed group, comprising a battalion of lorried infantry with tanks and guns, was dispatched from the Tobruk front. The employment of tanks in night operations in the Tobruk Salient in the early hours of that morning, already narrated, was probably intended to mask this departure of armour.

By contrast, Gott's message was sent at 9 p.m. and was "much delayed".[1] Beresford-Peirse did not reply till 2.45 a.m. He instructed Gott to hold the positions taken and added that he would himself review the situation after receiving the morning air reconnaissance reports. But Gott, who had a penchant for acting independently of higher formation, had already ordered the withdrawal. The outlying groups drew back from the escarpment above Salum and from Musaid before daylight.

On 16th May, during which the German forces were grounded for long periods by lack of petrol, the cruiser tank force withdrew as the Germans advanced. Early on 17th May the Germans reoccupied Salum. Halfaya alone remained in British hands, the Guards holding the top of the pass with support from artillery and a squadron of infantry tanks.

Military writers almost unanimously discount the achievement of operation BREVITY. Thus the official British *History of the Second World War* sums it up:

> Operation "Brevity" was therefore a failure; the only British gain was the Halfaya Pass.

It is probably true that the forces available were not sufficient to retain indefinitely all the initial gains, and that the decision to capture Capuzzo and Salum was not matched by a determination to accept risks to hold on to them. But if the Western Desert Command had attempted too much with too little, it had still gained much at little cost. The German casualties in men in the operation appear to have been as heavy as the British.

---

[1] I. S. O. Playfair, *The Mediterranean and Middle East*, Vol II (1956), p. 162, a volume in the United Kingdom official series, *History of the Second World War*.

There was a large bag of Italian prisoners. The Germans lost three tanks, the British five.[2] One military writer who may still be accorded some authority attributed importance to the gain. Commenting on the fact that the British now held the Halfaya Pass, Rommel later wrote:

> The Halfaya and Salum Passes were points of great strategic importance, for they were the only two places between the coast and Habata where it was possible to cross the escarpment—of anything up to 600 feet in height—which stretched away from Salum in a south-easterly direction towards Egypt. The Halfaya positions gave an equal command over both possible roads. In any offensive from Egypt, therefore, possession of these passes was bound to be of the utmost value to the enemy, as they offered him a comparatively safe route for his supplies. If, on the other hand, he were to attempt to attack Bardia without holding them, he would be thrown back on a supply route through Habata which would be vulnerable to attack and harassing action by us.[3]

On 16th May, the day on which Gott was withdrawing the armour from the frontier, General Wavell sent General Beresford-Peirse a memorandum reiterating that the policy must be to drive the enemy west of Tobruk and keep him there. It was essential, he said, that the landing grounds between Tobruk and Salum should be available for the use of the R.A.F. The forces necessary for this would be decided later, but provisionally the 7th Armoured Division and the 7th and 9th Australian Divisions were suggested. Rather contradictorily a staff conference held at Wavell's headquarters later in the day agreed that all the A.I.F. in the Middle East should be concentrated as soon as possible.

On 18th May Mr Churchill sent Wavell one of his animating messages. He commented favourably on operation BREVITY but asked: "What are your dates for bringing Tiger Cubs into action?" In the meantime trouble for Wavell was brewing in the north where the German forces in conquered Greece seemed to be gathering for further strikes. It was evident that an attack on Crete was impending, while German aircraft had begun using Syrian airfields and German technicians were known to be arriving in Syria. Wavell was induced by compelling pressure from the British Government to plan an invasion of Syria. By 18th May Blamey and the Australian Government knew that the 7th Division was likely to be transferred from the Western Desert for employment on this front. However the surrender of the Duke of Aosta on 19th May with the remnants of his army marked the virtual end of the East African campaign, while in Iraq the force dispatched by Wavell had almost reached the beleaguered R.A.F. station at Habbaniya without misadventure.

The message received in the early hours of 17th May by Colonel Evans just before his battalion left Airente to the effect that Post S8 had been "retaken" was not accurate. After night fell on the 16th contact had at last been made with Posts S8 and S9. It was discovered that the garrisons were still intact, with only two men wounded. Post S9, under Lieutenant

---

[2] Playfair, Vol II, p. 162. But the CO of the 4 RTR gives the loss as "some eight tanks" in B. H. Liddell Hart, *The Tanks*, Vol II (1959), p. 80.
[3] *The Rommel Papers*, pp. 136-7.

Reid,[4] had at one stage become closely invested. After the mortar bombardment which had preceded the attack, the enemy had managed to get into the anti-tank ditch surrounding the emplacement and had begun throwing bombs into the post but Reid had mounted a vigorous counter-attack, cleared the anti-tank ditch and driven the enemy off. In Post S8 Lieutenant Douglas[5] had seen enemy crawling in towards the post as soon as the bombardment ceased. These were immediately engaged with grenades and automatics. For about an hour the enemy persisted with attempts to get in close but withdrew after a repetition of failures, taking their wounded but leaving six dead men round the post and others farther out. One Australian in the post was killed and two were wounded.

On the way to the western sector, where his battalion was to mount the counter-attack next morning, Evans called in at Brigadier Wootten's headquarters. He knew already that Post S8 was in safe hands. Now he learnt that Post S9 was also intact. The first phase of his plan had thus become redundant; so, before moving on to his headquarters, he rearranged the artillery program, cancelling the bombardment of S8 and S9 for the first phase.

The nature of Evans' task had now changed from one primarily of recapturing recently lost ground and exploiting forward for consolidation to one of attacking a fully developed enemy position held since 1st May. A coordinating conference was held at 4.30 a.m., at which Evans decided to seek permission to extend his task, unexpectedly reduced to the capture of Posts S7 and S6, to include also exploitation to, and capture of, Posts S5 and S4. Wootten, with Lloyd's concurrence, gave approval before the operation began.

The attack was to be made with two companies forward: Captain Malloch's on the right, Major Perry's[6] on the left, each with a troop of infantry tanks. Each company was to take its first objective, leave one platoon in the captured post, and push on with two platoons to the next. The two reserve companies were to hold themselves ready to assist at Evans' direction. The artillery program included timed concentrations on the objectives and general fire and smoke on Ras el Medauuar. For the first time in Tobruk Australian infantry were supported by Australian artillery. The 2/12th Field Regiment (less three troops) had arrived in Tobruk on H.M.A.S. *Vampire* at 1 a.m. Zero hour for the attack was 5.30 a.m., just before first light, and the 2/12th gunners were in action supporting the attack when it started.

Colonel Evans saw his men crossing the start-line on time three minutes after machine-guns of the Northumberland Fusiliers had begun a sustained fire program. The field guns opened up as the men stepped forward. Four minutes later the enemy artillery replied with an even heavier bombardment. About 10 minutes after the troops had set forth smoke from the

---

[4] Lt A. L. Reid, MC, TX2105; 2/12 Bn. Insurance adjuster; of Hobart; b. Hobart, 6 Oct 1906.
[5] Maj J. A. Douglas, QX6097. 2/12 Bn, 19 MG Bn. Law student; of Townsville, Qld; b. Townsville, 14 Aug 1917.
[6] Maj W. H. Perry, ED, VX48549. (1st AIF: 10 Bn.) 2/23 Bn. Printer; of Malvern, Vic; b. Prahran, Vic, 10 Feb 1896.

screen laid across Medauuar, thickened by more smoke put down by German guns, began drifting down from the north. It reduced visibility to 50 yards. Evans moved back to his headquarters to await whatever good or sad news the day would bring.

On the right Malloch led his company southwards along the perimeter, as he had twice done in the Medauuar battle. During the approach the tanks held back from the infantry and veered slightly off course. When the smoke came down, reducing visibility first to 50 yards, then to 25, the tanks were almost blinded, lost contact with the infantry, became unsure of their whereabouts and eventually turned into S9, the front-line post next before that to be attacked—750 yards short of the objective. Here Malloch's reserve platoon strove to attract their attention and redirect them. The 9th Division, it will be remembered, had received no battle training when it became committed to front-line action and Evans' men were unaware, nor did Evans himself know for sure,[7] that a push button had been placed on the back of the Matildas for the express purpose of enabling infantry to call up the tank commander by a bell that rang 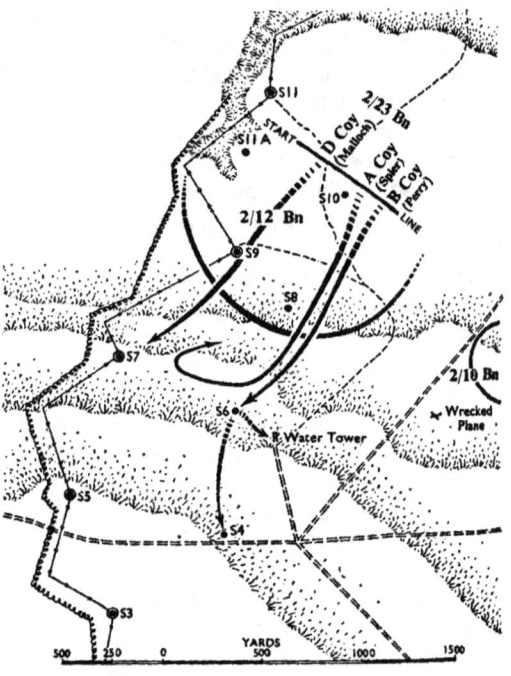 inside. The infantry beat on the outside of the tanks with rifle-butts and rocks without avail; the tanks remained closed-up and stationary. In time they turned round and ground their way back to the assembly area: all except one, whose spirited commander, with a courage that deserved to be rewarded by positive accomplishment, pushed on through the smoke but arrived lost in front of the 2/10th Battalion well to the left of the area of thrust.

Meanwhile Malloch's company was suffering heavy casualties from thunderclap air bursts of 88-mm shell fire 50 feet above the men. Malloch urged his platoons on without the tanks towards their objective across ground now overlaid with intense fire. The infantry, who before the attack had been much enheartened by knowledge that the tanks would be with them, felt badly let down, but pressed on desperately. Casualties

---

[7] As he stated in a report on the action written soon afterwards.

were severe. Malloch was wounded but remained to direct the attack on Post S7. Lieutenant Bowden's platoon on the left moved in first and pushed up the rise towards the post. Men fell away dead or wounded, but the intrepid Bowden, whose shoulder had been gashed open by shell fire, pressed on and the survivors followed. At the top of the ridge they assaulted and captured some German sangars. Bowden sent back, in succession, three men to tell Malloch the platoon was too weak to attack the post without reinforcements. Only the last of these reached Malloch, who then had no unwounded men to send back to summon up Lieutenant Anderson's[8] reserve platoon, which had inexplicably not arrived; for Anderson and his men had been vainly endeavouring to redirect the tanks.

Lieutenant Neuendorf's[9] platoon had meanwhile charged S7 from the right flank and overrun it. Neuendorf found the post to be completely covered by machine-gun fire from nearby sangars and took a section forward to clear them. Some sangars were cleaned out, but almost all his men were hit, and to right and left other machine-guns continued to spatter fire. Neuendorf sent back a runner asking for reinforcements and waited, with the survivors of his platoon, for help to reach him. But Anderson's platoon failed to get through the enemy's now greatly thickened fire-belt and withdrew to S11 just before 7 a.m. The wounded Malloch returned to Evans' battle headquarters to report the desperate situation.

While Malloch's company had been closing on S7, the left forward company commanded by Major Perry, also without tanks, had attacked Post S6; but the forward platoons became pinned down by fire from a near-by sangar. Lieutenant Jess[1] and three men threw in grenades, jumped into the position and silenced the machine-guns; but Jess was shot through the stomach and legs and could take no further part. The rest of the men then charged through and overran the post, capturing the German garrison of 19 men, including the officer-in-charge. When the stretcher bearers came up to the wounded Jess, he refused to be moved and directed them to rescue other men more likely to survive.

Major Perry wasted no time in pressing forward to his next objective. He left Captain Gahan,[2] with Morrison[3] (his sergeant-major) and Jess' platoon, in S6; Lieutenant Gardiner's platoon was sent out to deal with some enemy sangars at the top of the escarpment on the right flank; and Perry himself pressed on with Lieutenant Sheldrick's[4] platoon to Post S4. The assault on S4 succeeded after a desperate, hand-to-hand fight, in which most of the garrison was killed but four prisoners were taken. Perry fired the prescribed signal calling for reinforcements to be sent

---

[8] Capt G. G. Anderson, VX48780; 2/23 Bn. Salesman; of Prahran, Vic; b. St Kilda, Vic, 13 May 1919. Died of wounds 13 Jul 1942.

[9] Capt T. O. Neuendorf, VX48783; 2/23 Bn. Clerk; of Auburn, Vic; b. Royal Park, Vic, 13 May 1918. His twin brother, Lt K. O. Neuendorf, was also serving in the 2/23 Bn at this time.

[1] Lt C. McG. Jess, VX48792; 2/23 Bn. Clerk; of Toorak, Vic; b. Surrey, England, 15 Jul 1920. Died of wounds 17 May 1941.

[2] Capt S. M. Gahan, VX48379; 2/23 Bn. Bank clerk; of Caulfield, Vic; b. Ivanhoe, Vic, 8 Dec 1913. Killed in action 17 May 1941.

[3] Capt W. G. Morrison, VX30501. 2/23 Bn; BBCAU 1945. Tailor; of Coburg, Vic; b. Fitzroy, Vic, 27 Jul 1906.

[4] Lt G. A. Sheldrick, VX48319; 2/23 Bn. Estate agent; of Preston, Vic; b. London, 16 May 1905.

forward on attaining the objective, but unfortunately this went unnoticed and was not reported to Evans. Then Perry set out to return across the fire-beaten ground to S6 with the four prisoners (including an officer), leaving Sheldrick to hold Post S4.

Gahan and Morrison had in the meantime found S6 so completely covered by fire from positions on either flank that it became essential to find a more covered position until the area could be cleared. They moved out to an improvised defensive post in a stone structure near the Water Tower, a landmark east of Post S6. Sergeant Hook[5] arrived in thick smoke near S6 in a carrier loaded with ammunition, rations and additional weapons and found Captain Gahan and his men in this position. He returned bearing wounded in his carrier. Another carrier went on to take provisions and munitions to S4 but lost direction in the smoke, veered towards enemy positions, ran into machine-gun fire and returned without contacting Sheldrick.

Gardiner's platoon, which had moved out to clean up the enemy positions on the right flank while Sheldrick's platoon had been advancing on S4, was less successful than Sheldrick's. The men were forced to ground by cross-fire from the sangars, and Gardiner could make no progress. Gahan observed his predicament and took out a section of men to assist him, leaving Sergeant-Major Morrison in charge near the Water Tower. Eventually Gahan and Gardiner overcame the nearest sangars, but lost about a third of their men. Perry, returning from S4, was fired on from the same area. Finding eight of his men sheltering near the Water Tower, Perry led them in an assault on the sangars. He later described what happened in a letter from a prisoner-of-war camp:

> As we rushed the sangars we ran into Gahan, Gardiner and about 12 men who had attacked from a different angle but were not seen owing to the smoke. Just as we cleaned up these sangars, heavy machine-gun fire came from all angles. In a second only five of us were left standing. Immediately I ordered them into the sangars, each dragging a wounded man. Gahan and Gardiner were killed and as the light improved we saw we were almost surrounded. . . .[6]

About 7 a.m. Evans knew that the two forward platoons of Malloch's company had few effective men left, and that the company's reserve platoon was back at S11. He believed that Post S7 had not been taken. He had been informed that Post S6 had been captured and that two platoons had gone forward to carry out the next phase, the capture of S4. He decided to order his right reserve company (Major Spier) to attack Post S7 in conjunction with the tanks. Of the nine tanks originally allotted, eight were in the assembly area, but the commander informed Evans that only four of these would take part. An artillery plan was prepared and Evans gave his orders at 7.30 a.m. The tanks were to lead the attack on S7 and then to circle around the posts generally, breaking up enemy machine-gun positions and thus allowing the infantry to consolidate; they

---

[5] Lt P. R. Hook, MM, VX42081; 2/23 Bn. Station hand; of Hay, NSW; b. London, 25 Jan 1920. Similar tasks were carried out in this action by a second carrier commanded by Sgt C. G. Rigg (of Caulfield, Vic).
[6] Wilmot, *Tobruk*, p. 189.

were ordered to proceed past S6 and then turn right along the top of the escarpment to S7. Evans instructed that if the tanks did not continue on to S7 the infantry were to retire.

The tanks and infantry crossed the start-line at 7.40 a.m. Almost immediately the enemy opened up with intense artillery, mortar and machine-gun fire and, as S7 was approached, laid down smoke of greater density than before. The tanks did not go up to the escarpment past Post S6 as ordered but turned right, short of the post, to advance on S7, thus failing to neutralise the remaining enemy machine-gun nests on the escarpment. When they were about 100 yards from S7 the tanks swung around to the right and began to return: the infantry followed. The infantry saw enemy tanks coming up from the south and some attributed the decision of the British tanks to this development; but more probably the crews would have been prevented by smoke from seeing the approaching enemy tanks, which were not perceived from an observation post set up by Evans on the left of the area of attack. Both tanks and infantry came all the way back. Subsequently German tanks accompanied by infantry counter-attacked in the S7 area and rounded up the Australians scattered about in sangars, ground hollows and the post itself. Two later reports gave the time of this occurrence as 8.30 a.m.

By 9.5 a.m. most of Spier's company had returned. Evans reported to Wootten that his battalion had suffered heavy casualties in three companies and that he was breaking off the attack. Morshead went to Wootten's headquarters to discuss future action.

For Lieutenant Sheldrick, however, the action had not been broken off; nor for Sergeant-Major Morrison or Major Perry. Although completely surrounded Sheldrick was holding off the enemy from S4. He had sent messengers who had failed, however, to get through. Probably one of these was a wounded man who was seen to be picked up forward of S4 by two enemy and taken in to S5. Morrison and the remnants of Perry's company were still in the stone structure near the Water Tower, while Perry and the handful of men with him, using their rifles, were still keeping the Germans off the sangars that Gardiner's platoon had taken. But none of this was known at Evans' headquarters.

The men in the right-hand companies of the 2/10th Battalion, whose front was on the left of the battle area, had seen more of the action than Evans' battalion. About 8.35 a.m. enemy infantry guns and field guns situated behind the wrecked plane fired a creeping barrage moving eastwards towards the 2/10th companies. The garrison guns could not reply because it was believed that some of Perry's company might be in that vicinity. Behind the barrage German infantry and four medium tanks came into the Water Tower area from the west. The tanks, two on either side of the Water Tower, began firing on the 2/10th Battalion positions but the 51st Field Regiment then intervened and put both tanks and infantry to flight. One tank was disabled and a member of the crew took to his heels. Within four minutes tanks again appeared from the west and moved out of sight into a re-entrant south of the Water Tower.

They re-appeared clustering around S4 soon after 9 a.m. Unaware that Sheldrick was there, the garrison artillery again put down a concentrated bombardment that drove the tanks off. Lieutenant Scott[8] of the 2/10th Battalion later shot up enemy guns near the wrecked plane with a "bush" mountain gun.

About 9.30 a.m. Colonel Evans made arrangements with Major Bruer to reconnoitre the ground between Post S6 and the right company of the 2/10th in order to consider the possibility of advancing that battalion's right company positions to link up with S6. Evans and Bruer made a joint reconnaissance some time after 10 a.m. This vital ground was flat, exposed and hard; the distance to be covered, substantial. Bruer felt that he could not undertake the commitment without dangerously attenuating his right flank.

At 12.15 Evans arrived back at his headquarters. Nothing had been learnt meanwhile to shed light on what was the position in front. His observers reported an absence of movement around Posts S6 or S4; but unknown to Evans a German party of tanks and infantry, operating under cover of a smoke-screen, were about this time overrunning the positions occupied by Perry. They captured him and the men with him, of whom there were now only four survivors. In the meantime Corporal Carleton,[9] a company orderly-room clerk, had been endeavouring to carry back a message from Morrison. Carleton had made a brave, successful dash through machine-gun fire but had the misfortune, as he approached S8, to be fired on and badly wounded by the Australians in the post. After lying quiet for a time, he found the will to struggle on to reach Post S9 and deliver his message soon after Evans had returned. Carleton reported that Morrison was still holding out when he had left him much earlier. Morrison needed a signal line to enable him to direct artillery fire on to the surrounding enemy. A signaller, Private Clark,[1] volunteered to repair the line to S6 and set out with his field telephone from S10, knowing that he would have to crawl across more than 1,000 yards of bare, fire-raked ground. Evans now reported, in reply to inquiries from Wootten's headquarters, that Perry's company was in S6 but, until a runner who had gone out returned, the position could not be clarified: S4 and S7 were in doubt.

Morshead and Wootten had come to the conclusion that S6 could not be held while S7 remained in enemy hands. Wootten discussed with Evans the possibility of a further attack on S7, but Evans contended that it was essential to ascertain the position at S6 before reaching a decision. Evans nevertheless warned his reserve company commanders to rest their men in anticipation of an evening attack and ordered a check of strength, which indicated that 148 men could be made immediately available.

---

[8] Lt A. R. Scott, VX6330; 2/10 Bn. Regular soldier; of Frankston, Vic; b. Gibraltar, 22 Oct 1914. Killed in action 27 Aug 1942.

[9] Sgt F. L. Carleton, VX33476; 2/23 Bn. Shipping clerk; of Warrandyte, Vic; b. South Yarra, Vic, 25 Aug 1906.

[1] L-Cpl H. P. Clark, MM, VX48151; 2/23 Bn. Railway porter; of Burwood, Vic; b. Prahran, Vic, 29 Mar 1916.

Private Clark was meanwhile crawling along the line towards S6, repairing break after break, only to find the line dead on testing at each new break. But Morrison saw him coming, and sent out a man to repair from his end. When Clark repaired his thirteenth break (about 12.40 p.m.) he was rewarded by Morrison's answering voice. Morrison reported that he was troubled by machine-gun and anti-tank fire from 300 yards to the left and by snipers 150 yards to the right. Five of his men had been killed and five wounded, but he and 13 others were unharmed.

It was now possible to give Morrison artillery protection. Five minutes later three enemy tanks approached the Water Tower but were driven off by gunfire, which came down dangerously close to Morrison's position. About an hour later another thrust by five tanks was similarly stopped. Corporal Carleton reported from S9 that men were "lolling about" Post S7, which he therefore concluded to be in enemy hands.

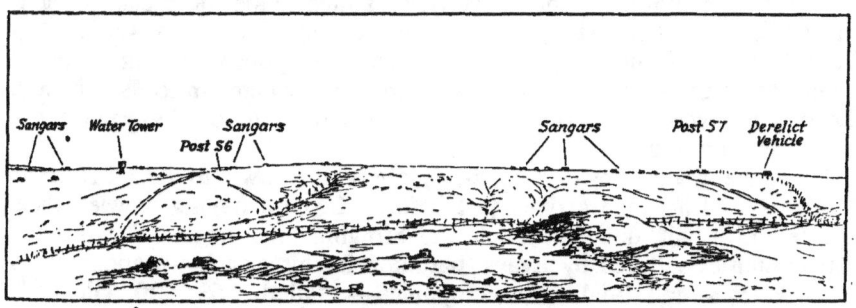

The Water Tower—Post S7, viewed from Post S10

About 4 p.m. Wootten gave instructions that Evans' battalion should attack again for Post S7 either in the evening or at next daybreak. But although Evans summoned his company and supporting commanders to report for reconnaissance at 5 p.m., he had concluded that a further attack with no greater strength than remained to him would be of no value. To hold Post S6 and S7 it would be necessary, in his opinion, not only to take and hold the overlooking ground, but also to secure the left flank. It was clear that the two posts were but points in a general, strongly-held enemy line running east-west and extending on either side. He therefore requested reconsideration of the decision. Morshead and Wootten considered Evans' representations and at 5.30 p.m. authorised him to withdraw his battalion after dark. It was decided, however, to establish a new line linking the right battalion in the Salient (at the time the 2/10th) with Post S8. Evans then ordered patrols and stretcher bearers to scour the battlefield after dark and arranged for a section of carriers to go out to Morrison when darkness fell, to bring in his wounded as he withdrew.

From 7.30 onwards enemy tanks could be heard. About 8.10 p.m., as the sun was setting, Morrison reported that they were 500 yards to his right rear. They closed in towards his position about 8.30 p.m. Evans asked for immediate artillery fire and ordered the waiting carriers to set out to Morrison's aid. The fire came down, the enemy tanks drew back, and the three carriers went on but in the gloom veered off course towards a German anti-tank gun position. One carrier was disabled; another stopped when its driver was hit. The driver of the disabled carrier, although wounded, jumped out and into the driverless carrier and drove it off. Of the six men comprising the crews, two had now been killed and two wounded. The drivers of the two mobile carriers returned with the dead and wounded.

Evans then instructed Morrison to bring in the fit men to Post S8 but to leave the wounded; to evacuate them, he said, would endanger more lives. For almost half an hour efforts were made, in communication with Morrison, to adjust the artillery fire to afford him maximum protection. At last, at 8.35 p.m., Morrison called over the telephone "Keep shooting on that mark."[2] The shelling forced the Germans in the closest sangars to leave their positions and at 9 p.m., as Morrison's men made the break, the artillery bombardment was stepped up to gunfire rate. Very lights were shot up from S8 to guide them in, and the enemy in response brought down fire around the Australian posts. Morrison's men never came in to S8. Although the distance was but 800 yards, there was no sign of the party three-quarters of an hour later.

From the Water Tower a pipe-line ditch ran down to Post S10. Here Morrison and his men arrived just before 10 p.m., having crawled about a mile and a half along the ditch and bringing their wounded with them. The casualties suffered by Evans' battalion in this attack—preponderantly from Perry's and Malloch's companies—totalled 163: 20 killed, 47 wounded and recovered and 96 missing. Of the missing there was evidence that at least 5 had been killed and 23 wounded. There are not many achievements by an infantry company in the 9th Division's history comparable with the capture by Perry's company of S6 and S4; but at the end of three days' operations, after attacks by both sides, the position at the right-hand hinge of the Salient remained unchanged. The final scene at Post S4 next morning—Sheldrick's surrender with no food or water and with ammunition expended—was mercifully not observed from the Australian positions.

Debatable questions may be asked about this operation. Should any attack have been mounted after it was discovered that S8 and S9 had not been lost? Should the objectives have then been limited, as at first planned, to S7 and S6, or was it necessary for the security of these posts to go farther? Could any intermediate objective have been held short of Medauuar itself? Were the orders Evans gave for the second phase a suitable prescription for a situation in which his left company was already committed to the assault on S4? Or, did his orders precisely limit his commitment to what was then feasible, thus saving his battalion from possible near-extinction in futile strife for the unachievable or untenable?

It is more instructive to consider what was done than to ask what should have been done. The concept of the operation was faulty because of the

---

[2] As recorded in battalion message log.

failure to appreciate (which Evans was the first to perceive) that the perimeter posts, the strongpoints in the old westward-facing defence system of the fortress, were not the key to the enemy's now northward-facing defence line. Amateurish methods were in evidence in this and the two preceding Salient counter-attacks—the methods of untrained units gaining their tactical lessons in the harsh reality of battle, in which failure is mercilessly punished. Infantry and tank sub-unit commanders did not reconnoitre or plan together. The *sine qua non* for cooperation between them in battle, a mutually understood method of intercommunication, did not exist. Evans, in his report on the actions, stated his opinion of the tanks' performance:

> The tanks tried hard but it is felt that topography is their trouble.

He also commented:

> When lost, tanks should not return immediately but should cruise about and look for the infantry. . . . In both attacks the tanks returned too early.[3]

But the infantry had similar lessons to learn.

The arrival of the 2/12th Field Regiment (Lieut-Colonel Goodwin[4]) was a useful reinforcement of the garrison's artillery. It was placed in the western sector under operational command of the 51st Field Regiment and given an assortment of guns of various calibres, including the garrison's main medium artillery, the troop of 60-pounder guns of first world war vintage. Captain Holmes'[5] and Captain Hamilton's[6] troops took over ten 4.5 howitzers which had been replaced in the 51st Field Regiment by twelve 25-pounders. Lieutenant McDermott's[7] troop, which arrived on the night of 20th May, relieved the 51st Field Regiment on 25-pounders, while Captain Feitel's[8] troop manned the 60-pounders. On 20th May the regiment suffered its first shelling and Lance-Bombardier Butler[9] was mortally wounded. A successful predicted counter-battery shoot was conducted in the early hours of 29th May by a 60-pounder gun from a pre-arranged forward position, neutralising a hostile battery in ten rounds. The diarist commented:

> The 60 pounders were somewhat short of ammunition but fortunately some more rounds have arrived. Artillery here is working under difficulties and we are in need of a flash-spotting and sound-ranging group to fix hostile batteries and an occasional sortie by Arty R[1] to present us with some air photographs and also to cooperate in some air shooting . . . more particularly as observation is poor in the salient

---

[3] Report on action of 2/23 Bn, morning 17th May 1941.
[4] Brig S. T. W. Goodwin, DSO, VX11. (1st AIF: 6 Bty AFA.) CO 2/12 Fd Regt 1940-43; CRA 9 Div 1943. Regular soldier; b. Ballarat, Vic, 6 Feb 1894. Killed in action 25 Oct 1943.
[5] Lt-Col D. L. Holmes, TX1514; 2/12 Fd Regt. Regular soldier; b. Sydney, 10 Jun 1909.
[6] Maj H. P. Hamilton, VX14797. 2/12 Fd Regt; BM (RAA) 3 Div 1943-45. Bank clerk; of St Kilda, Vic; b. St Kilda, Vic, 21 Dec 1911.
[7] Capt D. H. McDermott, VX13717. 2/12 Fd Regt, Pacific Islands Regt. Clerk; of Elwood, Vic; b. Elwood, 25 May 1912.
[8] Maj M. Feitel, MBE, VX22216; 2/12 Fd Regt. Manager; of East St Kilda, Vic; b. Melbourne, 20 Oct 1910.
[9] L-Bdr B. McD. Butler, VX33108; 2/12 Fd Regt. Schoolteacher; of Rushworth, Vic; b. Melbourne, 4 Jan 1908. Died of wounds 21 May 1941.
[1] Aircraft reconnaissance for artillery.

since the enemy occupy a ridge just inside the perimeter which commands the whole area both inside and out. Our O.P's, on a lower ridge, are therefore labouring under a disadvantage and most artillery shooting is in the nature of harassing fire and opportunity shoots, though some neutralisation by predicted fire is carried out.

Wootten's brigade remained in the Salient until 5th June, when Murray's brigade took over the sector. No more attacks were mounted but the line continued to be edged forward and strengthened. To close the gap between Post S8 and the right battalion position in the Salient, each battalion took a small side-step to the right on the evening and night of 18th May, the 2/10th Battalion taking over the left platoon area of the 2/12th, the 2/9th the left platoon area of the 2/10th and the 2/13th the left platoon area of the 2/10th. Later the same night Handley's company on the right of the 2/13th moved its right flank forward to within 400 yards of the enemy.

Having advanced his front on both flanks, Burrows began planning to push out the line of his centre company, swinging it forward 300 yards on the right and 50 yards on the left. On the night of the 27th Captain Gillan's[2] company moved out to establish itself on the new alignment. It proved impossible to complete the digging of the positions that night, so the men withdrew before daylight to their former line, intending to complete the job next day. The enemy appeared to know that something was afoot and increased his harassing fire: next day some 650 shells fell on the western sector positions. Enemy jumpiness was also evidenced later the same night when the 18th Indian Cavalry Regiment sent out a strong patrol, with 2-inch mortars and 18-pounders in support, in the western sector near the coast. A curtain of defensive fire from four batteries came down along the whole sector. The officer commanding the patrol, Captain R. J. Gretton, was killed.

In the evening Colonel Verrier and Colonel Burrows moved their headquarters forward (to be followed next day by a forward move of Wootten's headquarters) and after dark Gillan's company went out to complete the new 2/13th centre company positions and occupy them permanently. Gillan's men were well ensconced and just settling down to a meal when about 200 Germans came forward in apparent expectation of finding the positions ready for the taking. A covering patrol reported their approach. In a close fight the Germans, walking straight into an ambush, were engaged with every Bren gun and mortar to hand and fled to their own lines. Then Lieutenant Bucknell,[3] gathering six men, followed on the heels of the enemy to within 15 yards of their positions, threw in grenades to the front, engaged the flanks with Bren fire, and withdrew without harm. Agonised cries testified to deadly work.

Next morning five ambulances came up behind the enemy positions opposite and German stretcher bearers under cover of a Red Cross flag

---

[2] Maj H. G. Gillan, NX12336; 2/13 Bn. Accountant; of Broadwater, NSW; b. Innisfail, Qld, 17 Sep 1909.

[3] Capt E. R. Bucknell, MC, NX34714; 2/13 Bn. Station hand; of Graman, NSW; b. Longreach, Qld, 28 Apr 1917.

scoured no-man's land for wounded. Stretcher bearers went out from the 2/13th to help in the compassionate work but were also canny enough to take a close look by daylight at the enemy positions. Burrows' men were able to stand up and stretch their limbs while the work went on till a German Spandau burst, aimed at nobody, signalled that the truce was over.

On the right of the 2/13th Battalion, Colonel Martin's 2/9th Battalion, the veteran unit of the Salient, which had already pushed its positions far in front of the line it originally took over in rear of Bianca, advanced its line 150 yards to conform with Burrows' movement. The defences of Martin's front line were now excellently developed and completely wired and trip-wired.

The Salient sector had now been transformed from a breach in the front line, to be blocked off against further penetration, to a zone from which at every opportunity the enemy could be closely engaged and bruised. Almost every morning the patrol report of Wootten's headquarters listed more than 20 patrols that had operated in no-man's land during the preceding night, of which a number had always been in the Salient. Not all sought to harass the enemy, but many did, such as several led by Lieutenant Bucknell; for example, one morning Bucknell crept with a handful of men into a hollow on the edge of the enemy positions under cover of a mist and opened fire when visibility increased sufficiently for accurate aiming, throwing the enemy into momentary confusion as many were hit. It was by day, however, that the enemy was made to suffer most: the vigilant forward observation officers of the Royal Horse Artillery and 51st Field Regiment (and later the 2/12th Australian Field Regiment) were the chief executioners. If an enemy mortar or machine-gun disclosed its position by firing or a careless messenger revealed the likely whereabouts of an enemy headquarters, the retribution was almost instantaneous. Day by day unit action diaries and message logs recorded these occurrences, concluding with such words as "artillery engaged and scored a direct hit". The enemy scored direct hits too; often the sad call for stretcher bearers rang out. But the defenders knew they were inflicting greater casualties than they were receiving.

The day after Wootten's brigade left the Salient, an unsolicited testimonial to the Australian infantry was written by the commander of an enemy battalion opposite the sector then held by the 2/15th Battalion.[4] In a report written on 7th June Major Ballerstedt, commanding the *II Battalion* of the *115th Lorried Infantry Regiment,* wrote:

> The Australians, who are the men our troops have had opposite them so far, are extraordinarily tough fighters. The German is more active in the attack but the enemy stakes his life in the defence and fights to the last with extreme cunning. Our men, usually easy going and unsuspecting, fall easily into his traps especially as a result of their experiences in the closing stages of the Western Campaign [campaign in France].
> The Australian is unquestionably superior to the German soldier:
> i. in the use of individual weapons, especially as snipers
> ii. in the use of ground camouflage

---

[4] Before 2nd June by the 2/13.

iii. in his gift of observation, and the drawing of the correct conclusions from his observation
iv. in every means of taking us by surprise. . . .

The enemy allows isolated individuals to come right up to his positions, then fires on them.

Enemy snipers have astounding results. They shoot at anything they recognise. Several N.C.O's of the battalion have been shot through the head with the first shot while making observation in the front line. Protruding sights in gun directors have been shot off, observation slits and loopholes have been fired on, and hit, as soon as they were seen to be in use (i.e. when the light background became dark).

The enemy shoots very accurately with his high angle infantry weapons. He usually uses these in conjunction with a sniper—or MG. . . .[5]

If the Germans had anything to learn from the Australian infantry they learnt quickly. A month later Lieut-Colonel Ogle, whose battalion (2/15th) then held the British line in the same sector, wrote, in words that sound like an echo from Major Ballerstedt's report:

Mortar firing has been extremely accurate, in two cases the bomb falling right into the weapon-pit. . . . As an indication of accuracy in sniping, the only periscope in possession of the unit was hit as soon as it was raised above the post. In another case one man was shot through the temple when he raised his head above the parapet.

In many cases mortar fire and machine-gun fire was coordinated. If the enemy saw that his mortar had made a direct hit on the post he would follow it immediately with bursts of machine-gun fire. . . .

Our own troops have learned the following lessons from the German.

(a) Camouflage—of positions and of muzzle blast, for they have found it extremely difficult to locate his guns.
(b) Dummy Positions—so many sangars have been constructed that we cannot in confidence assume that he is occupying any one of them.
(c) Day Discipline—Practically no movement at all is seen. To the observer, the whole of the enemy territory appears unoccupied.

Each commander saw his opponents in the same light. Each followed the precept: make thine enemy thy teacher.

In the use of mortars the Australians were at a disadvantage because the British 3-inch mortar was outranged by both German and Italian mortars. Except for one or two captured Italian 81-mm mortars, for which ammunition was scarce, the infantry possessed no means of retaliation against the weapons that caused most of their casualties. The artillery was quick to silence enemy mortars if they fired in daylight but they mostly fired at night when the guns could not risk disclosing their positions by gun flashes merely to engage minor targets. Some counter-action was later taken with captured guns firing from forward night positions, and by the 2/12th Field Regiment on a greater scale with 4.5-inch howitzers. In the bluff and counter-bluff of the artillery duel the gunners disliked showing their hand to take on targets that should have been tasks for suitably equipped infantry.

During the attack by the 2/23rd Battalion there were several reports of evacuation of positions by the enemy under bombardment by the

---

[5] Appendix "A" to 9 Aust Div Intelligence Summary No. 74, 30 Jun 1941.

British artillery. The German command, with Teutonic thoroughness, immediately set about remedying the disclosed weaknesses by constructing a new line in rear of the positions then held. Night by night until the end of the month the Australians heard the sounds of working compressors. Captured documents later indicated that the new line was constructed by the German *33rd Engineer Battalion*.

The Axis forces disposed around Tobruk were:

	Formations	Remarks
Derna Road sector—north of the Salient	*Brescia Division* *16th Italian Artillery Regiment*	Probably five battalions west of Tobruk but only two close to the perimeter.
Salient sector	*I* and *II* Battalions, *115th Lorried Infantry Regiment*	Right of Salient (i.e. defender's right) *II Battalion 104th*, centre *I Battalion 115th*, left *II Battalion 115th*.
	II Battalion, 104th Lorried Infantry Regiment	
	Two oasis companies[6]	
	2nd Machine Gun Battalion	
	Two German artillery battalions	
	16th Italian Artillery Regiment	Three batteries.
	33rd Engineer Battalion	
	900th Engineer Battalion	
Pilastrino and El Adem Roads sector (east of the Salient)	*Ariete Division* (being relieved by *Pavia Division*)	Two lorried infantry battalions, one motor-cycle battalion.
	One regiment (*132nd*) plus one group of artillery (*46th Regiment*)	
Bardia Road sector	*Trento Division*	Two (lorried) infantry battalions, one motor-cycle battalion, one machine-gun battalion.

The *I Battalion* of the *18th Anti-Aircraft Regiment* and the *8th Machine Gun Battalion* (now brought up to the strength of three companies) were also employed in the siege; part certainly, but perhaps not all, of the latter battalion was in the Salient. The *5th Light Division* was near and west of El Adem, with some tanks at close call of the infantry, and portion of the *Ariete Division* was 25 miles west of Tobruk, where the division had about 80 tanks, of which three-fifths were medium tanks. Although supply difficulties doubtless dictated the employment of some of these forces at Tobruk, such as stationing the *Brescia Division* in substantial strength opposite the western outlet with the *Ariete Division's* tanks farther west, the invested forces were nevertheless tying down an equivalent force. Almost all Rommel's German mobile infantry and positional ground troops were absorbed in the task of defending the Salient.

Rommel still had his teeth well into the slice of the Tobruk perimeter

---

[6] Volunteer unmotorised mixed groups for independent desert roles.

he had snatched, but it was too much to chew. While he was left free to deploy a strong armoured striking force (about 80 tanks) near the frontier to meet any British thrust, the only German mobile infantry left to him to consolidate the results of any German eastward thrust or counter-thrust was one battalion of lorried infantry and one motor-cycle battalion. Tobruk was therefore providing the British Western Desert Force Command with an insurance against the worst consequences of failure if an offensive from the frontier were rashly or riskily ventured.

On the night of 20th May Tovell's brigade, which had been in reserve, relieved Godfrey's brigade in the eastern (Bardia Road) sector and on the 23rd May Godfrey's brigade changed places with Murray's brigade (less the 2/13th Battalion, but with the 2/1st Pioneers under command), which then went into reserve for a fortnight before taking over from Wootten's brigade in the Salient and the western sector. On the night of 1st June the 2/15th Battalion under Major Conroy[7] relieved the 2/13th Battalion, which was then granted four days' relief from front-line duty before it was due to return to the Salient when Murray's brigade took over that sector.

In early June a crisis arose in relation to the supply of a vital requirement. The daily usage of fuel and lubricants by the vehicles, tanks and other machinery in Tobruk was largely met in April and May by drawing on reserves. No bulk petrol was received, though 800 tons of cased petrol and lubricants were brought in. Adequate efforts to control consumption were not made in the first month of the investment, when the daily consumption averaged 46 tons. This was then reduced to about 30 tons. On 5th May "a high flying plane fluked a hit on a petrol dump which in turn ignited a diesel oil dump. The smoke went up thousands of feet and must have gladdened the heart of the pilot concerned."[8] On 25th May the *Helka* carrying 1,000 tons of bulk petrol for the garrison was sunk about 30 miles north-east of Tobruk. Another bulk shipment was arranged, due to arrive at 3 a.m. on 2nd June, and a lighter carrying 100 tons of cased petrol was to arrive on 1st June. In the early morning of 1st June the lighter caught fire while unloading; only 10 tons of petrol were saved. Meanwhile information was received that the departure of the tanker had been delayed for 48 hours in order to enable the R.A.F. to arrange better fighter protection. On 2nd June Morshead was informed that by the end of the day only 130 tons of petrol would remain.

Morshead's annoyance that the shortage should have been allowed to develop is evident in his diary. He wrote a personal letter to all commanding officers calling for economy, directed that all use of transport for taking troops to the beaches be discontinued, ordered that next day's indents should be only half satisfied and no issue be made on the following day and required that units should thereafter be held, if possible, to one-third of previous drawings. He apprehended that such a severe curtailment

---

[7] Lt-Col T. M. Conroy, ED, SX8886. 2/43 Bn; CO 2/32 Bn 1941-42, 2/5 Bn 1943-44. Industrial chemist; of Melbourne; b. Port Adelaide, 31 Jul 1906.
[8] War Diary, 2/17 Bn.

could not be sustained but noted in his diary that he was counting on reducing consumption to 20 tons a day.

On 2nd June a lighter escorted by a minesweeper left Mersa Matruh with 1,200 cases of petrol but next day it was reported that the minesweeper was adrift and the lighter proceeding unescorted. Later, after suffering air attack and incurring heavy casualties to her crew, the lighter returned to Mersa Matruh. Meanwhile the *Pass of Balmaha,* carrying some 760 tons of bulk petrol, making all of her maximum speed of 6 knots, was ploughing her steady way. " 'Pass of Balmaha' is due 2330/3 if she survives" noted the diarist of 9th Division headquarters on 2nd June. Though twice attacked on the voyage she arrived just after 11 p.m. on 3rd June, laid up heavily camouflaged throughout the next day and sailed safely for Alexandria at 2 a.m. on the 5th, having discharged her cargo and leaving the garrison with about 40 days supplies. On 5th June some of the stocks were lost by fires in three dumps caused by incendiaries dropped from aircraft, but before the end of the month *Pass of Balmaha's* gallant company brought her again to Tobruk. More than 1,400 tons of bulk petrol were received in June by this ship.

The relief of Wootten's brigade by Murray's brigade took place on the nights of 4th, 5th and 6th June. Responsibility for the sector passed from Wootten to Murray at 3 a.m. on the 5th. Of all Wootten's battalions the 2/9th was most deserving of rest, having held the Bianca sector of the Salient from the night of 4th May (after mounting a counter-attack on the night of 3rd May) to the night of 5th June, during which period it substantially advanced the front line of defence.

Mention must also be made of the dismounted squadron of the King's Dragoon Guards which had occupied the perimeter posts S27 to S21 (inclusive) in the Derna Road sector from 20th May to 4th June, when it was relieved by a company of the 2/1st Pioneer Battalion. The squadron had carried out its infantry role with spirit. On the night of 28th May Captain Llewellen Palmer[1] took out a patrol to interfere with the construction of an enemy line on his front. Captain Palmer's patrol got right into the enemy with the bayonet, driving them out in disorder, and Palmer himself killed four Italians. The fleeing enemy were caught by fire from their own neighbouring positions and, as Palmer's patrol withdrew, confusion reigned among the enemy who continued to fire at each other to the delight of the patrol.

The Derna Road sector was now held by the 2/1st Pioneers with left flank at S8 and S10; in the Salient the 2/13th Battalion was on the right, the 2/17th in the centre, and the 2/15th on the left. Colonel Burrows quickly reached the conclusion that the right of the Salient offered even greater opportunities for advancing the line than he had previously exploited on the left. Forbes' Mound, in the centre of his front, ran out into no-man's land like a promontory (or true salient) from which, on

---

[1] Lt-Col A. W. A. Llewellen Palmer, DSO, MC; King's Dragoon Guards. Regular soldier; b. 18 Nov 1912. (Palmer had been ADC to the Governor-General of Australia, Lord Gowrie, prior to the outbreak of war.)

either side, the line swept back in semi-circular bays. On the right of Forbes' Mound his line was as crooked as a dog's leg. From the right flank near S10 it extended in a south-easterly direction for about 700 yards, switched east for some 600 yards, then ran out at a right-angle due south for almost 1,000 yards to Forbes' Mound. Burrows conceived the idea of advancing the front on the right flank to the line of the more forward perimeter post S8, then running it south-eastwards practically in a straight line (with some minor curvature dictated by the contour of the ground) to the front of Nixon's Post and beyond. (This project was facilitated by the fact that the enemy during the previous month had similarly straightened out his opposing line on an almost parallel alignment, not, like Burrows, by pushing it out, but by constructing a straightened line just behind his forward troops, which were then drawn back on to it.) Murray entirely approved of Burrows' proposals and Morshead gave his authorisation, stipulating only that the entire move forward should be completed in two nights, not four as Burrows had proposed.

On the third night after his battalion's arrival each of Burrows' forward companies sent out observers to lie up during the day in no-man's land well forward of the front line on either side of Forbes' Mound. Engineers cleared routes through the heavily booby-trapped minefields the Germans had put down, and the positions to be dug were carefully sited and laid out. The engineers lifted 60 booby-traps on one night.

> Booby-traps took many forms. MT pits, and vacated weapon-pits contained quantities of Italian hand grenades, either loosely scattered or attached to pieces of flat board. These grenades were prepared to explode when disturbed. Explosives were attached to trip wires which when cut caused explosion, attached to or concealed in everyday articles, such as ration tins, loaves of bread, articles of clothing and so prepared that they exploded when stepped on. Technical details of these traps may be obtained from engineers.[2]

On the left of Forbes' Mound Captain Hill's company advanced its line some 350 yards on the night of 10th-11th June. On the next night Captain Daintree's[3] and Major Chilton's companies conformed, establishing new lines at distances varying between 250 and 500 yards forward of the old. On the two nights only two serious casualties (of whom one, an engineer, was killed) were caused by enemy fire. Heavier casualties resulted from booby-traps: four men killed and five wounded. These losses must have been greater but for the work of Corporal Hunt[4] who, before the line was advanced, located a minefield and took out eight men to clear it. The minelifting was carried out under persistent mortar fire and one bomb eventually found its mark: two of the party were killed, three wounded. Hunt extricated the casualties and returned undeterred the same night with another party to continue the work. Next night, when the positions were being dug, he returned once more and an enemy mortar

---

[2] From 2/13 Bn report of the operation.
[3] Lt-Col C. M. Daintree, NX12384; 2/13 Bn. Chain store manager; of Cremorne Point, NSW; b. Bowenfels, NSW, 11 Dec 1907.
[4] L-Sgt J. G. Hunt, DCM, NX14892; 2/13 Bn. Farmer and grazier; of Inverell, NSW; b. Inverell, 15 Apr 1912. Died of wounds 30 Nov 1941.

again attempted to range his party. Work was interrupted but, when no casualties resulted, was pushed on under persistent fire to completion.

In a report on the operation Burrows pointed out that the line had been shortened by about 600 yards, enabling company fronts to be held with only two platoons forward, thus giving added depth; the link with Post S8 had ended that post's isolation and strengthened the position of Post S10; closer touch with the enemy had been obtained. Another advantage appreciated but not specified by Burrows was that minefields laid by the enemy had been converted to the use of the defence.

Brigadier Murray was as interested in depth of defence and reserves on a brigade scale as Colonel Burrows was within his battalion and decided to take advantage of the shortening of the line to release one battalion from front-line duties and with it to constitute a brigade reserve. Accordingly, on 12th June, he called his battalion commanders to a conference to discuss this possibility, and at a further conference next day ordered the 2/17th Battalion to

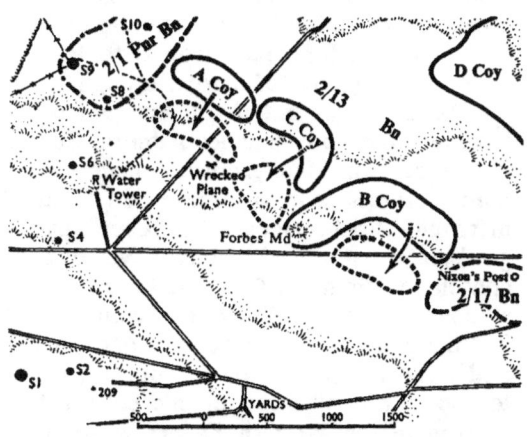

Advancing of line in north of Salient, 11th-12th June

come back into reserve on the night of 14th June. The 2/17th had three companies forward. The 2/13th was to take over the right company area, the 2/15th the remainder. The relief was effected without difficulty; in the heartlessness of war one man killed and two wounded was not a high price. A notable incident had occurred during the 2/17th Battalion's tenure in the Salient. On 8th June when 20 enemy aircraft strafed and bombed the battalion's positions (killing one man and wounding two), the Regimental Sergeant-Major, Warrant-Officer Brown,[5] manned a Lewis gun[6] mounted for anti-aircraft fire and brought down a plane.[7]

On 15th June the unrelenting Burrows surveyed the positions he had taken over on his left and could see no reason why they should not also be advanced to conform with his new line. From the junction at his old boundary the new front ran east to Nixon's Post. Why not swing the left forward to the south-easterly alignment? All that was necessary

---

[5] Lt D. McD. Brown, NX14415. 2/17 Bn, 1 Para Bn. Woolclasser; of Northwood, NSW; b. Chatswood, NSW, 9 Jul 1920. Brown was believed at this time to be the youngest RSM in the Australian Army.

[6] Obsolete light machine-gun.

[7] The war diary of the 14th Light Anti-Aircraft Regiment, describing the shooting down of planes this day, states "one of these, though obviously destroyed by A-A, is credited to inf, much to our disgust". On the other hand the war diary of the 1st R.H.A. notes: "Aust Inf brought down a plane by m.g. fire."

was that the neighbouring battalion should conform and any enemy objection be firmly overruled.

The static warfare to which the Tobruk front had now reverted, though smouldering at the hot point of close contact in the Medauuar Salient, and sometimes briefly flaring, presented a strong contrast to the swift movement of the war elsewhere. On 20th May German aircraft in their hundreds darkened the skies over Crete. On the same evening the airborne invaders gained a foothold on the Maleme airfield and by 23rd May had made their hold secure. The British force on Crete was thenceforward doomed. On 24th May, off the shores of Greenland, the *Bismarck* sank H.M.S. *Hood,* for which wound to British naval prestige and pride the later sinking of the *Bismarck,* though it redressed the tactical balance in the Atlantic, was but a sop and not a consolation. There was nothing, however, to counter-balance Admiral Cunningham's disastrous naval losses in the eastern Mediterranean incurred in supporting and rescuing the military forces sent to Greece and Crete. By the end of the month the mercifully brief campaign in Crete had ended. Only half the British garrison was retrieved. General Wavell could derive a little relief but less consolation from the fact that the risky expedition to Iraq had succeeded without becoming a dangerous commitment. The hostile Rashid Ali had fled the country. The adventure had prospered, it is now known, because Hitler too had drawn back from a commitment in Iraq, having decided to concentrate all effort on the conquest of Russia.

Even in the Western Desert where the British forces were operating comparatively close to their base, there was a falling back. After operation BREVITY Halfaya Pass was defended by the 3rd Coldstream Guards (with field, anti-tank and anti-aircraft artillery in support) and a detachment of nine infantry tanks of the 4th Royal Tank Regiment. It had been ordered that the pass was to be held, but the size of the force employed hardly indicated an intention to fight a major battle for its retention; such apparently was the inference drawn by the German Africa Command which, in planning operation SCORPION to recapture the pass, thought at first to enforce withdrawal by no more than a show of force on a wide front. The theory was never fully tested, however, for the scorpion carried a potent sting, which was effectively used. The German frontier force—the Herff Group—had strong forces including 160 tanks, but lacked sufficient fuel to employ them to full advantage. It was divided into four groups which in the end set out with the purpose not of feinting but of seeking battle.

The operation began on 26th May. On the right, the Wechmar Group, a mobile battle group strong in artillery, was to carry out the conventional right hook towards Deir el Hamra; in the centre the Cramer Group—the main tank force—was to thrust towards Sidi Suleiman, while on the left the Bach Group was to operate close in to the escarpment against infantry positions not readily accessible to tanks. A small divisional reserve was constituted, called after its commander, the Knabe Group. If the British obliged by offering battle, the Wechmar and Cramer Groups would concentrate. As the operation developed, however, the Bach Group alone encountered substantial opposition and this influenced the German commander during the afternoon of 26th May to switch the armour northwards with the object of crushing the British opposition at Halfaya. The movement was swiftly executed under cover of night and at dawn on the 27th the Knabe Group attacked the head of the pass, the Bach Group began to converge on the foot and the German armour appeared at the top of the escarpment to shell the coastal plain. Major C. G. Miles (4th Royal Tank Regiment) in command of the squadron led out his handful of tanks to distract the enemy while the Guards executed a good withdrawal, though some were caught at the foot of the pass by the Bach Group.

The cost that the British command required the enemy to pay for the recapture of Halfaya was minute in comparison with that soon to be incurred in an unsuccessful attempt to regain the pass; but the terrain so greatly favoured a force operating from the west that, unless a major battle with prospect of success could have been fought, the result of committing more forces to its defence might have been to increase the losses sustained more than those inflicted.

On 27th May Mr Churchill issued a minute to the Chiefs of Staff stating that it was imperative to prescribe from London the priorities and emphasis for future operations in the Middle East. In this document he stated (*inter alia*):

> In the Western Desert alone the opportunity for a decisive military success presents itself. Here the object must not be the pushing back of the enemy to any particular line or region, but the destruction of his armed force, or the bulk of it, in a decisive battle fought with our whole strength. It should be possible in the next fortnight to inflict a crushing defeat upon the Germans in Cyrenaica.[8]

Next day the Chiefs of Staff signalled Wavell their views. Their message agreed with the main points of Churchill's suggested prescription but placed greater emphasis on the need, having regard to the loss of Crete, to re-establish British air forces in the part of Cyrenaica between Salum and Derna. It was stated that this was imperative. Decisive success must be sought in the desert in a battle fought with all available strength. On the same day (that is, the day after Halfaya had fallen) Wavell issued to Western Desert Force his outline orders for operation BATTLEAXE. The offensive was to be planned in three phases: defeat of the enemy forces at the frontier and securing the frontier area; defeat of the enemy forces in the Tobruk-El Adem area; exploitation to Derna and Mechili. The Tobruk garrison was to play an active role. Wavell simultaneously warned the Chiefs of Staff that the measure of success that would attend the operation was doubtful.

On 4th June a meeting of the Commanders-in-Chief in Cairo (not attended by General Blamey) discussed the situation at Tobruk in gloomy terms. General Wavell said that the prospect of a blitz on the fortress in the near future was causing him anxiety, Admiral Cunningham spoke of

---

[8] Churchill, Vol III, p. 684.

the difficulty of keeping up supplies to the fortress, and Air Marshal Tedder said that little fighter support could be given. It was decided that nothing much could be done except to investigate whether sending ships to Tobruk every night could be avoided. Three days later, with the concurrence of the other Commanders-in-Chief, Cunningham ordered a temporary suspension of all shipping to Tobruk other than destroyers; these continued the nightly service. This decision in time led to some rationing in Tobruk and curtailment of ammunition expenditure.

Wavell had told the Chief of the Imperial General Staff that his tank strength, including those in Tobruk, was 230 cruisers (90 in workshops) and 217 infantry tanks (30 in workshops). Referring to the presence of two German armoured divisions and one Italian in Libya, he warned that by 1st September there might well be another two or three and that the enemy might also receive facilities to pass two or three through Anatolia to operate on his northern flank. He stated that it was therefore imperative, if Egypt were to be held, that further armoured reinforcements should be shipped at once and be ready for battle by the end of August.

On 6th June Wavell sent an appreciation of the possibilities of operation BATTLEAXE to the Chief of the Imperial Staff.[9] He pointed out that the enemy had now prepared defensive positions opposite Tobruk and that a break-out of the garrison, though still possible, would probably involve considerable casualties in tanks and men; therefore if the Tobruk garrison attacked during the first stage of BATTLEAXE and the main attack stopped at the end of that stage owing to casualties suffered by the armoured formations, the further defence of Tobruk would be compromised. The garrison would therefore have to contain the enemy in the first stage and make its sortie in the second stage when the main attack came within supporting distance.

Wavell's general appreciation of the prospects was not couched in optimistic terms. If both stages of the operation succeeded, the benefits, he said, would include the relief of Tobruk and the re-establishment of air bases between Tobruk and Salum. Success in the first stage only would delay the enemy advance on Egypt and probably prevent him from using air bases between Salum and Tobruk. If the attack in the first stage should fail, the position would be serious, since he had no reserve of armour. The fall of Tobruk might then be likely and the enemy would be placed in a strong position to invade Egypt in the late summer or early autumn. Wavell summed up:

> I do not anticipate complete failure in the first stage but our strength at the end of first stage may not enable us to carry out second stage and reach Tobruk.

At a meeting of the Middle East Commanders-in-Chief on 13th June, which Blamey attended, Wavell stated that once touch with Tobruk had been established he proposed to base a system of mobile defence upon the fortress but that, if our main forces were subsequently driven back eastwards, he proposed that Tobruk should be left ungarrisoned.

---

[9] GHQ Middle East war diary.

The date set for operation BATTLEAXE to begin was 15th June. The few days allowed by the time-table for the hastily reassembled 7th Armoured Division to train with the new tanks was a grossly inadequate preparation for battle. But although Wavell was under great pressure from London to bring the battle on as soon as the newly-arrived tanks could be got to the front, it is not to be lightly presumed that he fixed the date against his better judgment. The background to the problem was the prospective immediate improvement in Rommel's supply situation resulting from the German conquest of Crete, sure to be quickly converted into an air base, and the simultaneous weakening of the British fleet in the eastern Mediterranean. A better trained force attacking later might encounter a much stronger enemy, or the enemy attacking in concentrated force might choose the time and place of the engagement. Whether these considerations justified giving battle without proper training may be doubtful, but it may also be doubted whether a longer training period would have effected much improvement. Three main factors limiting the success of operation BATTLEAXE were the higher commanders' propensity to disperse the armour, their failure to combine the action of their force's tanks, field guns and anti-tank guns and their exposure of the infantry tanks, in attacks on fixed fortifications, to guns that outranged them. These faults persisted long after BATTLEAXE, as operation CRUSADER was to show.

Wavell planned to use some 200 medium tanks in the offensive, of which about half would be infantry tanks.[1] He estimated that the Germans had 100 medium tanks in the forward area and 120 in the Tobruk area, where there were also some 70 light German tanks and a few Italian tanks. Thus while the British might achieve a 2 to 1 superiority over German tanks at the outset, he inferred that it would be possible for Rommel to concentrate about 300 tanks against the British total of about 200.[2] If these do not appear very favourable terms for mounting an offensive, it must be remembered that for Britain the war was still a contest with a militarily stronger power. Neither Wavell nor any other British commander had yet been vouchsafed a general superiority of force in an important theatre of operations. Success depended on achieving momentary superiority at a decisive point. The situation was in fact better than Wavell appreciated, for the Germans had fewer than 200 tanks fit for action when the operation started and the British actually achieved a superiority of 4 to 1 in gun-armed tanks and 2 to 1 in troops for their attack on the frontier.[3]

---

[1] Playfair, Vol II, p. 171, gives the numbers used as 90 cruiser tanks and approximately 100 infantry tanks.

[2] Final estimate of German tank strength before the operation given in Intelligence summaries was—
    Frontier . . . . German 100 medium, 66 light
    Gazala—Tobruk—El Adem . German 76 medium, 46 light
                                         Italian 18 medium, 46 light
Figures in Morshead's diary which may have come from most secret sources, were:
    Frontier . . . German 62 medium, 36 light (including 26 Mk II)
    Tobruk, etc. . . German 116 medium, 66 light (including 46 Mk II)
                        Italian 18 medium, 46 light

[3] See Liddell Hart, *The Tanks*, Vol II, pp. 81-3.

The plan for operation BATTLEAXE was, as the historian of the Indian Armed Forces has remarked, "similar in tactics to that which had proved so successful a month before". On the right, the 4th Indian Division, with infantry tank support, was to assault Halfaya frontally, both above and below the escarpment, a second column of tanks and infantry comprising the main infantry tank strength (the 4th Armoured Brigade) was to be aimed through Point 206 at Fort Capuzzo and Salum, and the 7th Armoured Division with cruiser tanks was to advance on the left to the Hafid Ridge and beyond, hoping to draw the enemy armour, while its Support Group screened the flank.

The German Africa Command watched the development of the British preparations through the eyes of its Intelligence services and drew correct deductions. By 6th June the likelihood of an attack had been appreciated. It was noted by the German *Africa Corps* on 10th June that a planned relief of the *Ariete Division* by the *Pavia Division* had been completed but that "owing to the alteration in the enemy situation"—no doubt a reference to the advancing of the line in the Tobruk Salient—it was impossible to relieve the *5th Light Division* of its front-line responsibilities. The division remained in the El Adem-Acroma area as corps reserve. In the meantime three local defence positions were constructed astride the British line of advance, prepared for all-round defence, equipped with artillery and as many anti-tank weapons as possible and, "in accordance with the lessons learnt at Tobruk", carefully concealed in the hope that the British would run inadvertently upon them: one at Point 208 was on the Hafid Ridge, one was at Point 206 (south of Fort Capuzzo) and one at Halfaya. Both at Point 208 and at Halfaya a troop of 88-mm guns was dug in. Behind the bastion at Halfaya and the two fortified islands in the desert approaches, manned mainly by German troops, stretched a second line of Italian-manned strongpoints at Fort Capuzzo, Musaid and Salum barracks, and between the two main defence lines two further strongpoints were developed, at Bir Wair and Qalala. The guns in these chequered fortifications provided artillery defence in great depth covering the environs of the vital pass-heads. The mobile reserve of the German armoured force on the frontier, comprising the medium tanks of the *15th Armoured Division* with mobile infantry and medium (88-mm) and light anti-aircraft artillery, was stationed north of Capuzzo.

On 14th June the German command deduced that the British attack would open next day. Mobile reserve units in the Tobruk-El Adem area (including the *5th Light Division*) were ordered to be ready for action at first light and the *5th Light Division* was ordered to move a mixed tank and artillery unit to a position south of Gambut on the frontier approaches to the Tobruk front. The *Ariete Division* at Gazala, west of Tobruk, was alerted and the entire artillery at Tobruk was ordered to lay a barrage at moonrise.

It was now more than two months since the 9th Australian Division had withdrawn into Tobruk to deny its fortress and harbour to the enemy until the British command could organise a force to drive him back. The troops had understood that their sentence was imprisonment with hard labour until relieved, but had expected that the building up of a relief force would straightaway be put in hand. Information of the first thrust had not been imparted in a way to engender undue hopes and had been quickly followed by news of failure. But through the "grape-vine" communication network the men became aware of the impending June offensive and rumours of the assembling of a large British armoured force kindled great hope. Although extreme precautions to maintain secrecy were taken, the practising of roles on a large scale, together with far-reaching administrative arrangements, left few in ignorance.

The role of the Tobruk garrison in operation BATTLEAXE, as foreshadowed in Wavell's appreciation, was to contain the besieging enemy in the first stage (frontier operations) and to execute a strong sortie in the second stage to join forces with the formations operating from the frontier; but until these were within striking distance no move was to be made outside the perimeter. The junction was to be made at Ed Duda, a dominant hill eight miles south-east of the perimeter. Ed Duda overlooked the Trigh Capuzzo near its junction with the Tobruk by-pass route (later to be made a bituminous road) by which Axis transport bound for the frontier, having left the coast road to skirt the perimeter, rejoined it on the eastern side. The task of the garrison force therefore involved not merely breaching the defence ring to reach Ed Duda but maintaining an open corridor to that point. A similar plan was later to be adopted for operation CRUSADER but had then to be carried out through much more strongly developed defences.

Morshead's assignment confronted him with difficult problems. He was determined that the garrison's contribution should be formidable, but the need to allocate an adequate force to the sortie from his four infantry brigades competed directly with his responsibility for defending a perimeter of some 30 miles. While Tobruk was encircled he could not part with a large force to establish a stronghold at Ed Duda. Closer to the perimeter, however, he chose not to minimise the commitment but to strike with vigour.

The plan provided for the main sortie to be made by the 18th Brigade complete with supporting arms (including the 1st R.H.A.) and the 3rd Armoured Brigade. Simultaneously the 26th Brigade on the left was to make a sortie with one battalion (the 2/48th) to attack the enemy defences near the Bardia Road with the primary object of flank protection and dispersal of the enemy's defensive and counter-preparation fire. As a further diversion and stimulus to Italian nervousness on the left, a company of English commandos under Major Lord Sudeley[4] (and including among its officers Major Randolph Churchill, the British Prime Minister's son) was to make a landing behind the enemy lines six miles to the east of the perimeter. On the right of the sortie the 24th and 20th Brigades were to engage the enemy with fire. In a late development of

---

[4] Major Lord Sudeley; Royal Horse Guards. Regular soldier; b. 20 Apr 1911. Died 26 Aug 1941.

the plan, the 24th Brigade was to be on call to attack with two battalions on the right flank of the sortie. Another subsidiary operation planned in detail was for the 20th Brigade, if opportunity offered—which presumably meant, if the enemy thinned out in this sector or replaced the *5th Light Division* infantry with Italians—to attack with one battalion (the 2/15th) along the southern perimeter for Medauuar. A final operation planned, to be mounted if the enemy's grip on the perimeter loosened, was a sortie through the western gate along the Derna Road by the 24th Brigade with two battalions. Thought was given to possible enemy counterthrusts and the most likely points of penetration, counter-attack tasks were worked out, and Godfrey's and Tovell's brigades each had one battalion on call to carry them out.

Wootten learned of his assignment only one day after his brigade had moved into reserve. A week of intensive preparation followed and Wootten twice reconnoitred the area in front of the perimeter by carrier. His plan was to establish two battalion positions a little more than three miles out from the perimeter on either side of the "corridor"—the 2/9th Battalion at Bir Ghersa on the right, the 2/12th on the left—thus providing a protected zone in which the artillery would be sited, while the 2/10th Battalion went forward to seize and hold Ed Duda. The 7th Royal Tanks (with 15 infantry tanks) were to participate in Martin's and Field's attack. The rest of the 3rd Armoured Brigade—1st Royal Tank Regiment (about 20 old cruiser tanks), 3rd Hussars (19 light tanks) and King's Dragoon Guards (26 armoured cars)—with one company of the 2/10th Battalion was to precede the main body of the battalion as an advanced guard and seize Ed Duda if unoccupied or lightly held until the infantry arrived. If the offensive developed favourably, the 2/10th was to be prepared to come under command of the 3rd Armoured Brigade to participate in a wide sweep of the desert to a position west of Acroma; possibly the whole brigade might be so employed. The 18th Brigade had been made operationally mobile, largely with vehicles commandeered from the 18th Indian Cavalry Regiment.

All was ready by 15th June and the first situation reports received from the frontier, which according to fashion played successes up and failures down, reporting that Capuzzo had been captured but that Halfaya was "still holding out", gave promise of favourable development. The commencement of Wootten's operation waited on the receipt of the agreed signal, which was to be issued when the armoured forces from the frontier came within 20 miles. The signal did not come.

The best that can be said of operation BATTLEAXE is that it was not the complete failure it was at first adjudged, but it ended, as became the almost invariable pattern in the desert armoured conflicts, with the German forces in possession of the battlefield and thus able to recover their temporarily disabled tanks while for the same reason most serious British tank casualties became total losses.

The two columns operating against Halfaya and Fort Capuzzo were under the command of the 4th Indian Division (General F. W. Messervy). The 7th Armoured Division (General Creagh) was responsible for the inland flank. The Royal Air Force succeeded, by the costly method of continuous fighter patrols, in establishing local superiority over the battlefield notwithstanding that Rommel, on the eve of the battle, had appealed to the German Air Command for full support. The three British columns, though detected, were not hampered in their advance to the battle zone.

In the early morning the right-hand column, which was subdivided into two, advancing in part above and in part below the escarpment, attacked Halfaya. The force on the coastal plain, which comprised two battalions of the 4th Indian Division and six infantry tanks of the 4th Royal Tank Regiment, failed in its head-on assault; four of the tanks became immobilised on a minefield which, according to one account, "had not been gapped, as arranged".[5] The force operating above the escarpment, consisting of one infantry battalion (2/Camerons) and 12 infantry tanks of the 4th Royal Tanks, attacked the top of the pass without support from its artillery, which had become bogged in sand on the approach march. The 88-mm and anti-tank guns of the defence at first held their fire and then shot the British tanks to pieces at close range, accounting for 11 out of 12. Denuded of support, the Camerons could not press home the attack.

In the centre the 4th Royal Tank Regiment, weakened by the detachments allotted to the infantry force operating against Halfaya, was directed at the German strongpoints covering the approaches to Fort Capuzzo, while the main centre column to attack Capuzzo bypassed these positions. A fortification just north of the wire containing eight field guns was captured (but subsequently lost in a surprise counter-attack by German armoured cars). The attack on Point 206 initially made by one troop of tanks was repelled. In the late morning, however, the main centre column, speared by the 7th Royal Tank Regiment's infantry tanks, overran Capuzzo; the 22nd Guards Brigade consolidated.

On the left the advanced guard of the inland column (7th Armoured Division) had meanwhile been checked by heavy fire on the Hafid Ridge, but just before midday an attack by one squadron, supported by artillery, overran some enemy gun positions.

The German command had by this time inferred that the aim of the operation might be to wipe out the German frontier forces and relieve Tobruk. A reconnaissance battalion and an artillery regiment of the *5th Light Division* were set moving in the morning to the frontier for employment opposite Capuzzo. Permission was sought from the Italian command to use the *Ariete Division*; when this was given, the division was ordered to be ready to move at 3 p.m. Just before midday the rest of the *5th Light Division* was ordered to move to south of Gambut ready for future employment. About the same time General Neumann-Silkow (later recognised as one of the most competent commanders of armour in Africa), who had been recently appointed to command the *15th Armoured*

---

[5] Liddell Hart, *The Tanks*, Vol II, p. 83.

Division, became concerned at the loss of artillery at Point 206 and Point 208 and ordered the division's mobile armoured reserves to restore the situation in those areas.

Throughout the day the British inland column, including the cruiser tank regiments, spent its strength endeavouring to overcome the enemy on the Hafid Ridge, sparring with the tanks of Neumann-Silkow's division and running into German ambushes in the bewitching succession of ridges near Point 208, while in the centre a second weak attack on Point 206 in mid-afternoon penetrated the position but failed to consolidate its hold.

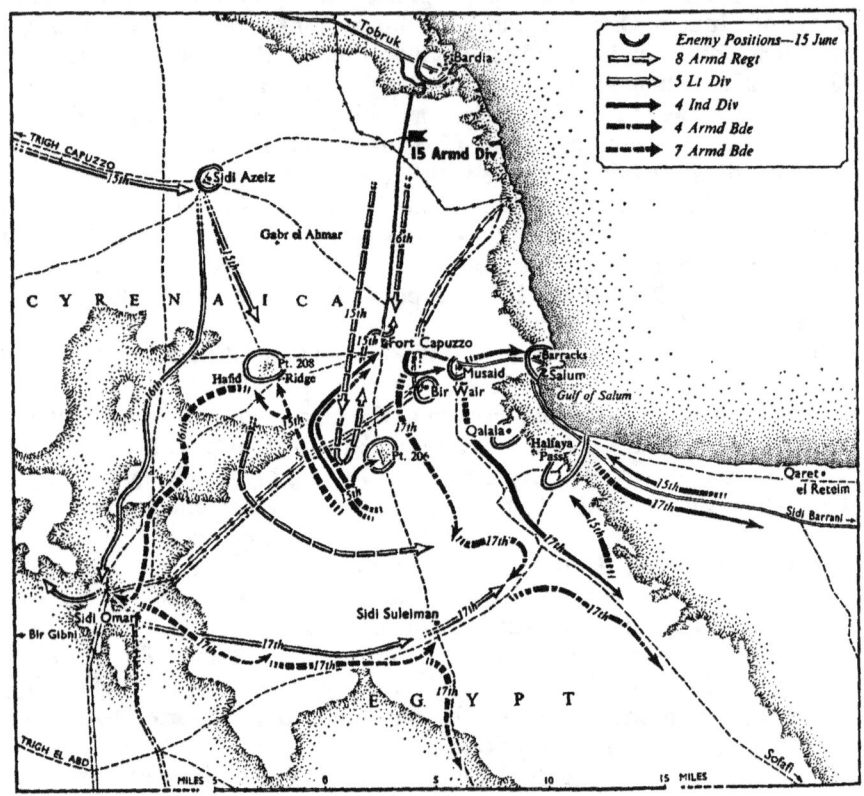

Operation BATTLEAXE

In the evening Point 206 was taken by a stronger attack and a German counter-attack at Capuzzo was repulsed, but on the inland flank the advanced guard of the *5th Light Division* appeared on the scene in the late afternoon and the 7th Armoured Division drew back from the Hafid Ridge when the Germans attacked with a strong tank force. The German tanks followed, engaging the British tanks at long range as they withdrew to south of the frontier wire, there to leaguer.

In brief, on the first day the centre thrust had succeeded, but both the attack on Halfaya and the left flank thrust had failed.

On the morning of 16th June the 7th Armoured Division had about 48 cruiser tanks fit for action, while the 4th Armoured Brigade's two infantry-tank regiments with the 4th Indian Division had some 40 infantry-tank runners. Although some German tank units had been engaged, the British forces had failed to come to grips with the German armour, which must therefore have been regarded as retaining most of its original tank strength, then estimated to include 170 medium tanks. Thus the conditions that gave some initial hope of success for the operation appeared to exist no longer.

The British plan for the 16th required the coast force again to attack for Halfaya frontally, the centre force without its tanks to exploit towards Bardia and the inland column to be strengthened by a junction of the 4th Armoured Brigade (infantry tanks) with the rest of the 7th Armoured Division, the intention being that both armoured brigades should operate together to destroy the enemy's armour at Hafid. The 7th Armoured Division's plan for the employment of the armour, however, handed over the vexatious task of subduing the Hafid Ridge positions to the Matildas of the 4th Armoured Brigade while the 7th Armoured Brigade and the Support Group were to "attack and smash" the armour that had come far south of the Hafid Ridge to engage the division during its withdrawal on the previous evening. But the German command chose to seize the initiative, in consequence of which the situation at first developed more favourably for the British than their plan warranted. The German mobile formations were ordered to attack at first light, the *15th Armoured Division* at Capuzzo, the *5th Light Division* against the British armour on the inland flank, with the intention of reaching Sidi Omar at 8 a.m. Rommel also ordered the *Ariete Division* to send a detachment to Ed Duda: it is possible that the over-all British plan was known to him from captured documents.

Owing perhaps to General Beresford-Peirse's much criticised order to the 4th Armoured Brigade to "rally forward", the British infantry were for once not caught without support from their own tanks when on the 16th the *15th Armoured Division* surprisingly attacked Fort Capuzzo before 5 a.m. The 7th Royal Tanks aided by the combined fire of the artillery and infantry-support weapons beat off the attack and the German *8th Armoured Regiment,* which appears to have begun operation BATTLE-AXE with some 80 tanks, reported after the action that it had only 33 runners. In view of this attack General Messervy refused to release the 4th Armoured Brigade to attack Hafid Ridge.

Meanwhile the Scots Guards had taken Musaid and later captured Salum barracks, though on the coast the renewed frontal attack on Halfaya by the 11th Indian Brigade failed. On the inland flank the two regiments of the 7th Armoured Brigade acting in concert successfully checked a German southward thrust.

This was the high tide of British success in the operation and caused the German command to fear that the British force operating from Capuzzo could break through to the Tobruk front. Rommel decided to attack the flank of this force by using the *5th Light Division* in a thrust at Sidi Suleiman, but embroilment of the division's tank regiment with the 7th Armoured Division and British shelling of the assembly area chosen prevented the mounting of the attack as originally planned.

From late afternoon onwards the battle developed unfavourably for the British. One of the 7th Armoured Division's two cruiser regiments joyfully pursued an unescorted German transport column. The regiments became separated; their artillery was withdrawn farther back. In the evening each regiment was successively attacked by German armour of the *5th Light Division* acting in combination with its artillery. The second engagement became critical but the German attack was halted by darkness. A third British infantry attack on Halfaya in the evening failed.

The two cruiser regiments of the 7th Armoured Brigade now had no more than 25 cruiser tanks fit for action while the 4th Armoured Brigade protecting the Capuzzo force had 29 infantry tanks. The British plan for the third day was that the two armoured brigades should join forces to smash the German armour. Rommel's counter-plan was that his two armoured divisions should start moving at 4.30 a.m. to join forces and attack through Sidi Suleiman to Halfaya. Such a thrust, if successful, would both end the isolation of Halfaya and cut in behind the British centre column.

At first light on the morning of 17th June the mobile group of the *15th Armoured Division,* taking 88-mm guns with it and employing them in a mobile role, brushed up against the 7th Armoured Brigade; soon afterwards the *5th Light Division* tanks entered Sidi Suleiman. Rommel's initiative and early start again dissuaded General Messervy from parting with the 4th Armoured Brigade.

General Creagh, from the 7th Armoured Division headquarters 25 miles behind the frontier wire, now spoke to General Beresford-Peirse, who was at his headquarters 60 miles back, suggesting that he come forward to take an important decision. Wavell had arrived at Beresford-Peirse's headquarters on the previous evening. Wavell and Beresford-Peirse flew to Creagh's headquarters but in the meantime Messervy had decided to withdraw from Capuzzo. When Wavell arrived, he authorised the withdrawal and the abandonment of the offensive. Notwithstanding Rommel's efforts to concentrate both his armoured divisions to trap the British force at Capuzzo, its withdrawal was well effected under cover of gallant action by the dwindling Matildas of the 4th Armoured Brigade.

In the BATTLEAXE operation the 12th Battery, 2/3rd Anti-Tank Regiment, was employed with the columns screening the south-west flank and rear of the attacking force. Major Argent's headquarters and Lieutenant Scanlon's troop were with the 60th Rifles, Lieutenant Cheetham's troop, less a section, with the headquarters of a Rifle Brigade battalion, Sergeant Hocking's[6] section with the Support Group headquarters and Lieutenant Rennison's troop with "Harry Column", which operated in the opening

---

[6] Sgt I. D. Hocking, NX59941; 2/3 A-Tk Regt. Warehouse assistant; of Sydney; b. Walcha, NSW, 18 Oct 1919.

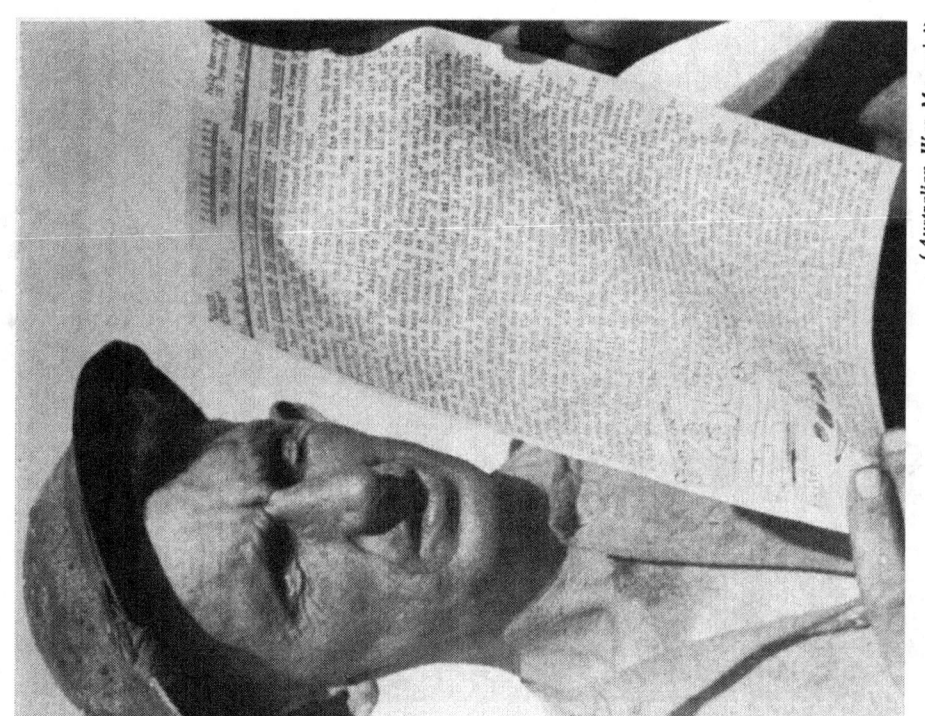

An Australian soldier reading a copy of *Tobruk Truth*.
(*Australian War Memorial*)

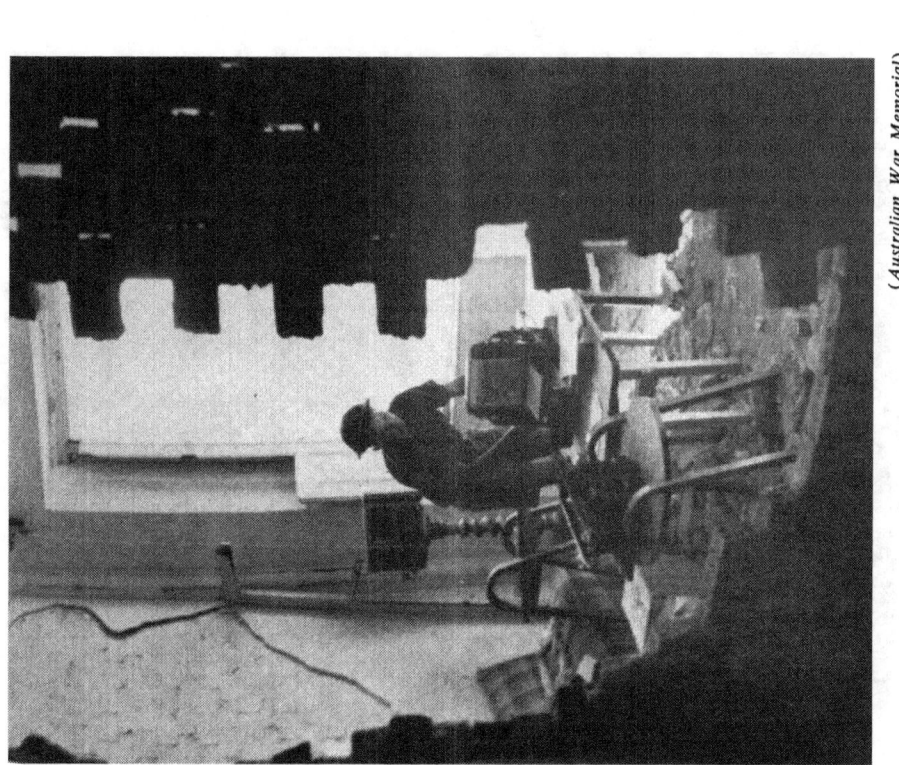

The printing press of *Tobruk Truth* which gave the garrison authentic news throughout the siege.
(*Australian War Memorial*)

(Australian War Memorial)
"Aldershot" ovens helped to keep the troops in Tobruk supplied with bread.

(Australian War Memorial)
Drawing water from a well in Tobruk.

(Australian War Memorial)

Loading stores and rations at a 9th Divisional A.A.S.C. supply depot. Note dispersion of supplies to minimise damage from air attack.

(Australian War Memorial)

A camouflaged headquarters at Tobruk, looking north-west across the plain towards the Derna Road.

(Maj O. M. Walsoe)

The "Garden of Eden" and a ration truck of the 2/13th Battalion after attracting enemy artillery fire. What appear to be bushes are the tops of fig-trees growing in a cavity around a well.

(Maj O. M. Walsoe)

Post R25, just forward of the "Garden of Eden", manned by the 2/13th Battalion.

phase along the Trigh el Abd to Bir Gibni in Libya, some 12 miles west-south-west of Sidi Omar. While on Harry Column's excursion, Rennison's troop destroyed three German armoured cars without loss to themselves. During the withdrawal on 17th June Harry Column was about seven miles south-east of Sidi Suleiman at 6 p.m. when 14 German tanks approached from the direction of Sidi Suleiman. Two guns of Rennison's troop opened fire and scored direct hits on the tanks, one of which burst into flames.

The British tank losses in BATTLEAXE were severe: of the 100 (approximately) infantry tanks engaged, 64 were destroyed or abandoned, of the 90 cruisers 23 were lost. According to German records only 12 German medium tanks were lost and the loss was counter-balanced by the capture of 12 usable British infantry tanks. From the official British history it would appear that about 100 tanks of those engaged were recoverable or still runners, while we now know the Germans were left with 81 undamaged or recoverable medium gun-armed tanks. But the German strength was at the time thought to be greater.

Churchill later commented critically:

> The operation seemed ill-concerted, especially from the failure to make a sortie from the Tobruk sally-port as an indispensable preliminary and concomitant.[7]

But although such a preliminary sortie might possibly have distracted the *5th Light Division* and delayed its mobile group's arrival on the frontier, few would agree that victory should have been sought on the frontier by risking the destruction of the Tobruk sortie force.

Four days after General Wavell had authorised the discontinuance of BATTLEAXE, he was informed by Mr Churchill that he was to change places with General Auchinleck, Commander-in-Chief of India. Later Churchill wrote that after BATTLEAXE he "came to the conclusion that there should be a change".[8] But there is evidence that this conclusion may have been reached before the BATTLEAXE failure—much of which flowed from faulty handling of arms and formations in a battle Wavell did not personally control. BATTLEAXE provided the pretext and the opportunity. General Kennedy has written that the exchange had been strongly mooted on 6th May and "finally decided" on 19th May. The Chief of the General Staff, Sir John Dill, did not at that time exactly espouse the Commander-in-Chief's cause:

> Dill had repeated his former advice: 'Back him or sack him.' Churchill had replied: 'It is not so simple as that. Lloyd George did not trust Haig in the last war—yet he could not sack him.' Dill had told him that Auchinleck, for all his great qualities and his outstanding record on the Frontier, was not the coming man of the war, as the Prime Minister thought.[9]

Nevertheless after BATTLEAXE General Auchinleck was appointed to succeed General Wavell without more ado. It may be doubted whether any other "coming man of the war" would have proved a better choice.

---

[7] Churchill, Vol III, p. 308.
[8] Churchill, Vol III, p. 309.
[9] J. Kennedy, *The Business of War* (1957), p. 119.

Auchinleck was an officer of the Indian Army whose active service in the first world war had all been in the Middle East, mainly in Mesopotamia. He had served with distinction in operations on the North-West Frontier of India, where in 1935 he had commanded a division of four brigades in action. In January 1940 he was appointed to raise and command the IV British Corps which was to join the B.E.F. in France. The choice of an Indian Army officer for this post was indicative of the high regard in which he was held by at least some senior officers of the British Army. In May, before his corps was ready to go to France, Auchinleck was given command of the Anglo-French forces in northern Norway. After the withdrawal of this force in June he briefly commanded the V Corps in England, and in July succeeded General Brooke as G.O.C. Southern Command. (Lieut-General B. L. Montgomery took over V Corps.) After four months in Southern Command, including the period when danger of invasion seemed most imminent, Auchinleck was appointed Commander-in-Chief in India, having had the experience, in less than a year, of commanding an Allied force in the field, two British corps, and the equivalent of a British army.

Wavell graciously agreed with the Prime Minister that "a new eye and a new hand" were required. Impressions that Wavell had become tired circulated and were later emphasised, though there is no evidence that the supposed weariness had impaired his powers of command and prompt decision. What is patent is that a change was imperative because he had lost the confidence of the British Government and because, lacking effective protection by the Chiefs of Staff, he would have been unable to plan future operations free of interference from Whitehall. His successor was to be better placed in this regard, for like Haig he could not be sacked—at least, not for some time.

On 20th June Wavell terminated the operational subordination of the Tobruk fortress to Western Desert Force headquarters and Morshead became directly responsible to the General Headquarters of the Middle East.

The news of BATTLEAXE's failure was inevitably received with great disappointment in Tobruk. The disagreeable fact that the prospect of early relief had disappeared and the success of any future attempt seemed problematic, its date distant and indefinite, could not but induce pessimism; but there is no evidence that the will to see the siege out was weakened. "We learn from the BBC news," wrote one unit diarist,[1] "that our troops after a three day battle 'to test the enemy strength' have retired to their original position. While this is a little disappointing we are more concerned with the pressing problem 'what has happened to our mail?'."

The fact that the Western Desert was the sole remaining land front on which Britain and her allies were engaged with the Axis forces tended to exaggerate the significance of the British reverse. If German forces could not be successfully opposed even on this front, where and how could

---
[1] War diary, 2/17 Bn.

a victory be won? What could halt the advancing shadow cast by German military power, portending to Britain and her allies a yet darker hour of total eclipse? What indeed but the overconfidence of one who harnessed uncurbed ambition to the shafts of the German war machine and drove it eastwards to destruction? A new cause for hope of victory in the end—and, for the Tobruk garrison, of relief in the intervening time—came when the news of Germany's declaration of war against Russia flashed round the world on 22nd June. That night, in hollows and caves and dugouts in Tobruk, all who could gathered round the radio sets (mostly given by the Australian Comforts Fund and unit funds) and heard the eloquent, inspired voice of the British Prime Minister denouncing the Nazi war machine, its "crafty expert agents", its "odious apparatus" and "behind all this glare, behind all this storm" the "group of villainous men" who planned "this cataract of horrors", declaring that there was but one aim and one single, irrevocable purpose, the destruction of Hitler and every vestige of the Nazi regime, declaiming in unforgettable words:

> We shall fight him by land, we shall fight him by sea, we shall fight him in the air, until, with God's help, we have rid the earth of his shadow and liberated its people from his yoke.

Next day the *Tobruk Truth* reported:

> As Mr Churchill ended, the crowd listening at Salvation Army Hall was stirred by a voice that called "a cheer for Winnie". Instantaneously another voice "The King". In less than a second the crowd was at attention—voices lifted as National Anthem sung.

But it is of interest that in most diaries and daily news sheets (which several units were now producing) the arrival of a mail delivery was accorded greater significance. "There's no doubt about it, when a mail arrives, our whole outlook changes," wrote the editor of *Mud and Blood*[2] next day, adding later "perhaps a little of our jubilation today is occasioned by the good news from overseas." The diarist of another unit remarked: "3,000 letters have arrived to our great joy. The unit is as happy as if it were going on leave. . . ." Another commented on the involvement of Russia: "All hope it may help our cause but few seem to expect the Russians to hold out for very long."

On 24th June German aircraft dropped leaflets over the garrison. The text ran:

AUSSIES

After Crete disaster Anzac troops are now being ruthlessly sacrificed by England in Tobruch and Syria. Turkey has concluded pact of friendship with Germany. England will shortly be driven out of the Mediterranean. Offensive from Egypt to relieve you totally smashed.

YOU CANNOT ESCAPE

Our dive bombers are waiting to sink your transports. Think of your future and your people at home. Come forward. Show white flags and you will be out of danger.

SURRENDER

---

[2] News sheet of the 2/23 Bn.

These brought to light many previously unrecognised gifts of humour. The diarist of Morshead's headquarters wrote more seriously that owing to the great demand for the leaflets as souvenirs "two copies are included as Appendix 46A". When the war diary was received at 2nd Echelon, however, it was noted that Appendix 46A was missing.

Morshead's prescription to counter the disappointment at the failure of efforts to relieve Tobruk was hard work. The construction of field works giving depth to the defence by units in reserve was intensified. In the front line "active patrolling and raids were encouraged still further. In short, we set out to besiege the besiegers".[3]

The possibility that the siege might be lifted had postponed Burrows' plans for a further advancement of the Salient line. Meanwhile his battalion was occupied in changing the sites of its company headquarters and improving the earthworks and wiring of the new positions, while day by day the enemy fired a substantial weight of shells on to the vacated positions, to the mutual satisfaction of the front-line troops of both sides. Colonel Crawford, whose 2/17th Battalion was in reserve behind the Salient, changed the location of one of his companies on 16th June and within a few hours had the pleasure of seeing 500 shells fall on the abandoned position. But although the enemy artillery became more active during the frontier offensive, there is no reference in any artillery or unit diary to the moonrise bombardment ordered by Rommel's headquarters.

When the expectation of relief faded Burrows began to press for acceptance of his plans. On 20th June Lieutenant Burrell and another man (Private Davidson[4]) went out 400 yards into no-man's land before first light to observe the area in daylight: Burrell reported that, though heavily booby-trapped, it could be occupied with advantage. On the next day Burrows went to Murray's headquarters, as the unit diarist expressed it, "to arrange further forward movement of left flank and to ensure cooperation from 2/15th Battalion". There was no problem, however, in ensuring the cooperation of Major Ogle, who assumed command of the 2/15th Battalion next day. Ogle entered enthusiastically into the project, not only immediately cooperating in putting into effect Burrows' plan but also later advancing some of the line his battalion had inherited from Burrows' battalion at the beginning of the month.

It was decided that the 2/13th Battalion should construct the new positions on the left of Nixon's Post and that the 2/15th Battalion should occupy them. This arrangement was logical. The positions would be in the 2/13th Battalion's area of responsibility until occupied by the 2/15th. Nevertheless the decision was not, in the jargon of the industrialist, "good human relations", for not even excellent leadership can get soldiers to perceive the justice of being required to dig other soldiers' trenches in most extreme danger, nor with the best morale in the world can weary troops

---

[3] 9 Aust Div Report on Operations in Cyrenaica.
[4] L-Cpl A. MacK. Davidson, NX35320; 2/13 Bn. Station hand; of The Rock, NSW; b. Goulburn, NSW, 2 Jan 1918. Killed in action 23 Jun 1941.

find for such tasks the will and energy they would be able to summon up if their own lives were to depend on their performance. The plan provided for Captain Handley's company of the 2/13th to dig the positions on the night of 22nd-23rd June and Captain Strange's[5] company of the 2/15th to occupy them next night. Simultaneously the 2/15th Battalion was to construct a new company area on the left and, in due course, to occupy it.

The work began on the night of 22nd June. Before the evening meal was taken, the explosion of a mine that wounded three men in the 2/15th Battalion to the left of the work area sounded a warning. At 10 p.m. the taping party moved out preceded by sappers to clear the route and before midnight work was under way. Wire and other stores began to be brought forward, but at 1 a.m. a carrying party of the 2/13th Battalion set off a booby-trap killing two men and wounding one. Enemy machine-guns then opened up on the scene of the explosion. For the rest of the night work had to proceed under unnerving fire. In the adjacent 2/15th Battalion area, while a platoon led by Lieutenant Harland was reconnoitring an area it was to occupy, a booby-trap exploded and wounded five men. Captain Strange's company suffered six more casualties, of which one was fatal. Two sections occupied a forward position on the left of this area next day.

The work of the 2/13th was not completed by first light. The posts had been dug to the insufficient depth of 30 inches and the front was only partly wired. Consequently engineers, digging parties, carrying parties and others had to carry on the work next night. It was decided that although the 2/13th Battalion would continue to supervise the arrangements, the 2/15th Battalion would provide the working parties in the area to be taken over. This work was to be done by Captain Strange's company. Ogle's plans were to bring the positions that night to a state of readiness for occupation by Strange's company on the succeeding night. He told his company commanders at an orders conference on the afternoon of 23rd June that Handley's company of the 2/13th would be manning the newly-dug positions from dusk. When Strange's company arrived, Handley's men would move out as a covering party until 4 a.m., when they would withdraw. He ordered: "2/15th Battalion will prepare new positions for occupation on the night of 24th June." One of two essential points to be stressed was that the positions *must* be occupied on the following night as the relief of the 2/13th had been postponed to allow this to be completed.[6] Apparently this was not fully understood by the 2/13th Battalion, which according to its diarist was still expecting that the 2/15th would occupy the positions at 4 a.m. on the 24th.

Ogle went out to the area as work began and remained until first light. The men moved out with dread to the death-trapped minefield. Soon after midnight two parties of 2/13th Intelligence men and sappers who

---

[5] Maj B. D. Strange, DSO, QX6222; 2/15 Bn. Departmental manager; of Townsville, Qld; b. Brisbane, 5 Apr 1913. Accidentally killed 20 Sep 1944.
[6] Based on notes for this conference from Lt-Col Ogle's personal notebook lent to author.

were working towards each other from the flanks had just met in the centre when a booby-trap exploded; 4 men were killed and 6 wounded. Thereupon an enemy mortar opened up, from which an exploding bomb killed 3 men and wounded 6. The work nevertheless was pushed on. It appears from the war diary of the 2/13th that that unit only became aware at 3 a.m. that the 2/15th did not intend to occupy the positions until the following night. By 4 a.m. they were adequately dug though still not completely wired. They were then occupied by Handley's company.

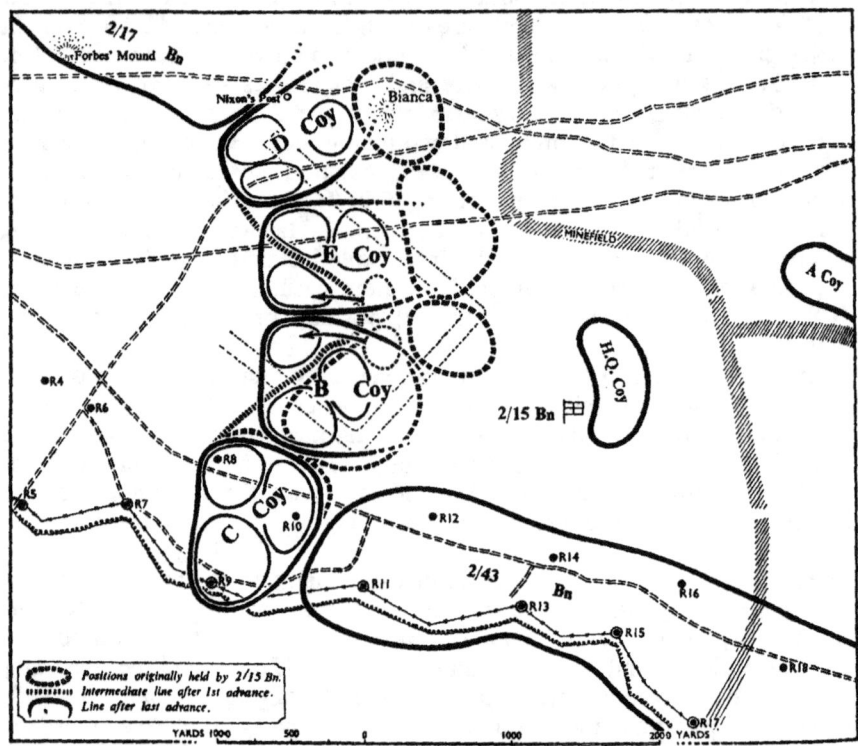

Advancing the left flank of the Salient, 29th June-3rd July

Intense precautions were taken to prevent a repetition of these losses next night and, by avoiding bunching, to minimise casualties should any misfortune occur. Strange's company relieved Handley's company without incident and by 4 a.m. on 25th June Captain Newcomb's[7] company[8] on Strange's left was also safely ensconced in its new positions, where the line had been brought forward to conform. During the morning reconnaissance parties from the 2/17th Battalion arrived at the 2/13th which was to be withdrawn from the Salient into brigade reserve.

---

[7] Maj S. P. Newcomb, QX6238; 2/15 Bn. Clerk; of Graceville, Qld; b. Toowoomba, Qld, 3 Nov 1909.

[8] "E" Company. To cope with its extensive front-line responsibilities, the 2/15th had temporarily adopted a five-company organisation.

Not every battalion commander agreed with Burrows that it was beneficial to advance the line so close to the enemy positions. A wide no-man's land has advantages for the defence if it is conducted with vigour and its patrols assert mastery. Some thought that the closer observation afforded to the enemy from his higher ground overlooking both the new defence line and its approaches outweighed the advantages secured, particularly since an intense and continuous strain was imposed on the men occupying these exposed, shallow earthworks. But the importance of denying Post S8, Forbes' Mound and Post R8 to the enemy, which predetermined the nearness to the German line both at each end of the Salient and in the centre, was a counter-argument in favour of advancing the front line to the flanks of these positions. In war those who do not push forward are often thrust back.

These arguments against more forward siting had less application on the left of the Salient, where the next adjustment was planned by Major Ogle. After he had swung his battalion's right flank forward to the new alignment running out towards Nixon's Post, the centre of his front was shaped like an elbow pointing inwards; in fact it followed the approximate alignment of a deliberately laid "elbow" in the original British minefield put down in this sector before the Medauuar battle. From the junction of Ogle's centre companies the line ran north-west on the right, south-west on the left. Ogle decided to cut the elbow off by siting his front along a north-south line joining the outer-platoon positions of the two centre companies. This involved advancing the front 700 yards in the centre. The operation, carefully planned, was to be conducted over five nights, allowing one night for an inter-company relief, and to be completed by the early

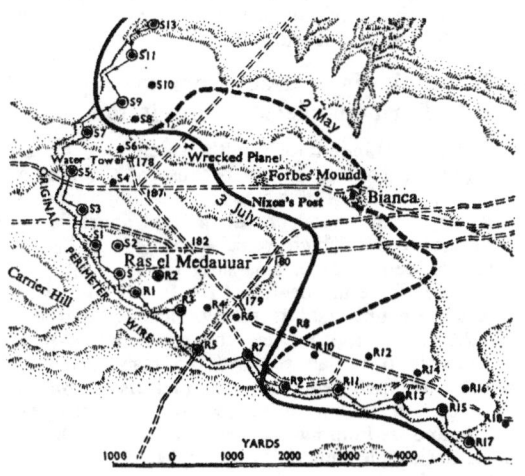

Shortening the Salient, May-July 1941

morning of 3rd July. On the first night the engineers, devitalising mines as they went, ran tapes from the existing positions forward to 30 yards in front of the line to be taken up, then laid tracks along the whole of the front to mark the siting of the new wire. Next night they devitalised mines and booby-traps within the new platoon positions, marking off the "safe areas". On the succeeding two nights the infantry dug the positions and erected the wire. The enemy, however, became restive on the night of the move forward: there was much movement along the whole Salient front and an increase in artillery fire elsewhere. An almost continuous night reconnaissance was conducted by enemy aircraft, using flares after the moon had set. It is more likely that the nervousness was set off by interception of messages passed in an exercise conducted that afternoon by the 3rd Armoured Brigade than by the 2/15th Battalion's activity.

Two months had elapsed since the second Axis assault had breached the perimeter. The prolonged front-line duty, the unchallenged domination of Tobruk skies by hostile aircraft, the intensifying heat, the unpalatable, unchanging diet, and the monotony began to produce noticeable effects, revealed both in a general lassitude and in a lessening of the *élan* that had characterised the patrolling and raiding activities of the first weeks of the siege. One battalion commander wrote in the unit war diary for June:

> All ranks are undoubtedly jaded, yet to go into a rear area only offers the usual digging tasks with no active patrolling. Some form of amusement is vitally needed to maintain a sense of balance, especially if we are to be here for many more months. We publish a daily paper of one sheet . . . which is very popular; but some form of relieving contrast is needed to tone up all ranks. Reinforcements would bring new blood and ideas, and training of them would then be undertaken, giving new zest to officers and N.C.O's.
>
> The spirit of the battalion is still good and the defences of its section of Tobruk are as secure as ever. But a calculating outlook has definitely crept in as regards the "joie de vivre" of raiding. I expect this will grow unless some event takes place to change our outlook.

The following extract from the report of the medical officer of a unit that had just completed a term in the Salient gives an objective picture:

> The high standard of health which had prevailed since leaving Palestine declined on entering Tobruk, chiefly because of the increasing heat, the difficulty in obtaining adequate quantities of water for washing purposes, and the innumerable flies. Gastro-enteritis became very prevalent, and sporadic cases B. Flexner dysentery occurred.
>
> Several cases which were suspected to be sand-fly fever were encountered and a few proved cases of relapsing fever.
>
> On the whole the health of the Battalion was still very good for although diarrhoea was almost universal it rarely incapacitated the patient for more than 24 hours. By 22 June 41, however, the continued exposure to arduous conditions and the unbearable heat had reduced the resistance of the men in the front line and the number of men reporting sick had risen considerably.
>
> Later, on moving into reserve, the men were able to get adequate rest and sleep, and swimming parties were arranged. The influence of this relaxation was soon noticeable and the general health and resistance rapidly improved.[9]

In the month ending 24th June the R.A.P. of this unit treated 360 cases of diarrhoea, 26 of dysentery and 16 of "fear state". There was, moreover, in all units, a number of men—particularly among officers and N.C.O's—who did not report from front-line duty for treatment of gastro-enteric disorders.

The lack of friendly aircraft in the skies over Tobruk did not conduce to the elation of the defence, but familiarity caused air attack to lose some of its awe for the great majority although bombs continued to take their toll of the emotionally less robust, particularly in the port and base

---

[9] War diary, 2/13 Bn, June 1941.

areas against which the raids were usually made. The front-line atmosphere is recaptured in this extract from a war diary:[1]

> A bomber which was later identified as ours flew over Tobruk harbour and then to Hill 209 where a bomb was dropped. This unusual occurrence stopped all activity for a while, no doubt both sides doubting their own insanity. (sic)

In June there were 134 bombing raids on the fortress, in addition to 39 reconnaissance flights.

In the hope that the siege would be raised, little but the barest essentials had been shipped to Tobruk in the weeks preceding BATTLEAXE. No fresh meat was received in June. In May, according to transportation records, 112 tons had been received, but there is no record of its consumption (except in hospitals). However the storeships *Miranda* and *Antiklia* put into Tobruk Harbour on the morning of 1st July, the *Miranda* with 150 tons on board. The arrival of fresh meat at forward units within a few days, in news jargon, "created a sensation". One diarist wrote:

> We hadn't tasted any for 3 months at the very inside. And was it appreciated? We smacked our lips after each mouthful and said "My, this is delicious." This did much to buck up our spirits.[2]

In June only 186 tons of other supplies (rations, medical supplies, hygiene requirements etc) were received. The month's shipment of comforts and canteen stores was 28 tons (for a garrison comprising approximately 28,000 operational and 5,000 non-operational men). This compared with 86 tons in May and 152 in July.

The virtual limitation of supplies to subsistence requirements no doubt contributed its influence to the intangible complex out of which attitudes developed. In June, however, the diarist of the 18th Brigade noted:

> An issue was made today of ONE orange per man, the first issue of fresh fruit in Tobruk . . .

and in subsequent months the provision of "wet" rations—fresh meat, vegetables and fruit—greatly improved. To compensate for vitamin C deficiency in the diet, two tablets of ascorbic acid per man were issued daily.[3]

The curtailment of supplies to essentials was generally regarded as warranted but another shortage during June directly impaired the force's fighting efficiency. The garrison's normal usage of ammunition was of the order of 40 tons a day, and of this no component was more important than 25-pounder high-explosive shell. Reserves by the end of May had fallen dangerously and the decision of the Commanders-in-Chief on 4th June to curtail further supply before BATTLEAXE necessitated strict rationing of the guns, except in emergencies. On 6th June the 25-pounders were limited to an expenditure of 10 rounds per gun. The daily average expenditure in June was little more than 5 tons, compared with an average from 11th April to 17th October of 17 tons.

---
[1] 2/17 Bn, 11 May 1941.
[2] War diary, 2/48 Bn, July 1941.
[3] For a general summary of health and morale factors at Tobruk see Allan S. Walker, *Middle East and Far East* (1953), in the medical series of this history, pp. 210-11.

The severe rationing caused many heart-burnings, all the more so because the enemy artillery was becoming more active. Especially exasperating were his shoots conducted with air observation from a Henschel aircraft with increased frequency—almost every day from mid-May onwards, by which time he had become aware that Hurricanes were no longer operating from the Tobruk airfield. The targets were often the garrison's gun positions. The observation aircraft usually kept beyond range of the heavy anti-aircraft artillery sited near the coast to protect the port, base area and water-supply. On 30th June the diarist of the 1st R.H.A. wrote:

> During the month the enemy have steadily been consolidating their positions, our forced economy allowing them to do so with greater impunity than they would otherwise be entitled to.

He found some consolation, however, in the observation that there was plenty of ammunition for the 149-mm Italian howitzers. Each of the three artillery sectors had these in use.

Early in July there was a disturbing increase in enemy shelling on the forward defence areas. More than 2,500 shells per day, about 1,500 in the western sector alone, rained down for a period of two days ending on 4th July, when the rate suddenly subsided to normal, after which the gunners resumed the barter of their wares on terms of approximately equal exchange.

Lack of ammunition also recurrently plagued Captain Feitel's troop manning the 60-pounders, but on the whole the shortage of British ammunition had a quite contrary effect on the 2/12th Field Regiment, firing its mixed bag of captured field pieces. These were called upon to make good some of the deficiency. "Each troop in the salient must now fire its 100 rounds per gun per day," commented the regiment's diarist on 12th June. Colonel Goodwin translated some captured range tables, which enabled greater accuracy to be obtained.

The remaining two troops of the regiment arrived on 4th June. Lieutenant Bromley's[4] troop was equipped with Italian 75-mm field guns, Captain Young's[5] with 100-mm. One section of Captain McDermott's troop, which had been relieving the 51st Field Regiment on 25-pounders, took over two of the 4.5 howitzers; the other was equipped with 149-mm guns. The latter equipment had a good range but proved difficult to handle owing to lack of knowledge of the various charges and to difficulty with the recuperator system. One of the guns had to be abandoned after two attempts to fire it.

The drawback of very restricted firing was partly offset in June by the proper organisation of counter-battery work. In the first month of the siege, this had devolved on the staffs of the regiments controlling the three artillery sectors. After 10th May, when a counter-battery section

---

[4] Maj L. F. Bromley, VX13688; 2/12 Fd Regt. Investor; of Burwood, Vic; b. Maffra, Vic, 30 Jul 1912.
[5] Maj V. L. Young, ED, VX13712. 2/12 and 2/6 Fd Regts. Electrical mechanic; of St Kilda, Vic; b. South Yarra, Vic, 22 Nov 1912.

commanded by Lieutenant D. W. Scrimgeour from the staff of the 4th Indian Division at Keren came to Tobruk, a coordinating counter-battery office was established at Royal Artillery headquarters; but it laboured under many disadvantages, of which the greatest was the lack of sound-ranging and flash-spotting equipment. On the night of 3rd June, however, a composite sound-ranging and flash-spotting battery of the 4th Survey Regiment was brought in and three nights later Lieut-Colonel Klein,[6] the counter-battery officer of I Australian Corps, arrived to take charge of the counter-battery organisation.

Klein displayed both drive and ingenuity in quickly establishing an efficient and flexible organisation.[7] His first step was to move the office to a site where living and working conditions and lighting were good and there establish an efficient telephone exchange and communication system. By 9th June the new control centre and observation network were fully operative and on 20th June the diarist of the 1st R.H.A. noted that a detailed counter-battery concentration table had been issued to each battery, enabling any enemy battery to be dealt with in an immediate and methodical way. Klein soon provided Feitel's 60-pounders with much to do.

A feature of artillery work at Tobruk was the number of tower observation posts used by both besiegers and besieged. Some on the perimeter were on poles, others were platforms on steel framework like giant scaffolds. On 26th June it was found that the enemy had erected 10 tripods and towers overnight. Their purpose caused much speculation because they were not used for observation on subsequent days.

The failure of BATTLEAXE had consigned the prospect of lifting the siege to the nebulous realm of "future operations". Whether Tobruk should continue to be held clearly required reconsideration. The problem was taken up by the Chiefs of Staff in London and the Commanders-in-Chief in the Middle East, in whose deliberations General Blamey participated as Deputy Commander-in-Chief. Morshead's chief staff officer, Colonel Lloyd, went to Cairo for consultation.

On 25th June the Commanders-in-Chief discussed a preliminary study prepared by the planning staff and agreed that Tobruk should continue to be held. General Blamey said that the morale was excellent, the defence strong and the garrison confident of resisting attack; Morshead wished, however, to have surplus men and units taken out. Next day the Commanders-in-Chief telegraphed their decision to the Chiefs of Staff. They said that Tobruk greatly influenced enemy action in the Western Desert because a prerequisite to enemy action against the Nile Delta was that the fortress should be either reduced or strongly contained; Tobruk had not yet been really strongly attacked on the ground and in the air but the

---

[6] Brig B. E. Klein, NX4. BM RAA 6 Div 1939-40; 2/8 Fd Regt 1940-41; CBO I Corps 1941-42; CCRA III Corps 1942-44; CRA 3 Div 1944-45. Regular soldier; of Swanbourne, WA; b. Perth, WA, 30 Jan 1900.
[7] See further Chapter 8.

enemy could probably produce the necessary forces for heavy attack in about two months' time; evacuation at any time would require the use of warships for four consecutive nights and would be a difficult operation hard to disguise: it had been decided to hold Tobruk "until supply difficulties or enemy intentions render evacuation desirable" but to reduce the garrison consistent with defence requirements, both to ease the supply situation and to allow of evacuation if necessary on two successive nights. General Blamey informed the Australian Government of the decision by cable.

It is difficult to see how it was thought that such a reduction in the garrison strength could be achieved, unless some diminution of the combatant force was contemplated at the very time when it was apprehended that the danger to the fortress was growing. Morshead had been continually asking to be rid of "bouches inutiles" but, by the time Blamey spoke, that had been largely accomplished. When the 9th Division withdrew into Tobruk, there were almost 10,000 prisoners of war and more than 2,200 Senussi, but when Blamey spoke the total of these remaining would have numbered fewer than 1,000 and week by week their number was being speedily reduced. Most of the prisoners had been removed within a few days of the commencement of the siege; by 13th April only 2,780 remained; by the end of May, despite the addition of more than 2,000 captured in the meantime, the holding had been reduced to 178. The removal of the Senussi was then put in hand. They were shipped out throughout June and by the end of that month there were only some 400 left. There remained some 1,150 dispensable Indian and native personnel in the base area, mainly in labouring units, used principally for stevedoring and other port duties. Including these the total strength of the base area after BATTLEAXE was 4,411 (18th June). It was only here that a significant reduction in strength could be effected.

Other than the prisoners of war the total strength at Tobruk (excluding Royal Navy) after BATTLEAXE was 28,231, of which 22,725 belonged to fighting units. Through most stringent economy these figures were reduced by 31st July to a total of 22,076[8] of which 20,679 belonged to fighting units. The ratio of 1,400 base area personnel to 20,700 in operational formations speaks for itself.

Brigadier Whiteley,[9] of the General Staff at Wavell's headquarters, accompanied Lloyd on his return to Tobruk. Whiteley informed Morshead that the next attempt to relieve Tobruk would not be made until superiority in tanks was assured. The garrison was to be prepared to hold out indefinitely and stocks of ammunition and supplies were to be built up to a reserve of 60 days. Plans for evacuation by sea were to be prepared but were to be made known only to the commander and his senior staff. Within a few days Morshead himself left by sea for Egypt, to arrive at Cairo just as command was passing from General Wavell to General Auchinleck.

---

[8] Excluding 46 prisoners of war.
[9] Gen Sir John Whiteley, GBE, KCB, MC. (1915-18: Lt to Capt, RE.) BGS Eighth Army 1941-42. Regular soldier; b. 7 Jun 1896.

The last meeting of the Chiefs of Staff over which General Wavell presided (and which General Auchinleck also attended) wrestled with the problem of supplying Tobruk. It was decided that an average of 230 tons per day would have to be shipped to avoid breaking into reserve supplies. Two schemes prepared by the staff and involving the use of destroyers and "A" lighters, an early form of tank landing craft, were considered, but Admiral Cunningham declined to exclude the possibility of running small ships into Tobruk. Air Marshal Tedder stated that the entire fighter strength of the Western Desert would be required.

The decision to ship 230 tons per day was an acceptance of a very serious commitment. Fortunately the target then set did not have to be met. It was found possible to limit the requirements to 170 tons per day[1] for a garrison of 25,000. The navy and small ships brought in 170 tons per day in July and almost as much in August, which not only fulfilled the essential requirements for a garrison then reduced to less than 25,000, but enabled reserves to be built up.

In Cairo Morshead pointed out that in determining the future operational policy for Tobruk a choice was involved between conducting a static defence of the perimeter and adopting a more active role of harassing the enemy and attacking his communications. He suggested that the provision of another brigade group and some additional tanks would enable him to operate in strength outside the perimeter so as to induce the enemy to withdraw portion of his force from the frontier; but General Auchinleck, having regard to his other commitments and the strength of his forces, found it impossible to accede to the request. Morshead was informed that the British armoured strength would not be restored until the end of July and that the policy meanwhile would be to avoid a major embroilment.

On 4th July Generals Blamey and Morshead conferred with Air Marshals Tedder and Drummond[2] and made arrangements for tactical reconnaissance sweeps to be flown from El Gubbi and Sidi Barrani and for Morshead to have the right to call on the services of the army-cooperation squadron operating with the Western Desert Force.

Brigadier Murray commanded the Tobruk garrison while Morshead was in Cairo. Morshead resumed command on 9th July.

A series of reliefs, planned before Morshead went to Cairo, had been put in hand. At the end of June the 2/48th Battalion had relieved the 2/1st Pioneer Battalion on the sector of the western perimeter running from the north edge of the Salient across the Derna Road to the head of the Wadi Sehel. Wootten's brigade (in divisional reserve) next changed places in the southern sector with Godfrey's brigade, which then relieved Murray's brigade in the Salient and took command of the 2/48th Bat-

---

[1] Later reduced—see Chapter 8.
[2] Air Marshal Sir Peter Drummond, KCB, DSO, OBE, MC. (1914-18: AAMC 1914-15, RFC and RAF, Palestine, 1916-18.) SASO, HQ RAF ME 1937-41; DAOC-in-C HQ RAF ME 1941-43; Air Member Training, Air Council, 1943-45. Regular air force offr; of Perth, WA; b. Perth, 2 Jun 1894. Killed in aircraft accident 27 Mar 1945.

talion, while Murray's brigade came into divisional reserve. Command passed in the Salient on 11th July. Tovell's brigade (less the 2/48th Battalion but with the 2/1st Pioneer Battalion under command) remained in the eastern sector. The assignment of defence sectors to brigades remained unaltered throughout July except in the southern sector where towards the end of the month Murray's brigade relieved Wootten's brigade, which returned to divisional reserve on 26th July.

No major operations were undertaken in July, but several strong patrol actions and raids were conducted.[3] Morshead encouraged these activities. After a successful raid by two fighting patrols from the 2/12th Battalion, commanded by Lieutenant Reid and Sergeant Russell,[4] he wrote Colonel Field:

My compliments and congratulations to you on the success of your fighting patrols last night. A really good effort in every way. Will you please convey my congratulations to all those who took part.

I am glad that you are seizing every opportunity to inflict casualties on our unneighbourly enemy and to harass him—it's good for him and also for us. And remember what the good Book says: It's more blessed to give than to receive.

Field's battalion carried out another raid on the night of 16th July in which Lieutenant Steddy's platoon inflicted about 20 casualties. While the Chestnut Troop was directly supporting Steddy's approach to his objective with a creeping barrage, the sector artillery staged a diversionary shoot designed to distract attention from the locality where the patrol was operating. All captured guns manned by the southern artillery group (1st and 107th R.H.A.) together with the "bush" guns manned by Wootten's brigade fired a concentration on an enemy trench system. In all, 14 guns (6 of them 149-mm howitzers) fired 1,220 rounds. Six guns failed to stay the course but the rest fired for two hours.

On the succeeding night raids were conducted by the 2/28th Battalion, the 18th Cavalry Regiment and the British commandos who were attached to the latter and occupied part of the perimeter in the Wadi Sehel. Morshead visited the 18th Cavalry Regiment in the afternoon before the raid and spoke to the men who were to take part. The 2/12th Field Regiment fired about 1,200 rounds in support. The 2/28th cleaned out three rows of sangars and the enemy was caused to put down defensive fire for four hours from the Derna Road to the sea.

These activities excited much comment from the German and Italian broadcasting stations. The Italians represented them as attempts to break out of an "unsupportable position", the Germans as "lively reconnaissance activity".

Patrols were now better equipped than in the early days of the siege. An important improvement was the provision of a limited number of Tommy-guns, which were issued to battalions towards the end of June. In mid-July the enemy began using a searchlight to detect patrols. The

---

[3] See Chapter 8.
[4] Capt N. H. Russell, DCM, QX2047; 2/12 Bn. Clerk; of Townsville, Qld; b. Claremont, WA, 18 May 1917.

first report of its use was in the early hours of 15th July. Thereafter it appeared almost every night in different localities. It was soon discovered that it was mounted on a vehicle. The searchlight exerted a cramping effect on many patrols but demonstrations were arranged to show that its effectiveness was limited to close ranges against patrols going to ground ahead of the sweeping beam or remaining motionless. Patrols discovered lengths of cable laid in various places which were believed to be used to provide the power, cut them frequently and removed several sections. A further development in the use of searchlights was reported in the divisional Intelligence summary on 22nd July:

> Enemy searchlight units operating nights 20/21 and 21/22 Jul, are reported to be using coloured screens in front of their lights. On night 20/21 Jul, green, blue and mauve beams were observed and on night 21/22 Jul, green and blue beams are said to have been used. It is known that amber or yellow beams are frequently used in foggy or misty atmospheres, but the particular properties of the other colours are not known.

Several Alsatian dogs were also observed in the Italians' positions. In July patrols often reported the barking of dogs from positions occupied by Italians in both the western and eastern sectors. It was believed that they were kept to warn their masters when a patrol was approaching. No evidence of their use to track patrols was forthcoming.

Towards the end of May the enemy began shelling the harbour with a gun that became known as "Bardia Bill". The origin of the name is obscure. It may have arisen because the gun seemed to fire from the direction of Bardia and was believed by uninformed experts, but not by Klein's counter-battery staff, to be fired from that fort; or it may have been inspired by the fact that it was believed in gunner circles that a heavy gun had been left undestroyed in Bardia when the British forces evacuated the town. It was not the only gun to shell the harbour but was often mixed up with other breeds. Its own heritage remained a mystery throughout the Australian occupation of Tobruk. Examination of an unexploded shell thought to have been fired from the gun led to the belief for a time that it was a French Schneider gun. On 17th July a German shell of still larger calibre—210-mm—believed to have come from a Skoda gun was found in the Wadi Auda, but it was not established that it came from "Bardia Bill". The shelling from the east still appeared to be coming from a gun having a calibre of 150 or 155-mm. The neutralisation of this gun became a major preoccupation of Klein's staff and of Feitel's troop manning the 60-pounder. The shelling of the harbour did not cause serious damage but continually interrupted the work of the port.

By the end of July Klein's counter-battery organisation was operating efficiently and smoothly. Observation posts established along the front were linked by direct line (not through an exchange) to the counter-battery office; battery command posts were also linked to the office by other direct lines. A sector control observation post selected the hostile battery to receive attention, and passed the bearing to the counter-battery officer, who then advised the other observation posts of the approximate bearings on which to look. The diarist of the 107th R.H.A. commented:[5]

> In one case, order to bombard was received at Battery Headquarters just three minutes after control OP picked up the flash of a new HB.[6] After this no more than three bombards were brought off. HB's only opened fire long enough to give Control OP his first bearing to them and then ceased.

On 17th July the rationing of ammunition expenditure was relaxed. Regimental commanders were permitted a discretion to increase the daily expenditure from 10 rounds to 20 rounds per gun, but hostile enemy batteries were still not allowed to be engaged unless firing with effect. The daily turnover of British artillery ammunition, seven tons and a half in the preceding week, was immediately increased by four tons. This reflected a more than proportional increase in effectiveness, since the discretion now accorded gave reasonable freedom to engage good opportunity targets.

Goodwin's regiment continued to experience difficulties with the recuperator systems of its Italian guns. The 75-mm guns alone performed satisfactorily. The 100-mm guns gave so much trouble that they were replaced in Lieutenant Tutton's[7] troop with 75-mm at the end of the second week in July, though one 100-mm continued to fire from the old troop position to maintain deception. On 19th July a premature shell-burst from a 149-mm gun killed 3 men and wounded 7 of McDermott's troop. The use of these guns was for a time discontinued, but by the end of the month two were again manned and were being fired with a long lanyard from behind sangars.

The base area and engineering staffs during this period were partly engaged in the problems of reorganisation necessary to enable the strength of base units to be reduced to the minimum. To a program already beyond their resources the engineers had to add the further work of preparing beaches and their approaches for possible embarkation and of accelerating the demolition program; this at the time when they were losing both Royal Engineer personnel and the services of the Indian pioneer and labour corps troops. The demolition scheme was thorough; it included arrangements for destruction of some ammunition dumps, all plant, machinery, quays, jetties and other port and base installations, power houses, water reservoirs, water tanks and all wells, pumping plants and water points. (Few, if any, of these demolitions appear to have been carried out in the next year when Tobruk was lost, a lapse doubtless attributable to intervening loss of continuity in command and the swift development of the crisis.) Large quantities of Italian ammunition were destroyed by explosion and sea-dumping. On 5th July some Italian ammunition dumped into the sea by the Army Service Corps blew up, killing Lieutenant Meggitt[8] and two drivers and injuring several others.

---

[5] Undated entry about 24 July 1941.
[6] Hostile battery.
[7] Maj J. K. Tutton, VX13685; 2/12 Fd Regt. Insurance clerk; of Hawthorn, Vic; b. Hawthorn, 2 Apr 1914.
[8] Lt N. P. Meggitt, QX17093; 9 Div Amn Coy. Commercial traveller; of Ashgrove, Qld; b. Ipswich, Qld, 12 Aug 1910. Killed in action 5 Jul 1941.

(H. J. Ferres)

Men of "B" Company, 2/13th Battalion, in Post R8 on the morning of 28th May 1941. This photograph was taken during a truce to allow the Germans, assisted by Australians, to recover their dead and wounded after attempts the previous night to take positions occupied by the 2/13th. In the background are the White House and a burnt-out "I" tank and beyond them the enemy-occupied R7.

(Australian War Memorial)

Bombs bursting among shipping in Tobruk Harbour, August 1941.

(*Australian War Memorial*)

Underground headquarters of the 9th Division at Tobruk, August 1941. *Left to right*: Lieutenant P. H. Bayley, R.N., Colonel R. C. Keller (commanding the 3rd Armoured Brigade), Captains S. H. Good and L. K. Shave, Major T. W. White, Colonel C. E. M. Lloyd, Captains H. K. Oxley and F. E. C. Loxton.

(*Australian War Memorial*)

The Figtree, a leafy landmark growing over a deep cavern, was used as a regimental aid post by the battalion occupying the western sector.

The improvement of the defences in depth was pushed on, and called for continuous work on the part of both the engineers and the infantry. Units drawn into reserve from Salient or other front-line duty, though allowed one or two days of rest and swimming, soon found themselves required to dig defences in the Blue Line and ancillary switch lines.

In the country lying to the south-east of the perimeter the enemy defended localities were sparse. In April General Rommel's first action, as his forces had come up to Tobruk, had been to order the closing of the eastern outlet by the Bardia Road. Here the enemy developed a strong defence line astride the road with right flank on the north firmly locked into the heads of the precipitous wadis that tumbled down from the plateau to the sea. In June and July this was held by *Bersaglieri* battalions of the *Trento Division*. South of these positions, however, the plateau running out from the perimeter to the Trigh Capuzzo was not at first strongly developed in defence. A more extensive chain of works and obstacles began to be laid down after 10th June, when the *Pavia Division* replaced the *Ariete Division* in the southern sector, but these were sited for the most part beyond machine-gun range at distances from the perimeter varying between 4,000 and 6,000 yards.

The inter-brigade boundary between the southern and eastern defence sectors of the fortress was on the west side of R55. In June Godfrey's brigade in the southern sector was responsible for the perimeter from R52-53 westward across the El Adem Road to the Salient sector boundary, Tovell's brigade in the eastern sector from R55 eastwards across the Bardia Road to the coast. Between these two roads important outposts were established and later strongly defended.

Before 10th June Windeyer's battalion on the right of Tovell's sector had patrolled by day with carriers south from the perimeter about R57 in great depth. One night four men patrolled extensively at a depth of almost five miles without opposition. On another night a patrol led by Lieutenant Beer[9] penetrated without a fight to the bypass tracks between the Trigh Capuzzo and the Bardia Road, which it mined. Soon after BATTLEAXE the Germans began constructing a bituminous road along this route, which was to assume great tactical significance in the November offensive.

Windeyer's battalion had established night standing patrols and listening posts beyond the wire. They were continued by Spowers' battalion, which took over the sector on 10th June. From 19th June onwards a screen of standing patrols beyond the wire and anti-tank ditch, usually 500 yards out, was established every night along the whole front of Tovell's brigade from Spowers' southward-facing right flank to the eastward-fronting positions behind the Wadi Zeitun.

A number of daylight observation posts were also established out in no-man's land. At first occupied by only one man, or only intermittently,

---

[9] Lt H. R. Beer, MC, SX10324; 2/48 Bn. Upholsterer; of Prospect, SA; b. Kensington, SA, 24 Sep 1920.

a few of these were later developed for local defence and held by a section of men continuously.

On 18th June Major Cox,[1] temporarily in command of the 2/32nd Battalion straddling the El Adem Road, ordered that from that day onwards his battalion was to maintain infantry observation posts in depth beyond the perimeter. Before dawn on 19th June Sergeant Richards[2] and three other men from this battalion went out to observe from an old walled camp some 3,500 yards south of R53. Three days earlier Lieutenant Fahey[3] had taken out three carriers to the camp and harassed an Italian working party, but the carriers had been abandoned after one broke down and two ran on to a minefield. While Sergeant Richards' patrol was observing, two Italians came up on motor-cycles and dismounted to examine the carriers. The patrol killed one and captured the other. On 23rd June the 2/32nd Battalion sent out another daylight observation patrol forward of Bir el Azazi. The walled camp and Bir el Azazi later became sites for permanent outposts, the walled camp becoming known as "Walled Village" and "Bondi", Bir el Azazi as "Plonk".

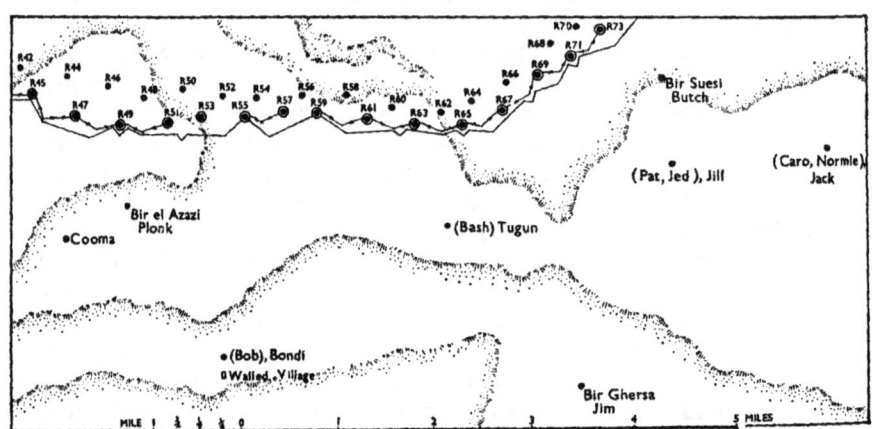

Tobruk outposts, eastern sector

On the left of the 2/32nd Battalion, across the brigade boundary, Colonel Spowers had one or two men observing almost every day towards the end of June at one place or another deep in the no-man's land south of the 2/24th Battalion.

Colonel Field's 2/12th Battalion, which relieved the 2/32nd in early July, continued the policy of manning daylight observation posts in the El Adem Road sector, but meanwhile the 2/24th Battalion had established a daylight patrol at the walled camp. On 7th July three men observing

---

[1] Col J. P. Cox, ED, WX3387. 2/28 and 2/32 Bns; DAAG 9 Div 1942-43; AAG I Corps 1944-45. Accountant; of Dalkeith, WA; b. Mount Lawley, WA, 8 Sep 1906.

[2] Lt E. J. Richards, MM, WX2162; 2/32 Bn. Electrician; of Cannington, WA; b. West Perth, WA, 10 Feb 1918. Killed in action 2 Nov 1942.

[3] Capt J. P. Fahey, TX2008; 2/32 Bn. Printer; of Hobart; b. Hobart, 4 May 1916. Died of wounds 25 Jul 1942.

from the camp fired on two Italians in a truck. Spowers thereupon decided to extricate the men by carrier and to maintain observation there next day with three carriers. But for a time the use of the site for an infantry O.P. was discontinued; it was re-established by the 2/9th Battalion in the third week of July.

The first step towards establishing a continuously manned infantry observation post in the eastern sector was taken by the 2/23rd Battalion on 27th June, when two men occupied for a few days an old well-concealed pit about 2,600 yards from the wire. The post, initially called "Pat" and later to become successively known as "Jed" and "Jill", was re-established on 5th July. The outpost "Caro", later successively called "Normie" and "Jack", was established at Trig 146 by Evans' battalion on 10th July and manned by six men from his carrier platoon. (The enemy position called "Jack" during the November offensive on the north of the Tobruk-Ed Duda corridor was to the west of Trig 146.) These outposts continued to be manned by the 2/1st Pioneer Battalion after it relieved the 2/23rd on 15th July. A protective minefield was laid around Jack on the night of 19th July.

It became evident early in the siege that Rommel intended to contain the garrison and protect his communications by hemming it in with tank-proof defences. Mines were laid down continuously nor did the work cease until the garrison broke out in the November offensive. The Salient was lavishly strewn with mines. North of the Salient belts were laid across the accessible plains between the scarps and wadis. In the open country to the south, work was pushed forward on laying down a continuous but undulating line of mines, in most places three rows deep, which appeared to be designed ultimately to girdle the southern perimeter completely from the Salient to the sea cliffs. The Australians' vigorous patrolling policy ensured (in default of air reconnaissance) that the fields were quickly discovered.

Towards the end of June the experiences of patrols demonstrated that sections of the field, mainly in the south, were not covered by fire. In broad daylight at midday on 1st July Spowers sent out a large patrol commanded by Captain Gebhardt to a minefield some 4,000 yards south of his front. Two trucks took out 30 men of the 2/24th Battalion and nine sappers of the 2/4th Field Company. Three carriers from Spowers' battalion and an armoured carrier of the 104th R.H.A. with artillery link provided protection. In a well-planned operation the patrol cleared a gap of 1,000 yards, disarming the anti-personnel mines and bringing back 504 "Teller" mines, which were relaid in front of the battalion position. Several later patrols committed similar excellent robberies, by night and day, but not on such a grand scale. For example, on 9th July Captain Baillieu[4] led a patrol from Spowers' battalion which carried in, from 4,000 yards beyond the wire, 120 25-pounder shells left at a gunpit that had been manned for the assault by the 6th Division in January, when Tobruk was captured. Spowers again, on 12th July, dispatched two officers

---

[4] Maj E. Baillieu, VX14039; 2/24 Bn. Company director; of Melbourne; b. Melbourne, 9 Dec 1912.

and 25 men (including 14 sappers from the 2/4th Field Company) in daylight to the minefield south of his front. One 5-ton and one 30-cwt truck were provided to transport the men and their stores and bring in the booty. Three carriers were added for local protection. Leaving at 2.30 p.m. and arriving at 3 p.m. they had more than an hour's uninterrupted minelifting before the enemy fired a few light shells among them. They returned unscathed having lifted 203 mines.

Next morning three carriers went out from the 2/24th Battalion soon after sunrise to the walled camp, picked up 34 mines left by earlier lifting parties and a few more from the field. This completed the clearing of a gap extending for 2,300 yards in this minefield, which Spowers could then have fittingly described as "a poor thing but mine own".

In June and July most A.I.F. units in Tobruk received their first reinforcements. Many of these were reported to have left Australia as late as April and some even to have enlisted as late as March. Commanding officers and unit diarists commented on their lack of training. The enlistment and continuous reinforcement of four A.I.F. infantry divisions together with base and line-of-communication troops at home and overseas was proving an ambitious commitment to meet in Australia from voluntary enlistment; the resultant shortening of the period between enlistment and front-line service left insufficient time for proper training. The 2/48th diarist commented on reinforcements received on 18th July:

None had fired a Bren or an anti-tank rifle or knew anything about a grenade.

Lack of a sense of the pressing urgency to train men and formations to battle-pitch afflicted the Middle East Command and also the staffs of some administrative formations of the A.I.F. beyond the reach of guns, both at home and overseas. Officers in charge of training battalions usually did their best under conditions that rendered impossible the carrying out of a comprehensive and systematic training program.

CHAPTER 8

LAST COUNTER-ATTACK AND A CONTROVERSIAL RELIEF

THE men of the Tobruk garrison had always thought that the term of their confinement would be the time taken to drive off the besiegers. In the midsummer month of July when the prospect of relief by a frontier offensive seemed indefinitely remote, General Blamey proposed another kind of relief: relief by sea. His request provoked a strong disagreement between the British and Australian Governments; but confidences were so well kept that to all but one or two of the Australians who were in the fortress the first intimation that their going thence had been the subject of controversy was the publication after the war of Sir Winston Churchill's *The Grand Alliance,* in which he gave his own account of the dispute. There he declared that it gave him pain to have to relate the incident, but to suppress it indefinitely would have been impossible. "Besides," he wrote, "the Australian people have a right to know what happened and why."[1] For that very reason it was unfortunate that, in relating the differences between the two Governments, Sir Winston Churchill quoted extensively from his own messages to successive Australian Prime Ministers but did not disclose the text of their replies.

If the Australian people had depended solely on Sir Winston Churchill's account for knowledge of what happened and why, they might have been left with some erroneous impressions. In particular it might have been inferred that when Mr Fadden's Government insisted that the relief of the 9th Division should proceed, it did so not because of a strong conviction based on broad considerations advanced by its military advisers but because it had been induced by "hard pressure from its political opponents" to turn a deaf ear to Churchill's entreaties. That this was Churchill's opinion is evident from a message sent by him in September 1941 to the Minister of State in Egypt in which he said:

I was astounded at Australian Government's decision, being sure it would be repudiated by Australia if the facts could be made known. Allowances must be made for a Government with a majority only of one faced by a bitter Opposition, parts of which at least are isolationist in outlook.[2]

The political aspects of the controversy have been discussed in another volume of this series.[3] It will suffice to say here that no Australian Government was influenced to the course it took by its political opponents. On the contrary the three successive Prime Ministers (who were the leaders of the three political parties in the Commonwealth Parliament) and their governments were in entire agreement. Throughout the controversy the three party leaders sat together on the inter-party Advisory War Council,

---
[1] Churchill, Vol III, p. 372.
[2] Churchill, Vol III, p. 369.
[3] See P. Hasluck, *The Government and the People 1939-1941* (1952), pp. 616-24.

to which the question was referred on several occasions. In the course pursued without deviation through two changes of government, the Australian political leaders were guided at each step, indeed impelled in most instances, by the representations of their military advisers—principally by General Blamey himself. The problem was military in origin; if it had political implications, they arose because the British and Australian Governments were in conflict on a military issue.

The conditions upon which the A.I.F. served under the operational command of the Commanders-in-Chief of overseas theatres of war were set out in General Blamey's "charter", of which the first operative paragraph read:

> The Force to be recognised as an Australian force under its own Commander, who will have a direct responsibility to the Commonwealth Government with the right to communicate direct with that Government. No part of the Force to be detached or employed apart from the Force without his consent.[4]

Before this document was issued, the British Government had been informed of the principles to be embodied in it, and had accepted them. The first volume of this series gave earlier instances of General Blamey's reliance on its terms to resist moves to employ parts of the A.I.F. in detached roles.[5] The Australian Government itself had already twice reminded the British Government (in November 1940 and April 1941) of the importance it attached to the concentration of the A.I.F. into one force under a single command. Furthermore Mr Menzies, when in London, had informed the Chief of the Imperial General Staff of his Government's concern at the dispersion of the A.I.F. On the same day (19th April 1941) Menzies cabled the Australian Government:

> I have told Dill that it is a matter of imperative importance from Australia's point of view that all Australian forces should as soon as possible be assembled as one corps under the command of Blamey.

On 1st May 1941, General Blamey cabled Mr Spender, the Australian Minister for the Army:

> On returning Egypt (from Greece) I find the A.I.F. distributed among several forces and ten different areas. This distribution was made to meet the emergency that arose mainly through the Italo-German advance in Libya as sufficient other troops were not available. . . . It will not be possible to collect the A.I.F. into single force for a considerable time and this is dependent on development of situation in Middle East.

A substantial part of the 6th Division was then in Crete, the 9th Division and one brigade of the 7th in Tobruk, the 7th Division less one brigade at Mersa Matruh, the 7th Divisional Cavalry Regiment in Cyprus; and there were also numerous smaller A.I.F. detachments throughout the Middle East.

The policy of concentrating the A.I.F. into one force had been complicated by another development. In March, after the composition of the

---
[4] Long, *To Benghazi*, p. 101.
[5] Long, *To Benghazi*, pp. 103-4, 109.

expeditionary force for Greece had been determined, Mr Menzies proposed that the 6th and 7th Australian Divisions and the New Zealand Division, all allocated to the expedition, should be formed into an Anzac Corps.[6] The suggestion was not immediately adopted; but, when the campaign in Greece brought the 6th Australian Division and the New Zealand Division together under the command of Blamey's I Australian Corps, the corps was renamed "Anzac Corps". The conclusion of that campaign and the piecemeal evacuation of the force from Greece dispersed the formation and dissolved the organisation; but then consideration was given to re-establishing the Anzac Corps as soon as regrouping became possible. On 8th May the Secretary of State for Dominion Affairs informed the Australian and New Zealand Governments that General Wavell had welcomed the suggestion that, on being re-equipped, the 6th Australian Division and the New Zealand Division should again be formed into an Anzac Corps; the British Government, he said, favoured the proposal and Wavell recommended that General Freyberg should command the corps. Mr Fadden, the Acting Prime Minister of Australia, telegraphed the proposal to General Blamey but pointed out that, on 18th April, the Government had telegraphed the Dominions Office asking that "subject to over-riding circumstances" the Australian troops should be reassembled as a complete corps under Blamey's command. He commented:

> The proposal now made would result in a splitting of the Australian force. The 6th Division would, with the New Zealand Division, have the right to be termed Anzacs which they so nobly earned in Greece together . . . but the 7th and 9th Divisions would presumably be excluded from this privilege, which may cause some heart-burning.

He sought Blamey's recommendations both on the reconstitution of the corps and on the appointment of General Freyberg to command it.

Blamey replied that efforts were being made in the Middle East to bring about a more permanent grouping of higher commands: the tentative proposals contemplated one corps headquarters generally for each two infantry divisions. He was strongly of the opinion that to group the three Australian divisions and one New Zealand division in two corps would strengthen their fighting value. He recommended that the 6th Division and the New Zealand Division should be grouped together as Anzac Corps; if this were agreed to, he would recommend that the 7th and 9th Divisions should form Australian Corps when they could be released from the Western Desert. He recommended that General Freyberg, "a bold, skilful and tireless commander", should command Anzac Corps, General Lavarack Australian Corps.

On 7th June, in a letter to Mr Menzies, General Blamey said that he had been troubled over the extent to which organisations in the Middle East had been broken up; but he recognised that necessity had forced the position from time to time. "I feel," he said, "that if we could get two corps established, Australian Corps and an Anzac Corps, and pull them together, it would help to establish the principle of working in fixed

---

[6] Long, *Greece, Crete and Syria*, pp. 69-70.

formations. This is the main reason for supporting the recommendations. . . ."

Meanwhile the Australian Government had become very concerned to discover that the 7th Division's cavalry regiment was in Cyprus. This disposition had been made without General Blamey's knowledge while he was in Greece; nor had the Australian Government been informed. In a cable sent on 13th June Mr Menzies reminded Blamey of the importance attached by the Government to the principle that A.I.F. units should serve in their own formations in the Australian Corps under Australian command, and stated that, while it was realised that the Commander-in-Chief might be taxed in the disposition of his forces to meet all contingencies, it appeared rather unfortunate that this small group of Australians should have been placed in Cyprus. Blamey immediately referred his Government's representations to Wavell, who agreed to arrange the earliest possible relief of the Australian unit.

On 17th June Blamey followed up this request with a memorandum addressed to the Commander-in-Chief in which he quoted the Prime Minister's telegram, referred to 10 other A.I.F. units (not including units serving in Tobruk) distributed in commands other than Australian and requested their return to A.I.F. formations. The staff of General Headquarters promptly made plans for the relief of these units, which it was proposed to complete by mid-July. General Smith, Wavell's chief of staff, submitted to Blamey the proposed reply of General Headquarters to his request and pencilled on it a note:

Deputy C-in-C—Do you approve of suggested reply in para 4 to GOC 2nd AIF?![7]

On 26th June General Blamey telegraphed to Mr Menzies a reply to a series of questions from him, including one on the future policy with regard to Tobruk. "Are you satisfied," Mr Menzies had asked, "that garrison at Tobruk can hold out? Should we press for evacuation or for any other and what course?" Blamey replied that he was satisfied that Tobruk could hold out for the present. He assured Mr Menzies that the problem of evacuating Tobruk, should it become necessary, was being considered; the navy was of the opinion that evacuation was practicable. There was no need to press for action since he had already asked for a plan. Colonel Lloyd, then in Cairo, did not feel any immediate anxiety.

The Government's curt reminder to General Blamey of its policy that all A.I.F. units should serve in the Australian Corps was further discussed by him in a letter written on 27th June to the Minister for the Army. He told Mr Spender that he hoped soon to have all the A.I.F. under Australian command. Existing conditions, he said, prevented its complete assembly in one force, but he hoped to have it in four main groups—Syria under Lavarack—Tobruk under Morshead—and the rest in Palestine (fighting organisations under Mackay and the remainder under Base Headquarters) "with the long view of ultimately getting it all together in Palestine or Syria". He said that, as Deputy Commander-in-Chief, he was having a

---

[7] The implication was, of course, that there was an incompatibility in Blamey's holding both posts.

very definite influence in restoring a proper sense of formation organisation, not only in the A.I.F. but in all the forces in the Middle East. Referring to the proposal to establish an Anzac Corps, he commented that it would be difficult to ensure that the A.I.F. would be kept under one command if the second corps were formed. Although this could be made to appear as an objection to "implementing" a second corps for some time, it need not be so at all: there was no longer any real objection to placing other Imperial forces under an Australian commander.

Some progress was made in terminating the small detachments of Australian units, but in mid-July it had still not been found possible to assemble in one place even one of the three Australian divisions with all its units. Their training as complete formations could not be undertaken.

It is clear from Blamey's communications to the Prime Minister and Mr Spender in the last week of June that he was not then contemplating an early relief of the 9th Division nor is there any evidence that he had considered requesting its relief until his senior medical adviser, Major-General Burston,[8] represented to him that there had been a physical decline in the condition of the Tobruk garrison.[9] Burston's opinion appears to have been based in the first place on his own observation that a few men from the garrison whom he had encountered in Cairo appeared to be considerably underweight; but investigations confirmed the impression. When General Morshead visited Cairo from 2nd to 8th July Blamey sought his views; Morshead told him that the garrison's capacity to resist a sustained assault was diminishing. Morshead's diary indicates that he lunched with General Burston and Colonel Fairley[1] on 3rd July. It is probable, though concrete evidence is lacking, that Blamey made up his mind to request the relief about that time. The fact that the Syrian campaign was drawing to its close—the armistice was initialled on 12th July—may have made the moment seem most opportune for drawing the A.I.F. together.

General Blamey's decision should be regarded against the background of the current war situation in the Middle East and elsewhere. If a seaborne relief were to be effected, it was desirable to undertake it at a time when the garrison was not under threat of imminent assault. The drive of the German armed forces into Russia continued unchecked. Hitler, it seemed, had taken in the flood a tide in the affairs of nations that led on to fortune. Not even the British Chiefs of Staff expected that onslaught to be long withstood; indeed not until the British winter offensive to relieve Tobruk was under way would any reliable sign be discerned of Russia's capacity to block the German armour's onrush and throw the intruders back. If Russian resistance broke, no longer would Germany be restrained from reinforcing her army and air forces in the Middle

---

[8] Maj-Gen Sir Samuel Burston, KBE, CB, DSO, VD, VX2. (1st AIF: 7 Fd Amb; SMO AGB Depot 1917-18.) DDMS I Corps 1940; DMS AIF in ME 1940-42; DGMS LHQ 1942-45, AMF 1945-47. Physician; of Adelaide; b. Melbourne, 21 Mar 1888. Died 21 Aug 1960.

[9] J. Hetherington, *Blamey* (1954), p. 118.

[1] Brig Sir Neil Fairley, KBE, VX38970. (1st AIF: 14 AGH 1916-18.) Director of Medicine LHQ 1942-45; Chairman, Combined Advisory Cttee to Gen MacArthur on Tropical Medicine, Hygiene and Sanitation, HQ SWPA. Physician; b. Inglewood, Vic, 15 Jul 1891.

East theatre by the exigencies of providing for commitments on the Eastern front. Whether the British would succeed in building up, before the threat to Tobruk was renewed, a sufficient superiority of force in the desert to take the initiative; if so, when the new offensive would be launched; whether it would then succeed: these were questions to which the answers could not be wrested from an enigmatic and comparatively distant future. On the other hand it seemed unlikely that in the immediate future either side would be able to assemble the resources for a major operation. If the present opportunity to effect a seaborne relief were not seized, no definite limit could be set to the 9th Division's expectant term of front-line service and incarceration.

On 18th July, in a letter to General Auchinleck of which the full text is set out below, General Blamey proposed that the Tobruk garrison should be relieved. It will be noticed that the first paragraph propounded an argument for relief of the entire garrison on the ground of the troops' physical decline, while the second paragraph advanced an additional reason for the relief of the garrison's Australian component.

1. It is recommended that action be taken forthwith for the relief of the Garrison at Tobruk. These troops have been engaged continuously in operations since March and are therefore well into their fourth month. The strain of continuous operations is showing signs of affecting the troops. The Commander of the Garrison informs me he considers the average loss of weight to be approximately a stone per man. A senior medical officer, recently down from Tobruk, informs me that in the last few weeks there has been a definite decline in the health resistance of the troops. Recovery from minor wounds and sicknesses is markedly slower recently.

It may be anticipated that within the next few months a serious attack may be made on the Garrison, and by then at the present rate its capacity for resistance would be very greatly reduced. The casualties have been considerable and cannot be replaced.

It would therefore seem wise to give consideration immediately for their relief by fresh troops and I urge that this be carried out during the present moonless period. The relief requires movement of personnel only.

2. With reference to the Australian portion of the Garrison; the agreed policy for the employment of Australian troops between the British and Australian Governments is that the Australian troops should operate as a single force.

Because the needs of the moment made it necessary, the Australian Government has allowed this principle to be disregarded to meet immediate conditions. But it nevertheless requires that this condition shall be observed, and I therefore desire to represent that during the present lull in active operations, action should be taken to implement this as far as possible. This is particularly desirable in view of the readiness the Australian Government has so far shown to meet special conditions as they arose.

3. The Australian Corps is probably the most completely organised body in the Middle East and will certainly be required for operations within the next few months.

The 6th Australian Division has been sorely tried, having fought continuously through Libya, Greece and Crete, and a considerable proportion of its units had to be detailed for Syria.

The 7th Australian Division has just completed the campaign in Syria and has suffered losses which have to be made good. It cannot be completed until 18th Australian Infantry Brigade, now in Tobruk, is relieved to join its own division and the 7th Australian Cavalry Regiment is freed from Cyprus.

The 9th Australian Division at Tobruk has been continuously in operations since March and has suffered considerable losses.

The drain on reinforcements has been heavy.

This Corps probably will be required in a month or two for further operations. If it is to render full value in accordance with the wishes of the Australian Government and as agreed by the British Government, it is necessary that action be taken early for its re-assembly in order that the formations and units may be thoroughly set up as quickly as possible.

4. The New Zealand Division has been through one campaign and is up to full strength.

The South African Division, under existing law, is confined to operating in Africa. It has had a prolonged rest from active operations.

I can see no adequate reason why the conditions agreed between the Australian and United Kingdom Governments should not now be fulfilled.

5. A copy of this memo is being despatched to the Prime Minister of Australia.

Blamey told Mr Menzies, in a cable sent the same day, that, in view of the garrison's continuous front-line service since March, he was of opinion that its fighting value was now on the decline and he was pressing for its relief by fresh troops, which could be made available "if will to do so can be forced on Command here"; he was also pressing for the collection of the A.I.F. in Palestine, to which the only real obstacle that could not be overcome was unwillingness to do so. It was most desirable, he said, that after any series of operations the troops involved should be given a respite to refresh them and to provide an opportunity to restore discipline and re-equip them. He suggested that Mr Menzies should take strong action to ensure the collection of the A.I.F. as a single force.

Mr Menzies cabled Churchill on the 20th:

We regard it as of first class importance that now that Syria Campaign has concluded Australian troops in Middle East should be aggregated into one force. This would not only give an opportunity refreshment, restoration of discipline and re-equipment after strenuous campaign but would also give immense satisfaction to Australian people for whom there is great national value and significance in knowing that all Australian soldiers in any zone form one Australian unit. This principle was fully accepted by both United Kingdom Government and ours when troops first despatched to Middle East. Problem has a particular bearing on garrison at Tobruk which has engaged in operations since March and is therefore in position of a force with continuous front-line service over a period of months, a state of affairs which must result in some decline of fighting value. If they could be relieved by fresh troops, move of personnel only being involved, reaggregation and equipment of Australian Imperial Force in Palestine would then present no major difficulty. I would be glad if you could direct British High Command in Middle East along these lines. The comparative lull now obtaining in Libya seems to make this an ideal time for making above move to which we attach real and indeed urgent importance.

The Chiefs of Staff telegraphed the text of Mr Menzies' communication to General Auchinleck with the comment:

Full and sympathetic consideration must clearly be given to the views of the Australian Government. At the same time we realise, as no doubt does the Australian Government, that the grouping and distribution of divisions must be subject to strategical and tactical requirements and to what is administratively practicable.

General Auchinleck replied that the two questions—the relief of the Tobruk garrison and the concentration of the A.I.F.—were under consideration. He fully agreed as to the desirability in principle but there were many difficulties, which he hoped might be overcome.

General Auchinleck had succeeded General Wavell in the Middle East Command on 5th July. Almost immediately he found himself subjected to pressure from Mr Churchill and the Chiefs of Staff to resume offensive operations in the desert at the earliest possible moment. Wavell had advised that no offensive would be practicable for three months but this was overlooked as soon as he was replaced by the commander who had struck Mr Churchill as more forward in outlook. One of Auchinleck's first decisions—the choice of the 50th Division to garrison Cyprus (which was associated with the promised relief of the 7th Divisional Cavalry Regiment)—caused Churchill much annoyance. On 15th July Auchinleck informed the Chiefs of Staff that he doubted whether it would be possible to hold Tobruk after September. On 19th July the Chiefs of Staff replied that they assumed therefore that any offensive to regain Cyrenaica could not be postponed beyond that month. Churchill added his own comment.

> If we do not use the lull accorded us by the German entanglement in Russia to restore the situation in Cyrenaica, the opportunity may never recur. A month has passed since the failure at Sollum, and presumably another month may have to pass before a renewed effort is possible. This interval should certainly give time for training.

Auchinleck refused to be hustled. Churchill was perturbed by the "stiffness of his attitude" and decided that the stimulation of personal contact was required to impart a less cautious mood.

On 23rd July (the day on which the Chiefs of Staff telegraphed to Auchinleck the text of Mr Menzies' message) the British Prime Minister invited the Middle East commander to come at once to London to "have a talk", adding that Blamey could act for him in his absence. Knowing that in London he was to be faced with strong pressure to mount in September another operation to relieve Tobruk by land, Auchinleck, even if he had so wished, could hardly have acceded, on the eve of his departure, to Blamey's request that the entire Tobruk garrison should be relieved by sea. Such a relief could not have been completed before late September. Auchinleck agreed, however, that as a first step the 18th Brigade might be brought out, thus enabling both the 6th and 7th Australian Divisions to be reconstituted as complete formations, and also that the possibility of a more extensive relief should be studied. By good fortune to replace the 18th Brigade there was available an eager, excellently trained brigade of Polish troops, the 1st Carpathian Brigade. Originally allotted to the expedition to Greece, this formation had been held in reserve since the loss of Cyrenaica.

General Auchinleck arrived in London on 29th July. On 1st August he telegraphed Blamey that General Sikorski, head of the Polish Government in exile, agreed to the use of the Polish contingent as part of the Tobruk garrison, but subject to certain conditions; if these could not be fulfilled Blamey was to wire alternative proposals. Blamey replied on the 2nd that the conditions would be fulfilled; the meeting of the Commanders-in-

Chief on that day had decided that a relief of the Tobruk garrison by the 6th British Division and the Polish contingent would be carried out during the moonless periods of August and September, two brigade groups being relieved each period. On 4th August, however, Blamey telegraphed Auchinleck again to say that, after further discussion with Admiral Cunningham and Air Marshal Tedder, he had agreed that the relief would be deferred till September, when a greater scale of air protection would be available.

Meanwhile Mr Menzies, who knew nothing of these interchanges, was perturbed that he had received no response from Mr Churchill to his telegram of 20th July. He telegraphed again on 7th August, asking for an early reply. After mentioning the Australian War Cabinet's concern at the Tobruk garrison's decline in "health resistance" and recalling that all three Australian divisions had latterly been much engaged in operations —the 9th at Tobruk continuously since March—he concluded:

As fresher troops are available I must press for early relief of 9th Division and re-assembly of Australian Corps.

The text of this message was telegraphed to General Blamey, who hastened to reassure the Australian Prime Minister. "Policy agreed to and plans prepared," he replied. "As scale air protection available not yet sufficient have felt obliged to agree to postponement to September, which will also give advantage of longer nights." From London the response was also reassuring. Viscount Cranborne, the Secretary of State for Dominion Affairs, replying in the absence of Mr Churchill (who had gone to the Atlantic meeting with Mr Roosevelt) told Mr Menzies that General Auchinleck had been directed to give full and sympathetic consideration to Menzies' first telegram. Auchinleck was now in London and Menzies' second telegram had been discussed with him. "We entirely agree in principle that the A.I.F. should be concentrated into one force as soon as possible," he said, "and General Auchinleck has undertaken to see to this immediately on his return. He does not anticipate any difficulty except in regard to Tobruk. He is as anxious as you in this connection to relieve this garrison."

By the end of the third week of July Morshead, as yet uninformed of these negotiations, was contemplating further operations to pinch out the enemy's salient. He intended that Godfrey's brigade should attack and capture both shoulders of the Salient simultaneously. The ultimate object, according to the divisional report, was to exploit their capture and thrust the enemy from the perimeter, but this final development had not been planned as an immediate follow-up operation.

It is not certain when Morshead reached the decision that Godfrey's brigade should mount that attack, but arrangements for preliminary moves that may have been intended to set the stage were put in hand on 20th July. Reconnaissance parties from Lieut-Colonel Lloyd's 2/28th Battalion spent that day with Lieut-Colonel Windeyer's 2/48th Battalion which held the perimeter from north of the Derna Road to the northern edge of the Salient. The 2/28th was destined to mount the attack on the northern shoulder from that sector, and the 2/48th, which was to carry out a subsidiary but important task on the left flank of the 2/28th, badly needed a rest. Two days later Lloyd's battalion relieved Windeyer's battalion, which came back to the Blue Line in the western sector. "The C.O. has been prevailed upon to take a spell," wrote the diarist of the 2/48th. "The men are tired today after their period of 3 weeks in the line."[2]

On 21st July Morshead visited his four brigade commanders and his headquarters issued orders to the 20th Brigade to relieve the 18th, which Morshead always liked to have in reserve for counter-attack in critical times. The 20th was to take over from the 18th on the southern sector on 27th July.

On the same day divisional headquarters issued general orders to all brigades to carry out raids relentlessly (but not without purposeful intent) and to endeavour to bring back prisoners and other identifications. From 22nd July the 2/28th Battalion, now holding the positions against the northern shoulder of the Salient, and the 2/43rd, which held the front opposite the southern shoulder, embarked on a systematic patrolling program designed to pin-point enemy positions, plot minefields and discover approach routes, along some of which minefields were devitalised. Soon orders for the capture of a prisoner were brought to bear upon these two battalions with pressing urgency. In the fourth week of July they sent out on an average two fighting patrols of platoon strength per night on this and other missions. Lieut-Colonel Conroy's 2/32nd Battalion on the right of the Salient also patrolled vigorously on its right flank.

The divisional report implies that it was found from these patrols "that the enemy were not holding their positions in great strength, and that extensive use was being made of mines and booby traps". A detailed scrutiny of the patrol reports has not yielded confirmation of the first part of this statement. The notion seems to have persisted from an impression gained at the beginning of June, when the 20th Brigade held the Salient line. All battalion commanders agreed at a conference at Murray's headquarters on 7th June that the enemy was thinning out his foremost defended localities "to straighten his line". These observations, however, were consistent with a falling back on a strong line of new constructions while some positions on the previous front continued to be lightly held. On 8th July, when Crellin's 2/43rd Battalion relieved Ogle's 2/15th Battalion on the left of the Salient line, Ogle reported:

> It is considered that the enemy is not holding the Salient by strength of numbers but by strength in automatic weapons and mortars. He is protected by the anti-personnel mines which he has sown. . . .

The belief that the enemy might be thinning out was sharply revived on the night of 25th-26th July when, after an unusually quiet day, patrols

---

[2] In the 14 weeks since the siege began the 2/48th had spent 65 days in the front line, only 3 days in divisional reserve, and the remainder as reserve battalion of a forward brigade.

from the 2/28th and 2/32nd Battalions found that some previously occupied enemy outpost positions were vacant. A patrol from the 2/32nd searched the Water Tower (where Sergeant-Major Morrison had held out during the attack by the 2/23rd), and found that area and the ground to the west unoccupied. When this patrol's report was received, Conroy sent out further patrols, which reported no signs of movement in positions known to have been previously occupied. Simultaneously, from the 2/28th Battalion, Lance-Corporal Monk[3] and three men searched the area west of the Water Tower and found it unoccupied. Brigadier Godfrey's reaction to these reports was quick, if optimistic. Colonel Lloyd was to send out a patrol at first light "to attack and capture" Post S7, and Colonel Conroy another, to seize S6 if unoccupied.

Lieutenant Taylor[4] and 10 men from the 2/28th Battalion set out for Post S7. Without difficulty they reached the mouth of a re-entrant leading up the escarpment on the east side of S7 but were then engaged by machine-guns posted on the slope ahead. The fire quickly thickened and the attempt had to be abandoned, the patrol members only extricating themselves slowly and with great difficulty.

Lieutenant Brownrigg[5] took out from the 2/32nd Battalion the patrol to seize Post S6 if unoccupied. Brownrigg and nine men reached the vicinity of the Water Tower without incident just before 6 a.m. but fire from the south soon afterwards indicated that the area of the objective was held defensively. Brownrigg's patrol spent the day observing from close to the Water Tower.

On the night of 25th July, an Italian prisoner was taken in a raid by British commandos near the coast west of the perimeter, but the great need was to get a German prisoner from the Salient. This was accomplished two nights later by a patrol from the 2/43rd Battalion led by Lieutenant Siekmann.[6] The patrol challenged and engaged a German working party coming down a road some 1,500 yards from the Australian positions. Several Germans were killed, but two fled. Sergeant Cawthorne,[7] though wounded twice, gave chase, killed one of these and captured the other. Enemy parties attempted to intercept the patrol as it returned, but were eluded. Questioning of the prisoner established that the Salient front was manned by the same three German lorried infantry battalions as before, and yielded information concerning the nature of the defences.

Morshead commented on the capture in a letter written to General Blamey next day:

> From a German corporal captured in a particularly good effort by a fighting patrol of the 43rd Battalion early this morning, we learned that even the Germans

---

[3] L-Cpl R. J. Monk, WX5533; 2/28 Bn. Farm labourer; of Bencubbin, WA; b. London, 8 May 1914. Died of wounds 3 Aug 1941.
[4] Maj A. L. F. Taylor, MC, WX3403; 2/28 Bn. Clerk of courts; of Katanning, WA; b. Coolgardie, WA, 3 Oct 1906.
[5] Lt C. Brownrigg, WX670. 2/11 and 2/32 Bns. Motor mechanic; of Norseman, WA; b. Geraldton, WA, 21 Mar 1919. Killed in action 28 Jul 1941.
[6] Capt D. C. Siekmann, MC, SX8896; 2/43 Bn. Salesman; of Kensington Gardens, SA; b. Adelaide, 29 Dec 1915.
[7] Lt C. H. Cawthorne, MM, SX5399; 2/43 Bn. Physiotherapist; of Adelaide; b. Lydd, England, 7 Dec 1907.

in the Medauuar sector—it is no longer a salient—are apprehensive of our activities, so much so that they stand-to throughout the whole night, and have done so for the past week. We are planning an attack on posts S7 and S6 on the German left flank and R7, R6 and R5 on their right flank in the near future.

Two days before this, Colonel Lloyd, Morshead's chief staff officer, had been summoned to Cairo. No record survives of the message summoning him, or of how it was conveyed to Morshead. Circumstantial evidence supports the inference that Morshead was aware that Blamey had broached the question of a relief but did not know what course the discussions had taken. Not yet an advocate in the controversy, Morshead, in the letter just quoted, spoke with pride of the garrison's spirit. He told Blamey:

> The troops are in wonderful heart, their morale never higher—the nightly raiding parties and fighting patrols, as well as the daylight carrier sorties, have contributed to this. Then the marked improvement in rations and canteen stores and the gifts of the Comforts Fund have also helped.
>
> The men understand the position perfectly, and are enthusiastic in their appreciation for all that is being done.

On the night of 30th July, the 2/48th Battalion relieved the 2/32nd Battalion, which then came into brigade reserve. Two nights later, "A" Company of the 2/32nd Battalion relieved "D" Company of the 2/28th, and became the reserve company in the 2/28th's sector thus freeing the 2/28th company from defence duties for employment in the projected attack.

The general plan for the operation by Godfrey's brigade was to attack the shoulders of the Salient by night from right and left simultaneously. In more detail the plan is well described in Morshead's own words:

> The plan for the 43 Bn was to capture Post R7 with two platoons, the third platoon occupying a position south of that post and outside the wire to deal with counter attacks. A fourth platoon acted as a carrying party. In the event of this attack being successful, the second phase would follow—this being the capture of Posts R5 and 6 by the covering platoon and one of the platoons from R7.
>
> The plan for the 28 Bn was the capture of (a) Post S7 by two platoons, one attacking from the west and the other from the north and (b) Post S6 by one platoon.
>
> Plans were made too for the exploitation of success by the attacking coys and also by the 32 Bn in reserve. The artillery support was by thirty-six 25-pounders, two 18-pdrs, nine 4.5 hows, eight 75-mms, four 105-mms, two 149-mms, two 60-pdrs and the "bush artillery". In addition, all available mortars including seven 81-mms and 4 platoons MG were used.

The diarist of the 107th R.H.A., whose commanding officer was a critic of attempts to retake the Salient, described the operation more pithily:

> This was a two platoon attack at each end . . . supported by twenty-one troops of artillery!

The operation was thoroughly planned. Captain McCarter's[8] company of the 2/43rd Battalion was relieved by the English commandos for three

---

[8] Lt-Col L. McCarter, MC, SX8974. 2/43, 2/32 and 2/28 Bns (CO 2/28 Bn 1942). Schoolteacher; of Kadina, SA; b. Adelaide, 26 Aug 1911.

days to practise the operation on a model of R7 which had been built into the Green Line defences of the fortress; Morshead watched them rehearse and was "much impressed by the manner in which they carried out the practice and the careful thought that had been given to the plan".[9] Unfortunately the company of the 2/28th Battalion to mount the attack on the right shoulder, under the temporary command of Captain Conway,[1] could not be afforded an opportunity for similar practice because the company of the 2/32nd which had to take over its front-line defence duties could not be made available to release it in time.

Of the two parallel fronts embaying the Salient in a double arc, the enemy line, on the inner side of the curve, was the shorter. Three German infantry battalions held the Salient against two Australian battalions and the left flank of a third. A battalion of the *104th Lorried Infantry Regiment* held the front opposite Lloyd's battalion, the *II Battalion* of the *115th Lorried Infantry Regiment* that opposite Crellin's battalion, with the *I Battalion* of the latter between. Depth was given by some Italian troops ensconced in rear, but the inference from patrol reports was that their main function was to construct defences.

For three months the enemy had laboured tirelessly to improve the Salient fortifications. Patrols brought back reports of working parties, both Italian and German, almost every night up to the time of the attack. Without air photographs it was impossible to pinpoint the defences behind the outer fringe. Morshead commented on this to General Blamey:

> Well before the operation I asked 204 Group for photographs of Medauuar, sent the usual reminders, and eventually the photographs were taken two days before the battle. I asked that they be dropped here and they agreed to so do on 1st August. I understand that they were flown up on that date, but the releasing apparatus failed. They were dropped next day, and found to be of the wrong area. However there are indications that from now on we can expect some cooperation from the Air Force.

It was known nevertheless that this tenaciously guarded territory was interlaced with earthworks set in minefields studded with anti-personnel mines. The sangars housing the German machine-guns were strongly built from sandbags and covered with earth camouflaged with tufts of coarse grass.

> They rise from the ground to a height of about 4'6" with crawl trenches connecting each. MGs are fired through loopholes about 6" from the ground. . . .[2]

Where Lloyd's battalion was to attack, the terrain greatly favoured the defence. The attackers' problem was brilliantly analysed a fortnight later in an appreciation written by Major T. J. Daly, Wootten's brigade major.

Ground

(a) The ground over which the attack must be made is in the form of an escarpment at the top of which is the objective and at the bottom of which are our FDLs. The enemy occupies a line running along the top of the escarpment which peters out about 1,000 yds East of Post S6 but continues for a considerable

---

[9] From letter to General Blamey already quoted.
[1] Capt R. A. E. Conway, WX3380; 2/28 Bn. Accountant; of Floreat Park, WA; b. Southampton, England, 23 Jun 1913.
[2] Report of the 2/17 Bn Intelligence section, 1 Jul 1941.

distance to the West of S7. This ground formation enables the enemy to observe all the ground between our FDLs and the objective from both flanks and his weapons are so sited as to enable him to produce heavy enfilade fire from MGs while the narrowness of the immediate front enables him to cover the area most effectively with arty and mortar fire. Between our FDLs and the objective there are no covered lines of approach. A number of small wadis provide slight protection for part of the way against flanking MG fire but these are thoroughly covered by mortars.

It is obvious, therefore, that failing the complete neutralisation of the enemy's defensive fire it will not be possible to advance over this country in daylight or, having advanced, to bring further troops across it.

(b) The capture of the objective presents us with a linear posn which, owing to the nature of the ground and the impossibility of either giving direct supporting fire or securing observation from our present posns, is virtually without depth. In addition it will be subjected to heavy fire from both flanks which, unless subdued, will also effectively prevent communication with the rear and the bringing up of necessary reserves and stores. Consequently it will be necessary to exploit fwd from these posns sufficiently far to give depth necessary to hold these posns, which from our present knowledge, would appear to be to the general line of the Acroma Rd. In addition exploitation to the East at least as far as the wrecked plane will be necessary in order to protect the left flank of the captured posn and to prevent it forming a narrow salient jutting out towards Ras el Medauuar. This will require a heavy arty preparation before being undertaken. Simultaneously, a front must be formed facing West to meet any threat from that direction.

Time and Space

 . . . In an attack carried out under these conditions exploitation during the hours of darkness must necessarily lead to an almost complete loss of control and it is doubtful if our force would be able to withstand a determined counter-attack at first light. On the other hand failure to exploit would greatly increase the difficulty of holding a line S6-S7 on the following day. . . .

Opposite Crellin's battalion the terrain afforded the German defence little assistance except commanding observation from the gentle, concave slope leading up to Medauuar; but it was known that the defences were intensively developed. The approach was barred to tanks by a continuous minefield with a screen of listening posts in front. The prisoner taken on 27th July thus described the defences:

Behind the minefield is a continuous belt of barbed wire, and behind the wire are more holes occupied by from 2 to 4 men. These holes are camouflaged with bushes to fit in with the surrounding country, and are all connected by crawl trenches. They are close together, varying from 3 to 4 metres apart to 20 and even 30 metres apart, depending on the nature of the ground. . . . The strongposts are surrounded by barbed wire, and Posts R7, R6 and R5 are held by about 30 men each, one company holding Posts R7, R6 and part of R5 and intervening fieldworks, while the rest of the R5 garrison is from a reserve company.

Lieut-Colonel Lloyd, whose battalion's task of capturing S6 and S7 with one company was perhaps the more formidable of the two, was the most widely experienced of the Australian battalion commanders in Tobruk. After hard service in the first A.I.F. in which he had reached the rank of captain he transferred in 1918 to the Indian Army, with which he served in the Second Afghan War and from which he retired in 1922. He returned to Australia and in 1936 had become a major in a militia battalion. Lloyd's plan was to employ two platoons in direct assaults on each post while a third gave right flank protection. The latter was to move outside the perimeter and engage the sangars on the escarpment west of S7, one platoon was to assault S7 from the area of S9 and the third S6 from the area of S8. On the left a platoon from the 2/48th, moving in rear of the platoon attacking S6, was to seize the Water Tower and the sangars to the east of it, while farther to the left that battalion's forward companies were to engage with fire the enemy positions on their front (within the arc S4 to R2). The 2/48th was to be ready on 10 minutes' notice to swing forward the right of its front to a new alignment linking the Water Tower with the existing front at Forbes' Mound. This in turn would require the capture and occupation of an enemy strongpoint beyond the wrecked plane and of another about 300 yards south-west of Forbes' Mound. The task of wresting, from a thoroughly alerted foe, the foremost fringe of a defensive zone developed in depth was a forbidding one.

Lloyd had one company plus one platoon available to capture the two posts that Evans had earlier failed to take in a battalion attack (albeit hastily mounted) using initially two companies. His plan differed from Evans' assault in two respects: on the one hand by providing for attack on a broader front, with a platoon neutralising the outer flank of each post attacked, but on the other hand by allotting one platoon to the direct assault on each post as against one company in Evans' operation.

For the attack on the southern shoulder Crellin's plan was that his assault company should use two platoons to attack R7 in converging assaults from right and left, while one platoon was to be held in reserve to meet enemy counter-moves from flank or rear or, if the operation developed propitiously, to exploit initial success by a further advance. The attack was to be made from a start-line laid outside the perimeter to the south of the objective. A platoon from another company was to carry bridges for crossing the anti-tank ditch, give flank support southward during the assault and be ready to assist in consolidation.

Crellin's assignment included exploitation by his assault company, on success of the first phase, to capture Posts R6 and R5, if there was a reasonable assurance of success. Godfrey's orders adopted the unusual but sensible course of requiring the company commander himself to decide whether that should be undertaken. If it were, the two flanking companies of the 2/43rd and, farther right, the left company of the 2/48th were each to push out a platoon to establish an outpost line as close as possible to a road that ran north-west and south-east across the enemy territory in front of S4 on the right, and R4 and R6 on the left. A feature of Crellin's plan was the provision for quick delivery of consolidation stores by five carriers, a trailer and an ammunition truck (with a reserve truck standing by). These were to assemble near R9, whence they would be able to reach R7 within five minutes of the call forward. They were to take forward two anti-tank guns and a 3-inch mortar, with their crews, as well as ammunition, wire, shovels and other stores.

Tanks were not to be used in either assault, for fear of prejudicing surprise, but two squadrons of cruisers and two troops of infantry tanks were to stand by under Godfrey's command to deal with counter-attacks or assist exploitation.

For Lloyd's assault artillery support was to be provided by the 51st Field Regiment less one section, one battery of the 107th R.H.A. and three troops of the 2/12th Field Regiment; for Crellin's assault by "B/O" Battery, one battery of the 107th and one battery and one troop of the 2/12th. Lieut-Colonel Goodwin was in charge of counter-battery fire. Four platoons of the Royal Northumberland Fusiliers were to provide machine-gun support, three with pre-arranged fire tasks during the assault.

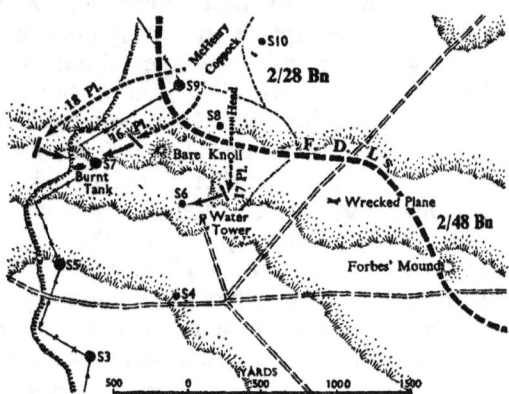

The 2/28th Battalion attack, 2nd-3rd August

The zero hour for both attacks was 3.30 a.m. on 3rd August. Silently, below the Salient's steep north shoulder, Captain Conway and his platoons, Lieutenant Overall with his sappers, and the Intelligence section men who were to lay the start-lines, got ready in the middle of the night. Conway's company had been relieved the night before from local defence duties by a company of the 2/32nd Battalion.

Lieutenant McHenry's[3] platoon was the first to move off, an hour before zero, followed by the rest 15 minutes later. The moon, which was three-quarters illumined, set while they were going forward to the places chosen for their start-lines. Captain Conway, who was to move into S7 when the success signal was shot, went to his battle headquarters at a feature called Bare Knoll.

For the attack on S7 McHenry's platoon was to advance from a start-line west of S7 outside the wire and give supporting fire while Lieutenant Coppock's[4] platoon executed a direct assault from a start-line near the bottom of the escarpment. When Coppock fired the success signal the engineers with McHenry were to blow the perimeter wire and McHenry would join Coppock.

All were ready when the bombardment from more than 60 guns opened up five minutes before zero. Enemy defensive fire from all arms sprayed down on the approaches before the platoons moved off. Coppock and his men advanced up the escarpment. Fire slashed them from front and sides, while "jumping jack" mines burst out of the ground they trod. The few survivors who reached the top, nearly all wounded, gave covering fire while the sappers moved in with their bangalore torpedoes, blew the

---

[3] Lt S. C. McHenry, WX3402; 2/28 Bn. Hotel keeper; of Perth, WA; b. Dublin, Ireland, 17 Sep 1904. Died 9 Nov 1958.
[4] Capt H. T. Coppock, WX3404; 2/28 Bn. Salesman; of Mount Hawthorn, WA; b. Perth, WA, 30 Aug 1908.

wire with a resonant boom and placed their bridges across the anti-tank ditch. Coppock and three men got across to the post, killed four Germans and took the surrender of six more, only two of whom were unwounded.

The Very light signal to call in McHenry's platoon should then have been given, but Coppock was unable to fire it because the sack carrying the cartridges had been shot from his back. A runner was sent to Conway but did not reach him.

Others of Coppock's platoon managed to get into the post. But from outside Lance-Corporal Anderson,[5] now twice wounded, continued firing with his Bren gun on the enemy sangars, until Coppock himself went out and dragged him in. About two hours later he died. Stretcher bearers toiled to get the wounded back to S8. The enemy lit up the area at short intervals with flares and began to close in. Coppock, dazed and wounded, when no help came set out to find Conway. Two signallers, White[6] and Delfs,[7] arrived having laid a line to the post, worked on a telephone but found the line dead.

Lance-Sergeant Ross[8] of the 2/13th Field Company, a born soldier and leader, who had joined in the work of removing the wounded, returned afterwards to the post to remove the bridges and assist in its consolidation. He found there a dozen men of whom only about five (including two signallers) were fit to fight.

Meanwhile from outside the perimeter Lance-Corporal Riebeling's[9] section of McHenry's platoon had given close support. But when the night moved towards dawn and no light signal came, McHenry withdrew his men within the perimeter and went to report to Conway.

The attack on S6 had proceeded with even less success. Lieutenant Head's[1] platoon reached the escarpment with few casualties. Behind it followed a platoon of the 2/48th Battalion under Sergeant Ziesing,[2] which then seized the weapon-pits and sangars east of the Water Tower without much trouble. But thenceforward Head's platoon was mown down by bullets, bombs, shells and mines. The engineers were shot before they could blow the wire round the post. Head, with the survivors following, pressed on but stepped on a booby-trap as he reached the wire and was wounded in the neck and legs. He had now only eight men with him, some of them seriously wounded. No platoon, no other men, stood by, waiting on his success signal, to reinforce his strength. Ought Head still have ordered his dwindling band to strive to reach that post through its

---

[5] L-Cpl K. C. Anderson, WX4639; 2/28 Bn. Salesman; of West Perth, WA; b. Kalgoorlie, WA, 19 Mar 1916. Killed in action 3 Aug 1941.

[6] Sig L. L. White, WX6701; 2/28 Bn. Battery hand; of Southern Cross, WA; b. Melbourne, 17 Jan 1917.

[7] Sig W. G. Delfs, WX6702; 2/28 Bn. Mine puddler; of Northam and Southern Cross, WA; b. Yarloop, WA, 30 May 1914. Died 1 Jul 1950. (White and Delfs enlisted together on 20 Jul 1940. Both were later taken prisoner on 27 Jul 1942 at Ruin Ridge.)

[8] L-Sgt N. D. Ross, QX2880; 2/13 Fd Coy. Bridge contractor; of Calliope, Qld; b. Dalby, Qld, 6 Nov 1914.

[9] Cpl E. C. Riebeling, WX6481; 2/28 Bn. Clerk; of Collie, WA; b. Collie, 11 Jul 1917.

[1] Capt J. M. Head, WX7644; 2/28 Bn. Regular soldier and farmer; of Wandin, Vic; b. Melbourne, 29 Dec 1917.

[2] WO2 F. G. Ziesing, SX3917; 2/48 Bn. Grocer's assistant; of St Peters, SA; b. Torrensville, SA, 19 Feb 1918. Died of wounds 26 Oct 1942.

uncleared obstacles and mines, subdue its garrison and, if yet some survived, to hold out if possible in case miraculous help might come in time? Their lives were his to command. Doubtless they would have done his bidding. Head led them back.

Colonel Lloyd, who had established an advanced headquarters on top of the escarpment between S12 and S13, waited long and in vain for the success signals. An hour passed, and another. No word came back. At last the passage of time itself, with not a single report received, seemed to spell failure. Accordingly he reported to Godfrey about 5 a.m. that both attacks had failed.

The carrying parties waiting to take stores and ammunition up to the captured posts, which had been assembled on the exposed shelf round S10, were now drawn back to cover because of the approach of dawn. Godfrey dismissed the waiting tanks, which then lumbered slowly back on their journey of some miles to their harbour. At 5.15 a.m. Windeyer was informed of the failure of both attacks by Godfrey's headquarters. Windeyer, doubtless with some feelings of relief, stood down the platoons waiting to advance his front to the intended new line and recalled Ziesing's platoon from the Water Tower. But at 5.20 a.m., unmistakably above Post S7, a green light burned in the sky, then a red, then another green. Fifteen seconds later came the same succession of lights—the signal for success at S7.

Conway had refused to infer failure from negative evidence; he had gone forward from Bare Knoll before dawn to find out the situation for himself. So Coppock, returning, had missed him at Bare Knoll; McHenry also. Coppock in his wounded, dazed condition subsequently became lost; McHenry went back to S9. Most of McHenry's platoon then moved down to the regimental aid post at S12. But Conway reached S7 with his sergeant-major and two other men, having meanwhile lost two men as casualties. Finding the post occupied by his own men, he fired the success signal.

Lloyd, who had no reserves for the attack and whose carrying parties had gone back, now attempted to get a platoon from the relieving company of the 2/32nd to reinforce the post and gave orders for stores to be taken forward in carriers. Learning that McHenry had returned, Lloyd also instructed him to go to S7 with the men at hand. McHenry with his platoon sergeant and two of his men set off at once, carrying more than 2,000 rounds of ammunition, and reached the post before dawn. But the 2/32nd platoon and the carriers bearing stores were not so quick off the mark; meeting with a concentration of artillery, mortar and machine-gun fire laid down on the approaches, they could not get over the escarpment to the post. A carrier was disabled and the stores were dumped in a wadi 300 yards from S7.

About 6.45 a.m. it was observed from Lloyd's battle headquarters that the area of S7 had been smoked by the enemy. In the captured strongpoint Conway and McHenry had only nine men fit to fight. What happened there, after Conway arrived, was described in a statement taken from Signaller White next day:

> The sapper, L-Sgt Ross, then rearranged the sandbags. He pulled out bags on his side and instructed us where to pull out and rearrange the bags so as to be able to fire and have protection. We could see the positions of the snipers—we arranged the bags so that we could fire at them.
> Dawn broke at about this time.
> The sapper took me and Sig Delfs to the other end post. . . . Lieut McHenry came to this pit with a Bren and two men were between us with rifles.
> The sapper came back to the north pit. There were two of us and the sapper in this pit. From this point there was a burnt-out tank on the right.

Just after dawn the Germans counter-attacked. They were seen coming out of a wadi to the east and moving south-westwards, whence they attacked from west, south and east, under covering fire from near-by sangars. White thus described the attack:

> At about 0600 hrs, the enemy came up the fence from my right—they scrambled through the fence and made for the burnt-out tank. The tank was about 150 yards to the west from the post. . . . They moved up in small groups and we engaged them. They went around the tank and came quickly towards us—all were knocked down—only about two crawled back through the wire. When this was taking place there was very heavy MG fire from a wadi from the east to the south.
> The sandbags were being cut by fire and the sand draining on to the Bren prevented it from firing more than single shots. I was using a German machine pistol which stopped for the same reason. I then used my rifle. As they were coming from behind the tank in twos and threes, single shots were enough. The sapper got a flesh wound from a bullet in the forehead—went below and dressed it and returned and continued firing.

The counter-attack was beaten off. German stretcher bearers later came out and Conway permitted them to collect their wounded. This was observed from Lloyd's advanced headquarters about 9.30 a.m. But Lloyd, a rugged soldier of the old school, who believed (though higher formation forbade) that commanding officers should direct the battle from the front line and that when his battalion was in action the cooks should fight beside the riflemen, interpreted this licence allowed by Conway as indicating not a truce but defeat. The impression was confirmed by one of his men who later crawled to the vicinity of the post and saw no movement.

The Germans did not allow the Australians similar liberties when attempts were made to remove the 2/28th wounded lying in Posts S9 and S10. Staff-Sergeant Lyall[2] was granted permission to take a truck under the Red Cross flag to the posts, but although the Germans allowed the vehicle to approach, they fired on the occupants when they dismounted, preventing evacuation of the wounded.[3]

By mid-morning the result of the attack for the northern shoulder of the Salient, as it presented itself to Godfrey and Lloyd unable to peer through the battle-fog, was that S6 had not been taken and S7, though recaptured and briefly held, had again been lost. In the early morning,

---

[2] WO2 W. K. McK. Lyall, MM, WX3789; 2/28 Bn. Stock inspector; of Perth, WA; b. Kalgoorlie, WA, 31 Mar 1901.
[3] Pte G. S. Skipworth of the battalion transport platoon was the volunteer driver of this vehicle.

however, Godfrey had instructed the 2/32nd Battalion to send a second company to the 2/28th Battalion to come under Lloyd's command so that he could continue operations if the situation proved better than was feared.

Of the 2/43rd Battalion's attack on the southern shoulder, as of the attack in the north, the enemy appeared to be forewarned. Probably the assembling troops had been seen in the moonlight through field glasses before they moved out to the start-line. When the garrison's bombardment began, enemy defensive fire came down as if by switch. Some of Captain McCarter's assault force were hit before they moved off. The sappers, and Lieutenant Tapp's[4] platoon carrying the assault stores, reached the perimeter wire south of R7 with the bangalores and bridges. The wire was blown on time, but before the objective was reached the bridges were shattered by the enemy bombardment and the men carrying them wounded. Gusts of shell fire swept down on the area where the wire had been gapped; but the men, as a close observer

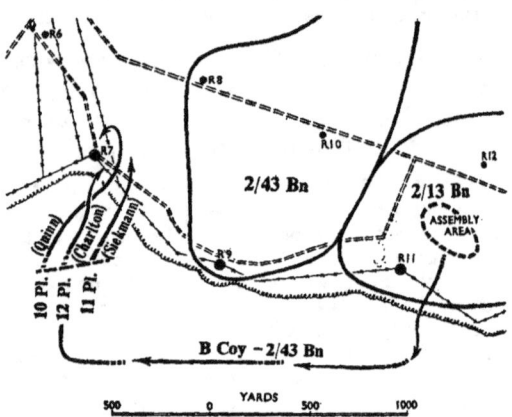

The 2/43rd Battalion attack on R7, 2nd-3rd August

said, "moved on as though it were a tactical exercise".[5] As the infantry approached the post, exploding grenades and booby-traps caused casualties to mount alarmingly. Some of the leaders were first to fall.

The left-hand platoon led by Warrant-Officer Quinn[6], going too far right, overshot the post, swung round and attacked it from the north. One section was silhouetted by flares and completely wiped out by mortar bombs. The other two sections got through the post wire and pressed on in dwindling numbers across a lethal mine garden to the edge of the unbridged, booby-trapped anti-tank ditch. Quinn had only seven others with him by the time he reached the ditch. Taking cover in it, they carried on the fight with grenades. Only three survived.

The route by which the left-hand platoon had attacked was that ordered for the right-hand platoon. The result was that the latter—Siekmann's platoon—keeping to the right of Quinn's, became closely involved in a fire fight with German flanking positions to the east and lost heavily. Siekmann extricated a handful of men and tried to get into the post but the defence weapons did not cease exacting their toll. Soon only two men

---

[4] Lt R. P. Tapp, SX8892; 2/43 Bn. Book-keeper; of Murray Bridge, SA; b. Murray Bridge, 8 Nov 1914.
[5] Quoted in 2/43 Bn war diary.
[6] Lt R. B. Quinn, MM, SX5547; 2/43 Bn. Leather worker; of Birkenhead, SA; b. Birkenhead, 9 Apr 1915.

were with him, one badly wounded. Siekmann and the other fit man, crawling, dragged the wounded man back.

Twenty minutes after the fight began Captain McCarter instructed Lieutenant Pollok's[7] platoon, which was in reserve, to take up the attack. Led by Sergeant Charlton[8] who had taken over command after Pollok had been wounded, the platoon practically re-enacted Quinn's assault and suffered similar attrition. Charlton also reached the ditch with only seven men, fought on from there, but lacked the numbers to carry the assault into the post.

All three assault platoons had spent their force. Captain McCarter saw that it was impossible to make more progress and ordered a withdrawal. He gave the order about 50 minutes after the attack had commenced. McCarter, though he had been twice wounded, remained at the wire gap to keep control until all returning sections had passed through. It was an orderly withdrawal and many wounded were carried out.

It had been a costly attack. The attacking infantry had numbered 4 officers and 139 men; their battle casualties were 4 officers and 97 men. In addition the supporting troops incurred five casualties (4 engineers and 1 driver wounded). Four were missing. Twenty-nine infantrymen lost their lives.

Early next morning the attention of observers within the perimeter was arrested by an unusual spectacle. Vehicles from both sides, carrying the Geneva emblem, drove out unmolested into the bare, fire-swept Salient near R7. Sergeant Tuit,[9] accompanied by stretcher bearers, took out the first vehicle from the 2/43rd at 7 a.m. Others followed in procession throughout the day. The Geneva Convention was seldom dishonoured in the desert war, though German Air Force attacks on hospital ships were frequent. On this occasion the Germans displayed a magnanimous solicitude for the wounded and their rescuers. They allowed the vehicles to approach within 200 yards, devitalised minefields to enable the wounded to be reached, brought out 4 wounded and 15 dead from the post, and gave Sergeant Tuit a drink. Tuit's humanitarian mission recovered 5 wounded and 28 dead.

But around Post S7, which remained isolated throughout the livelong summer day, neither side ventured any move before dusk. All approaches to the post were under enemy observation and close-range fire; it was impracticable to make contact in daylight except by a major operation. A sergeant of the 2/32nd Battalion, who kept the post under constant observation for two hours, reported just before 2 p.m. that he was certain that it was occupied by the enemy.

Nevertheless it was essential to obtain positive confirmation. Colonel Lloyd's plans for immediate action after dark were to send out two reconnaissance patrols. One, of five men under a senior N.C.O., was to ascertain

---

[7] Lt-Col J. A. Pollok, MC, SX8977; 2/43 Bn. Salesman; of Payneham, SA; b. Adelaide, 26 Nov 1916.
[8] Sgt T. Charlton, MM, SX6263; 2/43 Bn. Labourer; of Streaky Bay, SA; b. Durham, England, 15 Dec 1916.
[9] Sgt W. J. Tuit, SX8293; 2/43 Bn. Timber mill foreman; of Alberton, SA; b. Sandwell, SA, 8 Mar 1902. Died 4 Jul 1954.

and report on the situation at S6, including the condition of the wire, and to "endeavour locate and arrange for any of our wounded of this morning to be brought in". The other, to consist of an officer and six men including one N.C.O. and one sapper and to be commanded by Lieutenant Taylor, was to move out through S8 and reconnoitre S7 and its immediate vicinity. Taylor's task was—

to ascertain and report upon the following:
 (a) Who is in occupation of S7 and surroundings, i.e. whether enemy or own troops.
 (b) If enemy, whether Italian or German.
 (c) Estimate strength in weapons and manpower.

Should S7 be in our hands, then to contact and obtain full information as to numbers and names in occupation, commander etc. and other particulars that will help establish definite information.

Both these patrols were ordered to depart at 9.45 p.m. and to return not later than midnight. If Taylor's patrol reported the post not occupied by the enemy, Captain Cahill's[1] company of the 2/32nd Battalion was to send forward a fighting patrol of one platoon to reinforce the garrison. Another company was to provide a platoon as a carrying party. Both the latter patrols were to be ready to leave at 10 minutes notice.

About 8.15 p.m. Colonel Lloyd received a direction from Brigadier Godfrey to send out a fighting patrol at last light and at once sent his adjutant, Lieutenant Lamb,[2] to Captain Cahill to instruct him that the fighting patrol was to move out as soon as darkness fell. The sun set at 8.20 p.m. but still shone its beams onto a high, gleaming moon, which shed down its light with cruel brilliance. The 2/28th forward defences came under intense fire. The fighting patrol became disorganised.

At 9.50 p.m. the Very light signal by which Conway had notified the capture of S7 in the early morning was seen again above S7. Conway, who was under close attack, was calling for defensive fire but the signal was not so interpreted. About the same time the two signallers (White and Delfs) who had followed Coppock's platoon into S7 when it was captured suddenly appeared at Post S8. Each brought a copy of a message from Conway, whom they had left about an hour earlier:

Am at S7 with Lieut McHenry and 19 ORs including 9 very badly injured also some shock cases. The remainder of us are too fatigued to offer any resistance. We have seven prisoners here. We must have immediate help to hold Post S7.
 Amn—have about 1,200 rds. 10 new men could hold the post.
 Please send out help for injured. Have no bandages left. Require morphia tablets. Direct route 9-S7 appears clear. No enemy in vicinity except two snipers.
 2020 hrs 3 Aug 41
 R. A. E. Conway

Lieutenant Waring,[3] in S8 when White and Delfs arrived, endeavoured unsuccessfully to take a section forward immediately to Conway's help;

---

[1] Maj N. M. Cahill, VX12007. 2/32 and 2/43 Bns. Bank clerk; of East St Kilda, Vic; b. Bendigo, Vic, 24 Apr 1917.
[2] Maj L. Lamb, WX3424; 2/28 Bn. Chartered accountant; of Perth, WA; b. Perth, 17 Apr 1912.
[3] Capt E. Waring, WX3400; 2/28 Bn. Business manager; of Wembley, WA; b. Manchester, England, 7 Jul 1912.

the enemy strafed the area as soon as the movement was perceived. Meanwhile a patrol that had gone out at last light from the 2/48th Battalion to the Water Tower area had approached S7; it returned to report that Australian voices could be heard. Lieutenant Beer of the 2/48th then took out a patrol with the intention of occupying S6 if it should be unoccupied. Lieutenant Taylor subsequently set out from the 2/28th Battalion on his mission to S7.

Colonel Lloyd then had to endure another long wait. It was not until 1.25 a.m. that he received the report from Taylor's patrol. Taylor had seen about 50 enemy skylined on the northern side of S7 and inferred that the post was definitely in enemy hands, but Lloyd refused to accept this conclusion and ordered an attack for S7 by the 2/32nd men under his command. This was a difficult task to carry out in a moonlit area under continuous mortar bombardment with no place of assembly beyond the enemy's observation. Eventually the move off was deferred until after moonset (3.45 a.m.) and got under way just before 4 a.m.

The attack was made by two platoons, with a third acting as a carrying party, but failed. Lieutenant Payne,[4] whose platoon suffered 12 serious casualties in the assault, reached the wire but was there badly wounded in the stomach. Lieutenant Fidler,[5] commanding another platoon, was mortally wounded. In all 30 serious casualties were incurred.

At 4.40 a.m. Lieutenant Beer's patrol from the 2/48th, which was in the vicinity of S7 (his second patrol to the region that night), saw a green flare fired by the enemy. Thereupon all firing suddenly died down. The fight for S7 was over. Conway's attack had been made by 135 men (including the attached engineers); of these 83 had been killed or wounded or were missing; the company's fighting strength at dawn on the 4th was 4 N.C.O's and 28 privates. Conway had surrendered just before 11 p.m. when his ammunition was almost exhausted and the enemy having got into the anti-tank ditch surrounding the post was poised for a final assault.

Between 4th and 7th August the 18th Brigade relieved the 24th, which went into divisional reserve. On the night of the 8th the much tried 2/48th Battalion came into brigade reserve, the three forward battalions then being: right 2/12th, centre 2/10th, left 2/9th. Two nights later the 2/48th left the Salient, changing places with the 2/24th Battalion and becoming reserve battalion in the quiet eastern sector. Another unit to be allowed a well-earned rest was the 2/13th Field Company, which had been continuously in the Salient and western sector since May. It was replaced by the 2/4th Field Company on 12th August.

The months following the BATTLEAXE operation were a time of reconstruction and reinforcement for both the Axis and the British forces in Africa. When General Paulus reported back to the German Army Com-

---

[4] Lt L. J. Payne, WX2073; 2/32 Bn. Miner; of Maylands, WA; b. Dongara, WA, 1 Jun 1911. Killed in action 4 Aug 1941.
[5] Lt T. Fidler, VX14866; 2/32 Bn. Produce buyer; of Bullarto, Vic; b. Durham, England, 19 Jul 1908. Died of wounds 4 Aug 1941.

mand after the failure of Rommel's assault on Tobruk in May, the German Army Chief of Staff, General Halder, conceived a means of controlling the African field commander whose proclivity for becoming committed beyond his allotted supply resources was proving so vexatious. General Gause was appointed, with Field Marshal Brauchitsch's concurrence, "German Liaison Officer at Italian Headquarters in North Africa". Gause arrived in Tripoli on 10th June but found General Gariboldi, the Commander-in-Chief in Africa to whom Rommel owed nominal allegiance, not complaisant. The inherent threat to Gariboldi's illusory authority appears to have impressed him more than the intended curb on his intractable subordinate. Rommel, of course, was indignant, and protested to General Brauchitsch.

The stars in the Axis High Command firmament, however, favoured Rommel. While Brauchitsch and Halder, in fear that Hitler was committing Germany to undertakings for which her resources were insufficient, were setting up machinery to keep Rommel in check, Field Marshal Keitel, Hitler's right-hand man and subservient supreme commander, was discussing with General Cavallero, the Italian Chief of Staff, the mounting of an offensive against Egypt in the autumn by four armoured divisions, two of them German, and three motorised divisions, and the provision of the artillery reinforcements estimated to be necessary for the capture of Tobruk to be undertaken. Plans were also in hand to reduce Rommel's dependence on Italian infantry. Advanced elements of what was to become the *Division Afrika zbV*[6] (and later the *90th Light Division*) began crossing to Africa in June.

On the day after Gause set foot in Africa, there appeared the first draft of a directive from Hitler which provided for the further prosecution of the war after the invasion of Russia had felicitously ended. The proposal included attacks directed at the Middle East through Libya, Turkey and the Caucasus. This grandiose scheme was called "Plan Orient". Though its golden consummation was perhaps seen through a glass darkly, two early steps on the way were in immediate contemplation: the capture of Tobruk and the seizure of Gibraltar. The directive was followed up in an instruction from Halder to Rommel on 28th June: Rommel was required to submit a draft plan for an invasion of Egypt after the reduction of Tobruk.

The intention to drive forward aggressively did not well accord with a scheme to keep the field commander's head in check with long, tight reins. The repulse of the British mid-summer offensive, reported to the High Command with an honest magnification of the tank losses inflicted, had added lustre to Rommel's reputation. General Cavallero now came forward as an advocate for a single headquarters to control the operational forces in Africa, with Rommel in command. Hitler appears to have supported Rommel's claims. Eventually Halder had to give way.

Before this issue had been settled, Halder on 2nd July ordered Rommel

---

[6] *zur besonderen Verwendung*—for special service.

to submit a draft plan for the attack on Tobruk. Still conducting a rearguard action to prevent enlargement of the African commitment, he warned Rommel to expect no further reinforcements and imposed a collateral restriction that one complete armoured division was not to be committed to the attack on Tobruk but held behind the Egyptian frontier.

The task exactly fitted Rommel's aspirations but the annexed condition was not to his liking, as his plan submitted on 15th July demonstrated. He proposed to concentrate almost all the German forces in Africa for the attack, including the *15th Armoured Division* and part of the *5th Light Division*. The assault was to be preceded by 10 days of bombing to soften up the defences and was to be made against the south-east perimeter while a feint was made in the west. As in the two preceding attacks (and in the attack to which Tobruk eventually succumbed) it was planned to breach the perimeter with tanks at dawn—the Matilda tanks captured in BATTLEAXE leading the way—and to drive the armour through to the port and harbour. It was hoped to reduce Tobruk by mid-September to enable Egypt to be invaded in October.

The shape of the new Axis organisation emerged from a welter of top-level conferences, some of which Rommel attended in Germany and Italy at the beginning of July and early August. The flattering designation "Panzergruppe Rommel" at first adopted for the new force was sensibly changed, but this did nothing to cloud Rommel's new eminence. The Commander-in-Chief in North Africa remained Italian—an appointment in which General Bastico had replaced General Gariboldi on 23rd July. Prestige prevailed over commonsense and duality of control on the battlefield was perpetuated: an Italian mobile corps, to comprise the *Ariete Armoured* and *Trieste Motorised Divisions*, was to be under Bastico's direct orders. But all other ground forces in the operational area, both German and Italian, were allotted to Rommel's new command, renamed the *Armoured Group Africa*.

The forces under Rommel's command were to be grouped into two formations, the *German Africa Corps* and the *XXI Italian Corps*. The *Africa Corps* was to be built up to a strength of two complete armoured divisions and two infantry divisions, the infantry to consist of a German light infantry division in process of formation and the Italian *Savona Division* (the latter for static defence duties on the frontier). The Italian corps was to comprise four Italian divisions destined for employment mainly in the Tobruk-El Adem area: *Trento, Pavia, Brescia* and *Bologna*. Three of these—*Trento, Pavia* and *Brescia*—were already engaged in the siege, being stationed respectively opposite the eastern, southern and western sectors. The provision of a fourth division would free the German forces for offensive tasks as well as enabling the Italian divisions to be brought into reserve in rotation.

At the beginning of August, the High Command of the German armoured forces outlined the strategic objectives for the remainder of the year. These included strengthening the armed forces in North Africa to enable the capture of Tobruk, and simultaneously renewing the air attack on Malta. The directive declared:

> Provided that weather conditions cause no delay and the service of transports is assured as planned, it can be assumed that the campaign against Tobruk will begin in mid-September.[7]

An important gloss should have been added to the statement of that proviso. Whatever the weather, the Royal Navy was to prove a potent deterrent to fast reinforcement. Rommel was destined to wait two months to receive the major part of the promised forces with enough supplies and equipment to permit their active employment.

Nevertheless by mid-July the form of the projected assault had crystallised in Rommel's mind, which immediately revealed the necessity for preliminary operations the execution of which did not have to wait on the advent of reinforcements. The plan for an irruption directed at the bifurcate junction of the main south road from Tobruk with the Bardia and El Adem Roads, later generally known as "King's Cross", required that the assault force should be assembled on the plateau south-east of the perimeter and jump off from an area not so remote from the intended point of penetration as to involve a long approach march. In this region the Tobruk garrison had brazenly established outposts.[8] The first step was to remove them.

Towards the end of July the 2/1st Pioneer Battalion was on the perimeter on the left of the eastern sector and maintained small permanent garrisons in two outposts taken over from the 2/23rd Battalion. On 26th July, about two hours after midnight, the outpost "Normie" at Trig 146 repelled an attack by an Italian patrol of between 12 and 15 men. At 9 p.m. on the 28th Normie was heavily shelled and the five men in the post were forced to withdraw on the approach of enemy in substantial numbers.

At 10 p.m. Captain Ellis[9] with Lieutenant Williams[1] and 21 men set out to restore the situation. Two hundred yards from the post they were engaged and vigorously returned the fire, to keep the enemy's heads down. Ellis then moved his patrol to envelop the position in a flanking movement. The enemy shot up flares and close artillery defensive fire came down; but the patrol charged through and the enemy fled, their numbers being estimated at 100. The patrol pursued them for some distance, returned to the post, took possession of an Italian light machine-gun, 20 rifles, 36 grenades, flares and ammunition and left the five observers in occupation.

The enemy attacked Normie again on 30th July, this time in mid-afternoon. The men in the post retaliated, the 104th R.H.A. accurately

---

[7] Quoted in Churchill, Vol III, p. 491.
[8] Erroneously reported in the German narrative *Feldzug* to have been held since April.
[9] Capt H. L. Ellis, NX12412; 2/1 Pnr Bn. Accountant; of Sydney; b. Sydney, 17 Jan 1915.
[1] Maj C. G. Williams, ED, NX34898; 2/1 Pnr Bn. Departmental manager; of Scone, NSW; b. Wee Waa, NSW, 23 Jun 1911.

bombarded, and Lieut-Colonel Brown sent out two carriers with an officer and 10 men to help. The attackers were dispersed and a mortally wounded Italian was captured.

Interest in the south-eastern outposts next switched to the 2/23rd Battalion's sector, on the right of the 2/1st Pioneer Battalion. The use of the Walled Village area as an observation site had been discontinued but two other observation posts had been established in the region. On the night of 6th-7th August the 2/23rd established one at Bir Ghersa about 5,800 yards south of the perimeter. It was named "Jim". Another post, "Bob", was established north of the Walled Village, due west of Jim.

During the afternoon of the 7th two tanks and about 30 infantry were reported near the Walled Village. A patrol sent out in the evening to investigate came under mortar fire. On the 8th a patrol of three Italians approached Jim, unaware that the point was occupied, and were promptly captured. On the 9th, a very hot, windy day, Bob was heavily bombarded and the occupants withdrew under fire. A covering party was sent out to protect Jim and took up a position 400 yards to the north-west. Jim was usually manned by three infantrymen in charge of a non-commissioned officer, but Captain Leakey[2] of the Royal Tank Regiment, seeking experience and information, had received permission to take command of the post on this day. With him were Corporal Hayes[3] and Private Bennett[4] of the 2/23rd. Leakey and the two Australians saw 21 men approaching and deploying to attack, waited until they were only 100 yards away, called for artillery support from the 104th R.H.A., then opened fire with Bren and Tommy-gun. The Bren jammed, and while Leakey was putting it to rights, the enemy approached to about 30 yards away; the others kept them at bay with grenades. Soon the stoppage was freed and the three men with their two automatics poured devastating fire into the enemy, killing 20 and seriously wounding the other. The post was then mortared and shelled. Leakey and his men withdrew through the covering patrol, which later killed five men in a party passing by about 600 yards to the south. Subsequently patrols went out to scour the area for spoil and identifications and heard an enemy working party in the Bir Ghersa area. Next morning an infantry carrier patrol with an F.O.O. from the 414th Battery went out to Bir Ghersa and found it unoccupied.

"I am considering another attack on S7 and possibly other posts in that vicinity, using 18th Brigade," General Morshead told Lieut-General Smith, General Auchinleck's Chief of Staff, in a letter written on 9th August. Next morning Morshead's own chief staff officer, Colonel Lloyd, who had returned during the night from Cairo, reported to Morshead the stage reached in the planning for the seaborne relief: that it was expected that the relief would take place during the months of September and October and that the first formation to be relieved would be the 18th Brigade. The

---
[2] Lt-Col A. R. Leakey, DSO, MC; RTR. Regular soldier; b. 30 Dec 1915.
[3] L-Sgt C. B. Hayes, MM, VX43273; 2/23 Bn. Clerk; of Ferntree Gully, Vic; b. Blackburn, Vic, 26 Nov 1915. Killed in action 16 Jul 1942.
[4] Sgt L. Bennett, MM, VX46681; 2/23 Bn. Dairy farmer; of Terang, Vic; b. Terang, 23 Jul 1918.

purpose of Lloyd's visit to Cairo had been kept completely secret. Not one rumour escaped.

In the afternoon of the same day Morshead visited Brigadier Wootten at his headquarters, not to forewarn him of his brigade's impending relief, but to give orders that plans be drawn up for another attack on Post S7. The company of English commandos was to be placed under Wootten's command for employment on the flank of the attack. Two days later Morshead sent Lloyd to Wootten's headquarters to enquire how preparations were progressing. Next day he came himself. On a second visit on 14th August Morshead received from Wootten the appreciation of the problem written by his brigade major, Daly.

Meanwhile General Morshead had written to General Blamey on 11th August:

> I understand that the intention is that the 18th Brigade is to be the first to go so that it can rejoin the 7 Div. I had planned that it should be the last to go because it is the best brigade here as it should be seeing that it was formed nearly two years ago. During the process of relief the defence will be affected by the force being a mixed one and the new units being unfamiliar with the ground and the situation generally. Consequently I feel very strongly that the 18 Bde should be retained until the last and I trust that you will approve of this. The first units to send away should be the ASC personnel used as infantry—they have been in the line, in a very quiet sector it is true, since the beginning and without relief —and the Pioneer Bn which also has been employed as infantry.

Obviously it was unlikely that Blamey would entertain Morshead's proposal to defer the relief of the 18th Brigade, which would have introduced a new complication to the extremely difficult negotiations. He did, however, consider Morshead's other suggestion, that the relief should begin earlier than September, though on a smaller scale, and referred it to Admiral Cunningham, whom he found sympathetic. But General Auchinleck, now back from London, took charge of the matter, and forthwith ordered an immediate relief of the 18th Brigade and the 18th (Indian) Cavalry Regiment by the 1st Carpathian Brigade and Polish Cavalry Regiment. The relief was to be carried out in the approaching moonless period; the proposed deferment until September to wait on the build-up of air strength was overruled. Instructions that the relief was to be effected between the 19th and 29th August were received in Tobruk on 15th August.

Since Morshead's wish that the relief should begin in August had been granted, but not his recommendation that the 18th Brigade should be the last to leave, the proposed attack by that brigade on the right shoulder of the Salient could not proceed. After Morshead had left Wootten's headquarters on the 14th taking with him Daly's appreciation, Wootten had appointed Captain Coleman[5] to make an intense study of the enemy defences. On the 16th Wootten was summoned to divisional headquarters and took Coleman with him. But the reason for the summons was not to discuss the attack. On the contrary Wootten received orders to cancel

---

[5] Col S. T. G. Coleman, OBE, NX468. 2/1 Pnr Bn; 18 Bde and staff appointments. Regular soldier; b. Sydney, 5 Feb 1916.

(*Australian War Memorial*)
Sandbagged sangars close to and to the east of the El Adem Road. Tobruk, 1941.

Australian War Memorial)

Shells from the enemy long-range gun, known to the Tobruk garrison as "Bardia Bill", falling near anti-aircraft positions close to the town.

(*Australian War Memorial*)

A section of Australian troops on the move at Tobruk.

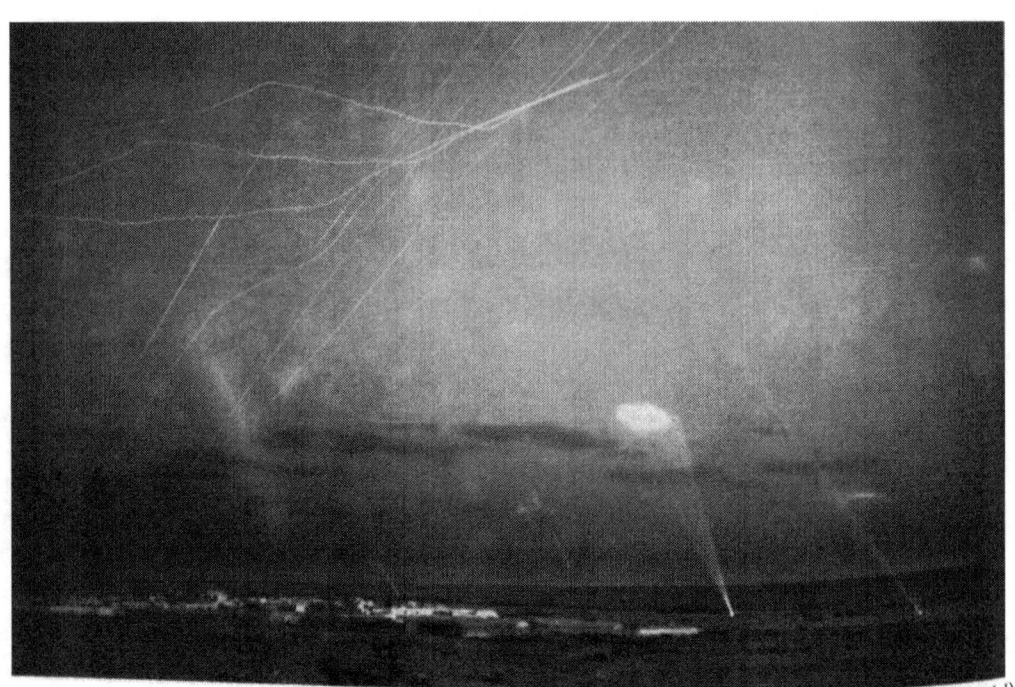

(*Australian War Memorial*)

Night air raid on Tobruk, September 1941.

the operation, was informed of the impending relief and was instructed to have advanced parties secretly made ready to leave. On the night of the 17th Lloyd went back to Cairo to superintend the administrative arrangements. He returned to Tobruk on the 21st, by which time the relief was proceeding.

The study of the projected operation made by Wootten and Daly had convinced them that the initial attack would have to be made by a full battalion at least, and probably two further companies. The 2/10th Battalion had been detailed for the main attack. It was proposed to attack Posts S6 and S7 simultaneously, subsequently exploiting to the general line of the Acroma Road and eastwards to Forbes' Mound. It was also estimated that a second battalion would be needed to hold on to the initial gains for reasons lucidly expressed in Daly's appreciation:

> If it is the enemy's intention to retain S7 and S6 then we may expect a series of counter-attacks in strength and strongly supported by artillery, mortars and possibly tanks etc, and should an attacking battalion have suffered heavy casualties, as seems likely in the light of the experience of previous attacks, it will be necessary to put a further battalion in to take over the fight.

If the operation had been executed, it would have imposed some strain on the loyalty of the infantry and their confidence in the command. The "grape-vine" communication network, which had failed to intercept one word or whisper connected with the relief, was fully tuned in to the attack preparations. Whether securing the objective, if achieved, would warrant the unavoidable casualties was widely questioned. For the sights had now been lowered; the prospect no longer included a step up from the foothold seized on the shoulder to the Medauuar summit, and then a closing of the ring on the original perimeter.

With the exception of Medauuar itself, the bristling ridge adjacent to S7 was the most troublesome thorn in the flesh of the defence. Its removal, even though Medauuar remained untouched, would have been a substantial easement. But it may be doubted whether Morshead's decision had been motivated by a simple weighing of the tactical gain against manpower loss; rather it symbolised the spirit of the great siege commander, the essence of whose defence was not a dazzling of the opponent by brilliant improvisations but a dogged, immutable determination to yield not an inch and never to admit defeat.

To have the 18th Brigade and attached troops ready for transport to Egypt a complicated series of reliefs was put in train and effected over the five nights from the evening of the 16th August to the morning of 21st August; but the reason was not disclosed. The 24th Brigade in divisional reserve replaced the 26th Brigade on the eastern sector; in the western and Salient sector the 18th Brigade, with one battalion (the 2/24th) of the 26th Brigade under command, was then relieved by the 26th Brigade, with the 2/1st Pioneer Battalion under command; the 2/24th therefore remained in the sector. Once more the 2/48th Battalion returned to the Salient sector, but this time as brigade reserve. The 2/1st

Pioneer Battalion took over the western perimeter; the 2/23rd went to the right of the Salient, the 2/24th to the left.

Because the 2/4th Field Company was to return with the 18th Brigade to its own division (the 7th), the 2/13th Field Company was ordered to change places with the 2/4th. Having no inkling of the reason, the diarist of the 2/13th was much aggrieved:

> Orders received that Company will move back into the western sector and that the 2/4 Field Company will again come out into reserve. This comes as a shock as the 2/4th Field Company had no fighting and practically all the activity in Tobruk has been in the western end. . . . The move is to be immediate and no explanations are given. The D.C.E. apparently had no say in the matter. . . . Our men are tired out and, although they don't like the prospect, they have not murmured.

Advanced parties of the Polish Brigade Group appeared in Tobruk on the 20th, having arrived by destroyer during the night. The cat was out of the bag. By nightfall the news had reached every nook within the perimeter. The 2/13th Field Company's diarist noted on the 20th:

> 18th Brigade Group plus certain other units . . . are to be relieved from Tobruk by a Polish Brigade. This is a bolt from the blue and rumours are rife.

In addition to the 18th Brigade Group and the 18th Cavalry Regiment, units earmarked for the August relief included the 51st Field Regiment and the detachments of the King's Dragoon Guards and the 3rd Hussars that had remained in Tobruk.

Although on his return from London General Auchinleck had ordered the immediate relief of the 18th Brigade and 18th Indian Cavalry Regiment, thus terminating the split-up of their parent formations (7th Australian Division and 3rd Indian Motor Brigade), he had deferred giving a decision on the proposal to relieve the 9th Division by the 6th British Division, to which the Commanders-in-Chief had approved in principle during his absence. If he was, as Viscount Cranborne had inferred, as anxious as the Australian Government to relieve the garrison, his enthusiasm does not appear to have impressed General Blamey so much as the general opposition to the project.

Blamey reported the latest developments to Mr Spender in a letter written on 18th August. The 7th Divisional Cavalry Regiment, he said, had at last been withdrawn from Cyprus and had rejoined the 7th Division. The relief of the troops in Tobruk had begun; the Polish Brigade would relieve the 18th Brigade in the next fortnight. In due course these reliefs would set free from Syria the 6th Divisional Cavalry Regiment and a composite brigade of the 6th (Australian) Division, thus enabling the re-assembly of the latter division to be completed. He continued:

> There has been a great deal of opposition to the relief of the troops in Tobruk and it certainly does present difficulties, but they can all be overcome. I am perfectly sure in my own mind that these are largely due to the Staff opposition to our desire to concentrate the three Australian divisions as a single command. It is quite certain, however, that if the relief does not take place within the next two or three

months the fighting efficiency of these troops will decline to a considerable degree. Signs of this decline are already showing and this is really the main reason why I have pressed the case so strongly. I may have to press further to get the 9th Division out.

Thus although by mid-August the brigade relief had been ordered and the principle of a divisional relief had not been countermanded, Blamey remained apprehensive that the relief of the 9th Division would not proceed unless further pressure were applied.

The August relief began in Tobruk on the night of 21st-22nd August, when two companies of the 2/9th Battalion and other details embarked for Alexandria and the 1st Polish Battalion came in. Nightly until the last relief convoy left on the morning of the 29th, the departures smoothly continued. The ships were usually alongside for about an hour and a half, during which about 150 tons would be off-loaded, 850 men disembarked, and an equal number taken on. Quick unloading and embarkation were facilitated by preparations the engineers had made for the secret purpose of a possible evacuation of Tobruk by sea. The jetties had been improved and new berths constructed beside the wrecks close to the southern shore; all skilfully camouflaged.

The infantrymen, the gunners, the Dragoon Guards, the Hussars, and the Indian cavalrymen turned infantry who clambered aboard the destroyers and left at dead of night, casting no longing, lingering look behind, had all made their contribution in effort, daring and endurance to checkmating Rommel and denying him Tobruk's vital port, but none a greater contribution, man for man, day by day, night by night, than the 18th (King Edward VII's Own) Cavalry Regiment. This Australian history has not detailed the regiment's exploits, which belong to its own country's chronicles, but they earned the warm praise accorded in Morshead's official report:

> It is appropriate to mention here the ascendancy which the 18th Cavalry Regiment had always maintained over the enemy. This unit, untrained for such duties, took up its allotted position in the front line as infantry practically from the time the defences were first occupied and remained there continuously until their time of embarkation at the end of August. By their fighting spirit, venturesomeness and constant alertness, these stalwart Indians succeeded in defending a very wide front for a long period, throughout which the enemy was made to feel and fear their presence.

The departure of the 18th Cavalry, as an Indian narrative recorded,

> ended the Regiment's long and very pleasant association with the 9th Australian Division. Treated in every respect as a unit of the A.I.F.; receiving the comforts from the Australian War Societies on an equal basis with the rest of the forward battalions, the Australian and Indian soldiers became firm friends. After the relief, men of the Regiment received letters from the Australians and, in some cases, from their families in Australia.[6]

---

[6] Historical Section (India), Narrative of 18th King Edward VII's Own Cavalry during the period they were under command of 9th Australian Division, Tobruk, 8 April 1941-26 August 1941.

While the August relief was proceeding, the weight of the enemy's impact on the defences appeared to be shifting from the west to the south and south-east. In August the 20th Brigade held the southern sector, the 26th Brigade the eastern. The likelihood that the *Bologna Division* would move up to the Tobruk front and relieve the *Trento Division* on the eastern front became known to the Intelligence staff early in August. The only surprise, when the change-over occurred, was that it took place a week later than expected. The relief itself excited no particular interest but the contemporaneous and subsequent increase in enemy shelling attracted attention.

In the first few weeks of the siege the reporting of enemy shelling was treated as primarily an artillery function but soon a system of daily very detailed reports from all units was instituted and enforced with particularity. At first these were used mainly for counter-battery purposes, but Morshead directed early in August that shelling reports should be analysed for daily incidence, trends, and maximum and minimum intensities. It was ascertained that in the 42 consecutive days ending on 6th August a daily average of approximately 650 shells fell on the three forward defence sectors. In the western sector the daily average for the period was 405 shells, the normal minimum on a quiet day 200. In the southern sector the intensity showed little variation within the limits of 150 shells minimum, 180 maximum; in the eastern sector it fluctuated greatly from day to day, with an average of about 80 and a maximum of 370.

The shelling reports gave daily tallies for each period of 24 hours ending at 8 a.m. Abnormal intensity was reported from the southern sector on 4th-5th August and again on 7th-8th August, when 500 shells fell. On the 13th, 14th and 15th the western sector reported daily tallies rising from 585 to 723 to 982 shells. A week later a further increase was noticed, accompanied by greatly augmented counter-battery fire. By the last week of August the daily norms established for June, July and early August, had become outdated and the main weight had shifted to the eastern and southern sectors. On 24th August the previously quiet eastern sector reported 400 shells. On the 25th 1,175 shells fell in the forward areas, of which 500 were in the eastern sector; next day 1,500, of which 700 were in the southern sector. On 29th August a sector peak of 1,000 was reached in the eastern sector where the rate continued in excess of 500 daily to the end of the month. Against the garrison's 80 guns (including the four 60-pounders, but excluding the bush artillery) it was estimated that the enemy now had 224 field guns and a marked numerical superiority in medium guns. The four ancient 60-pounders (of which seldom more than three could be got into action at one time) and the handful of unreliable 149-mm guns were known to be opposed by four medium batteries (each of 4 guns) and four heavy batteries.

Enemy medium-gun activity became pronounced towards the end of the month. The "harbour gun", firing from the wadis east of the perimeter, had become three guns of 155-mm calibre; after a week's silence they resumed their annoying activity on 19th August, as the sea relief was about to begin. The same day brought an unpleasant surprise when three 210-mm guns shelled Pilastrino. No shelling from equipment of that calibre had previously been suffered, although a solitary 210-mm shell had been found in the Wadi Auda in July. The projectiles weighed 248 lbs. Next day enemy 120-mm naval guns, which from time to time since mid-July had shelled the harbour and coast from the southern sector, put down five rounds gunfire. The 1st R.H.A. took up the gauntlet, and silenced them by firing an immediate bombardment from all troops and on the following day a howitzer manned by regimental headquarters personnel scored a hit on an ammunition dump in the southern harbour-gun area. These guns did not fire again in August. Shelling of the harbour ceased for two days but was resumed on the 22nd first by another battery of 105-mm guns firing at the extreme range of 20,000 yards and subsequently by the 155-mm guns of original "Bardia Bill" vintage firing from the east. These were counter-bombarded, and with evident success, for despite the unusual activity in the harbour practically no further shelling of the port occurred until the morning of 27th August, when 60 shells were fired in the face of vigorous counter-bombardment. The bombardment of the port was followed in the afternoon by an ingeniously planned raid of 40 bombers and 3 fighters against the harbour and heavy anti-aircraft gun sites. The enemy succeeded in sinking the whaler *Skudd 3* but the defenders' barrage sent three aircraft crashing, hit six others hard and damaged many more.

August was a month of increasing air activity, which was notable for the reappearance of the Stuka dive bombers in substantial numbers—35 in the attack on 27th August—and also for a tendency for the attacks to be directed largely against the anti-aircraft gun sites to the exclusion of strategic targets. The anti-aircraft gunners engaged almost 600 aircraft over Tobruk in that month. The climax to the aviator-gunner duel was a particularly brutal raid 15 minutes before midday on 1st September in which about 140 planes in all took part. Thirty Stukas attacked two heavy anti-aircraft guns and a formation of high-level bombers managed to drop more than 50 bombs on and around the site of a third, 15 Stukas dive-bombed the field gun sites, other high-level bombers attacked targets in the base area, while others again distributed their largesse with a certain impartiality over the forward defended localities, some bombs falling in the enemy lines. With the enthusiasm and inaccuracy of amateur duck-shooters the ground forces fired thousands of rounds into the path of the lower-flying aircraft, while the ammunition expenditure of the anti-aircraft regiments in the raid was—

        3.7-inch . . 1,006 rounds
        102-mm . .   111
        40-mm . . 1,200
        20-mm . . 3,000

One anti-aircraft gunner was killed and six wounded; five heavy guns were put out of action for four hours. Numerous planes were hit and at least four were believed to have been destroyed, though only one was seen to crash. But evidence, if not proof, of good shooting was perceived in the fact that only one other Stuka was seen over Tobruk in the rest of September.

In the southern sector at the beginning of August the 2/13th Battalion was on the right, the 2/17th on the left. Soon it became evident that the enemy was extensively developing the defences, particularly near the El Adem Road block. Gaps in the enemy minefield were gradually being closed, and patrols from both battalions reported progress regularly. They also created new gaps, as a patrol of the 2/17th did on 4th August, when 184 mines were lifted from the field and brought in.

The 2/13th Battalion's sector, which it held from 15th July to 18th August, lent itself to patrolling activity because the enemy defence works were sufficiently distant to allow patrols unperceived egress and unmolested approach, but not so far away as to make it difficult for patrol commanders to locate objectives exactly after a night march. Lieutenant Martin[7] came back from one of the first patrols with fresh and accurate information of an enemy minefield on his front. This was the start of a systematic series of reconnaissance patrols, many of them under Martin's leadership, by which the enemy positions were accurately pinpointed. Martin was soon in a position to penetrate the enemy's line at will and move freely behind his front at night. One night he closely observed the flashes of a heavy enemy gun shelling the port and base area. Lieut-Colonel Burrows planned to destroy the gun with a large fighting patrol. On a subsequent night Martin and another patrol commander took cross-bearings in no-man's land on its flashes while bearings were simultaneously taken from within the perimeter. On the night of 17th-18th August a patrol of 3 officers and 40 men from the 2/13th Battalion and 6 sappers from the 2/3rd Field Company, commanded by Captain Walsoe, went out to assault the gun positions. While one party under Lieutenant Bucknell covered an enemy strongpoint on the flank, Lieutenant Martin led the main assault party to the gun area but found only empty pits, though evidence of recent use was seen.

The air support accorded to the fortress, if less than Morshead's estimation of the due entitlement, had nevertheless improved, although the prohibition on the use of the Tobruk airfield except for an occasional prearranged reconnaissance sortie remained in force. On 3rd August, and again on 16th August, the R.A.F. bombed the harbour guns east of Tobruk. After Morshead's vigorous protest at the lack of timely air photography for the August Salient attack, the R.A.F. made exceptional efforts to meet his calls for reconnaissance. Soon photographs of considerable sections of the enemy defences were taken and a trained interpreter was attached to the fortress headquarters.

When air photographs of the enemy defences in the southern sector west of the El Adem Road were received by Lieut-Colonel Williams,[8]

---

[7] Capt J. B. Martin, NX13888; 2/13 Bn. Clerk; of Artarmon, NSW; b. Artarmon, 4 Jul 1919.
[8] Brig S. Williams, DSO, MC; CO 1 RHA. Regular soldier; b. 8 Jul 1896.

commander of the 1st R.H.A., he addressed a letter to Brigadier Thompson, the fortress' artillery commander, in which he drew attention to the arresting confirmation given by the photographs to the reports of patrols and stated that he wished the "enormous importance of deep patrolling by infantry to be placed on record".

> Although having had experience of various theatres of operations in the past (he wrote) I have never seen the great value of deep patrolling so forcibly brought out before. The continuous failure of air support, either by observation or photographs, added to the featureless nature of the desert set an apparently hopeless prospect of correctly deducing the enemy dispositions and activity beyond our limited zone of observation. It was simply through the fearless and meticulously thorough investigation of the terrain out of view and often deep inside the enemy defended localities, that we have gradually built up a clear knowledge of his defences and organisation.

Williams then went on to describe how the 2/9th Battalion's patrols had given most valuable information to the limit of the guns' range. The "climax" had been reached when the 2/13th Battalion "produced a series of most convincing detailed reports of the enemy dispositions, and it was highly satisfactory on receipt (after waiting nearly five months) of an air photo of that area to see with what astounding accuracy those dispositions had been fixed". The "continuously brilliant patrolling" had enabled the gunners "to strike deeply and accurately" and had "persistently impressed" them as "regular soldiers".

The Polish Carpathian Brigade was formed in Syria in April 1940 by order of the Polish Government in exile, which was then operating from Paris. Around its original nucleus—a commander and 32 staff officers—the brigade slowly took shape as patriotic Polish soldiers escaped from internment and prisoner-of-war camps and made their ways by diverse routes to Syria.

After the French Government had made a separate peace with Germany and it had become clear that the Syrian administration would remain loyal to the Pétain government, the brigade's commander (Colonel Kopanski) marched it, in June 1940, into Palestine to join forces with the British Middle East Command. There it continued to expand with a steady flow of recruits until the German conquest of Greece finally closed the main escape outlets from eastern Europe. Meanwhile the brigade staff had been expanded to the nucleus of a divisional staff.

The brigade's recruits had included a very high proportion of men who were commissioned officers in the vanquished Polish Army. Some of these were organised into a special unit, additional to the normal strength of a British brigade, called the Polish Officers' Legion;[9] others served in the normal units of the brigade as non-commissioned officers or in the ranks. Self-selected by initiative, sifted by adversity, culled of the weakhearted by surmounted barriers and motivated by insatiable hatred of their

---

[9] The Polish Officers' Legion did not accompany the rest of the brigade to Tobruk in the October convoys.

nation's oppressors, the band of eager, vengeful men who constituted the Carpathian Brigade were trained to a pitch that matched their ardour to fight.

When the brigade came to Tobruk under the command of Major-General Kopanski, it was a complete brigade group, including a cavalry regiment. The staff included a second-in-command, a chief of staff, two brigade majors, two Intelligence officers, ordnance and quartermaster staff on normal brigade scale, and a British military mission of seven officers.

General Kopanski arrived in Tobruk on the night 25th-26th August. Next morning General Morshead invited him and members of his staff to lunch, after which a conference was held to inform him that his brigade was to take over the southern sector a week later and that arrangements were to be made next day for advanced parties to move out immediately from the Polish units to their opposite numbers in the 20th Brigade.

The introduction to action of some Polish units had been even swifter. To enable the 51st Field Regiment to depart, the Polish field regiment, immediately on its arrival, was sent to the western artillery sector, command of which passed to Colonel Goodwin when the English regiment left. The anti-tank regiment relieved the 24th Anti-Tank Company and 9th Battery of the 2/3rd Anti-Tank Regiment in the same fashion, going straight to the guns. Also the cavalry regiment went at once to the perimeter in the western sector near the coast to change places with the 18th Indian Cavalry Regiment.

For a week the advanced parties of the Polish Brigade with the 20th Brigade were attached to all units and sub-units from headquarters down to platoons, mingling with the Australians as they carried out their duties, accompanying them on patrols, in some cases quickly forming enduring friendships and generally learning their ways. The barriers to communication imposed by speaking different tongues were surmounted by their strong motivation to learn and to do. They openly expressed displeasure (but in no disloyal sense) that they were to be posted to a sector where they were to be opposed not by Germans but by Italians. Theirs was a personal war. It was often noted that, when listening to news broadcasts about the Russian front, they appeared to be as pleased with announcements of Russian as of German casualties.

The relief of the 20th Brigade took place from 3rd to 6th September. The 2nd Battalion relieved the 2/17th on the perimeter on the night of the 3rd-4th, but Colonel Crawford remained with the Polish commanding officer to assist, and rear parties of each company stayed on for the next 48 hours to advise on the routine procedures of the defence system. Next night a similar relief of the 2/15th Battalion by the 3rd Polish Battalion took place. For the first time the perimeter of a complete brigade sector was then held by non-Australian infantry units. The brigade relief was completed on the night of the 5th-6th, when the reserve battalion, the

2/13th, was relieved by the 1st Battalion, whereupon the Polish Carpathian Brigade assumed command of the southern sector.

When General Auchinleck assumed command in the Middle East, it fell to him to decide two questions of the utmost importance: when the desert army was to be launched into another offensive; who was to be appointed to command it. From the moment of Auchinleck's assumption of his office, Churchill strove to have his own views on these questions accepted by the man he had chosen as Commander-in-Chief, but Auchinleck, less pliant than Churchill had hoped, exercised a commander's prerogatives, determined his course in the light of his own judgment, and held to it with infrangible will. Auchinleck had been told by General Dill that when Wavell had made the last desert attack before he was fully prepared "the fault was not Wavell's except in so far as he did not resist the pressure from Whitehall with sufficient vigour". Advised by the Chief of the Imperial General Staff himself that

> he should point clearly to the risks he is prepared to accept and those which he considers too great. He should demand the resources he considers strictly necessary to carry out any project and he should make it clear what he can and cannot do in their absence. . . .[10]

Auchinleck faced the Prime Minister, who pressed him to an early onslaught, with the blunt rejoinder that to launch an offensive with the inadequate means at his disposal was not "a justifiable operation of war". In London he declined to attack before November but agreed to set 1st November as the target date. Thereafter he did his utmost to adhere to this timing as one to which he was personally committed, yet later was prepared to endure the displeasure of the Prime Minister by a postponement beyond the date first set rather than order the advance with preparations incomplete and the supply dumping program unfulfilled.

Oddly enough, at the very time when the impetuous British Prime Minister, with the seeming support of a compliant if not insouciant Chiefs of Staff Committee, was striving to prevail upon General Auchinleck to embroil the Middle East forces audaciously and quickly in a renewed offensive, the violent but vague prospects of which appeared the more dubious the closer to the point of impact they were scrutinised, President Roosevelt and his emissaries were attempting to persuade Mr Churchill and his Service chiefs to curtail the reinforcement of the Middle East, urging that it was not a defensible position for the British Empire to hold. Their arguments were given a force their own logic could not provide by hints that the flow of American supplies might diminish or run dry if not directed to the regions that the detached strategists of Washington deemed most fruitful for their employment. Churchill's reply to Roosevelt, which failed to acknowledge the Olympus of the new world as the fount of omniscience or its right to direct men's struggles from afar, caused Roosevelt to "hit the roof".[11] But a battleship meeting of the two

---

[10] Quoted in J. Kennedy, *The Business of War*, p. 136.
[11] Kennedy, p. 155.

statesmen in the Bay of Newfoundland was soon arranged, for which Churchill hurriedly left London soon after Auckinleck had arrived. Amity was restored, after which the Americans gave bountiful aid to the Middle East in tanks, vehicles and other equipment and continued to do so unstintingly during the next year even in the face of calamitous reverses.

Before Churchill left London for the Atlantic meeting, it was decided to send out to the Middle East a second armoured division, which would not arrive there in time for the start of the offensive, though its advent was to be more welcome than could then be foreseen. But convoys bearing men and munitions to Auchinleck were already on their way, and 165 General Stuart tanks from the United States would reach him in time for the battle.

The date having been fixed, the commander had next to be chosen. This was a more difficult decision for Auchinleck to make (though not to sustain). It was not a question to which hard facts pointed the answer. On the day on which he assumed command, Churchill told him:

> Once Syria is cleared up, we hope you will consider Wilson for the Western Desert, but of course the decision rests with you.[1]

Seventeen days later, Churchill reiterated:

> We still think that Wilson should have the command of the next offensive, if there is to be one, unless of course you propose to take personal command yourself.[2]

Auchinleck's translation to a new command had denied him that insight into his principal subordinates' abilities that only long and close observation of performance in responsible appointments can provide. Success, if an unreliable criterion, yet the best to hand, pointed to Lieut-General Cunningham whose felicitous conduct of the difficult East African campaign had been characterised by firmness and vigour. It is not surprising that Auchinleck chose him in preference to the older Wilson and to others who had not yet won such laurels. Latter-day critics may inveigh against the appointment of a man who lacked experience of armoured forces to exercise command in a battle of armour; but if Cunningham had won mastery in his first enterprise in mobile war, they might no less aptly have pointed the moral that technical proficiency is but an aid and not a prerequisite to successful management and command. Moreover it was planned that the armour should be commanded by Lieut-General V. V. Pope, who had not long before been Director of Armoured Fighting Vehicles at the War Office; but Pope and his senior staff were soon to be killed in an air accident, with imponderable consequences. A commander endowed with Einstein's genius and Wellington's tactical skill and administrative ability would have been fully extended in the appointment and task to which Cunningham had been called.

The commander designate of the desert army about to be created left East Africa on 29th August for Cairo to report to Auchinleck who instructed him to prepare two detailed plans on the basis of two possible

---

[1] Churchill, Vol III, p. 354.
[2] Churchill, Vol III, p. 359.

courses. One of these was an ambitious inland thrust to strike the coast south of Benghazi and then seize that port; the other was a thrust along the coast towards Tobruk, with feints inland. With the two courses to study and innumerable possibilities to ponder, Cunningham was allowed one month to produce the plan for which Auchinleck waited, Churchill yearned, and the Middle East forces, listless for want of a goal, hankered. Cunningham's own headquarters were established on 9th September under the designation Western Army Headquarters.

The relief of the 18th Brigade had been successfully completed by 30th August and on that day Blamey so informed the Australian Government by cable, stressing the need for secrecy. On the same day the chiefs of staff of the three Services and some of their subordinates held a conference at the General Headquarters to discuss future policy for supplying Tobruk.

Throughout July and August the supply had been maintained under constant risk of attack at a delivery rate sufficient to conserve and augment the garrison's reserves. Two destroyers ran almost every night, moonlit or otherwise, between Matruh or Alexandria and Tobruk, "A" lighters plied slowly between Mersa Matruh and Tobruk, small ships between Alexandria or Mersa Matruh and Tobruk. The risks were air attack on the run, mining of harbours and approaches, shelling or bombing while entering or leaving Tobruk port or while berthed there, damage in quick berthing and get away in darkness in a wreck-strewn harbour (two destroyers damaged themselves against the oil jetty in July) and delay by bad weather or engine trouble to the lighters. Transporting military formations both in and out of Tobruk necessitated an increase in the destroyer service because destroyers fully loaded with stores could not at the same time carry a large number of troops.

For operation "Treacle"—the naval operation to effect the August relief—the nightly destroyer program was increased from two ships to three for some of the time, and to four during the height of the relief, the ships usually including one of the two fast minelayers, *Abdiel* and *Latona*, which had been experimentally used on the run in July. The extra ships effected the majority of the personnel reliefs whilst the others continued the normal provisioning program. Protection from air attack was given by augmented fighter patrols supplemented by anti-aircraft fire from a covering force of cruisers. The only naval casualties in the August relief operations were slight damage to the Australian destroyer *Nizam* by a near-hit and serious damage to the covering cruiser *Phoebe* at night by an aircraft torpedo, which necessitated her withdrawal from service for major repair in the United States. For comparison, on the normal run in July one destroyer had been sunk and three damaged by air attack.

The provision of fighter escort in August reduced the rate of loss to the small ships. Sinkings by enemy action were reduced to three. A trawler and a whaler were sunk by aircraft in the Tobruk region and a tank lighter by mine in Tobruk Harbour. A minesweeper was damaged off Matruh.

On 28th August Tobruk was warned that the nightly destroyer run was likely to be suspended during the coming moonlit period. Later the Commander-in-Chief Mediterranean signalled that the service would be suspended pending the result of the conference on future policy on the 30th.

The naval chief of staff proposed at this conference that in future the supply should be cut down to a minimum during the moon period and made up during moonless periods and suggested that the program for the moonless period in September (17th to 27th) should be one minelayer and three destroyers to run two nights in three, but with sailings staggered. This would permit of carrying 2,250 personnel reliefs in addition to stores—a scale insufficient to effect a complete brigade relief. The proposal, in substance, was to revert to the pre-relief scale of shipping but to provide the service over fewer days, in the safer moonless period. The Deputy Air Commander-in-Chief pointed out that broadly speaking the R.A.F. provided the same fighter cover regardless of the size of convoys; it would be to their advantage to reduce the number of convoys. At the conclusion of the meeting it was agreed to recommend to the Commanders-in-Chief that there should be no further big relief of the Tobruk garrison.

The 2,250 reliefs proposed for September may be compared with the actual arrivals and departures both before and during the relief in the following table:

Month	Arrived[a] Services Personnel	Evacuated Services Personnel Wounded	Others	Civilians	Senussi Libyans & Arabs	P.W.
April	4,783	1,686	4,501	148	—	9,432
May	1,695	1,516	2,184	—	—	2,405
June	1,862	1,233	1,777	—	1,839	135
July	2,217	825	5,114	—	405	20
August	7,237	1,246	4,934	—	—	40
September	6,913	889	5,499	—	—	8
October (to 20th only)	4,164	563	3,480	—	—	2

After this meeting, the Director of Medical Services raised objections to using the 6th (British) Division for the relief of the 9th Division on the ground that it had been in a malarial neighbourhood and also raised objections, on the same ground, to sending any other formation to that area to relieve the 6th Division. Five days later (4th September) Blamey telegraphed the Australian Government that it was being pressed upon him that a general relief of the garrison was not possible; nevertheless he had been asked to agree to the relief of the British artillery in Tobruk by the artillery of the 9th Division. He had refused, he said, because he took the view that this would mean that the 9th Division would remain there indefinitely.

---

[a] Includes relieving units, and normal reinforcements.

Despite Viscount Cranborne's reassuring telegram to Mr Menzies, Blamey's forebodings in mid-August had proved correct. Only a vicarious responsibility rests with Lord Cranborne, who was not a member of the War Cabinet, for the text of a message designed to placate the Australian Government, which represented that Auchinleck was "anxious to relieve the garrison" at a time when it was the British Government's intention to avoid, if possible, effecting the relief Menzies had requested. Lord Cranborne's assurances about Auchinleck's anxiety to relieve the garrison were true, at this juncture, only in the sense of a relief by land. It is hard to resist the conclusion that the message was intended to be read in another sense by the recipient. The impression conveyed was at variance with the British Government's intentions, which must be identified with those of the Prime Minister and Minister for Defence whose direction of the war it constantly endorsed. Churchill, the protagonist of opposition to the relief, revealed his own attitude (which may have accounted for his omission to reply to so important a communication from the Australian Prime Minister) in a telegram sent some weeks later to the Minister of State in Egypt. He was assuring the Minister that the British Government fully agreed with Auchinleck's opposition to the relief and strongly deprecated the "Australian resolve to quit the line at this juncture". "Moreover," he said, "I particularly stimulated Auchinleck when he was at home not to prejudice defence of Tobruk by making a needless relief."[4] Memories today would be an unsure guide to the intentions at that time of Mr Churchill, the Chiefs of Staff and General Auchinleck. Their actions, however, leave the impression that they were playing for time and are consistent with the supposition that by the beginning of August an intention had been formed to relieve the 18th Brigade by the Polish Brigade in August but to effect no relief of the 9th Division or to undertake that relief only if it proved impossible to mount the offensive as planned.

General Auchinleck had returned to Cairo in August determined, if possible, to mount the projected offensive by 1st November and to ensure that the entire energies both of the staff and of the fighting formations were applied without distraction to the solution of the administrative and supply problems and the completion of all necessary planning, training and preliminary movement. Planning for operation CRUSADER, as the offensive was to be called, had scarcely begun when the relief of the 18th Brigade was authorised, but was under way by the beginning of September when it became necessary to reach a final decision whether the relief of the 9th Division should proceed.

General Auchinleck found both his brother commanders-in-chief opposed to a further relief. Admiral Cunningham wished to avoid the added burden on his already overworked ships; to Air Marshal Tedder the question was bound up with the Royal Air Force's paramount task of winning, before the start of CRUSADER, sufficient air superiority to enable it to

---

[4] This statement also lends some support to a comment Blamey made 10 days earlier (on 8th September) in a letter to Mr Spender: "The real point at the back of the objections to the relief is that the Australians have great fighting capacity. They believe that they will hang on in any event."

maintain during the battle the degree of ascendancy over the battlefield necessary to support the ground forces and protect their communications. A contemporary staff study indicated that by November the two Axis powers might be able to employ about 650 aircraft (apart from transport planes) to support operations in Cyrenaica, of which about 300 might be German.[5] The British expected to have 544 available. If the British on balance held the advantage in the calibre of their aircrews and the efficiency of their maintenance organisations, the Germans could array against them fighter aircraft of superior performance and more quickly reinforce the theatre. Should the war in Russia continue to develop favourably for German arms, German aircraft alone might outnumber British aircraft when the time came. The R.A.F's primary aim, therefore, might prove very difficult to achieve. A decision to carry out a further relief would increase the frequency of the convoys requiring protection during the ten days of the moonless period. Since Tedder's policy for obtaining air superiority included provoking encounters by fighter sweeps, small-scale attempts by the enemy to interfere with the Tobruk convoys would accord with R.A.F. aims. But convoy patrols were not best suited to the purpose. They presented the enemy with the opportunity of momentarily concentrating stronger forces against a convoy than the R.A.F. could continuously maintain over it.

To General Auchinleck the continuance of the relief represented a substantial diversion of both physical and mental energy from the primary objective, particularly on the part of the planning and administrative staffs.[6] He did not think that the garrison's capacity to resist a sustained assault had been materially impaired; rather he believed that the 9th Division with its thorough knowledge of the ground and its confidence born of success would hold the fortress more securely than a relieving division, which might have to face attack before it had become firmly established. Moreover the Tobruk garrison would probably be required at some stage of the projected offensive to punch a hole in the defences ringing Tobruk in order to effect a junction with the forces operating from Egypt, as had been planned for BATTLEAXE. If the intended date for the commencement of the offensive (1st November) were met, such a sortie might have to be made in the first week of November; but the relief of the 9th Division could not be completed until the third week of October, which would allow the relieving formation little time for planning, preparing and rehearsing an attack. The dispatch of a battalion of infantry tanks to Tobruk to take part in the breakout operations was under consideration. If it were sent, the decline in the garrison's power of resistance would be offset. General Auchinleck therefore proposed to General Blamey that the 9th Division's artillery should be sent to Tobruk to make the division complete there rather than in Palestine, and that a further relief should be postponed.

In Australia Mr Fadden had in the meantime succeeded Mr Menzies as

---

[5] We now know that the enemy strength in operational aircraft at the start of CRUSADER was 536 of which 342 were serviceable.

[6] Field Marshal Sir Claude Auchinleck informed the author in July 1956 that this was his principal reason for opposing a continuance of the relief.

Prime Minister; but there had been little change in the composition of the Government except in the leadership. Menzies remained as Minister for Defence Coordination. In his message of 4th September Blamey told Fadden that, although the artillery relief had been sought, it had been pressed upon him that a general relief of the garrison was not possible; but the difficulties could be overcome with the will to do so; fresh British and Dominion formations were available. If the relief were not insisted upon, the decline in the fighting value of the 9th Division would be considerable, its period of recovery correspondingly long. Furthermore if Tobruk were attacked with strength and determination after one or two months of further decline, the division would not be fit to withstand the onslaught. General Auchinleck (Blamey averred) had been informed by Churchill when recently in England that he would make it right with the Australian Government if Auchinleck did not see fit to relieve the division. After the 18th Brigade's relief, the troops remaining would feel let down if not relieved, which would further detract from their morale. Unless the Australian Government took a very firm stand, he was convinced that the 9th Division would be left in Tobruk indefinitely in spite of his efforts.

On the next day Fadden telegraphed Churchill. He referred to previous communications between the two governments relating to the relief, to the latest proposal to send the 9th Division's artillery to Tobruk, and to a statement from Blamey throwing doubt on the possibility of a general relief of the garrison; in view of the decline in "health resistance" of the troops at Tobruk and the availability of fresh troops he reiterated his predecessor's request that the British Government should direct Auchinleck to give effect to the Australian Government's wishes. The Australian Parliament was meeting at the end of the month: when the withdrawal had been completed he wished to make a statement to it that the A.I.F. had been reconcentrated. It was, he said, a vital national question. There would be grave repercussions if a catastrophe occurred because of a further decline of the garrison and an inability to withstand a determined attack.

In *The Grand Alliance,* Churchill referred to this communication as though it put forward a new proposal made at an advanced stage of the preparations for CRUSADER. The truth is that it renewed an old request, and that the CRUSADER preparations had not yet crystallised into any sort of plan; nothing was yet settled except a tentative starting date.[7] "Auchinleck protested strongly against this change," wrote Churchill later, "pointing out the difficulties of the relief and the derangement of the plan for the new offensive. I tried to reassure the General:

Prime Minister to General Auchinleck   6 Sept 41

I am pretty sure the Australians will play the game if the facts are put before them squarely. We do not want either your supply of Tobruk or your other combinations to be hampered. If meeting their demand would do this, let me have

---

[7] General Cunningham's first plan, which differed materially from the earlier staff concepts, was not formulated until 28th September.

the facts to put to them. Australia would not tolerate anything shabby. Of course if it does not make any serious difference we ought to meet their wishes."[8]

The reasons advanced for discontinuing the relief do not appear to have impressed General Blamey. He wrote a long letter to Spender on 8th September outlining the "considerable difficulties" he had met in his efforts to assemble the A.I.F. as a single body. He had organised a temporary brigade to help in the Syrian fighting on the express condition that the units would be returned to their parent division as soon as possible. Two months had elapsed since the end of the campaign but still he had not got them back, although it could not be contended that there was a dangerous position in Syria. As regards Tobruk, he was meeting with the greatest opposition on all sides.

> The Englishman is a born casuist. A plan was made for the relief. Everyone agreed, the Air Force with reservations. The C-in-C was absent. In pursuance of the plan our 18th Brigade was relieved by the Polish Brigade and brought out without any great inconvenience. Then the Staff re-examined the position and they thought in view of the offensive plans . . . it would be easier to leave our 9th Division in. Then a crop of reasons were advanced and the C-in-C even went so far as to say it was not a "possible proposition". . . .

If the division were left in Tobruk very much longer, its decline would become very marked, and if the enemy were able to make an attack on a large scale towards the end of the year, he had grave misgivings as to the results. He felt sure that the Australian Government would not care to have another Greece and Crete experience.

Blamey next referred to the intended date for the commencement of the offensive. The earliest possible date was 1st November but he did not think it could take place so soon. He continued:

> You will see from what I have said that the present is a most propitious moment for the relief. The claim that it is a particularly difficult operation is not tenable in my view, as no great difficulty has so far been met in carrying out the part that has been completed. General Auchinleck will oppose the relief to the utmost, so I have endeavoured to set forth the position as it appears to me.
>
> I am becoming personally the most unpopular man in the Middle East over the matter. . . . I am pressing this matter again because I am convinced I am right. It is a short-sighted policy, but one that one frequently meets amongst the British, to use up a division until it is worthless for months afterwards. The 9th Division will need a considerable period of rest even if it comes out now. If its withdrawal is delayed very much longer, I would not like to say how long it will be before it is fit to take the field again.

Before replying to Churchill's request that he should be provided with the facts to put squarely before the Australian Government, General Auchinleck summoned General Morshead to Cairo. General Blamey forewarned Morshead by letter of the purpose of the summons and informed him of the views he was putting forward as to the physical condition of the troops and their capacity to resist a determined attack if their stay was prolonged.

---

[8] Churchill, Vol III, p. 367.

These are, I think, the views we formulated during your last visit. You are to stay with General Auchinleck and I think if you can spare the time it would be a good thing if you called in at my flat on your way down. You should arrive somewhere about 7.30 p.m. and I will await you.

Morshead left Tobruk for Cairo at 1 a.m. on 9th September in H.M.S. *Kipling*. The destroyer was bombed five times and slightly damaged on the voyage. When he arrived in Cairo he called on General Blamey on his way to the Commander-in-Chief's home.

On 10th September Morshead attended three conferences in company with General Blamey: first a conference with General Auchinleck and General Cunningham, presumably in connection with operation CRUSADER, next a conference with the three Commanders-in-Chief relating to the 9th Division's relief, finally one with the Deputy Chief of the General Staff, Major-General Ritchie[9] and the Deputy Quartermaster General, Major-General Hutchison.[1]

At the conference with the Commanders-in-Chief Morshead was asked to report on the physical condition of the garrison. He said that the troops were tiring; their health was good but medical officers had noticed that their stamina and their powers of resistance were weakening; this applied equally to British and Australian troops: he would be unhappy if, in the event that the 9th Division were relieved, British units had to remain. In his opinion to prolong the division's stay until November would impair the fighting efficiency of the force.[2] Auchinleck told Morshead that, while he wished to relieve the garrison, to do so would seriously endanger his plans. To compensate for any deterioration in fighting capacity through overstrain he would send forward a battalion of infantry tanks as quickly as possible. In any case he could consider relieving only the 9th Division because he had no troops to relieve the British units.[3]

Later in the day General Auchinleck sent Mr Churchill a long telegram in which he set out the factors bearing on the problem. The most undesirable factor, he stated, was that half of the relief would have to take place during the latter half of October,[4] when it was hoped to exert the maximum effort to gain air superiority and to complete preparations for making a sortie from Tobruk. It was conceivable that in certain eventualities the intended date for the offensive (1st November) might not be met, in which event some of the reasons against carrying out the relief would lose much of their force, but it was his firm intention to meet it if possible. During the recent relief of one brigade, nearly all the ships were attacked by aircraft. A continuation of the relief would throw an added burden on the destroyers, already burdened by the task of maintaining the fortress, and be undertaken at the expense of other naval operations. At least five

---

[9] Gen Sir Neil Ritchie, KCB, KBE, DSO, MC. BGS BEF 1939-40, Home Forces 1940; GOC 51 (Highland) Div 1940-41; DCGS ME 1941; GOC Eighth Army 1941, 52 (Lowland) Div 1942-43, XII Corps 1944-45. Regular soldier; b. 29 Jul 1897.
[1] Lt-Gen Sir Balfour Hutchison, KBE, CB. Dep QMG ME 1940-42; GOC Sudan and Eritrea 1942-43; QMG India 1944-45. Regular soldier; b. 12 Feb 1889.
[2] 9 Aust Div Report on Operations.
[3] Based on draft for 9 Div report, written in Morshead's hand.
[4] The second half of the relief, if undertaken, would have been completed by 26th October.

fighter squadrons were permanently employed escorting ships during the August relief as opposed to a normal requirement of three to cover normal maintenance shipping, and this was at the expense of offensive operations on which air superiority depended. The only suitable formation readily available to relieve the Australian division was the 6th (British) Division. If it were used, a plan to dilute it with Indian troops would have to be indefinitely deferred but this was not an insuperable difficulty.

Auchinleck adverted to the contention that the 9th Division had suffered a physical decline and impartially summarised:

> The health and morale of Tobruk garrison is very good but the power of endurance of the troops is noticeably reduced and this is likely to be further reduced as time goes on and I detect signs of tiredness in those in responsible positions. An alternative solution to relief would be to strengthen the powers of resistance of the garrison.

It was still "just possible", he continued, to relieve a brigade of the 9th Division with a brigade of the 6th Division in September but he did not favour that course because he was of the opinion that the breaking up of the 9th Division with its very strong *esprit de corps* and high morale would reduce the tactical efficiency of the garrison. An alternative to relieving an Australian brigade in September would be to send an infantry-tank battalion to Tobruk.[5] This would increase both the defensive power of the garrison and its offensive power in future operations. He felt confident that with this reinforcement Tobruk could resist an attack. He concluded:

> The matter has today been placed before the Minister of State and the other two Commanders-in-Chief at a meeting of the Defence Committee and they agree with my opinion that to attempt any further relief of the Tobruk garrison, however desirable it may be politically, is not a justifiable military operation in the circumstances and would definitely prejudice the chances of success of our projected offensive in the Western Desert. Subject to your approval I propose therefore definitely to abandon the idea of a further large scale relief of Australian personnel in Tobruk and to reinforce the garrison at once with an infantry-tank battalion.

Blamey telegraphed to the Australian Government an elaborate commentary on Auchinleck's message, in which he traversed Auchinleck's numerous arguments (including some not mentioned above) one by one. It must suffice here to indicate his comments on the three major contentions. He said that in the absence of a hostile fleet in the Mediterranean or of any proposed large-scale naval operations, the naval argument was not a sufficient reason for discontinuing the relief. That the provision of additional air cover would be at the expense of offensive operations for the purpose of obtaining air superiority was true, but since he had agreed to the relief's postponement from August to September because the R.A.F. then stated that they would be able to provide three extra squadrons in September, and when the great increase in air forces in the Middle East as already reported by him and the now reduced risk in Iraq and Iran were taken into account, the additional strain on the R.A.F. did not appear

---

[5] The alternatives were not mutually exclusive, however. The tanks were in fact sent in although the relief proceeded.

to justify unwillingness to proceed with the relief. With regard to the proposed sortie, after two or three more months the 9th Division, he said, would be quite unfitted for the task, which would involve continuous and severe fighting. In a subsequent message Blamey indicated that Morshead confirmed the last statement.

Mr Churchill telegraphed General Auchinleck's message to Mr Fadden in its entirety. He pointed out that in any case the relief could not be completed in time for Fadden to make the announcement he desired to the Commonwealth Parliament. If Fadden insisted that the withdrawal should take place, orders would be issued accordingly "irrespective of the cost entailed and the injury to future prospects". He trusted that Fadden would weigh very carefully the immense responsibility he would assume before history by depriving Australia of the glory of holding Tobruk till victory was won, which otherwise, by God's help, would be theirs for ever.

But the Australian Prime Minister stood his ground. His reply once more stressed the importance the Australian Government attached to the concentration of the A.I.F. in one corps, urged that the decline in the garrison's powers of resistance necessitated the relief, referred in detail to the several reasons advanced by General Auchinleck for deferring a relief, adopted in general the comments already received from General Blamey, and stated that the reference to a sortie from Tobruk had caused the Australian Government grave concern. In view of the responsibilities reposed in General Blamey as commander of the A.I.F. and the advice tendered by him, which was supported by the Government's advisers in Australia, he was bound, he said, to request that the relief and the reconcentration of the A.I.F. should proceed. In the light of the requests made over an extended period, any reverse suffered by the Tobruk garrison would have far-reaching effects. The Australian Government did not consider that the military considerations put forward by General Auchinleck outweighed the case for a relief.

In reply Churchill telegraphed Fadden (on 15th September): "Orders will at once be given in accordance with your decision." The Chiefs of Staff thereupon instructed the commanders-in-chief in the Middle East to take action to carry out the decision immediately.

Two days later Churchill telegraphed Auchinleck that he was grieved at the Australian attitude but had long feared the dangerous reactions on Australian and world opinion of seeming to fight all the battles in the Middle East only with Dominion troops.[6] Churchill who saw the contemporary scene as an enactment of history in which leaders and their peoples were playing out historic roles could not fail to be apprehensive of such a charge; but the implication that Australians had judged the issue in those terms was not warranted by anything their leaders had said; nor, in the lengthy private correspondence that passed between General Blamey and the Australian Prime Ministers and Minister for the Army on this

---

[6] Churchill made a similar implication in a message to the Minister of State in the Middle East on 18th September.

and related subjects, was any suggestion made that Great Britain or British soldiers had borne in the Middle East less than their due share of the day's burden. In fact Blamey had continually proposed other Dominion formations as possible reliefs; but this had appeared politically undesirable to others. It was not on the Australian side that such comparisons intruded on the consideration of a purely military problem. So important were questions of prestige in Churchill's eyes, on the other hand, that, overriding the advice both of General Auchinleck and of the British Chiefs of Staff, he insisted on sending to the Middle East, in the convoys arranged at that time, new regular British divisions instead of the reinforcements and drafts requested by Auchinleck to restore British units already there to full strength;[7] so important that the replacement in Cyprus of a British division not required for CRUSADER by an Indian division was being planned at the same time as the relief of the 9th Division was being opposed.[8]

General Auchinleck was no less grieved than Mr Churchill and wished to resign on the ground that he had failed to command the confidence of the Australian Government. It was indeed a most unsatisfactory situation that on a matter of policy within Auchinleck's sphere of command a decision should have been taken against his advice and on that of his deputy. The fact that the Australian Government had to rely on advice tendered at that level, however, was in part due to Mr Churchill's and the British Government's unwillingness to grant the Australian Government's request for representation on the British War Cabinet or the Defence Committee.[9] The Australian Government acted on the advice of its representatives at the highest planning level at which effective representation was conceded.

Although as Commander-in-Chief, Mediterranean, Admiral Cunningham had opposed the relief, Morshead's personal relations with him and his staff were most cordial. Morshead also established good relations with General Ritchie and attended a number of conferences with him and the directors of the various arms and Services. On 11th September, the day following the conference with the Commanders-in-Chief, Ritchie informed Morshead that two squadrons of infantry tanks were to be sent to Tobruk during the September moonless period. Morshead also learnt from Brigadier A. H. Maxwell, Auchinleck's chief artillery staff officer, that after the tanks had been shipped four 4.5-inch guns and twelve additional 25-pounders would be sent.

One subject discussed, on which Morshead held strong views, was the policy for the award of periodical decorations. He had been informed by Middle East Headquarters that he could make recommendations for a maximum of 20 periodical awards for inclusion in General Wavell's final despatch and could submit no more than 50 names for mention in despatches. He had earlier made a written request to be allotted 50 periodical awards. He attached a copy of the Order of Battle in Tobruk,

---

[7] Playfair, Vol. II, p. 292.
[8] This relief was carried out, in the month succeeding the last major Tobruk relief, by some of the ships used for the 9th Division's relief.
[9] See Hasluck, *The Government and the People, 1939-1941*, Appendix 10

listed 52 major units under his command and pointed out that all headquarters, units and services had been in contact with the enemy and subjected to continuous bombing and shelling, and that many new units and services, from the nature of their duties, had not had the opportunity to participate in immediate awards.

Morshead's pride in his command and the spirit imbuing his generalship shone through his submission:

I do stress that the following factors be considered in relation to the allotment for Tobruk:
- a. The importance of the operations at Tobruk as affecting the defence of Egypt.
- b. The unique characteristics of the operations in the period under review particularly in relation to the 9th Australian Division before the occupation of the Tobruk defences. The Division, provided with only a fraction of its armament and transport, sent to an area to train and be equipped, was almost immediately involved in major operations against a first-class enemy provided with every conceivable modern equipment. The avoidance of the enemy's initial blow, the equipment and organisation of the Division on the battlefield in contact with the enemy, and the defeat of his subsequent assaults are all unique and are deserving adequate recognition.
- c. The actions before Tobruk in April and May are the first in which armoured formations of the German Army have been defied and defeated.
- d. The general conditions under which Tobruk has been denied to the enemy for four and a half months. Throughout this period the garrison has been in continuous contact with the enemy under difficult conditions of terrain and climate and without the normal amenities of field service conditions. In particular the complete air monopoly enjoyed by the enemy over Tobruk has exposed all ranks to continuous air attack and permitted the unhindered direction of artillery fire from weapons of every calibre up to 8" on to the whole area.
- e. The maintenance of the offensive spirit of the Garrison under adverse conditions as manifested in the constant deep offensive patrolling, the execution of continuous raids and the delivery of spirited counter-attacks.
- f. The excellent cooperation between British, Australian and Indian troops, brought together in the first instance at Tobruk without design, but associated by the fortune of war in a common enterprise. From the beginning the garrison has been as one and the mutual respect and admiration engendered by joint service in difficult conditions has a deep significance in the future history of the Empire.

It is imperative that nothing be done to disturb in the slightest degree the maintenance of this bond. It is most desirable therefore that sufficient awards be placed at my disposal to ensure an equitable distribution as between British, Australian and Indian Units.

Morshead's personal representations were in the end effective. The 9th Division portion of the garrison, for example, received 134 mentions in General Wavell's despatch, and 83 in the first periodical list submitted by General Auchinleck.

Morshead returned to Tobruk on the evening of 17th September. Only one incident of importance had occurred there during his absence, an enemy attack in strength with about five tanks in the early hours of 14th September on one of the Australian observation posts outside the perimeter, which synchronised with a major excursion of the German armoured forces across the frontier into Egypt: Rommel's reconnaissance in force, an operation which was aptly named "Summer Night's Dream".[1] Born of fantasy and developing into an extravagant goose chase, the enterprise was to leave Rommel's mind clouded with an illusory picture of what his enemy was about.

Many lessons were to be learnt from operation BATTLEAXE, the first full-dress rehearsal of desert armoured warfare. The German commanders took them to heart. In the first place the weakness of the German frontier defences constituted by their open desert flank, which the attack had emphasised for the second time, was partly remedied. The flank could not be closed but it could be deepened, and Rommel immediately put in hand the construction of a line of forts south-westwards from Halfaya to Sidi Omar (a distance of some 25 miles) to be held in approximately battalion strength and provisioned with sufficient reserves for eight days' supplies. This disadvantaged an attacker from the east by forcing him to a wide detour and the establishment of a more exposed line of communications than that of the defence. In the second place the battle's lessons concerning the tactical employment of armour and the control of swift-moving battles were assimilated and effectively applied in intensive training. The commanders' battle headquarters were made mobile and travelled on wheels close to the tanks. Their wireless sets listened in directly to messages of battle units instead of waiting for relayed information to reach them through intermediate headquarters. Procedures for intercepting, interpreting and acting upon messages passed by the enemy during the battle were perfected. The vulnerability of tanks to gunfire—particularly to the high-velocity projectiles of medium anti-aircraft guns—was appreciated to be the critical factor. The employment of tanks and mobile artillery in close conjunction to attack tanks as well as to defend them was therefore adopted as a first principle of battle organisation.

By the end of August the German mobile units had been reorganised into two complete armoured divisions (with some cross-posting of units which in turn led to the internal jealousies normal to such arrangements). The better part of the personnel of three additional German infantry regiments had arrived, including the *361st Africa Regiment* which included a number of ex-members of the French Foreign Legion, and also a few of the heavy guns promised as siege train for use against Tobruk. So too had the *Trieste Division,* to make complete, at least in personnel, the Italian mobile corps.

The Axis supply and reinforcement situation was, however, far from satisfactory. While personnel continued to reach Africa by aircraft and destroyer, severe losses were suffered by the ships carrying their heavy equipment. After considering a detailed report from Admiral Raeder on the Mediterranean supply situation, Hitler determined on 22nd August, against Raeder's advice, to transfer German submarines from the Atlantic to the Mediterranean. Three weeks later he ordered the *X Air Corps* to

---
[1] The literal translation has been preferred to the idiomatic "Midsummer Night's Dream" because the term "Midsummer" seems incongruous when applied to an operation mounted as late as September 14th.

switch from attacking Egypt to providing air cover for the convoys supplying Africa.

The reorganisation of the Axis command structure had left Rommel's authority both as virtual German Commander-in-Chief in Africa and as the only Axis commander exercising effective operational control no more curtailed than it was before the German Army High Command had attempted to clip his wings. General Gause and his staff whom Halder had attempted to interpose between Rommel and the home authorities had become the nucleus of Rommel's new "African Armoured Group" command headquarters and Gause himself had become Rommel's chief of staff. It is greatly to the credit of both men, and particularly to that of Gause, who had earlier spoken to Halder of Rommel's "morbid ambition", that Rommel was able to write to his wife on 28th August:

> I am getting on famously with my new Chief of Staff—which is of tremendous importance to me.

After BATTLEAXE both British and Axis forces withdrew their armoured formations from the region of close contact at the frontier. The Germans screened their front with their two reconnaissance battalions, equipped with six-wheeled armoured cars. On the coast the British established their forward troops behind a minefield some six miles east of Halfaya; above the escarpment, also behind a minefield, they occupied a fortified locality (but not a strong defence line) hinged on North Point, some 25 miles back from the fortified enemy positions running from Halfaya to Sidi Omar. The ground did not lend itself to the establishment of a firm defence line.

The territory between North Point and the enemy forces constituted a wide no-man's land across which light mobile groups marauded and skirmished. Even on the coast where, walled in by the escarpment, the littoral shelf narrowed towards the Halfaya apex, the foremost positions permanently occupied by the British were beyond enemy artillery range. With a solitary exception, of which more later, British field guns were normally employed in a purely protective role against an enemy who almost never came within range, though commanders continually devised and executed ephemeral harassing plots. It is a strange reflection, and one which gives some point to Churchill's hardly controllable impatience, that on the only front, except Tobruk, on which the ground forces of two Powers involved in bitter war were in contact their armies airily shadow-sparred throughout the summer without landing a single heavy punch.

Doubtless the British intention was to mark their foremost patches of occupied desert with tactical signs to be read by the enemy as indicating: "Past this point you do not go without a battle." The occupiers' orders, however, were not to fight hard if the enemy came on in force but to withdraw on Sidi Barrani after the first brush. It goes without saying that the knowledge that the whole force would withdraw induced all commanders to prepare carefully for the event and to make sure that, should the order come, their own units would not become stranded, disorganised, or lost. Behind Sidi Barrani lay the Mersa Matruh port and rail-head, with defences developed like Tobruk to deny the enemy the port without a stiff fight and so to pose to British commanders the recurrent problem whether for that purpose to permit a substantial force to become encircled. The railway was being energetically extended westwards under the supervision of New Zealand railway construction engineers.

At Mersa Matruh a sizeable force was ensconced. During the summer the perimeter defence rested on the 1st South African Division (Major-General G. L. Brink) supported by a machine-gun battalion (the 2/2nd Australian, commanded by Lieut-Colonel Whitehead[2]), three field artillery regiments[3] and two anti-tank batteries. The artillery (field and anti-tank) was under the command of the artillery headquarters of the 9th Australian Division (Brigadier A. H. Ramsay).

When, in the brief halcyon interlude of March, the 9th Division had been sent west to garrison Cyrenaica with the intention that it should train for war there while lightly brushing aside any attempted interference by remnants of the vanquished Italian forces, the division's artillery, comprising the 2/7th, 2/8th and 2/12th Field Regiments, was kept at base. The decision, though intensely frustrating to these first-rate regiments imbued with the buoyant spirit of the unblooded, may have been wise. Lack of equipment was the reason. Until this was received, the regiments could not learn, however excellent their earlier training, the lessons of collective control under the worst possible conditions: the latter, in the contemporary war, included featureless terrain blurred by mirage or blanketed by dust, rough country that caused vehicle breakdowns, and inadequate maps, of which often none were available in Cyrenaica. There was no transport in Cyrenaica for learning these lessons; there was not enough to service and move units having operational tasks, whose artillery protection was therefore entrusted to regiments already in the region and trained in war.

But soon these idle, restless Australian regiments were needed for the second and third lines of Egypt's defence. Then trucks and guns were conjured up out of an empty ordnance; some were old enough to have been borrowed from museums. The regiments were married to their war equipment in camps in the desert close to Alexandria, briefly learnt the desert's first lessons in soul-destroying exercises on its sun-scorched, khamsin-seared fringes and were moved up one by one to Mersa Matruh. The 2/7th Field Regiment (Lieut-Colonel Eastick[4]) came in to Matruh on 23rd May, followed by the 2/8th (Lieut-Colonel Tinsley[5]) next day.

---

[2] Brig D. A. Whitehead, CBE, DSO, MC, ED, NX376. (1st AIF: OC 23 MG Coy 1917-18.) CO 2/2 MG Bn 1940-42, 2/32 Bn 1942; comd 26 Bde 1942-45. Engineer; of Sydney; b. Leith, Scotland, 30 Sep 1896.

[3] It is interesting that these three regiments had between them 88 guns as against the 80 guns of the five field regiments in Tobruk. On the other hand Tobruk was accorded a higher proportion of 25-pounders over obsolescent types until gun shortages were generally made good in the autumn.

[4] Brig T. C. Eastick, CMG, DSO, ED, SX3295. CO 2/7 Fd Regt 1940-43; CRA 7 Div 1943-44, 9 Div 1944-46 (comd Kuching Force 1945). Engineer; of Reade Park, SA; b. Hyde Park, SA, 3 May 1900.

[5] Brig W. N. Tinsley, DSO, NX372. (1st AIF: 8 Bn.) BM 9 Div RAA 1940-41; CO 2/8 Fd Regt 1941-43; CRA 9 Div 1943-44, 5 Div 1945, 11 Div 1945. Regular soldier; b. Richmond, Vic, 24 Dec 1898.

The 2/12th Field Regiment had meanwhile been dispatched to Tobruk. After BATTLEAXE, liaison tours were arranged to enable officers of the Australian regiments to see artillery in action on the front.

British field regiments, the 8th and 25th, had hitherto shared responsibility for the coast sector. At first it was the practice to move guns forward at night to shell Halfaya, withdrawing them before dawn. Later the sniping-gun stratagem was devised and put into effect to more fruitful purpose. A gun was manhandled before first light into a position in the sand-dunes, used to snipe at observed movement throughout the day and withdrawn after dark. Almost every day this was repeated, the object being to strain the enemy's supplies by causing him to shoot off more ammunition than the sniping gun fired. The score was reported daily in cricket jargon. Thus 195 for 10 meant, not that the whole side was out after 195 scoring shots, but that 10 rounds sent over had brought 195 returns. On 23rd July Lieutenant Fielding[6] of the 2/7th was permitted to act as observation post officer for the gun. He fired 28 rounds, effectively engaged a working party and vehicles on the pass and "probably destroyed one staff car".[7] Perhaps Rommel had chosen that day to swim at Halfaya Beach.

On occupying the Matruh defences the Australian regiments soon realised that, if they were to be called upon to use the positions for the purpose for which they had been constructed, there remained much scope for their improvement. Extensive works were quickly put in hand, new positions constructed, old reconstructed. The nick-name "Digger" was earned anew. After local security had thus been provided, there was more time to contemplate the wider scene, which was enough to turn the stomach. Outside the perimeter, a close horizon of high ground overlooked the harbour and defences. Gunners had only to imagine themselves "the other side of the hill", only to go up there for a look, to confirm their apprehensions.

Ramsay and his regimental commanders became advocates of a policy of extending the defence scheme for Matruh so as to deny to the enemy this dominating ground beyond the perimeter. Western Desert Force headquarters approved of the idea, to the great annoyance of General Brink, who saw that it would involve the South African division in endless digging at the expense of training for its future fighting role. It is easier to see in retrospect that General Brink was right than it was to determine priorities at the time. However much the Middle East Command may have acknowledged the paramount importance of training, the fact remains that, both before and after CRUSADER, it constantly so ordered priorities as to preclude the fulfilment of training requirements. It remained for General Montgomery later to restore rehearsal to its primacy in battle preparation. Yet who would say that the time spent that summer in constructing the El Alamein line should have been foregone?

---

[6] Capt A. W. Fielding, SX5271; 2/7 Fd Regt. Electrical engineer; of North Walkerville, SA; b. Adelaide, 1 Mar 1913. Killed in action 27 Jul 1942.

[7] D. Goodhart, *The History of the 2/7 Australian Field Regiment* (1952), p. 59.

In August and early September, the 22nd Guards Brigade was stationed opposite Halfaya in the coast sector, holding its front with three columns which, like bad neighbours, harried the enemy without making his life too unendurable: a way of life that did not quite fit their biblical four-letter code names—"Fait", "Hope" and "Char". Fait blocked the old road following the coast, Hope barred the Italian-built bitumen Victory Road a short distance inland, and Char masked the tracks that climbed the escarpment to North Point, the hinge of the main British forward position. With the exception of the water point at Buq Buq the ground held did not have much tactical significance. Above the escarpment were the Support Group at North Point, with the 4th Indian Division headquarters in the Sofafi area, and on the left flank the 7th Armoured Division, in what was known as the Playground. The 4th South African Armoured Car Regiment operated in front of the minefield.

In the last week of July the Australian field regiments were given their front-line assignments. On 27th July Captain Huggett's[8] troop of the 2/7th was sent to Siwa oasis, a 30-mile-long strip of verdant groves and pools on the edge of the great sand sea, which was the headquarters of the now renowned but then little known Long Range Desert Group. Simultaneously the 15th Battery (2/8th Field Regiment) commanded by Major Johnston[9] moved up to the frontier to become the artillery component of Char column. Major Johnston was given command of the column.

The 15th Battery remained with Char column until 30th August and was afforded several opportunities of engaging the enemy, the first being a shoot on 2nd September from a newly chosen position: three enemy armoured vehicles were engaged and put to flight. On the night of 30th August Major Ralph's[1] 16th Battery relieved the 15th, but Major Johnston remained behind as column commander.

On 25th August Major Argent's 12th Battery of the 2/3rd Anti-Tank Regiment, which had been with the frontier forces continuously for five months, came into Mersa Matruh and under Brigadier Ramsay's command.

On 2nd September Colonel Eastick's 2/7th Field Regiment (less "E" Troop at Siwa and "C" Troop, which remained at Matruh to calibrate guns just issued to it) moved out from Matruh, where it had been relieved by the 4th South African Field Regiment, and on the night of the 3rd took over responsibility for the artillery in the coast sector. Eastick was appointed commander of all the sector's artillery which, in addition to three Australian batteries of field guns,[2] included three anti-tank batteries and a light anti-aircraft battery. The 13th Battery was placed under the command of Fait column commander, the 14th of Hope column commander. The 16th Battery (2/8th Field Regiment) remained with Char.

Before the Australians' arrival the application of cricket rules to sniping-gun activities had been carried beyond the recording of the score. It

---
[8] Maj G. R. Huggett, WX1579; 2/7 Fd Regt. Cashier; of Lawley, WA; b. London, 30 Apr 1908.
[9] Lt-Col R. L. Johnston, ED, VX173. 2/8 and 2/7 Fd Regts (CO 2/8 Fd Regt 1943-45). Company director; of Caulfield, Vic; b. Melbourne, 9 Feb 1900.
[1] Maj M. R. Ralph, MBE, ED, VX13931. 2/8 and 2/12 Fd Regts. Accountant, of Windsor, Vic; b. Largs Bay, SA, 14 Jul 1906. Died 2 May 1963.
[2] The contemporary organisation provided for two 12-gun batteries per field regiment.

was "not cricket" to shoot up bathing parties and on Sundays the game was not played. But the Australians broke the rules and substituted an ungentlemanly kind of rounders.

On 5th September the 16th Battery took a turn at sniping-gun duty on the coast. A gun of Captain Roberts'[3] troop was taken across and was ready to fire by 2 a.m. Roberts decided to confuse the enemy by firing faked flashes from a pit 350 yards to the left rear of the gun. After some shooting up of vehicles on the pass in the early morning, the gun dispersed a bathing party. The deception at first succeeded and Bombardier Campbell's[4] flash-bang set-up received the first spate of the enemy's returns; but a shortage of flashes and inadequate synchronising arrangements gave the show away.

Captain Schrader[5] was the observation officer on the first morning the sniping gun was manned by a 2/7th gun-crew. For two consecutive days they fired the gun from an old pit that was well registered by the enemy, a fact of which the 2/7th had not been forewarned, though they should have been. On the second day, for a few rounds fired, they received 204 rounds right on the position and were lucky to escape without harm. Thereafter, by careful reconnaissance, better positions were selected. The 2/7th kept a sniping gun in action almost continuously throughout their stay and, unlike either their predecessors or their successors, succeeded in avoiding casualties. One day, 9th September, the gun was silent on orders from above, because "two generals" were visiting the sector.

Major Ralph succeeded Major Johnston as Char column commander on 10th September. On 13th September General Messervy visited the column and issued to Major Ralph a warning order that the coast sector was to be held on the line of the minefield behind Alam Barghut.

On 7th September Lieut-Colonel Tinsley assumed command at the 9th Divisional Artillery headquarters and became acting Royal Artillery Commander of Mersa Matruh fortress; next evening Brigadier Ramsay took passage for Tobruk by the destroyer convoy which was to bring Morshead back to Egypt to take part in discussions about the 9th Division's relief. Ramsay visited all Australian artillery units in the fortress. The diarist of the 2/12th Field Regiment recorded that he visited the regiment on the 9th and inspected troop positions. A few days later he informed the regiment of its projected reorganisation from a two-battery to a three-battery basis, the regiment's batteries to be the 23rd, 24th and 62nd.

Some interest attaches to the information Brigadier Ramsay brought to the 2/3rd Anti-Tank Regiment while he was in Tobruk. On 12th September he told the regiment that the 12th Battery, then in Mersa Matruh, would join the regiment in Tobruk. Four days later, after Ramsay had returned to Mersa Matruh (where he resumed command of the artillery on the 14th), he visited the 12th Battery. According to the historian of

---
[3] Maj T. L. Roberts, MC, TX2063. 2/8 and 2/2 Fd Regts. Accountant; of Hobart; b. Hobart, 3 Apr 1916.
[4] Sgt N. L. Campbell, TX1989; 2/8 Fd Regt. Forest surveyor; of Scottsdale, Tas; b. Launceston, Tas, 7 Sep 1910.
[5] Capt C. L. Schrader, SX9339; 2/7 Fd Regt. Survey draftsman; of Cowandilla, SA; b. Broken Hill, NSW, 10 May 1911. Killed in aircraft accident 1 Oct 1944.

the 2/3rd Anti-Tank Regiment, Ramsay congratulated the battery on its service with the 7th Armoured Division's Support Group and brought word that it was to go to Tobruk. In the light of the controversy then raging, it is interesting to speculate through what channel Ramsay received these instructions, and whether General Blamey knew of them.

Inactivity was no less abhorrent to General Rommel than to Mr Churchill. Lacking resources and denied authority to launch a full-scale offensive before Tobruk had been reduced, Rommel opted for the best substitute—a reconnaissance in force. A surmise by the German *Africa Corps* that the British would soon attack provided a pretext, the discovery of a supposed British supply depot in the forward area an objective. On 27th August he directed the *Africa Corps* to be ready at any time after 15th September to attack and destroy the dump at Bir el Khireigat and the British battle groups guarding it. Forces up to the strength of one armoured division might be employed. The title Summer Night's Dream given to the operation was apt, for the existence of the dump was an illusion, as Rommel's own Intelligence staff concluded in early September from observing that there was no anti-aircraft defence; but reveries of rich booty to be taken continued to stimulate the nominated participants, nor was Rommel to be deterred by lack of a dump. Depot or no depot the covering forces at Khireigat were to be attacked; one would have a discreet look at the dump in any case just to be sure.

Rommel's orders issued on 7th September prescribed that the attack was to be made on the 14th by the *21st Armoured Division* and the *3rd Reconnaissance Unit*. The British groups east and south-west of Bir el Khireigat were to be taken in rear; after they had been accounted for the *21st Armoured Division* was to deliver an attack on the British 7th Armoured Division farther east. The attack was not to be sustained beyond the day. The main body of the armoured division was to be back in its positions behind the front within 24 hours.

For the Axis troops detailed to launch a subsidiary raid on the coast sector, the day selected—a Sunday—must have seemed, whether by accident or design, a happy choice, for the sniping gun had not fired on Sundays. The apostate Colonel Eastick, however, had ruled that the Sunday Observance Act had no extra-territorial application. For the first time a sniping gun was in position when dawn broke that Sunday. Moreover the other three guns of the forward troop had been ensconced in an intermediate position not much farther back. Major Rogers[6] had registered fire from the new positions on the eve of dream day.

The main push took place, of course, on the plateau south of the escarpment. The British were forewarned. Forward units were told to expect an advance which, it was thought, would be "probably a demonstration, possibly to cover an attack on Tobruk". All were in readiness for a withdrawal as soon as the code words were passed. To a Tobruk defender the planned movement might have appeared to be in the wrong direction in the light of that interpretation; but even if an assault on Tobruk had

---

[6] Maj A. L. Rogers, ED, WX1578; 2/7 Fd Regt. Dentist; of Perth, WA; b. Perth, 8 Jun 1908.

eventuated, the gambit would probably have proved as good an opening move as any, for Rommel was to learn his first, sharp lesson in the dangers of massed movement against an enemy strong in the air. The broad, hot African day's harsh realities were to shatter his dream.

That Sunday morning the German armour surged confidently across the frontier in three columns, manoeuvred in brilliant encircling sweeps but failed to catch the will-o'-the-wisp Western Desert Force groups falling back to the minefield in the first step of the prescribed withdrawal. Empty desert mocked the Germans as they reached the supposed depot site, but South African armoured cars keeping watch, scurrying like beetles on the

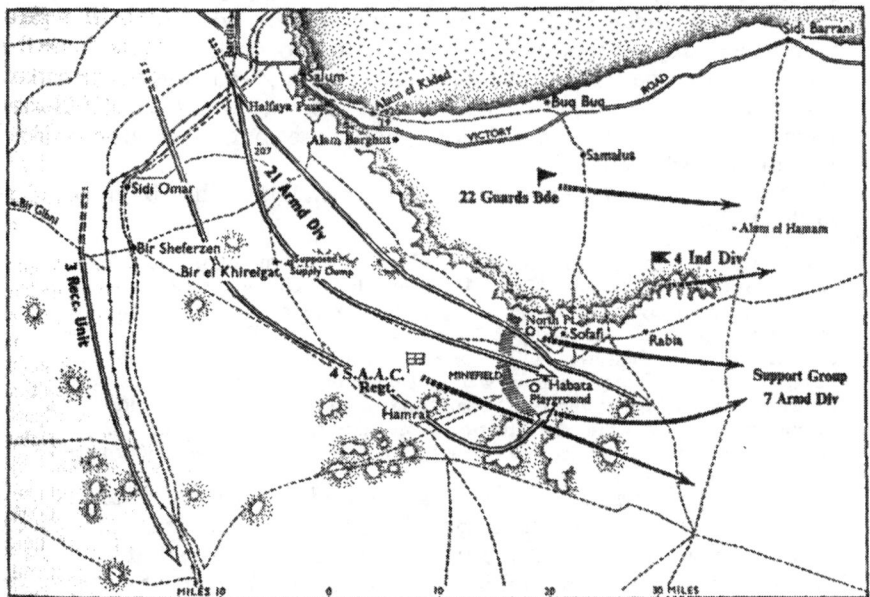

"Summer Night's Dream", 14th September

horizon's lip, invited them to continue the hunt for larger prey. The Germans drove on eastward but the British withdrew before them with outmatching speed. The North Point and Playground lairs were found empty. Through the British minefield the German armour drove on with "unperturbed pace, deliberate speed" until, near Sofafi, the chase came to an unmajestic stop in the afternoon when fuel ran out. Drawing together to replenish with an arrogant self-confidence begotten of past easy victories, the immobile German armour was caught huddled and defenceless by the Middle East air forces and scourged with fire and bomb-blast; the congested stretch of desert erupted with the concussion of carpet bombing. Chastened by their brief season in hell, with thirst unslaked by a dream booty of British whisky and tinned pineapple but with a bitter taste hardly relished of desert earth and stones and rock and fire, the Germans headed for home. After a lonely night on the wrong side of the wire, Rommel made a solitary ignominious exit from Egypt excellently described with German humour in the autobiography of his aide-de-camp. Rommel's return trip from a Sunday's motoring in a captured British command car was delayed by a puncture with which the master race had some difficulty in coping.

On the coast the Australian gunners do not appear to have been entrusted with information so secret as knowledge or a premonition of what the enemy was about to do. Throughout the preceding summer's night strange rumbles were heard in the direction of Halfaya, but (as already mentioned) the ordered routine for the Sunday was the same as for any other week-day. When the sniping-gun crew enquired from the British column commander what was the reason for the odd noises, he replied with a perhaps disproportioned sense of the poetic that it was "only the sea". This left the tension unrelieved until an Australian gunner remarked that it was the first time he had "heard the sea change gears".[7] Nevertheless, when morning came, Colonel Eastick set out on a routine periodic visit to the 13th Battery.

The early morning's excitement has been well described by the historian of the 2/7th:

> Up the coast road, from Alam el Kidad, an enemy patrol of 30 to 40 men engaged the Scots Guards on Point 19 at first light, killing a sergeant and wounding a guardsman. They were in turn engaged with mortars from Point 20, also by our carrier patrols, who scouted forwards as far as Kidad in full view of the enemy, and under shell fire. "B" Troop's O.P.O. on Point 20 (Lieutenant Phillipson[8]) engaged enemy infantry as they were dismounting from trucks, causing casualties. Considerable shelling of the coast road, and of the sniping gun's position, continued throughout the day, while the situation remained uneasily under control. The sniping gun broke all records by scoring 5 for 225 before the breakfast adjournment.

The spirited British reaction disorganised the enemy's Sunday coast excursion. He tried to filter forward, using ground cover, but was held at arm's length throughout the day. When Eastick arrived at the column, he found that line communication with the forward groups had broken down and directed that it must be reopened and kept open. Lieutenant Jones[9] and Gunner Tyson[1] went out and repaired the line. Their efficient work in keeping it operative throughout the day under continuous shelling was later recorded in commendatory letters from the 2nd Scots Guards to the regiment.

In Char column, commanded by Major Ralph, the routine tactical reports indicating that in the desert sector enemy tanks were in contact were read with some interest. While the forces above the escarpment were making ready to fall back on Sidi Barrani, Ralph called forward his third troop, which was at Sidi Barrani, and put it into a backstop position to strengthen the forward defences at the first holding line. When the early

---

[7] Goodhart, *History of the 2/7th Field Regiment*, p. 88.
[8] Maj E. C. Phillipson, SX3289. 2/7 Fd Regt, 1 Mil Landing Gp. Departmental manager; of Glenelg, SA; b. Parkside, SA, 31 Aug 1911.
[9] Maj A. G. Jones, WX3339; 2/7 Fd Regt. Property clerk; of Leederville, WA; b. Perth, WA, 28 Aug 1907.
[1] Sgt J. B. Tyson, SX4453; 2/7 Fd Regt. Clerk; of Streaky Bay, SA; b. Adelaide, 9 Oct 1918.

afternoon situation reports indicated how things were moving "up top", Ralph withdrew his foremost section from its harassing position (the forward section positions were known as "High" and "Dry"—this was High) to another covering the minefield.

Just after 6.30 p.m. the code word "Bicycle" (which had a specific meaning for each forward unit but generally meant "withdraw screening forces to main forward position") was received, to be put into effect at 7.30 p.m. Anxious moments preceded the withdrawal on the coast; large parties of enemy infantry were seen working forward through the sandhills. But the Scots Guards and Australian gunners made a good getaway as the swiftly-falling Egyptian night darkened the shore. In the intermediate position the guns put down a barrage as the forward detachment passed through, then the gunners brought their guns out of action and followed. Faith, Hope and Charity shamelessly quitted "the rough edge of battle".

At their first stop back, by which time the Germans were making tracks for home, Fait and Hope received the code words requiring them to fall back with the rest of the British force on Sidi Barrani, and resumed the withdrawal at midnight. Char, which had taken up an intermediate position around Samalus and Point 52, did not receive its recall code word till 4 a.m. Each column detached little rearguards comprising field guns, anti-tank guns and a platoon of infantry (Scots Guards) to hold vital points, which got ready to die for King, Egypt, Scotland, England and Australia. "A" Troop of the 2/7th provided the guns for the two detachments guarding the Buq Buq water point and cross-roads. "D" Troop of the 16th Battery remained with a detachment (commanded by Captain Mackay[2]) which placed itself astride the Sofafi track near Samalus. "C" Troop of the 2/7th was sent with another force, a company strong, to turn south at Sidi Barrani and advance along the escarpment track "to an area round Alam el Hamam to contact the advancing enemy columns".[3] Nineteen miles along the track, out in the blue and black of the Egyptian night they got ready to blunt the German armoured spearhead.

The Fait and Hope columns were in their assigned places near Sidi Barrani by first light; Char column, later apprised, by 8 a.m. The whole British withdrawal, if perhaps carried out in parts with more alacrity than dignity—"The Great Flap" and the "Hamra Scurry", as the self-critical British later humorously called it—was well executed and earned admiring comment in German records. The soundness of the dispositions taken up was not put to the test.

At 10.45 a.m., by which time the members of the German foray force were seeking elusive sleep in their sun-drenched Libyan leaguers, reports reached the Buq Buq detachment from inland that German tanks were approaching along the Victory Road. The water point was blown with 600

---

[2] Maj-Gen K. Mackay, MBE, NX12365. 2/8 Fd Regt; BM 26 Bde 1942-44. Comd Aust Force Vietnam 1966. Regular soldier; of Sydney; b. Sydney, 17 Feb 1917.
[3] War diary, 2/7 Fd Regt.

pounds of dynamite—"a lovely sight"—and the Buq Buq detachments drove "hell for leather" down the road to Sidi Barrani. Which left Captain Mackay's detachment in splendid isolation as Western Desert Force's sole outpost on the coast.

By the afternoon the coast was reported clear and just after 2 p.m. the three columns moved out to take up substantially their original positions, gathering in the Buq Buq detachment just arrived back. Huggett's troop from Siwa had rejoined the 2/7th after a "valuable experience" which included coming upstream against the backward flow of British transport. High had been reoccupied by the morning of the 17th, and the lone sniping gun had resumed its defiant barking.

The German forces had returned without booty and prisoners, badly battered. German claims that only one tank or only two tanks were totally destroyed may be compared with this description of the site of their ordeal by the historian of the 2/7th Field Regiment, which passed through it a fortnight later:

> Anyone who saw that graveyard, with burnt-out tanks and blown-up tankers, his dead still lying around, and with the detonated Jerricans strewn all over the desert, could hardly have known any doubt as to what stopped Rommel's reconnaissance in force.[4]

Be that as it may, the German armoured fighting strength was reduced from 110 tank runners a few days before Summer Night's Dream to 43 a few days after. One prize, however, was gained for their substantial expenditure of fuel, resources and life—a broken-down orderly room truck taken with its codes and documents undestroyed, which enabled Rommel and General Ravenstein to convince themselves that the ostensible purpose of the raid, the discovery of their enemy's intentions, had indeed been accomplished. But whatever the Germans may have learnt about British plans in force at that time, the documents could tell them nothing of what had not yet been given troubled birth, the plan for operation CRUSADER, the delivery pains of which had scarcely begun. Nor were they likely to glean much information about the forces arriving in the Middle East. It appeared from the documents that there were no British offensive plans or preparations. The jinn of Rommel's summer night's dream continued to bewitch him in the days that followed with illusions that he was safe from attack from the east while he made unhurried preparations to subdue Tobruk.

Two days after Fait, Hope and Char had resumed their unneighbourly bickerings under Halfaya, Colonel Eastick learnt that the 11th Indian Infantry Brigade was to relieve the Guards Brigade on the coast, the Guards were to become the forward brigade in the open desert above the escarpment, and the three Australian batteries under Eastick's command were to go with them. New orders were also issued that betrayed a stiffer attitude than those Rommel had captured. A Scots Guards' operation order issued on 20th September stated:

---

[4] Goodhart, *History of the 2/7th Field Regiment*, p. 93.

Men of the 9th Divisional A.A.S.C. manning Post Z84 near the mouth of the Wadi Zeitun on the eastern perimeter.

(Australian War Memorial)

Brigadier J. J. Murray, commanding the 20th Brigade, with his battalion commanders at Tobruk, September 1941. *Left to right:* Lieut-Colonels J. W. Crawford (2/17th), R. W. Ogle (2/15th), F. A. Burrows (2/13th); and Brigadier Murray.

(Australian War Memorial)

(Australian War Memorial)

Brigadier A. H. L. Godfrey, commanding the 24th Brigade, with his battalion commanders at Tobruk, September 1941. *Left to right*: Lieut-Colonel T. M. Conroy (2/32nd), Brigadier Godfrey, Lieut-Colonels W. W. Crellin (2/43rd), and J. E. Lloyd (2/28th). On the right is Lieut-Colonel A. G. Matthew, commanding the 104th R.H.A.

(Australian War Memorial)

Camouflaged hangars constructed by 9th Divisional Engineers at El Gubbi. September 1941.

Fait Coln will stand and fight on the line of the minefields as from 0630 hours 22 Sep. Previous plans for withdrawal on code words Bicycle etc. will be non-operative as from 0630 hours 22 Sep.

On 19th September General Freyberg visited the front on the coast sector, reconnoitring the New Zealand Division's probable future battleground; but no embargo was placed on the sniping gun, which "got plenty back" that day.

The 2/7th Field Regiment was relieved on the 22nd September. On the 24th Fait, Hope and Char columns ceased to exist on completion of the relief of the Scots Guards. Major Ralph reported to the artillery headquarters of the 4th Indian Division after attending to the closing down of Char column and was there informed that the 2/8th Field Regiment was coming forward from Mersa Matruh and that his battery would be reunited with the regiment in the Playground area.

By 26th September the 2/7th Field Regiment was at Sofafi. The 16th Battery, still separated from its regiment, had one troop in the North Point area and two in the Playground area and the rest of the 2/8th Field Regiment, moving up, was near Sidi Barrani. On the 27th, the 15th Battery occupied a forward position coming under the command of the 7th Armoured Division. The role of the Australian field regiments as key pieces in the new, stiffened British front was cheerfully described in the dry idiom of operation orders as being to support the main British positions at North Point and Playground "to the last man and the last round". The decision to stand and fight on the advanced line was not merely a change in the tenor of the operation orders. The construction of the emplacements and other works required to convert the chosen ground into a strong redoubt able to repel forceful assault was undertaken with more sweat and purpose than before. The eagerness of these blooded but unmauled artillerymen, stimulated by regimental pride and an instinct for self-preservation, gave them vigour for their tasks. Within a short time the 2/7th Field Regiment had constructed 40 emplacements. For the last few days of the month the two batteries of the 2/8th Field Regiment were busily engaged in laying out and constructing an interconnected system of gun positions and observation posts and in setting up an appropriate organisation. The progress of the work of the 16th Battery, now commanded by Captain Stevens[5] (Major Ralph having been accidentally injured), was later specially commended to Colonel Tinsley by the artillery commander of the 4th Indian Division as "far away in advance of the most optimistic expectations".

The staunch "stand-firm" outlook now inspiriting the British command seemed, however, to be associated with a willingness to call on a select few, if it came to the point, to offer themselves up in an ordeal of annihilation before help could reach them. The North Point and Playground fortifications, and the "Kennel" on the flank, looked formidable on the map but the forces holding them were puny. A statement in the 2/7th

---

[5] Maj F. D. Stevens, DSO, ED, VX13937. 2/8 and 4 Fd Regts. Salesman; of Hawthorn, Vic; b. Geelong, Vic, 7 Mar 1910.

Field Regiment's operation order that the North Point position was held by the 3rd Coldstream Guards and attached troops and the Playground position by the 9th Rifle Brigade and attached troops, with the 7th Armoured Brigade on the left flank, did not sound too unimpressive until one looked to the split-up of the holding force. It was divided into two columns, "Brother" column at North Point, "Sister" column at Playground. Each column maintained a detachment (known in the one case as "Little Brother" column, in the other as "Little Sister" column) which operated as a mobile advanced force at distances varying from about 15 to about 25 miles in front of the column position. Farther out the South African armoured cars continued to screen the front. Shorn of these detachments Brother and Sister columns were anything but big. Their main fighting strength at each of North Point and Playground holding positions was two infantry companies, two troops of field guns in a normal role, two troops of anti-tank guns and one or two troops of field guns in an anti-tank role. Engineers, anti-aircraft gunners and infantry protecting headquarters gave a little additional fire-power. The brigade reserve was one infantry company. But the force was efficient, keen and confident. More would not in fact be needed.

The 2/7th Field Regiment arrived before the Coldstream Guards and Colonel Eastick was given temporary command of Brother column from 26th September to 1st October. Major Munro's[6] 14th Battery was placed in support of Brother column, Major Rogers' 13th Battery in support of Sister column. The 16th Battery (2/8th), now under the command of the 102nd Anti-Tank Regiment, R.A. (Northumberland Hussars), was employed in an anti-tank role. The 13th and 14th Batteries each maintained a troop with its column's Little Brother or Little Sister. These two roving columns, whose home was the desert, seldom if ever leaguered two nights successively in the same place. Marauding by day in wide but ordered dispersion, huddled by night into a tight perimeter, they provided the troops of the 2/7th Regiment fortunate to be attached to them with unrivalled training in learning to be desert wise. Captain Dennis'[7] troop, allotted to support a column of cruiser tanks in a detached role, was similarly fortunate.

Colonel Tinsley and Colonel Eastick were informed at the beginning of October that their regiments were to be withdrawn from the desert to rejoin I Australian Corps in Palestine. Before the regiments reached Palestine, they were to put into effect the prescribed reorganisation into regiments of three batteries: the 2/7th would in future comprise the 13th, 14th and 57th Batteries, the 2/8th the 15th, 16th and 58th Batteries. Trained to battle-pitch and chafing to play an effective part in the fighting for which they had volunteered, the regiments were irked at the news. They had lost their chance of action when the 9th Division had been prematurely committed, because the policy of employing Australian

---

[6] Maj N. J. Munro, ED, WX3428. 2/7 Fd Regt and staff appts. Company secretary; of Perth, WA; b. Bunbury, WA, 27 Aug 1899.
[7] Maj W. J. Dennis, ED, SX9340; 2/7 Fd Regt. Constructional foreman; of Unley, SA; b. Port Broughton, SA, 6 Oct 1903.

forces in complete formations had been broken. Because that policy had been reimposed they were being denied the opportunity of further action.

The 2/8th was first to leave. It set off in a south-easterly direction in desert formation on 10th October, the first time in its history that the regiment had moved in its entirety on wheels. Eight days later it reached the end of its journey, Hill 69 in Palestine.

The 2/7th was vouchsafed a little more time in the desert to which it now felt it belonged, and made good use of some fleeting opportunities to engage the enemy. Captain Huggett's troop took over duty with Little Brother on 6th October and carried out a predicted shoot on the night of 7th-8th October. The target was a night leaguer for enemy vehicles to the south of the strongpoint at Point 207. The regiment's diarist reported rather vaguely that "the result of the shoot indicated that rounds fell in the area".

On 12th October "C" Troop, supporting the cruiser tanks, took part in a raid across the frontier wire south of Sidi Omar as part of a mixed mobile column of armoured cars, tanks and artillery, the object of which was to capture "prisoners, tanks, armoured cars and guns". "Guns" in the regimental diarist's concise language meant a battery of 105-mm guns at Bir Sheferzen, which "C" Troop was to silence should they attempt to fire.

A heavy mist enveloped the region at first light when the strike was made but did not muffle the clatter set up by the Australians' approaching gun tractors when they ground across a dump of discarded kerosene tins. When the mist cleared, no tanks or guns were seen: only five armoured cars. The surrender of one armoured car was enforced, ammunition and fuel dumps were destroyed and four prisoners taken.

There was a tragic side to the action. Twelve Hurricanes provided fighter cover but six were shot down by faster Messerschmitts. During the withdrawal there was a second dog-fight between Messerschmitts (one of which machine-gunned Eastick's vehicle) and Tomahawks. Eastick and a United States Army observer saw a parachuting British pilot shot out of his harness. A grave was dug. Eastick conducted a brief Christian burial service. There in the desert the airman was laid to rest.

That afternoon Eastick and his staff (and a number of important observers, including the American) set off for Little Brother headquarters to observe the last action his regiment would take against the enemy for many days. It was a scheme to which Eastick had given much personal attention, a combined strike at a ground target by field guns and bomber aircraft acting in cooperation. The artillery was to consist of the regiment's "E" and "F" Troops, the Fleet Air Arm was to provide the bombers, and the enemy camps at Point 207 were to be the target. The action was to start half an hour after midnight, by which time the bombers were to be over the troop positions. The artillery was to delineate the target by predicted searching fire, the aircraft were to unload bombs, incendiaries and flares for about a quarter of an hour, then after a pause of 15 minutes the guns were again to bombard the target for 15 minutes at rapid rate. It was the first operation of its kind in the frontier sector, though fire from the Tobruk garrison guns had been used to help R.A.F. bombers locate the German harbour guns. The operation was carried out to plan and without mishap, except to the enemy, though during the shoot the gunners had uneasy thoughts about the wisdom of opening fire a second time from a position that could well have been flash-spotted. Observers stationed at selected points reported "fires, as though vehicles were burning, and a large explosion, as if an ammunition dump had been hit".

On the next day, 14th October, the 2/7th Field Regiment assembled near Rabia, having handed over its responsibilities to the 1st Field Regiment, R.A. On the 16th it moved off en route to Palestine; but when it reached the Wadi Natrun near Alexandria three days later, it learnt that it was to proceed immediately to Cairo to become the duty regiment at the Royal Artillery Base Depot at Almaza. The invaluable opportunity presented to the regiment to perfect its training (and complete its equipment) was not at first appreciated.

The heavy air raid on Tobruk on 1st September was followed by an increase in the rate of bombardment of the fortress, not from the skies, where the enemy did not again appear en masse after the raid's hot reception (though air attack did continue on a heavy scale), but from the encircling guns. The disheartening restriction to 10 rounds per gun per day had of necessity been reimposed on guns of British manufacture. Then one day the main Italian ammunition depot was destroyed by bombing and the same restriction was placed on the Italian 75-mm and 100-mm guns. August had been a good month for ammunition supply: the destroyers, schooners, lighters and other small ships had brought in 1,456 tons. But deliveries to forward units in the month had totalled 1,354 tons, leaving an over-all increase in the reserves of only 100 tons. The August turnover of 25-pounder high explosive was 15,838 rounds (excluding super shot and smoke). At the end of the month the total stock holding was 101,993 rounds.

In an effort to achieve maximum effectiveness from the few rounds permitted, a new stop-watch procedure for counter-battery bombardment was introduced at the beginning of September. In a counter-bombardment the guns were fired seriatim but so timed that all rounds hit the target in the same instant. In addition an aggressive policy of planned shoots was instituted for which some relaxation of restrictions was permitted and adequate freedom was allowed for countering the ever more troublesome harbour guns.

The *Wolborough*, a large trawler converted to a storeship, with 110 tons of stores aboard, was due at Tobruk at 4.30 a.m. on 2nd September but, failing to make good her usual speed, came into the harbour at daylight. In the circumstances it did not avail to cover her with the skilful camouflage which usually successfully hid ships in port from the enemy. The harbour guns had a gala day, shelling with effect and delaying unloading. Two troops of the 104th R.H.A. bombarded them with 353 rounds; but afterwards the enemy counter-battery guns, which had of late shown more punch, effectively bombarded one of the 104th Regiment's troops, killing one man and wounding two others. How to cope with the growing menace with limited resources was a worrying problem, to discuss which a conference was held on 4th September. It was decided to ascertain from the navy, whenever the harbour was being shelled, whether damage of much account was being incurred; if so, to counter-bombard hotly and simultaneously to switch other guns from normal tasks to combat enemy counter-battery guns.

Two days later the harbour guns shelled the port and scored two direct hits on one of the jetties used by the destroyers, then turned their fire on to the same troop of the 104th and on the 2/12th Regiment's troop of 60-pounders. The challenge was accepted. The 25-pounders shot back 350 rounds and the 60-pounders 77 rounds. An ambulance was seen to leave the enemy gun area but none was needed on the home ground. On the following day the contest was renewed and the Royal Air Force bombed the harbour-gun positions. Subsequently one gun defiantly shelled the harbour. The 60-pounders and 25-pounders counter-bombarded and a duel between the harbour gun and Captain Feitel's 60-pounders ensued. "Honours to 60-pounders, who fired last," wrote the 104th diarist.

It was not enough, however, to preserve honour, if the tiresome guns were unsubdued. The army and air force had not succeeded, so the navy's help was sought. H.M.S. *Gnat,* of the Inshore Squadron, was directed to Tobruk to bombard the guns, but developed engine trouble. H.M.S. *Aphis* came up instead and carried out the task on the night 15th-16th September. Navy, army and air force combined in the operation to carry out a joint bombardment. The garrison guns shelled the target to indicate it to the R.A.F.; bombers illuminated it with flares; subsequently *Aphis* bombarded. For eight days the harbour-gun battery did not reopen fire, its enforced silence covering two-thirds of the moonless period in which the next relief took place.

At the beginning of September the enemy defences were still least developed in the south-east. The segment of no-man's land in the arc between the El Adem and Bardia Roads, from which Rommel had determined to attack, was screened by five garrison outposts maintained by the battalions holding the perimeter. At Bir el Azazi was the outpost Plonk, originally established by the 2/15th Battalion on 15th August. The others, from right to left, were Bob and Bash—renamed Bondi and Tugun on 15th September—and Jill and Jack (previously Jed and Normie). The eastern defence sector was now held by the 24th Brigade. Bob and Bash were manned by its right forward battalion—the 2/43rd; Jack and Jill by the left forward battalion—the 2/28th. Two small observation posts had also been established on the enemy side of the Wadi Zeitun, north of the Bardia Road.

At the other end of the perimeter, north of the Derna Road, where the rock-shelf was gashed by the cliff-walled Wadi Sehel, standing patrols were also maintained across the gorge on the enemy's side. As though for a warning, one of these was heavily shelled and shot up at dusk on 8th September, and subsequently attacked by a patrol, which was driven off. The shelling killed two in the outpost and wounded two.

On 18th August Brigadier Godfrey had issued an order instructing "that battalions adopt an active and aggressive patrolling policy" during their occupation of the eastern sector.

> Recce patrols will penetrate deeply to check location of enemy dispositions and minefields, and to collect information with a view to carrying out fighting patrols and raids.

Reconnaissance of certain areas was to receive particular attention. Battalion commanders were to consider opportunities, and submit plans, for "effective raiding both by night and day".

These were not empty words. Day by day the brigade Intelligence summary's dry, concise reports told of vigorous patrolling, with almost always some effective engagement to relate. A typical example was the joint action of two 2/28th Battalion patrols at the end of August whose assignment was to determine the flanks of an enemy position, pass round on either side, meet in rear and assault it. In the fight Lieutenant Hickey[8] was badly wounded in the shoulder by a mortar bomb and three other men received less serious wounds. Lieutenant Allen[9] commanded the raiding force.

> Enemy were chased out of two sangars and two Bredas destroyed. Enemy fire ceased at this stage, and patrol made a circuit of the area. Wire was encountered in front of other enemy posts. These were engaged from outside wire with LMG's and grenades. The patrol leader with 8/10 men then got under the wire (a DA[1] type fence) and attacked the posns. 2 LMGs were put out of action. At this time patrol comd decided to withdraw.... When at a distance from the enemy posns, the signal was sent up for carriers, which met the patrol and took back wounded. It is estimated about 15 to 20 casualties were inflicted on the enemy.

On the night of 13th-14th September there was a climax and anti-climax to this aggression. Godfrey's brigade had planned to execute two raids but the enemy also had plans. One of the Australian raids, to be carried out by the 2/32nd Battalion, then in brigade reserve, was to be made against an enemy strongpoint south-west of Bir Ghersa and about four miles and a half from the perimeter, in an area known as Dalby Square. A patrol from the 2/43rd was to prevent any intervention by enemy from the Bir Ghersa area. At the same time a strong patrol from the 2/28th was to raid an enemy strongpoint on the opposite side of Bir Ghersa, some 5,000 yards away to the north-east, known as White Cairn.

Captain Joshua[2] was to command the 2/32nd Battalion's raid on Dalby Square, which had been singled out as the first area for reconnaissance in Brigadier Godfrey's patrol instruction. Joshua had already led two

---

[8] Lt M. A. Hickey, WX5277; 2/28 Bn. Clerk; of Fremantle, WA; b. Fremantle, 5 Jan 1910.
[9] Capt J. L. Allen, MC, WX3305; 2/28 Bn. Regular soldier; of Dalby, Qld; b. Warwick, Qld, 6 May 1915. Killed in action 27 Jul 1942.
[1] Double apron.
[2] Lt-Col R. Joshua, MC, VX15117. 2/32 Bn 1941-43; CO 2/43 Bn 1943-44, 13/33 Bn 1944-45. MHR 1951-55. Bank officer; of Korumburra, Vic; b. Armadale, Vic, 6 Jun 1906.

patrols to Dalby Square, finding the objective strongly held. The attack had been carefully rehearsed.

Joshua's patrol, 60 strong including two infantry platoons, mortarmen, 8 stretcher bearers, and 7 sappers of the 2/7th Field Company, set out at 9 p.m. from R69 on a hushed night march and were not detected before they reached their forming-up place west of the objective. There they formed up for the assault. The engineers, who were to blow the wire, were 150 yards in front, Joshua with them; next was the leading platoon, Lieutenant Cronk's[3], with sections spaced at 30 yard intervals; the second platoon under Sergeant Reardon,[4] similarly deployed, was 30 yards behind; and company headquarters, with Lieutenant Cherrington-Hunter[5] in charge, was in the rear. A 2-inch mortar had been placed in a firing position farther north to neutralise the north-eastern post of the strongpoint.

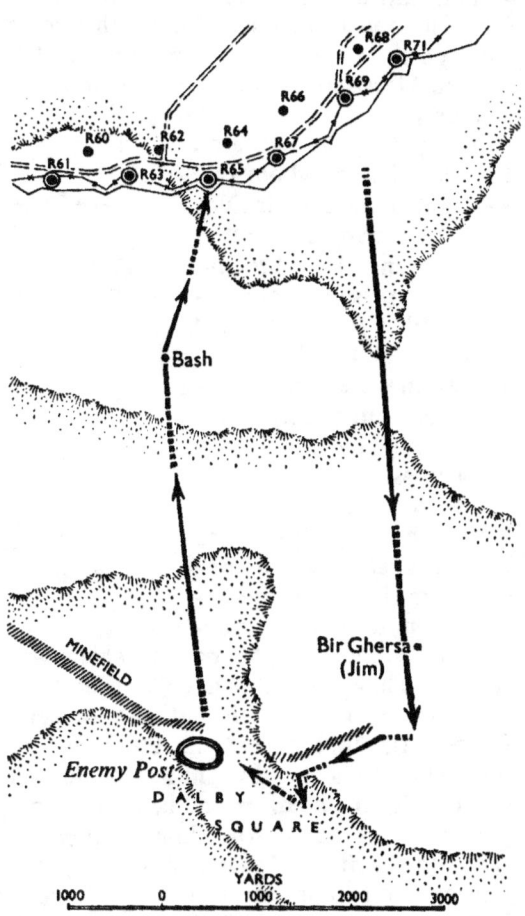

The 2/32nd Battalion attack on Dalby Square, 13th-14th September

As Joshua's force advanced on the strongpoint, some nervous spasmodic firing indicated that the enemy was unlikely to be taken by surprise, but nothing else occurred until the leading platoon was only 75 yards from the wire. Then mortars and more machine-guns opened fire. So loud was the resonance of gun-blasts and bomb-bursts sounding above the strident rapid clatter of the automatics that Cronk was undecided whether the wire had been blown. He pressed on, found the wire unbroken and put his men to ground while the engineers fired their

---

[3] Maj R. G. Cronk, MBE, MC, VX39719; 2/32 Bn. Clerk; of Shepparton, Vic; b. Wangaratta, Vic, 10 Mar 1918.
[4] Sgt J. D. Reardon, VX23304; 2/32 Bn. Clerk; of West Melbourne; b. Rutherglen, Vic, 11 Sep 1910. Killed in action 14 Sep 1941.
[5] Lt B. Cherrington-Hunter, VX27605; 2/32 Bn. Salesman; of St Kilda, Vic; b. Christchurch, NZ, 11 Mar 1918. Killed in action 14 Sep 1941.

bangalores. Then Cronk took his platoon in to the assault. But Reardon, whose platoon had also reached the wire, was hit; Warrant-Officer Harrison[6] came forward, rallied the men, and followed in. Each section set about its rehearsed task, but with limited success. One or two posts were assaulted and cleaned out, the engineers destroyed a 75-mm gun and a 47-mm anti-tank gun and some damage was done to another anti-tank gun; but soon Joshua and about a third of his men had been hit and many other posts in the strong-point continued firing with telling effect. Cronk ordered Harrison to collect the wounded. When that was done the force withdrew.

The patrol had suffered 28 casualties, of whom two were killed and five, including Cherrington-Hunter, were missing. They brought back two prisoners and estimated that they had killed about 20 of the defenders. Three times next night carriers went out to search for the missing men, but with no success.

The other raiding party, from the 2/28th, also brought back prisoners, one of whom had startling information to impart. Captain Johnstone[7] led the patrol, which was 27 strong and included two sappers. They reached White Cairn undetected and attacked at 11.30 p.m. in an assault from south and east. Sergeant Potter[8] led the right section, Lance-Sergeant Holmes[9] the other two on the left. Potter emptied the magazine of his Tommy-gun into a sangar near the cairn, then, using it as a club, hit an Italian on the head; but an exploding grenade knocked the gun from his hand, so, taking a grenade, Potter threatened an Italian, snatched his rifle and marched him off, to hand him over to an escort, who already had two prisoners in charge. Meanwhile the sections led by Holmes had come back with another prisoner after killing several Italians. By this time both Johnstone and Potter had been wounded in the head, but before the patrol withdrew Potter went back to the position his section had assaulted to see if there were any other wounded. There he found

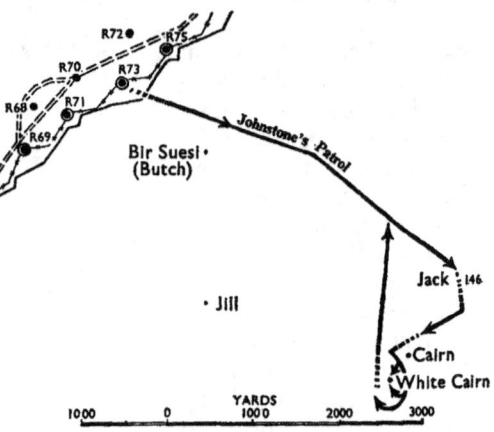

The 2/28th Battalion attack on White Cairn, 13th-14th September

---

[6] Lt A. J. Harrison, MM, VX22425. 2/32 Bn, 1 NGIB. Garage hand; of Prahran, Vic; b. Hay, NSW, 11 Feb 1915.
[7] Maj J. A. Johnstone, WX3427. 24 A-Tk Coy, 2/28 Bn. Commercial traveller; of North Perth, WA; b. Kalgoorlie, WA, 25 Jul 1916.
[8] WO2 A. K. Potter, WX6879; 2/28 Bn. Clerk; of Claremont, WA; b. Melbourne, 10 Jun 1920.
[9] Lt E. L. Holmes, WX7590; 2/28 Bn. Regular soldier; of Victoria Park, WA; b. Fremantle, WA, 21 Dec 1912.

Corporal Hagart[1] calling on three Italians to surrender. When they refused Potter and Hagart grenaded the sangar and rejoined the platoon.

Johnstone's prisoners, of which there were four including an Italian artillery officer of the *Bologna Division,* were dispatched back to divisional headquarters for interrogation. Several important documents were found on the captured officer, including his diary. There he had noted, in an entry dated 11th September:

> The strongpoint I am in (HQ of sub-sector), as indeed with all the other strongpoints, is divided into a number of independent centres of fire, each surrounded by its own wire and with its own munitions for six days (in case of siege).

On 13th September, the date of his capture, he had noted:

> I am C.O. of the O.P. of the 6th Battery (Rubicon) for the whole length (night and day) of the operations in connection with Pt. 146.

Point 146 was the outpost Jack maintained by the 2/28th Battalion. There was much more information to be obtained from the officer about enemy intentions, and the story he was to tell seemed an improbable one. The truck taking him to divisional headquarters slowly threaded its long way back by the rough, dusty, unlit desert tracks; when he got there, the interrogating officer steadily plied him with questions; the star-spiked wheel of the night sky continued its slow turning; minutes ran on into hours before the vital information he gave reached the battalion it most concerned.

That night at 1.30 a.m., just as the moon, in its first quarter, was rising, a call came through to the 2/28th Battalion on the line by which Jack O.P. used to report hour by hour through the night: "Sitrep Sitnor."[2] "Send help at once," an agitated voice was heard to say, against a hammering background of automatic fire, "they're within 20 yards of us." Two carriers which by a standing order stood by to rescue any outpost occupants in an emergency set forth immediately.

Jack was held by seven men, with Corporal France[3] in charge. A protective patrol of 12 men under Sergeant Lally[4] was in position 300 yards to the south. Lally had visited Jack just before the attack began; he was badly wounded while returning to his patrol, which tried to intervene but was driven off by fire from the flanks.

The enemy, who were Germans, had deployed a sizeable force which, after throwing in grenades, advanced against the little outpost in considerable numbers. One of France's men was killed and another wounded. The others slashed the Germans with automatic fire as they swarmed in but surrendered when their pits were about to be overrun. The historian

---

[1] Sgt P. C. Hagart, WX7153; 2/28 Bn. Boiler attendant; of East Guildford, WA; b. Subiaco, WA, 11 Feb 1918.
[2] Situation report, situation normal.
[3] Sgt W. L. France, MM, WX5279; 2/28 Bn. Clerk; of Perth, WA; b. Subiaco, WA, 16 Dec 1916.
[4] Sgt D. A. Lally, WX5288; 2/28 Bn. Apprentice panel beater; of Perth, WA; b. Fremantle, WA, 30 Nov 1919. Died of wounds 17 Sep 1941 at a German dressing station.

of the 2/28th records that Corporal France was taken to General Rommel who congratulated him on his courage and his men's effective resistance.[5]

When the two carriers reached Jack, fighting was continuing. The carriers brought back most of Lally's protective patrol and reported to Colonel Lloyd that the enemy was attacking in great strength; about 100 had taken part in the estimation of the members of Lally's patrol. Lloyd sent Lieutenant Masel out with a stronger force of carriers with instructions to attempt to fight through to the post, but Masel returned and reported that the fighting had ceased and that Jack was strongly held and guarded by from three to five tanks. Lloyd was at first dubious, but about this time divisional headquarters notified the result of the captured Italian officer's interrogation, which confirmed that the outpost was to be attacked in strength by German pioneers and engineers supported by six German and three captured Matilda tanks. The prisoner had also said that German troops with tank support would attack other garrison outposts on the next four nights.

Lloyd asked the 104th R.H.A. for harassing fire on Jack and the 104th R.H.A. put down five rounds' gunfire from one troop on to the area. The infantry wanted more but the artillerymen pointed out that their liberty of action was circumscribed by standing orders designed to conserve ammunition, which quite specifically limited the response to be given to infantry requests for support, except in a big attack. For instance, a call for defensive fire was to be answered by four rounds per minute per gun allotted to the task, to be fired over a maximum of two minutes. Brigadier Godfrey sent for Colonel Matthew, who subsequently ordered the 339th Battery to harass the area with up to 35 rounds per gun from two troops. The commander of the fortress artillery, Brigadier Thompson, placed Feitel's troop of 60-pounders under the command of Matthew as sector artillery commander and removed all ammunition restrictions.

At dawn there was a general stand-to in the sector. Preparations were made to repel an attack and six infantry tanks were moved up to a position by the Bardia Road. No attack occurred, but a daylight patrol confirmed that Jack was strongly held. Throughout the day shelling of the eastern sector was very heavy, and the tension was sustained in the evening when groups of tanks were seen around Jack and two made a demonstration against an observation post (Butch) at Bir Suesi, closer to the perimeter than Jack or Jill; others were heard along the front after nightfall. But the night brought no new attack on the outposts, nor did succeeding nights; possibly the enemy had appreciated the likelihood that his plans had been disclosed.

Captain Feitel's troop of 60-pounders had a busy day on the 14th countering the active enemy artillery. They counter-bombarded five batteries. Next day, however, the enemy conducted an area shoot with observation

---

[5] Rommel is recorded as saying that 102 casualties were inflicted. If this was correct, some were probably caused by artillery fire and mines, to which the Germans' bunching habits made them particularly vulnerable.

from aircraft and accurately shelled garrison troop positions. Ten men of the 2/12th Field Regiment were killed.

The dwindling but irrepressible rumours still circulating round Tobruk that all the Australians in the fortress would follow the 18th Brigade out were revived on the 17th September, when units scheduled to leave in the coming moonlit period were forewarned. The 2/1st Pioneer Battalion and the 24th Brigade less the 2/43rd Battalion, were to be relieved by the 16th British Brigade, commanded by Brigadier C. E. N. Lomax, the 2/12th Field Regiment by the 144th Regiment, R.A., the 2/3rd Anti-Tank Regiment and two batteries of the 3rd R.H.A. by the 149th Anti-Tank Regiment. The 2/7th Field Company was to accompany the 24th Brigade with other units normally attached to the brigade.

To enable Godfrey's brigade to change places with Lomax's brigade in divisional reserve, Murray's brigade relieved Godfrey's brigade between the 18th and 20th September in the eastern sector, which Murray's brigade then held for the first time; but before the last of the 24th Brigade Group had embarked, battalions of the 16th Brigade began to take over the eastern sector. The 20th Brigade returned to divisional reserve.

The 144th Field Regiment arrived in Tobruk on the night of the 18th September to relieve the 2/12th. The 2/12th Regiment's diarist noted:

Since its arrival in the area the Regt has fired approx. 56,000 rounds of which the 75-mm equipments fired 27,000 rounds. Total battle casualties to date: 24 killed and 24 wounded.

An advanced party of the 2/12th left for Egypt on the same night. While the 2/12th handed over to the 144th Field Regiment in Tobruk its mixed assortment of guns and ramshackle tractors and motor trucks, the advanced party of the 2/12th took over at Amiriya, near Alexandria, the 144th Regiment's equipment in its entirety, including twenty-four 25-pounder guns and 36 good tractors. Thus, as it left the battle area, the 2/12th received for the first time the equipment it had trained to use in Australia and which it and the other field regiments of the division had at that time been told would be issued to them as soon as they arrived in the Middle East. It is strange that while some Tobruk gunners were still using 18-pounders, regiments at Mersa Matruh and elsewhere in Egypt which had not been engaging the enemy had received their complete entitlement of the modern guns. But the Tobruk gunners' eyes did not see this, nor therefore did their hearts grieve.

The departure from Tobruk of the 2/1st Pioneer Battalion ended that unit's close association with the 9th Division. Since the battalion had established the left of the switch-line to block the German penetration on 1st May, it had shared front-line duties equally with the infantry battalions. When the 9th Division fought its next campaign, the place of the 2/1st would be taken by the 2/3rd Pioneers.

While the minesweepers and destroyers were ferrying the personnel of the incoming and outgoing units, the "A" lighters were busy bringing in the promised reinforcement of tanks. Twenty-nine were brought in during the September moonless period. The commander of the 32nd Army Tank Brigade, Brigadier Willison,[6] arrived in Tobruk on 17th September and next day his headquarters took over all the garrison's armoured forces from the 3rd Armoured Brigade. Between the 20th and 29th September the headquarters and three squadrons of the 4th Royal Tank Regiment reached the fortress.

This substantial if overdue reinforcement enabled Morshead to employ his armour less sparingly and to distribute some of the tanks closer to sector fronts where a call for their use might be expected. Hitherto, as he observed in the divisional report, having in mind no doubt the morning of the German assault on 1st May, "more than ordinary restraint had to be exercised to avoid over-hasty employment against attacks which might turn out to be feints". However Morshead was not given a completely free hand to employ the tanks. In order to conserve armoured strength for the forthcoming offensive, General Headquarters restricted their use to defence and counter-attack. Approval had to be obtained for their use in attacks; but it was never refused.

The September seaborne relief, called operation SUPERCHARGE by the Royal Navy, was carried out over the period from 17th to 27th September. Almost every night of the moonless period a convoy consisting of one fast minelayer and three destroyers came into Tobruk Harbour and departed within two hours of arrival. Two minelayers and as many as eleven destroyers took part in the relief, while the 7th Cruiser Squadron—the *Ajax, Neptune* and *Hobart*—acted as a covering force.

The much-feared intervention by Axis air forces did not eventuate. The only hostile action during the relief period recorded in the daily naval reports to Morshead's headquarters was an attack on 19th September on a convoy of three lighters bringing in the tanks from Mersa Matruh; a stick of bombs fell harmlessly half a mile from the convoy. In fact, such failures as occurred to meet the month's complete shipping program were due not to enemy action but to the inability of the gallantly-manned little old ships to perform their missions. This was a constant problem throughout the siege. For example, on 20th September three schooners were on their way to Tobruk: the *Maria Giovanni* with 50 tons of ammunition, 115 tons of stores, 2 tons of mail and 24 sheep; the *Hilmi* with 65 tons of ammunition and stores; and the *Khaid el Dine* with 121 tons of ammunition and stores. The schooner *Amin* was delayed with engine defects at Matruh, where her cargo had been discharged. On 21st September the Naval Liaison Officer at Morshead's headquarters reported:

> The schooners *Khaid el Dine* and *Hilmi* did not arrive this morning as scheduled. They met with a series of misfortunes and are now both back at Matruh. The *Khaid el Dine* apparently had no navigational facilities, her steering was unsatisfactory and she was making water in her forehold. She will be sailed to Alex with cargo left onboard, for these defects to be remedied. The *Hilmi's* engines failed at 2300/18 and she was becalmed all day of the 19th. She was sighted off Ishaila Rock a.m. 20th and was towed back to Matruh by *Kos XXI*.

---

[6] Brig A. C. Willison, DSO, MC; comd 32 Army Tk Bde 1941-42. Regular soldier; b. 2 Jan 1896.

The position as regards the *Maria Giovanni* is somewhat obscure. She should have arrived Matruh at 1100/20 but at 1950/20 NOIC Matruh made a signal stating that she had been sighted by *Kos XXI* (who was then picking up the schooner *Hilmi*) some 20 miles West of Matruh steering a N'Westerly course.
No further signals have been received, and it is not known whether she is proceeding direct to Tobruk, or whether she had over-shot the Matruh entrance.

On 24th September he again reported:

Maria Giovanni has returned to Matruh. She had constant engine trouble due to overheating and poor quality fuel. It is intended that she will sail again for Tobruk a.m. 15th Sept.

In operation SUPERCHARGE almost 6,000 men (including 544 wounded) were taken out of Tobruk and 6,300 brought in without incident. On the other hand supply deliveries in September fell short of the delivery rate in the preceding two months by more than 1,000 tons. This was not only because the cargo-carrying capacity of the destroyers was diminished by the requirement to transport troops but also because the relief coincided with the shipping of tank reinforcements to Tobruk, for which the lighters normally employed in carrying stores and ammunition were used, and with a wise confining of almost all shipping movement to and from Tobruk to the relief period when the R.A.F. was providing substantial protection. The suspension of shipping ordered in late August pending the holding of a conference on 30th August to discuss the supply of the garrison was continued after that conference. On 6th September the Naval Liaison Officer reported:

Activities of the Inshore Squadron are practically at a standstill for the present and there is little of interest to report.

The prudence of concentrating sailings within the moonless period was soon confirmed. A destroyer convoy arranged for 8th-9th September, in the moonlit period, which took Morshead to Cairo for the relief discussions, was attacked by bombers both on entering and on leaving the harbour and again on the return voyage, when two destroyers were nearly hit; another which three days later made a moonlit return passage was bombed in the early morning.

The current target rate for supply maintenance was 165 tons per day, including 20 tons per day of petrol, based on a nominal strength of 25,000. The supplies received in September fell short of target by approximately 32 tons per day. But the position was better than the over-all figures suggested. The most critical items were petrol, ammunition and consumable supplies (rations etc.). The *Pass of Balmaha* had brought in another cargo of bulk petrol, which exceeded the month's maintenance scale. Deliveries of consumable supplies at 1,349 tons were short of the target of 1,500 tons based on a nominal strength of 25,000 but almost exactly right for the actual ration strength. The ration position was in fact quite good. Two issues of fresh meat were made in September and at the end of the month the scale of issue for preserved vegetables was increased from 3½ ounces twice weekly to 3½ ounces daily, there being more than 80 days' supplies on hand. Ammunition delivered was 1,110 tons against a target of 1,200 tons, but by internal restrictions the month's expenditure was kept to 1,064 tons; about 60 tons of 37-mm, 75-mm and 18-pounder ammunition (not critical items) had been destroyed by air attack. The main deficiencies in the month's deliveries were in ordnance, engineering and amenities stores. Of these the engineering stores were the most important; but although the 259 tons received in September fell far short of the maintenance scale of 20 tons a day, the month's deliveries greatly exceeded the average for the preceding four months (180 tons).

After the September relief only two Australian brigades remained. No serious attempt was made to disguise the intention that their relief would follow. In September not only the relieving 16th British Brigade Group but also an advanced headquarters of the 6th (British) Division and advanced parties from the division's remaining brigades came to Tobruk. These were sent out to the areas nominated for their parent units to take over on arrival in the next month's relief convoys. Men of the Black Watch, the Durham Light Infantry, the Yorks and Lancs and other regiments fraternised with the diggers. So the Australians remaining in Tobruk no longer husbanded any doubt that the moon had only once more to wane and they would be off.

Notwithstanding the trouble-free execution of the September program, Churchill, or his advisers in Whitehall, or both, were however still obsessed with the notion that to proceed with the relief would pose a serious threat to the success of CRUSADER; or perhaps the fear was that continuance of the relief might set back by a week or more the date when the Prime Minister could announce to the House of Commons and the world the newly constituted Eighth Army's victorious advance to the relief of Tobruk and the wholesale destruction of the German armour in Africa. Of what account by comparison was the faint-hearted, unsoldierly plea that a division that had been under fire for six months was due for relief?

It was not deemed too late to reconsider the orders given, on the Australian Government's firm insistence, to effect a complete relief of the division. The question was reopened on the basis of possible prejudice to the achievement of air superiority. This was an issue on which the British Government, in the light of criticism of lack of air support in past operations, was particularly sensitive. "Air superiority" was an imprecise, not easily definable concept, though the consequences of the lack of it in operationable areas were not indefinable. Many factors ponderable and imponderable contribute to the attainment of mastery in the air by one side or the other at a critical place and critical time. On only one of these factors, the relative strength in fighter aircraft, could the relief of Tobruk have had much effect. In that respect Air Marshal Tedder's problem would have been less acute if the British Service chiefs had matched Churchill's enthusiasm for enterprise in Africa while Germany was heavily involved in Russia by dispatching to the Middle East while such involvement seemed likely to continue more fighter squadrons and some Spitfire aircraft.[7]

The context of the reopened discussions, however, was that Tedder would have only such resources as had been spared and that his pilots flying Hurricanes and Tomahawks were likely to be engaged by German pilots manning Messerschmitt aircraft that could fly higher and faster. Therefore it was not improbable that protection of the Tobruk convoys might prove costly. Even so, the extent to which the relief augmented the existing R.A.F. commitment tended to be exaggerated. The supply commitment of itself necessitated frequent destroyer convoys the number of which could not be much reduced because, on the one hand, the cargo load of destroyers was limited even when troops were not carried and, on the other, the port facilities could not handle larger convoys or bigger loads during the brief time in port. While some ships in a convoy berthed at jetties, others tied up beside submerged wrecks or anchored in midstream and unloaded into lighters.

On the hypothesis that there would be no further major relief the staff conference which had considered the Tobruk supply problem at the end of August had recommended a program of sailings on two nights out of every three in the moonless period. In the event, when the major relief did occur, two of the eleven nights in the moonless period were convoy-free: if there had been no relief, probably only one more night would have been convoy-free. Relief or no relief most of the moonless nights had to be utilised.

On 24th September, while the first phase of the divisional relief was still proceeding, the Chief of the Air Staff in London telegraphed Tedder:

> We clearly realise handicap that would be imposed on you by need to protect ships relieving Tobruk during October moonless period when you should be striving with all your strength to establish highest possible degree of air superiority. Rather than allow this handicap to prejudice success of future Army operations, in particular by necessitating postponement of land offensive, H.M.G. might attempt to persuade Australian Government to agree to discontinue relief operations after present moonless period.
>
> Whether H.M.G. decide to approach Australian Government or not depends on difference which discontinuance of reliefs would make to your prospects. Signal your appreciation on this point to be agreed with C-in-C.

Tedder's reply (dated 29th September) containing as it does an authoritative analysis of the air risk, which was the most important operational objection to the relief's continuance, deserves quotation in full:

> Relief of Tobruk has proceeded smoothly during September moonless period as up to date enemy have made no attacks. Provided the enemy remains inactive the very large amount of flying necessary for protective patrols to cover the shipping engaged on relief can continue without prejudicing future operations more than they are already prejudiced by the necessity for providing protective patrols over supply shipping. If, on the other hand, when the enemy gets wind of the relief operations, he should decide to concentrate against them we would be compelled to maintain much larger covering formations. This would involve using probably

---

[7] Almost 70 per cent of Britain's day-fighter squadrons were kept in Great Britain.

whole fighter force on an operation which is inevitably expensive since enemy has initiative. Heavy losses which may well be incurred under such conditions would seriously prejudice our chances of achieving air superiority before and during CRUSADER operations. Diversion of fighter force must also affect bomber and tactical reconnaissance operations. It depends therefore on the action of the German Air Force as to whether the continuance of the relief does in fact prejudice CRUSADER operations. The discontinuance of the relief would be a great help to Auchinleck and most welcome to C. in C. Mediterranean. As far as I am concerned it would certainly greatly increase our prospects of being in a favourable position vis-a-vis the enemy in the air if any further relief is now stopped.

Blamey and Auchinleck agree.

On the same day, Churchill telegraphed Auchinleck:

It may well be that you will be granted by the enemy the time you have asked. But every day's delay is dearly purchased in the wider sphere. . . . I hope to persuade the Australian Government not to hamper you by pulling out their last two brigades in the October moonless period.

Churchill reopened the question with Fadden in a telegram sent on 30th September. He mentioned that he and the Minister of State had with difficulty prevented Auchinleck from resigning because of the Australian Government's want of confidence: had their decision been based on political grounds, Auchinleck would not have felt the want of confidence implied. He trusted that all troops in Tobruk would be relieved in the great impending operation. The withdrawal of the Australians in October would certainly handicap the air force in their fight for air superiority; every day's delay in delivering the attack would make the task more difficult. The probable date of the offensive was early November and the period during which the two Australian brigades would be involved was very short. After mentioning the implication that Australian troops had been subjected to an undue burden and referring to British losses, Churchill said:

We feel that we are entitled to count on Australia to make every sacrifice necessary for the comradeship of the Empire.

The message was received in Australia on the day on which the Fadden Government was overthrown. While Mr Curtin, the leader of the Labor Party and new Prime Minister, was forming his Government, a reply was sent on 4th October over Mr Fadden's signature; it was, however, discussed with Curtin before it was sent. Fadden denied the imputation of want of confidence in Auchinleck's military judgment and the implication that the Australian Government thought Australian troops had borne an undue burden but, after "most full and careful further consideration", maintained the request that the withdrawal should continue. Churchill informed Auchinleck on 5th October that he could get no helpful response from the late Australian Government. He had not yet made contact with the new Australian Government but trusted that there would be no postponement of CRUSADER.[8]

---

[8] About this time, the Australian Government decided that it would not be practicable, because of manpower difficulties, to form two corps—an Anzac Corps and an Australian Corps in the Middle East.

After what he called a "suitable interval" Churchill made a final appeal to the new Australian Government on 13th October:

> I will not repeat the arguments I have already used, but will only add that if you felt able to consent it would not expose your troops to any undue or invidious risks, and would at the same time be taken very kindly as an act of comradeship in the present struggle.

Curtin replied:

> War Cabinet has considered your request but it is regretted that it does not feel disposed to vary the previous Government's decision which was apparently reached after the fullest review of all the considerations involved.

Auchinleck was therefore instructed that the relief was to proceed. Churchill's final word to the Australian Government was that he regretted their decision.

The initiative in requesting a discontinuance of the 9th Division's relief in October after it had been partially undertaken in September appears to have come not from Auchinleck, who had informed the Prime Minister in September that he did not favour a partial relief, but from Whitehall. The reason given was a continuing anxiety lest it might "prejudice success of future army operations, *in particular by necessitating postponement of land offensive*". But before the last exchanges had taken place, it had become clear, as had indeed appeared probable for some time, that for other reasons the commencement of CRUSADER would have to be deferred for at least a fortnight. Eventually 18th November was set as the starting date, to the great displeasure of Mr Churchill, which he made clear to Auchinleck in a telegram sent on 18th October:

> It is impossible to explain to Parliament and the nation how it is our Middle East armies have had to stand for 4½ months without engaging the enemy while all the time Russia is being battered to pieces. I have hitherto managed to prevent public discussion, but at any time it may break out. Moreover, the few precious weeks that remain to us for the exploitation of any success are passing. No warning has been given to me of your further delay, and no reasons. . . .

Within a year two further differences were to arise between the British and the Australian Governments concerning the employment of Australian formations; in both cases the Australian Government, in the face of great diplomatic pressure, again refused to yield to Mr Churchill's requests. That on the occasion of the Australian Government's insistence on the relief of the 9th Division no less than on the later occasion of its refusal of a division to fight in Burma, Churchill felt most aggrieved, he forcefully made known to the world when he wrote *The Second World War*.

The military issues in the instant case cannot be judged in simple terms of right or wrong; but the course taken by the successive Australian Governments can hardly be impugned, for an Australian Prime Minister who had disregarded or overruled Blamey's advice would have shouldered a grave responsibility. Nor can one call in question General Auchinleck's desire to concentrate all effort on the single purpose of launching the offensive with maximum force. If vindication were needed it is found in the fact that the margin between victory and defeat was never so slight as in that offensive.

General Blamey's approach to the problem must be assessed by weighing long-term against short-term considerations in the prosecution of war. He believed that a policy of regularly relieving formations from front-line duty required to be firmly pursued in the face of the always pressing exigencies of the moment. He also believed in the advice General Brudenell White had given the Australian Government at the commencement of the war, that the Australian formations could be most effectively employed as a single force, whereas Auchinleck's opinion was that it was not practicable to undertake the transfer of a complete corps from Syria to the desert or to find operational employment for the A.I.F. as an undivided force. Whether, if Japan had not entered the war, Blamey's opinion would have been vindicated in the desert campaigns of 1942 must remain an unanswered question. It must also be acknowledged that Blamey wished to avoid "another Greece and Crete experience".

How important, in retrospect, were the reasons for withholding relief? The military objection with most substance was that if the offensive were to be commenced on 1st November, the relieving formation would have little time to plan and prepare for the sortie from Tobruk. A possible solution was to defer the offensive for the short time necessary. The great danger, if this were done, was that the initiative might pass to the enemy. After two deferments CRUSADER was launched on 18th November; Rommel had planned to assault Tobruk on the 20th. But the main reason why that solution was not considered was Churchill's refusal to contemplate a postponement for reasons that took less account of the local tactical situation than of the course of the war on all fronts.

The most serious objection was that of the R.A.F. Even assuming that adherence to the target date of 1st November for launching the offensive was vital, this objection would not have presented itself in so acute a form if General Blamey's request for a relief had been acceded to at once when made and if, in the months immediately following, the relief had been carried out on a larger scale. Some deferment in putting the relief into effect having taken place, a small deferment of the date for opening the offensive beyond 1st November would have mitigated, though not completely solved, the R.A.F's problem. The R.A.F. was not in the event unduly extended.

A valid objection, which was not pressed, could also have been taken on naval grounds. To what extent was it justifiable to call for an additional effort from overworked destroyers to save the 9th Division from overstrain? There can be no final answer to that question, but it must be remembered that it was never certain that the intended relief by land in November would succeed.

That in the perspective of the war as a whole the close engagement of the enemy by the British forces in North Africa at the earliest possible moment was of great importance is undeniable. To Churchill other considerations did not matter. In the opinion of Blamey (which the Australian

Governments accepted) they were no less important. Either Government might have been proved wrong: the British, if CRUSADER had failed; the Australian, if the German Air Force had fought a major battle to prevent the relief. But presupposing the worst possible case, the possible weakening of the CRUSADER offensive that could have resulted from the relief could not have been of such magnitude in relation to the total resources to be employed as to be likely to affect the outcome. Much more would be at stake in the decisions the commanders on both sides would be required to take, and would often wrongly take, day by day, in a most fluid battle.

CHAPTER 9

PARTING SHOTS AND FAREWELL SALUTES

MANNING the Salient defences, which were so exposed, so close to those of the enemy, was still the most dangerous infantry duty to be performed day by day in Tobruk. The diarist of the 2/13th Field Company paid a special tribute to the 2/24th Battalion's work in the Salient in re-siting the tactical wire to obtain maximum advantage from its fire plan, which it did first on the left of the Salient (from 18th August to 1st September) and later on the right (from 8th to 25th September). In both sectors the 2/24th lost a number of men from anti-personnel mines.

Nevertheless the Salient was less dangerous than in the summer months because the defences had been gradually improved by deepening and more overhead cover had been provided. Also the front-line troops of each side had developed a certain amount of tolerance of the other and had unofficially adopted "live-and-let-live" attitudes to some extent. After sundown there was an unofficial truce for three or four hours, more strictly observed, it would appear, on the right of the Salient than on the left, during which both sides brought up their evening meal and undertook tasks on the surface (for example, repairs to wire) that were dangerous at other times. The end of the nightly truce was usually notified by a flare-signal.

There was a curious entry in the diary of the Italian officer captured on the night on which Jack was overrun. Against 1st September he had written:

During the night the British, perhaps having heard of the existence of German patrols, penetrate into the eastern strongpoint, wounding an officer and a soldier.

At this time, on the contrary "the British" knew nothing of patrolling by Germans. If the Germans had been patrolling effectively, they had no less effectively avoided trying conclusions with the garrison's infantry. It had been exceptional throughout the siege to encounter German patrols other than protective patrols about their own defended areas. On the night of 11th September, however, a patrol commanded by Sergeant Buckley[1] of the 2/48th Battalion, which was then on the left of the Salient, perceived a German patrol approaching the company's wire, waited till they were close and opened fire. Three Germans were killed and the rest scattered; but later one of these, apparently lost, came into an Australian post and was captured. He belonged to the *III/258th Battalion*. This was the first intimation of the presence at Tobruk of infantry of the newly-formed *Division Afrika zbV*. The divisional Intelligence summary surmised:

It is thought that they were brought over to release the Lorried Inf for their proper mobile role of supporting an armoured Div.

---

[1] Lt J. A. R. Buckley, MC, SX7985; 2/48 Bn. Insurance clerk; of Glandore, SA; b. Prospect, SA, 14 Jan 1911.

The 16th British Brigade's service in Tobruk was not its first contact with the A.I.F. It had already fought beside Australians in three campaigns: in Wavell's Western Desert offensive, in Crete and in Syria. The staff of the newly-arrived brigade immediately interested itself in the defence arrangements for the sector it was soon to take over. The critical eyes of regular soldiers apparently saw much to find fault with. "No defence scheme exists for Tobruch fortress," a brigade letter circulated on the 23rd September roundly asserted, and next day this deficiency was in part remedied by the issue of 16th Brigade Operation Instruction No. 1, together with a "Plan of Defence—Eastern Sector". Points in the instruction were:

Outposts will be re-occupied as O.Ps. Patrols will be offensive to prevent the enemy encroaching in no-man's land.

Thus the brigade approached its first operational task in Tobruk in a positive and aggressive spirit. Later its "continuous active patrolling and readiness to engage the enemy at every opportunity" were commended in the 9th Division's report; but it was not long before most of the outposts in no-man's land then occupied by garrison troops had been taken over by the enemy and converted to defended localities.

There was good reason for the 16th Brigade to be thinking in definite terms and in detail about action to meet an enemy attack. On 21st September, the day on which it became known that the 16th Brigade would take over from the 20th, Colonel Matthew of the 104th R.H.A. had issued an appreciation in which he examined the recent increase in the enemy's artillery strength in the eastern sector. It showed that opposite Matthew's 24 guns (including 2 anti-aircraft guns) the enemy had 71 guns. (The anti-aircraft guns had only 200 rounds each and were not normally manned; Matthew's purpose was to reserve them for defence against tank attack.) The enemy had 52 field guns against Matthew's 16 25-pounders, and 16 medium and three heavy guns against his four 60-pounders and two 149-mm guns. Matthew deduced that without help from guns in other sectors the enemy artillery opposite him could counter-bombard his guns on a one for one basis and still have sufficient uncommitted guns to fire a "three-hour barrage on 1,500 yards front". He made a further deduction: "There is now a possibility of an attack."

The looming danger was perhaps more keenly appreciated by the artillery than by the infantry. What struck the 20th Brigade, freshly arrived in the sector when Matthew wrote, and then holding it for the first time, was the enemy's remoteness. Nevertheless Colonel Crawford in an operational instruction issued on 19th September had stated that "the area has ceased to be a home of peace" and that "should an enemy attack develop it is appreciated that it will be upon positions south of the BARDIA ROAD". Brigadier Murray and Major Allan, his brigade major, were unhappy about the sector's defence arrangements. They were of the opinion that the second line (Blue Line) defence positions were congested when occupied by both a battalion of the divisional reserve and a battalion of the brigade reserve and were too remote from the perimeter to enable the brigade reserve battalion to intervene quickly if the perimeter was threatened. They recommended that a new position for the brigade reserve battalion should be developed closer to the perimeter behind the tactical (B2) minefield.

The policy of maintaining fixed outposts in no-man's land was considered at a brigade conference on 20th September. There were five of these outposts in the brigade sector: Bondi and Tugun in front of the right battalion—the 2/13th; Jill, Butch and Kim in front of the left— the 2/17th. Neither Bondi nor Jill were visible from the perimeter. It was decided that it would be better to maintain observation by daylight standing patrols sent out to varying points, and in the meantime to send out strong fighter patrols at night to observation-post localities already known to the enemy.

Colonel Burrows decided to put the new policy into effect in a manner intended to bait the supposedly reluctant enemy. On 21st September he ostentatiously withdrew the Tugun garrison in carriers in broad daylight, but sent out a fighting patrol to the area after dark for the entertainment of any enterprising squatters. This produced no result. So next morning two carriers and an armoured car with an artillery observation officer moved out to Tugun, then across to Bondi, from which enemy positions were shelled by observation. The enemy responded by shelling Bondi very heavily. But then orders were received that the 16th Brigade was to relieve the 20th Brigade. Advanced parties from the 2/Queen's arrived, and it was decided to cease stirring up trouble for others to face.

Its defence plan ready made, the 16th British Brigade relieved the 20th Australian Brigade in the eastern sector on the nights of 25th, 26th and 27th September and on the 28th the sector command passed from Brigadier Murray to Brigadier Lomax. The 2/Queen's was on the perimeter on the right, the 2/Leicester on the left; the 2/King's Own on the Blue Line in reserve.

As soon as the 20th Brigade had been relieved in the eastern sector it began to relieve the Polish Brigade in the southern sector. This relief was completed on 30th September. But the Polish Brigade's time in divisional reserve was as short as the 20th Brigade's. On the night of 1st-2nd October the Poles began to take over the western sector from the 26th Brigade, which came back to divisional reserve for a much needed rest after about eight weeks in the dreaded Salient.

In the western sector the 2/43 Battalion, which had earlier replaced the 2/1st Pioneer Battalion as fourth battalion to the 26th Brigade, remained in the sector and came under the command of the Polish Brigade. The Polish cavalry regiment, holding the Wadi Sehel sector, also remained, reverting to the command of its parent formation.

The 16th Brigade's first close contact with the enemy arose from hostile action by an enemy patrol, encountered about a mile south of the perimeter by a patrol of nine men from the 2/Queen's on the night of 2nd-3rd October. The enemy threw grenades. The Englishmen opened fire and, as the enemy withdrew, gave chase, but apparently with insufficient speed to regain contact. Next evening an even more unusual incident occurred. Posts in the Bardia Road sector (held by the 2/Leicester), opposite which the Italian defence line had been conveniently established beyond small-arms range, suddenly came under machine-gun fire from a distance of about 600 yards. A counter-bombardment by artillery and mortars quickly silenced the enemy weapons. "From this and other reports" the divisional Intelligence summary inferred that "the enemy is endeavouring to advance his FDLs in this area".

But interest was soon to switch from the eastern to the southern sector. On the night of the 5th-6th Lieutenant Cartledge[2] took out from the 2/17th Battalion a small patrol comprising himself, a sergeant and two other men. From one of the listening posts established beyond the perimeter on the eastern side of the El Adem Road the four men struck out due south for 2,400 yards until they were close to the enemy minefield. There they saw two enemy parties, each about 27 strong, apparently being guided through the minefield; then a third party, not quite so close, which they followed, at first crawling then swiftly walking. After going to ground and so eluding what appeared to be a roving protective patrol, Cartledge and the others moved in to within 100 yards of an Italian working party, about 50 strong, and opened fire with telling effect, which cries of distress made evident. After engaging for about 10 minutes the patrol was about to close when machine-guns on the flanks and light automatic weapons in front began to whip the desert around them. The four Australians, with ammunition almost exhausted, "scattered towards the north" as Cartledge afterwards said, and came back to the listening post along a pipe-line ditch.

Next night, from just before midnight to dawn, enemy tanks were observed on the front of the 2/17th Battalion near the pipe-line along which Cartledge's patrol had withdrawn, and to the west of Bir el Azazi, at which the outpost Plonk had been established. Plonk consisted of three alternative posts, one of which was normally occupied by seven men of the 2/17th Battalion, with a non-commissioned officer in charge. About 3,000 yards to the south-east of Plonk was the outpost Bondi, garrisoned by nine men of the 2/Queen's. Nine tanks were reported west of Plonk at the one time—more than had been observed when the enemy overran the outpost Jack—and Colonel Crawford of the 2/17th estimated that 14 tanks and 4 other armoured vehicles had been involved. They came within a mile of the perimeter. Crawford thought they were closer than they realised and planned to attack them with tank-hunting platoons and to counter-attack with tanks. It was believed that the tanks were operating to protect working parties rather than offensively, since they moved about noisily.

On the night of the 7th-8th the occupants of Plonk reported five tanks advancing from the south at 12.25 a.m. Others were observed near the pipe-line. Tank-hunting patrols went after the latter and one patrol scored

---

[2] Maj D. J. Cartledge, NX21913. 2/17 Bn 1941-43; 3 Div and 7 Bde 1944-45. Department manager; of Vaucluse, NSW; b. Ashfield, NSW, 21 Feb 1916.

hits on one tank with two "68" grenades. The Plonk standing patrol was normally relieved nightly, but this time was withdrawn without a relief. At dawn the 107th Field Regiment engaged the tanks at Bir el Azazi. Later the enemy heavily shelled the perimeter on either side of the El Adem Road and dive-bombed the troop positions of the 104th and 107th R.H.A. covering the sector. Fifty-one bombers escorted by six fighters took part in the raid. Two guns were put out of action and three gunners killed.

In the evening Brigadier Murray instructed Colonel Crawford to reoccupy Plonk. At last light a patrol of sappers went out and mined the route the enemy tanks had taken on the preceding two nights. Another patrol then set out to occupy the post. Part of this patrol was put to ground by three tanks but they later moved away and the post was entered. A garrison of eight men was left in occupation. Groups of tanks were again reported moving about throughout the night, in one instance accompanied by infantry. Some enemy tanks in the vicinity of the listening post were shelled, but did not move off. Next morning Plonk was heavily bombarded by enemy guns beyond range of the garrison's artillery.

The enemy tank activity seemed to indicate a more offensive intention than the mere protection of Italian working parties against patrols such as Cartledge's. Plans were therefore made, as the divisional report expressed it, "to put an end to this bolstered aggressiveness". It was decided to send out a squadron of 16 infantry tanks and 2 light tanks to Plonk at 9.45 p.m. under orders "to engage and defeat any enemy tanks met with". The 2/17th Battalion and an engineer party had the task of lifting the anti-tank minefield at Plonk and also the mines laid on the preceding night to trap enemy tanks. In addition two gaps were to be made in the perimeter minefield and to be protected by anti-tank guns. Elaborate precautions were taken to identify returning tanks. The identification password was "Welsh Washerwoman", apparently chosen as difficult for Germans to pronounce.

At dusk a patrol of two men was sent out from Plonk to the enemy minefield to the south. It found that a gap of 40 yards had been cleared and a white tape laid. The two Australians picked up the tape and fired on an enemy working party. About 10 enemy followed them most of the way back to Plonk.

Just after dark vehicle engine-noises were heard in the region of Bondi, to the south-east. Artillery defensive fire was put down around the post. Enemy tanks twice approached it before 9 p.m. but withdrew in face of defensive fire. Then the 2/Queen's lost communication with Bondi, but soon after 10 p.m. two men from Bondi came into Plonk with the disturbing news that the garrison of nine men had been overrun in an attack by German infantry and more than 30 tanks.

The squadron of Matilda tanks, which had at first waited on its start-line outside the perimeter for the 2/17th men who were to report that the Plonk minefield had been lifted, was meanwhile proceeding to Plonk under the guidance of Captain McMaster,[3] but moving slowly, so that high engine-noise would not disclose their approach. On the way the squadron met the two men of the 2/Queen's and learnt that Bondi had fallen, also that Plonk had been shelled and one man wounded there. The Matildas went on to Plonk at full speed. Soon after their arrival German tanks were heard coming from the south-east. The British tanks went out to meet them and got within 100 yards before opening fire. A close-range tank-battle developed; the British squadron commander was wounded and his tank disabled. After 15 minutes the German tanks made off and the British followed, but the Matildas were soon outdistanced. One of the British tanks, having mechanical trouble, had meanwhile retired to Plonk where it fought off five German tanks approaching from another direction. While this was occurring McMaster withdrew the infantry patrol from the Plonk positions, which were no longer mined, and brought it back to the perimeter. But soon after midnight a reconnaissance patrol went back and found the area all clear, so the post was reoccupied. The enemy tanks were heard at intervals during the rest of the night, but made no further attack.

Colonel Crawford was putting into effect the policy he had advocated when the 20th Brigade had gone to the eastern sector: to maintain forward observation posts but not to regard the localities taken up as ground to be denied to the enemy at all costs. To give up any ground without a fight in the face of a mere threat, however, was alien to Morshead's temper. On 10th October he directed that the 2/17th Battalion was to hold the Plonk area and to defend it. The brigade orders laid down that the outpost was to be held by two sections of infantrymen under command of an officer, and a section of anti-tank guns from the 20th Anti-Tank Company. Whether further protection should be afforded by additional fighting patrols or other methods was left to Crawford's discretion.

Crawford planned to send out the standing patrol at last light accompanied by two infantry working parties to erect wire, lay minefields and construct gun and weapon pits and by a covering party of one platoon to be stationed 300 yards to the south in order to prevent encirclement round the flanks. In addition to the anti-tank guns the standing patrol was to man four light machine-guns and two mortars. Captain Windeyer[4] was to be in tactical command, Captain Maclarn in charge of the working parties.

By 7.50 p.m. Windeyer and Maclarn had reached Plonk with their men but at 8.40 p.m. the enemy began to shell the area heavily. The bombardment was sustained and continued for more than half an hour. Several men were hit. Some were sent back by stretcher to the perimeter. Windeyer himself was wounded but remained in active command. The working parties were drawn back from the beaten zone, but when the shelling did not abate Windeyer attempted to resume the work under shell fire. Dust

---
[3] Capt I. F. McMaster, MC, NX12510; 2/17 Bn. Studmaster and grazier; of Cassilis, NSW; b. Randwick, NSW, 22 Dec 1907. Died of wounds 2 Nov 1942.
[4] Capt H. F. Windeyer, NX12224; 2/17 Bn. Solicitor; of Sydney; b. Hunter's Hill, NSW, 31 Mar 1914. Died of wounds 17 Oct 1941.

caused by bursting shells reduced visibility to five yards. The ground was stony, hard, and unyielding. Little progress was made.

About 9.20 p.m. the shelling was still continuing and telephone communication from Plonk to the 2/17th Battalion had broken down. It had been reported that German tanks had passed through the minefield gap to the north. Reports had also reached Crawford from his patrols that enemy parties had been observed at two points south-west of Plonk, and that German voices had been heard at both points. The 2/Queen's reported that tanks were pushing in their patrols.

Another half hour passed and still there was the sound of intermittent firing around Plonk but no further word had come back to Crawford. Just before 10 p.m. Lieutenant Reid[5] received orders to proceed to Plonk with all available men of his platoon, his main task being to protect the anti-tank guns. At 10 p.m., however, Maclarn came in and reported that both of the trucks carrying the anti-tank guns had been hit on the way to Plonk. He said that Plonk was "absolutely untenable". Maclarn went back to attempt to recover the anti-tank guns. Reid awaited further orders.

Meanwhile, out to the front, the battle clamour intensified. At 10.50 p.m. Crawford reported to Brigadier Murray that his patrols had been driven back from Plonk by very heavy machine-gun and artillery fire. As they had withdrawn the enemy artillery fire had crept after them until they were almost back to the perimeter. Enemy tanks were moving around the Plonk area.

Crawford now decided to send out Reid's patrol to Plonk to ascertain what the enemy was doing. Reid led out 15 men at 11.15 p.m., met and conferred with Captain Windeyer and then went forward with two men towards Plonk. He reported on his return:

> There were 11 large tanks and five carriers or troop carriers. These latter were small vehicles. The tanks were splayed. Parties were digging on a front of approximately 300 to 400 yards. We heard voices speaking Italian (can identify definitely). At least 30 to 40 men were digging spread over the area right on the line of Plonk. . . . Sounds of tank movements to the flanks and rear were audible.

Maclarn managed to recover both the damaged trucks, with their guns. One gun was out of action but was repaired by the following night.

The standing patrol's enforced withdrawal from Plonk was reported to fortress headquarters just before midnight. Major Hodgman[6] of Morshead's staff told 20th Brigade headquarters that, since the attempt to carry out the orders had failed, he "had no further task" for the 2/17th Battalion. About 3 a.m. the enemy opened a heavy bombardment of the 2/17th Battalion's forward companies; it was estimated that more than 2,000 shells fell in the next four hours. In the night's operations two men had been killed and nine seriously wounded by shell fire. Captain Windeyer was mortally wounded.

---

[5] Capt G. T. Reid, NX13893; 2/17 Bn. Grazier and cattle breeder; of Yass, NSW; b. Sydney, 27 Jun 1908. Killed in action 14 Sep 1943.

[6] Lt-Col S. T. Hodgman, OBE, TX2003. 2/12 Bn; 9 and 3 Divs; GSO1 I Corps 1944-45. Bank officer; of Hobart; b. Burnie, Tas, 18 Nov 1907.

In the no-man's land in front of the 2/Queen's, to the left of the 2/17th, the enemy was also active. The Queen's were establishing a new outpost, called Seaview, to be occupied as an alternative observation site to the overrun Bondi, but the locality was so heavily shelled that the working party was forced to withdraw. At the old Tugun outpost site also enemy tanks were discovered patrolling at 2.30 a.m., but by 5.30 had withdrawn.

Only in the western sector had the defending forces exhibited their normal mastery of no-man's land that night. A patrol from the 2/43rd Battalion ambushed an Italian patrol in the White Knoll region, inflicting fearful slaughter. The Italian patrol had been advancing in two groups; in the forward group, numbering 16, there was only one survivor.

About an hour before sunrise, as soon as the sombre landscape's contours were discernible, the garrison's artillery bombarded Plonk. Yelling and screaming were heard at once. Later there were sounds of picks and shovels being thrown onto a truck, and vehicles drove off to the south. At 6 a.m. Plonk was again bombarded, while a patrol was sent out to see if it was still occupied. About four men were observed walking about the post just after sunrise and were engaged by artillery and machine-guns. Concurrently the enemy guns carried out the customary dawn strafe of the 2/17th's defended localities but with exceptional intensity. Again, just before 8 a.m., eight men were seen at Plonk and engaged, and again the 2/17th's front was bombarded. But soon the warm day's haze and the dust stirred up by gunfire and tank movement and wind made observation of activity at Plonk impossible.

Between 8.30 and 9 a.m., first 6 tanks, then 17, then 20 were reported on the 2/17th Battalion front and some machine-gun fire swept that battalion's defences, which in this sector was unusual. The enemy reoccupied Tugun. A general attack seemed possible. A rehearsal for a planned attack in the Carmusa area by a company of the 2/15th Battalion in conjunction with tanks of the 32nd Armoured Brigade was cancelled soon after 9 a.m. and training cadres and conferences were stopped in order that the whole of the 20th Brigade could be kept in a state of instant readiness. At 9.45 12 tanks were reported hull-down just south of Plonk; but although the enemy continued to be unusually active, there was no attack.

Next night, the 11th-12th, was the culmination of the Plonk operations. Morshead ordered the 20th Brigade to attack and recapture Plonk, and to establish a new outpost in the Plonk area, but not at the site of the old outpost because it was appreciated that the previously held positions were registered by the enemy artillery. As the divisional report later stated:

any place in that vicinity offered as good observation as any other—the main object was to keep the upper hand and to put a stop to the enemy pushing our posts back and advancing his position.

The site chosen for the new post, to be called Cooma, was 1,500 yards south-west of Plonk. The forward troops were to be "C" Company of the 2/17th and any other 2/17th troops detailed and one squadron of the 4th Royal Tank Regiment. A company of the 2/13th Battalion was placed under Colonel Crawford's command as a reserve. The infantry attack on Plonk was to be preceded by a regimental bombardment by the 107th R.H.A.: at slow rate for 20 minutes and rapid rate for 10. The 1st R.H.A. was to put down smoke on the enemy minefield if the wind was favourable.

That night Lieutenant Reid led the 2/17th's assault force of two platoons out from the wire 10 minutes after the beginning of the slow bombardment of Plonk (which to him "appeared to be very poor"). The foremost tanks, all of which should have set off for Plonk 10 minutes earlier, were then just behind the perimeter wire. About half way to Plonk Reid halted his party for the tanks to come up and open fire. Apparently Reid did not know that the tanks which were following behind the first to arrive were strung out (as the movement orders prescribed) at a mile interval between tanks and making only five miles an hour, and that therefore considerable time would pass before the squadron could be assembled on the start-line. Meanwhile the enemy put down defensive artillery fire in front of Plonk and shelled the 2/17th's defences so intensely that, when the bombardment was heard at Brigadier Tovell's distant headquarters, two battalions—the 2/23rd and 2/24th—were made ready to come at call to the assistance of Murray's brigade.

After waiting in vain for the tanks to appear Reid sent back an orderly to report that he proposed to attack Plonk without them, but the orderly soon reappeared to say that he had found the tanks on their start-line. So Reid went back and learnt from the squadron commander that, having got forward late, he had thought it wisest to wait on further instructions. (The inference from the 20th Brigade war diary is that he had not referred to Crawford for these instructions till about 11.45 p.m.) Reid then reported to Crawford, who arranged to repeat the artillery preparation and to re-stage the attack 15 minutes after midnight with such tanks as were available, some having broken down.

Reid went out again to his patrol. Before the artillery program was repeated he and his men could hear digging and talking at Plonk and to the north-west. The bombardment for the attack opened slowly but intensified, the enemy replied with defensive fire, the Matilda tanks from the garrison approached, and Reid moved his patrol to about 300 yards from Plonk.

A tank action began just before 1 a.m. when the British tank commanders discerned enemy tanks about 100 yards ahead and opened fire. The battle was brisk and noisy, punctuated by tank gun reports and the rapid crackling of automatics. Fiery projectiles ricocheted in every direction as though from a carelessly ignited box of fireworks. Enemy tanks were found both in front and to the east and west of Bir el Azazi but the British tanks, though fired on wildly (but, in the darkness, not accurately) from ahead and right and left, advanced steadily onto the objective. The German tanks, still engaging, withdrew in front of the British.

The tanks moved slowly east (Reid wrote in his report) and defensive fire redoubled. My party waited and machine-guns from forward elements of enemy ceased and by the light of a flare I saw one of our tanks on or very close to Plonk. More of our tanks were firing across our front periodically and prevented me from going forward.

The firing ceased at 1.25 a.m., by which time the enemy had gone from Plonk, and for a brief interval no-man's land was quiet. Then one or two gun flickers were seen in the enemy territory and in a moment numerous guns were flashing in a wide semi-circle from west to south to east, their fire converging on Plonk. Never before at Tobruk had such an intensive bombardment been seen; the impressive artillery display struck the watching infantry with awe. While shells were rapidly pounding and exploding upon Plonk, another group of German tanks approached from the west. Again the British tanks drove them off.

It was clear to Reid that by entering Plonk he could achieve nothing but would lose his whole patrol. He sent one section back with a wounded man and with the rest made a sweep for some distance to the east, looking for a machine-gun nest from which fire had come before the British tanks overran Plonk, but failed to find it. Reid then sent back the rest of his men but waited forward for a time before firing (at 2 a.m.) the Very light signal to indicate success of the mission to clear the enemy from Plonk. When the light shot up into the sky, the enemy artillery, probably interpreting it as a signal that the position had been reoccupied, again bombarded.

While each side in turn had been pounding this small patch of desert the work of establishing the new outpost at Cooma had been proceeding. After overrunning Plonk the Matildas had come across to Cooma to protect the infantry and had shielded them from a group of enemy tanks; but later they withdrew within the perimeter. Shortly before 5 a.m. Brigadier Willison ordered the tanks to return to Cooma and to remain out during the day to protect the infantry post, but at 5.17 Crawford reported to brigade headquarters that, although it was getting light, the tanks had not yet reached the minefield gap. He requested permission, which Murray gave, to withdraw the tanks to the forward assembly area.

At sunrise on the 12th 19 German tanks and about half a dozen other vehicles were within view on the front of the 2/17th, mostly near Plonk, which the enemy had again reoccupied, and behind the old outpost a line of sangars could be seen stretching to right and left. Along this line working parties were seen throughout the day. By mid-morning it was reported that Plonk was defensively wired. By mid-afternoon, taking advantage of the mirage which prevented observation of artillery fire, the enemy had run wire south-east from Plonk to the sangar line. Orders were now given that until further notice a squadron of tanks was to provide protection each night for the Cooma outpost, leaving the perimeter at dusk, remaining stationary in close proximity to the post all night, and returning at dawn. In addition two troops of tanks were to be kept at hand throughout the day in a state of instant preparedness to go to the assistance of Cooma. The duty was at first performed by the 4th Royal Tank Regiment, but later for two days by the 7th.

On the evening of the 12th, about an hour after sunset but before the tanks to protect Cooma had left the perimeter, nine German tanks were perceived 90 yards west of Cooma. Crawford asked for permission to withdraw the Cooma patrol, and Murray consented. It came in at 7.30 p.m. For some hours enemy tanks patrolled round Plonk and Cooma and in front of the 2/17th, one or two approaching the perimeter wire. Infantry tank-hunting patrols were organised but failed to make contact. At 1 a.m. the British tank squadron went out. They failed also to make contact with the enemy tanks, but for an hour shot up his working parties. The enemy fired up to 20 anti-tank guns on fixed lines and an erroneous impression was gained in the perimeter that another tank-versus-tank battle was taking place. Meanwhile Cooma was being reoccupied and strengthened.

In the succeeding days, and for the rest of the time that Murray's brigade held the southern sector, Cooma continued to be occupied by the 2/17th and Plonk by the enemy. Each night the squadron of tanks went out to protect Cooma. The enemy, perhaps discouraged by experiences at Plonk, did not attempt to remove the garrison's latest observation post, from which his activities in developing a new defence line could be closely observed. The situation was discussed in an appreciation written on the 13th by Lieutenant Vincent,[7] the Intelligence officer of the 20th Brigade:

> That the enemy intended to push forward his general line in this and eastern sector (he wrote) was known since fall of Jack, though to what extent was unknown. It would seem that he is forming a general line from his strongposts on east of El Adem rd, eastwards south of Plonk, to Bondi.
> Until this new line is well established any large-scale action on the enemy's part in southern sector would seem unlikely.

Two days later the brigade Intelligence summary commented that events seemed to bear out these conclusions and added:

> Now that this is accomplished his activity appears to be concerned with consolidation. The move forward fills in the gap which previously existed between the Bologna and Pavia Divs and which was thought to be held in depth by a small armoured column of some twenty tanks.

What is surprising about the war of the outposts is not that the enemy succeeded in wresting Jack, Bondi and Plonk from the garrison but that the fortress troops with their main force confined within the fixed perimeter line managed to maintain these little strongpoints for so long and, as some fell, to establish others; with what audacity may be appreciated if it is realised, for example, that Bondi could not be seen from the perimeter and was almost three miles beyond it and had been established within the enemy's own minefield at a time when no armoured vehicles more formidable than infantry carriers were available to come to its occupants' rescue. In the latest episode the enemy had been forced

---

[7] Capt M. D. Vincent, NX13867; 2/13 Bn. Station overseer; of Merriwa, NSW; b. Sydney, 7 Apr 1912.

to a major expenditure of effort, not to mention ammunition (in comparison with which the tallies of the Halfaya sniper gun were insignificant), to establish a line of defences some 2,000 yards from the perimeter. Moreover, observations by the counter-battery staff indicated that

in addition to increasing his field artillery for the operation, the enemy also brought round three heavy batteries consisting of the 210-mm howitzers, a battery of 149/35's and an unidentified battery which may be one of the "Harbour Gun" batteries (155-mm).[8]

That week the enemy artillery strength in the southern sector was estimated to be 10 field, 12 medium and 3 heavy batteries—about 100 guns.

Although by a temporary concentration of force the enemy had effectively dominated the region in which he was establishing the new defence line, the policy of offensive defence and dominance of no-man's land was being maintained in the other sectors. On the night of the 12th a squadron of the Polish cavalry successfully raided enemy positions established at Points 22 and 32 on the bluffs running out to the sea west of Wadi Sehel. Early on the 14th a carrier patrol of the 2/King's Own in the eastern sector captured 10 Italians near Bir Suesi and on other nights strong fighting patrols of the King's Own and 2/Queen's successfully shot up enemy working parties.

The time was now approaching for the rest of the 9th Division to leave Tobruk. The final relief operation could prove more difficult than earlier reliefs, not only because several men of the 16th Brigade were missing from operations and it was therefore to be assumed that the enemy would realise that the relief was proceeding, but also because the changing over of units in forward areas would be hard to conceal.

It was more complicated than the previous ones as two complete infantry brigades together with divisional units had to be lifted each way, and it entailed a great deal of movement within the Fortress, as units had to be brought into reserve before they could be finally relieved.[9]

Furthermore, in the first two reliefs, incoming units were able to spend some time for acclimatisation in divisional reserve but on this occasion it would be necessary for some new units to go almost directly into forward positions.

The accompanying diagram shows the manner in which the reliefs were planned. A principle adopted in the previous reliefs was maintained: that an incoming unit should arrive at least one day before the departure of the one it replaced. Thus the number of units available for operational employment was at no time diminished.

As before, the relief was effected by a minelayer and three destroyers which came into Tobruk nearly every night of the moonless period. The first trip was made on the 12th-13th October, the rest on seven out of the nine nights from the evening of the 17th to the morning of the 26th. Most of the convoys brought in 1,000 men and took away a few less.

---
[8] Counter-battery Intelligence summary for week ending 13th October.
[9] 9 Aust Div Report on Operations, para 109.

The convoy on the night of the 12th-13th brought in the 1/Durham Light Infantry and took away, among others, advanced parties of the 26th Brigade Group. During the next three days the Durham Light Infantry relieved the 2/43rd Battalion, taking over the whole of its equipment. The fortress was now one battalion over-strength and the 2/43rd was freed for relief.

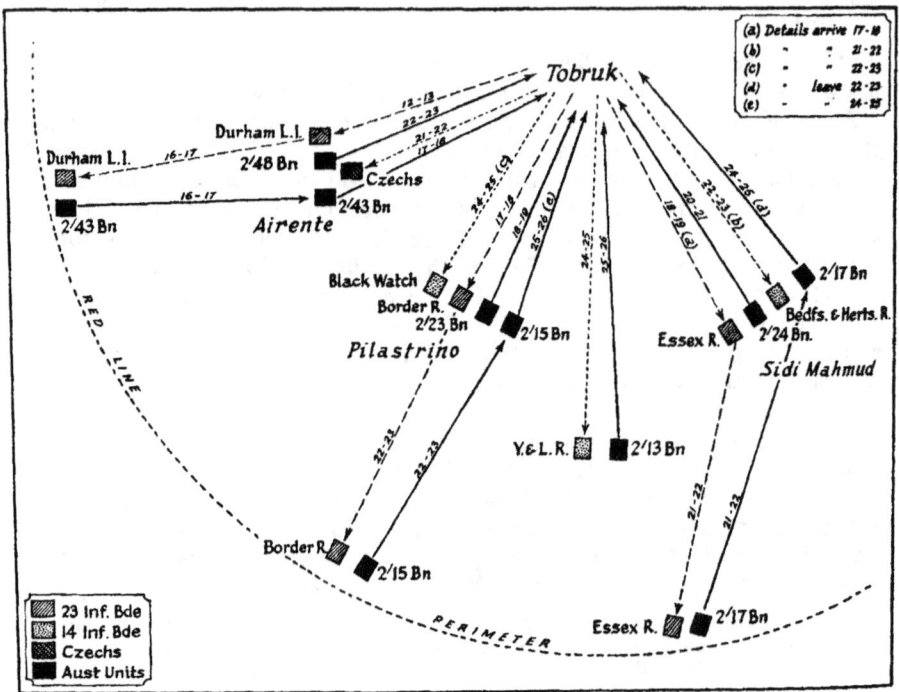

The main unit reliefs then proceeded. On the night of the 17th-18th, the 2/Border relieved the 2/23rd Battalion and the 2/43rd departed; also portion of the 2/Essex arrived and more advanced parties went out. On the night of the 18th-19th the main body of the Essex came in and relieved the 2/24th Battalion, while the 2/23rd Battalion and part of the 2/3rd Field Company departed. On the night 20th-21st, a field ambulance, an anti-tank company and a number of maintenance units arrived, and the 2/24th Battalion, the rest of the 2/3rd Field Company and the 2/11th Field Ambulance departed. On the night 21st-22nd October the 2nd Czechoslovakian Battalion and portion of the 1/Bedfordshire and Hertfordshire came in and a number of headquarters and maintenance groups went out.

Nobody appreciated more than Morshead how much the defence of Tobruk owed to the non-Australian units of the garrison, which had worked in such close integration with the Australian units now departing and which were for the most part to remain. While the reliefs were proceeding he visited them and their commanders. On one day he farewelled

(Australian War Memorial)

Major-General L. J. Morshead, G.O.C. 9th Division (left), with the new commander of Tobruk fortress, Major-General R. MacK. Scobie, shortly before the Australians moved out.

(Australian War Memorial)

The salute after the ceremony at which General Morshead unveiled the memorial at the Tobruk War Cemetery. Designed by Lance-Corporal R. L. Sands of the 2/4th Field Company, the memorial was constructed by the 2/4th and 2/3rd Field Companies in August-September 1941. After the war, because of signs of deterioration, the Commonwealth War Graves Commission erected a new monument with stone quarried from near the El Alamein Cemetery.

(Australian War Memorial)

Australians fraternising with Poles at Tobruk.

(Imperial War Museum)

Australian troops on a destroyer bound for Alexandria on 24th October 1941, after relief from Tobruk. In the background is H.M.S. *Jaguar*, also transporting troops from Tobruk.

the regimental commanders of the five field regiments and on another lunched with Lieut-Colonel Martin and addressed a parade of the 1/Royal Northumberland Fusiliers.

Major-General Scobie,[1] who had now been appointed to succeed Morshead as fortress commander, arrived in Tobruk on the night of the 20th-21st, and next day Morshead took him out to every brigade headquarters. The command of the divisional reserve passed on this day from the 26th Brigade to the 23rd British Brigade, the first of the two incoming brigades, which was now complete in Tobruk. The 23rd Brigade immediately began to change places in the southern sector with the 20th Brigade, which had to come into divisional reserve before relief, and in the evening the 1/Essex relieved the 2/17th.

The 22nd October was the last day of Morshead's command in Tobruk. He farewelled the 4th Anti-Aircraft Brigade, the Polish Carpathian Brigade, the 16th Brigade and the 32nd Tank Brigade. At 5 p.m. he handed over command to Scobie, then went to the shell-holed, bomb-scarred "Admiralty House", where he dined with the naval staff before departing in H.M.S. *Endeavour*.

Several British war diaries recorded Morshead's farewell visits with appreciation. It is unfortunate that the text of none of the addresses he gave has survived. We know what he said and wrote, however, in farewelling a number of units later in the war: there can be little doubt that the theme of these addresses would have been apt, the sentiment poignant and the English scholarly; in fine, that they would have been worthy of their occasions.

That night the relief of the 20th Brigade in the southern sector was continued, the 2/Border relieving the 2/15th Battalion. The rest of the Beds and Herts battalion and portion of the 2/Black Watch came in and the 2/48th and advanced elements of the 2/17th went out. Command of the southern sector passed from the 20th Australian Brigade to the 23rd British Brigade in the afternoon of the 23rd and the relief and withdrawal into divisional reserve of the 20th Brigade (less the 2/13th Battalion) was completed next night. Then on the night of the 24th-25th the rest of the Black Watch and the 2/York and Lancaster arrived and the main body of the 2/17th and the 2/15th less two companies departed. With the hand-over of equipment from the 2/13th to the Yorks and Lancs next day, all was ready for the final act of the controversial relief, the departure of the last contingent of Australians. Brigadier Murray paid farewell visits and at 5 p.m. handed over command of the divisional reserve to the 14th British Brigade. At the end of the day there was a dive-bombing attack on the harbour. When night fell, the relieving British units served a meal to the outgoing Australians, who then began moving off to their embarkation assembly areas.

---

[1] Lt-Gen Sir Ronald Scobie, KBE, CB, MC. Director of Mil Art RMC Duntroon, 1932-35; GOC 70 Div 1941, Tobruk Fortress 1941, Malta 1942; CGS ME 1943; GOC Greece 1944-46. Regular soldier; b. 8 Jun 1893.

The October relief had seemed to start inauspiciously when there was some shelling of the harbour on 17th October and very heavy shelling next day: Admiralty House, beside the harbour foreshore, received a direct hit. Yet the enemy did not show awareness that the relief was proceeding and made no intensive attack. Bomb and mining raids on the port and harbour were abnormally few and of less than normal strength.

A new threat to Tobruk shipping had developed, however, though at first its nature was not apprehended. On 15th October naval headquarters at Tobruk reported that two "A" lighters that had sailed on the night of the 11th had not reached their destination and must be presumed sunk. They had indeed been sunk, on the 12th, by one of the U-boats Hitler had transferred from the Atlantic to the Mediterranean, and which were now based at Salamis. Their operational assignment was to attack the shipping servicing Tobruk.

The Royal Navy was not attempting to conceal that its ships were operating in Tobruk waters but on the contrary was making full use of their presence to do damage to the enemy. H.M.S. *Gnat*, one of the garrison's best warrior-friends afloat, while escorting two "A" lighters to Tobruk, bombarded the harbour-gun battery on the night of the 18th-19th. Next night again she went out and gave the battery another pasting. On the succeeding night, the 20th-21st, *Gnat* sailed for Alexandria but the cruiser escort squadron for the relief convoys, the cruisers *Ajax*, *Hobart* and *Galatea*, carried on the work, bombarding the gun positions in company with two destroyers.

At 4.45 a.m. on the 21st H.M.S. *Gnat* was torpedoed about 60 miles east of Tobruk by the German submarine *U 79*. Her bows were blown off but she did not sink. The nightly relief convoy was at that time to the east of the *Gnat*, making good speed for Alexandria. Four destroyers, including H.M.A.S. *Nizam*, went to *Gnat's* assistance but not long afterwards the Commander-in-Chief ordered them to turn eastward because of threatened air attack. When the *Nizam*, which had part of the 2/24th Battalion aboard, turned in compliance with this order, a huge wave broke over the ship and swept 21 men of the battalion overboard. The *Nizam* turned again and went to their rescue; sailors dived overboard and helped to sustain them; but six men were drowned and two seriously injured, one mortally. Private Godden,[2] a strong swimmer, courageously helped two of the others who probably would not otherwise have survived. Eventually *Gnat* was taken in tow by the destroyer *Griffin* and brought to Alexandria under strong fighter escort. Next day three destroyers bombarded the harbour at Bardia in consequence of a report that an enemy submarine was unloading petrol there, and the cruiser squadron bombarded the petrol dump area at Bardia on the night of the 23rd-24th while four destroyers shot up enemy positions at Salum.

The October moonless period was now ending. On the night of the 25th the moon, almost in its first quarter, was not due to set until 10.27

---

[2] Pte E. Godden, VX24006; 2/24 Bn. Labourer; of Yarraville, Vic; b. West Melbourne, Vic, 29 Dec 1917. Killed in action 14 Sep 1943.

p.m. It was still shining and according fair visibility over the sea as the incoming Tobruk convoy—the last of the relief program—approached the enemy-held shores lying between Salum and Tobruk. The ships were the fast minelayer *Latona* and the destroyers *Hero, Encounter* and *Hotspur*. At 9.5 p.m., about 40 miles east of Tobruk, the convoy was heavily attacked by aircraft. A bomb hit the *Latona* and set her afire. The deck cargo of ammunition exploded, then her magazine blew up. Four officers, twenty naval ratings and seven soldiers were killed. The *Hero* and *Encounter* took off the survivors, the *Hero* being damaged by a near miss while alongside the *Latona*. There could be no question of completing the night's program, but the three destroyers managed to make Alexandria safely next day. Admiral Cunningham and the other Commanders-in-Chief decided that the risks involved "in present moon conditions" were too great to organise a special convoy to bring out the 968 fit and 10 sick or wounded Australians still in Tobruk. They advised the Chiefs of Staff in London:

> Completion of relief has therefore been indefinitely postponed.

Thus operations for the relief of the 9th Division concluded with the loss of some life and a fine ship.

In Tobruk, on the night of the 25th, Brigadier Murray and Major Allan, Major Dodds of Morshead's staff (who had been responsible for the efficient administrative arrangements for the relief) together with the 2/13th Battalion, two companies of the 2/15th, and rear parties of the divisional and 20th Brigade headquarters and supply staffs arrived at the embarkation assembly areas by the harbour side between 10 and 10.30 p.m. and waited for the convoy due to arrive about 11 p.m. At midnight they were still waiting. Half an hour later word was received that the move was cancelled. Between 1.30 and 2.30 a.m. dejected bodies of troops were marched to embussing points, placed on vehicles and taken to areas where they might snatch some sleep and be served breakfast in the morning: 20th Brigade headquarters to Fort Solaro, the 2/13th to Airente (Eagle Corner) and the 2/15th to Pilastrino.

Morshead received many congratulatory messages during the siege, most, but not all, sent after one or other of the garrison's critical actions had been fought. The extent to which they imparted a consoling sense of recognition is indicated by the fact that copies of them circulated from Morshead's headquarters were included in almost every unit diary. The concluding paragraph of the narrative of the siege in the divisional report referred to them:

> Messages of commendation and encouragement were received from the Parliaments of the Commonwealth of Australia and New Zealand, from the Prime Ministers of Great Britain, Australia and New Zealand, the Commanders-in-Chief, the G.O.C. A.I.F. and from many others. These messages were appreciated to an unusual degree; they heartened the whole garrison and inspired them to still greater efforts.

No plaudits hailed the 9th Division, however, as it left the battleground of its hard striving. If there had been some generous impulse to acclaim, perhaps the bitterness engendered by the controversy about the relief had quelled it, just as it tainted the last interchanges between the British and Australian Governments about the division's departure. On 26th October Churchill telegraphed Curtin:

> Our new fast minelayer, *Latona,* was sunk and the destroyer *Hero* damaged by air attack last night in going to fetch the last 1,200 Australians remaining in Tobruk. Providentially, your men were not on board. I do not yet know our casualties. Admiral Cunningham reports that it will not be possible to move these 1,200 men till the next dark period in November. Everything in human power has been done to comply with your wishes.

In a further telegram to Curtin sent next day Churchill detailed the casualties and concluded with the statement:

> We must be thankful these air attacks did not start in the earlier stages of the relief.

Curtin, who had meanwhile heard from Blamey that the relief had been "indefinitely postponed", replied on the 30th:

> You may be interested to know that Inspector-General Medical Services who recently returned from a visit to the Middle East and who saw first units of 9th Division to be relieved reported they had suffered a considerable decline in their physical powers. As condition remainder would have deteriorated further we are naturally anxious that those remaining should be brought away during next dark period as intended.

Perhaps there was less magnanimity in these messages than Burke would have thought wise but the friction remained on the political plane.[3] No sentiments of envy or disapproval were heard in Tobruk to weaken a bond between British, Australian, Indian and Polish fighting men that had been forged in the heat of battle by shared suffering and combined effort.

If the greatest single factor in repelling the German assaults and holding the besiegers off was the steadfast, efficient and brave work of the field artillery which for some of the time was solely and for the whole time preponderantly from the British Army; if the greatest call on deep resources of courage was laid most often upon the anti-aircraft gunners who stood to their guns day and night even when they themselves were the direct target of the strike; if the most dreadful burden borne by the defenders was the constant manning of shallow and sun-scorched diggings and weapon-pits in the regularly bombed, bullet-raked Salient, in which to stand in daylight was to stand for the last time; these judgments only illustrate that each man had his own job in the conduct of the defence. The spontaneous respect of all arms and services for the performance of the others and the loyalty with which they combined were the things that made Tobruk strong in defence and dangerous to its besiegers. General Auchinleck summarised the garrison's achievement in his despatch:

> Our freedom from embarrassment in the frontier area for four and a half months is to be ascribed largely to the defenders of Tobruk. Behaving not as a hardly

---

[3] "Magnanimity in politics is not seldom the truest wisdom"—Edmund Burke: Speech on Conciliation with America.

pressed garrison but as a spirited force ready at any moment to launch an attack, they contained an enemy force twice their strength. By keeping the enemy continually in a high state of tension, they held back four Italian divisions and three German battalions from the frontier area from April until November.

That such success was achieved was due most of all to Morshead's own insistence on an aggressive conduct of the defence; his determination that the enemy should be attacked wherever he came within reach; his single-minded rigid resolve, to which he adhered in the face of counsels for a more flexible defence, that his forces should never yield ground nor give quarter, that if any place was wrested from them, they should not relent until they recaptured it. There were some misjudgments. Sometimes the tasks prescribed could not be done with the means given. Nonetheless Morshead's policy left his opponent no other choice than to let the garrison forces keep their ground, at least until he felt able to mount a massive attack.[4]

Courageous patrolling had contributed not a little to that achievement. If during the siege some magic eye could have captured the comings and goings after dark around Tobruk, each night small groups of men would have been seen going forth into no-man's land from every part of the perimeter, some proceeding along the wire and anti-tank ditch, some covering ground close in and some—probably about thirty in all around the whole perimeter—thrusting deeply into enemy territory. Some went out at night to lie up for the next day, observing the enemy's defenceworks and activities. Others patrolled daringly in daylight.

When the historian thinks of these patrols, names and occasions emerge at random. Take, for example, a brief war-diary entry concerning the 2/24th Battalion: "B company patrols capture 6 officers, 57 other ranks". No wonder a German soldier noted in his private diary captured in mid-April:

> They already have a lot of dead and wounded in the 3rd Company. It is very distressing. In their camp faces are very pale and all eyes . . . downcast. Their nerves are taut to breaking point.

There was the sustained patrolling of the 18th Indian Cavalry Regiment: for example, the patrol on 27th May when Captain Gretton was killed and no fewer than three remarkable patrols by Captain Barlow. There were the brilliantly executed patrols by Lieutenant Harland of the 2/15th

---

[4] The 9th Division's casualties from 8th April to 25th October amounted to 749 killed, 1,996 wounded and 604 prisoners. The infantry losses during this period were:

	K	W	PW		K	W	PW
18 Bde				24 Bde			
2/9 Bn	57	205	—	2/28 Bn	29	92	28
2/10 Bn	39	130	6	2/32 Bn	26	95	3
2/12 Bn	39	172	9	2/43 Bn	48	152	8
20 Bde				26 Bde			
2/13 Bn	40	124	28	2/23 Bn	78	150	79
2/15 Bn	39	103	22	2/24 Bn	70	82	259
2/17 Bn	39	132	14	2/48 Bn	56	102	—
				2/1 Pnr Bn	45	63	9

In this period the artillery lost 44 killed, 106 wounded and 96 were taken prisoner, most of the prisoners being 2/3 A-Tk Regt, captured at Mechili; engineer losses were 30 killed, 112 wounded and 3 prisoners.

The total losses in the 9th Division and attached troops in the period 1st March to 15th December amounted to 832 killed, 2,177 wounded and 941 prisoners.

Battalion in the early siege days; the patrol led by Captain Llewellen Palmer of the King's Dragoon Guards, which created such confusion that the enemy continued fighting among themselves after the patrol had left. There was Lieutenant Beer of the 2/48th Battalion, whose patrol record few rivalled and who on the 29th-30th May with six others wearing sandshoes went out to the by-pass tracks (not yet a formed bitumenised road) at a distance of five miles from the perimeter, mined them and laid up there in ambush for an hour. They boldly began their journey in a captured car but had to abandon it when a wheel got stuck in a slit-trench.

Opposite each sector of the perimeter were localities beyond the wire which had been the scene of adventurous patrol activity. On the west of the perimeter near the coast, across the Wadi Sehel and beyond the garrison's "Cocoa" outposts, the most prominent landmarks were the Twin Pimples, looking like bare-topped rabbit warrens, though the inmates were Italians. Their nights were troubled; death often struck; but their most dreadful night was on 17th-18th July when 40 Special Service troops broke into the heavily-fortified position and overran it, killing all but one of those who did not flee, while a patrol of nine Indians attacked a flanking post. Next night a large Italian working party of well over 100 men, protected by Germans, was successfully shot up by a patrol of the 2/48th Battalion led by Lieutenant Wallis.[5]

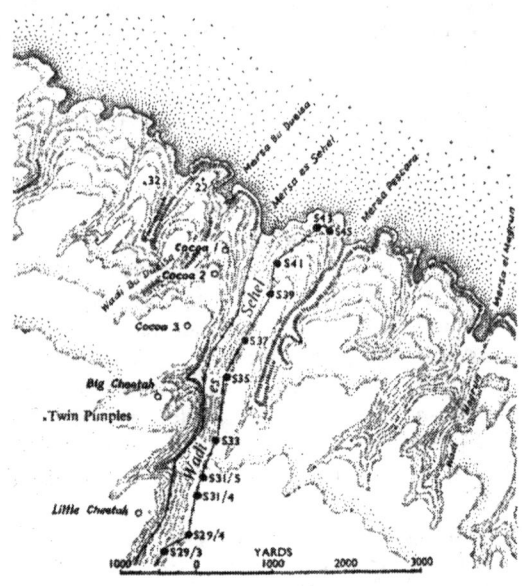

Near the head of the Wadi Sehel the main coast road entered the perimeter south of S21. Here the broken eroded ground provided good cover for the besieging Italians, but the road was under British observation. Vehicles bringing up their rations and supplies had to come by night. On 29th June Lieutenant Nicholls[6] of the 2/1st Pioneer Battalion led out a patrol of six at 9.30 p.m. to intercept the Italians' ration truck on its return journey; by that time they were expected to have relaxed their vigilance. The plot failed because the truck returned by another route. Nicholls then tried to intercept the carrying party but, failing again,

---

[5] Capt D. N. Wallis, SX8048; 2/48 Bn. Salesman; of Fullarton, SA; b. Adelaide, 24 Feb 1916.
[6] Maj H. W. Nicholls, MC, NX15737. 2/1 Pnr Bn, 1 Aust Para Bn and "Z" Special Unit. Clerk; of Leichhardt, NSW; b. Leichhardt, 22 Jul 1920.

decided to attack an enemy position which was manned by about 40 men and armed with three machine-guns and three mortars. Nicholls got close to the sentry undetected and grabbed him as he moved to give the alarm, whereupon his men rushed a sangar and dispatched its eight occupants with the bayonet. A mêlée developed as other enemy came to help their comrades, Corporal Raward[7] repulsed an attack by five but was himself mortally wounded. Private Evans[8] shot an enemy machine-gunner and with Private Jamison[9] got Nicholls' prisoner away.

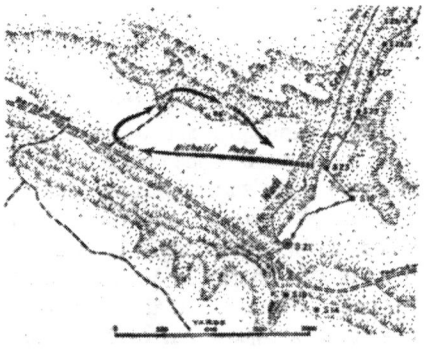

South across the Derna Road and towards the dreaded Salient, the perimeter from S19 to S11 ascended in turn two escarpments. West of S15 on the second escarpment was the feature well-named "White Knoll"; between the two escarpments were a number of enemy sangars and diggings. In this area Lieutenant Beer had one of his most successful nights when a small patrol under his leadership attacked the enemy in vastly superior numbers and brought back a talkative prisoner. On the night of 17th-18th July Captain Buntine's[1] company of the 2/28th Battalion raided enemy positions on the two escarpments. The company was divided into two for the raid. One platoon patrolled uneventfully along the northern escarpment. The main body, finding White Knoll unoccupied, established a base there, and Lieutenants Hall's[2] and Hannah's[3] platoons, with Lance-Corporal Booth[4] as forward scout, launched raids deeper into the enemy's rear, killing 19 of the enemy and wounding twice as many. Corporal France accounted single-handed for two enemy weapon-pits. Only one Australian was wounded.

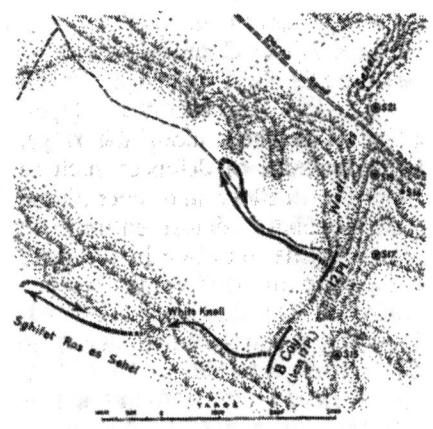

---

[7] Cpl L. V. Raward, NX28174; 2/1 Pnr Bn. Rigger; of Camperdown, NSW; b. Sydney, 9 Jan 1917. Killed in action 30 Jun 1941.
[8] Pte G. D. Evans, MM, NX25549; 2/1 Pnr Bn. Labourer; of Ganmain, NSW; b. Ganmain, 18 Jan 1914.
[9] Pte E. E. Jamison, NX23964; 2/1 Pnr Bn. Plumber; of Gladesville, NSW; b. Hollywood, Ireland, 21 Nov 1911.
[1] Lt-Col M. A. Buntine, WX3378. 2/28 Bn; CO 11 Bn 1942-43. Headmaster; of Perth, WA; b. Melbourne, 27 Dec 1898.
[2] Maj R. J. Hall, WX5262; 2/28 Bn. Shop assistant; of Kalgoorlie, WA; b. Kalgoorlie, 1 Apr 1919.
[3] Capt J. F. Hannah, WX6881; 2/28 Bn. Bank officer; of Subiaco, WA; b. Menzies, WA, 22 Jun 1919.
[4] Cpl F. O. Booth, MM, WX6545; 2/28 Bn. Plumber's assistant; of Wongan Hills, WA; b. Fremantle, WA, 9 Jun 1919.

In the Salient of bitter memory, patrolling against the close and strongly held enemy positions, webbed with booby-traps, was most dangerous. Corporal Weston[5] of the 2/48th and Lieutenant Bucknell of the 2/13th are two names to stand for many who more than once risked death there on night patrol but by stealth and quick action outwitted and killed their opponents. It was in front of this chalky knob, known as Forbes' Mound, that Corporal Leeson's[6] six-man patrol from the 2/32nd Battalion on the 24th-25th July stalked two German crews manning a machine-gun and a mortar. The Germans were moving their weapons from point to point in

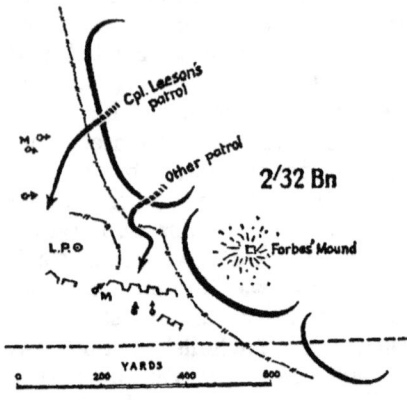

a truck to counter-attack another patrol of the 2/32nd which had become embroiled in a firefight with enemy unexpectedly encountered in sangars close to the Australians' wire.

From the southern shoulder of the Salient the perimeter ran for some distance east-south-east. Parallel to it, and some two miles to the south, ran a low escarpment which petered out near Bir el Carmusa where, as the name implies, there was a well and a fig tree. The enemy developed a line of defences along the ridge. For knowledge of defences such as these the artillery and operational staffs depended almost entirely on patrol reports until late in the siege when some air photographs became available. On the night of 22nd-23rd July a patrol of five men from the 2/43rd Battalion under a non-commissioned officer found a new minefield some 300 to 400 yards from the foot of the escarpment and followed the field in a westerly direction. Here is an extract from the patrol's report, which was accompanied by an excellent diagram of the minefield.

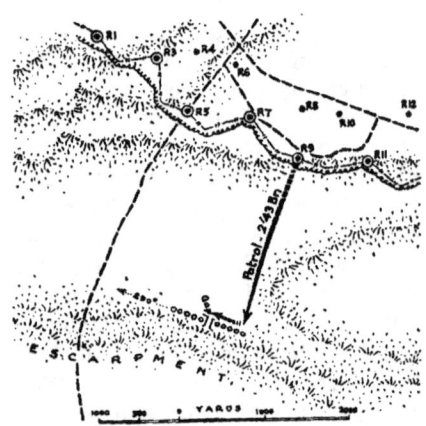

> The bearing of this field is 290°. At this point a gap of 10 yds occurs (39934251) —this gap is marked by trip-wires. The minefield then runs on a bearing of 340° and is composed of 2 rows of anti-personnel and 4 rows of Teller mines. The

---

[5] Sgt J. K. Weston, DCM, MM, SX7808; 2/48 Bn. Tractor driver; of Appila, SA; b. Adelaide, 8 Jan 1912.
[6] Sgt H. T. Leeson, DCM, QX3026; 2/32 Bn. Electrician's labourer; of Maryborough, Qld; b. Childers, Qld, 1 Sep 1918. Killed in action 31 Oct 1942.

spacing of this field is similar except that the AP mines are 9 paces apart, also the mines are staggered. One Teller and one AP mine were brought back. Recent tank tracks exist in the gap in the minefield.

Eastwards was the sector from R21 to R29 where the perimeter bulged out southwards onto the plateau and from which there was a clear view of the fig tree at Bir el Carmusa. On the night of 19th-20th July the 2/10th Battalion sent out two large patrols to operate against enemy positions around Carmusa while the 1st R.H.A. fired an effective artillery program in support. From R23 Lieutenant Ellenby[7] led out a patrol of 21 men including 2 sappers which assaulted the Carmusa strongpoint and inflicted numerous casualties. Ellenby and Private Booker[8] broke through the wire but Ellenby was shot down after he had flung seven grenades into the enemy weapon-pits. At Ellenby's command Booker blew the whistle signal to withdraw.

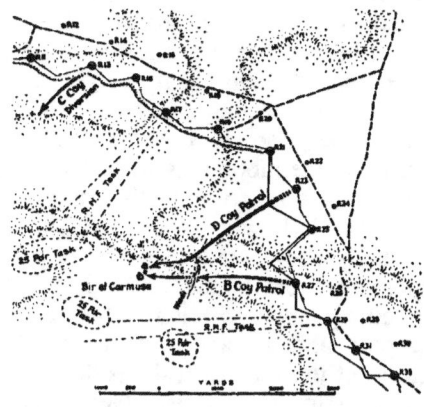

Private Fallon[9] carried Ellenby back to the Australian lines, a distance of 2,750 yards. The other patrol of the same strength, led by Sergeant Seekamp,[1] went out from R27 and was equally successful but encountered very heavy fire from more than 15 machine-guns and had three men wounded.

Farther east the El Adem Road issued from the perimeter between posts R41 and R43. It was from R41 that Lieutenant Haupt with two others of the 2/12th Battalion went out on 10th July to establish an observation post more than three miles from the perimeter. They occupied it for more than 15 hours and throughout one whole day made careful observations of the enemy's doings and the effects of his shelling.

On the night after Haupt returned, Lieutenant A. L. Reid and Sergeant Russell led out two fighting patrols, each of nineteen men, to raid an enemy position astride the road. Support was given by the guns of 1st R.H.A. and the machine-guns of the 1/Royal Northumberland Fusiliers. They drove out the occupants from one position, assaulted another and

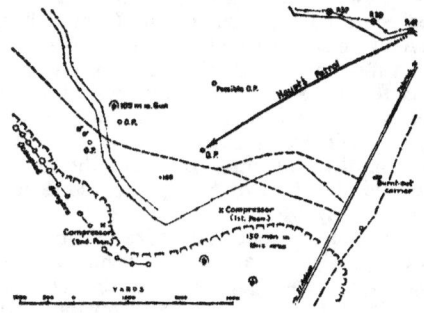

---

[7] Lt M. R. Ellenby, MC, SX1166; 2/10 Bn. Salesman; of St Peters, SA; b. Plympton, SA, 4 Jun 1918.
[8] Pte G. T. Booker, SX2562; 2/10 Bn. Switchboard operator; of Clarence Park, SA; b. Vancouver, Canada, 18 Apr 1920.
[9] Pte M. Fallon, SX1410; 2/10 Bn. Wharf labourer; of Port Lincoln, SA; b. Liverpool, England, 4 Nov 1897. Died 1963.
[1] Lt A. H. Seekamp, SX1192. 2/10, 39 and 2/6 Bns. Labourer; of Berri, SA; b. Berri, 20 Feb 1916.

brought back five prisoners, leaving the ground strewn with dead and wounded. Reid and nine others were wounded and three did not return. The Italian radio described the raid as a foiled attempt to break through the siege lines.

It was from R41, too, that Captain Bode[2] of the 2/15th Battalion led out his patrol of eleven men on 31st August to attack a strongpoint east of the road. Five patrols of the 2/15th had earlier reconnoitred the region, two of them led by Sergeant Patrick,[3] who accompanied Captain Bode. They moved out at 12.15 a.m. when the moon was within one hour of setting so that the night would be dark when they arrived. For the last few hundred yards they approached on hands and knees, formed up about 50 yards behind the post and advanced north. A flare went up, the Australians threw themselves to the ground and a Breda machine-gun opened fire. Next day Chester Wilmot heard Patrick tell Colonel Ogle what ensued.

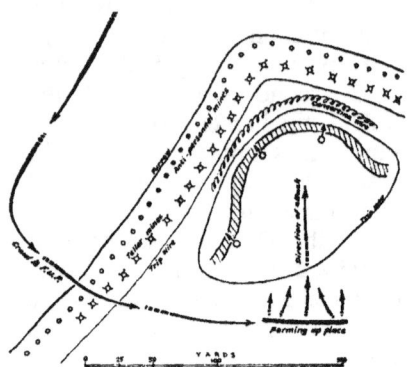

> The firing stopped and Captain Bode said "Come on boys, up and at 'em." We charged. Another flare went up behind us and the Ities must have seen us silhouetted against its light. They swung four machine-guns straight on to us and a volley of hand grenades burst in our path. For a few seconds the dust and flash blinded us, but we went on. In the confusion I ran past the machine-gun pit that I was going for, and a hand grenade—one of the useless Itie money-box type—hit my tin hat. The explosion knocked me down but it didn't hurt me. As I lay there, the fight was going on all around, and I could hear Ities shouting and screaming and our Tommy-guns firing and grenades bursting.
>
> I rolled over and pitched two grenades into the nearest trench and made a dash for the end machine-gun post. I jumped into the pit on top of three Italians, and bayoneted two before my bayonet snapped. I got the third with my revolver as he made for a dug-out where there were at least two other men. I let them have most of my magazine. Another Italian jumped into the pit and I shot him too. He didn't have any papers so I took his shoulder-badges, jumped up and went for my life.
>
> I cleared the concertina wire in front of the post, but caught my foot in a tripwire. Luckily it brought me down, for just then a machine-gun burst got the chap next to me. I wriggled over to him, but he was so badly hit I couldn't do anything to help. I took his last two grenades; crawled out through the booby-traps and then threw one grenade at a machine-gun that was still firing. As this burst, I made a dash for it, and a hundred yards out reached a shell-hole. I waited till it was all quiet again, and then came back.

At one stage Bode, though maimed with a bullet-wound in the hip, attempted to pull two Italians from a five-foot deep weapon-pit but an

---

[2] Capt F. L. Bode, MC, QX6225; 2/15 Bn. Mechanic; of Winton, Qld; b. Winton, 21 Apr 1914. Killed in action 1 Sep 1942.
[3] Sgt R. A. Patrick, MM, QX3000; 2/15 Bn. Dispatch clerk; of Rockhampton, Qld; b. Gladstone, Qld, 15 Dec 1919. Killed in action 1 Sep 1942.

Italian grenade exploded at his feet, temporarily blinding him. Corporal Isaacs[4] went to his leader's assistance, shot the two Italians and shepherded Bode out of the post. As the patrol returned Bode came in singing the old song "My eyes are dim, I cannot see; I have not brought my 'specs' with me." Three Australians, including Bode, were wounded; three were missing.

It was from this sector also that at 8 a.m. on 14th May Lieutenant Maclarn issued from the perimeter near R43 with four carriers taking with him an artillery forward observation officer. They proceeded south for 4,000 yards, and began to direct artillery fire on a tank and other targets. Soon two enemy tanks appeared, then others, making six in all. These engaged Maclarn's carriers, but Maclarn got them back safely to the perimeter, which was re-entered an hour and a half after their departure.

Farther east, opposite the southernmost portion of the perimeter, was the part of no-man's land in which many of the outposts came to be established. It was here that Captain Barnes[5] led ten men of the 2/9th Battalion to locate, cut and bring back portion of an electrical cable previously reported in the Sghifet el Adem. That was nearly 7,000 yards from the perimeter. The patrol proceeded from R53 by way of "White Post" (in the locality later known successively as Bob and Bondi) and the Walled Village, and then worked back and forth along the foot of the escarpment until it found the heavy black cable, which the men then cut under fire. At one stage entrenched enemy engaged the patrol with a machine-gun, a mortar and six light machine-guns. Although nearly four miles from the perimeter Captain Barnes charged the position, inflicting six casualties for two suffered, of whom one was missing.

The south-eastern sector of the perimeter from, say, R63 to R71 was one of the quietest in the early days of the siege though towards its end most activity by both sides was concentrated on this part of no-man's land, for here the British were planning a sortie, the Germans an incursion. The fighting for some of the outposts has already been described. Until late in the siege much of the patrolling in this sector was therefore done with carriers, some at night but mostly by day, and with this phase the names of Lieutenant Masel and Sergeant Rule, both of the 2/28th, will always be associated. A daylight patrol on 10th May by three carriers commanded by Captain Sudholz of the 2/43rd around Point 144 and Trig 146 provides an example of the daring way in which these lightly armoured vehicles were handled. The sketch shows the patrol's

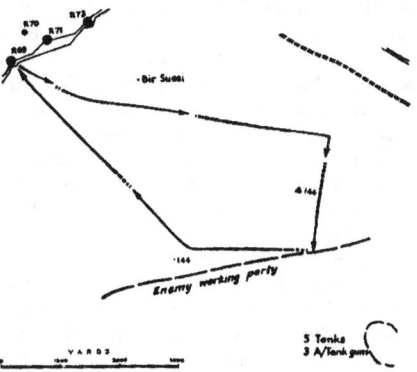

[4] Cpl R. A. N. Isaacs, QX6928; 2/15 Bn. Clerk; of Brisbane; b. Brisbane, 15 Jan 1920.
[5] Lt-Col E. Barnes, QX3615. 2/9 and 8 Bns; CO 19 Bn 1945. Clerk; of Cairns, Qld; b. Ingham, Qld, 31 May 1914.

route. The end of the southward leg of its course brought it upon an Italian working party constructing gun-pits and weapon-pits along a reverse slope. About 1,200 yards to the south-east five enemy tanks and three anti-tank guns were seen. The carriers shot up the working party and were in turn engaged by the tanks and guns. The patrol returned unscathed to report the construction of a new defence line.

Four and a half miles to the south of the perimeter lay Dalby Square, the scene of Captain Joshua's raid on the night 13th-14th September. The report of one of Joshua's preliminary reconnaissance patrols to the area is an excellent example of patrol reporting. Joshua took with him three N.C.O's of his own battalion (the 2/32nd), a sergeant sapper and a corporal and one other man from the 2/43rd.

> The patrol left R65 at 2130 hours, proceeded to BASH OP, and left there on a bearing of 160°. At 1450 yards a white cement obelisk was 50 yards on left of route. At 1900 yards (41944166) a drum with cask on top was 120 yards to left. After passing the cask a small recently constructed dugout was 80 yards to the right of the route. It was camouflaged with bushes, and in front were several rows of stakes 2 feet high, as if ready for wire. Telephone wires led into the dugout from the rear and a foot pad not well worn but recently used ran along the wires. A shovel was leaning against the dugout. At 3800 yards a road was reached. At 3900 yards (42004147) a spur of minefield was met; it consisted of a row of B4 web-type mines, joined together with loose string and hidden under bushes, with two rows of B2 box-type mines about 6 yards to the rear. Bearing of the field was 52°. Sounds of digging and voices were heard on an approximate bearing of 230°. Patrol is unable to estimate the distance but the sounds were a long way off. The patrol turned right and moved along the field for 250 yards, where this spur field met the main field. The engineer devitalised the web-type mines as the patrol moved. He did not touch the B2 mines. At the junction the main field had bearings of 335° and 160°. Patrol turned left and followed the field for approximately 400 yards, reaching a road which appeared to be much used, bearing of road is 300° (41994143). 200 yards west of the junction of road and field is a branch road, bearing 285°. Search was made 60 yards south and 60 yards east from junction of field and road, but no mines were found. Patrol commander and two others moved 100 yards westerly along the road and came to a recently used latrine indicated by a sign "MATTERCINE". 100 yards farther west along the road a sangar was seen (41974144), and party then turned to their right (northerly), and as they turned they heard an alarm from the direction of the sangar. The alarm resembled a blowfly in a spider's web, and was probably made by a wind instrument. Remainder of patrol approximately 200 yards away could clearly hear the alarm. No shots were fired immediately, but shortly afterwards the balance of patrol was fired on by LMG's (estimated 2) from the north-west of the patrol commander and approximately 400 yards from him (41944147). Another MG was to the south or south-west of the patrol commander and approximately 800 yards from him (41904140). This gun had a slower rate of fire. Some rifles were also fired and voices could be plainly heard. The time was then 0200 hours. Patrol withdrew to the junction of the two minefields, moved north 6450 yards meeting a road 40 yards south of the tank trap. Patrol moved 375 yards north along the wire to R69, reaching there 0515 hours.

An earlier excellent patrol in the same region was carried out by the 2/24th Battalion. Moving out from R67 at 9.30 p.m. on the night of 15th-16th July the patrol of two officers and 15 men led by Lieutenant

Hayman[6] investigated a minefield and, stumbling upon two enemy posts at a depth of 6,000 yards from the perimeter, assaulted them inflicting numerous casualties. Hayman and the other officer (Lieutenant Finlay[7]) and three of the men were wounded. One of the men, whose leg seemed to be broken, had to be left. He died later in an Italian hospital. Morshead asked that this patrol's exploits be "fully written up in next Mideast Summary".

Farther east and north was the Bardia Road and the precipitous Wadi Zeitun, held from 21st April onwards by dismounted Army Service Corps men. Here at midnight on 9th-10th July five men of the 2/23rd Battalion were led out by Private Stirk[8] on an adventurous patrol from Z101, the easternmost of more than 100 perimeter strongpoints east of Ras el Medauuar. They intended to take prisoners. The patrol descended the forward slopes of the bluff, passed round the next bluff and set up a base near the mouth of the Wadi Weddan. They patrolled 1,500 yards up the wadi, found no enemy, returned and moved their base to the next wadi to the east, near the 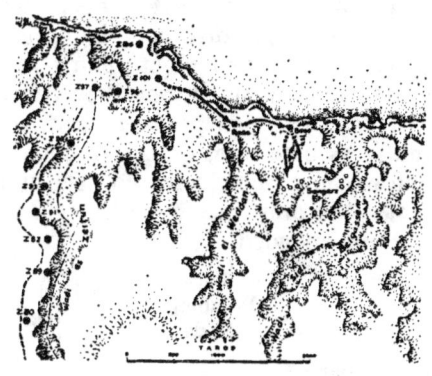 shore. From there they searched some sangars 600 yards to the south but, finding no enemy, returned to their base and waited there until first light.

At dawn Stirk took his men back to the sangars, which were still empty. Then they climbed up a headland ahead of their base to watch an enemy observation post, and saw some movement to the north-east of it. They pushed on 500 yards to the east where they halted a party of three enemy near the mouth of the Wadi Belgassem, two of whom held up their hands. The third made off but they shot him, badly wounding him.

Private Stirk and his four comrades arrived back at Post Z101 at 10.45 a.m. with their two prisoners.

The siege of Tobruk was not, like some famous sieges, a struggle for survival in the face of dire shortages of food or water or munitions. Shortages there were at times but never so acute that men were starving or guns without rounds to fire. For this the main credit must go to the Royal Navy's Inshore Squadron and the garrison's anti-aircraft artillery—the 4th Anti-Aircraft Brigade, commanded by Brigadier Slater. Moreover

---

[6] Capt P. S. Hayman, MC, VX14987; 2/24 Bn. Bank officer; of Elwood, Vic; b. Exeter, SA, 23 Nov 1916. Killed in action 11 Jul 1942.
[7] Capt J. T. Finlay, MC, VX40767; 2/24 Bn. Grazier; of Seymour, Vic; b. Melbourne, 16 Oct 1909.
[8] Pte F. A. Stirk, VX40798; 2/23 Bn. Labourer; of Carlton, Vic; b. Leicester, England, 22 Dec 1914.

the navy's efforts to keep the garrison supplied might have proved abortive or too costly if the anti-aircraft gunners' defence of the harbour and base installations had been less successful. This protective battle was won only by continually improving operating practice and developing new techniques to cope with each change in the enemy's method of attack; it was won by men in under-strength units handicapped by inadequate supplies of gun spares and signal equipment and a scarcity of external labouring assistance. Often the available gun-power was seriously reduced by enemy action; but the speed with which the workshop sections carried out repairs usually reduced the periods of extreme danger to a few hours.

Tobruk's anti-aircraft gunners had to deal with four main types of attack—daylight dive-bombing raids, daylight high-level attacks, night-bombing raids and night-mining raids. As the defenders improved their technique and fire power the enemy changed the method of attack. At first daylight raids predominated, more than half of them dive-bombing raids. As time went on the frequency of dive-bombing attacks diminished and of night raids increased. The trends can be seen in the accompanying table. On only one day during Morshead's command was no air raid warning sounded.

	Dive-Bombing Raids	Total Daylight-Bombing Raids	Night-Bombing Raids	Total Bombing Raids	Daylight Reconnaissances
April 10th-30th	21	41	11	73	27
May	17	60	22	99	58
June	6	58	76	140	39
July	4	91	43	138	46
August	11	55	77	143	39

At the beginning of the siege the anti-aircraft artillery in Tobruk comprised 16 mobile heavy 3.7-inch guns in action and 8 unmounted guns not yet brought into action, 5 mobile and 12 static 40-mm Bofors (of which 6 static guns were not yet in action) and 42 20-mm Bredas. As soon as four of the static 3.7-inch guns were brought into action, four heavy mobile guns were released for perimeter defence to deter dive bombers and artillery observation planes. They were, however, brought back to the harbour region whenever particularly vulnerable targets were in port.

The defensive air battle began with a struggle to defeat the dive bombers, which predominated in the early attacks. With the exception of Brigadier Slater, who had commanded the 4th Anti-Aircraft Brigade with the British Expeditionary Force in France, none of the anti-aircraft personnel in Tobruk had experienced dive-bombing attacks before the siege began. By 14th April, when the first large-scale dive-bombing attack was made, an elementary fixed horizontal barrage at 3,000 feet had been prepared to give protection to the ships and waterside installations. A serious weakness was immediately revealed: aircraft had penetrated unobserved before the barrage was fired. This was successfully countered by establishing an observation post on the escarpment overlooking the harbour. As further attacks developed, other weaknesses were discovered. There appeared to be gaps in the barrage; it had insufficient depth; it was often fired too soon, so that the bombers, discovering its edge, could dive under it. These defects were effectively remedied. The barrage was spread from 3,000 to 6,000 feet and made to swing back and forth across the harbour; the fire was intensified by repairing and bringing into action four captured Italian 102-mm guns. In August, three more of these were added. Pilots who still penetrated the barrage found themselves engaged accurately, and often fatally, by the 12 static 40-mm Bofors guns of the 40th Light Anti-Aircraft Battery, which were disposed singly around the harbour.

In mid-August the Royal Navy provided three 20-barrel parachute rocket projectors whose missiles contained a parachute which opened above the vulnerable area and trailed long strands of wire—like an octopus with long tentacles; at the end of the tentacles was a small bomb. The rockets were first used on 18th August and achieved great success in countering an attack by 18 dive bombers escorted by three fighters. The diving aircraft were completely upset. Two came in contact with bombs and one withdrew with a parachute entangled in its tail.

One of the enemy's counter-measures was to attack the gun-sites. Six guns were put temporarily out of action by these tactics, but none was destroyed. After the lesson had been learnt in May and June that the gunners' safest course in these attacks was not to take cover but to engage the attacking aircraft, it was seldom that an attack on the gun-sites did not result in the destruction of one or more aircraft shattered by direct hits. There were nineteen dive-bombing attacks on the guns from 10th April to 1st September, when the last such attack was made. The effectiveness of this policy in combating the dive bomber can be seen from this table.

Month	Number of dive-bombing raids	Number of dive bombers (Ju-87) engaged
April (last 20 days)	21	386
May	17	277
June	6	123
July	4	79
August	11	217
September	1	46
October (first 9 days)	2	57

When it became evident to the enemy that dive-bombing attacks were proving very costly but not very effective, he swung the weight of his attack into high-level daylight raids. Such raids were carried out daily from 11th April to the end of July. Towards the end of May their frequency increased. Sometimes 10 to 15 attacks were made in one day on the jetties and town area.

These attacks usually took place at heights between 18,000 and 25,000 feet. Observation was the first very difficult problem. Visibility was such that an attacking high-level bomber was seldom seen until it had dropped its bombs, and this from a height from which it could bomb accurately. Efforts were made to get telescopic observation by obtaining an early sound pick-up of the aircraft and predicting a future bearing in which telescopic search could be carried out within the range of likely altitude of approach but, owing to haze and clouds, these met with very limited success. The method next adopted was to attempt to bar the way although the plane could not be seen. A line on which fire was required was drawn just outside the line of bomb release for attack on the vulnerable areas in and around the harbour. Any aircraft approaching a position from which it could attack a target in these areas would be confronted with a barrage of shells bursting immediately ahead in its line of flight. The barrage was divided into four sectors, each the responsibility of one four-gun position. In September a system of decentralised control was developed, each gun position officer firing on his own initiative. As enemy aircraft developed deceptive methods of approach, extremely quick appreciation and decision were required. Some gun-position officers became remarkably adept in outwitting the enemy. The introduction of these barrages bordering the bomb-lines had an immediate effect on bombing accuracy. A large proportion of the bombs fell harmlessly north of the town; some were released over the sea.

After the end of July high-level daylight attacks became less frequent and were mainly confined to times when a particularly inviting target was in the harbour. The scale of night attack, on the other hand, steadily increased month by month from the beginning of the siege until it reached maximum intensity in late summer. The number of night bombers engaged each month was as follows:

April (last 21 nights) . .	32
May	74
June	132
July	126
August	205
September . . .	187
October (first 9 days) . .	152

In April and May most of the night raids were low-flying attacks made for the purpose of dropping "thermos" bombs. In June all night raids except one were high-level bombing attacks, but the scale was not yet heavy. On 21st July the first serious attempt was made to block the harbour mouth with mines. Two more attempts were made in the last week of July and these together with the now mounting scale of bombing attacks constituted a serious threat. On several occasions 50 enemy aircraft operated over Tobruk on one night. As the attacks developed, minelaying and bombing operations were mixed in the same raid to confuse the defence and render the detection of minelaying more difficult. The incidence of night attacks was uneven from week to week since most were made in the moonlit periods, during which the strain of fatigue and lack of sleep told heavily on the gunners.

Until the end of July, night raiders almost invariably approached singly and between 30 and 50 per cent of attacks were turned from their objectives by the barrages. When mine-laying attacks began, listening posts were established and a special barrage illuminated with searchlights was arranged over the ends and centre of the harbour, fired by 22 heavy and 13 light anti-aircraft guns. It was fired when aircraft were heard to be gliding towards the harbour and looked formidable and impenetrable. If fired in time, the raiders took care to avoid it.

From 10th April to 9th October 3,525 aircraft were engaged by anti-aircraft fire over Tobruk. Forty anti-aircraft gunners were killed and 128 wounded and more than 49,000 rounds of 3.7-inch, 3,700 rounds of 40-mm, and 75,000 rounds of 20-mm ammunition fired, in addition to the many thousands of rounds fired from captured Italian weapons. In the same period the headquarters of the anti-aircraft brigade reported 74 aircraft definitely destroyed, 59 probably destroyed and 145 damaged. No aircaft was reported destoyed unless seen to crash. On two occasions when captured documents enabled the brigade's reports to be compared with enemy records, its claims of damage were found to be substantial understatements. It is probable that some 150 enemy aircraft were destroyed.

Attacks by enemy aircraft caused considerable shipping losses on the Tobruk run, but otherwise the damage inflicted was not significant. Except in June, when the *Pass of Balmaha* delivered her 750 tons of petrol in the face of an intensely active enemy air force, the supply position was never critical.

All supplies for Tobruk were brought from ports in Egypt by small ships, some the fastest in the Royal Navy, some plying under sail. Above the seas through which they ploughed their dangerous courses past the enemy-held shore, trailing tell-tale furrows that gleamed white if the night was moonlit, the air forces of the enemy ranged at will and often unchallenged. Submarine attack was a constant danger.

As mentioned earlier, the responsibility for supplying the garrison devolved on the Inshore Squadron which was commanded by Captain Poland from 5th February until the end of the siege. When Rommel's forces first encircled the perimeter, the squadron comprised two destroyers, three river gunboats and other small craft, then used primarily in protective and counter-offensive roles rather than for provisioning. Although most categories of supplies were then held in sufficient quantity for the immediate future, there was considerable port activity. Merchant ships brought in armaments and some short items and evacuated unwanted personnel, wounded and prisoners, using the wreck-strewn harbour almost as much by day as by night.

Shipping using the harbour was subject to constant air attack on an increasing scale. The scarcity of fighters and the abandonment by the Royal Air Force of the use of the more western airfields made the provision of adequate shore-based fighter cover impossible. Losses were heavy. For example, between 12th April and 1st June, the Inshore Squadron itself lost a whaler, 2 armed boarding vessels, 2 minesweepers, a gunboat, a sloop and an anti-submarine trawler, and had four other ships damaged.

Consequently early in May it was decided to use ships of the 10th Destroyer Flotilla (in which were the five Australian destroyers *Stuart, Vendetta, Waterhen, Voyager* and *Vampire*) to provide a supply service. *Voyager* and *Vendetta* made an initial run on 5th May. For the rest of May, however, the destroyer service was on a limited scale because of naval commitments round Crete. Other ships were also used.

After Crete fell the scale of air attack on ships on the Tobruk run intensified. Hence, as recorded earlier, Admiral Cunningham found it necessary, after consulting the other Commanders-in-Chief, to order on 7th June a temporary suspension of all shipping except destroyers, which ran in supplies, off-loaded quickly and made the return run the same night. The destroyers continued a nightly service until 15th June; it was suspended while Operation BATTLEAXE was fought out; it was resumed on 18th June. At that time the Inshore Squadron had 4 destroyers, 3 sloops, 2 gunboats and a number of other small vessels, such as whalers, trawlers, minesweepers, auxiliary schooners and "A" lighters. For some time thereafter the destroyers worked in pairs, two coming in on two nights out of every three.

Some supplementation of the destroyer service by slower ships was necessary. The Royal Air Force was now able to provide better protection than had been possible when Cunningham had suspended the use of all ships except destroyers, but there was need for further improvement. The three Royal Air Force and two South African Air Force squadrons available operated with odds weighted against them. Enemy fighters had closer bases and outranged them. British fighters could patrol for one hour at a range of 100 miles, enemy fighters at a range of 150 miles. The Royal Air Force's most forward refuelling ground at Sidi Barrani was 100 miles from Tobruk.

The problem of providing the supply ships with adequate cover was brought to a head in the last days of June. On the 23rd the petrol carrier *Pass of Balmaha,* whose vital run at the beginning of that month had relieved the garrison in its greatest emergency, set forth from Alexandria on a replenishing mission escorted by the sloops *Auckland* and *Parramatta*. Accompanying her was the store-ship *Antiklia* escorted by the sloop *Flamingo*. The arrangements for fighter cover broke down. Next day the *Auckland* was hit by a bomb and sunk, the *Pass of Balmaha* damaged by a near miss. The *Waterhen* soon reached the scene and took the *Pass of Balmaha* in tow while the *Parramatta,* which had shot down two aircraft, returned to Alexandria with the *Auckland's* survivors. The *Antiklia* was sent into Mersa Matruh until a promise of fighter cover was given. On 27th June *Antiklia* tried again, but returned when heavy weather reduced her speed to 4 knots. On 29th June she and the store-ship *Miranda* set forth, making 6 knots, escorted by a sloop, a whaler and a gunboat. The *Waterhen* was hit by a bomb off Sidi Barrani on the evening of the 29th. The *Defender* took her ship's company on board and after dark took her in tow—and while doing so opened fire on an Italian submarine, which escaped by crash-diving. Later the *Waterhen* capsized and sank. On the afternoon of the 30th the store-ships' convoy was attacked by some 60 fighter-escorted bombers and dive bombers, which were driven off by relays of Royal Air Force and South African Air Force fighters. Each side lost two fighters. The two store-ships reached Tobruk safely, but two of the escorting vessels were damaged. The *Pass of Balmaha* also made Tobruk harbour safely and delivered her cargo.

The Royal Air Force could not afford to sustain fighter cover on the scale provided for the store-ships' convoy, nor could a continuation of the shipping losses suffered notwithstanding such cover be accepted. It was decided to discontinue the service of slow steamers, replacing them by eight "A" lighters, which had a speed of 10 knots. The first pair reached Tobruk on 7th July. At first they had a three-day turn round, arriving one night, unloading on the next and departing on the third. Despite the high frequency of daylight bombing attacks in July, it was soon decided to reduce the turn-round by daylight unloading under camouflage nets. Destroyer runs continued and trial sailings were made by the fast minelayers *Abdiel* and *Latona*. July was a good month for supply, more than 5,000 tons being delivered. A few runs were made by small merchant ships and schooners bringing in both ammunition and much-prized non-essentials, such as "comforts" and fruit.

Schooners were at first sailed into Tobruk on a volunteer basis for a single trip but it was soon evident that an organisation was needed to control and service their activities. In July the Western Desert Schooner Flotilla was constituted by Admiral Cunningham and placed under command of a Falstaffian adventurer, Lieut-Commander Duff. The outrageously unorthodox Duff took up his task with zest and relish.

There were a few ships (Duff wrote later) which ran the whole time, manned by Greeks and Levantines; there was one famous Rock Scorpion vessel, the *Jebel Kebir*; as well as a few Jewish-manned and Jewish-officered Palestinian vessels, which at first flew the Panamanian flag until they changed to the Red Ensign with the badge of the Holy Land; *Sophie, Atid* and others. But the best of the fleet were a few small British ships with entirely British crews, and wherever the White Ensign went, and to some places where it could not go, *Bantria*, a little Cunard "brig", *Volo, Kirkland* and *Rhodi* (she was an Italian prize) carried the Red Duster.

My first task was to organise my flotilla, to pick crews and officers from the very few spare people available, all of them survivors of sunk ships or recently discharged from hospital. I already had a nucleus in the captains of the bigger steel schooners; Lieutenant [A. B.] Palmer, R.N.R., a burly Australian, was skipper of H.M.S. *Maria Giovanni*, and Sub-Lieutenant [I. H.] Laing commanded H.M.S. *Tiberio*. A third schooner *Zingarella*, like her sisters a prize taken from the enemy, had been laid up for months, half-completed, because the dockyard authorities kept putting her back whenever a more important ship was damaged. Then there were eight wooden schooners, all of the usual *merkab* rig, lateen sails, two masted, and of about 200 tons, which had to be manned and fitted out.[9]

A few incidents from the chequered adventures of these weatherbeaten and unseaworthy vessels have already been related. One more, recounted by Duff, will suffice to illustrate the spirit in which the schooners were manned:

---

[9] Duff, *May the Winds Blow*, p. 345.

I was coming back from Mersa Matruh with five of our schooners. We were light, for we had only about half the cargo we could have carried, as the salvage we loaded for our return trip to Alexandria was not so badly wanted at the moment. As dawn broke we were a hundred miles or so from the Great Pass when the look-out reported a large Italian submarine on the surface about a couple of miles ahead. We were running in a rough line-abreast with all sail set before a light breeze on our starboard-quarters. . . .

From my earliest childhood I have had the ambition to hoist a certain signal to armed ships under my sole command, and now my chance had come—that foolish schoolboyish nonsense unworthy, I suppose, of a grown man. The signal was already bent on to our halyards.

"Signalman," I said.

"Sir," he replied.

"Hoist: *Engage the enemy more closely*, please."

"Aye, aye, sir. Hoist 'Engage the enemy more closely'," he answered, and the flags of the hoist fluttered aloft.

Each schooner had an ancient 3-pounder gun on her top-gallant-forecastle—one of the saluting pieces which *Medway* carried in peace-time—and with these pop-guns we went into action with our sails drawing full and our ancient auxiliary engines starting to pop as they warmed. I knew that it would be an almighty fluke if we sank our enemy with our pea-shooters, but there was always the chance that the Italians might surrender. If we had had only one twelve-pounder among the lot of us, I believe that they might have done so, fearing that they had fallen into a "Q" ship ambush, but, as it was, they saw that we could do them very little harm unless one of our tiny shells scored a hit and pierced their pressure-hull, which was extremely unlikely. But they broke off the action quickly enough, for none of the crew were at all anxious to remain on deck with the 3-pounder shells in the air, whistling in from five matronly forecastles.[1]

Supply continued in August on a comparable scale. The *Pass of Balmaha* delivered another cargo of petrol and the merchant ship *Lesbos,* anti-submarine trawler *Wolborough* and schooner *Maria Giovanni* between them brought in 570 tons of stores additional to the deliveries made by minelayers, destroyers and lighters. Better day-fighter protection reduced the losses from air attack, but since night attacks from the air were increasing and continuous night-fighter patrols could not be provided, destroyer sailings in the moonlit period were discontinued at the end of the month.

An account has already been given of the operations in August, including Operation TREACLE in which, covered by a force of cruisers, the two fast minelayers and the destroyers took more than 6,000 troops into Tobruk and brought out more than 5,500, including more than 600 invalids. In the September reliefs (Operation SUPERCHARGE), for which a covering force of three cruisers and still stronger fighter protection were provided, no damage was suffered, though there were two near-misses on destroyers. Vexatious enemy shelling of the harbour increasingly interrupted daylight unloading of the slower vessels but caused no serious loss or disruption. In September 6,308 troops, 3,330 tons of stores, 250 tons of petrol and 29 tanks were delivered to Tobruk, and 5,988 troops, including 544 wounded were taken out. Near the end of the month the auxiliary schooner *Tiberio* had a unique adventure. The Royal Air Force and

---

[1] Duff, pp. 349-51.

Fleet Air Arm had attacked a merchant ship in Bardia on 27th and 28th September. Two days later *Tiberio* was passing Bardia on a routine supply trip to Tobruk when she found herself being escorted by enemy fighters and shortly afterwards under attack by R.A.F. Blenheims. The enemy fighters drove off the unfriendly Blenheims but not before the *Tiberio* had received slight damage from a near miss.

In the final series of relief convoys (Operation CULTIVATE), on the last night of which the *Latona* was sunk and the *Hero*, while alongside her, damaged by a near miss, 7,138 troops were brought in and 7,234 (including 727 wounded) taken out. The losses of the Inshore Squadron were very heavy that month. The *Pass of Balmaha*, the merchant ship *Samos*, a whaler and two "A" lighters were sunk, a merchant and 4 small ships and the gunboat *Gnat* were damaged.

The Inshore Squadron performed its last service for the 9th Australian Division in the series of reliefs that began on 13th November, when the remaining Australians other than the 2/13th Battalion were taken out. The squadron's work of supply and off-shore bombardment continued thereafter both in support of Operation CRUSADER and in later operations of the Eighth Army, until the enemy was driven back to Tripoli.

In the period from 11th April to 9th December 1941 during which enemy forces were around the Tobruk perimeter, 26 naval vessels and 5 merchant ships were sunk and 4 warships and 4 merchant ships seriously damaged in operations connected with holding and defending Tobruk. General Auchinleck has recorded that the ships servicing Tobruk during the siege "transported 72 tanks, 92 guns and 34,000 tons of stores, replaced 32,667 men of the garrison by 34,113 fresh troops and withdrew 7,516 wounded and 7,097 prisoners of war".[2] Royal Australian Navy ships played their part. Australian destroyers—the five already mentioned of the 10th Flotilla and the *Nizam* and *Napier*—made 139 runs in and out of Tobruk. The sloops *Parramatta* and *Yarra* did escort duty, the latter only towards the end of the siege. When the *Parramatta* was sunk by torpedo off Tobruk on 27th November, Admiral Cunningham sent a message of sympathy to the Australian Naval Board:

> I deeply deplore the loss of H.M.A.S. *Parramatta*. This fine little ship had built up for herself a splendid standard of efficiency and achievements fully in keeping with the record of HMA ships in the Mediterranean.

Thus was the struggle to hold Tobruk waged not only around its perimeter and in the sky above its port and base but on its sea lanes and above them. The army in Tobruk could not have held its ground but for the devotion of men in small ships and of men flying obsolescent aeroplanes to protect the ships.

---

[2] Auchinleck, Despatch, p. 343.

CHAPTER 10

ED DUDA

TOBRUK on its desert coast had been enveloped in dust by every land-wind for centuries before the heavy transport and armoured vehicles of two armies had ground its arid fine-clay hinterland to light powder. Airente was the dustiest corner in Tobruk. There, after having been brought back from the embarkation point, the men of the 2/13th Battalion, some of whom had bedded down where they could—but most had not troubled—were greeted on 26th October with the densest duststorm suffered since the siege began. Visibility was only a few feet. The Durham Light Infantry Battalion did its best at short notice to serve the Australians with a hot breakfast.

At midday Brigadier Murray attended a conference with General Scobie to discuss the disposition of the remaining Australians. It was agreed that the two companies of the 2/15th Battalion would remain in the Pilastrino area and could be called upon to provide working parties. General Scobie proposed that the 2/13th Battalion should take over the perimeter in the western sector along the Wadi Sehel near the coast, to carry out the role which he had intended to assign to the Polish Officers' Legion, which was to have arrived in Tobruk in the ships that were to take the last Australians out, but now was not expected to arrive until destroyer convoys were resumed in the November moonless period. Brigadier Murray raised no objection.

Soon afterwards General Scobie visited Colonel Burrows at Airente and offered him a choice between the operational role indicated and a non-operational one. Burrows made the only choice a soldier could. Moreover he knew from his long experience that to have his men at work was the best way of keeping them out of mischief.

The battalion had handed over to the Yorks and Lancs all its equipment except what had been ordered to be carried on the man on embarkation: rifles, pistols and personal accoutrements. It was therefore directed to take over the equipment that had been drawn for the Polish Officers' Legion by the Polish Cavalry Regiment. When it moved forward it was to come under the command of the Polish Brigade, which was responsible for the western and Salient sector. The defences to be occupied constituted a two-company or squadron position; there was also a reserve squadron locality. It was decided that nucleus parties would go out that night to the Polish Cavalry Regiment then holding the area and that three companies would effect the relief on the succeeding night while the fourth waited until an area for it to occupy had been reconnoitred.

Some reorganisation was taking place to strengthen the western sector, in which the front-line units had always been very fully extended. After the Salient line had been shortened, this sector had been held with two battalions in the Salient, one battalion and a cavalry regiment on the western perimeter and one battalion in reserve. It had been planned that on the arrival of the Polish Officers' Legion, which would slightly augment the holding-unit strength beyond that in Morshead's day, the front-line strength would be increased by disposing the cavalry regiment in the centre of the Salient and extending the right flank of the Polish Battalion at the Salient's northern corner, thus removing the inter-battalion boundary from a very vulnerable region overlooked by the enemy positions around S7. By relieving the Polish Cavalry Regiment in the Wadi Sehel, the 2/13th would enable these redispositions to proceed. The perimeter between the Polish Battalion on the right of the Salient and the Wadi Sehel positions to be taken over by the 2/13th Battalion was held by the recently arrived Czechoslovakian Battalion.

The coast sector on the western perimeter was quite unlike anything the 2/13th had known in Tobruk. In other sectors in which it had done front-line duty, the perimeter had opened out onto a terrain which though ridged and uneven in parts was rather flat and featureless, but here the perimeter posts were cut into the cliff-face of a gorge, just below its rim. The wadi they overlooked was about 150 feet deep, with a wide, normally dry watercourse at the bottom.

There were a number of wells in the wadi bed and a pumping station that provided—notwithstanding that it was in no-man's land—a substantial proportion of the fortress's potable water. That the garrison had for so long drawn water from beyond its supposed confines was probably a result of the intensely aggressive patrolling of the Indian and Polish Cavalry Regiments which had kept the enemy on the defensive and deterred him from establishing a defence line or outposts close to the wadi.[1]

Additional protection to the sector and in particular to the pumping station was provided by five outposts: Cocoa 1, 2 and 3, Big Cheetah and Little Cheetah. These were situated on the plateau on the enemy side of the wadi but close to its verge.

The 2/13th advanced parties went out to the sector on the night 26th-27th October. Next morning Major Colvin,[2] Colonel Burrows' second-in-command, went forward to the Polish Cavalry headquarters. Although the preceding day's storm had to some extent abated, dust still shrouded the western perimeter. Major-General Kopanski visited the cavalry headquarters about 10.30 a.m. and informed Colvin that a prisoner captured on the night of the 25th-26th in the Wadi Sehel had stated that an attack would be made on the sector in the early hours of the next morning, the pumping station in the wadi being one of the principal objectives. This prisoner, a Libyan, was a civilian enemy agent—the first apprehended at Tobruk—and had been accompanied by another Libyan who, he said, had come straight from the Italian military Intelligence department at Beda Littoria. The captured Libyan said that he had been ordered by a Captain Bianco of the Italian Intelligence department to ascertain the dispositions in the western sector facing the Wadi Sehel.

---

[1] It is possible that the Axis command, expecting to capture Tobruk, preferred to leave its water-supply intact.
[2] Lt-Col G. E. Colvin, DSO, ED, NX12217. 2/13 Bn (CO 1942-45). Manager; of Roseville, NSW; b. Melbourne, 22 Apr 1903.

Kopanski came back to Airente with Colvin to discuss this information with Burrows. Soon afterwards Scobie arrived and the conference considered whether the relief should proceed as planned at the risk that the Australians might be attacked on the night of their arrival, before they knew the ground. Scobie concluded, however, that an attack on a large scale was improbable, and decided that the relief should take place. Burrows decided that as well as manning the positions to be taken over he would detach a platoon from the reserve company to guard the pumping station. In the early afternoon he went forward to the headquarters of the unit sector.

The relief, in accordance with normal front-line routine, was due to be effected after darkness fell; but at 3.30 p.m. Burrows ordered that the battalion come forward at once under cover of the dust storm then raging. The transport summoned without notice while the drivers were taking their meal arrived in driblets but by 5.45 p.m. battalion headquarters and the forward companies had arrived in the forward sector. The relief was completed by 10 p.m., and soon after midnight the last convoy of outgoing troops departed. The men stood to arms throughout the night to face the predicted attack, but none eventuated.

The 2/13th now held the perimeter from the sea to S33, with the Czechoslovakian Battalion on its left. Two companies were forward: Captain Daintree's on the right, also manning the three Cocoa outposts, and Captain Walsoe's on the left, also responsible for the Cheetahs. Captain Graham's[3] company was in reserve. In the evening of the 28th Captain Handley's company came into a deep reserve position in the Wadi Magrun.

So the men of the 2/13th Battalion settled down to weeks of front-line duty, mercifully uneventful, in the best sector they had known. The rugged gullies and headlands afforded plenty of cover. Moving up and down the wadis and hilly tracks the troops got beneficial exercise; all except those who could not be spared from perimeter defence bathed freely from the beaches of the Mersa Pescara and Mersa el Magrun. The weather cooled; the sun ceased to scorch. The men lost the languor and pallor that had seemed to afflict most of them at the height of the summer. But the *élan* in patrolling that had characterised their early action days was not in evidence, nor did Burrows press his men so much to offensive embroilments as he had in other sectors. Nevertheless they executed a number of deep night patrols, and some in daylight, particularly to the Wadi Bu Dueisa.

The 2/15th Battalion's two companies near Pilastrino, though not exposed to the front's dangers or the strain of night patrolling, were given some burdensome tasks and for a time subjected to less pleasant living conditions than the 2/13th; at the end of October, however, they moved to the Wadi Auda, known as Tobruk's most verdant place but, because of its water-installations, one of the most bombed. The 20th

---

[3] Capt H. T. Graham, NX12375; 2/13 Bn. Clerk; of Coffs Harbour, NSW; b. Ulmarra, NSW, 28 Nov 1917.

Brigade headquarters and the attached rearguard details from the 9th Division headquarters established themselves in the next wadi to the west, the Wadi Tberegh, which was more peaceful.

The Australians left in Tobruk accepted their disappointing situation philosophically. A soldier in the 2/13th wrote these verses which became the unit song—

> O, we're Bull Burrows' Bomb-Happy Boys
> Back up the line we must go!
> Once we were heading for Alex so fair,
> Something went wrong and we didn't get there. . . .[4]

And a ballad writer of the 20th Brigade headquarters wrote:[5]

> "The last of all to leave Tobruk"—
> We felt like heroes—donned our packs,
> We gave away our primus stoves
> And strapped equipment on our backs;
> We said: "It's something to achieve
> To be the very last to leave."
>
> We waited gaily on the wharf
> The inky darkness peering through,
> Some thought they saw the ships arrive
> Before they'd even passed Matruh;
> But soon we learned the game was crook—
> It seemed we wouldn't leave Tobruk. . . .
>
> Sometimes we even start to think,
> When in depression's deepest throes,
> That we are doomed to stay in here
> Till Angel Gabriel's trumpet blows,
> And Peter, taking one quick look,
> Says: "Enter! Last to leave Tobruk!"

The enemy's activities on other sectors and the conformation of his newly developed localities were evidence of the continuation of trends apparent in the last weeks of the 9th Division's command. The shift of operational pressure from the west to the south and east continued. On the last day of the divisional relief it had been reported that the small outpost at Cooma had disappeared and must be presumed lost. On the night of the 27th the party reappeared after an absence of nearly 48 hours, but also on that night enemy infantry accompanied by tanks were seen advancing on foot on the left of the Essex Battalion, which had replaced the 2/17th in the El Adem Road sector. The enemy approached within 300 yards and were then engaged by the infantry. Another party of enemy infiltrated through the wire at R51 and were inside for half an hour; no such penetration, so far as was known, had occurred since the full-scale assault on Medauuar in May. A few hours later two enemy were observed tampering with the perimeter wire close to R47.

Before the 9th Division departed, it had been presumed, from observations of the different behaviour by the troops opposed to the Polish

---

[4] By Pte M. N. Kirby of "C" Company, 2/13 Bn.
[5] Sergeant Hugh Paterson, son of A. B. ("Banjo") Paterson.

Brigade, that an enemy relief had taken place in the Salient. It was now thought that Italian troops might have replaced Germans there. This seemed to be borne out when it was observed that German artillery units had left the sector while batteries of similar guns had appeared in the south-east.

On the 28th the 1st R.H.A. reported that the enemy was busily registering targets—various forward posts—elsewhere than in the Salient while simultaneously the Salient was heavily shelled. Reports of these developments and particularly of the new patrolling pattern in the south-east caused Brigadier Murray concern. He suggested to fortress headquarters on the 28th that the 2/13th Battalion and the companies of the 2/15th should be organised into a composite reserve force and stationed at the vital junction of the El Adem and Bardia Roads, where they could serve as a back-stop against irruption from the south-east. The suggestion was rejected.

The first fortnight of November brought no notable change in the situation. One night the Polish Brigade staged a demonstration assisted by an artillery bombardment and an effective smoke-screen. It evoked an attractive display of flares of all colours from the enemy and a return fire of most satisfactory volume from guns firing from all angles. Special arrangements had been made to plot battery positions by flash spotting. On the night of the 9th the 1/Durham Light Infantry made a courageous attack on Plonk, but with a sad outcome. Though supported by three regiments of 25-pounders and a squadron of tanks, the attackers were handicapped by a difficulty experienced in earlier attacks: sufficient artillery was not available to neutralise both the objective and its flanks. The infantry were caught by flanking fire on the approach and, failing to keep up with the barrage, were badly cut up by small-arms defensive fire and booby-traps at the wire, which they failed to get through. Eight men were missing and fourteen wounded.

The enemy continued his close reconnaissance of the south-eastern perimeter. On the night of the full moon an infantry party 30 to 40 strong approached the wire between R63 and R65, a region in which the anti-tank ditch was only four feet deep. Some got into the ditch but withdrew after being engaged by the infantry on the perimeter. Six nights later, on 10th November, about 40 Germans were discovered inside the perimeter near Post R53. They were contacted by two platoons of the 2/Queens and driven off. One of the enemy patrol was killed and another captured. A week later the German *21st Armoured Division* was reported to be due south of the south-eastern perimeter at a distance of less than nine miles—as the diarist of the 1st R.H.A. recorded, "presumably to watch Tobruk more closely, possibly to launch an attack".

By the second week in November it was generally known in Tobruk that another offensive from Egypt with the object of raising the siege would be mounted very soon. On 7th November the 1st R.H.A. was withdrawn from sector defence responsibilities into divisional reserve and was made fully mobile; many other units had to hand over vehicles to make this possible. Preliminary reconnaissance and engineering work indicated that, as in the plans for BATTLEAXE, a garrison sortie in the south-eastern sector was projected.

To the Australians still in Tobruk the garrison's role in the offensive was of less interest than the enemy's intentions in the meantime. On 5th November sub-unit commanders had been informed that the remaining units and sub-units would be leaving in the convoys of the November moonless period. The 2/13th was warned that half of the battalion should be ready to leave by the 13th—a date which some of them did not deem well chosen; the remainder, including the forward companies, would leave two or three days later, after their relief by the Polish Officers' Legion had been effected.

During the succeeding week there was a revival of enemy high-level and dive-bombing attacks on artillery positions and forward defences and there were more reports of probing enemy patrols near and within the perimeter, which contrasted sharply with his normal conduct at night as experienced over six months. Apprehensiveness grew as to what he was plotting. Then one day Burrows was summoned to fortress headquarters. On the next, the 13th, he called a conference of his company commanders and informed them that the battalion's departure from Tobruk had been deferred till the night of 19th-20th November. In the meantime the battalion would have a role as part of the reserve in operations connected with the offensive from the frontier. When the garrison's sortie was made, the battalion was to be split in two—one half to remain to defend the perimeter by the coast, the other to go to Pilastrino to take up a back-stop position. The battalion was to leave Tobruk not by sea, but by land, it appeared, after the garrison had linked up with the frontier forces. The clock-like precision of the predicted timing was received with some scepticism.

Whereas the general outline of the projected operations was accepted readily enough (wrote an historian of the unit) dates had ceased to be significant; the "push" that had been promised for so long would have to be seen to be believed.[6]

On that night, and the next, all Australians remaining in Tobruk except the 2/13th Battalion were taken out.

Some mystery still surrounds the decision to leave the 2/13th in Tobruk for the CRUSADER operations. One of the few certain facts is that General Sikorski, the Polish Prime Minister and Commander-in-Chief, who was then visiting the Middle East, requested that the two companies of the Officers' Legion with which it had been planned to man the sector of the perimeter where the 2/13th was rendering vicarious service should not be sent to Tobruk. Sikorski desired that they should be held at base where the officers would be needed because of plans to form new Polish divisions in the Middle East. General Headquarters had the request under consideration by 8th November.

---

[6] Maj G. D. Evans in *Bayonets Abroad—A History of the 2/13th Battalion A.I.F. in the Second World War* (1953), p. 128.

Hence the Poles who were to relieve the 2/13th did not come to Tobruk. It may be presumed that General Scobie would have been unwilling to release the 2/13th Battalion until a replacement was forthcoming. Morshead's advice that the garrison should be reinforced with an additional brigade group if it was to make an offensive sortie had not been heeded or, if heeded, not accepted by the General Headquarters; to have adopted it would have created other supply, transportation and order-of-battle problems for the Middle East Command which, however, were not insuperable. The result, whether the reasons for not reinforcing were sound or unsound, was that Scobie's forces would be fully extended to effect the proposed sortie and his reserves depleted, as indeed his plan to block the key Pilastrino pass-head with but two companies of the 2/13th abundantly illustrated. It was decided that the 2/13th should stay.

There is no record that A.I.F. Headquarters was consulted about that decision or agreed to it. If there was such a reference, it is curious that G.H.Q. did not preserve a record of it. It would be even more curious if any officer of the A.I.F. had granted authorisation on a question that had been negotiated between governments at the Prime Minister level, without carefully ensuring that the decision, and the circumstances in which it was taken, were fully recorded. General Blamey was not in Cairo, having been recalled by the Commonwealth Government to Australia for consultation. The better inference, but only an inference, is that General Headquarters decided not to seek Australian concurrence but to present A.I.F. Headquarters with a *fait accompli*.[7] After all, the deferment of the battalion's departure was for only a week.

Only a week! There is no reason to suspect General Scobie of being insincere when he informed the 2/13th that it was to be sent out by road on the night of the 19th-20th November. That he should have thought there was a reasonable prospect of this reflects the optimism imbuing the British higher command with which Scobie had doubtless been infected in the course of the deliberations in which he had taken part before coming to Tobruk. The reborn army's confidence in the likelihood of success was never again surpassed—not even before El Alamein; fortunately so, for it was dangerous over-confidence.

Some explanation must be sought for such excessive optimism. Paradoxically it appears to have been born mainly of past failures. It had become the custom to attribute British defeats in the many reversals hitherto suffered by Allied arms to the fact that battle had always been joined in inferior force, that it had not yet proved possible to confront and fight the enemy on equal terms because he had started so many laps ahead in the armaments race. How often had it been said of the

---

[7] The nucleus of the 2/13th Battalion in Palestine was still making ready to receive the main body until Brigadier Murray arrived from Tobruk on 16th November and informed Major Turner (battalion 2 i/c) that the unit would not arrive for a few days, perhaps a week.
Further slight evidence that the arrangements were made below top level is furnished by a 2/13th Battalion report, which is so detailed as to suggest that it is based on contemporaneous notes, of General Scobie's address to the battalion on 14th December. "When our convoy failed to arrive, he had hoped to send us out the following month. However, when news was received that the Polish Officers' Legion was not coming to Tobruk, and in view of the forthcoming offensive from Sollum, he asked Brigadier Murray and Colonel Burrows if we would be willing to remain in Tobruk to relieve the shortage of troops in the garrison. . . ."

Tommy, the Digger, or the Kiwi, that man for man, he was the equal of his opponent, if not superior! When such had been proved the case, as often it had, it had been important for the maintenance of morale to stress the fact; when such had not been the case, it had still been found expedient to explain failure by attributing it to the arms, and not to the man.

This sentiment pervaded a message published to all troops who were to take part in the offensive—whether from Egypt or from Tobruk—in which the British Prime Minister said that he had it "in command from the King" to express His Majesty's confidence that they would do their duty "with exemplary devotion" in the approaching important battle, in which the Desert Army might "add a page to history" which would rank "with Blenheim and with Waterloo". "For the first time," declared the message, "British and Empire troops will meet the Germans with an ample equipment in modern weapons of all kinds."

The word "ample" was a modest description when the British forces' equipment and administrative resources were compared with the enemy's. Did not the British have twice as many medium tanks as their adversaries —sufficient tanks, in fact, to allot infantry support roles to the cumbrous Matildas and Valentines and still leave the armoured divisions with a comfortable majority of fast tanks for the engagement and defeat of the enemy armour? In artillery, did they not have a like superiority in the number of guns?

At midnight on 26th-27th September 1941, General Cunningham's Western Army Headquarters became Headquarters Eighth Army. Simultaneously Western Desert Force went out of existence and XIII Corps, its successor, was born. Within a few days a new armoured corps was established which, on 21st October, became XXX Corps. Thus a command structure of one army headquarters and two corps headquarters was established.

General Cunningham produced his first plan for operation CRUSADER on 28th September. The plan was much debated and to some extent redrawn before the Eighth Army moved forward into battle seven weeks later; but its main conceptions changed little.

Cunningham was not one to write "approved" to somebody else's plan. "There are two courses open to us,"[8] Auchinleck had earlier written: one, a main thrust along the line of the inland oases, bypassing Tobruk, to the enemy's rear, "whilst maintaining pressure and advancing as opportunity offers along the coast"; the other, a main thrust near the coast south of the escarpment, with two feints "from the centre and south". Cunningham chose a third course; historians and critics have suggested others. Cunningham's plan was to isolate, pin down and cut off the enemy positions by the coast, to feint along the line of oases towards Benghazi and to thrust with the main striking force south of Maddalena—which was perhaps about the direction of thrust Auchinleck earlier had in mind when he wrote of feinting "from the centre".

---

[8] Letter to Lieut-General Sir Alan Cunningham, 2 Sep 1941, quoted in Auchinleck's despatch, *Operations in the Middle East from 1st November 1941 to 15th August 1942*, p. 373.

The 1st Army Tank Brigade of Matildas and Valentines—approximately 145 of them—was assigned to the northern or coast force, to work in conjunction with two infantry divisions, the New Zealand and the 4th Indian. This force was the XIII Corps, commanded by Lieut-General Godwin-Austen.[9] It had the pedestrian role of prising out the enemy ground troops expected to be left stranded in the forward defences by the battle-tide's ebb when others had won the victory.

Cunningham's plan allotted the decisive roles to the three armoured brigades[1] equipped with 500 fast medium tanks—American Honeys, British Crusaders and older British cruisers—whose ingress into enemy-held territory was to be made well to the south of Rommel's fortified line that stretched from Salum to Sidi Omar. Lieut-General Norrie,[2] then commanding the 1st Armoured Division in England, had succeeded Lieut-General Pope as the commander of XXX Corps (which was to be the armoured striking force) after the plan had been framed.

The command structure bestowed on Cunningham, comprising an army headquarters, an armoured corps headquarters with a specialist signals organisation for communication with armoured formations, and an infantry corps headquarters with normal signals organisation, almost invited, if it did not predicate, a separate employment of the armoured and infantry formations. The decision to employ the infantry corps near the coast and the armoured corps in the south after outflanking the Salum-Sidi Omar line in itself divided the army's strength. But the fact that the two corps were to be deployed so distantly from each other that they could not be mutually supporting induced a further subdivision. Cunningham's plan provided for three forces: a northern force, as already described; a southern force, under the command of the armoured corps, to consist of the 7th Armoured Division (including two of the three armoured brigades), the 1st South African Division of two infantry brigades and the 22nd Guards Brigade, with additional anti-tank artillery and medium artillery; and a centre force comprising a reinforced armoured brigade, which was to operate between the northern and southern forces.

In Cunningham's first plan the centre force was to be initially under the command of the XIII Corps. This revealed its primary purpose: to protect the flank of the infantry corps. General Norrie was a contemporary critic of this detachment. There have been many critics since. Norrie pleaded that the armour should be freed from the obligation of protecting the infantry corps. Neither Norrie nor Cunningham's other critics, however, had to take the responsibility (political as well as military) of making and executing a plan which might have exposed the New Zealand Division or the 4th Indian Division, or both in turn, to the concentrated assault of two as yet unmauled German armoured divisions. To avoid splitting

---

[9] General Sir Reade Godwin-Austen, KCSI, CB, OBE, MC. (Served Gallipoli and Mesopotamia, 1915-1919.) Comd 14 Inf Bde 1938-39; GOC Somaliland 1940-41, XIII Corps 1941-42; Director of Tactical Investigation, War Office, 1942-43. Regular soldier; b. 17 Apr 1889. Died 20 Mar 1963.
[1] More correctly, according to contemporary war establishments, one armoured division (the 7th) plus one armoured brigade group.
[2] Lt-Gen Lord Norrie, GCMG, GCVO, CB, DSO, MC. (1914-18: BM 90 Inf Bde and 2 Tk Bde.) Comd 1 Armd Bde 1938-40; GOC 1 Armd Div 1940-41, XXX Corps 1941-42. Governor of Sth Australia 1944-52; Governor-General of New Zealand 1952-57. Regular soldier; b. 26 Sep 1893.

his armour Cunningham had either to run that risk or to devise a plan that would entail employing the armoured corps and the infantry corps closer together; but the course urged upon him—to concentrate his armour astride the enemy communications in the El Adem-Sidi Rezegh area—would have meant employing them farther apart. Cunningham's solution in his final plan was to restore the third armoured brigade to the armoured corps but to give to that corps the additional task of protecting the left flank of the infantry corps.

The conclusion General Cunningham drew from the staff's estimate of the relative tank strengths of the opposing armies ("about 6:4 in our favour") was thus stated in his "appreciation of the situation".

> It should be our endeavour to bring the enemy armoured forces to battle under conditions where we can concentrate against them a numerical superiority in tanks. Our armoured division [i.e. of two armoured brigades] will not have this superiority if faced with both the enemy armoured divisions, and one of our armoured brigades is weaker than one enemy armoured division. In order, therefore, to produce a superiority of tanks against the enemy, as long as the enemy divisions are within inter-supporting distance of each other, a similar condition must apply to our armoured division and our remaining armoured brigade.[3]

This states the principle Cunningham planned to follow more accurately and less unjustly than the impromptu statement attributed to him in a British narrative which it has become the fashion to quote in derogation of the general:

> [The enemy] must either concentrate his armour to defend Bardia or Tobruch, or divide his forces. If the enemy split his forces we could split ours.

The comment was no more than a recognition of the truism that if from each of two unequal quantities the same amount is taken away, the disparity of the remainders is increased (to the advantage of the stronger), or in the instant case that two British armoured brigades against one German armoured division gave better odds than three against two combined; but it is hardly just to quote it as implying that if Rommel were to employ his two armoured divisions in different directions, Cunningham intended as a matter of course to divide his own armour. Rather he was arguing that the enemy could not gain an advantage by splitting his.

Cunningham's final plan called for a triangular deployment of the three armoured brigades around Gabr Saleh, a convenient name on the map near the junction of the track from Bardia with the Trigh el Abd. An armoured force so disposed behind the enemy fortified line from Salum to Sidi Omar could strike north-west to Tobruk, north-east to Bardia or due north to cut communications between the Tobruk and Bardia-frontier zones, seizing supplies stored between the two fronts.

If the object of the excursion was to fight the enemy on ground of one's own choosing, Gabr Saleh may have appeared a curious and indifferent choice; but the real reason for selecting it seems to have been that to be disposed there was the most threatening posture the armour could take up and still meet (or meet half-way) Cunningham's requirements

---
[3] Quoted in Auchinleck's despatch, p. 374.

that the three armoured brigades should be kept "within inter-supporting distance of each other" while simultaneously protecting the flank of an infantry corps charged with the task of containing the enemy's frontier forces.

Of no less importance than the dispositions postulated by the plan which, if they had been adhered to, might have served well enough, were the basic concepts that underlay the thinking of the commanders and which were to exert a more potent influence on their actions than Cunningham's "appreciation". First there was the confident assumption that the destruction of the enemy armour would readily result from its engagement. "If all enemy armour is brought to battle," wrote Cunningham, "the conquest of the rest of Cyrenaica should not be difficult or slow." Hence "the essentials of a plan" as Cunningham saw them were not what a Tobruk defender would have expected:

(i) The enemy armoured forces are the target.
(ii) They must be hemmed in and not allowed to escape.
(iii) The relief of Tobruk must be incidental to the plan.[4]

Another opinion expressed by Cunningham was that "the relief of Tobruk would mean much more to [the enemy] than the loss of Bardia-Salum". From this observation the conclusion was drawn that the way to bring to battle the reluctant German armour seeking "to avoid meeting superior armoured forces" was to develop a threat in the Tobruk area. This belief was very widely held. "What will make enemy move out to meet us?" asked General Auchinleck, and answered his own question: "An obvious move to raise siege of Tobruk." It seems to have occurred to nobody that General Rommel was not one to abandon his own forces to destruction and that a serious threat to his frontier garrisons might have been no less efficacious.

Evolving naturally from the premise that "the enemy armoured forces are the target", the "seek out and destroy" terminology employed to denote the task of the armoured corps exerted its own influence. Writing later but echoing words Cunningham had used in his written instructions to Norrie before the battle, General Auchinleck thus described the initial role of the armoured forces:

> The three armoured brigades were concentrated in the 30th Corps and General Norrie was instructed to seek out and destroy the enemy's armour.

The phrase may have induced a happy hunting mood. It was hardly likely to call forth the restraint and imperturbability needed to bring the enemy to battle on ground one has both chosen and got ready.

The exercise of military command becomes real when the commander passes from stating a general purpose to determining courses of action that will accomplish it. But the proposition that the enemy armoured forces were the target was a notion from which neither a plan nor a guiding principle could be derived for the very reason that the target was mobile.

---
[4] Auchinleck despatch, p. 374.

Although Cunningham may have intended not only to stage-manage the first clash but also to provide a new formulation and fresh impulse at every turn of battle, the possibility that his forces might be committed as a result of decisions neither of his own making nor impressed with his will was inherent in the way he conceived the "essentials of a plan". With the precept "seek out and destroy" ringing in their ears, subordinate commanders were hardly likely to wait upon definitions of a master plan before engaging.

To exhort subordinate commanders to seek out and destroy their enemies might not have worked disastrously if they and the formations they commanded had been more than a match for their opponents, but experience was to prove that they were outmatched. Comparisons of the quality and quantity of each side's equipment, showing for example that the British had more but the Axis heavier guns or that the British were the stronger in tanks, the Axis in anti-tank guns, do not provide the main reason, which was that the Germans had, but the British lacked, a sound tactical doctrine for the employment of armoured forces. A separation of the operations and training functions at the higher levels of the British command structure may have contributed to this lack, for in the employment of armoured forces the commanders consistently failed to practise what the training staff had preached. The cardinal difference was that the Germans fought their tanks in close conjunction with guns and other arms whereas the British, notwithstanding that their tanks mounted a lesser variety of weapons than those of their opponents, for the most part expected their tanks to fight with little aid from other arms, except in set-piece operations. What this meant in practice is well illustrated by some comments made by the South African historians:

> The artillery of the British 30th Corps comprised one hundred and fifty-six field-guns. . . . Even if the infantry formations be excluded—and if their artillery is not to be taken into account, why were they in the Corps?—7th Armoured Division alone could muster eighty-four field-guns against sixty 105 and 150-mms of D.A.K.[5] However, when the Crusader operation came to be fought out in November of 1941, each British armoured brigade was committed separately, and 4th, 7th and 22nd Armoured Brigades went into action with twenty-four, sixteen and eight field-guns respectively. The sixteen mediums of 7th Medium Regiment R.A. were not with the armour at all, but had been assigned to 1st S.A. Division. . . . 7th Armoured Brigade had sixteen field-guns and four 2-pounders, and in the critical midday battle of 21 November this Brigade, less a regiment of its tanks, was called upon to engage the whole of D.A.K., which controlled forty field-guns, twenty mediums, sixty-three 50-mm and twenty-one 37-mm anti-tank guns—to say nothing of the 88s and the lighter anti-aircraft artillery.[6]

Not only did the Germans bring more guns to the fray. They had better anti-tank guns, they used them to better advantage and, as in operation BATTLEAXE, they used 88-mm anti-aircraft guns as anti-tank weapons, which could destroy a British tank from well beyond the reach of its 2-pounder gun.

In the first phase General Godwin-Austen's XIII Corps (New Zealand

---
[5] *Africa Corps.*
[6] J. A. I. Agar-Hamilton and L. C. F. Turner, *The Sidi Rezeg Battles 1941* (1957), pp. 54-5, a volume in the official war history of the Union of South Africa.

Division, 4th Indian Division, 1st Army Tank Brigade) was to prevent the enemy frontier garrisons from moving east or south while General Norrie's XXX Corps (7th Armoured Division, 4th Armoured Brigade Group, 1st South African Division and 22nd Guards Brigade) was to destroy the enemy's armoured forces, employing the armoured brigades, or at least two of them, to do so. In the next phase, *after the hostile armour had been destroyed*, the XXX Corps, using the South African division (of two infantry brigades) as well as the armoured brigades, was to break the siege of Tobruk by joining up with a sally force from the fortress; it was intended that the South Africans should seize Sidi Rezegh and the neighbouring ridges, the Tobruk forces Ed Duda—while the XIII Corps cleared the enemy from between the frontier and Tobruk. All would then be set to complete the capture of Cyrenaica, reduce the abandoned garrisons on the Egyptian frontier and proceed to the capture of Tripolitania.

That was not the way the battle went. In the first phase the British armoured corps, far from destroying the German armoured divisions, was itself almost destroyed. Moreover, before the German armour had even been encountered, Sidi Rezegh was seized with only one armoured brigade (plus a weak support group) and without the South African division. Soon the area became a battleground on which the German armoured divisions soundly defeated the British armoured formations and overran a South African brigade caught up in the mêlée. The British were thrust from the ground seized.

In the second phase the German armour charged around the battle arena and expended its strength in attacks on the XIII Corps. The latter took over the carriage of the offensive, fought its infantry in conjunction with its tanks (Matildas and Valentines), maintained pressure at the frontier and proceeded to effect a junction with the Tobruk garrison while the XXX Corps for the most part watched from the side-lines, rebuilding its tank strength.

In the third phase, the advance from Tobruk to recapture the whole of Cyrenaica, the British armour which had meanwhile re-established its superiority in numbers of tanks was again defeated. Operations intended to pave the way for an invasion of Tripolitania in fact so depleted British armoured strength that subsequently General Rommel was able to regain the initiative and retake the whole of Cyrenaica west of Gazala, where for a time a stable line between the two armies was established.

If the time spent by the German commander on reconnaissance in strength in mid-September (Operation "Summer Night's Dream") was not entirely wasted, it may be doubted whether his planning was any the better for it. Nothing was discovered to cause any modification of his plan to crush the British outpost at Tobruk which, as a symbol and a legend, was developing a moral significance to match its tactical importance. Nothing, it appeared, but his own intractable supply situation threatened to thwart his ambition to encompass its downfall.

It may have been more than a coincidence that Rommel issued his operational directive for the capture of Tobruk only three days before Hitler, on 29th October, made an announcement foreshadowing German naval and air reinforcement of the Mediterranean theatre and the appointment of Field Marshal Kesselring as Commander-in-Chief South. The German High Command made a serious attempt to achieve Axis supremacy over the seas across which the Germans and Italians supplied and reinforced their African front and the British provisioned Malta. In course of time the Axis supply situation in Africa was to improve to some extent, that of Malta to worsen greatly—a change resulting as much from the diversion of British resources from the Mediterranean and Middle East to the Far East as from German reinforcement of the region. But it was a gradual change, and for the rest of that year, when the supplies received by either army would influence the outcome of British efforts to raise the siege of Tobruk, the rate of delivery to Rommel's army was not increased but on the contrary halved. During the summer and autumn the supplies reaching the Axis forces in North Africa had averaged approximately 72,000 tons a month; of those sent about 20 per cent were lost on the way. But in November only 30,000 tons were received; more than 60 per cent was lost. In December, a month of almost continuous ground fighting, only 39,000 tons were received. British aircraft, ships and submarines all contributed to that result.

The striking British successes in November were due mostly to sinkings by surface ships, in particular by Force K (the cruisers *Aurora* and *Penelope* and the destroyers *Lance* and *Lively*) operating from Malta, which sank the seven merchant ships of a convoy on 9th November and a large tanker on 1st December; in December most sinkings of Axis shipping were effected by submarines.

The German submarines in the Mediterranean, as already noted, achieved early successes against British shipping on the Tobruk run. Soon they made their mark against bigger quarry and sank the aircraft carrier *Ark Royal* on 14th November and the battleship *Barham* on 25th November. These developments greatly intensified the urgent strategic need for the British land forces to secure ground for air force bases in Cyrenaica and Tripolitania.

Rommel's orders for the capture of Tobruk followed in the main his outline plan. It was hoped to make the attack between 15th and 20th November. The *Africa Division* (soon to be known as the *90th Light*) was to secure the sector of the perimeter bounded on the north-east by the Bardia Road and on the west by the boundary between the Pilastrino and El Adem sectors (which boundary was heavily overprinted on Italian maps of Tobruk then in use by both sides), including a supposed strongpoint at the junction of the Bardia and El Adem Roads. After the *Africa Division* had breached the perimeter, the *15th Armoured Division* (100 gun-armed tanks, including the 5 captured Matildas, and 38 light tanks) was to push on to the coast, also to seize the road-pass of Fort Solaro (so-called). The Italian *XXI Corps* was to "advance to the high ground west of Tobruk" to prevent a westerly or south-westerly escape of the foredoomed garrison. In deference to General Halder's requirement that the frontier flank be guarded, the *21st Armoured Division* was to be stationed south-west of Gambut, an ambivalent position that did not rule out its employment as a reserve for the attacking force if the assault did not prosper.

Notwithstanding the accumulating evidence of growing British strength and the deterioration in his own supply situation General Rommel adhered with single-minded purpose to his intention to mount this attack. He refused to regard the build-up of the Eighth Army as a ground for cancelling it, and his arguments in general were sound enough. An operation to subdue the fortress, if it succeeded, should be completed in three days, within which time, he maintained, the British could not effectively intervene. In thus limiting himself to only three days of grace Rommel seems to have allowed for the possibility that the British had a proper plan to intervene. But if the British command had such a plan, it was one of its better kept secrets.[7]

Rommel's calculation that the unwieldiness of the British forces would vouchsafe him three days free from serious interference was reasonable except in the contingency that the British began to move forward from their holding positions before the attack began, which could happen in either the not unlikely event that they had discovered or inferred that his attack was imminent or the most unlikely event that they had chosen to mount an offensive of their own on the same day or a day or two earlier. What was mathematically so improbable almost occurred. Early in November Rommel was planning to open his attack on Tobruk on 15th November, the very date on which the British forces were then scheduled to cross the frontier for the CRUSADER offensive. On the 11th, two days after the loss of the convoy destroyed by Force K but perhaps not because of it, Rommel's Quartermaster-General produced a curious document the purpose of which seems to have been to demonstrate that enough supplies were on hand—20,700 tons of ammunition in addition to that held by the frontier garrison and 4,609 tons of fuel (sufficient to last the 28 days ending on 12th December)—to mount an attack on Tobruk, but not enough for a big advance with distant objectives; moreover, because of the British neutralisation of the shipment of Axis supplies the army would have to live on its reserves. Presumably the conclusion to be drawn was: strike while you can; there is enough for a strike against Tobruk but for nothing else.[8] Simultaneously Rommel's Intelligence staff reported that no British preparations for attack, such as the establishment of supply dumps, had been discovered and that the enemy situation had undergone no significant changes. The possibility that the British might

---

[7] One author, writing as if his information were from an inspired source, has suggested, however, that when Auchinleck and Cunningham became "aware of this impending attack", they were tempted "to delay CRUSADER until Rommel was fully embroiled in Tobruk, and then strike him in the back". Correlli Barnett, *The Desert Generals* (1960), p. 88.

[8] Bayerlein, in *The Rommel Papers*, p. 155. "Rommel . . . feared that any lengthy postponement would only result in the balance of strength swinging even further against us."

be about to make a serious attack was considered but discounted with the reassuring deduction that they could not get their main bodies forward before the second night or attack decisively before the third morning. The Intelligence staff in Germany also issued an appreciation denying the likelihood of an early British offensive.

Whether by coincidence or not, this flurry of German paper-work coincided with a report by Rommel's nominal superior, General Bastico, to the Italian Supreme Command drawing an exactly opposite conclusion from the results of ground and air reconnaissance. Bastico's opinion was that the British were ready and indeed only waiting for the Axis forces to become involved in an attack on Tobruk to launch "a heavy offensive aimed at forcing a final conclusion".

On 14th November Rommel flew to Rome to attend high-level discussions about the Tobruk attack with the Italian and German staffs. There he appears to have won his point by shouting down his opponents and other doubters, such as Field Marshal Jodl, to whom he spoke by telephone. The formal authorisation of the attack was conveyed to Bastico's African headquarters and received there on 18th November. The 21st of November was fixed as the date for the assault.

The British offensive, however, had also been postponed. Otherwise the Eighth Army might have crossed the frontier while Rommel was still in Rome. In the months of the summer and autumn the South Africans had found, as had the Australians and New Zealanders on other occasions, that of all the army's needs few were accorded lower priority by the Middle East staffs than training; greater priority had been given to digging fixed defences in rear areas. At the end of October, the commander of the 1st South African Division, General Brink, reported that he could not be ready for an offensive before 21st November and demanded 21 clear days for training. A few days later he repeated this request to Auchinleck himself, in a conference which the latter held with Cunningham, Norrie and Brink on 3rd November. Auchinleck and Cunningham agreed to defer the opening of the offensive from 15th to 18th November provided that Brink would then be ready. General Brink asked once again for three more days of training to bring the date of the opening of the offensive to 21 November, but agreed, if this was impossible, to advance into battle on the 18th.[9]

Thus it happened that the British advanced before the Germans attacked. If Auchinleck had agreed to the further deferment requested by Brink, he might have had to do much explaining to Churchill.

Although the British plans and outline orders prescribed close coordination between the forces from the frontier and those inside Tobruk, no one seems to have informed the headquarters of Tobruk fortress that the onset of the offensive had been postponed for three days. Yet the garrison had a part to play and, by 6 p.m. on the day on which the Eighth Army would cross the frontier, had to be ready to start preparatory moves for

---
[9] Agar-Hamilton and Turner, p. 92.

a sortie at next first light. These timings were based on the optimistic assumption that the British forces might decisively defeat the German armoured divisions in one day, their first in Libya, though it was not really expected that an opportunity to do so would be presented or created before the second day.

Tobruk fortress came under the command of the Eighth Army on 30th October but was to be transferred to the command of the XXX Corps as soon as Operation CRUSADER started. The garrison's sortie was to be made at dawn on a day XXX Corps would nominate and notify by code word. On every day after the start of the offensive the XXX Corps was to send a code word to fortress headquarters before 6 p.m., which would be either "Tug" ("Don't attack tomorrow") or "Pop" ("Attack tomorrow").

Scarcely a unit in Tobruk was unaffected by the sortie plan, for according to the fashion of the day every combatant formation had either to fight or to feint. Orders were passed down to subordinate commanders in time for them to get their units ready by the appointed day but without time to waste. Command and staff problems were thrashed out over a sand-table model. On 13th November a rehearsal of the main sortie was conducted over similar ground. The infantrymen were inspirited to see the tanks that were to support them in the real show charge through to overrun the imaginary enemy. They were further encouraged when next day the fortress commander addressed them and told them that the sortie, though hazardous, would not be ordered until the relieving British forces had got the better of the German armour.

By 15th November all preparations had been made and from 4 p.m. many were at one hour's notice to move. But the day brought neither the promised code word ("Tug" or "Pop") nor any other news of the "push". On the contrary through the communications network grim warnings were passed that an Axis attack might be impending, in which parachute troops and seaborne troops in rubber boats might be employed. The information received at fortress headquarters indicated that the assault was likely to be made in the western sector near the coast.

At 4 p.m. Lieut-Colonel Zaremba, General Kopanski's chief of staff, called on Lieut-Colonel Burrows and informed him that divisional headquarters had received information suggesting that an enemy landing on the western beaches supported by parachute troops was possible. The 1st R.H.A., now fully mobile for the CRUSADER operation, was placed in support of the 2/13th Battalion for the night. Burrows stood his battalion to arms at dusk and established six fighting patrols along the beaches and headlands for almost three miles east of the perimeter. If an enemy force made a beach landing in the battalion's sector, a code word was to be passed. Captain Graham's company would at once occupy a defensive position to block penetration.

The night passed without alarms, the next day without news of the Eighth Army's advance. At dusk there was a similar stand-to, followed by similar protective measures, except that the 1st R.H.A. was withdrawn from the sector to stand by for its part in the CRUSADER sortie, which the fortress command had to be ready to mount as from that evening. The night was again uneventful except for some rain showers.

Next evening—the 17th—the 2/13th was again required to act as beach night-watchman. There was still no information of either the British drive or the German combined operation. A few more postponements, a few more nights of standing to arms, should suffice, it seemed, to make the 2/13th Battalion utterly miserable. The fact that there was no news from the frontier added to their discouragement; fortress veterans remembered that practically no information of BATTLEAXE had been passed down to them before that offensive's failure had been announced. But the elements themselves were to complete their discomfiture.

That night above Tobruk the skies which throughout the summer had shed not a drop of rain and had since bestowed only a few token showers were murky with heavy cloud. Lightning sporadically illuminated them. In time, with an accompaniment of thunderclaps, drenching rain fell, wadis quickly became coursing torrents—"*letti di torrenti temporanei*" as the Italian military maps described them—and crawl-trenches, weapon-pits, dug-outs, and other entrenchments, deep and shallow alike, were soon water-filled. Fieldworks had made no provision for drainage. At the Wadi Sehel pumping station men of the 2/13th Battalion carrier platoon who provided the standing patrol withdrew quickly but not according to plan, while their warning flares and rockets, triggered by torrent-borne debris striking the trip-wires, shot to the sky. Dawn brought a scene that seemed funny to some but not others when Australian patrols were discovered on the enemy side of the Wadi Sehel, waiting for the torrent to subside.

That morning in many of the frontal areas soldiers on both sides abandoned the holes in which they normally took shelter from each other's shell and shot, and stood about or sat around in scattered groups sprawled across the defended localities like ants flooded out of their nests. If the ethics of war required them to kill off their exposed enemies, a simple-minded solicitude for their own survival induced some deviation from first principle. In the Salient the Poles, fearing that daylight's disclosure of their plight would invite disaster, were determined to get the upper hand by shooting first. With machine-guns set up in improvised positions, they harassed the enemy as soon as they could be discerned in the dim light.

> The enemy did not respond by fire but began to hoist white flags asking for peace. When fire ceased the work of draining their positions and drying their clothes began and enemy went so far as to kindle fire in improvised blanket tents. We took advantage of it to make some warm tea for our troops.[1]

Some officers of the R.H.A. also made the best of the situation, visiting the Salient as observers "to make some observations which under normal conditions would have been impossible".

This was the opening day of the Eighth Army's postponed offensive. One would not have thought so in the western sector of Tobruk where the 2/13th Battalion, like most other units, awaited receipt of the code

---

[1] Polish Carpathian Brigade Group Intelligence Summary No. 71 dated 19th November 1941.

word signalling first action to be taken. As the compiler of the Polish Brigade's Intelligence summary remarked next day—

> The day of 18 of November was marked by exceptional inactivity of the enemy and own troops. Artillery shelling almost nil. . . . During the day a sort of truce was established, each side trying to remove the effects of the rain and subsequent floods. After dark the normal conditions became re-established.

On the 20th, however, it was reported in the same publication:

> The conditions on the salient yesterday were the same as on the previous day but this morning the old habits became re-established.

Old habits: one shoots to kill, that is.

In Tobruk the relief operations had no dramatic beginning. The garrison did not see the Eighth Army's westward advance on wheels that caught the imagination of those who took part, firing them with the eager confidence of men who believe they belong to an invincible army. One heard of a flare-up in another region. In the course of days the wind changed, the conflagration drifted closer; then one's own ground was threatened; there was real danger suddenly; one was in the fight, in the midst of it. But what was really happening out there beyond the perimeter nobody knew. The prescription for confidence was faith, hope and luck.

To the forces in Tobruk the offensive was an operation which from the start seemed behind schedule and always confused. Knowing their own tasks but not the master plan, conceiving the proposed link-up at Ed Duda with the Tobruk sortie force not as a merely incidental sequel to the planned destruction of the German armour but as the chief objective of the first phase of the offensive, they read the first situation reports with some puzzlement and judged the early progress more halting than audacious.

The code word "Tug" meaning "Don't attack" was received from the XXX Corps on the 18th and again on the 19th. The 2/13th received its first battle situation report on the evening of the 19th. It gave the dispositions of the armour as at 10.45 a.m. on the 18th (and even then inaccurately, by confusing Bir Taieb el Esem with Gabr Taieb el Esem). So far no British tanks were reported within 30 miles of Ed Duda.

A situation report received on the morning of the 20th purported to depict the situation on the preceding morning. The 7th Armoured Brigade was moving to Sidi Rezegh, the 22nd to Bir el Gubi. The 4th Armoured Brigade had engaged 60 tanks, which had retired northwards. The puzzling part of that report was that the South African division, which was expected to capture Sidi Rezegh at the same time as the garrison sally force snatched Ed Duda, was still deep in the desert south of El Gubi. In the early afternoon the garrison witnessed a fighter sweep by 40 British aircraft; the 104th R.H.A.'s diarist remarked that it was the first time they had seen anything like it. Gun flashes and tracer fire were subsequently seen from the Tobruk perimeter in the direction of Sidi Rezegh. It was reported that a big tank battle had occurred on the preceding day, the British having destroyed 27 enemy tanks for the loss of 20. British forces from the frontier were obviously in the neighbourhood and it seemed as if the offensive's objectives were being substantially achieved.

No further report came from the Eighth Army or XXX Corps; but a satisfactory outcome of the tank engagements could be presumed, for the code word XXX Corps sent that afternoon was not "Tug" but "Pop": the sortie was to be made on the morrow. Through the Tobruk telephone network other code words were passed to set in train all required action.

There was a close resemblance in the routes and final objective chosen and some similarity in the associated deception schemes between the plan devised by Morshead and Wootten for a sortie in BATTLEAXE and that put out by Scobie and Martin for the sortie of the 70th Division in CRUSADER. In fact the decision to seize Ed Duda with a sally force from Tobruk appears to have been adopted (or reborn) at an early stage of the CRUSADER planning. General Cunningham discussed some details of the project at a staff conference on 15th October which General Scobie attended before going to Tobruk to take command there. General Scobie is reported to have agreed to place a squadron of cruisers at General Brink's disposal for any westward move of the South African division[2] after the link-up at Ed Duda. This was advanced planning indeed, perhaps without full knowledge of the mechanical condition of the cruisers Scobie was to inherit or the clairvoyance to foretell that by the end of the first day of the sortie only eight of them would be runners.

The best that can be said of the sortie plan is that in some fashion it worked. Two of its features seemed to commend it rather as a course to take after defeating the enemy than as a way of defeating him. One was the necessity to detach part of the garrison force including practically all its tanks and an indispensable artillery regiment and to employ the detachment so distantly that if it was endangered the garrison would be unable to lend effective aid. The other was the requirement to open up a corridor through enemy-held territory and keep it open; this involved exposing to the enemy two flanks of almost maximum extension defended at almost minimum depth. By simple logic holding the corridor open necessitated later secondary operations to make the flanks safe, in fact a greater commitment than nominally undertaken.

It was assumed that surprise was unlikely to be achieved. The chances of obtaining it were diminished by plans for ancillary operations to precede the main thrust, which were intended to divert the enemy's attention from the sortie zone to other sectors but, if keenly executed, held promise of alarming and alerting him all round the perimeter.

The plan for the main sortie, like many ambitious projects, was in two parts; the first required much doing, the second much daring. In the first phase the striking force was to punch a gap through the encompassing enemy defences, converting the enemy strongpoints to its own use; in the second a mixed column of infantry and armour—the armour leading—was to sweep on to Ed Duda, seize that feature and hold it.

---

[2] Official report of GOC 1 SA Division, quoted in Agar-Hamilton and Turner, p. 65.

The composition of the main sally force, its order of advance and axis are shown in the diagram. The operation was not just a short attack across known ground to the front of that held. The main objective of the first phase, the strongly held and fortified locality called Tiger, was two miles and a half from the perimeter. The plan required that secretly by night men, tanks, guns, other weapons, stores and vehicles should be got across the perimeter's anti-tank obstacles and formed up for battle in no-man's land. For this eight bridges over the anti-tank ditch would be needed. Moreover Tiger was but one of a number of mutually supporting enemy localities. So before Tiger could be attacked, Butch had to be subdued, Jill overrun, and something would have to be done to neutralise Tugun, Lion, Cub and Jack. Then to reach Ed Duda a further advance of about five miles would have to be undertaken.

The first feint, to be carried out by the Polish Brigade in the western sector at 3 a.m., was a series of raids combined with an artillery bombardment. In this operation the 2/13th was to participate with a patrol of one officer and 12 men, which was to demonstrate against a strong Italian defensive locality known as Twin Pimples as though threatening attack while concentrated fire was laid along the front by mortars, medium machine-guns and light machine-guns. Other sorties—one of company strength and two of platoon strength—were to be made on the left of the 2/13th by the 1st and 3rd Polish Battalions. A second diversion was to be carried out by the 23rd Brigade in the area of the El Adem road-block.

The Tobruk garrison's great assault began with these diversionary operations in the early hours of 21st November. The Polish Brigade's operation went to plan, woke up everybody, deceived nobody and attracted a satisfactory if not lavish volume of retaliatory fire. The 23rd Brigade's diversion was quite successful to the extent that its purpose was to make a noise and stir up the enemy; but Plonk, the *pièce de résistance* of the brigade's task, was not captured.

The sally force's difficult forming-up outside the perimeter was achieved without interference from the enemy; the roar of supporting gunfire and enemy counter-bombardment from the 23rd Brigade's false strike drowned the clatter of its assembly. Zero hour for the infantry to advance in the most formidable attack ever made by the Tobruk force was 6.30 a.m. On the left of the sally port and not far out was Butch, which had to be neutralised or the route to Tiger would be murderously enfiladed. It was to be taken by the 2/King's Own. The centre strike, by the 2/Black Watch, was to be directed at Tiger through the smaller outpost Jill. The left prong was to reach out to Tugun, far to the left flank—an operation assigned to the 2/Queen's.

At 6.20 a.m. a bombardment of Butch began. Within 10 minutes the 2/King's Own supported by a squadron of the 7th Royal Tank Regiment (19 Matildas) announced its capture. They reported that the enemy, of whom there were 30 dead, were German and they sent back 10 live ones to prove it. And it soon became evident that this was no isolated pocket. A region thought to lie along the boundary of two Italian divisions and expected to be defended mainly by cross-fire from a few strong-points proved to be a German defensive area held in some density by unyielding and determined defenders. Most of these had moved in six days before. Moreover the localities called by code names and delineated in the plans accompanying the operation orders proved to be parts of a more extensive, unmapped and well-concealed defensive system, interlaced with unmarked minefields. Thus an area just to the north of Butch which was not one of the operation's objectives remained in enemy hands for several days.

At 6.30 a.m., sustained by a regimental tradition reaching back for more than 200 years, the infantrymen of the 2/Black Watch's assault companies stood up, all to face death, half to die. The tanks were not there, except for a squadron of cruisers not to be employed in the main assault. The time required to get them over the bridges crossing the anti-tank ditch had been underestimated. The infantry commanders made the right decision: to press on alone, making best use of what protection the timed artillery program would provide.

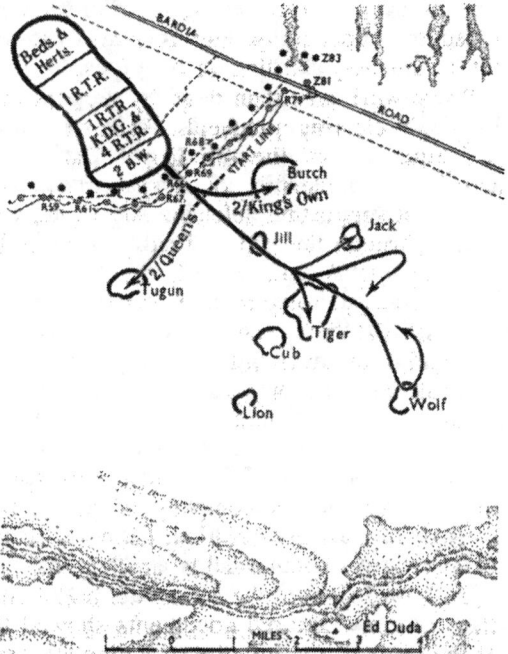

The break-out, 21st November

The action developed into a muddle redeemed by great leadership and utmost bravery. Jill, treated in the plan as a small detached post to be easily smothered in the advance of the leading company, proved a strong locality. Each effort of the Black Watch to get forward was murderously cut down until the lately arrived infantry tanks came across from Butch with a company of the 2/King's Own following. When Jill had been overrun, "there was nothing left of [the leading company of the 2/Black Watch] to carry on to Tiger".[3]

When the tanks of the 4th Royal Tank Regiment were assembled on the battlefield, they were unable to proceed because of a minefield to the west and north of Tiger. They were told to make "merry hell", which they did, with a resounding accompaniment from the guns of "A/E"

---

[3] Bernard Fergusson, *The Black Watch and the King's Enemies* (1950), p. 107.

Battery. The defence seemed momentarily neutralised and Captain Armitage, who had nosed his armoured command post forward, reported at 8.30 a.m. that he was "on the back of Tiger", which comprised 1,000 yards of infantry positions dug flush with the ground. The Black Watch were too extended, however, to make the concerted rush needed to exploit a fleeting opportunity, but continued to probe forward to the stirring but melancholy skirling of bagpipes.

Brave work was then done by sappers and men of the King's Dragoon Guards in clearing minefields. At last a sufficient gap was made and, while "C" Squadron of the 4th Royal Tank Regiment under the brilliant if unorthodox leadership of Major Goschen of "B/O" Battery attacked centres of supporting defensive fire to the east, the tanks of "B" Squadron surged through the gap and right through Tiger. Then, about three hours after the attack had started, the 200 men still remaining of the Black Watch charged forward and captured their objective at the point of the bayonet. Yet there was still work for the Black Watch to do. Machine-gun hail beat down intermittently directed from Jack to the north-east. A weak company was collected and with tanks of the 4th Royal Tank Regiment assaulted and took the place. When Captain Jones of the 104th R.H.A. reported there a little later to establish an artillery command post, he found only a handful of men, sent for reinforcements and personally took charge until a company of the 1/Bedfordshire and Hertfordshire arrived. In another operation, Lion—a defended locality to the south-west of Tiger—was bombarded by artillery and overrun by tanks, but not seized.

Jack was found to be a German battalion headquarters and communications centre. Captured documents showed that the sortie force had struck at the heart of the infantry of Rommel's assault force, who were all set to go and expected to assault on the morrow;[4] the 70th Division's attack had driven a wedge between the *Africa zbV Division* on the left and the *Bologna Division* on the right. There was also evidence that the enemy had been forewarned of the British attack. The warning, it now appears, had emanated from Rommel himself, who had called for three-hourly reports; which suggests that his excellent intercept service may have gathered some clue as to what was afoot.

A subsidiary operation by the 2/Queen's against Tugun on the right flank, planned concurrently with the main sortie but in insufficient strength, had not succeeded. The 2/Queen's, reinforced by a company of the Beds and Herts, later mounted a second assault in conjunction with a squadron of the 7th Royal Tank Regiment and managed to secure the eastern end of the locality, but the enemy hung on to the western end.

That morning's situation report from the Eighth Army, detailing its situation at 9 a.m., had said that the 4th Armoured Brigade was at Gabr Taieb el Esem and the 22nd north-west of Gabr Saleh, both "following up the retreating enemy armoured forces" in a north-westerly direction and that the 7th Armoured Brigade which, with the 7th Support Group,

---

[4] This intention, however, was no longer held at the German Armoured group command headquarters.

was at Sidi Rezegh had been ordered to intercept the retreating enemy. An encouraging message from XXX Corps received later in the morning, which indicated that the 5th South African Brigade was ten miles south of Sidi Rezegh, and confirmed that its support of the sortie operations would be forthcoming that afternoon, emboldened General Scobie to proceed with the second phase, the seizure of Ed Duda, notwithstanding the unexpected casualty rate suffered in the first.

The start-time was set first at 1 p.m., later at 2.30. By then the task force had assembled on its start-line, but Brigadier Willison, commanding the 32nd Army Tank Brigade, asked for more time to enable the participation of a number of tanks which had become embroiled in resisting local counter-attacks and in mopping-up operations in the corridor. Even after a postponement, he would only be strong enough, he said, if the attack were synchronised with operations by the South Africans. The postponement was agreed to. Shortly before 4 p.m., just as Willison's force was making ready for its delayed start, another message came from the XXX Corps suggesting that the operation be postponed because it would be impossible to provide support for the operation against Ed Duda owing to an armoured battle 16 miles to the south-east. Scobie, impressed no doubt by the apparent resilience of the retreating German armour, cancelled the sally.

It had been a day of great achievement. A wedge three miles deep had been driven through one of the strongest sections of the encircling defences. To secure the corridor against sniping and cross-fire, further operations would be required, but it was already possible for garrison forces to debouch into the open desert, whatever perils might lie beyond. Five hundred and fifty German prisoners (including 20 officers) and 527 Italian (including 18 officers) had been taken, but at great cost in loss of life. In the 2/Black Watch alone, there were 200 dead.

Next morning (22nd November) another message was received from the XXX Corps stating that their own troops at Sidi Rezegh were being heavily attacked. "Please attack Ed Duda as soon as possible," the message importuned, "and shoot up enemy tanks now on Trigh Capuzzo." This was not the kind of sortie General Scobie's planning had envisaged. He signalled that his heavy tank strength was much reduced and that if the operation failed, the safety of the fortress would be endangered, but added: "Will attack Ed Duda if you wish. Request immediate orders." The XXX Corps replied just after midday "Do not attack", adding with inverted logic "Situation improving".

In the CRUSADER planning the prerequisite for the sortie to Ed Duda was the defeat of the German armoured forces but on that day the British 7th Armoured Division was staring defeat in the face. The execution was to take place on the morrow.

As the great British army of the desert had set off westwards on wheels to cross the frontier, the storms that had caused torrents to flow in the wadis of Tobruk had swept towards the advancing forces, flooding airfields and grounding aircraft in the operational zone. No aircraft had reported to the German armoured group commander (General Rommel) the size of the British force coming towards him, or even detected its

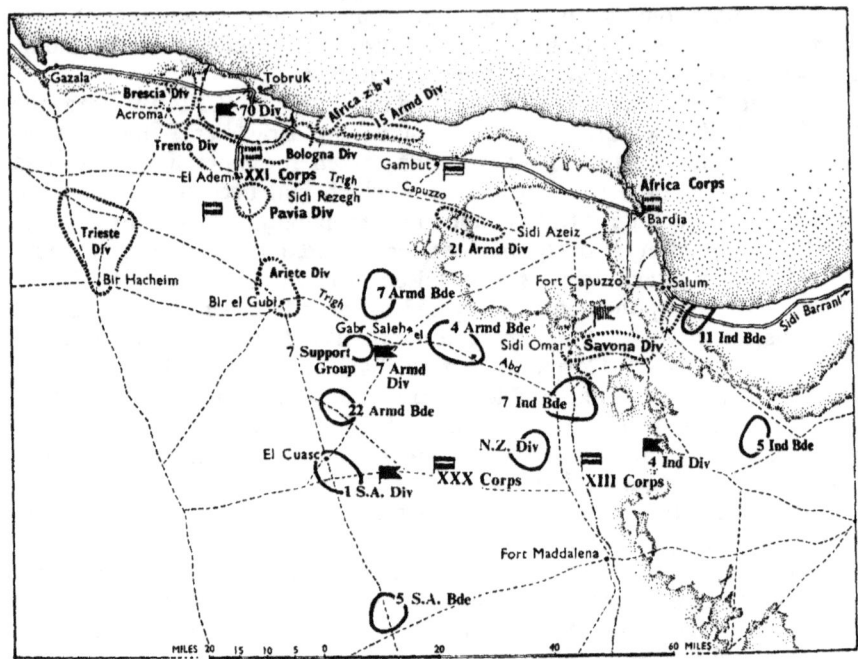

Dispositions, 18th November

presence. The British formations moved on the 18th to their designated first objectives unopposed except for one or two skirmishes with light enemy screening detachments. Never in a large operation had tactical surprise been more completely achieved since Gustavus Adolphus crossed the frozen Baltic; never had it been achieved to less purpose. So well had the British command and the elements concealed the move intended to provoke a disconcerted enemy to self-destructive reaction that none ensued. The old campaigner Rommel was not put about by early, scary reports of the magnitude of the British incursion and declined to authorise any counter-measures that might interrupt his advanced preparations to assault Tobruk.

The wait-and-see, your-turn-next tactic implicit in the Cunningham plan had brought the Eighth Army to a halt. What to do next? Seek out and destroy! While Cunningham deliberated subordinate commanders took the initiative. Late on the 18th General Norrie indicated Bir el Gubi and Sidi Rezegh as likely objectives for the next day's operations and early on the 19th General Gott, commanding the 7th Armoured Division, ordered the 22nd Armoured Brigade to attack the *Ariete Division* at

El Gubi, which was ground of the *Ariete's* own choosing, and well-prepared at that. Honours were about even in the battle. The British lost 25 tanks, the Italians 34, but when the action was broken off the Italians held the ground. Gott also ordered the 7th Armoured Brigade to reconnoitre towards Sidi Rezegh and later to seize a position there, which it did at good speed, overrunning the airfield and capturing 19 Italian aircraft.

Meanwhile the 4th Armoured Brigade had sent the 3rd Royal Tank Regiment with armoured cars of the King's Dragoon Guards on a foray, cavalry-style, to the north-east. The excursion, which developed into a

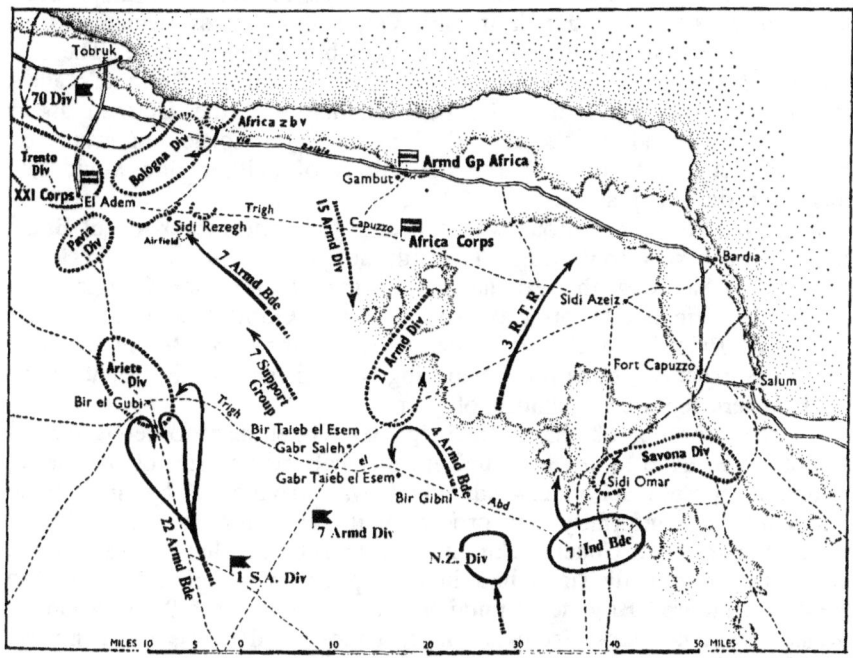

The capture of Sidi Rezegh airfield, 19th November

chase of the German *3rd Reconnaissance Unit,* stung the German command into the sort of reaction the CRUSADER planners had visualised. At the instance of General von Ravenstein (commanding the *21st Armoured Division*) General Cruewell (commanding the German *Africa Corps*) obtained General Rommel's permission to send a reinforced tank regiment (the *5th*) to strike at Gabr Saleh. Here was presented the first opportunity of inflicting defeat in detail on the German armoured forces. But at Gabr Saleh there was now only one British tank regiment, the 8th Hussars, with little more than 50 General Stuart tanks, a 12-gun battery of 25-pounders and four 2-pounders. The 5th Royal Tanks were not far to the east, but not exactly within inter-supporting distance. The divisional artillery was not to hand. The battle was joined about 2.30 p.m. and the 5th R.T.R.

came across in time to join in the fight, which was not broken off until night began to fall. The British armoured brigades, then slightly outnumbering their opponents in tanks, were not disgraced but the German group with its stronger artillery had had the best of it.

The armoured engagements had so far been inconclusive but in the next three days the battle moved swiftly to a calamitous climax. The 3rd Royal Tank Regiment's jaunt had convinced the German command of the necessity for strong counter-measures, though misleading it as to the purposes of the British and the location of their main strength. The *15th Armoured Division* on the coast east of Tobruk was directed to link up with the *21st Armoured Division*. Thus concentrated the armour would strike towards the frontier from Sidi Omar northwards, which was not in fact the region threatened by the British armoured force. The *15th Armoured Division's* move would inevitably postpone Rommel's attack on Tobruk, thus precluding the near chance that the German assault would be launched on the day Scobie made his sortie, an eventuality in which (it is safe to say) the operations of neither side would have gone according to plan.

While the German armour was concentrating, the dispersion of British mobile forces was continuing. The 7th Support Group was directed to move up to Sidi Rezegh next day to join the 7th Armoured Brigade and the South African division was sent to Bir el Gubi to release the 22nd Armoured Brigade so that it could also join the 7th. Before the latter move was executed, however, perturbing reports received by Eighth Army headquarters required a change of plan.

On the morning of the 20th Brigadier Gatehouse[4] ordered the 4th Armoured Brigade to advance and engage their adversaries of the evening before. A spirited action ensued, which was broken off by the German commander in conformity with orders for the concentration of his division at Sidi Omar. Then General Cunningham learnt from his intercept service that both German divisions had linked up and were planning to attack the 4th Armoured Brigade at midday. He summoned the 22nd Armoured Brigade to come across from El Gubi, a move which was not completed until late afternoon. At that moment of crisis help from another quarter was proffered to Gatehouse. General Freyberg, whose excellent New Zealand division was at Bir Gibni some seven miles away, could see no reason why it should be kept out of the fight. With General Godwin-Austen's approbation he offered the division with its complete artillery and its battalion of heavy tanks to Gatehouse, but Gatehouse preferred to fight his battle unencumbered by infantry. So the 4th Armoured Brigade, kept—in Rommel's phrase—pure of race, made ready to meet its sternest test alone. The attack, delayed and diminished in strength to one division by German supply difficulties, came in at 4.30 p.m. and again the fighting continued until nightfall stopped it, with the 22nd Armoured Brigade joining in before it ended. This second battle between British and German

---

[4] Maj-Gen A. H. Gatehouse, DSO, MC. (1914-18: Lt to Maj Tank Corps.) Comd 4 Armd Bde 1941; GOC 10 Armd Div 1942. Regular soldier; b. 20 May 1895.

armour was as inconclusive as the first but at its end the enemy camped on the battlefield, recovering his damaged tanks—none had been destroyed. The 4th Armoured Brigade, which had crossed the frontier with 164 tanks, had 97 left.

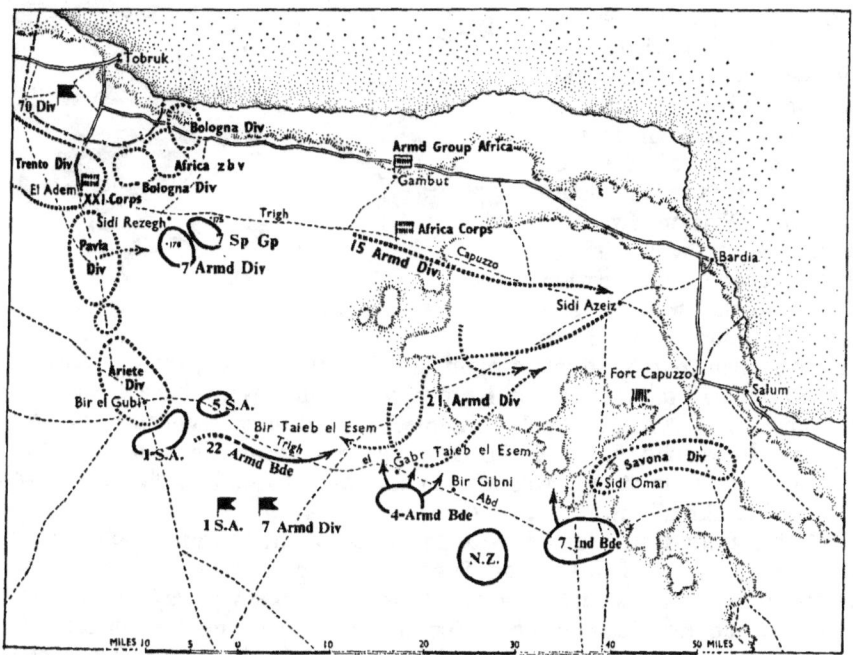

Situation, 20th November

That night General Rommel, believing the 4th Armoured Brigade to have been accounted for, ordered both German armoured divisions to proceed at once to the Tobruk front to deal with the British armoured force at Sidi Rezegh. The Germans were no longer doubtful of British plans. The B.B.C. had obligingly informed them. The British command had meanwhile transmitted the code word requiring the Tobruk garrison to break out on the morrow. If the Tobruk garrison and the German forces had both fully carried out their orders next day, Scobie's small sortie force would have reached Ed Duda about the same time as two German armoured divisions.

When the British irruption from Egypt had been first reported, Major-General Suemmermann had prudently ordered the *zbV Division* to form a front facing south. The front was a wide one necessitating the establishment of defended localities at widely-spaced dominating points. East of the Sidi Rezegh airfield, the *361st Infantry Regiment* established itself around Trig 175 on the escarpment running parallel to the Trigh Capuzzo and overlooking it from the south, while south-west of the airfield the *155th Regiment* established itself at the second escarpment which overlooked the steppe on which the airfield was sited. A powerful artillery group, with a battalion of Italian infantry of the *Bologna Division* for protection, was established on the escarpments near Belhamed; throughout the 20th it harassed the British.

General Gott visited Sidi Rezegh twice on the 20th. Between visits, he arranged with General Brink to send forward one of the two brigades of the 1st South African Division from El Gubi. Brink, who (it will be recalled) had earlier protested the need for further training refused to allow a night march, so when night fell the 5th Brigade, the one selected, halted some 17 miles from Sidi Rezegh, where they were due at 7 a.m. next morning. The XXX Corps' only medium artillery regiment had been allowed to remain at El Gubi. The South African division, then only one brigade group strong, was also to stay near El Gubi with the peculiar role of "masking" an armoured division, the *Ariete*.

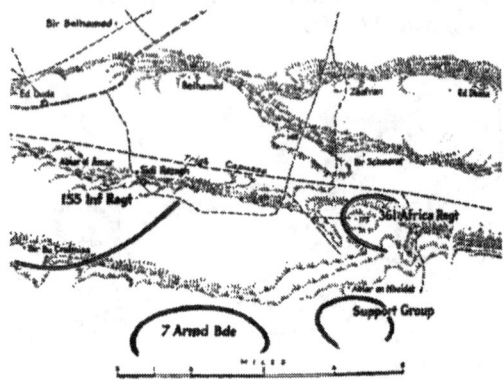

On his second visit to Sidi Rezegh, made in the evening, Gott ordered the 7th Armoured Brigade and Support Group to clear the ridge north of the airfield with an infantry attack and thus open a way to the Trigh Capuzzo and Ed Duda, where a junction was to be made with the 70th Division's sortie force next day (the 21st). The attack was made next morning at 7.45 (simultaneously with the early stages of the Tobruk sortie operations) without waiting for the South African brigade, which had been held up in muddy country. Three companies of the 1/King's Royal Rifle Corps and one of the 2/Rifle Brigade wrested the ridges from the enemy and the 6th Royal Tank Regiment passed through, all set for Ed Duda. There was an important observer of the engagement in the person of the German armoured group commander. With customary decisiveness Rommel mustered four 88-mm guns and sent them with the *3rd Reconnaissance Unit* to block the way. The 6th Royal Tank Regiment was shot to pieces; it saved only sufficient tanks to field one composite squadron. Meanwhile Gott had caught up with the South African brigade and halted it 10 miles short of Sidi Rezegh. Gott spent most of the day with the brigade, but curiously, to judge from the narrative of the South African historians, did not inform the brigade commander of the plan to employ it that day at Ed Duda in conjunction with the Tobruk sortie force.

The 7th Support Group's capture of the Sidi Rezegh ridge and the capture of Tiger and Jack by the Tobruk sortie force later that morning were the high-water mark of British success in the first phase of the offensive. The ebb set in swiftly. Farther east, about Gabr Saleh, the day had also seemed to begin propitiously. General Norrie thought the enemy had taken a hard knock the previous evening, and when the German armour disengaged that morning bent on smashing the British foothold at Sidi Rezegh, the 4th and 22nd Armoured Brigades followed up the seeming retreat, as Scobie had been told. The Germans made better pace at first, but the British caught up with the German rearguards and a running fight ensued until the British, having outrun their supplies, paused to refuel. The German divisions pressed on. By about 8 a.m. the van of the German armour was approaching the Sidi Rezegh area. Before the Black Watch, not far to the north, had taken Tiger, the gunners and infantry of the Support Group were fighting with their lives to hold their ground.

Meanwhile Norrie had suggested to Cunningham that the time was propitious for operations by the XIII Corps to reduce the Axis frontier positions. Norrie's optimistic interpretation of the previous day's armoured battles and of the German armour's westward move induced Cunningham to receive the suggestion favourably. Cunningham authorised but did not enjoin Godwin-Austen to start, but Godwin-Austen needed no prodding. So, impelled by a sure instinct that the cause could be advanced better by fighting than by standing idle, a corps commander exercising a delegated discretion set in train the operations that were to provide a fatal distraction for Rommel when victory was within his grasp, operations which were to be pertinaciously and staunchly prosecuted until the Eighth Army's fortunes had been retrieved.

Soon after the 7th Support Group had secured a lodgment south of Belhamed on the Sidi Rezegh ridges beside the Trigh Capuzzo, its eastern elements and its artillery group came under attack from the *21st Armoured Division*. For the rest of the day the 7th Armoured Brigade and the 7th Support Group fought both German armoured divisions in a confused battle in which the legendary Brigadier Campbell's bravery and resource helped stave off utter destruction, but not severe defeat. The stark result was that the ratio of British tank losses to German for the day was of the order of 15 to 1 and when night fell the 7th Armoured Brigade was left with only 28 tanks in running order. The 4th and 22nd Armoured Brigades had not pursued the enemy with sufficient alacrity to join the battle.

At his remote headquarters General Cunningham had a false picture of the situation, partly because many reports were slow to reach him, partly because many of them were wrong; most of his interventions in the swiftly moving battle were based on a view corresponding little with the actual contemporaneous situation but representing rather an erroneous conception of an earlier situation. The salient features of the battle situation that afternoon, as he conceived it, were that the German armour was in retreat and the Tobruk sortie force about to make for Ed Duda; his forces at Sidi Rezegh, he feared, might be insufficiently regardful of the critical importance of linking at Ed Duda with the sortie force. He told Norrie that evening that he must join up with the sortie force if it got to Ed Duda; to Cunningham (as he informed Norrie) this appeared to require only a short night march. Norrie and Gott, however, attached prior importance to clearing the German infantry from the escarpment south-west of the Sidi Rezegh airfield, which was a more realistic first step, if a bit one-sided. The 5th South African Brigade was moved up for that purpose.

On the night of the 21st there were divergent views in the enemy camp on the best course to take. Becoming aware of the convergence of more British armoured forces on the Sidi Rezegh front, the German commanders were cautious. The upshot was that one armoured division—the weaker *21st Armoured*—was ordered to Belhamed, to form, in conjunction with the *155th* and *361st Regiments,* a defensive front there which would block a British advance from Sidi Rezegh to link up with the Tobruk sortie force, while the other (*15th Armoured*) moved off into the open desert about 7 miles south of Gambut, under the erroneous impression that it would then be well-disposed to attack the British in flank. Unfortunately for the British it found the going difficult and so by chance was to be given an opportunity to strike a damaging blow.

On 22nd November the Eighth Army's great armoured force, which in the CRUSADER plan had been cast for the role of destroying the Axis armour, was itself decisively defeated. In the early morning there were desultory skirmishes and gunfire duels. The 7th Armoured Brigade and the Support Group's artillery sparred with the *21st Armoured Division* as it went into position near Belhamed; the 4th and 22nd Armoured Brigades with the *15th Armoured Division's* rearguards as it departed. In mid-morning the message asking Scobie to attack Ed Duda and shoot up the enemy tanks on the Trigh Capuzzo was dispatched. The situation was hardly suited to such an enterprise, which Gott's force was not poised to support, but in general the trend of operations seemed not unpropitious for the forces around Sidi Rezegh. Orders had just been passed to the 4th Armoured Brigade (which meanwhile had expended some energy and fuel in a wild goose chase) to advance to Trig 175 on the northern escarpment, and to the 5th South African Brigade to advance to Trig 178 on the southern escarpment. Later the 22nd Armoured was also directed to the Trig 178 region. Thus all were set for clearing the Sidi Rezegh area though not yet for getting to Ed Duda.

When Scobie was told, about midday, that the situation was improving, and that therefore he need not attack Ed Duda, there was nothing in the local scene at Sidi Rezegh to belie the message. The British plan for the afternoon provided that the 5th South African Brigade should clear the enemy from the southern (Trig 178) escarpment west of the British positions. But Rommel had made a different appreciation. In the early afternoon he ordered the *21st Armoured Division* to launch an immediate counter-attack to regain the airfield. The division's armoured regiment (the *5th*) was to attack from the west while its infantry (Knabe

Group) attacked from the north and the operation was to be supported by the powerful *Army Artillery Group* behind Belhamed.

The result of the afternoon's operations may be briefly told. The South African attack did not succeed but the German did. The Knabe Group struck direct at the Support Group and thrust it from the escarpment above the tomb of Sidi Rezegh. The emasculated 7th Armoured

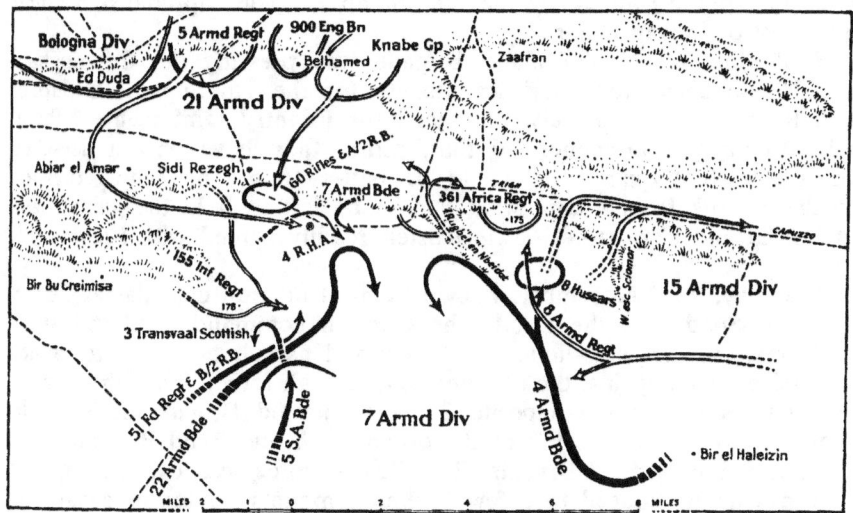

Defeat at Sidi Rezegh, 22nd November

Brigade took the first brunt of the armoured encounter: the 22nd Armoured Brigade counter-attacked, but while the British fire was directed mainly at the German tanks German 88-mm and 50-mm guns shot the British tank force to pieces. The 4th Armoured Brigade arrived too late to retrieve the disaster. By nightfall the 7th Armoured Brigade was reduced to 10 tanks, the 22nd to 24 and most of the Support Group had been overrun. Worse was to come. Cruewell had ordered the roving *15th Armoured Division* to the escarpment east of the airfield, which it did not reach before dark; but one tank regiment, sent ahead while the rest bedded down, bumped into the night leaguer of the headquarters and one regiment (the 8th Hussars) of the 4th Armoured Brigade, which it boldly surrounded and overran. The Germans captured the entire headquarters of the 4th Armoured Brigade except the brigade commander (Brigadier Gatehouse) who had the good fortune to be elsewhere, also 35 tanks and several guns. After the destruction of its command and communications system, the 4th Armoured Brigade became "temporarily useless as a fighting formation".

Meanwhile General Godwin-Austen had not been dilatory in setting in train operations by the XIII Corps. General Freyberg needed no spurring. On his initiative the 6th New Zealand Brigade (not the whole division as Scobie had supposed) had been dispatched along the Trigh Capuzzo on the 22nd to reinforce the British hold on Sidi Rezegh and, despite some delay caused by a direction from Norrie to change its attached Matildas for a squadron of Valentines, the brigade had made good but hard progress. In the meantime the XIII Corps had begun operating offensively on the frontier. One New Zealand brigade took Fort Capuzzo and Musaid, another mopped up around Bardia and cut its pipe-line while a tank and infantry attack by the 7th Indian Brigade captured Sidi Omar and most of Libyan Omar.

While the 6th New Zealand Brigade was pressing on, Cunningham and Norrie began to experience anxiety for the 7th Support Group at Sidi Rezegh and to perceive the need for infantry reinforcement there. Also Freyberg soon conceived that, rather than have only a detached brigade in that quarter, it would be better to get his whole division to the Tobruk front except what had to be left to hold the gains made at Bardia and Capuzzo. Godwin-Austen readily agreed with Freyberg.

Next day, 23rd November, known in the Lutheran calendar as *Totensonntag*—Sunday of the Dead—the German command employed about 160 tanks, several battalions of infantry and assault engineers to launch a massive attack against the depleted Sidi Rezegh force, of which the main components were the composite 22nd Armoured Brigade of 34 tanks (formed from what was left of the original 7th and 22nd Brigades) and the 5th South African Brigade. The British force was overrun and the British armour reduced to a few broken remnants no longer capable of challenging the *Africa Corps* to battle. The 5th South African Brigade ceased to exist as an effective formation. But the enemy victory was not won without cost. The Germans began the day with about 170 tanks; they ended it with about 100. They could not afford many such victories. And although next day the 7th Armoured Division's most effective tank formation could muster only 15 runners, the infantry of XIII Corps and the Matildas and Valentines allotted to their support still had a part to play.

Neither of the two messages sent to Scobie on the 22nd—first calling on him to attack Ed Duda to relieve a critical situation at Sidi Rezegh, then agreeing to a deferment of the attack because the situation was improving—had fitted his preconceptions of the CRUSADER plan. Knowing something was amiss, but not what it was, he decided to consolidate his outlet, mop up enemy remnants close to the corridor, extend his hold by capturing neighbouring strongpoints and maintain continuous pressure.

On the afternoon of the 22nd the 32nd Army Tank Brigade and the 2/Yorks and Lancs, with the 1st R.H.A. in support, took the strongpoint Lion, to the right of Tiger. In the evening Scobie heard that the enemy had recaptured Sidi Rezegh but other messages led him to believe erroneously that the whole of the New Zealand Division was proceeding to the Tobruk front. Next day consolidation west of the corridor continued. Dalby Square was captured and a counter-attack there withstood;

300 prisoners were taken. In another attack the western end of Tugun, to which the enemy had clung tenaciously, was captured.

The 25-pounders of the sortie force had fired about 400 rounds per gun on the 21st and again on the 23rd. That day Scobie asked for an ammunition ship, but was told that one could not be sent and he should conserve ammunition. Because of this and the necessity to husband his tank and infantry resources for an operation against Ed Duda he decided to limit field-gun action and curtail further exploitation. The fortress anti-aircraft guns, however, were used for a counter-battery shoot.

On the morning of the sortie the 2/13th Battalion had been split, battalion headquarters and two companies moving to the head of the Pilastrino road-pass, there to establish a back-stop defensive position, while the other two companies continued to hold the Wadi Sehel perimeter. Next day the battalion provided a grave-digging party on the Tiger battlefield, and on subsequent days guards at the neighbouring prisoner-of-war compound. On the morning of the 23rd a wrecked ship could be seen on the coast some distance to the west of the Wadi Sehel. It proved to be the *Maria Giovanni* which so often during the siege had brought canteen goods, wet and dry, and other comforts to Tobruk; this time the schooner had overshot the harbour and run into the shore. As the wreck was beyond field-gun range, efforts were made to shell it and destroy the cargo with anti-aircraft gunfire, but without success.

On the night of the 24th November the two 2/13th companies on the Wadi Sehel were relieved by troops from the Polish Brigade and joined the rest of the battalion at Pilastrino. No significance was attached to the reunion and for two days the men had little to do except ponder sceptically the reports of an offensive that seemed to have become bogged down. The course of the battle was viewed more optimistically at fortress headquarters, however, where it was inferred on the 24th from a study of intercepted messages that "the enemy's position was becoming extremely critical" and this seemed to be confirmed by a message received early next morning directing Scobie to get ready to attack Ed Duda in conjunction with the New Zealand Division. Stocks of 25-pounder ammunition were low—only 554 rounds per gun—but a ship provided in response to further urgent pleas was due to reach Tobruk on the night of the 26th with 600 tons.

By the morning of the 23rd the reports of British tank losses had forced Cunningham to acknowledge the stark truth that he had lost the armoured battle, and that the armoured force facing utter destruction was not the enemy's but his own. Whether to maintain the offensive or halt it was the one decision he could not take himself; there is little doubt, however, to which course he inclined. He asked General Auchinleck to come to the front. Cunningham's staff was presenting him with totals not only of British tank losses but of supposed German losses, based on grossly exaggerated reports. The situation was even worse than Cunningham thought.

In four days Eighth Army had lost some 530 tanks while the enemy lost about 100. Of 500 cruisers 7 Armoured Division retained fewer than 90, whereas the three enemy armoured divisions still had 250 tanks (170 of them German) of the 356 with which they had started the battle.[5]

Perhaps the exaggeration of enemy losses was just as well, for otherwise General Auchinleck might have found it more difficult to make the great and courageous decision which brought victory after defeat and for which he will always be famous. On 24th November he directed Cunningham to continue to attack the enemy relentlessly, using all his resources, "even to the last tank". Seldom in the annals of war has a single tactical decision been fraught with such great consequences. That the situation was not exactly as Auchinleck, for good reasons, conceived it is of less consequence than that his decision proved the right one for the situation that did evolve. No criticism can ever detract from his nobility in unequivocally declaring the grave risks his decision entailed and openly taking the whole responsibility for their acceptance.

Auchinleck issued a directive which re-affirmed that the immediate object was to destroy the enemy tank forces, the ultimate, the conquest of Cyrenaica, as a prelude to an advance to Tripoli. When one passes from his statement of the objects to his prescription of the method of achievement, one is arrested by the magnitude of the risks he took. The main method indicated was to recapture the Sidi Rezegh-Ed Duda ridge and join hands with the Tobruk garrison; in its practical application this meant that two New Zealand brigade groups and a small force of Valentines were to attempt what the XXX Corps had been defeated in attempting. But Auchinleck's indication of method merely endorsed what the field commanders were already doing. General Cunningham's preconception of the battle had been shattered; what he had originally regarded as only an incidental to the plan, the relief of Tobruk, was the only part of it that remained unattempted. This the formation commanders began to carry into effect almost as a matter of course, and as though unmindful that the prior destruction of the German armour had been declared a pre-requisite to its accomplishment.

The 6th New Zealand Brigade, pressing along the Trigh Capuzzo, had reached the vicinity of Sidi Rezegh airfield by the 23rd; New Zealand field and anti-tank gunners accounted for some of the German losses suffered in the *Totensonntag* battle. The 26th New Zealand Battalion at Garaet en Nbeidat was on the fringe of the battlefield, and that day the 25th and 24th Battalions had hard fighting with German infantry of the *361st Regiment* for possession of Point 175.

Godwin-Austen was told by Cunningham early on the 23rd that on the 24th he was to take charge of all operations to relieve Tobruk, including command of the fortress troops. Having little to spare from frontier commitments with which to help the New Zealand brigades advancing along the Trigh Capuzzo, Godwin-Austen thought of the two-brigade South African division, of which one brigade had not yet been committed. But

---

[5] W. E. Murphy, *The Relief of Tobruk* (1961), p. 108, a volume in the series *Official History of New Zealand in the Second World War 1939-45*.

there were others who had wanted the brigade's services. Norrie had summoned it to Sidi Rezegh; Cunningham had interfered to send one battalion group back to El Gubi to help the 22nd Guards Brigade "mask" the Italian *Ariete Division*. By sunset on the 23rd that brigade—Brigadier Pienaar's[6] 1st South African—was the only one that remained of the 1st South African Division.

The desolate scene at nightfall on the *Totensonntag* battlefield, south of Sidi Rezegh—the drifting smoke, the flickering fires, the sad groups of dejected men waiting to be gathered and imprisoned—symbolised the shattering of General Cunningham's CRUSADER dream. At dawn on the 24th the outmatched and battered 7th Armoured Division was all but defenceless. Nothing the British had left could try conclusions with the *Africa Corps'* armoured divisions or dispute their mastery of the desert between Tobruk and Salum in which both armies had their forward supply centres. The enemy could exploit the victory almost at will.

The German exploitation plan and its execution were both typical of Rommel. Relying on speed and surprise to unsettle and dislodge his enemy, he intended to drive the *Africa Corps* south-east at maximum speed, cross the frontier south of the Omars and then take in rear the British forces investing the German and Italian frontier garrisons.

By the evening of the 24th, leading elements of the *21st Armoured Division* were across the Egyptian frontier and making for the Halfaya Pass, though the *15th* had halted some distance west of the frontier and the *Ariete Division* was still not far from Bir el Gubi. On the 25th, the *21st Armoured Division's* tactical headquarters near Halfaya (under von Ravenstein) plotted an attack on Capuzzo but was unable to make mobile a sufficient force to mount it; the division's *5th Armoured Regiment* expended itself in unavailing attacks on Indian troops in the Omars. The *15th Armoured Division*, short of fuel and under air attack, probed into the rear areas of the New Zealand Division near Sidi Azeiz but accomplished little. The *Ariete Division* tried conclusions ingloriously with the 1st South African Brigade near Gabr Saleh.

Next day, the 26th, the *Africa Corps* did little but wrestle with its own supply difficulties until late afternoon and early night, when the *15th Armoured Division* operating from Bardia, and the *21st* from Halfaya, sent motorised battle groups against the two New Zealand battalions—the 23rd and 28th (Maori)—in the Capuzzo-Musaid-upper Salum area. The New Zealand battalions were not dislodged from their main holding positions.

So far the British command and troops had proved strangely unreactive and phlegmatic in face of the German commander's deep armoured thrusts. Though still hopeful of first snatching an easy prize or two on the frontier, Rommel realised by the morning of the 27th that it had become urgent to take his armoured formations back to the Tobruk front, whence Colonel

---

[6] Maj-Gen D. H. Pienaar, CB, DSO. Comd 1 SA Bde; GOC 1 SA Div. Regular soldier; b. Ladybrand, Orange Free State, 1893. Killed in plane crash 19 Dec 1942.

Westphal, left in command there by Rommel, had been sending a stream of increasingly apprehensive messages supplicating their help.

Norrie and Gott had admirably sustained their offensive outlook in face of the incredible decimation of their armoured regiments. The XXX Corps was organised into a number of "Jock" columns. This helped keep people's spirits up for a few days when the side was not winning, but later a continuation of the same policy was to allow the mobile forces to be satisfied with light sparring when some good slogging and close-in fighting would have better suited the New Zealand infantry advancing to Tobruk.

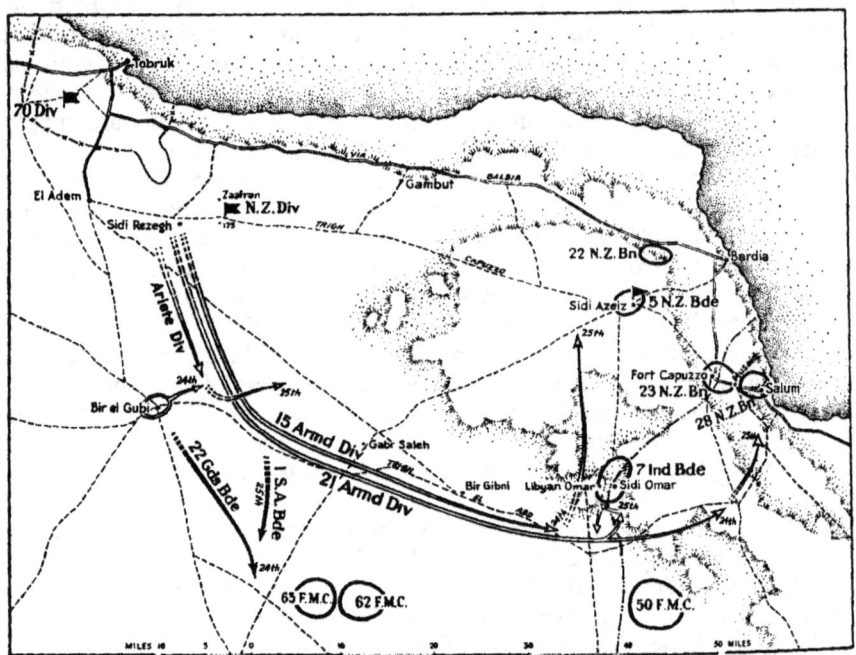

The German frontier foray, 24th-25th November

At first it was the obstinate British command's perverse tendency to underrate Rommel's power and belittle his efforts that robbed him of the success his enterprise deserved. So greatly had British reports overstated German tank losses, so greatly had Auchinleck's Intelligence service therefore under-stated the remaining German tank strength that he could not help but under-estimate the threat to his supply bases and lines of communication. But ultimately it was Rommel who robbed himself of that success by being blind to his enemy's Achilles heel. His threat to the vulnerable British supply and administrative areas did not become real because he sought other quarry, and Auchinleck's appreciation in his message to Cunningham and the Eighth Army (quoted below) "His position is desperate, and he is trying by lashing out in all directions to distract us from our object", though far from true, provided an interpretation with which Rommel's actions did not seem inconsistent.

One of the many paradoxes of the CRUSADER battle is that, while each army commander gave his striking forces tasks close to his enemy's forward supply and maintenance area, neither thought of his enemy's forward supply services as a primary target or went to special pains to discover their location. Rommel ordering the *Africa Corps* to make attacks on Capuzzo and Sidi Omar was no more mindful of the exposed British field maintenance centres than was the Eighth Army's staff, following on maps the New Zealand Division's progress towards Ed Duda, of the *Africa Corps'* vulnerable supply areas on the New Zealanders' northern flank. Yet both Auchinleck and Rommel gave much time and distracting thought to secondary operations along the line of oases from Giarabub to Gialo developed by the Eighth Army as a threat to Axis lines of communication in Cyrenaica.

Auchinleck spent two days at Eighth Army headquarters while Rommel was developing his eastward thrust but held steadfastly to his opinion that the Eighth Army had "only to persist to win".

His position is desperate (he told the army in a message before returning to Cairo) and he is trying by lashing out in all directions to distract us from our object, which is to destroy him utterly. . . . Give him no rest. The general situation in North Africa is excellent. There is only one order: ATTACK AND PURSUE. All out everyone.[7]

He returned to Cairo on 25th November, by which time he had decided that he could no longer repose confidence in General Cunningham who, in Auchinleck's opinion, had "begun to think defensively instead of offensively, mainly because of our large tank losses".[8] He chose his deputy chief of staff, Major-General Ritchie, whom he promoted to the rank of lieut-general, to replace Cunningham as army commander. Next afternoon General Smith, the Chief of the General Staff in the Middle East, arrived with Ritchie at Cunningham's headquarters bearing two letters from Auchinleck to Cunningham, and Smith informed Cunningham that he was to hand his command over at once to Ritchie. Never to be dismayed by misfortune was the theme of Auchinleck's substitution of Ritchie for Cunningham, which precept seemed to epitomise Ritchie's ill-starred exercise of command in the ensuing seven months.

The New Zealand Division (less the 5th Brigade) which with the 1st Army Tank Brigade (less one regiment) was advancing towards Tobruk by the Trigh Capuzzo route was too occupied with its own problems to be over-troubled by the disasters that had overtaken the 7th Armoured Division and 5th South African Brigade. On the 23rd the 25th New Zealand Battalion and part of the 24th and of the 8th Royal Tank Regiment (47 Valentines), were involved in heavy fighting with the German *361st Africa Regiment* in the 6th New Zealand Brigade's attack on Point 175, the capture of which was gallantly completed next day. On the

---
[7] Messages to CIGS and British Prime Minister quoted in J. Connell, *Auchinleck* (1959), pp. 372 and 373.
[8] Connell, p. 373.

25th the 4th New Zealand Brigade began clearing the enemy from the escarpment north of the Trigh Capuzzo on the right flank of the 6th Brigade and took Zaafran, while the 6th captured the Blockhouse and established two companies on the eastern edge of the Sidi Rezegh airfield.

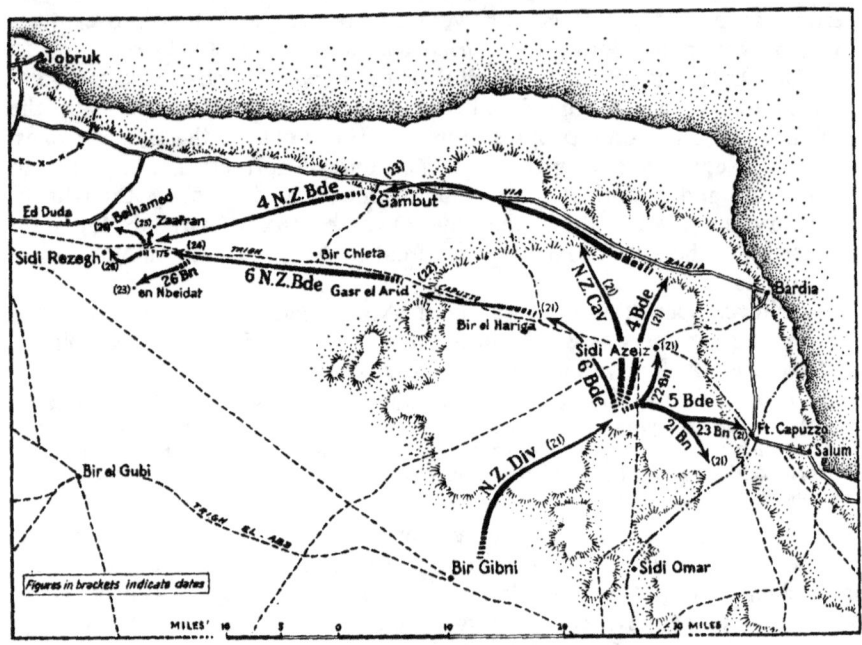

Westward advance of New Zealand Division, from 21st to 26th November

To General Freyberg the situation seemed propitious for a resumption of the plan to form a link at Ed Duda between the British frontier-based forces and the Tobruk sortie force. He heard from Godwin-Austen that Scobie had been preparing a sortie north-east of the "corridor" but had been told by Godwin-Austen that any sortie plan must include a "definite firm and secure junction" with the New Zealand Division at Ed Duda. Infected by the fantastic optimism of the intrepid but wishful-thinking British command and staff, who were incapable of recognising the battle signs of defeat, Freyberg sent Godwin-Austen a message to the effect that by first light next morning (26th November) the New Zealanders would be on a line from Ed Duda to Point 178 on the southern Sidi Rezegh escarpment. It was from the latter feature that as recently as the 22nd the 5th South African Brigade had been thrown back and counter-attacked by the German *155th Infantry Regiment*. In the admirable but incredible spirit of the day it seemed as if little more was needed than the order "fix bayonets, charge!" for the commanding Belhamed-Sidi Rezegh-Ed Duda triangle to fall to two brigades of New Zealand infantry and a few dozen army tanks.

It is surprising how long the comfortable official opinion that Rommel's armoured thrust to the frontier was "a last desperate effort" continued to colour the thinking and impair the judgment of commanders not only at the very top but also at command levels not entirely cut off from contact with the real situation. Scobie isolated in Tobruk could not fail to be misled, having no voice other than the biased and closely censored wireless traffic to tell him of what was occurring beyond the vision of his own forces' observation posts. His signallers, however, helped fill in the gaps left in official situation reports by intercepting signals not intended for his information.

Having learnt early on the 25th that his division would be expected to cooperate with the XIII Corps in capturing the Ed Duda-Sidi Rezegh area, Scobie ordered that a task force to comprise the 32nd Army Tank Brigade and the 1/Essex with supporting arms and to be commanded by Brigadier Willison should assemble that night. Soon after midday the fortress signallers intercepted a message from the army commander to the XXX Corps which indicated that the situation outside Tobruk was "very favourable". The army commander was quoted in the action log at fortress headquarters as saying "Enemy tank strength most frightfully low and getting worse; he is at his last or approaching last effort." A later message from Eighth Army headquarters said that 52 enemy tanks had been knocked out on the preceding day.

The situation outside as seen that day from within the fortress is thus depicted in a report issued from Scobie's headquarters at 6.45 a.m. on the 25th purporting to describe the state of the battle on the preceding day:

7 Indian Brigade and 42 RTR, Sheferzen area where small pockets enemy believed holding out. 5 NZ Brigade and 2 Squadron 44 RTR, area Bardia-Sollum-Capuzzo. Enemy still hold Bardia and Sollum villages. 4 NZ Brigade and 8 RTR Gambut-Bir Chleta. 6 New Zealand Brigade and 1 Squadron 44 RTR area point 175. 4 NZ Brigade engaging enemy in Gambut area. Small pockets enemy between 4 and 6 NZ Brigades. . . . 30 Corps situation this evening very confused. Gabr Saleh attacked by two columns each of 17 tanks. . . . Commander 13 Corps ordered to proceed with plan for relief of Tobruk. . . .

The Ed Duda force assembled at 8 p.m. and at 10.30 Scobie placed it on one hour's notice to move. A misunderstanding now sprang up between Godwin-Austen and Scobie that might not have occurred if the two commanders had previously been closely associated in jointly planning the relief operations or if their communications with each other had not been restricted to brief enciphered messages.

From the time of BATTLEAXE to the evolution of the CRUSADER plan, a junction at Ed Duda between frontier-based and fortress-based troops had been the keystone of all planning in Tobruk for garrison forces to participate in an operation to relieve the fortress. Every variation of the plan had made the garrison responsible for dispatching a mixed tank and infantry force to seize and hold Ed Duda. On the other hand, the planning both for BATTLEAXE and CRUSADER had also taken into account the possibility of other siege-raising operations by the garrison force, including a further sortie on the western sector. These were conceived, however, not as substitutes for the Ed Duda operation but as supplementary. Such a plan was made on 23rd November for a sortie by the Polish Brigade and one squadron of the 7th Royal Tanks to form a corridor through the enemy lines south of the Derna Road on the western sector. Its purpose is thus described in a 70th Division report.

> It appeared at this time that great success would be achieved . . . by passing any troops South African or New Zealand who might join hands on Ed Duda through the perimeter and out through a second corridor on the Western sector to cut the bypass road in the Acroma area.

For the junction at Ed Duda with troops from the frontier, however, Scobie and his staff had only one plan—Phase 5 of the set-piece sortie operation—which required the tank brigade to charge from the end of the corridor for about 7,000 yards to seize Ed Duda, and an infantry battalion, following soon afterwards, to hold that feature.

From the moment that he was given responsibility for the Tobruk front, however, General Godwin-Austen thought of the capture of Ed Duda as a task for the relieving force, not the Tobruk garrison. On 23rd November he wrote to General Freyberg concerning the sortie from Tobruk:

> I do not consider it has the reasonable chance of success we should offer it until we are ourselves firmly established on the Ed Duda position. I would ask you to let me know instantly when you are so disposed, using the codeword CURATE.

On the 24th Scobie signalled Godwin-Austen of the possible advantages of staging a sortie in the west where he thought that an easy success might be achieved that could unhinge the enemy. A message from Godwin-Austen crossed Scobie's message, the deciphered copy being received early next morning. Though partly corrupt Godwin-Austen's signal indicated that the New Zealand Division hoped to secure a given area (described by a corrupt group) on the morning of the 25th and that "the advance would then be on (1) Bir Amud[9] Sidi Rezegh (2) Ed Duda". Scobie was directed: "Be prepared to continue your operation to create a diversion." To its sender the message implied that the New Zealand Division would be responsible for taking Ed Duda, but Scobie was unlikely to read it that way and in fact appears to have construed it as a requirement to continue his sortie operations with the object of creating as much diversion as possible. He informed Godwin-Austen that, since it did not seem practical to attack Ed Duda without the certainty of cooperation from other troops in the Sidi Rezegh area, he had decided to undertake operations to widen the corridor as much as possible.

Next a long message, also corrupt, brought Godwin-Austen's reply to Scobie's earlier message and expressed Godwin-Austen's fear that the proposal to debouch near the Derna Road might prejudice the Ed Duda sortie. This message did not help remove the underlying misunderstanding about who was to take Ed Duda. It explained that Freyberg hoped to reach Ed Duda next night and that Scobie was to be ready to advance

---

[9] North of Belhamed.

on Ed Duda at any time after first light on the 26th. Corps headquarters would send Scobie the code word and the date but the time would be at Scobie's discretion.

Hard on this message, to keep the cipher sections busy, came another long one from the XIII Corps,[1] in which Godwin-Austen (probably taking Scobie as replying to his second message, not his first) was at pains to explain that he had had no intention of ordering Scobie to advance to Ed Duda till Freyberg had reached it, but that thereupon Scobie was to join forces with Freyberg "at all costs". In the meantime, subject to its not weakening his power to join forces, Scobie was to do his best to assist Freyberg by creating a diversion as soon as he received through corps headquarters the zero hour for Freyberg's attack on Ed Duda. Scobie replied that his forces were all set to cooperate. The corridor would be open if the New Zealanders got Ed Duda and a mobile mixed force would be ready for further cooperation next day.

Scobie had in fact settled the diversionary tasks at an orders conference at 8.45 a.m. The Polish Brigade had made a feint attack in the western sector early that morning; the enemy was not unnerved but on the contrary counter-attacked from the Twin Pimples area. It was therefore decided that the diversionary operations would be carried out in the corridor area and would be directed to mopping up on the corridor's eastern side, from which the enemy could direct fire against the flanks of a force advancing on Ed Duda.

Tobruk Fortress headquarters learnt in the evening that the New Zealand Division was to open its attack at 9 p.m.[2] Simultaneously the garrison forces launched tank and infantry operations with artillery support in the corridor to mop up enemy pockets at Butch (on the east of the corridor near the perimeter) and at Wolf.[3] Operations by a company of the 2/Leicester and a squadron of the 7th Royal Tanks in the wrecked plane area were partly successful, capturing two out of five sangars but the attack on Wolf by a company of the 2/Yorks and Lancs and the 4th Royal Tanks encountered much opposition; 150 prisoners were taken but the enemy strongly counter-attacked and recaptured part of the locality. About 7 a.m. next morning a second British attack recaptured Wolf and many prisoners were taken, but about 300 enemy escaped up the escarpment. From the corridor sounds of battle to the south and south-east had been heard after midnight and when it became light some shelling thought to be from 25-pounders was observed on Belhamed, and farther west, towards El Adem.

About 11 a.m. on 26th November the long awaited code word for the attack on Ed Duda was passed through Tobruk. It seems that the decision to mount the attack was Scobie's own and was made after interception of two messages from the New Zealand Division to the XIII Corps, the first stating that the 6th New Zealand Brigade had captured Sidi Rezegh

---
[1] Quoted in full in Murphy, *The Relief of Tobruk*, p. 247.
[2] This was probably ascertained from the intercept service.
[3] Carmuset Beludeah, south-east of Tiger. The old code-names have been used though new code-names Sneezy and Grumpy had been introduced for Tiger and Wolf.

and was on the way to Ed Duda and the second asking what time the Tobruk garrison would attack. Scobie replied immediately to the second that he had already made his diversionary attack. One can only conjecture that on further consideration he concluded that the basic principle of Godwin-Austen's instructions to him was that he should at all costs effect a junction with the New Zealand Division when it had reached Ed Duda and that inquiries from each division to corps headquarters about what the other was doing were not likely to promote this. Zero hour was fixed at five minutes after midday.

According to the Tobruk Fortress action log a message was received from the New Zealand Division before the Ed Duda force crossed the start-line to the effect that the New Zealand Division's forward troops were "held up at Sidi Rezegh and hill 2 miles NNE"[4] but (states the divisional narrative) it was too late, even if desirable, to postpone the attack.

Matildas of the 4th Royal Tanks (Lieut-Colonel W. C. L. O'Carroll), followed by the 1st Royal Tanks (cruisers and light tanks) and supported by the 1st R.H.A. charged across the four or five miles of flat desert separating the start-line from Ed Duda and climbed to the top of that feature; but as they went over the rise to descend to the by-pass road they found themselves facing enemy guns firing point-blank. The closer guns were silenced by the Besa machine-guns mounted on the tanks and the 1st R.H.A. did their best to neutralise others.

About 45 minutes later Brigadier Willison called forward the 1/Essex. Led by their carrier platoon, they "made a fine spectacle".

> The advance was carried out across the plain without interruption until the leading troops were about 200 yards from the near edge of the escarpment, where they were heavily bombed. This bombardment destroyed half the Carrier Platoon, about one platoon of "D" Company, killing the Company Commander (Major C. H. Robinson) and the Carrier Officer (Lieutenant C. H. Lawrence, M.C.), and inflicting about 35 other casualties. This did not check the advance, and all companies, on reaching the escarpment, debussed according to plan and went forward rapidly to seize their respective objectives.
> At this time the whole Tank Brigade had withdrawn to the left flank, and was formed up ready to support the battalion if required.[5]

The bombing resulted from an attack made by the R.A.F. in response to calls for support by the 4th New Zealand Brigade (then at Belhamed) which had nominated a bomb-line that placed Ed Duda in the target area, the raid being described as "most successful to date" in that evening's situation report.

The Essex soon dug themselves in for all round defence. The situation became most unpleasant when some German 210-mm guns, at first unable to traverse far enough round, were re-sited and then engaged both tanks and infantry with very damaging fire. Several local German counter-attacks were made before dusk and repulsed with the capture of about 70 prisoners.

---

[4] This is probably a paraphrase of Message O1 quoted in NZ Divisional Campaign Narrative Nov-Dec 1941, Vol 7, p. 879. A paraphrase of message 12 quoted on p. 878 is logged as having been received at 1.30 p.m.

[5] T. A. Martin, *The Essex Regiment 1929-1950* (1952), p. 80.

After dark several groups of Germans and Italians were ambushed while travelling along the by-pass road unaware that it had been cut.

At 1.30 p.m. Scobie's signallers had intercepted a message from Freyberg to Godwin-Austen which stated that the situation demanded that the Tobruk garrison exert its strongest pressure and that the New Zealand Division would endeavour to "reach Ed Duda" after darkness, which in the context of Godwin-Austen's instructions placed the onus on Scobie to dispatch his junction force at that time. But by 1.30 p.m. Willison's tanks were already on top of Ed Duda. The success of the operation was reported to Scobie at 2.45 p.m. Scobie then sent Freyberg a brief message. "We are on Ed Duda. Ensure not bombed."

Freyberg's plan had provided for a night attack on the 25th-26th by the 4th and 6th New Zealand Brigades to capture Belhamed and Sidi Rezegh, after which a force was to be pushed through to seize Ed Duda. The two brigades were to thrust westwards on either side of the Trigh Capuzzo, the 4th on the north side to take Belhamed, the 6th on the south to secure the Sidi Rezegh plateau. Because Belhamed was thought to be the more strongly held, the 6th Brigade was allotted the further task of dispatching a force to Ed Duda.

Even with their best will and utmost effort Freyberg's battalions could not be ready by 9 p.m., the zero hour he had over-optimistically prescribed. They got away to a late and ragged start to carry out plans too hastily made. The 4th Brigade meeting less opposition than expected overran Belhamed, which was not strongly held. The 6th Brigade had a confused and troublesome night, all the more so because the enemy was effecting a relief on the ground attacked in the course of a reorganisation of his front. The plan was to establish a firm base on the Sidi Rezegh escarpment plateau above the Trigh Capuzzo from which a force of two battalions (the 21st and 26th) with supporting arms would descend to the "Trigh" en route to Ed Duda. The 24th and depleted 25th Battalions managed to establish themselves in a defensive "box" on the plateau above the escarpment south-west of the Sidi Rezegh mosque, but the route of the Ed Duda force to the Trigh Capuzzo had not been cleared of enemy and confusion attended efforts to get it married up and started before dawn. So with Freyberg's approval the advance to Ed Duda was cancelled.

Dawn on the 26th found the New Zealanders at Sidi Rezegh disorganised and exposed to the close fire of an enemy ensconced on most of the ground of vantage but although many detachments had soon to be extricated and others were lost the New Zealanders clung throughout the day to their foothold west of the airfield and south-west of the mosque.

When Freyberg was told that a force from Tobruk had taken Ed Duda, he ordered his 4th Brigade (Brigadier L. M. Inglis) to effect a junction with the garrison force and his 6th Brigade (Brigadier H. E. Barrowclough) to complete the capture of Sidi Rezegh. A composite squadron of tanks of the 44th Royal Tanks set off for Ed Duda at 9.30 p.m.; fifteen minutes later the 19th Infantry Battalion followed, accompanied by 6 more tanks. The leading tanks approached Ed Duda just before midnight firing green Very lights for recognition. The infantry battalion arrived about an hour later after some light skirmishing on the way. In the meantime the weary, overtried battalions of Barrowclough's brigade, in bitter bullet-and-bayonet night fighting, slaughtered or winkled out most of the remaining enemy pockets on the Sidi Rezegh escarpment. But one German strongpoint remained on the escarpment, to the east of the mosque; another German locality lay midway between Belhamed and Sidi Rezegh.

Thus by dawn on 27th November the junction at Ed Duda between the Tobruk garrison and the frontier-based forces to which Godwin-Austen, Freyberg and Scobie had ascribed pre-eminent importance had been achieved. Yet the other pieces on the battle-board were oddly slow in arranging themselves into a pattern of victory. Scobie sent two "senior staff officers"[6] to Ed Duda in an armoured car hoping to make contact with the New Zealand Division only to find that despite the preceding night's consolidation by the New Zealanders there was no free passage across from Ed Duda to the rest of the New Zealand Division.[7]

Early on the 27th Godwin-Austen sent a message to Tobruk Fortress, the New Zealand Division and the 22nd Armoured Brigade directing that as soon as the position at Belhamed, Sidi Rezegh and Ed Duda was established the westward advance to the line Tobruk-El Adem-Bir el Gubi track would be continued. The New Zealand Division was to continue the advance along the escarpment, the Tobruk garrison to conform on the north. The interdivisional boundary, prescribed as inclusive to the New Zealand Division, was to be the escarpment running from Ed Duda to Point 162. The message continued:

TOBFORT will organise and dispatch mobile columns to clear areas between Tobfort and Gambut and establish strong picquets east of the road and track Gambut-463414 and will secure all landing grounds.[8]

Scobie sent Freyberg a message requesting that in view of these instructions his troops at Ed Duda should be relieved as soon as possible. Later Scobie signalled Godwin-Austen pointing out that he was much extended and stating that it was essential that this relief be arranged as soon as possible if he was to comply with Godwin-Austen's instructions. Soon afterwards Freyberg signalled Scobie:

We are holding firmly Ed Duda and Belhamed. Must know your forward troops and general line you hold. . . .

which created an unhappy and unfavourable impression in Tobruk, as if the New Zealanders were unsure of their bearings, and Scobie rather tartly rejoined:

Your infantry are not repeat not on Ed Duda which is feature in square 424409. . . . My next forward posts are in 419414 and 426415. . . .

---

[6] The war diary of the King's Dragoon Guards, which was to provide the armoured car, suggests that one of the two senior officers was Scobie himself.

[7] It is stated in Murphy, *The Relief of Tobruk*, that Scobie did not get word from Willison until after 1 p.m. of the presence of 44 RTR and 19 Bn at Ed Duda but a report from the Essex timed 8.20 a.m. is entered in the divisional action log and a map reference is given for the 19 Bn's location, which was also repeated in a situation report sent to all units during the morning.

[8] Deciphered at 70 Div slightly differently from at NZ Div.

Freyberg's message about holding Ed Duda firmly is difficult to understand. It is unlikely that he knew just where his 19th Battalion was. Probably his purpose was only to find out where Scobie's forces were. Perhaps some misreading of code names is at the root of the confusion and this possibly explains Scobie's next message to Freyberg:

> Confirm you hold Sidi Rezegh and the hill to the north. . . . Confirm your tanks and infantry are under my command. . . .

to which Freyberg replied that the 44th Royal Tank Regiment would have to return to the New Zealand Division but the 19th Battalion was available for the continued defence of Ed Duda.

These messages reflect their authors' blind spots for battle situations beyond the vision of their own forward troops, Scobie being unaware of the rigours endured by the New Zealanders and their near exhaustion and Godwin-Austen and Freyberg not comprehending how Scobie's resources had been stretched to the limit in holding a front of more than 40 miles even before he was given the superadded tasks Godwin-Austen had just ordained.

Though rightly wary of dangerously weakening Tobruk's defences by undertaking excursions, Scobie thought the enemy was cracking and suggested to Godwin-Austen late on the morning of the 27th that a general retreat could be imminent. But the rosy view of the battle was beginning to be dispelled by irrefragable evidence. Godwin-Austen visited the New Zealanders for lunch. First-hand reports of their heavy losses and recurrent warnings reaching him of the German armoured divisions' approach from the frontier region induced him to adopt a more cautious tone than the exuberant "all-out-for-the-chase" theme of his early morning directive, which had drowned his simultaneously sounded warning note. He now told Scobie that the New Zealand Division could do no more than hold the ground it had gained and that Scobie would therefore be responsible for "establishing the corridor and holding it open at all costs". Scobie replied that the corridor was already open and the garrison would do its best to maintain it so.

The 2/13th Battalion ensconced in the last ditch at Pilastrino while everybody else was advancing could not help but feel that its masters regarded it as unemployable except for such tasks as guarding prisoners, collecting dead and digging graves. About 12.30 p.m. on the 27th divisional headquarters instructed the battalion to send armed parties to the perimeter in the only two light vehicles it possessed and there to take charge of incoming prisoners. Soon afterwards this order was cancelled and a message from Scobie's battle headquarters stated that the deputy fortress commander, Brigadier Martin, was on his way to the battalion and directed the commanding officer to call his company commanders together. Martin arrived 15 minutes later and explained that the battalion was to be prepared to move on one hour's notice with the surprising role of issuing from the perimeter and advancing to Gambut along the Bardia Road.[9]

---

[9] i.e. main coast road (Via Balbia).

It was believed that about 1,000 Italians had given themselves up in that region and were being escorted into the perimeter and others in the east were gathering together as though waiting to be collected. A kind of mustering and picketing operation seemed to be in prospect.

About 5 p.m. Colonel Burrows was called to Scobie at his battle headquarters. Scobie told Burrows that the garrison had been warned to expect a German counter-attack from the direction of Bardia. Burrows' battalion was his only reserve and was to be ready to counter-attack any penetrating force at half an hour's notice. It was to take up a back-stop position blocking the Bardia Road. This would be convenient for another reason. If the German attack did not materialise, there would be an eastward thrust next day by the 32nd Armoured Brigade and 2/Queen's south of the Bardia Road and the 1/King's Own north of it. The 2/13th was to follow the 1/King's Own and continue the advance from Sidi Bu Amud to Gazala. This operation would start at 7 a.m. unless the dawn tactical reconnaissance indicated that a German attack was brewing.

When Burrows came out from Scobie's office he was told that while he had been conferring with Scobie his battalion had been moved up to a covering position astride the Bardia Road and in front of King's Cross; but Burrows arrived there in time to dispose the main body of the battalion. The next 24 hours were miserable, not because of any action but because it rained before the ill-equipped battalion could get comfortably settled.

The CRUSADER battle took a new turn on 27th November when Rommel reluctantly turned his back on the frontier and returned to the Tobruk front. For three days the great Eighth Army's offensive had dwindled to small-scale, mixed infantry and tank attacks by the equivalent of about three infantry brigades and three tank battalions, yet the pressure exerted by these forces had strained the Axis front at Tobruk so near to breaking-point that a large part of the combatant strength of both armies was soon drawn to the area of stress.

The German command was not single-minded that morning of the 27th. General Cruewell wanted the armoured divisions to return as quickly as possible to the Tobruk front; General Rommel, who had the last word, desired to win some quick successes first at the frontier. Typically the day's work for the German armoured formations began two hours before dawn. Soon after daylight the *8th Armoured Regiment* overran the headquarters of the 5th New Zealand Brigade at Sidi Azeiz. The main body of the *15th Armoured Division* (but less the *33rd Engineer Battalion*) then made its best time westwards along the Trigh Capuzzo; on this course, if its progress was not contested, it would take in rear first the rear headquarters of the XXX Corps and then in succession the respective headquarters of the XIII Corps, the New Zealand Division and the 1st Army Tank Brigade. Meanwhile the main body of the *21st Armoured Division,* issuing from Bardia by the main coast road, had bumped into the 22nd New Zealand Battalion at Menastir. The New Zealanders held on, forcing the

German formation to lose valuable time; next day it proceeded by another route. The *33rd Engineer Battalion* and supporting detachments, under Rommel's direct observation, daringly assaulted the 23rd New Zealand Battalion's positions at Capuzzo in the afternoon and drove a deep wedge into the New Zealanders' positions but failed to thrust them from their ground. After dark the attackers went west to rejoin their parent formation.

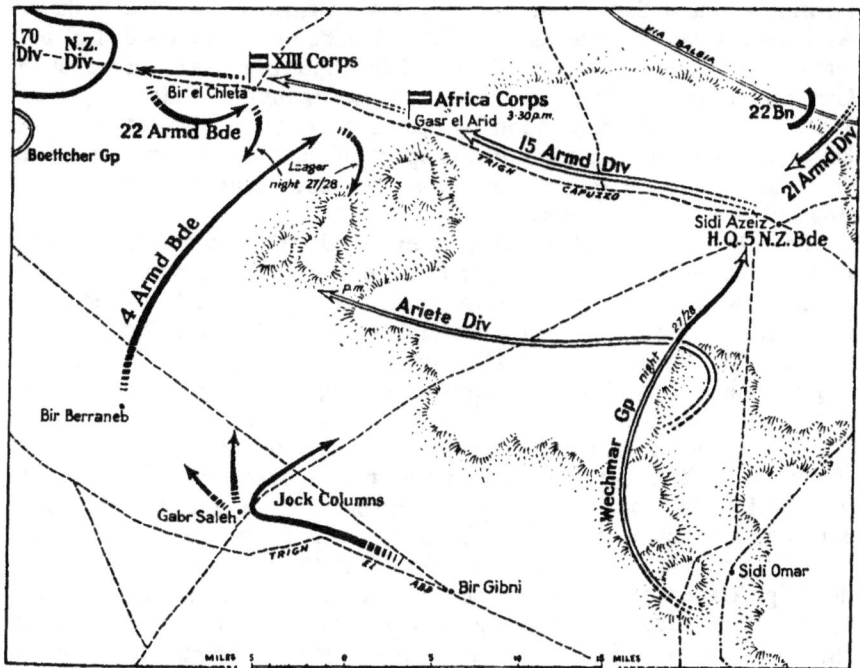

Movements of armoured formations, 27th November

Each army was following the course of the battle largely by intercepting its opponents' signal traffic. The British knew that the German armour was returning to the Tobruk front and higher commanders and headquarters gave Freyberg and Scobie and the other field commanders every warning. But the British command was hoist with its own petard. Eighth Army headquarters could not alert its people to the reality of a threat it had itself dismissed as unreal. So long had the Eighth Army's reports been nonchalantly depicting the two German armoured divisions operating on the frontier as roaming "columns of tanks and MT", not to be contemplated with undue alarm, that the warnings now issued failed to induce the infantry formation commanders to see the German armour's return to the Tobruk front as the grave and potent threat it was. Worse, practising self-deception, the British command itself saw the German westward move as prompted not by its real purpose of crippling attack but by an imagined one of evasion. The German columns were no more in retreat than on that earlier occasion when in presumed flight they had driven westward to Sidi Rezegh with the foolishly optimistic British armoured brigades in pursuit.

In the three days taken up by the *Africa Corps'* frontier foray the 7th Armoured Division, left to its own devices, had substantially reconstituted its strength by battlefield recoveries, workshop returns and new deliveries. The 22nd Armoured Brigade, which had been protecting the New Zealand Division's inland flank, had more than 40 British cruiser tanks, the 4th Armoured some 77 Stuarts; the 7th, also being re-equipped, had been temporarily withdrawn from battle. Gott had been forewarned of the German armoured divisions' westward moves by the intercept service. When he was told about noon by scouting armoured cars of the King's Dragoon Guards that a column was approaching Gasr el Arid, he ordered the 22nd Armoured Brigade to "stop the head" and the 4th Armoured Brigade to attack the flank.

The 22nd Armoured Brigade intercepted and blocked the German *15th Armoured Division* near Bir el Chleta about 1.30 p.m. In numbers of tanks the two formations were about equally matched but the British with only one battery of 25-pounders and one of 2-pounders were outgunned. The 7th Armoured Division was still employing its armoured brigades separately from its support group, whose artillery had been dispersed among a number of light-raiding Jock columns.

Later in the afternoon the stronger 4th Armoured Brigade joined in, giving the British equality in gun-power and superiority in tanks, and the R.A.F. intervened effectively with several bombing strikes. The battle honours were about even, but the British armour thwarted the German commander's attempt to get a foothold on the escarpment overlooking the Trigh Capuzzo from which he could attack the British forces opening up the Trigh route to Ed Duda. When it became too dark for another chukker, however, the British armoured brigades, having virtually won the day, quitted the ground and returned to their congenial leaguers. The oft-repeated injunctions "Attack", "Pursue", "Destroy" contained nothing about fighting for a tactical advantage. General Neumann-Silkow pushed on after dark to seize and secure the pass up the escarpment at Bir Sciafsciuf.

While in the 2/13th Battalion's command post in Tobruk the lie of the ground from Sidi Bu Amud to Gambut was being studied that night by lantern on the Gambut map, Rommel and Cruewell were in conference at Gambut, and Rommel according to the *Africa Corps* war diary was proposing to attack west or south-west from the area south of Sidi Bu Amud. That was where General Suemmermann had his headquarters; his infantry would join in. On this day a new name had been given to Suemmermann's battered *Division zbV Africa*, which its own performances would soon make famous: it became the *90th Light Division*.

If an illustration were required to give point to General Blamey's criticism of the British command for lacking a sense of organisation and failing to recognise the importance of employing formations complete, none better could be found than the use of the New Zealand Division in CRUSADER. When Freyberg asked for the return of his 5th Brigade, nobody went to much pains to see that his wish was granted. If another brigade were needed, then Ritchie, it should seem, was content that the 1st South African Brigade be sent.

It was decided on the evening of the 27th that the South African brigade should join the New Zealand Division, but the marriage was to prove difficult to consummate and from this arose some of the difficulties with which the New Zealand Division was soon to be beset. In the meantime the division lacked the manpower and the fire-power to consolidate on its vital ground and liquidate the remaining enemy pockets near by.

There was hope in Tobruk on the 28th, expressed in the planned operations to clear the enemy from the Bardia Road, that after ten days of battering since the offensive began the hold of the Axis forces on the surrounding desert was breaking. Rain and misconstrued reports from Ed Duda of enemy tank activity, however, delayed the start of these operations. At dawn Ed Duda was found to be quieter; the enemy had withdrawn from holding positions on the west side. Two companies of the 19th New Zealand Battalion were sent out to establish an outpost on the escarpment south of the Trigh Capuzzo and west of Sidi Rezegh where the Essex had maintained a patrol on the previous day and to ascertain whether some troops near by were hostile or friendly; but the patrol was recalled before its mission was completed.

For two days the 1st R.H.A. had suspected enemy on Belhamed despite the reported capture of the feature by the New Zealand Division. This morning the crystal clear vision afforded by the first light left no doubt that there was an enemy pocket on the north-west side of the feature, from which a grand-stand view would be had of the proposed sweep by the 2/Queens from Bir Belhamed through enemy positions east of the corridor to the Bardia Road.

About 11.30 in the morning Tobruk Fortress headquarters received a message from the XIII Corps to the effect that it was "vital to the advance of the New Zealand Division" that an area which was designated by map reference should be occupied and held from 2 p.m. that day. The area included the ground where the pocket had been observed. Probably the message intended no more than to ensure that the 4th New Zealand Brigade's northern flank should be looked after while the division concentrated on mopping-up operations to the south. The 19th New Zealand Battalion (less the two companies patrolling from Ed Duda) and a squadron of the 4th Royal Tank Regiment were detailed for the operation and the two patrolling companies were recalled to take their place. After a late start this force occupied the Belhamed escarpment in the early afternoon; a mixed group of Germans and Italians surrendered when the tanks got close. Subsequently the forces at Ed Duda lost contact with the Belhamed assault force and tank patrols sent out in the evening could not find them. Brigadier Inglis had sent the 19th Battalion detachment back that night to Zaafran. It was typical of the confusing liaison by the XIII Corps in this operation that after Scobie had responded to the corps' request to secure this area, the New Zealand Division was permitted to take under its command the troops Scobie had sent there for the purpose, without so much as a "by your leave".

On the 28th the New Zealanders in the Belhamed-Sidi Rezegh-Ed Duda triangle operated to mop up the two German localities near the Trigh Capuzzo that were still troubling them. In the afternoon part of the 18th New Zealand Battalion and a squadron of the 44th Royal Tanks overran the pocket between Belhamed and Sidi Rezegh, and the troublesome strongpoint on the escarpment east of the tomb was taken in a two-platoon attack by the 26th New Zealand Battalion.

Overlooking the Sidi Rezegh airfield and plateau from the south was the second escarpment on which the New Zealanders had of necessity left the enemy in undisturbed possession. Here the powerful *Artillery Command 104* (ARKO) of Major-General Boettcher had established itself after the reorganisation necessitated by the New Zealand advance. While the 18th and 26th Battalions were attacking the last two enemy pockets, a German attack from this escarpment was launched on the 24th Battalion and, by various ruses, achieved surprise and substantial success. Subsequent counter-attacks by tanks of the 8th Royal Tank Regiment did not fully restore the situation.

In the early part of the day the German armoured formations were scatttered, and some grounded by supply difficulties, but they were not much troubled by their adversaries. The 7th Armoured Division spent a futile day, nor did it accomplish its main task which was to deliver the 1st South African Brigade to the New Zealand Division at Trig 175; it suffered much in unprofitable skirmishing with the *15th Armoured Division* but unknowingly secured some advantage to the New Zealand Division by enticing the German formation southwards. Some elements of the German division overran the New Zealand main dressing station in the afternoon but allowed it to continue functioning. As the daylight was failing German advance-guards briefly clashed with a local defence group of the New Zealand divisional headquarters. By nightfall the *21st Armoured Division* had closed up on the headquarters area of the New Zealand Division and the XIII Corps; with the latter were headquarters elements of the XXX Corps. Godwin-Austen and Freyberg decided to move their headquarters into Tobruk that night and so notified Scobie. Freyberg kept with him outside Tobruk only the minimum staff for a battle headquarters. The 7th Armoured Division leaguered not far away to the south, by the Trigh el Abd, with the 1st South African Brigade near by.

The wishful belief that the besieging force might soon disintegrate was belied by the resistance encountered when the garrison's delayed operation to break through to the Bardia Road was launched. The operation was to start with the capture, on the east of the corridor, of Freddie and Walter, two posts in a chain of strong-points developed for the protection of the German by-pass road; but Freddie, to quote the diarist of the 1st R.H.A., "proved a hard nut". The attack was made by two companies of the 2/Queen's and "D" Squadron of the 7th Royal Tanks. The attacking infantry were disorganised by hostile fire. An enemy force on the right flank from which fire was disrupting the assault was attacked by nine cruiser tanks and some light tanks of the 1st Royal Tanks sent across from Ed Duda. Twenty enemy were captured and eleven enemy tanks driven off. Some of the tanks of the assault force then got onto the top of Freddie and circled round it and about 300 prisoners, mostly German, were taken. But five tanks were lost (mainly on mines), the artillery forward observation officer was killed, the exploitation operations were cancelled and towards dusk the assault infantry were withdrawn. The mere fact that the garrison was continuing to press the enemy, however, was a contribution to its prospects; it must be realised that the German infantry constituted the steel in the enemy's siege girdle round Tobruk. Those attacked were some of the few elements of the *90th Light Division* hitherto unmauled.

The development of the battle that afternoon made Scobie apprehensive about the situation at Ed Duda. There, after the cruiser squadron of the 1st Royal Tanks had been sent off to support the attack against Freddie and the one remaining squadron of Matildas of the 4th Royal Tanks had accompanied the 19th New Zealand Battalion to Belhamed, the 1/Essex had been practically unsupported. Late in the afternoon enemy activity had been observed on the Sidi Rezegh escarpment. On receiving a situation report from the New Zealand Division just before 6 p.m. Scobie gave instructions that the 16th Brigade would move the 2/13th Battalion to Ed Duda (the 2/13th having no transport of its own) and ordered Burrows to report to him for orders. Scobie told Burrows that the primary purpose of the battalion's move was to strengthen the defence of Ed Duda; the battalion was not to be employed without Scobie's authority, except in an emergency. Burrows returned to the battalion, gave orders for the move and then departed in his staff car to meet Brigadier Lomax at his headquarters at Post R69. Near the gap in the perimeter Burrows' car was intercepted by Brigadier Willison in another car, who told Burrows that Scobie was coming to meet him there. Scobie arrived about 15 minutes later and at the back of a truck which shielded the light from no-man's land produced a map and outlined the situation in the Belhamed-Sidi Rezegh-Ed Duda triangle which, he said, had the "double virtue" of dominating the enemy lines of retreat westward and affording strong-points in the link-up with British forces from the frontier. Corps headquarters was coming into Tobruk that night, which made it more necessary than ever to keep the corridor open and to ensure that Ed Duda was not cut off. There had been a disturbing report that the enemy might have taken Sidi Rezegh that afternoon in a counter-attack. There would probably be a New Zealand attack next day to recapture Sidi Rezegh and the 2/13th might have to assist. Orders would later be sent about that, but the main responsibility was Ed Duda.

I can remember, when that conference was over, the General's last words to us as we were standing there, before he turned to go away. "Whatever happens we *must* hold Ed Duda. Ed Duda must be held."[2]

By that time the unit convoy had arrived and was waiting at the gap. Soon it moved on, shielded by armoured cars in front and on the flank. Most of the men later commented on the strangeness of the emotions they experienced as they were driven out that night through the imprisoning wire into *his* territory, as though something that had unconsciously weighed on the mind had been lifted and an unbelievable freedom had suddenly become real. The convoy halted at Tiger (then officially called Sneezy) where the 32nd Army Tank Brigade had a headquarters or communications centre. Here a warning was received that the 2/13th Battalion was to support an attack next morning on Sidi Rezegh by Willison's armoured brigade and a New Zealand battalion, for which orders would be given after the battalion reached Ed Duda. The project is thus described in the 70th Division's operations report:

> A plan was made during the night by which the 19th New Zealand Battalion, assisted if necessary by 2/13th Australian Battalion, should be established on the spur which runs east from Sidi Rezegh with the support of the 32nd Army Tank Brigade.

At Tiger a supply column going to the New Zealand Division and a stronger escort joined the convoy, which moved off after a wait that was not as long as it seemed, for the battalion reached Ed Duda soon after midnight. The men jumped down from their trucks and were taken by guides to areas they were to occupy on Ed Duda's eastern slopes. The night was too cold for most to sleep. The besieged garrison's link through Ed Duda with the British forces operating outside seemed very real that night as long British and New Zealand convoys from headquarters and administrative units, emerging from the desert, came up the by-pass road, turned off at Ed Duda and proceeded in the direction of the Tobruk corridor.

At 4 a.m. Burrows attended a conference at Willison's tactical headquarters held to decide details of the attack on Sidi Rezegh. Here it was ascertained that the commanding officer and half of the 19th New Zealand Battalion were not available and a plan was made for the 2/13th to make the attack and moreover to establish itself on the ground to be taken. Burrows emphasised the need for daylight reconnaissance before attempting what seemed an ambitious enterprise and the 1st R.H.A. pointed out that the guns would have to be moved forward before the attack could be supported, so it was decided that it could not begin before 11 a.m. Concise orders for the operation were formulated:

> Enemy is in occupation of SW slope of Sidi Rezegh. Own troops 2/13 Battalion under command of 4 RTR for operation and will have tank support. New Zealand troops are to occupy remainder of Sidi Rezegh. *Intention* 2/13 Battalion will seize and hold high feature in squares 425405, 425406 and 425407.

---

[2] From letter written by the author on 4th December 1941. Scobie used the pronunciation "El Duda".

The orders went on to prescribe the method and to indicate the forming-up place, start-line, a start-time (11 a.m.), and limit to the depth of the attack.

The guides who showed the 2/13th companies to their bivouac areas on eastern Ed Duda that night warned that there would be shelling in the morning but the incoming veterans, thinking they had little to learn about shell fire, were insufficiently regardful. Just before dawn, as the escarpment ridges began to be outlined by a paling sky, a column of New Zealand heavy transport vehicles, reluctant to proceed to Tobruk without a guide, halted about the Ed Duda pass. Well dispersed, the trucks began moving. The report of a heavy gun and the shatter of an exploding shell sent muttering echoes travelling down the long line of the escarpment. Other bursts quickly followed. Huge lurid billows of black smoke mushroomed from the desert floor around the now fast-moving vehicles headed for Tobruk. These awe-inspiring explosions came from heavier artillery[3] than the Australians had become accustomed to in Tobruk. When the last vehicle disappeared, the enemy guns began with murderous effect to bombard the slopes on which the light of dawn had disclosed the 2/13th companies not properly dug in. To escape, men began making for the lee of the escarpment on the other side of the pass. The quick-thinking Burrows indicated to Lieutenant Maughan[4] an area some distance to the east, at the foot of the escarpment on its northern side, and told him to intercept the men there and direct them into defensive positions facing south, the headquarters to be at the foot of the escarpment, two rifle companies forward, two in rear. The rest of the men were then told to get moving in the same direction. The battalion was soon properly formed up and Maughan was both surprised and impressed on plotting the battalion's new map location, to discover that Burrows had utilised the impromptu movement engendered by the enemy, which could easily have become a rout, to get his battalion assembled in correct formation at the forming-up place designated for the Sidi Rezegh attack. The movement took the battalion temporarily beyond reach of shell fire, but within a short time the enemy had the area covered by an extraordinary variety of artillery weapons.[5] There was some cover, however, in diggings left by previous occupants, also in the deep tracks left by "I" tanks which came up to "marry" with the infantry; and many shells were duds.

About 7.30 a.m. Burrows reconnoitred the route to Sidi Rezegh in a light tank and, while doing so, captured two wounded Italians. The battalion's task looked a forbidding one; the objective seemed far away, the approaches to it bare and flat, with no cover. Some of the intervening terrain looked boggy from the recent rain. Soon, however, it was learnt that the 2/13th Battalion was not to make the attack. About 10 a.m. company commanders were told at an orders conference that the attack

---

[3] 210-mm guns, the projectiles of which weighed 248 lbs.
[4] Lt-Col D. W. B. Maughan, MC, NX 21195. 2/13 Bn 1940-43; HQ 20 Bde 1943-44; South-East Asia Comd 1944-45. Barrister-at-law; of Sydney; b. Woollahra, NSW, 7 Oct 1912.
[5] Including French guns (probably 100- and 150-mm).

would not take place for four hours and would then be carried out by the 19th New Zealand Battalion,[6] the 2/13th Battalion to be "in support".

The corps commander appears to have prompted this change of plan. Godwin-Austen had arrived at his newly established headquarters on the El Gubbi airfield in Tobruk at first light that morning and thereupon had sent off his much quoted (and misquoted) message to the effect that Tobruk was as relieved as he was. The seriousness of the situation, however, hardly justified poetic licence or misleading puns. Godwin-Austen was not slow in giving Scobie the benefit of the greater wisdom with which a commander of higher rank is necessarily endowed. Consequently Willison had been informed that Godwin-Austen wished to extend the corridor from "Grumpy to feature north of Prince Town"[7] and that the 2/13th was to be used for the purpose; therefore that battalion was not to be committed more than absolutely necessary in the Sidi Rezegh operation. In the meantime a report from the Eighth Army headquarters had stated that the 1st South African Brigade was moving north to secure Sidi Rezegh.

Soon after the changed orders had been conveyed to company commanders, observers on the escarpment saw vehicles and tanks moving on the ridge to be attacked. These began to advance towards Ed Duda. The squadron of Matildas moved out to meet them and the enemy drew back. The British tank commander, believing this a ruse to draw his tanks onto enemy guns, also withdrew.

Enemy activity at Sidi Rezegh continued and about 11.30 a.m. a large mobile force including tanks was seen descending the Sidi Rezegh ridge more than a mile to the west of the feature the 2/13th had earlier been planning to capture. Soon it seemed that the force was heading for the escarpment to the west of Ed Duda. Simultaneously warnings were being received from Eighth Army headquarters that the enemy was planning to attack the New Zealand Division from all sides.

The Eighth Army headquarters, as though enacting a compulsive ritual, persisted in interpreting the daily events of the battle as the thrashing out of a maimed and beaten enemy, and Ritchie's conception of the *Africa Corps*' activities this day was that it had become for the enemy a matter of life or death to drive the British from their positions astride his communications. Rommel and Cruewell, however, were thinking not so much of saving their own forces as of crushing Ritchie's.

A wrong interpretation of the enemy's motives would not have mattered, however, if the right action had been taken to counter his moves, for the problem of meeting the threat of an attack on the British force outside Tobruk was much the same, whether the enemy's designs were offensive or escapist. To make his attack costly to him it was necessary first to prepare the ground for defence and secondly to bring the maximum number of available men, guns, tanks and bombers into action. In preparing ground for defence—in the use of minefields, the placing of anti-tank guns in

---

[6] This is difficult to explain but it was known that the tank squadron at Belhamed was on its way back and it may have been thought that the 19th Battalion would accompany them.
[7] i.e. from north-east tip of corridor towards the Bardia Road.

relation to them and the siting of field-guns for effective anti-tank roles—Scobie's operations had compared favourably with those of other British commanders. But the reports and comments and exhortations emanating from the headquarters of the Eighth Army and from its commander did not induce the commanders in the XXX Corps to get their guns, tanks and infantry up to the battle zone nor did they encourage Godwin-Austen and Freyberg to link the two New Zealand infantry brigades and one British army tank brigade under Freyberg's command with the Tobruk garrison force in an interlocking and mutually supporting scheme of defence.

Keeping open a corridor for the passage of troops in and out of Tobruk was still for Freyberg, who loyally accepted Godwin-Austen's policy declarations, the paramount operational requirement and this necessitated that the New Zealand Division should continue to hold an east-west corridor (including the Trigh Capuzzo) to Ed Duda by retaining the two ridges running parallel to and on either side of the trigh: the Ed Duda-Belhamed-Zaafran escarpment, and the Sidi Rezegh-Point 175 escarpment. On the night 28th-29th, after the returning German armour had made its aggressive appearance to the east and south, the New Zealanders were redisposed to meet a threat from this direction; rather than getting closer to the Tobruk garrison's corridor strongpoints, the New Zealanders moved part of their forces away from it to establish defended localities on the eastern end of the escarpments at Zaafran and Point 175. Freyberg was encouraged to occupy this extended line by the belief that the 1st South African Brigade would join him next day.

The new commander of the Eighth Army had begun to make his wishes known but was far from getting them carried into effect. He wished the 1st South African Brigade to join up "as soon as the situation permitted" with the New Zealand Division; being thus contingently expressed, the wish was unlikely to be—and was not—realised. The situation did not "permit" the two British armoured brigades of the 7th Division (with at least 100 tanks) to get the 1st South African Brigade across to Freyberg and "circumstances" later prevented the armoured brigades from carrying out orders to protect the New Zealand Division from attack. Ritchie also wanted the excellent work of the Jock columns to be continued, which would increase the likelihood that the armoured brigades would operate with minimal artillery support, since on this score the field commanders agreed with him. In fine, despite Ritchie's exhortations and Norrie's and Gott's orders, the XXX Corps and 7th Armoured Division brought no effective help to Scobie and Freyberg on a day of developing crisis.

The German forces began operations on the 29th to a plan made by General Cruewell for a two-pronged attack on the British salient, his object being to drive the British troops operating south of Tobruk inside the perimeter. General von Ravenstein's *21st Armoured Division* was to attack through Belhamed to Jack, and General Neumann-Silkow's *15th* through Ed Duda to Tugun. The operations developed quite differently. Von Ravenstein was captured by the New Zealand Division in the morning near Point 175 and the *21st* did nothing effective for the rest of the day.

The *15th Armoured Division* drove west to Bir bu Creimisa on the escarpment to the south of Sidi Rezegh, then north-west to Bir Salem. This was the movement seen and reported from the Ed Duda escarpment just before midday. The plan to which the Germans were now operating, however, was a different one from General Cruewell's. Rommel himself was at Bir bu Creimisa and had taken charge. The plan was now to cut the New Zealand Division off from Tobruk and from the east. The *15th Armoured Division* was to capture Ed Duda and to drive thence eastwards by the northern edge of Belhamed. It was hoped that the *21st Armoured Division* would make a westward thrust by the northern edge of Zaafran to meet the *15th* and that the *Ariete Division* would capture the eastern edge of Sidi Rezegh.

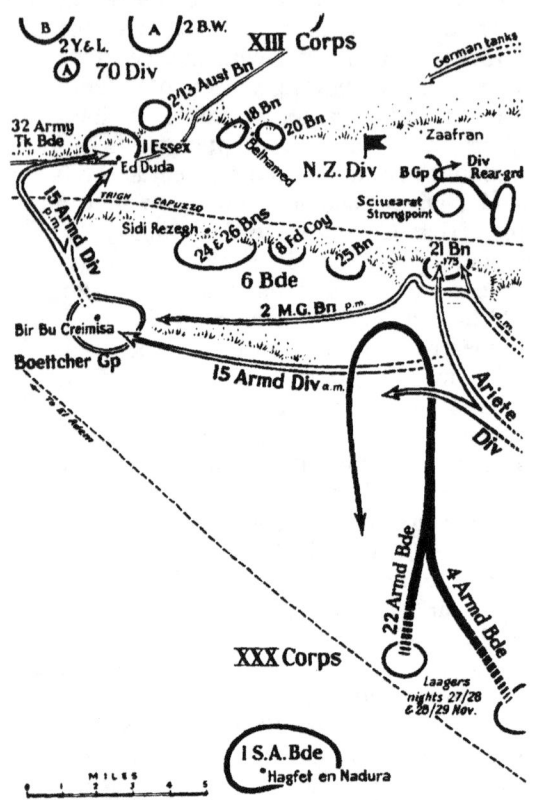

Attacks on Ed Duda and Point 175, 29th November

The *15th Armoured Division*, which was to carry out the thrust through Ed Duda, contained the main tank strength of the *Africa Corps*. The principal formations taking part were the *8th Tank Regiment* (both battalions), the *115th Infantry Regiment* and the *200th Infantry Regiment*. The transport of about half the *115th Regiment* got bogged near Bir Salem, however, and the *200th* attacked "Doc" (previously Dalby Square) instead of Ed Duda, so that only about a battalion of the *115th* participated in the attack on Ed Duda.

About 1 p.m. the *15th Armoured Division* began forming up to attack Ed Duda from the west. Captain Salt of the 1st R.H.A's Chestnut Troop broadcast a running description of their deployment and approach, and of the early development of the battle. The first German assault on the westernmost positions of the 1/Essex was thrown back by the infantry and anti-tank gunners. Colonel O'Carroll of the 4th Royal Tank Regiment ordered all tanks to the top of Ed Duda and those at hand went with him; about eight, including some acting as armoured command posts for the 1st R.H.A., went on to the main feature.⁸ For a time the German tanks stood off and bombarded the pits and sangars of the Essex infantry, neutralised their machine and anti-tank guns and cleared the minefields with patrols. Captain Salt's tank was hit and he was killed. Major Goschen's tank was also knocked out; Captain Armitage rescued him and his crew. This disorganised the artillery support, and about 4.30 p.m. the enemy started closing in from the west.

> It was late in the afternoon, and the sun was behind them. Three of our tanks came up on the side of our position, later joined by a fourth. They were Matildas. They started withdrawing in pairs, firing as they went. As the heavy tanks got nearer the position, the German light Mk. IIs moved up on our flank, and swept the area with machine-gun fire. . . . Some posts continued firing. The German tanks, twenty of them, fanned out and formed a line right across the middle of the battalion position. Our four tanks had cleverly withdrawn behind us to a hulls-down position. . . . It was starting to get dark . . . they had halted just short of where our tanks could engage them.⁹

The loss of Ed Duda was reported to Burrows about nightfall when he was called to a tank in direct communication with Willison's headquarters. The possibility of a counter-attack by the 2/13th Battalion was discussed. Burrows indicated that he was prepared to attack infantry but not tanks. The issues were hammered out at a conference at Willison's headquarters about 8 p.m.; it was conceded that 2/13th would not be expected to attack against tanks without tank support. The 2/13th Battalion was to counter-attack at Ed Duda with two companies and provide one company to protect the 1st R.H.A's gun area near Belhamed. The rest of the battalion was to be organised to hold the escarpment where the battalion was then situated.

The 2/13th headquarters were on the escarpment about 1,000 yards north-east of the Ed Duda pass. "C" and "D" Companies were detailed for the counter-attack, but when it appeared that the outlying "D" Company would not reach battalion headquarters by the time prescribed for leaving, Burrows issued a last-minute order that "B" Company (Captain Graham) would take its place and move off with "C" Company (Captain Walsoe). The two companies were then assembled by platoons in column of route at the foot of the escarpment on its northern side. A troop of 25-pounders was firing directly over their heads from behind a ridge to the north-east but the night was otherwise quiet. The guns stopped firing and almost as they did so a shell landed in the middle of a closely-bunched platoon of Graham's company, killing or wounding almost all.

It was necessary for Burrows, so as to be on time at the rendezvous, to order the rest of the column to march past. As the men did so with exemplary discipline, heart-rending cries from the stricken platoon assailed

---

⁸ Not all the tank commanders managed to comply with this instruction. The charge is made in a British narrative that some non-participation arose because a tank commander "had been seized as a suspect by the 2/13th Australian Infantry Battalion and not released until 9 p.m." On the likelihood that any such irresponsible action was taken by the experienced, earnest and realistic Australians, no comment is offered.

⁹ Martin, *The Essex Regiment 1929-1950*, pp. 635-6. From a description by Lieutenant P. P. S. Brownless.

them. They were then led in silence round the foot of the escarpment to a start-line laid for an attack south-west on both sides of the "pimples" of the Ed Duda feature. The forms of enemy tanks could be identified through binoculars on the objective some 500 yards away. Burrows refused to allow the attack to proceed. The start was postponed while he went back to Willison's headquarters. Only one conclusion was possible. If Ed Duda was to be retaken, the German tanks would have to be dislodged; if Willison's tanks could not do this, there was no other way. It was decided that it would have to be a close-in tank-to-tank and man-to-man fight without artillery support. This may have been influenced by the fact that the 1st R.H.A's "A/E" Battery had withdrawn to Tiger after dusk and Colonel Williams had ordered "B/O" Battery back in the belief that the by-pass road was not blocked. The 4th R.T.R., however, was maintaining a block just forward of the 2/13th with three tanks and the 44th R.T.R. was maintaining another to the east. It was decided that the battery's departure could no longer be delayed.

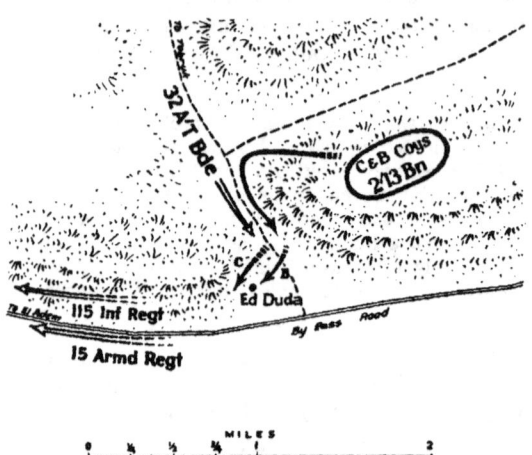

So, while in the desert not far to the south Gott's armoured brigades again spent an untroubled night in a leaguer off the battlefield, Willison's tanks, which had been in the thick of the fight for nine days, came forward with devotion and pluck to try conclusions with the main tank force of the *Africa Corps*.

Accounts of the battle are difficult to reconcile. Some misunderstandings have arisen because descriptions of incidents have been read as descriptions of an entire engagement, which was a long one. The tanks fought for about three hours, the infantry for about fifteen minutes. The battle began when eight Matilda tanks approached the Ed Duda escarpment from low ground in front and fought the German tanks skylined above. The contest provided a most spectacular fireworks display. Streams of small-arms tracer fire, which seemed to issue from holes in the hill, and fiery marbles spat out by automatic cannon converged on the British tanks' hulls and ricocheted from them like splashing molten metal. The Matildas stabbed back with rapid Besa machine-gun fire. Sharp exchanges of 2-pounder or 50-mm shot rang out; some tanks and vehicles on either side caught fire. The British tanks outnumbered by about three to one continued to engage, but the worrying question was whether all or most had been immobilised. Soon it was answered when some were seen to advance a short distance. Then it was puzzling to observe the same tanks withdraw. But they returned to the fray. In the end the puzzle of the battle was that the German tanks, after having appeared to have the upper hand, withdrew and did not come back. The Germans later blamed the receipt of a wrongly coded message purporting to recall the *8th Armoured Regiment*, but the battle had been decided before the message was received. British tank crews had for once fought German tanks in an action in which the Germans could not employ their guns to weight the odds against the British; at the end the outnumbered British were there, the Germans gone.

At one stage it had been planned to delay the infantry attack until the moon set behind the western ridge but when it appeared that the German tanks had departed Willison and Burrows decided to attack at 1.30 a.m. German war diaries make it plain that complete surprise was achieved because the attack was made without artillery support (as though an offence against the ethics of war had been perpetrated). Burrows, however, was more interested in frightening than surprising the enemy and told the men to call out "Australians coming" as they assaulted. In the same spirit the Matildas advancing on the flanks soon had their tank engines roaring at full throttle and were firing wildly when on the move. Unfortunately battles often do not proceed according to plan. Soon the enthusiastic British tank gunners were shooting up the charging Australians, mistaking them for retreating Germans, and the ignorant Germans, despite the Australians' shouted attempts to identify themselves, were crying out "Engländer kommen".

The following are extracts from an account written by a soldier about two months after the battle:[2]

> Captain Walsoe fired a green Very flare and the attack started with two platoons of B company on the left and C company on the right. C company had first to ascertain whether the men to their front belonged to the Essex Battalion or were Germans. . . . Soon however a German was captured. Colonel Burrows moved with the men telling them to call out "The Australians are coming" when they charged. The men went forward at a steady walking pace until they sighted the enemy. There was no need to advise them to shout when they went in: shouting, yelling, coo-eeing like madmen, they charged with the bayonet. The enemy seemed stupefied. There was no concerted resistance. Those who did not run either threw themselves on the ground or held up their hands. . . . As the attack progressed through the enemy's positions Germans could be heard running in front . . . calling out "Englander kommen". . . . The advance was continued to a distance of 500 yards beyond the top of the opposing ridge, but though Germans were heard running and shouting in the distance the men were recalled, since it would have been unwise to have gone further. Small pockets of enemy were soon mopped up and the companies withdrew to the southern slope of Ed Duda. B company sent out a patrol and took another 15 prisoners from a post on the left flank. . . .
> Enemy motor transport was heard moving about in confusion but could not be captured in the darkness, but a motor cyclist was stopped by a burst of TSMG fire and captured.

---

[2] Cpl Thompson of 2/13 Bn Int Sec.

Although at the moment of assault the men charged with vigour and elation, Walsoe and Graham kept their companies in hand and platoon commanders and section leaders maintained control. Organised resistance was met only on the fringes, and there, by initiative and with confidence in night fighting based on patrol experience, the Australians kept on top. On the right, for example, Sergeant Searle[3] put in a quick charge and subdued a pocket of enemy that opened fire when challenged. Two men near by who were slow to stand up and surrender were about to be dispatched with the bayonet when they identified themselves as Australian stretcher bearers captured by the enemy that evening. On the other flank Private Ferres[4] firing his Bren gun from the hip and leading three other men assaulted a troublesome enemy post and took the surrender of 25 Germans. The prisoners taken in the attack—almost all by the Australians —numbered 167. Only 7 Australians were wounded, two mortally.

The Australians were quickly reorganised to form a compact two-company front in the centre of the Ed Duda position, where they prepared for an immediate counter-attack. What was needed was to get below ground at once and be concealed as much as possible by dawn, but only one or two picks or shovels could be found. Infantry could hardly have been placed with less protection in a more vulnerable position than these men on Ed Duda at the very hinge of the Tobruk corridor; but no immediate counter-attack was made.

Meanwhile the main 2/13th Battalion defensive position on the ridge to the east, which had been depleted by the dispatch of two companies to the counter-attack and a third to protect the artillery, had been strengthened by the acquisition of the two companies of the 19th New Zealand Battalion that had remained with the Ed Duda force. They now came under the command of the 2/13th and moved into position alongside the Australians.

Thus about two squadrons of tanks and two companies of infantry had snatched back from the *Africa Corps* almost the only important acquisition it had won by its exertions at Rommel's direction in the six days since it had trampled exultantly on the armoured brigades and infantry battle-groups of the XXX Corps. The commanders of both sides continued fighting the battle under strange misconceptions, Rommel imagining the British to be aware how roundly they had been beaten and believing that the New Zealanders would therefore be withdrawing into Tobruk, Ritchie still imagining the German armour to have been so weakened that it was trying to escape to the west. Rommel suffered from a further misconception that the British armour might soon intervene in force, so the German commander decided to press on quickly next day with plans to cut off and destroy the New Zealand forces on the ridges south of Tobruk. Ritchie shared his illusion. "Stick to them tonight," he had enjoined Gott, but Gott's armoured brigades, conforming to their convenient routine, had returned to a night leaguer at a reasonably safe

---

[3] Capt J. E. Searle, DCM, NX21876; 2/13 Bn. Bank officer; of Cudal, NSW; b. Bathurst, NSW, 10 Mar 1919.

[4] Cpl H. Ferres, MM, NX17484; 2/13 Bn. Labourer; of Paddington, NSW; b. Sydney, 12 Dec 1919.

distance from the battle. The two brigades were being organised into one composite brigade under Brigadier Gatehouse's command.

Rommel's orders for the 30th were "to complete the ring" round the New Zealand Division but oddly enough, and fortunately for the 2/13th Battalion, completing the ring did not include retaking Ed Duda. The main task was to capture Sidi Rezegh. In the meantime, Major-General Boettcher, who had been commanding the German heavy artillery at Bir bu Creimisa, was appointed to command the *21st Armoured Division* in succession to Major-General von Ravenstein.

Ritchie's overnight orders to the 7th Armoured Division for the next day were to "chivvy the rear" of the German *15th Armoured Division*. Later orders to General Gott required him to harass and destroy the enemy "as opportunity occurred' so as to protect the 1st South African Brigade, which was to recapture Point 175. Just before first light, the orders were changed so far as the 1st South African Brigade was concerned, when Pienaar was told to take his brigade farther west, in the Ed Duda direction, to the area south of the Sidi Rezegh airfield and not far east of the region from which Rommel was planning to launch his main attack. Later, however, Norrie told Pienaar to go to Sciafsciuf far to the east of Point 175 before mounting the escarpment, then to attack 175 from the east.

Godwin-Austen's proposals for the 30th were cast in strangely similar mould to his suggestions on preceding days. From outside Tobruk he had asked Scobie to create diversions to help Freyberg; from inside he now called on Freyberg, after Ed Duda had been attacked, for diversionary operations to help Scobie; but later when the insecurity of Ed Duda appeared to have been redressed, he reverted once more to the old BATTLE-AXE plan of advancing from Ed Duda to El Adem. As soon as Freyberg had made contact with the South African brigade and was satisfied that the present position could be held, the New Zealand Division was to advance to the El Adem-Bir el Gubi road.

Norrie's activities this day were almost solely concerned with getting Pienaar's brigade to the New Zealand Division. It had been the intention on the 28th and again on the 29th that Pienaar's brigade should join Godwin-Austen's and Freyberg's force, but the Axis armoured forces coming back from the frontier region had been operating across the desert to the south of the New Zealanders that Pienaar would have to cross if he was to go to them by a reasonably direct route. The orders reaching Pienaar had been chopped and changed but none of them had adequately coped with the problem of effecting the junction without exposing Pienaar's thin-skinned forces to armoured ambush. Norrie may have felt that he bore some responsibility for the failure. "I decided," he subsequently reported, "to make myself personally responsible for ensuring that there was no repetition of the two previous days." So as to be free to concentrate on this himself, he even went so far that afternoon as to place Gott temporarily in command of the rest of the corps. To have got Gatehouse's composite armoured brigade to intervene might have been more useful.

To have got both brigades up to the battle together might have been one way of "ensuring that there was no repetition of the two previous days", but apparently was not considered.

So on 30th November, one week after the *Totensonntag* battle, the day on which Rommel was to bring to bear against Freyberg's New Zealanders all the strength, armoured or otherwise, the German *Africa Corps* could muster, Ritchie told the 7th Armoured Division to "chivvy up" the rear of the *15th Armoured Division,* Norrie told the 7th Armoured Division to protect the South African infantry brigade while it regained Point 175 (and later personally conducted the brigade to the eastern part of Freyberg's front), Gott told Gatehouse to "maintain the corridor" to the New Zealand Division near Point 175 and to protect the South African brigade and Godwin-Austen told Freyberg to start a westward advance as soon as the South African brigade joined him and he felt secure.

When the defence of Ed Duda was reorganised after the successful counter-attack, Walsoe's and Graham's companies were left under the command of Lieut-Colonel Nichols[5] to form a composite battalion with the headquarters and "C" Company and the remnants of "A", "B" and "D" Companies of the 1/Essex. Burrows returned to command the rest of his battalion on the ridge to the east of Ed Duda and was told that the two companies of the 19th New Zealand Battalion would be under his command.

Although the Australians had been reading the battle reports rather sceptically they had not expected to find on going out to Ed Duda that the German armour was still traversing the desert at will, as it had throughout the siege. Now the battalion had been made responsible for developing defensive localities on exposed ridges in the face of a boldly thrusting armoured force. Although the 1st R.H.A. had come forward again and its Rocket Troop, which Captain Daintree's company was protecting, was sited in an anti-tank role, there were no anti-tank guns with the Australians and Burrows and his staff were worried at the lack of defence against tanks.[6] Importunate demands were made for mines to be provided. The staff at Scobie's headquarters, though at first taken aback at the number sought, were sympathetic and helpful.

When dawn came on the 30th the Australians with the Essex battalion were astonished to see a busy German bivouac on the desert flats to their front.

> There were bell tents, repair shops, field kitchens sending up their smoke, soldiers marching about in small groups, panzers moving about the encampment and staff cars coming and going (wrote Major Colvin some years later).[7]

It took a little time for everybody to make sure that this apparition was not of British origin while an impatient forward observation officer,

---

[5] Maj-Gen J. S. Nichols, DSO, MC. (1915-18: Lt Border Regt.) CO 1/Essex 1940-41; Comd 151 Bde 1942; GOC 50 Div 1942-43. Regular soldier; b. 5 Jul 1896.
[6] According to the War Diary of the 104th RHA there were 73 anti-tank guns in the corridor on 30th November.
[7] *Bayonets Abroad,* p. 153.

Captain G. C. Etches of the 1st R.H.A., fretted and waited. When fire on the camp was authorised, it was quickly laid low in smoke and dust and flame by a bombardment from "A/E" Battery. The enemy artillery (Mickl Group, previously the Boettcher Group) at once retaliated against both the 1/Essex and the 2/13th positions with heavy and punishing fire, which had to be endured for a good part of the morning. In the meantime about 40 tanks began approaching from the west. Twelve came up to within 3,000 yards, were shelled and withdrew. At 8 a.m. about 35 medium tanks were reported to be "standing off watching"; about ten minutes later they were bombed by the R.A.F. Later two enemy tanks came forward, probably to inspect four damaged tanks which had been left on Ed Duda when the enemy had fled during the night. Harassed by the British artillery as they approached, the tanks nosed their way into Walsoe's company's positions and called on the men to surrender. This was one ruse that could not succeed against siege-trained Australians. A cat-and-mouse game began but the two tanks suddenly made off as though sensing that they were being trapped. Subsequently the German tank force moved off to the south, then round to the east, in the direction of the New Zealand Division.

Two or three vehicles were captured on the by-pass road in the morning. At "B/O" Battery's position covering the road, which it had occupied at 9.30 a.m., the British gunners and Australian infantry protecting them captured a mixed bag, including an Intelligence officer of one of the German armoured formations and a lorry well stocked with enemy canteen stores. A section under Corporal McKellar[8] ambushed an artillery command vehicle with useful maps, plans and instruments.

In mid-morning Burrows attended a conference at Willison's headquarters at which it was decided that the two companies of the 19th New Zealand Battalion would change places with the two 2/13th Battalion companies then at Ed Duda under command of the 1/Essex, and that the 2/13th Battalion would maintain the localities previously held by the New Zealand companies. Orders were given for a very complicated relief operation devised to ensure that no locality would be left vacant during the change-over. Later in the day a feature in rear of the 2/13th called Bir Belhamed (not to be confused with Belhamed, which was on the same escarpment as the 2/13th but farther east) was occupied by advanced parties of the 1/Bedfordshire and Hertfordshire, who completed the occupation after dark and also placed a company on either side of the road below the escarpment.

The tragic fact that no single-minded purpose was activating the British mobile forces lying in the desert to the south of the ridges on which Freyberg's two infantry brigades and the foremost battalions of Scobie's sortie force had been so boldly but dangerously disposed enhanced the very danger of their situation. Not only did the expectation or hope (however slight it was becoming) that the 1st South African Brigade might recapture Point 175 fatally tempt Freyberg to maintain an insecure arrange-

---

[8] Sgt R. V. McKellar, MM, NX21667; 2/13 Bn. Printer; of Hornsby, NSW; b. Grenfell, NSW, 9 Nov 1914.

ment of his forces and Godwin-Austen to sanction it; the mere possibility that the South Africans or even the legendary 7th Armoured Division might do some of the things known from intercepted messages to have been suggested to them left the defenders on the escarpment uncertain whether forces manoeuvring in the desert to the south were friend or foe. Thus the diarist of the 1st R.H.A., which that day had about 48 guns under command including batteries of the 104th and 107th R.H.A., complained of a confusing general "sitrep"[9] which had ended with the statement "It is not safe to shoot south of Duda unless we can identify; quite safe to shoot east" and commented that a large force which at 3.50 p.m. was moving east towards Ed Duda but at nightfall put in a damaging attack on the New Zealand brigade near Sidi Rezegh had received "little opposition from our artillery" because it was not certain that they were not British.

Observers on the ridges around Ed Duda saw and heard the signs of a distant battle about Sidi Rezegh but nobody could tell what was happening. Nothing was discerned to dispel vague premonitions that an enemy who was palpably displaying such initiative was in the ascendant. So menacing seemed the extensive movement as night approached that the proposed change-over on Ed Duda between the two companies of the 19th New Zealand Battalion and Walsoe's and Graham's companies was cancelled. The night was devoted to mine-laying and energetic digging to improve prospects of survival. Up to midnight nothing was known in Tobruk, not even at XIII Corps headquarters, of the course of the fighting near Sidi Rezegh.

Gatehouse's composite 4th/22nd Armoured Brigade spent 30th November, the first day of its existence, in shadow-sparring with the *Ariete Division* and with figments of the German *Africa Corps*. Its activities, which hardly seemed to conform with Gott's order that it should maintain the corridor to the New Zealand Division near Point 175, did not interfere with German preparations to encompass the New Zealand Division's destruction nor deter the Italians from shelling the New Zealanders from Point 175. In the morning Pienaar experienced the usual changes in his orders until Norrie decided about midday to take the South African brigade under his personal command and to see it personally onto the Trigh Capuzzo escarpment at Bir Sciafsciuf, the route to which lay well to the east of the battle area. There it was to turn west and attack Point 175. Later Norrie reported: "I more or less personally led the 1st S.A. Brigade with a flag in my Recce Car and got on the escarpment ahead of anyone else."[1] The escarpment was reached just before 4 p.m. No further advance was attempted before dark, though preparations were made for two columns to begin an advance at nightfall with the object of retaking the dressing station near Point 175 against possible light opposition.

The German *15th Armoured Division* had started late on its mission of capturing Sidi Rezegh as the next step towards cutting the New Zealand

---
[9] i.e. situation report.
[1] Quoted in Agar-Hamilton and Turner, p. 393.

Division off from both Tobruk and Egypt. By somebody's blunder the whole division had started to move to El Adem in the early hours of the morning but was later halted at Bir Salem.[2] In the late morning, as observed from Ed Duda, the division moved round to north of Bir bu Creimisa.

The headquarters of the *Africa Corps* had been established near Bir bu Creimisa and there in the early afternoon Rommel issued his final orders for the assault on the New Zealand Division. The Mickl Group with five tanks from the *15th Armoured Division* was to attack Sidi Rezegh; simultaneously the *Ariete* was to close in from the east. The *90th Light Division* was to attack Belhamed from the north and the *15th Armoured,* at Cruewell's suggestion, would advance to the so-called "saddle" between Ed Duda and Belhamed with the object of linking with the *90th Light* on the northern side of Belhamed. In other words the *15th Armoured* was to pass along the plain just at the foot of the ridge on which most of Burrows' battalion and the two New Zealand companies under his tactical command had made their precarious lodgments and establish itself astride the ridge to the east of them, where the by-pass road crossed it. Destiny seemed to be plotting an exciting evening for the two 2/13th Battalion patrols being briefed at that time to patrol during the night to the by-pass road.

Undistracted by the British armour's over-cautious skirmishing, the Axis armoured forces closed in on the New Zealand Division between 4 and 5 p.m. Neumann-Silkow, however, with a sound tactical instinct for the kill, joined in the attack on Sidi Rezegh on the left flank of the Mickl Group instead of advancing into the "saddle" east of Burrows' positions. This saved the Australians but sealed the fate of the 6th New Zealand Brigade around the Sidi Rezegh mosque. The 24th and 26th New Zealand Battalions were overrun and the 25th Battalion near the blockhouse was hard-pressed by the *Ariete Division*. Brigadier Barrowclough wished to bring what was left of the 6th Brigade including its artillery and machine-guns behind the shelter of the Tobruk sortie force's established positions.

The New Zealand Division's situation was indeed perilous. The overrunning of Barrowclough's infantry had left the way unbarred to most of the divisional artillery lying south and east of Belhamed and to Belhamed itself. In the east the German *21st Armoured Division* had exerted pressure and was closing up astride the Trigh Capuzzo; behind the *Ariete Division* but farther east the 1st South African Brigade was now on the escarpment. After dark a mobile striking force of two companies with a third as flank protection set out from the South African Brigade for Point 175 but the force ran up against elements of the *21st*, including the *3rd Reconnaissance Unit,* and did not reach its objective.

That night several Eighth Army commanders of high rank made decisions and issued orders influenced by varying degrees of awareness of the

---

[2] The explanation that Neumann-Silkow inferred from a message in which a wrong call-sign had been used that the division was required to move to El Adem is difficult to accept, but none other can be suggested.

calamitous possibilities indicated by the day's set-backs and vacillations. Some messages sent evoked a corresponding action, some did not.

To Freyberg whose homespun philosophy imposed on every soldier, every unit and every commander a simple duty to accept sacrificial losses

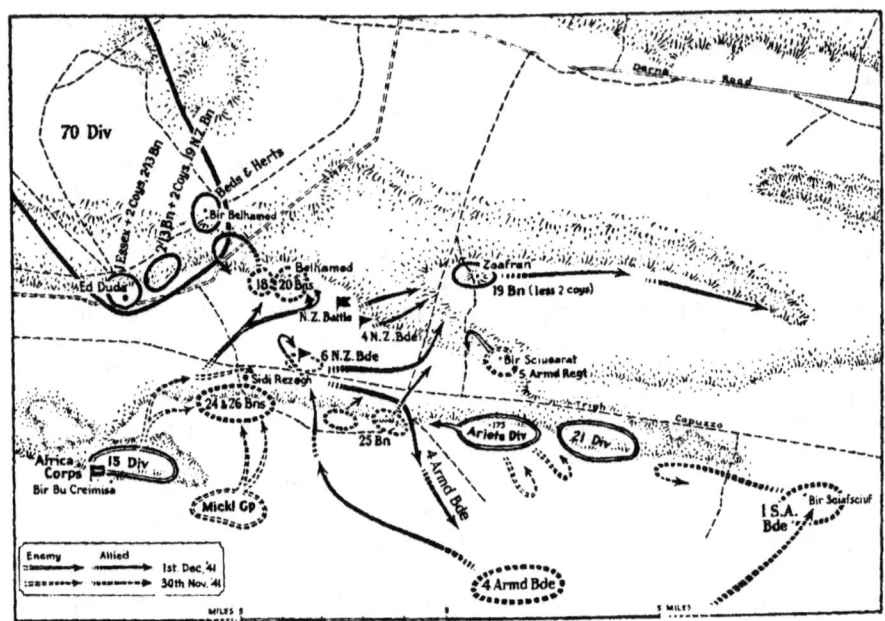

30th November-1st December

when necessary for the common cause, it was plain that the New Zealand Division remained under an obligation to fight for the ground it held, across which the link with the Tobruk garrison was to be maintained. Thus Barrowclough's withdrawal proposals were not accepted. On the other hand Freyberg's close view of the situation's hard facts told him that both the South African infantry and the British armour would have to join battle at once alongside the New Zealanders if the aim was to be achieved. He sent Brigadier R. Miles, his chief artillery officer, on an urgent mission to Tobruk to explain this to Godwin-Austen. He sent two liaison officers to Pienaar, whom he believed to have been placed under his command, with the following message:

> Sidi Rezegh was captured by the enemy this afternoon. Our position is untenable unless you can recapture it before dawn 1 December. You will therefore carry out this task at once.

Miles did not reach the XIII Corps headquarters in Tobruk until after midnight and the officers sent to the 1st South African Brigade headquarters did not arrive until 1.40 a.m. Norrie had camped for the night close to Pienaar's headquarters and soon Pienaar woke Norrie to discuss Freyberg's message. Norrie and Pienaar agreed that to recapture Point

175 before dawn was not practicable. The attack would be resumed at dawn.

Soon after Miles reached the headquarters of XIII Corps in the early hours of 1st December Godwin-Austen began to convey his thoughts and orders by slowly transmitted wireless messages. The headquarters of both the Eighth Army and the XXX Corps (of which Gott had temporary command) heard from him that it was essential that the 7th Armoured Division should concentrate every effort on destroying the enemy tanks east and west of the New Zealand Division. Freyberg was told that the XXX Corps had been asked to concentrate the 7th Armoured Division's efforts on this, that if the South African attack for Point 175 and Sidi Rezegh succeeded the gains were to be consolidated; if not, the New Zealand troops were to be withdrawn behind Ed Duda while the division continued to hold Belhamed. In effect this meant: "Hang on while the South African brigade tries to re-take the lost ground and 7th Armoured Division sets about destroying the enemy tanks. If they can't do this, hold on to Belhamed but give up whatever else is necessary beyond the reach of the Tobruk fortress guns." The alternative to such an instruction would have been to order the New Zealand Division to withdraw immediately (which there was hardly time to do before the next blow would fall); but Godwin-Austen had no real option to order thus. How could he have taken the responsibility of assuming that the 1st South African Brigade and 7th Armoured Division could not, or would not, intervene with decisive effect? Godwin-Austen had perceived that his dilemma had wide implications affecting not only the New Zealanders but also the forces Scobie had thrust out beyond the tank defences of the Tobruk perimeter. At 7.55 a.m. on 1st December he sent this message to the Eighth Army headquarters:

If 1 SA Bde fail secure firm footing on Pt 175-Sidi Rezegh escarpment and if our armd forces continue be unable prevent enemy armd forces from attacking tps holding corridor defs, situation may shortly arise in which decision will have to be taken whether or not essential withdraw to original perimeter rather than continue expose tps holding corridor to tk attack on both sides. Unable give accurate figures, but our total "I" tk runners now most unlikely exceed 20. Further offensive action by 70 Div would dangerously weaken garrison and incur serious risk total loss of Tobruk as long as enemy tks able operate in strength on my front. Request Staff Officer able give decisions on behalf Army Comd on above points be sent here soonest possible. Meantime intend continue hold Ed Duda and Belhamed.[3]

The tale of the morning's orders is completed by a message sent at 4 a.m. by Gott to Gatehouse telling him briefly that the enemy had captured Sidi Rezegh, the New Zealanders were being attacked by tanks from east and west and the South Africans were "south-west" of Point 175, and giving him this order:

You will reconnoitre Sidi Rezegh area first light and counter-attack enemy tanks at all costs, subsequently rally south of Point 175.

But time was running out. The enemy was already stirring, the dawn very near.

---

[3] Quoted in Agar-Hamilton and Turner, p. 404.

There was some fuss in the early hours of 1st December about infiltration in the corridor between Butch and Tiger, but at first light this proved to be an isolated enemy party, which was quickly mopped up by the 32nd Army Tank Brigade. At dawn ground mist hid the plateau to the south of the Ed Duda ridges and before it cleared heavy artillery fire began to fall around Belhamed. It was soon evident that the New Zealand positions there were under attack. The 1st R.H.A. did their best to send officers to the battle area but two tanks ran onto an enemy minefield and another was stopped by anti-tank fire. Major Goschen went out in a truck but, after it had run onto a mine, was hit in the shoulder by a bullet. About 8.30 a.m. Major Loder-Symonds reported that the infantry on Belhamed were without tank support and being overrun. He asked regimental headquarters to try to have some tanks sent up.

Godwin-Austen had called a conference at his headquarters at 9 a.m. to consider Miles' report of the New Zealand Division's situation and his own instruction to Freyberg to withdraw the New Zealand Division to the area north of Belhamed if the South African attack on Point 175 failed. By that time reports of the 1st R.H.A's unhappy observations of events at Belhamed had been received. It was decided that if Belhamed was lost, plans would have to be made for withdrawing in darkness from Ed Duda and the forward posts in the corridor.

About 9.30 a.m. it was learnt at Scobie's headquarters that the New Zealand infantry on Belhamed had begun withdrawing towards the garrison's posts in the corridor and instructions were given to rally them and employ them in the forward posts. Meanwhile an enemy attack from the east on the left shoulder of the corridor (on the post known then as Dopey, previously Butch) had been repulsed and it was reported that about 50 enemy had been killed and 50 captured.

The 18th New Zealand Battalion, on the side of Belhamed facing the Ed Duda ridge, withstood the German assault for some time, but later gave ground and began to withdraw westwards. By this time Loder-Symonds had two mobile observation posts operating and was able to cover its withdrawal; the guns of "B/O" Battery quickly turned back some German tanks that moved round to the New Zealanders' western flank, trying to cut them off. As the New Zealanders came back through his battery positions, Loder-Symonds sought out their commander, whom he found to be a spirited leader, told him that the guns would stay and give his men good protection against tanks provided that they "remained just in front of the guns" and pointed out that the enemy minefield "was now well placed for our own use".[4] The New Zealand colonel took Loder-Symonds at his word, reconnoitred the ridge west of Belhamed with him and established his battalion there. Soon afterwards a convoy of remnants of the New Zealand Division's artillery including a troop of the 6th New Zealand Field Regiment came down the by-pass road. According to the diarist of "B/O" Battery, "Loder-Symonds then got the N.Z. guns into action alongside 'B' Troop, making eight guns in line, and they

---
[4] "B/O" Battery war diary.

were shot by Captain Hay as an eight-gun troop". Next, in case the R.H.A's "B" Troop should be forced to withdraw by an attack from the open flank, the Rocket Troop were ordered to take up a position at Bir Belhamed from which support could also be given. This they did. They were later heavily shelled, a gunner being killed and five others wounded, but the guns remained in position until after dark.

From the 2/13th Battalion's positions on the Ed Duda-Belhamed ridge, part of the German tank assault on Belhamed could be observed through field-glasses. The 18th New Zealand Battalion's subsequent withdrawal was watched. At 10 a.m. an enemy column at the foot of Belhamed was reported to be moving towards the 2/13th area. Later some movement —then thought to be of German troops—was discerned on the ridge beyond the by-pass road. The battalion's position seemed precarious, being overlooked not only from the Trig 157 ridge on the west but from Belhamed in the east and also to some extent from the south. At 10.30 a.m. the battalion was notified that the enemy had taken Belhamed and that a conference was to be held at 11 a.m. at Willison's headquarters to consider the situation.

The crisis of CRUSADER had been reached. The offensive that had been almost smashed on *Totensonntag,* but which the spirited fighting of Scobie's and Freyberg's infantry and army tank brigades had kept going, was now verging towards pitiful and ominous failure. The dangerously exposed New Zealand Division had been stripped of most of its outer defences. The armoured divisions of the *Africa Corps* were closing in to crush it.

By a custom that had often helped them win battles the Germans had made their preliminary moves in the dark, striking at Belhamed at 6.30 a.m. before the sun's warm touch dissolved the morning mist. Had Gatehouse reconnoitred Sidi Rezegh at first light as, with scarcely adequate notice, he had been ordered to do, he would still have been too late to strike the Germans in the back before they attacked. About 9 a.m., by which time he had completed a dismal visual reconnaissance from the Sidi Rezegh plateau's southern edge and the Germans had secured Belhamed, Gatehouse's leading tanks (of the 8th Hussars and 5th Royal Tanks) were coming over the edge of the northern Sidi Rezegh escarpment to contact the most southerly troops of Barrowclough's 6th New Zealand Brigade. "Attack the enemy relentlessly using all your resources, even to the last tank," Auchinleck had written. "Counter-attack enemy tanks at all costs," Gott had ordered. Gatehouse told Lieut-Colonel Drew, commanding the 5th Royal Tanks, to get in touch with the New Zealand commander and make a plan to attack against the enemy tanks.

In war many must fight and many die to the orders of a few. The stage had been set, orders given, first moves made for British and German armour to clash in the climactic battle of the campaign. Yet there was no such battle, no last fight at Sidi Rezegh between the armoured forces for better or for worse, with tanks burning, men dying, blood draining into sand. In the main, what the British tanks did and did not do that day was what Gatehouse ordered them to do and not to do. It does not seem right, however, to judge his orders or their performance in terms of correspondence or non-correspondence with Gott's initial instruction to counter-attack the enemy tanks "at all costs". One must first ask whether that instruction meant what it said.

To demand the performance of a task "at all costs" (which involves disregarding the loss of precious life) is a commander's prerogative which should be used only sparingly and in an extremity, but commanders in the Eighth Army were developing a loose habit of ordering tasks to be carried out "at all costs" in circumstances in which to be entirely unregardful of losses would not have been justified. Such orders unfairly placed responsibility for any non-performance on the recipient, who was still expected to exercise his command prudently and with a proper discretion that was ostensibly denied him. Thus, despite Gott's categorical orders, Gatehouse, the armoured commander on the spot on 1st December, was not really expected by Gott to counter-attack at all costs. That Gott intended to allow him some discretion, though perhaps not as much as in fact he exercised, is evident from the published messages that passed between them.[5]

It is also evident that Gatehouse did not regard himself as under obligation to commit his tanks to blind charges at the enemy wherever seen but rather as personally responsible for saving both his men and their equipment from rash enterprises seemingly enjoined by the literal sense of orders written for execution in a situation no longer pertaining. The situation when Gatehouse's tanks descended the escarpment north of the Sidi Rezegh airfield to the battle zone offered many opportunities for engagements of doubtful outcome. The New Zealand Division had already been thrust from its ground at Belhamed and Sidi Rezegh. The 1st South African Brigade's second and stronger attack on Trig 175 had failed to penetrate to that feature through the *21st Armoured Division's* screen blocking the approaches from the east. To Gatehouse's immediate north, across the Trigh Capuzzo, was the hastily improvised defensive position taken up in the dark by the remnants of Barrowclough's brigade (excluding the 25th Battalion still at the blockhouse). North of them again were the 8th Royal Tanks (five "I" tanks) and farther north the 44th Royal Tanks (seven "I" tanks). This extremely thin red line covered a field and anti-tank artillery screen in a wadi. Mainly there, some forty 25-pounders were still in action and stoutly manned, a force to be reckoned with, but the New Zealand Division had little else—the battalion at the blockhouse, half a battalion at Zaafran (the 19th less the two companies near Ed Duda), divisional cavalry, engineers and other staunch but small bodies.

Against the battered and depleted New Zealand Division Rommel had concentrated almost the entire strength of the *Africa Corps*. The ring was relentlessly closing. Rommel called the area within it the *Kessel*—the kettle,

---

[5] See Murphy, *The Relief of Tobruk*, pp. 447-55.

or cauldron—thus appropriately symbolising his intentions. In the west, opposite Barrowclough, and now Gatehouse, were the *8th Armoured* and *200th Infantry Regiments* north of the Trigh Capuzzo and the powerful Mickl artillery group and the *115th Infantry Regiment* south of it. The great strength of this force lay not in its tanks but in its numerous and varied artillery, which the staunch New Zealand field regiments and whatever guns Gatehouse had brought with him could not oppose on equal terms. To the north was the *90th Light Division,* with a part to play in exerting pressure; in the east was the *Ariete Division.* Behind it, astride the Trigh Capuzzo and under orders to take up positions of all-round defence, the *21st Armoured Division* "closed the ring".

Not all this, nor very much of it, was known to Gatehouse; but once in the kettle he did not like its simmer. The record of his messages to Gott shows that he was impressed with the number of enemy guns "of all sizes" and particularly with the "very large stuff" and also that he soon concluded that it was too late to halt a New Zealand withdrawal or to reverse the battle's course. Gatehouse did not choose to counter-attack the German tanks in the face of such gun-power. Barrowclough had no option but to withdraw to Zaafran and Freyberg had independently decided that the withdrawal of what was left of his division was inevitable, a course which (he inferred from a message) was endorsed and expected by higher formation. Gatehouse's brigade at first covered the New Zealand withdrawal, which Gott had indicated to him was Norrie's wish. Later, however, Gatehouse signalled Gott:

Starting evacuating leaguer as arranged. After 2 miles on a point just E of aerodrome we were attacked by Italian tanks from in front, German tanks on right flank. Column we were protecting disappeared NE, could not protect them as had no contact. Consider responsibility over towards column. . . .

The German *15th Armoured Division* got ready to meet a counter-attack by Gatehouse's force with its numerous tanks. After midday the British armoured brigade moved off to the south and replenished but did not return to the *Kessel* that day. The New Zealand historian has commented:

To the men of 6 Brigade the whole episode was puzzling. They were thankful for the timely help of the Stuart tanks when capture had seemed inevitable and full of admiration for the tank crews who lingered under heavy fire to escort them to safety. But they were mildly surprised that the British armour disappeared so quickly from the scene and disappointed that such a strong force made such a small impression on the battle as a whole. They had expected the tide to turn, but it continued to flow against them.[6]

No doubt the British "top brass" had put Gatehouse in "a nasty position", as he called it. No doubt a counter-attack would have been costly. But CRUSADER could not be won if everybody drove off the battlefield yielding the initiative entirely to the German armoured divisions and permitting them to concentrate superior force against the British infantry battalions one by one. The Germans had been scraping the barrel to find

---

[6] Murphy, p. 455.

forces to attack the British and New Zealand forces in the Ed Duda-Sidi Rezegh-Belhamed triangle. The *90th Light Division* was organising a battalion from men rescued from the New Zealand prisoner-of-war compound and was able to do nothing effective. The depleted *115th Regiment* had not recovered from its defeat at Sidi Rezegh. For some days the *21st Armoured Division* had been in poor condition and the day before had been looking on the situation "in an unduly pessimistic light" and sending "alarming reports", as the diarist of the *Africa Corps* noted. Apart from his well-sited and influential medium and heavy artillery, the only battleworthy assault troops of much account available to Rommel at the beginning of this critical day were the two tank battalions of the *8th Armoured Regiment,* with about 40 tanks, the *2nd Machine Gun Battalion* and the *15th Motor Cycle Battalion.* Before the British armoured brigade had arrived on the scene, these had fought a strenuous action against the 20th New Zealand Battalion and 6th Field Regiment. Probably the *15th Armoured Division* could not have mustered two dozen medium tank runners. The British armoured brigade with its 115 tanks left this force free to continue bringing pressure for the rest of the day on the ill-used and over-tried New Zealand Division.

About the time when Gatehouse ordered his armoured brigade to resume its return journey, Cruewell directed the *15th Armoured Division* to continue its attack eastward through Zaafran. To allow time for the *8th Armoured Regiment* to refuel and replenish and for the *2nd Machine Gun Battalion* to withdraw from western Belhamed opposite the 18th New Zealand Battalion, Neumann-Silkow fixed the start-time at 4.30 p.m. So the New Zealand gunners, who had planned to withdraw from their wadi and from Bir Sciuearat at 5.30 p.m. as twilight darkened to full night, were attacked about 50 minutes before that time. In the wadi, standing by the guns in their last fight, were the five Matildas of the 44th Royal Tanks; at Bir Sciuearat, a few Valentines of the 8th Royal Tanks also fought in the last action. The guns were under close attack and continued firing, some at point-blank range, up to the moment they were withdrawn. Most were extricated but some had to be abandoned, the sights only taken. Then the weary German *8th Armoured* and *200th Infantry Regiments* settled for the night on the field of their second won battle, only to receive a sharp rebuke from General Cruewell who said that he had named Zaafran as the objective and knew of no order to halt. He told Neumann-Silkow to "move on to Zaafran at daybreak and capture it".

At 6.45 p.m., after the main body had waited for more than an hour for the rearguards, the survivors of the New Zealand Division, assembled in orderly columns, crossed their last start-line in the CRUSADER campaign in a disciplined withdrawal, passed through a gap in the rearward enemy screen, and went east and south to Bir el Chleta. General Norrie saw them there. Thence they drove south-east on the first step of their journey back to Egypt to rest, rebuild, and refit. They reached Bir Gibni by 3.30 a.m. next day. By that time the 1st South African Brigade was at Taieb el Esem, the 4th Armoured Brigade in its night leaguer at Bir Berraneb, some 24 miles from Ed Duda. There was no substantial British force closer than that to Scobie's corridor. The *Kessel* had been emptied, the attempt to relieve Tobruk smashed.

The Eighth Army had been dealt a telling rebuff but Rommel had not restored the situation to what it was before the British offensive began. The Tobruk garrison's protrusion from the perimeter to Ed Duda remained. In the frontier region British troops were besieging the Axis garrisons from Salum to the Omars, and at Bardia. A substantial British force about the Trigh el Abd threatened the Axis flank. Whether the German commander could continue to attack the outlying British infantry battalions and brigades with his armoured divisions and to confront British armoured formations with a superior power of artillery on the battlefield would depend as much on his opponent's decisions as his own.

"Ritchie has gripped battle completely and is thinking far ahead," Auchinleck told Churchill on 30th November. Ritchie had now been in command of the Eighth Army long enough to take full charge of the battle. It is a measure of the archaism of the army's command methods that on 1st December he went to the XXX Corps headquarters to see Norrie not knowing that Norrie was elsewhere and that the big decisions that day were made without reference to him, such as that the 4th Armoured Brigade would counter-attack to help the New Zealand Division, then that it would not counter-attack, that the New Zealand Division would withdraw from the battle and that the 4th Armoured Brigade would leave the battle zone before the New Zealand Division had been extricated. A decision on the further question whether the Tobruk "appendix" (as the ground seized in the sortie operations was called) should be abandoned had been referred to him early in the morning but his reply was not sent for twelve hours.

It appears that Ritchie spent most of that critical day at XXX Corps headquarters, where he studied the situation map and framed an outline plan for future operations. The map must have been fairly up to date—no doubt more so than at his own headquarters—because it showed the enemy armour lying surrounded by anti-tank guns in what Ritchie called "the valley between Sidi Rezegh and Belhamed" and Ritchie made the observation, as though the armour had not just gone there, that it was important to draw it out into the open and "never leave it alone". The last part did not exactly fit the day's actual program for the 4th Armoured Brigade or any other formation. The main features of Ritchie's plan, which with a covering letter he left in an envelope for Norrie, were to attack El Adem with a brigade of the 4th Indian Division and to raid enemy supply lines between Tmimi and Acroma with armoured car columns.[7] Another point stressed was that an imagined but non-existent enemy supply line from Bardia to enemy forces west of it should be blocked. (Rommel's main concern on the same day was to get supplies

---

[7] British armoured cars were so vulnerable that such raids did not constitute a serious threat to enemy communications.

into Bardia, not out.) When Ritchie got back to his own headquarters he signalled Godwin-Austen that to continue to hold the Ed Duda appendix would assist "future operations for relief of Tobruk . . . being planned now", but he did not encourage Godwin-Austen to think he would get much help from outside Tobruk in the immediate future.

> You are however sole judge of whether any such positions are too exposed to offer reasonable likelihood of successful and prolonged resistance for at least a week and you may therefore adjust the defence of the appendix as you consider necessary even so far as to withdraw to the original perimeter.

The voice of Auchinleck seems to ring out in this well-phrased, lofty declaration, which is perhaps not surprising, since Auchinleck had arrived at Ritchie's headquarters that day. He stayed for the next ten.

Other decisions made were to recommend continued use of the equipment of the 7th Support Group in Jock columns, and to place under the command of the XXX Corps the 1st South African Brigade, 22nd Guards Brigade and, as soon as their relief at the frontier by the 2nd South African Division could be arranged, the rest of the 4th Indian Division.

At 11 a.m. on 1st December Burrows, Nichols (of the 1/Essex) and O'Carroll (of the 4th Royal Tanks) attended a conference at Willison's headquarters to review the defence arrangements in the light of the loss of Belhamed. It was a meeting of practical men who briskly reached the decisions they deemed appropriate. None thought that the enemy's occupation of the ridge and hill to the east so changed an always dubious prospect of successful defence as to necessitate a less bold stance. It was decided to proceed that night with the projected reorganisation and relief, twice ordained, twice cancelled, by which the two 19th New Zealand Battalion companies were to change places with the two Australian in Nichols' composite battalion force on Ed Duda. The Australians would then assume undivided responsibility for all defended localities on the escarpment between Ed Duda and the by-pass road. The main anxiety was the width of the front and the increasing risk of attack in rear. Plans were made to withdraw the mortar detachments and carriers from support of the 1st R.H.A. so as to free them for employment in a mobile role to thicken up the positional defence. The New Zealand battalion was to provide two mortar detachments and the crews of four carriers to come under Burrows' command and operate with Australian-manned mortars and carriers. Burrows announced these arrangements and plans for the night relief at a conference at 11.30 p.m. which was attended by the New Zealand company commanders as well as Burrows' company commanders (other than Walsoe and Graham who were still under Nichols' command).

During the morning three more half-hearted enemy attacks—one against Jill and two against Jack (renamed Happy)—were made against the eastern side of the corridor. Subsequently, probably about midday, the 1/Essex received a warning order directing the battalion to prepare to withdraw from Ed Duda after dark if Belhamed fell to the enemy. Colonel Nichols' soldierly inclinations were affronted. True, Belhamed had been seized, but

(Australian War Memorial)

Salum bay and township. The road winds up the steep escarpment through Halfaya Pass to Salum Barracks at top left.

(British Official)

Men of the 19th New Zealand Battalion and a Matilda of the 4th Royal Tank Regiment at Ed Duda after the link-up.

(*Australian War Memorial*)
Looking towards Tripoli, Syria, from the plateau above the Chekka tunnel. Chekka village is in the valley in the middle distance.

(*Capt M. D. Vincent*)
An Australian soldier looks across the border of northern Syria into Turkey at Djerablous where the Baghdad railway crosses the Euphrates River.

enemy attacking troops encountered that morning had been reported as having shown little offensive spirit. More determined troops had previously been ejected from Nichols' territory. He deplored any suggestion of withdrawal. The duty officer at the 70th Division battle headquarters noted that he reported at 12.40 a.m.:

> Troops at Ed Duda are ready to resist attack from any direction. Defences getting stronger every hour.

Other units, according to the 70th Division's report, made suggestions for further operations to restore the situation outside. Scobie told Nichols that he admired his spirit and "informed Commander XIII Corps that he proposed to hold on unless ordered to withdraw".[8] Godwin-Austen concurred.

Thus a step Ritchie was ready to authorise was not taken and Godwin-Austen, encouraged if not actuated by the resoluteness of Nichols and other forward commanders, decided not to withdraw after dark from Ed Duda but to remain steadfast at the end of the corridor and to accept the risks entailed in maintaining an offensive and defiant posture. Rommel had already ordered an advance to the Omar-Salum-Bardia front next day and if Ed Duda had been given up it is hard to believe that he would not have subsequently concentrated his main forces on the frontier, with imponderable consequences, instead of splitting them as he did between the frontier and the edge of the Ed Duda salient. Perhaps no other action by a British battalion commander during Operation CRUSADER so decisively affected its course and outcome as Nichols' protest.

Shelling of the ridge and flats occupied by the 2/13th Battalion intensified after the enemy had captured Belhamed, where presumably he had established observation posts overlooking the battalion's ground. The mortar platoon's return about midday and the withdrawal through the battalion area of a troop of New Zealand field artillery both attracted enemy attention and provoked strafing. About 1 p.m. Burrows went across to Bir Belhamed to contact the 1/Bedfordshire and Hertfordshire there, acquaint them with his situation and discover theirs and that of the 18th New Zealand Battalion near by. Then as a result of enemy movement on the north and west sides of Belhamed a warning was given that an attack on Ed Duda was expected. Burrows returned but the attack did not develop. Later in the afternoon enemy infantry and three tanks advanced from the east as though to cut the corridor in rear of the battalion and a heightening of artillery fire in the west indicated a possible converging thrust from that quarter, but the force attacking from the east did not press on when shelled. Soon afterwards, while Burrows was speaking to his second-in-command (Major Colvin) and acting adjutant (Lieutenant Maughan), a 210-mm shell hit a rock near by and although the detonation failed to fragment the projectile, which continued bouncing down the hill, Burrows was severely wounded and Colvin, who had been thrown down by the blast, momentarily dazed. Maughan believed both

---

[8] 70th Division report.

Burrows and Colvin to have been incapacitated and, after making arrangements with Captain Goode,[9] the Regimental Medical Officer, sent for Captain Daintree to take command; but when the anxious Daintree reported to battalion headquarters, not a little perturbed by the lurid message summoning him, he found an outwardly confident and completely recovered Colvin in charge. In view of enemy threats to the rear, Colvin made some dispositional changes and called Captain Gillan forward from rear battalion headquarters in Tobruk to take charge of Headquarters Company fighting troops which, in addition to the mobile detachments, included a substantial group built around the anti-aircraft and pioneer platoons and others released from specialist functions because of lack of equipment.

As soon as it was dark the changeover of companies at Ed Duda took place without incident but not far to the east there was troublesome infiltration between Belhamed and Bir Belhamed. A German infantry advance against the 1/Bedfordshire and Hertfordshire, supported by a heavy volume of small arms fire, was checked, and the New Zealanders drove off a party that simultaneously approached their headquarters. One company position at Bir Belhamed was penetrated, however, and isolated English pockets anxiously held to their ground throughout a confused night. At first light some Germans were captured but the enemy reorganised and about 9 a.m. a sizable force of infantry assault engineers and anti-tank gunners made a crude attack. The Beds and Herts showing cool discipline held all fire until the enemy were close and then engaged them with crippling effect. The Germans turned and made for the ridge to the north only to run into sharp fire from the New Zealanders, who effectively disrupted a none too orderly withdrawal. Once again a German assault on the Tobruk sortie force had gained nothing but had cost the German command many killed, wounded and captured. Some had been taken prisoner twice within a fortnight. Many of them belonged to a newly formed infantry unit of the *90th Light Division,* called after its commander the Kolbeck Battalion, which was composed largely of men released from the New Zealand prisoner-of-war camp overrun in the German counter-offensive on 28th November.

Throughout the rest of 2nd December not a little anxiety was experienced by units in the corridor, on the fringes of which the enemy's armoured battle groups had been operating almost unchecked for three days with momentous success. Reports of enemy excursions and tank movement coming in first from one quarter and then another kept commanders and their staffs on edge. What a different picture clairvoyance would have given of the enemy on the other side of the hill—broken-spirited infantry, tanks grounded for overhaul, and a desperate commander lacking reserves to follow up his success with strong blows. So the day brought no crisis. Never since he had come to Africa had Rommel so greatly needed to be unmolested for a few days.

---

[9] Maj P. C. R. Goode, MC, SX9183. RMO 2/13 Bn; DADMS 9 Div. Medical practitioner; of Lower Mitcham, SA; b. Port Lincoln, SA, 13 Sep 1916.

When the XIII Corps headquarters had telegraphed Eighth Army headquarters on 1st December "Request SO able give decisions on behalf Army Comd . . . be sent here soonest possible", Godwin-Austen doubtless intended to suggest that Ritchie should himself come, for the decisions required were well beyond the authority of a mere staff officer; the irony in the wording of the request, we must presume, was unintended. Ritchie duly came on 2nd December. He had received meanwhile a message from Godwin-Austen who expressed disappointment at the 7th Armoured Division's failure to attack the enemy armoured forces which were thus free to operate against the "appendix" and suggested that he would be better placed to exert pressure "in direction of El Adem" if only the 7th Armoured would attack the enemy tanks.

Neil flew into Tobruk yesterday and cleared up future plans with Godwin-Austen very satisfactorily, I think . . . (wrote Auchinleck on 3rd December to his chief of staff in Cairo, General Smith). Godwin is quite confident he can hold the "appendix" without undue risk of its being pinched out, which is good news. He says it is very strongly held, and they have wire and mines, besides quite a number of "I" tanks. In fact, he is starting at once to work forward from its western face towards El Adem, which is *good*. He is relieving some of the more tired troops in the salient by the Poles.[1]

Ritchie's planning with Godwin-Austen had an impact on the 70th Division late in the evening of 2nd December when

orders were received from 13 Corps to effect that 70th Division would soon be required to carry out an advance along the Northern edge of the escarpment from Ed Duda and that one Brigade Group must be prepared for this eventuality.

13 Corps were informed that 70th Division was already more than fully committed and that it was not possible to disengage a Brigade Group for this further operation. The thinning out of the perimeter by the withdrawal of one more battalion was however considered a justifiable risk and consequently it was decided to withdraw one battalion from the western sector and relieve 4 Border by it. The Polish Brigade, therefore, with II. E Czechoslovak Battalion under command would then hold half the perimeter—nearly fifteen miles of front. The 4 Border were to relieve 2/13 Australian Battalion at Ed Duda who in turn were to relieve the 1 D.L.I. in the southern sector. The latter were to come into reserve at the North of the corridor ready for this further advance.[2]

Scobie's plan, elaborated in the 70th Division Operation Order No. 24 issued next day, was to cooperate with the XXX Corps in attacking El Adem by mounting two operations from Tobruk on the night on which the XXX Corps force, advancing north from the Trigh el Abd, was to attack El Adem. One of the operations was to be a westward advance along the line of the escarpment from Ed Duda to El Adem by a force comprising two battalions, a squadron of tanks, a field regiment, an anti-tank battery and a machine-gun company; the other, a sortie from the perimeter to Bir el Azazi to capture the strongpoint previously known as Plonk[3] and exploit as far as the "walled village". The latter was to be

---
[1] Connell, *Auchinleck*, p. 388. By "the salient" Auchinleck meant the Ed Duda salient.
[2] 70 Div Operation Report, Part II, pp. 16-17.
[3] Confusion has been caused by the fact that "Plonk", the old codeword for this locality, continued to be used after its supersession by a new codeword "Snowwhite" had been ordered. For example in *Bayonets Abroad*, Snowwhite and Plonk are treated as two localities. Henceforward the locality will be referred to by its place-name Bir el Azazi.

carried out by the 2/13th Battalion "employing not more than one company, with one squadron of 'I' tanks to be provided by 1 Army Tank Brigade". These two localities on the old boundary between the *Trento Division* and the *Bologna Division* were the main supports of an enemy north-south defence line covering the Tobruk-El Adem road. The preliminary arrangements included an extensive reorganisation of brigade responsibilities, the original perimeter being divided into two sectors. The Polish brigade's responsibilities were extended to include the perimeter from the sea in the west to posts R34 and R35; the rest of the perimeter was the responsibility of the 16th Brigade. This released the 23rd Brigade which, with the 104th R.H.A. in support, was to take command of all troops on the Ed Duda feature as soon as the 4/Border had relieved the 2/13th Battalion. The 14th Brigade with four battalions (including the 18th New Zealand Battalion) under command and the 1st R.H.A. in support was to remain responsible for holding the corridor, excluding the Ed Duda feature.

"Abnormal lull on front still prevailed" was the 2/13th diarist's entry for 10 a.m. on 3rd December. As the day progressed the enemy became more active and in the late morning his tanks appeared to be reconnoitring near Bir Belhamed. But they withdrew when tanks of the 32nd Army Tank Brigade moved towards them. Moreover the Australians were developing a feeling that victory was in the air, which came from seeing plenty of evidence of British air superiority for the first time in the battalion's nine months of service in forward areas—another instance in which a wider vision might have modified the impression, for the most striking recent event in the desert air war was a damaging Stuka attack on the 5th South African Brigade made on the preceding morning. The Ed Duda ridge had been reconnoitred by two Me-109's in the evening.

Soon after midday a message received through the 1/Essex instructed 2/13th Battalion to send advanced parties ("to include down to platoon representatives"), to the 1/Durham Light Infantry as soon as possible; the unit was warned to be prepared to move by 4 a.m. next morning. There must have been some failure to direct this message to the commanding officer for nothing appears to have been done until a party from the Borders arrived at battalion headquarters at 4 p.m. The 2/13th Battalion advanced party left at 5.30 p.m. and arrived at 7 p.m. at the headquarters of the Durham Light Infantry on the left of the El Adem Road sector of the perimeter.

Soon after the Borders' advanced party arrived, artillery activity around the extremity of the "appendix" was stepped up by both sides. The enemy shelling was concentrated on the strongpoint Doc on the outer right flank of the sortie salient. Colvin and his staff

watched another attack on our right rear but unfortunately this time Dalby Square [Doc] fell to the enemy. For sheer temerity and bold enterprise one had to credit the enemy with his success. About three companies bowled along in vehicles, almost concealed by their own dust, dismounted, and went into action immediately.[4]

---

[4] *Bayonets Abroad*, p. 156.

The main party of the 4/Border arrived at 1.45 a.m. on 4th December and immediately relieved the 2/13th Battalion, which then left in the transport that had brought the English battalion.

> Never did we think during all those months (a soldier of the 2/13th wrote soon afterwards) that we would ever wish to return to Tobruch but we were very ready to climb on the trucks which at 0300 moved off towards the perimeter.[5]

The convoy slowly threaded its obscure way back and arrived at its destination at 5.30 a.m. The men, miserable with the cold of a wind that had penetrated clothes to chill raw flesh, were at once taken by guides to their defensive positions. The battalion was to hold the perimeter from Post R37 to Post R59 with three companies forward and one in reserve. The divisional operation order required the 1/Durham Light Infantry to move to its dispersal area in the convoy that brought the 2/13th. This it did not do but remained in the forward area, which became undesirably congested for the amount of cover available.[6] Probably this situation resulted from some indecision or late change of intention in relation to a plan for an early advance to be made westward from Ed Duda towards El Adem by a battalion of infantry accompanied by tanks. An order had been issued assigning this task to the 2/13th Battalion but it was subsequently decided to use the 1/Durham Light Infantry. Then mounting enemy activity at Ed Duda as the 2/13th was moving to its positions on the perimeter necessitated a postponement of the plan.

On 30th November Rommel had been visited at his headquarters at El Adem by his nominal superior, General Bastico. They agreed that the battle was developing into one of attrition, that their scope for effective action was limited by shortages of equipment, supplies and men and that quick replenishment was essential. Although they had been told they could expect no early deliveries of tanks and other vehicles, both subsequently sent requests to Rome for urgent deliveries of heavy equipment.

The point of the discussion noted in the German battle report, however, was an assertion by Rommel that his troops had "also" suffered severely and one may surmise that the necessity for the comment arose from remarks directed to the plight of the Italian and German garrisons on the frontier, to whose relief the discussion about supply problems was also pertinent. In fact Bastico had recently been wrestling with the intractable problems of supplying them by air lift or submarine to Bardia. That Bastico and Rommel discussed their unhappy situation there can be little doubt. Early on 1st December, when Rommel called at Cruewell's headquarters just after the German attack against the New Zealand Division had begun, he spoke of the British trying to starve out the Salum front, which had food "for only two days" and of the necessity "to make a push, at least with a strong advance-guard".[7]

---

[5] 2/13th Battalion's "Unofficial History".
[6] According to a 2/13th narrative, 1/DLI was "waiting for orders to move".
[7] See Murphy, p. 474.

Messages sent out from Rommel's headquarters in the late afternoon and evening indicated that hard on the heels of the advance-guard Rommel intended to launch a two-pronged eastward advance, with the *Africa Corps* in the north and the *Ariete* and *Trieste Divisions* in the south, the latter spearheaded by the *33rd Reconnaissance Unit*. Rommel came forward in the evening to Point 175 with the reconnaissance unit. He impressed on Cruewell that the advance was to start as soon as the *Kessel* had been emptied out. "Take food to Bardia," he said. Next day the kettle was empty. That the forces sent east were so small and so late in moving off is indicative of how close the Germans were to exhaustion. They were confident, from the tenor of British signals intercepted on 1st December, that an attack by the British armour was unlikely before the 3rd. Cruewell urged that only by committing the whole force, not detachments, could a quick and decisive success be gained by thrusting east, though he agreed with Rommel that the tanks could not be used since they had to be grounded for maintenance. Overruling as usual the protests of his underlings, Rommel adhered to his decision that the operation would commence with parallel thrusts by two German advance-guards, one advancing by the Via Balbia, the other by the Trigh Capuzzo. The northernmost column, to be provided by the *15th Armoured Division* and commanded by Lieut-Colonel Geissler, was to comprise a battalion battle group of all arms based on the *15th Motor Cycle Battalion,* fresh from its victory at Belhamed. The southernmost, to be provided by the *21st Armoured Division* and commanded by Lieut-Colonel Knabe, was to be of similar strength, except that it was given three tanks. General Neumann-Silkow was given overall command of both advance-guards. A "reinforced regiment" was to follow, but not the whole corps, because the remainder, including the *90th Light Division* and the army artillery, was to join with the Italian ground forces (*XXI Corps*) "in the elimination of the enemy in the Ed Duda position". Geissler's and Knabe's forces assembled on their respective routes on the 2nd and set out at dawn on the 3rd.

The Eighth Army's forces in the region into which the German columns were advancing had been reorganised in the preceding two days. On the morning of 29th November Lieut-Colonel L. W. Andrew, commanding the 22nd New Zealand Battalion, received orders from General Messervy of the 4th Indian Division, who was in command in the frontier region, to form a headquarters and assume command of the 5th New Zealand Brigade. This was not as a preliminary to meeting Freyberg's (and Godwin-Austen's) request for the brigade to be returned to the New Zealand Division, then about to face attack on the vital ground of Sidi Rezegh. The underlying reason was Ritchie's anxiety to intensify measures to prevent the enemy from getting supplies from Bardia to the Tobruk front, and the appointment was a preliminary to a redeployment of forces for that purpose. Two brigades (the 5th Indian and 5th New Zealand) instead of one were committed to masking the Bardia perimeter, which task was thus accorded a higher priority than the reinforcement of Sidi

Rezegh or the release of a second Indian brigade for operations on the Trigh el Abd axis. The reorganisation on the Bardia front took place on 1st and 2nd December, 5th New Zealand Brigade covering the northern perimeter and the main coast road with two battalions forward facing east and one in reserve. The divisional cavalry was to patrol to the west. Similar westward patrolling was to be done farther south about Sidi Azeiz on the Trigh Capuzzo by Goldforce, a mixed force of cavalry and artillery from the Central India Horse and the 31st Field Regiment, with other arms. East of Goldforce was the 5th Indian Brigade.

On the morning of 3rd December a New Zealand mobile column of cavalry and infantry sighted the approach of Geissler's force and gave the alarm to Andrew's brigade. Similarly a column of the Central India Horse reported the approach of Knabe force. The Geissler force, flushed with victory, under-estimated its enemy, deployed, and confidently attacked but was disastrously defeated. What was left of the *15th Motor Cycle Battalion* was reorganised into one company and took up a blocking position. Knabe force was more fortunate but became locked in long-range duels with Goldforce and the Support Group's Jock columns. Knabe felt too insecure to move to Geissler's help and in the evening was ordered to break contact and withdraw to Gasr el Arid.

The New Zealand Division's total contribution to the defeat of Rommel's army in Operation CRUSADER has not always been adequately acknowledged. Not least of the New Zealanders' achievements was the rebuff administered to Geissler's force just when it lay in the balance whether the centre of the fighting would shift to the east or west. It is of interest to consider how much of the depletion of the fighting strength of the *15th* and *21st Armoured Divisions* and the *90th Light Division* between 18th November and 4th December was due to losses inflicted by the New Zealand Division and the Tobruk garrison.

That evening the German staff decided to reinforce the drive to the frontier by sending the rest of *15th Armoured Division* to Gasr el Arid early next morning to join the *Ariete Division* and Knabe force; but part of the *21st Armoured Division's* artillery together with *8th Machine Gun Battalion* and an engineer battalion were kept back for a second attack on Ed Duda. The junction with Knabe was duly made and the force, though bombed on the way, drove on to the east, forcing Goldforce to withdraw. In the north the 5th New Zealand Brigade was now ideally situated for destruction by the usual German tactic of isolation and attack in superior force and Neumann-Silkow planned to advance against the brigade's positions in the afternoon.

At the Eighth Army headquarters from which Ritchie (Auchinleck with him) was directing the British operations by remote control, the appearance of this sizable force near the frontier was not regarded with equanimity. The 2nd South African Division which had relieved the 4th Indian Division at Sidi Omar at 9 a.m. that morning was warned and at 11 a.m. an order was sent to Norrie's headquarters that the 4th Armoured

Brigade was to be withdrawn. To ponder this stroke of cautious generalship, it will be necessary to advert to the situation on Norrie's front.[8]

As soon as Norrie returned on 1st December to resume command of his corps after his hapless tour of duty as South African fugleman, he acquainted himself with Ritchie's plan to regain the initiative by attacking El Adem. His first reaction was to seek assurances that this was to be no "half-cocked show"[9] by which presumably he meant that the show should have more backing than had been given to Godwin-Austen's and Freyberg's push to Sidi Rezegh. Having received assurances on this point he allowed the 4th Armoured Brigade a day of make-and-mend at Bir Berraneb after its day's excursion to the Tobruk arena, cancelled Gott's less ambitious plans for flank-threatening moves and began to get units ready for the thrust. Norrie planned to secure the Bir el Gubi area first and then to attack El Adem from the south.

El Gubi was held by a battalion of *Fascist Youth* and a reconnaissance unit armed with Italian light and medium tanks and light artillery. On 3rd December the 11th Indian Brigade was moved up to Bir Duedar, south-east of Bir el Gubi, and the 1st South African Brigade sent out a number of harassing columns. At short notice the Indian brigade with a field battery, a regiment of medium artillery and a squadron of "I" tanks executed a difficult night march of 47 miles and at dawn on 4th December launched a surprise attack from the west and south-west over necessarily unreconnoitred ground. The 2/5th Mahratta successfully captured one strong-point but an attack by the 2/Camerons on another held by the battalion of *Fascist Youth* was repulsed. Simultaneously the 4th Armoured Brigade using 98 of its 126 tanks clashed with a detachment of the Italian reconnaissance unit two or three miles north of El Gubi, claiming 11 M13 tanks destroyed, and armoured cars of the King's Dragoon Guards and of South African units raided dumps and columns of vehicles north-west and north-east of El Gubi.

A further attack in the evening on the stubborn locality defended by the *Fascist Youth* failed. Norrie had meanwhile received Ritchie's request for help against the tanks approaching the frontier from the direction of Sidi Azeiz. Norrie protested against conforming to Rommel's every movement, but was told to move back the 7th Armoured Division's "centre of gravity" to where it had been; so the 4th Armoured Brigade returned for the night to its favourite leaguer at Bir Berraneb, which was some 20 miles from Bir el Gubi.

Perhaps nobody was better placed to weigh the emergent risks than General Messervy who had relinquished command in the frontier region as late as 9 a.m. that morning but who now had one of his brigades (the

---

[8] Auchinleck's outlook this day is indicated by the following passages from his letter to General Smith on 4th December (see Connell, p. 391). "He *may* think we have shot our bolt. . . . He may underestimate our tank strength (160 cruisers and M.3s [sic] this morning) as we have not done much for two days. If he does think this, I think he will go for Bardia-Capuzzo-Sidi Omar with a view to joining up with the Germans in Halfaya and establishing himself on the flank of the L. of C. of our main concentration at Gabr Saleh. . . . If he does this it should suit us very well, and I do not think he will get very far."

[9] Agar-Hamilton and Turner, p. 438.

11th) fully committed at Bir el Gubi at the other extremity of the wide battle arena. Norrie came to discuss the perplexing developments with him and together they motored to Gott's headquarters. Norrie and Messervy, like Scobie, Nichols and O'Carroll, preferred accepting risks to stepping back, and they chose to accept them with even more temerity, for their troops at El Gubi were less firmly placed than Scobie's at Ed Duda. The move-back instruction had referred only to armour; only armour went back. And the efforts to complete the capture of El Gubi by the infantry were intensified. An attack at dawn was ordered.

At 2.30 a.m. on 5th December Ritchie signalled Norrie that he had changed the policy for future operations and that, owing to enemy movements towards Bardia, he had decided that it was essential to "reduce frontier area prior to tackling Tobruk, thus reducing possibility of enemy refuelling from Bardia and operating in our rear". Norrie was to discuss with a staff officer, who would arrive that day, a plan for carrying out this policy, which had been substituted for previous orders. It may be doubted whether Auchinleck, who had earlier formed the opinion that "the situation was really in hand",[1] approved of this nocturnal enunciation of a startling reversal of priorities. Be that as it may, nobody with the Bir el Gubi force called "halt" or "about turn", and it was soon discovered that the danger to Ritchie's lines of communication had passed. In fact Neumann-Silkow's menacing force had been withdrawn some hours before Ritchie sent the signal announcing his pessimistic change of policy.

By daylight on 5th December the German threat to the frontier had vanished. The guarded stance the Eighth Army had adopted to meet it still seemed good, however, at least until Rommel's armour made its next appearance. Auchinleck commented to General Smith at Cairo:

... his thrusts towards Capuzzo seem to have been half-hearted and to have petered out under the attacks of our "Jock columns".... These "Jock" columns of which more and more are being organised are just what we want.... I am pretty sure Rommel will use the last of his armour in an attempt to throw us off our balance. He tried before, you remember, and very nearly succeeded. If he tries again he will find us very much on our toes I think, and not up against the ropes. Neil is very wisely keeping the bulk of our armour centrally placed ready to counter-attack north, north-west or north-east. It is *not* being tied to the infantry. I am very glad that the 4th Indian Div is now leading the offensive.[2]

The Indian division was indeed leading the offensive, and by a good 20 miles too, and though the 4th Armoured Brigade at Bir Berraneb was to be ready to counter-attack in any direction, whether the brigade would arrive anywhere in time if it left the initiative to the enemy was a question to which its past performance might have suggested that a yes answer could not be given with assurance.

Gott had command of the 11th Indian Brigade as well as of the 4th Armoured. The Indian brigade made its third attack at Bir el Gubi at dawn on the 5th and again failed. A fourth attack in the early afternoon also failed. In the meantime reconnaissance reports received by Gott

---
[1] Connell, p. 393.
[2] Letter to General Smith, 5th December 1941. Connell, pp. 392-3.

indicated that something might be afoot at Hagfet en Nezha, between El Adem and El Gubi. Gott wished, however, to leave the 4th Armoured Brigade at Bir Berraneb "for administrative reasons"—a euphemism to cover the desire of the armoured commanders to be freed at that juncture from participation in the fighting so that they could practise a new system of leaguering.[3] Norrie deferred to Gott's wishes although, now relieved of embarrassing supplications to deal with enemy columns in rear, he pressed Gott to begin the advance to El Adem with the 4th Armoured Brigade early next morning; to which Gott agreed. Thus Norrie, to borrow his own phrase, was allowing his show "to go off half-cocked".

While the Australian troops were journeying back to the perimeter on the night of 3rd December, shelling could be heard in the direction from which they had come. At first light a heavy assault on Ed Duda developed from the west, south and south-east. The 4/Border found themselves under attack on terrain they had never seen in daylight. A thrust from the west against the 1/Essex was made by enemy approaching above and north of the escarpment, but was broken up by defensive fire, and the mobile defence with carriers manned by crews provided by the New Zealanders proved its worth in mopping up. Soon afterwards enemy attacks against the Bir Belhamed positions from the north and against the 18th New Zealand Battalion from the east were also driven off but a thrust from the south-east to the left flank of the 4/Border secured a foothold across the by-pass road. The Essex and one company of the Borders counter-attacked in conjunction with the 4th Royal Tanks. All ground lost, down to the foot of the escarpment, was recovered and the company of the 4/Border accompanying the tanks drove through the enemy positions to a depth of 1,000 yards; but 15 Matildas, which represented most of the remaining "I" tank strength of the 32nd Army Tank Brigade, were knocked out by 88-mm guns that had been brought forward to within effective anti-tank range, and thick machine-gun fire from the flanks then pinned down the Borders, prevented anybody from approaching, or escaping from, the tanks and gave the enemy control of the ground. The Germans seemed to be preparing to thrust from Belhamed along the ridge with the aim of linking up with the force attacking the 4/Border. The 18th New Zealand Battalion was bombarded by mortars and two tanks advanced against the New Zealanders' positions; but both were knocked out, one by the minefield and one by a New Zealand gun, and the attack was not pressed home.

Ed Duda and the salient of which it was the shield were the most important gains the British had managed to retain against Rommel's counter-offensive. When Ed Duda came under attack, Godwin-Austen deemed the time appropriate to issue an order of the day to "General Scobie and all ranks engaged in the establishment and defences of the Tobruk corridor".

You are fighting the battle which will result in the reconquest of Cyrenaica. Your magnificent efforts . . . are beyond all praise. . . . This is a bitter fight which will

---

[3] Liddell Hart, *The Tanks*, Vol II, p. 139.

be won by those who stick it longest. We must if it is humanly possible continue to hold Ed Duda. We shall then be able to cooperate with 30 Corps and help to turn the scale in the decisive battle shortly to be fought.

For the garrison force the loss of tanks was very serious and indeed dangerous, reducing its mobile reserve's strength to the perilously low state of early siege days. When another counter-attack by the 4/Border failed to overcome the enemy's echeloned machine-guns, it was decided to launch a two-battalion attack as soon as it was dark, using the 4/Border and the 18th New Zealand Battalion. The report of the 70th Division comments:

> In the heavy fighting that had taken place communications to these distant battalions had been cut and consequently many hours were spent in arranging the details for this coordinated attack, which it was hoped to start early, so that the majority of the tanks might be recovered during the hours of darkness. By 2000 hours it was realised that the enemy was withdrawing from the forward slope and this enabled tank recovery to start at once. Commander 14 Brigade decided that the attack as originally planned would not be necessary and only strong fighting patrols were sent forward. These achieved the object and by first light 5th December the enemy had vacated his positions and many enemy wounded were taken prisoner. The anti-tank guns which had caused so much damage to the "I" tanks the day before were captured.[4]

On 4th December and the succeeding night, the 2/13th had what would have been called in more normal times a quiet day of perimeter duty: a little shelling, normal protective patrols at night and two special patrols reconnoitring for future operations. But next morning opened with two hours of what the battalion's diarist called "fairly heavy shelling". The battalion's shelling report for the day indicates that as accurately as could be estimated between 1,500 and 1,700 shells fell on the battalion, whose Intelligence officer thought this was counter-preparation fire against an expected attack on Bir el Azazi.[5]

The rest of the day was uneventful until late afternoon when the 1/Durham Light Infantry was ordered to leave at once and these orders were associated with the usual rumours that there were signs of an enemy withdrawal. It was also said that the English battalion was to take part next morning in an advance to El Adem.

Hard upon the Durham Light Infantry's summons came an order to the 2/13th Battalion to launch a company attack on Bir el Azazi, reputed to be the enemy's strongest outpost. The Australians were not very pleased that the attack previously planned to be made in conjunction with tanks was now to be made without them. A bombardment program arranged by the garrison's artillery and aimed principally at the guns responsible for the morning strafe was the occasion for the order, which was a typical example of the unduly rosy view of a demoralised enemy sometimes taken by headquarters staff.

16 Brigade (said the divisional instruction) will take advantage of the artillery concentrations to send a strong fighting patrol from the 2/13th Battalion to Plonk

---
[4] 70th Division report, pp. 224-5.
[5] It is quite likely that from interception of messages the enemy knew of the plan to attack this feature.

to inflict casualties and take prisoners and if enemy withdraws establish an OP at Plonk.[6]

The neighbouring Bondi (or Queen) was also to be raided but not occupied, by another battalion. Major Colvin made a plan to give his assault parties maximum support, using his mortar and carrier platoons with all weapons available from his support company, but the acting brigade commander, Lieut-Colonel R. F. C. Oxley-Boyle, cancelled the operation about 7.30 p.m.

The day had been a memorable one for the garrison and particularly those who had been in close contact with the enemy from Ed Duda eastwards. At Ed Duda not only had the force which had attacked on the preceding day been withdrawn, but the defences previously held by the enemy had been abandoned. Soon from all round the perimeter, but mainly from the east, reports were received of unusual enemy movement, most of it from east to west. A patrol with anti-tank guns and a platoon of machine-guns was pushed out to the Trigh Capuzzo. All enemy columns coming within range of the garrison's artillery and machine-guns were engaged.

> Great damage was seen to be inflicted as [the enemy columns] tried to pass through the bottleneck between Ed Duda and the next escarpment, and at times it was reported that complete confusion reigned.[7]

The 23rd Infantry Brigade took command of all troops at Ed Duda and plans were completed for the 1/Durham Light Infantry, 104th R.H.A. and other units allocated to the westward thrust to assemble during the night so that by first light they would be ready to start the advance along the escarpment running west from Ed Duda to be made in cooperation with "the advance of 4th Indian Division from the south towards El Adem".

Just before dark a Polish officer who had been commanding a troop of anti-tank guns in the corridor reported that he had driven as far north as the Bardia Road and had found Freddie and Walter unoccupied. It was decided to send out fighting patrols during the night to these and other localities and occupy them if the report proved correct.

Everything was set for a busy night of patrol activity, artillery bombardment and preparation for the El Adem push, when at 8.30 p.m. the headquarters of XIII Corps instructed Scobie to cancel the advance to El Adem. The reason given was that enemy action had necessitated a cancellation of the attack by the XXX Corps.

On the morning of 4th December Rommel's army divided its efforts, as we saw, between an eastward thrust by the main strength of the German and Italian mobile forces and an assault on Ed Duda by what remaining force he could muster. Neumann-Silkow's force quickly brushed aside Goldforce and made ready for its unenviable task of destroying British frontier detachments one by one until it became too weak to continue the process. The attack on Ed Duda, however, did not prosper. It was

---

[6] 70th Division Operation Instruction No. 29 of 5th December 1941.
[7] 70th Division report.

a four-pronged affair: from the west the infantry of the Mickl Group, from the south engineers from the *200th* and *900th Engineer Battalions,* from the south-east the *8th Machine Gun Battalion* and from the east little bits of infantry from the *90th Light Division.* The concerted attacks from such diverse starting points were ill synchronised. Only that of the *8th Machine Gun Battalion* (against the 4/Border) had any success. As against this puny gain the Germans had been unsettled by aggressive raids made by a Jock column (Currie column) from Bir bu Creimisa to Sidi Rezegh, in which several anti-tank guns and a number of prisoners had been taken.

There is nothing more remarkable or puzzling in the CRUSADER story than the extent and suddenness of the change in Rommel's plans between the morning and evening of 5th December. Within so few hours the commander whose intention, when the day was young, had been to lop off the Tobruk garrison's ill-protected protuberance at Ed Duda, smash through to Bardia and open a way to Sidi Omar, had decided not merely to abandon both enterprises so as to concentrate the German and Italian armour against the British forces threatening his flank, but also to give up the whole territory between Tobruk and the Egyptian frontier including the defence line opposite the eastern face of the perimeter. What seems astonishing is not so much the retraction of the administrative and maintenance organisations while there was yet time as the sudden withdrawal of the holding infantry on the eastern siege front. Rommel's decision to concentrate his mobile forces—both Italian as well as both German armoured divisions—near El Gubi seems to have been made about midday. An intriguing if unlikely explanation of the sudden haste to join battle at El Gubi is that the German intercept unit had provided him with up-to-date reports on Ritchie's message to Norrie. As soon as Norrie was pressed to draw his armour back from El Gubi, Rommel drove all his armour in that direction as fast as he could. The German battle report does not support the surmise but the timing does. Ritchie and Rommel each reacted to each other's threats but Ritchie had reacted first.

The first instructions for the withdrawal of artillery and other operational units from east of Tobruk were given about mid-afternoon. No doubt Rommel had ruminated on the rehabilitated British armour's dark purposes after its brief appearance at Sidi Rezegh, learnt of the British attack at El Gubi, received Intelligence reports of the 2nd South African Division's arrival at the frontier and the 4th Indian's on the Trigh el Abd; but a decision so final and symbolic as to lift the siege, if only temporarily, requires more explanation. Perhaps he had contemplated his own forces' pusillanimity when attacking the weakly held Ed Duda ridges. But probably the explanation must be found in the arrival that day of a staff officer from the Italian High Command (Lieut-Colonel Montezemolo) to inform Bastico and Rommel that the only supplies they could expect before the end of December would be limited to deliveries of petrol, food and medical stores. Rommel did not see Montezemolo until next day but may have learnt the gist of his bad tidings.

However Rommel probably heard at the same time of Hitler's "Directive 38" of 2nd December which had placed an air fleet and defences to be transferred from the Russian front under Field Marshal Kesselring's command and given them the prime task of achieving mastery of the air and sea across the narrows so to ensure the safety of communications between Italy and North Africa. His current shortages might necessitate a withdrawal, but steps now being taken held promise of a brighter New Year.

Orders recalling the forces operating against the frontier were issued from Rommel's headquarters to the *Africa Corps* at 12.50 p.m. and to the Italian *Mobile Armoured Corps* ten minutes later. Neumann-Silkow received his order at 1.45 p.m., in time to save the 5th New Zealand Brigade from attack. At 7.30 p.m. the *90th Light Division* was ordered to "the sector Bir Salem-Ed Duda-Belhamed", which seems to have been liberally interpreted as authorisation not only to withdraw from the eastern perimeter (including Freddie and Walter) but also to break contact in most of the sector named to be held. The *Bologna Division* also evacuated the eastern sector during the night.

By dawn on the 5th Neumann-Silkow's division was two to three miles west of Ed Duda and the *21st Armoured Division* was five miles west of El Adem. In mid-morning Rommel indicated that his intention was to push on to the *Fascist Youth Battalion* north (sic) of Gubi. There contact was to be made with the Italian *Mobile Armoured Corps* in preparation for attacks next day against British supply dumps south of the Trigh el Abd. In view of the weakness of the German armoured formations (tank strength about 50 tanks), Rommel intended the Italian *Ariete* and *Trieste Divisions* to join up with the German armour before it advanced into contact with the British formations.

Rommel as usual wanted to strike with speed but the Italian armour kept him waiting. After three hours and a half the *Africa Corps* advanced to El Gubi without the Italians, and to the Germans' surprise encountered the hapless 11th Indian Brigade, which was overrun just before dusk, while the "centrally disposed" 4th Armoured Brigade left by Gott's choice 20 miles away addressed itself to another night of trouble-free and well-practised leaguering.

Thus the XXX Corps was constrained to postpone the dawn attack on El Adem, as Scobie had been informed. The night of 5th-6th December at El Gubi, moreover, was one of great confusion for both the British and the Germans. At first light the partly reorganised 11th Indian Brigade withdrew and was pursued by most of the German armour into the area of the 22nd Guards Brigade, who might perhaps have met the same fate but that Cruewell received an order from Rommel at 8.30 a.m. telling him to go over to the defensive until the arrival of the Italian armour. The British 4th Armoured Brigade was not encountered, as it had shrewdly moved to the area where Italian tanks had previously been engaged and then took up a defensive position north-east of El Gubi behind an armoured car screen. For the rest of the day there was some skirmishing, each side being wary of the other, but nothing much of importance occurred except that General Neumann-Silkow was killed. The British artillery bombardment and air attack, however, were taking a steady toll. The Germans' and Italians' battle prospects, heavily weighted against them by the bleak supply outlook, would deteriorate further unless a quick success was gained.

Early on the morning of 7th December Ritchie directed Norrie to begin an advance as soon as the situation seemed favourable and to let Godwin-Austen know so that he could cooperate with his thrust from Ed Duda to El Adem. "Our armoured brigade standing off ready to go in if opportunity offers," wrote Auchinleck to Smith. But the enemy did not offer the opportunity and later in the morning Gott said he thought the enemy was thickening up. Norrie informed everybody concerned that he could not continue with the advance to El Adem.

At 9.30 a.m. on 7th December Rommel announced at the headquarters of the *Africa Corps* that he would have to abandon the Tobruk front and go back to the Gazala position if the enemy was not beaten that day. No orders or plans likely to have that outcome were given out, however, whereas several arrangements connected with withdrawing were put into effect. In the early afternoon orders were issued for a disengagement after dark, and in the late afternoon supply columns started moving back. At nightfall the 4th Armoured Brigade, adhering to its convenient custom, drew back to a leaguer 5 miles south-east of El Gubi. Contrary to German expectations, the disengagement of the *Africa Corps,* according to the German narrative, passed off without incident and according to plan.

In mid-afternoon Ritchie ordered Godwin-Austen to proceed with the Tobruk garrison's thrust against El Adem, whether the XXX Corps took part or not.

On the Tobruk front car patrols went out at dawn on 6th December to clear the road-block on the Bardia Road and infantry patrols occupied the strongposts Freddie and Walter. Other patrols probed south-east to the Bu Amud area. There was no news from outside Tobruk and Scobie was restless, feeling that the enemy was slipping away and valuable time being lost.

In mid-afternoon armoured cars of "C" Squadron of the King's Dragoon Guards made contact near Ed Duda with a column of the 11th Hussars and a meeting took place between Major Loder-Symonds and Brigadier Campbell of the Support Group. Loder-Symonds' battery engaged targets in conjunction with the support group column. Another Jock column achievement this day was the liberation by Wilson column of the captured New Zealand dressing station near Point 175, which had been left stranded by the battle-tide's westward ebb. After dark a small column from the 2nd South African Division arrived in Tobruk, having journeyed from Menastir by the main coast road.

It had been laid down that the clearing of stragglers from the coast and hinterland between Bardia and Tobruk would be the responsibility of the 70th Division west of Gambut, and of the 2nd South African Division east of Gambut. On the morning of the 7th Scobie sent out a mobile column to mop up between Tobruk and Gambut. The column was out all day and returned at 6 p.m. with much valuable information and 50 prisoners. Other salvaging parties went out.

In particular "Bardia Bill", the heavy gun which had so constantly shelled the harbour in the past month and had become a by-word among the garrison was discovered intact together with the German Master Gunner who had refused to leave his gun. . . .[8]

When it was learnt that Norrie did not intend to attack El Adem on the morning of 8th December, Godwin-Austen called a conference at which it was directed that the 70th Division would carry out its advance to El Adem alone "in order to create a diversion and so reduce pressure in the area south of El Adem".

The 2/13th Battalion's reconnaissance patrols on the night of the 5th-6th indicated that Bir el Azazi was still held by an alert enemy. During the morning of the 6th enemy movement was observed in rear of the strongpoint. An order was received to mount the attack that night, and tanks were to be provided, in accordance with the original orders; but later the operation was again cancelled. At 10 p.m. harassing artillery fire was laid down in rear of Bir el Azazi and for three hours after midnight the enemy responded with intermittent shelling of the 2/13th's positions.

Sitnor[9] was the comment made next morning when once again the battalion received an order to proceed that night with the attack on Bir el Azazi. The day was uneventful but not cheerful, for the history of assaults on Plonk was mainly of failures. The start-line was laid on time at 8.30 p.m. but nothing else was on time. The transport arrived late and then was inadequate; one company had to hasten forward by foot over a great distance. The infantry were not in position at 9 p.m. when the supporting machine-guns and artillery opened up, nor had the tanks even reached the minefield gap on the perimeter from which they were to be guided forward. So the attack was postponed until 9.30 p.m., then to 10.30 p.m. and, when the tanks had still not arrived, until a time to be fixed. The tank commander did not arrive until 1 a.m. and his tanks were then at the wrong gap—Gap L instead of Gap 23. The action log kept at 70th Division battle headquarters had the following entries:

2230 Reported that because of the failure of the tanks to arrive, 2/13 Bn attack had not taken place.
2240 GOC told Commander 16 Brigade that the attack was to take place later in the night, as soon as tanks could be found, but without artillery support.
2345 Tanks still not arrived. GOC tells 32 Brigade urgency of finding them.
Tanks now arrived. Zero hour for Snowwhite 0200.
0120 Brigade Commander to Division. Tanks had not arrived but the officer was there and the tanks were at Gap L. Told attack was to proceed with a still later Z hour.

Lieut-Colonel Oxley-Boyle arrived at 2/13th Battalion headquarters at 1.30 a.m. with orders that the attack was to proceed at 3.30 a.m. in

---
[8] 70th Division report.
[9] Abbreviation for "situation normal".

conjunction with the tanks but without artillery or machine-gun support (presumably because this would endanger operations of the 2/Queen's against the outpost Queen, previously known as Bondi). The effect of these many changes on morale was not tested in action because the brigade commander decided at 2.15 a.m. that a start-time of 3.30 would be too late; an earlier start would be impracticable because the tanks were still some 5,000 yards from the start-line. A reconnaissance patrol was sent out and reported later that there had been some movement at Bir el Azazi. The fighting patrol of the 2/Queen's was driven off from the neighbouring Queen with the loss of nine men.

Next morning there was a complete absence of movement from the direction of Bir el Azazi. Two patrols sent out soon after midday on the 8th approached the strongpoint from either side and found it unoccupied. Soon afterwards a standing patrol was placed there. The Queen's similarly occupied Queen but then patrolled north towards Bir el Azazi without notifying the 2/13th whose standing patrol had to exercise much restraint.

It had been intended that the 2/13th Battalion's attack on Bir el Azazi on the *Trento Division's* left flank would synchronise with the collision with its right flank by the force advancing to El Adem. The advance mounted by the 23rd Brigade was timed to start at 8.30 p.m. with an advance of the 1/Durham Light Infantry to Point 157, whereupon the 4/Border was to pass through and secure Point 162. The operation proceeded without opposition until the 1/Durham Light Infantry had advanced some 5,000 yards. Here the *Pavia Division* had established a rearguard position which was tenaciously defended but overcome after midnight by an attack made in conjunction with tanks of the 32nd Army Tank Brigade. The 1/Durham Light Infantry took "150 prisoners and many guns but lost 11 killed and 25 wounded". The 4/Border, with some New Zealanders attached, then advanced to Point 162, which was taken without further opposition. Thus it was the Tobruk Fortress garrison itself that in the end broke the enemy's hold, though this was only made possible because the XXX Corps had drawn away the enemy's main force.

The night of 7th-8th December marked the end of a phase not only of Operation CRUSADER, but of the war. With the seizure of El Adem the cautious Auchinleck was willing for an announcement to be made to the world that Tobruk had been relieved and so 7th December is usually regarded as the last day of a siege which is commonly said to have lasted 242 days, though as we have seen it had ceased to be effective before that date. Tobruk was not relieved; rather, the siege was abandoned; it does not seem of consequence to determine the precise moments when it began and ceased to be effective or to define its duration more accurately than a few days less than eight months.

The disengagement of the German and Italian mobile forces on the night of the 7th-8th as a result of the German commander's decision to abandon the Tobruk front and stand next at Gazala changed the character of the desert campaign. But contemporaneous events far from the desert had even more far-reaching consequences. When Hitler had attacked

Russia, Britain had acquired an ally, but not a sympathetic one. On the morning of 7th December she had no other; by the morning of the 8th, after Japan had almost simultaneously attacked Pearl Harbour and British territories in the Far East, the British had acquired a new strong ally with common ideals. But although Britain's ultimate victory had by that one stroke become almost assured, the immediate consequence to the war in Africa was a worsening of Auchinleck's supply position in comparison with that of his adversary.

By dawn on 8th December the 70th Division was very much extended. Scobie did not know that a general retreat had started; indeed the situation report he received from the outside world told him that the El Adem line was very strongly held. He decided that the safest course would be to keep the initiative by maintaining the offensive on all fronts. On the 8th and the succeeding night the main operations were directed to clearing the El Adem Road; on the 9th, having heard that the 5th New Zealand Brigade was to take part in an advance along the by-pass road, he sent out the 2/Leicestershire to occupy Point 156 "so that at least the reconnaissance parties of the 5th New Zealand Brigade on arrival could view the ground for their subsequent advance from this commanding feature". There contact was gained with the 7th Indian Infantry Brigade of the 4th Indian Division. On the night 9th-10th December the Medauuar Salient was captured in a night attack. Next morning the Polish Cavalry Regiment advanced along the Derna Road to the junction with the by-pass road and by noon that day Acroma had been taken.

The 2/13th Battalion played a minor part in this vigorous exploitation. On the evening of 9th December the battalion took over the perimeter from R17 to R40. At first light on 10th December it occupied the enemy locality south of the Salient known as Bir el Carmusa and on 11th December moved again to take over the Twin Poles area—in daylight!

> During this period we experienced a feeling of great relaxation—pass-words, situation and shelling reports, stand-to's and restrictions on lights being dispensed with. . . . It was now possible for the troops to take time off to visit, in daylight, their patrol objectives.[1]

Late on 13th December the 2/13th received the first of several warning orders to leave Tobruk. It was intended that the battalion, departing at first light on 15th December, should escort 1,800 prisoners of war to Egypt. At 3 p.m. on the 14th December a parade "as regimentally correct as circumstances would permit" was held to enable General Scobie to farewell the battalion. Standing orders forbade unit parades owing to the risk of air attack, so the assembly was limited to officers and N.C.O's; no doubt somebody commented that in the circumstances the choice of the personnel to attend was apposite. Though small it was an impressive parade. In an address of some length General Scobie paid tribute to the 9th Division's services in the defence of Tobruk, recounted the course of

---

[1] *Bayonets Abroad*, pp. 157-8.

events that had necessitated the battalion's employment in the battle, described its counter-attack as "brilliant and masterful" and expressed his deep regret at the wounding of its gallant colonel. The General's tribute and courtesy were then acknowledged by the traditional general salute. The felicity of the occasion was slightly marred by an incident at 3.15 p.m., drily but concisely recorded by the battalion's diarist:

> Message received while G.O.C. was addressing battalion cancelling proposed move.

The battalion eventually left Tobruk at 7.30 a.m. on 16th December, issuing from the perimeter by the El Adem Road and proceeding to a point on the escarpment south of El Adem. The convoy then traversed the recent battlefield to a gap in the frontier wire at K62 which was reached at 4.15 p.m., Lieutenant Martin's navigation taking it to the gap with absolute accuracy. The battalion bivouacked at the frontier and proceeded next day to rail-head. Soon after 9 a.m. on the 18th the battalion entrained— "30 men to a goods van"—and 60 hours later it reached camp at Hill 69 in Palestine.

Casualties suffered by the 2/13th Battalion while under the command of the 70th Division were 39 killed and 36 wounded.

Australian ground forces did not take part in the desert campaign after the end of the siege until more than six months had elapsed, by which time Tobruk had fallen to the enemy. In the intervening months of mainly unsuccessful endeavour the desert fighting recedes into the background of the Australian story.[2]

Despite its prestige value Tobruk, like Bardia, was little more than a military outpost in a barren province destitute of crops or good pasture, but Cyrenaica supported a prosperous Italian colony whose protection was in fact the prime reason for these outposts' existence before the war.

On 7th December the Italian Supreme Command had agreed that the siege should be given up but had suggested to Bastico that an attempt to defend Cyrenaica should be made and that if some of it had to be given up, at least Benghazi should be retained, covered by a force holding Agedabia. A retreat to Tripolitania should be considered only as a last resort. The decision, however, was correctly left to the man on the spot who, in Bastico's eyes, was Bastico. He visited Rommel on the 8th and they agreed that an attempt would be made to stand at Gazala where a defence line had been developed from the coast at Ain el Gazala to Alam Hamza. Next day the *90th Light Division* began to move back to Agedabia and the *Brescia* and *Trento Divisions* to withdraw from the western perimeter of Tobruk.

When on the morning of 8th December it became apparent that the Axis forces were in general retreat, Norrie directed the 7th Armoured Division to the track junction south of Acroma, known later as Knightsbridge, and ordered the 4th Indian Division to advance along the escarpment

---

[2] Australian aircrew continued, however, to play a leading part in operations—see J. Herington, *Air War Against Germany and Italy 1939-1943* (1954), in the air series of this history.

west from El Adem. On the 10th, as we saw, the Indian division made contact at Acroma with advance-guards from the Tobruk force.

It was decided on the 9th that as from the 11th Godwin-Austen's XIII Corps would take command of the advancing forces while Norrie's XXX Corps (though better equipped, as he pointed out, to control mobile operations) was to be in charge of operations to reduce the abandoned Axis garrisons on the Egyptian frontier. In the pursuit the British commanders did not drive their forces very hard—not as hard as Rommel would have driven them had the commands been reversed. The 5th New Zealand Brigade (though without Freyberg's knowledge) was brought forward from the frontier on the 9th to spearhead the next stage of the advance and married for that purpose with the 1st R.H.A. and the 32nd Army Tank Brigade. After some brushes the New Zealanders reached Gazala on the 13th. They closed up on the right of the line. The Polish Brigade came up in the centre before Bir en Naghia. Arriving by the inland route the 5th Indian Brigade was directed at Alam Hamza from the south-east, while on its left flank was the 7th Indian Brigade. The British armour, despite its superiority, continued to eschew head-on conflicts; the German armour, despite its attrition, to deal out heavy blows. The 17th Indian Brigade was attacked by tanks on the 13th and part of its artillery overrun.

A tussle began between Godwin-Austen and Gott, Godwin-Austen calling for the German armour to be attacked and destroyed, Gott wishing to influence the battle by threatening the German rear. Gott was to have his way. The plans for the 15th December were for a frontal attack by the infantry on the Gazala line and a left-hook by the armour in rear of the enemy. The upshot was that the infantry as usual bore the burden of the day. Their attack—made by the Maoris and Poles—succeeded, but south-west of Alam Hamza the *Africa Corps* counter-attacked and overran the 1/Buffs. The 4th Armoured Brigade moved to Bir el Eleba. Godwin-Austen continued to exhort Gott to get to grips with the enemy. But Gott and Gatehouse did nothing that day or the next likely to involve trying doubtful conclusions with the enemy, though on the 16th raids made at Gatehouse's bidding by two detachments from the 4th Armoured Brigade on the enemy's rear caused the enemy considerable alarm.

The moves of the 4th Armoured Brigade convinced Rommel, who believed it to be making for Mechili, that he could no longer stand at Gazala. Since Rommel and Bastico were at loggerheads on this issue General Cavallero and Field Marshal Kesselring flew across from Rome to resolve the disagreement. On the morning of the 17th, after two meetings with Cavallero, Rommel agreed to attempt to form a front at Derna and Mechili but warned that if this line were by-passed, he would have to go back. When that afternoon a column of the 7th Support Group was observed from the air to be moving towards Tengeder, he ordered a general retreat to western Cyrenaica.

If Gott and Gatehouse had intended to force Rommel's withdrawal by keeping the 7th Armoured Division in being and unmauled as an ever-present threat to his flank and rear, the outcome justified their judgment. But the German armoured force had also been kept in being. When the next encounter took place, it would fight at less of a disadvantage.

British occupation of a string of airfields of which the most eastern was that at Mechili was the most important immediate reward for the army's victory. The German Air Force's planned reinforcement of the Mediterranean theatre, however, was beginning to take effect with the arrival of *Fliegerkorps II*. At sea German U-boats continued their sinkings though British ships sank three U-boats in the Mediterranean in November and December. Small ships sunk on the Tobruk run in the same two months were the H.M.A.S. *Parramatta,* H.M.S. *Salvia, Chantala* and *Chakdina* and the merchant ships *Shunten, Warszawa* and *Volo.* Others were damaged. On 14th December a cruiser was sunk by a U-boat off Alexandria and on the 19th a cruiser and destroyer were lost and another cruiser badly damaged in a minefield near Tripoli. Almost simultaneously the battleships *Valiant* and *Queen Elizabeth* were put out of action in Alexandria Harbour by explosives placed by Italian "human torpedoes". Losses on this scale would have been serious at any time. Just after Japan's entry into the war they were virtually irreplaceable. For example between 9th December and 3rd January all Australian ships in the Mediterranean were recalled. H.M.A.S. *Hobart* was first away on the 9th, the day after Pearl Harbour.

About 600 men were aboard the *Chakdina* when she was sunk on the night of 5th December. They were mostly wounded British, New Zealand and Australian troops and included some prisoners of war. About a third were rescued. Among the lost was Major Goschen of the 1st R.H.A.; among the rescued, Major-General von Ravenstein.

CHAPTER 11

IN PALESTINE, SYRIA AND THE LEBANON

THE troops brought out from Tobruk in the minelayers and destroyers of the relief convoys disembarked at Alexandria, stayed for about 24 hours at Amiriya and then entrained for the A.I.F. Base Area in Palestine. The 24th Brigade[1] and other units, including the 2/12th Field Regiment, the 2/3rd Anti-Tank Regiment and the 2/1st Pioneer Battalion, arrived in Palestine during the last week in September; the brigade went to camp Kilo 89. The 26th Brigade, followed closely by the 20th Brigade,[2] arrived a month later; both settled in at Julis. General Morshead arrived at divisional headquarters at Julis on 30th October.

On arrival in Palestine each unit was allowed two days of rest, free from parades and duties. The men received lavish issues of beer and of comforts provided by the Australian Comforts Fund; they relaxed and enjoyed the good food, and the amenities of the permanent camps. Thereafter the normal rigid camp routine was reimposed, units were re-equipped and preparations for training were started. Daily leave to Tel Aviv and Jerusalem was granted on an ample scale. Later, two days of leave were allowed to those centres, and four days to Haifa. Still longer leave to Cairo was instituted for men with sufficient pay credits.

General Morshead toured Syria early in November and on his return went to the Delta, and then to Kenya for a month's leave. At Alexandria he met Brigadier Murray and elements of the division (other than the 2/13th Battalion) that had been left in Tobruk after the cancellation of the last relief convoy and had just been brought out. At Cairo Morshead was invested by General Sikorski, Prime Minister of the Polish Government in exile and Commander-in-Chief Polish Forces, with the *Virtuti Militari* (5th Class); the 26th Brigade provided the band and the guard of honour at the ceremony.

Axis agents were said to be attempting to provoke rebellion in Palestine and to be disseminating rumours that British forces there were at low strength. To counter this propaganda the British command instituted patrols to villages and the 9th Division was made responsible for them in the Gaza area. Patrols of company, or half-battalion, strength, led by a band where possible, would march to the outskirts of a village and wait there while an officer and interpreter called on the mayor or mukhtar, inviting him to take coffee with the officer-in-charge and seeking permission for the patrol to march through the centre of the village. Invariably the village dignitary would request an official call by the officer and others, and hospitality would be reciprocated, while the band played in the village. Motorised patrols of platoon strength were sent on similar missions to outlying small villages.

---

[1] Less the 2/43rd Battalion which came out from Tobruk in the next series of reliefs, rejoining the brigade a month later.

[2] Not including Brigadier J. J. Murray and those elements of the division which had been left in Tobruk after the last relief convoy was cancelled.

A company of the 2/17th Battalion was dispatched to Broumane, Syria, for guard duties at Ninth Army headquarters. Considerable demands, too, were made on the division to supply guards at base installations. The interference with training entailed in meeting these requirements caused General Morshead to approach General Lavarack, commanding I Australian Corps, with the request that the guards be supplied by base troops. Training, beginning with individual and sub-unit training, soon became the division's main occupation, with leisure hours often spent in sport. Three Australian crews took part in a regatta at Tel Aviv in which Jewish and Palestinian Police crews participated. Soccer and hockey teams from the 20th Brigade toured Palestine for a week, meeting R.A.F. teams at various stations.

On 20th December the 2/13th Battalion reached Palestine from Tobruk. An elaborate welcome was staged but had to be cancelled because the train was late. The division was now approaching full strength, reinforcements having been steadily absorbed. The divisional cavalry regiment and the 2/8th Field Regiment had rejoined; the 2/7th Field Regiment, however, was still acting as depot regiment at the School of Artillery, near Cairo. The divisional engineers, less the 2/7th Field Company, were in Syria under the command of X Corps. To put into effect an alteration in War Establishments relating to the organisation of anti-tank artillery, the brigade anti-tank companies were disbanded. Members of the 20th and 24th Anti-Tank Companies were absorbed into the 2/3rd Anti-Tank Regiment; the men of the 26th Anti-Tank Company were later taken into the 4th Light Anti-Aircraft Regiment. The health of the troops was improving, but medical opinion was that they were not yet fit for a 20-mile march or sustained operations.

By the time the siege of Tobruk had been raised, at a cost in men and material so much in excess of every prediction, the Eighth Army's resources not only of armour and motor transport but also of infantry had become severely strained. On 10th December the Ninth Army was directed to have a division ready to move to the Nile Delta for reinforcement of the General Headquarters reserve. Ninth Army headquarters nominated the 7th Australian Division but requested that it should be replaced in Syria by the 9th Division as soon as the move took place. General Blamey demurred to the latter proposal, pointing out that the 9th Division had been an untrained formation when it had been committed to operations and that it was essential that its training should be undertaken before it was given other duties. General Headquarters did not press the issue, presumably because General Freyberg had already made a proposal to transfer the New Zealand Division to Syria, which had been agreed to.[3]

The future deployment of the 7th Division, however, was to be determined by events of greater consequence then occurring far from Cairo. The day on which Japanese armed forces had landed in Thailand and Malaya and struck from the air at Pearl Harbour, Wake Island, Guam,

---

[3] J. L. Scoullar, *Battle for Egypt* (1955), pp. 5-6, a volume in the series *Official History of New Zealand in the Second World War 1939-45*.

Hong Kong and Ocean Island, had dawned three days before Middle East Headquarters had asked the Ninth Army to nominate a division for the reserve. A fortnight later the Japanese forces were at the Perak River, having captured the northern end of the Malayan Peninsula; a landing had been made in North Borneo; Hong Kong was soon to fall; the Philippines had been invaded. The reinforcement of the Far Eastern theatre had become the Allies' most pressing strategic problem. It was patent that a call might be made to dispatch from the Middle East any forces that could be momentarily spared (including some or all of the Australian divisions). On 21st December, Middle East Headquarters cancelled the plan to move the 7th Division to Egypt. About a week later new warning orders were issued: to the 7th Division to move to the Gaza area "for training", and to the 9th Division to relieve the 7th in Syria. General Blamey no longer raised objections.

Early in the New Year the British Government proposed to the Australian Government that two Australian divisions should be dispatched from the Middle East to the Far East and on 6th January the Australian Government notified its concurrence.[4] Next day orders were issued for the projected relief of the 7th Division by the 9th to proceed at once.

The 9th Division was to relieve the 7th Division in the northern parts of Syria and the Lebanon, assuming operational responsibility for an area exceeding 1,200 square miles adjoining the Turkish border. The 20th Brigade was to relieve the 18th Brigade in the frontier region, the 24th Brigade to relieve the 21st around Madjlaya, three miles to the south-east of Tripoli, and the 26th Brigade to take over in Tripoli from the 25th. Other 9th Division units were to relieve their counterparts of the 7th Division. Advanced parties left Palestine on 9th January and main bodies commenced the move on the 11th, departures continuing daily thereafter until the 18th.

Bitterly cold weather prevailed as the convoys, leaving Palestine, wound their way northwards along the Lebanon coast to Tripoli, and the troops, mostly in open trucks, were too miserable to admire the beauties of an ever-changing landscape—green hillsides, ribbed with whitish rock, which shelved down to a cobalt sea, red roofs topping neat stone dwellings in the villages and the soft azure of distant mountains under a veil of snow, gleaming white at the skyline.

The relief was to begin with the foremost units and outlying detachments on the frontier, so the 20th Brigade was the first to move. On the 13th the 2/17th Battalion reached Tripoli and immediately set out for Afrine, a village about 20 miles north-north-west of Aleppo to relieve the 2/12th Battalion, the 2/13th Battalion followed to relieve the 2/9th Battalion at Latakia and two frontier outposts. The 2/15th Battalion, relieving the 2/10th, arrived a day later. The battalion was quartered in barracks and tin huts at Idlib, less two companies which occupied barracks at Aleppo. Brigade headquarters were established at Aleppo.

---

[4] Long, *Greece, Crete and Syria*, pp. 549-50.

Units of the 24th Brigade arrived in the Tripoli area on 15th and 16th January, and brigade headquarters opened at Madjlaya. The 9th Division headquarters, with Brigadier Tovell temporarily in command,

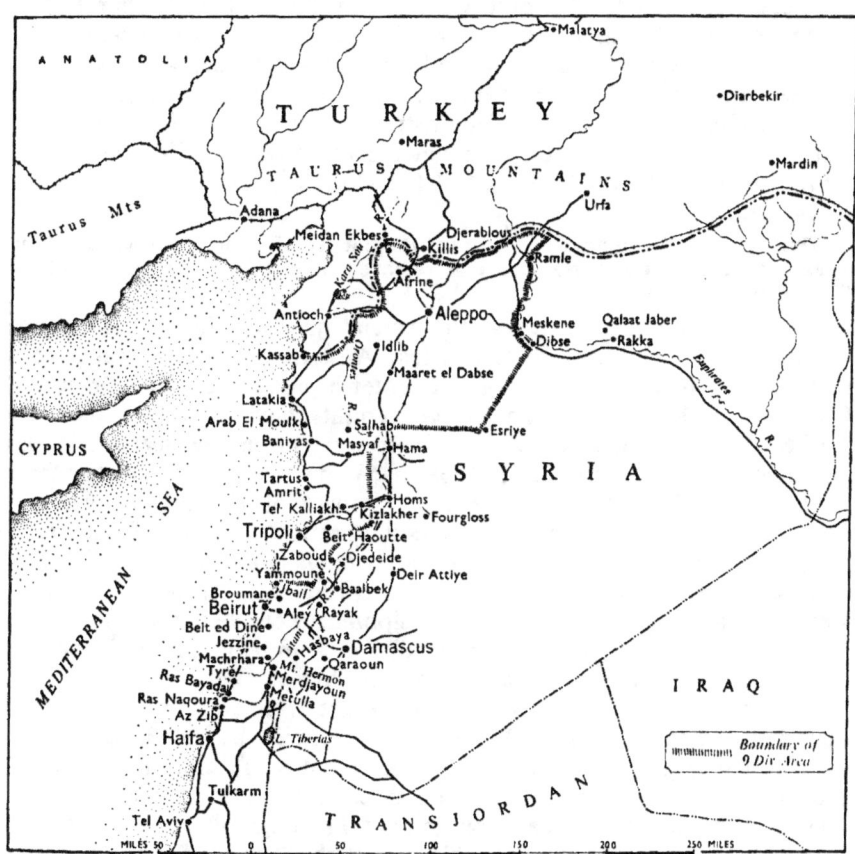

Turkey, Syria and the Lebanon

opened in Tripoli on the 16th. General Morshead had gone to I Australian Corps headquarters at Aley, where he remained until General Lavarack, the corps commander, left for Lake Tiberias to embark on a flying-boat for the Far Eastern theatre on the 19th. General Morshead then went with a small staff to the Ninth Army headquarters at Broumane and established a headquarters there to administer command of the remaining corps units still in Syria and to settle claims and finalise contracts made with civilian contractors by the outgoing corps.

The move of the division was completed with the arrival in Tripoli of the 26th Brigade on 18th and 19th January. The divisional artillery (less the 2/7th Field Regiment still in Cairo[5]) and other divisional units had also arrived and were encamped or billeted in the Tripoli area.

---

[5] The regiment arrived at Aleppo on 10th February.

The British occupation of Syria in the summer of 1941 had removed the danger to the Middle East of a German penetration bypassing Turkey to the south, driving a wedge between Palestine and Turkey and building a bridge of entry to the oilfields through Syria; but the threat of an incursion through Turkey persisted. The danger, which had seemed very real in the previous autumn, had abated with the unexpected success of the Russian winter counter-offensive, but it remained to be seen whether the German forces would demonstrate once more their exceptional resilience and prove capable of renewing the advance. Churchill summed up the situation for the President of the United States in a paper prepared in December 1941:

> While it would be imprudent to regard the danger of a German south-west thrust against the Persian-Iraq-Syrian front as removed, it certainly now seems much less likely than heretofore.[6]

How the Turks might react was the crucial question. Much might depend on the military situation in Cyrenaica. Ankara became a focal point of diplomatic activity, espionage and counter-espionage by both Britain and Germany, of some of which lively accounts have been published. The Turkish Government was understandably wary of entanglements. Although an outcome to the war which left Germany the victor might create a threat to Turkish independence, while the prospect of British victory evoked no such spectre, yet a too open collaboration with the British might bring the day of possible loss of independence much closer. Therefore Turkish relations with Britain, though cordial and secretly cooperative, were cautious.[7] British arms and equipment were being supplied to the Turkish Army, which, however, was still far from being modernised or able even on its own ground to halt a German Army.

The problem of resisting a German thrust from the north, if it should materialise, was intractable. The strategy followed by the British Government rested largely on the hope that the threat would not materialise. The topography of the northern and north-eastern flank clearly indicated a tactical solution, but political geography and strategy inhibited its execution. The wide mountain barrier stretching from the Aegean Sea to the Persian Gulf roughly in the shape of a boomerang, behind which, between the Black and Caspian Seas, the Caucasus Mountains provided a second barrier, was the obvious ground on which to block a German advance before it could reach the plains of Syria and Iraq. This meant that the battles to defend Syria and Iraq against a German thrust through Turkey should ideally be fought in Turkey. British planners conceived that defensive positions should be held covering the arc Mardin-Diarbekir-Malatya-Maras-Adana, utilising the barriers constituted by the Taurus, Masab and Malatya Mountains.

There were good reasons to hope that, with no immediate threat from the Caucasus, Turkey might actively resist a German invasion from Thrace.

---

[6] Churchill, Vol III, p. 575.
[7] High-level staff talks by British and Turkish commands, arranged for Cyprus in August 1941, were suddenly cancelled by Turkey when it was discovered that Germany knew of the arrangements through a leak in Ankara. The talks were relegated to representations by British Service attachés at Ankara.

There were reports of reinforcements of Turkish forces across the Bosporus. Such reinforcement, though a good omen politically, the British regarded as militarily unjustifiable. Although there was some fear that, if the Germans seized the Strait of Istanbul by an airborne operation, the Turks might deem resistance to be futile, the consensus of Allied opinion in Turkey was that they would fight an invading force in Anatolia. Several schemes of counter-action had been considered at planning level, some envisaging the employment of armoured forces in Turkey; but, as between the possible courses entertained, the likelihood that the required resources could be made available for any one scheme varied in inverse proportion to its adequacy to meet a serious threat. The least improbable course with the resources available, but also the least propitious one, was a plan to send an air striking force of 24 R.A.F. squadrons accompanied by a "protective" ground force of four infantry brigade groups, anti-aircraft artillery and ancillary troops to Anatolia, where a number of aerodromes had already been prepared for their use and dumps of stores and materials established.[8] It is not easy, however, to conceive of circumstances in which even that would have been practicable. Indeed, by the third week of January, General Auchinleck, reviewing the situation in the light of the prospective diminution of his ground and air strength by the dispatch of forces to the Far East, had decided that his resources in the foreseeable future would be insufficient to permit him to do more against a strong invading force than wage a defensive battle on a line through central Persia and Iraq and southern Syria, yielding to the enemy the strategically sited airfields farther north.

The Ninth Army's plan for the defence of the Suez Canal and the Middle East base from the north, in the event that no advance into Turkey should be undertaken, provided for delaying actions near the Turko-Syrian frontier while the main British forces were to pivot on a system of defensive areas on "fortresses" in the Lebanon and northern Palestine, a scheme of defence which General Blamey strongly criticised.[9] The responsibility for the construction and defence of two of these—Tripoli and Djedeide fortresses—had originally devolved on the I Australian Corps, which had also been made responsible for the demolition and holding positions along the frontier.

The responsibility for defence of the Turko-Syrian frontier, and for mounting, if the necessity arose, delaying actions in conjunction with a planned withdrawal on the Tripoli fortress, had now fallen to the 20th Brigade (Brigadier Windeyer), which was deployed on a front extending over 100 miles, not taking into account the distance to outlying detachments around Azaz or to an isolated post on the Euphrates.[10] Under brigade

---

[8] Turkey had agreed to the entry of British air forces, but not ground forces.
[9] See Long, *Greece, Crete and Syria*, p. 536.
[10] Three command changes had occurred within the brigade in a week. Brig Windeyer succeeded Brig Murray, posted to Australia, on 12th January; Maj Turner was promoted and appointed to command the 2/13th Bn on 15th January succeeding Lt-Col Burrows, wounded at Ed Duda. On the 19th Lt-Col M. A. Fergusson assumed command of 2/17th Bn vice Lt-Col Crawford, who was transferred to a command in Australia, but he was succeeded in that command by Lt-Col N. W. Simpson on 7th March. Murray, Burrows and Crawford had each held their commands since the formation of the brigade at Ingleburn in April 1940.

command was the 9th Divisional Cavalry Regiment at Aleppo, less three troops at Djerablous where the Baghdad railway crosses the Euphrates; also the 2/9th Field Regiment, 42nd Field Company R.E., and ancillary units, all at Aleppo. Throughout the brigade's area there were detachments of Free French forces, which were exclusively responsible for patrolling

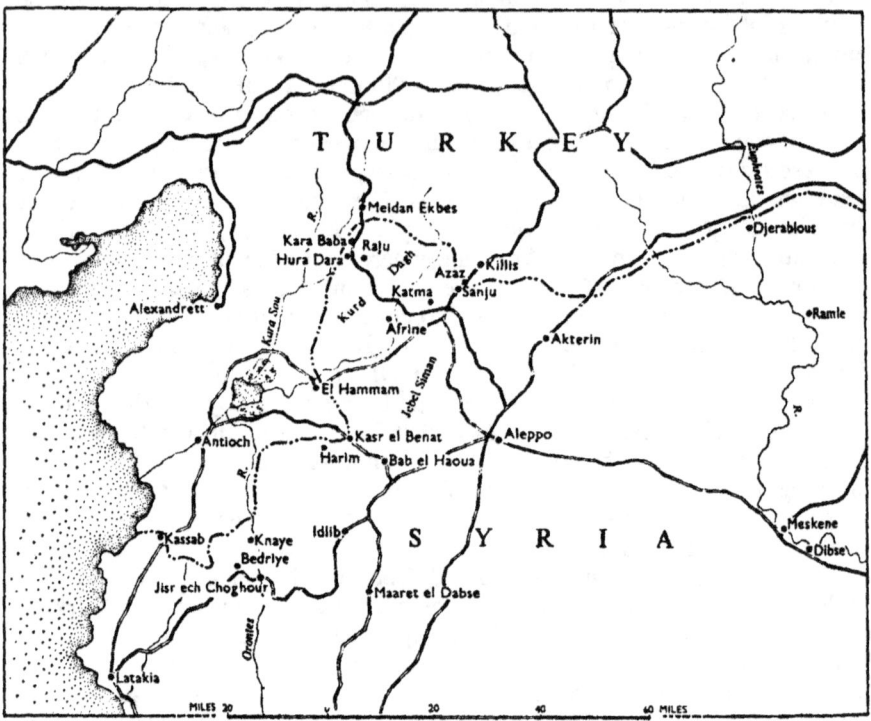

the frontier and primarily responsible for internal security, airfield defence and coastwatching.

The task of the brigade in the event of German attack through Turkey was to cover the withdrawal of base and line-of-communication installations from Aleppo, of the R.A.F. operating from airfields in northern Syria, and of the Free French forces. Subsequently it would itself withdraw into the Tripoli fortress.

The 2/17th Battalion was on the right flank of the 20th Brigade, with "A" and "B" Companies disposed along the Aleppo-Meidan Ekbes railway from Raju to Meidan Ekbes on the frontier, the main concentration being around Raju to protect the demolitions at the two tunnels and viaduct. It was essential, in the event of an enemy thrust from the north, that the use of the railway be denied to the enemy, and it required protection meanwhile from saboteur bands known to be active there. "D" Company was at El Hammam, a frontier village to the south. "C" Company's headquarters was at Azaz, to the east and rear of the remainder of the battalion, but still adjacent to the frontier; the company had a section at Sanju on the Aleppo-Killis road, a platoon guarding the Katma tunnel on the Aleppo-Meidan Ekbes railway and a platoon at Akterin, on the Aleppo-Baghdad railway, some 30 miles across country accessible only by devious tracks.

The brigade headquarters and administrative units were based on Aleppo, as well as the centre battalion, the 2/15th, which was mainly quartered in barracks in Aleppo and Idlib but maintained frontier posts at Bab el Haoua, Harim and Knaye.

From Aleppo to Latakia is about 100 miles as the crow flies, much farther by road, and there the 2/13th Battalion was operationally employed in a detached role, blocking the coast route from Turkey. Battalion headquarters and two companies were encamped not far from the town, one company went initially to Bedriye, a village adjacent to the frontier about 40 miles north-east of Latakia, on the Aleppo Road, and another company went to quarters at Kassab in the mountain fastnesses of the frontier near the coast. Later the outlying companies were drawn back to Latakia for training, except that one platoon was left at Kassab to show the flag to the Turks.

Commanders of formations and sub-units down to platoon leaders were soon busy on reconnaissance. The troops took a keen interest in the country, its historical associations, its customs and the novel and sometimes quaint styles of dress of the inhabitants, with whom they quickly established friendly relations, notably at Afrine where the Kurds were very cooperative and on occasions gave information about the whereabouts of bandits.

Very little work on defences was required and the brigade was committed to a program of training, which, however, the weather during January to some extent frustrated. Storms lashed the coast during the last week of the month; two vessels were driven ashore at Latakia, and tents and huts of the 2/13th Battalion were blown down. Snow fell over most of the brigade area on the 27th, cutting off communication with the frontier posts, except the parties on the railway.

The division held Tripoli fortress, the pivot of the northern defence scheme, with two brigades, the 24th (Brigadier Godfrey) and 26th (Brigadier Tovell), the 24th on the right. The battalions of the 24th Brigade moved into winter quarters on arrival, but maintained sections forward in occupation of the sector defences. The 2/28th Battalion, the right battalion in Section "B", took over the area previously occupied by the 2/14th Battalion around Srar, one company being in a position 24 miles forward of battalion headquarters. With the exception of the reserve company, movement of the rifle companies had to be completed by pack-mules owing to incessant rain and the inability of vehicles to move on the tracks. The 2/43rd Battalion, based at Arbe, occupied a shorter front on the left of the 2/28th Battalion and were on the eastern slopes of Jebel Tourbol, around Kafr Aya, with the Nahr Barid gorge between them and the forward company of the 2/28th. The brigade's third battalion, the

2/32nd, was in the reserve area around El Ayoun and took over security duties.

The headquarters of the 26th Brigade, which held the coast sector, were established in the Legoult Barracks, in which the 2/48th Battalion was also quartered. The 2/23rd Battalion occupied the adjacent Beit

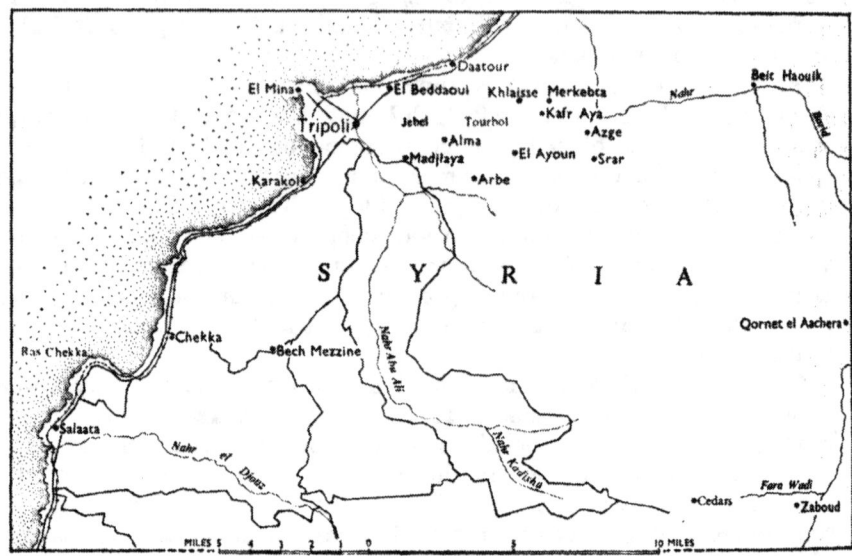

Ghanein Barracks. The two battalions quartered in barracks sent companies daily to their allotted forward positions to work on the defences; the moves were made on foot owing to lack of transport, causing a loss of two to three hours of working time daily. Later, when tents became available, camps were made in company forward areas. The 2/24th Battalion was under canvas in the foothills east of Madjlaya, two companies moving 10 days later to bivouac in forward positions on the arc, Azge-Kafr Aya-Khlaisse, around the north-eastern and eastern slopes of the Jebel Tourbol, with "A" Company of the 2/48th Battalion in positions on the plateau behind them. Officers and men alike were struck by the similarity of the defences being prepared around Tripoli to those on the Tobruk perimeter. Profiting by their experience in Tobruk, they re-sited some positions and adopted the "Tobruk" type of defence positions in preference to the text-book type.

The A.I.F. maintained no school in the Middle East to train cadets for commissioned rank. Men chosen for promotion were sent to the Middle East Officer Cadet Training Unit (O.C.T.U.), for which the A.I.F. and other Dominion contingents were allotted a proportion of each monthly intake. The mingling of men from the various components of the Middle East forces in this and other training schools was a potent force in imparting a sense of unity and common purpose to a heterogeneous army.

At the O.C.T.U. the cadets were tested in leadership qualities, given a grounding in tactics and unit administration and smartened up by barrack-square drill in the strictest British Regular Army tradition. The cadets attending in February 1942, who included a due proportion of Australians, found themselves, in addition to undergoing the prescribed course of indoctrination for their future responsibilities, participating in activities not included in the syllabus—the staging of a *coup d'état*.

This history is no place to unravel the Gilbertian complexities of Egyptian politics of that day and earlier days. King Farouk, then aged only 22, was believed to have pro-Italian sympathies. The maintenance of a strong government friendly to the Allied cause was of prime importance to the British. The Egyptian Prime Minister, Sirry Pasha, had evinced unexceptional loyalty to the Anglo-Egyptian treaty, but lacked support in the country. The resignation of his Finance Minister at the end of the year had weakened his government. Confronted with a demand for his resignation from the King, who was nurturing and exploiting a grievance at not having been consulted about a recent suspension of diplomatic relations with Vichy France, and troubled by student demonstrations in the streets which were believed to have been inspired from the palace, Sirry Pasha resigned on 2nd February.

The British were not found unprepared or wanting in a situation Machiavelli would have relished. A mixed brigade of British, New Zealand and South African units had already been moved into Cairo to "maintain order" and on the day after Sirry Pasha's resignation Sir Miles Lampson, the British Ambassador, called on the King and proposed a course that may have surprised His Majesty. It was necessary, he represented, in order to ensure internal security, to have a government that commanded a majority; so Nahas Pasha was the man to appoint, Nahas Pasha, leader of the Wafdists, the traditionally anti-British party whose policy was to rid Egypt of the Anglo-Egyptian treaty and all that went with it— the occupation of Egyptian territory by alien forces and the special "mixed courts" to try suits involving Europeans. The King was not immediately compliant.

At the O.C.T.U., meanwhile, the course of instruction of the Middle East Force's budding subalterns had taken on a bias for exercises in mobile battle-column tactics, with tanks, such training being carried to the point that a column would be ready to move at 10 minutes' notice. One day the cadets were told that they would thenceforth practise with live ammunition.

At midday on 4th February Sir Miles Lampson delivered an ultimatum to the King to the effect that the required action to appoint Nahas Pasha must be taken by the end of the day. That evening detachments from the mixed brigade surrounded the Abdin Palace. At 8.30 p.m., the commandant of the O.C.T.U. paraded the cadets, informed them of the ultimatum and of its expiry at 8 p.m. and told them that they were to proceed to the palace to force the issue. Headed by military police, the column, which included light tanks and guns, drove straight to the palace, pushed open the gate and deployed in the courtyard, while the royal guard ceremoniously presented arms. Soon after 9 p.m. the British Ambassador arrived by car and entered the palace. After about 15 minutes, he returned and drove off. Nahas Pasha was invited to form a government.

Before accepting, Nahas Pasha presented a letter to the British Ambassador in which he said:

> It is quite understood that I accept the task on the basis that neither the Anglo-Egyptian treaty nor the situation of Egypt as a sovereign and independent country permits the Ally to interfere in the internal affairs of the country and particularly in the formation and dismissal of ministries.

The impeccable Government of His Britannic Majesty was only too happy to assent to these irreproachable sentiments, the Ambassador in his reply confirming that it was the policy of His Majesty's Government to secure sincere collaboration with the Government of Egypt, as an independent and allied country. The excellent compact was democratically validated in elections held immediately afterwards, which the Opposition conveniently boycotted.

Whence the British Government derived its faith that Nahas Pasha would provide the secure, collaborative government so greatly needed may be known only to the inscrutable Sphinx; but the faith was not misplaced. The "Incident of 1942" was shrouded in official secrecy until after the war ended, when it was recalled and became symbolic to Egyptian nationalists of the incompatibility of foreign military occupation with national sovereignty and independence. Britain's resort to brazen power politics in an hour of crisis no doubt provided impetus after the war to the movement to end the British occupation. But the causes of the movement were more deep-seated, the end inevitable.

Early in February General Morshead spent five days reconnoitring the 20th Brigade area, after which he visited the Ninth Army commander and, having doubtless in mind the 9th Division's experiences in withdrawing to Tobruk, expressed his dislike at being compelled to rely for his divisional reserve on a brigade having such a role as that of the one based on Aleppo. It might not get back, he said; and, if it did, would not know the country. Since six weeks' warning of an invasion was anticipated, why not blow the demolitions early and be assured of getting the brigade back, foregoing any delay that covering the demolitions might impose, he argued. As for covering landing grounds, how long would the air force use them? On past experience, General Morshead contended, they would give them up in the early stages. He suggested that he should leave one battalion in the Aleppo area and withdraw the rest of the 20th Brigade Group to Tripoli.

Morshead was concerned at the lack of opportunities for training afforded troops in the fortress area. Because of slow progress in construction of the defences, the Ninth Army had issued instructions that during February six days a week should be devoted to work on the defences, instead of three days to defence work and three to training as hitherto.

(Australian War Memorial)

In Syria at the time when the 9th Division was relieving the 7th Division.

(Imperial War Museum)

The Nahr el Kelb in Syria, showing bridges under construction by the Australian Railway Construction and Maintenance Group. The bridge on the left is for rail traffic, the other for foot and vehicular use.

Crusader tanks of the 9th Divisional Cavalry Regiment at the Amiriya water-point on their way to the El Alamein front, July 1942.

British vehicles dispersed to minimise damage from air attack off the main coast road a few miles west of El Alamein, July 1942.

Morshead objected to the new order; he was supported by General Blamey and General Wilson agreed that the training of the division would continue and that civilian labour could be employed under unit supervision on defence works. Morshead noted: "We've been digging since April almost and it is of paramount importance that we have time for training. We must also be equipped."[9] He broached to General Blamey "this eternal question of equipment".[1]

Another proposal of General Wilson—that the 20th Brigade be employed as army reserve—was also vetoed by General Blamey, who insisted that the command of the complete division must remain with General Morshead.

Except for one day of torrential rain in the 2/13th Battalion area, the weather improved during February and warmed towards the end of the month. The troops were in good health and spirits, and there was little reaction to the scant but sombre news of the Japanese advances and the air raid against Darwin; or to false rumours that Sydney had been bombed; but one remark addressed to the commander of the 24th Brigade reflected a developing uneasiness: "Are you sure we are not wasting our time here? It's a good spot but they might be needing us at home soon."

There was some fraternisation between Australians and the Free French forces at command level, but not much below. The relationship could be said to be "polite". Fraternisation between British and Turkish frontier detachments was encouraged by the former but the Turks would not approach British posts during daylight; after dark, however, they showed themselves anxious to be friendly and eager to partake of Australian cups of tea.

Measures were taken by General Morshead to ensure that the reputation of his troops as a fighting force should not be tarnished by their behaviour as occupation troops. Careful regulation of leave, watchfulness by the divisional Provost Corps who set a high example in dress and deportment, and tight discipline all had their effect, but most troops needed no discipline to force them to conduct themselves well. Unit pride and a strongly-developed pride in the division, which good formation and unit commanders always strove to create, alone sufficed. Two senior officers from divisional headquarters were informed

> that the conduct of the troops in Tripoli at the present time is a great credit to Australia. The civilian population in the past have been afraid of soldiers generally, but our troops have impressed them with their bearing, manners and good behaviour to such a degree that civilians are not now afraid but friendly towards soldiers.[2]

---

[9] General Morshead's diary.
[1] The weapons and AFV's held by the division expressed as a percentage of the war establishment were:

	16 Jan 42 per cent	12 Mar 42 per cent		16 Jan 42 per cent	12 Mar 42 per cent
TSMG	56	9.6	Medium MG	31	5
LMG	78	69	Heavy MG	85	85
2-in mortars	46	—	2-pdr A-Tk guns	75	75
3-in mortars	35	—	Carriers	61	61
Boyes A-Tk rifles	84	84	Light tanks	90	90

These shortages were in addition to 42 TSMG, 225 LMG, 44 MMG, 26 3-inch mortars, 24 spigot mortars, and 16 each of 2-pdr and 25-pdr guns requested by the 9th Division at the instigation of the commander of the Ninth Army, as being required for the defence of Tripoli fortress and not received. At 31st March the division was 50 per cent deficient in motor transport.

[2] War diary, "A" Branch HQ 9 Div, Feb 1942.

The officer commanding No. 255 Section British Field Security Service, stationed at Aleppo, reported on 31st January:

A good impression has been made on local people by the determination of the new [20th] Brigade to establish a good record for behaviour in public.[3]

Unsolicited testimony to good behaviour by Australians also came in from some café proprietors and shopkeepers. No longer were continual complaints of the A.I.F's behaviour being received by the Australian command from General Auchinleck, General Maitland Wilson and the Spears' Mission. Cases of delinquency of one kind or another continued to occur, of course. At this period the most prevalent offence was that of being found in one of the prohibited villages, which included most of those in the Tripoli area. Later disposing of government property in the flourishing black market was to become the most frequent crime. Severe measures were taken to stamp it out.

Throughout the division, unit tactical exercises were carried out in the field. To free troops for participation in battalion exercises, some minor alterations were made to dispositions in the frontier region and at Tripoli several thousands of civilians were employed on defence works to release troops for training. Nevertheless they were still required to work on the Tripoli defences for three days weekly. Apathy and some positive antipathy to digging tasks were displayed and progress was slow, but the men showed more enthusiasm for training. Firing courses were carried out on rifle ranges in brigade areas and practical wire-crushing training was included, also practice with the new spigot anti-tank mortar. Battalions cooperated with each other in tactical exercises. One battalion would defend its sector of the Tripoli defences against attack by another and at a later date would attack its sector while the other battalion defended it. The troops thus became thoroughly acquainted with the terrain they might have to defend. The 2/3rd Anti-Tank Regiment, having received 32 guns, constructed an anti-tank practice range at Amrit and, by batteries, carried out shoots there. During February cadres from units of all arms proceeded to Australia to help train reinforcements for the division.

Rumours of an imminent German attack on Turkey were reported from the Balkans and it was also reported that Italian officers in Greece had spoken of an intention to stage small-scale raids on the Syrian coast. Although the rumours were suspect and believed to have been disseminated in order to excite British uneasiness for the northern flank while an Axis offence was being prepared in Libya, the 26th Brigade was nevertheless ordered to maintain a mobile group of one rifle company, one section of carriers and one platoon of machine-gunners ready to move at half-an-hour's notice to reinforce protective detachments at the port of Tripoli and at Chekka.

Troops manning the frontier posts stopped many letter-carriers attempting to cross the border, apprehended Turkish deserters and prevented some

---

[3] Later the 20th Brigade was relieved by the 6th New Zealand Brigade. The New Zealand historian, Scoullar, afterwards wrote that the New Zealanders . . . "were ordered through talks and routine orders to be on their best behaviour at all times, the high standard of conduct of the 20 Australian Infantry Brigade . . . being cited as an example to be followed." *Battle for Egypt*, p. 33.

smuggling, particularly of sheep skins, the price of which had risen to such an extent that it was assumed the skins were being procured for winter clothing for German troops on the Russian front.

On 22nd February General Blamey summoned General Morshead to Cairo and informed him that he would become G.O.C., A.I.F. (Middle East) on Blamey's departure for Australia. Morshead returned to Tripoli and again pressed General Wilson for a third brigade for the defence of the fortress. On 3rd March he returned to Cairo and spent the next three days in consultation with Blamey concerning his future responsibilities. With General Auchinleck, General and Lady Freyberg, and other senior officers of the fighting Services, he farewelled General and Lady Blamey early on the morning of the 7th when they left Cairo airport on their flight to South Africa on the way to Australia. For security reasons Morshead's appointment was not announced, nor was his promotion to lieut-general gazetted, until three weeks later. The strength of the A.I.F. in the Middle East at that time was about 45,000 of whom, however, approximately 10,000 belonged to the 6th Division and I Australian Corps and were awaiting embarkation.

The I Australian Corps, having detached the 9th Division and a proportion of corps units to remain with it in the Middle East, had embarked for the Far East in a succession of convoys from 30th January onwards. The corps commander (General Lavarack) and small parties of officers had flown to Java ahead of the main body. Two days after the fall of Singapore on 15th February, the Australian Government, on the strong recommendation of Lieut-General Sturdee, the Chief of the Australian General Staff, requested that all Australian forces then in transit or about to sail to the Netherlands East Indies should be diverted to Australia, and that the 9th Division and other A.I.F. units in the Middle East should be recalled at an early date. The forces alluded to as being "in transit or about to sail" comprised the I Australian Corps headquarters and the 6th and 7th Divisions and attached corps troops with the exception of a machine-gun battalion and pioneer battalion and other small units (numbering in all some 2,900 men) which had already disembarked in Java. The Australian Government's reasons for making the request were set out at great length in messages to the British Government. In summary, relying on the wise counsel of General Sturdee who in retrospect is seen to have been less swayed by contemporary crises, and to have made a sounder, more detached assessment of the strategic problem presented by Japanese aggression in South-East Asia and the South-West Pacific than either the British or the American Chiefs of Staff, the Australian Government contended that the policy of the Allies should be to "avoid a 'penny packet' distribution of our limited forces and their defeat in detail", to secure Australia as a base as a first step, to accumulate Allied forces there, and later to lodge a counter-offensive in strength. The background of the request, the dismal weakness of the military forces then available in Australia to resist invasion, and other relevant facts are related in detail in the next volume of this series. There an account is given of Mr Churchill's efforts to obtain the Australian Government's agreement to the employment in Burma of part of the Australian forces (consisting of most of the 7th Division) then moving through the Indian Ocean and of the ensuing conflict between Mr Churchill, strongly supported by the President of the United States and the British and American Chiefs of Staff on the one hand, and Mr Curtin, adopting the advice of the Australian Chief of the General Staff on the other, in which Mr Curtin had his way.

Mr Curtin was informed on 18th February by Sir Earle Page, the Australian representative to the United Kingdom War Cabinet, that the Pacific War Council had recommended that the 6th Division (then embarking in the Middle East) and the 9th Division should be returned as fast as possible to Australia and the 7th Division be diverted to Burma but that before the 9th Division was moved, the 70th British Division should be sent from the Middle East to the India-Burma theatre. It is apparent that what was in contemplation concerning the 9th Division was a return, not in the immediately foreseeable future, but in a matter of some months, after urgent calls on shipping had been met. It was on the next day that Mr Curtin informed Sir Earle Page that the Government had decided not to agree to the diversion of the 7th Division to Burma, but before the decision had been communicated to the British Government the Secretary of State for Dominion Affairs informed the Australian Government that an additional American division would be sent to Australia to augment the forces already proposed to be sent there. The Secretary of State asked:

> In these circumstances would it not be wise to leave destination of 6th and 9th Australian Divisions open? More troops might be badly needed in Burma.

On 23rd February, General Sturdee discussed this suggestion in a memorandum to the War Cabinet and urged that the Government should adhere to its decision that both the 6th and 7th Divisions should be returned to Australia. In regard to the 9th Division he commented:

> No date has been mentioned for its departure from Syria and it is most improbable that it could be made available for operations in any country outside the Middle East until late May. . . . The date of its departure can be much later if other moves take priority of shipping or the British Government is piqued at the Australian Government's firm demand for the diversion to Australia of the A.I.F. originally destined for Java. . . . The most that I feel we can offer is that the return of the 9th Division be delayed for a short period if the services of an American division is made available.

The Australian Government, accepting Sturdee's advice, maintained its insistence that the 6th and 7th Divisions should return, and in so doing greatly offended Mr Churchill. Acting on a suggestion made by Sir Earle Page, Mr Curtin then attempted to heal the breach and to show his Government's desire to be cooperative, without derogation from its overall policy or unjustifiable risk to Australian security, by offering on 2nd March to make two brigade groups of the 6th Division available temporarily for the defence of Ceylon; but he added that the Australian

Government made that offer "relying on the understanding that the 9th Division will return to Australia under proper escort as soon as possible".

A shortage of food had developed in Syria to such an extent that it posed a threat to internal security. The Spears' wheat plan, initiated in the autumn, had for a time eased the situation, but hoarding of wheat and flour and, to a less extent, of other foodstuffs, had continued and caused prices to rise to levels far beyond the reach of the average Syrian. Suleiman Murshed, the Alaouite leader, was said to have a hoard of wheat in his village and a report that he was to receive 200 tons from the United Kingdom Convention Commissioner for distribution among Alaouite peasants in the hills led to some apprehension that this consignment would merely swell his store. A modification of the Spears' plan was introduced providing for flour to be sold by the U.K. Convention Commissioner to the poorer classes at important centres. This was only a palliative for it did not strike at the root of the trouble by controlling the wartime profiteer. Axis propaganda among the Arabs made much play of price rises and provoked demonstrations.

From the time of their first engagement, all civilians employed on roads, defence works and the Beirut-Tripoli railway had been issued with about 10 pounds of flour weekly to ensure that they would be fit for manual labour. The 2/17th Battalion supervised the issue of 5,000 pounds of flour to the poor in the Raju area which were supplied by the American Red Cross in response to the battalion's representations.[4]

In the middle of March the greater part of the New Zealand Division arrived in Syria. One brigade occupied the Djedeide fortress; another relieved units of the 20th Australian Brigade Group in the Aleppo area. The 20th Brigade then concentrated around Latakia. The 9th Division had thus been relieved of a considerable area of responsibility; there were no longer any Australian detachments east of the Orontes River.

This concentration was effected in pursuance of General Auchinleck's "plan of deception". Bearing as Commander-in-Chief a unique personal responsibility for the military security of the Middle East bases, and acutely conscious, as he always was, of the danger latent in an inadequately guarded northern flank, Auchinleck emphasised that it was

of paramount importance that we avoid disclosing our weakness or our intentions to the enemy, to Turkey or to the local populations, because by so doing we may encourage the enemy to attack, drive Turkey into submission, and bring about a serious security situation.[5]

---

[4] Australians of all ranks were deeply impressed by the plight of Syrian children. The 9th Division headquarters sent a cheque from canteen profits for £P25 (£A31.5s.) to a fund for the poor and sick children of Tripoli. Personnel of the 2/24th Field Park Coy considered that there should be a school for the children of Alma, a village in the southern foothills of Jebel Tourbol. The parents were unable to pay a teacher, so the officer commanding the unit convened a meeting of the shop and barkeepers of the village, the priest and the prospective teacher at which it was decided (mainly by the OC) that the barkeepers should pay the salary of the teacher. School began in a few days.

[5] GHQ MEF Operation Instruction No. 112, 23 Feb 1942.

General Morshead was highly sceptical of the efficacy of the many ruses used to create illusions of strength and wished to see more attention given to getting the men ready to fight. He noted in his private diary:

I am sick to death about the importance attached to prestige and the flying of the flag. All to impress wogs and doubtful Free French!

He told his brigade and other commanders: "We must train the men to give them confidence begotten of knowledge and experience." The 20th Brigade's relief from other responsibilities, however, served Morshead's purposes as well as Auchinleck's. The brigade immediately embarked upon an intensive program of battalion and brigade field exercises. This was the first occasion on which it had undergone field training, the first occasion in the 22 months since its formation that it had been given an opportunity to conduct exercises in the field with troops.

Morshead became concerned about a field security service report that there was unrest among his command. "Unrest" was perhaps too strong a word to use. Battalion commanders had without exception reported that the morale in their commands was good. Yet evidence that some men were becoming unsettled could not be gainsaid. An uneasiness about their current employment, which had been aggravated by lack of mail from home, was apparent in a number of rumours and stories which, though usually regarded as apocryphal, were continually recounted, such as a supposed accusation by an Australian women's journal that men were volunteering to remain in the Middle East while Australia was in danger, a rumour that American troops had been sent to Australia and a story that Australian girls had written to men in the Middle East rejecting them in favour of brave militiamen who had stayed to defend their homeland. The sentiment underlying the masochistic repetition of these stories was undoubtedly one of rejection by the men of their role of passive employment in a Middle East backwater. Evolving as it did out of their particular complex situation, it cannot be regarded as indicative of an attitude to circumstances not then existing, such as for example, their further operational employment in Africa.

The A.I.F. Entertainment Unit opened its Syrian tour on 10th March at Beirut with the revue "All in Fun" under the direction of Jim Gerald.[6] General Maitland Wilson, General Morshead, the President of The Lebanon, the American Consul-General (Mr C. van Engert) and other notabilities were present. This show, the best the troops had seen in the Middle East, was subsequently played in all Australian areas in Syria. There were also nightly cinema shows in each brigade area. Trips were arranged to the snowfields and places of historic interest and leave to Tripoli and Beirut was maintained. In the evenings, for units not engaged on night exercises, table-tennis, chess, draughts, boxing tournaments and euchre parties were arranged. Short-wave broadcasts of news bulletins prepared by the Department of Information in Australia were re-issued

---

[6] Lt-Col J. Gerald, NX70922; AIF Entertainment Offr 1941-42. Actor and entertainer; of Bellevue Hill, NSW; b. Sydney, 1 Jan 1891.

through the Palestine Broadcasting Service at Jerusalem and Radio Levant at Beirut.

The battalions in the Tripoli area were now engaged in "live out and train" exercises of three days' duration, carrying out tactical movements by day and bivouacking for two nights under "alert" conditions. The men, appreciating the break from camp or barrack routine, participated keenly, and were stimulated to take an intelligent interest in the manoeuvres by being brought into the picture beforehand and having mistakes discussed and explained to them afterwards.

In mid-April the 20th Brigade was transferred from the Latakia area to Tripoli, where it relieved the 26th Brigade on the coast sector of the perimeter north of the town. The 26th Brigade then became divisional reserve and moved into tented camps among the olive groves around Bech Mezzine, about nine miles south-south-west of Tripoli. The 9th Divisional Cavalry Regiment stayed at Latakia. The battalions of the 20th Brigade marched the 95 miles from Latakia to Tripoli in four days and a half, battalions leaving Latakia on consecutive days and bivouacking nightly. The enthusiastic reception of the troops by villagers along the way indicated a friendly regard for the A.I.F.

Frequent tactical exercises were carried out in the field both with and without troops. One battalion held an exercise relying completely on pack-mules for transport. Another held a four-day bivouac exercise in which Hurricane fighters of No. 451 Squadron R.A.A.F. cooperated. The artillery regiments, when not engaged on the construction of their field positions, conducted exercises and shoots in the country east of Tel Kalliakh, and also participated in training exercises with officers of the infantry brigades. The divisional engineers went by companies to Kishon near Haifa for bridging exercises.

The 1942 grain crop in Syria was an abundant one and more than sufficient for local needs. To ensure that the harvest should not be bought and stored by merchants who had the market cornered, it was decided, with the concurrence of local authorities, that the Spears' Mission would acquire the crops as they stood and harvest them under military supervision. To this end volunteers with wheat-harvesting experience were called for from the division and the men required were forthcoming, but the division was destined to leave Syria before the harvest.

There was a scare on the night of 24th-25th May. The whole of the 20th Brigade and the mobile and coast defence detachments of the division were alerted. At 9 o'clock it was reported that four boats had landed troops near the Nahr Sene. Later Free French watching posts reported that two warships, probably destroyers, and three fairly large transports were seen moving towards the coast in the vicinity of Arab el Moulk. There were other highly-coloured reports from coastwatching posts but nothing transpired and at 6.30 a.m. the alert ended. Ninth Army headquarters subsequently announced that a British convoy of which the naval authorities at Tripoli had not been informed had been proceeding north along the Syrian coast. Though 50 miles away, the convoy had been visible as a result of peculiar atmospheric conditions, which included temporary illumination from a large meteor.

The War Office had authorised the granting of 28 days' leave during the summer to all officers and men serving under British command in the Middle East, with free travel to and from an approved leave centre. Troops stationed in Syria or the Lebanon were not permitted to take their leave in Palestine or Egypt. The Ninth Army headquarters stipulated that the leave be taken in two periods of 14 days. General Morshead authorised leave for the A.I.F. on the prescribed scale but directed that it be taken in seven-day periods in order that as many troops as possible should have some leave before anything could occur to interrupt the program. It proved a wise decision; the scheme had been in operation for only four weeks when the division moved to Egypt. Leave camps were established at Beirut and Damascus, but Beirut was preferred, Damascus being extremely hot and, after a few days of sightseeing, having little to offer. At Beirut the camps were near the city and close to the sea. Cool breezes, bathing and a complete freedom from duties made the stay very enjoyable. Accommodation at the camps was free; but other ranks were allowed a choice of accommodation at reasonable cost at hotels or "pensions" controlled by the Australian Comforts Fund. Ten per cent of each unit went on leave weekly, approximately 1,500 from the division.

In parts of south Lebanon there was evidence of native unrest among the Arabs, some of whom were armed, and the Ninth Army requested the dispatch of a small force to "show the flag". This was provided by the 2/24th Battalion, and consisted of one rifle company, with mortar, machine-gun, provost and medical detachments; it was commanded by Major Tasker. Its route included the villages of Beit ed Dine, Jezzine, Machrhara, Qaraoun and Merdjayoun, with diversions to Hasbaya and Tyre. Company exercises were carried out in the affected area and close-order drill near the villages. The expedition was away five days.

Meanwhile, in the desert west of Tobruk where the opposing armies had been sparring with each other around Gazala from static defence lines for more than four months, intense fighting had broken out and the Eighth Army appeared to be in danger of being thrust from its ground. The possibility that the day might not be far distant when the 9th Division, which had seen no action for seven months, might be required to fight again was in the minds both of the planning staffs and of every soldier of the division. To fit it for such a role, training in motorised battle deployment in a desert terrain, which the division had never had an opportunity to practise, was an urgent need. A program for training each brigade in turn was arranged.

On 5th June the 24th Brigade Group, having earlier been relieved by the 26th Brigade Group on the right forward sector of the defences, moved from the Tripoli area to Fourgloss, east of Homs, and for the next fortnight underwent extensive exercises in motorised deployment and movements in "box" formation, bivouacking in the desert at night. No.

451 Squadron R.A.A.F. cooperated with low-level strafing runs. Conditions were exacting; the days were extremely hot and the sun beat down mercilessly on the shelterless plain, from which the vehicles churned up clouds of stifling dust; yet the nights were cold. Hardest to endure of all was the severe rationing of water to three-quarters of a gallon a man for all purposes, including vehicles. One battalion, the 2/28th, alleviated the shortage when it discovered a small wadi showing signs of dampness and, by digging to depths varying from two to six feet, obtained about 1,000 gallons of good water.

At first, formation of unit "boxes" was practised by battalion groups. This was followed by evolutions by the entire brigade group. To see more than 600 vehicles neatly deployed in the prescribed order with a front of 3,500 yards and a depth of 6,000 was most impressive. The artillery units carried out range shoots as well as participating in formation movements. The syllabus culminated in a demonstration in two phases. The first was an attack by the 24th Brigade Group on a simulated German lorried-infantry column; the second was designed to demonstrate the defensive fire that could be brought down by the group's supporting arms; live ammunition was fired at screens representing an attacking column. Over 400 officers from British formations and Allied forces watched the demonstration, which was described in a broadcast running commentary.

The group returned to Tripoli on 23rd June and relieved the 26th Brigade Group so that the latter could be released for similar exercises. The 20th Brigade was under orders to follow in due course. In the event only the 24th Brigade completed the training.

For the British Commanders-in-Chief in the Middle East, the most important consequence of the Japanese onslaught in December 1941 had been that reinforcements and supplies intended for the Middle Eastern theatre were diverted to the Far East, and formations already in the Middle East were sent to the new theatre of war, including, as we have seen, the 6th and 7th Australian Divisions. It was in the air that the reduction in strength had most effect on operations in the early months of 1942. By April about 180 bombers and 330 fighters had been dispatched to the Far East.

Partly because his forces were thus weakened, partly because faulty methods of handling tanks and guns still thwarted the Eighth Army's designs, General Auchinleck was unable to exploit fully, in the six months after Tobruk was relieved, the opportunities afforded by his victory in the CRUSADER offensive. Moreover the problem of sustaining Malta weighed each month more heavily on the Commanders-in-Chief and imposed a severe strain on their diminished naval and air force strength.

After the German and Italian forces abandoned the Gazala line in mid-December, they next stood at Agedabia, in the plain south of Benghazi. British mobile forces entered Benghazi on Christmas Eve, while to the south the Guards Brigade made contact with the German forces on 22nd December. When, on 6th January, the 1st British Armoured Division arrived in the forward area, the Axis forces retired to the Tripolitanian frontier region. Meanwhile, near the Egyptian frontier the isolated German garrisons at Bardia, Salum and Halfaya were reduced and taken in the first 17 days of January.

Rommel received strong reinforcements of tanks, armoured cars and supplies of all kinds from a convoy which arrived in Tripoli on 5th January, and on the 21st launched a counter-attack which took the British by surprise. The German commander was able to retain the initiative in the fighting that ensued. By 6th February the British had been driven back to Gazala, having lost great quantities of stores and equipment. The 1st Armoured Division, for example, had lost 90 tanks—three-fifths of its full establishment.

At Gazala Lieut-General Ritchie succeeded in establishing a stable line behind a minefield running from the sea to the strongpoint of Bir Hacheim on the desert flank about 45 miles to the south. Tobruk was the forward base and the ridges running back towards Tobruk were fortified against penetration.

The opposing armies maintained a static front on the Gazala line for three months and a half, during which the plight of Malta became ever more desperate. Some success in provisioning Malta had been achieved in January, when the R.A.F. could operate from airfields in Cyrenaica. Of a convoy of four supply ships sent early in February under escort, however, not one arrived. Another convoy bearing 26,000 tons, which was fought through in March with skill, bold action and extreme courage, suffered grievous loss. Only 7,500 tons reached the garrison of Malta.

Malta's perilous situation underlay a conflict then developing between Mr Churchill, with some support from the Chiefs of Staff, and General Auchinleck. From the end of February the irrepressible Prime Minister brought continued pressure on the Commander-in-Chief to renew the offensive. While Churchill feared that if the Cyrenaican airfields were not recaptured Malta would be lost, Auchinleck averred that to launch an offensive with the forces available would incur a risk of their piecemeal destruction and could endanger the security of Egypt. Eventually the Middle East Commanders-in-Chief were over-ruled from Whitehall and the Prime Minister, in the name of the War Cabinet, the Defence Committee and the Chiefs of Staff, telegraphed on 10th May instructions to launch an attack at the very latest before the June dark-period convoy to Malta.

It had already become apparent, however, that an enemy offensive might be expected before the British forces could be made ready to attack. On 26th May General Rommel launched an onslaught on the Gazala position, thrusting with his armour around the southern flank of the British forward defence line. Although Rommel held the initiative in the first few days and achieved considerable local successes, while the British command repeatedly committed the error of permitting isolated formations to become separately engaged and failed to mount an effective counter-stroke, the Axis forces after a week's exertions had failed to dislodge the Eighth Army from its ground and had lost almost one third of their effective tank strength.

In the early hours of 5th June, General Ritchie launched an operation aimed at closing the German armour's supply route but, after some initial successes, the assault force was repulsed with great loss. Sensing the discomfiture of his enemy, Rommel reverted to the assault. First he concentrated his forces against Bir Hacheim. This strongpoint, on the southern flank of the British position, and now isolated, was held by the 1st Free French Brigade. After a most heroic defence for five days against continuous assault from the ground and the air the position had to be abandoned. The garrison fought its way out on the night of 10th June.

Ritchie still attempted to hold a line from Gazala to Tobruk. The defence rested on a number of strongly-held fortified localities in dominating positions. On 12th June, however, the German armour struck at the British armour in the centre of this line, between the Knightsbridge and El Adem boxes, routed the three British armoured brigades of the 7th Armoured Division and remained in possession of the battlefield. Next day the British suffered further losses.

Ritchie had to abandon Gazala to save his weakened force from piecemeal destruction. General Auchinleck authorised this course, but ordered Ritchie to hold a line west and south-west of Tobruk through Acroma and El Adem and directed that he was not to permit Tobruk to become invested. Whether or no it was practicable to hold the German and Italian forces on that line, Ritchie, influenced, it should seem, by Gott's advice, made no serious attempt to do so, but withdrew to the Egyptian frontier most of the forces released by the abandonment of the Gazala bastion. Meanwhile Mr Churchill had asked Auchinleck for an assurance that there would be no question of giving up Tobruk. Under pressure from above and below, Auchinleck authorised Ritchie to permit "isolation" of the fortress for short periods. Rommel was in fact allowed to invest Tobruk without interference worthy of remark. On 17th June the reorganised 4th British Armoured Brigade was engaged and completely defeated. Rommel swiftly planned an assault to reduce Tobruk and the British command now lacked the means of effective intervention from outside.

The attack was launched on the 20th. The *German Africa Corps* assaulted in the south-eastern sector with infantry and about 40 tanks after a heavy dive-bombing and artillery bombardment and the tanks quickly penetrated through to the defenders' gun-line. By the early afternoon they were bombarding the harbour from the top of the escarpment and by the evening the port was in their hands. Effective resistance or escape being no longer practicable, the garrison commander (Major-General H. B. Klopper), wishing to avoid further bloodshed, surrendered the fortress next morning at dawn. About 35,000 men, including four infantry brigades (two South African, one British and one Indian) and a tank brigade, were taken prisoner.

Most defenders of Tobruk from Morshead's days have pondered this debacle, asking themselves whether they could have repelled the assault to which Tobruk at last succumbed. That onslaught cannot be directly compared with any they themselves withstood. There were significant differences between Morshead's dispositions in the south-eastern sector and those adopted by the defenders on that day. The brigade holding that sector had three battalions forward on the perimeter, one—the 2/7th Gurkhas—behind the Wadi es Zeitun. If any of these were overrun, the vital crossroads in rear (King's Cross) and the road to the port would lie open. Morshead always held one battalion back in this sector, using it, together with a battalion of the divisional reserve, to constitute a second defence line in an arc covering the crossroads. Another battalion (at Fort Airente) could be moved up at short notice from below the escarpment. He insisted that units of the line should not be tied down to the defence of the perimeter on the fringe of the precipitous Wadi es Zeitun, which he held lightly with Army Service Corps spare personnel employed as infantry. Such arrangements, however, though influential, could not of themselves determine the outcome of an engagement such as occurred, in which an armoured force numbering more than 100 tanks (outnumbering the defenders by about 2 to 1) was cast for the decisive role. The speed of the collapse appears to have been mainly due to sluggishness in bringing reserves into battle, and to failure to confine the enemy to a narrow bridgehead.

Immediately after the fall of Tobruk Ritchie withdrew the Eighth Army to Mersa Matruh, and Rommel pressed on in pursuit. By 25th June his advanced elements were in contact with the British forces masking the Matruh defences. On that day Auchinleck relieved Ritchie of command of the Eighth Army, assuming personal command.

The army was now organised as follows: the X Corps (Lieut-General Holmes[7]) was in charge of the static defences of the Matruh fortress, having under command the 10th Indian Division (which had just arrived in the desert) and the 50th Division. The XIII Corps (Lieut-General Gott) was responsible for the left flank, having under command the remnants of the 1st and 7th Armoured Divisions and the motorised New Zealand Division (less one brigade), also newly arrived. The XXX Corps (Lieut-General Norrie) was at El Alamein, 120 miles to the rear, organising a defensive position with the 1st South African Division and 2nd Free French Brigade Group. On taking over command Auchinleck immediately decreed an extensive re-organisation of formations into battle-groups, of which the basic principle was to use the artillery in a mobile role as the main weapon and the infantry as local defence for the artillery. Whatever the scheme's merits, its inauguration on the very eve of battle was perhaps inopportune.

Auchinleck decided not to commit the army to the task of holding Mersa Matruh, lest the X Corps within the port's perimeter defences

---

[7] Lt-Gen Sir William Holmes, KBE, CB, DSO; GOC X Corps 1941-42. Regular soldier; b. 20 Aug 1892.

should share the fate of the Tobruk garrison. His overriding aim was to keep his force intact. But he intended, by fighting a mobile offensive battle with battle groups in the area between Matruh and El Alamein, to confront his enemy with a novel situation and hoped thus to halt his advance in that region. What occurred, however, was more in the nature of a precipitate withdrawal than an offensive defence. On the evening of the 26th June the German forces made a breach in the minefield south of Matruh. Next day the *21st Armoured Division,* passing to the north of the New Zealand division at Minqar Qaim, attacked it in rear (from the east) while the *15th Armoured Division* converged on it from the west and the German *90th Light Division* cut the road between the British XIII Corps and the X Corps. General Gott ordered the withdrawal of the XIII Corps and in consequence the X Corps was left isolated at Mersa Matruh. The situation was in part retrieved by great gallantry. That night the New Zealand division, in the epic battle of Minqar Qaim, broke through the German ring and retired with little loss to El Alamein. The next night the 50th Division and the 10th Indian Division fought their way out of Mersa Matruh. Although the break-out was successful, these formations suffered severely and had to be withdrawn soon afterwards from the battle area to reorganise.

News of Tobruk's fall profoundly shocked the men of the 9th Division, who had so stoutly defended it. To some it seemed that their efforts, and those of lost comrades, had gone for nought. Some commanders addressed their men in an effort to combat their sombre mood. The relentless advance of Rommel's forces towards Alexandria continued meanwhile and the thought that the division might soon follow the New Zealanders to the desert was ever present.

At intervals during the three months preceding the British withdrawal to El Alamein, the Australian Government had broached with the British Government the question of the 9th Division's future employment. In a message to Mr Curtin on 10th March 1942 Mr Churchill had quoted a message from the President of the United States in which the President had informed him that the United States was prepared to send two additional divisions to the Pacific area, one to Australia and one to New Zealand, the decision to do so having been taken, so Curtin was informed, on the basis of (*a*) the President's recognition of the importance of the continuing security of the Middle East, India and Ceylon, (*b*) the need for economising in shipping and (*c*) the President's agreement with the British Government's view that the Australian and New Zealand divisions then in the Middle East should remain there; upon this, it was stated, the sending of the two additional American divisions was conditional. Churchill said that he hoped that in these circumstances the Australian Government would consent to leave the 9th Division in the Middle East: he added that the two brigades of the 6th Division soon to arrive in Ceylon would be sent on to Australia "as soon as the minimum arrangements for this all-important point can be made".

Next day the Australian Chiefs of Staff recommended that the proposal be accepted. They pointed out that the American division would reach Australia as soon as the 9th Division could arrive, that considerable shipping would be saved if a move of the 9th Division from the Middle East and another division to the Middle East to replace it were avoided, and that acceptance might hasten the return to Australia of the two brigades of the 6th Division then earmarked for Ceylon.

But the Government did not come to an immediate decision. On 20th March Curtin telegraphed Churchill that the question was still under consideration, being related to other aspects of Australian defence, including naval and air strength. The Australian Government may have been playing for time until it had an opportunity to consult General Blamey, whom it intended to appoint Commander-in-Chief of the Australian Military Forces, but who was still overseas. Blamey was due to leave Capetown by the *Queen Mary* on 15th March and to reach Australia on the 23rd. There was, moreover, a hint of coercion in this and previous communications from the British and American Governments that displeased the Australian Government, the dispatch of American forces to Australia having been represented (and, in the latest instance, the return of Australian forces in Ceylon obliquely suggested) to be conditional upon Australian agreement to the employment of Australian formations elsewhere. The Government's objection to this mode of negotiation between cooperating allies was conveyed to the President of the United States by Dr Evatt, the Australian Minister for External Affairs, who had arrived in the United States on 20th March. Dr Evatt subsequently reported to the Government that the President had stated that American forces were being, and would continue to be, dispatched to the Australian theatre unconditionally, and that the Australian Government's right to decide the destination of the A.I.F. was not questioned.

General MacArthur had arrived in Darwin from Manila on 17th March. Mr Curtin announced next day that the Australian Government had nominated him as Supreme Commander in the South-West Pacific Area. General Blamey's appointment as Commander-in-Chief of the Australian Army was made on the 26th; soon afterwards he was also appointed Commander of Allied Land Forces in the South-West Pacific. Mr Curtin at once consulted General MacArthur on the 9th Division's future employment. MacArthur advised that the division might be permitted to remain in the Middle East provided that the naval and air strength of the Australian base were augmented: to conserve shipping the aim, in his opinion, should be to move troops from non-operational to operational areas rather than from one operational area to another. General Blamey, however, urged that the division should be returned to Australia as soon as it could be replaced in the Middle East and shipping be made available. The Government's decision was conveyed to Mr Churchill in a telegram sent by Mr Curtin on 14th April, in which he alluded to most of the issues involved:

> The Government's view is that all Australian troops should be returned to Australia but it appreciates the difficulties at this stage in giving effect to its wishes, in regard to the 9th Division, owing to the shipping position. . . . It is therefore prepared to agree to the postponement of the return of the division until it can be replaced in the Middle East and the necessary shipping and escort can be made available for its transportation to Australia.[8]

Although on 1st April the Australian Government had received from Mr Churchill an unsolicited undertaking that in the event of large-scale invasion of Australia by Japanese forces the British Government would divert to Australia a British infantry division due to round the Cape towards the end of April or beginning of May and an armoured division that would be following it one month later, the British Government was not willing to provide, in circumstances indicating no imminence of such a peril, the augmented naval and air forces for which General MacArthur was pressing. MacArthur's immediate reaction was to seek additional land forces, with an eye to those two divisions. On 28th April Curtin telegraphed Churchill that, because additional land and air forces could not be provided from elsewhere, he had been asked by MacArthur to request that the two divisions rounding the Cape be diverted to Australia; the Australian Government, he said, supported General MacArthur's request. The British Government would not agree; which could hardly have surprised either Mr Curtin or General MacArthur, who then told the Australian Government (on 2nd May) that he felt impelled to ask for the early recall of the 9th Division and strongly recommended that the British Government should be asked to state a definite time for its return. General Blamey supported MacArthur's recommendation. These representations were communicated to Dr Evatt then in London, who in a reply (dated 8th May) indicated his intention to discuss this and other matters related to Australian defence with Mr Churchill on the following Monday; but succeeding reports from Dr Evatt contained no further reference to the question, and it would seem that no specific request for the return of the division was then addressed to the British Government. On 28th May Dr Evatt suggested that if such a request were to be made, it should be made from Australia. On 30th May General Blamey represented in a memorandum addressed to the Government that a decision on the retention or otherwise of the 9th Division had become a question of pressing importance because general decisions on organisation and the allocation of manpower in Australia hinged on whether or not reinforcements were to be sent to the Middle East. The problem was further discussed at the Prime Minister's war conferences on 1st and 2nd June, when General MacArthur and General Blamey renewed their requests for the division's return.

---

[8] Although the inadequacy of the Allies' dwindling shipping resources was the most limiting factor to the Allies' capacity for swift and effective reaction to the new dangers created by Japanese intervention, yet the stringency was not so great as practically to deny any option in the use of the resources. At this very time, a substantial volume of shipping was allocated to the mounting of an operation against Madagascar undertaken by the British Prime Minister against the advice of the Chief of the Imperial General Staff.

The war situation was rapidly changing, however, both in the Middle East and in the Pacific and discussions initiated when the Allies were devoid of resources to oppose the advancing Japanese forces in the South-West Pacific on land or sea or in the air were being carried on at a time when Rommel's swift advance was threatening to place the Middle East base and oilfields in more imminent peril than the Allied base in Australia. The losses suffered by Japanese naval forces in the battle of Midway Island from 3rd to 6th June put an end to Japanese naval dominance in the Pacific seas. On 11th June General MacArthur announced that in consequence of the damage suffered by the Japanese Navy in the Coral Sea and Midway Island actions, the security of Australia was now assured. In the desert of North Africa, on the other hand, the development of the battle during June seemed to portend a major defeat, which might even involve the loss of the Middle East naval, military and air bases towards the end of the month. MacArthur and Blamey both advised the Australian Government that it should not press for the return of the 9th Division at that time. Their recommendation was adopted by the Australian War Cabinet on 30th June and endorsed by the Advisory War Council on 1st July.

Already on 25th June orders had been received at the headquarters of the 9th Division that the division should move to Egypt as soon as possible. Secrecy was to cloak the move and an elaborate deception plan was evolved. No titles were worn, A.I.F. and divisional signs were obliterated, Australian-type hats hidden,[9] unit signposts left in position, 9th Division wireless-telegraphy traffic was simulated after its departure, interpreters travelled with units to Egypt and later returned to Syria. Anyone enquiring concerning the move was told it was a training exercise.

Some of the troops averred that their destination was Australia, but as the journey proceeded it became patent that they were bound for Egypt. Few were deceived by the security precautions, not even the inhabitants of Tripoli who scorned any suggestion that the division was going anywhere but to Egypt—had not advanced divisional headquarters travelled south by the coast road? The populace knew, moreover, that tan boots were peculiar to the A.I.F. From the villages of Syria to the streets of Cairo, the troops were greeted with cries of "Good luck Australia".

The 26th Brigade, first away, left at 6 a.m. on 26th June and travelled by way of Homs, Baalbek, Rayak, Tiberias, Tulkarm, Gaza, across the Sinai Desert to the Canal and Cairo; the whole journey was completed in motor transport. Instructions were received en route that the division would be responsible for the defence of Cairo, but before the main bodies reached Cairo orders had been changed.

Main divisional headquarters and divisional troops left Tripoli on the 27th and, travelling by the coast road and the Sinai Desert, reached Amiriya about the same time as the 26th Brigade. The 24th Brigade Group left on the night of the 27th-28th by the same route as the 26th Brigade

---

[9] With the exception of the men of the 26th Brigade who wore hats to Homs and thereafter steel helmets.

until Tiberias was reached, when the main body was diverted to Haifa to entrain, a road party continuing on by the 26th Brigade's route. The rail party detrained at sidings to the west of Alexandria in the afternoon of 1st July, the road party arriving some hours later.

The remaining brigade, the 20th, now in the frontier area, was not to move immediately but to await relief by the 17th Indian Brigade. The 2/15th Battalion was dispatched hurriedly by road and rail to Tripoli for the defence of that town, the commanding officer, Lieut-Colonel Ogle becoming commander of Tripoli fortress. Late on 29th June, however, the 20th Brigade received orders from the Ninth Army not to await relief but to move to Egypt early next morning. The 9th Divisional Cavalry Regiment also left Latakia for Egypt that day.

All units got away on their journey at extremely short notice and their onward movement was most efficiently organised by the staffs and units of Ninth Army and the British line-of-communications organisations. Whatever the future might hold for them, the men welcomed the end of garrison duties in Syria.

CHAPTER 12

AT EL ALAMEIN UNDER AUCHINLECK

ON 30th June Rommel's army was pressing on towards the last British defences west of the Nile Delta—the partly-prepared El Alamein position which obstructed the 30-mile neck of desert between the sea near El Alamein and the Qattara Depression. For some days troops allotted to its defence had been digging, wiring and laying mines while past them poured the transport of a retreating army.

A system of fortified locations had been laid out there and partly constructed in the months preceding the launching of the CRUSADER operation. The most developed stronghold provided all round defence for an area surrounding the El Alamein railway station and extending from the coast across the main road and railway and south into the desert for a few miles.

North of El Alamein railway station the coast road travelled along a low rise which lay between the railway and the narrow strip of salt marsh and sand dunes bordering the sea. To the immediate south only two noteworthy features emerged from a slightly undulant waste of sandy desert: the low ridges of Miteiriya and Ruweisat. South of Ruweisat the desert floor became rougher and was broken by sharp-edged escarpments and flat-topped hills nowhere rising to more than 700 feet. Cliffs defined the southern border of the desert tract on which the Eighth Army had chosen to stand; below them lay the waterlogged Qattara Depression, deceptively covered with a brittle sun-baked sand crust. South of the Qattara Depression, which could be bypassed only far to the west, and then only by going far to the south, stretched the soft and shifting sands of the Sahara, impassable by conventional military vehicles.

The plan for defending the El Alamein positions had long provided for three defended areas, or "boxes" to use the terminology then current, one about El Alamein, one about Bab el Qattara about 15 miles to the south and a third round Naqb Abu Dweis at the edge of the depression. The El Alamein Box had been dug and partly wired and mined; the Bab el Qattara position had been dug but not mined; at Naqb Abu Dweis little work had been done. Each box lay astride one of the three main lines of approach from the west: the El Alamein Box was astride the main road and railway, the Qattara Box astride the Barrel track leading from Fuka to the Cairo-Alexandria road, and the Naqb Abu Dweis Box astride passable country along the escarpment north of the Qattara Depression.

In the month since Field Marshal Rommel's offensive had opened, the strength of the Eighth Army had been drastically whittled away. When Rommel attacked at Gazala it had comprised two armoured divisions (1st and 7th), four infantry divisions (1st and 2nd South African, 5th Indian and 50th British), and the 1st and 32nd Army Tank Brigades; the 10th Indian Division, 1st Armoured Brigade and 11th Indian Brigade were under orders to join it. On 1st July the army possessed only one complete infantry division (the 2nd New Zealand[1]), one depleted infantry division (1st South African), one fairly effective armoured division (the 1st), two brigade groups (9th and 18th Indian), and numbers of battle groups or columns formed from the 7th Armoured and 5th Indian and 50th British Divisions. One complete and rested infantry division was on the way forward—the 9th Australian.

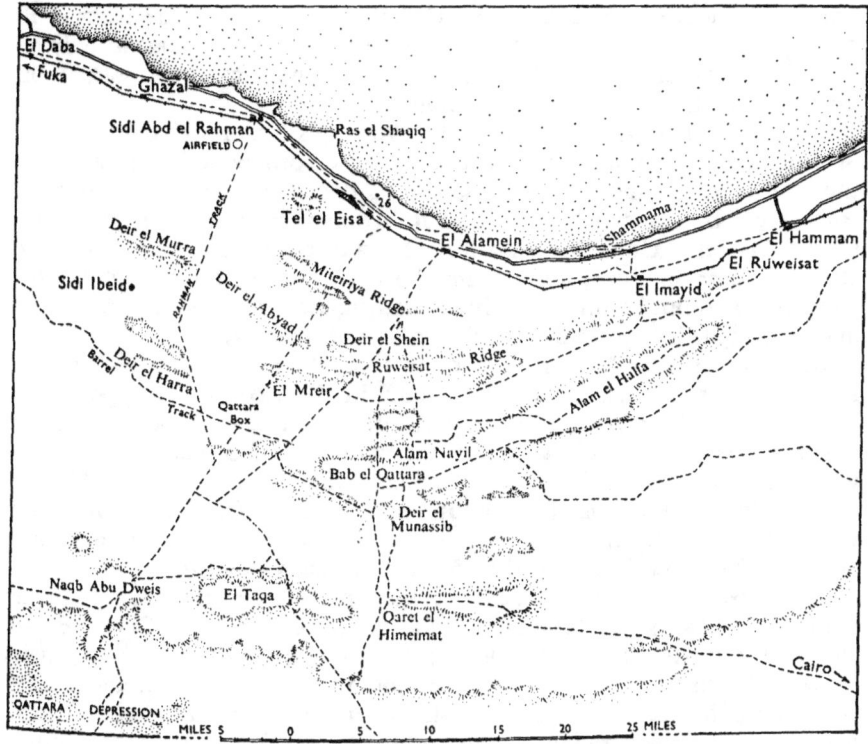

El Alamein

On 1st July the 1st South African Division was on the right of the British line with its 3rd Brigade occupying the El Alamein Box. The 18th Indian Brigade, newly arrived from Iraq, and under command of the 1st South African Division, was about Deir el Shein. The 1st Armoured Division was deployed between the El Alamein defences and the eastern end of Ruweisat Ridge. In the XIII Corps area to the south the 6th New Zealand Brigade was forward of Bab el Qattara with the remainder of the division some 10 miles to the east. The 5th Indian Division with one brigade—the 9th—was at Naqb Abu Dweis and the 7th Motor Brigade between it and the 6th New Zealand with patrols forward.

---

[1] On the 8th the "New Zealand Division" was renamed the "2nd New Zealand Division". The 1st, 4th and 5th New Zealand Divisions comprised the home army; the 3rd was in Fiji. As a deception measure the New Zealand base units in the Middle East were now named the 6th New Zealand Division.

General Holmes' X Corps headquarters had been sent back on 30th June to command Delta Force, which was being formed to defend Alexandria and the western edge of the Delta should the forward positions be lost. It was to Delta Force that the 9th Australian Division had just been allotted.

The 9th Division, the only battle-hardened formation at General Auchinleck's disposal that was thoroughly rested, was over-strength in men but gravely short of equipment. It was deficient in transport; the tanks of the cavalry regiment were obsolete and 22 below the establishment; only one field regiment had all its vehicles; only one anti-tank battery had 2-pounders, and there were no 6-pounders.

General Morshead, with Colonel H. Wells, his senior staff officer, arrived at Cairo on 28th June, reported to G.H.Q. for orders and was there given the task of defending the Cairo sector of the Delta with his division and some local bodies capable of combat in emergency, such as the Officer Cadet Training Unit. Morshead next reported to the headquarters of British Troops in Egypt and sought the written plans for the defence but, as these could not be immediately located, made a personal reconnaissance and that night issued preliminary orders from the map.

In Henry Wells, Morshead had been allotted a worthy successor to Lloyd, who had been his chief of staff in Tobruk. When appointed to the A.I.F. in 1940 Wells had 20 years of varied staff service behind him and had passed the staff college in the company of British officers beside whom he was now serving. He had demonstrated his energy and efficiency on the staff of I Corps throughout the operations in Greece and Syria. He had joined Morshead a few weeks after the withdrawal from Tobruk and they had now been together for about seven months.

It is interesting to note that on 29th June, after a busy day preparing plans, Morshead spent the night at the home of Mr R. G. Casey, British Resident Minister in the Middle East. The part in Middle East affairs played at this period by Casey, a notable Australian parliamentarian accorded Cabinet status by the British Government, belongs more to British war history than Australian. It must suffice to mention here that in addition to exercising responsibilities in relation to civil affairs and to the Middle East Supply Centre, which coordinated the administration and distribution of both military and civilian supplies, he was brought into consultation whenever the military situation in the Middle East seemed so critical as to have political implications. At a later stage, for example, we shall find him visiting General Montgomery's headquarters during the battle of El Alamein at a time when the British Government became restive at Montgomery's failure to achieve an early break-through. General de Guingand, referring to Casey's role in Auchinleck's time, wrote later:

> I felt that Auchinleck did not make the best use of the Minister of State. I believe he thought, possibly unconsciously, that the politician was critical of his handling of the situation. It was a pity, because Casey was out to help, and would have responded wholeheartedly to the full confidence of the Commander-in-Chief.[2]

---

[2] De Guingand, *Operation Victory*, p. 127.

At a conference at G.H.Q. on 30th June Morshead received orders cancelling the division's role as last-ditch defenders of Cairo and directing it to go at once to Alexandria. Meanwhile G.H.Q. had sent orders direct to Brigadier Tovell to take his 26th Brigade Group to Amiriya. These orders reached Tovell before he had received Morshead's earlier orders about the defence of Cairo.

These were the days of what later became known as the "Cairo flap", a widespread apprehensiveness that followed warning orders to headquarters in the Cairo and Delta district to prepare for a move and the hurried departure of the fleet from Alexandria. General de Guingand and others later wrote of the alarm and despondency caused by the burning of voluminous documents and records.[3] The warning orders have usually been represented as precautionary only. Morshead's diary notes of the conference on 30th June suggest that at that time the possibility of a move of Middle East Headquarters was not so unlikely.

> Conference at GHQ. Owing to withdrawal to El Alamein line and attacks on it by Rommel, plans made for the defence of the Delta and Cairo, and for moving of GHQ eastwards. 9 Aust Div ordered to Alexandria forthwith. Holmes appointed command Delta Force but as doubt whether he was captured or not I was appointed in event his not arriving.

General Holmes did arrive and was given the command.

The division's move to Alexandria was described in its report:

> It was a journey that few will forget. The opposing traffic moved nose to tail in one continuous stream of tanks, guns, armoured cars and trucks or jammed sometimes for hours, holding up the divisional convoys at the same time. One block alone lasted from 0400 hrs to 0900 hrs on 1 July but fortunately no enemy aircraft attacked.

The historian of an artillery regiment thus described the journey:

> Congestion on the Desert Highway that night considerably hampered the progress of the guns, going up. There were long delays, accidents owing to bad visibility. To clear the road-blocks, lame ducks had to be pushed off the bridge of bitumen into the yielding sand. Sometimes the retreating columns were not only nose-to-tail, but two and three abreast. All their personnel except the drivers—and often the drivers, too—slept where they sat. There were bits and pieces of broken units—here and there an anti-tank gun, here and there a Bofors, here and there a 25-pounder.[4]

On 1st July Morshead left Cairo at 2 a.m., arrived at Amiriya at 8 a.m. and established his headquarters first at El Mex, "but being unventilated caves and funkholes moved to camp at Sidi Bishr—an awful place".[5] He then gave to the two leading brigades, just arrived, their precise tasks of denying the enemy the approaches to Alexandria from the west and south-west. The 24th Brigade was to occupy the right sector with its flank on the coast and the 26th Brigade was to be on the left. The 24th Brigade

---
[3] "There was a run on the Cairo banks from June 30th to July 2nd," wrote Lord Casey. "As a precaution we decided to burn all non-essential papers on Wednesday, July 1st, which, with some originality, came to be called Ash Wednesday. Foreign diplomatic posts and some civil organisations were evacuated from Cairo on July 1st and 2nd."—*Personal Experience 1939-46* (1962), p. 112.
[4] D. Goodhart, *The History of the 2/7 Australian Field Regiment*, p. 151.
[5] General Morshead's notebooks.

(Brigadier Godfrey) took under command a motley force that had been assembled in its area, comprising the remnants of the headquarters of the 150th Brigade, the 1st Northumberland Fusiliers (the machine-gun battalion that had been part of the Tobruk garrison in 1941), and 600 troops from five units, including 120 Czechs and 30 naval men. Some land-based naval guns were to be used for anti-tank defence. The brigade was to hold a line constructed by the Polish Brigade in 1940 and 1941 to cover the isthmus north of Lake Maryut. Its three battalions occupied the line on the 1st. By the 2nd the 26th Brigade too was in position, and all units were digging busily. The 2/48th Battalion recorded that its men were working in relays, some digging while others slept; and that, in common with other units round Amiriya, it was completing its war establishment in weapons and other gear by salvaging large quantities of equipment left there by previous occupants.

Dispositions, 24th and 26th Brigades, 1st July

Morshead spent 2nd July in reconnoitring with Brigadier Tovell, Brigadier Godfrey and Colonel Wells the areas his two brigades had been ordered to defend. He was disconcerted at the preparations so far made and determined that civilian considerations were not to interfere with the establishment of proper defensive positions in a warlike manner. The ground to be held was too extensive for the troops available, but could be reduced by flooding, which would interfere with the local salt industry. Morshead set the engineers channeling to let the sea in and sought Corps approval, but the situation at the front became more stable before it was necessary to press the point. Morshead's notes on his visits to the 24th and 26th Brigades on 2nd July indicate that his orders included the removal of all civilians from the areas taken up, the discontinuance of any works being done by Egyptians, the clearing of fields of fire by cutting down palm trees and fig trees in the areas, and the demolition of a building.

Although General Auchinleck hoped to halt the enemy advance at El Alamein, he was also determined, come what may, to keep his army in being. If the El Alamein area was lost he would fight farther back on the approaches to the Delta. If these were lost he would fight on the Suez Canal with part of his force while part withdrew along the Nile. Plans were prudently made for such operations. Inevitably they became known to some, and subtly affected their morale.

Among Auchinleck's subordinate commanders there were several opinions about the immediate prospects. General Norrie, of XXX Corps, has since said that to him "Alamein was the last ditch, and it was a real case of 'Do or Die', with every chance of stopping the enemy whose armour had been reduced to a mere shadow of its former self".[6] General Gott, on the other hand, seems to have thought more of the alternative. On the 30th he showed Brigadier H. K. Kippenberger, of the New Zealand division, a letter from Lieut-General Corbett,[7] the Chief of Staff at G.H.Q., in which Corbett wrote that "the Chief" had decided to save the Eighth Army, and that the South Africans would retire through Alexandria and the rest through Cairo. Norrie wrote later that Major-General Pienaar of the 1st South African Division had been "openly saying that he thought it was wrong to stand at El Alamein, and that the best place was to go behind the Suez Canal".[8]

The spirit in which General Auchinleck prepared to confront the enemy at El Alamein, however, was not downcast, even though he had with wisdom been planning a course to follow in the event of yet another failure. On the contrary, with his exceptional talent for perceiving his enemy's difficulties, he judged that Rommel might over-reach himself (as the German High Command had also feared) and the opportunity be presented, not merely to halt him, but to throw him back. Auchinleck had on paper sufficient strength to take the initiative. He was resolved to seize it. Not all his battered formations were dispirited, least of all the New Zealanders, fresh from their break-out at Minqar Qaim. He had some battle-hardened but rested formations and some fresh troops from England.

Indeed, all was not well on the Axis side. The enterprising Germans, as they moved up to the El Alamein defences on the 30th, had only 1,700 first-line infantry and 55 tanks forward. Rommel was perilously short of supplies and largely dependent on what he had captured during the advance from Gazala. On the other hand he knew that his enemy was receiving men and weapons in large numbers and at last "there were already signs, in the new British tanks and anti-tank guns, of a coming qualitative superiority of British material. If this were achieved, it would clearly mean the end for us".[9]

It seemed, therefore, that Rommel's only chance of victory in the African war, was to press on as fast as he could drive his overtaxed troops. On the morning of the 30th he ordered the *Africa Corps* and the *90th Light Division* to thrust forward before dawn next morning between the El Alamein position and Deir el Abyad. The *90th* was then to wheel

---

[6] Quoted in J. A. I. Agar-Hamilton and L. C. F. Turner, *Crisis in the Desert* (1952), p. 275, a volume of the South African official history.
[7] Lt-Gen T. W. Corbett, CB, MC. (1916-18: Staff Capt and BM.) GOC IV Indian Corps 1942; CGS ME 1942. Regular soldier; b. 2 Jun 1888.
[8] Agar-Hamilton and Turner, p. 276. On the other hand, Major-General F. H. Theron, the senior South African administrative officer in Cairo, found General Pienaar, though pessimistic, "indomitable in spirit and determined to fight" (p. 277).
[9] *The Rommel Papers*, p. 245.

northward and cut off the El Alamein Box while the *Africa Corps* swung south and took the XIII Corps in the rear. The Italian *Trento Division* was to attack El Alamein from the west and the *Brescia* to follow the *Africa Corps*. The *XX Italian Corps* with its one armoured and one motorised division was to deal with the Qattara Box. The Axis army was in new country. The advance would not only start in the dark but have to be made over unfamiliar ground.

Meanwhile in accordance with the tactical theories then in vogue on the British side, numbers of mobile columns had been formed. Two, each built round a battalion and two batteries of artillery, were formed in the South African division; only the 3rd South African Brigade was left in the box, whose eastern side was now undefended. The 50th Division was organised into three columns each possessing eight field guns. The 10th and 5th Indian Divisions also formed mobile columns.

On the 30th the British northern rearguard passed through the El Alamein Box. The leading troops of the *90th Light* followed and halted a few miles from the box where they were shelled and bombed. They made ready for the big attack ordered for the next day.

Events had moved so swiftly that Rommel's Intelligence staff had an inaccurate picture of the British dispositions. They placed the X, not the XXX Corps, in the northern sector, and the 50th Division in the Alamein Box. They did not know that the 1st South African Division was forward. They placed an Indian brigade at Deir el Abyad instead of Deir el Shein and were unaware that two South African brigades were in the gap between Deir el Shein and Alamein. They placed the whole New Zealand division, instead of only one brigade, in the Qattara Box, and had the 1st Armoured Division west of that box whereas it was in process of moving into reserve about Ruweisat Ridge having only just arrived back from Mersa Matruh. In fact, coming back to El Alamein on the afternoon of the 30th, the 1st Armoured Division bumped against the *Africa Corps* in its assembly area for the attack Rommel was preparing to launch next day.

The British commanders expected the Germans to attack on the 30th-1st and to thrust with their armour somewhere between the El Alamein Box and Bab el Qattara. If the attack fell on the northern gap, between the box and Deir el Shein, it was planned that the 1st Armoured Division (Major-General Lumsden[1]) would counter-attack from the north and the New Zealanders from the south. This plan was made at Eighth Army headquarters without appreciating that the 1st Armoured was dispersed as well as weary and in no shape to fight a battle next day.

The tired Axis forces attacked as planned on the 1st but made little headway. As a result of heavy going, a dust storm and powerful air attack the *Africa Corps* bogged down. The Corps then found, to its surprise, that Deir el Shein was occupied. Here was the fresh 18th Indian Brigade supported by nine Matilda tanks. The Germans became involved in eight hours of bitter fighting with the brigade which, unsupported by the British

---

[1] Lt-Gen H. Lumsden, CB, DSO, MC. (1916-18: Lt, RA.) Comd 28 Armd Bde 1941-42; GOC X Corps 1942-43; Mr Churchill's personal representative on GHQ SWPA 1943-45. Regular soldier; b. 8 Apr 1897. Killed in USS *New Mexico* in Lingayen Gulf, 6 Jan 1945.

armour, despite the optimistic prescriptions of army headquarters, was at length overrun and virtually destroyed; but the advance had been delayed and valuable time for counter-measures gained. Soon the *Africa Corps* had only 37 tanks running out of 55 that had opened the attack.

That afternoon the *90th Light Division* came under the fire of all three artillery regiments of the South African division. The Germans halted and dug in but at 3.30 p.m., under persistent artillery fire from the South Africans' guns to the north and east, the over-tried Germans began to panic and many men fled. At the end of the day the *90th Light's* diary recorded: "The situation has been clarified and a rout prevented, but the advance has broken down under concentrated enemy fire." Next morning Rommel ordered the *Africa Corps* to abandon the southward advance and reinforce a renewed effort of the *90th Light* to cut off the El Alamein position.

General Auchinleck was not unsettled by the disheartening loss of the 18th Indian Brigade. Although he had decided earlier that day that he was holding too wide a front and that the boxes at Naqb Abu Dweis and Bab el Qattara, garrisoned respectively by the 5th Indian and 2nd New Zealand Divisions, would have to be abandoned, on the night of the 1st he ordered preparation for a counter-attack from the south by the XIII Corps, employing the 1st Armoured Division and the New Zealand division.

Next morning the Axis infantry attack on the South African positions in the north was resumed at first light in dutiful compliance with the German commander's exacting orders, but the *90th Light* had lost heart and no real assault was made. The Italian *X Corps* (*Trento Division* and *7th Bersaglieri*) to their north did no better. At midday, noting the continued northward concentration of the German forces, General Auchinleck confirmed the orders to the XIII Corps to attack the enemy's flank and rear. In the afternoon the 1st Armoured set off on a preliminary move to the south-west but collided with the armour of the *Africa Corps* moving east, bent on its similar mission against the South African sector. The two armoured forces fought each other inconclusively until nightfall. In the south the Italian armoured forces, discouraged by air attack, had made no move.

Next day, 3rd July, marked the end of Rommel's attempt to hustle the Eighth Army back from El Alamein before it could get settled. Rommel called for another effort from his flagging formations, though significantly they were told to probe for weaknesses first, and the over-spent *90th Light Division* was permitted to dig in where it was. Once more the *Africa Corps,* which had only 26 tanks in running order (as against more than 100 in the 1st Armoured Division), was to thrust east to break in behind the South Africans, while the Italian *XX Corps* was to carry out the attack ordered the day before. Auchinleck's plan was that the XXX Corps should hold its ground against the expected attack in the coast region while the XIII Corps threatened the enemy's rear by executing the prescribed attack from behind Deir el Shein.

In the morning, probing for weak spots, the *Africa Corps* again bumped into the 1st Armoured Division, which then took up hull-down positions. The two armoured forces slogged it out astride the Ruweisat Ridge for the rest of the day. In the late afternoon, goaded by Rommel's blunt and peremptory injunctions, the *Africa Corps* forced its way a short distance past the South African positions on their southern flank, but its will to fight on was spent.

Although the 1st Armoured Division could not disengage to carry out its intended left hook, the day was marked by a signal victory in the south which a New Zealand historian has described as "an outstanding episode in the Dominion's military history".[2] Setting out in the morning for Alam Nayil, a typical cliff-walled outcrop emerging from the desert between the Ruweisat Ridge and the Qattara Box, the *Ariete Division* first brushed against the 4th Armoured Brigade and then came under fire from four New Zealand batteries.

This fire seemed so to disconcert the Italians that the 4th New Zealand Brigade (Brigadier J. R. Gray) attacked the Italian armoured division from the south. The leading battalion—the 19th—led by its carrier platoon advanced with fixed bayonets and captured some prisoners in an outlying group, and then made a systematic attack on a larger body of Italians of whom about 350 surrendered; 44 medium and field guns and many vehicles were captured there. Major-General Inglis, temporarily commanding the New Zealand division, at once ordered his 5th Brigade (Brigadier Kippenberger) to cut off the remainder of the *Ariete* at El Mreir. The brigade came under fire from the *Brescia Division* at El Mreir and eventually dug in.

That night Rommel realised that he had driven his staunch but dwindling forces to a standstill and decided to discontinue his attack on the makeshift British defence line for at least a fortnight. The fighting strength of each of his divisions, he reported on the 3rd, was no more than 1,200 to 1,300 men; the *Africa Corps* had only 36 serviceable tanks; he was short of ammunition.

On the morning of 4 July 1942 (wrote von Mellenthin of Rommel's staff, after the war) the position of Panzerarmee Africa was perilous.[3]

Auchinleck, while aware that he had the upper hand, evinced less clairvoyance than usual and does not appear to have fully appreciated the enemy's plight. Although on the night 4th-5th July he issued confident orders that the Eighth Army would "attack and destroy the enemy in his present position", the confidence wore a little thin in the eyes of the New Zealanders next day when they received an order giving a new plan for withdrawal should the line collapse: the XXX Corps was to retreat by the coast to Alexandria, the XIII Corps (including the New Zealand division) inland to Cairo.

There followed a week of missed opportunities for the British, and thereafter more weeks of costly and mismanaged operations, yet for most

---

[2] Scoullar, *Battle for Egypt*, p. 167.
[3] F. W. von Mellenthin, *Panzer Battles 1939-1945* (1955), p. 129.

of that time Auchinleck was able to call the tune to both armies. The fault lay more in the execution of his plans than in their conception. Auchinleck had stepped down from the highest plane of command to undertake the day-to-day control of a formation that he had not first fashioned, tempered and hammered to perform its tasks in the way he desired. In the first place, its control and communications mechanisms were not geared or tuned to execute surely and swiftly the kind of flexible operations Auchinleck wanted; some parts of his command structure needed replacing, others redesigning. The kind of direct communication through report centres which Montgomery later instituted was needed to project a more accurate picture before the commander. In the second place the interpretations given to Auchinleck's directions by the staffs of some subordinate headquarters, particularly Gott's and Lumsden's, resulted in orders that bore to the Commander-in-Chief's conceptions but a shadowy resemblance, in which their original purpose was sometimes scarcely discernible.

On the 4th a series of confused and indecisive actions took place. Tanks of the 22nd Armoured Brigade probed along Ruweisat Ridge and overran part of the *115th Infantry Regiment* (of the *15th Armoured Division*). Some hundreds of Germans made as if to surrender, but their would-be captors were driven off by artillery fire. The *Africa Corps'* war diary reported the *15th Division's* situation that day to be "most serious". In retrospect it seems not unlikely that a resolute thrust from Ruweisat would have broken through.

That night Auchinleck gave the orders quoted above that the Eighth Army would "attack and destroy the enemy in his present position". This was to be done by the XIII Corps which was to press round the enemy's south-west flank and threaten his rear towards the coast road. But nothing much was achieved by the corps on the 5th, and for the Germans it was another precious day of reorganisation and of improvement of defences. On succeeding days, as the New Zealand historian has remarked:

Numerous plans were made by Army and Corps for action against the enemy's rear and flank. Orders to execute them were never given.[4]

At 3 a.m. on 3rd July, the senior staff officer of X Corps, Brigadier Walsh,[5] telephoned orders to the headquarters of the 9th Division near Alexandria that the division was to be formed into battle groups. One brigade group (less one battalion) was to be sent forward at once. Colonel Wells pointed out that the brigades lacked much essential equipment and that only one of the three field regiments was reasonably complete. Having been advised by General Blamey before his departure from the Middle East that the piecemeal employment of Australian detachments severed from the main formation should not be permitted, Morshead flew up to the Commander-in-Chief's tactical headquarters, and sought an interview with Auchinleck. Before leaving, however, he gave directions that the 24th Brigade (less the 2/28th Battalion) should be prepared to move by 5

---
[4] Scoullar, p. 192.
[5] Maj-Gen G. P. Walsh, CB, CBE, DSO. (1918: Lt, RA.) BGS X Corps 1942; Chief of Staff Eighth Army 1944; ALFSEA 1945. Regular soldier; b. 30 Jun 1899.

a.m. next day provided that deficiencies in equipment and transport could be made good. After the war Morshead said that Auchinleck spoke to him very brusquely at the interview, and that the conversation went as follows:

Auchinleck: I want that brigade right away.
Morshead: You can't have that brigade.
Auchinleck: Why?
Morshead: Because they are going to fight as a formation with the rest of the division.
Auchinleck: Not if I give you orders?
Morshead: Give me the orders and you'll see.
Auchinleck: So you're being like Blamey. You're wearing his mantle.

Auchinleck, who was in no position to allow operational plans to be delayed by differences which could only be resolved satisfactorily to his wishes, if at all, by the slow process of inter-Governmental representations, agreed that the whole of the 9th Division should be brought forward as soon as practicable and employed under Morshead's command. Morshead was ready to agree to the temporary detachment of a brigade group of the 9th Division to the XXX Corps on this basis. After seeing Auchinleck, Morshead met Norrie of XXX Corps, stayed at his headquarters for three hours, and then flew back in a Lysander aircraft to his headquarters on the Alexandria racecourse.[6] Meanwhile Wells had been busily completing arrangements for the equipment of the 24th Brigade. Some of the needed equipment was brought forward during the day.

At midday the division came under the command of the XXX Corps and on the 4th the 24th Brigade Group (less the 2/28th Battalion) moved forward with many stops and starts on a road still crowded with vehicles moving eastward. By nightfall the 2/43rd was digging in on Tel el Shammama and the 2/32nd was halted near by. The staff of XXX Corps informed Godfrey of the 24th Brigade that he was to keep his group mobile in readiness for a quick move. Meanwhile the 2/28th Battalion remained at Amiriya, and the 20th Brigade had taken over the defensive position in front of Alexandria vacated by the 24th.

The Australians, with their memories of Tobruk where the enemy had commanded the air, were gladdened by the constant evidence of Allied air superiority. Numerous fighter formations and light bomber formations (of Bostons and Baltimores) with wheeling fighter escort passed overhead each day; but German fighters were still to be reckoned with, and there were many dog-fights, with honours often divided.

The request for an Australian brigade had come down from Auchinleck because he believed that Rommel might be about to withdraw; Auchinleck had given orders to prepare for a pursuit. Morshead chose the 24th Brigade as the one to be sent forward because that brigade alone had completed its training in mobile operations. Exploitation to El Daba was an optimistic feature of the plans not only for this operation but also for

---

[6] The entry in Morshead's diary on the same date states: "This detachment cuts completely across the policy of the Australian Government and A.I.F."

most other major operations in which the division was to be engaged in the coming month; but on no occasion did the exploitation take place.

On the 5th, Auchinleck decided that he was not able to thrust the XIII Corps towards the enemy's rear and instead ordered both corps to converge on Deir el Shein. Rommel had meanwhile withdrawn the *Africa*

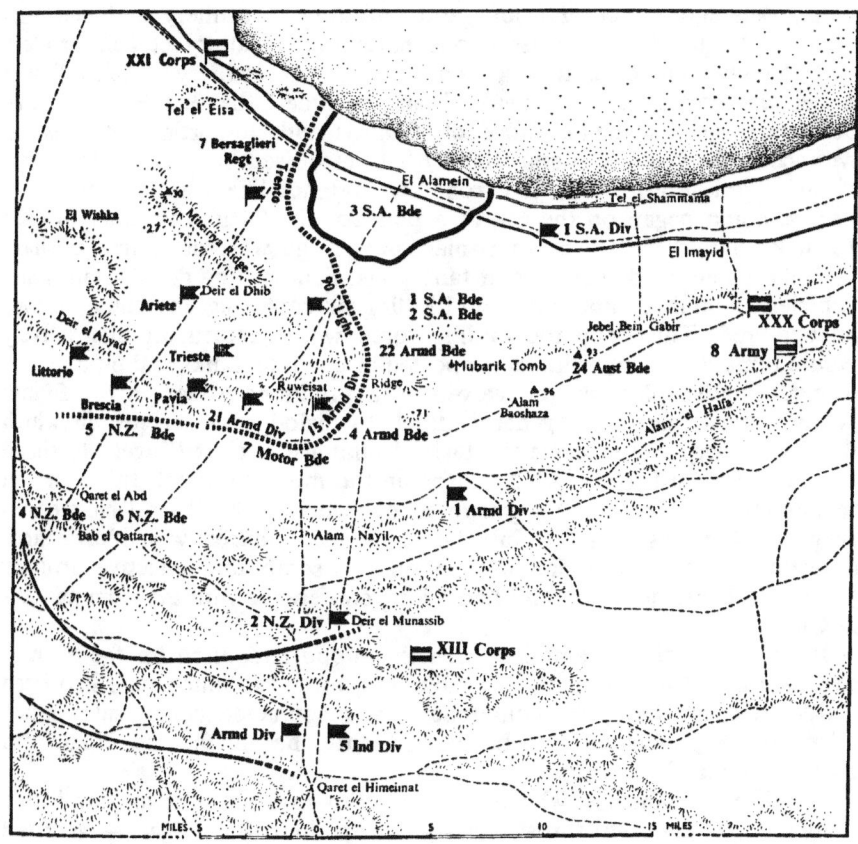

Situation, noon, 5th July

Corps, XX Corps and *90th Division* from front-line positions. The front was now held with the Italian infantry of the *X* and *XXI Corps* so that his striking force could be rested and reorganised in preparation for a resumption of the offensive later on.

On 5th July the 24th Australian Brigade moved to Ruweisat Ridge (the 2/32nd about Trig 96 and 2/43rd about Trig 93) with the task of establishing a firm base from which the 1st Armoured Division and various columns comprising "Wall Group" (under Brigadier R. P. Waller) might operate. In its new position the 24th Brigade, directly under the command of XXX Corps, relieved the headquarters of the 50th Division and a force known as "Stancol" which moved back to the Delta for reorganisation. The composition of "Wall Group"—an assortment of units from various formations, brought together "pending reorganisation"—illustrates the degree to which the commanders were still thinking in terms of improvised columns. Waller was nominally the C.R.A. of the 10th Indian Division. One column—"Robcol"—comprised one battalion, one field regiment, detachments of anti-tank and anti-aircraft artillery and machine-gunners. "Squeakcol" possessed one battalion, a battery of field artillery and detachments of anti-tank and anti-aircraft artillery. "Ackcol" was under the command of Squeakcol and included the 3rd R.H.A., three companies of Coldstream and Scots Guards and supporting detachments. Morshead, on whom General Blamey had impressed his aversion to improvised organisation, toured the front and did not like what he saw.

Discussion began on the 6th of a plan for the 24th Australian Brigade to make a raid with two companies on a ridge west of Alam Baoshaza with the object of damaging anti-tank guns, demolishing derelict tanks and vehicles, obtaining information and killing or capturing any enemy troops encountered. This done the raiding force would return, or alternatively would remain and consolidate, supported at dawn by tanks and 6-pounders. The alternative plan was conceived as a preliminary step in the Eighth Army's latest plan for a general attack to dislodge the enemy, in which the XXX Corps would have the task of taking Ruweisat Ridge. Morshead had gone forward to the XXX Corps on the morning of 5th July and had reconnoitred the area of the proposed operation with General Norrie and Brigadier Godfrey. On 6th July he again reconnoitred with Norrie and, objecting to the consolidation plan on the score that effective artillery protection could not be given,[7] had a long conference with the Commander-in-Chief.

Brigadier Godfrey maintained that the support required for the alternative plan could not be made available and, after "so much time had been fruitlessly spent during the conference that reconnaissances by subordinate commanders . . . could not be carried out", he sought and obtained a postponement of 24 hours.[8]

The New Zealanders, who had a contemporaneous part to play in the army's larger plan—to thrust westward with their 4th Brigade—were not informed of the postponement. On the contrary, just as the brigade was setting forth, the division received an emergency operations message indicating a possibility that the enemy might be pulling out to withdraw westwards and telling the division to be ready to drive through deeply into the enemy's rear. The 4th New Zealand Brigade carried out its original orders with élan, shooting up the *Littorio Armoured Division* in its leaguer before breakfast and playing merry hell. Before the end of the forenoon, however, the volatile mood at army headquarters was exhibited in new orders to the New Zealand division, this time to draw back from the Qattara Box to a position from which its guns could reach the Ruweisat

---
[7] So Morshead told the author after the war.
[8] Report on Operations 24 Aust Inf Bde, 3-29 July 42.

Ridge; this doubtless pleased Morshead. What caused the army commander's renewed anxiety for the gap between his two corps at this moment is a matter for speculation, but he appears to have recast his thoughts as to how the next phase of the battle would be fought. The plan for a two-pronged thrust south of the Ruweisat Ridge had been abandoned.

By the 7th Auchinleck, having concluded that his plan to drive through the southern flank of the Axis army had failed, had decided that he would use the fresh 9th Australian Division to attack on the northern flank, where, he was convinced, only Italian troops would be encountered. The 26th Brigade Group (less one battalion) had been moved up on 5th and 6th July to positions giving depth to the defence on the coast sector. Divisional headquarters moved forward on the 7th to an area near El Imayid station and resumed command of the 24th and 26th Brigades, leaving a reserve group holding the Alexandria defences. Next day a "tentacle" from Army Air Support Control joined divisional headquarters; another "tentacle" was operating with the 24th Brigade. These tentacles not only reduced the delay in obtaining air support but enabled information about the enemy to be swiftly passed to divisions and brigades.

The "Reserve Group" at first included the 20th Brigade and all units and detachments not included in the two-battalion brigade groups sent forward, but the 20th Brigade Group (again less one battalion) was called forward a day later and by 8th July the "Reserve Group", which was put under the command of Colonel H. Wrigley of the Reinforcements Depot, comprised the 2/13th, 2/28th, 2/32nd and 2/3rd Pioneer Battalions, some other units and detachments and the "left-out-of-battle" personnel from the units sent forward. In future each unit was to leave out of battle a certain number of officers and men of all ranks, who were to remain in the "B" Echelon area when the unit went into battle; thus if a unit had very heavy losses there would be a nucleus round which it could be re-formed. In an infantry battalion, for example, the second-in-command, 6 other officers and 61 others of specified ranks or qualifications were left behind; this was a minimum, as it was also laid down that an infantry battalion was not to go into action with its rifle sections of greater strength than one N.C.O. and seven men. Within a week each of the infantry battalions left behind was called forward to rejoin its brigade, leaving its "L.O.B." personnel at Alexandria.

When visiting the XXX Corps headquarters Morshead had learnt from Norrie himself that Norrie was returning to England and would be succeeded by Major-General Ramsden[9] of the 50th Division. Morshead would not have been surprised therefore when Ramsden called at his headquarters at 6 p.m. on 7th July to tell Morshead of his new appointment. In his diary for that day Morshead wrote: "Ramsden has been commanding the remnants of his division (50 Div) remaining forward = 3 companies

---

[9] Lt-Gen W. H. C. Ramsden, CB, CBE, DSO, MC. (1916-18: Capt to Maj, E York Regt.) Comd 25 Bde 1939-40; GOC 50 Div 1940-42, XXX Corps Jul-Sep 1942, 3 Div 1942-43; Comd British Troops, Sudan and Eritrea 1944-45. Regular soldier; b. 3 Oct 1888.

plus various artillery groups."[1] This entry suggests an initial uneasiness on Morshead's part, who would not have appreciated being subordinated to a colleague whose responsibilities immediately before had been less than Morshead's. Nor was the situation made easier by the fact that Morshead, by virtue of his responsibility for the whole of the A.I.F. in the Middle East, held the rank of lieut-general, which had not yet been conferred on Ramsden. In the subsequent operations Ramsden did not win Morshead's confidence and Ramsden found Morshead an intractable subordinate. Morshead said after the war that Ramsden twice complained to Auchinleck about his attitude.

On the 7th the role of the 24th Australian Brigade was amended to provide for a raid by one company with a detachment of engineers. The task was given to Captain Jeanes' company of the 2/43rd (Lieut-Colonel W. J. Wain) with 4 officers and 64 others, plus 20 sappers and 6 stretcher bearers. By 10.30 p.m. on the 7th the raiders had formed up at Point 71, whence they moved off at 11 p.m. After 1,400 yards the leading platoon (Lieutenant Grant[2]) reported the presence of enemy troops about 800 yards to the north-west and promptly attacked; the other platoons fanned out to right and left and joined in.

Under fire from a variety of weapons Lance-Sergeant Curren's[3] platoon thrust forward for about 700 yards destroying guns and vehicles and taking prisoners. Grant's platoon moved a similar distance and its sappers destroyed three disabled British tanks—one Honey and two Grants—and a gun. Lieutenant Combe's[4] platoon destroyed a gun and tractor. Private Franklin[5] in Curren's platoon, who acted with great dash throughout the attack, recaptured a British carrier, killing two Germans, and drove it back to his own lines. By 3 a.m. the company was back at Point 71. Throughout the raid the enemy fired wildly and sent up many flares. Soon flares, blasting guns and blazing tractors illuminated the area. When it was over one Australian was missing and seven had been wounded, four anti-tank guns, one field gun, three damaged British tanks and six tractors had been destroyed, and at least 15 enemy troops had been killed and 9 prisoners taken—all Germans of an anti-tank unit. The raid had an inspiriting effect on the division and on neighbouring troops.

On the enemy side the raid produced far stronger repercussions than the attackers realised. The commander of the *15th Armoured Division* threw in the divisional reserve to counter what was regarded as a serious attack. Before dawn 19 tanks of the *21st Armoured Division*—half the available total—were moved to the area where a threat of deep penetration had apparently arisen. Next day Rommel ordered that officers of forward units must stay awake all night to avoid being taken by surprise.

---

[1] Ramsden had had wide experience in command at most levels, as the preceding footnote shows. He had seen active service in France (15 months) in the 1914-18 war, on the North-West Frontier of India between the wars and again in France in 1939-40.
[2] Maj E. C. Grant, MC, SX10270; 2/43 Bn. Regular soldier; of Woodville Park, SA; b. Rose Park, SA, 2 Jan 1910.
[3] Sgt W. B. Curren, MM, SX5911; 2/43 Bn. Labourer; of Winkie, SA; b. Richmond, SA, 29 Apr 1912. Killed in action 28 Jul 1942.
[4] Capt G. D. Combe, MC, SX6977; 2/43 Bn. Parliamentary officer; of Adelaide; b. Gumeracha, SA, 12 Jun 1917.
[5] Cpl D. Franklin, MM, SX6842; 2/43 Bn. Butcher; of Barmera, SA; b. Ashton, SA, 14 Dec 1917.

(*Australian War Memorial*)

The railway cutting at Tel el Eisa, the scene of bitter fighting by the 2/23rd Battalion on 22nd July 1942.

(*Australian War Memorial*)

Tel el Eisa railway station.

(*Imperial War Museum*)

On the night 14th-15th July 15 trucks approached "A" Company, 2/48th Battalion, near the Tel el Eisa cutting. After a fight 7 trucks were destroyed, 32 Germans captured and arms and ammunition salvaged. Next morning the Australians found that six of the vehicles had black crosses painted on the sides and were flying white flags. The seventh was an ambulance.

(*Capt G. H. Yates*)

Members of the 2/28th Battalion searching for traces of men missing in the attack on Ruin Ridge in July 1942. This photograph was taken in November after the area had been recaptured.

The fourteen days' respite from offensive tasks tentatively vouchsafed —on 4th July—to the Axis Army's few and stalwart but overtaxed German troops was soon curtailed. The prime motivator, it should seem, was Mussolini who had come across to Africa on 29th June to be there when Egypt fell to Axis arms, and perhaps to lay the foundations for a second Roman empire in a region where Caesars had once fought and loved, and who had announced on 6th July from his headquarters far from the fighting line that if there was no further attack for ten or fourteen days the chance of exploiting British unreadiness would be lost and the light forces available would prove insufficient to push through to Cairo and the Suez Canal. On the other hand taking the shorter coast route and capturing Alexandria, he thought, would bring splendid prestige. A top-level discussion ensued of the alternative merits of Cairo and Alexandria as targets for a resumed offensive, but Cavallero and Rommel decided that the best course was to cut the Red Sea supply route by striking through Cairo, thus avoiding the many obstacles to an advance through the Nile Delta. The Axis forces had somewhat recovered their tank strength, having some 50 German and 60 Italian tanks. The *21st Armoured* and *90th Light Divisions* and the *Littorio Division* were assembled opposite the centre of the XIII Corps, where they were joined by the *3rd* and *33rd Reconnaissance Units* brought up from the far south. They were told to advance to Alam Nayil and strike north on 9th July. To the north of them, astride the Ruweisat Ridge, were the *15th Armoured Division* and the *Trento Division* of the Italian *X Corps*. Farther north, where the 9th Australian Division was soon to operate, the Italian *XXI Corps* held the line with the *Trento* and *Sabratha Divisions*.

As mentioned, Auchinleck had decided to abandon the Bab el Qattara Box, and on the night of the 7th-8th the New Zealand division had withdrawn. The Germans did not become aware of this until next afternoon. Their patrols in the evening confirmed that the box had been abandoned; but to Rommel this appeared too good to be true and, on the 9th, in dutiful compliance with the Field Marshal's admonitions made in person at *Africa Corps Headquarters*, a full-scale attack on the "strong-point" was made by the two armoured divisions assembled for the offensive—one German and one Italian—using infantry, assault engineers, heavy artillery and tanks. The planned advance to Alam Nayil that morning was left to a detachment comprising part of the *5th Armoured Regiment*, which was turned back by New Zealand artillery fire.

Having chosen to attack in the north, Auchinleck had ordered Ramsden to take the ridges of Tel el Eisa and Tel el Makh Khad, just south of the coast road. When these had been captured Auchinleck proposed that battle groups would advance south on Deir el Shein, and raiding parties attack the forward landing grounds about El Daba. The capture of Tel el Eisa was to be undertaken by the 9th Division; the 1st South African Division was to take Tel el Makh Khad. The 44th R.T.R. with 32 Valentines was placed under Morshead's command and the 1st South African Division was given 8 Matildas. The raiding force to make the foray towards

Daba comprised one squadron of tanks and one troop of armoured cars supported by a troop of field guns and another of anti-tank guns.

Where the black ribbon of the coast road issued from the Alamein Box, it traversed a flat, with a salt-marsh on the right, and continued on past a smooth-sloped white hill rising on the right to a height of almost 80 feet (Hill 26), which was the southern extremity of an elongated hill-feature stretching back across a saddle (Point 23) to a still higher feature, Trig 33. Below the steep southern side of Trig 33, the ground began to rise again gradually to rolling ground across the railway, shown on most maps as a ridge named "Tel el Eisa". In a generally flat terrain the double-humped hill (Point 26—Trig 33) lying between the sea and the road and railway was the dominating feature near the coast, providing as it did good observation not only southwards to the Miteiriya Ridge over the ground in front of the Alamein Box but also into much of the Eighth Army's territory. On the other hand it shielded the coast tract against observation from farther west. The 9th Division's task was to seize it and exploit south to the Tel el Eisa Ridge across the railway.

General Morshead conferred with General Ramsden and with General Pienaar of the South African division on the 8th, and on the 9th issued his orders for the attack, which was to open in the early morning of the 10th. The 26th Brigade was to capture and hold the features which have just been described. The brigade plan required the 2/48th Battalion to take the first objective, Point 26, and then to move on to the Point 23 saddle. Then the 2/24th Battalion, with the tanks, was to come up on the right over the sand dunes, swing left and take Trig 33. The 2/24th was then to exploit to East Point 24 south of the railway. The 9th Divisional Cavalry with one field battery under command was to be at 30 minutes' notice to move forward from 8 a.m. on the 10th onwards.

Formidable support was to be given by artillery and aircraft. The division had the 7th Medium Regiment under command plus its own three field regiments, and such guns of the South African division as could bear were placed under the command of Brigadier Ramsay, Morshead's artillery commander.[6] There would be an air sweep over the area from 7.30 a.m. on the 10th plus bomber and fighter-bomber attacks.

Morshead's tactical headquarters opened in the El Alamein fortress on the 9th and at dusk that day the attacking battalions moved to their assembly areas within the western perimeter of the fortress. Each battalion had under command a troop of anti-tank guns, a platoon of machine-gunners and some engineers, and, in support, a squadron of tanks.

The 2/48th Battalion, which was to open the operation by capturing Point 26, was commanded by Lieut-Colonel H. H. Hammer, who was to prove one of the most original and magnetic leaders of the A.I.F. When war broke out he was a major in a country light horse unit in Victoria. That was not a promising situation for one eager to obtain appointment to one of the first-formed divisions but Hammer "got away" in 1940 in

---

[6] As the 9th Division was attacking through the South African area the South African division came under operational command of the 9th Division for the period of the attack.

the Base Depot (A.G.B.D.). Thence just after the first Libyan campaign, to the pained surprise of the proud and veteran 16th Brigade, he was appointed its brigade major and served with it in Greece, and seven months thereafter. This colourful and buoyant commander, who had led the 2/48th since January 1942, gave his battalion a motto, "Hard as nails", when he came to it, and the men gave it back to him, smarting under his strong hand until in action they found that his tight grip, his sureness and his quick decision protected them.

Hammer's plan provided for an attack on Point 26 on a two-company front. To achieve surprise he decided that the first phase would be executed without artillery support and as silently as possible. There would then be artillery concentrations on Point 23, and the two other rifle companies would move through to the second objective. In the third phase the two companies on the left were to swing left to the Tel el Eisa station area and hold it.

On the move to the assembly area trucks carrying the 2/48th bogged in the salt-marshes beside the track and the consequent delay deprived the troops of the few hours of sleep the plan allowed for. The silent advance began at 3.40 a.m. A lone areoplane was circling above.

> Suddenly the night was lit up like day. The plane had dropped a parachute flare directly over the leading companies. The men froze, expecting the impact of a terrific outburst of fire. None came, and then the forward companies gathered momentum as they advanced, working their way along the ridge on either side of the crest.[7]

Before dawn broke, the Italians garrisoning Point 26 awoke to discover that they had been captured. Then a barrage of an intensity not heard before in the desert announced that the Eighth Army was making its first advance since the battle-tide had turned against it on the Tripolitanian frontier after CRUSADER. To veterans of the Great War, according to the *Africa Corps'* war diary, it recalled the "drum-fire" of the Western Front. Artillery concentrations descended on Point 23 and, as daylight was breaking, smoke screens were put down on Trig 33. As soon as the guns ceased the two rear companies passed through and took Point 23 against only light opposition, capturing some prisoners including the commander of the *7th Bersaglieri Regiment*. Some of the prisoners were caught in bed. So far—4,500 yards from the start-line—there had been no Australian casualties.

At 7.15 a.m. two companies swung south and, now under heavy shell fire, moved on Tel el Eisa station, 2,500 yards to the south-west. Captain Bryant's company on the right and Captain Williams'[8] on the left attacked with great dash. One platoon of Bryant's company, for instance, charging with fixed bayonets, overran a battery of four guns, capturing 106 prisoners, mostly German. Here Corporal Hinson[9] led his section with

---
[7] J. G. Glenn, *Tobruk to Tarakan* (1960), p. 107, a history of the 2/48th Battalion.
[8] Capt C. F. Williams, MC, SX10317; 2/48 Bn. Clerk; of Renmark, SA; b. Semaphore, SA, 20 Jan 1914. Killed in action 22 Jul 1942.
[9] Cpl J. Hinson, DCM, SX7429; 2/48 Bn. Trimmer; of Plympton, SA; b. Manchester, England, 5 Apr 1919. Killed in action 31 Oct 1942. In one of the tank attacks on the evening of the same day, Hinson placed a sticky grenade on one tank and took prisoner the crew of another knocked out by anti-tank fire.

bayonets fixed straight at two guns that were firing point-blank and whose crews did not surrender until the Australians were in the gun-pit. The companies reached the station, dug in and patrolled forward covered by

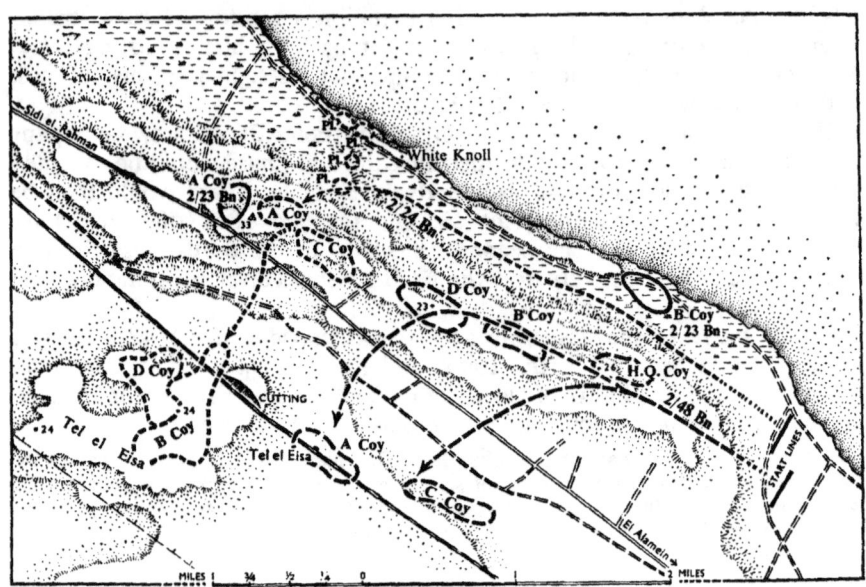

10th-12th July

the tank squadron until, about 9 a.m., six guns of the 2/3rd Anti-Tank Regiment arrived. About 40 dive bombers attacked Hammer's headquarters on Point 26 ridge at 9.45, but everyone was well dug in and there was only one casualty. There were five more dive-bombing attacks that day by from 30 to 40 aircraft but little damage was done.

In the approach march the trucks carrying the 2/24th also got bogged in soft sand some miles from the forming-up ground, but largely as a result of the drive and energy of their commanding officer, Lieut-Colonel Spowers, whose tall familiar figure inspired confidence in everyone, the troops reached the start-line ahead of time. At 4.30 a.m. the 2/24th's attack opened. There was little resistance until Point 26, already held by the 2/48th, had been passed on the left, but thereafter opposition increased. Throughout the advance Lieutenant McNamara's[1] platoon preceded the main body with the "commando role" of clearing the dunes of any enemy troops; the carrier platoon also ranged ahead. The carriers charged and overcame machine-gun posts and two anti-tank gun detachments whose Italian crews did not fire a shot.

At White Knoll a strong nest of machine-guns was encountered but was overcome by McNamara's men and the carriers, reinforced by a

---

[1] Capt J. F. McNamara, MC, VX30994; 2/24 Bn. Auctioneer; of Yarrawonga, Vic; b. Yarrawonga, 25 May 1909. Killed in action 8 Dec 1943.

platoon from the reserve company. By 6.35 the men were digging in on Trig 33, whence Lieutenant Bell[2] led his platoon forward and took four heavy guns and 100 Italian prisoners.

The plan provided that Captain Snell's[3] company, which had followed the main body from the start-line in trucks, should exploit to eastern Point 24, supported by two troops of tanks and by fire from a machine-gun platoon. Both tanks and machine-guns, however, were far to the rear, "hopelessly bogged" in the salt-marshes, so Spowers ordered the company to dig in on the reverse slope of Trig 33 and remain there. That afternoon at 5 o'clock 18 enemy tanks attacked across the salt-marsh to the west but most of them bogged and 14 were knocked out by anti-tank and artillery fire. Gunner McMahon[4] towed his gun into action forward of Trig 33 and, even after three of his crew had been wounded and he himself hit in the leg and hand, continued to fire. He destroyed two tanks. Nine more tanks appeared on the southern slopes of Trig 33 and five of these were knocked out by the anti-tank gunners. The 2/24th Battalion lost 6 killed and 22 wounded in the day and took more than 800 unwounded prisoners and much equipment.

The 2/48th were also counter-attacked by tanks, though in smaller numbers; five, which appeared south of the railway line at 11 a.m., drove off the tanks that had been supporting the battalion. There the infantry had to endure very heavy shell fire, from which they sheltered in trenches that could be dug only a few inches deep because the ground was so rocky.

At 11.30 a.m. the 9th Divisional Cavalry (Lieut-Colonel H. E. Bastin) set out astride the main road to exploit to Sidi el Rahman and return to El Alamein station, but on high ground north of Tel el Eisa station the leading squadron came under artillery fire and found themselves threatened by the tanks that were engaging the 2/48th. Three hours later a bombing attack destroyed a carrier and caused seven casualties. The regiment was withdrawn during the afternoon.

At 2.30 p.m. ten tanks again attacked towards the 2/48th positions near the railway and ran over some of the shallow trenches in which the men lay. When they had passed some of the men hurled sticky grenades at them. Sergeant Haynes[5] jumped out of his trench and planted a sticky grenade in a tank and then fell wounded. Fire from the field and anti-tank guns prevented the tanks from crossing the railway line and forced them back.

Thrice more the enemy tanks attacked, getting in amongst the slit trenches of both Bryant's and Williams' companies, but both companies, encouraged by the unflinching example of their commanders, held all their positions. On the last occasion the tanks reached the defenders' positions near the station, but withdrew after the anti-tank guns had

---
[2] Lt H. E. Y. Bell, MC, SX9328; 2/24 Bn. Share farmer; of Cummins, SA; b. Folkestone, England, 29 Jul 1912.
[3] Maj H. W. Snell, VX48636; 2/24 Bn. Manager; of Oakleigh, Vic; b. Leongatha, Vic, 17 Aug 1919.
[4] Bdr J. T. McMahon, DCM, NX40595; 2/3 A-Tk Regt. PMG linesman; of Narrabri, NSW; b. Narrabri, 24 Mar 1919.
[5] Sgt R. N. Haynes, SX8466; 2/48 Bn. Motor driver; of Hyde Park, SA; b. Mt Gambier, SA, 13 Dec 1919.

knocked out six of the ten. When one crew leaped out and sought to escape Sergeant Longhurst[6] of the 2/2nd Machine Gun Battalion tried to fire on them, but they were behind a slight rise. Longhurst then lifted the entire gun and tripod and, with the help of another man, brought fire to bear on the enemy, who promptly surrendered.[7]

Just before dusk, after two hours of shelling, the enemy mounted a further attack on the forward companies with both tanks and infantry. The tanks overran the forward posts of Williams' company on the right. Hammer had anticipated such an attack and had arranged for a counter-attack to be launched by a force, commanded by Major Tucker, of one company (Captain Shillaker's[8]) plus two platoons. Williams' company was in a critical position when the counter-attack went in at 8.30 p.m., but as soon as Captain Shillaker's company arrived it charged, firing from the hip, and forced the enemy back across the railway. In this counter-attack Sergeant Derrick,[9] who in the initial attack had led an assault on three machine-gun posts and captured many prisoners, attacked two tanks with sticky bombs and damaged them. When the fight was over Shillaker's company had lost only one man killed and one wounded but 13 were missing from Williams' company. By the next morning the 2/48th had suffered 39 casualties, but they had taken 89 German prisoners and 835 Italians and captured 27 guns of 35-mm to 75-mm calibre. In all the brigade knocked out 18 tanks and took 1,150 prisoners.

Farther south, on the 9th Division's left, the South Africans reached Tel el Makh Khad, cleared it of enemy and then withdrew to the Alamein Box.

The German command reacted sharply to the attack of XXX Corps. At the main headquarters of Rommel's army on the coast only a few miles to the west the "alarming news" was received that the *Sabratha Division* (whose infantry comprised only two regiments each of two battalions) had been put to flight. Lieut-Colonel von Mellenthin in charge at Rommel's headquarters was "startled to see hundreds of Italians rushing past the Headquarters in the final stages of panic and rout.... It was clear to me ... that *Sabratha* was finished[1]—their artillery was already 'in the bag'—and something must be done immediately to close the road to the west."[2] He collected "headquarters troops" which included machine-guns, anti-aircraft guns, and some infantry reinforcements who happened to arrive, to plug the gap, which he later strengthened with the main body of the *382nd Regiment* of the *164th Division*, which was in course of arriving by air.

Rommel himself, who was in the south at Qaret el Abd to superintend the launching that day of his renewed offensive to reach Cairo and had heard the drumming of guns in the north with foreboding, also acted quickly. "To restore the situation the Commander-in-Chief brought up a quickly-formed battle group of *15th Armoured Division* and his headquarters' battle group (Kiehl Group). This force was to attack

---

[6] Lt A. W. Longhurst, MM, NX25154; 2/2 MG Bn. Clerk; of Campbelltown, NSW; b. Campbelltown, 17 May 1917. Killed in action 15 Apr 1945.
[7] The weight of a Vickers gun and tripod was 94 pounds.
[8] Capt R. S. Shillaker, MC, SX10306; 2/48 Bn. Cadet engineer; of St Peters, SA; b. Henley Beach, SA, 26 Feb 1919.
[9] Lt T. C. Derrick, VC, DCM, SX7964; 2/48 Bn. Orchardist; of Berri, SA; b. Medindie, SA, 20 Mar 1914. Died of wounds 24 May 1945.
[1] Early in August a proposal to disband the *Sabratha Division* was being discussed but, at the request of the German High Command, it was retained on the order of battle. "In view of the experience gained in Russia," said a signal to Rommel's headquarters, "in order to fool the enemy intelligence service, even the most depleted division is not to be relieved."
[2] Mellenthin, p. 130.

the enemy's southern flank and cut him off from Alamein stronghold. The battle groups advanced to the attack about midday but made very slow progress owing to terrific shell-fire from Alamein stronghold."[3] Meanwhile the *Africa Corps* was told to make only a limited advance in the south. The two battle groups employed in the north had 15 or 16 German tanks.

Early on the 11th "Daycol", a raiding force built round a squadron of the 6th Royal Tanks, manning Stuarts, was sent out from the Alamein fortress towards Miteiriya Ridge to threaten the enemy's line of communications. The column included a troop of 6-pounders, a troop of 25-pounders and a troop of armoured cars, all British; the 57th Australian Field Battery, a platoon of the 2/2nd Machine Gun Battalion and a platoon plus four carriers of the 2/23rd Battalion. It left its start-line at 5.30 a.m. Half an hour later, just short of its objective, it came under fire from about two companies of infantry. These were swiftly overrun and 400 Italians surrendered. But in the early afternoon a heavy artillery duel developed and at 1.30 Daycol withdrew, having destroyed eight Italian field guns and other weapons and taken 1,024 prisoners.

At 4.30 a.m. that day the 2/24th set out to capture East Point 24 which it had been unable to secure in the attack made the day before. It had formidable support: the fire of three Australian field regiments and one South African, and of the 7th Medium Regiment, and the support of a squadron of the 44th Royal Tank Regiment with 8 Valentine tanks, which were to assist in the later stages. Captain Snell's company made the attack, reached the objective without a single casualty and took 500 prisoners. The tanks covered the company while it dug in. Thereafter the company was lashed with intense artillery and mortar fire and by the end of the day 25 men had been killed or wounded. At 6 p.m. Spowers decided to reinforce Snell. He appointed Major Budge to command all troops on Point 24 and at dusk sent Captain Monotti's[4] company forward. That day one company of the 2/23rd moved up to join the 2/24th and one joined the 2/48th.

All day the 2/48th had been under heavy shell fire but had toiled on, improving weapon-pits and laying mines. Every concentration of enemy troops had been dispersed by heavy and accurate artillery fire.

A danger faced by those moving about in the thinly-held battle area was starkly illustrated by a misadventure to a group of officers who were returning from a conference at the 26th Brigade's headquarters in the small hours of the 12th. This included Colonel Spowers who was returning to his battalion, Major Wheatley[5] of the 2/2nd Machine Gun Battalion, Lieutenant Mulgrue of the 2/3rd Anti-Tank Regiment and a driver, all in a jeep. They did not arrive at their destination and next day examination of the jeep's tracks showed that the driver, who had been following a track at the edge of the sand dunes fronting the sea-shore, instead of turning off to the left just east of battalion headquarters, had continued

---

[3] Battle report of the *Armoured Army of Africa*.
[4] Capt F. R. Monotti, VX48808; 2/24 Bn. Articled law clerk; of Bendigo, Vic; b. St. Arnaud, Vic, 15 Feb 1917.
[5] Maj M. I. Wheatley, NX12343; 2/2 MG Bn. Grazier; of Camden, NSW; b. Goulburn, NSW, 7 Apr 1915.

on into enemy territory. Later it was learnt that all had become prisoners. Three nights later Captain Tivey[6] of the 2/23rd Battalion drove into enemy territory at the same point and was captured.

The battle report of the *Armoured Army of Africa* gives the German version of the XXX Corps' operations on the 11th including those of the 2/24th Battalion against Point 24:

> Early next morning the enemy again attacked after a very heavy preliminary bombardment. In this attack two *Bersaglieri* strongpoints, which had held firm the previous day, fell very soon. A battalion of *Trieste* which was committed to plug a gap was overrun and wiped out. This made the situation so serious that almost the whole of the army artillery had to be committed in the northern sector. Before evening all the other battalions of the *Trieste Division* were brought forward to the Point 21 area to seal off the advance. Reconnaissance Detachment 3 was moved into the area south-west of Point 23[7] to prevent the enemy from breaking through to the west. "I was compelled to order every last German soldier out of his tent or rest camp up to the front," Rommel wrote later, "for, in face of the virtual default of a large proportion of our Italian fighting power, the situation was beginning to take on crisis proportions."[8]

On 11th July Rommel decided to smash the British penetration with a strong counter-stroke using the *21st Armoured Division*. He brought the division up from the south on the 12th and decided to capture the Alamein Box next day and cut off the Australians on Tel el Eisa. "The attack was to be supported by every gun and every aeroplane we could muster."[9]

In the meantime Auchinleck, noting that Rommel was transferring armour to the north, set in train preparations for an attack from the south and centre in the Ruweisat Ridge region similar to the operation which had been in contemplation when the 24th Brigade's raid in that sector was being planned. The staff of Eighth Army, however, did not know that although one of the enemy's armoured divisions and about 30 German tanks (approximately two-thirds of the total German tank strength) were in the north, the bulk of his armoured forces were still in the south under the firm command of the *Africa Corps* (Lieut-General Nehring) and poised to undertake the projected offensive as soon as the detachments in the north returned.

On the 12th the 9th Division enjoyed freedom from ground attack until the late afternoon but suffered artillery bombardment of mounting intensity as the afternoon wore on, particularly on the ridges of Hill 33. About 6 p.m. German infantry attacked in waves along the whole of the front of the 2/24th Battalion, of which Major Budge had assumed command, but were met by sustained artillery fire from the 2/8th Field Regiment and British howitzers. Captain Anderson's company of the 2/23rd Battalion, with which the 2/24th had been reinforced, bore the brunt of the attack, fighting from exposed ground forward of Trig 33.

---

[6] Maj E. P. Tivey, VX15648. 2/23 Bn; LO 26 Bde. Stockbroker; of Melbourne; b. Melbourne, 10 Mar 1909. Died 26 Mar 1943.

[7] For Point 23 read Point 24. German maps commonly gave spot heights as one metre lower than the current British maps. So did some older vintage British maps.

[8] *The Rommel Papers*, p. 253.

[9] *The Rommel Papers*, p. 254.

Private Buckingham,[1] maintaining fire though with little cover, had first one and then another Bren gun shot out of his hands. Corporal Knight[2] of the 2/2nd Machine Gun Battalion played a gallant part which inspired the men fighting from their shallow pits around him. Knight and his men carried their guns forward under fire to an exposed position on top of the hill. There they blazed away at the enemy, Knight often standing nonchalantly in front of his gun positions to pick out targets. He moved his guns seven times; nor were they ever pin-pointed by the enemy. But there were many casualties in the company and Anderson was mortally wounded when his trench was hit.

By 9 p.m. the attack—by Germans of the *104th Lorried Infantry Regiment*—had died down. It was estimated that they left 600 dead and that the machine-gun platoon had accounted for most of them. Captain Harding[3] took over command from Anderson and for the next five days led this battered company in most resolute defence of its vital ground.

On the morning of the 13th the 26th Brigade was warned to expect a strong attack by the *21st Armoured Division*. Rommel's plan for the day, however, was not to overrun the Australians but to cut them off by enveloping their rear, and although East Point 24 withstood two assaults with the aid of the concentrated artillery fire of five regiments, the main onslaught was made on the South African division south of the Alamein Box. As before, the South Africans held their ground.

On this day of anxiety the 9th Division received an order to move south to a position south-east of Jebel Bein Gabir, leaving the 26th Brigade under the South African division, but next day, after preliminary reconnaissances and moves, the order was countermanded: only the 20th Brigade was to go. The reason for these orders was not known then at divisional headquarters, but they resulted from Auchinleck's preparations for a renewed thrust in the centre of the front along the Ruweisat Ridge. Auchinleck's headquarters, the location of which was kept secret and never shown on any map, was to the rear of the chosen area for attack, and thus vulnerable should an enemy counter-thrust succeed in piercing the British front. The locality to which the 20th Brigade was to move was one of the mined defensive areas known as "boxes" and was just to the rear of Auchinleck's headquarters.

Rommel ordered the *21st Armoured Division* to attack the Australians again on the 14th. The night of the 13th-14th brought signs that an onslaught was coming: the forward troops reported infantry and guns moving into position and the artillery fired on many targets. In midmorning of the 14th enemy infantry edged closer to the cutting area and to the southern slopes of Trig 33 and three German tanks came up near Captain Mollard's[4] company of the 2/24th to cover a party of engineers

---

[1] Pte E. L. Buckingham, VX47187; 2/23 Bn. Presser; of Malvern, Vic; b. Wonthaggi, Vic, 9 Apr 1920.
[2] WO1 V. H. Knight, DCM, NX16912; 2/2 MG Bn. 3 Bn RAR, Korea. Ship's storekeeper; of Sydney; b. London, 9 Feb 1915.
[3] Capt W. C. Harding, MC, VX38918; 2/23 Bn. Designer; of West Preston, Vic; b. Johannesburg, South Africa, 11 Mar 1913. Killed in action 22 Jul 1942.
[4] Maj K. F. Mollard, DSO, VX48771. 2/24 and 2/32 Bns, "Z" Special Unit. Oil company representative; of Lae, NG; b. Melbourne, 20 May 1915.

who set about lifting the minefield. The infantry weapons could not counter the standover tactics of the tanks and no anti-tank guns were able to bring effective fire to bear on the German tanks in the positions where they had halted. Defensive artillery fire was called down, which was probably effective since the attack was not further pressed for some time. In mid-afternoon, however, and again as night fell, German infantry and tanks, using close infiltration tactics, attacked the two companies on East Point 24, the tanks crumbling the weapon-pits when they could. One incident must suffice to illustrate the spirit in which the defence was conducted. When two Bren-gunners were crushed in their pit, Private Dwyer[5] leapt up and, while the fire-fight was at its height, dug them out in plain view of the enemy. The first attack was repelled by keeping the upper hand in the fire-fight—the tanks were kept closed up, one commander who poked his head up to have a look being promptly shot dead—and the defenders hung on against the second attack until night blinded the tanks and action ceased. Budge, realising that in their isolation and with flanks exposed the two depleted companies could not withstand sustained attack, ordered their withdrawal at 9.30 p.m., and having no transport they came out on foot. The anti-tank gunners took the breech-blocks from their guns; later they returned with towing vehicles and brought the guns out.

Some of the German tanks engaged in the attack on Point 24 afterwards moved across the front of the forward companies of the 2/48th about Tel el Eisa station. Failing to draw fire, eight of the tanks crossed the railway line and advanced on Point 26. They were then engaged by field guns, swung west to avoid this fire and came within close range of two Australian anti-tank guns. A brisk fire-fight developed in which all neighbouring infantry joined. Some tanks burst into flames and the rest soon withdrew. The 2/3rd Anti-Tank Regiment reported having destroyed seven of them in quick succession; four of these were hit by Sergeant Digby's[6] gun and three by Bombardier Muffett's.[7] Tanks of the 1st Army Tank Brigade were hurried forward ready to give support next morning. Dawn revealed ten burnt-out German tanks left on the battlefield.

Rommel had intended to renew the attack on Tel el Eisa in some strength on the 15th but the attack launched by Auchinleck on Ruweisat Ridge forced him to reduce the scale of the assault. Auchinleck's general intention, as stated in his orders, was to break through the enemy's centre and destroy the enemy forces deployed north of Ruweisat Ridge and east of the El Alamein-Abu Dweis track. The XXX Corps was to take the eastern part of the ridge, then attack southward from Tel el Eisa and take the Miteiriya Ridge. The XIII Corps was to advance by night to Trig 63 at the western end of the ridge and then exploit to the northwest. On the 14th it was decided to make the attacks that night; the two corps were ordered to reach their objectives by 4.30 a.m. on the 15th.

---

[5] Pte A. J. Dwyer, MM, VX52935; 2/24 Bn. Labourer; of West Coburg, Vic; b. Coburg, 24 Aug 1919.

[6] WO2 K. N. W. Digby, WX10078; 2/3 A-Tk Regt. Clerk; of York, WA; b. Kellerberrin, WA, 22 Oct 1920.

[7] Sgt A. J. Muffett, NX33750; 2/3 A-Tk Regt. Dairyman; of Scone, NSW; b. Coonabarabran, NSW, 5 Mar 1920.

The orders of the XIII Corps and 1st Armoured Division giving effect to this clear if over-simplified directive had enunciated more limited objectives and purposes, however, and had discarded as though it had been useless or pious embroidery, the statement of the broad intention which should have given impulse and cohesion to the forces operating. Conferences had been held but had not produced a common understanding of how the formations were to work together. The New Zealanders thought that they had a promise of close and firm armoured support when they got on their objective, whereas General Lumsden's understanding seems to have been that the armour need not come up unless nor until there was a call for its assistance. The two armoured brigades were not told to get up on the New Zealand division's flanks but only to be prepared to move. As the New Zealand historian has commented:

> Moreover, the instruction to both brigades that they "will be prepared to move" implied a waiting role and allowed the brigade commanders a discretion which, with fateful consequences, they exercised in the operation.[8]

In the XXX Corps sector the assault was made by the 5th Indian Brigade. The leading battalion was held up east of Trig 63 and the second, which had come under very heavy fire, had to retire.

The 2nd New Zealand Division made the attack in the XIII Corps sector with its 5th Brigade on the right and 4th on the left. Setting out at 11 p.m. it reached minefields a little after midnight and soon the men were under machine-gun fire and illuminated by enemy flares. They pressed on leaving many posts—more than they knew—to be mopped up later. Shortly before dawn the 5th Brigade was on its objective but with its left battalion in some confusion; the 4th Brigade had reached its objective on the left but was also somewhat scattered. At dawn the New Zealanders were awaiting the arrival of the tanks of the 22nd Armoured Brigade, but both this brigade and the 2nd which was to support the Indians were well to the rear awaiting orders.

Among the enemy troops inadvertently bypassed by the New Zealanders were about eight tanks of the *8th Armoured Regiment*. In the half-light of dawn, these came in on the 22nd New Zealand Battalion, which at first mistook them for the expected British tanks, and attacked. Eventually, after a fierce fight between German tanks and New Zealand anti-tank gunners, about 350 New Zealanders were taken prisoner.

In the morning, General Nehring commanding the *Africa Corps* and in charge on the southern front reported the attack at Deir el Shein to Rommel, who ordered German units to converge on the area of penetration: the *3rd Reconnaissance Unit* and a battle group of 100 infantry (with supporting arms) of the *21st Armoured Division* from the north and the Baade Group (a battle group of 200 riflemen with supporting artillery) and *33rd Reconnaissance Unit* from the south. At 5 p.m., the group from the north and the *33rd Reconnaissance Unit*, together with tanks at hand of the *15th Armoured Division*, opened a counter-attack.

---

[8] Scoullar, p. 223.

The Baade Group failed to get to the battle. The New Zealanders were too thin on the ground to cope with the onslaught and the British tanks behind them were still awaiting orders. The New Zealand 4th Brigade was overrun. At 6.35 p.m. some tanks of the 2nd Armoured Brigade went

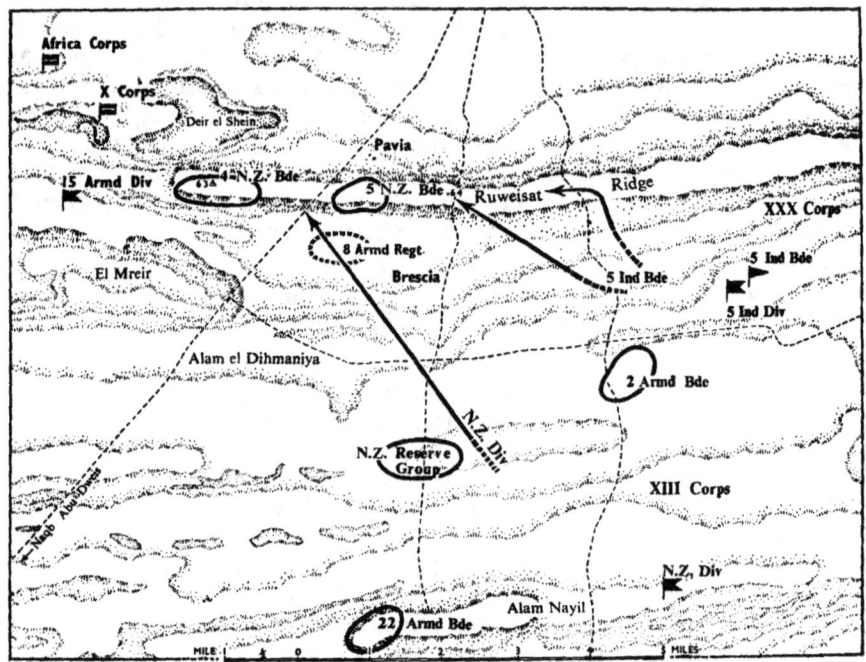

The attack on Ruweisat Ridge, 14th-15th July

forward to the edge of the battle and gave some support. At 10 p.m. General Gott of XIII Corps authorised Inglis to withdraw to a line from Trig 63 to a position south-west of Alam el Dihmaniya. The New Zealand division's exposure to the German armour and the failure of British armoured brigades (whose tank strength so greatly exceeded that of the Germans) to be there alongside to give battle left an aftermath of bitterness and distrust of the armour and also of the commanders responsible.

Up to a point the British attack had been a brilliant success. Some 2,000 men of the *Brescia* and *Pavia* had surrendered, and in Rommel's words the "line south-east of Deir el Shein collapsed"; but the success was not exploited and Nehring's prompt counter-attack turned it into a costly reverse. The 2nd New Zealand Division lost 1,405 killed, wounded or missing.

> The fundamental fault was the failure to co-ordinate infantry and armour (wrote Brigadier Kippenberger later). . . . The attitude of the armour commanders at that period was not helpful, but I do not think we of the infantry did nearly as much as we could or should have done to ensure that we fought the battle together.[9]

---

[9] H. K. Kippenberger, *Infantry Brigadier* (1949), pp. 173-4.

Meanwhile the 20th Brigade Group (Brigadier Windeyer) had moved on the afternoon of the 15th to the defensive positions close to General Auchinleck's tactical headquarters. Late that night a liaison officer from Eighth Army was sent to Windeyer's headquarters with orders that the brigade was to move at 5.30 a.m. next morning in three battalion groups, each in mobile box formation, to a position (Mubarik Tomb) behind the 5th Indian Division, against which an enemy counter-attack was expected. There the brigade formed next morning a hastily improvised and dangerously exposed defence line. These orders were given without Morshead's knowledge. When Morshead learnt what had occurred, he telephoned General Auchinleck and said that he was dumbfounded that Auchinleck should have done this; it was opposed to their agreement, he said, and opposed to Morshead's charter. Auchinleck agreed to return the brigade, but soon afterwards sent news that he was being attacked heavily, whereupon Morshead agreed that the return of the brigade should be deferred, but asked to have it back as soon as possible. The brigade was released and returned to the 9th Division on the 17th.

On the 15th the 26th Australian Brigade had been fairly heavily engaged when Rommel resumed the attack with the forces left to him after sending reinforcements to Nehring. During the night of the 14th-15th patrols of the 2/48th could hear German voices and the engines of vehicles on their front near Tel el Eisa railway station. These were fired on, and in the morning it was discovered that 15 German vehicles were close to the wire and two machine-guns and two anti-tank guns had been established at or near the railway station. There was a sharp fight in which 32 Germans were captured and others killed. The vehicles were captured but later destroyed after the ammunition and equipment they contained had been salvaged. That night a patrol from the neighbouring company of the 2/48th had attacked a German party lifting the minefield, taking seven prisoners.

Meanwhile in front of the 2/24th Battalion dawn on the 15th had revealed 10 enemy tanks and infantry in 70 troop carriers approaching Trig 33. At 7.30 a.m. after an intense artillery barrage an attack was made by some 35 tanks and about seven companies of infantry. The tanks came up to the foot of Trig 33 and fourteen tanks reached that feature but the following infantry were driven back by the 2/24th and later the tanks withdrew to dead ground. At 8.15 a.m. there was a second attack from the north with 25 tanks and this too was beaten off with the help of a counter-attack by light tanks of the 44th Tank Regiment. A third attack without tanks was repulsed after about half an hour's fighting. A fourth attack by both tanks and infantry at midday was broken up by artillery and machine-gun fire. Ten German tanks were destroyed in the day and the Australians took 63 prisoners.

At 4.15 a.m. on the 15th the *5th Armoured Regiment* was ordered to continue the attack against the Australians with such sub-units as were available. The *II/104th Battalion* advanced across the railway north-west of the cutting at 5.50 and at 8 o'clock 12 tanks of the *5th* began thrusting from the west north of the railway and by 2 p.m. reported that it had reoccupied the "former positions" but was being prevented by artillery fire from moving up heavy weapons.[1]

Later that afternoon this advance had to be broken off and the *5th Armoured Regiment* moved south-east to meet the attack "south-east of the El Alamein Box" leaving one battalion of the *104th Regiment* to hold on in the northern sector. The *5th* was ordered to attack in the south-east at 4.30 on the 16th.

That night plans were made to recapture the double Point 24 feature next morning (the 16th) with two companies of the 2/23rd and five tanks. The attack succeeded brilliantly at first. Captain Cromie's[2] company with two troops of the 8th R.T.R. set out at 5.20 a.m. At the railway cutting an enemy post brought two forward sections under heavy fire at close range. Lance-Corporal Bell[3] promptly led his section to a firing position on the flank and himself moved out under fire and attacked the post with grenades and sub-machine-gun. Bell and his men swiftly silenced the post, which was manned by 30 Germans. By 6.30 a.m. Cromie's company had taken East Point 24.

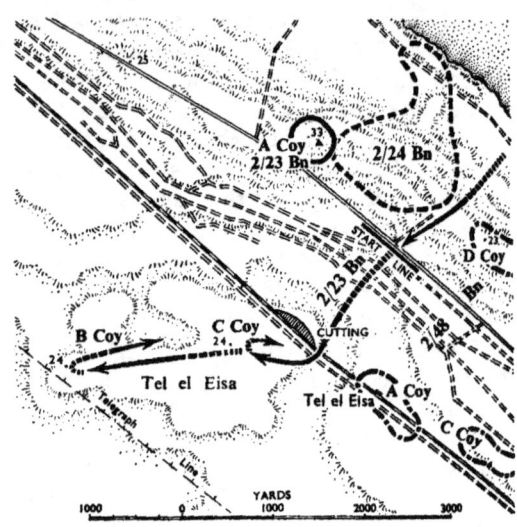

Captain Neuendorf's[4] company passed through Cromie's with three troops of the 44th R.T.R. and advanced under continuous shell, mortar and small-arms fire. Neuendorf, wounded in the hand, advanced calmly in front of his men exhorting them and controlling movement, keeping his company never more than 50 yards behind the leading tanks; when he ordered his men to lie he would remain standing. By 7.45 a.m. West Point 24 had been taken. On the objective, Neuendorf went through a belt of fire to give first aid to a wounded man and, while returning, was killed by a shell. The attackers had taken 601 prisoners of whom 41 were Germans, including three colonels, one a German.

The two companies were at once subjected to intense and accurate artillery, mortar and machine-gun fire and soon 90 of the 200 men engaged had been killed or wounded. The prisoners were all sent back and, at

---

[1] The only "former positions" that could have been occupied by the tanks that afternoon were on the double Point 24 feature south of the railway. There was no tank penetration that afternoon of the 9th Division's territory.

[2] Capt R. C. Cromie, VX43892; 2/23 Bn. Wheat farmer; of Rupanyup, Vic; b. Rupanyup, 25 Mar 1914. Killed in action 22 Jul 1942.

[3] Sgt J. W. Bell, MM, VX42867; 2/23 Bn. Labourer; of Merino, Vic; b. Ballarat, Vic, 2 Aug 1916.

[4] Capt K. O. Neuendorf, VX48799; 2/23 Bn. Clerk; of Auburn, Vic; b. Royal Park, Vic, 13 May 1918. Killed in action 16 Jul 1942. (His twin brother, Lt T. O. Neuendorf of the 2/23 Bn, had been taken prisoner on 17 May 1941.)

11.30, Lieut-Colonel Evans, after moving about the whole area to see for himself, ordered a withdrawal because the area was commanded by the enemy and he could perceive no tactical value[5] in it, he had no artillery support or Vickers guns, no anti-tank guns had arrived and casualties were mounting. The withdrawal "was carried out in a most soldierly and able manner without further casualties".

The 2/23rd Battalion's attack overran the sole remaining battalion of the *Sabratha Division* and a portion of a German battalion (*I/382nd Infantry Regiment*). The new situation, which the *Africa Corps* reported as "critical" at 7.25 a.m., caused Rommel to send for reinforcements from the *Africa Corps* in the south, which was just starting operations to exploit its victory at Ruweisat. From the south came the *33rd Reconnaissance Battalion*, the Briehl Group from *90th Light Division* and a battalion of the *104th Regiment*. At 9.50 a.m. the *21st Armoured Division* reported that flanking fire from the right made an advance impossible. At 1.40 p.m. the division ordered the *5th Armoured Regiment* in the south to go over to the defensive. The commander of the *104th* now had under command his *I* and *III Battalions* and also the recently-arrived *382nd Regiment* (of the *164th Division*), so that a formidable force of armour and infantry had been assembled round Tel el Eisa to envelop Evans' two companies.

This action marked the end of the first phase of the 9th Division's operations, in which one brigade, without heavy loss to itself, had taken and held the high ground west of the El Alamein fortress and north of the railway, inflicted about 2,000 casualties on the enemy and taken 3,708 prisoners.

The price paid by the Germans and Italians was exacted very largely by the accuracy and intensity of our artillery and machine-gun support (said the divisional report). This was the first time that the divisional artillery and machine-guns had fought beside their own infantry and for most it was their baptism of fire. . . . This was the first occasion on which direct air support was available to the division. . . .

The divisional artillery was under the command of Brigadier Ramsay whom we previously saw in command of the artillery at Mersa Matruh. Ramsay had served in the ranks of the artillery in the first A.I.F., had been commissioned after the armistice and by 1930 was commanding a field regiment (then still named a "field brigade"). When war broke out he was commanding the artillery of a division; he dropped a step in rank to form the 2/2nd Field Regiment and before coming to the 9th Division had been in command of the medium artillery of the corps. He was a schoolmaster and university lecturer and destined to fill the most senior posts his branch of the teaching profession offered.

The 9th Division was not to be permitted to rest. The thrustful Auchinleck had decided to relieve enemy pressure in the centre at Ruweisat by attacking next day on each flank. The northern blow was to be delivered by the 24th Australian Brigade, attacking with two battalions forward: it

---

[5] The downs south of the railway extending from the double Point 24 feature back to the Qattara Track region had some tactical importance in that if held by the enemy the salient north of the railway was dangerously narrow. An isolated lodgment on Point 24, however, was an embarrassing and weakening commitment.

was to capture Makh Khad Ridge and then exploit southwards for about 5,000 yards towards Ruin Ridge. The 2/32nd Battalion was to take Trig 22 (Makh Khad Ridge) in a silent night attack, and at dawn the 2/43rd was to pass through, followed by a squadron of Valentines of the 44th R.T.R., and capture Ruin Ridge 5,000 yards farther south. The tanks of the 44th plus a squadron of the 9th Divisional Cavalry with Crusader tanks were to protect the left flank and if necessary to assist at Trig 22. The attack was to be supported by the combined artillery of the 9th Australian and 1st South African Divisions and two British artillery regiments.

The 2/32nd Battalion which had the opening role had been commanded since February 1942 by Lieut-Colonel Whitehead, who had previously been in command of the 2/2nd Machine Gun Battalion, which he had formed and taken overseas. Whitehead had been commissioned in the regular army in 1916 and had served in France where in 1917 and 1918 he had commanded a machine-gun company. Staff service followed until 1922 when, in common with other outstanding young officers, he resigned from a service that seemed to offer few prospects and became a businessman. He served on in the militia and in 1939 was commanding a light horse machine-gun regiment.

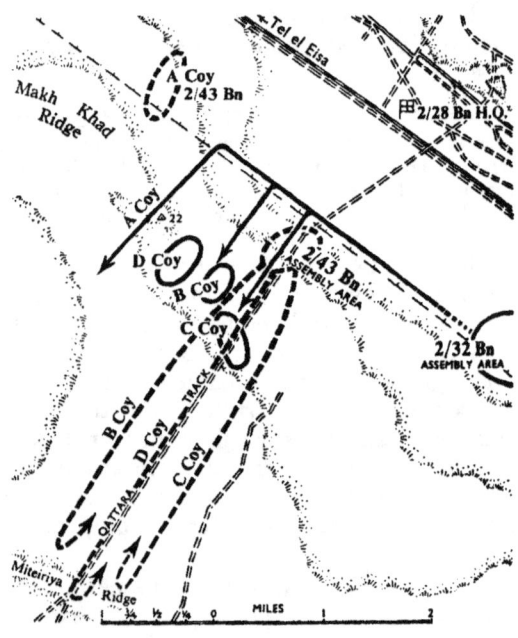

The 2/32nd attacked with three companies forward. They left the forming-up place at 2.30 a.m. on the 17th and within a quarter of an hour were under fire from artillery, mortars and machine-guns. The commander of the right company (Captain Forwood[6]) reported at 5.15 that he thought he had overshot the objective—Trig 22. (In fact he was a good 1,500 yards beyond it to the south-west.) The centre and left companies secured their objectives. The battalion had taken some 160 prisoners. The three companies were on a front of 2,500 yards with gaps between them and there were strong enemy forces between Forwood's company and Trig 22 where anti-tank guns and Lieutenant Cameron's[7] platoon of the 2/2nd Machine Gun

---

[6] Capt K. B. Forwood, SX5005; 2/32 Bn. Draftsman; of Adelaide; b. Albany, WA, 30 Dec 1909.
[7] Lt-Col R. W. Cameron, DSO, ED, QX6262. 2/2 MG Bn; HQ 9 Div. Bank officer; of Brisbane; b. Brisbane, 12 Dec 1916.

Battalion had been established. By 7 a.m. the crest of Trig 22 had been lost. Whitehead ordered his fourth rifle company, less a platoon, to counter-attack, and by 7.45 it had regained the crest. At 8.45 the objectives were all secure. The squadron of the 9th Divisional Cavalry protecting the 2/32nd's right, which was commanded by Captain Fyffe[8] and had 7 tanks and 15 carriers, manoeuvred under direct enemy observation and anti-tank fire and knocked out some anti-tank guns and machine-gun posts. This was the regiment's first tank action.

Meanwhile the 2/43rd (Lieut-Colonel Wain) had moved through at 6 a.m. on a two-company front with a third company 500 yards in rear astride the Qattara track. The leading companies advanced at the rate of 100 yards to the minute under severe shelling and reached Ruin Ridge about 7 a.m. The left company (Captain Gordon[9]) met strong resistance and had to fight its way through extensive enemy positions in broken ground. In the left section all were wounded except Private Dean[1] who fought on alone with a Bren and eventually rejoined his platoon 1,000 yards farther on. Gordon's company took 400 prisoners. When it reached its objective on Ruin Ridge at 7.3 a.m. it found that 19 enemy guns were firing across its front from only 300 yards away. Gordon led out the left platoon and some men of company headquarters and captured the gun positions, taking 150 more prisoners and damaging or destroying three of the guns; they could not destroy the rest unless they were to use up all their anti-tank grenades, which they refrained from doing, knowing that enemy tanks were around.

The right company (Captain Hare[2]) advanced 2,500 yards across ground torn by shell fire before meeting with small-arms fire from an enemy position. The troops marched on, firing from the hip, and the enemy surrendered. About 1,000 yards farther on machine-guns and an anti-tank gun were encountered. The Australians attacked from a flank and about 50 Italians ceased firing and stood up; the anti-tank gun fired two more rounds, whereupon its gunner was killed. When the objective was secured seven tanks and about 400 other vehicles could be seen beyond. Corporal Yendall[3] went forward alone under observation by the enemy, pinpointing the enemy's position and directing his platoon's fire on to it.

From 7.10 onwards the company was attacked by tanks and infantry; but the 2/43rd now had no anti-tank gun support and ammunition was running low. The field artillery could not help because communications had broken down. Colonel Wain proposed an advance against a collection of enemy vehicles and guns 800 yards to the front, but the squadron of the 44th R.T.R. had only six tanks left and its commander said that he

---

[8] Capt H. G. Fyffe, MC, VX42774. 9 Cav Regt; 2/9 Cav (Cdo) Regt. Grazier; of Tocumwal, NSW; b. Melbourne, 20 Mar 1908.
[9] Lt-Col J. D. Gordon, MC, SX9822; 2/43 Bn. Warehouseman; of Grange, SA; b. London, 15 Apr 1918.
[1] Cpl H. J. Dean, MM, SX5282; 2/43 Bn. Butcher; of Minnipa, SA; b. Kadina, SA, 14 Sep 1908. Killed in action 2 Oct 1943.
[2] Capt A. I. Hare, MC, SX8897; 2/43 Bn. Schoolteacher; of St Peters, SA; b. Ballarat, Vic, 3 Mar 1908. Killed in action 1 Nov 1942.
[3] Sgt G. L. Yendall, SX6259; 2/43 Bn. Farmer; of Ceduna, SA; b. Nairne, SA, 26 May 1904. Corporal O. R. Yendall, a younger brother, had been killed at Tobruk the previous year. Two other Yendall brothers were serving with the 2/43rd.

could not support an advance. Wain therefore, with Godfrey's concurrence, ordered a withdrawal which eventually placed the 2/43rd on the Makh Khad Ridge on the left flank of the 2/32nd. The 2/43rd had destroyed 13 guns and 12 machine-guns and three heavy mortars.

The action around Trig 22 was meanwhile intensifying. The enemy began to shell the ridge heavily a quarter of an hour after the 2/32nd had recaptured the crest. Air-burst shells proved specially lethal; the diggings were so shallow, and without head-cover. At 10 a.m. tanks and armoured cars attacked but were driven off by fire from 2-pounders and a captured Breda manned by Corporal Leeson, who knocked out three vehicles before the enemy shot his gun out of action and wounded him. Leeson repaired the gun and remained to fight on, engaging vehicles and low-flying aircraft.

Mounting pressure necessitated some withdrawals and re-locations but the front was stabilised, except for a post the enemy had succeeded in establishing on Trig 22, and the 2/32nd was in touch with the 2/43rd on its left. In the evening Brigadier Godfrey gave Whitehead permission to reorganise on a line covering the track that followed the telegraph poles and linking with the 2/43rd's positions astride the Qattara track.

The 24th Brigade had taken 736 prisoners who included men from both infantry regiments of the *Trento Division,* from one regiment of the *Trieste,* and from the *7th Bersaglieri Regiment* (corps troops). It had achieved more that day than the local tactical importance of the ground taken would signify. The operation had far-reaching effects.

"Early that morning," wrote the diarist of the *Armoured Army of Africa,* "2 strong battle groups of both brigades[4] of 9th Australian Division attacked south-west along the Qattara track from the area Makh Khad . . . overran the right wing of *Trieste Division* and the *Bersaglieri* strongpoint of *XXI Corps* and pushed forward quickly to area north of Sanyet el Miteiriya. A strong force had to be brought up from the central sector to seal off this penetration. . . . *Panzerarmee* was thus forced to abandon its attempt to win back *X Corps* old positions in the central sector."

The 24th Brigade's attack had pierced the fronts of the *Trento* and *Trieste Divisions.* The former had lost an artillery unit, the latter a battalion. But Rommel had at hand the reserves he had called for after the 2/23rd Battalion's attack on the preceding day and at once sent in the *33rd Reconnaissance Unit,* part of the *3rd,* and a battalion of the mobile Baade Group (detached from *104th Infantry Regiment*), with the Briehl Group in support. Of no less importance, he summoned up more troops and ordered Nehring to go over to the defensive. The *90th Light Division* was told to withdraw an infantry regiment from its front and send it north. The divisional commander decided that he could not pull out a whole regiment but dispatched the *1/361st* northward at 3.15 p.m.

On the 17th the enemy round Tel el Eisa was not happy although the 26th Brigade was not pressing hard. The *5th Armoured* and *104th Regiments* were withdrawn to their positions of the previous day and in the course of this move the *II/104th Battalion* lost heavily and was greatly dispersed.

Rommel wrote to his wife that day: "The enemy is using his superiority, especially in infantry, to destroy the Italian formations one by one, and the German formations are much too weak to stand alone. It's enough to make one weep."[5]

---

[4] The German command believed that the division had four battalions at El Alamein and two in the "Amiriya positions".
[5] *The Rommel Papers,* p. 257.

Thus for the third time the 9th Division's aggression had caused the enemy to call off an intended thrust at the centre.

About 5 p.m. on the 17th enemy tanks launched a stronger attack than hitherto against the junction of the two Australian battalions. The defence on the 2/32nd front was encouraged by the outstanding gunnery of Lance-Sergeant Daley[6] who, though twice wounded, kept his gun in action and knocked out six tanks. But two forward platoons of the 2/32nd's left company were overrun, 22 men were taken prisoner and the two battalions lost contact. In the words of the brigade report, "an ugly situation seemed to be developing"; but a stable line was soon formed about 1,500 yards farther back along the telegraph line with the Qattara track marking the junction of the two units.

At 7.10 p.m. Major D. R. Jackson, Godfrey's brigade major, returned from the forward battalions with news that the front was firm. Thereupon Godfrey ordered Major Cox, acting in command of the 2/28th, to attack that night and regain positions from which the other battalions had just withdrawn.

The 2/28th had only three rifle companies available — one was escorting prisoners. The three moved off on a front of 1,000 yards at 12.20 a.m. on the 18th and reached the objective about 1.30 a.m. They encountered only a few enemy infantry, and one tank, which was destroyed. The battalion had two men wounded. By 5 p.m. sappers commanded by Lieutenant Murray[7] of the 2/7th Field Company working under small-arms and artillery fire—"pretty hot conditions", wrote the diarist—had laid 2,500 mines across the front and added more during the night of the 18th-19th.[8]

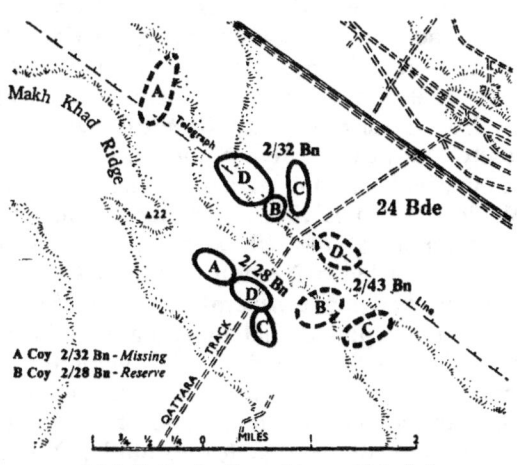

24th Brigade dispositions, 18th July

The brigade was now in a triangular formation with 2/28th as the apex and with the other two battalions based on the line of the telegraph posts. It was not the best of dispositions because Point 22 jutted in between the right flank of the 2/28th and the front of the 2/32nd. Obviously further moves would have to be made, and at sunrise on July 18th a carrier patrol was sent out by 2/28th to seek further information. This patrol found the Spandau which was still firing its occasional bursts. It was sited inside a minefield and was manned by a lone German—a giant of a man

---
[6] Sgt D. A. Daley, DCM, NX40585; 2/3 A-Tk Regt. Station hand; of Biniguy, NSW; b. Moree, NSW, 6 Aug 1916. Died 20 Aug 1949.
[7] Maj E. D. Murray, MC, QX19162. 2/7 Fd Coy; GSO2 (Engrs) War Office 1944-45. Engineering student; of Blackall, Qld; b. Blackall, 29 May 1919.
[8] A common practice at this time was to lay out belts of mines on the surface immediately an objective was taken to check any immediate tank counter-attack. They would be buried as soon afterwards as practicable.

whose face was set in an expression of grim determination as he maintained the principle of defence to the last man and the last round.

The carrier patrol also discovered that a German reconnaissance party in tanks and armoured cars was making a study of Makh Khad Ridge. A few minutes later the first airburst shell detonated above the 2/28th, and for the remainder of the day there was little respite. The battalion suffered more casualties on July 18th from 88-millimetre airburst than it had done from artillery shelling during its entire six months in Tobruk.[9]

Although there were exchanges of fire on the 18th, the enemy did not attack.[1]

By the 18th the *15th Armoured Division* had only 9 serviceable tanks, the *21st* only 19. The *90th Light Division* was ordered to move into the northern sector. Its diarist recorded that, owing to the "complete collapse" of the *Brescia, Trieste, Sabratha* and *Pavia Divisions,* "a temporary crisis" had arisen.

On the evening of the 17th the 2/48th Battalion had staged a diversion aimed at disrupting the enemy's preparations on Tel el Eisa Ridge. At dusk three sections of carriers set out, under Sergeant Jacka,[2] crossed the railway line near the station, drove to East 24, on to West 24, and then returned. Artillery and machine-guns and mortars fired in support throughout the raid and the carriers spent 3,400 rounds engaging several posts, some from a range of only 40 yards. During the raid there was only one casualty, but at the rallying point on their return one section ran into its own minefield suffering six casualties and damage to three carriers.

While the 9th Division had been attacking in the Makh Khad Ridge area, columns of the 7th Armoured Division in the far south, though endowed with but a fraction of the XXX Corps' weight of numbers and fire-power, had made several offensive thrusts and won some successes. The division reported that the enemy was thinning out in that region.

Adhering to the principle of envelopment from either flank, General Auchinleck issued an order on the evening of the 17th calling for a renewal of the flank attacks about the end of the month and for constant pressure meanwhile in all sectors; for example, XXX Corps was to destroy the Italians on its front. Next day, however, he issued a very different order. Now he planned to attack as soon as possible—about 21st July—at the centre, in the Ruweisat Ridge region, where the German main strength lay, with cooperating thrusts in the south against the left flank and into the enemy's rear. The XIII Corps would break through at Deir el Shein, Deir el Abyad and Buweibat el Raml and thrust westward; then the fleeing enemy was to be pursued to Daba and Fuka. Simultaneously, to prevent the enemy from concentrating against the main thrust, the XXX Corps was to mount a new offensive in the north. In the few ensuing days before the army struck, much of the staff's time was taken up with elaborate planning for the pursuit phase.

---

[9] P. Masel, *The Second 28th,* p. 73.
[1] In the fighting on the 17th and 18th the 2/32nd lost 10 officers and 234 others killed or wounded and the 2/43rd 7 and 81.
[2] Sgt C. R. Jacka, MM, SX7996; 2/48 Bn. Traveller; of Renmark, SA; b. Caltowie, SA, 2 May 1912.

No marked change had occurred in the enemy situation to explain so great a change of concept, plan and expectation. In searching for clues to the new-born optimism, one notes that the Eighth Army had intercepted Rommel's instructions to his forces in the centre to go over to the defensive; perhaps *90th Light Division's* embarrassment at being ordered to send a regiment north was also known. Moreover Auchinleck had available two fresh formations: the 161st Indian Motor Brigade from Iraq and the 23rd Armoured Brigade Group just arrived from England—the latter had arrived in the desert only as planning for the attack began. Auchinleck had 61 Grant, 81 Crusader and 31 Stuart tanks in the 1st Armoured Division, 150 Valentines and a few Matildas in the 23rd Armoured Brigade in addition to the close cooperation tanks of the 1st Army Tank Brigade. Rommel was believed to have only 31 German tanks (actually 38) and 70 Italian (actually 59). In air support, artillery and also in infantry strength, Auchinleck had, over his enemy, a remarkable superiority.

The XIII Corps plan for the initial assault required the 161st Indian Brigade to attack west along the Ruweisat Ridge for Trig 63, and the 2nd New Zealand Division, attacking from the south, to take the eastern part of the El Mreir depression, a locality to the south and south-west of Trig 33, but with a gap between. In the second phase the 23rd Armoured Brigade was to thrust westwards through the gap into the enemy's headquarters and administrative area. This meant thrusting at the heart of the *Africa Corps* between its two armoured divisions. It was a role for which the eager spirit of the unblooded 23rd was suited, but not its tanks, nor the obsolescent little 2-pounder guns they mounted. The experienced armoured brigades were being husbanded for the pursuit when the defeated enemy fled, but it was odd that, in the battle intended to turn the scales, the faster and, in part, better armed tanks were to give close protection to the infantry and the slow Valentines and Matildas to break through.

The attack opened early in the night of the 21st. On the right the South African division seized a depression on the Indian brigade's right flank; the Indian right battalion broke into Deir el Shein, but was thrown back; the left battalion was held up short of Trig 63. On the left the 6th New Zealand Brigade took its objectives. Again the New Zealanders were attacked at dawn by tanks; again tank support at dawn, which the New Zealanders understood to have been promised, had not been provided; again, despite planning attention to this very point and arrangements for closer liaison, a common intention between cooperating infantry and armoured units as to the method of operation had not been achieved. The New Zealanders lost 700 men including the brigade commander (Brigadier G. H. Clifton) who, however, escaped later in the day.

At 8 a.m. the reserve Indian battalion attacked, reaching Point 23, and the 23rd Armoured Brigade set off westward to win its laurels, losing tanks as it went, to mines, anti-tank guns, and tanks, but pressing on always in Balaclava spirit until each regiment reached its objective some three miles and a half west of the Indians' forward infantry; by then one regiment had only 15 tanks left, the other 12. This gallant, though costly and imprudent thrust threw the enemy into confusion, but he did not flee and the XIII Corps had no further punches planned for the day. About midday the survivors of 23rd Armoured Brigade were withdrawn with support from the 2nd Armoured Brigade; they had only 7 left of the 87 tanks with which they had set out, though more than half of those lost were later recovered.

Some further efforts were made by the XIII Corps that afternoon and night but the disaster could not be retrieved. The New Zealand division had lost 904, including 69 officers; after the accumulated losses of the two ill-planned and ill-concerted Ruweisat battles it required extensive re-organisation. The division was also "sourly discontented"[3] and General Inglis wrote to General Freyberg:

> I have flatly refused to do another operation of the same kind while I command. I have said that the *sine qua non* is my own armour under my own command.[4]

The XIII Corps had not been fighting the Eighth Army's battle alone on that hard, disappointing day. The tasks undertaken by the XXX Corps were scarcely less formidable or ambitious. In addition to the seizure by the South African division of a depression to the north of Deir el Shein, the corps' orders required a two-brigade infantry attack by the 9th Division followed by thrusts by armour and infantry no less daring than that prescribed for the 23rd Armoured Brigade, first 6,000 yards west then 4,000 yards south. The division was required to advance on all its fronts, to the west in both the north and the centre, and also to the south—onto the Miteiriya Ridge. Inevitably this required a number of thrusts that were not closely inter-supporting and a dispersion of the available artillery support over a wide front. The 1st Tank Brigade and the 50th R.T.R. were placed under the division's command and the South African artillery was to assist.[5]

The 9th Division's attack was to be in three phases with two hours between the first and second phases to allow two field regiments to move forward to support the later phases. In the first phase the 26th Brigade on the right in the Tel el Eisa area was to make two thrusts—one straight out from the westernmost protrusion of the line at Trig 33, beside the coast road, to seize the next high feature, Ring Contour 25 (Baillieu's Bluff), the other southwards across the road and railway again to capture the high rolling ground of the double Point 24 feature (or Tel el Eisa Ridge)—while the 24th Brigade striking out from the Tel Makh Khad region was to take the dominating ridge behind the double 24 feature

---

[3] Scoullar, p. 370.
[4] Scoullar, pp. 367-8.
[5] In *The Desert Generals*, at p. 209, Corelli Barnett represents Auchinleck's plan for this offensive as being first to drive into the centre (Ruweisat) and three days later to "drive the German left flank off the Miteiriya Ridge, the key to the defence; the armour would then break through before Rommel could disengage himself from the earlier battle with 13th Corps". This prescient, deliberate, straight-left right-hook tactic does not accord with the way the battle was fought, with the XXX Corps striking at dawn the first day and planning a break-through, nor is it easily reconcilable with the spate of orders and instructions then issuing from many other formations. There was, of course, another thrust by the XXX Corps three days later but the reason given for it in Auchinleck's despatch is not the same. "Having failed in the centre," he wrote, "I decided to attack in the north with the aid which the possession of Tel el Eisa Salient would give me."

(from Cairn to Trig 22 on the map). When these objectives were taken, the 9th Divisional Cavalry would have the role of delaying any move by the enemy between the two brigades. In the second phase the 50th R.T.R. was to take Point 21 on a ridge to the west of the 24th Brigade's first objective, which would then be held by the 2/28th Battalion and in the third phase the 50th R.T.R. was to seize Trig 30 on Ruin Ridge, which the 2/43rd Battalion would then take over. To free the 2/28th for its westward thrust, the 2/13th Battalion was placed under command of the 24th Brigade and was to relieve the 2/28th during the night before the attack. The 20th Brigade Group was to be prepared to exploit towards Daba from the night of the 22nd-23rd onwards.

Morshead was extremely critical of the tasks laid upon his division in the operation and took strong exception to the plan. The following note appears in his diary for 21st July:[6]

> 2 hours conference with Ramsden, during which I objected strongly to scope of my attack to take place tomorrow and several changes in timings. As result Commander-in-Chief sent for me and conference held at XXX Corps. Present Commander-in-Chief, Ramsden, D.C.G.S. (Dorman-Smith[7]) who took down notes! Commander-in-Chief explained plan of 13 Corps' attack. I did not like our plan because of wide dispersion and difficulty to support and pointed out that our immediate objectives were much more difficult than realised by Army and Corps. Commander-in-Chief according to Ramsden was very annoyed and perturbed but he did not show it. He stressed that he realised he must have a willing commander. I stressed that my concern was a task which was reasonably certain of success and could be held and supported, and that my job too was to minimise casualties. Altogether it turned out to be rather like a family party.

This was almost certainly the interview described in *The Desert Generals* which the author of that work represents as occurring on 22nd July and relating to orders for 24th July—which could hardly have been true since the 9th Division's orders for the attack a few days later were in substance orders to repeat an abortive attack about to be launched that very afternoon of 22nd July (just after the alleged time of the interview).[8]

In the few days before this operation began the forward battalions of the 9th Division had patrolled strenuously and there was little rest for anyone. The diarist of the 2/48th recorded that it was almost impossible to sleep by day because of the heat and flies, while the nights were occupied with digging and patrolling. The troops were very tired. Some relief was

---

[6] This date refutes the implied and highly suppositive criticism of Morshead, based on the account in *The Desert Generals*, appearing at p. 81 of *The Second 28th*, by Philip Masel.

[7] Maj-Gen E. E. Dorman-Smith, MC. (1914-18: Lt to Major Northumberland Fusiliers.) DCGS GHQ ME 1942. Regular soldier; b. 24 Jul 1895.

[8] "Auchinleck," wrote Barnett, "was visiting 30th Corps H.Q. with Dorman-Smith after lunch on 22nd July, when General Ramsden, commanding 30th Corps, told him the news. . . . Ramsden explained that Morshead had been questioning his orders for 24th July, saying that his division had done enough attacking. 'His main reason,' in Ramsden's words, 'was *no* confidence in our armour.' Ramsden said that he had done his best 'to stop this bloody-mindedness without result'. Morshead, he told Auchinleck, had insisted that 'he must refer to his government'."

The author states that this "at first . . . shattered his (Auchinleck's) self-control" and that Auchinleck ordered Ramsden to have Morshead report to him immediately but Ramsden suggested that Morshead should come up for tea. "Auchinleck thought for a moment, and at that moment the swift rage abated with equal swiftness. The Australians must be got into action and anger would not do the trick. He took Ramsden by the arm and, in his usual deep voice, agreed that Morshead should come for tea. Time passed, Morshead arrived, Auchinleck was gruffly charming, they all, in a thoroughly British Commonwealth manner, had tea."—*The Desert Generals*, p. 212.

being given by sending one man from each forward section to spend the day on the beach.

On the night of the 19th-20th a company of the 2/28th with 20 sappers of the 2/7th Field Company made a large-scale raid on enemy diggings about Trig 22. The patrol left at 12.25 a.m. and returned at 3.40. It encountered a tank which Sapper Gilson[9] destroyed with a No. 73 grenade, killing three or four men in or round the tank.

The 26th Brigade was not relieved for the attack but had still to hold the salient in the north. Since the 2/24th and 2/48th Battalions had therefore to continue holding their fronts, they could spare only two companies each for their tasks and would be without reserves to reinforce if all did not go well. The brigade plan required two companies of the 2/24th and one of the 2/23rd to thrust beside and parallel to the coast road—the 2/24th companies to Ring Contour 25, the 2/23rd to Kilo 109 on the old track just south of the new main road—the 2/23rd Battalion (less the company mentioned) to take East Point 24 and, when this was secured, the 2/48th to take West Point 24.

In fine, 26th Brigade was to attack the defences by which the enemy blocked access along the main coast road which led into the enemy's main headquarters area and on to Mersa Matruh, Tobruk and Tripoli—the enemy's only supply line. As in the XIII Corps, the Eighth Army's offensive was striking not at the enemy's weak points but where he was likely to be strongest. With after-knowledge denied to the commanders who directed the battle, it seems that to strike beside the road with only three companies of infantry supported by two batteries of artillery was indeed optimistic.

Major Weir,[1] summoned up from Alexandria on the preceding day to take command of the 2/24th Battalion, had called in at brigade headquarters on the way and was troubled at receiving orders to mount an attack next morning. As the 2/24th assault companies were waiting before dawn next morning for the start time to arrive, a Very light was accidentally fired, which probably alerted the enemy. When the attack started, the enemy artillery opened up almost immediately and

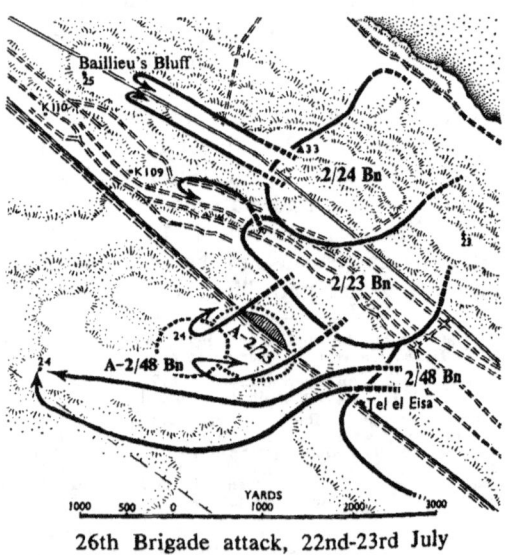

26th Brigade attack, 22nd-23rd July

---

[9] Spr J. F. Gilson, QX10630; 2/7 Fd Coy. Labourer; of Maryborough, Qld; b. Ipswich, Qld, 23 Mar 1920.

[1] Lt-Col C. G. Weir, DSO, ED, VX48424; 2/24 Bn (CO 1942). Departmental manager; of Mentone, Vic; b. Malvern, Vic, 30 Jul 1908.

the companies went forward through devastating machine-gun fire. Captain Baillieu's company on the right took heavy casualties. Captain Baillieu and his second-in-command (Captain Austin[2]) were in turn wounded and evacuated and the assault developed into uncoordinated platoon actions. Most sections got on or near their objectives only to find them swept by constant intense fire from flank or rear; but though unable to deal with it, they hung on. Soon all the officers had been hit except Lieutenant Austin[3] who, having rejoined the battalion only the day before, found himself in charge, scarcely knowing the men; but with the help of the only surviving N.C.O., Lance-Sergeant Annear,[4] Austin was able to exercise command.

On their left Captain Mollard's company lost touch with Baillieu's but managed to get onto its objective, on Ring Contour 25, which was also well covered by enemy machine-guns. There the ground was so rocky that they had difficulty in digging in. Sergeant Hughes,[5] observing that two Spandaus were troubling one of his sections, crawled forward and with two rifle shots hit the No. 1 of each gun. The No. 2's immediately replaced them, but with his next two shots, Hughes hit both, putting their guns out of action. Then Hughes tried to carry out the wounded leader of the section that the Spandaus had been engaging, but the man was shot and killed on Hughes' back. Captain Mollard soon decided that his objective was untenable and side-stepped to the right towards Baillieu's company, where he held on in a less exposed position.

Major Weir decided about 6.45 a.m. that the two companies, which he could not reinforce, would have to be withdrawn and ordered them back, obtaining Brigadier Tovell's concurrence as soon as possible. At first difficulty was experienced in informing the right company but telephone communications were in time restored. When Lieutenant Austin received the order, he sent Sergeant Annear back with the survivors but stayed behind to assist in recovering the wounded and in so doing was himself wounded. The withdrawal order did not reach some outlying sections, who fought on until late afternoon and were overrun. Five officers of the 2/24th had been wounded and 20 other ranks killed; and 39 wounded were brought back; 14 other men known to have been wounded were missing; 6 were missing believed killed; and 15 others were listed simply as missing; 7 who had been wounded remained on duty.

The 2/24th believed that the 2/23rd's company was to attack simultaneously for Kilo 109 and Captain Mollard had been much concerned, on the approach to his objective, at being unable to make contact with it. The company's orders, however, were to start its advance only when the success signal was sent up over Ring Contour 25. This the company

---

[2] Maj G. Austin, VX25783; 2/24 Bn. Retired grazier; of Boggabri, NSW; b. Geelong, Vic, 27 Aug 1903.
[3] Capt A. G. Austin, MC, VX27754; 2/24 Bn; Intell Corps 1944-45. Schoolteacher; of Brunswick, Vic; b. Brunswick, 20 Sep 1918.
[4] Sgt G. M. P. Annear, VX46774; 2/24 Bn. Dyer; of East Malvern, Vic; b. South Yarra, Vic, 10 Feb 1906.
[5] Sgt W. T. Hughes, DCM, VX42434; 2/24 Bn. Dairy farmer; of Foster, Vic; b. Newport, Wales, 16 Sep 1907.

did when the signal was given, under "terrible enemy fire", and Captain Mollard, looking back from the ring contour, saw them struggling forward in dire straits.

The main attack of the 2/23rd south of the railway line had been made simultaneously, with two companies forward, behind a heavy artillery concentration. Round East Point 24 the dust made it impossible to see more than a few yards and a fierce fight developed. The success signal was fired at 6.20 by which time 24 German prisoners had been sent back.

At 5.55 news reached the 2/48th on its start-line—the railway at Tel el Eisa station—that the other battalions were on their objectives, whereupon it moved off round the left of the 2/23rd towards West Point 24, the right company (Captain Williams) going straight to the objective, the left (Captain Kimber) swinging out to come in on the left flank. The men soon came under intense shell and mortar fire but continued to advance, keeping formation and leaving a trail of fallen men on the desert. Wireless communication broke down. Almost a mile from the railway the advancing companies found themselves under fire from the enemy's forward positions. Soon the right company had lost all its officers. In the left company only one remained and he was out of touch; the company sergeant-major, Sergeant Pryor,[6] took command and led it forward. When the right company arrived within 100 yards of the enemy positions it was pinned down by accurate and intense artillery and machine-gun fire, particularly from the left. Private Gurney[7] leapt up and charged across the bullet-swept ground, killed the three Germans manning a machine-gun post with his bayonet, then dashed on to a post 30 yards away, bayoneted two more Germans and sent back a third as a prisoner. Then a grenade hurled at Gurney blew him off his feet, but he got up, picked up his rifle, and charged a third post. He was bayoneting more Germans when a burst from another machine-gun killed him.[8]

Wounded men returning through battalion headquarters reported that their companies had been cut to pieces but Hammer thought the survivors would be pressing on and ordered a section of carriers forward to give support and obtain accurate information; so heavy was the fire, however, that the carrier crews had many men wounded and could not get through; nor could the vehicles carrying supporting weapons.

Hammer asked for support from tanks and at 11 a.m. nine arrived. Alacrity in getting help to his men was what the dynamic and resourceful Hammer expected of the tanks. His subsequent report on their response must be read with the reservation that the defence has not been heard.

> The tank commander was given the task of supporting the attacking companies on to the objective (wrote Hammer). He asked for 30 minutes to move but the tanks actually took 4¼ hours to cross the railway line—the time lag seemed almost impossible to explain. On crossing the line they found a small enemy minefield,

---

[6] Capt W. E. Pryor, DCM, SX7338; 2/48 Bn. Builder's labourer; of Mitchell Park, SA; b. Rosebank, SA, 11 Sep 1915.
[7] Pte A. S. Gurney, VC, WX9858; 2/48 Bn. Electrician; of Victoria Park, WA; b. Murchison Goldfields, WA, 15 Dec 1908. Killed in action 22 Jul 1942.
[8] Gurney was posthumously awarded the Victoria Cross.

withdrew, held a conference, and moved forward to attack again. Two tanks moved gingerly forward and were knocked out by an enemy anti-tank gun, the only one seen in the area. The tanks then withdrew completely.

About 7 a.m. Private Hogan,[9] who was with the left company, and had been wounded in the arm, had been left to guard nine Germans. Fire was so intense throughout the day that Hogan could not escort the prisoners back. They were within easy reach of their own weapons and only about 200 yards from their own lines but by his aggressive attitude and alertness, Hogan, though frequently sniped at from not far away, kept them under control for 14 hours and after dark brought them to battalion headquarters.

About 8 a.m. the Germans had meanwhile opened a heavy counter-attack on the 2/23rd companies at East Point 24. The enemy made some progress against the left company (Captain Cromie) but it continued on fighting for three hours. Part of the other (Lieutenant McRae[1]) was able to hold the enemy at bay. Evans sent forward his acting second-in-command (Major Urquhart[2]) in a carrier to tell the men at East Point 24 to hang on while the remaining company ("A") came up to support them. Then Evans learnt that the 2/24th was withdrawing from the Ring Contour and his company advancing on Kilo 109 was out in the blue. At 8.30 "A" Company (Captain Harding) began moving to East Point 24. Urquhart had meanwhile reached East Point 24 but was killed on the way back, and so Evans did not know how matters stood. Out there, where doubt and anxiety brooded in many minds, a splendid job was being done by Corporal McCluskey[3] in charge of a carrier whose initial task was to take a mortar detachment forward. Having done so, he returned for a load of ammunition, traversing hundreds of yards of shell and bullet-swept ground, and stopping several times to pick up wounded men. When he had gone back and delivered his mortar bombs he saw that communications were obscure and travelled the whole battalion front establishing contact between the company commanders. Again he loaded his vehicle with wounded but on the way back his carrier was hit. He was thrown out and stunned but regained consciousness, repaired his damaged carrier, still under fire, and carried on.

A runner from the company away to the right that had been advancing on Kilo 109 brought Evans news that the men were pinned down by withering fire, the company commander (Lieutenant McKoy[4]) had been killed and the other officers and half the company were casualties. Evans arranged a smoke screen to cover the withdrawal of the survivors and 30 men got back. Lieutenant Clarke[5] who had taken over the command

---

[9] Pte J. S. Hogan, WX10224; 2/48 Bn. Miner; of Kalgoorlie, WA; b. Fremantle, WA, 8 Jun 1909.
[1] Maj E. H. McRae, VX48791; 2/23 Bn. Bank officer; of Werribee, Vic; b. Bairnsdale, Vic, 9 Apr 1916.
[2] Maj G. F. Urquhart, VX48258; 2/23 Bn. Accountant; of Yarram, Vic; b. Denham, England, 5 Nov 1910. Killed in action 22 Jul 1942.
[3] Cpl J. McCluskey, VX27400; 2/23 Bn. Motor transport driver; of Camperdown, Vic; b. Caramut, Vic, 26 Aug 1904.
[4] Lt A. N. McKoy, VX26764; 2/23 Bn. Manager; of Albury, NSW; b. Albury, 14 Sep 1908. Killed in action 22 Jul 1942.
[5] Maj K. C. Clarke, MC, VX37109. 2/23 Bn; HQ I Corps and NG Force 1943-44; BM 17 Bde 1944-45. Salesman; of Brighton, Vic; b. Adelaide, 5 Feb 1916.

of this company was himself wounded in the foot and could not walk. Rather than delay the withdrawal he remained and was brought in after dark by a fighting patrol.

After 8.30 a.m. radio communication with the left company of the 2/23rd had ceased. It fought on until 11, when a few men filtered back and reported that the commander, Captain Cromie, was dead, the second-in-command wounded and all other officers wounded and evacuated, but that the recently arrived "A" Company was barring further German progress towards East Point 24. Evans organised some 80 men to hold the battalion's main positions between Trig 33 and the Tel el Eisa cutting.

The pressure on the left of Evans' front was also felt on the right of Hammer's where the leaderless "D" Company had lost cohesion, though scattered remnants clung to their ground throughout the day. Here, late in the afternoon, was a section of men led by Private Ashby,[6] who had earlier taken command of his section in the assault and with them had overrun several posts. Ashby and his men saw a Valentine tank knocked out. Germans near by rushed across and took the crew and two members of Ashby's section prisoner but Ashby opened fire with such accuracy that all the Germans were killed or badly wounded, so that their prisoners escaped.

In the late afternoon, the anxious Hammer at last got some information from the front when Sergeant Pryor, commanding his "B" Company, came on the air to say that they were holding on, though he could not say where he was because all maps were with dead or wounded officers. Hammer at once organised an emergency force from all available headquarters and Headquarters Company men and some 50 reinforcements who had just arrived, released his "A" Company (Captain Shillaker) from its defences, and sent it, plus a platoon of machine-gunners and a troop of anti-tank guns, to the aid of Pryor's men. Just as they were setting forth, however, Pryor reported that he and his men had been surrounded, but would fight their way out. Shillaker's company pressed on and met them coming back, then only 15 strong. Hammer ordered Shillaker's company to re-occupy East Point 24, which they did during the night, consolidating with wire and mines.[7]

At the end of the day "A" Company of the 2/23rd was digging in near the railway cutting but two of the platoons were out of contact and Captain Harding was missing and believed to have been killed. In the battalion about 100 had been wounded and 50 were missing. Eleven officers had been killed or were wounded or missing, and the casualties among N.C.O's totalled 43.[8]

As the sun was setting on that desperate day on which these companies of the 2/23rd and 2/48th—infantry of finest mettle—after fighting so valiantly, and suffering so severely in casualties (not by capture but by

---

[6] Sgt H. H. Ashby, DCM, SX10570; 2/48 Bn. Labourer; of Kongorong, SA; b. Mt Gambier, SA, 12 Oct 1921.

[7] In this two-company attack the 2/48th had lost 3 officers killed and 4 wounded, 46 others killed and 59 wounded; 3 men were missing.

[8] In the past week the battalion had lost 270 killed or wounded, and about 50 were not accounted for; all the company commanders had been killed, all their replacements had become casualties.

death and maiming) had been thrust from much of the ground they had taken, it seemed they might have fought to no avail. Yet by holding on to what they could, they had accomplished their assignment. By the morning of the 23rd it was evident that the enemy had withdrawn from round both East and West Point 24. The depleted 2/23rd was reorganised with only two rifle companies, one of which remained on East Point 24 while the other was between that point and the 2/24th. The 2/48th extended the line eastwards along the railway for some 3,500 yards.

The 24th Brigade's operations on the 22nd had met with mixed fortune. The 2/32nd Battalion's objective—Trig 22—was known to be strongly held and patrols had tested a strong-post equipped with anti-tank guns and machine-guns along the telephone line to the north of the line of advance. Whitehead persuaded Godfrey to leave one company of the 2/43rd under his command for the attack; his own battalion, after the losses on 17th July, had been reorganised into three rifle companies each about 90 strong and weak in N.C.O's.

The attack was made with three companies forward and the start-line, which was 1,700 yards from the objective, was crossed at 5.30 a.m. after the supporting artillery had been firing for 15 minutes. Captain Sudholz's company of the 2/43rd on the right was the first to be fired on; after 600 yards it was halted by heavy fire from the right and dug in; Sudholz was mortally wounded. The centre company's commander, Captain O'Mara,[9] was killed soon after the advance began and Lieutenant Bennett[1] took command. It gained its objective taking some 20 prisoners, but was soon pinned down by fire. The left company captured three anti-tank guns in its attack but was held to the edge of the escarpment below Trig 22, where it dug in. Lieutenant Cameron, commanding the supporting machine-gun platoon, established his left section forward of the left flank and at 6.30, armed with only a pistol, charged a German machine-gun that was firing from a sangar and had caused many casualties. The machine-gunner fired until Cameron reached the post, then stood up and was shot by one of Cameron's men. Cameron then turned the Spandau on to the Germans until it jammed.

On the right wing the 2/43rd company was under fire from two field guns in a fortified post. Whitehead decided to send his reserve company (Lieutenant Davidson[2]) to attack it, with support from artillery and mortars. Davidson's men subdued the post and the surviving enemy troops retired north-west; later in the darkness engineers sallied out and damaged the two guns. At 9.45, after an enemy artillery bombardment, tanks and armoured cars struck at the centre company. Bennett and others were killed, part of the company was overrun and 66 men were taken prisoner. Eventually the tanks were driven off by artillery fire.

The tanks and armoured cars and two mobile guns next attacked round

---

[9] Capt M. J. O'Mara, WX507; 2/32 Bn. Station overseer; of Guildford, WA; b. Fremantle, WA, 27 Nov 1910. Killed in action 22 Jul 1942.
[1] Lt A. M. Bennett, VX12706; 2/32 Bn. Bank officer; b. Melbourne, 25 Mar 1911. Killed in action 22 Jul 1942.
[2] Maj J. J. G. Davidson, QX6092; 2/32 Bn. Regular soldier; of Red Hill, Qld; b. Murwillumbah, NSW, 14 May 1913.

Trig 22 and a long fight followed in which two armoured cars and the two mobile guns were put out of action. Finally the line was sited so that anti-tank guns could cover both sides of Trig 22, and further positions were chosen in ground suitable for digging and back from the crest. The brigade had taken 57 prisoners up to this stage, all German from the *I/155th Infantry Battalion.*

Morshead visited Godfrey at his headquarters several times during the day. Waiting there in mid-afternoon for news that the 24th Brigade had accomplished the first phase, Morshead learnt just before 3.45 p.m. that the 2/32nd's hold on its ground was now secure and the 24th Brigade therefore ready to start the exploitation phase. On the other hand, as we have seen, the situation in front, on the double Point 24 feature, was fluid and obscure. Morshead conferred with Ramsden and the decision was made to cancel both phases of the ambitious thrusts by armour and infantry 2,000 yards west and 4,000 yards south, but to continue with the plan to exploit southward, with the object of gaining a footing on Ruin Ridge by dusk and consolidating during the night on the reverse slope.

As the 2/28th Battalion had been assembled and made ready to advance for the westward exploitation, Morshead decided that it should undertake the southward thrust, instead of the partly committed 2/43rd Battalion originally assigned. The 50th R.T.R. with one squadron forward on a front of 600 yards, carrying one platoon of the 2/28th and engineers and followed by a second squadron 700 yards behind, was to advance at 6 miles in the hour to Ruin Ridge. This spearhead was to be followed by a troop of 6-pounders and a machine-gun platoon, after which would come the 2/28th Battalion on foot moving at 2 miles in the hour, and then the remainder of the 50th R.T.R. group. The tanks were to halt in hull-down positions on the objective and were not to withdraw until the main body of the 2/28th had arrived. The 50th R.T.R. had 52 Valentines in all.

Since Ruin Ridge had been similarly attacked only 4 days earlier, the enemy was unlikely to be unexpectant and the time for planning preliminary moves and giving orders was extremely brief. It was 5 p.m. before Major Cox of the 2/28th and his adjutant left brigade headquarters after receiving oral orders for an attack to start at 7. And between 6 and 7 o'clock a disturbing report arrived at Godfrey's heaquarters from an aircraft on reconnaissance that along 1,000 yards of Miteiriya Ridge 500 enemy vehicles were dispersed, infantry were digging in, and there were at least 20 gun positions. Godfrey passed the information on to Colonel Wells at divisional headquarters.

A penalty was to be paid for too much haste. There was no time for reconnaissance—scarcely sufficient even to pass quick orders down and get the men to the start-line. The platoon to ride on the tanks arrived just in time but got mixed up trying at first to mount the first wave of tanks instead of the second.[3] The tanks, with the infantry aboard but not the

---

[3] The 50th R.T.R. recorded that "the carrier platoon" did not arrive in time, and so some 50 infantrymen were carried on the second wave of tanks but soon had to drop off because of the heavy fire. The notes of the verbal orders made by Godfrey's brigade major say that two infantry platoons and engineers were to ride on the second squadron of tanks. The carriers did arrive in time to accompany the tanks.

sappers, set off.[4] Some 20 tanks were disabled by running onto a known minefield which, with better preparation and passing of orders, should have been avoided. The rest, accompanied by the carriers, pressed on to a further ridge which the tank commanders, having covered the distance prescribed for them, believed to be Ruin Ridge but perhaps may have been still some distance short. Some enemy were dislodged and sent back. The tanks waited for the 2/28th to come up.

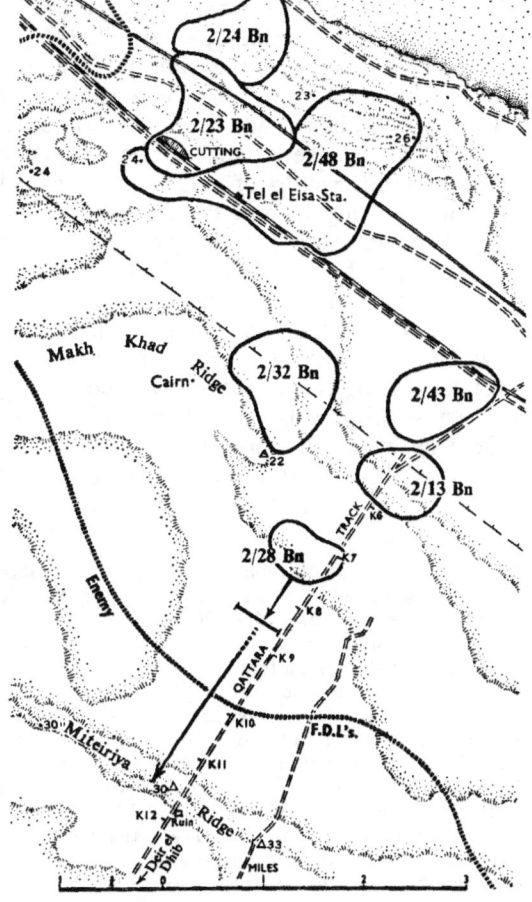

The rest of the infantry, hurrying forward, came up late to the start-line but then strung out and attacked in perfect extended-line formation. "I watched advance of 2/28th Battalion," wrote Morshead in his diary, "and all the indications of success were present."

No news arrived until 10.45 p.m. from the 2/28th —its wireless van had been destroyed soon after crossing the start-line, but in the meantime, two hours earlier, about 50 German prisoners had arrived back in the 2/13th Battalion's area. Line communication was then established and at 11.45 p.m. Cox reported having reached a ridge with a ruin on the left; the tanks had withdrawn and the infantry were now getting into position on the reverse slope. Ten Italian tanks were visible.

The 2/28th had taken 59 German prisoners including members of all three infantry regiments of the *90th Light Division* and five Italians from the *Trento,* but had lost 2 officers and 52 others.

When the tanks returned, and leaguered farther back than had been

---

[4] The diary of the 2/7th Field Company asserts that the commander of the regiment ordered off the 16 sappers who had been detailed to ride on the tanks, that the sappers warned the tanks to keep to the west of the road but they crossed to the east and had 28 tanks damaged on the minefields there.

intended, Brigadier Richards[5] of the 1st Tank Brigade, evidently suspecting that they had not reached the objective, went forward to investigate, and at 1.30 a.m. returned and announced that the 2/28th was some 3,000 yards short of Ruin Ridge. From this and other reports—five minutes later, for instance, Lieutenant Ligertwood,[6] the F.O.O. with the 2/28th, reported that he considered them 2,500 yards short of the objective—Godfrey concluded that the battalion was deployed west of the road on a front of about 400 yards between Kilos 8 and 9.

That was substantially correct. Some ruins encountered during the advance had deceived some officers into thinking they had reached Ruin Ridge though far short of it. There the men had been ordered to halt, the battalion had dug in and the Intelligence officer had gone on to tell the tanks they were too far forward and to instruct them to return, which they did. For the raw 50th R.T.R. it had been an unhappy introduction to battle; the regiment recorded the loss of 23 tanks.[7] No explanation can be given of the battalion's premature stop, evincing failure to keep prescribed distances firmly in mind and to check with care distances covered, except the effects of extreme fatigue, accentuated by constant air-burst shelling of the battalion over the preceding days.

Godfrey went forward about 4.30 a.m. with Richards, reached the 2/28th at dawn and ordered Cox to widen his front, put patrols well forward, make contact with the 2/32nd at Trig 22, and try to get as far forward as possible; by 9.23 the two battalions were in contact.

"If the results of this day's fighting were disappointing from the point of view of objectives gained" (says the divisional report) "there was some consolation in the report from XXX Corps that the enemy had found it necessary to move the entire *90 Light Division,* less some infantry but supported by elements of three Italian divisions, to hold his battered left flank."

The war diary of the *90th Light Division* described how their enemy, attacking south-west of El Alamein before dawn on the 22nd, penetrated a gap between the *1/155th* and *1/361st* Battalions and captured nearly a whole company of the *155th.* After bitter fighting the Briehl Group, with the support of tanks from the *21st Armoured Division,* counter-attacked and threw the enemy back with a loss of 23 tanks of which 12 fell to the Briehl Group.

The daily report of the *Armoured Army of Africa,* after referring to the losses as particularly heavy and the position as being extremely critical, added: "It is questionable whether the whole front will be able to be held any longer against such heavy pressure."

The 9th Division which alone, it is pertinent to remember, had achieved valuable gains in the Eighth Army's costly and abortive offensive was soon to be called upon for a further effort. General Auchinleck, knowing that his adversary was becoming gradually stronger and that time was therefore precious, was resolved, as he later wrote in his despatch, "to go on hitting the enemy whenever and wherever I could" and decided to attack again as soon as a new offensive could be prepared.

---

[5] Maj-Gen G. W. Richards, CB, CBE, DSO, MC. (1916-18: Lt, Royal Welch Fusiliers.) Comd 4 Armd Bde, 1 Tank Bde, 23 Armd Bde during 1942. Regular soldier; b. 4 Jul 1898.

[6] Capt W. L. Ligertwood, MC, WX1585; 2/7 Fd Regt. Solicitor; of Hawthorn, SA; b. Hawthorn, 22 Feb 1916. Died of wounds 30 Oct 1942.

[7] Liddell Hart, *The Tanks,* Vol II, p. 206.

(*Australian War Memorial*)
Mr Winston Churchill in jovial mood as he emerges from the mess tent at 9th Division tactical headquarters with General Morshead during his visit to the Western Desert, 5th August 1942.

(*Australian War Memorial*)
A 2/2nd Machine Gun Battalion position at El Alamein, August 1942.

(Australian War Memorial)

General Sir Claude Auchinleck, Commander-in-Chief, Middle East (right), and Lieut-General W. H. C. Ramsden, commanding XXX Corps, awaiting the arrival of Mr Churchill at 9th Division Headquarters, 5th August 1942.

(Imperial War Museum)

An Australian officer interrogating a German officer captured at El Alamein, July 1942.

The object of the renewed attack, which was to be made by the XXX Corps, was to break through the enemy's front on the Miteiriya Ridge between Ruin Ridge and Deir el Dhib, thrust north-west and achieve a decisive victory. The corps was strengthened by the addition of the 1st Armoured Division less an armoured brigade, the 4th Light Armoured Brigade and the 69th Infantry Brigade (of the 50th Division). The plan provided that the 1st South African Division would make a wide gap in the enemy's minefields south-east of Miteiriya. By night the 24th Australian Brigade was to take the eastern end of Miteiriya and thrust north-west, while the 69th Brigade passed through to Deir el Dhib and made gaps in any further minefields; through the gaps the 2nd Armoured Brigade would advance to El Wishka followed by the 4th Light Armoured Brigade which would raid the enemy's rear areas. This plan, which required two converging attacks, one southward, one westward, to be made from different places, exhibited a point of weakness in that the two thrusts would not be mutually supporting unless or until both were successfully accomplished. Moreover the corps plan as developed in detail seemed to conflict with Auchinleck's orders to the corps to "avoid committing armoured formations in isolated action against superior enemy armoured forces".

Auchinleck wished the new offensive to open on the night of the 24th-25th but Ramsden thought the South Africans were too tired for a battle by that date, and the commander of the 69th Brigade wished his men to have more rest. Ramsden and Morshead agreed that the attack should be postponed to the 26th-27th and a request to that effect was approved.

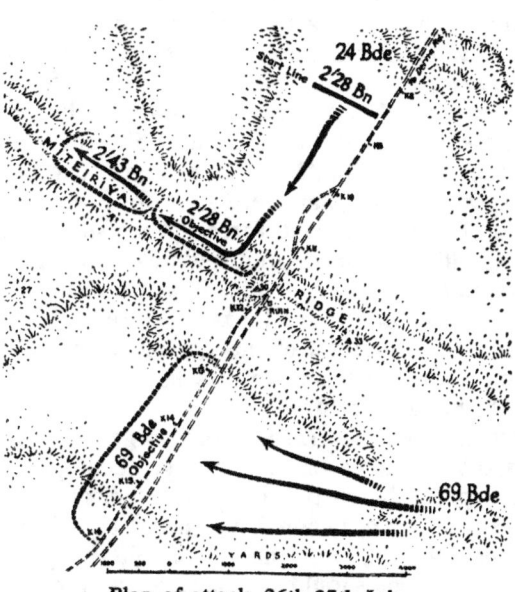

Plan of attack, 26th-27th July

The 24th Brigade Group's plan provided that the 2/28th Battalion Group, covered by artillery concentrations, would take Ruin Ridge and establish a strongpoint between the 24th Brigade's left flank and the right of the 69th Brigade. When the 2/28th and the 69th Brigade had attained their objectives the 2/43rd Battalion was to advance and capture the ridge to the west of the 2/28th, with the support, if necessary, of the 50th R.T.R. If not committed to this task the 50th R.T.R. was to attack westward and capture the area from Trig 30 to Point 27 near

El Wishka. The 20th Brigade Group was to be ready to join in the pursuit should the enemy withdraw.

On the 26th Auchinleck issued a Special Order of the Day:

> Behind El Alamein
> 25 July 42.
>
> To all ranks EIGHTH ARMY from C-in-C.
>
> You have done well. You have turned a retreat into a firm stand and stopped the enemy on the threshold of EGYPT. You have done more. You have wrenched the initiative from him by sheer guts and hard fighting and put HIM on the defensive in these last weeks.
>
> He has lost heavily and is short of men, ammunition, petrol and other things. He is trying desperately to bring these over to AFRICA but the Navy and the Air Force are after his ships.
>
> You have done much but I ask you for more. We must not slacken. If we can stick it we will break him.
>
> STICK TO IT.
>
> C. J. E. AUCHINLECK
> General.

By the evening of 25th July the British Intelligence believed that few Italian troops were left in the front line. The *Trieste* was thought to be west and south-west of Tel el Eisa and the *Trento* west of Miteiriya. These Italians were about 9,100 strong with 70 medium or field guns and 45 anti-tank guns, 15 armoured cars and perhaps 12 tanks. From the north the forward German units were believed to be: two battalions of the *382nd Regiment*, the Kiehl Group and *33rd Reconnaissance Regiment*, the *361st Regimental Group* (two battalions), the Briehl Group, and the *200th Regiment*. These totalled about 3,580 men and had from 106 to 120 guns in support including 26 to 29 88-mm weapons.

It was known that German troops were holding an area north-east of Ruin Ridge with light forces possessing a high proportion of machine-guns, anti-tank guns and a few field guns. An area south-west of the ridge was more strongly held and it was realised that, particularly to the south, the enemy would have tanks at close call. There was a minefield parallel to and generally east of the Qattara track on which many tanks had foundered in the previous two attacks and it was suspected that there was also one to the west of it.

On the 24th Morshead issued a general staff instruction which declared that the division's battle cunning, developed to a high degree in Tobruk, had "gone a bit rusty". He instructed, among other measures, that officers on reconnaissance should not make it obvious to the enemy that they were so engaged, that information should be got down to the troops swiftly, that the troops should be made to appreciate that supporting tanks could not remain on the objective for long without risking undue losses, and would leave the objective and rally in rear of the infantry; the tanks' task in attack was to destroy the machine-guns—the infantry's main enemy—the infantry's task to destroy anti-tank guns and artillery which might hold up the advance of tanks.

The 2/28th Battalion had carefully planned and reconnoitred for its second attack on Ruin Ridge. The battalion crossed the start-line—between

Kilo 8 and Kilo 9—punctually at midnight 26th-27th July in bright moonlight with two companies forward on a front of 800 yards. The rate of advance was 100 yards in two minutes. Lieut-Colonel McCarter, commanding the battalion since the 23rd, had warned his officers that during the advance fire could be expected from the flanks and told them that the men must answer it by firing from the hip without changing direction or halting.

Eight hundred yards from the start-line the battalion came under fire from field guns, mortars and machine-guns. Among the casualties were the commander of the right forward company (Captain Carlton[8]), and the commander (Captain Stenhouse[9]) and one other officer of the right rear company. The vehicles bearing the supporting arms were fired on by anti-tank guns as soon as they began to advance and, when about Kilo 10, were halted by a minefield. Soon five vehicles, including three carriers, had been knocked out and some began burning.

By 1.10 a.m. the leading companies were on Ruin Ridge. The left rear company cleared its objective with a bayonet charge. Soon McCarter's headquarters had been established about 900 yards north-west of the ruin. But all attempts to get the telephone cable past the minefield under heavy enemy fire had failed and the battalion's wireless set had been destroyed. When the men began to dig in they found the ground hard and rocky and could only make shallow trenches about a foot deep. Three company commanders had then been wounded. The whole area was under heavy fire. And efforts to deal with the German weapons pouring enfilading fire across the minefield had failed.

As soon as a narrow gap had been made in the minefield six anti-tank guns, two carriers and a machine-gun truck had passed through, but now four vehicles were in flames there, brightly illuminating the surrounding terrain and blocking the gap. The remaining vehicles carrying supporting arms then returned to the assembly area, and the surviving carriers—five out of ten—began ferrying back about 50 wounded men and escorting back the prisoners, of whom 115 Germans and 12 Italians were eventually brought out. An urgent request for ammunition for the 2/28th was received by the 2/43rd, then occupying the 2/28th's former positions, but did not reach Major Simpson,[1] in charge of the 2/28th's "A" Echelon vehicles, who had already gone forward to the start-line. Learning from Captain Masel, in charge of the carriers, that the battalion was on its objective, Simpson decided to attempt to take the ammunition through. He went ahead of the "A" Echelon transport with the ammunition trucks and drove "hell for leather" past the burning vehicles and through the mined area under bombardment by guns on the flanks. Seven or eight vehicles which swung right and followed the tape reached the objective,

---
[8] Capt W. A. Carlton, WX3401; 2/28 Bn. Clerk; of North Perth, WA; b. Perth, 22 Jul 1910.
[9] Maj T. R. Stenhouse, ED, WX3406; 2/28 Bn. Clerk; of Leederville, WA; b. Perth, WA, 27 Jul 1915.
[1] Maj B. Simpson, WX3386; 2/28 Bn. Barrister and solicitor; of Perth, WA; b. West Perth, 24 Feb 1906.

but others hit mines and became easy targets for the enemy anti-tank guns. Blazing vehicles lit up the area almost like day.

When all men wounded in the advance had been evacuated, Captain Priddis,[2] the regimental medical officer, whose regimental aid post was established in the assembly area, went forward with his stretcher bearers to the minefield to tend wounded men he had heard were still lying there, and continued administering to them in the beaten zone of enemy guns and the glare of burning vehicles until a German patrol took him and eleven patients prisoner.

The wireless set of the F.O.O. with the 2/28th, Captain Fielding of the 2/7th Field Regiment, was ineffective because of interference, and all other sets had been destroyed, so McCarter asked Fielding to return in his carrier to brigade headquarters and try to bring forward the ammunition trucks and telephone cable. On the way back Fielding twice challenged vehicles which turned out to be those of enemy troops who had closed in behind the ridge. He was killed when firing with his Tommy-gun on the second truck. The carrier was then disabled by a mine, but the driver, Gunner Manning,[3] made his way under fire through the minefield, reached brigade headquarters and delivered the message he had heard Fielding receive. Godfrey ordered the 2/43rd Battalion to send its ammunition truck to the 2/28th while the artillery bombarded the German gun covering the minefield, but the attempt to get through failed.

Brigadier Godfrey had seen the success signals and knew of the messages sent back calling for ammunition. But apart from what Manning could tell him, the only information Godfrey received during the night came from a liaison officer, Lieutenant Head, whom McCarter had sent back at 2 a.m. to arrange communication by line or wireless. To Godfrey Head described the advance to the objective and reported that when he left the battalion it was consolidating but under fire from machine-guns on the left, an anti-tank gun and machine-guns on the right and a light gun in front of Ruin Ridge.

Dawn and the inevitable counter-attack were a dismal prospect for the 2/28th Battalion. Unless the lethal minefield block was forced and help brought quickly or the 2nd Armoured Brigade could break through after the 69th Brigade's converging attack and arrive from the east, the West Australian battalion would be in dire peril.

At 2 a.m. the 69th British Brigade had advanced, but soon the leading battalion—the 6/Durham Light Infantry—came under fire and some men took cover in old slit trenches. "From this time onwards," wrote the leader of a liaison patrol from the 2/28th, Lieutenant Rule, "the advance became disorganised and was made worse owing to the East Yorkshire Regiment passing through and mixing with 6 DLI." Part of the brigade forced a small gap through the enemy's front but in general the attack became dis-

---

[2] Capt K. W. Priddis, QX19059; 2/3 Fd Amb and RMO 2/28 Bn. Medical practitioner; of Coonabarabran, NSW; b. Trangie, NSW, 3 Jul 1913.
[3] L-Sgt A. R. Manning, MM, WX4838; 2/7 Fd Regt. Cabinet maker; of Victoria Park, WA; b. Perth, WA, 4 Jun 1915.

ordered. Then the enemy counter-attacked and both battalions were overrun.

The 2nd Armoured Brigade had been due to advance at 7 a.m. following the 69th Brigade, but at dawn its commander decided that the South Africans had not cleared a gap in the minefield wide enough to permit its tanks to move through. At 7 a.m. Morshead's headquarters learnt that the brigade had fixed a provisional Zero hour for 7.30, but at 7.40 they were told Zero would be 8.15. At that time the artillery program for its advance opened.

At daylight on 27th July at 24th Brigade Headquarters the situation, though gravely perturbing because the 2/28th Battalion's communications had been cut, did not appear irretrievable. The battalion was where it should be and had had time to consolidate its ground. The armoured thrust due to start at 7 should reach it soon, before Godfrey could bring help. But when Godfrey heard of the deferment of the armour's attack, he ordered the 2/43rd at 7.29 a.m. to send a force including two carrier-borne mortars to destroy the guns covering the gap in the minefield. The force moved out about 8 a.m. but the guns were silent, so it bombarded the southern part of the minefield. Godfrey also sent Lieutenant Cook[4] of his staff to try to make contact with the 2/28th, but Cook did not return. His vehicle was hit and wrecked and he had to take cover near by, remaining out there until the morning of the 28th. About 8.25 a.m. the 1st Army Tank Brigade was asked to get ammunition forward to the 2/28th in two tanks, but by the time the commander of the 50th R.T.R. reported for orders the situation had changed and the regiment was asked to attack to relieve the battalion.

At 8.45 a.m. it had been learnt that the 2nd Armoured Brigade's advance had still not begun. Then suddenly, at Godfrey's headquarters, the 2/28th Battalion's wireless came on the air and began at 9.4 a.m. to pass a message. It was brief—only four words—but graphic. "We are in trouble." In the next three-quarters of an hour a number of messages calling for artillery support were received and the guns fired on the areas indicated by McCarter, with one 10-minute interruption, when it was feared that the fire would fall on the 2nd Armoured Brigade. At 9.30 a.m., however, the 9th Division learnt that the armoured brigade had been held up on a minefield.

All night, near Ruin Ridge, anti-tank gun and machine-gun fire had lashed the minefield gap but the 2/28th, though constantly harassed by fire, had confidently awaited the 2/43rd Battalion and the 69th Infantry and 2nd Armoured Brigades.

Soon after 3 a.m. McCarter ordered Lieutenant Harrod[5] to take out some men and silence a 50-mm anti-tank gun that was causing most of

---

[4] Lt J. T. Cook, WX2071; 2/32 Bn. Assistant assayer and surveyor; of Shenton Park, WA; b. Bendigo, Vic, 20 Nov 1907.
[5] Lt E. C. Harrod, WX11017; 2/28 Bn. Clerk; of East Fremantle, WA; b. Kalgoorlie, WA, 30 Jan 1917.

the damage to vehicles in the gap in the minefield. Harrod led out four men but found that the gun was strongly protected by infantry, of whom two fresh truckloads were then arriving.

When no response came from Captain Fielding's mission to get ammunition, Staff-Sergeant Lyall was sent back at 4.30 a.m. on the same errand but his vehicle struck a mine. Lyall and the driver of his truck got through eventually to 2/43rd Battalion headquarters, and reported the battalion's situation and its need for ammunition and anti-tank gun support to Brigadier Godfrey by telephone.[6]

Just before dawn 18 trucks unloaded German troops on McCarter's right flank. His battalion was out of communication, with no means of calling for artillery support and short of ammunition. The fire-fight became hotter but the 2/28th kept the upper hand. About 9 a.m. Captain Allen's company saw tanks and armoured cars to the south-east. Thinking they were the expected British tanks, Allen drove out to meet them, but they proved to be German and Allen was killed. As if by a miracle, the signaller just then finished repairs to the battalion's pack wireless and made contact with Godfrey's headquarters. As the counter-attack came in, McCarter sent the series of messages already mentioned calling for artillery support, which soon came, and the Australian anti-tank gunners fought off the tanks and armoured cars, destroying eight of them. A 6-pounder gun on the right of the 2/28th's position was served by the battery sergeant-major of the 12th Battery, McIlrick.[7] He and his team of two fought the gun until it was knocked out, and McIlrick killed.[8]

At 9.43 a.m. McCarter signalled to Godfrey's headquarters "There are tanks all around us," and a minute later, "You had better hurry up. Rock the artillery in."

The 50th R.T.R. began its attack to relieve the pressure on the 2/28th at 9.55 a.m. but met with disaster. The leading tanks reached Point 30 and a ridge near the Ruin but saw no Australian troops and were forced back by fire from a ring of anti-tank guns; 22 tanks were knocked out of which 10 were recovered later. The men of the 2/28th witnessed the debacle.

At 10 a.m. the cheering news was received at Morshead's headquarters that the 2nd Armoured Brigade was dealing with an enemy pocket behind the 69th Brigade and was preparing for a full-scale attack, probably north through the 2/28th, but at 11.40 a message arrived that the armour "was not playing until infantry guaranteed the mines clear". At midday the division was told that the attack had not started because the armoured brigade could not find the gap; "50 minutes later," wrote Morshead afterwards, "we heard that they had discovered the gap but what they did

---

[6] Lyall next day gathered the impression that his report had been disbelieved but it was included in Godfrey's report as authentic.

[7] WO2 A. A. McIlrick, MM, NX59950; 2/3 A-Tk Regt. Ironworker; of St Peters, NSW; b. Dulwich Hill, NSW, 17 Sep 1912. Killed in action 27 Jul 1942.

[8] Four months later McIlrick's gun was found on Ruin Ridge with a heap of 19 used shell cases beside it in the gunpit and a semi-circle of six knocked-out tanks.

with it we never heard. Anyhow our battle had already been finished 3 [sic] hours before."[9]

The 6th R.T.R. had been checked by heavy fire before it got through the minefield. Eleven enemy tanks appeared but did not then attack. It is not of consequence to follow further the course of an operation which could no longer achieve its purpose. About 3 p.m. the commander of the 1st Armoured Division, Major-General Fisher,[1] ordered the 6th R.T.R. to withdraw when it was dark. At dusk the 11 enemy tanks advanced but were checked and the 2nd Armoured Brigade withdrew, the 6th R.T.R. having lost three of its 41 tanks in the course of the day.

Godfrey had received the last signal from the 2/28th Battalion at 10.3 a.m. It said simply: "We have got to give in."

> Right up until 1000 hours (wrote the historian of the battalion) there had been no thought of surrender. The tanks were closing in from three directions, and Don Company on the forward left position was the first to be overrun. Immediately WO2 Fred Holding[2] of "A" Company . . . jumped from his pit to exhort his men to keep firing. As the tanks closed in on Battalion Headquarters a Bren gunner ran to an exposed position to open fire. His .303 bullets were useless against thick steel and he was shot down by one of the other tanks. The loss of this life convinced Lieut-Colonel McCarter of the futility of further resistance. He stood up in his weapon-pit, and with an upward wave of his hands signalled to his battalion to end the hopeless struggle.
> Many of the men of the 2/28th were in tears as they were formed up into a column and marched off to captivity. The bitterness of the moment was aggravated when the column trudged into the artillery concentrations which were still being fired, and more casualties were suffered.
> The final opposition did not end until early afternoon. One platoon from "C" Company, commanded by Lieutenant John Draper,[3] was occupying a position on the forward slope of the ridge and well out on the right flank. Unaware of the surrender and believing that the battalion had withdrawn to safety, this platoon fought until it was finally overrun by the tanks of the Briehl Group.[4]

The survivors were marched about five miles behind the German lines, then taken by truck to Daba.

Two officers and 63 other ranks of the 2/28th were known to have been killed or wounded, and 20 officers and 469 men were missing. The 69th British Brigade lost about 600 men.

After the battle the 2/28th was regrouped, for the present into two echelons: "A"—the operational element—comprised 98 all ranks organised

---

[9] The following are comments made by General Auchinleck on this operation in his Despatch:
"The South Africans experienced great difficulty in clearing gaps in the enemy minefields sufficiently safe and wide to be acceptable to the commander of the 1st Armoured Division. . . . The immediate cause of the failure of this operation was the delay in getting the tanks forward to support the 69th Brigade, but the fundamental cause was, as before, the lack of enough fresh well-trained troops." Despatch, pp. 366-7.

[1] Brig A. F. Fisher, CBE, DSO. (1918: Lt, RA.) Comd 4 and 22 Armd Bdes; GOC 1 Armd Div Jul-Aug 1942. Regular soldier; b. 11 Jul 1899.

[2] WO2 F. W. Holding, DCM, WX7386; 2/28 Bn. Clerk; of Bassendean, WA; b. Subiaco, WA, 19 Jun 1913.

[3] Lt J. W. Draper, WX10568; 2/28 Bn. Accountant; of Perth, WA; b. Perth, 23 Feb 1911.

[4] P. Masel, p. 89.

in two platoons; "B", 105 all ranks, comprised mainly administrative people and drivers.[6]

The 2/28th thrust struck the *1/361st Battalion* and the *I/200th* (both of the *90th Light Division*). The division reported that its positions were penetrated for five to seven kilometres and its forward battalions had heavy losses; part of the *1/361st* was wiped out. The advance of the 50th R.T.R. was halted by the *I/115th Battalion* and the *33rd Reconnaissance Unit* and artillery. Rommel ordered the usual swift counter-attack. The Briehl Group (the *3rd Reconnaissance Unit*, an infantry battalion and anti-tank guns) and the *33rd Reconnaissance Unit* were ordered to thrust north and the *II/200th Battalion* to thrust east, and a battle group of the *Africa Corps* comprising a tank unit, the *I/115th Battalion* and artillery was sent at 6.30 a.m. to the Deir el Dhib area. After the action *90th Light Division* reported having taken about 700 prisoners, mainly Australian, and knocked out 20 to 25 tanks.

So ended General Auchinleck's last attempt to dislodge Rommel's army from the El Alamein line. Auchinleck's efforts to exhaust the enemy forces had succeeded in exhausting his own. For more than a month afterwards neither of the opposing armies at El Alamein launched a major attack. Neither was strong enough. Rommel, commenting later, said of the situation after the failure of the attack by the XXX Corps:

It was now certain that we could continue to hold our front, and that, after the crises we had been through, was at least something. Although the British losses in this Alamein fighting had been higher than ours, yet the price to Auchinleck had not been excessive, for the one thing that had mattered to him was to halt our advance, and that, unfortunately, he had done.[7]

Auchinleck knew it would be necessary to pause and build up greater strength before attacking again. He reported to London to that effect, in a message that attributed part of his difficulties to the mixed composition of his forces which forebade detaching subordinate Dominion units and formations from parent formations.

On the afternoon of 27th July, the day of the disaster to the 2/28th Battalion, Dorman-Smith, Auchinleck's Deputy Chief of the General Staff, had placed before the general a comprehensive appreciation of the situation together with proposals for reorganisation of the Eighth Army to prevent the repeated failure of the armour and infantry to cooperate effectively.[8]

In the course of this paper Dorman-Smith expressed the opinion that the Axis forces were not strong enough to attempt the conquest of the Delta "except as a gamble and under very strong air cover". On the other hand none of the formations in Eighth Army was sufficiently well trained for offensive operations. The army's best course for the present

---

[6] From 17th to 27th July the 2/28th lost 30 officers and 700 other ranks killed, wounded, captured, missing or sick. There remained, including the left-out-of-battle detachment, about 260 officers and men. More officers soon arrived who had been sick, at schools or in staff appointments. Among these were the C.O., Lieut-Colonel Loughrey, and Major C. H. B. Norman. General Morshead ordered that, wherever practicable, other battalions should allow West Australians to transfer to the 2/28th and in this way more than 100 trained riflemen joined the battalion. Thus the unit was rebuilt (as a little more than a year before three battalions lost in Crete had been) round a sturdy nucleus of experienced soldiers. About half of the remaining reinforcements, however, were drawn from other arms and services and at first their training had to be quite elementary.

[7] *The Rommel Papers*, p. 260.

[8] The appreciation is printed in full in J. Connell, *Auchinleck*, pp. 937-44.

was to combine a defensive policy with raids and other offensive gestures. "The cover plan should be such as would induce the enemy to strike prematurely, i.e. mid-August, say, between August 10 and 20. Meanwhile the army front should be strengthened, and so held that at least one formation could come into reserve and train." It should be prepared to fight a defensive battle in the area El Alamein-Hammam. "To meet an enemy's sortie developing into manoeuvre by the southern flank" the army should organise and train a strong mobile wing based on the 7th Armoured Division. Eventually—perhaps in the latter part of September—the army would have to renew the offensive and this would probably mean a breakthrough about El Alamein. "The newly arrived infantry divisions and the armoured divisions must be trained for this and for pursuit." Auchinleck accepted this appreciation and its proposals.

Also on 27th July Auchinleck had made yet another change among his senior subordinates, calling forward Brigadier de Guingand, since February Director of Military Intelligence at G.H.Q., to replace Brigadier Whiteley as senior staff officer on Eighth Army headquarters. De Guingand has recorded that he was "considerably shaken", having had no experience as a general staff officer in the field, and indeed having filled no post that was closer to a battle than G.H.Q. in Cairo. He tried to evade a task for which he considered himself unqualified but Auchinleck sharply ordered him forward and he went to an appointment in which he was to prove perhaps the most brilliant and successful of his kind on the British side.

It would be interesting to know what de Guingand thought of the prophetic appreciation which, on the day of his arrival at Eighth Army headquarters, was presented to the Commander-in-Chief by Dorman-Smith. We have his comment on another scheme produced about the same time, the so-called "O.P." (observation posts) scheme, according to which the artillery was to be linked up and controlled from the O.P's, thus to be concentrated in support of any threatened sector or sectors. De Guingand thought that "there was a great danger of the guns being driven hither and thither and confusion setting in".

The various plans being worked out represented the state of mind of Eighth Army, or at least their High Command, at that moment (he wrote afterwards).[9] They were still looking over their shoulder. Other defensive positions far to the rear were being reconnoitred . . . if there is too much of this sort of thing it is most unlikely that the troops will fight their best in their existing positions.

Of his first days at Eighth Army headquarters de Guingand wrote: "I very soon found I was becoming overwhelmed by having to examine a number of such plans and schemes, both defensive and offensive."

On 29th July Auchinleck discussed future policy with General McCreery,[1] his adviser on armoured warfare, and proposed that in future each infantry division should include an armoured brigade and that the

---

[9] De Guingand, pp. 132-3.
[1] General Sir Richard McCreery, GCB, KBE, DSO, MC. (1915-18: Lt, 12 Lancers.) GSO1 1 Div 1939-40; CGS ME 1942-43; GOC Eighth Army, Italy, 1944-45. Regular soldier; b. 1 Feb 1898.

Crusader tanks should be grouped in a light armoured division. "McCreery resisted these suggestions so stubbornly that Auchinleck . . . told him that there was no further use for him if he could not fall in with his Commander-in-Chief's intentions."[2]

Morshead shared de Guingand's uneasiness at the fluctuating state of mind of the High Command. "Auchinleck thought in terms of brigades and Jock Columns and was continually alternating between optimism and depression," he said later. "I used to ask Wells 'How is the barometer this morning?'"[3] In Morshead's diary for 5th August, the day on which the British Prime Minister visited his headquarters in the desert, appears this cryptic entry:

> Appreciation by XXX Corps. In effect we are to turn our shoulders eastwards!

Morshead's diary entry for the next day (6th August) records that the corps commander visited him to talk of attack. The subsequent diary entry reads:

> He could not really give me the factors which brought about such a complete somersault (the barometer of Eighth Army has been wildly oscillating ever since our arrival). No stability, a wealth of plans and appreciations resulting in continual TEWTS. Fighting always in bits and pieces and so defeats in detail. Formations being broken up automatically—it has been difficult and unpleasant keeping 9th Div intact.
> General Wavell came to see me and we had a long talk. . . .

On 29th July Morshead on the occasion of a visit by Ramsden to his headquarters told his corps commander that he was not disposed to make any more attacks until he could be sure that the British armour would fight. He expressed the same views in writing on 4th August when he sent to the XXX Corps the report of the 24th Brigade on the attack on Ruin Ridge and listed "the factors contributing to this disaster". These included the encountering of an uncharted minefield 900 yards from the objective, inability to establish communication, the occupation of an exposed position with both flanks open, and the failure of the 1st Armoured Division to join the battle. "It is vital that on the next occasion," Morshead wrote, "our armour restores our lost faith in them. . . . Until we can be certain about our armour we must have more limited and less exposed objectives than those in recent operations. The only justification for recent objectives was that our armour would effectively operate."

Criticism of the armour by the infantry of the Eighth Army was unfortunately becoming fashionable. Some of it was merited but some unjust. There was a tendency to lay upon the armour the whole blame for failures that were in part infantry failures. Some criticisms rested on an unstated premise that an infantry formation could not be expected to hold to its ground against enemy tanks unless friendly tanks were alongside. Many of the German attacks, however, were made with not a large number of tanks and many such were successfully resisted in the 9th Division because its troops were imbued with the teaching Morshead had drummed into

---

[2] Connell, p. 684.
[3] Interview with General Morshead, 5 Apr 1955.

them in Tobruk to lie low, hold to their positions, deal with any accompanying infantry and let the guns behind deal with the tanks if they passed. This prevented tanks from achieving sweeping successes and reduced them to a slow process of prising out infantry by twos and threes, in which they seldom persisted for long.

More criticism than praise of the tanks operating with the 9th Division has appeared in the story just told, but only because commanders were more prone to write reports of what went wrong than of what went well. The division was particularly well served by the 1st Army Tank Brigade whose commander, Brigadier Richards, was an old personal friend of Colonel Wells and worked closely with him to achieve effective cooperation. Some criticisms were made, moreover, by Australian commanders who lacked the knowledge and experience to appreciate the problems and limitations of tanks in battle. It was Richards himself who first sorted out what had gone wrong in the 2/28th Battalion's first attack on Ruin Ridge and it is as well to remember that it was the infantry in that operation who failed to make the rendezvous.

It could not be said, however, that the armoured formations as a whole served the Eighth Army well in the battles just described. It is remarkable that the British won most of their successes by infantry attacks, the Germans most of theirs by armoured counter-attacks. German armoured formations almost always arrived where most needed, British almost never. The fault lay not in the men manning the tanks but in the commanders and the methods they used. Two defects stood out. First, the respective commanders of infantry and armoured divisions fighting a common battle made decisions independently without common purpose. Either the commander of an infantry division operating with armoured support would have to be given command of the armour or the corps commander would have to be in closer contact with the battle, exercising quick and effective command. Secondly, armoured formations were continually delayed or held up at minefields, the gapping of which had been made the responsibility of infantry formations. On a battlefield extensively sown with mines it was essential that armoured formations should be made fully responsible for clearing their own paths forward and be given also the trained men and equipment necessary to do the job. These defects were to receive attention in the days ahead and steps were to be taken to remedy them.

If the Eighth Army was uneasy in the last days of July and first days of August, its confidence was not undermined. It had stopped the enemy. It had thrown him on the defensive. It had wrested the Tel el Eisa hills from him—not a step perhaps so much as an edging forward for a foothold from which to lunge out on the long arduous trek to Tobruk, Benghazi, Tripoli and Bizerta. The long ebb of British military fortune had ceased. The tide had turned though the set the other way was not yet discernible.

Despite the virtual loss of a battalion, the 9th Division emerged from the battles fought at El Alamein under General Auchinleck, and perhaps uniquely so, a more self-confident formation than before, and a more efficient one. It was capable of being brought to a still higher pitch of effectiveness provided that replacements for men lost in battle continued to come forward.

It will be recalled that when, in May, the Australian Government was considering whether to ask for the recall of the 9th Division to Australia (eventually to decide that the request should not be pressed because of the developing crisis in the Western Desert) General Blamey had pointed out that decisions on organisation and manpower allocation in Australia hinged on the decision to be reached concerning the 9th Division.

On 10th May Morshead had pointed out to General Blamey the need to consider the division's future reinforcement. Blamey replied on 29th May that in view of the acute manpower position in Australia, he regretted that he could not send any further reinforcements at present. At that time the total strength of the A.I.F. headquarters and units remaining in the Middle East was about 29,300 of whom 21,500 belonged to operational units. In addition there were 3,400 reinforcements in, the Middle East, making a grand total of approximately 32,700. By the time the division returned to active operations, the grand total had decreased to 32,300 including 3,200 reinforcements. It was estimated that these reinforcements, though adequate to replace about four months and a half of wastage under normal conditions, would amount to only one and a half months' supply under conditions of intense activity such as were then contemplated for the division. On 14th July the Adjutant-General in Australia therefore recommended the dispatch of about 6,000 reinforcements in three successive batches. A request for further reinforcements was received about the same time from Morshead.

The provision of reinforcements on such a scale would inevitably react on the build-up of forces in Australia and was therefore the subject of much discussion. On 16th July Mr Curtin informed the British Government of the difficulties that would face the Australian Government in maintaining the flow of reinforcements from Australia to the 9th Division. On 24th July Mr Churchill cabled Mr Curtin the text of a commentary by the British Chiefs of Staff on the possibility of withdrawing the 9th Division from the Middle East. The Chiefs of Staff pointed to the danger to the oilfields of the Middle East from a possible German break-through in the Caucasus, the extent to which the Middle East had been denuded of forces to meet the threat from Japan, and the efforts being made to reinforce the Middle East from the United Kingdom. It was their opinion that to withdraw the 9th Division "at the present time or indeed during this year (1942)" would endanger the safety of the vital Abadan oilfields, without which it would be impossible to maintain the British position in the Middle East and the Indian Ocean and might prove impossible to meet Australia's oil requirements, 60 per cent of which came from there.[4]

---

[4] In Barnett, *The Desert Generals*, there is a quotation from a telegram said to have been sent by Churchill to Auchinleck on 12th July reading as follows: "The only way a sufficient army can be gathered in the northern theatre [of the Middle East] is by your defeating or destroying General Rommel and driving him at least to a safe distance. If this were accomplished before the middle of September, the Australian divisions [sic] could return to their station in Palestine and Iraq [sic]."

Moreover the division's transportation to Australia and replacement would involve a dangerous and unjustifiable shipping commitment. Mr Churchill said that he hoped that the Australian Government would be able to overcome the reinforcement difficulties; if not, he suggested that it would be necessary to fall back upon the expedient of making wastage good by breaking up ancillary units.

Japanese forces had been in New Guinea since the first week of March, when they had occupied Lae and Salamaua. On 21st July the Japanese made a landing at Gona, on the north coast of the massive island's eastern peninsula, in the territory of Papua, posing a threat, soon to be realised, that an advance would be made across the peninsula to strike at the Australian administrative centre at Port Moresby. The Torres Strait dividing Papua from the Australian mainland is only 90 miles wide.

It was against that background that Churchill's communication was considered by the Australian War Cabinet on 29th July. Next day Curtin replied to Churchill that it was disappointing that the review of the Chiefs of Staff dwelt at some length on the strategical position in the Middle East without mentioning the position in the Pacific. It was the desire of the Australian Government that the Commander-in-Chief of the South-West Pacific should have at his disposal all the Australian forces it could provide; therefore it would do no more than agree to an extension of the period for the temporary retention of the 9th Division in the Middle East. As General Blamey had advised against the breaking-up of ancillary units, approval had been given to the sending of reinforcements.

By the end of July, after four weeks' operations, the 9th Division had suffered 2,552 battle casualties (including 127 officers). On 31st July Curtin approved of the early dispatch of 3,978 reinforcements, being sufficient for two months at the intense activity scale; he told the Advisory War Council, however, that there was to be no departure from the principle that all A.I.F. forces abroad should return to Australia for employment in the South-West Pacific.

About a month later Morshead, presumably looking ahead to the division's likely requirements when the Eighth Army launched its next offensive, suggested to Australian Army Headquarters in Melbourne that the two months' reinforcements coming forward were not enough. In a cable sent on 27th August he represented that on the basis of recent experience it was essential to have available in the Middle East three months' reinforcements at the "intense activity" rate. To achieve this, 3,569 personnel would be required after making good existing shortages and after taking into account the 4,000 reinforcements already in transit. In addition, one month's reinforcements at the "intense activity" rate (2,544 personnel) should also be dispatched to allow for wastage during the period that would elapse before the arrival of the additional reinforcements. In brief, the early dispatch of 6,113 men was sought. It was also requested that thereafter monthly reinforcements be provided at the normal scale.

When Morshead's message arrived in Australia, the operations being fought to resist the Japanese attempt to take the whole of Papua had reached their most critical stage. On the Owen Stanley Range's jungle trails the outcome of the desperate fighting to halt and turn back the Japanese force advancing on Port Moresby hung in the balance, and at Milne Bay the Australian forces (including the 18th Brigade in its first operation since leaving Tobruk) had sustained some temporary rebuffs from the Japanese invading force. The need to employ more battle-hardened formations, and therefore A.I.F. formations, against the Japanese forces in Papua and New Guinea was plain and pressing. Moreover the high sickness rate in tropical warfare at that time, before the problem of malaria control had been solved, was aggravating the manpower problem.

General Blamey recommended to the Commonwealth Government that, if it intended the 9th Division to remain in the Middle East, Morshead's requests should be met. About the same time, however, Blamey represented to the Government that there was a need to increase the land forces in the South-West Pacific Area by a corps of three divisions. Mr Curtin on 11th September made similar representations to the President of the United States. On the same day Curtin approved of the dispatch of the 6,000 reinforcements Morshead had requested but informed General Blamey that the future of the 9th Division was at present under discussion with President Roosevelt and Mr Churchill. Before these reinforcements embarked other developments were to cause Curtin to reverse his decision.

CHAPTER 13

ALAM EL HALFA AND "BULIMBA"

AT the turn of the month the planning of Eighth Army headquarters reflected an unhappy ambivalence, as though the command was as apprehensive as it was hopeful. The respite from offensive operations afforded formation and unit commanders by the lull after the abortive attacks on 27th July was partly taken up by reconnaissances of possible holding areas in rear, and routes to them. Such prudent precautions against unexpected calamity were dispiriting.

Early in August the 9th Division was directed to give up the ground captured by the 24th Brigade on the Makh Khad ridges. The fortifications of the Alamein Box were to remain the main holding positions. Auchinleck's intention was to reduce the number of troops committed to holding the front; his policy was to discontinue the offensive for the present and to prepare for "a new and decisive effort", perhaps about the middle of September.

An operation order issued by the 9th Division on 1st August expressed the opinion that the Germans would build up a striking force as soon as possible, which might be ready to operate during the second half of August. The XXX Corps would hold its ground, reorganise to give greater depth in defence and create a reserve for the counter-offensive. The 24th Brigade was to withdraw into the El Alamein Box and the 20th and 26th Brigades were to change places over two nights, the 20th to be in position from Trig 33 to Point 26 by the morning of 3rd August, linking those positions with the El Alamein fortifications and protecting the area with minefields.

Similar reorganisation was effected in other sectors. As the army settled down to undertake a prolonged defence of the ground it held, the 9th Division (with the 50th R.T.R. under command) held the coast sector, on its left the South African division linked with the 5th Indian Division astride Ruweisat Ridge, the New Zealand division held the right flank of the neighbouring XIII Corps and part of the 1st South African was in rear of the 9th.

In June, July and the first half of August decisions were made in Washington, London and Cairo which greatly affected the future conduct of the war in Africa. When the British Prime Minister and General Sir Alan Brooke, Chief of the Imperial General Staff, visited the United States in June, they succeeded in persuading Roosevelt and the American Chiefs of Staff to reconsider their insistence that the main Allied effort in the European war should be a cross-channel operation to be mounted in the autumn. Churchill's polemic skill compelled notice to be taken of the British thesis that hard facts precluded operations in France until greater forces and resources could be assembled, while on the other hand an enlargement of operations in Africa offered promise of major victory. In a memorandum to the President of the United States Churchill asked questions that the American advocates of early, direct assault in France found hard to answer. He pointed out that no responsible British military authority had been able to devise a plan to invade Europe in 1942 with prospect of success.

"Have the American staffs a plan?" he asked. "At what points would they strike? What landing craft and shipping are available? Who is the officer prepared to command the enterprise? In case no plan can be made . . . what else are we going to do? . . . It is in this setting and on this background that the French North-West African operation should be studied."

Another decision made in Washington was of more immediate import to the Middle East command. The ill-wind that had taken the tidings of the fall of Tobruk to Churchill and Brooke in Washington presented the Eighth Army with a fulfilment of its greatest need in fighting equipment, tanks that could match the best German tanks in gun-range, mobility and dependability, for Roosevelt and General Marshall responded by magnanimously offering to send to the Middle East 100 self-propelled guns and 300 Sherman tanks, which had just been issued to the American armoured division. If Churchill's past arguments with Wavell and Auchinleck about launching newly-arrived tanks into battle could be taken as a pointer, it would not be long before he would again be calling upon the Middle East command to expedite the mounting of a major offensive.

When Churchill and Brooke returned from the United States, the Eighth Army was about to make what then seemed a last stand at El Alamein. Churchill desired to fly out at once to the Middle East but was persuaded by Brooke to wait till the situation had stabilised. And on 15th July, Brooke obtained from the Prime Minister permission to visit the Middle East alone.

In the next fortnight General Marshall, Admiral King and Mr Harry L. Hopkins visited London to finalise Allied strategy for the year and on 28th July agreement between the two nations to mount an invasion of North Africa and defer the invasion of Europe was at last attained.

Meanwhile news of Auchinleck's failure at Miteiriya Ridge and his decision to revert to the defensive had reached London. Churchill who was always desirous of making the main decisions in the conduct of the war determined at once that he must himself take the action necessary to put aright what seemed amiss in Cairo. The King and the War Cabinet agreed. Brooke was informed on 30th July, the eve of his departure, that Churchill would be following him to Egypt. Next day Stalin invited Churchill to visit him in Moscow. Churchill immediately accepted and decided to combine both journeys. He cabled Stalin that he would fix from Cairo the date of his visit to Russia.

Churchill also invited Field Marshal Smuts and General Wavell to attend the discussions in Cairo. There was no mistaking the mood in which the British Prime Minister set forth on his mission. On 1st August he sent the following message to General Brooke at Gibraltar:

> How necessary it is for us to get to the Middle East at once is shown by the following extract from Auchinleck's telegram received yesterday:
> "An exhaustive conference on tactical situation held yesterday with Corps Commanders. Owing to lack of resources and enemy's effective consolidation of his positions we reluctantly concluded that in present circumstances it is not feasible to renew our efforts to break enemy front or turn his southern flank. It is unlikely that an opportunity will arise for resumption of offensive operations before mid-September. This depends on enemy's ability to build up his tank force. Temporarily therefore our policy will be defensive, including thorough preparations and consolidations in whole defensive area. In the meantime we shall seize at once any opportunity of taking the offensive suddenly and surprising the enemy."

Churchill arrived by air in Cairo on 3rd August and in the evening conferred with Generals Brooke and Auchinleck. "He is fretting that there is to be no offensive action until September 15th, and I see already troublesome times ahead," Brooke noted in his diary.[1] The main discussion concerned the future command of the Eighth Army. It was agreed that Auchinleck should not continue to combine his office of theatre commander in the Middle East with direct command of the Eighth Army in the field. Brooke proposed General Montgomery as the army commander. Churchill proposed Gott, although, as Brooke commented, Churchill was selecting Gott without having seen him. A round of conferences followed on the 4th. Brooke again pressed for the appointment of Montgomery but the Prime Minister demurred on the ground that Montgomery could not arrive in time to advance the date of the next offensive.

A big strategical problem facing the Middle East commanders was whether to concentrate on holding the Persian oilfields against a possible German advance in the late summer or to concentrate on holding Egypt. "We have not got the forces to do both," the Middle East Defence Committee had said in a telegram to London on 9th July, "and if we try to do both we may fail to achieve either. We request your guidance and instruction on this issue."

At one of the conferences at Cairo on the 4th Brooke explained to Churchill, Smuts, Wavell, Casey and the three Commanders-in-Chief that the Chiefs of Staff considered that to defeat Rommel would be the best contribution the Commanders-in-Chief could make to the security of the Middle East, but that, if the Russian southern front broke, they must hold the Abadan oilfields area even at the risk of losing the Egyptian Delta. Churchill said, however, that he was not prepared to divert any forces from Egypt until a decision had been reached in the Western Desert. The meeting agreed to this policy.

Next day Churchill and Brooke visited the Eighth Army. Churchill drove first to the 9th Division's headquarters, where he arrived at 9 a.m. accompanied by Generals Brooke, Auchinleck and Ramsden and Air Chief Marshal Tedder. There he met the Australian brigadiers, senior staff officers, and heads of services and drove through the areas of the 2/3rd

---
[1] Quoted in A. Bryant, *The Turn of the Tide* (1957), p. 439.

Pioneer Battalion and 26th Brigade, stopping to speak to men on the way. Morshead noted in his diary that the British Prime Minister was most congratulatory and said that the division had stemmed the tide and done magnificently.

The visit to the Eighth Army provided opportunities for both Churchill and Brooke to see something of Gott. Churchill was confirmed in his view that this man with the "clear blue eyes" was the commander he needed. Brooke's misgivings were confirmed.

By 6th August Churchill had determined that General Auchinleck must be replaced. He first offered the new Middle East Command to Brooke but he declined. Brooke has since stated that he felt he could best serve the Prime Minister as Chief of Staff, but sometimes the reason and motive for a difficult personal choice are not fully evident when one makes the decision.

After further discussions Churchill (on 6th August) sent a telegram to London seeking War Cabinet approval of a reorganisation of the Middle East Command and a series of transfers of senior officers. He proposed a reorganisation of the Middle East Command into two commands—a Near East Command comprising Egypt, Palestine and Syria and a Middle East Command comprising Persia and Iraq. Auchinleck was to be offered the new and relatively inactive Middle East Command and General Alexander[2] the Near East Command. Alexander who had previously been appointed to command the British army to take part in the projected Allied landings in French North Africa, should be replaced in that command by General Montgomery. General Gott should command the Eighth Army; and Generals Corbett (C.G.S. at Cairo), Ramsden (XXX Corps) and Dorman-Smith (D.C.G.S.) should be replaced. Churchill added that Smuts, Brooke and Casey approved of these proposals. The War Cabinet agreed, though at first it raised objections to the division of the command. If the Prime Minister's personal selection of a field commander at the second level of command in an operational theatre was unorthodox, Brooke's endorsement gave it at least formal correctness. On the 7th, however, an aircraft in which Gott was travelling to Cairo was shot down. Gott was killed. Thereupon Churchill proposed that Montgomery should command the Eighth Army and the War Cabinet agreed.[3]

"Strafer" Gott was widely mourned in the Eighth Army by the commanders, staff officers and men who had come to know him in the course of the army's battles but were as yet unaware to what purpose he had been summoned to Cairo. Many of these later contended that, when the mantle was placed on Montgomery's shoulders, it was merely to execute a plan that Gott had made. Yet, in the after-knowledge afforded by historical research, Gott's potent influence on both the decisions of the army command and their execution in the campaigns that preceded his death appears

---

[2] Field Marshal Rt Hon Earl Alexander, KG, GCB, GCMG, CSI, DSO, MC. GOC 1 Div 1938-40; GOC-in-C Southern Comd 1940-42; GOC Burma 1942; C-in-C ME 1942-43, Allied Armies in Italy 1944; Supreme Comd Mediterranean Theatre 1944-45. Governor-General of Canada 1945-52. Regular soldier; b. Co. Tyrone, Ireland, 10 Dec 1891.

[3] The warm discussions leading up to these changes are described in Churchill, *The Second World War*, Vol IV (1951); A. Bryant, *The Turn of the Tide*; and J. Connell, *Auchinleck*.

to have contributed as much to the army's defeats as to its victories. His virtues were his character, impressive bearing and ability to inspire others with confidence in himself, rather than the capacity, possessed by Montgomery in abundant measure, to conceive the form of successful battle action and to get commanders, staff and combatants to work efficiently, train and fight to the conception.

In the preceding year Churchill had been impatiently critical of Auchinleck because of his refusal to be hastened in mounting the offensive intended to relieve Tobruk and destroy the German Army in Africa. Now, despite Auchinleck's recent success in halting Rommel by seizing the initiative and forcing him onto the defensive, Churchill was again impatient because Auchinleck was proposing not to mount another offensive before mid-September. That would seem to have been the main factor prompting Churchill's decision to remove him from command. Yet the successors Churchill chose soon came to the same conclusion as Auchinleck, and eventually decided that the offensive should not be resumed until much later than Auchinleck had suggested.

After the new appointments had been announced, among those of Auchinleck's subordinates who wrote to him expressing regret and gratitude was Morshead, who said:

I am very sorry and very surprised that you are going away, and every single member of the A.I.F. will be as regretful as I am, for we all hold you in the highest regard.

You have always been particularly kind and generous to me, and I shall always remember with gratitude your consideration and encouragement both while in Tobruk and ever since, and your having me to stay with you on several occasions.

I hope that your new appointment will be worthy of you. Whatever and wherever it is I should be not merely content but very privileged to serve under you.

"I looks towards you" Sir, and wish you all you wish yourself.

Auchinleck understandably declined the proposed "Middle East" appointment on the ground that he considered the new command arrangement faulty in structure and likely to break down under stress. He went to India, took some leave and then set about writing his despatch.

It had long been evident that Alexander, seven years younger than his predecessor and indeed four years younger than Montgomery, was destined for high command. Alexander, unlike most of his seniors, collaterals and his immediate subordinate, had held no staff appointment until he was 39; his service in the first world war was almost entirely in the infantry; he was commanding a battalion in France at the age of 25. Brooke, Wavell, Wilson, Montgomery, for example, had seen only brief regimental service or none at all in that war. In the 1930's Alexander had led a brigade in operations on the North-West Frontier of India, and in France in 1939 and 1940 had commanded the 1st Division (Montgomery commanded the 3rd) and finally the rearguard at Dunkirk. Writing long afterwards about critical days in France in May 1940 Brooke, then a corps commander in the B.E.F., wrote:

It was intensely interesting watching him [Alexander] and Monty during those trying days, both of them completely imperturbable and efficiency itself, and yet two totally different characters. Monty with his quick brain for appreciating military situations was well aware of the very critical situation that he was in, and the very dangers and difficulties . . . acted as a stimulus . . .; they thrilled him and put the sharpest of edges on his military ability. Alex, on the other hand, gave me the impression of never fully realising all the very unpleasant potentialities of our predicament. He remained entirely unaffected by it, completely composed and appeared never to have the slightest doubt that all would come right in the end.[4]

After Dunkirk Alexander had been a corps commander in Britain in 1940-41 and then was given the vital Southern Command. When the defence of Burma was collapsing in March 1942 he was hurried out to take over and he commanded during the retreat to India. Montgomery had become a corps commander in England in 1940 and late in 1941 had been promoted to South-Eastern Command.

Alexander arrived in Cairo on 8th August and, after he assumed command on the 15th, chose General McCreery as his chief of staff. McCreery, a cavalry officer, had been Alexander's G.S.O.1 when he commanded the 1st Division in France in 1939 and early 1940, and when the Germans attacked in May 1940 he was commanding the 2nd Armoured Brigade. General Lumsden had been appointed to command the XIII Corps in Gott's place.

On the 10th Churchill had handed Alexander a handwritten directive:

1. Your prime and main duty will be to take or destroy at the earliest opportunity the German-Italian Army commanded by Field Marshal Rommel together with all its supplies and establishments in Egypt and Libya.

2. You will discharge or cause to be discharged such other duties as pertain to your Command without prejudice to the task described in paragraph 1 which must be considered paramount in His Majesty's interests.

Alexander implied in his despatch written later that he found the Eighth Army disheartened and discouraged and lacking in confidence in the high command. His first step in restoring morale was "to lay down the firm principle, to be made known to all ranks, that no further withdrawal was contemplated and that we would fight the coming battle on the ground on which we stood".

Montgomery arrived in Cairo on 12th August. After seeing Auchinleck and Alexander that day he went next morning at Auchinleck's suggestion to the Eighth Army to spend the two days before Alexander and he were due to take over their appointments. The senior staff officer of Eighth Army, Brigadier de Guingand, was well known to Montgomery, and they had worked together before the war. Montgomery summoned de Guingand to meet him in the desert outside Alexandria, and together they drove out to the headquarters of the Eighth Army. On the way, at Montgomery's request, de Guingand described the situation and outlined some matters that he thought needed Montgomery's attention. Among these were:

(a) The dangerous "looking over the shoulder" defensive policy.
(b) The unsound fashion that prevailed of fighting in battle groups or "Jock Columns" as they were called, and not in divisions as the army had been trained to fight. Only in this way could the army develop its full strength.

---

[4] Quoted in Bryant, *The Turn of the Tide*, pp. 107-8.

(c) The unsatisfactory headquarters set-up.
(d) The fact that Army and Air Headquarters were not together.[5]

Montgomery had the staff assembled on the night of his arrival and addressed them. In de Guingand's words, "the effect of the address was electric—it was terrific! And we all went to bed that night with a new hope in our hearts, and a great confidence in the future of our army".[6]

Montgomery said that Alexander and he had been given a mandate to destroy the Axis forces in North Africa. Any further withdrawal was out of the question. He would not be very happy if Rommel's expected attack came within the next two weeks; after that he would welcome it. He would immediately start planning a great offensive. The expression "battle groups" would cease to exist; divisions were to fight as divisions. He would form a reserve "corps d'élite" consisting of two armoured divisions and the New Zealand division (motorised). He would not attack until he was ready, whatever the pressure and from whatever quarter.

When Montgomery arrived Ramsden was temporarily in command of the Eighth Army and both corps were temporarily commanded by Dominion generals—the XXX by Morshead and the XIII by Freyberg. Montgomery, although not due to take over until the 15th, sent Ramsden back to his corps and then wrote a signal to Middle East Headquarters stating that he had assumed command of the army.

"I will give you two simple rules which every general should observe". It is some three years before Montgomery came to the Middle East, Wavell is speaking, and his subject is "The General and his Troops". He proceeds to state his two rules. "First, never to try to do his own staff work; and, secondly, never to let his staff get between him and his troops."

From the very moment of his arrival at the Eighth Army Montgomery carried both rules to their extreme application. He declined to exercise command through a clutter of paper-work. When de Guingand set out to meet Montgomery that first day, he took with him a paper laboriously prepared to present his views on what was wrong. Montgomery told him to put the paper away. "Tell me about it!" he enjoined. We see him next morning bundling off the unfortunate staff officer who came to him with the morning's situation and patrol reports.

Far from letting his staff get between him and his men, Montgomery set out assiduously to attract their attention, to show himself often to them and to make himself easily recognisable, not only as a commander but as a man of individuality; to implant in their minds an image of himself as an energetic, realistic and efficient commander. Morale was the number one factor in war, Montgomery always declared. Experts in logistics might disagree, but it was an expedient and efficacious belief for one who could influence his men to fight but had no power to energise the production and delivery of the material means. So Montgomery's efforts were directed to giving his officers and men a belief in the army they belonged to, a quite unqualified confidence. That, he knew, only success could give them;

---
[5] De Guingand, *Operation Victory*, p. 135.
[6] De Guingand, pp. 136-7.

but a spirit of optimism could be nurtured meanwhile, and would grow. The first step was to make them believe that they would win their battles. He himself exuded confidence, for he had no doubt that he was an absolutely first-rate commander, and he was determined that there were to be no failures.

Having arrogated to himself two days of command not rightly his, Montgomery went out, saw the ground, and then set off to see and talk with Freyberg and other commanders. On the 14th he visited the 9th Australian Division, met the senior officers, went forward to the 20th Brigade, viewed no-man's land and the enemy's front line from Point 24, and then visited the 24th Brigade headquarters for 10 minutes. He called for and was issued with a "digger" hat, which he wore for some time before deciding to adopt a beret as his distinctive head-dress. Montgomery then asked for and was given a "Rising Sun" badge for the hat, claiming an entitlement to wear it on the ground that his father had been Bishop of Tasmania.

The hat was brought to him while he was at Brigadier Windeyer's headquarters on the occasion of that first visit. Montgomery tried it on without denting it, looking rather odd. While Montgomery was talking to others present about hats, Morshead took Windeyer aside, suspecting that the new army commander's idiosyncrasies might strike Windeyer as rather comic, if not surprising, and told him: "This man is really a breath of fresh air. Things are going to be different soon." A few days later Morshead summoned the brigadiers to meet him at Windeyer's headquarters. Windeyer recalled the conference many years later:

> I am quoting Morshead's words as nearly as I can remember them:
> "I have had a long talk with the new army commander. It was refreshing. He is making some changes. There are some things, four things especially, he wants understood.
> First, this line will be held. There will be no further withdrawals and plans for withdrawals are cancelled. We will hold our present position until he is ready to attack. That is good news.
> Second, formations are not to be broken up. There will be no more battle groups or 'Jock columns'. Divisions will fight as divisions and brigades as brigades. That I am sure we are pleased to hear.
> Third, the word 'box' is not to be used; it is banished from the military vocabulary. He doesn't want to create the impression that the army is boxed up. That you will understand too.
> His fourth point is perhaps not quite so easy: he says that the word 'consolidation' is also to be banished. It is a handicap to the momentum of an attack. When his attack begins he does not want it to seem that he intends it to come to a standstill. He intends to keep going. He suggests 're-organise' is a better word than consolidate."

A point Morshead may not have mentioned to his brigadiers, because it did not concern them, was that Montgomery had also told his senior commanders that he was a firm believer in the chief of staff system and would always act through the chief of his staff. This contrasted with the methods adopted by his predecessor, whose employment of the clever Dorman-Smith in the role of Deputy Chief of the General Staff in the field, and as a close collaborator in directing operations, had introduced, whatever benefit came from it, a questionable dualism of staff function.

Montgomery further made it clear to his commanders that orders were to be acted upon, not debated.

On another visit to the division made soon afterwards Montgomery, seeing some gunners beside one of the new anti-tank guns, asked them what they thought of the gun and was told that they had not fired it; they had been forbidden, they said, to practise with live ammunition because it was so scarce and reserved exclusively for battle use. Within a day or two an order came down from Army Headquarters that every six-pounder gun was to fire off half its ammunition stocks in practice. "Unless the men are trained to shoot," said Montgomery's memorandum, "we shall do no good on the day of battle however great the number of rounds we have saved ready for that day."

When the commander of the 51st Highland Division, General Wimberley,[7] informed General Montgomery soon after the division's arrival that he was troubled at having been told that flashes were not to be worn in his division because Middle East security rules forbade formation and unit identifications on dress, Montgomery at once told Wimberley to let his men wear their flashes.

Other instances could be found, but those given must suffice to illustrate the methods by which Montgomery almost instantly had an extraordinary effect on the Eighth Army, giving it revived hope, a better tone and a new confidence. With an orator's instinct—not with rhetoric but with telling words followed up by action that showed he meant what he said—he told his army the things it wanted to hear, that it would never go back but fight where it stood, that it would surely attack again when ready, but not before, and that tactical methods which had failed—the "boxes" and the small improvised battle groups—would be discarded and the vocabulary signifying them banished. His influence was felt first and most dynamically at the higher command level but percolated down to the front-line soldier as the thoroughness of the army's preparations and the purposefulness of the training and rehearsal soon required of all formations and units came to be experienced. No army was ever more confident, none ever had a higher morale, than the Eighth Army when it next attacked.

Montgomery soon took the wise step of concentrating his whole headquarters at Burg el Arab close to Air Vice-Marshal Coningham's[8] Desert Air Force headquarters. Alexander then set up a small tactical headquarters of his own, also alongside.

In order to strengthen the army against Rommel's expected attack Montgomery asked for and was promptly given the recently-arrived 44th Division because he wished to place it on Alam el Halfa Ridge which could become the keystone of resistance to a wide turning movement

---

[7] Maj-Gen D. N. Wimberley, CB, DSO, MC. (1915-18: Lt to Maj, MG Corps.) Comd 152 Bde 1940-41; GOC 51 Highland Div 1941-43; Comdt Staff College 1943-44; Director of Inf, War Office, 1944-46. Regular soldier; b. 15 Aug 1896.
[8] Air Marshal Sir Arthur Coningham, KCB, KBE, DSO, MC, DFC, AFC. AOC Desert Air Force 1941-43, NW African Tactical Air Force 1943, Second TAF 1944-45; AOC-in-C Flying Training Comd 1945. Regular air force officer; of Wellington, NZ, and Cookham Dean, England; b. Brisbane, 19 Jan 1895. Killed in aircraft accident 30 Jan 1948.

when the next enemy blow fell. He then got Alexander to agree to have General Horrocks[9] flown from England to command the XIII Corps; later Lumsden was transferred to the command of the X Corps.

Churchill visited Egypt again on the 19th on his way home from Russia. "A complete change of atmosphere has taken place . . ." he reported. "The highest alacrity and activity prevails"; and he found that Alexander "cool, gay, comprehending all . . . inspired quiet, deep confidence in every quarter."[1]

In due course news of the appointments to high commands in the Middle East made after Mr Churchill's first visit reached Australia. When General Blamey learnt of the first round of changes, including the promotion of Major-General Lumsden to a corps command, he drew Mr Curtin's attention to the appointments, in a letter dated 21st August 1942, asserting, but without derogating from the officers concerned, that none of them had had "the same experience of desert warfare or the same success in any warfare" as General Morshead, who, he said, could not but feel humiliated at having inexperienced English officers in command over him.[2] The disregard invariably shown by British authorities in the Middle East in this respect, said General Blamey, was notorious, and this latest example had aroused ill-feeling in the Australian Army. He asked the Prime Minister to make representations to London that the claims of Dominion commanders for higher command should not be disregarded. He also cabled Morshead assuring him of his fullest confidence and informing him that he was referring this question of higher command appointments to the Prime Minister.

Morshead replied that it had been made abundantly clear that Dominion commanders were ineligible for corps commands even when the corps consisted wholly of Dominion troops; soon after Major-General Ramsden had been appointed to the command of XXX Corps, then consisting of the 1st South African and 9th Australian Divisions, he had informed Morshead that Major-General Briggs,[3] who had only recently been appointed to command an Indian division in another corps, would take over the XXX Corps if Ramsden became a casualty.[4] Morshead also

---

[9] Lt-Gen Sir Brian Horrocks, KCB, KBE, DSO, MC. (1914-19: Lt to Capt, Middlesex Regt.) GOC 9 Armd Div, XIII Corps, X Corps, IX Corps and XXX Corps. Regular soldier; b. 7 Sep 1895.
[1] Churchill, Vol IV, pp. 466, 469.
[2] Montgomery was chief staff officer of a division by the end of the first world war and, as mentioned, had commanded a division in the British Expeditionary Force in France in 1940 and later a corps and then an area in England. Ramsden had commanded a brigade in the BEF, and the 50th Division in the Middle East until appointed a corps commander in July 1942. Horrocks had commanded a battalion in the BEF and, temporarily, a brigade in the last days round Dunkirk; then a division in England. Leese had been DCGS of the BEF and later commanded a brigade and then various divisions in England. Morshead had commanded a battalion in France from 1916 to 1918, a brigade in England and Africa in 1940 and 1941, a division since February 1941, and had been fortress commander in Tobruk. Freyberg had commanded a battalion from 1915 to 1917, a brigade in France in 1917 and 1918, and the New Zealand division from 1939 onwards. He had been in effect a corps commander on Crete in 1941.
[3] Lt-Gen Sir Harold Briggs, KCIE, CB, CBE, DSO. (1915-18: Lt to Capt, Indian Army.) Comd 7 Indian Bde 1940-42; GOC 5 Indian Div 1942-44. Regular soldier; b. 14 Jul 1894. Died 27 Oct 1952.
[4] Morshead did command the corps for two short periods while Ramsden acted as army commander, but it appears that his command was more nominal than real. "I have theoretically been commanding XXX Corps for last four days," he noted in his diary for 13th August. A diary entry on 3rd August relating to an earlier period of command reads: "I am now temporarily in command of XXX Corps. All I do is to spend night at Corps Headquarters."

mentioned that when Gott was killed Freyberg had administered the XIII Corps for a few days, but then Horrocks, who had commanded a machine-gun battalion in France but had had no operational experience since, had been appointed to that command.[5] Morshead added that he was too interested and occupied with his own command to bother about personal feelings.

Blamey wrote a second letter to Curtin, telling him of the additional facts mentioned by Morshead and again suggesting that he raise the matter with the authorities in the United Kingdom. No Australian commander, he said, had any desire to be appointed to the command of troops of the United Kingdom except when they were fighting in the same formations as Dominion troops; but where that was so, failure to recognise the claims of proved Dominion commanders placed a severe strain on good relations between senior officers. Curtin then cabled Churchill expressing the Australian Government's concern that Morshead's claims for consideration appeared to have been disregarded. Churchill replied that Morshead had been carefully considered when the recent appointments were made and his undoubted qualifications would be taken into account in any further change. He added that the Chief of the Imperial General Staff had instructed Montgomery to consider the desirability of giving Morshead a corps; this, said Churchill, would have been agreeable to himself, for he had formed a high opinion of Morshead's bearing and spirit when he had visited his headquarters at El Alamein.

Meanwhile Morshead had informed Alexander (on 5th September) of his exchange of cables with Blamey and of Curtin's cable to Churchill. A few days later, in a cable to Blamey, he reported Alexander's reaction:

> He replied highest commands in Middle East were open to Dominion commanders and that appointments of corps commanders in August were made at a conference of Prime Minister, Commander-in-Chief and General Montgomery in Cairo. He was good enough to say he thought I had some qualifications for corps command, adding that war would last long time and opportunity would come.

On 13th September, three days after Churchill had cabled Curtin that Morshead's qualifications would be considered in any further change, Montgomery informed Morshead that Lieut-General Ramsden was being replaced as commander of the XXX Corps by Lieut-General Leese,[6] who was due to arrive by air from the United Kingdom that day. In a cable sent next day informing Blamey of this, Morshead said that he had asked Montgomery whether he was aware of Morshead's earlier conversation with Alexander. Montgomery had acknowledged that he was. Morshead reported Montgomery as saying that both the Commander-in-Chief and he

---

[5] Horrocks wrote in his autobiography: "How would I shape as a corps commander, I wondered? It was a big step up from command of the 2nd Battalion, The Middlesex Regiment during the withdrawal to Dunkirk, which was the last time I had been on active service. My subsequent promotions to brigadier and divisional commander had been made during training in the United Kingdom."—*A Full Life* (1960), p. 103.

[6] Lt-Gen Sir Oliver Leese, Bt, KCB, CBE, DSO. (1914-16: Lt, Coldstream Guards.) Dep CGS BEF 1940; GOC 15 (Scottish) Div 1941, XXX Corps 1942-43, Eighth Army 1943-44; C-in-C Allied Land Forces South-East Asia 1944-45. Regular soldier; b. 27 Oct 1894.

were of opinion that as Morshead was not a regular soldier he did not possess the requisite training and experience.[7] He continued:

> When asked whether 9th Australian Division had ever failed to do what was required of it he replied it was superb. Admitted he did not know me or anything about my service and said if Leese became casualty during operations I would then command corps. Montgomery who has revitalised Eighth Army is quite friendly but just doubts capacity any general who has not devoted entire life to soldiering.[8]

Morshead stated that he had told Montgomery that he was presenting the case of Dominion officers generally rather than pressing any personal claims. He told Blamey that he was very content and happy with his present command and appointment.

Blamey (who had been a regular from 1906 to 1925) wrote to Curtin that Morshead's account of his interviews revealed an "attitude of unconscious arrogance" and "the repugnance of the British Command to accept Dominion officers, however successful in higher command" because "they had not been turned out on the British pattern". If these were strong words, yet the facts seemed to support Blamey's contention. An unexpressed reason for not preferring Morshead may have been that Auchinleck and Ramsden had found him a difficult subordinate. The considerations mentioned by Blamey did not apply to the case of Freyberg who, though he showed no ambition to leave the New Zealand division for higher responsibilities, could have been considered for a corps command but was not, for a long time to come. Freyberg was an ex-regular officer and Guardsman with an unsurpassed record of both gallantry and operational command; his seniority as a regular major-general had been above that of Alexander, Montgomery, Wilson and Auchinleck and only nine months below Wavell's.[9] Yet at the close of the African campaign, Freyberg was still only a divisional commander, although he had temporarily commanded a corps for a fortnight just before the surrender of the Axis forces; indeed it was not until February 1944, after Freyberg's division, in three years of fighting under his command, had successfully carried out more major operational tasks than any other Allied formation, that he was made a corps commander, after representations had been made by the New Zealand Government to the British Government against his repeated supersession by British commanders of less experience.

---

[7] Montgomery may not have been aware that in France in 1918 the Canadian and Australian corps, outstanding both for their fighting ability and their staff work, were commanded by citizen soldiers. To most British regulars the idea of a citizen soldier commanding even a division seems to have been unwelcome and disturbing. It is interesting, however, that eventually Montgomery's senior administrative officer, Major-General Miles Graham, and his senior Intelligence officer, Brigadier E. T. Williams, were civilian soldiers. It appears that there was an odd difference between Montgomery's views about the qualifications needed in formation commanders and in staff officers. De Guingand wrote: "In 21st Army Group a number of important posts were held by young ex-civilians. . . . Montgomery backed youth and the 'clever chap' and this policy paid him enormously."—*Operation Victory*, p. 473.

[8] More convincing evidence can hardly be imagined of how swiftly Montgomery had exerted an invigorating influence throughout his vast command than that Morshead, no more than a month after Montgomery had taken charge and in the very course of commenting adversely on his attitude to non-professional commanders (including Morshead himself), should have spontaneously averred that he had "revitalised" the Eighth Army.

[9] Seven years earlier, on the eve of Freyberg's retirement from the British regular army, he had been a major-general of three years seniority, while Horrocks was a brigade major. Writing of the Battle of Mareth (March 1944) Horrocks generously described Freyberg as a general "who had forgotten more about soldiering than I was ever likely to know".

There was nothing dishonourable in all this. It was merely that the men at the top of the British Army hierarchy tacitly assumed that they would direct the operations of all the formations committed to a theatre in which they exercised command, regarding the role of Dominion commanders as merely one of commanding their own formations; nor would the point have occurred to them, until it was brought to their attention, that a corps such as XXX Corps, holding its front with two Dominion divisions, might as appropriately be commanded by a Dominion commander.

There can be little doubt that a main factor determining the selection of the officers chosen for key posts in the Middle East at this time was the opinion of the Chief of the Imperial Staff, General Brooke. They had all served under him: Alexander, Montgomery, McCreery and Horrocks in France, Leese in England.[1] That Brooke chose well is unquestionable.

While the appointments to higher command were under discussion, Morshead was considering who should command the 9th Division in the event of his becoming a casualty. He felt that, of the officers available, Brigadier Ramsay would be the best choice. Since Tovell was senior to Ramsay, he recommended in a cable to Blamey on 31st August that Tovell should be recalled to Australia for higher appointment. He told Blamey that Tovell's brigade had done splendidly in recent operations and that Tovell had always given full and loyal support. Blamey replied that Tovell should be returned to Australia, but owing to the claims of others could not receive a higher appointment. He also said that he intended to send a major-general to be Morshead's second-in-command. Morshead demurred to the latter suggestion. He did not, he said, see the need for a deputy. He had every confidence that Ramsay would command the division efficiently if the need arose. Should Blamey still decide to send a deputy, he asked to be first consulted about the person to be appointed, for it was essential that he and Morshead should work well together. Blamey did not reply immediately. In the meantime, on 12th September, Tovell had handed over his command to Brigadier Whitehead, whom Morshead had promoted to be his successor. Blamey reverted to the question of a deputy when cabling Morshead with reference to Leese's appointment to the command of XXX Corps. He said that the suggestion had been made partly as a camouflage "of possible developments at some future date"—an oblique reference, presumably, to the possibility of the division's recall to Australia. He had intended sending Major-General J. E. S. Stevens (then commanding Northern Territory Force), but, on receiving Morshead's views, had withheld action. If Morshead now agreed with him, he would be glad of a panel of names of officers whom Morshead would prefer for the appointment. He doubted if Ramsay was sufficiently experienced for the responsibility involved. Morshead replied that he would now be glad to have Stevens as his deputy.

Curtin's and Blamey's protests and Morshead's representations appear to have eventually had some effect. Morshead's diary records that Alexander's Chief of Staff, McCreery, called on him on 4th October and had

---
[1] See Bryant, *The Turn of the Tide*, p. 239.

a general discussion. Next day Montgomery visited Morshead and, in the course of a long discussion about the forthcoming battle, informed him that he would command the XXX Corps if Leese became a casualty.

The period over which the first of these changes in command had been taking place was one of static defence while the Eighth Army was getting ready to counter the onslaught Rommel was expected to make in mid-August. For the forward infantry and the engineers, who were laying mines, digging and patrolling, it was not a restful time. By night they slept in broken watches, each taking his turn to keep guard or patrol the wire; in addition one full night's sleep in three might be lost by men employed on deep patrolling. By day the heat, the intermittent shelling and the ubiquitous flies drove sleep away. The flies! The divisional cavalry recorded on the 9th that they were so bad that the midday meal had been practically dispensed with. It was midsummer. A number of unburied dead still lay on the battlefield when the 20th Brigade took over the forward positions. A strenuous policy of burying and cleaning up was adopted and within a fortnight the fly menace was under control.

The 20th Australian Brigade had two battalions forward: the 2/15th (Lieut-Colonel Ogle) on the right and the 2/17th (Lieut-Colonel Simpson[2]) on the left, with the 2/13th (Lieut-Colonel Turner) in reserve. On 3rd August, the day on which the brigade took over the front, Brigadier Windeyer laid down a policy of aggression. The enemy, he ordered, was to be fired on whenever seen, and harassed by patrols and raids. The first patrol in compliance with this direction set out from the 2/15th at 9 p.m. on the 4th. It comprised Captain Cobb[3] and 12 others. When they reached their objective about 1,500 yards north of Point 25 (Baillieu's Bluff) they were challenged and found themselves in the midst of a German position.

By this time (wrote Cobb in his report) everyone knew that surprise had been lost. All talking and digging had ceased and they were waiting for us. I placed the two Brens and then told the others we were going to crawl forward to the ones we had seen go to ground. No questions were asked. We crawled for about 60 yards, Corporal Else[4] and three men on my right, Corporal Cooper[5] and three men on my left, when we heard the bolt of a Spandau ripped back about 15 yards in front. I pitched my 69 at him and he fired at the same time. One bullet got me through the leg, one got Munckton[6] through the foot and one got Cooper, who was the slowest to get to his feet, in the body.

Private Munckton and I then followed the others into where the Spandau just fired from. The gun was not firing but there was movement in the fairly large trench behind it. Munckton emptied his rifle into it and at the same time Corporal Else yelled out "I've got a prisoner and all my men are safe." McHenry[7] yelled out

[2] Maj-Gen N. W. Simpson, CB, CBE, DSO, ED, NX12221. DAAG 7 Div 1941-42; CO 2/17 Bn 1942-44, 2/43 Bn 1944-45; Comd 29 Bde 1945. Bank officer; of Cremorne, NSW; b. Sydney, 22 Feb 1907.
[3] Capt W. W. Cobb, MC, QX6223; 2/15 Bn. Grazier; of Winton, Qld; b. Brisbane, 6 Jun 1917. Killed in action 23 Oct 1942.
[4] S-Sgt A. Else, MM, QX5495; 2/15 Bn. Farmer; of Pullenvale, Qld; b. Brisbane, 20 Aug 1916.
[5] Cpl R. C. Cooper, QX11442; 2/15 Bn. Inspector and oil depot keeper; of Townsville, Qld; b. Townsville, 6 Apr 1911. Killed in action 4 Aug 1942.
[6] Pte M. L. Munckton, QX5938; 2/15 Bn. Labourer; of Miles, Qld; b. Toowoomba, Qld, 3 Jan 1919.
[7] WO2 W. R. McHenry, QX5766; 2/15 Bn. Drover; of Charleville, Qld; b. Charleville, 19 Jan 1918.

"Corporal Cooper dead, Munckton hit and has left for home." Lance-Corporal Morris[8] who was Cooper's fourth man was having a merry time with his Tommy-gun on the left flank in another doover. I ordered the patrol to withdraw and moved over to where Corporal Else and party were. Just then the prisoner had a bit of a scuffle and threw himself to the ground—shamming dead. Private Woods[9] reminded him that he was alive with his bayonet and he jumped up and moved off with us. We had gone about 10 paces when someone fired from the ground at us with a Tommy-gun. I got him twice with my pistol from about ten feet but not before he had put one into my arm and killed our prisoner. After we'd gone through the prisoner I began to realise that the bullet through the arm was going to be a different matter than that in the leg. I told Else to take the patrol back and got Private Pickup[1] to give me a hand along. Just as we reached the Bren gunners I blacked out and Corporal Else threw me over his shoulder, got his men together —or rather apart—and moved off. From then on for about 1,000 yards they took it in turns to carry me until some particularly close medium machine-gun fire forced us to ground. I found when I got to my feet I was feeling much better and was able to walk most of the way into the road. At the road fortunately we found an Iti stretcher and I rode home in state on that.

Every man on the patrol knew, when the surprise was lost, that we were in for it —but no one hesitated or asked any questions. Corporal Else did an outstanding job. He carried out his orders to the letter in obtaining a prisoner and controlling his men. He remarked when I told him that I could stumble along behind that he'd carry me home even if I were b—— well dead. He frequently changed direction going home to keep the patrol out of the heaviest MMG fire and kept the men alert and moving. . . .

For the second night in succession Private McHenry did an excellent job. His sense of direction is always reliable. He moves like a cat. Can see and hear men moving and talking in about ten different places at the same time.

An intensive program of supporting fire from machine-guns, artillery and mortars had been prearranged to begin at the moment when surprise was lost and this had the desired effect of simulating an attack on a broad front, thus confusing the enemy and causing the laying-down of his defensive fire plan. Thus enemy shells and machine-gun fire passed harmlessly over the heads of the withdrawing patrol to fall on the distant targets of Point 25 and Trig 33. Cobb decided that there was a continuous line of enemy defence works from the coast to Point 25. The prisoner was from the *125th Regiment* (part of the *164th Division*) newly arrived from Crete.

Until the 7th the enemy appeared to be unaware of the 9th Division's withdrawal from the El Makh Khad positions. That day, however, enemy aircraft made a reconnaissance of the area and Morshead decided that outpost positions should be occupied there to prevent close enemy observation of the El Alamein and Tel el Eisa defences. At 11 p.m. on the 7th a company of the 2/13th, which had been maintaining a series of posts south of the railway and north of Makh Khad linking with the Alamein Box defences, occupied Trig 22, around which a protective minefield belt was at once laid by the 2/13th Field Company. A patrol, 1,800 yards farther forward, drew flares and long-range fire. The same night the 2/43rd placed a company with anti-tank guns and machine-guns astride

[8] L-Cpl J. A. Morris, QX7674; 2/15 Bn. Shop assistant; of Herberton, Qld; b. Watsonville, Qld, 19 Jul 1918.
[9] Cpl W. A. Woods, DCM, QX8178; 2/15 Bn. Stockman; of Nambour, Qld; b. Bangalow, NSW, 15 Oct 1910. Killed in action, Korea, 11 Mar 1951.
[1] Pte V. G. Pickup, QX13771; 2/15 Bn. Rubber worker; of Brisbane; b. Brisbane, 4 Sep 1922.

the Qattara Track east-south-east of Trig 22. On the next night the 2/43rd took over from the company of the 2/13th at 22 and occupied the Makh Khad Ridge from about Cairn to a position astride the road round Kilo 6. Patrols went forward 2,000 yards that night but saw no movement and next night patrols with sappers attached went 3,000 yards—half way to Ruin Ridge—still without finding minefields or seeing the enemy.

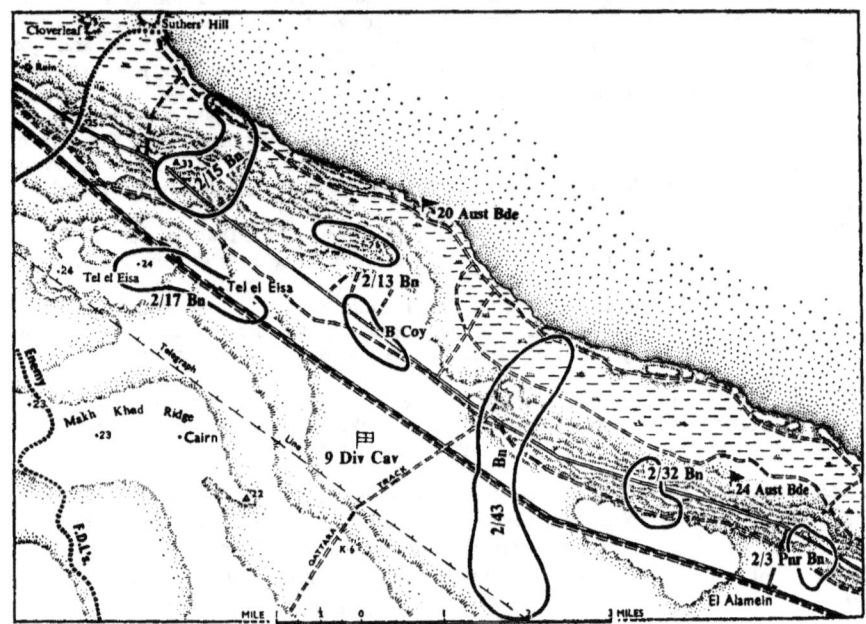

Dispositions, noon 7th August

On the night of the 10th-11th the 2/15th sent out a patrol to probe west of Point 17 for some 2,600 yards ahead of the forward companies to a locality which earlier patrols had established to be the usual route taken by German working parties. Captain Angus[2] led the patrol which was 17 strong. After 2,400 yards an enemy working party of about 40 men was seen moving north about 75 yards away. Other parties were observed moving about but were too far away to be attacked advantageously. After the patrol had waited patiently for some 30 minutes, a party of 25 Germans approached. When they were only three or four yards away Angus threw a grenade as the signal for every man to open fire; the patrol had two Brens, four sub-machine-guns and six rifles. Every German was killed or wounded and one of the wounded (from the *125th Regiment*) was carried back; one Australian was wounded and another was missing. Here again a previously planned heavy fire support plan was used to confuse the enemy and cause him to lay down his defensive

---

[2] Capt W. Angus, MC, QX6243; 2/15 Bn. Bank officer; of Warwick, Qld; b. Edinburgh, Scotland, 9 Oct 1917.

fire and the patrol returned unmolested by the enemy fire, which passed well overhead.

While the 2/15th Battalion's patrols were aggressively fighting the enemy behind his own lines between the railway and the coast, the 2/17th was patrolling along the railway line and to the south of it, where the enemy defences were more distant from the Australian lines. The 2/13th Battalion was also pushing out patrols through the 2/17th Battalion front in a south-westerly direction.

A patrol of the 2/17th led by Lieutenant Norton,[3] a particularly accurate and reliable officer, which was out from 9 p.m. on the 13th August to 3.30 a.m. next morning, made the deepest penetration so far effected in their sector—5,500 yards. At 4,090 yards the patrol was fired on by a Spandau but its bullets flew high. In the next 800 yards trip wires were encountered and at 5,478 yards a breast-high wire on long pickets, which gave a warning rattle when struck by the patrol's scout. A sentry challenged. The patrol went to ground for a few minutes, moved forward again, was again challenged, then charged, and was met by fire from men in trenches, to which the patrol replied with grenades, sub-machine-guns and rifles. After an exchange of fire lasting two minutes Norton withdrew his men without having a single casualty.

Next night the 2/17th sent out two patrols, one to follow up Norton's, the other to probe a locality on the south side of the railway line where the enemy had been reported (by a group of officers investigating from no-man's land without authority) to be developing a defensive position. The latter patrol, which was the deepest, was led by Lieutenant Thompson[4] and its task was to move 6,000 yards parallel to the railway line, then south-west for 1,400 yards and thence back to the start-point. After about 4,000 yards the patrol, 12 strong, passed through two fences into a "most extensive" but unoccupied position with a pill-box and trenches. Just then about 50 enemy troops approached unawares. The patrol opened fire at 20 yards range, inflicted some casualties and then withdrew north to the railway line. Thompson was hit by grenade splinters but no other Australian was harmed. Thompson having been stunned, Corporal Monaghan[5] coolly and skilfully extricated the patrol. The patrol was important as confirming the existence of a strongly-held locality about 500 yards south of the railway and 5,500 yards from Tel el Eisa station. This was now named Thompson's Post, a designation that was not apt to describe a defended area of considerable extent.

The other patrol again probed the general area covered by Norton's patrol and discovered that the enemy had closed a gap in his wire and was working hard with compressors, picks and shovels. These patrols showed what the enemy was doing to command the coast road from the south.

---

[3] Capt E. O. Norton, NX34884; 2/17 Bn. Grazier; of Walcha, NSW; b. Kyogle, NSW, 19 Oct 1909. Killed in action 25 Sep 1943.
[4] Capt J. K. Thompson, NX56431; 2/17 Bn. Grazier; of Cassilis, NSW; b. Killara, NSW, 29 Dec 1911.
[5] Cpl S. C. H. Monaghan, NX21689; 2/17 Bn. Company secretary; of Nowra, NSW; b. Nowra, 16 Jul 1916.

A patrol of the 2/13th Battalion which probed forward of the 2/17th's positions on the night of the 14th-15th comprised Lieutenant Edmunds,[6] a reinforcement officer leading his first patrol, and seven others. Edmunds pointed out to his men a constellation on which any man who became separated was to march. The patrol moved out stealthily for 2,800 yards and went to ground near an enemy working party. Edmunds went forward and returned with the information that there were enemy-occupied positions on either side. After a wait Edmunds moved the patrol towards one working party. An enemy sentry stood up and challenged. Edmunds gave the order to charge and hurled himself at the sentry but was shot. Corporal Humphries[7] took command but was killed while leading the men out. The men scattered but the survivors, except one man who became a prisoner, made their way back separately, guided by the constellation Edmunds had with forethought pointed out.

The divisional cavalry was patrolling by day, and on the 15th it was decided that members of patrolling companies of the 2/13th should go out with the cavalry to study the country west and north of East Point 23 in daylight.

Information from a prisoner suggested that Italians occupied a dominant feature, which faced Trig 33 across the saltmarsh, named Cloverleaf (from the shape of its contours on the map) and Germans the feature on the coast to the north-east, later named Suthers' Hill. Major Suthers'[8] company was given the task of raiding the hill. If the opposition was not too strong, he was to leave one platoon there and raid Cloverleaf with the other two. The company set out but about 400 yards from Suthers' Hill Lieutenant Newton's[9] platoon walked into a field of booby-traps and Newton and 10 men were hit. A flare was fired from Cloverleaf and voices were heard from Suthers' Hill but no shots were fired. Unable to find a way round the field of booby-traps the company withdrew.

A patrol of 19 under Lieutenant Adnams[1] of the 2/43rd and including Captain Bakewell[2] of the 2/3rd Pioneers set out from between Cairn and Trig 22 in a south-westerly direction at 11.15 p.m. on the 16th under orders to penetrate some 4,000 yards. After 2,600 yards had been covered a working party could be heard and 800 yards farther on minefields were encountered. German voices were audible. Four Bren gunners were left here and the patrol went on, reached diggings occupied by at least 50 men, threw grenades, grabbed three men (Italians) and shot or bayoneted at least 12 more. Soon after they had begun to move back, they came under fire from a mortar and at least eight machine-guns firing on fixed lines. It took the patrol about an hour to get clear, and Bakewell and the four

---

[6] Lt I. G. Edmunds, NX56579; 2/13 Bn. Salesman; of Queenscliff, NSW; b. Newcastle, NSW, 2 May 1915. Killed in action 14 Aug 1942.

[7] Cpl W. Humphries, NX23250; 2/13 Bn. Labourer; of Campsie, NSW; b. Moree, NSW, 2 Feb 1913. Killed in action 14 Aug 1942.

[8] Lt-Col R. A. Suthers, QX6221. 2/15 Bn; BM 18 Bde 1945. Solicitor; of Townsville, Qld; b. Kingaroy, Qld, 10 Mar 1916.

[9] Lt R. Newton, QX5694; 2/15 Bn. Jackeroo; of Stanthorpe, Qld; b. Stanthorpe, 9 Aug 1920.

[1] Capt W. T. Adnams, WX11418; 2/43 Bn. Salesman; of South Perth, WA; b. London, 4 Jun 1912.

[2] Capt L. N. Bakewell, SX9501; 2/3 Pnr Bn. Sharebroker's clerk; of Prospect, SA; b. Unley, SA, 18 Apr 1916. Died of wounds 17 Aug 1942.

(Australian War Memorial)
A roadside security sign in the Australian sector at El Alamein, October 1942.

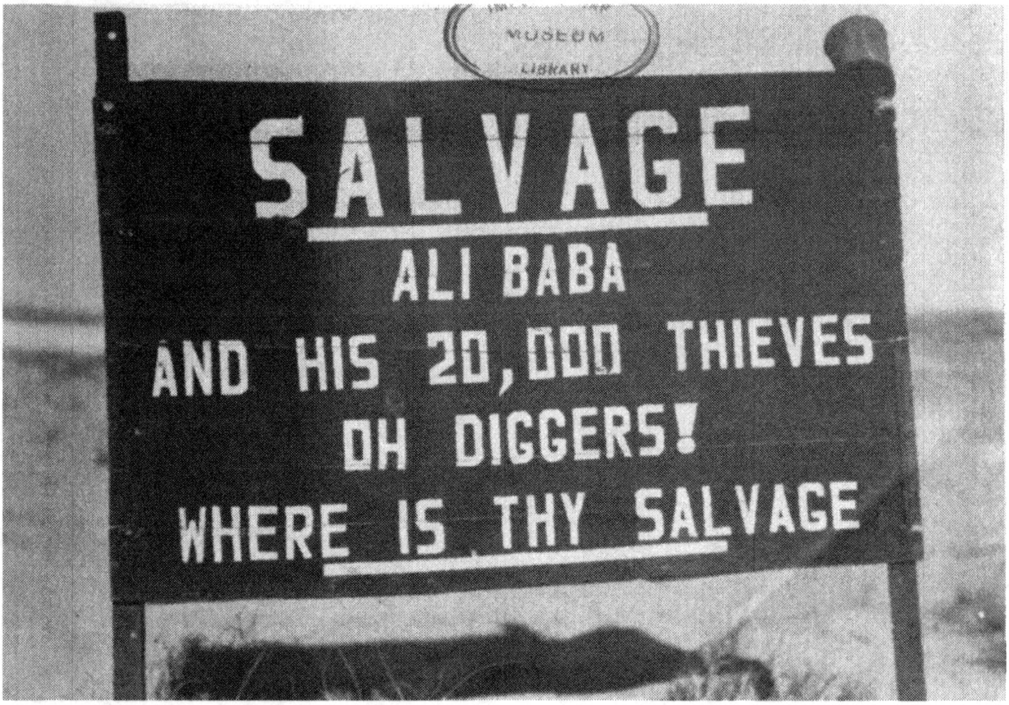

(Australian War Memorial)
An Australian salvage notice near El Alamein. The reference to "Ali Baba Morshead and his 20,000 thieves" is said to have originated in a German broadcast announcing the arrival in the Western Desert from Syria of the 9th Australian Division.

(*Australian War Memorial*)

Brigadier D. A. Whitehead who commanded the 26th Brigade in the October offensive at El Alamein.

(*Australian War Memorial*)

Brigadier A. H. Ramsay, commanding the 9th Divisional Artillery at El Alamein.

(*Australian War Memorial*)

Brigadier R. W. Tovell, commanding the 26th Brigade, with his battalion commanders, September 1942. *Left to right*: Lieut-Colonels C. G. Weir (2/24th) and B. Evans (2/23rd), Brigadier Tovell and Lieut-Colonel H. H. Hammer (2/48th).

Bren gunners were then missing. Captain Hare led a party out to find the missing men. It was discovered that Bakewell had been wounded by a booby-trap. The Bren gunners carried him for 200 yards but then left him at his own request, and because his wounds were so serious. All the other missing men were found or made their own ways back, three of them having been wounded.

Australian patrols established bit by bit that German sub-units were bolstering Italian units. Night patrols heard both languages being spoken in adjacent places, and German and Italian weapons were fired from positions close together. The Australian battalions maintained their mastery of no-man's land but the enemy reacted by closely wiring and booby-trapping all forward positions within the range of normal patrolling so that it became difficult to effect deep penetrations unless a large and carefully planned raid was made.[3]

On 22nd August the enemy's "political warfare" experts raised the 9th Division's spirits by arranging for aircraft to scatter leaflets over the divisional area. They measured 6 by 8 inches and were headed with the divisional insignia—a platypus over a boomerang. One set read: "Aussies! The Yankees are having a jolly good time in your country. And you?" The other read: "Diggers! You are defending Alamein Box. What about Port Darwin?" The leaflets were treasure trove indeed and eagerly collected for sale to others as mementos or to post home.

On 19th August Alexander confirmed his spoken instructions to Montgomery with the following written directive:

1. Your prime and immediate task is to prepare for offensive action against the German-Italian forces with a view to destroying them at the earliest possible moment.
2. Whilst preparing this attack you must hold your present positions and on no account allow the enemy to penetrate east of them.

Alexander ordered that this decision be made known to all troops.

By the 20th Montgomery had been in command for eight days and his new policies were having their effect in the forward units. An operation order by Morshead on 17th August announced that the division would defend its present forward defended localities at all costs and that this was to be impressed on all ranks immediately. Next day a divisional staff instruction stated that in the Eighth Army the word "box" was not to be used to describe a defended area, and the term "battle group" was not to be used. On the 19th Godfrey informed his colonels that, in accordance with the army commander's policy, the 2/43rd's positions would cease to be "outposts" and become "forward defended localities".

On the 22nd extracts from a memorandum from Montgomery were sent to all commanding officers. One extract expressed alarm at the prevalent idea that units and sub-units could not be assembled in compact bodies

---

[3] On 11th August the Australian war correspondents stationed in Egypt visited General Morshead and complained of difficulties in their relations with GHQ in carrying out their work. They told Morshead that the Press had received instructions to "pipe down" on Australians who, it was said, had been given too much publicity. They cited Press reports that the "Allies" had recaptured Tel el Eisa, lost by "Australians" the previous day. Morshead later complained to Alexander about this.

to be addressed by their commanding officers or sub-unit commanders; apparently it was feared that the enemy might see such an assembly and shell it or attack it from the air. "I consider," wrote Montgomery, "that if a unit is to be welded into a fighting machine that will fight with tenacity in battle, then it must be assembled regularly and the men addressed personally by their officers." He also said that he favoured performances by concert parties in the areas of the forward divisions and added that he wished weapon training to be carried out in forward areas with live ammunition.

Many equipment shortages were being remedied, though requisitions for wire to protect the forward infantry positions, most of which were not wired, continued to remain unfulfilled. The divisional diary recorded on the 19th that more Crusader tanks were expected for the cavalry regiment to bring it to its full establishment of 28 tanks; battalions were to have four Vickers guns and eight 2-pounder anti-tank guns.[4] Since early in August the 2/3rd Anti-Tank Regiment had had 64 6-pounders; its 2-pounders were being handed over to the infantry.

Officers and men who had served in the first world war or the militia welcomed the restoration of a medium machine-gun platoon to battalion war establishments, recalling that there were two such platoons in the support companies of Australian battalions until the formation of the first A.I.F. division, when a more recent British establishment was adopted. Then Vickers guns were grouped in machine-gun battalions, which became corps troops, on the scale of one such battalion per division in the corps. This reorganisation may have been prompted by first world war experience, but A.I.F. experience in the 1939-45 war evidenced no need to place medium machine-guns under corps control.

In a sense the defeat of the Axis forces in Africa was a victory of the sea war. Both armies' supplies came mostly by sea. The fortunes of the British army commanders depended more on what they received and what their enemy was prevented from receiving than on their own manoeuvres. They never for long had the better of their adversary on the field of battle except when they were blessed with a preponderance of armaments and resources. Some of Rommel's greatest victories, even so, were won when he was outmatched in all but skill.

There were three courses open to Rommel after Auchinleck's spirited counter-attack in July had failed by never so fine a margin to snap the strained Axis line. He could disengage to entice the British from their fixed defences, and revert to a battle of movement in which his formations excelled; he could try once more to envelop his enemy's forces in the

---

[4] On 2nd September Morshead reported to Blamey (to whom he cabled brief reports at fairly frequent intervals) that he was considering replacing one rifle company in each infantry battalion with a support company with 8 anti-tank guns, 8 Vickers guns, 6 mortars and carriers. The anti-tank platoons (with 2-pounders) had been formed when the division arrived at Alexandria. The machine-gun platoons were formed about the second week in August. These, however, were incorporated in the headquarters company of battalions, which still retained four rifle companies.
The 20th Brigade diarist recorded on 3rd September that each battalion then held two Vickers guns and six 2-pounder anti-tank guns and thus had the nucleus of the proposed support company.

El Alamein positions if only he could build up the requisite strength; or he could settle down to hold fast to the El Alamein line by defence in depth, a course that could offer no prosperous final outcome.

Mellenthin has recorded that disengagement, together with a withdrawal of all the non-mobile formations to Libya, was considered early in August by the general staff of the *Armoured Army of Africa* but there were reasons other than tactical for not adopting that course.

> The British excelled at static warfare, while in mobile operations Rommel had proved himself master of the field. So long as we did not remain tied to a particular locality we could hope to hold up a British invasion of Cyrenaica for a long time. But Hitler would never have accepted a solution which involved giving up ground, and so the only alternative was to try and go forward to the Nile, while we still had the strength to make the attempt.[5]

The "only alternative" required an improvement in the dispatch of men, equipment and supplies and their safe delivery to Rommel's army. In July and August deliveries were stepped up. The Germans were using 500 transport aircraft to bring across men and supplies. In April, May and June 22,900 men were flown in for the army, 6,600 for the air force; in July and August 24,600 for the army, 11,600 for the air force. In addition to the *164th Division*, the *Ramcke Parachute Brigade* was brought across from Greece. As replacements for the *Pavia* and *Sabratha Divisions*, rendered ineffective in the July fighting, two new Italian divisions, the *Bologna* and the *Folgore* (a parachute formation), were arriving forward. Another fresh division, the *Pistoia*, had arrived but remained in Libya.

The German army formations were low in numbers when August opened. Only about half the units of the *164th Division* had arrived. The *90th Light Division* had only 51 per cent of establishment; the two armoured divisions, the *15th* and *21st*, only 61 and 68 per cent respectively. By 15th August, however, the German war diary recorded that the German formations were then at 75 per cent of full strength, compared with 30 per cent on 21st July.

With respect to supplies brought by sea the picture was gloomy. In July only 6 per cent of such supplies had gone to the bottom, but in August 25 per cent of the general military cargo and 41 per cent of the fuel were lost on the way.[6] Further grave difficulties were experienced in delivering to the front such supplies as were landed. On 1st August Rommel made representations to the German High Command concerning these problems and their remedy. He asked for barges and three coasters and recommended continuous air protection of his coastwise shipping. More unloading equipment was required for Tobruk. German staff, for effective regulation of railway traffic, and German locomotives and waggons were needed. The shortage of vehicles should be remedied by deliveries to Tripoli and Benghazi.

The shorter Axis supply route could be utilised to reduce temporarily the disparity in strength between the contending armies but Rommel could

---

[5] *Panzer Battles 1939-1945*, p. 136.
[6] Based on summary of shipping losses from German and Italian sources.—Playfair, Vol III (1960), p. 327.

expect the situation again to become worse in September when the supplies sent from America and Britain after Tobruk fell reached Egypt. He must therefore attack in August.

On 7th August Rommel informed the commanders of the *Africa Corps, XX Italian Corps* and *90th Light Division* of plans for a renewed offensive. The *21st* and *15th Armoured Divisions* were then withdrawn in succession to rearward positions to prepare for the onslaught. On 19th August the German commander told his subordinates that he would probably attack in the moonlit period at the end of the month, and three days later he issued the preliminary orders. Moonlight was needed for the armour to make the initial penetration by night.

The two critical items of supply were tanks and fuel. The *Africa Corps* had accumulated 203 medium tanks of which more than half were the formidable "Specials", including Mark IV Specials which outmatched any tank of its opponents. The *XX Italian Corps* had 281. This was largesse not enjoyed since the first weeks of the Gazala offensive. But fuel was short. On the day Rommel issued the preliminary orders, he reported to General von Rintelen that if the attack was to be made about 6,000 tons must reach Libya between 25th and 30th August. A promise to send 10,000 tons, of which half would be for the army and half for the air force, was received. On the 27th the *Africa Corps* had only enough fuel to carry its tracked vehicles 100 miles and its wheeled vehicles 150 miles, but on the 30th more stocks arrived, the *Luftwaffe* gave the army 1,500 tons, and a shipload of 730 tons reached Tobruk. Rommel had enough fuel to launch his offensive, but not enough for further operations. However, the formations to make the assault had already begun to move.

A defensive position in the desert was usually established by resting one flank securely on the sea and holding a front strongly some distance to the south; behind the front a line of defences facing south was usually developed, with gaps filled by armoured formations to threaten the flank and rear of an enveloping force. El Alamein was no exception, since the Qattara Depression was too far from the sea for all the ground between to be strongly held. When the Battle of Alam el Halfa began the front was firmly held from the coast to Alam Nayil with three Dominion and one Indian divisions; south from Alam Nayil, where the New Zealanders' left flank was refused, the continuation of the line was held with light mobile forces.

Three ridges ran back from the firm front: El Miteiriya, Ruweisat and Alam el Halfa. Like Auchinleck and Dorman-Smith before them, Alexander and Montgomery saw that the key to defence against attack from the south was to base the rearward defence of the southern flank on the southernmost of the three ridges—the Alam el Halfa, behind Alam Nayil.

Auchinleck had lacked sufficient forces to hold a firm front southwards from the sea-shore beyond Tel el Eisa to Alam Nayil while at the same time providing for defence against an enveloping enemy attack launched south of Alam Nayil. Hence had flowed the indecisiveness, which had angered Morshead, as to whether to hold the shortest possible front, resting the main defence on the Alamein Box, or whether to extend the ground to be firmly held to include the Makh Khad ridges and other territory forward of the box.

Montgomery's policy of "what we have we hold" had settled that the more extended front would be held but had involved tying down more troops to frontal defence. His inland flank was not strong despite the occupation of the Alam el Halfa Ridge by two brigades of the 44th Division which had been called forward. Particularly was this so at the flank's hinge at Alam Nayil where, until the evening of the unexpectedly late German attack, the New Zealand division's southern flank was held by the inexperienced 132nd Brigade. That evening the 5th New Zealand Brigade changed places with the 132nd in a routine brigade relief which was carried out while the German armour, getting ready to strike, was known to be assembling near by.

At the end of August the northern sector from the coast to Deir el Shein was held by the *164th German Division* and the *Trento Division* with their regiments interspersed so that an Italian regiment normally was flanked by German ones. From the north the front-line regiments were: *125th German Regiment, 62nd Italian Regiment, 382nd German Regiment* (these three faced the 9th Division), part of *361st German Regiment, 61st Italian Regiment, 433rd German Regiment*. From Deir el Shein southwards were the *Bologna* and *Brescia Divisions*, stiffened by German groups including units of the *Ramcke Parachute Brigade*, and the *Folgore Division*. Behind the front line in the southern sector were concentrating (from north to south) the *90th Light Division, Ariete, Littorio, Trieste, 21st* and *15th Armoured Divisions, 3rd* and *33rd Reconnaissance Units*. The German formations totalled about 41,000 officers and men; the Italian about 33,000.

Auchinleck's appreciation, and Montgomery's, that a German attack in the south could best be resisted by defending the Alam el Halfa Ridge was to prove correct. Rommel decided to skirt the front as far south as Alam Nayil, which he thought to be too deep and strongly held to be swiftly penetrable, and planned to attack between Alam Nayil and Qaret el Himeimat with the *Africa Corps* (two armoured divisions) and *Reconnaissance Group* on the right, the *XX Italian Corps* (two armoured divisions) in the centre and the *90th Light Division* on the left. When these had thrust through the British front they were to wheel northward and advance to the sea. It was an ambitious plan which required the *Africa Corps* to travel seven miles between 11 p.m. on 30th August and 6 a.m. on the 31st through minefields of unknown extent.

The initial attack would thus fall on the weak 7th Armoured Division (7th Motor Brigade and 4th Light Armoured Brigade). If the Axis forces broke through to the south and swung north, they were bound to clash with one or more of the three armoured brigades of the 10th Armoured Division. They would be faced (from their left) by the 5th New Zealand Brigade, which was settling in on the New Zealand division's turned-back left flank, then—though with a wide gap between—the 22nd Armoured Brigade, then farther to the right the two infantry brigades of the 44th Division ensconced on the Alam el Halfa Ridge, with the 8th Armoured

Brigade forward of the ridge about Trig 87. If they pushed through the gap behind the New Zealand division, they would come up against the 23rd Armoured Brigade in front of the Ruweisat Ridge. The brunt of the attack would therefore be borne by the XIII Corps which comprised the formations named above. Montgomery, looking ahead to his own offensive, instructed Horrocks that he must not allow his corps and particularly the 7th Armoured Division to get mauled. The Desert Air Force was to attack the enemy's forward troops day and night, and also to do all it could to prevent the German Air Force from playing an effective part in the battle.

By 23rd August the British staff expected that Rommel would attack in the moonlight period between 25th August and 1st September and it had been decided that, as an immediate counter-stroke, a raid would be made in the north near the coast road towards the enemy's vulnerable supply routes as soon as his attack was launched. This was to be carried out by the 20th Brigade which was to seize a sector of the enemy's defences with one battalion and hold it as a firm base from which a small armoured force would raid enemy transport on the main supply tracks leading south from Sidi Abd el Rahman. The operation was to be called BULIMBA.

At 10.20 a.m. on 30th August sentries of the 2/17th found a British soldier who told a remarkable story and incidentally provided detailed information about the defences west of Point 23 where BULIMBA was to take place. He was Private A. G. Evans of the 1/Sherwood Foresters, who had escaped from Tobruk after its capture and made his way to Salum, thence eastwards, keeping south of the road. He had lived by stealing scraps of food and searching old dugouts. Arabs had helped him. "Nobody took any notice of me," he said, "although on one occasion I went by mistake into a German camp, but as I had an Italian water-bottle and made a movement with my hands that I had seen Italians make, they did not stop me." For the past fortnight he had been in the enemy's area forward of the 2/17th's positions, either hiding in a dugout or making attempts to get safely through the enemy's wire, minefields and working parties. Finally he succeeded.

About 11.30 p.m. that night the enemy began shelling and mortaring the 2/13th Battalion's positions near the sea. Captain Walsoe, whose company occupied a tongue of sand dunes between the seashore and a salt-marsh lying at the foot of Trig 33, reported at 12.30 a.m. that at least a company of the enemy were in the salt-marsh moving towards battalion headquarters and also penetrating the wire of his own defences. Almost simultaneously Lieutenant Appleton,[7] whose carrier platoon, holding static positions on Point 5, barred the enemy's access to battalion headquarters, reported that Germans were trying to get through his lines. Several small enemy groups attempted to work their way forward but were shot up. A fierce small-arms fire fight developed, but after about an hour

---

[7] Lt F. C. Appleton, NX14765; 2/13 Bn. Commercial traveller; of Haberfield, NSW; b. Haberfield, 18 Oct 1911. Killed in action 22 Sep 1943.

the enemy ceased to return the fire. Later the area was shelled. A German prisoner taken in this raid, who belonged to the *III/125th Battalion,* said that 80 men had taken part.

Just before 4.30 a.m. a similar raid was launched against Captain Sanderson's[8] company holding the ground to the south of Trig 33. Sanderson called for defensive fire, which the Australian artillery brought down close to the forward positions, but the enemy continued to press the attack for some time and Sanderson's reserves of ammunition were running low before it was broken off. The Australians later brought in several prisoners.

Another unsuccessful raid was made on the front of the 24th Brigade. At 12.30 a.m. men of Captain Minocks'[9] company of the 2/43rd reported that about 80 enemy troops were approaching. The 2/7th Field Regiment shelled them but they passed through the minefield and reached the wire. A close fire fight developed before they were driven off. Then at 4 a.m., Minocks' men came under fire from six machine-guns. Defensive fire was again brought down and the enemy made off. A patrol at first light found fresh blood on the ground in six places and signs that wounded had been dragged away. One prisoner was taken—a German of the *I/382nd Battalion.*

These were among several diversionary attacks from the coast to Ruweisat Ridge intended to divert attention from the main thrust farther south, beyond Alam Nayil, where the main enemy force was then moving eastwards.

Rommel hoped to achieve surprise, but since the British expected the attack to be made in the moonlit period the Desert Air Force watched the southward movement of his armour. At dusk on the 30th the forces concentrating for the offensive were attacked from the air. This was only the first of a series of tribulations. When the *Africa Corps* reached the first minefield about 2 a.m. on the 31st it was in some confusion, again under attack from the air, and under fire from the 7th Armoured Division. Progress was slow; General Nehring was wounded and Colonel Bayerlein took command of the corps until General von Vaerst took over later in the day. The attackers were delayed by bad going, unexpected minefields and renewed air attack, and when Rommel arrived forward at 9 a.m. he postponed the attack, originally planned for 6 a.m., to midday to allow time for re-fuelling, and reduced the distance the corps would have to travel by ordering that it would attack the western part of Alam el Halfa, not the eastern part as planned.

The axis of the German advance was thus switched close to the left of the main concentration of British armour instead of widely by-passing all of it except the isolated 8th Armoured Brigade, which was out in front of the ridge opposite the centre of the 44th Division. Despite the postponement of six hours the German armoured divisions were late, the *15th* starting at 1 p.m. and the *21st* (whose commander, Major-General von

---
[8] Capt R. G. Sanderson, NX12335; 2/13 Bn. Bank clerk; of Taree, NSW; b. Enmore, NSW, 9 Sep 1912. Killed in action 24 Oct 1942.
[9] Capt J. W. N. Minocks, SX8889; 2/43 Bn. Viticulturist; of Glossop, SA; b. Adelaide, 30 Nov 1919. Killed in action 2 Nov 1942.

Bismarck, was killed during the day) about 2 p.m. They were soon being hit hard by the British guns and tanks, and at dusk Vaerst decided to cease the attack.

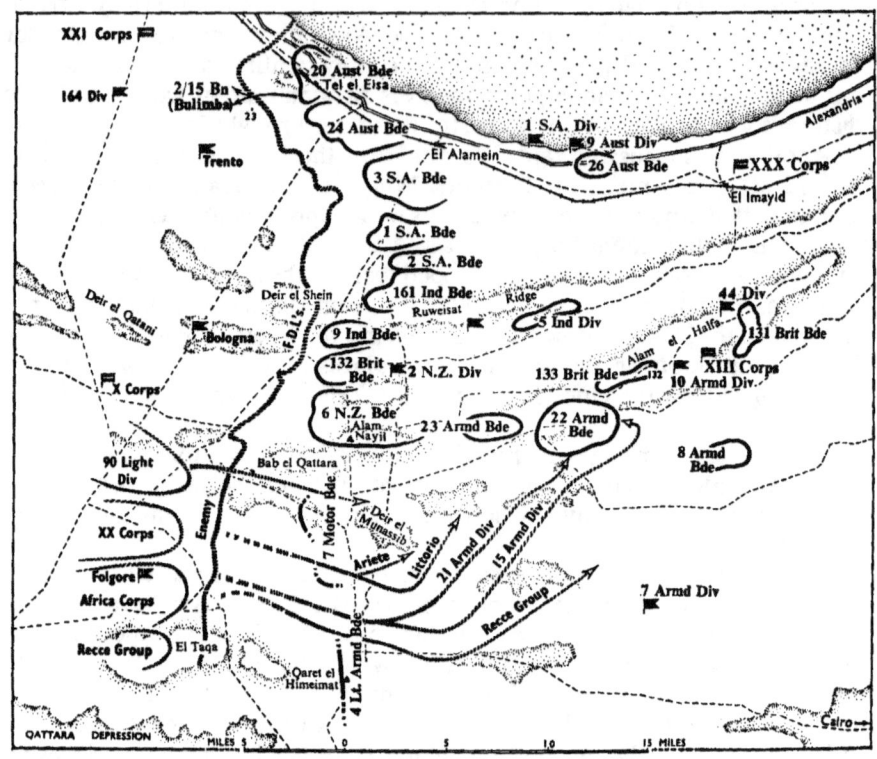

The Battle of Alam el Halfa, 30th-31st August

As soon as Montgomery's staff had discerned the position and intentions of the *Africa Corps,* the 23rd Armoured Brigade was moved into the gap between the New Zealand division and the 10th Armoured Division. When night fell the air force lit up the desert with flares and attacked the enemy's vehicles without ceasing, and soon clouds of smoke were rising from petrol fires and burning vehicles.

On the 1st the *Africa Corps* made little progress and was struck hard by day-bombers. The *21st Armoured Division* did not move, perhaps for want of fuel, but the *15th* again tried to work round the flank of the main concentration of British armour. Throughout the day the German armour was "under constant bombardment from guns and aircraft".[1] Montgomery ordered the 2nd South African Brigade to move to a position north of Alam el Halfa, and warned the New Zealand division to prepare to attack southward across the enemy's line of communication.

---

[1] Mellenthin, p. 140.

By the end of the day the air attacks had severely damaged the *3rd* and *33rd Reconnaissance Units* on the enemy's right flank and they were in a bad way; but the *15th Armoured Division* was still threatening Point 132. According to the *Armoured Army of Africa's* diary, however, petrol supplies were now assured only until 5th September. "The position was so serious that it was necessary to break off the offensive for the time being and go over to the defensive."

Next day Montgomery was offered the opportunity to attempt a dramatic counter-stroke in force behind the German armour sprawled to the south of the XIII Corps; but the army commander who had earlier warned Horrocks to husband his armour for a later offensive was apparently still of the same mind. He decided to continue with the infantry attack being prepared by Freyberg to close the gap where the enemy had penetrated but to hold his armour to its defensive role. Optimism was shaping the plans as much as farsightedness, however, for the attack was directed to proceed with such forces as had been allotted, in the expectation that it would succeed. The attack, to be made by Freyberg's own 5th and 6th Brigades and the 132nd British Brigade, was to open on the night of the 3rd-4th. Freyberg was to advance three miles southward in the first phase and a further three miles in the second. The initial thrust was to be made by the 132nd Brigade on the right and 5th New Zealand Brigade on the left, each with a squadron of Valentines.

Montgomery was doubtless wise not to hustle Freyberg into an earlier hasty attack—as it was, there was hastiness in some of the preparations— but the enemy had meanwhile been strengthening his defences at his most vulnerable point. The raw 132nd Brigade left the start-line about an hour late, on the night of the 3rd, and came under heavy fire which wounded the commander; the units fell into some confusion. The 5th New Zealand Brigade reached its objective after hard fighting and defeated two counter-attacks. Montgomery and Horrocks agreed with Freyberg, however, that a renewed attack was unlikely to succeed and that his brigades should withdraw (the 5th had had 275 casualties and the 132nd 697). This they did that night. More effective than the counter-attack was the continued onslaught of the air force. By 4th September the *Africa Corps* had had 170 vehicles destroyed and 270 damaged by air attack, and petrol supplies were now gravely depleted.

In the next few days the enemy withdrew as he had planned, and was not pressed. He was left in advantageous possession of the British minefields where the front had been breached and of Himeimat—an eminence 700 feet high that dominated the landscape in the southern parts of El Alamein. Horrocks protested at this but Montgomery firmly declined to contest the ground taken.[2] "The impression we gained of the new British commander, General Montgomery," wrote Rommel, "was that of a very cautious man, who was not prepared to take any sort of risk."[3]

In their attack the Germans lost 1,859 killed, wounded or missing and

---
[2] Montgomery, *Memoirs* (1958), p. 110.
[3] *The Rommel Papers*, p. 280.

the Italians 1,051; 49 tanks were destroyed. The British lost 1,750 killed, wounded or missing and 67 tanks. Mellenthin later described Alam el Halfa as "the turning point of the desert war, and the first of the long series of defeats on every front which foreshadowed the collapse of Germany".[4]

While the German attack was in progress the 1st South African Brigade had carried out a raid supported by heavy artillery fire and collected 56 prisoners of the *Trento Division*.

A diversionary attack by part of the *Ramcke Brigade* on the 9th Indian Brigade at Ruweisat Ridge penetrated the defenders' positions and led to a counter-attack by infantry and a squadron of tanks. The *Ramcke* lost 11 killed or wounded and 49 were missing.

The 9th Division's diversionary attack—Operation BULIMBA—was launched by the 20th Brigade just before dawn on the first day of the battle. West Point 23 had been chosen as the sector of the enemy's line to be secured for a bridgehead for several reasons; it was distant from the commanding Sidi Abd el Rahman features which were strongly held by the enemy and also was partly defiladed from enemy positions to the south; it gave observation over the desert for several miles; and the "going" between the Australian forward positions and the objective was suitable for wheeled vehicles.

The 2/15th Battalion (Lieut-Colonel Ogle) had been chosen to establish the base, and a force built round a squadron of the 40th Royal Tanks and commanded by Major McIntyre[5] of the 9th Divisional Cavalry was to conduct the raids. McIntyre's force and appropriate detachments of other arms were to be under Colonel Ogle's command. The 2/15th had been relieved on the coast sector of the front by the 2/13th Battalion on the 20th and 21st August and was in brigade reserve. Preparations were to be completed before the night of the 25th-26th after which, on receipt of the codeword BULIMBA, the sub-units concerned would immediately assemble. Elaborate air support and support by the divisional artillery and the 7th Medium Regiment were arranged. In the first phase the force would seize and hold, at dawn, enemy defences round West Point 23; McIntyre's detachment would then exploit southward returning at 3 p.m. when the whole force would retire.

Zero hour was fixed at 5.35 a.m. so that the leading infantry and engineers would reach the minefield at first light. At first the attack was to be silent. The artillery concentrations, by two field regiments and one medium battery, were to open fifteen minutes later.

By 5.15 on 1st September the infantry were out of their trucks and were quietly forming up on the taped start-line 1,000 yards ahead of their own forward defended localities and 2,500 yards from the objectives. They moved off exactly on time with two companies forward on a 600-yard front, and reached the outer wire of the enemy's minefield just before the artillery fire lifted. Captain Bode's company on the right came under the

---
[4] Mellenthin, pp. 136-7.
[5] Lt-Col A. E. McIntyre, OBE, ED, VX14742. 7 and 9 Cav Regts; CO 2/9 Armd Regt 1943-45. Grazier; of Beaufort, Vic; b. Skipton, Vic, 20 Mar 1904.

enemy's defensive fire, lost men, pressed on for a while, but was pinned down. Captain Snell's[6] company on the left was more fortunate; following closely behind the shelling, it crossed the minefield without difficulty. Three mine-lifting parties, each of six men from the 2/13th Field Company, immediately began clearing gaps in the minefield, which extended over a front of about 500 yards.

Led with great dash by Snell, the company reached its objective. When a section leader was killed Private Bambling,[7] firing his gun from the hip, led the survivors to the enemy positions. He killed five and took the surrender of an officer and 10 others. With two men he then attacked

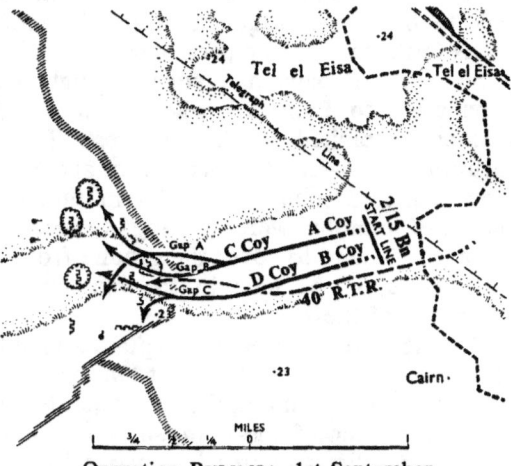

Operation BULIMBA, 1st September

another post 50 yards away and was hit thrice. While he was lying wounded a tank arrived. Bambling pointed out the enemy post and the tank knocked it out with two rounds, killing five and taking 14 prisoners. "So far as is known," said the battalion report, "this was the only tank that produced any aimed fire against enemy positions."

Corporal McLachlan's[8] section came under fire from an enemy post on the left. He bayoneted three men in this post, then, taking a sub-machine-gun from a wounded man, attacked a second post and killed its four occupants. He next attacked another post 200 yards ahead, killing four Germans with grenades, and then, having no ammunition left, assaulted four Germans using his Tommy-gun as a club; one of these attacked him but he knocked him out with a kick and disposed of the rest with a grenade. Snell's company took 39 prisoners and estimated that they had killed about 100, but their own losses were 2 officers and 35 others.

Colonel Ogle, whose headquarters had been established about 150 yards within the minefield, had meanwhile been informed by radio that Bode had been killed and his company was pinned down by machine-gun fire. Ogle moved to that flank in his carrier, but it struck a mine. He was seriously wounded, and sent a message back ordering Major Grace[9] to come forward and take command. Grace arrived at Ogle's headquarters

---

[6] Maj L. Snell, MC, QX6226; 2/15 Bn. Clerk; of Bowen, Qld; b. Bowen, 4 Sep 1915.
[7] Cpl R. H. Bambling, DCM, QX6943; 2/15 Bn. Labourer; b. Gympie, Qld, 15 Aug 1916.
[8] Sgt H. F. McLachlan, DCM, QX5634; 2/15 Bn. Station hand; of Boggabilla, NSW; b. Inverell, NSW, 5 May 1916.
[9] Col C. H. Grace, DSO, ED, NX457. HQ 7 Div 1940-41; 2/15 Bn (CO 1943-45). Office manager; of Sydney; b. Sydney, 17 Jul 1909.

about 6.45, and Ogle handed over. All companies were at that time out of communication.

After Ogle had been taken out his wireless operator, Trooper Hill,[1] remained in the disabled carrier and continued to operate his set as a rear link to brigade headquarters and forward to Grace's headquarters 600 yards farther west. The carrier was again hit by a shell but Hill carried on.

Suthers' company had gone through the wire behind Snell's and was soon close to Point 23 where it took 15 to 20 prisoners; thence the platoons exploited south and west. The commanders of two platoons thrusting west—Lieutenants Exton[2] and Heatley[3]—and their sergeants were wounded, and soon Suthers learnt that the commander and sergeant of the third platoon were missing. Suthers ordered a withdrawal through the enemy's wire to cover the ground from the wire to Point 23 but at that stage none of the men in the platoons were able to emerge from the other side of the wire.

The right rear company (Captain Angus) had reached its objective with relatively light losses. Warrant-Officer Walsh[4] did sterling work, making his way to and from battalion headquarters under heavy shell fire to inform the commander of the company's position and then going out some 50 yards under fire to carry in a wounded man.

The sappers had meanwhile been opening gaps 30 to 50 yards wide in the minefield, now under heavy fire. Gap "A" was cleared by 6.5 a.m. The men of Lance-Sergeant Yarrow's[5] party at Gap "B" were all hit in the first 10 minutes, but Yarrow completed his gap and then worked on the adjoining one. There Yarrow was hit again but remained on duty until he was relieved; he was then carried out by two prisoners. Gaps "B" and "C" were opened and marked by 6.20 a.m. A tank had tried to pass through Gap "C" before it was completely cleared and when no sappers were left unwounded to warn it. It struck a mine. The incident appeared to undermine the tank commanders' confidence in the sappers. Lieutenant Overall, in charge of the engineers, told the commanders of several of the remaining tanks that the gaps were open but for some 30 minutes none advanced. At 7.5 Suthers had asked for tanks to help him get forward to Point 23. Grace sent an officer back to bring the tanks forward and eventually four tanks were led through the gaps by sappers who walked in front of them, but not before two other tanks had suddenly turned at right angles in the field and run on to mines. The commander of the squadron, Captain J. L. Lumby, was killed soon after he got his own tank through the field. The four tanks reached Grace's headquarters and were directed towards Point 23, but they halted half way and declined to move without orders from their own commander.

---

[1] Cpl J. D. Hill, SX9379. 9 Cav Regt; 2/12 Cdo Sqn. Farm hand; of Frances, SA; b. Frances, 10 May 1920.
[2] Lt R. D. Exton, QX19142; 2/15 Bn. Company representative; of Brisbane; b. Brisbane, 18 Jul 1911. Killed in action 1 Sep 1942.
[3] Capt W. C. Heatley, QX6231; 2/15 Bn. Jackeroo; of Townsville, Qld; b. Townsville, 12 Jul 1920.
[4] Lt S. R. Walsh, DCM, QX835; 2/15 Bn. Lecturer; of Stanthorpe, Qld; b. Stanthorpe, 16 Apr 1918.
[5] WO2 W. H. T. Yarrow, DCM, QX4973; 2/13 Fd Coy. Farmer; of Cleveland, Qld; b. South Shields, Durham, England, 25 Nov 1911.

Meanwhile three carriers of the 2/15th had gone forward to support Suthers' company. About 7.30 two more tanks, led by the second-in-command of the squadron, went through the gap and were directed to collect the other four and help Snell's company to resist a counter-attack which seemed imminent. The leader's tank with two others went to the crest of a ridge running north-west from Point 23 but was immediately knocked out and he was killed. The remaining two tanks came back to rejoin the others and all remained near battalion headquarters.

By 8.40 Grace still knew nothing of Bode's company except that it had been under heavy fire and had reported an hour and twenty minutes earlier that it was running out of ammunition; he knew that Snell's had reported heavy losses and was also short of ammunition; Suthers' company was reported to have been reduced to 12 men; Angus' company had had only light casualties but was a platoon short having lent one to the exploitation force. Dust and smoke were making it impossible for the artillery officers to engage targets with observed fire. Grace concluded that the position his men had gained could not be held with such depleted companies against an organised counter-attack, and therefore decided that the raiding force could not safely be sent out and that the battalion should be withdrawn. He ordered the withdrawal to begin at 9 a.m.

When Windeyer learnt that the withdrawal had been ordered he thought that the decision was premature; the threatened counter-attack had not begun and might be broken by artillery fire, or might already have been broken. He sent Grace a message that no withdrawal was authorised unless the troops were forced off the position; but the battalion was already on the move before the message reached Grace.

Despite tumultuous fire and mounting casualties the withdrawal was executed in exemplary order and in a manner that drew admiring comment from those who watched it, including Windeyer: first Suthers' company, then Angus', then Bode's, then Snell's. The wounded were brought in except for some men in Snell's company too badly wounded to be carried. In the withdrawal the devoted Warrant-Officer Walsh carried out the wounded man he had brought to safety earlier in the day. During the carry of 500 yards the man was hit again. Walsh dressed this second wound and carried the man home.

In the operation 140 German prisoners were taken, mainly from the *I* and *II Battalions* of the *382nd Regiment,* and it was estimated that at least 150 were killed. The 2/15th Battalion lost 39 killed, 109 wounded and 25 missing. Among the missing (he had in fact been killed) was Captain Bode, described in Morshead's cabled report to Australia on BULIMBA as "one of the best officers in the division", an opinion widely shared. In his report Windeyer wrote:

> Although the operation did not achieve all that was hoped it was no doubt a solid blow to the local enemy. Considered simply as a raid it resulted in the capture of 104 prisoners and the inflicting of a great number of casualties on the enemy . . . it is conservatively estimated that upwards of 100 were killed in close infantry fighting and others killed or wounded by artillery and small arms fire.

Our troops fought with the greatest bravery. No man left the engagement before the order to withdraw and their battle discipline and determination were of a high order.

The operation was the first planned attack on a battalion scale against German troops on their now strongly fortified El Alamein line; and it showed that Australian troops could drive the Germans from the extensively wired and mined defences they were laboriously developing, but that a penetration on the narrow front of a single battalion could not be held. This point was made in a frank summing-up by an engineer, Major Gehrmann, who commanded the 2/13th Field Company in the raid.

It is my firm opinion, frequently voiced prior to the operation, that the action was doomed to failure before it started because:
1. The force was too small.
2. The front was too narrow.
3. The flanks were insecure.
4. The proposed penetration was too narrow.
5. The information was too scanty.
6. The operation was unsuitable for tanks.

But the efforts of the 2/15th Battalion in BULIMBA were not in vain, for the knowledge gained and the lessons learnt were utilised when the next attack was planned. As the historian of the 2/7th Field Regiment wrote:

Long before the end of August, it was realised within 9 Aust Div that interlocking keys of cooperation were essential, as between infantry, artillery, armour. Such keys would have to be cut to a precision-tool scale of efficiency not previously envisaged, if the combination lock of Axis minefields, defensive firepower, and rapidly counter-attacking armour was to be forced. BULIMBA, following on Ruin Ridge, taught that these bitter lessons could no longer be ignored. . . . As usual, the initial infantry attack . . . was successful. . . . The battalion then came under heavy small arms, mortar, and shell-fire, and, as at Ruin Ridge, the gaps made in the minefields were too narrow and the counter-fire too strong. The bridgehead could not be kept open.[6]

The July operations had ended with the infantry bitterly critical of British staff work and the British armour. Two months had passed. New and inspiring commanders had taken over. A successful defensive battle had been fought. The German armour had been defeated. Yet, in the diversionary attack that accompanied the main battle, misgivings about the degree of support the infantry could expect from armoured units had been revived. Conversely tank commanders still mistrusted infantry commanders who, they thought, did not understand the limitations of their tanks or that they could not operate to good purpose under the nose of anti-tank guns that outranged them unless steps were taken to neutralise the guns. It was clear that more training and indoctrination would be needed.

Montgomery's conduct of the Alam el Halfa battle differed from earlier defensive battles (of which one, the battle at Gazala, bore in some respects a close resemblance) in that the army was kept compact and armoured

---

[6] Goodhart, *The History of the 2/7 Australian Field Regiment*, p. 192.

formations were stationed alongside infantry divisions, with benefit of some support from their guns.

Alam el Halfa (wrote Alexander in his despatch) was the last throw of the German forces in Africa, their last chance of a victory before, as they calculated, our increasing strength would make victory for them impossible. It was hard to realise it at the time, but the moment when the *Africa Corps* began to retreat, slowly and stubbornly, from the sandy scrub of the Deir el Agram, marked the first westward ebb of the tide which had carried the Axis arms so far to the east, an ebb which was about to begin to the north as well in a few months from then on the Volga Steppe and in the Caucasus. To me at the time the great features of the battle were the immediate improvement in the morale of our own troops, and the confidence I felt in General Montgomery, who had handled his first battle in the desert with great ability. The valuable part played by the R.A.F. during the battle was a good omen for future air support. I now felt sure that we should be able to defeat the enemy when we were ready to take the offensive.[7]

Apart from a few violent interludes during the Battle of Alam el Halfa, the 9th Division's period of duty on the right of the Alamein front line during the late summer was remarkably quiet. The 2/13th Battalion, after its relief of the 2/15th Battalion, had carried out extensive patrols (in which Lieutenant Heslop[8] and Sergeant Morris[9] figured prominently) by which an accurate picture of the enemy's foremost defences was built up. Some particularly daring one-man patrols were executed by Lieutenant Madden,[1] who more than once played hide-and-seek with enemy sentries. Lieutenant Fairbairn[2] and Sergeant Slaughter[3] observed an enemy post for one whole day from underneath a derelict truck within a stone's throw from it. The post was raided next night, but without success.

The 2/17th, who had been longer in the line, also maintained their policy of vigorous patrolling, which was carried out in greater depth. Captain Hamer[4] of 20th Brigade Headquarters made a brilliant analysis of the reports of the two battalions and information derived from air photographs and built up a composite picture of the order-of-battle and defensive lay-out in front of the brigade, which was later published in the Intelligence summaries of the higher formations. At that stage the 2/13th was on the extreme right, the 2/17th to their left and the 2/15th (now commanded by Lieut-Colonel Magno[5]) from a reserve position was patrolling the gap between the 20th and 24th Brigades. The 24th Brigade had the 2/32nd (now commanded by Lieut-Colonel Balfe) on the right,

---

[7] *The African Campaign from El Alamein to Tunis, from 10th August 1942 to 13th May 1943*, pp. 846-7.
[8] Capt R. W. Heslop, NX70750. 2/13 Bn; HQ 20 Bde; HQ 26 Bde 1944-45. Bank officer; of Kogarah, NSW; b. Kogarah, 9 Jan 1921.
[9] Lt F. W. Morris, NX18256. 2/13 and 2/6 Bns. Grazier and horsebreaker; of Denman, NSW; b. Muswellbrook, NSW, 22 Dec 1913. Killed in action 9 Mar 1945.
[1] Lt J. E. Madden, MC, NX15077; 2/13 Bn. Regular soldier; of Armidale, NSW; b. Warialda, NSW, 5 Feb 1920. Died of wounds 26 Oct 1942.
[2] Capt M. T. Fairbairn, NX13864; 2/13 Bn. Jackeroo; of Moree, NSW; b. Sydney, 15 Nov 1917.
[3] Capt S. R. Slaughter, NX7709; 2/13 Bn. Newspaper reporter; of Manly, NSW; b. Toogoolawah, Qld, 11 Nov 1916.
[4] Lt-Col Hon R. J. Hamer, ED, VX13528. 2/43 Bn; HQ 20 Bde; GSO2 (Ops) HQ 9 Div 1943-44; GSO2 War Office 1944-45. MLC, Vic, since 1958; Minister for Immigration, Vic, 1962-64, for Local Government since 1962. Student; of Toorak, Vic; b. Kew, Vic, 29 Jul 1916.
[5] Lt-Col C. K. M. Magno, NX12306. 2/17 Bn; CO 2/15 Bn 1942. Shipping clerk; of Mosman, NSW; b. Kew, Vic, 6 Sep 1910. Died of wounds 30 Oct 1942.

the 2/28th in the centre and the 2/3rd Pioneers on the left; the 2/43rd was manning the western face of the Alamein defences.

After the Battle of Alam el Halfa the enemy became increasingly active and defiant in carrying out defence preparations by night. Thus on 9th September the 20th Brigade reported:

> His working parties appear well protected by covering parties and he sends out strong patrols with the intention of engaging ours.

And next day the 2/13th recorded that the enemy appeared to be trying to attract the attention of its patrols by the tapping of tools on stones, coughing, lighting cigarettes and so on.

On the night of the 10th-11th Lieutenant Thomas[6] of the 2/28th led out a patrol 22 strong to reconnoitre in the area of Point 23 east of the Qattara Track, ambush the enemy, inflict casualties and take prisoners.[7] At Point 23 a covering party was deployed and Thomas and four others moved on. After covering about 400 yards they were fired on by a party to their rear, and then challenged in guttural English. Thomas threw a grenade and ordered his men to make off, but when they reached home it was found that three were missing. They arrived later unhurt from the South African division's area: the other patrol had been South African and Thomas' grenade had wounded three of them. Later the South African division said that the error had been theirs.

On the 12th Morshead met General Wimberley of the recently arrived 51st Highland Division which was to be "affiliated" with the 9th Division to enable it to gain desert and battle experience as quickly as possible. Each infantry, cavalry, artillery and engineer unit of the 51st was linked with the corresponding unit of the 9th. The association was welcomed most warmly by all. After a party from the Black Watch had arrived at the 2/32nd Battalion the battalion diarist wrote:

> All ranks of the battalion view the affiliation with such interest and pleasure that it is felt that—wherever practicable—an exchange of officers and NCOs of different formations should be a matter of regular policy.

The 2/43rd was equally enthusiastic and thought that the idea should be extended to affiliation with armoured units:

> It is suggested that if some troops from English armoured formations could visit and live with A.I.F. infantry units for 3 or 4 days much would be done to overcome inter-arm prejudice.

The Highlanders also found the association beneficial:

> The Australians had a very different type of discipline from ours, but in the line our men learned very valuable lessons from those fine troops. The Aussies kept their weapons scrupulously clean and always free from sand. Their slit trenches were prepared with the utmost care, and each trench was completely equipped with such things as grenades. Before a party left on patrol each member of it was searched thoroughly for any identification marks. By night silence was enforced and no

---

[6] Lt E. Thomas, WX11087. 2/28 Bn, 2/1 Gd Bn. Bank officer; of Perth, WA; b. Perth, 24 Jun 1910.

[7] Since 9th September the 2/28th Battalion, re-formed after its losses on Ruin Ridge on 28th July, had been in the line about 670 strong and in fine fettle.

lights were allowed. When a patrol returned from its job a complete account of its investigation and acquired information was recorded on a map, and such maps combined with air-pictures gave the most detailed information of the enemy's minefields and other defences.[8]

On 8th September Morshead went to the XXX Corps to administer command of the corps for a week while General Ramsden was on leave in Cairo. On 13th September Montgomery informed Morshead that Lieut-General Leese would assume command of the corps on the 15th. On the 16th Leese and Morshead with their senior staff officers reconnoitred the front from Point 17 to Tel el Makh Khad in preparation for a move forward of the 24th Brigade for the ostensible purpose of gaining better observation of enemy territory and enabling the brigade to harass the enemy more effectively. The true reason (though this was known to few at the time) was to secure the ground from which it was planned to launch the infantry attack in the forthcoming offensive. Already the brigade had begun to work at night on new positions there and, on the night of the 18th-19th, the 2/32nd and the 2/28th occupied them without incident. This move advanced the forward defences of the brigade up to 2,000 yards so that the southernmost company of the 2/28th was about eastern Point 23 south-east of Kilo 8 on the Qattara Track. "The whirr of five compressors is loud enough to wake the dead but the enemy sleeps on," wrote the diarist of the 2/28th.

The South African division moved forward in conformity with the 9th on the same night and for the same reason. Two nights later the South Africans sidestepped and took over the 2/28th's positions up to and including the Qattara Track.

Significant changes in military terminology were introduced in the Eighth Army in late September when it was decided to bring into immediate use a common vocabulary for British and United States forces. Uniformity had been obtained, it was evident, by adopting American terms; to achieve it the veteran partners of the alliance had sensibly swallowed their pride and adopted the diction of the ally who might soon have to bear the main burden, but it was sad to see words and phrases that had become part of the everyday speech of soldiers removed with a stroke of the pen from a time-honoured military vocabulary. Thus, on 21st September the 9th Division informed all its formations that the Zero hour for an attack would henceforth be known as H hour, the day on which operations started would be referred to as D day, the day before D minus 1 and subsequent days D plus 1, D plus 2 and so on.[9]

Later the rhythmical and whimsical British phonetic alphabet was replaced by the dull and dreary American one. "Ack" became "Able", "Beer" became "Baker"; "Ink Johnnie", "Monkey Nuts", "Orange Pip"—from which "O Pip" became the colloquial term for an observation post—and "Uncle Vic", to take a few examples, were replaced by unimaginative substitutes. The anti-aircraft artillery, always known as "the Ack Ack",

---

[8] J. B. Salmond, *The History of the 51st Highland Division* (1953), p. 31.
[9] British practice had been to nominate the subsequent days D1, D2, D3 etc.

should now by rights have been called the "Able Able", but who could call them that? How difficult it was for battalions to bring themselves to call their Don companies "Dog Company"! Whoever would call the Toc O, Tare O or even Tare Oboe?

The 9th Division developed in its summer fighting at El Alamein a unity of spirit it had not entirely achieved before. The men were developing confidence in Morshead as their commander and an affection for him they never had in Tobruk. An unobtrusive man, Morshead used none of Montgomery's methods to appeal to their imagination. Their identification of themselves and of the division with its stern but soldierly leader was touched off by an article in the *A.I.F. News* on 15th August, based on despatches by three war correspondents, Kenneth Slessor, Ronald Monson and William Munday, which carried the following heading and opening paragraph:

THEY CAN TAKE IT—"ALI BABA
MORSHEAD AND HIS
20 THOUSAND THIEVES"

"Ali Baba's twenty thousand thieves," as the Berlin Radio calls Lt-Gen Sir Leslie Morshead's men in the Western Desert, have accepted the title as readily as they accepted Deutschlandsender's description of them as "Rats of Tobruk".

The Eighth Army as a whole was likewise developing confidence in its jaunty but resolute commander, who had not only predicted that he would repulse the enemy's onslaught but had done so. Time was moving on ineluctably to the day when it would be the Eighth Army's turn to strike. As the plan unfolded, as each part was revealed, as the clock-work timing became evident, as the thorough preparations and competent administration manifested themselves, the morale of the army was uplifted and its spirited soldiers, no longer perplexed by past failures, became aware that they belonged to an efficient army, and a great one.

CHAPTER 14

LAUNCHING THE BATTLE

IN September and October the Eighth Army rapidly gained strength. In the first nine months of 1942 2,453 tanks and 2,709 guns had reached the Middle East. In the first eight months there had arrived from the United Kingdom 149,800 men for the land forces, including two divisions of infantry and one of armour, 32,400 men for the R.A.F. and 9,800 for the navy. In addition some reinforcements had been received from India and the Dominions. From India 32,400 men had come, mainly as reinforcements, and there had been smaller numbers of reinforcements from Australia, South Africa and New Zealand.

Between 1st August and 23rd October 41,000 reinforcements joined the Eighth Army and, Alexander recorded, over 1,000 tanks, 360 carriers and 8,700 vehicles were sent forward. In September and early October the army's artillery was strengthened not only by the divisional artillery of the newly-arrived 8th Armoured and 44th and 51st Infantry Divisions but by two medium and six field regiments. By the third week of October the guns in the Eighth Army included 832 25-pounders, 32 4.5-inch guns, 20 5.5-inch, 24 105-mm; also 735 6-pounder and 521 2-pounder anti-tank guns.

The Eighth Army commanded a powerful superiority of tanks. By 23rd October 1,029 were ready for battle and there were some 200 replacements standing by and about 1,000 in the workshops. The German armoured divisions, on the other hand, had only 218 serviceable tanks (and 21 under repair) and the Italian divisions 278 when the battle opened.[1]

In the first half of September 318 Sherman tanks arrived at Suez and with these General Alexander intended to equip three of his six armoured brigades.[2] For the first time the Eighth Army had been given tanks which could match the enemy's in range and manoeuvre and outshoot all his tanks except the formidable Mark IV Specials, of which he had no more than 30.

The successful pursuit of the defeated Axis army would require far more vehicles than had been available hitherto. They were now available. By 23rd August the Eighth Army had the equivalent of 46 general transport companies and six tank-transporter companies; seven more general transport companies were in reserve.

More than 500 aircraft were available to Air Vice-Marshal Coningham to support the army whereas the Axis air forces could deploy only about 350 based in North Africa, though support could be given from Crete and quick reinforcement from Italy was possible; nor did Coningham have any fighters to match the German Messerschmitts F and G. By late

---

[1] Light tanks totalling about 50 are not included in the Axis figures.
[2] General Horrocks has pointed out that the fighting part of the Sherman tank was of British design. Three hundred were made initially, but after Pearl Harbour they were issued to the 1st American Armoured Division. When Tobruk fell President Roosevelt agreed to Mr Churchill's request that they be sent to the Middle East. See Horrocks, *A Full Life*, pp. 132-3 and Churchill, Vol IV, p. 344.

October the Desert Air Force was organised into No. 211 Group (with 17 fighter squadrons), No. 212 Group (8 fighter squadrons), No. 3 S.A.A.F. Wing (3 day-bomber squadrons), No. 232 Wing (2 day-bomber squadrons), No. 12 American Medium Bombardment Group (3 squadrons), No. 285 Wing (3 reconnaissance squadrons and 2 flights). Other squadrons, including some equipped with night-bombers, and long-range fighters, were available to give direct support to the army.

While supplies in such abundance were reaching the desert army after the battle of Alam el Halfa, Montgomery's confidence in the outcome of the attack which he was planning for their employment was growing, but Churchill was becoming impatient to see them used earlier than Montgomery or Alexander planned. In the background was the ever-deepening peril of Malta, whose scanty supplies, supplemented meagrely in August at appalling cost, were likely to be exhausted by October. However General Brooke deterred the British Prime Minister from pressing Alexander to attack before he was ready and the messages from London inquiring as to the intended date of the offensive were in surprisingly mild terms.

The original intention of the Middle East Command to open the British offensive in September had to be revised after the Battle of Alam el Halfa. Alexander and Montgomery had decided that it would be necessary to attack by night in order to penetrate the enemy's formidable defences and that to clear the minefields and deploy the armour a night of bright moonlight would be required. When the Alam el Halfa fighting had died down the September full moon was only three weeks away. That was quite insufficient time to allow for the training, extensive preparations and detailed planning required for the kind of stage-managed, large-scale army attack that Montgomery intended to launch. Alexander and Montgomery were determined that the army and especially the armoured corps should have sufficient time for training. Full moon was on 24th October and, with Montgomery's agreement, Alexander chose the 23rd as the opening date of the offensive.

Montgomery had a hand in preparing Alexander's message to the British Prime Minister notifying this decision.

I remember Alexander discussing the Prime Minister's signal with my chief (wrote de Guingand later). Montgomery took a sheet of paper and wrote out very carefully four points on which to base a reply. These were:

(a) Rommel's attack had caused some delay in our preparations.
(b) Moon conditions restricted "D" Day to certain periods in September and October.
(c) If the September date were accepted the troops would be insufficiently equipped and trained.
(d) If the September date were taken, failure would probably result, but if the attack took place in October then complete victory was assured.[3]

Another consideration that affected the timing was that the Allied invasion of French North Africa was to begin on 8th November. It was desirable that there should be a decisive victory over the Axis forces at El Alamein just before the invasion so as to impress the people of French

---
[3] *Operation Victory*, p. 158.

North Africa and the Spanish dictator, General Franco. The date chosen by Alexander and Montgomery for their offensive preceded the projected date of the invasion by just under a fortnight.

> I was convinced (wrote Alexander later) that this was the best interval that could be looked for in the circumstances. It would be long enough to destroy the greater part of the Axis army facing us, but on the other hand it would be too short for the enemy to start reinforcing Africa on any significant scale. Both these facts would be likely to have a strong effect on the French attitude. The decisive factor was that I was certain that to attack before I was ready would be to risk failure if not to court disaster.[4]

The Middle East Commanders-in-Chief planned two operations for the purpose of aggravating Rommel's supply difficulties while the Eighth Army was getting ready to attack. Raids were to be made on Benghazi and Tobruk with the object of destroying or damaging port equipment and fuel storages. On 13th September attempts to raid installations were made at Tobruk by both overland and sea-borne parties and at Benghazi by a column from Kufra. Both raids failed.

Nobody understood better than Montgomery that to possess abundant supplies was not enough. The requirement was to employ them with effect. The Eighth Army's plan would be more than a statement of tasks to be accomplished on the first and succeeding days of an attack. Those would be only the culminating moves in a series of closely correlated operations taking place for weeks before. The plan would embrace a thousand and one things, and more, that had to be done before the first shot would be fired. First an administrative network and supply system had to be designed, set-up, concealed from the enemy, and so placed as to best serve the forces where they would fight. Then special training had to be devised and carried out to prepare all arms and services for the exact tasks they would be expected to perform. And while the army was making ready the enemy was to be made unready by every conceivable ruse.

The design of the administrative lay-out and the location of supply points and forward dumps had to be subservient to a tactical plan, which had to be settled first. The tactical plan in turn had to fit the ground and meet the situation presented by the enemy's defensive measures.

From the time when the front stabilised itself after Auchinleck's attacks had failed to turn Rommel's advance into a retreat, the Axis forces had been preparing a strong defence line from the sea in the north to the Taqa plateau in the south. The operational task that confronted General Montgomery and his army was incomparably more difficult than anything previously essayed in the Middle East, for Rommel was turning to his own advantage the closed-flank defensive potentialities of El Alamein which had caused the British four months before to stand there against his drive to the Nile delta and the Egyptian capital. And the German commander whose tactical skill had so far been mainly demonstrated in swift manoeuvring of armoured mobile forces showed now (as he did later in organising the defence of the French coast) that, if the occasion demanded,

---

[4] Alexander, despatch, p. 850.

he would fully exploit the possibilities of static defence to entangle an advancing enemy. Realising after Alam el Halfa that air-power could tip the scales if he tried conclusions with the British armour in a war of movement, he adopted an entrapping, spider-web scheme of defence.

> We saw to it (he wrote) that the troops were given such firm positions, and that the front was held in such density that a threatened sector could hold out against even the heaviest British attack long enough to enable the mobile reserve to come up, however long it was delayed by the R.A.F.
>
> Coming down to more detail, the defences were so laid out that the minefields adjoining no-man's land were held by light outposts only, with the main defence line, which was two to three thousand yards in depth, located one to two thousand yards west of the first mine-belt. The panzer divisions were positioned behind the main defence line so that their guns could fire into the area in front of the line and increase the defensive fire-power of their sector. In the event of the attack developing a centre of gravity at any point, the panzer and motorised divisions situated to the north and south were to close up on the threatened sector.
>
> A very large number of mines was used in the construction of our line, something of the order of 500,000, counting in the captured British minefields. In placing the minefields, particular care was taken to ensure that the static formations could defend themselves to the side and rear as well as to the front. Vast numbers of captured British bombs and shells were built into the defence, arranged in some cases for electrical detonation. Italian troops were interspersed with their German comrades so that an Italian battalion always had a German as its neighbour.[5]

The defences, nowhere weak, were much more strongly developed in the northern part with which the 9th Division was to be concerned than in the south. The main defended zone in the north was some 6,000 yards wide and traversed laterally by two main lines of defence protected by minefields between which secondary minefield belts were laid in a random rectangular maze. Between these secondary fields were diagonal lanes of unmined ground so located that tanks advancing along them would expose their vulnerable sides to anti-tank guns. Behind the main defensive belt was an anti-tank gun line comprising both guns and dug-in tanks. These guns were carefully concealed, and firing, as they did, with flashless charges, were practically impossible to spot even when in action. Rommel laid great store on the ability of his "devils' gardens" to block a British advance but Kesselring has recorded that he had less faith in their efficacy.[6] No tank force could penetrate that triple defence barrier. The long-range concealed anti-tank gun was in fact beginning to relegate tank forces to the cavalry role that a temporary invulnerability had enabled them for a time to surpass.

Montgomery made two plans for the battle. The first was given out on 15th September, the second on 6th October; but the second was built onto the framework of the first so that none of the planning, preparation and training so far done was wasted.

Both plans recognised that a condition imposed by the enemy's preparations was that the initial onslaught would have to be made by a strong infantry assault force. In Montgomery's original plan the further development of the operation rested on the major premise, not inappropriate to

---

[5] *The Rommel Papers*, pp. 299-300.
[6] *The Memoirs of Field Marshal Kesselring* (1953), p. 135.

conditions in which tanks were becoming highly vulnerable, that to force the enemy to attack the British armour on ground of its own choosing (though it might be a lucky attacking force that found itself free to choose its own ground) offered better prospects of success than to employ the armour in launching attacks on the enemy armour.

The traditional desert tactic of making the initial penetration far from the coast where the defences were weakest or non-existent and then attacking the enemy on the inland flank was discarded. The original plan prescribed a two-pronged attack, the main weight of which was to fall on the heavily defended area in the north.

> This plan (wrote Montgomery later) was to attack the enemy simultaneously on both flanks. The main attack would be made by 30 Corps (Leese) in the north and here I planned to punch two corridors through the enemy defences and minefields. 10 Corps (Lumsden) would then pass through these corridors and would position itself on important ground astride the enemy supply routes; Rommel's armour would have to attack it, and would, I hoped, be destroyed in the process. . . . In the south, 13 Corps (Horrocks) was to break into the enemy positions and operate with 7th Armoured Division with a view to drawing enemy armour in that direction; this would make it easier for 10 Corps to get out into the open in the north.[7]

Here we see a prominent and finally decisive role assigned to the *corps d'élite* of armour (now the X Corps) that Montgomery had announced he would form on the day he took command of the Eighth Army.

The fact that the enemy held Himeimat with its commanding observation of all assembly areas in the south suited the plan in some respects since it would enable the enemy to observe deceptive measures which would simulate an intention to attack in the south. Conversely enemy possession of Himeimat would not have suited a plan for a real "left-hook" operation.

The Eighth Army had acquired a great deal of detailed information about the enemy defences from ground patrols, from air photographs and, in one important locality, from the BULIMBA Operation. Patrols provided little information of what lay beyond the spiked outer fringe of the defence girdle and the approaches to it. The detailed information came mainly from the very skilled Army Air Photograph Interpretation Unit, which produced traces and overprint maps of enemy defences; but so much detail was provided that there was a risk of believing that little had been missed. Enemy forethought, however, enabled many of the inner minefields to be hidden from the alert eyes of the interpreters. These fields were laid chiefly where the low "camel-thorn" scrub was thickest and presented on air photographs a mottled pattern that hid the disturbance of the surface. Wind-drift of shifting sand soon completed the mines' concealment.

The army's planning took account of the formidableness of the enemy defences, but even so its picture could not be complete and it could not be aware of the extent to which the girdle of defences was interlaced with strips of mines. The plan, of course, could only be based on overcoming the defences as they were known. They were described in a series of Intelligence summaries produced in the second week of October, which

---
[7] Montgomery, *Memoirs*, p. 118.

indicated that from the coast to Deir el Shein the defence system was from 3,000 to 7,000 yards in depth. There were two main defensive belts about 3,000 yards apart often with little between them, but with east-west "dividing walls" of defensive positions connecting the two main north-south belts at intervals of 4,000 to 5,000 yards, and forming a series of "hollow" areas, probably intended for defensive fire tasks, and as traps for attackers, who would be exposed to enfilade fire while in an angle of minefields formed by the junction of a dividing wall with the second belt of defences.

The summaries described the defences near the coast and near the road and railway, which latter were shown to be in considerable depth and strongly developed, and indicated that farther south (in the zone which the 9th Division was to attack) there was a strong buttress position about West Point 23. The second defensive belt ran parallel to the first, along the reverse slope, to Miteiriya. South from the Miteiriya hollow to Deir el Shein there were other strong and extensively wired positions. Southwards from Deir el Shein the defences were less continuous and from Himeimat southwards they were less developed still.

The immensity of the Eighth Army's onslaught, as Montgomery had conceived it, caught the imagination of the commanders and staff as it was successively disclosed to each command level in strict conformity with a carefully timed program. Montgomery saw to that by personally making the exposition to all commanders from the corps commanders down to the battalion commanders. The men were also to have their imagination fired and their confidence excited to a high pitch when, in their turn, they were to be told by their commanders. An attack in the north by four infantry divisions. A similar attack in the south by the better part of two infantry divisions. Two armoured divisions to break through at dawn in the north; another one in the south. There would be about a thousand tanks (and as many again available to replace them). There would be an opening barrage, so they were told, by close on a thousand guns.

Montgomery's corps and divisional commanders were first told of his plans for an offensive on 15th September when they were summoned with their chief staff officers to his headquarters to hear him expound his original plan, which he had set out in a memorandum of instructions for the battle signed by him on the 14th. As well as outlining the tactical plan Montgomery's memorandum contained instructions concerning secrecy, training, and the development of morale. The plan was not yet to be disclosed to anybody else except the artillery commanders; the memorandum was not be copied nor anything committed to paper; and for the present all orders were to be oral.

The operation was to be called "Lightfoot". It was designed to trap the enemy forces in the defences they then held and to destroy them there. The plan in outline provided that the enemy was to be "attacked simultaneously on his North and South flanks". The attack on the northern flank was to be carried out by the XXX Corps with the object of breaking into the enemy defences between the sea and the Miteiriya Ridge (part of which was included in the objectives) and forming a bridgehead which would include all the enemy main defended positions and his main gun areas. (The objectives of the XXX Corps were delineated on a trace. "These," stated the memorandum, "include the main enemy gun areas.") The whole of the bridgehead was to be thoroughly cleared of all enemy guns. The main armoured force—X Corps—would be passed through the bridgehead "to exploit success and complete the victory". On the southern flank the XIII Corps was to capture Himeimat, to conduct operations from there designed to draw the enemy armour away from the main battle in the north and to launch the 4th Light Armoured Brigade round the southern flank to secure Daba, capture the enemy supply and maintenance organisation there and deny him the use of the airfields thereabouts.

The break-in was to be effected in moonlight and supported by a great weight of artillery. For the main break-in, the XXX Corps would employ four infantry divisions—the 9th Australian, 51st Highland, 2nd New Zealand and 1st South African—and one armoured brigade, the 23rd. The New Zealand division's task would be to capture and hold the western end of the Miteiriya Ridge. The operations of the XXX Corps were designed so that the armoured divisions of X Corps would be able to pass unopposed through gaps made in the enemy minefields and be launched into territory to the west of them. The X Corps would then "pivot on the Miteiriya Ridge, held by its own New Zealand division, and . . . swing its right round" until the corps was positioned on ground of its own choosing astride the enemy supply routes. It was "essential for the success of the whole operation" that the leading armoured brigades should be deployed and ready to fight by first light.

Further operations would depend on how the enemy reacted. "The aim in the development of further operations," wrote Montgomery, "will be based on:

(a) The enemy being forced to attack X Corps on ground of its own choice.
(b) X Corps being able to attack the enemy armoured forces in flank.
(c) The fact that once the enemy armoured and mobile forces have been destroyed, or put out of action, the whole of the enemy army can be rounded up without any difficulty."[8]

A combined operation was to be organised with the object of landing a small force of tanks, artillery and infantry on the coast near Ras Abu el Guruf. (This was cancelled in the second plan.)

To the 9th Australian Division and doubtless to all the other infantry divisions the plan was most inspiring both in its broad concepts and in many of its details. The operations of Eighth Army so far experienced by the division had seemed to amount too often to "sending a boy on a man's errand". The infantry tasks in an army attack had usually consisted of one or two separate attacks on a two-brigade front or less (often much less) to seize an objective which then had to be held with open flanks. Now the division was to take part in an attack to be made by four infantry divisions in line abreast. Previous night attacks had required the

---

[8] Montgomery's memorandum dated 14th September.

infantry to be out in front at dawn, there with their meagre anti-tank artillery to await the inevitable tank counter-attack. Now the plan required the army's *élite* armoured corps to be out in front at dawn. How often, in previous attacks, had narrow breaches been made in minefields, only to be closed by enemy counter-action or sometimes blocked by a single vehicle's immobilisation. Now the mine-clearing forces had been enlarged and on each axis of advance two gaps would be made in each minefield, and one would be widened as soon as possible to 24 yards.

Some of the commanders of the armour, however, harboured doubts. The detailed planning, as it came to be revealed, took much account of the perplexing problem of minefield clearance; but the problem of the concealed, flashless anti-tank gun had received less attention. The plan was based on the expectation that almost all the anti-tank guns in the main assault region would be first smothered by the infantry night advance, but the armoured commanders were not so sure. It was to be discovered in the battle that in fact there was an anti-tank gun network farther back;[9] but even though the armoured formation commanders lacked such complete foreknowledge of what the battle would reveal, they were nevertheless apprehensive that optimism might have prevailed over realistic judgment and that, before the armoured force could reach the enemy supply routes through a heavily defended zone and there invite attack by the German armour, most of its tanks might be shot to pieces. Such apprehensiveness was evident, for example, in an instruction put out for the battle by the 1st Armoured Division, which warned the 22nd Armoured Brigade (which was to debouch near the Australian division's objectives) that it was imperative that its strength should not be dissipated against the anti-tank guns but be reserved to destroy the enemy armour.

Montgomery himself began to be assailed with doubt that his plan was sound in so far as it aimed to win the battle by relying on his armour to defeat Rommel's. On 6th October, two weeks and a half before the date set down for the attack, he changed the plan:

> My initial plan (he wrote later) had been based on destroying Rommel's armour; the remainder of his army, the un-armoured portion, could then be dealt with at leisure. This was in accordance with the accepted military thinking of the day. I decided to reverse the process and thus alter the whole conception of how the battle was to be fought. My modified plan now was to hold off, or contain, the enemy armour, while we carried out a methodical destruction of the infantry divisions holding the defensive system.[1]

Montgomery called the contemplated operations to destroy the enemy infantry in their defences "crumbling operations". The new approach dealt with the one incompletely answered question in the first plan. "What if the enemy should not attack the armour on the ground it was to take up?" Under the new plan, the enemy armour would not be able to stand by while his infantry was systematically destroyed. Montgomery still aimed,

---

[9] "It had been expected that 30 Corps objective was west of all the enemy minefields and west of his field gun areas. In fact hardly a field gun was captured in 30 Corps attack and at least one minefield was in the area west of the objective." Report on Operations, 9 Aust Div, El Alamein, 23 Oct-5 Nov 1942, p. 15.

[1] Montgomery, *Memoirs*, p. 119.

however, to get the armour out in front. The operation orders soon to be issued were to require the armour to pass through the bridgehead by dawn on the first day and deploy beyond the infantry objectives.

Thus the new plan was not really a reversal of the old. Only a change of emphasis had been introduced, which laid heavier tasks on the infantry. And the notion of "crumbling", which signified attacking the enemy with infantry to encompass his destruction rather than to wrest ground from him for the tactical advantages thereby gained, was to exert later an influence on the battle with important consequences to the 9th Division.

Montgomery then and later declared that the change of plan sprang from his apprehension that his troops were insufficiently trained for the tasks he had laid upon them. "It is a regrettable fact," he wrote, in the course of a four-page paper issued to senior staff and commanders down to divisional commanders, "that our troops are not, in all cases, highly trained. We must therefore ensure that we fight the battle *in our own way*, that we stage-manage the battle to suit the state of training of our troops, and that we keep well balanced at all times so that we can ignore enemy thrusts and can proceed relentlessly with our own plans to destroy the enemy." That a lesser standard of training was required to fight the battle according to the second prescription rather than the first is not instantly perceptible; but in other respects the original tasks had meanwhile been lightened—the attack by the 4th Light Armoured Brigade on Daba had been cancelled and the original objective for the thrust in the north had been reduced so as to avoid the strong defences in the coast region.

As mentioned the plan was revealed to successive levels of command by a timed program: to artillery commanders on the same day as the divisional commanders and their chief staff officers, to brigade commanders and senior engineer officers on 28th September, to battalion and unit commanders on 10th October, to company, battery and other sub-unit commanders on the 17th, to all officers on the 21st—two days before the battle, and to the men on that day and the next. Nobody was to be told of the plan in advance of the time prescribed for him to be told. From the 21st all leave was cancelled. The area occupied by Eighth Army was then sealed off and nobody was allowed out of it.

The expansion and large-scale re-equipment of the Eighth Army involved a parallel expansion and reorganisation of the supply services. This was particularly true of base workshops handling the servicing of tanks going forward and the maintenance and return of tanks sent back from the front. Soon after the plan was announced on 15th September small carefully camouflaged and dispersed dumps began to appear close to the front in the forward areas. There were dumps of supplies of all kinds, but mainly of ammunition. So far as possible petrol and ammunition were stored underground. Convoys of trucks delivered their loads in darkness; afterwards the vehicle tracks were obliterated. More than 300,000 rounds of field and medium artillery shells were concealed close to the positions from which the guns would fire when the attack opened.

In the 9th Division's area 600 rounds per field gun were moved up by night, dug in and camouflaged. Petrol supplies amounting to 7,500 tons had to be dumped forward. All captured German "Jerricans" were called in from the infantry formations and given to X Corps to ensure that its initial reserves of petrol would not suffer the losses through leakage invariably experienced with British containers.

Other diggings appeared, for no purpose evident at the time. Here would be set up the tactical headquarters of the formations. Other diggings again were preparations for the casualty stations and other medical services.[2] Provision was made for the evacuation of prisoners of war. Pipe-lines were extended and new water-points established.[3]

Utmost attention was given to concealment and deception. The intention to attack could not be hidden, but it was hoped that the day and the place could be kept secret. The aim of the "cover" plan was to create an illusion that the army would not be ready to attack until November and that the main attack would then be made in the south.

So far as possible administrative and supply arrangements that could be watched by the enemy espionage network at Cairo and Alexandria were so ordered that wrong conclusions could be drawn, and clandestine arrangements were made for information to reach the enemy that the army would not be ready by October. Leave to Cairo and Alexandria for forward troops was instituted on a considerable scale and was continued up to almost the eve of battle, the last parties selected being (without their knowing it) men to be left out of the battle. So that the stopping of contracts for fresh supplies might not lead to an inference that an attack was about to be launched, such contracts were stopped for a period early in October when no operations were pending, and for that time the whole army went on to hard rations. An air force bombing and strafing program similar to the one that was to precede the real offensive was carried out in September so that when it was repeated in October the enemy need attach no special significance to it. Infantry patrolling was kept general to ensure that no indication was given of a particular interest in any part of the front.

The construction of a dummy pipe-line (with ancillary installations) leading out to the south was undertaken to deceive not only as to the place of attack but as to the time. The pipe-line was visible from Himeimat and the work proceeded at a pace to indicate that it could not be completed by the October moon. Vehicles dragging chains to raise the dust were driven up and down the southern road to simulate heavy traffic serving that region.

Nothing could prevent the enemy's observing from the air the desert's changing face or noting the assembly, on its bare floor, of hundreds of guns and tanks and thousands of vehicles. The aim was not to disguise the fact that they were being assembled (rather it was advertised) but

---

[2] The AIF's medical organisation for the battle is detailed in Chapter 17 of Volume II of the medical series of this history—*Middle East and Far East*, by A. S. Walker.

[3] *Pipe-line to Battle* (1944), by Major Peter W. Rainier, is a lively book in which an account is given of some of this work.

to hide from the air camera their later movement when they would deploy for battle. Early in the planning each unit had to state the number of vehicles it would require for an attack followed by a short advance. The assembly of all vehicles and tanks required was planned and then, to conceal the movement of the immense concourse of vehicles into assembly areas on the day before battle, the planners ordained that by 1st October the number and arrangement of vehicles on the floor of the desert should appear the same from the air as it would on that later day after they had moved. This was achieved by erecting dummy vehicles to the required number and in exactly the places where the real vehicles would be both before they had moved, and after. The dummies were to be so constructed that they would shelter and conceal the real vehicles, which were to be driven into position beneath the dummies. Thus, for example, when the armour of the X Corps moved up from the south to assemble in the north for battle, it would leave one set of dummies and come to another, and the tanks' tracks would be carefully obliterated. Meanwhile a busy simulated wireless traffic would continue to be emitted in the south by the signallers of the inoperative 8th Armoured Division. No change in the number or placing of vehicles would show up on the enemy's air photographs.

The arrangements made in the 26th Brigade's area can serve as an illustration of how it was done. Vehicles and dummies equal in number to the total required on D-day were placed in the area by 1st October. All available "A" and "B" Echelon vehicles were brought forward and the balance was provided by dummies. An officer was appointed to control the area and ensure that dummies could not be detected from the air. The dummies were in vehicle pits interspersed among real vehicles, and drivers had to live near them and not with their real vehicles. Vehicles were allowed to move in and out of the area, but it had to be made to appear that the dummies were also moving in and out. When it was the turn of a dummy to move it was collapsed and a real vehicle was run in and out of its pit so as to produce a track plan suggesting that all the vehicles were real. At the end of each day some real and dummy vehicles changed places.

By requiring the X Corps to pass *en masse* through the four-division front of XXX Corps into enemy territory the plan would superimpose the armour's approach routes and communications on those of the infantry corps. This required the construction for X Corps of six roads leading up to the assault zone from well in rear and later to be continued on through the enemy's defended area after it had been captured by the infantry. The six new tracks for X Corps were to be known as Sun, Moon, Star, Bottle, Boat and Hat tracks. The XXX Corps was to use the existing roads up to the existing forward unit areas—on the night and day before the battle the two tracks to the right of the main bituminised coast road were to be made one-way only routes (i.e. both forward only)—but the 9th Divisional Engineers had to construct four routes from the main road across to the infantry assembly areas on the right of the corps front, whence also they would be continued on up the axes of advance into the enemy territory when taken. They were to branch left off the main road just in rear of the Tel el Eisa station. These routes—named Diamond, Boomerang, Double Bar and Square tracks—were to be the lines of communication to the infantry in the sector in which the 9th Division was to fight. On the day before the attack all these routes were marked with pictorial signs depicting their names—which were also indicated at night by illuminated signs shining backwards.

From the air the six broad tracks for the X Corps would appear like arrows on the face of the desert pointing from a long way back to the area of assault.[4] Therefore, until the last possible moment, work was done only on disconnected parts in the most difficult stretches. The rest of the work was completed almost overnight two nights before the attack.

"As you train, so you fight" might well have been made the Eighth Army's motto while it was preparing for battle. The program included special training in critically important aspects of the operation and realistic rehearsal of actual tasks by everybody. The most important tasks were first closely studied and then reduced as far as possible to a drill.

Three problems received specially close study: cooperation in offensive operations between infantry and tanks closely supporting them; clearance of minefields; and ensuring not only that the infantry would go to the right place in the right time in a night attack but that the vehicles bringing up their ammunition and stores afterwards would both be able to get forward and know where to go.

A study of close cooperation between infantry and tanks in attack had begun before the planning for Operation LIGHTFOOT got under way. At the suggestion of Brigadier Richards, battalions of the 9th Division when not in the line carried out exercises with a regiment of the 1st Army Tank Brigade. After a reorganisation of the armoured formations was effected, Brigadier Richards became the commander of the 23rd Armoured Brigade which was to support the 9th Division and other divisions of the XXX Corps in LIGHTFOOT and, in accordance with Montgomery's instruction that "tanks that are to work in close cooperation with infantry must actually train with that infantry from now onwards", the training was continued and extended to cover the additional problems of clearing minefields and attacking through them with tanks and infantry in a night attack.

At the direction of the Eighth Army's Chief Engineer (Brigadier Kisch), a drill for minefield clearance was worked out first (and appropriately) in the armoured corps and then made standard for the whole army. A school of mine clearance was then established. The minefields were the enemy's main obstacle. Their clearance was the most difficult problem to surmount in the task the Eighth Army had been set. In the main the fields consisted of buried anti-tank mines but were "booby-trapped" at random with the extremely lethal "S" type (anti-personnel)

---

[4] When the German general, von Thoma, was captured near the end of the battle, he was asked whether these routes had attracted attention. Thoma said that they had been noticed but their significance had been missed.

mines whose prongs protruding from the ground and surrounding web of trip wires were easy to miss. Some fields were mined with buried aerial bombs. The dreadful anti-personnel minefields were less extensive.

The mine-lifting job was done in logical stages. First, the field had to be detected; then its home and far boundaries were established and marked, and a centre line for the lane to be cleared was also marked. Next the outer edges of the lane were marked and the field was cleared of "S" mines. Finally the anti-tank mines were lifted and the cleared gap was marked with lights and signs.

Electronic detectors were used for mine detection when available, but they were not always available. Then reliance was placed on highly experienced, skilled and alert—and brave—engineers to "smell" the mines, after which individual mines in a field had to be located by prodding with bayonets.

A reconnaissance party headed by an officer followed the infantry into the attack, reeling out a tape for the working parties to follow, located the home edge of the field, planted there a stake with a rearward shining coloured light and proceeded through the field, stooping and lightly brushing the ground with the backs of the hands to feel for trip wires, and continuing meanwhile to unreel the centre-line tape until the far edge was located, when another stake with a coloured light would be hammered in. Two men, required by the drill-book to be tied to each other to keep them the right distance apart (eight feet), laid parallel tapes on either side of the centre line to mark the outer boundaries of the lane to be cleared. All tapes were pinned to the ground.

Other groups, well spaced and echeloned back to avoid unnecessary casualties from bunching, traversed the field, simultaneously with the lane-edge working parties, to clear the lane of anti-personnel mines, the removal of which required cool nerves and deft fingers. Provided that there were sufficient men, the lane was then cleared of anti-tank mines by parties working from both ends simultaneously towards. the centre. Different coloured rearward shining torch-lights on stakes were used to indicate the sides of the lanes and the home boundary of the minefield. Some modifications of procedure were adopted in the battle when it was found that the minefields were much deeper than expected.

Men operating an electronic detector had to stand erect as they swept it from side to side in a circular motion. All other detection work was done by men crawling the full length of the gap, side by side, sweeping lightly with their hands and actually touching their neighbours.

This was the main method to be adopted but other equipment and methods were used to a limited degree, mainly in the armoured divisions and the New Zealand division. The measures taken are summarised in this extract from the 9th Division's report on the battle.

(a) Hand lifting of minefields by sappers, based on Eighth Army minelifting drill.
(b) The Spiked Fowler Roller, which was fitted in front of each track of a proportion of the tanks of some armoured units.

(c) The newly developed "Scorpion" which consisted of a small roller fitted to operate in front of a tank and which could be rotated by an auxiliary engine fitted to the tank. Small lengths of trace chains were fitted to the roller so that when it was revolved the trace chains threshed the ground in front of it thus exploding any mines or booby-traps which lay in the path of the tank. By this means a gap of the approximate width of the tank could be cleared.[5]

(d) Minefield gaps were marked with the normal gap marking signs for daylight use and by small electric torches by night. The torches were erected on metal stands and were used in horizontal pairs after the style of the gap signs, one colour showing the minefield and therefore danger, whilst the colour alongside showed the gap and safety. These pairs of lights placed at intervals along each side of the gap proved effective. Groups of three lights were used to indicate the near and far edges of the gap and by the use of different colours the various gaps could be indicated. Different coloured lines of lights (shaded from the enemy direction) were also used to mark the routes to the gaps, starting lines and centre lines of units so that by night the battlefield, while remaining unchanged when viewed from the enemy's direction, appeared as a fairyland of coloured lights when viewed from our side.[6]

It was appreciated that the mine-lifting tasks to be done in the battle were too big for the number of engineers held on the strength of formations as prescribed by their war establishments. Mine task forces were therefore built up by giving men from other units to engineer units of the assault formation for the battle. Both army engineers and base engineers were called upon. Men from field park companies would in some instances soon find themselves in the van of assault forces. In the 9th Division a company of the pioneer battalion was absorbed into the 2/13th Field Company, doubling its strength.

It was laid down that the armoured formations would be responsible for clearing their own routes forward. Some mine task forces of the armoured formations (but not of those allocated to be employed with or close to the 9th Division) had protective detachments to mop up any by-passed enemy posts that might snipe at mine-clearing parties.

In the 9th Division, the engineers began training for their tasks six weeks before the battle opened, finally carrying out dress rehearsals on minefields imitated from enemy fields shown in aerial photographs. From early September onwards patrols of two to four sappers with an infantry covering party went forward each night to examine some part of the enemy's minefield. "For the first time in the history of 9 Aust Div RAE specialised equipment was available for an operation," says the report of the chief engineer of the division. This included Scorpions, described above; pilot vehicles,[7] trucks carrying rollers in front which would explode mines; mine detectors; and perambulators, which carried detectors on a framework mounted on bicycle wheels and were pushed in front of gap-clearing parties to find the edge of the field.

A similar if more straightforward battle-drill had to be worked out for the infantry battalions. The ground-work for many of the procedures

---

[5] By 23rd October 24 Scorpions were ready.
[6] 9 Div report, pp. 3-4.
[7] Heavily sand-bagged trucks, which made the first trip up to and through minefields to test that no mines had been missed.

(Australian War Memorial)
A tank, with a false truck body attached, as part of the British deception arrangements before the El Alamein battle.

(2/28 Bn war diary)
A dummy light anti-aircraft gun position in the coastal sector.

(2/28 Bn war diary)

Australian positions near the sea, El Alamein, September 1942.

(Australian War Memorial)

A church service in the sand dunes at El Alamein, September 1942.

that were adopted was done in the New Zealand division. Some of the most acute problems to be solved for a night attack to great depth were to ensure that, despite casualties to key personnel, the attack would be continued in the right direction, at the right pace and for the right distance, that information of progress would get back (not only to keep the formation and army commanders in the picture, but also to enable anti-tank guns, tanks, ammunition and consolidation stores to be sent forward at the right time) and that vehicles and men to come forward later would get to the right place.

In the 9th Division's attacks, which were usually planned for two-company fronts, guide parties were provided both at the centre line of the battalion's axis and on each of the two company axes. The drill ensured that the whole group knew what distance had to be covered, what distance had been covered at each bound and the direction to be maintained. It also covered the marking of the battle centre line both with tapes and with stakes holding rearward shining lights and the establishment, along the centre line, of report and traffic-control centres in direct communication with forward headquarters, both for calling the vehicles forward and for controlling their movement to prevent clustering near minefield gaps before they could be cleared.

As an additional insurance against loss of direction resulting from casualties to officers or others carrying compasses the idea was conceived that anti-aircraft tracer fire could be used to help. On 19th October two Bofors guns 1,000 yards apart were fired out to sea from the 20th Brigade area to test whether they could be safely fired over the heads of the infantry. The idea appeared practical and was approved by the divisional commander. One section of the 4th Light Anti-Aircraft Regiment was given the task of firing their guns at intervals along the axis of advance of the assaulting battalions.

The 9th Division's battle orders prescribed that the capture of each objective would be "reported by the quickest means available and repeated by all the alternative means which exist". The means included light signals, line and radio telephony, wireless telegraphy and (for emergencies) pigeons.

"All formations and units will at once begin to train for the part they will play in this battle." So Montgomery directed in his battle instructions issued on 14th September to outline the general plan. "Time is short," he continued, "and we must so direct our training that we shall be successful *in this particular battle*, neglecting other forms of training." Time was short indeed; and since the 9th Division still had to defend its front, the brigades would have to be relieved and trained in succession. The 26th Brigade was then in reserve, so its preliminary training was put in hand at once.

Intense, rigorous and almost continuous training was instituted for units not in the line with a twofold purpose: teaching what had to be learnt, and making the men hard and battle-fit. They cursed their masters then, but in retrospect fully approved when, at the time appointed, the realism and purposefulness of the training were revealed to them.

> This was supposed to be one of those well known rest areas (wrote a battalion historian). The troops grinned cynically whenever they heard the words. In a rest area you either dug holes all day and guarded dumps all night or you trained all day and guarded dumps all night. This rest area was different. You trained all day and then you trained all night. Not every day and every night—but almost.[8]

Battle drills were first taught to companies and sub-units by day and repeated the same night. They were repeated again in whole unit exercises by day and by night. Then infantry units and their supporting arms carried out joint exercises. Finally full-scale and full-dress rehearsals were conducted by brigades and their supporting arms and services, the men performing their long wearisome tasks—including advances for some 6,000 yards—heavily loaded with the full accoutrements of battle; the trucks, loaded with ammunition, bogged as often as not. The rehearsals avoided none of the difficulties. Defences and minefields were laid out exactly as they were expected to be encountered, except that for security reasons all tasks and the defence lay-out were reversed from left to right. The 26th Brigade, for example, which in the real battle would penetrate deeply on a narrow front, then form a firm flank facing right, was required in the rehearsal to advance the same distance and form a firm flank facing left. Thus when each unit entered the battle on the first night, it was to carry out an operation which it had fully rehearsed in detail. And during the battle a comment frequently heard from the men was, "it's just like an exercise".

On the 22nd and 23rd September the 26th Brigade relieved the 20th Brigade in the coast sector. The relieving officers and men told their counterparts in the 20th of the intense training in night attack exercises they had been undergoing and of the tactical plan to which the exercises had conformed. The 20th Brigade men soon found themselves rehearsing night attacks, but to a different tactical plan. They did not guess that this was because they were rehearsing their own different task in the forthcoming battle.

The 24th Brigade, which had had little rest since the brigade's first attack on Makh Khad Ridge, was relieved on 2nd and 3rd October by a brigade of the 51st Highland Division to afford it a brief spell before the battle. Soon, on the nights 12th-13th and 13th-14th October, the 24th Brigade returned to front-line duty, this time on the coast sector, where it relieved the 26th Brigade which then resumed its training for the biggest operational task it had yet attempted.

From 2nd October onwards each brigade of the 51st Division spent about one week in the line on the left of the divisional front, coming under command of the 9th Division. At midnight on 20th October the command of the southern sector of the divisional front passed to the

---

[8] Major H. Gillan in *Bayonets Abroad*, pp. 257-8.

51st Division, which was then in the area from which it was to move in to the attack.

By late October the Eighth Army was organised thus:
XXX Corps (Lieut-General Leese)
  23rd Armoured Brigade Group (Brigadier Richards)
  51st Division (Major-General Wimberley)
  9th Australian Division (Lieut-General Morshead)
  2nd New Zealand Division (Lieut-General Freyberg)
  1st South African Division (Major-General Pienaar)
  4th Indian Division (Major-General Tuker[9])
XIII Corps (Lieut-General Horrocks)
  7th Armoured Division (Major-General Harding)
  44th Division (Major-General Hughes[10])
  50th Division (Major-General Nichols)
X Corps (Lieut-General Lumsden)
  1st Armoured Division (Major-General Briggs[1])
  10th Armoured Division (Major-General Gatehouse)
  8th Armoured Division (Major-General Gairdner[2]) which comprised only a headquarters and some divisional troops. Because it was then incomplete its formations and units had been transferred to other formations.

The army had more than 220,000 men and would muster on the day of battle more than 900 tanks and about 900 field and medium guns.

In the Axis forces there were now four German and eight Italian divisions in Egypt. In the *Armoured Army of Africa* were the *Africa Corps* (*15th* and *21st Armoured Divisions*), *90th Light Division*, *164th Light Division* and the *Ramcke Parachute Brigade*. In the three Italian corps—*X, XX,* and *XXI*—were the *132nd* (*Ariete*) and *133rd* (*Littorio*) *Armoured Divisions*, the *101st* (*Trieste*) *Division* (motorised), the *185th* (*Folgore*) *Division* (parachute troops), and the *17th* (*Pavia*), *25th* (*Bologna*), *27th* (*Brescia*) and *102nd* (*Trento*) *Divisions* (infantry). The *Young Fascists Division* garrisoned the Siwa oasis and the *16th* (*Pistoia*) *Division* was just across the Libyan frontier at Bardia. The Axis forces were about 180,000 strong, of which a little less than half were Germans; there were some 77,000 other Italian troops elsewhere in North Africa. They had more than 500 tanks, of which more than half were Italian.

The enemy's forward positions were now held, from the north, by *XXI Corps* (*164th Light, Trento* and *Bologna Divisions* and two battalions of the *Ramcke Brigade*); then *X Corps* (*Brescia, Pavia, Folgore Divisions* and two battalions of the *Ramcke*); the *33rd Reconnaissance Unit* was on the southern flank. The *15th Armoured* and *Littorio Divisions* were behind *XXI Corps* and the *21st Armoured* and *Ariete Divisions* behind *X Corps*.

In reserve along the coast were the *90th Light Division* and the *Trieste Division* about Daba, and the *288th Special Force* and *588th Reconnaissance Unit* in the Mersa Matruh area.

In each corps sector of the front German units were interspersed with Italian so that for their defence girdle (to abuse the metaphor of Brigadier Williams,

---
[9] Lt-Gen Sir Francis Tuker, KCIE, CB, DSO, OBE. (1914-18: Lt to Capt, Indian Army.) GOC 34 Indian Div 1941, 4 Indian Div 1942-44, Ceylon 1945. Regular soldier; b. 14 Jul 1894.
[10] Maj-Gen I. T. P. Hughes, CB, CBE, DSO, MC. (1916-18: Lt Queen's Royal Regt.) GOC 44 Div 1942, XXV Corps 1943. Regular soldier; b. 21 Dec 1897.
[1] Maj-Gen R. Briggs, CB, DSO. (1915-18: Lt to Capt, King's Own Regt.) Comd 2 Armd Bde 1941-44; temp GOC 1 Armd Div 1942-43; Director Royal Armd Corps, War Office, 1943-47. Regular soldier; b. 19 Jan 1895.
[2] Gen Sir Charles Gairdner, KCMG, KCVO, CB, CBE. (1916-18: Lt RA.) GSO1 7 Armd Div 1940-41; GOC 8 and 6 Armd Divs 1942; CGS North Africa 1943; Prime Minister's Representative in Far East 1945-48. Governor of Western Australia since 1951. Regular soldier; b. 20 Mar 1898.

Montgomery's senior Intelligence officer, by mixing it with another) the German command had fashioned a corset strengthened with German whalebones.

Field Marshal Rommel had been in poor health for some time. When the battle of Alam el Halfa was fought he had been so ill that he could scarcely get in and out of his tank. On 22nd September he handed over his command to General Stumme, who had been commanding an armoured corps in Russia and earlier had commanded one in Greece, and left next day for Europe to recuperate, having first told Stumme that he would return if the British attacked. The *Africa Corps* had meanwhile been placed under the command of General von Thoma, also from the Russian front.

Appreciating the delay that British air power could impose on the movement of armour, Stumme and von Thoma decided—not long before the battle—to split the armour and hold it behind the lines in two groups, one north, one south, so that quick counter-attacks could be launched in either sector without a long approach march. It was thought likely that an attack by moonlight would be made in October.

Early that month the enemy was trying to guess where the attack would fall. It seemed unlikely that it would be in the far south. On 7th October the diary of the *Armoured Army of Africa* recorded that the probable directions of the British attack were (*a*) along the coast road, (*b*) about Deir el Qatani, (*c*) at and south of Deir el Munassib. Next day, however, a new appreciation predicted that the main attack would fall between Ruweisat and Himeimat, but that there would also be attacks in some strength astride the coast road.

Although Montgomery's second plan was a fundamental change from the first in that the process of destruction of the enemy had been "reversed", the orders to which the battle was actually fought bore, superficially at least, a remarkably close resemblance to the original plan. The XXX and XIII Corps were still required to deliver two simultaneous heavy blows at the enemy by moonlight—the heaviest and decisive blow to be aimed in the north—and the armour was still to debouch. Both infantry attacks would start at 10 p.m. on 23rd October and were designed to overrun the enemy's minefields and gain possession of his defences, including the field gun areas, so as to facilitate the passage of the armoured formations to the enemy's rear before dawn. Infantry "crumbling" operations would be developed on subsequent days in attacks from north and south to pinch out the enemy forces holding the centre. Depending on the progress of the battle, orders might also be given to pinch out the German forces between the northern flank and the sea.

The plan required the XXX Corps to attack with four infantry divisions forward—from right to left, the 9th Australian, the 51st Highland, the 2nd New Zealand and the 1st South African—and to take its final objectives by 3 a.m. so that the armour would be able to pass through before dawn. The final infantry objectives were depicted by a map-line (running, from the right, at first due south, then about south-south-east then about east-south-east) which was to be known in the army plan as the Oxalic line. When the infantry objectives had been taken the X Corps was to proceed through two bridgeheads and up to the Oxalic line and then advance beyond it by two bounds—the first bound (Pierson) being about 2,000 yards forward of the final infantry objectives—to secure on the second bound the high ground about Tel el Aqqaqir and establish there, with tanks, motorised infantry and anti-tank guns, a firm base astride the enemy's communications to his forces in the south. The object was to force the Axis armour to attack the anti-tank guns and armour of X Corps.

In the north of the XXX Corps front, in which the 9th Division was most interested, the 2nd Armoured Brigade was to lead the armoured

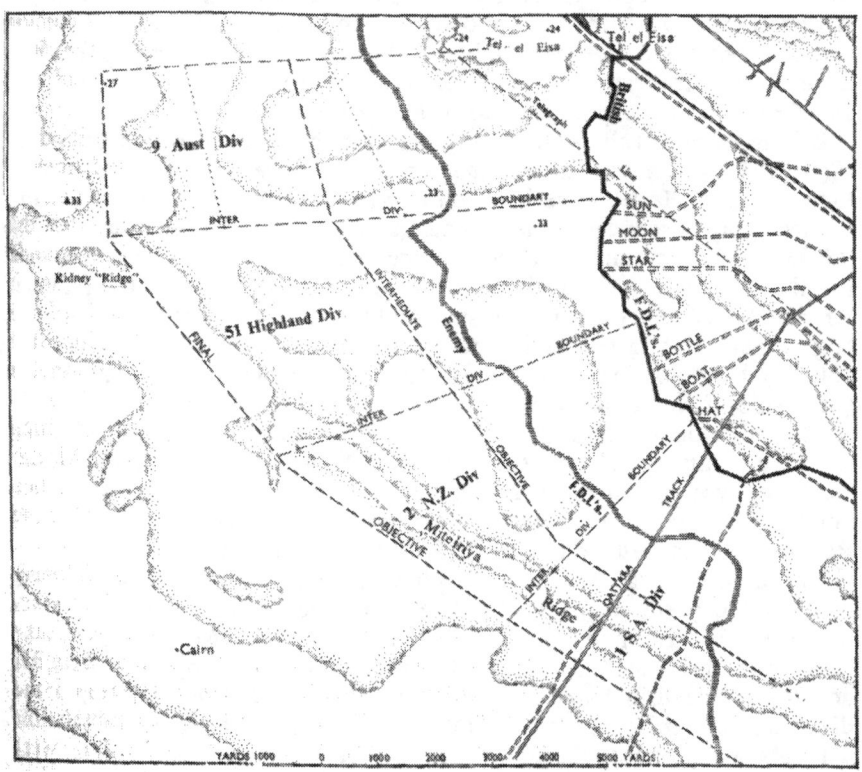

XXX Corps' objectives, 23rd-24th October

advance to the first bound, whereupon the 2nd Motor Brigade would come up to protect its flank for the move to the second bound.

In addition to the four infantry divisions the XXX Corps would have under command the 23rd Armoured Brigade Group of four tank regiments to give close support to the infantry battalions in the assault and later crumbling operations. The 9th Australian, 1st South African and 51st Highland Divisions each had a tank regiment attached for the operation. The wish of the New Zealanders to have their own armour under command had been granted and the 9th Armoured Brigade (with 122 tanks) had been incorporated in the division, which then comprised two infantry brigades (the 5th and 6th) and one armoured brigade.

The New Zealand division had been nominated as a component of the *élite* X Corps. Though under command of the XXX Corps for the opening assault, the division was intended to operate later with the X Corps.

In the south, the XIII Corps was to employ the 44th Division to make two gaps in the old British minefields (known as January and February) of which the enemy had retained possession after the Alam el Halfa battle, and then to pass the 7th Armoured Division through to the enemy's rear, where it was to operate as a threat so as to keep the German armour stationed in the south from moving north, but was to avoid becoming heavily committed. On the right of the main corps operation the 50th Division was to operate in the Munassib depression, and on the left the 1st Free French Brigade was to attack for Himeimat.

The most vulnerable part of the northern bridgehead would be its deep right flank, which would face the most fully developed defended area of the whole Axis front, covering the main road, to the north of which strong artillery was ensconced in the dunes near the coast. The selection of the 9th Division to mount the attack on the right of the line, though not made for that reason alone, was none the less a compliment. The 1st South African Division had similar responsibilities on the southern flank of the corps' front but if successful would not have an open flank, since the new front would link with the existing front where it protruded on the south side of the area the South Africans were to attack.

The additional troops placed under the command of the 9th Division for the operation included the 40th R.T.R., and the 66th British Mortar Company with eighteen 4.2-inch mortars;[3] and in support for certain periods were to be six troops of corps field artillery, the 7th Medium Regiment and a battery of the 64th Medium Regiment.

The division's tasks were to capture an area of the enemy's defences about 6,000 yards deep and 3,300 yards wide (whose western boundary was the 867 grid line) so as to facilitate the passage of the X Corps through the bridgehead,[4] to exploit westward from the objective to Trig 33, and to form a firm flank facing north. About 3,000 yards separated the division's forward defended localities from the foremost enemy minefields. The final objective of the division was almost three miles and a half west of the wire at Point 23, where the enemy defences would be first encountered.

One of the problems was to maintain the momentum of an advance which would have to penetrate for such a distance through heavily mined and strongly held defences developed in depth. This was tackled by phasing the attack and, on the 9th Division's but not on all other fronts, by using fresh troops for successive phases. The XXX Corps attack was to be made in two phases; in the first phase the "Red Line", about 3,700 yards from the final objective, would be captured. For the second phase, start-lines would be laid in territory wrested from the enemy in the first phase. In the divisional plan the two phases were again each subdivided into an intermediate and a final objective, making in all four objective lines to be

---

[3] These were mortars designed primarily for chemical warfare which could also fire a very heavy H.E. bomb. As there was a small stock of these in the Middle East it was decided to use them to support the 24th Brigade's feint attack, thus releasing guns for the main battle. The mortars fired the entire Middle East stock in doing this.

[4] The northernmost lane to be used by the armour was to be near the boundary of the 9th Australian and 51st Divisions.

taken in succession. The battalions that were to open the assault were to take the first two objectives, whereupon fresh battalions would pass through to take the last two. Each battalion except the 2/17th decided to use two companies to take its first (or intermediate) objective, passing through two fresh ones to take the final objective. As each company took its objective, it was to remain on it and develop it for defence. Thus momentum was to be achieved with fresh troops coming through in four waves. The first phase of the assault was to be made with three battalions, the second with two, the first phase being in greater strength to make sure that the initial penetration could be firmly held as a base from which to launch the second phase.

The division's attack was to be made on a two-brigade front with, on the right, the 26th Brigade (Brigadier Whitehead) less the 2/23rd Battalion, and on the left the 20th Brigade (Brigadier Wrigley). The 24th Brigade (Brigadier Godfrey) would continue to hold the existing front near the coast.

The 26th Brigade was to have under command a composite force which was to hold the gap between the right rear of Whitehead's open right flank, as it would rest when the brigade faced north on completion of the attack, and the left flank (near the road and railway) of the defences that the 24th Brigade would continue to hold. The composite force was to be commanded by Lieut-Colonel Macarthur-Onslow[5] and comprised a company of his own machine-gun battalion, a company of the pioneer battalion, a squadron of the divisional cavalry and anti-tank detachments.

As the 26th Brigade, on completion of its assault, would have to form a long firm front on the northern flank as well as a front to the west, it was given a narrower front to attack than the 20th Brigade. The 26th Brigade was to attack with one battalion up in both phases, the 20th with two up in the first phase, one in the second. The latter battalion (the 2/13th) would thus have to attack on the widest front and to the full depth of the divisional objective.

The role of the 24th Brigade was, in addition to holding the existing defences in the coast region, to carry out a diversionary operation beginning at Zero and designed to draw enemy artillery fire on to its area, and to maintain one battalion at call as a divisional reserve.

The 2/23rd Battalion and the 46th R.T.R., which were to be detached from their parent formations, were detailed as corps and divisional reserve, with perhaps a semi-mobile role. They bivouacked and trained together for a week before the battle. The 9th Divisional Cavalry Regiment (less the squadron with the composite force) was another mobile divisional reserve.

The 40th R.T.R. was to be placed under command of the 20th Brigade. The tanks were to move along the divisional centre line until the enemy's main forward positions had been passed and were then to move south-west in support of the 2/13th Battalion in their attack on the enemy's

---

[5] Lt-Col E. Macarthur-Onslow, DSO, ED, NX12629; 2/2 MG Bn (CO 1942-45). Flying instructor; of Camden, NSW; b. Goulburn, NSW, 1 Oct 1909.

positions about 2,000 yards south-west of Trig 33 and in their final exploitation to Trig 33.[6]

The 40th R.T.R. was then to rally to the rear of the objective and come under command of the 26th Brigade but was not to be employed by that brigade without reference to divisional headquarters "unless the situation will not permit this, in which case the action will be reported immediately".

The rate of advance was to be 75 yards a minute to the enemy minefield and thereafter 100 yards in 3 minutes. These timings (in adhering to which the infantry were first given exhaustive practice) were set to enable the foremost troops to "lean" on the artillery barrage. At Zero plus 55 minutes there would be a pause of 15 minutes to pass companies through, and at Zero plus 115 a pause of an hour to pass the battalions through to take the second objective. The signal for the opening of phase two would be the quickening of the rate of artillery fire. At Zero plus 235 there would be another pause of 15 minutes to pass companies through; at Zero plus 310 minutes the infantry should reach the final objective.

Montgomery's battle-plan laid great store on the shock effect of a barrage from the army's massed artillery. No more painstaking work was done before the battle than in the preparation of the fire-plan. All guns supporting the infantry assault had to move forward to new positions for the battle, which had to be chosen and surveyed, and because the guns could not range on targets beforehand, the setting for every gun for every target to be engaged in the battle had to be calculated from data.

Great though the army's array of artillery was, there were not sufficient guns for an efficient creeping barrage across the whole assault front. The program therefore provided for successive timed concentrations on known targets, though with creeping barrages on areas where specific targets were not indicated. Starting at 20 minutes before the Zero hour for the infantry advance, there was to be a bombardment of the enemy's gun-sites for 15 minutes. During that time the divisional artillery would be under corps command. At Zero it would come under divisional command and fire concentrations continuously (but at varying rates of fire) for the five hours and ten minutes allowed for the infantry to take their objectives, with pauses in lifts to correspond with the pauses prescribed for the infantry advance to allow following companies and battalions to pass through those in front and resume the advance.

Two searchlights were established at accurately surveyed points behind the corps artillery and were to send up stationary beams on the night of the battle. These were intended to serve two purposes: first, to indicate two known points from which position could be plotted by re-section—for this they proved to have been too close together and also too far back to be plotted on most of the maps carried forward; secondly, to indicate the commencement of phases of the artillery plan (which could be useful if a synchronised watch were destroyed) by swinging the beams inward at the moment of commencement.

---

[6] 23 Armd Bde Group Report on "Lightfoot".

Throughout the battle the bringing down of defensive artillery fire was to be greatly simplified and speeded up by dividing the enemy's territory into small areas each of which was labelled with a code name—Galway, for example, Broome, Wexford, Fremantle and so on. As soon as a call for attention to one of these places was sent back to the guns, several regiments would promptly concentrate their fire on it.

The main task of the engineers was to see the infantry safely through the minefields. The 2/7th Field Company was placed in support of the 26th Brigade and the augmented 2/13th Company in support of the 20th. The 2/3rd Company had the tasks of preparing, marking and maintaining traffic routes. Each company in support of an assaulting brigade had to provide detachments with each forward infantry company, provide and fire Bangalore torpedoes, make and mark gaps in the enemy minefields along the axis of advance, widen these gaps to 24 yards, make more gaps as required, and also assist the infantry to lay Hawkins mines.[7]

On the last few nights before the attack sappers moved out over the axis of advance dealing with all isolated minefields east of the main ones. In this period 203 mines were disarmed but left in position. As a result of this preparatory work there was a clear area right up to the start-line, and on the night of battle the mine-clearing parties had to deal only with the main fields.

The division was to go into battle better armed than ever before. The anti-tank defence showed the greatest improvement. The 2/3rd Anti-Tank Regiment had 64 6-pounder anti-tank guns—really first-class weapons for their task—and there was a good supply of the Hawkins anti-tank mines which could be quickly and easily laid. Most battalions furthermore had eight 2-pounders in their anti-tank platoons. The 9th Divisional Cavalry had 15 Crusader tanks, 5 Honeys and 52 carriers.

The infantry were much stronger in automatic weapons than ordained by war establishments at the beginning of the war. On the one hand there were the re-introduced machine-gun platoons, with 6 guns per platoon; on the other, the many salvaged weapons. There were 71 Spandau machine-guns in the division—the 2/3rd Pioneers had no fewer than ten—63 Bredas of calibres ranging from 6.5 to 47-mm, 15 81-mm mortars, 5 Besa machine-guns, and other weapons.

On the eve of battle the strength of the battalions ranged from 30 officers and 621 others to 36 officers and 740 others; the war establishment was 36 officers and 812.[8]

The draft of reinforcements dispatched from Australia on Morshead's representations had arrived on 10th October, but it was decided, having regard to the standard of earlier drafts, that there would be insufficient

---

[7] The Hawkins mine or grenade weighed two pounds and a half, could be thrown as far as 25 yards and could cut the track of a tank or disable a truck. It was used both as a grenade and a static mine.

[8] On 20th October Colonel Hammer of the 2/48th had pointed out to his brigadier that his battalion was 5 officers and 228 others below strength and asked that the number to be left out of battle be reduced or even eliminated. He said that 2 officers and 23 others were on the way back to the unit or were at schools, and 7 and 184 would soon be available from hospital and implied that these would suffice for an "L.O.B." group.

time before the battle began both to harden them sufficiently after the long sea voyage and to train them to a proper standard for battle.[9]

When everything had been prepared and all had been trained, it remained to reveal the plan first to the leaders and then to the men and to explain their individual tasks in it. The briefing of commanding officers, and later of company commanders and junior leaders, was carried out at divisional headquarters on an accurate large-scale model of the ground which had been made by the engineers and kept guarded in a building at headquarters.

"Morale is the big thing in war," the army commander had declared, in his original instructions for the battle.

> We must raise the morale of our soldiery to the highest pitch; they must be made enthusiastic, and must enter this battle with their tails high in the air and with the will to win.

The disclosures of the plan stage by stage downwards were made occasions for evoking the enthusiasm for which Montgomery was striving. Morshead expounded the plan to his commanding officers on 10th October and in the address he gave before he explained the operational tasks there were many echoes of Montgomery's sentiments and expressions.

> It will be a decisive battle (Morshead wrote in his notes for the conference), a hard and bloody battle and there must be only one result. Success will mean the end of the war in North Africa and an end to this running backward and forward between here and Benghazi. . . .
> No information about the operations to be disclosed to anyone likely to be taken prisoner. . . . No information therefore to be given to anyone in 24 Brigade.
> Wednesday 21st October and Thursday 22nd October will be devoted to the most intensive propaganda to educate attacking troops about the battle and enthusing them. Tell them that if we win, as we will, turning point of the war. . . . We must go all out and every man give completely of his best. No faintheartedness. Imbue with fighting spirit.
> We must go into the battle with our heads high and the will to win . . . it will be a killing match. . . . If you have anyone you are not sure of, then don't take the risk of taking him in. Give him some job other than fighting.
> We must all apply ourselves to the task that lies ahead, work, think, train, prepare, enthuse. We must regard ourselves as having been born for this battle.

Montgomery himself, in two conferences held on successive nights three or four days before the battle, addressed all senior officers and commanding officers in the army (who were forewarned not to smoke in his presence) about his plan, his reasons for changing it, the aim of the initial assault ("fighting for position and the tactical advantage"), the "dog-fight"—or "crumbling" operations—(which could last for more than a week), the army's "immense superiority in guns, tanks and men", the need to sustain pressure in a battle in which they could outlast the enemy, the importance of morale and the way to get it. As these men sat before Montgomery— these down-to-earth commanders to most of whom he had been perforce a distant and somewhat enigmatic figure—as they listened to his precise

---

[9] This draft proved to be much better trained than earlier drafts, most of the training having been carried out by officers of the division sent back to Australia for that purpose.

and clipped but confident speech and perceived his mastery of his subject and the occasion, as they heard from him how strongly the odds of battle were weighted in their favour, as they learnt that this attack was not to be one to be made by two brigades or so but one in which the whole army's forces would be arrayed, they developed instantly a strong confidence in the army commander himself and in his plan.

Thus enthused the commanding officers addressed the men in their units a day or two later, and read to them Montgomery's personal message in which he said (with a suitable injunction to the "Lord mighty in battle") that the Eighth Army was ready to carry out its mandate to destroy Rommel and his army, and would "hit the enemy for 'six' right out of North Africa".[1] That the men were inspirited and imbued with a confidence they had never before experienced, there could be no doubt. Emotionally charged anticipation was evident when in some instances they began chanting army songs, old and new, as they were moved off in trucks to their pre-battle assembly areas.

One aspect of the plan troubled Morshead: that the infantry to make the initial assault, for which the start-lines were to be laid in no-man's land, would have to move out the night before to an area near their forming-up places which was under enemy observation by day and would have to spend there a whole day out of sight in shallow slit trenches. He directed that all commanders should be warned of the possible lowering effect on morale.

On 10th October General Leese, after sounding out General Freyberg and finding him agreeable, had written to Generals Morshead, Wimberley and Pienaar to tell them that he wished to advance Zero hour from 10 p.m. to 9.30. Morshead had opposed this. He wrote:

> The troops will have lain "doggo" in slit trenches all day. I cannot conceive anything psychologically worse than such solitary confinement in a tight-fitting, grave-like pit awaiting the hard and bloody battle. There must be some relaxation before the fight.
>
> To avoid giving the show away to the air these troops will not be able to emerge until close on 1900 hours. Then they have dinner—in the semi-darkness—and they do not want to be rushed off as soon as they have eaten. During the day they will have been ungetatable for final instructions and advice—however long and thorough the preparations there are inevitably those very last instructions which a platoon commander gives to the whole of his platoon. All this could be done by 2030 but 2100 would be preferable as it would avoid any chance of last minute rush and excitement. Then we have the approach march of two miles and it will take up to an hour by the time the battalions are in position on their start-lines.
>
> To sum up, we will be demanding much of our men and we want them to start off in a proper frame of mind; we could be ready by 2120 hrs but I would much sooner have the extra 20 mins up my sleeve. This would further ensure getting A Echelon vehicles forward from Alamein in time.

In the event the infantry advanced at 10 p.m.

All day on the 23rd October the harsh sun and the flies tormented the restless assault troops in their slit trenches. By midday, the 2/17th

---

[1] There is an excellent example of one of these addresses in *The Second Twenty-Fourth* (1963), edited by R. P. Serle, pp. 195-7.

Battalion diarist noted, the men were getting unsettled and it was impossible to keep them under cover in their cramped positions.

> Men were confident and ready for job ahead (he wrote). Every man in the battalion knew his job and just what was required of him. No matter what happens or who gets hit there will be someone who can take his place and do his job. Our men are certainly entering this action with the "aggressive eagerness" required by the army commander.

Sprawled across the landscape farther back were others, waiting to move forward. There was scarcely any movement on the face of the desert until late afternoon when suddenly it became alive with vehicles emerging from their camouflage and lining up to join at the prescribed time the columns of traffic that had suddenly filled the roads. For 30 miles or more behind the forward defences, vehicles hurried eastwards along every road or track, old or new, leading to the front, in continuous parallel streams.

So, as the sun was setting, the Eighth Army moved to its battle stations, the 9th Australian Division on the right, then the 51st Highland, 2nd New Zealand, 1st South African and 4th Indian Divisions;[2] coming up behind these the 1st and 10th Armoured Divisions (and with the latter the 1st and 104th R.H.A., who had been with the 9th Division in Tobruk)—many of their units bearing names with an illustrious record in British military history; then farther south, the 50th and

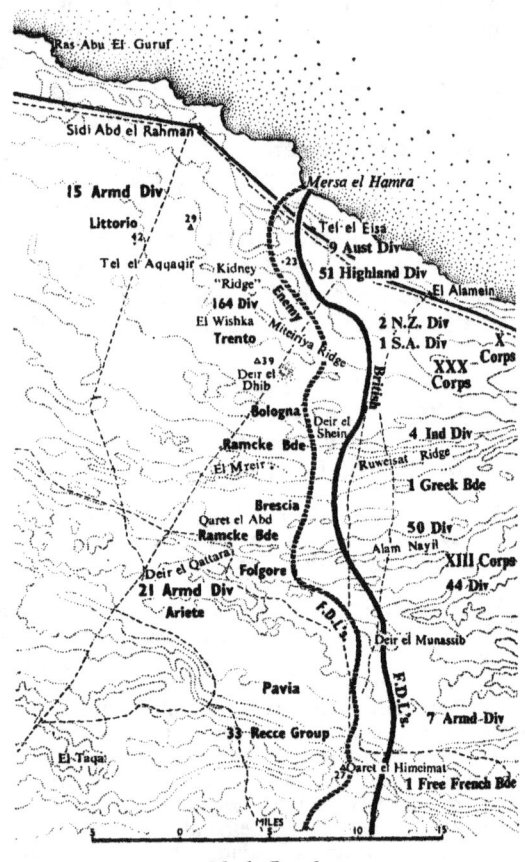

23rd October

44th British Divisions, the former including a Greek brigade and behind them the 7th Armoured Division—the "Desert Rats"—and on the left of the line the 1st Free French Brigade Group. The call to the battle was a roll-call of the Empire, that grand but old-fashioned "British Common-

---

[2] The 4th Indian Division's 5th Brigade had fought alongside Australians in Syria.

wealth of Nations", fighting its last righteous war before it was to dissolve into a shadowy illusion. And it was a summons to which expatriate forces of oppressed nations had responded, freely choosing to fight alongside.

That night General Morshead wrote to his wife:

> It is now 8.40 p.m. and in exactly two hours time by far the greatest battle ever fought in the Middle East will be launched. I have settled down in my hole in the ground at my battle headquarters which are little more than 2,000 yards from our start-line. I have always been a firm believer in having HQ well forward—it makes the job easier, saves a great deal of time, in fact it has every possible advantage and I know of no disadvantage. At the present time I can see and hear all the movement forward to battle positions—it is bright moonlight, tomorrow being full moon. . . .
>
> A hard fight is expected, and it will no doubt last a long time. We have no delusions about that. But we shall win out and I trust put an end to this running forward and backward to and from Benghazi. . . .
>
> The men are full of determination and confidence. Going round them, talking with them, and addressing them I have noticed an air of quiet and confident purposefulness that augurs well, even though these grand fellows have never once failed to respond fully.
>
> In the preliminary and opening stages of a battle a commander can do little or nothing. He merely waits and hopes. It is only as the battle develops that he can really act. From then on he is a very busy man. . . .

The night of 23rd October was clear and illumined by a brilliant, almost full moon. As soon as it was dark a hurried hot meal was served to the men out in front, start-lines were laid and the routes to the forming-up positions taped. As the leading battalions moved forward, following the tapes, a cool southerly breeze was blowing.

The noise of the Eighth Army's transport, which had been reverberating like city traffic as night fell, lessened in time, then ceased. A strange, sustained quietness reigned between the opposing armies. In the deceptive peace the illusion was created that time stood still; but one by one, unarrested, the irretrievable minutes moved on. In silence the men who were to go forward waited as the moment came ever closer when the guns in concert would strike the first chord of their harsh overture to battle.

When the hour for action was drawing near, a throbbing, at first half imagined, then faintly heard, stole through the night and grew into rhythmic, surging sound. The bomber aircraft that were to support the army's assault approached from the east and passed over. A few distant points of light then flickered unimpressively from the desert on the British side; they came from the muzzles of the long-range guns opening up in advance of the shock moment so that their first shells would fall in the same split second as those from the massed field artillery. In an instant, at the stroke of 9.40 p.m., flashes from hundreds of guns were seen sparkling in a long line across the desert. As a quiet interval follows a lightning flash before the thunder roll is heard, so the sound of the guns took time to reach the infantry. Seconds seemed to be drawn out into minutes while flickering gun flashes continued to play silently up and down the line, and only the droning rhythm of the aircraft then flying above the enemy positions could be heard until the sound wave crashed with a roar of furious hammering from the sharp, staccato reports of guns pounding at a combined firing rate of some thousand rounds per minute. The rapid bark of the guns almost masked the dull crunch of aircraft bombs and shells exploding in the enemy gun-line but the resonant clang of heavy mortar bombs bursting closer to the front on Cloverleaf opposite the 24th Brigade rang out clear and loud above the gunfire.[3]

For fifteen minutes the counter-battery bombardment continued unabated. Suddenly the guns were silent. There was a breathless stillness, as if their force was spent. Above the Eighth Army's hidden battle array two searchlights pointed long, still fingers into the sky. Five minutes passed. At 10 p.m. the two beams swung inward, intersected and stopped, forming a pointed arch dimly seen in the moonlit vault, like a remote symbol of crossed swords. At that instant the British guns opened a barrage of unimaginable intensity, eclipsing their first performance, and to the urgent drumming of the guns the infantrymen stepped out from their start-lines in slow, measured paces at the even rate of 75 yards per minute. A continuous stream of glowing tracer shells, in seeming slow motion, sailed in the air over the heads of the advancing Australians and pointed the direction of their attack. White and coloured flares shot up into the sky above the enemy wire. The moon shone down. The fight was on.

Well practised in exercises in keeping to the exact speed required, the infantry maintained, as they advanced, a straight extended line on either side of their company guide group, which set the speed and direction. In the centre of each advancing battalion the unit guide party was marking the centre line with stakes driven in at intervals of 100 yards, on each of which was placed a rearward shining torch emitting a coloured beam; various colours were used to differentiate the centre lines of different units. Later the road for following tanks and vehicles would be taken along the centre line to the left of the stakes. The signallers meanwhile were running their lines forward well to the right of the stakes, to be clear of later vehicle movement. Not far behind the guide parties the engineers followed, ready to come right forward as soon as a minefield was struck, and instantly to commence clearing a gap. Farther back again were other groups which, as they advanced, established traffic control points which would later be in direct communication with battalion headquarters and would control the movement forward, as required, of tanks or vehicles carrying ammunition and consolidation stores.[4] An efficient administrative machine was set in motion behind the infantrymen as they moved into the fight.

Those infantrymen going forward did not conform to the popular image of agile, lightly-clad men, each with a weapon in his hands. In addition

---

[3] There were 908 field and medium guns in the Eighth Army. The attack by the XXX Corps was supported by 408 25-pounders and 48 medium guns. There was a gun about every 17 yards. The average rate of fire was two rounds per gun per minute. The XIII Corps used 136 guns. On the XXX Corps front the enemy had about 200 field and 54 heavy and medium guns.

[4] Some conception of the density of the traffic up to and away from the battlefield on D-day may be given by mentioning that a typical battalion would have 31 carriers and 57 other vehicles on the move.

to their weapons they were loaded with ammunition in excess of standard battle scale, a few grenades, a pick or shovel, four sand-bags, personal kit, two days' rations and an emergency ration. Those assigned the deeper objectives would have to advance some three miles carrying this load, and, still burdened with it, they would have to fight.

Right along the front of the XXX Corps the enemy's front-line defences were breached and the objectives for the first phase successfully taken but it was soon found that the job of minefield clearance was much bigger than expected.

On the extreme right of the corps attack the 2/24th Battalion (Lieut-Colonel Weir) advanced with two companies forward—Lieutenant McNamara's on the right and Captain Serle's on the left. One small minefield was encountered on the start-line and cleared without difficulty. The enemy soon opened defensive fire with mortars and machine-guns and one of the supporting 25-pounders was dropping its shells short. At 10.30 the two companies reached the minefield while the artillery concentrations were still falling just beyond and went to ground until the barrage lifted while the engineers came forward and blew gaps in the wire with bangalores

When the leading companies passed through they encountered several enemy posts, which were attacked one by one. Soon both company commanders had been hit. McNamara was able to carry on. When Serle was hit his company was heavily engaged but pressed on, and later Lieutenant Greatorex[5] whose platoon had been busily rounding up Italians took charge. After waiting 20 minutes for the barrage to lift McNamara reached the intermediate objective without great opposition but Greatorex's men on their left were held up until some machine-gun posts were silenced. They were on the objective at 11.10.

At 11.30 Major Mollard's company and Captain Harty's[6] passed through to attack for the final objectives, which they took just on midnight without meeting strong opposition. The battalion had lost four killed and 39 wounded, and had taken 43 German and 35 Italian prisoners, six light guns and 16 machine-guns.

Meanwhile the sappers were working feverishly to clear lanes through the minefields so that anti-tank guns and vehicles laden with ammunition, mines and consolidation stores could be got forward. At 11.20, after 35 minutes work under fire, two eight-yard gaps had been cleared in the first minefield but ten minutes later another field of five rows was met. Enemy artillery and mortar fire was heavy and some sappers were hit, but by 12.5 a.m. gaps had been completed. This was the main field but farther on two more fields were found and had to be gapped.

In the first phase the 20th Brigade attacked with the 2/17th (Lieut-Colonel Simpson) on the right and the 2/15th (Lieut-Colonel Magno)

---

[5] Capt A. G. W. Greatorex, MC, WX11512; 2/24 Bn. Farmer; of Pinjarra, WA; b. London, 4 Feb 1905.

[6] Capt E. P. Harty, VX46436; 2/24 Bn. Accountant; of Double Bay, NSW; b. East Melbourne, 6 Apr 1914.

on the left. Major Brien's[7] company on the right of the 2/17th (which attacked with three companies forward) met heavy opposition and many men were hit, including Brien himself, mainly while overcoming two strong positions. One of these was knocked out and the occupants killed by a section of four men led with great dash by Corporal Harris.[8] (Though hit in both thigh and shoulder Harris continued to lead his section until the following night when he was again wounded.) Lieutenant Hannaford[9] took command of Brien's company and the men reached their objective on time. The centre company and the left one too reached their objectives without excessive casualties; by this time the battalion had lost 15 killed and 47 wounded and 14 others were not accounted for.

The 2/15th on the left took its intermediate and final objectives with relatively light losses but the audacious Captain Cobb, whose company was leading on the right, was among those killed. In all 5 were killed and 40 wounded.

The sappers with the 2/17th did not have undue difficulty in making gaps in the minefield but the area through which the 2/15th advanced was found to be alive with anti-personnel and anti-tank mines and it was not until 12.30 a.m. that a lane had been cleared.

The massive, rapid artillery bombardment—at an average rate, on the XXX Corps' front, of some 900 rounds per minute—had continued unabated while the foremost battalions were advancing to their objectives and still continued to pound the enemy defences beyond the objectives during the hour allowed for the following troops to pass through and launch their attack for the second objectives, at the end of which time, as though a sudden anger had impelled the artillery to its utmost exertion, the rapidity of the brutal bombardment sharply increased, signalling the commencement of the second phase.

The success of the XXX Corps' attack for the first phase augured well for the second, but it was soon to be found that the first line of defence which on British maps of enemy defences had bristled with obstacles and weapons of every kind was but a comparatively lightly held outer line to cover the main line of defence sited in rear at considerable depth.

On the right flank the 2/48th Battalion (Lieut-Colonel Hammer), coming up along the 2/24th's centre line, had seen the 2/24th's success signal go up just before it reached its start-line for the second phase. At 12.38 the battalion began to advance with two companies forward—Captain Robbins' on the right, Major Edmunds'[1] on the left—towards the enemy's second line of defence. The defences were wired, mined and booby-trapped but these obstacles were efficiently dealt with. At first there was stiff resistance. In Robbins' company Lieutenant Lewin[2] was hit. Sergeant

---

[7] Maj L. C. Brien, NX12298; 2/17 Bn. Oil company representative; of Temora, NSW; b. Cowra, NSW, 11 Feb 1906. Died 4 Dec 1948.
[8] L-Sgt E. Harris, DCM, NX21416; 2/17 Bn. Pastoral worker; of Coonamble, NSW; b. Coonamble, 23 Jun 1910.
[9] Lt R. A. Hannaford, NX20774; 2/17 Bn. Wool buyer; of Clifton Gardens, NSW; b. Sydney, 9 Jul 1918. Killed in action 29 Oct 1942.
[1] Maj G. S. Edmunds, SX10316; 2/48 Bn. Clerk; of Adelaide; b. Adelaide, 16 Jun 1917.
[2] Capt R. W. Lewin, WX6926; 2/48 Bn. Saddler; of Maylands, WA; b. Northam, WA, 15 Jan 1919.

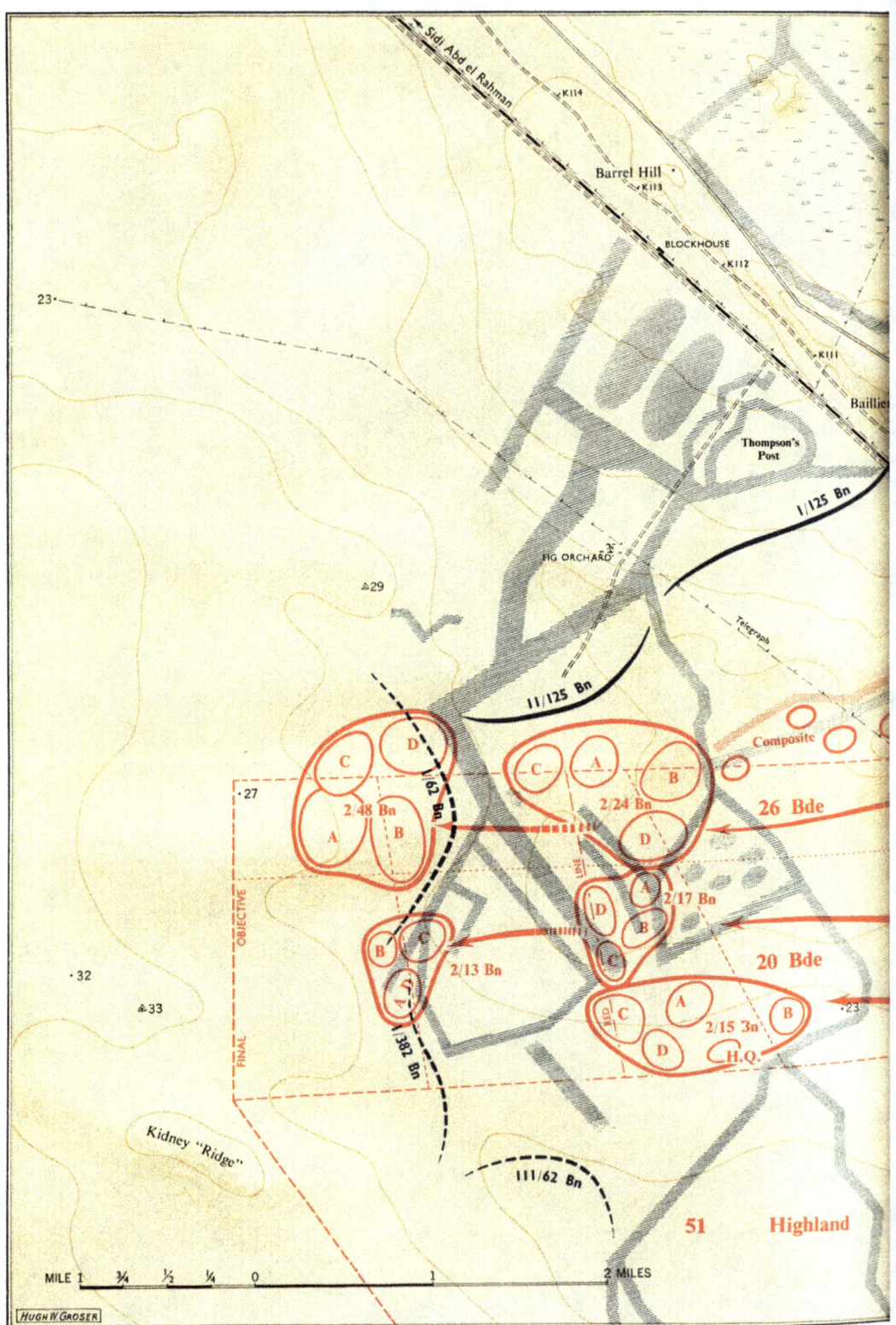

Dawn,

24th October

Kibby[3] took over the platoon and Robbins ordered him to attack a troublesome enemy post holding up the advance and pinning down Kibby's platoon. Kibby promptly dashed forward firing his Tommy-gun and silenced the post, killing three men and taking the surrender of 12 others. The advance was resumed.

The forward companies halted 2,500 yards from the start-line and the rear companies (Captains Bryant and Shillaker) passed through and advanced to the objective 1,400 yards farther forward. The smoke and dust raised by the bombardment had formed a dense pall and the Bofors guns, firing four rounds every five minutes along the centre line, were a great help. The success signal was sent up at 3.45 a.m. The 2/48th had advanced 3,900 yards from its own start-line and 6,900 yards from the brigade start-line. Patrols sent out to cover reorganisation met no opposition but although Major Edmunds' company had established contact with the 2/13th Battalion on the intermediate objective the companies on the final objective could find no sign of the 2/13th on their left.

The 26th Brigade's attack on the Eighth Army's northern flank had succeeded brilliantly. Reorganisation to form a firm front to the flank was at once put in hand. The ground on which the companies dug in on the northern side was for the most part beyond the boundary of the objective prescribed in the orders. In the 2/48th Robbins' company on the right faced north, Bryant's company, which was the right corner peg of the Eighth Army's new front, faced both north and north-west and on its left Shillaker's company faced west. On Shillaker's left flank, however, the ground was still held by the enemy. Meanwhile the toiling engineers had been unrelentingly pushing their mine-free lanes forward through ground constantly harassed by fire from the enemy's unattacked positions opposite the northern flank. As soon as the way was clear Major Tucker brought in the vehicles with consolidation stores, and the men, toughened by Hammer's hard training policy, put up a tremendous effort to get the often-rehearsed job done. "We were perfectly reorganised by dawn," wrote Hammer, in his report of the battle, "with 2,400 Hawkins laid and dug-in very solidly." All supporting weapons were in place and all men dug-in with galvanised-iron overhead protection against airburst.

The 2/24th Battalion, which had been not quite so pressed for time, had also reorganised facing north, pushing the left-rear company (Harty's) forward and left into the gap between the 2/24th and the 2/48th and likewise pushing out the right-rear company to cover the right flank beyond which the composite force had established its strong-points in the old no-man's land to link with the coast sector defences.

Lieut-Colonel Macarthur-Onslow's composite force was in position by 2 a.m. and digging in on a line 3,500 yards long through East and West minefield begun by the 2/3rd Pioneers on the two nights before the battle Point 24 and farther west. Six posts had been established covering a

---

[3] Sgt W. H. Kibby, VC, SX7089; 2/48 Bn. Fibrous plasterer; of Glenelg, SA; b. Winlaton, Durham, England, 15 Apr 1903. Killed in action 31 Oct 1942.

and finished on the 23rd-24th. There was no interference by the enemy except for some artillery fire.

The 20th Brigade's task in the second phase was assigned to the 2/13th Battalion (Lieut-Colonel Turner), with the 40th Royal Tank Regiment in support. Unlike Hammer, Turner had no open flank and did not have to worry about holding a long front to the north, but his battalion had to advance to the same depth as Hammer's and on a wider front—2,400 yards as against 800. Having regard to what was known of the enemy defences, Turner had allotted in each phase a frontage of 900 yards to the right company and of 1,500 yards to the left. The frontages were too great to be effectively covered by a straight infantry company attack, so various strong-points selected from the overprint maps were given as special tasks to platoons and fighting patrols. The attack had been rehearsed as one of cooperation between infantry and tanks, tanks being needed to help mop up so wide an area. It had been expected that the main minefield to be traversed in the first phase of the corps attack would be 250 yards deep and the plan allowed for this (and more) to have been cleared before the second-phase attack began. However the route to the start-line of the 2/13th and 40th R.T.R. was traversed by many secondary minefields so that mines had to be cleared for almost 1,600 yards. The lanes could not be made ready for the tanks despite Herculean efforts by Major Gehrmann's 2/13th Field Company, so the battalion attacked on time but without the tanks.

In the first 1,700 yards Captain Handley's and Captain Cribb's[4] companies encountered as expected only small outposts, from which the occupants made off,[5] with the exception of one strongpoint which Sergeant Carson's[6] platoon had been detailed to attack. Carson led out his platoon on the required bearing to the post, which was overcome with grenades and the bayonet, contacted the 2/48th on his right, and then had his platoon ensconced in an adjoining position. Having heard enemy fighting on the left he set out to find his company headquarters, encountered a German post and captured single-handed nine German prisoners.

Meanwhile, from Captain Cribb's company on the left, Sergeant Easter had set out with his platoon to contact the neighbouring Gordon Highlanders and take part in a joint attack with that battalion on a strongpost and anti-tank gun locality on the inter-divisional boundary. Much later Easter returned to report that he had contacted the Gordons and led his platoon with them in an attack on their next objective, which however did not succeed.

By 3 a.m. Captain Wilson's company and Captain Sanderson's had passed through, but still the tanks had not got forward. These companies came up against the enemy's defence line and soon met intense fire from the front and flanks and suffered heavy losses.

---

[4] Maj B. G. Cribb, NX12443; 2/13 Bn. Flooring manufacturer; of Hornsby, NSW; b. Eastwood, NSW, 3 May 1914.
[5] Rommel later wrote that part of the Italian *62nd Infantry Regiment* in this sector left the line and streamed back to the rear. *The Rommel Papers*, p. 303.
[6] Lt A. B. Carson, NX14764. 2/13 Bn and 2/9 Cdo Sqn. Shipping clerk; of Vaucluse, NSW; b. Newcastle, NSW, 10 Jan 1917.

Wilson's company ran into crossfire from a line of German posts. Soon Wilson and the commanders of two of his platoons were wounded and their platoons pinned down. The third platoon, led by Lieutenant Pope,[7] charged and overcame one post whereupon some of the enemy shouted in English, as a ruse, "Hold your fire. We are coming in."[8] The Australians ceased fire whereupon some Germans ran back and re-occupied some of the positions. Lieutenant Treweeke[9] took command of the company and twice attacked the nearest centre of resistance, succeeding on the second attempt in overcoming it; 12 Germans were killed and 23 surrendered. Treweeke decided to wait until the tanks came up before continuing the attack.

Sanderson's company, on the left, had also been in a fire-fight and taking casualties. Sanderson saw some Germans approaching as if they wished to surrender, ordered his men to cease fire and stood upright. He was immediately shot down. Lieutenant Norrie,[1] though wounded, took command and ordered the men to assault but as he led them forward was also killed. Lieutenant O'Connor,[2] also wounded, took over and after calling for volunteers led 12 men from his platoon against one of the posts. After hand-to-hand fighting the post was overcome, but not before O'Connor had been wounded again, this time mortally. Nearly all the N.C.O's had been killed or wounded and the survivors, under the only remaining officer, Lieutenant Bissaker,[3] were withdrawn to the intermediate objective where Captain Cribb later absorbed them into his company.

Meanwhile Colonel Turner had sent Captain Cribb back to bring up the tanks. Brigadier Wrigley warned the 2/17th to have two companies ready to move forward to help the 2/13th but when it became evident that they could not reach the area before daylight, the 2/13th was ordered to dig in where it was. At dawn the forward companies which were skylined on a slight crest came under heavy fire and were forced to withdraw to dead ground a short distance back. Soon the tanks arrived in line ahead. The infantry pointed out the troublesome posts that were still unsubdued near by and the tanks promptly destroyed them.

While the attack had been proceeding, the 24th Brigade had carried out its diversionary operations. Just before midnight a group of 50 dummies which had been earlier placed in no-man's land forward of the 2/43rd and 1,000 yards from the enemy's forward positions were raised by remote control and illuminated from time to time by sweeping searchlights to simulate men moving in to the attack, so as to invite retaliatory fire, which the enemy brought down in abundant measure.

---

[7] Maj H. W. Pope, MC, NX59159; 2/13 Bn. Law student; of Vaucluse, NSW; b. Sydney, 19 Mar 1920.

[8] Perhaps it was not a ruse. The German for "Stop firing. We are coming over there" sounds much the same.

[9] Lt F. S. Treweeke, NX56181; 2/13 Bn. Grazier; of Bourke, NSW; b. Mosman, NSW, 13 Aug 1912. Killed in action 28 Oct 1942.

[1] Lt E. F. G. Norrie, NX56159; 2/13 Bn. Accountant; of Pymble, NSW; b. Sydney, 28 Aug 1918. Killed in action 24 Oct 1942.

[2] Lt C. A. O'Connor, NX66681; 2/13 Bn. Despatch clerk; of Stanmore, NSW; b. Petersham, NSW, 12 Sep 1914. Died of wounds 24 Oct 1942.

[3] Lt F. S. Bissaker, NX57392; 2/13 Bn. Accountant; of Cabarita, NSW; b. Burwood, NSW, 30 Jul 1914. Killed in action 29 Oct 1942.

A reinforced platoon of the 2/43rd, under Lieutenant Thomas,[4] set out to raid enemy positions east of Kilo 110. After covering 600 yards under increasingly intense fire the patrol blew two gaps in the enemy wire, penetrated to its objective and there destroyed an anti-tank gun and inflicted about 30 casualties. After the withdrawal had been ordered, Thomas and two others were hit. Lance-Corporal Bingham (2/3rd Field Company) began to carry Thomas out. On the way Bingham shot a German with his pistol, then bailed up three others who helped him carry Thomas back. A total of five German prisoners were brought in; one Australian was killed, 8 were wounded and 7 were missing.

From Trig 33 the 2/28th sent out a raiding party 34 strong. Lieutenant Barnes'[5] platoon with sappers and others, advancing under fire and in the light of flares, broke through several belts of the enemy's wire and reached its objective. There one forward section got into the strongly-wired enemy post and silenced a machine-gun, but the other failed to break through the wire. Barnes, who had been seriously wounded, ordered a withdrawal. Sergeant Moore[6] took command and ably organised the rescue of the wounded and withdrawal of the survivors. The stretcher-party carrying Barnes was later hit by a mortar bomb and the stretcher was smashed, but Barnes managed to make his own way back. Moore organised a rescue party and brought in other wounded. Of the 34 men on the raid, 3 had been killed and 9 wounded. Two were missing.

The 24th Brigade's operations achieved their aim of drawing artillery fire, which came down on them for four hours. Prisoners taken later in that sector declared that they thought that they had defeated part of the main attack.

In the attack so far the 9th Division had taken 127 German prisoners, all from the *I/382nd Battalion* and 264 Italians mainly from the *I* and *III Battalions* of the *62nd Regiment*.

Elsewhere on the XXX Corps front the assaulting infantry had had similar experiences to those of the Australians. The first objectives were taken in about two hours without great opposition but again minefields proved to be much more extensive than expected and the strongest resistance was encountered in the second line.

The Highland division, which had a wider front than the Australian but employed seven battalions and a reconnaissance regiment (plus, like the Australian division, a tank regiment) compared with the five battalions available for the Australian task, attacked "six-up". Only on the two flanks was a second battalion to pass through at the first objective to attack for the final objective. Except on its left flank the division, which suffered many casualties from aerial bomb minefields, was unable to break through the intermediate objective of the second phase, about which was a line of staunchly held strongpoints. On the left, however, the 7/Black Watch, in perhaps the most hard-fought and successful battalion action of the

---

[4] Lt L. H. Thomas, MC, SX5289; 2/43 Bn. Farmer and grazier; of Burra North, SA; b. Burra, 2 Oct 1908.
[5] Lt G. Barnes, WX8189; 2/28 Bn. Coal miner; of Collie, WA; b. Keswick, England, 24 Feb 1917.
[6] Lt G. McI. Moore, MM, WX865. 2/11 and 2/28 Bns; FELO 1945. Law clerk; of Kalgoorlie, WA; b. Kalgoorlie, 25 Dec 1914.

night, took the final objective at the north-west extremity of Miteiriya Ridge.

On the Highland division's left, the New Zealand division had also taken its final objectives along and beyond the Miteiriya Ridge except on its left flank, where the front held receded towards the South African division. Farther left the South African division was short of the objective on its right adjoining the New Zealanders but had got onto the objective on the left flank of the corps front.

If the army commander's plan to get armoured formations of the X Corps through the bridgehead and astride the enemy's communications before dawn was to be accomplished on any part of the front, the best chance (as is more evident now than while the action was being fought) was along the Miteiriya Ridge where four contiguous battalions (one Highland and three New Zealand) had secured the final objective.

The X Corps had assigned the northern corridor (Sun, Moon and Star tracks) through the Australian and Highland divisions' bridgehead to the 1st Armoured Division, the southern corridor (Bottle, Boat and Hat) through the Miteiriya Ridge to the 10th Armoured Division. The chance of an armoured break-through would therefore depend on the 10th Division's progress through the mine-sown bridgehead. Here its reinforced sapper squadrons, fully conscious of the vital urgency of their mission, were being tormented by harassing fire and sniped at from by-passed posts, as they struggled in a race against time to get their lanes through. This they just managed to do, but some time was then lost in getting messages back to the armoured brigades because of destruction of communication links by enemy fire. As the tanks in the van of the leading regiments of the 8th Armoured Brigade issued out over the crest of Miteiriya Ridge with the following tanks strung behind them in long columns, the sky was paling and the German guns began to pick them off one by one, just as the armoured commanders had feared. There were some gallant duels then which are not the concern of this history, but the armour was soon withdrawn. The tanks of the New Zealand division's 9th Armoured Brigade crested the ridge, but there were still mines beyond.

To the north, where the battlefield was even more thickly mined, the 1st Armoured Division's mine task force had no chance of clearing lanes through before dawn to the XXX Corps' objective. At first light the sappers were still toiling to make gaps behind the foremost infantry. As the dawn sharpened the desert's outlines the leading tanks deployed where they were among the infantry (the Queen's Bays about the Sun track partly among the Australians) and attracted the fire of every gun within range, both on themselves and on their unarmoured neighbours. One or two tanks were hit.

All this looked odd to the infantry who knew that the armoured formations were to go beyond to challenge the enemy's armour to a decisive battle, if necessary fighting their way out,[7] but did not understand the

---

[7] The 1st Armoured Division's operational instruction had stipulated that the 2nd Armoured Brigade would be prepared to overcome possible enemy resistance during its passage through the enemy positions to the XXX Corps' final objective.

folly of pushing tanks out across uncleared minefields under the nose of anti-tank guns nor appreciate that the tanks had been ordered to deploy where they were to safeguard the infantry against an enemy armoured counter-attack at dawn.

In the south, on the front of the XIII Corps, the 44th Division established a bridgehead through the minefield "January" but by dawn was

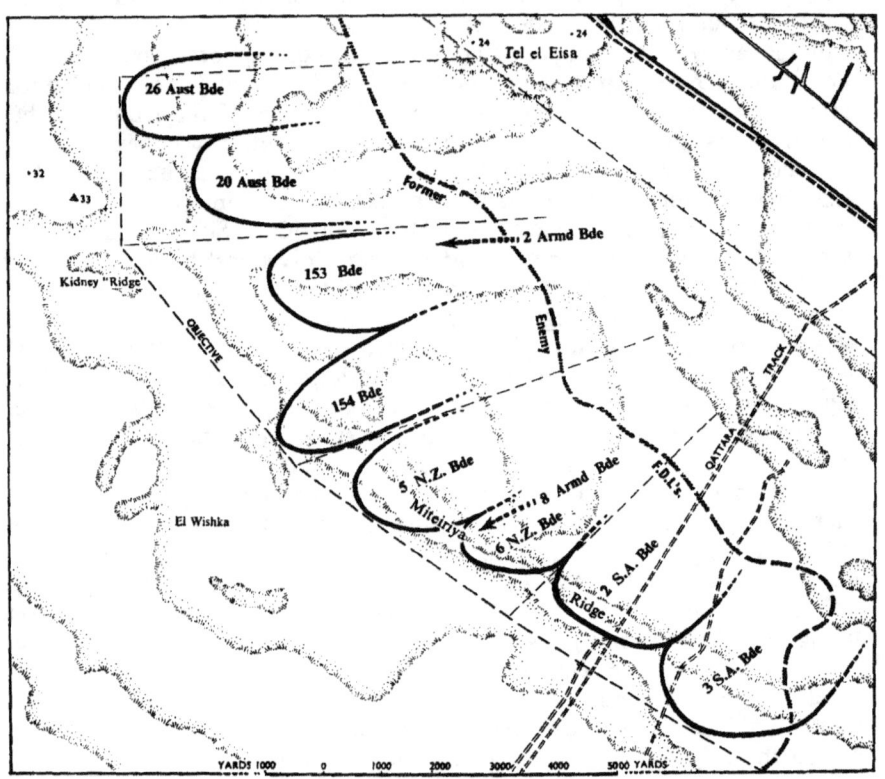

XXX Corps, dawn 24th October

only a short way through deeper "February" beyond. Farther south the stalwart Free French attacking Himeimat got the upper hand in the bitter infantry fight but could not get their anti-tank guns and consolidation stores through soft sand up the steep slopes. The Kiehl Group, which Stumme had stationed on his extreme right flank, counter-attacked with tanks and forced a withdrawal. The enemy retained Himeimat and took advantage of its boon of commanding observation to direct his artillery fire.

When the sun lit up the desert on the morning of the 24th, the enemy, if he had been able to observe the situation clearly through the battle-fog and tumult, would have seen the front of the 9th Australian and 51st Highland Divisions in the shape of a bay between two headlands. Southwards from where the 26th Brigade's positions jutted out on the extreme right flank, the front-line receded across the front of the two divisions but came out again on the left flank of the Highland division. Continuing south on the New Zealand front it remained out beyond the corps' objective—the Oxalic line—in front of the Miteiriya Ridge until the left New Zealand battalion was reached, when it again receded in from the Oxalic line on the New Zealand division's left flank and across the South African division's front to come out again to the objective on the left flank of that division and of the XXX Corps' bridgehead. All along that front the infantry were waiting to meet the expected armoured counter-attacks. The armour of the X Corps had failed to get out beyond the Oxalic line to place itself astride the enemy's supply routes in a challenging posture.

Farther south, on the front of the XIII Corps, the February minefield lay unbreached, blocking the way of the 7th Armoured Division to the enemy's rear.

General Stumme's headquarters, however, knew little of all this. The British bombardment had cut all the Axis communications. Few reports came back out of the turmoil though it was evident that the line had been deeply breached.

German narratives describe the opening of the bombardment along the whole front at 9.40 p.m. on the 23rd and record that it slackened in the south but increased in the north. The British attacked on a front of about five miles. Between the railway and the coast road the attack was halted by the *125th Panzer Grenadier Regiment*. (This "attack" presumably comprised the diversionary raids by the 24th Australian Brigade.) By 2 a.m. the British had crossed the minefields, overcome the outposts and were pressing on the main defence line. The pressure fell mostly on the *382nd German Regiment* and the *62nd Italian Regiment*, whose battalions were interspersed opposite the 9th Australian, 51st Highland and 2nd New Zealand Divisions, each division facing about one German and one Italian battalion. Parts of the three Italian battalions were wiped out by artillery fire and the survivors soon overrun. The Germans at first stood firm, under fire from both flanks.

As the attack progressed the battalions of the *382nd German Regiment* on the Australian and New Zealand fronts were also overrun. The attack was halted by the *115th German Regiment (15th Armoured Division)* manning the second line of defence. By dawn the *62nd Regiment* had been virtually destroyed and the *1/382nd German Battalion* (on the 9th Division's front) and *II/382nd* (on the New Zealand front) had been overcome.

Taking a staff officer with him Stumme set out in the morning to see for himself what had happened, but drove too close to the front and came under fire. The staff officer was killed and the driver turned and drove off. Stumme held on to the outside of the truck but suffered a heart attack, from which he died there on the face of the desert. Bereft for a time of a commander, the Axis forces effected no major redispositions. The *90th Light Division* remained in reserve by the sea, the *21st Armoured Division* remained in the south behind the unbreached minefields in front of the XIII Corps and the *15th Armoured Division* which, with the *Littorio Armoured Division*, was opposite the XXX Corps, took upon itself, according to invariable German habit, to counter-attack the enemy bridgehead on its front.

On the first night of the battle the Eighth Army had not accomplished what its commander had ordered. Only one of the three bridgeheads for the armour had been secured and cleared of mines to the prescribed depth, and that too late. None of the three armoured divisions had pushed through to the enemy's rear. Only one had made an attempt to do so.

Montgomery's second plan was less ambitious than the discarded first plan. The change had been made, he declared, because his troops were insufficiently trained for the tasks he had set them. But the assault forces were well trained for the tasks they were given on the night of 23rd October, and fully rehearsed. No troops could have been better spirited. Montgomery had seen to that himself. What the orders prescribed and the forces faithfully and with great sacrifice strove to do was not accomplished because the tasks Montgomery had laid on the infantry divisions and minefield task forces of the armoured divisions for that night were still too great for them to undertake. That, at least, was an opinion held afterwards at XXX Corps Headquarters.

An outstanding lesson of these operations is that the depth and frontage of the advance ordered for night 23-24 October, and in one or two other instances, was in fact too great against the opposition which was to be expected.[8]

Montgomery may have suspected as much himself when he wrote in his notes for his addresses to commanding officers before the battle that the whole affair would last about 10 days, and on further consideration altered "10 days" to 12.

---

[8] From draft XXX Corps report, dated 21st November 1942, submitted to 9 Aust Div before it left the desert.

CHAPTER 15

THE DOG FIGHT

THERE is no absolute measure of success or failure in war. Though a nation may win a war, when peace ensues it may find itself at a disadvantage. Of the success or failure of a military enterprise as such, however, final victory or defeat is the last judgment. Judged as a contribution to the outcome of the battle, the first night's attack at El Alamein was the foundation of the victory, though judged only in terms of the objectives prescribed, the attack had not succeeded.

As observed in the last chapter, the main reason for the XXX Corps' failure to take all its objectives up to the Oxalic line had been that the plan had asked too much of the infantry. Not even with unexampled skill and valour could tasks of such magnitude have been completely accomplished. Likewise the main explanation of the 8th Armoured Brigade's failure to debouch into the enemy rear even though its bridgehead to the Oxalic line had been cleared was that the plan had demanded the impossible in requiring the armour to give battle on ground of its choosing in the enemy's rear without becoming embroiled on the way, for the ground chosen and the routes from the Oxalic line to it had been fortified by the enemy against tank attack, contrariwise to the assumptions on which the plan had originally been based. To ordain that the armour should give battle on ground of its own choosing was one matter; to expect it to attack ground prepared by the enemy to resist armoured attack, quite another.

Faced with the problem that the bridgehead had failed to span the enemy's zone of anti-tank defence the Eighth Army had several courses open to it to persuade the enemy's armour to join battle so that it might be destroyed. The existing bridgehead could be extended to overreach the remaining tank-proof localities, a new bridgehead could be pushed through on a weaker part of the front, or the enemy could be enticed, by the methodical destruction of his infantry from the existing bridgehead, to launch attacks against ground already prepared in tank defence, as Montgomery's exposition of his second plan had foreshadowed; or some combination of these courses might be tried. These possibilities should be kept in mind as the subsequent course of the battle is followed.

On the morning of the 24th the attention of the armoured commanders, the corps commanders and the army commander himself was attracted to the Miteiriya Ridge sector where the Oxalic line had been reached and lanes for the passage of armour cleared. General Freyberg, forward in his tank in the early morning, was perturbed at the reluctance of the 10th Armoured Division's tanks to push forward. Unable to contact Lumsden, he sent a message to Leese, who thereupon came forward to see Freyberg. Leese and Freyberg reconnoitred the front together and then returned to Freyberg's headquarters to confer by the "blower" with Montgomery. There Lumsden soon joined them, having seen nothing that morning, it may be presumed, to diminish his dislike of issuing in line ahead through minefield lanes to attack an enemy gun-line. Freyberg, whose counsel the higher commanders probably valued more highly than anybody's, thought that the attack should be resumed that night, which may have helped the corps commanders to reach the same conclusion. Montgomery probably needed no prodding to decide that the risks could, should and would be accepted. Montgomery told Lumsden that the 10th Armoured Division was to get out into the open and manoeuvre beyond the Miteiriya Ridge.

In outline Montgomery's orders for the continuation of the battle were, with some modifications, to carry out by the morning of the 25th such of the tasks ordained for the 24th as had not been completed. The 9th Australian and 51st Highland Divisions were to secure the rest of the Oxalic line, the armour was to debouch by night and advance to the Pierson bound. The action of the armour, however, was not to be dependent on completion of the infantry tasks—the armoured divisions were to fight their own way forward. The 1st and 10th Armoured Divisions were to advance westwards, the 9th Armoured Brigade and the New Zealand division's cavalry (armed with Honeys) southwards, all four armoured brigades to link on the Pierson bound. The thrust of the 9th Armoured Brigade was to prepare the way for later southward infantry thrusts by the New Zealand division. The 133rd Lorried Infantry Brigade from the 10th Armoured Division was to take over the part of the New Zealand front adjoining the Highland division. De Guingand later recorded that Lumsden was "obviously not very happy about the role his armour had been given" and Montgomery wrote that he told Lumsden to "drive" his divisional commanders.[1] In the XIII Corps the 44th and 7th Armoured Divisions were also to carry out their tasks uncompleted on the first day.

By daylight that morning the 9th Division's front had erupted with fire of every kind—fire from field guns, machine-guns, mortars and snipers directed at the infantry, high velocity fire aimed at the tanks, and fire from British tanks and guns in rear engaging targets. The pandemonium was to continue—with some periods of great intensity—for several days.

Soon after sunrise the forms of enemy tanks could be seen approaching from the west. The German *15th Armoured Division* was coming in to make its first attack on the bridgehead. By 7.15 a.m. the tanks were reported about 1,000 yards west of the 2/48th's left forward company and also forward of Trig 33. The battlefire quickened. Soon the three Australian field regiments and the 7th Medium Regiment were firing pre-arranged concentrations on the areas into which the German tanks had moved and some Shermans in rear of the Highland division's front and of the left flank of the Australians' front were also engaging them. A little later lorried infantry appeared west of the 2/48th. In time the enemy armour drew back from its first encounter with the XXX Corps artillery and the Shermans' long-range gunfire, leaving several tanks burning on the battlefield. Some Shermans were also burning.

---

[1] De Guingand, p. 200; Montgomery, *Memoirs*, p. 129.

The first big day-bombing attack by the Desert Air Force was allotted to the 9th Australian Division, which chose as target an enemy headquarters area 1,500 yards north of the northern flank of the attack. The bombing was timed for 8 a.m. The division had to indicate the target by smoke shells and to define the line of its own northern defences with blue smoke (from candles captured from the Germans). Although these signals were given, the 18 aircraft, flying at 18,000 feet and probably misled by the smoke on the 9th Australian and 51st Highland and 1st Armoured Divisions' common battleground, dropped their 2,000-pound bombs on the 2/13th Battalion, 3,000 yards south of the target and 1,500 yards south of the blue smoke. But only four men were hit.[2] It was an unfortunate prelude to very close and effective cooperation throughout the battle between the ground and air forces. Later that morning the R.A.F's "tankbuster" squadron of heavily gunned Hurricanes attacked the Kiehl Group and reported that it had knocked out 18 of the Kiehl Group's 19 tanks.[3]

On the northern flank the prospect at daylight had at once revealed that the tactical key to the security of the flank was Trig 29, north of Hammer's battalion. Whitehead's brigade, by comparison with other fronts, was faced by a less subdued enemy infantry, which the main artillery storm of the night assault had by-passed. Enemy artillery to the north was also active though most of its shelling was behind the forward battalions, but soon the enemy began patrolling to find the flank of the penetration.

Meanwhile sappers were busy throughout the day widening lanes, bringing the Diamond, Boomerang, Double Bar and Square tracks up to the foremost localities and clearing minefields from congested areas. In the evening hot meals were brought right up to the forward troops.

On the Highland division's front the lanes of the northern corridor for the armour were being pushed forward. By 9.30 a.m., the tanks were deployed about the double Point 24 ridge to the south of the Australian sector and in action there. One successful daylight infantry attack by the Scottish was made in the centre of the division's front on an enemy locality that had resisted during the night and in the late afternoon tanks of an armoured regiment cleared other defended localities to extend a mine-free lane to the Oxalic line. Towards sunset the enemy armour (*15th Armoured* and *Littorio Divisions*) attacked out of the sun, the main weight being directed more against the Highland than the Australian front. The gunfire battle furiously quickened and the Australians saw "Priests" in action for the first time. The firing continued until dark. Twenty to thirty tanks were destroyed on either side; but the Germans had to destroy British tanks in about the ratio of four to one if they were to retain a chance of avoiding armoured defeat, and that they did not do.

On the New Zealand front, tanks of the 9th Armoured Brigade and some of the 8th Armoured had fought a force of 30 to 40 enemy tanks during the morning until most of the British tanks had been knocked out.

---

[2] The blue smoke was not visible above about 9,000 feet. Thereafter aircraft supporting the division did not bomb from such high altitudes but in consequence were at times effectively engaged by enemy anti-aircraft guns.

[3] This claim later proved to be exaggerated.

The survivors then took up advantageous hull-down positions behind the crest of the Miteiriya Ridge.

At 4 p.m. the commanding officer of the 2/13th Battalion, Colonel Turner, and the adjutant, Captain Leach,[4] were wounded, Turner mortally; both had to be evacuated. Major Colvin[5] was promptly brought forward to take over and, on the way, received orders from Brigadier Wrigley for the renewed attack up to the Oxalic line, which was to open at 2 a.m. next morning. The 20th Brigade was to capture the ground originally assigned to the 2/13th on the first night, but the task was now to be carried out by two battalions, the 2/17th on the right, 2/13th on the left. The attack was to be made with full artillery support. After the Australians had secured their objective the 7/Rifle Brigade was to pass through, take Point 32 and form a bridgehead for the tanks beyond the Oxalic line.

Colvin found the 2/13th practically without officers, and General Morshead agreed to allow all left-out-of-battle officers to be sent forward. Early that night Sergeant Easter of the 2/13th, who had a reputation for cool and reliable judgment under fire, returned from a patrol which had failed to find any sign of the 1/Gordons on the battalion's left.[6] He expressed the opinion that there would not be much opposition to the night attack. Thereupon Colvin conferred with Colonel Simpson of the 2/17th and it was agreed to make a silent attack without artillery support. The 40th Royal Tank Regiment was to support the attack.

The attack by the two battalions was timed to open at 2 a.m. on the 25th. Just before it began a single enemy plane, probably looking for the armour, dropped a flare and then bombed the start-line, but without causing harm. The 2/17th on the right advanced with two companies forward, took the objective without having to fight for it and began to dig in. The battalion's vehicles came forward but soon afterwards were shelled and bombed by aircraft. An anti-tank gun portee was set alight there and also an ammunition vehicle in the 2/13th's area, both providing most unwelcome illumination. Some enemy posts near by began harassing the 2/17th with machine-gun fire as reorganisation proceeded. In the right company Lieutenant Wray[7] was a steadying influence walking through it all pipe in mouth while carrying a heavy load of mixed ammunition for one of his sections which had reported that it was running short. A vehicle in charge of Sergeant Cortis[8] of the machine-gun platoon was hit and set alight, but Cortis coolly off-limbered a gun, got it into action,

---

[4] Maj S. R. Leach, MBE, NX13645. 2/13 Bn and "Z" Special Unit. Regular soldier; of Sydney; b. Melbourne, 12 Nov 1910.

[5] This was the second time Colvin had taken command of the battalion during a battle.

[6] This report does not indicate that 1/Gordons had not secured their intermediate objectives but that in the morning there were misconceptions in units as to the map location of ground taken up during the night. Most prominent identifiable features were outside the ground covered by the large-scale maps carried and features shown on the map were difficult to identify. For instance the location of Kidney Ridge near the boundary of the Australian and Highland divisions was debated for days and inspection of the ground after the battle showed that the 2/13th were closer to Trig 33 than they reported.

[7] Lt G. R. Wray, NX58449; 2/17 Bn. Salesman; of Chatswood, NSW; b. Napier, NZ, 19 Jun 1906.

[8] Lt J. F. Cortis, DCM, NX13746. 2/17 and 36 Bns. Insurance officer; of Bellevue Hill, NSW; b. Bathurst, NSW, 7 Jun 1917.

engaged some of the enemy posts and silenced them. Captain McCulloch[9] of the left forward company was killed by machine-gun fire and the company's only remaining officer wounded; Sergeant Williams[1] took command. The men were very weary and jaded, having been without sleep for 48 hours and throughout that time frequently under intense fire.

On the left the 2/13th had encountered machine-gun fire after about 500 yards but advanced through it. The right company surprised two posts and took the occupants prisoner. By 3.15 a.m. the troops were digging in on the objective with patrols out. The enemy began to lash the forward companies with machine-gun fire from close in front, but the 40th Royal Tanks came up behind and effectively engaged the enemy nests with tracer machine-gun fire. At 4.50 a.m. contact had been made with the Gordons on the left. By 7 a.m. shallow digging had been completed and supporting arms sited.

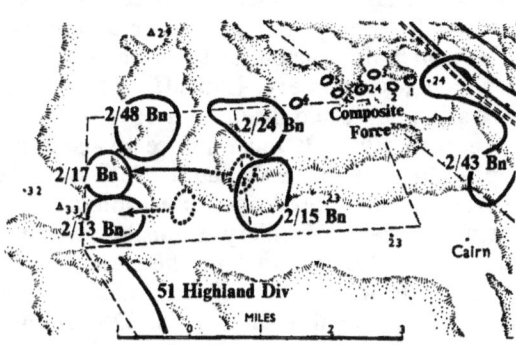

Dawn, 25th October

Before dawn the air was raucous with the noise of tanks approaching from the rear but the 7/Rifle Brigade had not yet appeared when the horizon showed the first signs of approaching day.

The break-out battle was soon to reach its climax. On the Highland front the main tank force of the 1st Armoured Division (2nd Armoured Brigade) had been moving up to the Oxalic line except on the division's left where an enemy strong-point, which the division had lacked the strength to attack, still held out to the right of the gallant 7/Black Watch. It was beyond the Highlanders, however, where the southern bridgehead reached across the Miteiriya Ridge, that the battle's most dramatic developments had been occurring that night. An hour and a half had been allowed to the sappers to clear lanes forward for each armoured regiment before, at 10 p.m., the guns fired the barrage behind which the three armoured brigades of the 10th Armoured Division were to debouch. The time proved all too short and the enemy, as could hardly have been otherwise, was expectant and ready for counter-strokes.

The 8th Armoured Brigade, in the centre, encountered the greatest misfortune. On one lane (Hat track) the enemy captured the mine reconnaissance party and the exit was covered by at least one 88-mm gun. The lane was abandoned. It was then decided that two regiments, the Nottinghamshire Yeomanry and 3rd Royal Tanks, would use the Boat track but

---

[9] Maj E. M. McCulloch, NX12408; 2/17 Bn. Articled law clerk; of Mosman, NSW; b. Rockhampton, Qld, 9 Sept 1917. Killed in action 25 Oct 1942.
[1] S-Sgt E. M. Williams, NX16214; 2/17 Bn. Clerk; of Summer Hill, NSW; b. Melbourne, 24 Jun 1905.

enemy aircraft reconnoitred with flares when the bombardment opened and the Notts Yeomanry were bombed with high explosive and incendiaries and shelled, so that the lane was soon illuminated by burning vehicles, in the light of which the column was harassed by enemy fire. It was decided that this lane was also unusable. The commander of the 10th Armoured Division, General Gatehouse, who was on the Boat track, had seen all this. Lumsden called for a report from Gatehouse.

Irreconcilable accounts have been given of the incidents that followed in which Montgomery, Lumsden and Gatehouse figured and the "friction of war" manifested itself and to which perhaps too much publicity has since been given. It must suffice to recount some salient facts that do not appear to have been disputed. Gatehouse feared that daylight would find his regiments exposed and vulnerable and likely to be shot to pieces by the enemy's anti-tank artillery. Lumsden, who had no authority to break off the attack, reported this to army headquarters, which was also keeping closely in touch through report centres and by analysing what could be heard of the much-jammed radio traffic. De Guingand concluded that "a feeling in some quarters was creeping in which favoured suspending the forward move, a pulling back under cover of the (Miteiriya) ridge" and decided to take what was apparently regarded as a risk even on that battlefield. He woke the army commander and called a conference with the corps commanders for 3.30 a.m.

Three of the four armoured brigades to make the advance to the Pierson line had encountered no insuperable difficulties or problems beyond those to be expected in such a difficult operation. It is understandable, therefore, that the army commander should have decided that the operation should proceed, for he could expect at least some 400 tanks to debouch. He gave very firm instructions that they should. The original orders were partly changed, however, presumably in recognition of the fact that only one of the 8th Armoured Brigade's three lanes—the Bottle track on which the Staffordshire Yeomanry were to debouch—was regarded as usable. One of the brigade's three regiments was to advance and link with the New Zealand division's 9th Armoured Brigade but the rest of the brigade was to remain on the Miteiriya Ridge and improve the gaps. After the conference Montgomery kept Lumsden behind and (he has since written) "spoke very plainly to him . . . any wavering or lack of firmness now would be fatal. If he himself, or the Commander 10th Armoured Division, was not 'for it', then I would appoint others who were."[2]

Gatehouse was no less averse than Morshead to accepting orders to commit his troops to operations which he thought unjustifiable but by comparison was less advantageously placed, not deriving his authority directly from a government. Lumsden wished Gatehouse to receive the instructions from the army commander himself. Gatehouse had gone back to his main headquarters so that he could be contacted by telephone, and there Montgomery telephoned him. Montgomery spoke "in no uncertain

---

[2] Montgomery, *Memoirs*, p. 130.

voice" and nettled Gatehouse by ordering him "to go forward at once and take charge of his battle".[3]

The orders were masterful. It remains to see what effect they had on the battle. On the left of the 9th Division's area dawn on the 25th revealed the Queen's Bays deploying among the infantry close to the end of the bridgehead, the tank commanders, dressed with great individuality for the hunt and bedecked with colourful cravats, standing up in their cock-pits unperturbed by the battle-fire's cacophony and coolly surveying the terrain. There and for some considerable distance to the south the armoured brigade's tanks sat about the foremost defended localities, the target of a vigorous bombardment, as if the limit of their advance had been reached. However hard and however often the "GO" button had been pressed on the army control panel, its impulses were not motivating these tanks whose commanders, though as brave as they were bizarre, evinced no intention to advance "at all costs" to the Pierson bound. Their presence there to do battle was not very welcome to the infantry who regarded the ground of the armour's choosing as their own. Meanwhile about 6 a.m. part of the 7/Rifle Brigade had arrived in rear of the 2/13th's forward companies where their vehicles attracted heavy fire, having insufficient space between the minefields for proper dispersal.

> The enemy gunners were not too proud to shoot at sitting ducks. The carnage was terrible to watch. . . . It was not long before a flood of casualties swamped the 2/13th R.A.P. which was already working at full pressure to cope with the unit's own casualties. Captain Phil Goode and his men were equal to the occasion.[4]

Other Rifle Brigade vehicles which, as the Australians read the map and ground, appeared to have made not for Trig 33 but Point 29 farther south, were also stricken near Kidney Ridge behind which the Highlanders' forward line had been established. Farther to the right, in front of the 2/17th Battalion, enemy infantry formed up to attack but were halted by artillery fire.

In the southern part of the XXX Corps front, however, the armour had advanced to places near the Pierson bound. The 24th Armoured Brigade on the right believed that it had two regiments on its objective (the third was in reserve behind the Miteiriya Ridge), though probably they were not in fact so far forward. The 8th, which had been pressing forward on its hard task while the generals had been conferring, had got all three of its regiments out by the Bottle track before the revised orders from Eighth Army Headquarters reached it. The Staffordshire Yeomanry, which had debouched first, was about the El Wishka ridge where soon after dawn concealed 88-mm guns put in hand a systematic destruction of its tanks.

The sappers of the New Zealand division had cleared and marked their lanes on time. The divisional cavalry ("Honey" tanks) on its way from the Oxalic line to its objective two miles to the south in an area southwest of El Wishka was soon met by intense fire. By 1.45 a.m. the regiment

---

[3] Montgomery, p. 130.
[4] *Bayonets Abroad*, p. 274. The 7/Rifle Brigade were also shelled by some British guns.

had lost 5 tanks and 4 carriers. It withdrew at dawn. The 9th Armoured Brigade had passed through the gaps at 2 a.m. (one regiment using one of the lanes abandoned by the 8th Brigade) and advanced south and south-west almost to the Pierson bound.

In the deep south the operations of the XIII Corps had been less successful. The February minefield was cleared but a wide bridgehead had not been secured and the tanks of the 7th Armoured Division's 22nd Armoured Brigade were shot up by anti-tank guns near by while trying to debouch. Thirty-one tanks were lost and the exits blocked. A successful infantry attack was made in the Munassib Depression, but was very costly in loss of life.

The armoured battles that day, though on balance advantageous to the Eighth Army, achieved less than Montgomery had hoped. In the course of the day most of the tanks were withdrawn from the positions they took up in the early morning. On the right the Bays, who seemed unable to locate where the fire directed at them was coming from, soon withdrew to some place beyond the Australians' ken (where they were in action later in the day); but farther south, in front of the Highland division, tanks of the 2nd Armoured Brigade remained out with the 24th Armoured Brigade to their left. On the left Gatehouse withdrew the 8th Armoured Brigade behind the Miteiriya Ridge about 7 a.m. when he learnt of the casualties it was taking. The main body of the 9th Armoured Brigade, which was in a depression overlooked by enemy on El Wishka and enduring damaging fire, remained out until the afternoon, when it was withdrawn behind the Oxalic line. It had suffered 162 casualties and many of its tanks were knocked out (all but 11, however, were recovered later).

Probing attacks rather than hammerhead punches were made by the Axis armour throughout the day all along the front, which was what Montgomery wanted. The 1st Armoured Division lost 24 tanks but claimed the destruction of more than twice as many of the enemy. In the struggle for armoured superiority the scales had been tipped further to the advantage of the British. The following tables enable a comparison to be made of British and Axis tank strengths approximately from formation to formation as they were disposed from north to south on the 23rd and 25th October (progressive totals being shown in brackets).

EIGHTH ARMY (AS AT MIDDAY)

(The table does not include a substantial number of tanks—e.g. cavalry units—in other than armoured formations.)

	23rd October		25th October	
	Formation Totals	Progressive Total	Formation Totals	Progressive Total
North:				
1st Armoured Division	169		149	
10th Armoured Division	280	(449)	167	(316)
9th Armoured Brigade	122	(571)	92	(408)
23rd Armoured Brigade	194	(765)	135	(543)
South:				
7th Armoured Division	214	(979)	191	(734)

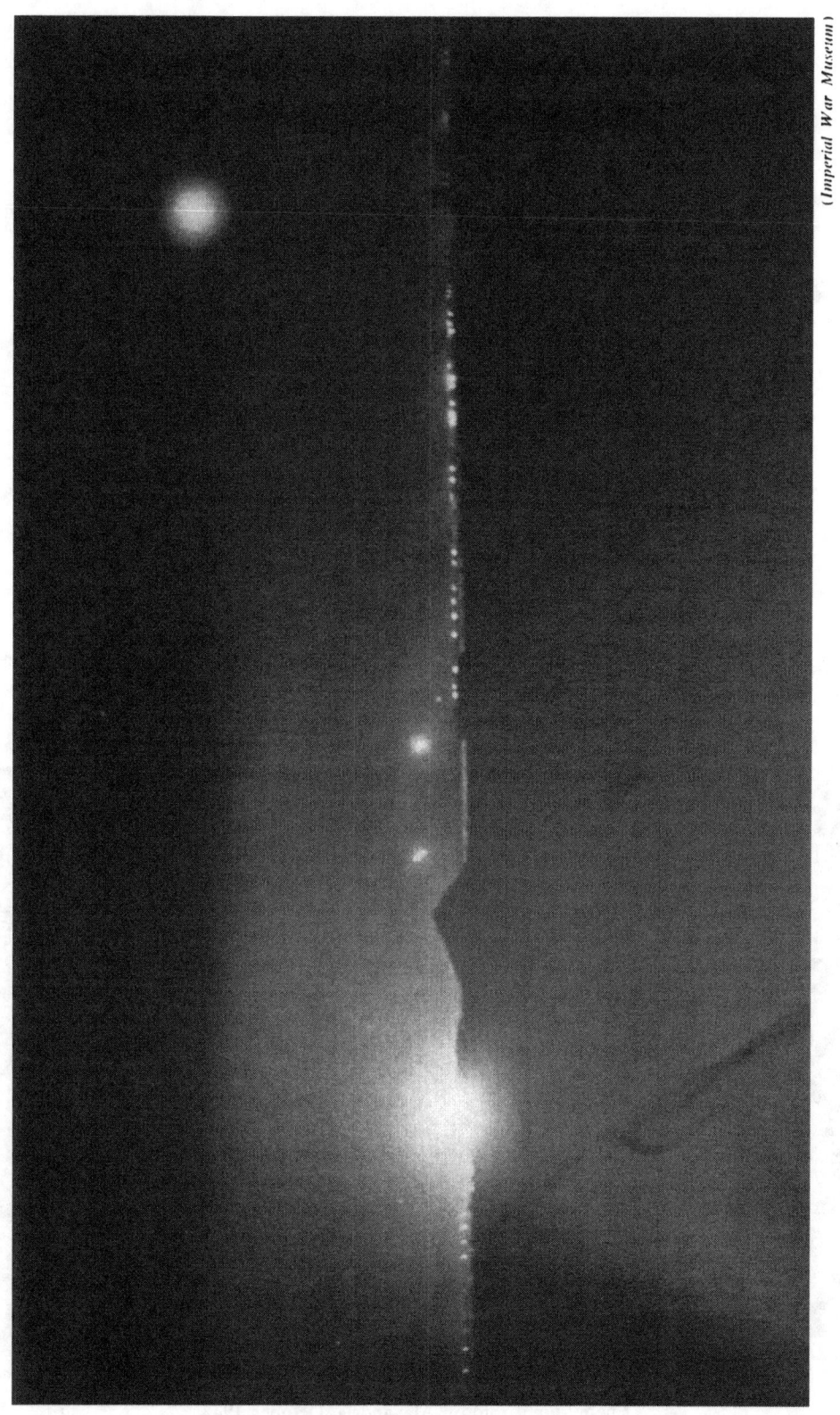

El Alamein, 9.40 p.m. 23rd October 1942. The silence of the desert was broken by the Eighth Army's opening artillery barrage. *(Imperial War Museum)*

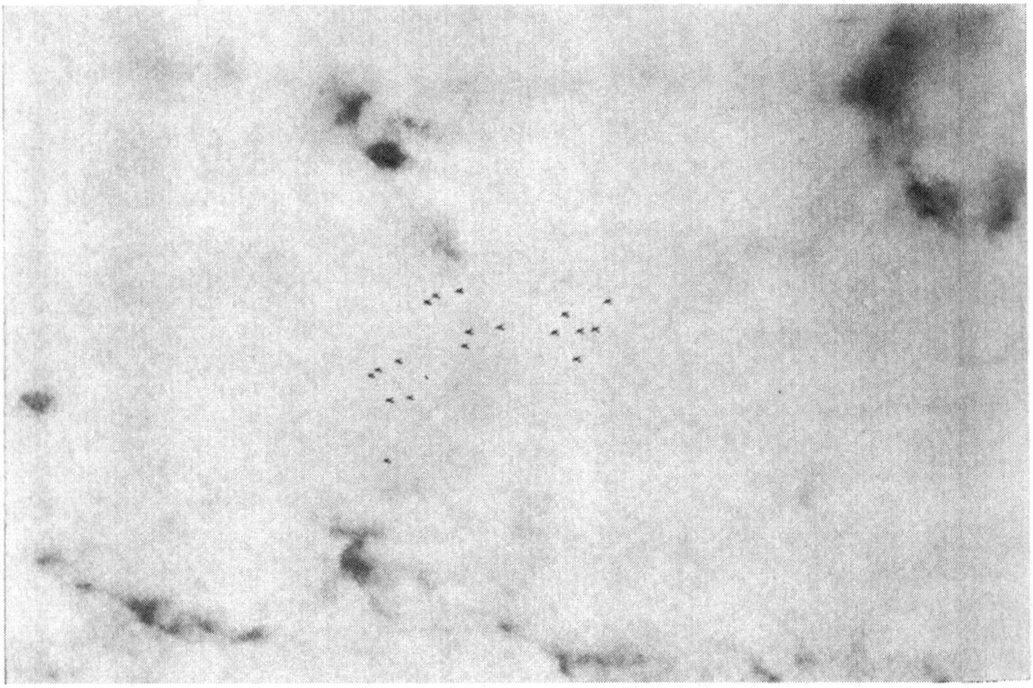

(Australian War Memorial)

British bombers over the battle area on the first day of the advance at El Alamein. Usually flying in a formation of eighteen, they were nicknamed "The Football Team" by the Australians.

(Lt-Col G. C. Burston)

Enemy night raid on Alexandria, October 1942.

TANK LOSSES

AXIS FORCES

	23rd October		25th October	
	Formation Totals	Progressive Total	Formation Totals	Progressive Total
North:				
15th Armoured Division	112		37	
Littorio Division	115	(227)	108	(145)
South:				
21st Armoured Division	137		122	
Ariete	129	(266)	125	(247)
Total North and South (excluding Trieste)		(493)		(392)
German armoured formations	249		159	
Italian armoured formations (excluding Trieste)	244	(493)	233	(392)
Trieste	34	(527)	34	(426)

Although the figures are not exactly comparable, if one regards the critical tank strengths in the armoured break-out battle of X Corps as those of its two armoured divisions plus the 9th Armoured Brigade on the one hand and of the two German armoured divisions on the other, the fall in the British strength from 571 tanks to 408 may be compared with the German fall from 112 to 37 in the *15th Armoured Division* opposite X Corps and from 249 to 159 overall.

Nevertheless the German anti-tank cordon had not been prised open. The armoured brigades had been unable to establish a firm base on the "chosen" ground onto which they had debouched because they had taken with them only light mobile infantry (used mainly to muster prisoners) who could neither seize the gun areas nor firmly hold the ground.

On the broader level, the men of the 10th Armoured Division had proved Montgomery's belief that, with their own resources, they could fight their way through to an objective, but the enemy guns had shown that they could not stay there by daylight alone.[5]

The 9th Division had its share that day of the enemy counter-attacks on the bridgehead. On the northern front a German patrol was shot up in the early hours of the morning by the 2/48th Battalion and later, about 1.20 p.m., a strong infantry attack on the battalion was launched but defeated by artillery and mortar fire. Another attack on the 2/48th by about 300 infantry was thrown back towards the end of the day.

Attacks in which tanks were employed were made from the west against the 20th Brigade. Just after 7 a.m. 12 tanks followed by infantry in 50 troop carriers hove into view but were halted by fire from the artillery and the foremost British tanks. In the early afternoon tank attacks were made almost simultaneously on the 2/17th and 2/13th Battalions. The tanks were first seen on the 2/17th front where a remarkable fire-storm was soon raging. Deterred by the intensity of their reception they came to

---

[5] C. E. Lucas Phillips, *Alamein* (1962), p. 231.

a halt beyond two-pounder range, but 15 were hit by heavier weapons. The enemy put down a smoke screen through which another wave of tanks emerged to attack the 2/13th Battalion front. Colvin instructed the anti-tank gunners to hold the fire of their well-concealed 2-pounder guns until the tanks were within short range. About 800 yards from the foremost defences some tanks halted hull-down; the rest drove on. So well did the gunners bide their orders that it looked as if the tanks would pass through the front-line unopposed. Sergeant Bentley[6] commanding the anti-tank platoon waited until the foremost was 40 yards away, then fired, whereupon the other anti-tank guns opened up and the first wave, all hit, came to a stop. In all 17 tanks were destroyed—nine by Lieutenant Wallder's[7] troops of the 2/3rd Anti-Tank Regiment, five by Bentley and two by Private Taylor.[8] The other tanks drew out of range but then waited while the infantry got ready to assault.

The enemy pressed the attack for an hour and a half on the 2/13th front and a further half-hour against the 2/17th. The intense fire that accompanied it took many casualties. The 2/17th, for example, lost 12 killed and 73 wounded through the day. Throughout it all the artillery observation post officers, Captain Jones with the 2/13th, Lieutenant Rodriguez[9] with the 2/17th, stood up to observe and direct the gunfire.

On the morning of the 25th Freyberg persuaded Leese and Montgomery to cancel the proposed southward infantry attacks of the New Zealand division. Freyberg thought that the main infantry attack had not failed by much to pierce the enemy's defence girdle and that therefore a further westward infantry attack on the pattern of the first should be made to extend the bridgehead. Again the top commanders conferred at the New Zealand division's headquarters. Montgomery decided about midday to cancel the New Zealand division's "crumbling" operations because (according to Montgomery and de Guingand) they were likely to prove very costly, and instead to start "crumbling" on the northern flank, using the 9th Australian Division. The armour was to be withdrawn except on the north of the XXX Corps front (where the 1st Armoured Division took the 24th Armoured Brigade under command) and in the far south the XIII Corps was to go over entirely to the defensive.

Montgomery's decision to attack in the north has usually been represented as a calculated switching of the direction of attack initiated after the failure of that morning's armoured sortie so as to retain the initiative and keep the enemy dancing to the Eighth Army's tune. It was not as clear-cut as that, however, for although the final orders for the switch were then given, the decision to begin the northward crumbling had been

---

[6] Lt A. R. Bentley, DCM, NX21473. 2/13 and 2/10 Bns. Clerk; of Leichhardt, NSW; b. Leichhardt, 24 Nov 1915.

[7] Lt A. F. Wallder, MC, WX5057. 2/28 Bn, 2/3 A-Tk Regt. Wool trade; of West Perth, WA; b. Perth, 29 Jan 1914.

[8] Pte J. D. Taylor, MM, NX16920; 2/13 Bn. Carpenter; of Liverpool, NSW; b. Ardlethan, NSW, 21 Dec 1916.
After both this and later attacks Taylor went out under fire and destroyed abandoned enemy tanks with grenades.

[9] Lt-Col T. A. Rodriguez, OBE, MC, WX174. 2/7 Fd Regt; RAA 7 Div; BM RAA 9 Div 1944-45. Metallurgist; of Perth, WA; b. Claremont, WA, 5 May 1908.

foreshadowed earlier; and before the dawn that morning had revealed the peril to which the 8th and 9th Armoured Brigades had been exposed, Lieut-Colonel Hammer of the 2/48th had given his company commanders preliminary instructions for an attack to be made on Trig 29 next night. The 9th Division's written operation order was issued at 1 p.m. The explanation of this switch given in the division's report on LIGHTFOOT probably puts it in better perspective:

> The only portion of the original plan still untried was the tentative portion for the cutting off and capture of the enemy between XXX Corps' northern flank and the sea. Orders were given to 9 Aust Div through XXX Corps for this to proceed.

The 9th Division's instructions were to begin attacking northwards towards the sea with the ultimate object of destroying the enemy forces in the salient that had been formed by the advancement of the Eighth Army's northern flank. The 1st Armoured Division was also to continue its attack west and north-west and if possible to get to the rear of the enemy in the salient. Written instructions by the XXX Corps on the 25th required the 9th Division to attack and seize the Trig 29 area that night. As a diversion the 1st South African Division was to carry out at 10 p.m. an artillery program simulating an attack in its sector.

The tactical value of the hill known as Trig 29 had been appreciated before the battle opened. It dominated the northern flank, being the highest ground thereabouts, though by only 20 feet. The already too broad frontage of the first night's attack could not be extended to include the hill but it had been chosen as the first exploitation task on that front. Morshead warned Brigadier Whitehead on 24th October to be ready to take Trig 29 and the warning, as we have seen, was passed down in turn to Lieut-Colonel Hammer and, by him, to his company commanders.

The 9th Division's task was to seize not only Trig 29 but the spur and the forward slopes of the high ground running out to the east of it. In effect the northern front was to be advanced about 1,000 yards. It is of some interest to observe that the fronts to be defended on completion of the task by the division's five bridgehead battalions (four up and one in depth) would extend on the west for about 5,000 yards and on the north for 4,000 yards.

The orders required Whitehead's brigade to advance its whole northern front from Trig 29 on the left to the front edge of the enemy's defence line on the right. North-east from where the 2/48th Battalion's right company now sat, a strong enemy switch-line ran up to Thompson's Post as a second line of defence against an attacker breaking through the front wire where it ran out to Point 23 (as the 2/15th did at BULIMBA) and then thrusting towards the coast road. The junction of the switch line with the front wire was an easily recognisable feature on ground and map—the Fig Orchard, which was down the forward slope of the ridge of which Trig 29 was the summit. The orders to the 26th Brigade were to employ the 2/48th and 2/24th Battalions—the 2/23rd still being held as a reserve behind the composite force—to seize Trig 29, the spur on the eastern side of Trig 29 pointing to the Fig Orchard, and the orchard itself. The

20th Brigade was to relieve the 2/48th on the part of the front it then held and the 24th Brigade to relieve Macarthur-Onslow's composite force of three of its posts so that it could extend its front to link with the 2/24th Battalion on its objective. Whitehead allotted the left objective, the Trig 29 area, to the 2/48th and the Fig Orchard to the 2/24th.

Colonel Hammer of the 2/48th made a bold and original plan of fire and quick movement for what was to prove a model battalion attack executed with precision, vigour, and great courage. He planned to advance on Trig 29 under cover of a barrage with two companies forward and, just as the barrage lifted, to rush a third company on to the objective in 29 carriers and other vehicles. Ten carriers were to carry the two leading platoons of the mobile company; four carriers towing 37-mm anti-tank guns were to follow, and after them a troop of 6-pounder anti-tank guns with the third platoon mounted on the portees.[1]

After the 2/48th had begun to attack, the 2/24th was to form up in part of the area of the first phase of the 2/48th's attack and thrust northeast, rolling up the flank of the switch line. Macarthur-Onslow's force was to push its line of defensive posts northward to conform with the 2/24th's new front.

A counter-attack was expected on the 2/48th's front but did not develop. At dusk an enemy group was seen near the forward companies and fired on. Several Germans were killed and three captured including the acting commanders of the *125th Regiment* and of that regiment's *II Battalion*. The battalion commander had a map of the area to be attacked that night showing the enemy's minefields and the disposition of his troops. The map showed that the track leading to Trig 29 along which Hammer's carriers were to advance was free of mines; this was confirmed by Hammer's interrogation of the prisoners. Interrogation also established that the Germans had just reinforced Trig 29.

To have captured the map was rare good fortune. When it was studied at Whitehead's headquarters it revealed that the planned axis of the 2/24th's attack ran straight along the leg of a minefield. The forming-up place and bearing of attack were therefore altered so that the sappers, instead of having to clear mines to a depth of 1,000 yards or more, would require to make only one gap 200 yards deep.

The 2/17th relieved the 2/48th at 10 p.m. on the 25th. The barrage opened at midnight and the leading companies of the 2/48th moved forward on foot, Captain Robbins' company on the right, Captain Shillaker's on the left. They pressed on through enemy defensive fire—which became particularly heavy on the right—to their intermediate objective some 200 yards short of Trig 29, and halted. Then the carriers under Captain Isaksson moving four abreast with Captain Bryant's company aboard charged through with synchronised timing onto the smoky dust-shrouded centre objective as the barrage stopped.

---

[1] **Hammer** who initiated this novel procedure had served for some years before the war in a motorised machine-gun regiment.

When the carriers reached the spur the infantry leapt out and charged, one platoon moving left and one right while one went straight on to Trig 29. The surprised defenders were overcome but only after sharp hand-to-hand fighting. When Corporal Kennedy,[2] for example, led his section against enemy posts that were engaging them with small-arms fire and grenades, the blast from a grenade knocked one of his men down; Kennedy helped him to his feet, dashed forward and killed two Germans with a grenade and farther on charged and bayoneted another German.

Bryant ordered one of his platoons to attack a troublesome post. Corporal Albrecht,[3] leading his section to attack it, found that it was a dug-in tank. Albrecht charged forward and knocked out the crew with grenades, and though wounded by shell fragments and covered with blood, continued to lead and control his section, refusing to be taken back until it was firmly dug in.

Captain Robbins' company on the right had taken heavy casualties from fire about 400 yards from the start and soon Robbins was the only remaining officer. The company pressed on nevertheless and secured its objective 1,100 yards from the start-line, taking 38 German prisoners.

Captain Shillaker's company also had to fight its way to the objective. Lieutenant Taggart[4] and four others in his platoon were killed attacking a series of posts that were holding up the company. The platoon became pinned to the ground and soon was only seven strong. Two of these, Private Gratwick[5] (aged 40) and Corporal Lindsey,[6] jumped up and raced forward to assault. Gratwick, with rifle and bayonet in one hand and a grenade in the other, charged the nearest post, threw in one grenade, then another, then jumped in with the bayonet. He killed all the occupants, including a complete mortar crew, then charged a second post with rifle and bayonet but, as he closed on it, was killed by a burst of machine-gun fire. Shillaker saw that Gratwick had unnerved the enemy and at once moved in and the whole position was quickly captured. The men began digging in very rocky soil.

As soon as the objective had been taken Colonel Hammer contacted Major Tucker and asked him to bring forward the vehicles loaded with consolidation stores, which were being held back along the track some 500 to 600 yards to the east of the point from which the attack had started. Just at that moment a stray shell hit a mine-laden truck which with five other trucks also loaded with mines exploded with an astounding detonation. Tucker was at first dazed, but soon got the undestroyed vehicles moving and sent Captain Potter[7] back to "B" Echelon. Potter

---

[2] Cpl R. F. Kennedy, DCM, SX7092; 2/48 Bn. Labourer; of Halbury, SA; b. Echunga, SA, 17 May 1921.
[3] Cpl K. G. Albrecht, DCM, SX7830; 2/48 Bn. Labourer; of Kingston-on-Murray, SA; b. Waikerie, SA, 20 Aug 1917.
[4] Lt C. E. Taggart, WX10083; 2/48 Bn. Bank officer; of Nedlands, WA; b. Perth, WA, 19 Mar 1915. Killed in action 26 Oct 1942.
[5] Pte P. E. Gratwick, VC, WX10426; 2/48 Bn. Prospector; of Port Hedland and Perth, WA; b. Katanning, WA, 19 Oct 1902. Killed in action 26 Oct 1942. Gratwick was awarded the Victoria Cross for this action.
[6] Cpl B. W. A. Lindsey, WX9894; 2/48 Bn. Bank clerk; of Kojonup, WA; b. Bridgetown, WA, 4 Nov 1912.
[7] Maj J. D. Potter, SX10258; 2/48 Bn. Regular soldier; of Prospect, SA; b. Riverton, SA, 15 Jun 1909.

returned with five composite reorganisation stores trucks. By first light 2,000 mines had been laid. Bryant's company was facing north, Shillaker's west. Edmunds' company, on the battalion's left, facing west and north-west, had linked with the 2/17th Battalion in the 2/48th's old positions. The battalion was now firmly established, though only shallow trenches had been dug and everyone was very weary.

Meanwhile at 12.40 a.m. the two leading companies of the 2/24th had crossed the start-line, striking north-eastwards on the right of the 2/48th. It had been realised that an advance of 3,000 yards along a line of enemy posts was a difficult assignment but the army's Intelligence service expected them to be held by Italians. On the contrary they proved to be mainly held by Germans, and where there were Italians there were usually Germans with them.

Major Mollard's company on the right attacked along the frontal wire with one platoon in front of the wire and two on the left behind it. They fought their way forward without any serious check until less than 100 yards from the company objective when they were held up by a strong-post. This was assaulted and taken but not before Mollard had received a disabling wound. The post was found to have a garrison of more than 40 mixed Germans and Italians and to house an 88-mm gun. Captain Mackenzie[8] led the company forward to its objective.

The left leading company under Lieutenant Geale[9] had to advance the prescribed distance then move left, contact the 2/48th Battalion and dig in on the north-east spur of Trig 29. This the company did but Geale was badly wounded and Lieutenant Doughan,[1] the only surviving officer took over. Doughan was wounded later in the day and Sergeant-Major Bailey[2] then took command. A number of posts were taken. Sergeant Berry[3] was foremost in the affray in the attack on three of these and took two positions single-handed.

Captain Harty (on the right) and Lieutenant Greatorex followed up the centre-line, then led their companies through the forward companies towards the Fig Orchard. Each had to overcome three posts on the way. Harty's company took the Fig Orchard post, which was found to be a headquarters with offices sunk in the ground to great depth. Greatorex's company overshot the Fig Orchard and came up near the outer edge of the defences covering the big defended locality known as Thompson's Post. Both companies were troubled by anti-tank and mortar fire from a post 300 yards ahead. Harty and Greatorex reconnoitred to plan an assault. Greatorex was wounded (for the second time that night) and Sergeant-Major Cameron[4] taking charge of his company got permission

---

[8] Capt I. S. Mackenzie, VX40762; 2/24 Bn. Grazier; of Avenel, Vic; b. Trawool, Vic, 26 Apr 1918.
[9] Capt F. B. Geale, VX38879. 2/24 Bn and "Z" Special Unit. Radio dealer; of Lilydale, Vic; b. Korumburra, Vic, 4 Jun 1909.
[1] Lt C. A. Doughan, NX66683. 2/24 Bn; Torres Strait Lt Inf Bn. Timber surveyor; of Campsie, NSW; b. Kogarah, NSW, 8 Nov 1915.
[2] WO2 L. K. Bailey, VX33882; 2/24 Bn. Transport driver; of Warracknabeal, Vic; b. Warracknabeal, 27 Dec 1917.
[3] Sgt G. T. Berry, DCM, VX31716; 2/24 Bn. Labourer; of Korumburra, Vic; b. Foster, Vic, 15 Mar 1919.
[4] WO2 F. M. Cameron, MC, VX27602; 2/24 Bn. Transport driver; of South Yarra, Vic; b. Victoria, 8 Mar 1913.

to withdraw it—now numbering only 14 of the 63 who started—to alongside Harty's.

The 2/24th had carried out a methodical destruction of the enemy as prescribed by the master plan, to which the number of enemy dead and of prisoners bore witness,[5] but Colonel Weir, after going forward,

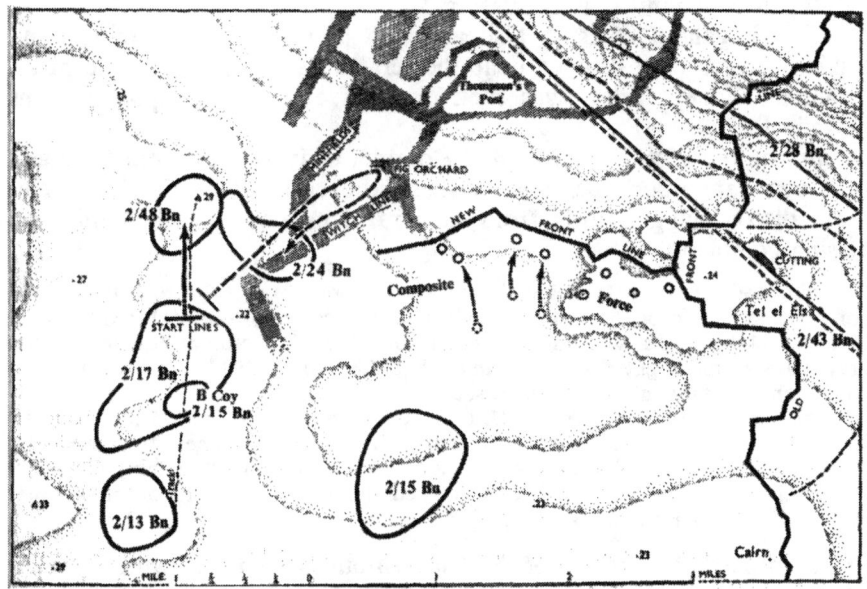

Dawn, 26th October

decided at 4 a.m. that the battalion was too depleted to hold the extended front on which his men were digging in. The forward companies were therefore withdrawn about 1,000 yards where by 5 a.m. they had consolidated behind a reverse slope running north-west from Point 22 to Trig 29. On the right flank the composite force, which had been held up in its advance by fire from Thompson's Post, found itself in an exposed situation.

On that night of much action the enemy launched an attack with infantry and a few tanks against the 2/13th Battalion, following up by dark the daylight attack that had failed. Three tanks were knocked out by Hawkins mines and Treweeke's company knocked out two tracked troop carriers when they were within 60 yards. Artillery and infantry-weapon fire broke up the attack. At dawn the 2/17th discerned 12 enemy tanks sitting on a ridge to the north-west, where they remained all day, harassing the Australians with guns and small-arms fire and knocking out vehicles. On the left of the divisional front the 1st Armoured Division made its morning visitation and the Australians saw 30 Sherman tanks engaging the enemy.

---

[5] By the end of the 26th October the 2/24th had taken 143 German and 26 Italian prisoners, two 88-mm guns, five smaller guns and 18 machine-guns, but had lost 10 killed, 102 wounded and two missing.

No foolhardy attempt was made to push through the enemy gun-line and behind the coast salient.

On the 25th-26th the division had taken a total of 173 German prisoners, all from the *I, II* or *III Battalions* of the *125th Regiment* and 67 Italians of the *Trento* and *Littorio Divisions*. The 26th Brigade reported its casualties for the night as 4 officers and 51 others killed, 20 officers and 236 others wounded and missing.[6]

The 51st Highland Division also attacked that night overcoming some remaining centres of resistance near the left of its front which, except on the right at Kidney Ridge, was then clear of enemy strongpoints about the Oxalic line.

At dusk on the 25th Field Marshal Rommel arrived back from Germany to take over, at Hitler's personal request, the conduct of the battle and received discouraging reports from General von Thoma, who had been exercising command.

"Our aim for the next few days," he later wrote, "was to throw the enemy out of our main defence line at all costs and to reoccupy our old positions, in order to avoid having a westward bulge in our front." Rommel listened to the artillery barrage that night and learnt that "Hill 28" (Trig 29)[7] had been taken—"an important position in the northern sector".

"Attacks were now launched on Hill 28 by elements of the 15th Armoured Division, the Littorio and a Bersaglieri Battalion," wrote Rommel, "supported by the concentrated fire of all the local artillery and A.A. Unfortunately the attack gained ground very slowly. The British resisted desperately. Rivers of blood were poured out over miserable strips of land."[8]

Attracted partly by activity of the 1st Armoured Division, which seemed to the enemy to be directed north-west towards the coast road, the Axis forces directed their main efforts on the 26th and 27th to breaking their enemy's new front on the northern flank. The attacks started on the 26th and were mounted with increasing frequency and vigour on the 27th, a day of many stresses for the Eighth Army but no disaster, during which the artillery was continually called on for defensive fire.

The 27th was marked by a day-long continuous struggle (wrote a battalion historian). . . . Those who were there that day may recall the extraordinary rising and falling waves of sound. All the different weapons appeared to be co-ordinated to produce a definite rhythm ranging from diminuendo to deafening crescendo and it went on hour after hour.[9]

---

[6] The "missing" in these operations were usually killed or severely wounded men who could not be accounted for.

[7] British writers consistently regard Hill 28 in *The Rommel Papers* and German narratives as referring not to Trig 29 but to the Kidney feature, the little ridges of which, however important, were not a hill. In the passages in *The Rommel Papers* in which Hill 28 is first mentioned, the description of the action can be made to appear to fit the facts by applying either interpretation. That interpretation, however, cannot be reconciled with German accounts of later thrusts from Trig 29. (The Australian attack on Trig 29 was finally planned from a German map of Hill 28!) In adopting this misinterpretation British authors have unwittingly belittled the effects of the 9th Division's efforts. Hence one author, in a book in which through insufficient knowledge the 9th Division and its efforts are elsewhere disparaged, has stated that "the Australian attack on Point 29 that night seems to have caused (Rommel) much less concern than the Highland Division's attacks and the subsequent cautious attempt by 2nd Armoured Brigade to exploit them". It would be fairer to say that Rommel saw the actions of all three formations as constituting in combination a threat of north-westwards attack.

[8] *The Rommel Papers*, p. 306.

[9] Major H. Gillan in *Bayonets Abroad*, pp. 277, 279.

The enemy vigorously bombarded the 2/24th and 2/48th in their newly seized positions on the morning of the 26th and more heavily still on the morning of the 27th but several of the guns were counter-bombarded with the help of observation from Trig 29 and forced to move back. There, on the most heavily shelled ground on the whole front, Lieutenant Menzies[1] maintained an observation post with little cover for several days, directing the fire that broke up many counter-attacks, some while the enemy was forming up. The value of Trig 29 was now plainly evident: from it one could see 4,000 to 5,000 yards in every direction.

The enemy's first effort against Trig 29 was made on the afternoon of the 26th, when 300 infantry moved into positions 1,500 yards to the north but were dispersed by gunfire. The 2/48th Battalion had three field regiments and one medium regiment on call at that stage and was able to defend itself with devastating fire.

The western front of the 20th Brigade was also attacked on the 26th. Three attacks by infantry and tanks, the main weight of which fell on the 2/13th, were repulsed on the afternoon of the 26th.

The subsequent continuation of the northward Australian attack is usually ascribed to Montgomery's having "spent the day of the 26th in detailed consideration of the situation".[2] It was, however, no more than a further implementing of the direction to attack northwards given on the 25th, though the consequential army regrouping no doubt resulted from Montgomery's day of pondering. Morshead had been instructed on the 25th to plan further northward operations to be mounted after the attack on Trig 29 at midnight on the 25th-26th. Montgomery, attended by Leese and Lumsden, held a conference at Morshead's headquarters at 11.30 a.m. on the 26th to hear his proposals. "On previous day," Morshead recorded in his notebook, "I had received orders to 'go north' and to have my firm plans ready today. The army commander fully approved plans without alteration." The 9th Division's attack was to be made on the night of the 28th. But first, on the night of the 26th, further thrusts were to be made to the west near the boundary of the Australian and Highland divisions. The 7th Motor Brigade was to capture two features in the Trig 33-Kidney Ridge area known as Woodcock and Snipe.

That day in the course of a tour of the XXX Corps front Montgomery spoke to several formation commanders. Freyberg still advocated another broad-front infantry attack but represented that if his own depleted division mounted the attack, it would then be unfit for its intended role in the exploitation phase.[3] Montgomery also visited Wimberley; it is unlikely that Montgomery found him much more anxious than Freyberg to mount another large-scale attack. By dawn that morning the Eighth Army had lost 6,140 men killed, wounded or missing. It had expended much of its

---

[1] Lt R. W. J. Menzies, MC, WX2677; 2/7 Fd Regiment. Clerk; of East Claremont, WA; b. Fremantle, WA, 23 Jan 1918.
[2] Montgomery, *El Alamein to the River Sangro* (1946), p. 22.
[3] From 23rd October until the 28th when it was withdrawn the New Zealand division lost 266 killed, 876 wounded and 37 were taken prisoner. Up to 6 a.m. on the 28th the 9th Division's casualties were 142 killed, 852 wounded and 73 missing (most of whom would have been killed or severely wounded).

strength; but although some ramparts had been taken, the strong enemy front showed no sign of collapse. The impulse to break the deadlock would have to come from the army commander himself. A new strong punch would be needed.

By the evening of the 26th Montgomery had decided that the New Zealand division should be withdrawn into reserve and rested, that the 1st Armoured Division should also be drawn into reserve for refitting and relieved by the 10th and that he would rely on the 9th Division's northward attack to retain the initiative. Consequently a substantial regrouping was to be effected on the night of 27th-28th. The northward shift of the 9th Division and the withdrawal of the New Zealand division would greatly extend the front to be held by other formations. The XIII Corps was directed to make available all the infantry it could spare for operations in the north and to extend its front to include the South Africans' sector. The 4th Indian Division was to relieve the South Africans and they in turn to relieve the New Zealanders, who would be withdrawn. The 51st Division was to relieve the 20th Australian Brigade thus enabling the 9th Division to have one brigade freed from holding duties and available to attack.

These instructions were given by Leese to Morshead and the other divisional commanders on the night of the 26th. It has been said that Leese was anxious as to how the proposals would be received, but he already knew Morshead's plans. He told the divisional commanders that the stalemate must be broken and that Montgomery had decided to follow up the Australians' success by a further thrust to the north. The Australians must draw everything they could on themselves. "He glanced at Morshead and saw no flicker of hesitancy disturb that swarthy face."[4] Just after these orders had been given, however, Morshead received a cable sent from Australia two days earlier, the full import and intention of which were not very clearly expressed, but which could have been construed in a way which would have critically prejudiced Montgomery's plans to break the stalemate.

On 14th October the Australian Government had considered two documents relating to the defence of Australia: a statement by the President of the United States to the effect that a superior naval force concerned solely with the defence of Australia and New Zealand could not be provided, and a memorandum from General Blamey drawing attention to the weakness of the Australian land forces available to resist an invasion if a naval reverse were suffered. The War Cabinet asked the Chiefs of Staff to report on the forces needed to defend vital areas on the Australian mainland. Next day, however, having been told that General MacArthur was of the opinion that the time had now come for the return of the 9th Division, the War Cabinet decided to press for the division's return and to cancel the approval previously given for the dispatch of 6,000 reinforcements.

---

[4] Lucas Phillips, *Alamein*, p. 258.

On 17th October Mr Curtin sent a cable to Mr Churchill (and a copy to President Roosevelt) requesting the early return of the 9th Division and setting out in detail the reasons for making the request. In brief they were:

> Australia was at present 22,000 men short of the number required for the present order of battle in Australia.
>
> From 7,000 to 8,000 personnel per month were needed to replace wastage against a prospective intake of 1,100 per month. Eight infantry battalions had therefore been disbanded and a further decrease of eleven battalions was contemplated.
>
> The extreme tropical conditions in New Guinea caused a heavy wastage of combatant personnel.
>
> Three Australian divisions were already in New Guinea. No further Australian formations could be sent there because of the depletion of forces available for the defence of the mainland.
>
> Thus it would not be possible to maintain the flow of reinforcements needed by the 9th Division in the Middle East; if left in the Middle East, the division would, in a few months, cease to be an effective fighting unit. General MacArthur had expressed apprehension at the shrinkage of Army combat troops consequent on the reduction of Australian formations.

The Government, the message stated, would not consent to the breaking-up of the 9th Division "by replacement of wastage from ancillary or other units" in the Middle East; but the division could be built up in Australia by disbanding other formations. The Government had consulted its Advisory War Council, which had come to the unanimous conclusion that the division's return should be requested.

On 20th October the Australian High Commissioner in London (Mr Bruce) informed the Australian Government that the British Chiefs of Staff were examining the problem with a view to the 9th Division's return at the earliest possible date but, owing to the operation which was then imminent and the part in it that had been allocated to the division, the date of its withdrawal from the front line depended on developments in the immediate future. Mr Curtin replied on the 22nd that it was essential that the Commander-in-Chief, in his use of the division, should have regard for the fact that reinforcements could not be provided either by dispatch from Australia or breaking up units in the Middle East. There the matter had stood when the battle (of whose planning Curtin knew nothing) opened next day.

On 24th October a message had been sent from Australia to General Morshead informing him of the Australian Government's request for the early return of the division to Australia and stating that he was being informed of this so that he might safeguard the Government's decision. This was the message that reached Morshead just after he had attended the conference at which Leese had announced Montgomery's intention of continuing the northward advance. Morshead replied to the Australian Government that he would see the Commander-in-Chief as soon as possible. This he did at 11 a.m. next morning, the 27th October, at Montgomery's tactical headquarters.

After the interview, Morshead reported to the Australian Government that Alexander had not hitherto been informed of its decision but had said that he could not consider the division's release at that time, as it was the main pin of the operations and without it the battle would collapse; of all the formations in the Middle East, it was the one (Alexander had said) that he could least afford to lose. Morshead added that Alexander had undertaken to arrange its relief as soon as the operational situation permitted but had drafted a signal to London which concluded as follows:

> 9th Australian Division playing very conspicuous and important part in present operations and it would be quite impossible to lose their magnificent services until present operations are brought to a successful conclusion.

In reply, the Australian War Cabinet instructed Morshead to ensure that the Government's wishes were kept constantly in mind; which Morshead assured them that he would not fail to do.

Next day (the 28th) Churchill telegraphed Curtin:

> You will have observed with pride and pleasure the distinguished part which the 9th Australian Division are playing in what may be an event of first magnitude.

Just after 4 a.m. on the 27th an attack on the 2/13th was made by "at least a company of infantry" just in front of 15 tanks. "Put down Fremantle urgently" was the message to the artillery recorded in the battalion's Action Log. The concentrated bombardment, with the infantry fire-curtain in front of it, broke up the attack. A second attack was easily repulsed. Later that morning a patrol under Lieutenant Pope was sent out to clear the front for 400 yards. Covered by the patrol, Private Burgess[5] took a telephone and cable 300 yards farther out and observed the front from a derelict tank, sent back reports which enabled enemy salvage parties to be engaged, also an 88-mm gun to be bombarded (which the enemy then withdrew) and later, having seen a group of the enemy, went across towards Kidney Ridge near by and guided back a carrier of the 7th Motor Brigade, which rounded up 30 prisoners.

It was on the afternoon of the 27th, after the enemy had reconnoitred the ground with four tanks, that the pressure on Trig 29 became intense.

> The next effort by the enemy (wrote the historian of the 2/48th Battalion) commenced near Sidi Rahman Mosque, where a great many vehicles began assembling. Word of this was passed back, and our bombers came in and straddled the area, leaving spirals of black smoke curling skywards. . . . Two hours later enemy troop carriers moved into dead ground 1,400 yards from our front, and were engaged by indirect fire from our guns. Thirty minutes later, enemy infantry estimated at one battalion strength formed up and advanced towards our troops. A great wall of fire was put down by our three regiments of artillery to check them, and the battalion joined in with mortars, machine-guns and rifles. Trig 29 and the surrounding area now came under a terrific bombardment as the Germans supported their attack. The position became so clouded with dust and smoke that the order was given for the mortars and artillery to cease fire in order to give the machine-gunners a clear view of the enemy. The Germans were driven back, and commenced to dig in eight hundred yards from the forward troops. Very heavy casualties had been inflicted. The night was filled with cries of the wounded. Patrols sent out later reported that the battlefield was strewn with enemy dead.[6]

---
[5] Cpl J. A. Burgess, NX20755; 2/13 Bn. Butcher; of Pambula, NSW; b. Pambula, 3 Oct 1917.
[6] J. G. Glenn, *Tobruk to Tarakan*, pp. 156-7.

The Germans' left wing came up against the left of the 2/24th Battalion, where an attack with infantry and tanks was pressed with some determination but broken up by a combination of artillery bombardment and mortar and machine-gun fire. The right wing of the German attack came in on the 2/17th Battalion but was beaten off 400 yards out from the forward infantry. Simultaneously the enemy also attacked the Kidney Ridge area with a powerful armoured thrust.

The so-called Kidney Ridge was a depression with raised lips around which the enemy had developed a powerful locality. Its continued resistance was the main reason for the 1st Armoured Division's failure to advance much beyond the Oxalic line to attack behind the salient as the Australians had hoped. The 51st Highland Division and the 1st Armoured Division had been cooperating in attempts to clear the area but these had been attended with much misfortune mainly because of a misreading of the map in one of these two divisions. Throughout that day, ensconced with 19 6-pounders on the left front of the ridge, men of the 2/Rifle Brigade had been in a position with little cover to which, owing to the same error, they had been misdirected; they were now cut off in rear. By the time of this last and heaviest attack by the enemy the desert around their outpost (appropriately named Snipe) was littered with tanks destroyed by them in earlier attacks. The attack was made straight at them and they broke it too, having knocked out in the day some 60 or 70 tanks and self-propelled guns, of which at least 32 were irrecoverable.[7]

That night the 2/Rifle Brigade withdrew after a relieving battalion of the 133rd Lorried Infantry Brigade had also lost its way. A second battalion of that brigade, which was to take another locality, also dug in on the wrong site and was overrun next day. By repelling strong armoured assaults without even field artillery support, the 2/Rifle Brigade had demonstrated that if the infantry front were pushed firmly forward and protected by anti-tank artillery the German armour could not throw it back. The 1st Armoured Division, however, in its efforts to secure Kidney Ridge was repeating errors of earlier days by sending out battalions to hold localities with open flanks when an advance on a broad front was needed. The efforts failed tragically, and the enemy was still on Kidney Ridge at the end of the month.

South from Kidney Ridge the remaining centres of enemy resistance about the Oxalic line had been cleared up on the night of the 26th-27th by the Highland, New Zealand and South African divisions. Thus the bridgehead originally planned to be seized had been captured, and had been extended in the north; but the enemy maintained an unbroken front to the west and the direction of the Eighth Army's attack had now been switched to the north.

On Rommel's return the enemy's defence had assumed the character of vigorous forlorn-hope attacks, which suited Montgomery who preferred the enemy to counter-attack rather than await attack on his own ground. Rommel's first morning at the front revealed the 1st Armoured Division concentrating near Kidney Ridge after

---

[7] The commanding officer, Lieut-Colonel V. B. Turner, was awarded the Victoria Cross.

night attacks had been made there and at Trig 29, which he interpreted as efforts to advance northwards to the coast road. He therefore ordered the *21st Armoured Division* and part of the *Ariete* to a position south of Tel el Aqqaqir ready to counter-attack. Artillery from the southern sector was sent north. The *90th Light Division* was ordered forward from Daba and, with the *361st Battle Group*, was put into the line south of Sidi Abd el Rahman on the night 26th-27th October, with the *159th Battle Group* west of Trig 29 and the *200th Battle Group* between Ghazal and the coast.

The strong counter-attacks on the 27th had resulted from orders by Rommel for attacks by the *90th Light Division* against Trig 29 from the north and by the *21st Armoured Division* against Kidney Ridge from the south. Infantry drawn from the *15th Armoured Division* and *164th Division* were to assist. The attack at Trig 29 was made by the *155th Battle Group* which advanced only to 500 yards west of that objective. The heavy British artillery fire halted the infantry and Rommel ordered that the troops should go over to the defensive on the ground then held. The *155th* dug in to the north-west of Trig 29, while the *361st Regimental Group* of the *90th Light Division* took up a holding position astride the railway line southeast of Abd el Rahman.

The policy, laid down by Montgomery on the 26th, of continuing the attack northwards towards the sea on the 27th and succeeding days, appears to have been originally embarked on as a crumbling operation with the general object of destroying the enemy in the salient by the coast, and not with the specific intent that the armour should debouch there. At that stage a break-out point does not appear to have been indicated, nor indeed had the planning evinced any haste to get ready for a chase. No immediate intention to break out along the coast road is suggested by the written orders nor by the narrative dealing with this stage in the 9th Division's report:

With the Army Commander's brief direction to "Attack North", consideration was given to the staging of a further attack in this area on the night 27th-28th October. On the arrival of XXX Corps Operation Instruction No. 85 of 26th October, which ordered a policy of mopping up, and the completion of the capture of the final objective by all divisions on 27th October, it was decided to plan the further attack northwards on the night 28th-29th October—one night later.

In the plan submitted to the army commander by Morshead on the morning of the 26th, however, his intention had been to attack at once to seize and open up the main road from the enemy's front-line westwards for three kilometres. Perhaps it was the contemplation of this plan that implanted the idea later tentatively adopted that the armour might next debouch along the coast road. A subsidiary object of Morshead's plan was to secure the road and the area south of it for use by the division's vehicles, thus shortening its long and exposed supply and evacuation routes.

The plan was an ambitious one. The task was to be accomplished in progressive phases and required the employment of all three brigades. For the operation the 23rd Armoured Brigade less two regiments was also placed under Morshead's command and the artillery of the 51st, 2nd New Zealand and 10th Armoured Divisions and of three medium regiments was to be in support. Including the division's own artillery there would be 360 guns.

In the first phase, the 20th Brigade was to secure the flanks of the northward advance. On the right the 2/13th Battalion was to advance along the switch line and establish itself south of Thompson's Post. On the left the 2/17th Battalion was to hold on to Trig 29 and the 2/15th to extend the western flank northwards by striking north from there. In the next phase, to be carried out by the 26th Brigade, the 2/23rd Battalion and 46th Royal Tank Regiment were to strike north-east from near Trig 29 to cut the main road about Kilo 113 and establish a firm base. Then the 2/48th was to advance eastwards alongside the road to attack in rear the enemy's front line defences astride the road and capture them. The 2/24th would follow the 2/48th and capture Thompson's Post from the north. Finally the 24th Brigade, as well as maintaining a firm base behind the original coast defences, was to capture the enemy's outpost covering the main road in the Kilo 109 area and also the area north of the 2/48th's breach, between the main road and the sea. For the attack the 2/3rd Field Company was to be in support of the 24th Brigade, 2/7th Field Company and 295th British Field Company in support of the 26th Brigade, and the 2/13th Field Company in support of the 20th Brigade.

Although the artillery provision was liberal, the guns were ill-sited to support the operations except those planned for the 2/13th Battalion (which were also to be supported by timed enfilade fire by the machine-guns of Macarthur-Onslow's composite force). To support the northward advance the guns had to fire concentrations in enfilade; to support the attack eastwards, they had to fire in the face of the advancing infantry. For the latter phase the plan provided for timed concentrations about 200 yards deep receding ahead of the infantry.

Morshead discussed his detailed orders with Leese on the morning of the 27th and had a further discussion on the operations with Montgomery in which he "stressed need for armour to support us on our left flank". Morshead recorded in his diary that Montgomery agreed that these were the proper tactics but doubted whether the armour would manage it.

Morshead outlined his plan to his brigade commanders and others at a conference at 2 p.m. on the 27th. That afternoon Brigadier Windeyer resumed command of the 20th Brigade after an absence due to severe illness. Morshead's final oral orders were given at a conference at 7 a.m. on the 28th and confirmed by a written operation order later in the morning. The attack was to be made on the night 28th-29th and the 20th Brigade, after its relief by the 152nd Highland Brigade, was to relieve the 26th so as to be in position to open the attack.

It may be readily assumed that on the 27th Alexander had discussed with Montgomery other matters than the future of the 9th Division, which may have had some bearing on developments on the 28th. So far all operations ordered and executed had been within the compass of the modified LIGHTFOOT plan expounded by Montgomery in his memorandum of 6th October:

The task of 30 Corps and 13 Corps will be to undertake the methodical destruction of the enemy troops holding his forward positions.

30 Corps will walk northwards from the northern flank of the bridgehead, using 9th Australian Division, and southwards from the Miteiriya Ridge using the New Zealand, South African and 4th Indian Divisions. . . .

> I hope that the operations outlined . . . will result in the destruction, by a crumbling process, of the whole of the enemy holding troops.
> Having thus "eaten the guts" out of the enemy he will have no troops with which to hold a front. . . . When we have succeeded in destroying the enemy holding troops, the eventual fate of the Panzer Army is certain—it will not be able to avoid destruction.

By the morning of the 28th, however, Montgomery had decided that a new break-out thrust would be made as soon as the 9th Division had completed its next "crumbling" phase. About 8 a.m. on the 28th Montgomery conferred with Leese and Lumsden and told them that he planned that the XXX Corps should then drive westwards along the axis of the road and railway to Sidi Abd el Rahman while the X Corps was to exploit westwards from the Australian left flank, holding off the enemy armour from XXX Corps. In brief, a break-out operation between Trig 29 and the sea was envisaged, and the front from Trig 29 southward was to go over to the defensive. It is remarkable that, if this break-out plan had been executed, the armour's seaward flank would have been closed when it emerged and it could have manoeuvred in only one direction.

Before advancing along the road axis it would have been desirable if not essential, in order to provide a safeguard against enfilade fire from the hillocks near the sea, to capture first not only the road and railway to the north of the 9th Division and all ground south of the railway but also the whole area between the road and the sea. That indeed was the underlying and ultimate purpose of the next operation planned for the 9th Division, but the enemy defences between the road and the sea were not within the scope of the operation's immediate objectives.

Later that morning Lumsden and Freyberg each had a long conference with Morshead, and Freyberg was subsequently warned by Montgomery that on completion of the Australian attack the New Zealand division should be ready to take over the sector and make an advance along the coast.

The relief of the 26th Brigade by the 20th Brigade on the night of the 27th-28th was made difficult by strong enemy counter-attacks on both the 2/24th and 2/48th Battalions at the time set for their reliefs and still more difficult by the late arrival of the 2/Camerons to relieve the 2/13th. The latter, which was to have proceeded across by foot, had to be fetched by transport waiting to take out the 2/24th, and was only just in time to complete the relief by dawn. The 2/17th on Trig 29 had previously been severely counter-attacked that morning and in the early afternoon but had driven the enemy off.

Both battalions of the 20th Brigade opened their attack at 10 p.m. on 28th October. The 2/13th on the right was a depleted unit, with rifle companies averaging only 35 of all ranks, and an exhausted one, after five sleepless nights. It had attacked on two successive nights, been counter-attacked on the next two, and on the night preceding this attack had been on the move, arriving only just before dawn in an area overlooked and constantly shelled by the enemy. The troops crossed a start-line laid farther back than the plan provided but soon caught up with the barrage and had to pause until it lifted. The attack by the 2/24th on the 26th

October had cleared the enemy from the ground covered in the first phase except for some isolated survivors who offered no resistance, but the enemy, apparently aiming behind the shell-bursts of the British barrage, brought artillery fire down on the battalion transport and in the midst of the rear companies. The Fig Orchard, which was the first objective, was reached in 50 minutes. Captain Gillan's company dug in close behind the orchard with battalion headquarters near by. Soon Lieutenant Barrett's[8] company and Lieutenant Vincent's passed through and continued down a track leading towards the coast. They took up position some 800 yards from Thompson's Post, after having to move back about 50 yards because the protective artillery barrage was too close. Captain Burrell's company then patrolled deeply ahead but without making contact.

With companies barely stronger than platoons, the battalion's attack with two companies forward had inevitably been on a narrow frontage. The path taken missed enemy positions on the left flank, which now became troublesome, heavily mortaring battalion headquarters and Gillan's company. Moreover the whole area was found to be strewn with anti-personnel mines. Casualties were mounting and it fell to Gillan's company to deal with two enemy posts which were mainly responsible. The first patrol of 10 men under Lieutenant North[9] met with disaster when a mortar bomb landed in its midst, killing or seriously wounding all except the commander. North returned and organised a second patrol to bring his men back. Colonel Colvin had meanwhile ordered Gillan to send out another patrol with firm orders to subdue the other post. Corporal McKellar, who was given the task, moved with ten others through a minefield, attacked with grenades two machine-gun crews giving covering fire to a mortar crew, and captured the guns and their crews. Next they rushed and overcame the mortar crew some 30 yards away and returned with their prisoners carrying the captured weapons. After one more post was silenced by patrol action it appeared that local opposition had at last been subdued. Meanwhile Burrell's company had returned and dug in a short distance behind battalion headquarters.

On the left the 2/15th attacked northward from Trig 29. As the battalion was forming up it was heavily shelled and Colonel Magno and his adjutant were wounded, Magno mortally. Strange took command and led the battalion in a vigorous, well-executed attack. Advancing through machine-gun and mortar fire they encountered posts manned mainly by Italians 900 yards from the forming-up place, overcame them and secured their objectives. In the attack 89 Italians were killed and some 130 Italian and German prisoners were taken. No minefields were found and the vehicles had no difficulty in moving up. The battalion dug in. It had lost 6 killed, including Captain Jubb,[1] a company commander, and 36 wounded; 3 men were missing. Soon after first light two enemy tractors

---

[8] Capt R. J. Barrett, NX70729; 2/13 Bn. Builder; of Coffs Harbour, NSW; b. Norwood, SA, 5 Apr 1909.
[9] Maj S. C. F. North, NX14978; 2/13 Bn. Store manager; of Taree, NSW; b. Singleton, NSW, 20 Sep 1919.
[1] Capt W. H. V. Jubb, QX6244; 2/15 Bn. Bank officer; of Brisbane; b. Strathfield, NSW, 21 Sep 1917. Killed in action 28 Oct 1942.

approached towing anti-tank guns. The guns and 22 Germans with them were promptly captured.

The fresh 2/23rd (Lieut-Colonel Evans) and the 46th Royal Tanks (Lieut-Colonel T. C. A. Clarke), who were to execute the advance to the main road, had trained together for semi-mobile operations. To gain surprise and save time Evans planned to advance to the objective with his assault troops (one company) mounted on the tanks and two companies following on his own carriers and those of the 2/24th. By the time the 20th Brigade attack began all were lined up ready at the forming-up place, there to await that brigade's success signal. An alerted enemy was also ready. When the barrage opened and the advance started the tanks and carriers and the men mounted on them were exposed to sharp fire. Some of the tanks, not having the assistance of moonlight as broad as that laid on for the earlier attacks, missed the marked gaps in the home minefield and were immobilised. Others, according to the diarist of the 2/23rd, moved right and left contrary to instructions to search for others gaps and "an extremely confused situation" developed, into which the enemy pumped shot and shell from weapons of every kind. In the left company, in which casualties were severe and all the officers wounded, the company sergeant major, Warrant-Officer Joyce,[2] rallied the survivors and led them forward without the tanks to overcome the foremost enemy positions in hand-to-hand fighting and take 40 prisoners; but elsewhere the attack did not progress.

It was decided to re-set the attack and the sappers were directed to widen the gaps, but much time was lost. "The difficulties of this period," states the 9th Division's report, "were added to by communications between the commanding officers of 2/23rd Battalion and 46th Royal Tanks breaking down and the headquarters of 26th Brigade and 23rd Armoured Brigade, which were situated close to each other, not being in touch." So no doubt it appeared to the staff at divisional headquarters. Evans had lost touch because Clarke and most (if not all) of his squadron leaders had been wounded. Whitehead and Richards had gone forward together to keep closer touch.

After the gaps had been widened the advance was resumed until the tanks again reported mines. Engineer sweeping operations were undertaken but failed to discover any. It was 12.55 a.m. before the tanks moved forward again, but then they came under fire from six 50-mm anti-tank guns, whereupon they dispersed taking their infantry with them. The enemy became very active and casualties mounted fast.

The operation was developing into the type of muddle for which there were several derisive epithets in common army parlance. Colonel Evans gathered what men he could—only 60 or 70—and organised an attack which at 3.15, after a hard fight, took the main German position with its six guns and 160 men.[3] About that time another group of infantry

[2] Lt K. D. Joyce, DCM, VX40737; 2/23 Bn. Labourer; of Korumburra, Vic; b. Yarram, Vic, 11 Jan 1915.
[3] "The battle raged at this point with tremendous fury for six hours, until finally II/125th Regiment and XI Bersaglieri Battalion were overrun by the enemy. Their troops, surrounded and exposed to enemy fire from all sides, fought on desperately." *The Rommel Papers*, pp. 311-12.

and 15 tanks, who were out of touch with Evans, advanced east of Evans' position towards the railway. After 800 yards they came under fire from German guns, including one 88-mm; nine tanks were knocked out and many of the infantrymen were hit. At 4 a.m. Evans reported that he was digging in about 1,000 yards forward of the original F.D.L's because he had so few men and was not in touch with any responsible officer of the 46th R.T.R. The 2/23rd had suffered very severe losses in the attack, having lost 29 killed, 172 wounded and 6 missing. The casualties included 2 majors, 4 captains, and 10 lieutenants.

Meanwhile Brigadier Whitehead had made a new plan: to attack with the 2/24th and 2/48th Battalions from the area firmly held by the 2/15th. General Morshead made the 40th R.T.R. available to him; but the 23rd Armoured Brigade could not at such short notice give a definite time for the 40th's arrival at the forming-up place and it became apparent that the fresh battalions would probably have insufficient time to reorganise on their objectives before daylight. Morshead therefore postponed the attack and ordered Whitehead to ensure that the 2/23rd was securely established and made contact with the 2/13th on its right and 2/15th on its left: the 2/24th and 2/48th were to return to their lying-up areas. The few tanks of the 46th R.T.R. still in running order—only eight— were withdrawn.

Dawn on the 29th found the 2/13th Battalion in an isolated, rather precarious position, with open left flank and a gap of 400 yards (protected, however, by an enemy-laid minefield) between the two left companies; opposite the gap were known enemy fortified posts, which might be still occupied. Behind the battalion there was an open flank for almost 1,000 yards.

From 7 a.m. onward heavy and accurate artillery fire fell on the battalion headquarters. Three shells penetrated the dug-outs; the third wounded and incapacitated Colonel Colvin, killed the adjutant, Lieutenant Pinkney,[4] and wounded the anti-tank officer, Lieutenant Gould.[5] Captain Jones, the command post officer, notified the catastrophe to Windeyer's headquarters and the two forward companies through his radio links. The Intelligence officer (Lieutenant Maughan) who was the only officer left on the headquarters, asked brigade headquarters to find Major Daintree, the second-in-command, and in the meantime Captain Gillan had come across from his company to take charge. Major Daintree could not be found. Later it was ascertained that he had been wounded while organising the transport and evacuated. Thereupon Windeyer asked Morshead to make available Captain Kelly, a former adjutant of the unit, who was then serving on divisional headquarters. Morshead agreed and promoted Kelly to the rank of major. Kelly arrived in the afternoon and took command. Finding that the four rifle companies had between them only about 100 men, he reinforced them with men from "B" Echelon and

---

[4] Lt E. M. Pinkney, NX27934; 2/13 Bn. Bank officer; of Canberra; b. Epping, NSW, 24 Jul 1916. Killed in action 29 Oct 1942.
[5] Capt N. S. Gould, NX34768; 2/3 A-Tk Regt. Building contractor; of Wahroonga, NSW; b. Wollstonecraft, NSW, 6 Jul 1913.

the Headquarters Company. Gillan later wrote: "To the dazed and battered troops, it was like a shot in the arm to see Major Joe back in the fold."[6]

It was against the 2/15th and the 2/17th, however, that the enemy's main efforts were directed on the 29th. Fourteen tanks stood hull-down

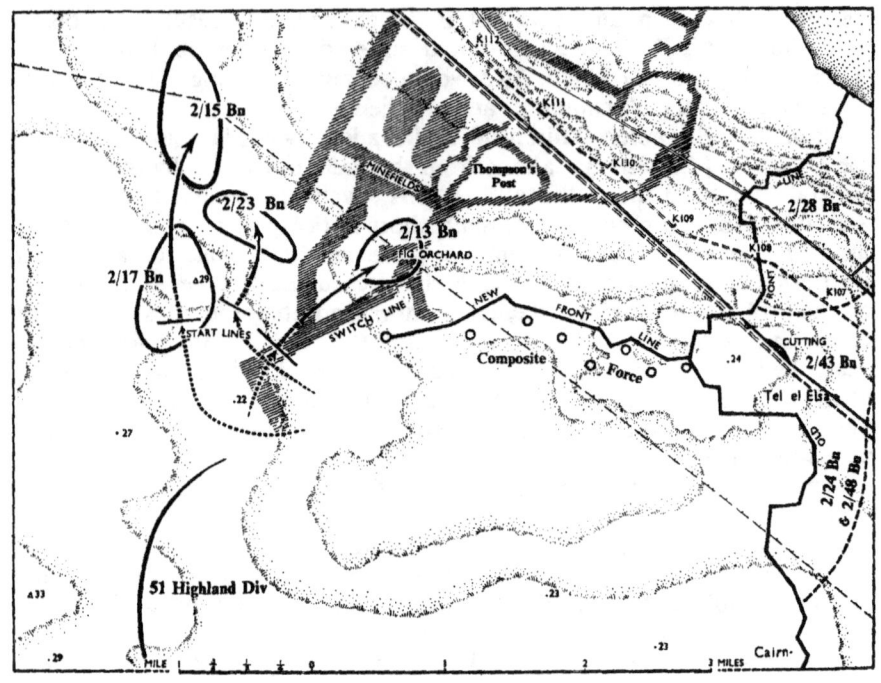

Dawn, 29th October

near Trig 29 all day and the whole area came under tempestuous fire. After dawn it became evident that the enemy had only a confused idea of the Australian positions; several enemy vehicles drove into the Australian lines and were destroyed or captured. Later in the morning enemy infantry and tanks formed up and two counter-attacks in which both tanks and infantry were employed were directed at Trig 29—one in the morning, and another in the early afternoon. The afternoon attack, which was made with greater determination, was sustained for three-quarters of an hour. Both were repelled, but on the second occasion not before six of the Australian anti-tank guns had been knocked out. At 5 p.m. the 2/15th and 2/17th sustained a still more determined attack launched at the junction of the two battalions; it was pressed until darkness fell. In coping with these attacks Colonel Simpson and his supporting artillery were greatly assisted by reports from Captain Dinning,[7] who had moved across from his company headquarters to an exposed observation post

---

[6] *Bayonets Abroad*, p. 285.
[7] Maj J. H. Dinning, MC, NX14374; 2/17 Bn. Buyer; of Croydon, NSW; b. North Sydney, 9 Aug 1914.

on Trig 29 to watch the enemy's moves. It could be seen that dreadful casualties had been inflicted on the attackers. As the light faded the enemy could be observed digging in at distances varying from a quarter of a mile to a mile from the Australian front. Shortly after midnight one more attack against the 2/15th and 2/17th was thrown back. Later an Italian officer drove up with a truckload of Italian wounded to the 2/17th Battalion's R.A.P. which was then crowded with wounded from the 2/15th.

Several more attacks were to be made before the enemy gave up the attempt to dislodge the 2/15th and 2/17th Battalions. The Australians' training in quick and thorough consolidation together with effective artillery protection had provided the answer to the German practice of counter-attacking quickly rather than deliberately. The enemy, unless able to counter-attack within two hours or so of the capture of a position, had little hope of breaking the front of these battalions, depleted though they were, except by a deliberate set-piece operation.

At 11 a.m. on the 29th the 20th Brigade assumed responsibility for the whole northern sector and the 2/23rd Battalion was placed under Brigadier Windeyer's command. After learning of plans for a renewed attack by the 26th Brigade on the 30th-31st, Windeyer ordered the 2/23rd to advance its positions 1,000 yards on the night of the 29th so as to link the north-east part of the 2/15th with the 2/13th. This was done without incident.

On the 28th, after noting the northward movement of British forces, Rommel had decided to withdraw still more German mobile forces from the southern sector and place them in the northern. By the end of that day the *15th Armoured Division* had only 21 serviceable Mark III or IV tanks; the *21st* only 45; the Italian divisions had a total of 196. Since the battle opened the number of Germans reported missing totalled 1,994, of Italians 1,660. In the *164th Division* two battalions of the *382nd Regiment* had been wiped out and the third had lost about one-quarter of its strength. One battalion of the *115th Regiment* was now only 40 strong.

The main German units to the east of the positions taken up by the *90th Light Division* west and north-west of Trig 29 were the *I* and *III Battalions* of the *125th Regiment* holding the original front from Thompson's Post across the railway and road to the sea and the *II/125th Regiment* in positions behind the original front line between the Trig 29 spur and the railway.

The Australian attack on the 28th-29th had breached the German line between the *II/125th* and a battle group (*155th Regiment*) of the *90th Light Division* and overrun the *XI Bersaglieri*. Parts of the *15th Armoured Division* and the *Littorio Division* were moved up to counter-attack.

The *90th Light Division* assumed command of the northern sector next day, taking the *125th Regimental Group* under command, and was ordered to form a new line, to be dug as quickly as possible and firmly held, from 10 kilometres south of Sidi Abd el Rahman to the coast four kilometres east of Sidi Abd el Rahman. (This was a line running from the south-west corner of the 9th Division's sector in a north-north-easterly direction—skirting the flank of the 2/15th Battalion—to the coast north of the 2/23rd Battalion.)

The attacks on the 2/15th and 2/17th Battalions on the 29th were made by the *200th Battle Group*, which had been ordered by the *90th Light Division* to recapture Bir Sultan Omar and then to re-establish the German line west of Trig 29 breached by the 2/15th Battalion's attack. The counter-attack failed but the remnants of the *II/125th* were extricated while it was proceeding.

The campaign narrative of the *Armoured Army of Africa* recorded that the heavy casualties suffered by the divisions of *XXI Corps* (*164th Infantry* and *Trento*) had made it necessary to commit almost the whole of the *Africa Corps* little by little to bolster up the northern sector.

It is interesting to see, from the enemy order of battle after the re-grouping on the 29th had taken place, the extent to which Rommel had denuded the other sectors to meet the threat posed by the 9th Division's operations.

The apparent stalemate in the battle had caused uneasiness in London where it had been expected that the best generals the English army could produce, launching an attack with an enormous superiority of men and munitions, would by now have obtained the so passionately desired victory, which was to redress Britain's record of military disasters in the desert before the joint American and British task force made its landing in North Africa. "I had my own doubts and my own anxieties as to the course of events," Brooke has recorded, "but these had to be kept entirely to myself."[8] On the 29th Churchill, now alarmed that the battle might not after all prove "an event of first magnitude", drafted a telegram ("not a pleasant one") to Alexander, called an urgent Chiefs of Staff meeting to which Field Marshal Smuts was invited, and berated Montgomery to Brooke:

> He had done nothing now for the last three days, and now he was withdrawing troops from the front. Why had he told us he would be through in seven days if all he intended to do was to fight a half-hearted battle? Had we not got a single general who could even win one single battle?

At the meeting Brooke defended Montgomery. To the criticism that for three days Montgomery had done nothing, Brooke

> pointed out that he had withstood a series of fierce counter-attacks in which Rommel had suffered heavy casualties. . . . As to the charge that Montgomery was withdrawing formations, had his critics forgotten, he asked, that the first principle of all offensive tactics lay in promptly creating new striking reserves for the next stage of attack.[9]

Smuts supported Brooke's interpretation of the reports and the Prime Minister agreed that the disturbing telegram should not be sent. Instead another was dispatched which merely told Alexander that the situation justified "all the risks and sacrifices involved in the relentless prosecution of this battle" and that he would be supported in "all the measures . . . to make this a fight to the finish".[1]

On the same morning Mr Casey and General Alexander, attended by his chief of staff, General McCreery, visited General Montgomery's headquarters to discuss what report should be sent to London on the progress and prospects of the battle. Casey's proper inquiries were apparently received with some pique but Montgomery spoke with confidence, recalled his prediction that the "crumbling might take ten or twelve days" and declared that he was certain of success. The meeting also discussed

---

[8] Bryant, *The Turn of the Tide*, p. 513.
[9] Bryant, pp. 512-13.
[1] Churchill, Vol IV, pp. 534-5.

Montgomery's plans for a new break-out thrust. The army commander's intention, de Guingand has recorded,

was to launch this attack as far north as possible. Some of us felt, however, that better results would be gained by adopting a more southerly axis. The further north we went, the more Germans, mines and prepared defences would we meet.[2]

Montgomery has also stated that "such was indeed my design at the time". McCreery expressed the opinion that the break-through should be attempted farther south.

During the morning the Intelligence service had deduced that the *90th Light Division* had concentrated about Sidi Abd el Rahman, which induced Montgomery to discard his plan at once. He would continue the attack in the north but break through at the junction between the *90th Light* and *Trento Divisions* and on the northern flank of the *Trento*.

But we had now achieved what Bill Williams had recommended. The Germans had been pulled against our right and were no longer "corsetting" the Italians. The Germans were in the north, the Italians together in the south; and the dividing line between them appeared to be just to the north of our original northern corridor. I at once changed my plan and decided to direct the final blow at this point of junction, but overlapping well on to the Italian front. I took this decision at 11 a.m., the 29th October.[3]

The break-out operation was to be a decisive attack, called SUPERCHARGE and the plan, written that day, provided that it should be delivered on the night of 31st October-1st November. The intention was to destroy the enemy's armour, force him to fight in the open and use up his petrol, get astride his supply route, force him from his forward airfields and thus "bring about the disintegration of the whole enemy army". The main infantry break-out was to be commanded by General Freyberg and was to be executed by a specially composed "New Zealand" division to comprise two British infantry brigades—the 151st (from the 50th Division) and the 152nd (from the 51st Highland Division)—plus a Maori battalion (under command of the 151st) and the 9th Armoured Brigade. The armoured thrust, which was to be made through the New Zealand division's new bridgehead, was to be carried out by the 1st Armoured Division, which would then comprise the 2nd and 8th Armoured Brigades and the 7th Motor Brigade. There were later some modifications to the original plan, including extending the depth of the initial penetration (to 6,000 yards). Moreover General Freyberg soon came to the conclusion that the two days allowed were insufficient for properly planning and mounting so large and complex an operation and Montgomery agreed early on the 31st to postpone the attack for one day to the night of 1st-2nd November.

It was essential to maintain relentless pressure on the enemy until the break-out operation took place and it fell to the lot of the 9th Division to do so by renewing its northward attacks. There were two purposes of immediate advantage that this might accomplish: to open up

---

[2] De Guingand, p. 206.
[3] Montgomery, *Memoirs*, p. 132. In fact, the point of junction proved to be farther south, so that the attack overlapped well on to the German front.

the main road from the enemy's original front-line as planned for the previous attack or to strike north from the division's already protruded left flank to the sea and cut off all enemy forces to the east. Now that the break-through would be effected farther south, the opening of the road was not of paramount importance. Morshead decided to do both.

The plan for the next attack was therefore even more ambitious than the last. The operations to open the coast road were to be much the same as before except that not one but two battalions were to thrust back eastwards along the road through the enemy's front-line to clear it and the battalion on the left was then to turn left and advance north to clear the enemy's forward defences between the road and sea, which were previously to have been taken by the 24th Brigade. As before the 24th Brigade would capture the outpost locality covering the road at Kilo 109. Four battalions were to be used, one to cut the road, two to clear it and one to push through to the coast from where the road was cut, thus isolating the enemy holding the dominating ground north of the road.

As before, Brigadier Whitehead was to be in charge of the attack, which was to take place on the night of the 30th-31st October and would be carried out by his 26th Brigade less the 2/23rd Battalion, but with the 2/32nd and 2/3rd Pioneer Battalions under command and the 40th Royal Tanks in support. The 2/23rd Battalion, which held part of the front of the 20th Brigade, would provide the base from which the attack would be launched. The 2/32nd's role was to be similar to that of the 2/23rd in the earlier attack. With an anti-tank battery and two platoons of machine-guns under command, it was to capture the enemy's positions astride the main road about Barrel Hill[4] (Point 11) and form defensive flanks to north, north-west and west. Behind this screen the 2/24th and 2/48th would form up and then advance eastward and capture the enemy's defences not only astride the railway and the main road but also for 1,200 yards north of the railway. This done the 2/24th would attack Thompson's Post, advancing south-west from the road, while the 2/48th attacked through Cloverleaf to the Egg feature on the coast. In the fourth and final stage the 2/3rd Pioneer Battalion was to pass through the 2/32nd and advance northward from Barrel Hill to near the coast, mop up and finally reorganise facing east and west. The outline plan provided that the Pioneers should have the support of a battery of anti-tank guns and a platoon of medium machine-guns.

The vehicles of the attacking units would have to cross the railway embankment. The engineers planned to blow up the rails and push the earth of the embankment away with a bulldozer. A second field company —the 2/3rd—was attached to the brigade because the engineer tasks were to be so heavy. The artillery, to be controlled by Brigadier Ramsay, comprised 12 field regiments and 3 medium with a total of 360 guns.

Morshead issued his outline plan at 5 p.m. on the 29th and gave Whitehead his final plan and orders at 7 a.m. next morning. Morshead's

---

[4] There was a navigation beacon on the hill, with an eight figure reference on the barrels for identification.

notes for the latter conference indicate that he had then decided that the 26th Brigade should be relieved by the 24th Brigade on the night of 31st October-1st November and that he intended so to inform Whitehead. He also noted later: "Whitehead does not want any tanks."

Between half an hour after midnight and dawn on the 30th, the 2/15th Battalion had been attacked four times. At one stage a penetration was made and the enemy almost reached the anti-tank guns. All attacks were finally repulsed and the line re-established. It had become very evident that an aggressive enemy had been reinforcing his strength in front of the 2/15th, close to where the 2/32nd was to establish the base for the 26th Brigade's operations, and Morshead, who knew also that the 2/24th and 2/48th were reduced to less than half strength, came to the conclusion that any one of these three battalions might need help from reserves to complete its task. The 2/3rd Pioneer Battalion was therefore to be available as a reserve to help any one of them; only if not so required was it to carry out the role of cutting the enemy's communications north of the coast road. The 2/3rd Pioneer Battalion therefore received instructions (aptly described by its historian as the "IF" plan) that it was to be ready to help the 2/32nd Battalion to take its objective if required; if not, then to be ready to help the 2/24th take Thompson's Post, if required; if not then to be ready to help the 2/48th take the defences from the road to the sea; if not required for any of these things, then to carry out its original role of advancing north from the firm base to the coast.

Thus, in the new plan's ultimate development, the earlier plan's purpose of opening the road remained the prime object; the object of cutting what would then be the enemy's only escape route by the sea-shore assumed secondary importance and was made contingent on the 2/3rd Pioneer Battalion's not being required to help with the prime object. To the 2/3rd Pioneer Battalion, which with only three companies (the fourth having to remain with the composite force) would be fighting its first action as a unit in an infantry role with such indefinite, and indeed bewildering, prospects, it was not consoling to learn that the anti-tank guns and machine-guns previously allocated to its support would no longer be employed in that role; for obviously the location of these important arms for securing the firm base could not be left to be determined by the uncertainties that would decide the role of the Pioneers.

The 2/32nd Battalion (Lieut-Colonel Balfe) assembled for its attack on the night of the 30th, for which the accompanying barrage was to begin at 10 p.m. Before it started two officers of the battalion had been wounded by a sniper while reconnoitring—Major Joshua (who nevertheless carried on) and Captain Jacoby,[5] wounded mortally. The two leading companies, commanded by Captains Huitfeldt[6] and Eacott,[7] set

---
[5] Capt P. R. Jacoby, VX12704; 2/32 Bn. Articled clerk; of South Melbourne; b. Perth, WA, 21 Apr 1917. Killed in action 30 Oct 1942.
[6] Maj H. Huitfeldt, VX12707. 2/32 Bn and Movt Control. Tramway clerk; of St Kilda, Vic; b. Enita, Flinders I, Tas, 2 Jul 1909.
[7] Maj D. F. Eacott, WX293; 2/32 Bn. Truck driver; of West Midland, WA; b. Mandurah, WA, 11 Jan 1916.

off ten minutes after the barrage began but, encountering no strong opposition, soon caught up with it. The railway line—the intermediate objective—was reached in good time; 175 prisoners, nearly all German from the *I/361st Battalion*, had been taken. After a pause on the railway line to re-form the advance continued against heavier opposition, and casualties mounted. After the forward troops had crossed the railway Colonel Balfe and his wireless operator were on the railway line when six Germans moved forward, evidently to surrender. One drew a pistol and shot Balfe in the arm. Balfe emptied his revolver into the Germans and made off.

When the final objectives had been reached, two companies remained in reverse slope positions covering the road while two moved left and occupied an area south of the railway facing west. The engineers were clearing mine-free tracks leading forward and had begun breaking down the 12-foot railway embankments to enable vehicles to cross, but the truck bringing their explosives and equipment had not arrived and they were reduced to doing the job with shovels and using Hawkins mines for explosive charges. Within the area captured by the 2/32nd Battalion was a blockhouse which had been used by the enemy as a main casualty station. Three German medical officers and their orderlies remained on duty. Field Marshal Rommel had always enjoined a scrupulous adherence to the rules of war. True to these traditions and those of their service, the German doctors and orderlies toiled that night and in the following days to minister without discrimination to the wounded of both sides as they were brought in. There they were soon joined by the 2/32nd's medical officer, Captain Campbell,[8] and his men and by Captain Grice[9] and his section of the 2/11th Field Ambulance.

The 2/48th Battalion under Lieut-Colonel Hammer, the 2/24th under Lieut-Colonel Weir and the 2/3rd Pioneer Battalion under Lieut-Colonel Gallasch[1] set off in turn from the Trig 29 area, at 10.30, 10.40 and 11.00 p.m. respectively, in the wake of the 2/32nd Battalion, and each had some action on the way. Two platoons from separate companies of the 2/3rd Pioneers assaulting separately, and saved just in time from mistaking each other for the enemy by the inimitable profanity of their language, attacked one troublesome post to the left of the track leading to the 2/32nd and overcame it in close hand-to-hand fighting, taking more than 50 prisoners.

The battalions dug in near the 2/32nd while waiting to go forward, the area being harassed by fire. A platoon of the pioneers went over to help the engineers with their task of gapping the railway embankment. The enemy had begun closing in from the west and was soon raking the gap with fire. A platoon of the pioneers and a company of the 2/32nd

---

[8] Maj W. H. Campbell, MC, NX12163; RMO 2/32 Bn. Medical practitioner; of Cremorne, NSW; b. Sydney, 15 Feb 1913.

[9] Maj K. J. Grice, VX39204. 2/11 Fd Amb; 2/7 AGH. Medical practitioner; of Melbourne; b. Brisbane, 23 Mar 1915.

[1] Col A. V. Gallasch, MC, NX35132. (1st AIF: Capt 27 Bn.) 2/3 Pnr Bn (CO 1941-43); Area Comd Nadzab 1943-44. Bank officer; of Sydney; b. Gladstone, SA, 7 Jun 1893.

independently attacked the positions mainly responsible with eventual success and again some misunderstandings were sorted out by descriptive language.

Casualties were coming fast. Balfe was hit a second time and carried out and Major Joshua took command of the 2/32nd. A German 88-mm gun shot up many carriers and vehicles attempting to bring ammunition and stores forward and many did not get through, including those of one company of the 2/32nd. About 3.45 a.m., after three hours work by 50 men, the crossing over the railway was complete and the "A" Echelon vehicles of the 2/32nd companies north of the railway crossed over; but the enemy was now pressing along the railway from the west and bringing heavy fire to bear on the gap. The 2/32nd had been unable to link with the 2/15th on the left. The ground that the 2/32nd had taken up will henceforth be called the Saucer because that is what it was to look like when dawn revealed their situation to the men of the 2/32nd and that is what they, and others who later went there, called it. In the next two days the Saucer was to become the focal point in the struggle between the two armies.

The 2/24th and 2/48th, numbering scarcely 450 men between them, had meanwhile set off on their desperate eastward advance of 2,250 yards, marching to the sound of the guns—not to the distant sound of the enemy's, but in the face of the close, harsh bombardment of their own—and were strewing the desert way of a long fight with fallen wounded and dead, yet sustaining still their forward progress, their soldierly spirit suffusing the performance of their task with a greatness transcending its purpose. The start-lines had been laid north from the railway to Barrel Hill, but not before the 2/48th had fought for the ground by clearing a neighbouring post. The barrage opened at 1 a.m. Because the battalions were to advance into the receding barrage, they had to keep 600 yards back from the fire-beaten zone, losing much of the benefit. There was some confusion at the start. The start-line was both harassed by enemy fire and shelled by the supporting artillery, who nevertheless were doing their best to carry out a most difficult task. The 2/48th were early at the forming-up place and, finding it under fire, moved forward and took cover. The 2/24th arriving subsequently but seeing nothing of the 2/48th thought they must have already started and pressed on. A fiasco at the very outset of the attack was averted by Captain Summerton, a liaison officer sent from 26th Brigade headquarters to ensure that the two battalions linked up. Arriving at the start-line but finding neither battalion on it, Summerton went forward along the 2/48th Battalion centre-line and found Hammer, who irately inquired where Weir's battalion was and instructed Summerton to find Weir. Summerton returned to the start-line and proceeded along the 2/24th centre-line until he encountered a man with a radio set. Summerton then spoke to Weir who agreed to put his battalion to ground until Hammer's battalion came up, whereupon Summerton moved across and reported to Hammer, attracting ill-aimed fire from the 2/48th on the way. Consideration was given to organising a re-start with a repetition of the artillery program but, as that would involve much delay, both battalions moved on from where they were, intending to catch up with the barrage. Both adopted the now conventional procedure of advancing with two companies forward to an intermediate objective and then passing the rear companies through to complete the task. Both were

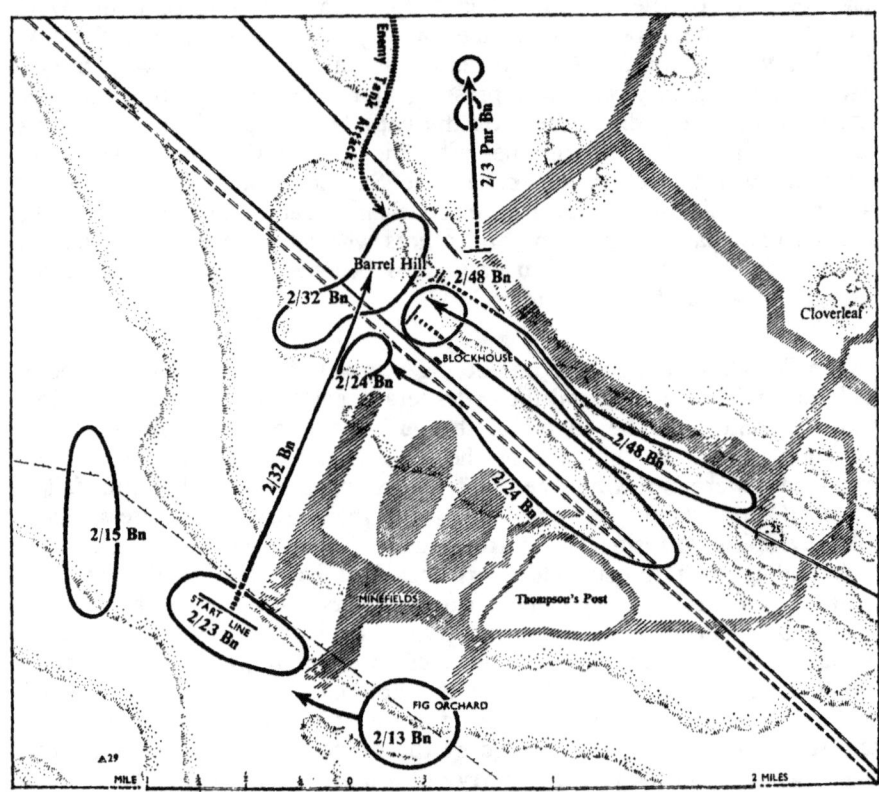

30th-31st October

soon knocked about by fire from anti-tank guns, heavy mortars and machine-guns; both successfully took their intermediate objectives (though not without fighting) but then found themselves advancing with ever-dwindling strength against ever-stronger opposition. As they fought their way on and one or other battalion or company heard its neighbour in trouble to right or left, groups from one crossed to the other to help.

In the 2/24th, which advanced with one section south of the railway line on the open right flank, the heaviest opposition was encountered on the left. Captain Harty's company on the right had, by comparison, an easier passage.

Lieutenant Kearney's[2] company on the left had a stiff fight in which Sergeant Dingwall[3] commanding the left platoon led his men against three posts in succession and overcame them. Then the other two platoons attacked a troublesome enemy strong-point on the left and Dingwall joined in, storming the post's 88-mm gun and capturing it.[4] Captain Mackenzie's and Lieutenant McLeod's[5] companies (McLeod's on the right) were meanwhile following up. Mackenzie's company was caught by enfilade machine-gun fire which cut down several men and badly wounded Mackenzie. Lieutenant Nelson[6] took command and soon had to come to the help of Kearney's company, held up in front of the first objective. Some of the 2/48th also came over to help and the post was overrun, whereupon the following companies passed through.

McLeod's company fought its way forward under increasingly heavy fire but this came mainly from posts in front of Nelson's company, which had been held up by a German strongpoint; soon Nelson was wounded. The company sergeant-major, Sergeant Alleyne, took command and led the men through the wire but he too soon fell mortally wounded. Lieutenant McLeod brought his company across to help. Corporal Anderson[7] charged one post single-handed, spattering the occupants with light machine-gun fire and killing all, but as McLeod's men moved into the assault on the strongpoint anti-tank and heavy machine-guns firing point-blank put them to ground. McLeod, calling on his men to cover him, charged the gun crews with Bren gun firing but was shot down and killed. Sergeant Lewis[8] who had taken command of the left company continued the attack in conjunction with men from McLeod's company, overran another post and then with only nine men dug in to hold the ground he had taken. When McLeod was hit, Warrant-Officer Cameron rushed to his assistance but was also wounded. Finding McLeod dead and himself again in command of the company, the wounded Cameron led back the survivors, numbering only eight, to contact the rear company, where they dug in, covering the front between the road and railway.

Colonel Weir decided to concentrate his meagre force and, when they were gathered in, led them, 84 strong, to a position due north of Thompson's Post. There they dug themselves in for all round defence. While there he received a message from brigade headquarters telling him that it had been reported—and how incredible it must have seemed to those

---

[2] Lt E. A. J. Kearney, VX42900; 2/24 Bn. Shearer; of Tarrington, Vic; b. Melbourne, 5 Jul 1915. Killed in action 31 Oct 1942.
[3] Lt L. J. Dingwall, DCM, VX32809. 2/24 and 2/1 Bns. Truck driver; of Drouin, Vic; b. Kyabram, Vic, 21 Nov 1918.
[4] This was probably the post attacked by Lieutenant Barnes' raiding party in the first night's diversionary operations.
[5] Lt E. McLeod, VX52893; 2/24 Bn. Carpenter; of Bairnsdale, Vic; b. Lucknow, Vic, 15 Dec 1907. Killed in action 31 Oct 1942.
[6] Lt F. R. Nelson, SX6481; 2/24 Bn. Linotype operator; of Hyde Park, SA; b. Adelaide, 3 Sep 1914.
[7] Cpl J. H. Anderson, DCM, VX34703; 2/24 Bn. Tractor driver; of Marnoo, Vic; b. Rupanyup, Vic, 22 Jul 1917.
[8] WO2 K. T. Lewis, VX34467; 2/24 Bn. Farmer; of Tongala, Vic; b. Wickepin, WA, 31 Jan 1914.

men!—that Thompson's Post was unoccupied;[9] the proposed barrage had therefore been cancelled and Weir was instructed to verify the report. Responding with fine leadership to a fearful mandate, Weir made himself the patrol leader and set out with 15 men to find out.

No less arduous had been the 2/48th Battalion's road to its objective. Major Edmunds' company on the right and Captain Bryant's on the left led the advance. As they reached the road they ran into deathly fire, but with numbers dwindling pressed on and with hard hand-to-hand fighting for almost two hours forced their way through the enemy positions to the intermediate objectives. In the right company casualties came fast: Lieutenant Caple[1] was killed assaulting a post, another platoon commander, Lieutenant Butler,[2] was badly wounded and evacuated. Sergeant Ranford[3] having taken command of his platoon led assaults on two posts, overcoming both, and on the second occasion damaging beyond repair two machine-guns and an 88-mm gun. Ranford, badly wounded, continued to lead his platoon, then only seven strong, until hit again.

The reserve companies also had to fight their way forward to the intermediate objective, having to deal with unsubdued enemy posts on the edge of the depleted forward companies' path. Passing through they took the full force of the enemy's mortar and machine-gun fire. Captain Shillaker leading the right company was soon badly wounded and Lieutenant Hamilton[4] was killed. Sergeant Derrick led the company forward but it was forced to ground near the objective. Captain Robbins' company on the left swung out to avoid a minefield and continued the advance, but the rest of the battalion lost touch with them.

After Caple had been killed and Butler wounded, Edmunds ordered Lieutenant Allen[5] to deal with mortar and machine-gun posts that had brought his advance to a stand-still and as Allen led a successful bayonet charge against them in the face of whipping fire, Edmunds resumed the advance with only six men. Allen's platoon took 15 prisoners but suffered severely; it was reduced to three men (including himself). On Allen's right Edmunds led his six men in an assault on another post but was badly wounded by machine-gun fire as they moved in. Allen, who was also wounded, was the only officer remaining to command the company's survivors, then numbering only five.

---

[9] This information was based on two patrols earlier that night by Lieutenant Pope of the 2/13th Battalion, an experienced and reliable patrol leader, who was asked to verify that Thompson's Post was still occupied. On the first occasion he went to the edge of wire and fired into the stronghold without response. Needing engineers to break through the outer obstacle, he returned and with a strong patrol including sappers broke through the wire and in the light of enemy flares moved under steadily increasing fire across the enemy positions, which were unoccupied. "Thompson's Post", however, was an extensive defended locality which Pope's patrol probably penetrated about 1,200 yards south of where the 2/24th was to attack.

[1] Lt S. S. Caple, WX9756; 2/48 Bn. Bank clerk; of Perth, WA; b. Fremantle, WA, 9 Apr 1913. Killed in action 31 Oct 1942.

[2] Lt G. J. Butler, SX12499; 2/48 Bn. Financier and money lender; of Perth, WA; b. Perth, 19 Aug 1910. Died of wounds 23 Nov 1943.

[3] Sgt R. F. G. Ranford, DCM, SX7410; 2/48 Bn. Station hand; of Davington, SA; b. Davington, 29 Oct 1917. Killed in action 20 Nov 1943.

[4] Lt B. Y. Hamilton, WX201; 2/48 Bn. Bank officer; of Claremont, WA; b. Fremantle, WA, 4 Feb 1918. Killed in action 31 Oct 1942.

[5] Capt K. F. Allen, MC, SX12498; 2/48 Bn. Insurance inspector; of Hayhurst, SA; b. Keswick, SA, 26 Apr 1915.

Battalion headquarters, coming up between Shillaker's and Robbins' companies, also passed through the original two forward companies and continued up the centre, but soon found themselves well ahead of the forward companies and began taking casualties from enemy fire from positions near the final objective. The Regimental Sergeant Major, Warrant-Officer Legg, led an assault by five men on a post but four were lost.

Meanwhile Captain Bryant, the only senior company commander apart from Robbins (who was still out of touch), brought up what was left of the two companies that had taken the first objective and took charge, amalgamating his with Shillaker's company (now commanded by Derrick who, though he had been hit, was still carrying on) to form a composite company of 45 men, and then, accompanied on the right by Lieutenant Allen commanding the few survivors of what was Edmunds' company, resumed the advance, organised a charge with grenades and bayonet, and overcame the post that had held up Derrick's men.

Hammer had heard no word from Robbins, whose company had pressed on close to the objective, because Robbins had been killed and all his platoon commanders and his headquarters men had been either killed or wounded. The company had been caught in open ground as it approached the end of its advance and 16 men were killed assaulting the objective. When Robbins had been killed and the officers commanding the other two platoons severely wounded, Sergeant Kibby took command and organised an attack on the objective with the survivors, perhaps a dozen men, in two converging groups. The attackers were forced to ground within 20 yards of it. Kibby jumped up and charged, hurling grenades which silenced the post, but not before he had been caught by the enemy's fire, which cut off the life of a soldier whose gallantry in this and earlier actions at El Alamein could not have been surpassed.[6] So was the left objective assaulted on the ground that Major Mollard's company of the 2/24th, attacking from the other side, had briefly captured some months before.

Colonel Hammer called a conference of all who were now acting as commanders of what remained of his battalion and ordered that the men were to dig in and hold the ground they had attained. The battalion, now reduced to 41 men, had no communications, all signal sets having been shot up and lines mutilated. He decided that he would make contact with the 2/24th Battalion to see whether it would be feasible to hold the ground where he was, north of the road, while the 2/24th held ground south of the road. Handing over command to his adjutant, Captain Reid,[7] who had been thrice wounded, Hammer set off alone, armed only with a pistol, to find the 2/24th. Later he returned, having been shot through the face, but with two prisoners. He had found the headquarters of the 2/24th, but Weir was not there. He then ordered a

---

[6] Kibby was awarded the Victoria Cross for his actions at El Alamein in the period 23rd October-31st October 1942.
[7] Capt W. R. Reid, SX10245; 2/48 Bn. Bank officer; of St Peters, SA; b. St Peters, 21 Feb 1920. Killed in action 31 Oct 1942.

withdrawal to the blockhouse, saying that he believed the 2/24th would also be withdrawing.

Colonel Weir's patrol to Thompson's Post had penetrated the outer wire without incident but was fired on soon afterwards at short range. One man was killed; another was wounded as the patrol quickly withdrew. Private O'Brien,[8] a stretcher bearer, turned back, however, and brought the wounded man out. The fire showed Thompson's Post to be very much occupied.

When Weir returned to his battalion's firm base, he was given an oral message to the effect that, because Hammer's battalion was so depleted, Hammer proposed to withdraw; so Weir decided to do likewise. Hammer, on the other hand, had decided to withdraw only because after making contact with the 2/24th while Weir was absent leading his patrol to Thompson's Post he had gathered that Weir had decided to withdraw. Still it was all for the best, and both battalions came back just before dawn to the Saucer. On the way, however, the 2/24th passed through a minefield of aerial bombs, two of which detonated. There were 28 casualties; Lieutenant Kearney and 11 others were killed and Colonel Weir so badly wounded that Captain Harty (who was a temporary captain of only three months' standing) had to take command. The devoted O'Brien moved fearlessly among the wounded, dressing all 16. Later two of the battalion's carriers came up and brought out these and other wounded just before first light.

Harty led back the 54 survivors of the 2/24th to the 2/32nd Battalion's base where they took up a position on the left of the 2/32nd Battalion. Weir was taken to the casualty station at the blockhouse and Major Gebhardt took command after first light. Of the 206 men (including only five officers) with which the 2/24th had entered the attack, 42 had been killed and 116 wounded (though some of these were still carrying on); two men were missing. The battalion had taken 48 German and 14 Italian prisoners and a formidable array of weapons: one 88-mm gun, two 50-mm guns, two 20-mm guns, 12 Spandaus, one medium mortar, one light mortar, and seven howitzers.

Hammer had also withdrawn his few—his very few—to the base at the Saucer, where they dug in just to the east of the 2/32nd Battalion. The 2/48th Battalion had taken some 200 German prisoners. It had lost 47 killed and 148 wounded and 4 were missing. Among the 18 officers who took part in the attack only four now remained alive and unwounded. On 23rd October this battalion had 30 officers and 656 other ranks; of these 21 officers and half the men had since been killed or wounded.

The prisoners taken by the division in the operation totalled 544 of which 421 (including 7 officers) were German and 123 (including 5 officers) were Italian.

Hard though the infantry had toiled that night, still harder had been the labour of the stretcher bearers who had been tending the wounded

---

[8] Pte J. P. O'Brien, DCM, VX56822; 2/24 Bn. Pottery hand; of West Brunswick, Vic; b. Violet Town, Vic, 23 Feb 1920.

(9th Division war diary)

"Scorpions", manned by Australian engineers, at El Alamein. Scorpions were tanks fitted with rotating drums to which were attached chains which flailed the ground and exploded mines thus clearing a passage through enemy minefields.

(Australian War Memorial)

Captured enemy anti-tank guns at El Daba, November 1942.

(Imperial War Museum)
A German tank destroyed during operations at El Alamein, with the burnt and blackened body of a crew member near by.

(Capt G. H. Yates)
Feeding captured Italians at the prisoner-of-war cage at El Alamein.

under fire all along the battalions' long trail and bringing them back to the blockhouse in the Saucer. A high proportion of the 264 wounded in the two battalions were stretcher cases. Only 6 men were not accounted for that night and it is believed that not one of them was a wounded man left untended. Meanwhile the centre of greatest activity was the blockhouse—a long prison-like building used to house railway gangers in peacetime—where Captain Campbell, Captain Grice and the German doctors and their respective orderlies were together tending the wounded.

In the early hours of the 31st an important reinforcement reached the small Australian force of three depleted battalions astride the main road—one which was soon to play an important and possibly decisive role in a battle which was of some moment to the Eighth Army's prospects of a successful break-out. The 289th Battery R.A., a battery of Rhodesian anti-tank gunners manning 6-pounders who had earlier been sent up from the XIII Corps to help with operations in the north and were now attached to the 2/3rd Anti-Tank Regiment, had been allotted to the 2/32nd Battalion's support. In the dark their commander sited three troops (one being still in reserve) to cover, on the right, the approaches to the crossing from north and west—this troop's guns being on either side of the crossing—and on the left, to prevent close envelopment of the 2/32nd Battalion's left flank and rear by tanks moving round the front of the battalion's protective minefield and through the gap between the 2/32nd and 2/15th Battalions. Here were two troops, one close to the railway and one farther out, in the gap.

Also in the Saucer next morning were three troops of Major Copeland's[9] 9th Battery of the 2/3rd Anti-Tank Regiment—Lieutenant Kessell's[1] in support of the 2/32nd Battalion on its northern flank, "B" Troop and "C" Troop (in support of the 2/24th and 2/48th Battalions) being south of the railway.

For more than four hours the 2/3rd Pioneers, awaiting their summons to their first battle, had listened to the close and far bombardment of the battleground and the crackling automatic-fire signalling the hard fight of the 2/24th and 2/48th Battalions. When dawn was not far off, Colonel Gallasch asked for orders. A signal was received at 4.30 a.m. telling him by code word to attack at 4.25 a.m. and carry out his original task. Already the bombardment had opened. The company which had to advance farthest would only have what little time was left before dawn to complete an advance of some 3,000 yards and then seize and dig in on the ground it was to hold.

Compelled to commit the cardinal sin of hastening men into battle, Gallasch started his two forward companies at 4.35 a.m. from a start-line that ran east from Barrel Hill. The third had to consolidate near by.

---

[9] Maj G. F. Copeland, NX35091. (1st AIF: Dvr 3 Army FA Bde.) 2/3 A-Tk Regt. Company manager; of Parramatta, NSW; b. Sydney, 21 Sep 1898. Killed in action 1 Nov 1942.
[1] Capt J. S. Kessell, NX70914; 2/3 A-Tk Regt. Law clerk; of Drummoyne, NSW; b. Drummoyne, 19 Jan 1913.

The leading company (Captain Owens[2]) advanced through heavy fire and perhaps a bit off course but reached the area of the first objective on time, having advanced 1,500 yards and taken some 30 prisoners and three machine-guns. It dug in and Captain Stevens'[3] company passed through at 5 a.m., its objective being close to the coast. This company was soon halted by the supporting barrage, which was 200 yards ahead (some shells were falling short, about where the company was). The barrage remained stationary on that line. Already a lightening of the sky indicated the approach of day. The battalion had no communications to the rear; the signal officer had been badly wounded earlier; nor was there an artillery Forward Observation Officer; his truck had been blown up. When the bombardment showed no sign of ceasing Stevens decided that, since he could not reach the dunes and consolidate there before daylight, his men should dig in where they were, about a mile from the start-line and some 1,200 yards from the objective. Major Rosevear's[4] company had meanwhile consolidated in front of the forward slopes of Barrel Hill, but north of the road.

The greatest needs of the Pioneers, not having the anti-tank and machine-guns originally allocated to them, were good artillery support and their own support weapons and ammunition, but the forward companies had no artillery link and their "A" Echelon vehicles carrying their ammunition and heavier weapons had been held back at Tel el Eisa; and there, by standard battle procedure, they would continue to be held until the word summoning them forward was received.[5] It did not come. (The transport was at Tel el Eisa because it had been hoped to move it forward by the coast road after the road had been captured!) The system may have been operating perfectly, but both watchfulness and initiative are sometimes needed to break through a system when it fails to achieve the prime object. That was not done for the Pioneers except by two men (one a sergeant) in charge of trucks, who broke away and drove their two trucks at best speed to arrive forward with their precious ammunition loads before it was fully light. There was some for Owens' company but none for Stevens'. The situation in which the 2/3rd Pioneers now found themselves has been thus described by the unit's historian.

It was now quite light and the Pioneers' predicament soon became apparent to them and to the enemy. They were in a saucer, with the enemy holding the high ground on three sides of them and indeed in positions from which they could bring fire even into the rear of most of the battalion, whose supporting weapons were still on trucks held up on the other side of Tel el Eisa. What they could have done with those weapons and also with the additional anti-tank guns and machine-guns originally to be provided was nobody's business. . . . There they were, with no support and little ammunition, shooting at targets which mostly they could not see whereas the enemy could see every move and almost every man.[6]

---

[2] Maj G. Owens, WX1193. 2/3 Fd Coy and 2/3 Pnr Bn. Structural engineer; of South Perth, WA; b. Belfast, Ireland, 10 May 1918.
[3] Maj J. W. C. Stevens, SX9039; 2/3 Pnr Bn. Clerk; of Norwood, SA; b. Adelaide, 25 Feb 1920.
[4] Maj H. G. M. Rosevear, MM, SX8264. (1st AIF: L-Cpl 12 Bn 1916-18.) 2/3 Pnr Bn. Cost accountant; of Black Forest, SA; b. Launceston, Tas, 6 Jun 1900. When he enlisted under the name of H. G. Brown in 1916 Rosevear gave his year of birth as 1895.
[5] This procedure was necessary to avoid holding the transport columns stationary in the lanes through the minefields farther forward.
[6] *Mud and Sand*, p. 309, the official history of the 2/3rd Pioneer Battalion.

There we shall leave the 2/3rd Pioneer Battalion—the right flank of the Eighth Army—with its thin barrier of two companies reaching out for about a mile across the saltmarsh to the north and precariously hinged on its third company at Barrel Hill—the brittle wedge cutting off all the Axis forces in the coast sector; there for the time being we shall leave them while we see what was happening on "the other side of the hill".

On the morning after the 26th Brigade's previous northward attack Rommel had concluded that it would not be possible to hold the El Alamein position indefinitely and had therefore given instructions for preparations to be made for a withdrawal to Fuka. By the evening of 30th October reconnaissances and preliminary arrangements had been made. Rommel expected a British break-through thrust at any moment. His plan was to meet and delay it with his armoured and mobile forces so as to cover the withdrawal of his infantry next night. By the evening of the 30th his petrol supplies had improved, so he then issued orders to the *21st Armoured Division*, which had been dug in to the west of the XXX Corps sector, that it was to become mobile next morning and hand over to the *Trieste Division*.

In forming its second defence line the *90th Light* had disposed the *361st Regiment* from the coast to the main road inclusive and the *200th Regiment* south of the road in front (and west of) the 2/15th Battalion. In the first phase of the operations on the night of the 30th-31st the Australian attack came in near the junction of the right flank of the *125th Regiment* (*164th Light Division*) and the left flank of the *361st Regiment* (*90th Light Division*) to which most of the prisoners taken by the 2/32nd Battalion belonged. Next the main weight of the Australian attack (i.e. by the 2/24th and 2/48th Battalions) fell on the *125th Regiment's* left flank; the *357th Italian Light Artillery Regiment* was overrun and all but one of its guns lost. Hearing and glimpsing the carriers bringing supplies to the 26th Brigade, the Germans reported and their command believed that a "strong force of British armour" had participated in the attack.[7] The Australian attack to the coast had driven a wedge which cut off the *125th Regiment* in the coast sector.

In the morning further reports reached Rommel that 30 British tanks had reached the main road and were attacking the *361st Regiment's* left flank. From the minaret of the Sidi Abd el Rahman mosque, which the Germans used as an artillery observation post, a dress-circle view could be obtained of the coast sector where the Australians had dug in. "I immediately drove up to Sidi Abd el Rahman," wrote Rommel, "and set up my command post east of the mosque." Rommel ordered an attack on the wedge to be made by the *21st Armoured* and *90th Light Divisions* and gave the command of the operation to General von Thoma. The attack would not be able to start until the *21st Armoured* had completed handing over to the *Trieste Division*.

A situation map showing the 9th Division's dispositions at dawn on the 31st, if one could then have been correctly drawn from the scanty information available, would have presented a vastly (and gravely) different picture from that expected to be seen on completion of the operation. The coast road was not open nor were the well-developed defences north and south of it cleared. It is strange that it could have been expected that they would be. The overprint map and all other information had given clear warning that the defences about the road were formidable. There are some indications that a belief had been

---

[7] German reports are often misread because the German word "Panzerkraftwagen" and its abbreviation are always translated as "tank" or "tanks" whereas the literal translation is the English term "armoured fighting vehicle(s)" which compendiously included carriers and the abbreviation for which—AFV—was in common use by the British.

nurtured that the enemy was thinning out and might by then have been demoralised; but if there was some evidence to that effect there was more plain evidence to the contrary. A plausible explanation but not a sound exculpation later given for Morshead's and the divisional staff's underrating of the enemy defence was that the enemy had been inspirited to put up an unexpectedly strong opposition because the diversionary operations mounted by the 24th Brigade on the night on which the offensive opened had misled the enemy troops there into believing that by standing fast they had succeeded in throwing back a full-scale attack; but in the preceding days many Germans not so inspirited had displayed plenty of fight. "Crumbling" had indeed been continued and relentless pressure on the enemy maintained; at the cost, however, of crumbling two fine battalions, than which there were none better—British or German—in Africa, nor probably in the world.

Neither at Morshead's headquarters, nor at Whitehead's below the forward slopes of Trig 29, could an accurate picture be formed that morning of the situation to the north, where four weak battalions were soon to face a fiery ordeal. South of the 2/3rd Pioneer Battalion's outstretched arm was the 2/32nd Battalion, holding a line from the road at Barrel Hill south across the railway (disposed with about half the battalion on each side of the railway), beyond the left flank of which there was a gap of about a mile to the 2/15th Battalion. Behind the right of the 2/32nd Battalion's positions south of the railway was the little band of men comprising the 2/48th Battalion, dug in facing north and east, with one post just north of the railway, and behind the left positions of the 2/32nd was the likewise depleted 2/24th in two localities about 200 yards apart. Major Gebhardt had come forward to the 2/24th at first light to take command.

Dawn revealed that an enemy locality had been penetrated and there were many isolated pockets which were quickly mopped up. The 2/32nd Battalion took some 200 prisoners. Major Rosevear's company of the Pioneers, which found itself in the midst of an enemy position, took 47.

The two isolated companies of the 2/3rd Pioneer Battalion received the enemy's first attention. Captain Stevens' company, holding no ground of vantage, and under observation from the enemy on the sand-dunes, was in the worst position. Stevens sent a patrol of 17 under Lieutenant Dunn[8] to some dunes out in front to enfilade the enemy from the flank. Some of the men were cut down by fire. Lieutenant Dunn extricated the patrol but not before all the N.C.O's had been killed or wounded, and more casualties were suffered as they came out. Dunn was badly hit and Captain Owens went out and carried him back. Only four out of the 17 returned unwounded. Stevens' company was pinned down, any move attracting fire, until about 10.30 a.m. when the fire ceased and a German officer approached under a white flag and advised surrender, as the alternative to annihilation. He was told, "If you want us, come and get us";

---

[8] Capt R. L. Dunn, NX46688; 2/3 Pnr Bn. Business manager; of Newcastle, NSW; b. Richmond, Vic, 17 Jun 1915.

some other remarks not in the best taste were also addressed to the envoy. After he had withdrawn the Germans completed the company's encirclement and continued to lacerate it with fire throughout the morning.

Greater efforts were being made by the enemy to force the issue against the men in the Saucer to the south of Stevens' and Owens' companies, but the Australians had meanwhile received an important reinforcement. In the early hours of the morning the 40th R.T.R. (Lieut-Colonel J. L. T. Finigan) less one squadron had been slowly moving northward, as sappers cleared a path for them, behind the enemy's original front-wire, by the track past the Fig Orchard which ran north to the railway along the western edge of Thompson's Post. About dawn, and not without mishaps, Finigan brought his squadron past Thompson's Post and up to the 2/48th Battalion, by which time he had received orders that he was to support that battalion. There is some evidence that the purport of Finigan's assignment was that Hammer and he should organise an attack on Thompson's Post. Be that as it may, Finigan carried out to the letter his orders to support Hammer's battalion and his tanks stayed beside the 2/48th through the day, two troops—no more had space for manoeuvre between the minefields—going into hull-down positions north of the railway.

The first German counter-attack was made about 11.30 a.m. Fifteen German Mark III and Mark IV tanks advanced north of the road and swung in between the road and railway near the Barrel track while infantry advanced on their right flank. The Rhodesians' guns and the Valentines engaged them. The German tanks probably expected a "walk-over" and panic but met strong fire and steady defence and soon withdrew. The infantry attack was smashed by artillery and other fire.

Meanwhile Stevens' company of the Pioneers had become more closely invested and had exhausted its ammunition stocks. Stevens visited Owens and between them preliminary arrangements for a withdrawal were made. Owens had telephone communication with Gallasch and sought authority for the withdrawal but Gallasch refused. About that time, soon after midday, and before Stevens had returned to his company, some German light tanks went over to help their infantry subdue Stevens' unreasoning men, putting down a smoke screen to cover their advance. The men tried to extricate themselves; some got away, by which time Gallasch had authorised their withdrawal, but others were captured. In the meantime Owens had sent back a depleted platoon with the wounded, but remained in his position with the other two platoons and the headquarters of the other company. Later this group was in turn attacked by the tanks, which overran the positions, grinding them in; most were taken prisoner. Owens, who had at first eluded the enemy, went back to care for a wounded sergeant and was captured. Stevens, by feigning to be dead all day, escaped later in the night. The Germans soon freed the Pioneers' German prisoners and made their captors captive. The count at the end of the day showed three officers and 43 others to be missing. Rosevear's company in front of the ridge next came under fire and attack, but meanwhile Major

Copeland had redisposed the 6-pounders of the 2/3rd Anti-Tank Regiment and Lieutenant Kessell's troop went into positions covering Barrel Hill. In this action against the 2/3rd Pioneers there were several notable instances of chivalrous consideration given by the Germans in withholding fire from men helping or carrying wounded.

The main attack on the Saucer was made in the early afternoon, again coming in from the northern side of the ridge. While the 6-pounders engaged the German tanks to the north, Valentine tanks south of the railway came forward to meet them. Two of the Rhodesian 6-pounders were put out of action but other Rhodesian guns knocked out four German tanks. The German tanks fought their way forward, knocking out many Valentines, and overran Captain Eacott's company of the 2/32nd Battalion, grinding in the infantry positions and taking prisoner most of the company's survivors. During the action the enemy attempted to bring forward an 88-mm gun but it was knocked out by an anti-tank gun and the trailer set alight.[9] On each side several tanks were knocked out (but more British than German) and a Valentine and a German Mark III were in flames. In this action an anti-tank gun of the 2/3rd Regiment was put out of action. All the crew were killed or wounded. Of the three wounded Gunner Schwebel[1] was the least disabled, though severely injured in arms and legs. Schwebel managed to get the other two wounded men across to the blockhouse. Typifying the spirit of the defence, he returned to the gun and had it ready to fire before the next attack. It was then hit again, whereupon Schwebel seized a Bren gun and fought with the infantry.[2]

It was decided to bring in the reserve squadron of the 40th R.T.R. The squadron arrived at Windeyer's headquarters. Captain Williams[3] then guided the tanks forward under fire, at first in a jeep and later on foot, to the 2/15th Battalion, whence most went on. Soon afterwards, however, the Valentines were withdrawn from the Saucer. No other comment need be made on the performance of the commanders and crews of the Valentine tanks in the fighting on 31st October than that of the historian of the 2/48th Battalion, which had earned the right to judge how others fought: "The courage of these men," he wrote, "made their action one of the most magnificent of the war."

About 4 p.m. the German tanks attacked again from the north but eight were stopped by gunfire and as the day ended they withdrew. They had, however, achieved part of their object by pushing the British off the road, for in a lull in the fighting towards 5 p.m. Rosevear's company, isolated by the earlier break-through behind them, was withdrawn. That left the international blockhouse with its tireless workers in effect in a no-man's land. From it the enemy had permitted casualties to be evacuated

---

[9] This gun was later taken back to Australia.
[1] Gnr A. H. Schwebel, NX52317; 2/3 A-Tk Regt. Mechanic's assistant; of Canley Vale, NSW; b. Erskineville, NSW, 19 Jan 1923.
[2] Next day Schwebel carried a wounded man 500 yards to the dressing station. He tried to return to his post but was detained when it was found that a bullet had passed through his head.
[3] Lt-Col B. Williams, MC, QX6200. 2/15 Bn; 20 Bde 1941-42; various staff and air liaison appointments 1942-45. Traveller and salesman; of Hamilton, Qld; b. Sandgate, Qld, 14 Mar 1914.

throughout the day. When darkness fell the Pioneers reorganised and dug in close to the railway embankment on its south side. In the attacks on the Saucer that day, the Germans had repeatedly brought up infantry with their tanks but on each occasion the concentrated gunfire of the defence had dispersed the infantry.

Rommel had ordered the *Africa Corps* to attack between the road and railway so as to release the *125th Regiment*, now practically cut off by the Australian thrust northward. The *Africa Corps* formed a battle group comprising about 15 tanks plus self-propelled guns, under Major Pfeiffer. It was to move to Sidi Abd el Rahman by 11 a.m. and thrust along or south of the railway. Later Rommel ordered that as the Australians had crossed the railway behind the *125th Regiment* Pfeiffer was to attack north of the line to relieve it.

A counter-attack in the early morning by two companies of infantry of the *361st Regiment* was halted by tank and infantry fire but the counter-attack by the Pfeiffer Group and *361st Regiment*, which opened in the early afternoon, at first succeeded swiftly, 150 prisoners being taken and 18 tanks destroyed. Farther on the advance was halted by the defenders' tanks and infantry. By 5.15 the *90th Light Division* reported contact with the *125th Regiment* on the coast but slow progress along the railway. By 7 p.m. the counter-attack had been halted. The *580th Reconnaissance Unit* was keeping the corridor to the *125th* open on the coast; but there was no contact with it along road and railway and the *361st Regiment*, pinned down by the British artillery fire directed from observation posts overlooking its whole area, could not reorganise until darkness fell.

Although contact with the *125th Regiment* had been effected along the sand-dunes near the sea, the British salient at Barrel Hill still posed a threat that they might again be cut off and therefore beyond reach if a quick withdrawal should become necessary when the British launched their unexpectedly delayed breakthrough attack.

It was not until late afternoon that it was known at Morshead's headquarters just how weak the depleted battalions at the Saucer had become. It then became obvious that their strength was insufficient to maintain the defence of the place against a violently reacting enemy, but to have given up the ground seized would have accorded neither with the army commander's plan nor with Morshead's character. The relief of the 26th Brigade by the 24th as previously contemplated would have involved, if all had gone according to plan, merely a change-over between battalions which would then have been alongside each other; a relief at the Saucer, the most hotly contested ground on the whole front, where an attack might well occur while units were changing over, was another matter. But Morshead at once decided that it must take place. The orders were issued about 7.30 p.m. The relief, effected at night with transport using circuitous routes, was completed by 3.30 a.m., which reflected some credit on the division's standard of staff work and training. The exhausted enemy did not attack while it was proceeding.

Brigadier Godfrey took over command of units in the Saucer from Brigadier Whitehead. The 2/28th Battalion—which Lieut-Colonel Loughrey had rebuilt after the Ruin Ridge disaster and moulded in so short a time into a first-rate combatant unit—relieved the 2/24th Battalion; the 2/43rd Battalion (Lieut-Colonel Wain) relieved the 2/48th.

The 2/32nd (now back in its own brigade) and the 2/3rd Pioneers were not relieved. Brigadier Godfrey established his command post in the Saucer.

The changes in dispositions that had been made in the Saucer under pressure of attack during the afternoon had not been known when the relief orders were issued, so that the fresh battalions arriving there by night found their instructions inapplicable and the situation confused. Colonel Loughrey acted with great vigour in consulting other commanders and having his companies quickly disposed, by his own siting, in tenable positions interlocking with the other units' defences. The improvised dispositions adopted in the dark in a precarious situation on unreconnoitred ground were—in the words of a unit historian—"the ultimate in unorthodoxy",[4] but were to be proved next day and found not greatly wanting by the ultimate test of severest attack. The defended locality's front-line (facing west) comprised one company of the 2/43rd astride the main road, then on its left two companies of the 2/28th between road and railway, then on the left of the railway the depleted 2/32nd Battalion, holding a flank out towards the 2/15th defences; the other three companies of the 2/43rd were in depth behind the two forward companies of the 2/28th, and the other two companies of the 2/28th were in depth behind the 2/32nd Battalion. Farther still to the left was the 2/3rd Pioneer Battalion. The 2/43rd faced east and north (with its northern flank platoon on Barrel Hill), the 2/28th and 2/32nd northwest and west and south-west. Thus it was astride the road itself that the defence had least depth. The men dug themselves in as best they could but the ground was in many places unyielding nor had they any head cover.

The anti-tank defence was improved by disposing a troop of the 12th Battery's guns with the 2/15th to cover the gap between that unit and the 2/32nd. (It was further strengthened next day when the reserve troop of the Rhodesian Battery was driven in helter-skelter and established south of the railway as an attack was imminent.) A minefield had been laid on the north-west side and the front was enfiladed from the 2/15th positions by machine-guns also brought forward during the night.

The survivors of the 2/24th and 2/48th, who had suffered more casualties during the day, were taken back to the original front-line on the coast sector (the defences opposite to which were still occupied by the enemy) to sleep the night and muster next morning at their saddest rollcalls ever.

Dawn on Sunday 1st November in the Saucer revealed to the incomers numerous enemy all around them, at distances only 800 to 1,000 yards away. The Germans were doubtless no less surprised than the Australians at what daylight revealed.

The enemy promptly opened fire with small arms, mortars, 88-mm guns firing airburst shells, and a variety of field guns. Most of the fire came from the west and north-west but some from the north-east and south-east. An artillery duel soon developed in which, of course, the Germans fared

---

[4] P. Masel, *The Second 28th*, p. 108.

worst, not only because they had fewer guns but because those they had were alarmingly short of ammunition. However it was the enemy's turn next, it seemed, when at 8.40 a.m. 30 German dive bombers, escorted by 15 fighters, were seen making for the Australian position; but they

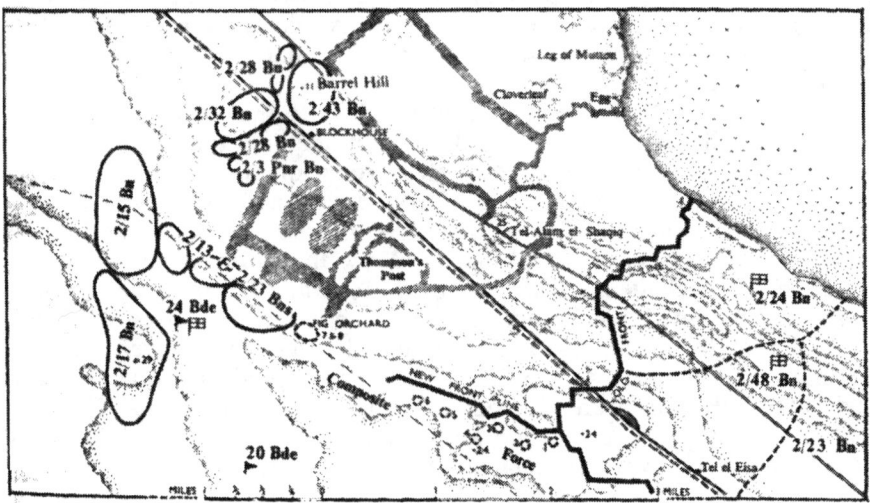

Dawn, 1st November

were intercepted by British and American fighters and jettisoned their bombs on their own troops. Seven were shot down. The enemy's infantry were seen assembling about 10 a.m. and at the same time it was reported that the British Intelligence service had intercepted a message from Field Marshal Rommel ordering the *21st Armoured* and *90th Light Divisions* to attack the Barrel Hill salient along the axis of the road and railway. The terms of the message indicated that Rommel thought only one strongpoint remained, which would not withstand a resolute attack. Morshead drove down to the tempestuous Saucer and conferred there with Brigadier Godfrey.

Later in the morning more troops were seen moving south-east from Sidi Rahman. Against this dangerous British outpost presumed to be so weakly held the Germans at midday opened an attack which they were to sustain and press without much avail throughout that long day and into the night with a succession of determined and most desperate attempts to fulfil their commander's injunction to destroy it. The brunt of the attacks came in between the road and railway on the 2/43rd and 2/28th Battalions, but the 2/32nd were also in the fire fight and, good neighbours as they were, judged it better to give than to receive. Their mortars were busy throughout the afternoon and very effective.

The first attack, made in the late forenoon by about a battalion and a half of infantry in conjunction with numerous tanks, was supported by sustained artillery, mortar and machine-gun fire. At least eight 88-mm guns were firing air-burst over the Australians. Both then and throughout the day the number of tanks employed could seldom be estimated because of the dust and smoke. As the assault was coming in, the enemy was attacked by a "football team" of bombers answering a call from the division. At 12.45 six tanks were closing in on the 2/43rd from the north-west. By 1.25 one platoon of the north-east company had been thrust off Barrel Hill but the position was regained by prompt counter-attack. Anti-tank fire had knocked out three German tanks and one 88-mm gun north of the 2/43rd.

In front of the 2/28th tanks advanced close to the forward companies, went into hull-down positions and fired mainly on the anti-tank guns. All four guns of Lieutenant Kessell's troop of the 2/3rd Anti-Tank Regiment were knocked out. Soon 12 6-pounders and two 2-pounders had been put out of action. The forward troops who, in the opinion of the battalion's diarist, were "not impressed by the close proximity of the tanks" met the challenge with sustained, accurate fire from all weapons. Casualties mounted but about 2.30 p.m. the German tanks apparently realised that their infantry could not get through and backed out. The Germans had singled out the Rhodesians for special attention. Eight of their anti-tank guns were put out of action. In a lull Major Copeland sent Lieutenant Wallder's troop across the railway to replace them and Wallder managed to get his guns into action under the enemy's observation and fire.

At 3.25 p.m. the enemy resumed the tank and infantry attack against the 2/43rd and 2/28th. This assault came in from the northern side and was pressed home against the north-west company of the 2/43rd commanded by Captain Hare, overrunning a platoon on Barrel Hill, which was captured. Hare was killed. Sergeant Joy, whose platoon had been partly overrun, reorganised his men and regained all the lost positions but one and eventually the enemy withdrew. On the 2/28th's front the attack had fallen mainly on Captain Taylor's company and Captain Newbery's,[5] both of whom proved inspiring leaders. The 2/28th had no artillery Forward Observation Officer nor line communication to the rear and therefore the artillery fire could not be directed to best effect. Some ground was given up but the attack was withstood and the forward companies held on.

Some of the German tanks pushed on past the Australian position down the road to the east towards Thompson's Post. Later—about 3.50 p.m.— 27 tanks were observed north of Thompson's Post. At the same time enemy infantry began forming up astride the road and railway about a mile or so to the west of the Australian positions, but were effectively shelled. The enemy next began probing, apparently seeking weak spots, after which an advance against the 2/28th was made by infantry riding on tanks and with several self-propelled guns coming forward to support, but the German infantry were quickly persuaded by accurate Australian fire to go to ground. Two self-propelled guns were soon knocked out.

---

[5] Brig J. C. Newbery, CBE, ED, WX3391; 2/28 Bn. Chartered accountant; of Perth, WA; b. Perth, 22 Jul 1911.

By 5 p.m. the enemy appeared to have accepted failure of that attack but half an hour later tanks and infantry formed up to assault from the east while from the other side about 100 infantry advanced with determination between the road and railway. These were halted by steady fire and the attack from the east did not develop.

From about 7.15 p.m. brigade tactical headquarters was shelled continuously for about half an hour. Eventually it received a direct hit which mortally wounded Brigadier Godfrey, wounded Lieut-Colonel Risson, the chief engineer of the division, killed Major Copeland of the 9th Anti-Tank Battery and Captain Bishop[6] of the brigade staff, mortally wounded Major Trenwith[7] and wounded Major Carter[8] (both of the artillery). The brigade major, Major Jackson, took charge and kept the headquarters operating.

At dusk, adopting the traditional German tactic of advancing out of the setting sun, tanks and infantry half concealed by dust and smoke attacked from the west while a simultaneous thrust was made from the north-east; covering fire was given from the ground seized on Barrel Hill. The force attacking from the north-east comprised at least three tanks and 15 lorry-loads of infantry. Again the attacks failed to penetrate the defensive fire.

The German onslaught continued after dark. An assault supported by an artillery bombardment was made at 8.30 p.m. and withstood, but the fire fight continued. Colonel Evans, appointed to take over the command of the brigade, arrived at 9.30 p.m. Soon afterwards all line communication to the Saucer and throughout most of the division was cut by British tanks moving forward through the divisional area. Still the fire continued to rage in the Saucer.[9] Before it died down at 2.30 a.m. next morning an intense British gun barrage had opened up farther south. Operation SUPERCHARGE had begun.

The 20th Brigade was harassed by shelling throughout the 1st. When the German attack opened at midday the 2/15th, now commanded by Major Grace, was heavily shelled and the other battalions were also under intermittent fire. In the 2/17th an outstanding company commander, Captain McMaster, was mortally wounded.

On the afternoon of 1st November Colonel Macarthur-Onslow of the composite force had been warned to send machine-guns, anti-tank guns and two platoons of Pioneers to strengthen the right flank of the 2/43rd between the railway and the main road. The thin-skinned vehicles could not get through in daylight. When Captain Williams[1] (2/2nd Machine Gun Battalion) reached the 2/43rd, Colonel Wain told him that as a result of the counter-attacks his battalion and the 2/28th were in so

---

[6] Capt K. E. Bishop, SX3713. HQ 9 Div and 24 Bde. Regular soldier; of Rosewater Gardens, SA; b. Mile End, SA, 25 Oct 1916. Killed in action 1 Nov 1942.
[7] Maj R. G. Trenwith, VX13679; 2/12 Fd Regt. Electrical engineer; of Oakleigh, Vic; b. Richmond, Vic, 8 May 1910. Died of wounds 1 Nov 1942.
[8] Maj A. A. C. Carter, DSO, VX13696; 2/12 Fd Regt. Technician; of Balwyn, Vic; b. Maidenhead, England, 12 Apr 1899.
[9] "While it was usual at all times for some lines to be out from shell fire or traffic, notwithstanding heroic work by linesmen," says the brigade report, "this was the first time when all lines, including the line to division and all laterals, were cut."
[1] Maj E. C. Williams, QX6271. 2/2 MG Bn; DAQMG 9 Div 1945. Oil company representative; of Rockhampton, Qld; b. Atherton, Qld, 26 Aug 1916.

confined an area that it was not advisable to bring so large a force forward; instead the detachment was sited in support between both battalions. It reached its position at 3.30 a.m. on the 2nd.

During the rest of the night of the 1st-2nd the battalions of the 24th Brigade were reorganised so as to give each battalion more room and to bring a reserve battalion back into a position in depth. The 2/43rd was now north of the railway with the composite force detachment to the east, the 2/32nd south of the railway with the 2/28th to the east. The 2/3rd Pioneers were on the left of the 2/32nd and linked with the 2/15th.

Throughout that fiery first day of November the infantry had received formidable support from the Desert Air Force, though targets were hard to find because of the dispersal of the enemy's vehicles. Time and again the "football teams" of 19 bombers flew over in immaculate formation for pattern bombing and came back again and again, though a number were shot down. Fourteen attacks were made in the sector.

Stark evidence of the severity of the fighting was found next day when a patrol of the 2/32nd Battalion counted 200 enemy dead in front of that battalion's positions. The saltmarsh beyond Barrel Hill was so closely pock-marked with shell holes that it would have been difficult to find a square yard that had not been cratered.

In the fighting in that area from 30th October to 2nd November the four battalions of the 24th Brigade had 487 casualties, most of which were received before Operation SUPERCHARGE began. The 2/43rd had 43 killed (and 7 missing), the 2/32nd 21, the 2/28th 13 (and 10 missing), the 2/3rd Pioneers 14 (and 46 missing).

Thus had the 9th Division carried out its "crumbling" mandate to attack northwards and to draw into the northern sector and upon itself as much of the enemy's fighting strength as possible while the Eighth Army was making its preparations for SUPERCHARGE. That was the division's contribution to the final break-out.

If SUPERCHARGE had been launched a little farther south so as to miss entirely the right flank of the *90th Light Division,* which had been disposed opposite the 9th Australian Division, very few German troops other than of the armoured formations would have been encountered in the break-out. Merely to have drawn into, or kept in, the northern sector the 88-mm guns that were employed against the 24th Brigade all day on the 1st and to have destroyed two of them was in itself a tangible contribution to victory in the battle, for these guns, of which the enemy had not many, were his only effective artillery against the Sherman tanks.

Rommel had ordered a resumption of the counter-attack by parts of the *21st Armoured* and *90th Light Divisions* on the 1st to re-establish contact with the *125th Regiment* and *X Bersaglieri* in the coast sector. It was to open at 11 a.m. and Point 24,[2] 10 kilometres south-east of Abd el Rahman, between the road and railway, was the objective. The *125th Regiment* was to prepare to withdraw some time from the night of the 1st-2nd onwards. The *90th Division* reported, however,

---

[2] Ring Contour 25, east-north-east of Thompson's Post, on which Sergeant Kibby had led the final assault.

that Point 24 was still in German hands. The counter-attack succeeded in thrusting the enemy back over the railway and gaining contact with the *125th Regiment* there. The forward troops of the *90th Light* were then along the railway facing south with the right flank of the *125th* on their left.

The plan for Operation SUPERCHARGE required the XXX Corps to launch an infantry attack to punch a corridor through the enemy defences to the west of the northern end of the original bridgehead. Through the corridor X Corps was to pass an armoured force into open country beyond, fighting its way forward if necessary.

The task of XXX Corps was to attack from the Tel el Eisa area on a front of some 4,000 yards and penetrate westward to a depth of 6,000 yards whence armoured and infantry patrols would thrust farther west to cover the break-out of the armoured divisions. In the van of the X Corps, armoured cars were to be launched through the bridgehead before dawn and fan out north-west, west, south-west and south, destroying everything they met. The first objective of the armoured thrust of X Corps was to be the general area Point 46-Tel el Aqqaqir—the old "Skinflint" line, the original objective of X Corps for the morning after the offensive opened.

It will be clearly understood (said Montgomery's directive) that should 30 Corps not succeed in reaching the final objective . . . the *armoured divisions of 10 Corps will fight their way to the first objective.*

The XXX Corps was to hold the 2nd New Zealand Division in readiness to take over the area of X Corps' first objective so as to free the X Corps for offensive operations against the enemy's armour or for a movement north-west towards Ghazal.

Determined leadership will be vital (said Montgomery's order); complete faith in the plan, and its success, will be vital; there must be no doubters; risks must be accepted freely; there must be no "bellyaching".

General Freyberg, as already mentioned, had been given the command of the infantry break-out operation, using his own New Zealand division but employing two British brigades and his Maori battalion as the infantry. On the right the 28th (Maori) Battalion was placed under the command of the 151st Brigade to take a suspected enemy position beyond Trig 29 and link with the 20th Australian Brigade to the north-east. The break-through was then to be made by the 151st Brigade on the right and the 152nd on the left, each with a regiment of tanks under command. The 9th Armoured Brigade, also under Freyberg's command, was to pass through the infantry objective, continue the advance for some 2,000 yards and break into the enemy's defences about the Rahman track. The 1st Armoured Division, now including the 2nd and 8th Armoured Brigades and 7th Motor Brigade, was to follow up the 9th Armoured Brigade's attack, cross the Rahman track and defeat the enemy's armour. The 51st Highland Division was to attack with one battalion on the left flank of the 2nd New Zealand and take Point 32. The attack was to be supported by 13 field regiments and 3 medium regiments. On the eve of battle the 1st Armoured Division had 271 fit tanks, the 9th Armoured Brigade 132, the 23rd Armoured Brigade 111, the 7th Armoured Division (less the 4th Light Armoured Brigade, now detached) 84; the 7th Armoured Division was not participating in the thrust. The 4th Light Armoured Brigade had 74 (including 53 Stuarts).

The strengths of the enemy formations on the eve of SUPERCHARGE were believed to be as follows: *15th Armoured Division,* 6,000 men, 25 tanks; *21st Armoured Division,* 8,000 men, 125 tanks; *164th Division,* 6,800 men; *90th Division,* 7,800 men; *101st (Trieste) Division,* 4,600 men, 30 tanks; *102nd (Trento) Division,* 2,400 men; *132nd (Ariete) Division,* 4,300 men, 140 tanks; *133rd (Littorio) Division,* 4,200 men, 60 tanks.

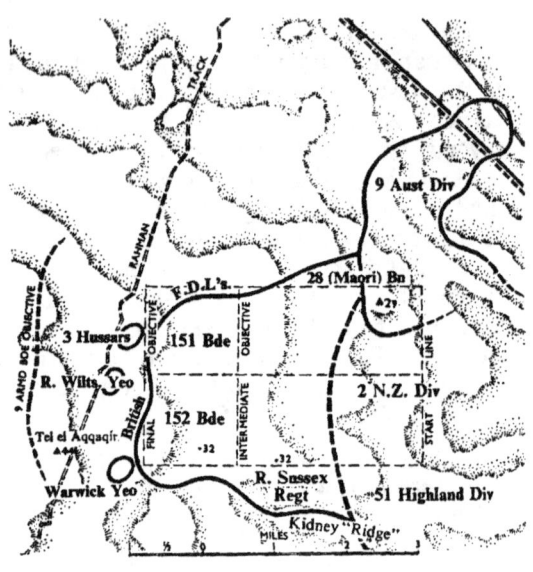

Supercharge, 2nd November

German records give the numbers of tanks available on 1st November as: *15th Armoured,* 56; *21st Armoured,* 49; *Trieste,* 27; *Ariete,* 124; *Littorio,* 38. The enemy therefore had 105 German tanks and 189 Italian with which to oppose the 403 tanks of the 1st Armoured Division and 9th Armoured Brigade which would be employed initially in the break-out.

A force of 87 bombers opened the bombardment. At 9.15 p.m. they attacked targets round Tel el Aqqaqir, Sidi Abd el Rahman and Ghazal. There were big explosions and fires; later it was learnt that at *Africa Corps* headquarters the signals system had been put out of action.

The attacking battalions of the 151st and 152nd Brigades moved from the start-line on time at 1.5 a.m. on the 2nd with the 8th and 50th R.T.R. close behind. The supporting barrage was fired by 192 guns in depth on a front of 4,000 yards, and an additional 168 guns shelled positions in front and on the flanks. The 152nd Brigade on the left took its objectives by 3.44 a.m., on time, but the 151st met strong opposition and it was 5.53 before it was able to report with certainty that it was on the final objective. The Maori battalion also had taken its objective—the strong-point west of Trig 29—after hard fighting, and on the left flank the 2/Sussex and 5/Sussex had taken the enemy strong-point "Woodcock" on Kidney Ridge.

By the time the three armoured regiments of the 9th Armoured Brigade had reached the infantry objectives, however, their strength had been reduced from a total of 132 tanks to 94. The next phase of the 9th Armoured Brigade's advance was postponed half an hour to 6.15 because one regiment arrived late, having been delayed by enemy action on the way and by various other troubles. The 3rd Hussars were to attack on the right, the Royal Wiltshire Yeomanry in the centre, and the Warwickshire Yeomanry on the left. The 2nd Armoured Brigade of the 1st Armoured Division would be coming up behind to follow through.

The battles fought that day by the armoured regiments debouching from the SUPERCHARGE bridgehead were not great field victories, but they were the finally decisive engagements of the Eighth Army's offensive. Not for two days did the enemy front break; but that it would eventually break had been rendered certain by the end of the day. That was not clear then, to the men who fought the actions, as it is today. Some experienced defeat, others felt baffled, not seeing beyond the rim.

If the British armour owed any battle debts to the New Zealand infantry, the 9th Armoured Brigade paid them dearly and liberally that morning in heroism and in blood. Directed by the Eighth Army's plan and exhorted by their own resolute commander to proceed along a course which (to snatch another's phrase soon to be quoted) led only to victory or death, they strove for a victory that was not to be theirs. All three regiments of the brigade attacked intrepidly and vigorously. At first they carried all before them.

The 3rd Hussars on the right, who had to advance one mile and three-quarters to a position west of the Rahman track, captured many prisoners and guns on the way but in the day's first light were met by close-range anti-tank fire near the Rahman track and took heavy punishment. The Wiltshire Yeomanry in the centre succeeded in crossing the Rahman track before dawn but came under fire from all sides when it became light. Their tanks—mainly Crusaders mounting only 2-pounders—charged and overcame many guns and infantry positions but were soon shot to pieces by other guns more deeply sited and by a tank column of the *21st Armoured Division*. Soon the regiment was reduced to 9 tanks, its commanding officer, second-in-command and three squadron leaders having all been wounded. The Warwickshire Yeomanry on the left (who moved too far south) also ran into destructive gunfire short of their objective and were soon reduced to seven tanks. The three regiments had destroyed at least 35 enemy guns but of their 94 tanks 75 were lost that day, most before the arrival of the 2nd Armoured Brigade, in the van of the 1st Armoured Division. The 9th Armoured Brigade, for all its valour, had perforated and fractured the enemy gun-line but had not broken through it.

The Royal Dragoons (armoured cars) broke out into the open, got well behind the enemy's lines and began destroying dumps and vehicles and cutting telephone lines.

The 2nd Armoured Brigade arrived late after an advance of great difficulty and confusion—too late to help the 9th in its hour of greatest need or to sustain the momentum of its thrust and exploit it. The orders authorised and, if read as a literal and unequivocal command, enjoined that it should still follow the same path, but General Briggs and Brigadier Fisher decided to deploy to meet an enemy counter-attack between the front of the bridgehead and the Rahman track (except that Fisher insisted that his brigade was already across the track). In the end the fortunes of Eighth Army probably prospered more by the course they took than if they had fought their battle from the master's printed word. Though the 1st Armoured Division was not yet "astride the enemy's supply routes", it was near enough, and the enemy did attack in force in the late forenoon in the way Montgomery had planned from the outset. The battle continued through the day, and by nightfall it was believed that 66 enemy tanks had been knocked out—not an exaggerated claim like those made in CRUSADER, for in fact 77 German and 40 Italian tanks had been put out of action. The Axis forces could afford these losses less than the British their heavier losses. Still the enemy's front had not been broken open and most British commanders other than Montgomery were beginning to wonder how that could ever be done. The Eighth Army was not hitting Rommel for six, nor even penetrating his outfield to the boundary.

That morning Montgomery had ordered the creation of a new infantry reserve of four brigades comprising one brigade from each of the 2nd New Zealand, 4th Indian, 50th (Durham) and 51st Highland Divisions and the dispatch of the 7th Armoured Division from the southern to the northern front. Since the British armour had not yet fallen upon the enemy's rear, it was decided to strengthen the corridor at once and therefore to broaden it. The broadening was to be done mainly on the left (south) side and was to be effected by the 51st Highland Division. During the day the troops in the break-out corridor were reorganised so that the New Zealand division assumed responsibility north of the 299 Northing grid line and the 51st Division south of it. The South African division took over the 153rd Brigade's sector to enable that brigade to relieve the 151st Brigade, which went into reserve.

In the evening two southward attacks speedily mounted by the 51st Highland Division were successful. One was made by the 2/Seaforth Highlanders and the 50th R.T.R. and the other by the 133rd Brigade, the former against a defended locality on high ground almost two miles west of Kidney Ridge, the other against the area of the Snipe episode. No German forces were encountered (for which some credit can be given to the 9th Division) but 160 prisoners from the *Trieste Division* were taken at Snipe.

General Lumsden tackled the main problem of breaking through the enemy's gun-line by deciding to attack it with his infantry of the 7/Motor Brigade. His plan was to breach the gun-line on the Aqqaqir Ridge by forcing a gap with infantry north-east of Tel el Aqqaqir on a front of two miles, through which the 1st Armoured Division would advance about three miles and a half; then the 7th Armoured Division was to pass through on the morning of the 3rd to Ring Contour 45 and thence to the

(Imperial War Museum)

Positions of the 24th Brigade, west of Tel el Eisa, under enemy shell fire late in the afternoon of 1st November 1942.

(9th Division war diary)

A Sherman tank used during the Eighth Army offensive at El Alamein. This tank had received several hits and had retired because of a casualty in the crew.

(*Australian War Memorial*)

Scene of a decisive tank battle near the Blockhouse, west of Tel el Eisa. In the foreground are knocked-out British tanks; eighteen German tanks were accounted for in the same action.

(*Maj W. G. R. Hall*)

German 88-mm gun and tractor destroyed in the Trig 29 area, El Alamein, by fire from "F" Troop, 2/7th Field Regiment, on 28th October 1942.

(2/28 Bn war diary)

Abandoned German positions at Ring Contour 25 in the 9th Division's sector at El Alamein, November 1942.

(Australian War Memorial)

Transport moving in the wake of Rommel's retreating army in the Western Desert, 13th November 1942. In the foreground a captured truck transporting prisoners to the rear has bogged.

(Australian War Memorial)
The ceremonial parade of the 9th Division at Gaza Airport, 22nd December 1942. The divisional cavalry regiment was on the right of the line which extended for almost a mile.

(Australian War Memorial)
General Sir Harold Alexander took the salute as the men swung past the saluting base.

Ghazal railway station. Thus the movement was not to be an encircling one but still north-west, towards the coast and main road. The attack by the 7/Motor Brigade's three battalions was made at 1.15 a.m. on the 3rd but except on the left was only partially successful. The two battalions in the centre and on the right were withdrawn before dawn.

The daylight operations on the 3rd began with a break-through attempt by the 4th/6th South African Regiment's armoured cars, with which Montgomery had hoped to repeat the successes of the Royals, but they were unable to break out to the enemy's rear. The main tank thrust of the day was made south-westwards by the 8th Armoured Brigade but they clashed with the *Ariete Division* and were again halted by the enemy's well-sited 88-mm guns. Superficially the situation on the second day after SUPERCHARGE was like that on the second day after LIGHTFOOT. By the end of the day the 1st Armoured Division had lost another 26 tanks and was still blocked. There were a number of signs that the enemy was close to breaking point but the Eighth Army was also fairly near the end of its tether.

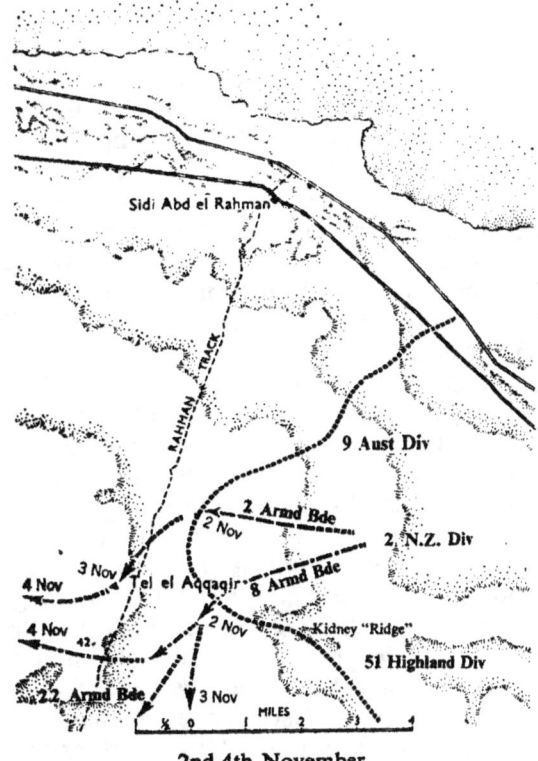

2nd-4th November

The launching of SUPERCHARGE had soon alleviated the pressure on the 24th Australian Infantry Brigade in the Saucer.

The enemy's first moves after daylight on the 2nd did not seem propitious. About 30 enemy tanks moved up on the right flank of the 2/15th Battalion just beyond range of its anti-tank guns—though one which strayed too close was hit—as if the intention was to strike at the right hinge of the SUPERCHARGE corridor where it adjoined the 20th Brigade, but the German tanks were engaged by the 8th Armoured Brigade on its move forward and later moved away. Soon afterwards Morshead went down to the Saucer and conferred there with Evans and Windeyer, perhaps having in mind the possibility of cutting off the enemy by the coast; but no further hard tasks were given to the tired battalions.

Otherwise, apart from sporadic well-directed shelling, the 2nd was a quiet day in the Australian sector, though more movement than usual was observed in the enemy positions to the north near the coast. When news of the initial success of the new offensive began to arrive, General Morshead ordered Brigadiers Whitehead and Evans to take strong offensive action to prevent the enemy in the coast sector from extricating themselves. So on the night of the 2nd-3rd the three battalions of the 24th Brigade each sent out a strong fighting patrol of two officers and about 40 men. The 2/43rd's was led by Captain Minocks and Lieutenant Perkins.[4] It was to penetrate beyond Barrel Hill, ascertain whether the enemy was thinning out, and take a prisoner so as to identify his unit. It went out at 9 p.m. behind a barrage. On reaching the crest of Barrel Hill the men were lashed with fire and forced back after losing four killed, including both officers, and 10 wounded. Four others were missing, believed killed.

The 2/32nd sent out two officers—Lieutenants Richards[5] and Hayes[6] —and about 40 men. They succeeded in bringing back four prisoners, but Richards was killed and Hayes wounded.

The 2/28th sent out two patrols, each about 20 strong. Lieutenant Boekeman's[7] patrol's tasks were to inflict casualties, take prisoners and discover the enemy's strength. It set out parallel to the railway line. After 150 yards the enemy sent up a flare and opened fire. The patrol pressed on another 450 yards and was then put to ground by machine-gun fire from directly ahead. Boekeman decided that the fire was too high, ordered a charge, and led the assault himself, shouting "Australia"; the others joined in. The attackers soon overcame five weapon-posts, bayoneting or shooting at least 15 Germans. Boekeman's men occupied the captured weapon-pits and thence grenaded a further line of pits. Machine-guns and a light gun then opened up from a position 100 yards to the rear and the patrol promptly withdrew, having had two men wounded.

The 2/28th's other patrol, led by Lieutenant Allan,[8] was less successful. Its task was to probe 2,000 yards north-west. At 1,200 yards the patrol reached the enemy's forward positions and pressed on under fire, overcoming posts and taking prisoners. After about 2,000 yards the centre of the patrol was halted by machine-gun fire and grenades but the men on both flanks went on and were soon out of touch. Allan was wounded by a grenade and ordered the men to get out. The patrol slowly withdrew in some confusion. Soon the Germans were closing in from all sides. Corporal Booth, himself wounded, ordered German prisoners to take turns

---

[4] Lt S. A. Perkins, WX5574; 2/43 Bn. Farmer; of Williams, WA; b. North Fremantle, WA, 14 Apr 1906. Killed in action 2 Nov 1942.
[5] Lt E. J. Richards, MM, WX2162; 2/32 Bn. Electrician; of Cannington, WA; b. West Perth, WA, 10 Feb 1918. Killed in action 2 Nov 1942.
[6] Lt E. D. P. Hayes, WX17030; 2/32 Bn. Farmer and grazier; of Toodyay, WA; b. Perth, WA, 18 Mar 1910.
[7] Lt R. Boekeman, MC, WX6837; 2/28 Bn. Tobacconist; of Quairading, WA; b. Katanning, WA, 30 Sep 1908.
[8] Lt R. T. Allan, WX6888; 2/28 Bn. Clerk; of Claremont, WA; b. Subiaco, WA, 9 Sep 1919.

carrying Allan back; but first one, then another, and then a third were hit by German fire and both Allan and Booth were captured.[9] When the patrol returned 10 men were missing.

Despite the vigour and valour with which these patrols penetrated deeply across the enemy's routes of withdrawal from his positions near

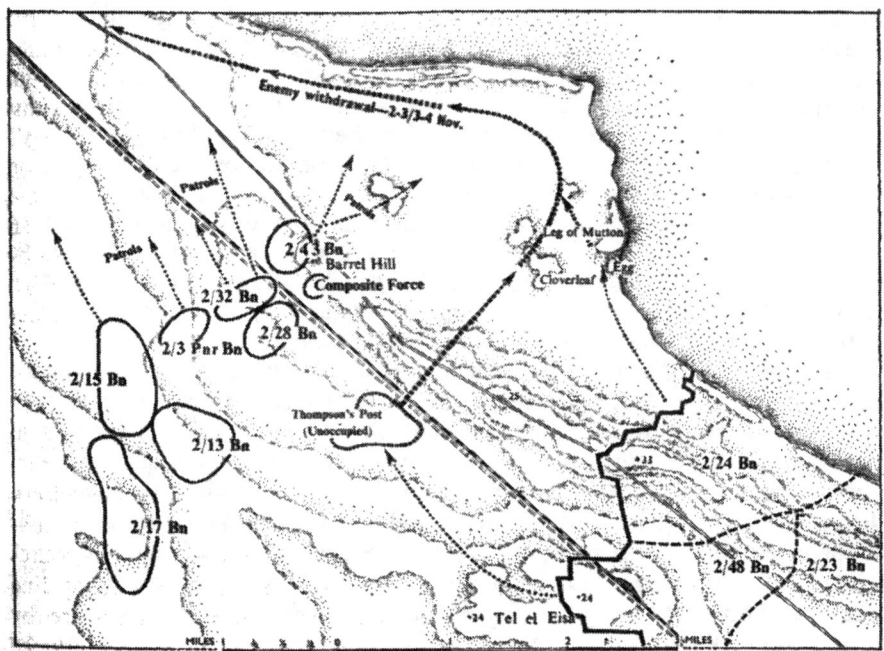

Dawn, 3rd November

the coast, their action alone could not have sufficed to disrupt an organised withdrawal. The sound of heavy vehicles could be heard through the night (2nd-3rd), which suggested that it was to protect the first stage of a withdrawal that the enemy had put up such a dogged opposition to penetration of his ground.

For the 9th Division the 3rd November, the second day after SUPER-CHARGE, was "a day of extensive daylight patrols, both in carriers and on foot". The 2/43rd patrolled north and north-east from Barrel Hill and found that the enemy had withdrawn. No enemy movement was seen between Barrel Hill and the coast. The enemy's forward defences seemed to be 1,300 yards west of the forward company of the 2/43rd. A German straggler who was captured said that part of the enemy's force had been withdrawn from the high ground near the road.

The 2/15th Battalion sent out a carrier patrol under Captain Yates north-west to find the enemy, and also exchanged fire with infantry posts about 2,000 yards forward. Later the battalion advanced its forward

---

[9] They were recovered at Mersa Matruh on 8th November.

positions about 1,000 yards so as to keep in contact with the enemy and link with the Maori battalion's front on the left.

The 2/17th reported that the enemy had abandoned his positions forward of the battalion during the night and withdrawn towards Abd el Rahman. The 3rd November, according to the battalion's diarist, was the first day since 23rd October on which the battalion had not been shelled; the strain had been eased and "all felt that the beginning of the enemy withdrawal or collapse had begun". The men were able to move about without danger and many went forward seeking souvenirs from German diggings. Carrier patrols ranged about and towed in enemy guns.

The Desert Air Force constantly bombed and strafed the enemy's vehicles and defences. That morning 93 tons of bombs were dropped on Tel el Aqqaqir area alone. In the day the Desert Air Force flew 1,094 sorties and dropped 199 tons of bombs; its fighter squadrons lost 16 aircraft. The enemy managed to turn on two dive-bombing raids, one by 20 and the other by 30 escorted Ju-87's. British fighters strafed the 2/43rd and 2/32nd in the afternoon; perhaps the fluidity of the battle farther south was some excuse. There were no casualties.

Interrogation of a prisoner revealed that all heavy weapons and anti-tank guns of the *125th Regiment* in the coast sector had already been withdrawn and it was anticipated that the enemy would endeavour to complete the extrication of his forces next night. Morshead issued instructions in the early afternoon which provided for further offensive operations. From the original front-line the divisional cavalry regiment with an attachment of engineers was to open up, and to clear of mines, all five routes (including the main road) that led westwards from the old front line between Thompson's Post and the sea, and was also to reconnoitre by day the enemy defences in that area. From the area of the Saucer attacks were to be made during the next night or early next morning on the enemy to the north-west—by the divisional cavalry north of the road and by the 24th Brigade and 40th R.T.R. south of the road.

By the end of 2nd November the German divisions were very weary and their strength in both tanks and infantry was dwindling alarmingly. Again the Italian armour and infantry had proved disappointing and, according to the *Africa Corps'* records, the *Littorio* and *Ariete Divisions* had begun to retreat.

Rommel decided on the 2nd that he should begin to withdraw to Fuka, which reconnaissance had confirmed to be a very suitable delaying or holding position. On the night of the 2nd-3rd he proposed to withdraw his *X Corps*, the *Ramcke Brigade* and *XXI Corps* to a line El Taqa-Qaret el Abd-Deir el Harra-Qatani. To the north the armoured divisions were to hold on a line from Deir el Murra to Sidi Abd el Rahman.

On the 3rd the mobile forces were to withdraw fighting to a line about half way from Rahman to Daba. After a further withdrawal the army would occupy the Fuka position. Infantry were to be trucked back to Fuka while the mobile forces formed a rearguard. It was evident, however, that there was now not enough transport to move all the infantry.

On the night of the 2nd-3rd and the morning of the 3rd preliminary moves for the Axis forces' withdrawal to a line about the Rahman track to Deir el Harra and thence to El Taqa were put in hand. The formations were warned to prepare for a further withdrawal. The transport of the infantry of *XXI Corps* to Fuka was ordered. Early in the afternoon, however, just after the withdrawal had been set in motion an order from Hitler arrived at Rommel's headquarters:

"It is with trusting confidence in your leadership and the courage of the German-Italian troops under your command that the German people and I are following the heroic struggle in Egypt. In the situation in which you find yourself there can be no other thought but to stand fast, yield not a yard of ground and throw every gun and every man into the battle. Considerable air force reinforcements are being sent to C.-in-C. South. The Duce and the Commando Supremo are also making the utmost efforts to send you the means to continue the fight. Your enemy, despite his superiority, must also be at the end of his strength. It would not be the first time in history that a strong will has triumphed over the bigger battalions. As to your troops, you can show them no other road than that to victory or death."

Immediately after this cheerful message had been received, the withdrawal orders were cancelled. Officers were posted on the coast road to stop the vehicles already moving west. All formations were ordered to defend their present positions. In some Italian units commanding officers experienced difficulty in reversing the direction of movement of their men, whose spirit had not been uplifted by the German leader's exhortation.

To Hitler's directive Rommel sent a frank reply:

"The Italian divisions and 1st Air Force Brigade in the southern sector have been ordered to shorten the line by withdrawing behind the line El Taqa-Bab el Qattara—south of Deir el Murra and defending this line to the last. The German divisions in the northern sector are very heavily engaged in the Deir el Murra-Sidi Abd el Rahman sector against a superior enemy force. All German troops that could possibly be raked up have been thrown into the fight. Casualties so far amount to 50 per cent of infantry, anti-tank and engineer units and about 40 per cent of artillery. Africa Corps now has 24 tanks. Of the Italian XX Corps, the Littorio Armoured Division and Trieste Motor Division are almost wiped out. The Ariete Armoured Division was brought up from the southern sector on the night 2nd-3rd November and committed in close cooperation with the Africa Corps. We will continue to do our utmost to retain command of the battlefield."

After unwillingly issuing these new orders Rommel sent off a staff officer to Hitler's headquarters to report that "if the Fuehrer's order were upheld, the final destruction of the German-Italian Army would be a matter of days only" and that they "had already suffered immense harm because of it".[1]

By noon on 3rd November Montgomery had decided to shift the main weight of the Eighth Army's attack from a direct approach in the north to an enveloping movement southwards from the SUPERCHARGE bridgehead, where the defences were expected to be weaker. The main defended localities on the Aqqaqir Ridge, about Tel el Aqqaqir and for 7,000 yards to the south, were to be seized by infantry. There the 7th Armoured Division (Major-General Harding) was to penetrate the Rahman-El Harra line and advance into the enemy's rear. In the evening, having received from the Desert Air Force and other sources reports of enemy movements connected with the commencement of the subsequently halted withdrawal (but not knowing about Hitler's victory-or-death order), Montgomery reached the conclusion that Rommel was about to make a general retreat, probably to Fuka, and therefore ordered the rest of the armour to be ready to drive northwards towards the coast road, while the New Zealand division was to advance west in the 7th Armoured Division's wake in

---
[1] *The Rommel Papers*, pp. 322-3.

preparation for a move against the Fuka escarpment from the south. The armour was again operating in three divisions, the 8th Armoured Brigade having returned to the 10th Division.

The infantry attack was to be made by the 51st Highland Division (to which had been added one of Montgomery's reserve infantry brigades, the 5th Indian) and the 23rd Armoured Brigade (less two regiments). The Indian brigade, in an operation to be launched at great depth, was to make the breach on the left, 7,000 yards south of Tel el Aqqaqir. The objectives in the centre and on the right were given to two Highland battalions.

The infantry operations for this attempt to break through began at 5.45 p.m. on the 3rd when the 5/7th Gordons attacked for the centre objective but without artillery support because, owing to a chronic inability of armoured formations to read the map, the locality had been erroneously reported to be already clear of enemy. The attack was broken short of the objective.

The Eighth Army's operations on 4th November opened at 1.30 a.m. with the long advance of the 5th Indian Brigade which

> mounted a speedily prepared attack and quickly reached the Rahman track on a four-mile front, piercing the softer part of the screen to the south and thus outflanking the stronger resistance in the north.[2]

The dawn attack on Tel el Aqqaqir by the 7/Argyll and Sutherland Highlanders succeeded with only light casualties suffered. A headquarters was captured. Then the taut, overstrained Axis defence ring sprang open, and the collapse was swift.

The 1st Armoured Division turned north-west to fight the last engagement with the German armour at El Alamein, and was held up by tanks and anti-tank guns not far beyond the Rahman track, where the two German armoured divisions had stationed themselves to execute Hitler's stark order. The 10th Armoured Division's 8th Armoured Brigade thrust west but did not push far past Tel el Aqqaqir. The 7th Armoured Division on the left crossed the Rahman track, struck north-west and fought and won a battle against the *XX Italian Corps*, including the *Ariete Division*. The 4th Light Armoured Brigade also debouched about Tel el Aqqaqir. The New Zealand and Highland divisions and other units appointed for the chase pressed with much mingling through the minefield gaps to get into the open. About midday the commander of the German *Africa Corps*, General von Thoma, was captured.

In the afternoon the 8th Armoured Brigade was ordered to advance on Daba by night to arrive there by dawn and by nightfall the armoured cars of the Royal Dragoons and the 4th/6th South Africans were both in the Fuka area, doing great damage and taking many prisoners.

By late afternoon the enemy was in full retreat. At 5.30 p.m. Rommel authorised a general withdrawal. That was the end of the battle of El Alamein and the opening of the pursuit. The depleted *90th* and *164th*

---
[2] P. C. Bharucha, *The North African Campaign 1940-43* (1956), p. 461, a volume in the series *Official History of the Indian Armed Forces in the Second World War 1939-1945*.

Light Divisions and the remnants of the German armour extricated themselves from the northern sector. The Italians in the south, lacking transport, had to be abandoned.

On the morning of the 4th the 9th Division found that only stragglers remained in the coast salient, but the enemy was then still holding a line about a mile west of the Australian positions. During the night, in addition to carrying out the prescribed patrolling program in conjunction

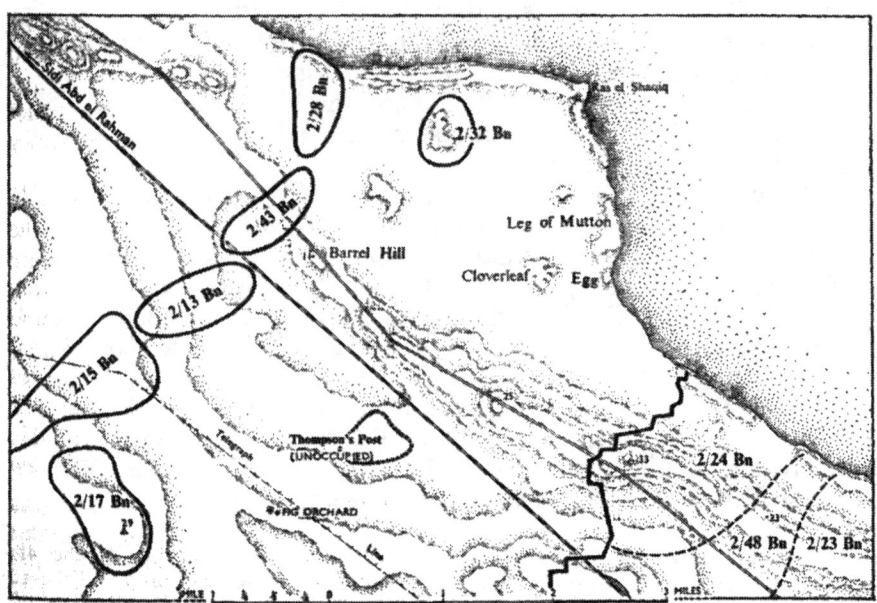

Dawn, 5th November

with the divisional cavalry, the 24th Brigade had established a line of three posts from Barrel Hill to the sea to cut off all enemy to the east. It was soon evident, however, that the enemy had extricated nearly all his troops and patrols of the 9th Divisional Cavalry Regiment established that he had abandoned his original front line from Thompson's Post across the railway and road to the sea. By 12.30 p.m. the 26th Brigade, advancing from the old Australian front line, had occupied Cloverleaf which had been the core of the enemy's original defensive position on the coast sector. A company patrol of the 2/28th Battalion moved north from the Saucer to the coast then back 1,500 yards and found two German stragglers. In the afternoon the 2/43rd sent out a strong patrol which penetrated 1,000 yards before coming under fire.

It was decided to advance the front that evening and night close up to the new enemy line, the new Australian line to run north-east from the 2/15th Battalion's front to the coast. The 2/13th was to come in between the right of the 2/15th and the railway, the 2/43rd to continue the line across the road, with the 2/28th holding from the right of the 2/43rd to the coast; the 2/32nd to be to the rear. When Major Williamson,[3] who was now in temporary command of the 2/43rd Battalion (Colonel Wain having been injured by shell blast), held an "orders group" conference to give instructions for the forward move, a shell landed in the midst of the group, killing 3 officers and wounding 4. The redispositions of all units were subsequently carried out without incident.

Patrols on the night of the 4th-5th from the 2/15th Battalion made no contact. At dawn on the 5th it was found that the enemy had gone from the 9th Division's front. A carrier patrol from the 2/15th, led by Lieutenant Brown,[4] followed up swiftly and captured 143 Germans who were waiting for transport at Sidi Abd el Rahman. A mobile company from the 2/15th was then ordered to occupy the high ground round Sidi Abd el Rahman, which it did without opposition, and the divisional cavalry was ordered to make for Ghazal.

Later the cavalry regiment (mounted, it will be remembered, partly in Crusaders and Honeys) was ordered to advance to Daba, clearing the intervening area of the enemy, and to hold Landing Ground 105 until the arrival of the 151st Brigade of the Highland division advancing from the south-east. This it did, handing over Daba and the landing ground to the Highlanders that evening. The 2/3rd and 2/13th Field Companies were sent to clear the landing grounds between Rahman and Daba of mines, and by the evening had declared them all safe. At 5.30 p.m. the 2/15th reported the last prisoners taken by the 20th Brigade and probably by the division—5 Germans, and 3 Italians of the *Toscana Division* (Wolves of Tuscany), then arriving from Greece.

Kesselring had arrived at Rommel's headquarters on the morning of the 4th November and he and Rommel exchanged sharp words since Rommel believed that Hitler's earlier order had been based on reports sent back by the air force.

"In actual fact," wrote Rommel later, "the Fuehrer's order had been based on other, quite different grounds—as was to become increasingly clear as time went on. . . . It was the custom at the Fuehrer's HQ to subordinate military interests to those of propaganda. They were simply unable to bring themselves to say to the German people and the world at large that Alamein had been lost, and believed they could avert its fate by a 'Victory or Death' order. Until this moment we in Africa had always had complete freedom of action. Now that was over."[5]

On 4th November the *Africa Corps* had at first held the British armour. The *90th Light Division* halted the attackers astride the coast road. But the British tanks (i.e. 7th Armoured Division), thrusting south-westward, broke into the *XXI Corps* and soon men of the *Trento* and *Bologna Divisions* were in full retreat. When these British tanks turned northward they struck the open flank of the *Ariete Division* which after putting up a stern defence reported that it was surrounded. By 2 p.m. the *Africa Corps*' front had been pierced in many places.

At 5.30 Rommel ordered a general withdrawal to Fuka to avoid complete encirclement. In a report to Hitler and the Supreme Army Commander he said that the enemy in the northern sector had almost wiped out the forward troops. The Italian

---

[3] Maj H. J. Williamson, ED, SX8891; 2/43 Bn. Salesman; of Da Costa Park, SA; b. Mt Gambier, SA, 27 Apr 1911.
[4] Capt J. F. S. Brown, MC, QX6934; 2/15 Bn. Salesman; of Montville, Qld; b. Montville, 2 May 1917.
[5] *The Rommel Papers*, p. 324.

troops had no more fighting value and some had been abandoning strong positions without orders. Mobile warfare offered the only opportunity of halting the enemy. If permission were granted he would make "a fighting withdrawal platoon by platoon to a new position running south from Fuka".

That night Mussolini authorised withdrawal to Fuka but required an assurance that the non-motorised formations would be extricated. Next day a message was received from Hitler approving Rommel's decision to withdraw.

The three abandoned divisions of the *X Italian Corps* (*Pavia, Brescia* and *Folgore*) had no option but to surrender. Only relatively few men of the other five Italian divisions managed to get away.

Rommel has described the calamitous situation in which his army then found itself. The traffic on the coast road between Fuka and Matruh was in "wild confusion". Overhead the R.A.F. "reigned supreme, flying one attack after the other against every worthwhile target". His own headquarters were twice bombed and then were under fire from several British tanks. He ordered withdrawal to Matruh "with a heavy heart, because of the German and Italian formations still on the march". He and his staff then moved off on a "wild helter-skelter drive through another pitch-black night. . . . At that time it was still a matter of doubt as to whether we would be able to get even the remnants of the army away to the west. . . . The bulk of the Italian infantry had been lost. . . . The only forces which retained any fighting strength were the remnants of the 90th Light Division, the Afrika Korps' two divisions—now reduced to the strength of small combat groups, the Panzer Grenadier Regiment Africa and a few quickly scratched together German units, the remains of the 164th Light Division. Tanks, heavy A.A. guns, heavy and light artillery, all had sustained such frightful losses at El Alamein that there was nothing but a few remnants left."[6]

The Eighth Army had been presented with some chance of cutting off a sizable proportion of Rommel's battered forces, whose withdrawal had been unduly delayed by Hitler's intervention, for there were defiles in rear and limits to the speed at which the enemy's soft-skinned vehicles could retreat along the clogged main road and few available subsidiary tracks. Such fruits of victory, however, are seldom earned without good planning and organisation, some audacity, great drive, and exceptional effort. None of these qualities was sufficiently displayed.

The 8th Armoured Brigade found the difficulties of the ordered cross-country night march to Daba insurmountable or the task too trying or themselves too tired. They soon halted for the night.

During that night (4th-5th November) there was much changing of orders. So bemused had the fatigued commanders and staffs become by the difficulties of breaking through that they were not balanced for the chase. In the event the 8th Armoured Brigade made for Galal and cut off some of the enemy. The 2nd Armoured Brigade made for Daba and found the enemy gone; the 22nd Armoured Brigade also moved up on their left in the same direction, to cut the road near by, but halted when they found themselves too late for the enemy. Later in the day these and other formations, moved westward for varying distances on varying courses but despite problems created by his fuel shortages Rommel was never in danger of being encircled.

Some of the pursuing formations were delayed by real difficulties, some by imaginary ones, some by their own lack of impetus. None evinced

---

[6] *The Rommel Papers*, pp. 339-40.

the initiative or drive needed to snatch the prize. Later the seasonal rains fell and the pursuit bogged down. The probability that this might occur any day was just one overlooked reason for moving with utmost speed.

There we shall leave the Eighth Army, for the 9th Division was not to accompany it to Tobruk, Tripoli and Bizerta.

News that the enemy had not merely withdrawn a bound but was in flight and that there had been mass surrenders in the south filtered through late that afternoon of 5th November to the Australians, numbers of whom had been "scrounging" in the enemy's abandoned positions. Many flares, which the Germans and Italians used prolifically, had been found. One or two were fired after dusk. This touched off throughout the 9th Division's area, as night fell, a spontaneous Guy Fawkes' fireworks celebration of the victory, in which light signals and flares of every kind, both British and German, were shot into the sky.

British tanks entered Matruh on 8th November, the day on which the combined Allied landing took place in North Africa. A great victory had been won though some of the fruits had not been gathered. In England everybody from Prime Minister to charlady was overjoyed. The churchbells were rung.

The Eighth Army's losses in winning the victory were 13,560 killed, wounded or missing, but about twice as many of the enemy were captured.[7] The enemy left more than 1,000 guns and all but about a dozen of his tanks on the battlefield or the withdrawal route—about 450 tanks were left in the El Alamein area.

The 9th Division's casualties in the battle were about one fifth of the total casualties of the Eighth Army. The final figures established after the war, when the "missing" had been dissected into prisoners of war, died of wounds and presumed dead, indicated that the number killed was more than 50 per cent in excess of the number then so reported. The division's casualties from 23rd October to 5th November, as finally established, were:

Killed	Wounded	Prisoners of War	Total
620[8]	1,944	130	2,694[9]

The Battle of El Alamein was fought in three phases. The first two nights and days were a striving to accomplish the plan for the armour

---

[7] Prisoners taken by the 9th Australian Division numbered: German—24 officers and 1,290 others; Italian—31 officers and 575 others.

[8] Includes died of wounds and presumed dead.

[9] The losses suffered by the Australian infantry battalions in the battle were:

20th Brigade			24th Brigade		
	Officers	Others		Officers	Others
2/13 Bn	20	266	2/28 Bn	2	44
2/15 Bn	14	138	2/32 Bn	10	181
2/17 Bn	12	244	2/43 Bn	10	147
			2/3 Pnr Bn	6	115

26th Brigade		
	Officers	Others
2/23 Bn	16	191
2/24 Bn	21	348
2/48 Bn	21	325

For the 24th Brigade the losses are only those suffered on 30th and 31st October. The divisional engineers lost one officer killed and 5 wounded, 17 other ranks killed and 86 wounded.

to debouch into the open on ground of the Eighth Army's choosing. In the next seven nights and days—the crumbling operations—the army faced and thrusted north; except in the first two of those days, the western front became in effect a defensively held flank to the 9th Division's northward thrust. In the last three days the army again advanced westward, reverting to the aim of getting the armour astride the enemy's communications, and on the third day it succeeded.

In the first phase of the battle the 9th Division bore with the other assault formations its share of the heavy fighting; in the long second phase —the dog-fight—the division bore the main burden of the attack; in the final phase, though not heavily committed, it was engaged on all three brigade fronts. The severity of the action is not easily imagined today. In the second phase, for example, the Germans made and the Australians withstood no less than 25 attacks against Trig 29.

The biggest contribution to the division's success in defending the ground captured by it was made by the artillery of its own field regiments in conjunction with the field and medium regiments of other formations. Innumerable infantry counter-attacks were broken up by artillery fire before they could be pressed. The artillery also made an immeasurable contribution to the success of the infantry attacks. Another notable feature of the battle was the Eighth Army's dominance in counter-battery work, which reduced night firing by enemy guns to a minimum. The 6-pounder anti-tank gun, on the other hand, proved to be by far the most effective static weapon against tanks.

Throughout the battle, by day and by night, some artillery action was occurring all the time, and heavy action for most of the time. In the 12 days of the battle the Eighth Army's artillery fired more than one million rounds of 25-pounder ammunition, at an average daily rate of 102 rounds per gun (159 per gun on the XXX Corps front). The 354 25-pounders on the XXX Corps front fired 577 rounds per gun on the first night. The total rounds per gun fired on the XXX Corps front for the whole battle averaged more than 1,900 rounds. The Australian regiments fired almost 50 per cent more than the corps average, which reflects the 9th Division's big share of the fighting.

The Eighth Army accomplished a Herculean labour though perhaps its efforts may not have always been directed to best advantage. Perhaps the army's purposes would have been better promoted if the 9th Division had advanced west instead of north, at least after Trig 29 was taken, or if, after it had been decided not to launch SUPERCHARGE from the coast road, the division had advanced entirely northwards and not at all to the east. But had the division done either of these things it might have had to face an even stronger enemy reaction. It is not profitable to peer long into the dark of actions that were not fought.

On another score, the criticism may be levelled that to plan a methodical destruction of an enemy in well-prepared defences is not in itself tactically justifiable and that the process was carried beyond the point at which the consequential advantages to be thereby gained justified the cost. Was there some touchstone then to discover that point clearly in the fog of the battle?

General Montgomery has also been criticised for his predilection for breaking through so far north near the source of Rommel's southward communications. Strong grounds exist for contending that the decision to do so was a tactical error; but if SUPERCHARGE had achieved the success expected of it, the decision to strike hard at the base by the shortest route would have been acclaimed. Perhaps the battle could have been won without laying such hard tasks on the troops but the Eighth Army as it was before Montgomery remoulded it could not have accomplished the tasks that won the victory.

General von Thoma's comment on Montgomery can be fittingly applied to his conduct of the battle:

I thought he was very cautious considering his immensely superior strength but he is the only Field Marshal in this war who won all his battles.

In modern mobile warfare, the tactics are not the main thing. The decisive factor is the organisation of one's resources—to maintain momentum.

What most distinguished General Montgomery's operations from those of his predecessors (some of whom, it should be remembered, had to divide their attention between the army's problems and wider responsibilities) was that his over-all plans derived their soundness from the soundness of the parts, which in turn was developed by thorough training that fitted men, units and formations for their tasks. The one-time revising author of the British Army's standard text-book on infantry training saw to it that commanders, staff and men learnt their roles by realistic rehearsal.

Comparisons have sometimes been made between the Eighth Army's achievements in the first desert offensive under Generals Auchinleck, Cunningham and Ritchie and in its second offensive eleven months later under Generals Alexander and Montgomery. Except that the fighting was against the same enemy commander at the same time of year and over similar terrain, such comparisons are not valid, for in respect of the problems presented and methods used the two offensives were almost as dissimilar as the battles of Thermopylae and Trafalgar. In General Auchinleck's offensive the Eighth Army debouched across a part of the frontier that was virtually undefended into open desert where there were vast spaces over which the armoured formations could manoeuvre unhampered by fortifications or obstructions. When General Alexander's offensive was mounted, however, there was no open flank; the areas within reach where armour could manoeuvre were very limited, and the routes to them blocked.

To Auchinleck and Montgomery, each in his time, was given a general superiority of arms, munitions and equipment over his adversary, but Montgomery had two pronounced advantages not given to Auchinleck. One was the mastery of the skies. Although in Auchinleck's time the Desert Air Force had the edge on the enemy, it could not exercise such a pronounced influence on the ground battles. Montgomery's other main advantage was his more effective tank-destroying armaments, but this was greatly offset by the enemy's ability at El Alamein to site his 88-mm guns to best advantage.

It is more to the point to compare the early summer battles at El Alamein with the autumn battle. Although the summer battles had by attrition halted the enemy advance, the several operations that in their aggregate effect had achieved this strategic reprieve were often individually failures in relation to their immediate aims. As a throwing-back operation, Auchinleck's counter-offensive did not succeed, and indeed most forward steps taken had to be retracted.

Auchinleck, the Commander-in-Chief, was a director of operations, Montgomery, the Army Commander, a managing director. Auchinleck, less cautious and deliberate than Montgomery, may have been a better tactician; but because Auchinleck more often than not had bad managers whereas Montgomery managed well, Montgomery's operations were, in their final outcome, more successful.

General Alexander and General Montgomery called on General Morshead on 4th November to express their appreciation of the 9th Division's part in winning the victory. General Leese toured the division's battlefield on the 5th, meeting many of the officers; several other of the army's senior commanders likewise called on Morshead before they left El Alamein to participate in the pursuit. Then congratulatory messages began to pour in and were promulgated in orders. They included tributes from the Governor-General of Australia, the President of the United States, General Blamey, General Montgomery and General Leese. Montgomery said that Morshead's men had been magnificent and the part they had played was beyond all praise.

The recognition of the importance of the 9th Division's fighting accorded in these messages, which were published throughout the division, profoundly revived and renewed the morale of the battle-weary troops, most of whom had lost several dear comrades in the ordeal. No tribute was more appreciated than the letter Leese wrote to Morshead on 6th November:

> Now that we have a pause in the fighting I would like to write a line to congratulate you on the magnificent fighting which your Division has carried out, and to thank you personally for your great co-operation and sound judgment during the battle.
> I would be very grateful if you would explain to the men the immense part they have played in the battle. It is perhaps difficult for them quite to realise the magnitude of their achievement as the main break-out of our armour was accomplished on another part of our front, thus could not be seen by them. But I am quite certain that this break-out was only made possible by the homeric fighting over your Divisional sector.
> When it was no longer possible for the crumbling process to go on in the South you will remember that the Army Commander decided to continue with his crumbling policy in the North. This led to five days bitter fighting on your front. During this time your Division attacked four times and were counter-attacked incessantly by enemy infantry and tanks.

The main mass of heavy and medium artillery was concentrated on your Divisional front. It was obvious that the enemy meant to resist any advance along the coastal route, and as we now know, they concentrated the whole of the Panzer Corps against you in the Northern area.

Your fighting gave the opportunity for the conception of the final break-through in the centre, but this could never have been carried out if your front had been broken. The final break was, in my opinion, a very bold conception by the Army Commander, and one which he could never have carried out unless he was certain of the valiant resistance that would be put up by your Division. If the Germans could have broken your Division, the whole gun support of the attack would have been disorganised and its success vitally prejudiced.

It has been for me a very proud occasion to have an Australian Division serving in the Corps and I am very happy that this is to continue in the subsequent advance.[1]

Those fortuitous last few words about the subsequent advance may have had a more far-reaching effect than their author could have expected, for it was extraordinary that, when the division was at first left out of the pursuit, no spontaneous rumour arose that it was destined for Australia. The Australian Government's request for its return had been kept a close secret. In point of fact the division's future employment was still being debated between those who were directing the Allied war effort from Washington and London on the one hand, and the Australian Prime Minister and the Allied Commander-in-Chief of the South-West Pacific on the other, as will shortly be told.

The wide recognition given to the men's achievements was reciprocated by them in their recognition of Morshead as a worthy leader. He had won both their confidence and their respect. Frequently they had seen him about the battlefield, from dawn on the first morning when he had visited the 20th Brigade after it had failed to secure the Oxalic line to that last fiery day before SUPERCHARGE was launched, when he had gone down to the Saucer; he had also been seen frequently by others in the field ambulances, which he had constantly visited during the battle, as later he often visited the base hospitals. Morshead had likewise a deep respect for the fighting men, but never forgot others. "Don't forget to say a good word to the cooks," he told his commanders at a conference soon after the battle.

On the morning of the 6th November, the advanced headquarters of the 9th Division moved back to the main headquarters position near El Alamein, and units moved across to bivouac areas allotted to them near the coast between Sidi Abd el Rahman and Tel el Eisa. Their first task, energetically put in hand, was to make the area both hygienic and safe. Unburied dead of both sides, but mainly of the enemy, were collected and reverently buried, the refuse around old Italian positions was cleared away, and a thorough combing of the area was instituted, to rid it of mines. A storm on the night of 6th November filled dugouts with water and blew down tents and hastily-erected bivouacs, but nobody seemed to

---

[1] General Horrocks wrote in his autobiography: "The success of Supercharge was largely due to the 9th Australian Division, who had carried out continuous attacks night after night in a northerly direction. . . . After the battle I went to see General Morshead . . . to congratulate him on the magnificent fighting carried out by his division. His reply was the classic understatement of all time. He said: "Thank you, General. The boys were interested." *A Full Life*, p. 140.

mind. Nothing could impair the men's sense of relief and release from battle involvement. In the following week a great deal of work was carried out in salvaging equipment from the battlefield.

Morshead was summoned to Leese's headquarters on the 6th and upon his return called his formation commanders to a conference at which he issued orders that the division less two brigades was to be prepared to move to Mersa Matruh from the 9th November onwards, and possibly later to Tobruk. Nothing came of the project, nor of a later one, appropriately called "Operation Hollywood", that a party representing the division should be present at the formal entry into Tobruk. The force was to have comprised 630 officers and men from all branches of the service and to have been commanded by Lieut-Colonel Colvin of the 2/13th Battalion, who had commanded the same battalion in the last days of the siege.

On 13th November the division was warned that it was to be prepared to move forward to Sidi Haneish at any time from the next day onwards, but two days later it was removed from the command of the XXX Corps when the latter was given responsibility for the conduct of operations west of Benghazi. Next day General Morshead received this signal from General Wimberley of the Highland division:

> Have just heard with the greatest regret that you are leaving 30 Corps. We hope this will be very temporary as we do not at all like not having our friends and instructors near us.

Since the division was no longer on call for operational employment, Morshead decided that a program of progressive training six days per week, starting with individual training, and to include training of staffs and commanders, should be instituted at once. He gave instructions to that effect to brigade and unit commanders at a conference on 17th November, and a confirmatory written instruction was issued on the same day. Weapon training with live ammunition and instruction with live mines were to be included. In the subsequent execution of the training, interest and a sense of realism were created by using former enemy defences for tactical exercises.

The plans of General Headquarters for the 9th Division's employment in the immediate future appear to have involved its return to Syria. General Alexander visited General Morshead on 19th November. The notes in Morshead's notebook made in anticipation of the Commander-in-Chief's visit indicate that Morshead intended to oppose this proposal vigorously and in particular a proposal (such as General Blamey had previously vetoed) to detach one brigade from the division. Among some of the arguments that Morshead intended to advance were that the Commander-in-Chief had previously promised that the division would return to Palestine on being withdrawn from the desert, that all the division's installations, services and camps were there and that Australians were no good as garrison troops or as pseudo-policemen. "We shall be of infinitely greater service, whether in the Middle East or Australia," he noted, "if we have an uninterrupted period of training, and training as a division."

Morshead also intended to discuss the question of leave for his troops. The upshot of the conference was that Alexander agreed to the division's return to Palestine and the granting of leave immediately. The first leave passes were issued to men applying for leave to visit friends in hospital.

A week later advanced parties left for Palestine, and for the next four days the troops were busy packing equipment and rehearsing speedy methods of embussing. It was ordered that all enemy equipment was to be handed over, which caused some annoyance; captured tents and mobile kitchens, among other things, had greatly added to the men's comfort. Requiem Masses and Memorial Services were held at El Alamein Cemetery by most units, and on 30th November the move began.

The division journeyed to Palestine in 12 convoys, two leaving daily, each bivouacking by the roadside on the next three nights, and reaching the Gaza area on the fourth day. The leading convoys passed through the heart of Cairo; the troops, in their exuberance, fired captured coloured signal rockets and discharged smoke bombs in the main streets and some, having a liking for collecting the national head-dress of the Cairenes as souvenirs, whisked tarbooshes from the heads of indignant citizens as the trucks passed along.[2] Consequently the later convoys were re-routed round the city.

By 9th December the whole division, with the exception of a few Bren carriers delayed on the railway, was established in the Australian base camps between Gaza and Qastina. Leave to Tel Aviv, Jerusalem, Haifa and Cairo was instituted. There has been so much adverse comment about the behaviour of Australian troops on leave that a paragraph published in routine orders throughout the division is noteworthy.

G.O.C. Cairo Area[3] has stated that during recent leave, 9th Australian Division troops were the best behaved in Cairo. As a mark of his appreciation, he has arranged to welcome the first draft of 100 personally at Cairo Main Station on 7th December and to turn out the band of a Highland Regiment and provide refreshments for the first five drafts.[4]

Soon after his arrival in Palestine General Morshead visited the 6th Australian General Hospital at Gaza. After this there was such an influx of visitors to the hospital that the authorities had to restrict their numbers and units were given a daily quota. However patients at the hospital, if fit to travel, and patients of the Australian Convalescent Depot were allowed to visit their units in camp.

It has already been intimated that the war leaders of Great Britain and the United States showed reluctance to agree to Mr Curtin's firm request that the 9th Division should return forthwith to Australia.

---

[2] One incident had a regrettable consequence. A convoy passed the University as the students were leaving and one or two smoke bombs fell among them. In the ensuing panic one student was struck by a motor-vehicle, and fatally injured.

[3] Maj-Gen J. I. Chrystall.

[4] 9 Aust Div "A" Bch War Diary, Dec 1942. In October Chrystall had sent the following signal to Morshead: "I much appreciated behaviour your troops on leave Cairo. Not one single word from C.M.P. and turnout and deportment beyond reproach. It is a pleasure to have them here."

(*Imperial War Museum*)

Stowing kits on to a lighter for trans-shipment to the *Queen Mary*, one of the ships which transported the 9th Division home. Port Tewfik, January 1943.

(*Australian War Memorial*)

Troops of the 9th Division aboard the troopship *Nieuw Amsterdam* anchored off Addu Atoll, one of the small islands in the Maldive Group in the Indian Ocean, where the homeward bound convoy refuelled in February 1943. The *Queen Mary* (right) and *Aquitania* can be seen behind the rigging.

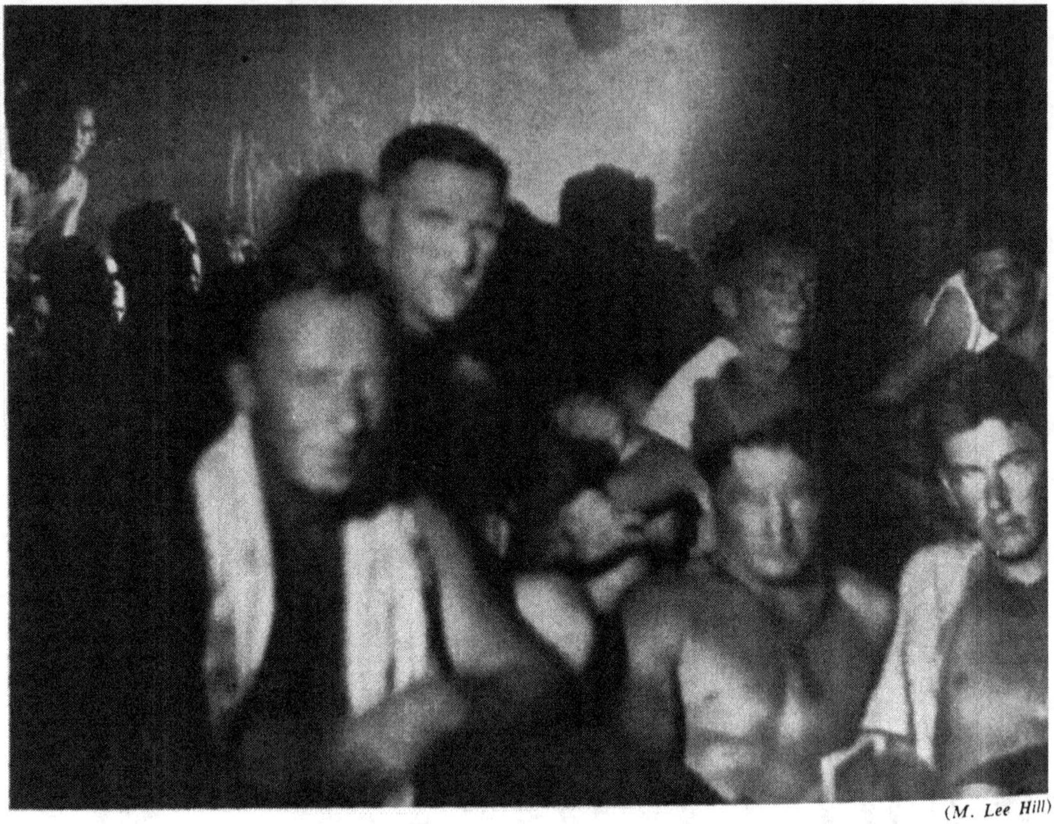

(M. Lee Hill)

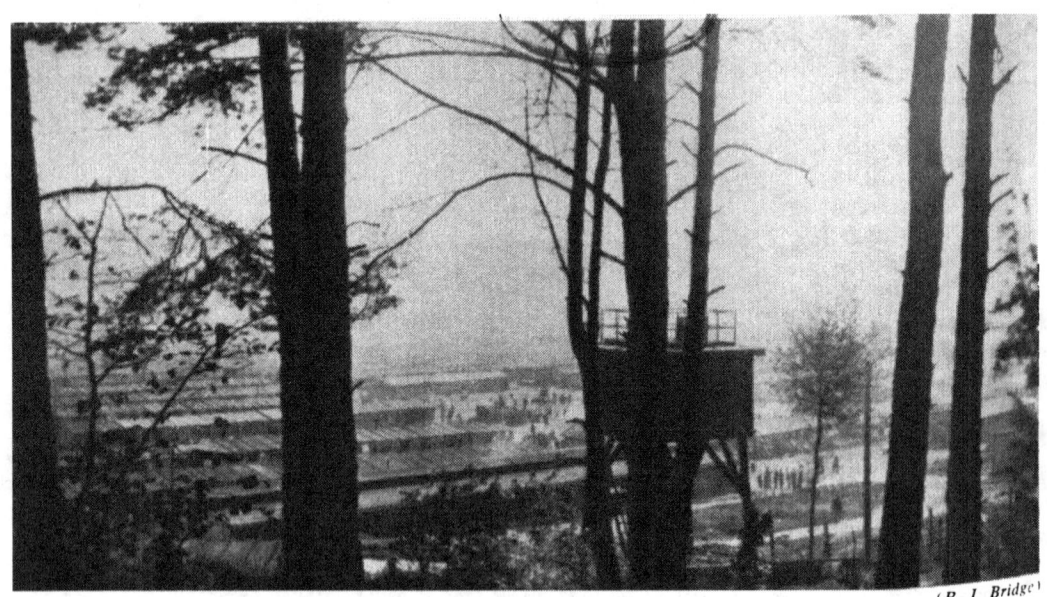

Prisoners of war in transit by cattle-truck from Italy to Germany.

(R. I. Bridge)

Stalag 383, Hohenfels.

On 29th October, after the receipt of Morshead's message, Mr Curtin had cabled Mr Churchill that it was of vital importance for the Government to get the 9th Division back; plans being made in the South-West Pacific were based on its being returned in good shape. He sought Churchill's personal interest in securing the fullest cooperation of all concerned to this end. He also cabled the Australian High Commissioner in London, Mr Bruce, asking him to ensure that the division was not committed to another phase of the campaign. But on 1st November Curtin received a letter from President Roosevelt in which, while expressing his appreciation of the Australian Government's concern at the absence of its forces in the Middle East, Roosevelt stated that he was convinced that the common cause would be best served by leaving the A.I.F. in the Middle East. He could dispatch a United States division from Hawaii to Australia and assumed that this would obviate the need to call back the 9th Division; however it must be appreciated, he said, that the United States division might later have to be diverted to another area where its employment would be of greater advantage to the defence of Australia.[5] Curtin referred the President's letter to General MacArthur, who nevertheless advised that the Government should still press for the division's return.

On 16th November, Curtin replied at length to President Roosevelt and indicated that his Government regarded the future employment of the division as absolutely governed by the obligation to fulfil the conditions previously laid down for its present use in the Middle East. Four days later the Australian Government heard from Bruce in London that planning of shipping for the return of the division had been held up pending further representations for its retention in the Middle East; but on 21st November it seemed that the Government had had its way, for Morshead cabled on that day that Alexander had told him that a firm decision had now been made that the division would return to Australia. A later cable from Churchill indicated that the division could not take its heavy equipment with it owing to demands on shipping and their effect on offensive preparations against the European powers. The Australian Government then sought General MacArthur's and General Blamey's comments on what difficulties this would involve.

Before these comments were available the Australian Prime Minister received on 3rd December a further letter from President Roosevelt, which again cast doubt on the 9th Division's employment in the immediate future. While affirming his belief that the division should return at the earliest practicable date, Roosevelt stated that this date would depend upon two factors: first, the division should remain in the Middle East until the pursuit of Rommel's forces had ended in final victory—a phrase which of course meant until the end of the African campaign; secondly, it should not be returned until its movement could be accomplished without too serious a drain on shipping. He thought the operations in the

---

[5] At this time there were four American divisions in Hawaii—24th, 25th, 27th and 40th.

Middle East would be concluded early in the year, when he would advocate its return; but the movement should include only personnel.

On 4th December, General Sturdee, the Australian military representative at Washington, cabled that the American Joint Chiefs of Staff had been considering the division's future employment and appeared to be opposed to its return on military grounds, but might make a decision on other grounds. Meanwhile the Government had been advised by MacArthur and Blamey that the essential point was to secure the division's return as soon as possible; the necessary equipment could be made available, if necessary, from American resources. On 8th December Curtin replied to Roosevelt's most recent letter. After referring to the high rate of manpower wastage in tropical warfare and detailing the forces available in Australia, he said:

> I wish you to know that we shall cooperate in the plan that you have outlined, which, as we see it, does not envisage the utilisation of the 9th Division for any further operations in the Middle East or adjacent areas. We look forward, therefore, to the fulfilment of the understanding that the 9th Division shall be returned to Australia as early as possible in the New Year.

He also suggested that about 3,500 tons of equipment should be brought back in the transports, including infantry weapons and a few items of specialised vehicles and stores. A summary of the message was cabled to Churchill.

Curtin's essay in dialectics concluded the discussion. No attempt was made to dispute his interpretation. On 15th December Churchill informed Curtin that shipping would be arranged at the end of January for the return of the 9th Division with minimum equipment. "The 9th Australian Division," he said, "would carry with them from the African desert a splendid reputation, and the honour of having played a leading part in a memorable victory for the Empire and the common cause."[6]

On 17th December a new divisional colour patch was issued. It was shaped like a "T" but with the vertical stroke shortened. There was much speculation as to the origin of the "T" shape and some years later Morshead was asked to comment. He wrote:

> The "T" stood for Tobruk. The 9th Division was hurriedly formed and wore a collection of colour patches—oblongs, squares, circles, ovals. After coming out of Tobruk I decided we should have the one form but, knowing how attached the men were to their old colour patches, the change had to be unanimously accepted. If not, then there would be no change. Finally, but not altogether readily, it was accepted, nothing as far as I was concerned having been indicated that the "T" stood for Tobruk, nor, when informing the Commander-in-Chief in Australia, the late Field Marshal Blamey, of the change, did I make reference to Tobruk, but explained that a common colour patch was necessary and I had decided, as all other simple forms from

---

[6] Two days later (17th December) General MacArthur, who had not heard that the division was soon to return, wrote to General Blamey to propose drastic steps: "It is my opinion," he said, "that this division . . . will not be returned to you within any reasonable time. I regard it as essential that the Australian Expeditionary Force should include three Infantry Divisions. As a means of accomplishing this purpose, would it not be possible to build up an A.I.F. Division in Australia by transferring as soon as possible a heavy cadre involving the majority of the officers of the 9th Division, detailed by name, from the Middle East to Australia. . . ."

squares to circles, had long since been bespoken, on the combination of two oblongs, the larger one on top.[7]

General Morshead accompanied General Alexander when he opened the Haifa-Beirut railway on 20th December. In the building of this strategic rail link, which traversed the hilly Syrian coast with many miles of cuttings, embankments and tunnels, a major part of the work had been carried out by the Australian Railway Construction and Maintenance Group.[8] Two days later a divisional parade was held at Gaza Airport. General Alexander, at Morshead's invitation, took the salute.

The pride that the 9th Division had developed in itself and in its reputation was exemplified on that field in Palestine on the 22nd December by the smartness of the turn-out of every man and the exemplary marching and arms-drill of every unit at the parade.

"On a perfect day, in a setting of green fields—a vast contrast to the scenes of their exploits—over 12,000 officers and men of the 9th Australian Division formed up in line of units in close column: an inspiring phalanx three-quarters of a mile long, the massed bands of the division drawn up in the rear.

"Clustered around the dais were the blue and gold uniforms of naval officers, beribboned generals from several Allied nations, the lighter blue uniforms of the R.A.F., the dresses of women guests, among whom were Lady Tedder and Mrs R. G. Casey who had flown from Cairo, the robes of four Sheiks and of the Governor of Sinai and here and there the tailored suits of diplomats.

"Flanking the dais were barriers behind which were nursing sisters from the near-by 6th A.G.H. in their scarlet capes and snow-white veils, V.A.D's, W.A.A.F's, detachments from every A.I.F. unit in the Middle East not included in the 9th Division, recent reinforcements and, lastly, but proudest of all, the wounded in hospital blues who had come to watch their mates 'bung on a show'. In front of the spectators was a row of white flags, each bearing the new 'T'-shaped colour patch of a unit of the division.

"A cloud of dust heralded the approach of the car bearing General Alexander and General Morshead. On their arrival, the order 'General Salute' by the acting divisional commander, Brigadier Ramsay, brought the rattle and slap of the 'Present'. The Australian flag was broken at the mast and in rotation the bands played a slow march for the Salute and the inspection, which General Alexander carried out standing in the back of an open car at the salute while the car traversed the whole of the front of the division.

"The long inspection completed, the men, now somewhat jaded, having been up since an early hour, and more than an hour on parade, listlessly resigned themselves to what might prove a long harangue, but with General Alexander's words, 'And great deeds have been done' there was an imperceptible stiffening of shoulders; heads were held perhaps a little

---

[7] *Stand-To*, March 1952.
[8] See Appendix 2.

higher as the general went on to extol their prowess as fighting men. They saw, not the assembled crowd to their front nor the rolling Gaza plains beyond, but as if through a haze, the sangars of Tobruk, the ridges of Tel el Eisa. There were memories of the brackish water, the myriads of flies and fleas, the interminable diet of bully beef, the oily margarine; nostrils filled again with the stench of death and the acrid fumes of explosives; they heard again the cries and groans of the wounded and dying, the scream of Stukas.

"At the conclusion of the address[9] General Morshead took command of the parade. His order calling the parade to attention was probably the first order a large majority of those present had heard him utter. Then followed the tribute of thousands of fighting men to their dead—The Salute to Fallen Comrades. On the execution of 'Present Arms' all ranks, other than those armed with rifles, saluted. The flag was lowered as massed buglers sounded the Last Post, the last wailing note echoing and re-echoing away in the distance, almost, it seemed, as if reaching those rows of crosses at El Alamein. Then Reveille, and the flag was raised. The massed bands played *Advance Australia Fair* and moved forward to a position opposite the dais whence to play the marchers past the saluting base.

"The division then marched past by groups in close column. Units moved to forming-up points at the end of the runway down which they marched, 40 abreast; showing that Australians' parade ground discipline could equal their battle discipline. On past the saluting base, where General Alexander took the salute, they went; then wheeled away to assembling points where they had their midday meal before returning to the camps."[1]

The next two days were spent mainly in preparations for Christmas festivities, and many parties were held in officers' and N.C.O's messes. Christmas Day was spent in the traditional army manner; after church services a bounteous dinner was provided, rations being generously

---

[9] "Officers, warrant officers, non-commissioned officers and men of the Australian Imperial Force; these great days we are living in are a time for deeds rather than words, but when great deeds have been done there is no harm in speaking of them. And great deeds have been done.

"The Battle of Alamein has made history, and you are in the proud position of having taken a major part in that great victory. Your reputation as fighters has always been famous, but I do not believe you have ever fought with greater bravery or distinction than you did during that battle, when you broke the German and Italian Armies in the Western Desert. Now you have added fresh lustre to your already illustrious name.

"Your losses have been heavy indeed and for that we are all greatly distressed. But war is a hard and bloody affair, and great victories cannot be won without sacrifice. It is always a fine and moving spectacle to see, as I do today, worthy men who have done their duty on the battlefield assembled in ranks on parade, and those ranks filled again with young recruits and fresh reinforcements.

"To these future warriors I extend a warm welcome and greet them as brothers in arms who have come to join the forces in the Middle East which it is my honour to command.

"What of the future? There is no doubt that the fortunes of war have turned in our favour. We now have the initiative and can strike when and where we will. It is we who will choose the future battlegrounds, and we will choose them where we can hit the enemy hardest and hurt him most.

"There is a hard and bitter struggle ahead before we come to final victory and much hard fighting to be done. In the flux and change of war individuals will change. Some will come; others will go. Formations will move from one theatre to another, and where you will be when the next battles are fought I do not know. But wherever you may be my thoughts will always go with you and I shall follow your fortunes with interest and your successes with admiration. There is one thought I shall cherish above all others—under my command fought the 9th Australian Division."

[1] From the account written by Mr A. E. Field of the War History staff.

supplemented with poultry, pork and the usual trimmings by the Australian Comforts Fund and grants from regimental funds. In a number of instances officers acted as mess orderlies in the men's messes.

Boxing Day was also a holiday, but on this day commanding officers were called to a conference and informed that the A.I.F. was to move from the Middle East. The movement was allocated the code name "Liddington". Camp routine and training were resumed next day and quiet preparations for Liddington began under the strictest security measures. Those who needed to know of a projected move were told that the immediate destination would be Egypt, which was not incorrect as the port of embarkation would be there.

General Morshead left by air for Cairo with General Alexander, and later flew on to Eighth Army headquarters at Marble Arch beyond Agheila, also visiting General Leese at the XXX Corps headquarters and General Freyberg at Nofilia. Morshead's visit was considered by some as an indication that the Australians would rejoin the Eighth Army for the advance into Tunisia, while others predicted that the division would train in Egypt for amphibious landings in Sicily and Italy. This theory gained some credence from the fact that senior officers were attending courses in combined operations on the Suez Canal.

As preparations for Liddington proceeded, however, it became progressively more apparent that a long sea voyage was ahead and that the direction would be south from the canal zone. Tanks, guns, and other heavy equipment were returned to ordnance depots and on 16th January the move to the canal area began. A divisional report centre was set up at Qassasin, and on each convoy's arrival there vehicles were handed over to British authorities. After a day or two in this camp each group entrained for staging camps at Port Tewfik or El Shatt in the embarkation area to await arrival of the transports. Embarkation began on 24th January and continued until the 31st.[2]

As embarkation on each transport was completed, the vessel moved out, later to rendezvous off Massawa on the Eritrean coast. The ships were crowded, with little space for assembly, so the troops settled down to a routine of instruction, lectures, sport and P.T., to the extent that the limited deck-space allowed.

The convoy that assembled at Massawa was composed of the troopships *Queen Mary, Aquitania, Ile de France, Nieuw Amsterdam* and the armed merchant cruiser *Queen of Bermuda*. It left Massawa on 4th February closely escorted by a cruiser and several destroyers. Five days later the convoy broke formation and anchored off a group of small islands to re-fuel and take in water. The location of this secluded re-fuelling point was not disclosed to the troops. It was the Addu Atoll, a ring of coral islets in the Maldive group which, under the designation of "Port T", had been developed since 1941 as a secret anchorage for the British and

---

[2] A total of 30,985 Australians embarked in the convoy, of whom 390 were AANS and VAD, leaving 622 (AIF) in the Middle East. This latter figure was reduced weekly until the end of March 1943 when fewer than 20 AIF personnel remained.

Allied naval squadrons in the Indian Ocean. Re-fuelling continued throughout the night and the convoy was again under way by midday on the 10th.

Soon after leaving Addu Atoll the troops were enthralled when they saw the British Eastern Fleet—battleships and cruisers with attendant destroyers—lying a mile or so off course, a magnificent spectacle. A signal flashed from the flagship by Aldis lamp to the *Nieuw Amsterdam* read: "G.O.C. from C-in-C. Rommel will be relieved but the Japs will have the jim-jams. In case I don't sight you again, au revoir until we meet in Tokyo." Led by the *Queen Mary*, the big fast ships sailed on southwards unescorted into the southern Indian Ocean, bearing the men of the 9th Division to their homeland.

* * * *

EPILOGUE

The date is 28th September 1959, the place Sydney. A funeral procession passes slowly through hushed streets. Thousands have come there. These men were once soldiers. Formed into unit groups, wearing their medals, they stand to attention now, silent while their great leader passes. He does not heed their tribute. Morshead is dead. Morshead who took a random collection of units, unhappily divorced from their parent formations, and moulded them into a proud, well-nigh unconquerable division. Morshead whose sense of duty and grasp of object made him always sure and firm and steadfast. Morshead never in doubt, never cast down; who never countenanced failure, never forgave, but never forgot to praise. Morshead who drove men almost to the point of desperation yet at the end won their acclaim. Whenever men speak of the 9th Australian Division's feats at Tobruk and El Alamein, this great and resolute commander will be remembered. Its victories were his.

APPENDIX 1

PRISONERS OF THE GERMANS AND ITALIANS

By A. E. FIELD

The author of this appendix served in 1914-1918 with the King's Own Scottish Borderers and was awarded the D.C.M. and M.M. In 1940 he enlisted in the 2/6th Field Company, serving with that unit as a sapper and later a sergeant in Libya, Syria and Java. He was a prisoner of the Japanese from 1942 to 1945.

During the service of the A.I.F. in the Middle East campaigns of 1941-42, 7,116[1] officers and men were taken prisoner. Of these, 21 were captured before 28th March 1941 when the withdrawal from Cyrenaica began. From that date until the investment of Tobruk 507 Australians fell into enemy hands; of these the 2/13th Battalion lost 87, the 2/15th Battalion 162, the 2/3rd Anti-Tank Regiment 96 and the 2/8th Field Ambulance 42. Twenty-seven members of the 2/3rd Field Company also entered captivity during this phase.

During the siege of Tobruk 467 Australians were taken prisoner. The biggest losses were suffered by the 2/24th and 2/23rd Battalions when the enemy penetrated the positions at Ras el Medauuar during the second unsuccessful attack on Tobruk on 1st May.

In 1942 during the second visit of the 9th Division to the Western Desert 946 Australians were captured, including 697 of the 24th Brigade Group during July. The greatest losses in this month were sustained by the 2/28th Battalion in its attack on Ruin Ridge when 489 were taken prisoner.

Practically every unit of the 6th Division was represented in the 2,065 captured during the campaign in Greece, the heaviest losses being in the 6th Divisional A.A.S.C. (225) and the 2/6th Battalion (208).

The engagements on Crete provided the largest number of Australians so far taken prisoner in a single operation. It is difficult to assess the maximum number that actually were in enemy hands because of the chaotic conditions in the assembly areas after the fighting ended. A large number who were virtually prisoners of war walked out of the concentration areas—they could not be described as camps—and although many were eventually recaptured, there were also many who escaped from the island, some to reach Egypt direct and others via Greece and Turkey.

---

[1] This total includes one (Pte G. H. Bamford, 2/33 Bn) who died of dysentery while a prisoner of the Vichy French in Syria. A total of 175 men of the A.I.F. were taken prisoner by the Vichy forces in the Syrian campaign, but, with the exception of Bamford, all were returned to their units on the signing of the armistice. Three officers and a warrant-officer of the A.I.F. were in a party of British officers and N.C.O's numbering 65 evacuated from Syria by air before the armistice. One plane-load of 13, which included Capt E. F. Aitken, 2/2 Pnr Bn, was forced to land on the island of Scarpanto in the Dodecanese and returned to Syria on 30th August 1941 by way of Rhodes, Athens, Corinth, Brindisi, Montalbo P.W. Camp and Toulon. The main party was landed at Athens, later transported to Salonika and eventually repatriated to Syria, but not before they had by train traversed Greece, Yugoslavia, Austria, Germany and occupied France to Toulon and thence by ship back to Beirut where they arrived on 15th August. This party included Lt G. B. Connor, 2/33 Bn, and Lt W. I. Summons and WO2 T. Hulse, both of 2/2 Pnr Bn. The Vichy French commander and others detained as hostages were not released until arrival of the party from Scarpanto—see G. Long, *Greece, Crete and Syria*, pp. 519-21.

The number that was eventually recorded as being taken prisoner on Crete was 3,109; of these 517 were of the 2/11th Battalion, 493 of the 2/1st Battalion and 410 of the 2/7th Battalion.

The unenviable distinction of being the first member of the A.I.F. to be taken prisoner in the second world war goes to Sergeant K. W. Walsh of the 6th Divisional Cavalry Regiment, who was captured by Italians at Giarabub on 26th December 1940, whilst the first Australian soldier to be captured by the Germans in this war was Lieutenant Rowley of the 2/5th Battalion.[2]

The combatants among the prisoners taken during the withdrawal to Tobruk in April 1941 were promptly marched away, but the 42 men of the 2/8th Field Ambulance remained near the scene of their capture for two days caring for British and German wounded in tents or in the open using medical supplies from their own vehicles. Later they were taken to Derna where they operated a hospital for wounded men, mainly Germans from the Tobruk perimeter.

The line of evacuation of prisoners of the Axis forces in North Africa was, generally, Derna (when capture was near to, or east of that town), Benghazi to Tripoli, with embarkation at either of the two latter places for the sea trip to Italy. When prisoners were taken by the Germans they were soon handed over to the Italians, the North African theatre being Italian "territory". The journey of three or four days to Tripoli was made in trucks into which the prisoners were packed with room only to stand, exposed to the sun and dust-storms with few stops between the nightly staging camps. At Benghazi, where the stay sometimes lasted days or even weeks, the prisoners were accommodated in bomb-damaged buildings or in a transit camp on the outskirts of the city. Between Benghazi and Tripoli the first night was usually spent at El Agheila at a ruined aerodrome, and the following night at Misurata where the men were quartered in an Italian-built Arab settlement consisting of several hundred squat, stone huts of two or three rooms each, devoid of furniture or appurtenances but certainly not of fleas! Around Tripoli there were three prisoner-of-war camps, two in use mainly as transit camps, while a third, at Gargaresc, was a work-camp, about which more will be said later.

The first batch of Australians to reach the Tripoli area were those captured at Er Regima and Mechili and they, after a four days' stop at Benghazi, reached Sabratha, some 30 miles beyond Tripoli. Here they stayed for a few days during which they received the Italian soldier's usual food. On 4th May, together with other British prisoners captured about the same time, they left for Italy, embarking at Tripoli for an uneventful crossing during which there were few complaints about the food. After disembarking at Naples they were taken to Capua, another transit camp. There they spent a week in tents; rain fell during the whole period and living conditions were very uncomfortable.

---

[2] See Long, *To Benghazi*, pp. 285, 291.

At Sulmona was the next camp, known later as Campo PG78,[3] where there were already a number of British officers and other ranks including a few Australians. The officers and other ranks were each in separate compounds, the former in brick buildings, the latter in stone huts with cement floors; all had been used to house Austrian prisoners during the 1914-18 war. Conditions there were an improvement on those experienced hitherto; food was better, hot showers were available, walks into the mountains were organised and playing-cards (later banned), draughts and other table games were available. Lieut-Colonel Munro of the 2/3rd Anti-Tank Regiment became Senior British Officer and he instituted a system of contributions from officers according to rank to help out the other ranks who were receiving rations only. Those other ranks who received pay for working also contributed to the fund. Red Cross food parcels and clothing were also issued. One diarist[4] recorded on 28th May "We get olive oil, lettuce, onions and a ration of sugar fairly often. Also we sleep between bed sheets", whilst another related that "life was almost bearable". The camp hospital was woefully short of medical supplies; any patients gravely ill were transferred to a civil hospital in Sulmona.

The majority of the officers who were in the camp at this period remained there until June 1943 and much the same conditions obtained, except that food became scarcer and prices higher. On 17th July 1941 all Australian other ranks were given a few hours' notice to leave and were transferred to a camp near Bolzano in northern Italy, known as Campo Prato. Here they were housed in a winery equipped with three-tier beds and overcrowded. The medical situation was similar to that at Sulmona, but at the hospital in Bolzano, sufferers from beri beri and dysentery were given injections with favourable results. An extract from a diary for 23rd July reads:

> Trouble for the first time—over the insubordination of the troops. Thirty of the boys went to gaol for 20 days. We soon got used to the Camp Commandant and he to us. He was a good old bloke in many ways and the boys had nothing to say against him. He used to let us go for walks two or three miles from the camp and we always got our Red Cross parcels and fags. We got one parcel each once a week. We also got writing paper, and letter cards once a week.[5]

It was also possible to send radiograms through the Vatican City Radio.

Owing to the congested nature of the area there was no sport or exercise other than walks, and to combat boredom the men played "two-up" and held concerts. The Italians made efforts to suppress gambling but with little success. All kinds of food, cigarettes or even clothes were staked in the games. A narrator drily remarks "Imagine backing a tail for a tin of jam at Thomo's".[6]

---

[3] Abbreviation of *Campo concentramento di prigionieri di guerra*. These permanent camps were not numbered until early in 1942.
[4] Pte H. Stephenson, NX19374; 2/13 Bn. Labourer; of Wollongong, NSW; b. Northumberland, England, 27 Sep 1919.
[5] Pte H. Stephenson.
[6] Pte C. H. Jagoe, 2/13 Bn in the 2/13 unit history, *Bayonets Abroad*. Thomo's was a notorious two-up school in Sydney.

Towards the end of October another move found this party of Australians at Campo 57, Gruppignano, in north-east Italy. There they were joined a day later by a draft of 200, also from North Africa, mainly men of the 2/23rd and 2/24th Battalions. The camp, into which all Australians were being drafted, was situated in a wide plain surrounded by mountains and was a large compound of barbed wire containing wooden huts about 90 feet long by 30 feet with concrete foundations. The camp was then in the course of being divided into two compounds, but was capable of further sub-division as the camp population increased. Sanitation was at first inadequate but was gradually improved by the prisoners themselves.

Beds were in timber-framed tiers of two, already bug infested. Winter was now setting in, snow lay on the ground and prisoners, many still clad only in tropical clothing, were acutely affected by the cold, accentuated by the numerous and long drawn-out check parades which were the fiendish delight of the camp commandant, Colonel Calcaterra of the Italian Carabinieri. Calcaterra was a dyed-in-the-wool Fascist, who was formerly in charge of an Italian police district, and a sign over his office door read: "The English are cursed, but more cursed are those Italians who treat them well." There were few among his camp guards who did not carry out the implication of this message. Men were awarded 30 days' detention—both the minimum and maximum penalty—for minor offences such as failing to salute an officer passing at a distance, or failing to stand to attention at Retreat even though they had not heard the faint bugle call. Men were frequently handcuffed in the cells for up to four hours a day. Not only were the cells always full, but there was usually a long waiting list for detention. Punishments were summarily awarded, no opportunity being given the accused to offer an explanation. Many pinpricking regulations were imposed and several fatal shootings took place including one of an Australian,[7] who was shot at point-blank range while being led away by two companions to prevent further altercation between the guard and his victim.

One instance of Calcaterra's wrath is worthy of record if only to exemplify the sense of humour that never deserted the average Australian even in the direst circumstances. Calcaterra, inspecting the morning check parade, came upon an offending beard and ordered that all beards were to be removed. The murmurs and demeanour of the rest of the men conveyed to the commandant that the order was not popular and likely to be disobeyed. Thereupon Calcaterra ordered that not only beards but also hair on the head should be removed. Remonstrance by the camp leader, Warrant-Officer Cotman,[8] who was vociferously supported by the rest of the parade, further incensed Calcaterra who worked himself into such

---

[7] Cpl E. W. Symons, WX1982; 2/32 Bn. Butcher; of Kalgoorlie, WA; b. Prahran, Vic, 7 May 1907. Killed while prisoner of war 20 May 1943. "Sox" Symons, a well-known identity in the unit was captured near Post S7, Tobruk, on 4th August 1941 when he, with another stretcher bearer, went into enemy-held territory after a counter-attack in search of missing men of his battalion.

[8] WO1 A. A. S. Cotman, PX8; 2/15 Bn. Planter; of Abau, Papua; b. Garstang, England, 24 Jul 1907.

a state that the prisoners' attitude changed from resentment to open amusement, bringing Calcaterra almost to apoplexy. He rushed out of the camp and returned with all available guards with fixed bayonets; a machine-gun was mounted and small hand-carts loaded with handcuffs were wheeled into the compound. Those who refused the ministrations of the barber were handcuffed. As the refusals increased more handcuffs were called for. Half way through the proceedings one humorist, on leaving the barber's chair, bleated like a sheep and scampered away jumping a non-existent hurdle in imitation of a sheep being released. This was taken up by others until the compound resembled a burlesque of a shearing-shed yard. Eventually "shearing" was completed, the handcuffed ones were led away to the cells and the camp quietened down. That night after the camp seemed at rest, a plaintive "baa" came from one of the huts, and was taken up from hut to hut until the camp was in a pandemonium which continued almost throughout the night. The climax arrived the next morning when Calcaterra discovered that those placed in detention for refusal had not been shorn! His wrath then fell on his guards.[9] Some months later the malcontents were removed to another camp—ironically, the best in Italy.

Later, the 500 Australians in Campo 57 were joined by a further draft from North Africa including 450 New Zealanders. In January 1942 a Red Cross clothing issue, including British battledress, was made, and, apart from the continued harsh discipline, conditions improved. Red Cross food parcels were issued weekly when available, but the camp suffered the reduction in rations which was general throughout Italy in March 1942. At Easter the commandant presented each prisoner with a sweet and wished him a happy Easter. Mail was arriving from Australia and some were receiving private parcels. A parade in commemoration of Anzac Day was held, to which the Italians sent a beautiful wreath. On the same day about 200 Australians moved out to various work-camps in the Vercelli district where they were engaged mainly in rice farming. Until April 1943 the prisoners at Gruppignano did no work other than the necessary camp chores, but they received one *lira* a day to supplement the rations. This was usually spent on vegetables. By October 1942 there were more than 1,200 Australians in the camp including two Australian medical officers, Major Binns[1] and Captain Levings,[2] 1,000 New Zealanders, a few Cypriots, Indians and one Chinese merchant seaman whom the Italians classed as an Australian.[3]

Benghazi prisoner-of-war camp was merely a transit camp from which prisoners captured in the German offensive of April 1941 or taken during the siege of Tobruk were staged en route to Tripoli. Up to September 1941, when the camp was suddenly emptied, conditions were comparatively

---
[9] Recounted by J. L. Brill, "It Happened in an Italian Prison Camp." *Stand-To*, April 1950.
[1] Lt-Col R. T. Binns, OBE, ED, SX9123. 2/8 Fd Amb 1940-41; MO Campo 57 (Italy) 1941-42; OC Med Div 101 AGH 1943-45. Medical practitioner; of Hazelwood Park, SA; b. Unley, SA, 12 Jun 1901.
[2] Capt E. W. Levings, OBE, NX70155. RMO 2/3 A-Tk Regt; MO Campo 57 (Italy). Medical practitioner; of Leeton, NSW; b. Wyalong, NSW, 16 Jan 1902. Died 17 May 1947.
[3] For the medical aspects of Campo 57 see A. S. Walker, *Middle East and Far East*, pp. 401-4.

good. The quarters provided in stone barracks with concrete floors were clean and not overcrowded. Rations consisted of two loaves of bread at 10 a.m., stew with fresh meat at noon, and rice or macaroni at 6 p.m., lemons twice weekly, olive oil three times a fortnight and 35 cigarettes each Monday. Having little to do but keep the camp clean the men spent the day playing chess, cards, studying or reading. Educational groups were formed to study a diversity of subjects, the philosophy lectures, given by an Australian clergyman serving in the ranks,[4] drawing audiences of up to 200.

This camp came into use again in November 1941 after the British offensive when thousands of prisoners fell into German hands. It was then woefully overcrowded and conditions were chaotic. Over 6,000 British troops were held there during December; as the British advance neared Benghazi they had high hopes of being freed, but a last-minute evacuation by sea prevented their liberation.

A party of 300, which included about 100 Australians, left Benghazi in June 1941 for Tripoli, being transported overland in motor trucks. These were mostly men who had been wounded and taken prisoner in the German offensive of April or in the counter-attacks at Tobruk or Salum and had recovered in Derna hospital. The party also included men of the 2/8th Field Ambulance who had conducted the hospital at Derna under Italian administration. At Tripoli they entered Campo 59, a stone barracks which had formerly served as a training centre for Italian naval cadets. A few days after arrival, control of the camp was taken over by the Germans from the Italians and its designation became *Feldpost 12545*. What had amounted almost to indifference by the Italians towards their captives now changed to brutality. Reveille varied from 2.30 to 4 a.m. according to the whim of the commandant. A cup of "coffee", slice of bread and a spoonful of jam comprised breakfast and then the men were hustled out in parties of 80 by the shouting guards to work 15 to 20 hours on the docks loading shells or bombs or unloading and stacking cases of supplies at a depot some 18 miles away, whither they were transported in trucks. Each had a small tin of sardines and bread for dinner, worked again till dark, sometimes till 11 p.m., and then went back to camp for a ladle of stew and bread and then bed. Pay was three *lire* a day, but was of little value. Razor blades, cigarettes and stationery could be bought at the canteen, but there was nothing to assuage hunger. Protected personnel were forced to work.

Sleep on most nights was interrupted by the crash of Allied bombs on Tripoli and the response of anti-aircraft batteries. On one occasion the camp kitchen was hit, but there were no casualties. For four months these continued, seven days a week, the only respite being one day on which all men remained in camp to de-bug their quarters. No man could have continued on the rations issued were it not for food stolen at Fatma, where the supply dump was situated. By numerous ruses and subterfuges

---

[4] Chaplain Rev E. N. Broomhead, SX5729. 2/8 Fd Amb, 2/5 AGH. Methodist minister; of Buckleboo, SA; b. Glenelg, SA, 31 Aug 1910. Author of *Barbed Wire in the Sunset* (1944).

the party working there fed themselves on chocolate, tinned milk, tinned meat and biscuits and every day returned to camp carrying food for those on other parties. Punishment of men who were caught was severe, but the thieving continued; their lives depended on it. The men on the docks and petrol dumps too were doing their part: hundreds of shells, bombs and cases of munitions "fell" into the harbour and petrol was allowed to pour out into the sand, and sugar (stolen from Fatma) was placed in full drums.

Eventually, of course, the wholesale depredation of the stock at Fatma was discovered and prisoners were no longer employed there. This caused a serious decline in health, but the consequent hardships were somewhat alleviated by the removal of the camp commandant, who, it was discovered, had been selling camp rations on the black market in Tripoli, and his replacement by a young German. This fanatical devotee of Hitler still retained a sense of human kindness. Although the seven-day working week still operated, hours were reduced to 10 or 12 daily and sometimes even to 8. Punishment of those undergoing detention was relaxed, camp concerts were encouraged and Divine Service, hitherto forbidden, was permitted. The working parties were now arriving back in camp early enough to have a swim in the sea from the beach adjoining the camp and this relieved the lice problem considerably. Working parties, too, were sometimes met on return to camp with a small gift of cigarettes, sweets or dried fruit.

This state of affairs, however, lasted but one month and the young man was replaced by a worse bully than the first commandant. He ordered that no prisoners were to sit down, except during the meal break, from the time they left camp till their return, nor were they to smoke while away from camp and then not after dark, which left little time in which one could smoke. He went from work-party to work-party to see if his orders were enforced, which they were not. The guards had acquired a grudging admiration for the prisoners for the way they had retained their morale during the regime of the first commandant and were now disposed to leniency; some even kept watch while their charges had a surreptitious smoke or rest.

Rations were progressively reduced, mainly on account of a general shortage; the Royal Navy and the R.A.F. were seriously hindering the enemy supply ships which had previously been arriving in weekly convoys of 10 to 15 ships. At one period 14 weeks elapsed without a single ship arriving at Tripoli. Christmas Day 1941 was spent working extra hours as punishment imposed because a complaint had been made to the commandant about a shooting incident on a working party. He ordered half rations and extra work for three days. This meant that the Christmas Day rations were: a bun for breakfast, two sardines for dinner, a ladle of soup at the day's end. In spite of this and despite the German ban on singing, the prisoners sang carols as they were driven through the streets of Tripoli to work on Christmas morning.

Ten days later, the British forces being once more in Benghazi and moving towards Tripoli, the whole camp was shipped away, first to Palermo in Sicily and eventually a few to Campo 52 at Chiavari near Genoa, but the majority to Gruppignano. The journey through Italy was in comfortable railway carriages.

The camp *Feldpost 12545*, Tripoli, was visited by a representative of the International Committee of the Red Cross on 15th August 1941, during the regime of the first commandant and the report submitted after the visit is a striking example of how prisoner-of-war camps under control of the Axis Powers were "window-dressed" for visits by representatives of the Protecting Power or the International Red Cross.[5] The report began with a flowery description of the location and surroundings of the camp, reminiscent of a brochure extolling the tourist attractions of any tropical country. It then went on to say, *inter alia*,

> On the beach . . . two roofs mounted on high pillars of wood, permit the prisoners in their hours of leisure to enjoy the sea air and at the same time be sheltered from the rays of the sun. Thus they enjoy their siestas, lying on the soft sand . . . lavatories which are sprinkled several times a day with lime and creosote . . . here also the hygiene is perfect. . . . The cooks have at their disposal abundant supplies of excellent quality, they prepare the food according to the taste of the prisoners who are obviously quite satisfied. . . . The prisoners who wish to have a second helping may ask for it and are never refused. Also at breakfast they receive coffee, bread and jam without limitation. Fruit and vegetables play a great part in the feeding of prisoners and are checked thoroughly every day by the Commandant and the camp doctor. . . . The daily ration contains a quantity of 4,500 calories per man. The vitamins A, B, C, D and E are furnished in a quantity more than sufficient. Fruit and vegetables are abundant. Work is a distraction for the prisoners and procures for them a remuneration which considerably improves their condition. . . . I also visited the camp at Fatma . . . the men work from 7.30 a.m. to midday, the midday meal is followed by a rest and work is started again at 2 p.m. and then finished again at 6 p.m. and this second period is interrupted by another rest of about 1½ hours towards 4 p.m. The discipline at the camp is satisfactory; there has been no need to inflict punishment up to this time.

All the above statements were at variance with the facts, as attested by a former inmate[6] and corroborated by statements of other prisoners who were there.

On 16th August 1942, the Italians embarked a number of Allied prisoners of various nationalities at Benghazi for shipment to Italy. Probably about 2,000 prisoners were crammed into the five holds of the *Nino Bixio*, a freighter of 8,400 tons, on her maiden voyage; these included about 200 Australians captured at El Alamein three or four weeks previously. The Australians together with 300 New Zealand and English troops were crowded into No. 1 (front) hold, half on the top portion and half below. The hatch cover was closed until the vessel was under way and then only partially opened to allow access to the latrines. With half

---

[5] On the other hand it should be noted that in October 1944 when ICRC representatives requested permission to visit Stalag XVIIIA, Wolfsberg, the day before the date arranged, the Germans agreed.

[6] A typescript of *Barbed Wire in the Sunset* by the Rev E. N. Broomhead was forwarded to the War Crimes Commission, London, as evidence in its investigations and an affidavit sworn by the author as to the truth of his statements.

of the men suffering from dysentery much misery was caused while the hatch was closed. At 3 p.m. on the second day out, the *Nino Bixio*, which was accompanied by another ship and two escorting Italian destroyers, was torpedoed by an Allied submarine. One torpedo hit the engine-room, another exploded in the crowded No. 1 hold, causing awful carnage. A survivor[7] from the bottom of the hold later described the scene:

> The bottom portion of the hold immediately flooded to about twenty feet. Timber and metal came crashing down everywhere and quite a lot of men, who were not killed by the explosion, were trapped by this falling debris. The two steel ladders leading to the top part of the hold were blown to bits, which left us no way of getting out of the hold. Survivors from the top portion found ropes somewhere on the ship and eventually all survivors [from the bottom hold] were landed on to the deck. Some men from the bottom, naturally thinking the boat would sink, tried to get through the jagged hole where the torpedo had passed out the other side of the ship. Some of these were cut to bits as the swell washed them against the jagged edges of the steel plates.

There was some panic aft among the Italian guards and crew and most of these jumped overboard, being joined by some Free French and Indian prisoners. A number of these perished almost immediately, others scrambled on to rafts and met with varying fortunes. Some on rafts drifted helplessly without food and water for long periods before being picked up and returned to Benghazi. One Australian[8] died on a raft after drifting for nine days. On the *Nino Bixio* the wounded were brought up on deck and made as comfortable as possible. The unwounded survivors paid tribute to the fortitude of the wounded, some of whom were very badly injured. The stricken ship wallowed helplessly all night, the other vessels having dispersed at the time of the attack, but at first light one of the destroyers returned and took *Nino Bixio* in tow to Navarino in southern Greece where the wounded were taken off. Of the 504 originally in No. 1 hold, only 70 remained. The survivors were kept on the ship for four days to carry up as many dead as was practicable and to identify them if possible. During this period a few Italian army biscuits were their only food, but, as a survivor put it, "everyone was too dazed by the shock to worry about food". Of the 201 Australians on board at Benghazi 37 were killed or drowned. After a short stay at Corinth the uninjured were shipped to Bari in Italy, where they entered Campo 75, then being used as a main transit camp for British prisoners from North Africa.

Most Australian officers who were captured in North Africa sooner or later found themselves at Campo 78, Sulmona, a permanent camp for both officers and other ranks. As previously stated when the Australian other ranks were transferred to another camp in October 1941 the officers remained, later being joined by others taken prisoner in the El Alamein operations. The officers were quartered in two compounds, one known as Top Camp, the other as Lower Camp. The former was composed of 48

---

[7] Sgt G. O. Norton-Knight, NX53869; 2/3 A-Tk Regt. Stud overseer; of Bowral, NSW; b. Sydney, 4 Jan 1913. Another brother, Bdr M. O. Norton-Knight, was also a survivor of the bottom hold. A third brother, Gnr O. P. Norton-Knight, was wounded and captured at Ruin Ridge in July 1942 and died in an Italian hospital on 25 Aug 1942.

[8] L-Cpl J. L. Paterson, WX7016; 2/28 Bn. Clerk; of Perth, WA; b. Aberdeen, Scotland, 5 Apr 1916. Died while prisoner of war 26 Aug 1942.

rooms each containing two officers. In Lower Camp there were five dormitories of about 100 by 15 feet each occupied by 18 officers. Each officer was allotted a wire mattress, bed sheets, three blankets, dressing-table, small table and chair. Each room or dormitory contained a stove and was lit by electricity. Later, with the influx of more prisoners, accommodation inclined to become cramped. The Australian officers were quartered in Top Camp, although there were English officers of higher rank living in the Lower Camp and enjoying less privacy and comfort. The Italians paid captive officers at the same rate as the equivalent rank in the Italian Army,[9] but deducted a messing charge which in August 1941 was 420 *lire* per month but had in six months risen to 630 *lire* and continued to rise progressively, although the quantity and quality of the food supplied likewise continued to diminish. With the increased cost of supplementary food, hardship was caused to those of lower ranks, particularly when there was a breakdown in the delivery of Red Cross parcels; it was then agreed that messing charges be met by a contribution proportionate to rank. The officers also contributed, again according to rank, to a fund to assist other ranks who were receiving rations only. The Australian officers also sent all available funds at Christmas 1942 and 1943 to the Australians at Gruppignano.

Study groups covering a multitude of subjects were organised and excellent theatrical performances were staged; the officers' productions were shown also in the other ranks' camp and the other ranks reciprocated by bringing their shows into the officers' compound.

Tunnelling with a view to escape was a favourite pastime and seven different tunnels were dug, but all discovered by the Italians before actual escape was possible. A library was in existence and officers were allowed to order books once a month from Turin. Newspapers were permitted after December 1941.

In June 1943 the majority of the Australian officers captive with the Italians were at Sulmona, and, with a few isolated exceptions, all Australian other ranks at Campo 57, Gruppignano, or at a work-camp near Vercelli, 50 miles from Turin. In view of the impending invasion, camps in southern Italy were cleared and the occupants sent north out of possible operational areas. At Sulmona the prisoners' hopes of an early release, which had been mounting as rumours of landings spread, received a rude shock when they were paraded and those captured by the Germans ordered to fall out. Very few did, as it suggested a move to Germany. However, shortly afterwards they were informed that they were to be moved to a camp in northern Italy. With a few exceptions all the officers were sent to

---

[9] The amount received per month by British and French officers was:

Second-Lieutenant	750 *lire*
Lieutenant	950 ,,
Captain	1,100 ,,
Major	1,300 ,,
Lieut-Colonel	1,400 ,,
Colonel	1,600 ,,

The exchange rate of 72 *lire* to the £1 was incompatible with existing conditions.

Campo 19 at Bologna.[1] They were allowed to take with them all their possessions, including the vast library and their private and communal food stocks.[2] At Bologna conditions were not as good as the ones they had left, but excitement, conjecture and the hope of early freedom dissipated thoughts of discomfort. Some were irritated by a tightening of discipline (by the Senior British Officers—not the Italians) and, despite an order by the Senior British Officer that everyone was to remain in camp until relieved, many were preparing food supplies in haversacks in readiness for a break if necessary. Parties from other camps farther south continued to arrive until there were 900-odd officers and 300 other ranks in camp and these were organised into well-planned groups, supplied with the necessary food, maps and so on, and allotted certain areas for dispersal and rendezvous.

Article III of the armistice read:

All prisoners or internees of the United Nations to be immediately turned over to the Allied Commander-in-Chief, and none of these may now or at any time be evacuated to Germany.

Elaborate arrangements had been drawn up as early as March for the recovery and evacuation of prisoners in the event of an armistice with Italy and most camp leaders had received the War Office instruction that in such event all prisoners were to remain in camp until the arrival of Allied forces. This order was issued on the assumption that Allied forces would occupy Italy, or the major portion of it, almost immediately after the signing of an armistice and was intended to expedite the evacuation of the released prisoners, but the military situation pertaining on 8th September was entirely different to that assumed earlier. As late as one week before the signing of the armistice on 3rd September, detailed plans, based on the tentative arrangements of March, were drawn up at a conference at Allied Headquarters, and on 7th September, the day before promulgation of the armistice, the War Office informed the Mediterranean branch of the War Office Intelligence section that arrangements for dealing with prisoners of war in the event of an Italian collapse were under review.

It was a week later, however, before a B.B.C. broadcast informed prisoners that it was not their duty to remain in the camps but to escape. It was then too late; of those who had obeyed the War Office order to remain or had been prevented by the Italians from leaving their camps, 25,000 British prisoners had already been evacuated to Germany, including those at Gruppignano where the Germans, with the connivance of the notorious Calcaterra, had quietly rounded up the camp almost intact two days after the armistice announcement. The policy of the British authorities regarding the procedure to be adopted by prisoners at this period has

---

[1] Maj M. I. Wheatley, 2/2 MG Bn, and Lt J. C. Guest, 2/3 Lt A-A Regt, were among the rear party left behind. Wheatley later escaped from the camp and reached Allied lines.

[2] In December 1941 the stock of Red Cross parcels was exhausted and none arrived for six months. It was then decided to build up a reserve of non-perishable foods. The wisdom of this paid excellent dividends during the transition to Germany.

been bitterly criticised by former prisoners of war. "It had been a ghastly blunder," wrote one. . . . "Thousands of men had been cheated of the freedom they had so anxiously awaited for so long."[3]

Two days after the Germans had taken over the camp at Gruppignano they began evacuating the prisoners to Germany, staging them in some instances in Austria. Strong guards accompanied every batch and dire threats were issued as to the consequences of any attempt to escape, including a demonstration of a flame-thrower. Of the Australians at Campo 57 the majority went to Stalag XVIIIA/Z at Spittal or to Stalag VIIIA, Gorlitz. Calcaterra, the commandant of Campo 57, it might be mentioned in passing, was killed by Italian partisans soon after the Italian collapse, thus being spared arraignment on charges before an Allied War Crimes Tribunal.

At Bologna when the news of the armistice arrived, the Italian guards were more demonstrative than their charges, smashing their rifles and donning civilian clothes preparatory to leaving for home. The atmosphere was electric, with everyone wondering what was to happen next. It was known that Germans were in the area. They had been seen by prisoners while on the controlled walking trips which were a feature of this camp, but most thought the Germans would be too occupied to worry about prisoners; moreover the Italian commandant had promised to give news of any hand-over. Whether he had been notified or whether he played false was not known, but at 4 a.m. next morning, 9th September, the Germans arrived in force, entered the camp, arrested the Italians, and took charge.

The prisoners had previously cut the perimeter-wire at the rear of the camp as an emergency exit and, on the arrival of the Germans at the main gate, the alarm was given and a mass exodus was made to the gap at the rear. Here the men were met by a burst of machine-gun fire and grenades. One was killed and several wounded, but most of the firing was aimed overhead. Several escaped, including Lieutenants Harrod and Ellis[4] who, befriended by Italians and Czechs, remained at large until reaching Allied lines on 29th July 1944. The great majority were herded back into the compound, packed tightly together, and surrounded by machine-gun detachments. Eventually they were allowed to return to their huts, and two days later were moved to Modena, 20 miles distant, being allowed to take with them only what they could carry. They loaded themselves from the reserve food stocks, destroying all surplus food and clothing. At Modena they were loaded into cattle-trucks, their first experience of the German method of transporting troops; then began a journey akin to those experienced by the 6th Division prisoners from Greece, described later, but in this instance there was no shortage of food although no rations or water were issued on the journey of three days. During the 12-hour wait in the trucks in Modena yards, attempts were made to escape through the cordon of S.S. guards patrolling the train. One of the

---
[3] Uys Krige, *The Way Out* (1946), p. 181.
[4] Capt C. C. Ellis, WX7519; 2/28 Bn. Regular soldier; of Melbourne; b. Melbourne, 3 Sep 1917.

successful ones[5] boldly walked across the yard in full view of everyone, vaulted the fence and walked with an Italian civilian down the street—to freedom. He succeeded in reaching Switzerland.

Once the train was on the move, each truckload became a potential escape party and holes were cut or forced in practically every truck. In all 102 prisoners were missing when the train arrived in Germany, of whom approximately 50, including 13 Australians,[6] reached Switzerland. Nine other Australians were known to have jumped from the train but were recaptured. One escaper wrote:

> The truck's floor was coated by a few generations of cattle manure and on lifting this we discovered that some of the wooden planks had rotted. . . . It took until dark to prise out a plank, leaving an opening large enough for one man to get through. An officer crawled through under the truck and undid the sliding doors: unfortunately the train stopped and in the subsequent inspection the Germans discovered the unlocked door and were heard to remark: "The fools inside don't realise that the door is unlocked." They locked it again and when we were moving again the task had to be repeated. With the door open and no interruptions from our over-confident guards, we drew lots to jump—Dad and I were ninth on the list. There was some discord between those willing to attempt to get away and those unwilling to do so. Eventually while moving slowly up a hill Dad and I jumped, after dropping a pack of food. It was then about four o'clock in the morning and we found ourselves near Le Viss, just outside Trento.[7]

The two Sharps for the next seven days travelled over the mountains, reaching Switzerland safely through the Bernina Pass.

Those who remained on the train were first placed in Stalag VIIA, Moosburg, then Fort Bismarck, Strasbourg; their sojourn in these overcrowded camps varied from a few days to a few weeks before they were sent to permanent camps at Oflag VA, Weinsberg, or Oflag XIIB, Hadamar.[8]

Those in the work-camps around Vercelli, whither several hundred Australians had been transferred from Gruppignano, were fortunate in that few Germans were in the area and their Italian guards, as gratified as their captives that the armistice had been signed, either deserted their posts or allowed their charges to leave. Moreover Vercelli was within reasonable distance of the Swiss border. In all, 400 Australians reached Switzerland safely from these work-camps in the Vercelli area, some arriving there by the middle of September; others preferred to stay with their new-found Italian friends in their homes or joined the so-called partisan bands, some of which were quite inactive.

---

[5] Lt E. A. Paul, NX27654; 2/3 Pnr Bn. Bridge carpenter; of Bondi, NSW; b. Sandgate, Qld, 12 Oct 1903. Died 22 Oct 1946.

[6] Capt H. J. Kroger, 9 Div HQ; Lt B. B. Grogan, 2/23 Bn; Lt R. S. Donnan, 2/15 Bn; Lt J. C. Morish, 2/3 Fd Regt; Lt D. A. MacDonald, 2/13 Bn; Lt H. A. Peterson, 2/13 Bn; Lt T. W. Elliot, 2/12 Bn; Lt J. L. Mair, 2/24 Bn; Lt R. H. Jones, 2/8 Bn; Lt F. Sharp, 2/3 A-Tk Regt; Gnr K. W. Sharp, 2/3 A-Tk Regt; F-Lt R. S. Jones, RAAF; F-Lt F. F. H. Eggleston, RAAF.
Gnr Sharp, the son of Lt Sharp, was permitted by the Senior British Officer to travel as an officer in order to be with his father in any escape plan.

[7] K. Sharp in *Stand-To*, January 1952. (Gnr K. W. Sharp, QX10358; 2/3 A-Tk Regt. Projectionist; of Toowoomba, Qld; b. Newcastle, NSW, 17 Oct 1920.)

[8] Oflag is an abbreviation of *offizierlager*—officers' camp; similarly stalag is an abbreviation of *mannschaft-stammlager*—a camp for men other than officers.

This was not so, however, in the case of Private Peck[9] and a few others of the A.I.F. whose deeds with the partisans in Italy were renowned both there and in Switzerland. Peck had a remarkable escape record. Between 1st June 1941, when he was taken prisoner at Sfakia, Crete, and 14th February 1942 he had escaped four times before being transferred to a prisoner-of-war camp on the island of Rhodes. He was there charged as a suspected spy. Before his trial in May, he with six others knocked out the guard, climbed the wall and set off for Turkey in a boat which was sunk in a storm. Picked up by an Italian destroyer, Peck was taken to Italy where for the next 12 months he was in four different prisoner-of-war camps. In June 1943 he escaped by climbing the wire at dusk but a month later was recaptured at the Swiss border, returned to Vercelli camp and sentenced to 30 days "camp discipline", but was placed in a prison. He was returned to camp on the day of the secret signing of the Italian armistice and on the day of promulgation, 8th September, he escaped as did many others. Peck then organised parties of Allied prisoners of war for movement to Switzerland and joined the partisans. In February 1944 he was arrested by the Gestapo in an act of sabotage and sentenced to death, but he appealed. Whilst awaiting hearing of the appeal in San Vittore gaol, Milan, he was detailed to an unexploded-bomb disposal squad. When performing this duty in Lambrate railway yards there was an air raid; the guards ran and so did Peck—in the opposite direction. Travelling by train to Laveno and by steamer across Lake Maggiore he contacted partisans at Intra and they assisted him to reach Switzerland on 22nd May. Six weeks later he returned to the partisans in Italy and remained with them for four months before re-entering Switzerland.

With the liberation of southern France, the Allied rescue organisation was able to operate in the area north and north-east of Turin, where numbers of prisoners were still living with civilians or fighting with the partisans. In October 1944 a party of 25, which included 9 Australians[1] who had been in Campo 106, Vercelli, was guided over the passes to Val-d'Isere, in France, where American forces were in occupation. They were later evacuated to Naples for repatriation. Approaching winter made similar evacuations impossible. One party perished in a blizzard in the Alps. There were still a few Australians at large in Italy at the end of hostilities. Eight were known to have been shot by Fascists during April and May 1945.

Before the Italian collapse very few escapers had succeeded in reaching Switzerland and these were accommodated with no difficulty until arrangements could be made for their repatriation. Under the Hague Convention of 1907, prisoners of war who escaped from custody into neutral territory were free men, but were expected to leave the neutral country as soon as

---

[9] Lt J. D. Peck, DCM, VX9534; 2/7 Bn. Farmer; of Crib Point, Vic; b. Sydney, 16 Feb 1918.
[1] Ptes C. W. Clarkson, J. C. Nelson, J. Fitzgerald, R. L. Vigar, H. G. L. Wainewright (all 2/28 Bn); Pte F. S. G. Hungerford (2/15 Bn); Pte I. H. St G. Sproule (2/32 Bn); Pte E. A. W. Morley (2/48 Bn) and Gnr R. Paton (2/3 A-Tk Regt).

possible. (They were in a different category to military personnel entering a neutral country to evade capture—these were liable to internment.) But the influx of escapers and Italian refugees[2] immediately after the Italian armistice became a serious problem to the Swiss authorities; there was not only the food question to be considered, but also the possibility of undesirables mixing with the genuine seekers of asylum, and the menace to Switzerland's neutrality with so many Allied troops free in the country. In consequence Britain agreed to let sufficient food and clothing pass through the European blockade to supply the escapers, and arranged to ensure the *bona fides* of all British escapers and to set up a military organisation for their concentration and control.

As the points of entry into Switzerland were scattered, nothing more than a preliminary medical examination was carried out until the escapers were sent to Wil in the north-east of Switzerland where the headquarters of British troops was situated. Here they were medically and dentally examined, issued with British uniforms and clothing and subjected to a thorough interrogation about their movements and every phase of their life from the time of their capture to their arrival at the Swiss frontier. They were then sent to detachment camps where the usual army issue of personal requirements was made. The detachments were each from 200 to 250 strong and were all within a radius of 10 to 20 miles of headquarters, generally in a small rural township, the billets usually being schools or factory buildings. Later the Senior British Officer arranged for the taking over of large hotels in the mountain tourist resorts of Adelboden, Arosa and Montreux, where, in addition to enjoying excellent accommodation, the men were able to participate in snow and ice sports, a number becoming quite proficient at these pastimes. The feeling of the Swiss population was definitely pro-Allied and the generosity and hospitality extended to the Australians were most marked.

Officers were allowed 15 Swiss francs a day and from this had to provide board and accommodation. Cost of living was high and most officers found it difficult to manage on the allowance. The troops were rationed on the same scale as Swiss troops which was a trifle better than that received by civilians. In addition they received an allowance of 60 *centimes* a day for the purchase of fruit or vegetables, these being the only unrationed food commodities. Escapers could not be forced to work but it was considered in the best interests of the men that they should engage in some form of civilian employment. A work-camp was opened and its occupants worked on a forest clearing scheme and a land draining project. Smaller contracts included farm work. Men working received 90 francs a month of which the worker was paid 2 francs a day, the balance being paid into an imprest account. Some men obtained employment in their own civilian type of work such as printing or watchmaking. In May 1944 a comprehensive trade training scheme was initiated, the subjects including all branches of the building and engineering trades, farming

---

[2] A Swiss source stated that about 20,000 escapers and refugees entered Switzerland between 8th and 24th September 1943.

and languages. Materials were supplied free by Swiss firms and stationery and text books by the Y.M.C.A. and International Red Cross. Language teachers were remunerated with funds supplied by the War Office. Ten days' leave was granted every three months to all ranks, with a rail warrant and, to other ranks, a subsistence allowance of seven francs a day. This leave could not always be taken by other ranks, however, because of the scarcity of invitations to private homes. Weekend and nightly leave was also available. The senior A.I.F. officer in Switzerland, Captain Kroger,[3] with others gave lectures on Australia to Anglo-Swiss clubs, universities and at villages in almost every canton with a view to stimulating migration, it being considered the Swiss would make excellent Australian citizens.

In addition to the A.I.F. officers mentioned previously there were also in Switzerland, Lieutenant Peterson, who escaped from Campo 5, Gavi, and Lieutenant A. Hunter,[4] a South African who was visiting Australia at the outbreak of war and enlisted as a private in the A.I.F. Taken prisoner in April 1941 in Greece he escaped in July and before recapture lived for four months in various Greek homes during which time he trained Greek officers in the use of the Bren gun and grenades. In addition to taking part in two unsuccessful tunnel schemes Hunter actually escaped seven times from various prisoner-of-war camps in Greece and Italy but in each case was recaptured soon afterwards. At the time of the Italian armistice he was transferred from Bologna in Italy to Fort Bismarck, Strasbourg, Germany. On arrival Hunter learned that they would be there for a short time only and he and another officer[5] prepared to hide in the fort. A month later when due to leave they hid for 15 hours in a small bricked-off part of a passage and eventually got clear of the fort. Three days later they reached France but, being warned of the presence of Germans, climbed into the mountains and, keeping parallel with the road, reached the village of Luvigny. Here arrangements were made for them to cross into Switzerland.

Articles 68 and 74 of the Geneva Convention provided for the setting up of mixed medical commissions to select candidates for repatriation by exchange of the maimed, incurable or other seriously ill prisoners. Very early in the war the I.C.R.C. drew the attention of belligerent nations to these provisions and, although negotiations with the Italians were slow, by March 1941 66 Germans and 1,153 British Commonwealth prisoners had been selected as eligible for repatriation. Arrangements went ahead for the exchange to take place at Dieppe, but, a few days before the fixed date, the Germans suddenly broadcast by radio that they would only agree to repatriation on terms of numerical equality. Britain would not agree and so the arrangements fell through—a bitter disappointment to the men

---

[3] Maj H. J. Kroger, VX1580. 6 Div AASC, 9 Div HQ, I Corps. Schoolteacher; of Kew, Vic; b. Caulfield, Vic, 27 Jun 1906.
[4] See Long, *Greece, Crete and Syria*, p. 167.
[5] Sqn Ldr G. T. Chinchen, MBE, DFC, 250704; 3 Sqn. Clerk; of Geelong, Vic; b. Gardenvale, Vic, 31 Jul 1915.

concerned, who reached the French coast, only to be returned to the prison camps.

The first exchange of seriously sick and wounded between the British and the Italians was on 7th April 1942. Two hospital ships took the respective nationals to Smyrna, in Turkey, where the exchange of 340 Italian disabled and 579 protected personnel for 60 British sick and wounded and 69 protected personnel took place. The eleven Australians in the party were to go to Egypt, the English by train through Europe to England. One Australian had an intense desire to travel through Europe and visit England. He wrote:

> The little Italian colonel saw me. "Ah, Pastore!" he said, "You go to Egypt! You are Australian." I gave him two packets of tea that had *not* been used before.[6] "No, Signore!" I said, "I go to England!" And it was so! I crossed Europe to England for four ounces of tea![7]

The second and third repatriation exchanges between Britain and Italy included no Australians, but the fourth, carried out, also at Smyrna, on 2nd June 1943, provided an exchange of 2,676 Italians (447 disabled, 2,229 protected personnel) against 435 British (142 disabled, 293 protected personnel), which included 80 Australians (44 disabled, 36 protected personnel). A fifth exchange, a triangular one, involving Britain, Italy and Germany was arranged for September 1943 at Lisbon but was upset by the Italian armistice. The British prisoners were on the point of leaving Italy for Lisbon but instead were sent to Germany in the wholesale evacuation and languished many months more in prison camps before being repatriated. The Germans for exchange reached Lisbon and were disembarked there. The Italians, not enjoying conditions of reciprocity, were not allowed to land at Lisbon and were diverted to Algiers, from which port they eventually reached Italy.[8]

GREECE AND CRETE

When the German *40 Corps* marched into Greece through the Monastir Gap and met units of the I Australian Corps, no provision had been made by the Germans for the reception of prisoners of war; nor did they, when prisoners continued to fall into their hands, make much attempt to provide properly for those captured. Indeed, although it was 12 months after the withdrawal of the British forces from Greece before the last of the captives were evacuated from that country, any provision made for the accommodation of prisoners was of no more than a transitory nature. Consequently those unfortunate enough to be taken prisoner, were exposed to much hardship and consequent deterioration in health, which in many cases proved to be permanent.

---

[6] British prisoners after using the tea from their Red Cross parcels, dried the leaves and repacked them, to be used as bribes to guards or sold.
[7] Broomhead, pp. 146-7.
[8] Details of exchanges quoted from *Report of the International Committee of the Red Cross on its Activities during the Second World War (September 1, 1939 to June 30, 1947)*, (1948), Vol I. This organisation arranged details of transfers at exchange ports and representatives travelled with prisoners from the detaining country until handed over to their own authorities.

The first Australians to fall into enemy hands in this campaign were captured on the night of 10th-11th April near Vevi.[9] These men, together with those captured during the next few days, were concentrated at Florina, where they were packed into cattle-trucks and taken north through Yugoslavia. They reached a prisoner-of-war camp at Marburg (Maribor) near the Austrian border, some 9 or 10 weeks later, having staged for varying periods at Skoplje, Nish and Belgrade. Throughout this period hunger was rampant and dysentery prevalent. No provision was made, even in the staging camps, for anything but the most primitive sanitation. Soon after arrival at Stalag XVIIID, as the camp at Marburg was designated, they were given a hot bath and their clothes were de-loused. They were photographed and fingerprinted, issued with prisoner-of-war numbers and identification discs, and for the first time registered as prisoners of war. It was some weeks, however, before they were given a postcard to send home. After a fortnight in this camp those who were fit were drafted out to work-camps. Of approximately 250 Australians who left Florina only 85 now remained fit for work; a number had been left behind at each stop in Yugoslavia suffering from dysentery, jaundice, beri beri or malaria.

At the *arbeitskommando,* or work-camp, each prisoner received a blanket, a Serbian or French uniform, strips of rags in place of socks, German underwear of *ersatz* material, a face towel, cake of soap and a weekly ration of 10 cigarettes. The prisoners worked from 7 a.m. to 5 p.m. digging a canal, with an hour off for a midday meal. After 5 p.m. and after noon on Saturday they could volunteer for work on neighbouring farms, for which they would be paid with food supplies by the farmers. The weekly pay for the canal work was 4.70 *Reichmark*.[1] There were no medical facilities at the work-camps, but at the stalag there was a hospital, sadly lacking in medical supplies.

After the evacuation of prisoners from Florina, nearly all British[2] troops subsequently captured eventually passed through Salonika. Those becoming captive in northern Greece went there direct, probably after concentrating at Larisa or Lamia. Whilst awaiting removal to the concentration points they were held in a diverse assortment of places, maybe an open field, empty houses, schools or even a cemetery.

The majority of prisoners captured in the southern areas were first concentrated at Corinth, where, too, prisoners from Crete were later congregated. The centre at Corinth already held 4,000 Italians who had been taken prisoners by the Greeks and who the Germans decided would still remain under guard.

By 6th May nearly 8,000 British prisoners (including 350 officers) were packed into a sandy area of about 15 acres near an aerodrome on the outskirts of Corinth. Inside the perimeter were old stone buildings

---

[9] See Long, *Greece, Crete and Syria,* Chapter 3.
[1] At the exchange rate agreed by Britain and Germany of 15*Rm* to £1 sterling.
[2] The term "British" throughout this appendix includes British Army troops, Empire troops, Cypriots and Palestinians.

and verminous wooden sheds lacking ventilation. The prisoners slept on stone floors; no beds or blankets were provided.[3] An open-trench latrine over 200 yards long was the only pretext to sanitation and dysentery was rife. Until the advent of older troops, unfit for front-line service, as guards, who proved more reasonable than their predecessors—paratroopers, Austrians and young S.S. guards in turn—the prisoners were subjected to the free use of rifle-butts on the person and there was unnecessary shooting in the compound resulting in some casualties.

A typical day's ration of about 800 calories[4] included a small quantity of dried fish, verminous lentils and a hard army biscuit, with a very little sugar or honey. It was possible to supplement this by gifts from, or purchases through, the Greek Red Cross; water was scarce, the daily ration being one quart obtained from primitive wells.

After the visit of an International Red Cross delegate, Dr Brunel, rations improved both in quality and quantity. Prisoners were allowed to go in parties to bathe, easing the personal hygiene problem. After the German attack on Crete, the camp commandant closed the camp market, reduced the already inadequate rations and imposed harsher discipline as a reprisal for alleged British atrocities to German paratroops in Crete, charges which later were admitted to be untrue.

On the arrival at Corinth of some of the prisoners of war from Crete early in June the transfer of those already there to Salonika was commenced. Batches of several hundreds went by train from Corinth to Gravia, then made a 25-mile march, which included the 4,000-foot Brallos Pass, to a siding near Lamia, where the captives were herded into cattle-trucks for the rail journey north to Salonika. Some parties went through Yugoslavia to Austria or Germany direct but the majority were staged at Salonika in a transit camp known as Frontstalag 183, their stay there varying from a few days to six months. This evacuation continued for a week, and by 11th June Corinth was cleared of most British prisoners. A number managed to evade the guards during the march between Gravia and Lamia and to escape into the hills where they were befriended by Greek peasants, but most escapers were gradually recaptured after varying periods and experiences. A few were able to get clear away and eventually rejoin their unit in Palestine via Turkey or islands of the Dodecanese group.

After the surrender in Crete those who did not succeed in evading capture were gradually concentrated near Canea where Australians, English, New Zealanders, Cypriots and Greeks straggled in, hungry, foot-sore and dispirited, until there was a mass of upwards of 15,000 Allied prisoners herded in a small sandy area, where they lay down in any available space. Water was scarce, shelter nil, except for a few small tents; there were no blankets, and food was at an absolute minimum, the main

---

[3] Prisoners taken at Tolos, however, had been equipped by the Germans with one blanket and a greatcoat before they left for Corinth.
[4] 2,250 calories were considered necessary to maintain normal health and 3,400 when engaged in manual work: *ICRC Report on its Activities during the Second World War*, Vol I, pp. 335-7.

source being what could be scrounged, by authorised parties, from former British dumps. Poultry, rabbits and in one instance a bullock, were also brought in and shared communally. Several narratives refer to a donkey that strayed into the camp area and was dispatched and devoured as food. The stench in the area surrounding the camp was overpowering, many bodies lay unburied and prisoners were set to work by the Germans as burial parties. Some were also forced to work on an adjacent aerodrome. Many escaped from this camp and some succeeded in reaching Egypt or Palestine, but as no records were made of the inhabitants of Dulag Kreta, as the camp was called by the Germans, it is impossible to tell who came under the categories of "escaped prisoners" or of "evaders".

The removal of Allied prisoners from Crete was partly by air and partly by sea. Most of the wounded and sick were flown by returning German troop-carrying aircraft to Athens where they were cared for at near-by Kokkinia in the 2/5th Australian General Hospital. Some uninjured prisoners, mostly officers, were also flown to the mainland of Greece, but the main body was shipped in parties of up to 1,000 on small coastal trading boats with primitive or no sanitary provision. Many were now suffering severely from dysentery which accentuated the misery of all. The first Australians to be shipped off left Suda Bay at the end of June, soon after Germany attacked Russia. Rations were issued on embarkation to last the period of the voyage. These were woefully inadequate and the men were ravenously hungry, with the result that few were able to make their rations last over the three to five days' voyage. Then they went on to Salonika by train. The first Australians from Crete arrived at Salonika towards the end of June when there were 7,000 Allied captives in the camp, including about 1,500 Yugoslavs and parties continued to arrive during the next few weeks, swelling the camp population to more than 12,000.

Bad as were conditions hitherto experienced those awaiting the captives at Salonika were infinitely worse. The accommodation—dilapidated barracks built during the Turko-Grecian wars and infested by fleas and bugs—was pitifully inadequate and many slept in the open; very few had any bedding and 50 per cent were without even one blanket. Indiscriminate firing by brutal and "trigger-happy" German guards caused casualties, kicking and use of rifle-butts and belts were common. Many were still suffering from dysentery, and now malaria added to the troops' misery. No one was allowed to the latrines after dark and several were shot for so doing, as also were two British officers discovered on the parade ground after nightfall, although they answered the guard's challenge and surrendered to the patrol. In one month seven British were shot; the bodies of two shot while scaling the wire were left hanging there for 24 hours as a warning. A camp hospital was established but, apart from drugs brought in by medical personnel who were prisoners, the only medical supplies available were a little quinine, the issue of which ceased after a few days, and some paper bandages. Charcoal, ground in the camp, was the only treatment available for dysentery cases. The Greek

Red Cross was unable to supply any drugs or medical supplies but did provide milk, eggs, fruit and special diet for the sick. The daily rations were: for breakfast a cup of mint tea and a slice, about four ounces, of black bread, always stale and sometimes mouldy; at midday, about a pint of thin watery lentil soup or alternatively two ounces of dried salty fish; and at night another cup of mint tea and half to three-quarters of a Greek army biscuit. This, without variation, was the ration for six weeks, and on this nearly all under the rank of sergeant, irrespective of fitness, were forced to work each day on the docks, railway sidings or timber yards of Salonika. Some guards were sympathetic towards those obviously too weak for heavy work, but in the main there was much bullying, kicking, and knocking with rifle-butts by the bellowing guards. There was some amelioration for the working parties, however, because by going out of camp they were able by devious and diverse means to obtain food and tobacco.

Many took the opportunity while on working parties to escape as also did some from the main camp, with varying fortunes. Some were recaptured and found themselves back in the same camp. Others got away to Turkey and freedom. For example, Gunner Brewer[5] escaped from the camp and after being befriended in Salonika by Greeks set off eastwards, where he contacted some monks who took him and others who had reached this point to Turkey by boat. Four months after escaping, he arrived back in Egypt where he volunteered to return to Greece to help in evacuating British soldiers still hiding in the Salonika area. For over six months he worked behind the enemy lines using the many useful contacts he had made in Salonika in helping others to escape. In another instance Sergeant Brown,[6] with two others, escaped by digging under the floorboards. They too were sheltered in Salonika by friendly Greeks and finally left for Turkey in a caique, but, chased by Germans, they were forced ashore. Brown spent the winter in the hills with other escapers, supported by the local villagers. When food became scarcer, the party split up and Brown with an Englishman and a Cypriot went in search of another boat; this they found and reached the Middle East via Turkey on 13th May 1942.

The only credit due to the Germans in their behaviour towards the prisoners of war at this period is for their treatment of the badly wounded. Not only were these spared the tortuous rail journey from Athens to Salonika, but also they were kept in the infamous camp for no more than a few days. The blinded, amputees and seriously sick were embarked at Athens for Salonika in the Italian hospital ship *Gradisca* and the treatment from Italian doctors and nurses on board was beyond reproach. These patients went north to Germany by hospital train. The less serious cases were shipped on small cargo boats on which food and treatment

---

[5] Capt F. N. T. Brewer, MM, NX3461. 2/1 Fd Regt, 2/3 Indep Coy, 2/3 Bn. Mechanic; of Wauchope, NSW; b. Edendale, NZ, 19 Nov 1918.
[6] Lt C. S. Brown, MM, NX4120; 2/1 Bn. Salesman; of Mosman, NSW; b. Bristol, England, 27 Sep 1912.

were reasonable, although the accommodation was overcrowded. Regarding the treatment of the prisoners in the camps and in transit, it might be urged in extenuation that the Germans were embarrassed by the influx of 25,000 Commonwealth troops captured in Greece and Crete whom they had to control and feed at the end of a long supply line and in an occupied country the inhabitants of which were completely uncooperative, but no excuse can be found for the neglect of the authorities administering the camps or for the uncontrolled brutalities of the guards. Few of the prisoners realised that the camps they had so far experienced were no more than transit camps and that eventually things would improve, but as each successive move had produced a worsening of conditions they can be forgiven for seeing little hope for the future. Many had disposed of their personal effects to buy, at highly inflated prices, extra food which was in most cases, ironically, British army rations. The calorific value of the daily ration issued was as low as 850. At a later date it was stated in a report by representatives[7] of the Protecting Power that:

> The Australian physician is Captain Playoust[8] who stated . . . the prisoners are beginning to come around. They were formerly badly undernourished in Crete and Greece. This conclusion was agreed with by chief German physician, Oberstabsarzt Dr Soebald.

As the move from Corinth to Salonika had conformed to a general pattern, so too did the transfer from Salonika north to Austria and Germany. From 10th June 1941 onwards parties of prisoners usually 1,000 strong were herded into cattle-trucks, designed to accommodate *40 hommes ou 8 chevaux*,[9] but into which were crowded an average of 35 officers or in the case of other ranks, 55, and in at least one case up to 66.

Rations for three or four days, according to the contemplated length of the journey, were issued, and consisted only of biscuits and tinned meat. Those in possession of water-bottles could fill them before leaving; replenishment was impossible for several days. Invariably the journey took seven days or longer owing to delays caused by the movement southward of German troops (the trip to Lubeck on the Baltic took nine nights and eight days). Sometimes the doors of the trucks were locked and the small apertures wired or barred; sometimes one door was left open. There was scarcely room for all to lie down, and sleep, on the hard floors and with the jolting of the primitive trucks, was difficult. The cold draughty nights after hot summer days, or in winter the freezing temperatures over the mountainous country, made the journey in itself a torture, but the most serious features were the scarcity of water and the absolute absence of sanitary facilities. Doors were not opened for periods of up to 24 hours. With many of the men still suffering from dysentery or like complaints, conditions may be better imagined than described. Some used eating utensils as sanitary receptacles, some had no eating utensils.

---

[7] Gordon Knox and Dr Howard Fishburn, Americans, in a report on Stalag XIIIC, September 1941.
[8] Capt R. A. Playoust, NX185; 2/1 Fd Amb. Medical practitioner; of Mosman, NSW; b. Sydney, 14 Jan 1900. Died 24 Aug 1962.
[9] 40 men or 8 horses. French rolling-stock was so labelled.

At some stops Yugoslavs handed food to the prisoners—bread, eggs, bacon fat and so on—through the windows of the trucks. At Salzburg German Red Cross workers met one of the first trains at 1.30 a.m. with cups of hot *ersatz* coffee, and next day at Munich Red Cross workers provided soup and a slice of bread for lunch and coffee and a slice of bread in the evening. Prisoners on later trains were less fortunate.

Despite warnings of reprisals by shooting there were escapes from practically every train. For example in June 1941 four Australians, including Corporal Lesar[1] and Private Sayers,[2] by the use of their boots forced the steel bars from the ventilators and jumped from the train as it was travelling between Belgrade and Zemun in Yugoslavia. For eight weeks they were sheltered by peasants and later introduced to adherents of the partisan movement. Their several attempts to leave Yugoslavia for Turkey were frustrated by a Chetnik leader. Lesar and Sayers thereupon served with the Chetniks for six months when they were permitted to report to a British paratroop detachment, with which they were employed, Lesar for 14 months as an interpreter, Sayers for 10 months, before both were evacuated to Bari, Italy, reaching Australia in September 1944. Private Boon,[3] who had made a similar escape from a train, stayed with the Chetniks for several weeks until, believing their leader was preparing to collaborate with the Germans, he went to Prokuplje, later linking up with other escapers at Brus in October 1941. With another man he spent over a year moving from one partisan group to another endeavouring to obtain assistance in leaving Yugoslavia. Eventually in March 1943 they located the British paratroop detachment and until evacuated to Italy 14 months later, they also were employed by them.

A favourite method of escaping from these trucks en route to Germany was by cutting, with smuggled tools, a hole in or near the door and reaching outside to release or remove the bolt fittings. Two Australians who escaped in this manner were Sergeant Kilby,[4] with 14 others and Sergeant Dyer[5] with 12 others. Both reached the Middle East safely by way of Turkey. The quick thinking of Warrant-Officer Barrett[6] led him to freedom. He was among a party that left Salonika on 9th July and while alighted at a town in Austria to change to another train, Barrett jumped into the empty brake-van of a train moving in the opposite direction; 25 hours later he found himself at Belgrade where he left the train and approached some cottages. He was succoured by the inhabitants and after three weeks with sympathisers during which he wandered freely around Belgrade with them, he was smuggled into a truck under a tarpaulin

---

[1] S-Sgt H. Lesar, MM, VX11469; 6 Div HQ. Clerk; of Bonbeach, Vic; b. Merricks, Vic, 6 Dec 1922.

[2] Sgt W. F. R. Sayers, MM, VX35920; 2/6 Bn. Trainee diesel engineer; of Castlemaine, Vic; b. Castlemaine, 1 Feb 1920.

[3] Capt W. J. Boon, MM, NX3814; 6 Div Postal Unit. Catering manager; of Wiseman's Ferry, NSW; b. Kettering, England, 15 Oct 1908.

[4] WO2 H. E. Kilby, MM, NX8575; 2/1 Bn. Cook; of Balmain, NSW; b. Balaklava, SA, 10 Oct 1905.

[5] Lt J. Dyer, MM, NX2776; 2/1 Bn. Optician; of Albury, NSW; b. Woodlark I, TNG, 6 Sep 1911.

[6] Lt F. A. Barrett, DCM, NX18434. 2/1 Bn, "M" Special Unit. Clerk; of Croydon, NSW; b. Sydney, 3 Sep 1911. Killed in action 24 Oct 1943.

and so reached Greece. After numerous setbacks and adventures he reached Turkey on 12th September and safety a month later, bringing back interesting information about enemy activities. It would be impossible to estimate how many escaped from these trains. Few, however, managed to finally reach Allied territory. Of those who were not immediately recaptured, the majority were picked up when endeavouring to make their way back to southern Greece.

Some were shot while trying to escape from trains. For example, Signalman Avery[7] who had been at large on Crete for some weeks in June before being wounded and captured there was shot while trying to escape from a train travelling north from Salonika. However, despite threats by the Germans there were no shootings as reprisals for the continued escapes although almost invariably those left in the trucks from which escapers had made their way were subject to kickings and rifle-butt jabs from the infuriated guards.

The first parties to leave Salonika were composed mainly of officers and the first trainload, containing some Australians, reached Oflag VB at Biberach, Bavaria, on 16th June. The new arrivals, having more or less resigned themselves to accept the conditions they had experienced since capture, here received a shock, albeit a particularly pleasant one. They found a well-organised camp, hot showers, sufficient food to stave off hunger and such luxuries as clean bed linen, towels and eating utensils. Moreover, the friendly welcome and generosity of the officers of the three British armed Services already in the camp were a morale-booster which was badly needed. Quarters were modern concrete buildings, divided into rooms which were not over-crowded. These contained steel-framed two-decker beds with wooden slats—a type to become well known to many officers and N.C.O's in the next four years. For the first time since capture they were free of vermin. The German rations issued were the best yet experienced and were properly cooked in the camp kitchen, but for two or three months few Red Cross supplies were available. Pay in *Lagergeld* (camp money) was credited regularly and letter-cards issued for writing home. Educational classes were well organised and facilities were available for sport and exercise. To the newcomers all this seemed a pleasant dream but it must be stressed that such a state of affairs existed only through the hard work, organisation and tactful approach of the camp leaders to the German authorities.

On the arrival at Biberach of more officers from Salonika, some of the inhabitants of the camp were transferred to Tittmoning; amongst these were six Australians.

An escape committee was in operation at Biberach, the newcomers being permitted to assist but, as a rule, not to engage in the actual escape. During the next three months numerous breaks were made, mainly by men in disguise or concealed on vehicles leaving the camp, and on 14th September 26 escaped by means of a tunnel. In October the Germans,

---
[7] Sig J. L. Avery, NX14080; 6 Div Sigs. Shop boy; of Dawes Point, NSW; b. Sydney, 2 Mar 1921. Killed while prisoner of war 2 Oct 1941.

because of the number of escapes and the proximity of the camp to the Swiss border, transferred the officers to Oflag VIB at Warburg, where British officers from all parts of Germany were being concentrated. The majority of officers from Crete on leaving Salonika were destined for Oflag XC, near the Baltic port of Lubeck. Nearly 100 Australian officers arrived there during July and stayed until October when they too were transferred to Warburg. At Lubeck the accommodation and facilities generally were much like those at Biberach, but the excellent camp organisation was missing, as was Red Cross food. The German rations, consisting mainly of potatoes and bread, were so sparse that the loaves were carefully measured to ensure that each person got his full share. Patients in the camp hospital received a half-litre of turnip soup and four slices of black bread daily plus *ersatz* coffee, sugarless, twice daily. The effect of these rations, following the starvation diet of the past few months, was so severe that, on arrival at Warburg, the men from Lubeck were given double Red Cross issues for a period to enable them to regain some of their lost weight. The only medical supplies issued by the Germans at Oflag XC were "Karlsbad" salts, iodine and paper bandages.

Included in the trainloads of other ranks leaving Salonika during July were approximately 700 for Marburg, and about 900 for Wolfsberg, 50 miles to the north-west and over the border. Those arriving at Stalag XVIIID, Marburg, were less fortunate than those going to other camps, for it was merely another transit camp very little better than the one at Salonika. The few buildings were verminous and dirty. The new arrivals were quartered in tents and slept on the bare ground while new buildings were being erected. The Senior British Medical Officer considered the camp to be overcrowded beyond safety. Medical facilities provided by the Germans were crude. At this stage the menu was: 4.30 a.m., cup of *ersatz* coffee; 11.30 a.m., one pint of potato or cabbage soup; 5 p.m., half a pound of black bread and approximately half an ounce of margarine or jam. There were shootings by trigger-happy guards for breaches of discipline. Conditions improved somewhat after a visit by the Protecting Power representative, but by this time a large percentage of the occupants had been drafted out to various work-camps in the area. Those who went to the work-camps were employed on various projects—roads, railways, factories or odd jobs about the town—while many were hired out to farmers, with whom they worked long hours but usually fared better for food. Fraternisation between civilians and prisoners was punishable with dire penalties; nevertheless many friendships developed. Early in September a Red Cross consignment arrived which gave a great fillip to morale, and with continued regular supplies an ample diet was ensured.

There had also been an improvement in conditions in the stalag, more particularly in the camp hospital where British doctors had secured bedding and blankets for the sick. The seriously ill were transferred to the civilian hospital in Marburg, where they received excellent treatment from the Yugoslav doctors and nurses. Nevertheless, visitors from the American

(M. Lee Hill)

"Anzac Avenue", Stalag 383.

(W. Dryvynsyde)

The costumes and props, all made in the camp, used in the presentation of this play at Oflag VIIB, Eichstatt, demonstrate remarkable ingenuity in improvisation by the prisoners of war.

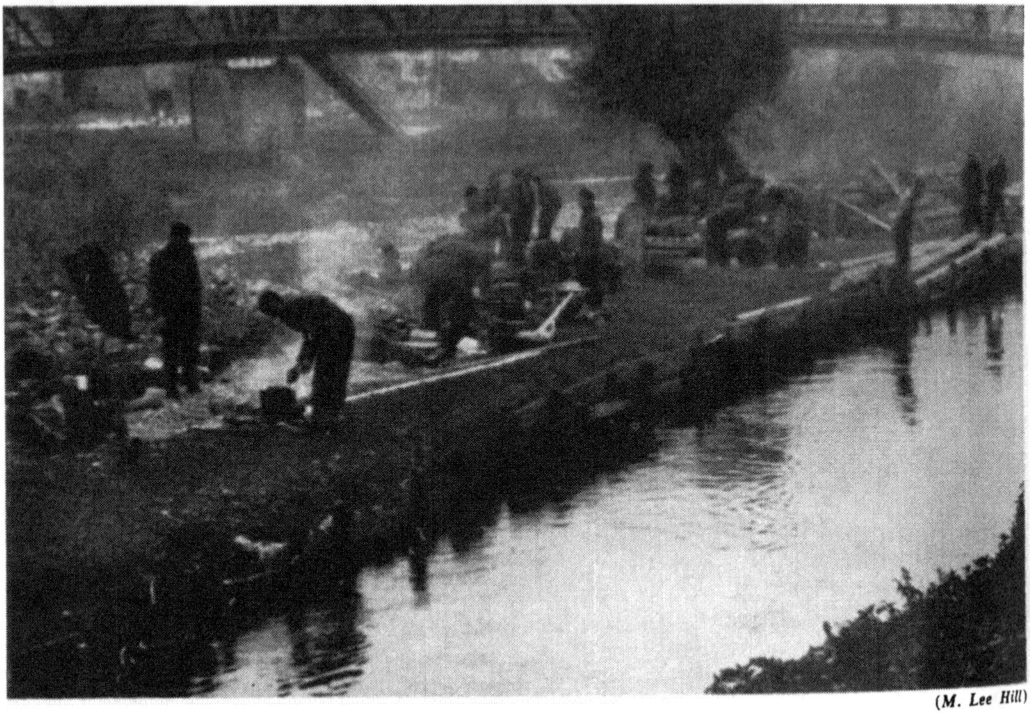

(M. Lee Hill)

Forced marches. Men from Stalag 383 halt for a meal at Etehausen during their journey south.

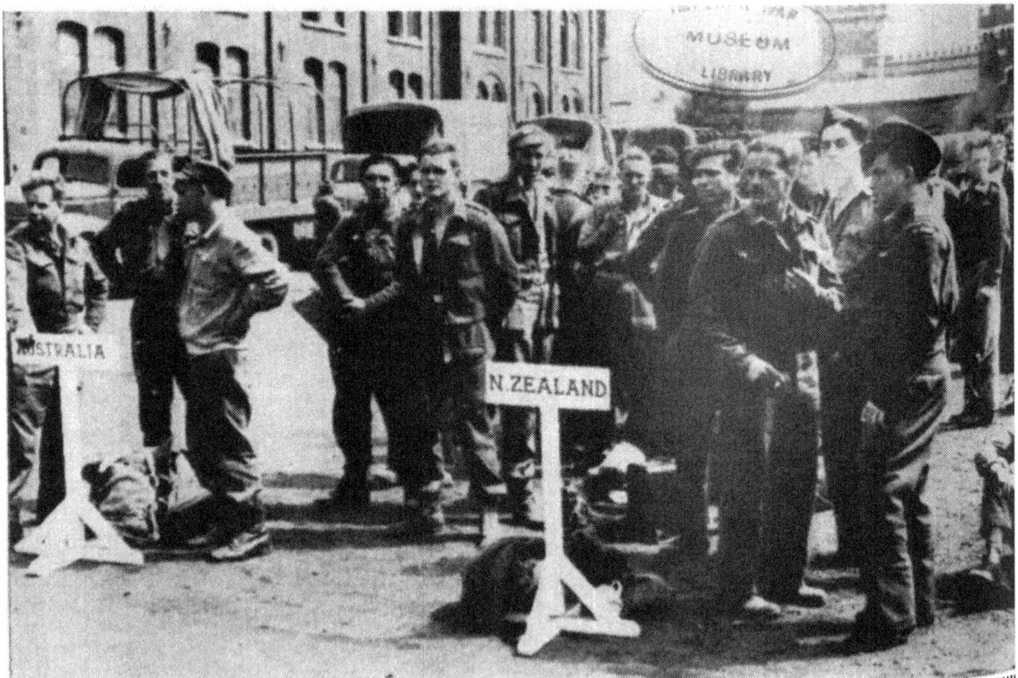

(M. Lee Hill)

Recovered prisoners of war at a transit centre at Brussels, Belgium, whence they were flown to the United Kingdom.

Embassy and the I.C.R.C. in October reported conditions as deplorable, with everything in disorder and badly organised, and said that the camp was a real danger to the health of the prisoners.[8] By the end of 1941, letters and parcels were arriving from home and concerts and theatrical shows were taking place, the Germans being particularly cooperative. Books were also coming into the camp in increasing numbers but physical recreation or exercise was limited owing to lack of space, there being room for one basket-ball court only. But it was still a bad camp and there was an outbreak of typhus early in 1942, the Russians being the worst sufferers. Several months later all British prisoners had been moved —those available for work to various work-camps, and non-working N.C.O's, medical personnel and unfit to Stalag XVIIIB (later XVIIIA/Z) at Spittal, Austria. It was not until the visit of the American Embassy officials in October that N.C.O's were aware that under the Geneva Convention they could not be forced to work and they were now asserting their rights. So far as British prisoners were concerned, the camp at Marburg had been "dissolved because it did not reach the standard of other main camps in the Salzburg district".

The Australians who were sent to Wolfsberg from Salonika were installed in Stalag XVIIIA situated just outside the town, which was set in a broad green valley backed by slopes of fir-trees and snowcapped mountains. Here they found some sort of organisation. In order to keep the camp free of vermin the trainloads as they arrived were temporarily placed in eight large tents. Here they were searched and had a hot shower and their clothes were fumigated; they were also registered in camp records. As further trainloads arrived those who had been through the delousing process were transferred to work-camps to make room for the new arrivals. Those remaining were accommodated in brick stables converted into barracks with three-tier bunks complete with palliasses and blankets. The hygiene and sanitary provisions were improvised though primitive. The food here, supplemented by Red Cross parcels, was ample, although the German ration had been reduced when Red Cross consignments arrived. With sufficient food, a clean camp and a bracing climate there was a gradual improvement in health. The British prisoners, of whom about 850 were Australians, soon organised themselves into a strong community. A "man-of-confidence"[9] was elected whose duties included camp administration and control and liaison with the Germans on all matters affecting the prisoners' welfare. He also was a liaison agent of the International Committee of the Red Cross. This committee was most appreciative of the efforts of the camp leaders.

The most important work done by camp leaders was in the help given to prisoners. . . . The camp leader was responsible for ensuring the issue of supplies precisely according to the wishes of the donors, and for rendering an account to Geneva,

---

[8] W. Wynne Mason, *Prisoners of War* (1954), a volume in the series *Official History of New Zealand in the Second World War 1939-45*. This 546-page book is one of the main published sources for this appendix.

[9] The term "man-of-confidence" is a literal translation of the French "homme-de-confiance" which appears in the French text of the 1929 Geneva POW Convention, its equivalent in the English text being "representative". More often than not they were called "camp leaders".

supported by documents such as detailed receipts, issue vouchers etc. . . . Throughout the war years, the Committee was able to appreciate how hard these men must have worked and with what devotion and human understanding they applied themselves to the task of maintaining a regular flow and issue of relief supplies to PW. The duties of camp leaders were also useful in other important connections; for instance they gave valuable assistance to the Committee in making up lists of PW. . . . Thus in each camp the leader became a centre of information, always on hand to give help or counsel, to mediate where he thought some useful purpose would be served and to deal with the PWs' many and various worries. . . . When a PW died it was the camp leader who wrote to the bereaved family and expressed the sympathies of his comrades. And it was the camp leader who saw to the tending of the grave.[1]

The camp leader at Stalag XVIIIA from December 1942 was an Australian, Warrant-Officer E. J. Stevenson.[2] Elected by his fellow prisoners of war, he retained the position as chief representative of 11,000 English, Australian, New Zealand, Canadian, South African and American prisoners until the end of the war.

The camp leader usually had an assistant who relieved him of responsibility for discipline, and in addition there were hut commanders who supervised the inmates of their hut and were responsible to the camp leaders. The working detachments were formed into companies, each detachment having a leader responsible to the company leader, who in turn was answerable to the camp leader, but communication between the camp leader and the working detachments outside the camp was difficult and often the cause of complaints to the representative of the Protecting Power. Amenities gradually were increased and improved. Books came into the camp in August 1941 and afforded a much-needed relief to the monotony. A small stage was erected and theatricals were undertaken.

During September mail arrived from England, but none for the Australians or New Zealanders. It was, however, a link with the outside world —and the Tommies shared their news. With the approaching winter, the lower temperatures were causing hardship to the majority, who were without underclothing and socks and had only worn-out boots (during the summer many had worked without boots in order to conserve them). The quarters were damp and comfortless with very little light. The washing and sanitary arrangements had not been improved although improvement had been promised. Conditions in the work-camps depended mainly on the type of the German N.C.O's in charge and of the civilians for whom the men worked. One labour detachment, including 52 Australians, working on the construction of a dam at Lavamund was housed on the site "in three wooden barracks, simple but sufficiently comfortable, well aired and lighted, easily warmed by stoves".[3] The tiered beds were of wood but a man's only bedding was a palliasse and one blanket. The men received a ration slightly heavier than in the stalag but not as much as that laid down for manual work. However, the Red Cross parcels, now arriving regularly, made up the deficiency. The I.C.R.C. representatives were not

---
[1] *ICRC Report on its Activities during the Second World War*, Vol I, pp. 344-5.
[2] See Long, *Greece, Crete and Syria*, p. 167.
[3] ICRC report, Drs Descoeudres and Rubli, 25th October 1941.

satisfied with the condition of the clothing, lack of underclothing and socks and stated the boots were in a terrible state. When reporting on the infirmary attached to the work-camp they reported that many were sick because of lack of clothing. Supplies of British battledress had arrived at Stalag XVIIIA in September 1941, but owing to a dispute between the Germans and the camp leaders over control of the issue it was withheld until January 1942, the prisoners finally having the last say. A British doctor was permanently at the camp, but in the majority of work-camps lack of treatment of injuries was a cause of serious complaint by the medical officers in the stalag who eventually had to treat them.

The prisoners worked day and night shifts; each man working an actual 10 hours and a half with a full day off each week. Pay was at the general rate for prisoners of 70 *pfennig*[4] a day. Certain specialists and good workmen received double pay. No overtime was paid. Two other work-parties visited at the same time by the I.C.R.C. representative were grouped in one camp. One party of 180 British, including 70 Australians, was employed on a housing project. They were placed in wooden barracks divided into rooms in which 16 were billeted. The employing firm issued them with four blankets each in addition to their own. This was one camp where the sanitary accommodation was reported as adequate. There were no complaints about the food. This camp was declared by the inspecting delegate to be "a model camp" and was replete with flower and vegetable gardens and ample space for sport.

Other work-camps in the area were not as good. Six hundred men, of whom 180 had been passed for light duty, were sent to two camps—Gruppenstein and Lassach. At Lassach they were employed on road-making over a steep mountain, working an actual 10 hours a day with half-an-hour's march to and from the camp. They were continually harassed to "Hurry, hurry", by the civilian gang-boss, each boss having an allotted quota to complete. Once weekly the sick were marched to Malnitge to a civilian doctor who refused to treat Australians or New Zealanders remarking "You volunteered to shoot my brother. Get out!" This problem was overcome by exchanging coats with Englishmen. The doctor wrote a prescription and the patients bought the medicine or supplies from the local chemist with their own funds. This was not an isolated instance of prisoners having to buy medical supplies. At one work-camp the men had to pay for the medicines and dental treatment they received.[5] At other work-camps connected with Stalag XVIIIA, Wolfsberg, prisoners were employed in brickworks, paper mills, a glass factory and at farms and forestry camps.

On 10th August 1941 about 1,000 Australians left Salonika for Hammelburg, 50 miles east of Frankfurt-on-Main, arriving there seven days later after a train trip similar to those already described. On arrival at Hammelburg station a German medical officer refused to allow the guards

---

[4] About 11d.
[5] ICRC report, 24th October 1941.

to start the four-mile march to the camp, Stalag XIIIC, until the prisoners had been fed. They were thereupon issued with a large ladle of soup and a loaf of bread between five. At the camp they were deloused and allowed a hot shower. Their clothing and boots were taken from them and they were issued with a conglomeration of French, Belgian and Serbian uniforms, two pairs of cotton underpants, a pair of wooden clogs and, instead of socks, two sets of *Fusslappen*, strips of material to wrap around the feet, known in the vernacular as "toe-rags". The Australians were quartered in what had been a large storage barracks equipped with double-tier beds. Food was the standard prisoner-of-war ration but slightly more generous than in some camps. Those from Greece considered the food very satisfactory. The British man-of-confidence was Warrant-Officer Brown[6] and the British medical officer, Captain Playoust. Officials of the American Embassy in Berlin visited the camp in September and reported among other things, "that adequate treatment was available in the camp infirmary; the Australians find this camp a veritable paradise compared with Crete and Greece, but they are not in a position to make accurate criticisms from long experience" and "the Australian prisoners here should be visited again when they have time to find their feet". The visitors stressed, however, the lack of warm clothing, including uniforms and boots. Soon after arrival at Stalag XIIIC 900 Australians were dispersed among various work-camps attached to the camp and their employment included road-making, farm work and the building of dikes along and near the Rhone River.

In February 1942 the I.C.R.C. representatives after a visit to the stalag reported[7] that, although the clothing position in the main camp had improved somewhat, it had deteriorated in the work-camps. Nearly all the prisoners had only one uniform in which they must work, the few exceptions receiving working clothes from their employers. In the wet winter this was a serious menace to health. Red Cross parcels were being received and the Australians were forwarding them individually to men in work-camps. In the main camp the leader in an unwitnessed interview with the delegates complained that "the camp was overcrowded, the sanitary installations insufficient and the general hygiene of the camp left much to be desired". In these matters the delegates concurred. On the other hand, the leader stated, "the food is good and the attitude of the Germans could not offend any critic". The I.C.R.C. delegates said in their report that heating, lighting and ventilation in the huts were insufficient and that the infirmary was too small. A French dentist was operating, but had had to suspend the supply and repair of dentures owing to lack of materials; this seemed to be the position in most camps throughout Germany. Mass was celebrated every Sunday at the camp. The library comprised 4,500 books (all languages) but card and indoor games were insufficient.

In one of the last batches of prisoners to leave Salonika in the summer

---

[6] WO1 W. R. Brown, MBE, WX270; 2/11 Bn. Dairyman; of Perth, WA; b. Perth, Scotland, 16 Oct 1900. Died 22 Sep 1961.

[7] ICRC report, Drs Schirmer and Masset, 3rd February 1942.

of 1941 was a party of approximately 1,000 Australians who arrived at Stalag VIIA, Moosburg, near Munich, on 20th August. Here they found conditions comparatively good. The camp already housed some thousands of French prisoners, who received the Australians with friendliness and sympathy, taking up a collection of food for them. One Australian[8] records that the Germans "did everything they could to relieve our condition on arrival. They gave us an easy time for the first few days." These men had been cooped up in cattle-trucks for six days during which the doors were only opened once, when they were let out for a quarter of an hour's exercise and a drink of tea. An incident on this journey could have led to a post-war friendship between a German and an Australian. At a stop in Yugoslavia Sergeant Roffey[9] was endeavouring surreptitiously to exchange a gold ring for food and water. He was observed by the N.C.O. in charge of the German guard, who, after explanations had been given, purchased food for the Australian, refusing to accept the ring in payment. On two subsequent stops the German gave his adopted friend food, coffee, beer and fruit. At the last stop before the destination the German *Feldwebel*[1] went to the truck and told the Australian he was going on ahead to make arrangements for their arrival and asked for the prisoner's home address so that he could write to him after the war. Roffey gave his address and offered the ring in repayment of the German's kindness. The German took the ring and stated he would return it after the war. On arrival at Moosburg, the *Feldwebel* slipped 10 *Reichmark* into the Australian's hand, remarking "These will be very useful to you in your camp. Do not say where you got them." Almost 12 months later the same German, on leave in the district from the Russian front, called at the camp to see Roffey and wanted to take him to his home, if the commandant would permit. Permission was refused, however, as Roffey had been found, some time previously, to be in possession of maps. The German N.C.O. again visited Roffey, stating he was on draft for Russia, but this was the last Roffey heard of him.

The quarters at Stalag VIIA consisted of groups of huts, each group containing two large dormitories, each with 200 beds in tiers of three. The palliasses were filled with wood-wool and two blankets a man were issued, although some were unlucky and only received two half-blankets. It was suspected that a French prisoner in charge of the blankets had sold many and made up his count by halving some of the remainder. A few days after arrival the men were issued with French uniforms in fairly good condition. The I.C.R.C. delegate complained during a visit in November that the British were wearing uniforms which were incongruous. "Many of them are dressed in uniforms from other units and that hurts their pride."[2]

---

[8] Gnr D. Lang, DCM, VX6693. 2/8 Bn, 2/4 Lt A-A Regt. Agricultural student; of Brighton Beach, Vic; b. Elsternwick, Vic, 21 Oct 1921.
[9] Lt G. C. de F. Roffey, EM, NX2646; 2/1 Bn. Clerk; of Maroubra, NSW; b. Balmain, NSW, 21 Mar 1914.
[1] German equivalent of sergeant-major.
[2] ICRC report, Dr Exchaquet, 25th November 1941.

The rations consisted of the standard cup of *ersatz* coffee for breakfast, cabbage and potato soup and a thick slice of bread for dinner, or sometimes instead *sauerkraut* and two potatoes in their skins and for tea cabbage and potato soup or carrot soup. Twice weekly a small amount of margarine was issued. On Sundays breakfast and dinner were combined. No one had seriously considered escape from the stalag as it was learned from the French that better prospects of escape existed in the work-camps.[3] After a month in the camp most of the new arrivals were drafted to work-camps in the Munich area, where they were employed in timber mills, railway yards, on railway permanent-way maintenance and in cleaning garbage from the streets of Munich.

Transfer to work detachments was favourably regarded by the prisoners for various reasons; escape was easier, food was better, and there were more opportunities to sell the contents of Red Cross food parcels to civilians, thereby accumulating an escape fund. Fifty cigarettes fetched 20 *Reichmark* or more, while four ounces of tea changed hands for anything from 10 to 20 *Reichmark*. Moreover bugs and fleas were less prevalent. The favourite occupation was cleaning garbage from the streets of Munich, which made it possible more or less to roam at will in the city; indeed prisoners stated that with a two-ounce tin of tea or a small cake of soap they received preferential treatment at the brothels of Munich.

Prospective escapers from these work-camps were afforded an excellent opportunity of reaching Swiss territory—if their luck held. A train left Munich nightly for Switzerland and those working in and around the marshalling yards were able to acquaint themselves of the layout and where the train was being made up. On 26th November Corporal Parker[4] with two others made their escape from a work-party in the area and went to the marshalling yards where they separated. Parker hid in some shrubs on the outskirts of the city until nightfall. When he returned to the yards and found the train bound for St Margrethen, the first station over the Swiss border, he strapped a ladder, which he found on the side of the train, underneath a carriage and travelled the entire journey, which lasted 25 hours, resting on the ladder. On reaching St Margrethen he gave himself up to the Swiss police and five days later was handed over to the British Military Attache at Berne, reaching England in mid-July 1942.

In March 1942 Gunner Lang had figured in a similar escapade. He had previously managed to accumulate maps stolen from the walls of stationary trains, and with escape in view he and a companion had been hoarding articles of civilian clothing, money and food. In the evening of 30th March they scrambled through the wire surrounding the work-camp and made their way to an old house where their stock of clothing was concealed. Hiding in the rafters until 2 a.m. they then made their way through the outskirts of the city, passing over a flood-lit bridge in the

---

[3] On 13 July 1942 it was recorded that "of the 41 British troops in the detention barracks at Stalag VIIA, 36 of them are Australians who have tried to escape from kommandos".

[4] Lt J. A. Parker, DCM, NX3653. 2/1 Fd Coy, 1 Base Store Coy. Turner and fitter; of Coff's Harbour, NSW; b. Coff's Harbour, 10 Jun 1918. Died of injuries accidentally received 3 Oct 1944.

process, to the marshalling yards. Other British prisoners at their work-camp who were awaiting removal to prison for their attempted escapes had previously told them of the exact location of the siding in which the Swiss train was made up. This they eventually found and they dived into the shadows beneath the coach directly behind the engine. Lang, by removing his overcoat, managed to squeeze himself on to a structure running parallel with one of the wheels. Throughout the journey the wheel at times rubbed against his shoe but did no damage. His companion succeeded in wriggling on to a section of the brake with his body lying parallel to the axle. A crouched position had to be maintained in order to keep his feet from the wheels. The weight of his body had a tendency partly to apply the brakes and at Munich station an engineer, fuming and cursing, worked for 15 minutes within five yards of him. At 7 a.m. the next morning the train pulled out of the station and, 12 hours later, after having at times reached a terrific speed, arrived at St Margrethen. Here a police official noticed a part of Lang's clothing alongside the wheel and ordered him out. He and his companion then emerged. After spending a week in prison at St Gall where they were well treated by the Swiss police, they were taken to Berne and handed over to the British Legation, who arranged for their repatriation via unoccupied France, the Pyrenees, Spain and Gibraltar to England where they arrived on 15th June.

A touch of humour surrounds the term "camp wives", an appellation in vogue in Stalag VIIA at this period. For convenience in apportioning rations, and economy in broaching tinned food from Red Cross parcels, small syndicates of a few men were formed and each syndicate would share everything that came its way. One member of each group would by devious and various means refrain from joining working parties, remain in camp and do the household chores of the group and have the evening meal ready for the remainder of the syndicate on their return. It was amusing to see these "wives" in the late afternoon returning to their barracks from a walk around the camp or from their shopping at the camp black market to prepare the evening meal for their "menfolk".

Two theatrical troupes gave performances in the Munich work-camps on Saturday and Sunday. More literature was needed and table games were particularly lacking. Discipline was applied to the camp in a rather severe fashion. At the time of the evening roll-call police dogs were unleashed in the camp so that the men were obliged to enter the huts. Many prisoners were treated at the infirmary after being bitten. Red Cross parcels arrived in sufficient numbers to permit the issue to each prisoner of one parcel a week.

On the occasion of a visit of the I.C.R.C. delegates to Stalag VIIA in November 1941 the Germans put on a cinema show for prisoners, showing propaganda films intended for civilian consumption, including supposed battle scenes on the Russian front and also a film of operations on Crete, where many of the audience were captured. The prisoners loudly cheered the German successes (which were many) and hissed whenever

Allied forces were shown. When Australian prisoners of war were shown being marched away on Crete, the audience hissed loudly and cried "barbarians", "uncivilised cannibals"—epithets which they knew were associated with the advertising of the film in Germany. This ridicule greatly incensed the camp authorities.

At the end of February 1942, the stalag was without hot showers for a fortnight because Russian women employed in the working parties came into the camp for de-lousing and bathing. There was a large compound in the camp entirely inhabited by Russians, desperately overcrowded with prisoners of war and civilians, among whom were women and children. The Russians were very badly treated, especially with regard to rations. In the diaries of British prisoners in Stalag VIIA, the entry "another Russian shot at the wire" is unhappily too prevalent. The Russians were so desperate for food that they took any risk to get into the British or French compounds to beg scraps of food, and if discovered near the wire separating the compounds were shot by the guards without warning or question. After the arrival of Red Cross parcels at this camp the Australians periodically took up collections of food and cigarettes and at great risk smuggled them into the Russian compound.

Back in Salonika conditions had slightly improved. By September 1941 the drafts northwards had reduced Frontstalag 183 to a few who were too seriously wounded to be moved and a small medical staff, plus a number of escapers who had been recaptured in the area. These escapers included men who had escaped in Greece and some who had got away from the trains in transit to Austria and Germany. Early in September a trainload consisting of 900 convalescents and 100 repatriation cases and including some Australians left Salonika for Stalag VIIIB, Lamsdorf, in Silesia. The journey in closed goods vans, with slats removed for light and ventilation, took 9 days and 10 nights. No sanitation or water was available for the first 36 hours after which a stop of 10 minutes was made at dawn and dusk. At Belgrade 14 prisoners were removed to hospital in a deplorable condition. On arrival at the stalag, snow two feet deep was on the ground. Accommodation was in ancient wooden huts, dark, cold, and infested with bugs and fleas, erected for a prisoner-of-war camp in the first world war and now in bad condition.

The hospital, although equipped for almost any type of operation and fully staffed by British medical officers and orderlies, was hopelessly overcrowded and depended largely on the British Red Cross for medical supplies and dressings.

Bad as these conditions were they afforded the newcomers the same pleasant contrast as had been experienced by the officers who earlier had gone to Biberach, for here again was organisation—this time the result of the efforts of two British Army warrant-officers. A second trainload arrived from Salonika in October and one member of the draft recorded "on 20th October our arrival at Lamsdorf seemed to afford a glimpse of another world—a well-organised camp, food in plenty, prisoners smart in new battledress and a high morale",[5] while another who was in the camp wrote that "the bearing of the British soldiers who were captured in France and their generosity and organisation was the biggest factor in improving morale". Organised recreation was well under way, implemented by equipment and materials supplied by the World Alliance of Y.M.C.A's. Gardening produced much needed vitamins as well as mental relaxation. Football, baseball and hockey were played, while table games, handicrafts, education classes, theatricals and music were all provided. An excellent orchestra had been performing for some months. After many representations the Germans had conceded half a hut for a church and similar space for a theatre and the educational classes.

Attempts to escape from Stalag VIIIB were not considered worthwhile on account of its location, and escape activities were confined mainly to the work-camps of which there were 66 attached to the stalag. A number of men escaped from the most undesirable work-camps, more with a view to being returned to the stalag as punishment than of attaining freedom. One Australian[6] got under way from a working party in April 1942 and travelled in a coal-truck hidden by coal for three days before recapture and return to Lamsdorf. He escaped again in July from another working party and reached Vienna, some 200 miles away, only to be arrested and again returned to Lamsdorf.

Mention has been made of the 2/5th Australian General Hospital which set up a hospital at Kokkinia near Athens for the reception of sick and wounded prisoners of war. As the patients became sufficiently fit to travel they were evacuated to Salonika and thence to Germany.[7] In mid-November practically all the remaining patients were evacuated by the Italian hospital ship *Gradisca* to Salonika where they remained a few days before being sent by hospital train into Germany. There were also German wounded on the train which dropped off its occupants at various hospitals en route.

The 2/5th A.G.H. staff left Kokkinia on 4th December for Salonika and on 14th December the last party of this unit departed from there for Thorn, in Poland, reaching Stalag XXA after a 12 days' journey in horse-trucks. Fortunately for this party Red Cross parcels had reached Salonika early in November and each prisoner was issued with a parcel before entraining. This at least assuaged their hunger during the trip.

Stalag XXA was situated in an old fortress surrounded by a dry moat. The quarters were mostly underground, damp and depressing, the weather intensely cold. Conditions generally were much the same as at other stalags during the period, although here the guards were of a stricter type and several shooting fatalities occurred. There were about 7,000 British prisoners from all parts of the Commonwealth in the camp when the

---
[5] Mason, p. 88.
[6] Cpl H. Cooper, MM, VX9921; 2/1 CCS. Farmer; of Footscray, Vic; b. Richmond, Vic, 19 Mar 1905. Cooper in 1943 made two more escapes before finally reaching freedom. He then fought with the Maquis.
[7] See A. S. Walker, *Middle East and Far East*, pp. 409-10.

Australians arrived and they included some 700 non-commissioned officers who had insisted, in face of strong opposition by the Germans, on their rights under the Geneva Convention and had refused to work. They had been transferred here from various other stalags.

By the end of 1941 most Australians captured in Greece or Crete had reached base or permanent camps in Germany or Austria and were becoming more settled. Red Cross parcels were arriving, some camps certainly receiving a more regular supply, and perhaps some a more liberal supply, than others, but they were undoubtedly relieving the food shortage considerably. These parcels were packed in various countries—Britain, America, New Zealand, Canada, Argentine, and a few in Brazil and Turkey. The absence of Australia from the list led many of our prisoners to believe they were being neglected by their homeland. That was far from being so. Australia subscribed generously to the International Committee of the Red Cross for this purpose, but by arrangement with the United Kingdom Government refrained from actually supplying or packing the parcels.[8] The individual food parcels consisted of such items as: stew (meat-roll or Spam), vegetables, tea (coffee or cocoa), sugar, jam, margarine or butter, biscuits or rolled oats, cheese, chocolate (soap or sweets), tinned fruit, herrings or salmon, condensed milk or "Ovaltine", a pudding, salt and pepper, bacon and cigarettes. The Scottish parcels were the only ones to contain rolled oats, and were popular with intending escapers—it was a good escaping ration.

Even the containers of these commodities were put to good use, many men constructing from them their "blowers", or individual fireplaces. These blowers were an integral part of prisoner-of-war life, which during their evolution had emerged from the primitive two stones on which rested a billy, to an intricate contraption of continuous draught with high-pressure blower. Competitions were held, type against type and operator against operator, to boil water in the shortest time. It was possible to boil a quart in under two minutes. In one camp, the commandant used to proudly display his camp's blowers to visiting generals.

A diarist in Stalag VIIA records "a continuous stream of Germans [guards] coming and going from our barracks. They come to exchange bread and other foodstuffs for tea and cigarettes from the Red Cross parcels."[9]

By October 1941 most Australian army officers captive in Germany were at Oflag VIB, Warburg. This camp, situated on a high exposed

---

[8] Between 1941 and 1946 the Australian Government and the Australian Red Cross had contributed 4.16 per cent of the world total of 27,246,624 Swiss francs for ICRC war work. In addition Australia had made two direct shipments to Russia valued at £20,000. ICRC Report, Vol I, pp. 124-5.

[9] British NCO's in Stalag VIIA at this period who later were transferred to Stalag 383, Hohenfels, saw this barter between guards and prisoners grow to fantastic proportions at the latter camp. Almost every conceivable commodity was smuggled in by the guards for cigarettes—bread (particularly), flour, eggs, parts for wireless sets, even a girl for the night (1,200 cigarettes). For 120 cigarettes a guard would allow 4 or 5 prisoners to scale the wire at night to steal building material from a new camp for firewood. This was pushed through the wire to waiting confederates.
On another occasion, sentries were bribed with cigarettes to negotiate with a shepherd for the purchase of six lambs; these were hoisted, one by one, by means of a long pole, over the great double stockade while the guard in the nearest watch-tower assisted with his searchlight.

area, had been vacated by civilian workers and the tumbledown huts were infested with rats and mice and the bedding flea-ridden. In a short time it was overcrowded with 2,500 officers and 450 orderlies—up to 16 officers were quartered in a space of 21 feet by 12 feet. Delegates of the I.C.R.C. described it as "the worst camp we have seen in Germany", and together with representatives of the American Embassy recommended that 1,000 officers should immediately be moved elsewhere. The Germans then began the erection of 10 new brick buildings and promised that "some hundreds of officers would be moved shortly". Rations were on the same sparse scale as in other camps but there was an ample supply of Red Cross parcels, there being a reserve stock of 18,000 in December. Outdoor recreation was available and there was plenty of space for football, netball and the like. With books brought in from various camps a library of 4,000 volumes was established and an orchestra was functioning. A pantomime, "Citronella", produced at Christmas time, was a hilarious success. The advent of winter, considered by the Germans to be the most severe for 40 years, curtailed outdoor recreation with the exception of ice-hockey. Organised indoor recreation provided for symphony concerts, performances by three dance bands, educational courses on innumerable subjects, and theatricals. Officers of the 51st Highland Division taught Highland and Scottish Country Dancing and this did much to keep men fit and in good spirits.

A camp exchange market had been established, designated "Foodacco Ltd", where a surplus of any commodity could be bartered for almost any requirement. By the New Year, vermin had been almost eradicated, extra fuel stoves had been provided and each man had an extra (Red Cross) blanket. In February 250 senior officers, of whom 14 were Australian, were moved to Oflag IXA/H, Spangenberg, where their existence continued in much the same tenor as at Warburg, but with improved accommodation.

As a result of alleged ill-treatment of German officer prisoners on board the *Pasteur*, en route from Suez to South Africa, the Germans in September 1942 carried out reprisals on all British officers at Oflag IXA/H, and ordered that "all personal and common luggage including sanitary and cosmetic articles such as soap, sponges, toothbrushes, towels, razors, etc., knives, forks, scissors of every description to be taken away; all badges of rank, all ribbons, decoration cockades and braids to be removed and all officers to be deprived of the services of their orderlies". The orderlies were moved to another camp and the heavy baggage stored in the town; the officers were left with nothing more than what they were wearing, plus sheets and blankets. The Germans were nonplussed at the spirit in which the reprisal was taken. Outwardly the officers carried on as usual except that everyone sported a beard, and these were the subject of competitions and sweepstakes. Swiss delegates of the I.C.R.C. who visited the camp during this period reported: "The spirit is splendid. . . . The sight of nearly four hundred bearded officers in plain uniforms is of course shocking, but the air of manliness and dignity with which they bear themselves makes a great impression." Notwithstanding letters of complaint and protests by the United Kingdom Government the reprisal order remained in force for two months after which the camp resumed its normal activities.

At Warburg, the new buildings were still unfinished in April 1942 and very little improvement had been made in the sanitary or washing arrangements; moreover, although the issue of Red Cross parcels had dwindled to one fortnightly, the German meat ration was reduced on the excuse that too many food parcels were being received. Warburg was finally cleared of prisoners in September 1942, almost 12 months after its condemnation by visiting delegates. During the occupation of Oflag VIB, numerous escape attempts were made; one source states that over 50 tunnels were found by the Germans; although two officers reached the Swiss border, no attempt was completely successful. A particularly daring mass escape was attempted about this time. Just at dusk about 100 officers, having succeeded in fusing the searchlights, rushed the wire with four ladders and got out of the camp. Most of them were recaptured almost at once but a few got away.

With the closing of Warburg camp, several Australians were in the party of 450 that went to Oflag IXA/Z[1] at Rotenburg near Spangenberg. This draft comprised those aged over 35, protected personnel and candidates for repatriation on medical grounds. Another party of 400 went to Oflag XXIB at Schubin in Poland while the remainder, approximately 1,800 and including the majority of the Australians, went to Oflag VIIB at Eichstatt.

The camp at Rotenburg was a modern stone building, formerly a girls' school, equipped with central heating, although scarcity of fuel restricted the usefulness of this amenity. The food position here was better than at Warburg, but only because there were ample Red Cross parcels. The area available for exercise and physical recreation was somewhat cramped, but walks on parole into the picturesque surrounding country were a pleasant substitute. Later the school gymnasium was opened and cinema shows, theatricals and the excellent library provided ample indoor recreation. There was a surfeit of medical officers and padres here—33 of the former and 20 chaplains. Despite their applications to be moved to camps where they could be of service, no action was taken, the German view being that they caused too much trouble with complaints about conditions.

When Oflag VIB, Warburg, was closed the 1,800-odd officers transferred to Oflag VIIB at Eichstatt comprised the younger and more junior officers, and no doubt this, together with their demeanour towards authority and the number of attempted escapes from Warburg, influenced the Germans in the precautions taken on the journey to Eichstatt and the subsequent tightening up of regulations and discipline at the new camp. During the train journey, the officers' boots were taken away each night, and on arrival at Oflag VIIB they were subjected to a stringent search. The

---

[1] The "Z" denotes *Zweiglar*, or branch camp.

Eichstatt camp was an old cavalry barracks set in beautiful surroundings, and had in its grounds two makeshift tennis courts, a playing field and vegetable gardens.[2]

Within a short time a strong theatrical group was in existence and the German authorities organised cinema shows.

In August 1942 British troops were obliged for operational reasons to bind the wrists of some of the Germans captured during the raid on Dieppe. A copy of the order authorising this procedure was captured by the Germans. Germany protested that Article 2 of the Geneva Convention had been violated. Unfortunately a similar incident occurred in a commando raid on Sark in the Channel Islands on 4th October, and the German High Command ordered that, as a reprisal, all British taken prisoners in the Dieppe raid should be handcuffed for a portion of each day. On 8th October 107 officers and 20 other ranks in Oflag VIIB, mostly Canadians, were fallen out and marched to the castle where their hands were tied with rope and remained so for 12 hours daily. The commandant stressed that the order came from the High Command, while others of the camp staff made it obvious that they were disgusted with the order. Britain retaliated by manacling a similar number of German prisoners, whereupon Germany replied by applying the order to three times the former number. This involved some Australians and New Zealanders, whose Governments made lively protests through the British authorities, Australia being concerned that the controversy might affect the treatment of Australians in Japanese hands. Protracted negotiations ensued, in which the Swiss Government and the I.C.R.C. both offered to help to find a solution. It was realised that Germany held the greater number of prisoners and therefore the advantage in competitive reprisals.

The shackling by rope had now been replaced by handcuffs and had spread to other camps. In addition to 380 of all ranks handcuffed at Eichstatt, 1,250 at Stalag 383, Hohenfels, 2,300 at Stalag VIIIB, Lamsdorf, and a few at Stalag IXC, Badsulza, were similarly treated.

In December the Swiss Government and the International Red Cross, having heard that Germany intended to relax the shackling during the Christmas period, appealed to both sides to free their prisoners from handcuffs for Christmas and to continue the concession for an indefinite period. On 12th December both the British and Canadian Governments removed handcuffs from their prisoners and never again put them on. The Germans, however, freed the prisoners' bonds only on Christmas Day and New Year's Day, insisting, before revoking the order, that the British issue a general order forbidding the binding of prisoners and the possession of bonds for this purpose. Britain would not relent to the extent of completely withdrawing the order authorising the binding of hands, asserting that such measures would be taken only in a case of operational necessity.

---

[2] An inmate, Capt W. H. Travers, 2/1 Bn, recorded in his diary that in the summer months of 1943 the tonnage of vegetables grown in the gardens amounted to: Tomatoes 3.4, onions 2.45, beetroot 1.87, carrots 1.55, marrow .65, in addition to 30,000 lettuce and large numbers of cucumbers, radish and spinach. All were divided equally among the prisoners.

The suggestion that a similar order should be issued to the Australian Army was viewed with concern by General Blamey, Commander-in-Chief of the Australian Military Forces, who pointed out that, as all Australian military operational forces had been withdrawn from the European and Middle East theatres, orders issued to the British Army did not apply to Australian forces. He considered that an endeavour should be made to regard the matter as one affecting only the European theatre of war. He wrote:

> I consider that the orders issued to the British Army, no matter how secretly promulgated, if repeated in the South-West Pacific theatre, would be immediately grasped by the Japanese to cover up their atrocities committed in the past and provide them with propaganda and excuses for any sort of inhuman action to our prisoners of war which we know from past experience they have no hesitation in carrying out.[3]

Reports received by the Protecting Power revealed that the manacling was being carried out in a humane manner and that strict policing was not enforced. Meanwhile prisoners had found it simple to make a key to unlock the handcuffs and were wearing them only when under observation. The guards had formed the habit of leaving the requisite number of handcuffs in each room each morning and collecting them at night. At Eichstatt the Germans provided chains 18 inches to 2 feet long with a handcuff at each end. The practice was for prisoners to tuck one end of the chain into each trouser pocket. If a German officer appeared the prisoner would put his hands into his pockets so that the officer would conclude that they were duly handcuffed.

The British War Office, in February 1943, issued an order forbidding the general tying-up of prisoners and from then on the numbers handcuffed in German camps gradually decreased until on 22nd November 1943 the procedure was discontinued. The German Foreign Office stated that the suppression of shackling had been based on communications by M. Pilet Golaz of the I.C.R.C., who "permitted the conclusion that the British authorities had taken measures to prevent a recurrence of the Dieppe incident although without formal declaration of guarantee".

Eichstatt, even before the shackling period, had not been a happy camp. In spite of reasonably good quarters and ample Red Cross parcels, the petty restrictions, imposed by a strict camp staff intent on ensuring security, tended to make conditions irksome. At first the contents of tins in Red Cross parcels were all opened and emptied into containers, but this did not last—it took too long. In November five prisoners escaped by posing as a German N.C.O. and a German sentry, with rifle, marching three "phoney" Frenchmen out of the camp to the dentist. Next day the whole camp was on a check parade in the snow lasting five hours, and this was followed by two night parades, each lasting for two hours. For several months there were regular night parades. The five-hour parade

---

[3] Letter to the Minister for the Army, 8th April 1943.

was repeated in June 1943 when 65 prisoners[4] escaped through a tunnel. All were eventually recaptured and transferred to Oflag IVC at Colditz, considered by the Germans to be escape-proof.

At the end of 1941 the majority of Australian other ranks in German hands were settled in permanent camps in Germany or Austria or in work-camps attached to the stalags. Eighty-six per cent were contained in five camps—approximately 1,000 in each of Stalags VIIA, Moosburg, XIIIC, Hammelburg, and XVIIIA, Wolfsberg, while VIIIB, Lamsdorf, and XVIIID, Marburg, each held between 600 and 700.

Conditions were much the same throughout, the degree of comfort or discomfort depending on the attitude of the particular German camp commandant towards his charges, or, in the work-camps, the treatment received from the German N.C.O.-in-charge or the employer. On large constructional jobs of a military nature where sabotage was possible full opportunity was taken to carry it out, and naturally the treatment of prisoners deteriorated. Private firms employing prisoners on large-scale building projects or in factories sometimes provided good quarters, working clothing and in isolated instances, a bonus, but in the main the chief causes of complaints in work-camps were inadequate protection against the cold in the quarters and lack of enough clothing to provide a dry change. In the mornings many men had sometimes to put on clothes still wet from the previous day. Those employed in road gangs seemed to be the worst sufferers from overwork and the "hurry-hurry" tactics of the supervisors. A certain amount of work had to be done, regardless of conditions or difficulties. Farm work probably provided the greatest variation of conditions experienced by prisoners; employers ranged from the tyrant who worked men excessively long hours and treated them little better than beasts of burden to the farm family who accepted the prisoner as one of themselves. Australians were well thought of by German and Austrian farmers. Men in the work-camps suffered other disabilities than those mentioned: their mail, both inward and outward, was spasmodic; Red Cross parcels were less regular owing to the lack of communication between them and the base camp; medical treatment was hard to obtain. Long working hours precluded recreation even had the facilities existed, but, in compensation, the men had a certain sense of freedom, saw fresh faces and had opportunities to "scrounge". Moreover their daily round was more normal than that of the men cooped up behind barbed wire—a psychological factor more beneficial than was probably realised.

Conditions in the stalags described previously in this chapter remained much the same up to the collapse of Italy in September 1943. There was, however, generally some improvement. After strong protests by the Australian Government and through the devoted efforts of delegates of the

---
[4] Seven were Australians: Capt R. R. Baxter, 2/5 Bn; Capt A. D. Crawford, 2/1 A-Tk Regt; Lt J. W. K. Champ, 2/6 Bn; Lt M. A. Howard, 2/7 Bn; Lt C. I. C. Dieppe, 2/1 Bn; Lt G. Bolding, Gd Bn, I Corps; Lt J. R. Millett, 2/11 Bn.

I.C.R.C., complaints regarding sanitation, overcrowding, lack of clothing and amenities, and the brutality of the guards had produced some improvement. Also the particularly bad camp at Marburg had been closed. The always inadequate German ration never improved and, with the advent of food parcels, even this was reduced—a practice adopted throughout Germany. More latitude was afforded prisoner-of-war medical officers in treating their own sick but they were dependent almost wholly on the Red Cross for medical supplies. Collective punishments, such as withholding mail for one or two weeks, or the withdrawal of amenities, were imposed, often on the slightest pretext. On occasions, usually after an escape scare, the Germans required all containers in a food parcel to be opened and the contents emptied into one receptacle, thus a man might walk away with a conglomerate mess of sardines, powdered coffee, sugar, jam, condensed milk, dried fruit, salmon, oatmeal, dried eggs, meat stew, butter and vegetables. This they would thoroughly mix and eat with a spoon. They called it "glop". In other cases more reason was shown and the various foods were emptied into separate containers for communal cooking.

The prisoners' own organisations in the stalags had now had time to get under way and, with more cooperation from the Germans than hitherto, were able to arrange comprehensive educational courses and lectures, theatrical and concert groups, organised outdoor sport and, in most camps, a news-sheet or magazine. Much ingenuity was shown in the production of these literary efforts, also in the ruses to circumvent the censor. Individually, too, the men were able to add to their own comfort by improvising articles of furniture, shelves and the like. Tea and cigarettes became mediums of currency; large numbers of cigarettes changed hands at "the tables" on the spin of a coin or the roll of a dice.

In April 1942 a number of Australians and New Zealanders were sent from Lamsdorf to work in a coal-mine at Oehringen in Poland. The quarters were at the pit-top and were very primitive; as three shifts were worked, sleep was continuously interrupted. Underground the civilian overseers, aided and abetted by the civilian miners, tried to boost production by bullying methods and the free use of pickhandles, but, after a number of fights, the civilians realised that the Britishers were not to be trifled with and by the end had developed a friendly admiration for the prisoners.

In October 1942 the British N.C.O's who had gone from Warburg and Wolfsberg to Stalag XVIIIB at Spittal (now re-numbered XVIIIA/Z) were transferred to Stalag 383, Hohenfels in southern Bavaria, which was being formed as a new N.C.O's camp; Spittal became a medical and dental centre and convalescent camp for prisoners in Stalag XVIIIA, Wolfsberg, and its attached work-camps. Wolfsberg at this stage had 26,000 prisoners of all nationalities under its control, including about 1,200 Australians.

By the end of 1942 there were nearly 4,000 N.C.O's at Hohenfels, of whom over 500 were Australians, some of whom had come from Stalag XXA at Thorn in Poland. The camp had been built for officers, and instead of being crammed into large barracks the N.C.O's found themselves allotted small huts holding up to 12 each, with larger barracks for theatricals and indoor amusements. There were ample sports and exercise areas, and with Red Cross parcels arriving regularly to supplement the standard German ration there was little to complain of; for most it was the best camp they had been in. Although the winter was cold in the extreme, the coal ration could be supplemented by wood from a near-by forest. Later, when the coal ration was discontinued, the greatest hardship at this camp was the shortage of fuel, which was virtually restricted to what could be found in the camp itself. Fence-posts gradually disappeared until there were no fences between compounds; rafters and floor-joists in the huts were reduced to a bare minimum; but the classic "fuel-drive" concerns a sentry-box which stood outside the main gate of the stalag. A German-speaking prisoner lured the sentry along the wire to discuss an attractive barter proposition and eight men opened the gate and grabbed the box, which was nine feet high and weighed about three hundredweight. Under cover of darkness they took it to their hut and within a short time it was broken into small pieces and hidden in an underground room, where it remained undiscovered during an intensive search by the Germans the next day, when the floors of every hut were lifted.

Several orchestras were in existence and a choir of 500 voices performed on occasions. A stalag "university" was organised and its classes, in addition to the activities of a number of clubs and societies—there were over 50 of them—provided profitable occupation.

Writing of conditions at Stalag 383 in June 1943 an Australian N.C.O.[5] said:

> It is the temporary home of 4,300 non-working NCO's and I think it must be the best camp in Germany. We have extensive playing fields, theatres, even dance rooms, educational classes on every subject under the sun, our own internal newspaper and many little conveniences I do not intend mentioning here. The Germans leave us pretty much to ourselves and but for searches which are caused through the activities of the "Moles" we would only see the enemy on morning check parade. We've even got a swimming pool 22 yards long with its Polo Club. We are free to do anything we like inside the barbed wire and there is plenty of room to do it in.

As previously mentioned, Hohenfels was one of the camps where shackling was introduced. But after the first week or two it did little to interfere with the normal routine of the camp. Shackling conditions were relaxed here perhaps earlier than at other camps, and later, with the acquiescence of the Germans, the men took the shackling by roster.

Hohenfels being a non-working camp, the N.C.O's incarcerated there found it hard to pass away the time once the more conventional means of recreation had palled. Thus, in amusing themselves, if they could ridicule or bewilder the Germans, so much the better. "Crazy Week" which

---

[5] Sgt W. P. Skene, NX3649; 2/1 Fd Coy. Commercial traveller; of Greenacre, NSW; b. Sydney, 19 Feb 1901.

was staged at this camp was a good example of this kind of project. It started when a prisoner, flying his home-made kite, observed a guard agape with astonishment at a grown man engaged in so childish a pursuit. A fellow-prisoner then joined in and the two staged a squabble resulting in kicked shins and in one sitting down and bawling his head off. The guard hurried off to report and other prisoners joined the fun—playing ring-a-roses, making daisy chains and so on. The German reaction was so satisfactory that it was decided to put on a full-scale "Crazy Week".

There were greatcoated Napoleons gazing darkly through the wire, cocked-hatted Nelsons peering up through telescopes, bands of painted Indians whooping through the roads, men riding invisible bikes, leading imaginary dogs, playing marbles, marching to a Chinese band, staring in bunches at the watch-towers—doing anything in fact, to get the Huns bewildered. In the sweltering heat, fellows would come on parade in coats and balaclavas and stand shivering next to others dressed in handkerchiefs.[6]

The "holiday train" was the crowning idiocy. This was a burlesque of a holiday excursion train leaving a London terminus for a seaside resort and left the Germans with every type of expression other than a laugh. The train was a row of huts.

It left for England twice a day at times announced throughout the camp, and passengers were warned to be on time and have their tickets ready. Whistles would blow in the Stalag, men would grasp suitcases and kitbags and rush from all parts of the camp, giving up their tickets at the barrier and crowding into compartments where they could get a seat at the window. Once inside, they would crane their necks out, smoke would belch from the funnel, late arrivals would dash desperately through the barrier, urged on by guard and porters, and, finally, the waving of a red flag would close the platform. As the train steamed out for Blighty, there would be wavings and counter-wavings from passengers and friends, last messages would be bawled out frantically and, as the guard announced the time of the next train, the crowd would disperse to their huts, leaving the extra Jerries in the watch-towers to work things out.[7]

After staff talks in Berlin, the commandant sought the views of the man-of-confidence, who rose swiftly to the occasion; undoubtedly there was madness in the camp, he declared, and it was becoming widespread. Was that surprising in view of the way in which thousands of prisoners were cooped up behind wire, with never a walk beyond it? How about walking-out parties while good weather held? Faced with the alternative of mass insanity the commandant was prompt to concede the request. Parole walks were instituted, and "Crazy Week" ceased, much to the relief of Germans and non-participating prisoners alike.

The theatre played a large part in the lives of prisoners in Stalag 383. Starting in a makeshift manner with revues and concert parties, the movement grew until there were two permanent theatres—one for vaudeville, the other for plays, comic opera and Shakespeare. The presence among the camp's inmates of professional dressmakers, tailors, carpenters, scene-

---

[6] M. N. McKibbin, *Barbed Wire Memories of Stalag 383* (1947), p. 76.
[7] McKibbin, p. 76.

painters and so on enabled shows to be produced with full and authentic costumes and stage properties; the house manager in an evening-dress suit (tailored in the camp), usherettes in neat little skirts and pill-box hats who collected thousands of cigarettes for the stage funds, and an orchestra of more than 20 pieces, all helped to transport the audience temporarily to other worlds.

Such plays as *Night Must Fall, Dinner at Eight, The Late Christopher Bean, I Killed The Count, The Cat and the Canary,* to name but a few; the Savoy operas, including *The Gondoliers, The Yeomen of the Guard, H.M.S. Pinafore,* and *The Mikado,* were faithfully produced, as was *The Merchant of Venice* for which the Germans lent the complete costumes from the State Theatre of Berlin—perhaps on account of its anti-Semitic theme. The commandant so enjoyed *The Mikado* that he waived roll-call for three days. The "female" characters in the various productions and their dresses were masterpieces of make-up and ingenuity and left the Germans simply agape. The commandant and his staff would leave just before the final curtain, after which the orchestra would strike up the National Anthem,

and never would it be sung more heartily than by those Stalag audiences, whose nostalgia for home had been quickened by the Theatre.[8]

Australians in Stalag 383, in common with compatriots in other stalags and oflags, complained bitterly at the sharp practice of some Australian booksellers who had been commissioned by relatives and friends of prisoners to send parcels of books to them. They were infuriated on opening these parcels to find that they sometimes contained children's books when they knew well that their friends had paid in good faith for vastly different kinds of books, and that the firms in question were using this means to unload unsaleable stock.

The mass transfer of prisoners from Italy to Germany after the Italian armistice had its repercussions in almost every stalag in Germany and Austria. Stalags XVIIIC, Markt Pongau, and XVIIIA/Z, Spittal and Stalag VIIA, Moosburg, became transit camps choked with prisoners who, however, stayed little longer than a week before being drafted on to one or other of the stalags in Germany. Practically all these received their quota from Italy and consequently became acutely overcrowded until provision was made for the setting up of further work-camps. Of the Australians transferred from Italy, about 250 went to Stalag VIIIA at Gorlitz in Silesia, some to Wolfsberg, but the majority to Stalag VIIIB, Lamsdorf. Conditions at Lamsdorf have already been described; they had, however, shown some improvement since the appointment of a new German commandant. The sudden influx had brought the number administered by the camp to more than 30,000, of whom 10,000 were in the stalag itself, with men sleeping on tables, forms or the floor. Consequently all camp services and amenities were likewise overtaxed. The increased demand

---
[8] McKibbin, p. 87.

on the German commissariat had caused a reduction of rations and the food parcels had necessarily to be shared among a larger number of prisoners. This, however, was only temporary.

In order to cope with the large number now at Stalag VIIIB and to simplify administration of the numerous work-camps under its control, the German authorities opened two new stalags, one at Sagan, to be known as Stalag VIIIC; the other at Teschen, on the Polish border, which was given the number by which Lamsdorf camp had hitherto been known, Stalag VIIIB, Lamsdorf being renumbered Stalag 344. Very soon a large percentage of prisoners from these three stalags were drafted out to work-camps, many going to the Silesian coal-mines. Very few were experienced coal-miners but within a short period they were working on the coal face for long hours. Accidents were numerous owing to inexperience. Fortunately for the prisoners the Swiss delegates viewed with concern the conditions of work in the mines and kept a close watch on them.

A feature of German prisoner-of-war camps wherever they held British troops was the celebration of anniversaries of notable events, and the national days and public holidays of the various Commonwealth countries. These events varied from a simple recognition of the day being celebrated to an elaborate affair lasting several days, depending on the personality of the German commandant. The Anzac Day marches at Hohenfels will be long remembered by those who participated, while the Whitsuntide carnival at Stalag 344, Lamsdorf, lasting three days was a milestone in the history of that camp. Saturday and Sunday were devoted to sports, an arts and crafts exhibition and a theatrical production. The culminating event was on Monday: a procession of tableaux of various subjects for which prizes were given. A special prize was awarded for the Cenotaph.

It was very simple—representing the Navy, Army, Air Force . . . but when the procession stopped, the Cenotaph was lifted and there sat Britannia! The band struck up *Rule Britannia* and everyone was spellbound at such a thing happening in a P.O.W. camp.[9]

Stalag VIIIA at Gorlitz was an old-established prisoner-of-war camp with conditions similar to those at Lamsdorf and, when Australians and others arrived there from Italy, it held French, Belgians, Yugoslavs and Russians. The portion of the camp occupied by the new arrivals was in bad shape, many doors and windows being missing, and there was a shortage of beds and palliasses. The water-supply was poor and, as usual, sanitation inadequate. The French and Belgians were generous with gifts of tobacco and food from their parcels and this tided the newcomers over the difficult first few weeks until Red Cross supplies arrived. Under good leadership it was not long before the camp had shown vast improvement and possessed the amenities usual in other British camps. Within the next three months many prisoners had been drafted out to work-camps, supplying labour for coal-mines, stone-quarries, sugar, glass or paper factories,

---

[9] From the diary of Cpl F. E. Anderson, NX46224; 2/3 Fd Coy. Builder; of Mayfield, NSW; b. Wallsend, NSW, 23 Sep 1910.

or for railway and building-construction jobs. Quarters outside the base camp were better and, in addition to the larger workers' ration, they could obtain by barter eggs, vegetables and other food. New arrivals were agreeably surprised to find they could attend a cinema on a free Sunday morning and swim or play football in the afternoon. One party of 200 Australians and New Zealanders were sent to a railway-construction job at Oderberg, near Raciborz on the Polish-Czechoslovakian border too far from Gorlitz camp to remain under its control, but the Germans ensured that ample Red Cross parcels reached this party, otherwise they could not have stood up to the work. The private construction firm required them to work for 11 hours and a half daily, but they had Saturday mornings and Sundays free, which was most unusual for German *arbeitskommandos*.

The first repatriation exchange of prisoners between Britain and Germany took place in October 1943 at the ports of Gothenburg (Sweden), Barcelona (Spain) and Oran (Algeria) simultaneously. In all 5,195 British and American prisoners and 5,265 Germans were involved. The British included 539 Australians (191 disabled or sick and 348 protected personnel). Of these 28 were exchanged at Gothenburg and went to the United Kingdom whence they embarked for Australia via America. The remainder travelled from Germany by hospital train to Marseilles and thence to Barcelona by ship. After the exchange, the sick and wounded embarked on a hospital ship and the protected personnel on a troopship for Alexandria. From the Middle East they travelled by the hospital ships *Oranje* and *Wanganella* to Australia.

News of the Allied landing in Normandy on 6th June 1944 brought great joy to the prisoners in Germany. Each oflag and stalag had its secret wireless-receiver and prisoners had the news within an hour or so of the landing, and the two-hourly bulletins broadcast by the B.B.C., were avidly awaited.[1] In Stalag 383 a special underground news-sheet was issued and read in all huts. A diarist[2] in that camp wrote: "The Germans who patrol inside the camp are just as eager as we are for news of the Second Front so a temporary peace is more or less arranged between us and them if we will give them the news! It is humorous to see a German ducking into a hut to hear what news has just been broadcast from the B.B.C."

Despite advances on both fronts, the failure of the plot against Hitler, the reverse at Arnhem, and the determination of Germany to fight on boded ill for an early cessation of hostilities and, with the arrival of autumn, prisoners resigned themselves to another dreaded winter in captivity.

Physically conditions were much the same as in the previous year: the oflags were overcrowded, causing a strain on sanitary facilities and a shortage of water in most camps, but the lack of accommodation for

---

[1] The smaller work-camps which had no wireless-receivers were kept informed through an organisation in their parent stalag.
[2] Lt Roffey.

indoor recreation and study, particularly in officers' camps, was the worst feature. At Eichstatt there was a library of over 15,000 volumes and in the spring of 1944 parole walks became a regular feature; there were occasional cinema shows and in one instance a visit to a travelling circus. At Oflag VA, Weinsberg, to which about 40 Australian officers went after the evacuation from Italy, a big improvement had been made since the early part of 1944. The water-supply and bathing facilities had been increased, sanitation and lighting improved and more facilities for sports provided. Thanks to generous supplies of sports materials, books and stationery from the World Alliance of Y.M.C.A's there was ample scope for recreation and pastimes. By June over 200 had applied to sit for recognised examinations. The appointment of a new German commandant had, too, in the opinion of the delegate of the Protecting Power, helped to improve matters considerably. The inmates of this camp felt some concern regarding the lack of adequate protection from air raids. The few slit-trenches at first available were insufficient for the size of the camp and of a design that provided little protection. Near the camp were factories for the manufacture of aircraft wings and machine-gun parts and consequently it was felt that cover in the event of air raids was essential. During 1944 the trenches were improved and extended and during a raid the prisoners could either use them or stay in their barracks. The Protecting Power had been asked to press for the removal of Oflag 79, Querum (near Brunswick), to a safer location.

The wholesale transfer of prisoners from the stalags to the various work-camps eased to some extent the acute overcrowding experienced in the previous three months. Lamsdorf (now Stalag 344) was an exception, however, and accommodation and all facilities were still inadequate for the 10,000 prisoners still in the British section of the base camp although over 9,000 had been dispersed among the 235 work-camps administered by the stalag. The Germans intended moving 4,000 air force, Canadian and American prisoners to other camps but only 500 actually left. This, however, was sufficient to obviate the use of beds on or near the floor. The Germans at this camp were now showing more cooperation in the provision of outdoor recreation and theatrical entertainments, maybe to ingratiate themselves with the prisoners, but more probably with a view to distracting the prisoners' minds from the discomfort and deficiencies of the camp.

The new Stalag VIIIB at Teschen had on its strength about 12,000 British of whom about 600 were Australians. About 11,500 of the prisoners were spread among the 66 work-camps attached to the stalag. In the base camp itself the barracks and conveniences were old and primitive, but lighting, heating, cooking and bathing facilities were satisfactory, although there was lack of space for recreation. The Swiss delegate did not hide from the German authorities the deplorable impression made on him by the stalag. He received the answer that the new camp would soon be finished. He noted there were two British doctors in the camp and also two chaplains but that in their visits to the hospital the chaplains encountered difficulties and that they were no longer permitted to visit the work-camps. He also noted that in recent months the British had lost by theft the equivalent of 367 parcels and 201,000 cigarettes. The delegate's report concluded: "However, considering present conditions of accommodation, Stalag VIIIB must be considered insufficient. Moreover conditions of work in the detachments in this area are often hard."[3] Since few toothbrushes, combs, razor blades and so on were arriving at the camp, pro rata distribution to the work-camps was impracticable, and the camp leader therefore made up some special packages of these items for prisoners who had not for some time received private parcels from their relatives or friends. As the majority of work-camps in this area provided labour for coal-mines, soap was an essential commodity but of this there was an acute shortage. Parcels from the Argentine did not contain soap and nearly 13,000 Argentinian parcels had been received in the camp during August.

The second offshoot from Lamsdorf, Stalag VIIIC at Sagan, was much smaller than either Lamsdorf or Teschen, with only about 70 Australians there in a total of two or three thousand Britishers. About 500 remained in the stalag, the balance being spread over 20 or so industrial work-camps.

In addition to the Silesian coal-mines there were in this district many factories and industrial concerns, as well as forestry camps and railway and construction works. The prisoners working in the factories found the wide range of jobs at first interesting and novel. They usually were working alongside civilians of both sexes and of various tongues—mostly forced labour. The prisoners lived either at the factory or close by, the midday meal being cooked on the job. A medical orderly and an interpreter were always included in any British party of over 50 strong. Factory work was comparatively easy and the men were not too tired to enjoy the free evenings, with swimming or sports in the summer and, in the winter, cards, darts or reading. Some, too, spent the evenings with women met at work during the day.

Early in 1943 the Red Cross Society informed prisoners that arrangements had been made whereby they could remit a portion of the amount in credit in their paybook to next-of-kin through the paymaster in London. A number of Australians took advantage of this and the money was being paid in Australia within 10 weeks of the prisoner signing the application form in the stalag. Later a similar scheme was operated by which prisoners could order monthly supplies of tobacco from London, the price being debited in the prisoners' paybooks. By similar remittances every man in Stalag 383, Hohenfels, was able to subscribe to a "special fund" amounting to over £5,000 which, by means of ingenious code

---

[3] ICRC report, Dr Rossel, 26th August 1944.

letters between a sergeant in the stalag and Mr Duncan Sandys,[4] was used to purchase a Spitfire fighter plane. The prisoners' joy was unbounded when they were informed that their fighter had been christened "Unshackled Spirit" and that it had been in action. A similar Spitfire fund was raised in Oflag VIB.

With the advent of summer, coupled with the possible approach of Allied forces, more prisoners planned escapes. Many attempts to escape from the work-camps were made, and quite a few were successful. The escapers found that the demeanour of civilians towards prisoners of war at large had changed considerably and not a little help was given them, especially once they had succeeded in reaching Yugoslavia. The civilians around the work-camps, too, were more friendly to the prisoners who now had no difficulty in bartering tea, coffee, chocolate or cigarettes from their parcels for fresh food and vegetables. It was generally conceded, also, that at this stage the German guards were showing more consideration to their prisoners although the Gestapo, as the year wore on, became more active and aggressive with security searches.

One successful escape story concerns two Australians, Privates Brudenell-Woods[5] and Irvine[6] who had been transferred by the Germans to Lamsdorf from Italy. With the idea of escape in mind they volunteered for work and were sent to a work-camp at Kunau. With two other prisoners they spent a fortnight perfecting plans. On 28th June they gained access to the Red Cross store by removing a panel from one door, securing a key to another and climbing over a third. Previously they had removed bricks from the outer wall, merely leaving a thick layer of plaster; breaking through this they reached the outside of the camp. For eight days they walked towards Hungary. Then a farmer gave them civilian clothes and promised a guide to Yugoslavia. When, several weeks later, the guide had not appeared and the other two escapers had already departed, Brudenell-Woods and Irvine crossed the border into Czechoslovakia, where they wandered about to avoid recapture. Eventually they were directed by partisans to Handlova, where their evacuation to Italy on 18th September, was arranged.

Two other Australians, Sergeants Brough[7] and Berry,[8] and a New Zealander[9] while at Stalag XVIIIA/Z, Spittal, planned a similar escape. In March 1944 the three succeeded in being sent to a small work-camp at Spitzendorf near Graz. A month later they had no trouble in unlocking the door of their farmhouse billet while the guards were asleep. As they had been unable to obtain civilian clothes they travelled at night only.

---

[4] Rt Hon Duncan Sandys, MP. RA 1939-41. Financial Secty to War Office 1941-43; Chairman of Intergovernmental Council for Empire POW's 1942-43; Parliamentary Secty, Ministry of Supply 1943-44; Chairman War Cabinet Cttee for defence against V-weapons 1943-45; Minister of Works 1944-45. B. 24 Jan 1908.

[5] Pte B. Brudenell-Woods, MM, NX13848; 2/13 Bn. Horticulturist; of Mona Vale, NSW; b. Inverell, NSW, 16 Feb 1914.

[6] Pte W. R. Irvine, MM, NX5322; 2/4 Bn. Carpenter's labourer; of Orbost, Vic; b. Orbost, 22 Jul 1901.

[7] Sgt E. J. Brough, MM, VX17575; 2/32 Bn. Butcher; of Drouin, Vic; b. Drouin, 16 Feb 1920.

[8] Sgt A. Berry, MM, WX2075; 2/2 Bn. Farm hand; of Leederville, WA; b. Perth, 4 Mar 1917.

[9] Pte E. L. Baty, DCM; 4 NZ Fd Amb.

The River Drau was crossed on an improvised raft and after eight days of severe winter weather they reached Yugoslavia where they met partisan soldiers who guided them to the British Military Mission. A month later they were evacuated by air to Italy reaching Bari on 9th June 1944.

One inveterate escaper was less fortunate. Sapper Steilberg[1] between May 1941 and October 1943, had escaped from stalags and camps no fewer than four times, remaining at liberty for up to 14 days. In February 1944 he and two companions cut the wire at a work-camp at Brux and crawled through unobserved but were recaptured four days later whilst sleeping in a barn. In the next seven months Steilberg made two similar attempts from work-camps. After the last attempt he was placed in a concentration camp at Fort Terezin until April 1945. On 21st April he escaped from the evacuation march, reaching the American lines four days later.

In the spring of 1944 the British Military Mission in Yugoslavia reported that there was "a steady slow trickle" of escapers from the camps in southern Austria. They were being assisted by friendly Austrians around Graz and Marburg and on reaching the River Drau were able, with the aid of Yugoslav partisans, to reach the mission's headquarters.

In March 1944 the Germans opened another camp for British non-working N.C.O's at Thorn in Poland—Stalag 357. British N.C.O's went there from camps all over Germany and Austria. The Germans intended that there should be no escapes from the trains that took the N.C.O's to their new camp. Australians who went there from Stalags XIIIC, Hammelburg, and XVIIIA/Z, Spittal, described how one-third of a truck was well wired off in the form of a small compound in which 14 prisoners travelled, the remaining two-thirds of the truck being occupied by seven guards. The prisoners had their boots, belts, braces and ties removed and all were handcuffed throughout the journey, which lasted four to five days. No man was allowed out of the compound during the whole time. The new arrivals were agreeably impressed with the conditions; although the well-spaced barracks were overcrowded, pending completion of the camp, there was ample bedding, lighting and other facilities, also a large sports field. For four months the camp held only 1,000, but in July, when 3,000 air force N.C.O's arrived from Heydekrug, the facilities became inadequate. In August before accommodation for the latest arrivals had been completed the whole camp was moved to Fallingbostel near Bremen, retaining the number Stalag 357.

A second exchange of prisoners between the Allies and Germany was arranged for 17th May 1944 at Barcelona. Four trainloads left Germany for Marseilles and went on to Barcelona by ship. The *Gripsholm* bringing 450 Germans from the United States picked up a similar number at Algiers and reached Barcelona on the appointed day. Two days later she left carrying 1,043 British and American repatriates, including 61 Australians

---
[1] Spr W. H. C. Steilberg, BEM, NX1164; 2/1 Fd Coy. Labourer; of Harbord, NSW; b. Port Macquarie, NSW, 7 Oct 1919.

(42 medically unfit, 19 protected personnel). The Australians were disembarked at Algiers, going from there by hospital ship to Alexandria, and returning home as berths on ships became available.

In the middle of 1943 it had become apparent that the Germans could no longer employ British defeats as propaganda material among British prisoners and a new approach was necessary. They turned from the abortive effort to convince British prisoners of Britain's error in fighting Germany to an attempt to gain sympathy (and eventual assistance, of course) for Germany's fight against Russian communism. *The Camp*, a small four-page weekly newspaper for general distribution to camps, printed in English, edited and published in Berlin, found it hard to provide convincing news for its readers. From the early days of its publication the paper had run a weekly article entitled "The German Point of View" in which it tried to prove how superior the German race was to the British and their Allies, but the article under that heading for August 1944 merely claimed for America a victory over Britain's ideas at the Bretton Woods conference. The paper had its usual padding of crossword puzzle, English sporting items and results, a weekly military survey and home news in brief. It also contained a list of awards for gallant services in Italy, culled from the *London Gazette* of a month before, a long report of a speech by Goebbels, and an announcement that Lord Gowrie was retiring from the office of Governor-General of Australia.

In January 1945 appeared a description of how a mayor in England had shaken hands with a German prisoner and in February a statement by repatriated German prisoners "that the attitude of British P.O.W. camp officers and guards left nothing to be desired". This of course fooled no one, and even more futile was the attempt, in May and later, to form a "British Free Corps" to fight against the Russians. A circular[2] was sent to all prisoner-of-war camps but there was only one known instance of an Australian volunteering. At Stalag 344, fights occurred between Australians and 72 British prisoners who had accepted the German propaganda.

A much more ingenious scheme was the setting up of "holiday camps" in 1943. One for other ranks was at Genshagen, near Berlin, and one for officers in Berlin. The Germans insisted that each stalag should send a quota to them, the Germans themselves detailing the officers who were to go. The objects of the camps were "to promote a better feeling between

---

[2] The circular said:
"As a result of repeated applications from British subjects from all parts of the world wishing to take part in the common European struggle against Bolshevism, authorisation has recently been given for the creation of a British Volunteer unit. The British Free Corps publishes herewith the following short statement of the aims and principles of the unit.

"(1) The British Free Corps is a thoroughly British volunteer unit conceived and created by British subjects from all parts of the Empire who have taken up arms and pledged their lives in the common European struggle against Soviet Russia.

"(2) The British Free Corps condemns the war with Germany and the sacrifice of British blood in the interests of Jewry and International Finance, and regards this conflict as a fundamental betrayal of the British people and British Imperial interests.

"(3) The British Free Corps desires the establishment of peace in Europe, the development of close friendly relations between England and Germany, and the encouragement of mutual understanding and collaboration between the two great Germanic peoples.

"(4) The British Free Corps will neither make war against Britain or the British Crown, nor support any action or policy detrimental to the interests of the British.
                                              Published by the British Free Corps."

the opposing nations when the war is over", to give men "a better outlook and relaxation from the tragedies of war" by educational, physical and social activities, and to form "a spiritual centre where the men could be brought closer to Him who alone can bring peace to this suffering world".[3] The prisoners went to the camp in drafts of 200, their stay lasting four weeks. It may well be imagined how pleasant a respite it was to men from coal-mining or other arduous work to be entertained by German musicians and opera singers and with films and lectures. There were outings to Potsdam and facilities for outdoor and indoor sports. Naturally there was ample food—from Red Cross sources! The irony of this was not lost on the prisoners. In 1944 the officers' holiday camp was moved to a castle at Steinburg, an old-world town near the Danube in Bavaria. The Senior British Officer in each oflag was now able to choose who should go, but it was incumbent on each oflag to send its quota. The castle was situated in country ideally suited for pleasant walks, which were taken in small parties accompanied by guides rather than by guards. The interpreters were university men; there was a good library, with, of course, a few propaganda volumes thrown in for good measure. A subtle touch was the employment of first-class photographers from whom photographs were readily obtainable for sending home, and the issue of plenty of letter forms.

The strategic bombing of Germany had reached its zenith by the autumn of 1944 and the sight or sound of the armadas of aircraft overhead passing to or from their targets was a source of joy to most prisoners—but not to those in work-camps around the industrial centres where their sleep was continually interrupted by the crash of bombs near by or the thunder of the anti-aircraft batteries, not to mention the accompanying danger. There were many complaints to delegates of the Protecting Power about the inadequacy of air-raid shelters available for prisoners and the refusal, in some instances, of guards to allow prisoners on working parties to take shelter during day raids. In December 1944 Allied aircraft bombed the main camp at Stalag XVIIIA, Wolfsberg, destroying several barracks and killing about 50 prisoners.

A further exchange of prisoners, the third with Germany, took place at Gothenburg in September 1944. From the collecting centres the Allied prisoners for repatriation went by hospital trains to Sassnitz on the Baltic, where they embarked on Swedish ferries for the 60-mile trip across the Baltic to Trelleborg. After two pleasant days in transit camps at Gothenburg, where they were shown every consideration by the British Consul and the Swedish Red Cross, they embarked for Liverpool; 107 Australians (10 protected personnel) were in the total of 2,560 Allied repatriates exchanged for 2,136 German nationals brought from England, Canada and the United States. The Australians were met at Liverpool by officers of the A.I.F. Reception Group, U.K., some going to hospitals and the

---

[3] The quotations are from *The Camp* of 20th February 1944.

remainder to the newly established transit camp of the group at Eastbourne whence they proceeded on 28 days' leave. The next, and what proved to be the last, exchange of prisoners took place in January 1945 at Kreuzlingen in Switzerland and involved 5,000 Germans and 2,500 Allied prisoners of whom 102 were men of the A.I.F. In all, a total of 427 maimed or medically unfit and 811 protected personnel of the A.I.F. were repatriated from German camps and a total of 91 from Italian camps.[4]

At the end of January 1945 there were approximately 5,300 members of the A.I.F. in German prison camps or in work-camps attached to them. Some 240 A.I.F. officers were spread among eight different oflags, with about 100 at Oflag VIIB, Eichstatt. The approximate distribution of other ranks was: Stalag XVIIIA, Wolfsberg, 1,500; Stalag 344, Lamsdorf, 1,000; Stalag XIIIC, Hammelburg, 700; Stalag VIIIB, Teschen, 600; Stalag 383, Hohenfels, 500; Stalag 357, Fallingbostel, 300; Stalag VIIIA, Gorlitz, 200. The remainder were dispersed among other stalags in groups varying from 5 to 60. At Stalag 357, Fallingbostel, and at Oflag VIIB, Eichstatt, the Germans in January staged a reprisal for alleged ill-treatment of German prisoners at a camp in Egypt. All palliasses, all but two blankets and 90 per cent of all stools and tables were taken away. All common and recreation rooms, except the Roman Catholic chapel at Eichstatt were closed. After a visit to Eichstatt the I.C.R.C. inspector stated:

> It is useless to expatiate at length on the present conditions of the British prisoners at this Oflag. They are very severe, the prisoners being forced almost always to remain on their feet all day and possessing only the frames of their former wooden beds, with a few cross pieces as base. . . . With the present cold weather, the rooms are very damp and the conditions of accommodation are so much worse.[5]

From about November 1944 onwards the supply of food parcels dwindled to nothing because of the disruption of the German railway system by Allied bombing. Consequently in January 1945 the I.C.R.C. sent weekly from Geneva a fleet of motor trucks, painted white with a large Red Cross on sides and top, carrying consignments of parcels direct to prison camps or to the columns of prisoners trudging across Germany in the long marches forced on them by the Germans. The men in the camps were overjoyed at the sight of "the white angels", the prisoners' name for the food trucks; so were the men on the march, but because of lack of knowledge of the location of the marchers or of their destination from day to day it was seldom that the trucks found the columns.

---

[4] Two protected personnel, Dvr C. W. Croucher and Dvr K. H. Griffin of the 2/1 Fd Amb, were among about 2,000 British prisoners assembled at Rouen in 1941 for repatriation. However, due to a breakdown in negotiations between the British and German Governments, the proposed exchange of prisoners was cancelled. With the help of French sympathisers they were among a group who escaped from a woodcutting party at Rouen in January 1942 and, after many adventures in unoccupied France, were recaptured when they were attempting to reach Spain by way of the Pyrenees and imprisoned at St Hippolyte du Fort. The two Australians spent a month there before being transferred to Fort de la Revere whence they finally escaped in September, reaching Gibraltar by fishing boat the next month.
A detailed account of their experiences, written by Griffin, was published in instalments in Stand-To, commencing in the Sept-Oct 1962 issue.
[5] ICRC report, Mr Mayer, 29th January 1945.

The transfer of prisoners from Heydekrug and later from Thorn, previously mentioned in this chapter, was the first step in the planned evacuation of prisoners from areas likely to be in the path of a Russian advance. But the launching of the Russian drive early in 1945 caused the German High Command to expedite the move of prisoners back into Germany, and some from Stalags XXB at Marienburg, XXA at Thorn and the punishment camp at Graudenz were moved westward towards

Brunswick early in January. The Russian advance from the Vistula, however, gained such impetus that these camps were overrun and the prisoners remaining there fell into Russian hands. At the same time the many work-camps scattered along the Polish and Silesian borders were similarly threatened and hasty preparations were made for evacuation, which had to be on foot because of lack of petrol and the strain on the German railway system consequent on the Russian advance.

On 19th January the men at Milowitz, a coal-mining camp in Poland, at a few hours' notice were set off on a march which took them through Upper Silesia and Czechoslovakia into Bavaria. They were kept on the move almost to the end, except for a 10-day halt when approaching Nuremberg, where they were billeted in a disused pottery factory and forced to work cleaning up bomb damage. They reached Regensburg on the Danube only to be bombed by Allied aircraft when crossing the bridge; 25 prisoners were killed. The whole party, about 1,400 strong, scattered, some making off on their own and others later returning to the column. On 27th March, after having travelled about 800 miles, they were put into a canvas camp near Landshut and more or less left to fend for themselves until an American armoured division arrived a fortnight later.

The stories of the marches of the various columns are much of the same pattern. The men invariably started off loaded with as much warm clothing, Red Cross food and personal possessions as they could carry. Some obtained or improvised sleds on which to drag their belongings. But many found the loads too heavy for long marches through snow feet deep or rain and slush, in their low physical condition. Sleds collapsed or became bogged, and at each succeeding stop there were many who made a re-appraisement of their carrying capacity and dumped everything but food and the barest necessities. All groups suffered the same forced pace in the early stages to get clear of the approaching Russians, the same struggle through snow feet deep on the back roads and country lanes, the crowding into leaking barns at night with no heating or lighting or means of drying clothes, the blistered and frost-bitten feet, the chills and digestive disorders caused by eating raw vegetables and the eventual weakness from lack of food. Fortunate were those who could at night get into a stable or barn containing horses or cattle to obtain comfort from the warmth of the farm animals' bodies, which also helped to melt the ice formed on the prisoners' clothes. The columns were kept for the most part away from the main roads which were choked with fleeing refugees and military traffic. The marches were begun in the dead of winter and wintry conditions were experienced through almost their whole extent. One party had a terrible night march through a blizzard. Exhausted men had to be helped along by their comrades and some were drawn on the sledges. An occasional rifle or revolver shot in the darkness meant that another poor Russian prisoner had been mercilessly killed because of his inability to keep going.

Fortunately most camps were able to issue a reserve of Red Cross parcels at the beginning of a march, for the rations issued by the Germans en route were totally insufficient. At first, in Poland and later in Czechoslovakia, civilians in the villages and smaller towns gave the prisoners bread and in some instances hot food, but the German people were too embittered by the incessant Allied bombing to have any sympathy for the marchers, wretched as their condition was. When their stock of Red Cross food had been consumed, the men were forced to steal what and where they could in order to supplement the irregular issues of about four ounces of bread, a few potatoes and a helping of soup, with an occasional addition of tinned meat or sausage. It was the custom in this part of the world for farmers to store potatoes and turnips in earth-covered mounds in the fields and it was from these heaps that the marchers, at great risk of reprisals from the guards, stole the main part of their food, eating the potatoes or turnips raw on the march. Some were able to obtain scraps of oil-cake, a compressed cattle-food, from farms.

It was noticeable that the men who had been employed on heavy work in the work-camps were in a better physical condition to stand up to the rigours of the marches. Many of the guards, of whom there were 50 to each 1,000 prisoners, were in no better condition than the prisoners; although their gear was carried in vehicles and they had better rations and billets each night, a number had to fall out and were left behind. The guards carried rifles and grenades and in some columns had brought with them police dogs from the camps. As the weary weeks wore on the marches produced in some guards a sense of apathy that boded well for prisoners on "scrounging" forays or making attempts to escape, while the more sadistic types became more brutal, causing many casualties by shooting or by the free use of rifle-butts. One guard who was known to have shot four prisoners later received retribution at the hands of American troops.

The first of the large camps in eastern Germany to be evacuated was Stalag 344, Lamsdorf, the prisoners receiving two hours' notice to leave on 22nd January. They marched out in eight columns, each of about 1,000 strong, and by nightfall the camp contained only the convalescent and lightly sick. A delegate of the I.C.R.C. who witnessed the departure reported that the prisoners "were in high spirits, full of expectation to be overtaken by the Russians", whose gunfire could be heard rumbling in the distance. Not all of them were in this frame of mind, however; at least some were glad to be moving away from the Russians. Gorlitz was the destination of the men from Lamsdorf and the 150-mile tramp was completed in about a fortnight. A week after arriving at Gorlitz they were moved on again, travelling westwards through Saxony and Thuringia to reach Meiningen, 60 miles north-east of Frankfurt, early in March, many sick from stomach disorders and fatigue. One column of 1,000 prisoners which left Lamsdorf arrived at Gorlitz only 600 strong; the remainder had been left behind sick, exhausted or suffering from severe frost-bite. Of these many reached Gorlitz days later in vehicles.

The 2,000-odd prisoners who had been left behind at Lamsdorf remained there for a further three weeks, with the Russian advance gradually moving towards them. The camp followed its usual routine except that there was no interference by the Germans, the prisoners' administration taking over the stores. On 21st February they were packed in parties of 40 to 50 in cattle-trucks and began a 10-day railway journey across Czechoslovakia into Bavaria. They were able to take plenty of Red Cross food with them, their worst hazard being attacks by Allied aircraft. Reaching Hammelburg safely, they stayed in the overcrowded Stalag XIIIC for three weeks before setting off on foot for Nuremberg or Moosburg. The more seriously sick or injured left Lamsdorf by train (as usual, 40 to a cattle-truck) for Stalag XVIIB at Krems in Austria which they reached after a week's journey under extremely bad conditions.

It was the original intention of the Germans to clear Stalag 344 at Lamsdorf in order to use it as a transit camp for prisoners evacuating Stalag VIIIB, Teschen, and the many work-camps in Upper Silesia but the momentum of the Russian drive precluded this, and the columns from Teschen and the southern *arbeitskommandos,* instead of travelling north, were forced to move westward.

The general direction of these columns, and also of some that had left Lamsdorf, was over the mountains of eastern Sudetenland, bypassing Prague, to Koniggratz and Karlsbad. The extremely cold weather experienced by these columns when in the mountain ranges caused many cases of frost-bite, necessitating amputations in 25 cases in one hospital alone—at Oberlangendorf. The intention had been to form these columns into two groups, one to remain in north-western Czechoslovakia, the other to be dispersed in areas around Munich, Nuremberg and Stuttgart. The Allied threat from the west, however, eliminated the two latter centres. Some columns stayed in Czechoslovakia and were put to work, but the majority eventually arrived in the Moosburg area to become part of a huge throng of prisoners of all nationalities estimated by some sources to number up to 100,000.

The next camp to get under way was Stalag VIIIC at Sagan. Leaving on 12th February the men marched to Spremberg, a distance of about 50 miles, expecting to be entrained there. Instead they had to walk 300 miles to Duderstadt, spending nights in the open in rain and snow.

By the middle of February the overcrowding at Gorlitz had become acute as a result of the influx from Lamsdorf and other camps to the east. Men were sleeping on floors, tables or wherever they could find space to lie. The camp hospital was filled with patients suffering from frost-bite, pneumonia and other complaints contracted on the march—patients whose condition would have been less serious had they been allowed to receive treatment when and where they became sick instead of being forced to complete the journey in a slower column. Doubtless the condition of these men had influenced the British camp leader at Gorlitz to protest to the Germans against a plan to move the whole camp on foot in the existing weather, but despite protests, the scarcity of food (the reserve of Red Cross food at Gorlitz had been issued to the men from Lamsdorf on their arrival) and the lack of transport for the sick, the march from Gorlitz began on 17th February. The first column to leave, after being issued with two days' rations, moved off in a heavy snowstorm and covered 20 miles on the first day. The distance covered was later reduced to a daily average of 12 miles, which distance became general in most columns. One of the marchers in this column, referring to the second morning, later wrote:

> I am awake before dawn, stirred by a cold that penetrates even the stupor of exhaustion. Others are moving about, stamping feet and rubbing hands in an attempt to restore circulation to frigid limbs. The guards have given no thought to

sanitation, and we stamp impatiently by the door awaiting their pleasure. Dawn finds us a sorry lot. Many are crippled by blisters and are unable to march any farther, while others suffer from cramps, torn tendons and muscles. Those fit to continue the march move up to the front; the remainder, about a hundred strong . . . are again quartered in the barn to await the orders of the authorities controlling the march. It transpired that, after resting for a day, they were marched at a slower rate. Only in cases of extreme illness were casualties loaded on to carts.[6]

The absence of hot meals on the march called for improvisation and the "travelling-cooker" was evolved with which to cook stolen vegetables. A bucket with holes punched in its base and having a long wire handle was the receptacle for the fire. A billy containing the food was placed over the flames and both bucket and billy suspended from a long pole which was carried by two men. There were several days on which the first column from Gorlitz received no rations at all; these were the days when the "cookers" were appreciated.

On arrival at Duderstadt on 8th March the prisoners were accommodated in Stalag XIC, long-disused brickworks of three stories, cold, draughty and full of brick dust. There was one water pump and one primitive latrine for the 1,000 men then there, but more were still to come. In the next three days two additional columns arrived. Dysentery broke out. Fires and light were forbidden and no one was allowed out after dark. The whole building was infested with lice and fouled by previous columns. There was no provision for the treatment of the seriously ill and 50 died of dysentery or pneumonia. "Cases of dysentery are mounting: the pile of the dead at the gate, most of them unidentified, grows larger."[7] The task of the medical officers was alleviated towards the end of March by the sending of a train of cattle-trucks containing the less seriously sick to Fallingbostel, where the reprisal order depriving British prisoners of their palliasses and furniture was still in force.

The march was continued from Duderstadt at the end of March, the columns heading in a north-easterly direction towards Magdeburg. The prisoners soon saw evidence that the end was approaching. Large formations of Allied planes were continually flying over them, and they witnessed from a hill-top near Halberstadt a mass air raid. They also saw, from a distance of less than a mile, the launching of a German A-4 rocket bomb, but neither prisoners nor guards realised what it was. One column from Duderstadt wandered for a week in the direction of Brunswick, being able to obtain almost no food on the way. The food shortage in Brunswick was so acute that the column leader was allowed to try to arrange for Red Cross food from the I.C.R.C. depot there; fortunately it was obtained, for soon afterwards the prisoners were ordered to move again, this time away from American forces who had reached Duderstadt on 9th April and were advancing towards Magdeburg. Another column on its way to Brunswick had reached Ditfurt where it halted. A long column of trucks pulled up ahead of the prisoners causing great excitement and hopes. The

---

[6] J. L. Brill, "Forced March to Freedom", *Stand-To*, March 1950.
[7] J. L. Brill.

hopes were short-lived however; the trucks were loaded with fully-armed S.S. troops, halted for an hourly rest!

The mass evacuation of prisoners from camps in eastern Germany and Poland had begun early in the New Year, and by February about 250,000 Allied prisoners of war were straggling westwards in columns and groups of varying sizes across Germany and Czechoslovakia. About 100,000 were in the north, travelling in a general direction towards Hamburg and Bremen; another 60,000 were trekking across central Germany towards an area bounded by Berlin, Leipzig and Brunswick; and more than 80,000 were moving through northern Czechoslovakia headed for Bavaria. By March, Stalags IIIA, Luckenwalde; 357, Fallingbostel; XIIIC, Hammelburg; VIIA, Moosburg, and to a lesser extent, XIIID, Nuremberg, and XIA, Altengrabow, had become large reception camps for wandering columns. Conditions in all these camps were bad: food and Red Cross supplies were short, camp facilities were overtaxed to the utmost degree, and every available inch of space had to be used for accommodation. At Hammelburg the last 2,000 prisoners to leave Lamsdorf were crowded into a group of small huts that was normally the camp infirmary. None was as bad, however, as the temporary transit camp at Duderstadt, previously described.

When on 7th March the First American Army forced the bridgehead at Remagen on the Rhine, it was only 35 miles from Oflag XIIB, Hadamar, and, as the Allied forces built up on the west bank of the Rhine for the final onslaught into Germany, the German High Command, adhering to its policy of moving prisoners away from the advancing Allies, ordered that some camps near the Rhine be evacuated eastwards. In addition to the prisoners static in oflags and stalags, there were some columns in the area which had marched from eastern Germany. These were now forced to march in an easterly direction.

The first camp to move was Oflag XIIB. The prisoners were transported by motor lorries on 21st and 22nd March to a transit camp at Lollar, some 40 miles distant, to await rail transport. The train awaiting them was bombed, so they stayed at Lollar and were still there when the 7th American Division overran the village on 29th March. The former prisoners were billeted in houses in the village and were well fed and amply supplied with French wines—German loot from France. They were in England on 4th April having been flown via Le Havre.

Stalag XIIIC, Hammelburg, was hurriedly evacuated as an armoured column from General Patton's Third American Army was rapidly approaching the area. This turned out to be a flying column sent forward for the purpose of releasing some 200 American officers at the camp, including the general's son-in-law. The armoured column took aboard some Americans from the camp on the night of 27th March but was ambushed while returning to their main force and lost several tanks and suffered severe casualties. The wounded were the next morning taken to the stalag hospital. It was nine days later before the prisoners of war remaining at the stalag were released.

Columns left the stalag in the early afternoon of 27th March and continued marching nearly all night, covering more than 25 miles. They continued the march in a south-easterly direction towards Moosburg, were billeted each night in reasonably comfortable accommodation, and fared quite well on food collected in the country they passed through. A variety of hand-drawn vehicles were improvised or "acquired" to carry their belongings and, averaging about 10 miles a day, they experienced no great hardships. Red Cross food was sent out to them from Stalag XIIID when they were near Nuremberg and loaded "white angel" trucks were awaiting when they reached the end of their march at Gutersberg on 22nd April after travelling about 230 miles. Five days later an American armoured column reached them. For the next few days the former prisoners wandered around the countryside eventually reporting to an American Army headquarters at Mainburg, where arrangements were made for their evacuation by air from Regensburg.

Towards the end of March the right arm of the pincer-movement encircling the Ruhr was approaching Kassel and nearing Oflags IXA/H and IXA/Z at Spangenburg and Rotenburg respectively. On 28th March the prisoners at Rotenburg were ordered to march east. Bed sheets sewn to form the letters "PW" were carried and laid out whenever Allied aircraft approached the column. They obtained plenty of good, fresh food by bartering cigarettes and soap as they went along. Averaging about 10 miles a day they just kept clear of American forces until 12th April when, near Halle, the Americans made a quick thrust and the prisoners found themselves in the middle of an artillery duel. The German guards deserted the column and next day the prisoners were liberated by the Americans and almost immediately flown to England.

Oflag IXA/H was evacuated on 29th March, the prisoners marching out at 5 p.m. and continuing throughout the night. The columns from this camp adhered to the practice of night marching until their liberation seven days later. They moved in much the same direction as the Rotenburg columns but took a more northerly road. On 3rd April they were camped at Legenfeld adjacent to a German artillery battery, still in action. A German parachute battalion was bivouacked in a wood near by and German wounded and stragglers were streaming through. Next day a pitched battle was going on around them and for a while the military position was obscure. The officers from Spangenburg disarmed their guards and in turn made them prisoners. Some also assisted the Americans to man road-blocks. Later in the day they were moved by American trucks back through a breach in the German lines to the headquarters of an American regiment that had contacted them. But they were not out of the wood yet. The Americans had had to evacuate Legenfeld and the regimental commander was apprehensive that Germans retreating from Kassel might threaten from the rear, so the former prisoners were formed into companies and armed with German rifles. Fighting was still going on in the next village. Eventually German resistance was overcome and the former prisoners guarded the German prisoners. On 9th April they were flown out from a near-by airfield and ferried by air to England.

It would appear that the delay in evacuating prisoners from the most westward of German prisoner-of-war camps was due, to some extent, to the German commandants' desire to remain and fall into American hands. This might have been the reason why prisoners at Oflag VA, Weinsberg, were not transferred eastward until 31st March, although the Americans were sitting on the west bank of the Rhine only 40 miles away. The evacuation from Oflag VA was to be by train and the German authorities agreed to move by night only, to mark the roofs of the trucks of the train with the Red Cross, Union Jack and letters "PW", and to allow the prisoners to disperse during the daytime. They left on the night of 31st March with Stalag VIIA, Moosburg, as the destination; the journey of 150 miles took four nights, the intervening three days being spent picnicking in fields beside the railway track. Owing to the slowness of the Allied advance in this sector these prisoners had to wait another month for liberation.

At Stalag 357, Fallingbostel, an effort was made to move the occupants to Lubeck, and on 6th April they set off on foot for that place, short of food but happy, being satisfied that the end could not be far away. By "scrounging" and bartering they fed better than they had done for some time. The German guards took little interest in their duties and many men wandered off. Those who did not were liberated by a British spearhead in that area on 18th April. At Stalag XIB, Fallingbostel, which held 20,000 prisoners of all nationalities, the German commandant handed over the camp to the prisoners' administration leaving only a token guard. Senior prisoner N.C.O's then took complete control, even to the issuing of leave passes for the German guards. On the morning of 16th April tanks of the 8th Hussars, a British armoured regiment, arrived at the camp gates. This regiment also liberated prisoners in the adjacent Stalag 357; these comprised the sick who had been left behind and others who had hidden when the columns were marched out on 6th April.

In mid-April the Americans were moving on Colditz, where Oflag IVC was situated. The Germans were offering considerable resistance here and the prisoners could hear the noise of battle for several days before the Germans ordered them all out into the woods. The Senior British Officer refused to obey. Later in the day the village was shelled. The American guns had been trained on the castle containing the oflag when a French flag and the Union Jack were noticed waving from windows and the order to fire was cancelled in the nick of time. The prisoners were liberated next day, 15th April. On 17th April 5,500 N.C.O's in Stalag 383 at Hohenfels set out on foot for Moosburg. A thousand or so sick remained to be transported by road and these with several hundreds who hid in the camp, remained there till the American forces arrived on 22nd April. The marchers did not get far; after three days forced marching they had three days' rest at Kosching, near Ingolstadt, where their guards deserted and where the prisoners remained until taken over by the Americans.

The day after the marchers left Hohenfels three Australians, Sergeants Roffey and Murphy,[8] and Corporal Walker,[9] who had hidden, left the camp on a foraging expedition and saw how German organisation had completely broken down. Small bands of civilians, prisoners of war, German soldiers (including officers) and foreign workers were raiding and looting what foodstuffs they could find. A chance remark brought the Australians into conversation with two English-speaking German officers, who eventually procured a car and drove the prisoners to a near-by ration store. After loading the car with foodstuffs they repaired to the officers' mess. Here the Germans proposed that if the Australians would promise to get them through the American lines before handing them over as prisoners of war, they, the Germans, would drive them there and give them every assistance. The Germans had a dread of being sent to work in the saltmines, which they had been assured by their propaganda would happen if they were captured by the Russians. Details of a plan were worked out in readiness for the time when the exact position of the American forces could be ascertained. Eventually, the Australians, now joined by a fourth,[1] took up residence in the officers' mess and awaited events. About midnight the prearranged signal was heard, but the Australians were astounded to find one of the officers hysterically waving a pistol. He explained that his fellow conspirator had suddenly exclaimed "God! What am I doing. I must do my duty," and had dashed out to the car and driven away to Regensburg where they had been ordered to report some days before. The Australians tried to calm him, explaining the Americans would be there in two days, but they were unsuccessful and, still waving his pistol, he rushed out into the night. The Australians then returned to the stalag and awaited the arrival of the American troops.

The Germans were endeavouring to get all prisoners in northern Bavaria to Stalag VIIA, Moosburg, and some were already there or in surrounding villages, while from other camps columns were heading towards Moosburg. The last camp to set out for Moosburg was Oflag VIIB, Eichstatt. They left on 14th April loaded with food and belongings but had not gone farther than a few hundred yards when they were attacked by Allied aircraft and suffered serious casualties.[2] The attack was precipitated by a German sentry in a watch-tower opening fire on an American plane. The column returned to camp and did not make another start until the next night; thereafter all movement was by night. The men arrived at Stalag VIIA in good condition after spending nine days on the road.

Moosburg was now very crowded and all facilities were hopelessly overtaxed. The German rations were infinitesimal but the I.C.R.C. had

---

[8] Sgt J. T. Murphy, VX4744; 2/7 Bn. Labourer; of Merbein, Vic; b. Mildura, Vic, 13 Aug 1919.
[9] Cpl A. M. Walker, VX5500; 2/7 Bn. Golf club maker; of Lower Plenty, Vic; b. Wonthaggi, Vic, 21 Nov 1913.
[1] Cpl A. E. Matthews, VX5175; 2/7 Bn. Clerk; of Geelong, Vic; b. Geelong, 9 Nov 1920.
[2] Twelve killed, 42 wounded including 4 seriously.

established a depot for Red Cross food parcels at the camp, so there was ample food except for bread and fresh vegetables. The officer prisoners at the camp, among whom were nearly 3,000 British, feared a move to the "Redoubt" area around Salzburg, but news of an agreement between the Allies and the Germans that there should be no further moves of prisoners allayed their fears. On 26th April the German commandant handed over the administration of the camp to the senior officer prisoner and most of the guards left. Next morning there were skirmishes near the camp between the retreating Germans and American advanced columns and on the 29th American tanks entered the camp. Unsuitable flying conditions hindered the air evacuation of the prisoners, but within the next fortnight several thousand a day were leaving the near-by airfield at Landshut.

In Austria the prisoners in German camps had experienced the same privations in the early months of 1945 as had those in Germany proper, but a Red Cross relief train from Switzerland had established a depot at Landeck and thence, from late March onwards, food parcels were distributed to the Austrian camps. At this time there were 36,000 prisoners of all nationalities in Stalag XVIIIA at Wolfsberg or the attached work-camps; some 10,000 were British, including about 1,500 A.I.F. These men did not experience the forced winter marches endured by their compatriots in eastern German camps; in fact, when they did move, it was in pleasant spring weather, there was no acute food shortage, and the march was an agreeable change from the monotony of prison-camp life.

The Germans planned to move as many British prisoners as possible from eastern Austria westwards to the Salzburg area. By the middle of April some columns were already on the move and by the end of the month, when a train-load of sick left Wolfsberg for Markt Pongau, practically all other British prisoners had left on foot. Those in the work-camps east and south of Wolfsberg were also on the march; all columns headed for Markt Pongau, where the first arrived on 23rd April. In the next few days hundreds arrived at Stalag XVIIIC, the camp at Markt Pongau, which the Germans estimated as having a capacity of 4,000 to 5,000. With the camp population swollen to 13,000 the overcrowding was similar to that in other camps. Some columns did not get as far as Markt Pongau; this was fortunate as the food problem would have become serious with a bigger influx. Although fighting was still continuing in adjacent areas the German guards left Markt Pongau on 2nd May and control of such a huge mass of men became difficult. On 6th May several hundreds broke out of camp and looted a goods train. A Swiss Red Cross representative stationed at the camp reported that order had been restored by the camp leaders without any serious clash with civilians, but it was considered advisable to send a medical officer to Salzburg to contact American forces, and a party of American troops arrived next day. A British recovery team, which included representatives of all Commonwealth forces, arrived on 17th May. Three days later the evacuation began—by lorry to Salzburg where the air-lift to France and on to England began.

The speed of the Russian advance in January 1945 prevented the Germans from moving all prisoners from the camps in Poland and eastern Germany. The outlying work-camps were overrun and in some main camps the sick were left with medical personnel to tend them. Consequently a number of British prisoners found themselves in Russian hands. In addition there were some who had escaped from the marching columns and had made their way back to the Russian lines. The British Military Mission to Moscow arranged with the Soviet authorities for the early repatriation of released British prisoners through Odessa. The Russians, however, wanted to work the former prisoners in the same way that released Russian prisoners were being worked by SHAEF.[3] Some Commonwealth Governments strongly opposed this and it was not until after agreement had been reached at Yalta in February between the Soviet and Commonwealth Governments for the "care and repatriation" of their respective former prisoners of war that British liaison officers were allowed on Soviet territory.

Arrangements, however, did not work smoothly; the movements of British liaison officers were considerably restricted, and although the Russians had established collecting points there was little organisation, probably due more to the chaotic conditions then prevailing in Poland than to any intentional Russian neglect. From the collecting points the ex-prisoners were directed back to Lvov in the Ukraine or Volkovysk farther north, from where they were sent on to Odessa. It was only at the two points mentioned that the British contact teams were allowed. Conditions were poor on the long train journey to Odessa, but no worse than for Russian soldiers or civilians travelling at the time. By February 1945 over 2,600 British released prisoners including about 50 Australians were on their way to Odessa, where a transit camp was being set up in a school building.[4] Here conditions were good; there was ample Red Cross food and medical attention was good. The men were allowed to go out under escort ("for their own protection"). The first ships carrying repatriates left Odessa in March.

When it was apparent in April 1945 that the collapse of Germany was imminent, an organisation, conceived as early as September 1942, began operations under SHAEF for the recovery of Allied prisoners of war in German hands. A branch of SHAEF known as P.W.X. was set up to control these operations.

It was considered advisable, in the interest of discipline and of the troops themselves, that contact officers should take charge of the former

---
[3] Supreme Headquarters Allied Expeditionary Force.
[4] In all 4,300 British released prisoners passed through Odessa, including 150 AIF.

prisoners in the camps as soon as practicable after liberation. These officers were to instruct the troops to remain in the camps or, if not in a camp, to report to the nearest transit centre; to explain to them the arrangements for their repatriation; to provide their immediate requirements and amenities, and generally assist in keeping them contented while awaiting evacuation to the United Kingdom. At the request of the War Office, Australia, in common with other Dominions, appointed her own liaison officers to assist with the repatriation scheme in general and her own nationals in particular.

Australia appointed 18 officers for this work—thirteen from the A.I.F. and five from the R.A.A.F. The senior Australian liaison officer[5] and one R.A.A.F. officer were attached to P.W.X. at Versailles, the others being attached to the headquarters of the various formations in the field. A unit, designated A.I.F. Reception Group (United Kingdom) formed in Melbourne in June 1944, commanded by Brigadier E. Gorman, sailed for England via the United States in July and established its headquarters first at Haslemere camp near High Wycombe in Buckinghamshire and later at Eastbourne, a seaside resort on the Sussex coast, where there were comfortable billets and all the amenities associated with a prosperous watering place. One transit camp and four reception camps were also established in the same area. Similar organisations were set up in England by the R.A.N. and R.A.A.F.

As the Allied advance from the west continued, the liaison officers in the field moved forward with the formations to which they were attached and, as prisoner-of-war camps were liberated, Australian prisoners were contacted and assisted in their evacuation by motor transport to airfields whence they were flown to England. In view of the bad physical condition of many of the men it was decided to expedite the air evacuation of the prisoners with all possible speed. Drafts were sent from the assembly centres to the airfield and were emplaned in groups irrespective of nationality. This method prevented the various liaison officers from contacting a number of their own nationals; but instead they assisted ably in the movement of all prisoners. After the German capitulation a large number of aircraft was made available for the air-lift of prisoners and the operation was stepped up considerably; more than 20,000 were evacuated by air in one day and most Allied prisoners were flown out of Europe within the next few weeks. After the main evacuation had been completed the liaison officers searched for stragglers in their areas. Some were recovered in this way and information was obtained about the fate of some who had died or had been killed by the Germans.[6]

Only the former prisoners from the few camps in north-western Europe were flown direct to England; the large majority staged for a few hours or overnight in Belgium or France, usually Brussels or Reims. The fol-

---

[5] Lt-Col J. S. Smith, VX138754. (1st AIF: Capt 4 FA Bde.) Staff appts LHQ; and SLO SHAEF, 1945. Club secretary; of Melbourne; b. Elsternwick, Vic, 5 Apr 1886.

[6] At 15th June 1945 about 120 men of the AIF were unaccounted for. This number was reduced to 9 and later the deaths of the 9 were presumed.

lowing description of the procedure at a Recovered Allied Military Personnel Reception Centre at Namur (Belgium) is typical. The centre was in an American L. of C. area and staffed by Americans with Allied liaison officers attached. The repatriates arrived at Namur either by plane, by train, by hitch-hiking or in stolen German cars. On arrival at the centre they were provided with coffee, cigarettes or chewing gum, and while waiting for particulars to be taken could read magazines and listen to music. After the documentation all clothes were removed and fumigated. A hot shower was followed by spraying with a special disinfectant powder, then the men were medically examined and completely outfitted with new clothing. A Red Cross parcel was issued containing cigarettes, confectionery, writing materials, toilet requisites, socks and handkerchiefs. Interrogation by Military Intelligence followed. An advance of pay of £5 was made before men were transported by truck to a billet which accommodated 2,500 and had a canteen and Red Cross centre. All meals were eaten at the billet. Next day the repatriates were entrained for Brussels, usually leaving that city by air for England on the following day. At the end of April this centre was processing repatriates at the rate of 200 in the hour and this number could have been increased with the addition of more medical officers.[7]

By 4th April the A.I.F. Reception Group had already handled the men of the A.I.F. involved in the last two exchanges of prisoners with Germany as well as repatriates from Italy and Switzerland and a few from Russia, and was prepared for an influx from German camps when, on that date, the first solitary repatriate from Germany arrived. From then onwards there were almost daily arrivals of up to 30 in number until about 20th April when the daily arrivals numbered about 100. The tempo gradually increased until the week ending 15th May when just over 1,000 arrived during the week, the peak being on 11th May when 55 officers and 603 other ranks were received by the group. Thereafter the rate of arrivals decreased until, at the end of June, there was only a dribble.

When the repatriates reached the airfields in England, usually in the Home Counties, those needing urgent medical treatment were sent to hospital. They reported to the reception group headquarters on discharge from hospital. The fit were drafted according to nationality and branch of the service to the appropriate transit camp, the A.I.F. Transit Camp, as mentioned, being at Eastbourne. Attached to A.I.F. Reception Group was a dental unit, cash office, provost platoon, postal unit and detachments of the Australian Canteen Services and the Australian Red Cross, the latter also representing other Australian philanthropic organisations.

On arrival at the transit camp repatriates were immediately provided with a meal and accommodation and later were allowed to send a free cable home and were presented with a Red Cross "welcome" parcel. They were then subjected to very thorough medical and dental examinations, given advances of pay and issued with Australian uniforms. Double rations

---

[7] From a report by Capt C. F. W. Baylis, Australian liaison officer.

were issued, with very substantial additions from the Australian Red Cross. Double ration cards were also issued when the repatriates went on the first 14 days of their repatriation leave, the balance of 46 days usually being withheld until arrival in Australia. For this leave, free rail passes were issued to any part of England, Scotland or Wales. Unbounded hospitality was showered on the men whether in hamlet, town or city. When leave was over the repatriates reported back to the transit camp, and were allotted to one of the reception camps; as far as practicable all men from one Australian State were in the same reception camp. Here everything was done to interest, entertain and keep the men fit by means of films, physical training, sports, instruction in the newest weapons, and by dances, lectures and so on. Many took the opportunity of continuing university and other courses interrupted by their enlistment. Embarkation for Australia was arranged as speedily as possible. Large-scale embarkation began in May 1945, when two batches of approximately 800 each left Liverpool. Similar numbers followed during June, and in July nearly 2,000 left. A draft of about 600 on 22nd August followed by a small one on the 30th completed the transfer of repatriates from Germany to Australia, except for a few who had been allowed to attend special courses in the United Kingdom and those who had requested discharge there.

APPENDIX 2

THE HAIFA-BEIRUT-TRIPOLI RAILWAY

By A. E. FIELD

Syria does not lend itself easily to railway construction. Very little such work was undertaken between the two world wars. In 1940, however, the possibility of Allied occupation of the Lebanon, and the hope that Turkey would join the Allies, made it very desirable that there should be a direct link between the standard gauge line from the British bases in Egypt and Palestine then terminating at Haifa, and the northern Syrian system ending at Tripoli. Earlier the French administration had considered the linking of Haifa and Tripoli by a route along the coast, but the project had been shelved for fear that the port of Haifa would benefit at the expense of Beirut. In 1940 and 1941 Middle East Command had surveys made of various routes as far as the Lebanon border. From a map study the first route favoured was from Haifa round the north of the Sea of Galilee to Rayak where the proposed railway would join the Homs-Aleppo-Turkey standard gauge line. This was ruled out because it involved very heavy cutting in basalt. The next possibility considered was an extension of the line northwards from Haifa along the coast to the Litani River and thence inland to Metulla-Rayak, but the route could not be explored before the conquest of Syria in July 1941. It then became evident that much heavy bridge work would be necessary in the Litani gorges which would not be economically justifiable as a wartime project. Finally, after a quick appreciation made at the end of August 1941 of the country between Beirut and Tripoli by Colonel Simner[1] and Lieut-Colonel K. A. Fraser of the Australian Railway Construction and Maintenance Group, a coast route from Haifa to Tripoli was chosen which, although it involved considerable tunnelling—including one tunnel of nearly a mile at Chekka headland—and several major bridges, had definite advantages over the alternative routes in that the rock cutting was not in basalt, a good all-weather road ran adjacent to the planned route and the provisional French plan was available. Moreover the route would serve Beirut and the Chekka cement works.

On 12th September 1941, No. 1 Section of 1st Railway Survey Company[2] set up camp at Az Zib and commenced a location survey around Ras Naqoura and Ras Bayada. Five weeks later they handed over the task to the South African Survey Company, G.H.Q. Middle East having allotted the Haifa-Beirut section of the line to the South African Engineering Corps. No. 1 Section then moved north to Maameltein and began a survey from Jounie to Heloue. Meanwhile No. 2 Survey Section, which

---

[1] Brig K. N. Simner, OBE. Dir of Railways ME 1940-41; Dep Dir Transportation ME 1941-42, Persia and Iraq 1942-43. Regular soldier; b. 5 Sep 1898.
[2] A unit of the Australian Railway Construction and Maintenance Group RAE. Henceforth units of the group will be referred to as follows: Headquarters, 1st, 2nd or 3rd Survey Company; 1st, 2nd or 3rd Construction Company.

had arrived at Heri, was concentrating on a topographical survey of the Chekka headland with a view to siting a line around it—a particularly difficult task. Colonel Simner decided to tunnel the headland and asked for a South African tunnelling company raised from miners of the Rand to carry out the work.[3] The survey of the tunnel length was taken over by the South African survey section and No. 2 and No. 3 Australian Survey Sections then completed the survey of the rest of the line. The arrival of the South African survey section is described thus by a narrator:

> They arrived without a knife, fork or spoon—thought they were to stay at hotels. I didn't even laugh, to my everlasting satisfaction; took them by the hand up to an A.I.F. "Q" bloke I knew in Tripoli and persuaded him to cut the "bull" and imagine they were A.I.F., so got [them] tents, blankets, personal and cookhouse gear and arranged for rations.[4]

The plan for construction was developed as the survey and work progressed. The line was to be a first-class military railway of standard gauge. The ruling grade was fixed at 1 in 50 and minimum radius of curvature at 10 chains. Passing loops were constructed every five miles. Formation was 16 feet wide on banks and 15 feet in cuttings. To economise in bridging, road crossings were level with the rails. Where possible the line was located so as to avoid demolition of houses. Where this was unavoidable, houses were pulled down and compensation paid to the owners or, in a few instances, new buildings were erected by the construction companies.

The South Africans started work at the Haifa end in December 1941 and the Haifa-Beirut section was opened for traffic in the following August —86 miles of standard gauge railway, the last five miles of which had been constructed by No. 1 Construction Company. This had involved the crossing of the Beirut-Damascus narrow gauge railway, the erection of a bridge over the Beirut River, of three 100-feet spans and the construction of the Beirut marshalling yards, for which about five miles of track was laid.

Early in 1942 the Australian construction companies, hitherto scattered over Egypt, Transjordan, Palestine and Syria, were concentrated on the route of the Beirut-Tripoli section, which was to be their task. They were allotted the following sections:

No. 1 Construction Company—Nahr Rhadir to Maameltein Cave.
No. 1 Section, 1st Survey Company—Maameltein Cave to Kilo 166.7.[5]
No. 2 Construction Company—Kilo 166.7 to Fadaous.[6]
No. 3 Construction Company—Fadaous to El Mina (less the section embracing Chekka tunnel).

At the outset, the only tools available were picks, shovels and crowbars. Imagine the dismay of men recently arrived from the Sinai Desert, where

---

[3] The 61st South African Tunnelling Company was allotted the task.
[4] Quoted in "The Haifa-Beirut-Tripoli Railway", by Major Eakins in *Royal Engineers Journal*, June 1952, from which much of the material in this narrative has been derived.
Maj D. H. Eakins, VX12698. Rlwy Constr and Maint Group; DAD Directorate Railway and Road Transportation 1943-45. Civil engineer; of Balwyn, Vic; b. Canterbury, Vic, 12 Dec 1898.
[5] The distances given are from Haifa.
[6] Later 2.6 kilometres of No. 2 Company's section, including the Ibrahim bridge, were taken over by No. 3 Company.

an 8-foot cutting in sand was a major job, when confronted with their first task in Syria—a quarter of a mile of hard rock excavation 30 feet deep, followed by a bank 80 feet high, then another rock excavation 35 feet deep; a bank of 46 feet and one more rock cutting of 35 feet, all within a mile. But plant gradually arrived: first a bulldozer that was worked night and day for six months, then compressors, drills, Decauville track and waggons until, by the end of September, the group was well equipped.

The group, with various attachments, was about 1,000 strong. Labour was drawn from two sources: the African Auxiliary Pioneer companies comprised of natives from Basutoland, Bechuanaland and Swaziland, of whom there were about 2,000, and local civilians. The latter, of various types and capacities, numbered at one stage up to 8,000, and included women, children and men of all ages. They were transported by motor lorries daily to and from their villages in the mountains. It was found economical at one stage to dismiss all those under 17 and over 70 years of age. The skilled workers of the civilian work-force were highly competent, particularly the stone-masons who displayed all the pride of craftsmen in their work. The unskilled civilians were of the usual Middle East standard, proficient in every known trick under the sun for receiving the maximum for a minimum of effort. The value of the South African natives was never very great. They had enlisted in an army, felt they should fight not work, and showed much more interest in military drill and parades. Cooks were observed instructing their helpers in the intricacies of rifle drill with ladles and brooms instead of rifles. Their fondness for drill

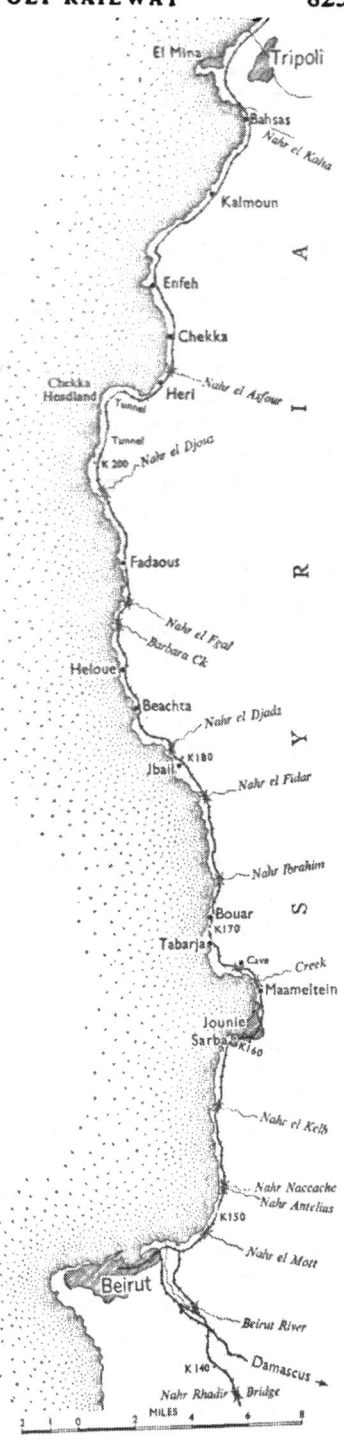

was used on one occasion in consolidating the track. A detachment of Basutos were marched at the double several times over a length of bank; the compression amounted to one inch in thirty after two passages.

From Dora, outside Beirut, the line followed the old tramway to the Nahr el Kelb. This stretch necessitated bridges at the Nahr el Mott (2 spans of 33 feet); at the Nahr Antelias (2 spans of 34 feet and one each of 27 and 20 feet) and a single 20-feet span bridge at the Nahr Naccache. These bridges were of similar construction. Foundations of the caisson type were put down to a depth of about 12 feet below water level on to clean sand. Piers were of concrete and the superstructure was launched from the shore by skids on to falsework and lowered to the piers. At the Nahr el Kelb a bridge was erected consisting of one 70-feet through-span and two 100-feet lattice-girder through-spans. Pier caissons and the southern abutment were sunk to a depth of 24 feet below water level and considerable water was encountered, necessitating the use of all available pumps. At 9 feet below water level a stratum of heavy loam was met, holding up the sinking of the caissons by extra skin friction. The caissons were allowed to fill with water and gelignite charges dropped into the caisson wells. This had the required effect and sinking proceeded to the prescribed depth.

Timber not being available for concrete formwork, it was decided to face the piers and abutments with masonry, laid in 10-inch courses in 4-feet lifts to act as formwork for the concrete core.[7] No scaffolding was necessary, because the stone was laid from inside the piers. At the Kelb headland difficult rock excavation was necessary. The Beirut-Tripoli road had been cut out of the rocky promontory and the railway had to be routed farther inland where the rock excavation was 70 feet deep. Disposal of spoil from the cutting across the road—the main artery of the forces in the Lebanon—was slow on account of heavy traffic. The lack of motor-trucks with tipping bodies was a severe handicap which added considerably to the time taken on formation. Frequently spoil was left on the sides of cuttings and banks had to be built from borrow pits.

From the Nahr el Kelb the line traversed fairly easy country through orchards and banana plantations to Sarba headland, whence it again followed the tramway route to Maameltein. From this point to Bouar there was much heavy rock cutting. At Maameltein headland 35,000 cubic yards of limestone rock had to be excavated and removed by hand which took six months to complete with three shifts working. The spoil plus an additional 5,000 cubic yards was used in the formation of the railway and for road diversions. Maameltein Creek was bridged with two spans one of 60 feet, the other 36 feet. At Maameltein Cave a 44-feet deck span was provided over an opening in the rock below the surface level. The span which came complete from India was hoisted from the road level on to its bearings by a light steel derrick.

Formation through Tabarja and Bouar was in dark chocolate soil through banana plantations interspersed by many small water channels

---

[7] This method was used on all major bridges on the Beirut-Tripoli section.

and irrigation ditches. In many instances these ditches were carried under the line by syphons. Precast concrete pipes of from 30 to 80-cm diameter were used, and strengthened by a casing of a minimum of six inches of concrete.

For the bridge at the Nahr Ibrahim, two lattice through-spans, one of 100 feet and another 70 feet, had been fabricated in South Africa, but the smaller span had been sunk en route and the Middle East through-span substituted did not match the lattice work of the larger span. The northern abutment was founded on rock; the southern abutment, founded 13 feet below water level, and the pier, 20 feet below water level, were of the caisson type. A heavy flow of water was encountered in the pier and a diver and grab were requisitioned to clear the cutting edge and remove the spoil. Masonry was again used as formwork, but in this case was notable for the fine work of the masons. In addition to the usual white stone, some of a slate-blue colour was supplied to this job and the masons arranged the colours in a most artistic pattern.

The erection of the bridge over the Nahr el Djouz was of exceptional interest because it was the first time an attempt had been made in the field to launch a unit construction railway bridge by the cantilever method, using a launching nose. The bridge had 3 spans of 80 feet each. While the piers and abutments were being completed, trackwork adjacent to the abutments was laid. The first span was assembled together with the launching nose on three bogies on the track. When the piers were complete, the span and nose were hauled across until No. 1 span was in position above the opening provided for it. The dismantling of the 53-foot launching nose 70 feet in the air by the aid of a flying-fox was a difficult operation and to obviate a recurrence with the second span, the officer-in-charge obtained permission to launch No. 2 and No. 3 spans together, thus bringing the nose on to the northern abutment for easy dismantling. The two spans with the launching nose were assembled on bogies as before, the track laid on No. 1 span now in position and the long assembly hauled across to rest on temporary supports on No. 2 pier until lowered by gantries to rest on the piers and northern abutment. The experiment was a complete success and was the method used later on other bridges, notably that at the Nahr el Fidar, which required four 75-foot deck spans on high piers, the highest being 62 feet from foundation level. Here all four spans and launching nose were coupled together and hauled across in one operation. The assembly, launching, jacking down and dismantling of the nose took only 389 man-hours.

Another bridge of interest was the 80-foot deck span over the Nahr el Fgal, a wadi 69 feet deep. The high abutments with their extensive splayed-wing walls involved much stone facing and 2,000 tons of concrete. Major bridges were also erected at Barbara Creek, the Nahr el Djouz, the Nahr el Asfour and the Nahr el Kalta. At the more important bridges, provision had been made in piers for demolition chambers for use should the necessity arise.

Further heavy rock cutting was encountered north of Beachta, and north of Enfeh and along the Tripoli road from Kalmoun. Because of a general shortage of detonators and fuses, shots were larger than is usual in railway work and this caused damage to near-by houses, telephone wires and the slopes of the cuttings.

Because there was no room for expansion of the existing marshalling yards at Enfeh, a terminal yard for the new traffic was established at Bahsas. Here a marshalling yard, reversing triangle, coal stage, and water column were installed, also a 500-foot long platform and approach roads. The Bahsas yards were constructed on sand near the sea and from there to the junction with the Tripoli-Aleppo standard gauge railway, the line was located through orchards in sandy country. This enabled No. 3 Company speedily to complete the earthwork and platelaying at the Tripoli end with the result that the line from El Mina to Chekka, with four passing loops and a spur to the Chekka cement works, was opened to traffic on 22nd July 1942.

The 61st South African Tunnelling Company handed over the main Chekka tunnel plus a small one of 90 feet near by to the Australians for platelaying at the end of September 1942 and then left for tunnelling operations at the Haifa end of the line. In the exceptionally short period of eight months they had driven the main tunnel 4,800 feet through rock at a level 100 feet lower than the 1,500-foot road tunnel on the main coast road. Working three shifts they had maintained air power, ventilation, water and electric light services along the whole length of the work without interruption—a praiseworthy achievement indeed.

Of the track laid by the construction companies, about two-thirds were 75-lb flat-bottomed American rails, the balance being bullhead English 85-lb rails. The former were laid on single steel tie plates fastened with dog-spikes. The bullhead track was supported on cast-iron chairs spiked to the sleepers and fastened with local timber keys, which if not driven home tight and kept so, went to alleviate the natives' chronic shortage of firewood. Sleepers, spaced at 2 feet 5 inches, were of Indian hardwood and American pine. Local and Turkish pine was used in loops and station yards.

About 70,000 cubic yards of ballasting was obtained by local contract and the remainder in various ways. In some instances, stone was napped to size on the formation; in others it was transported to the site by donkeys, while long lines of gaily-dressed women carried ballast, some of it picked to size, in baskets to the formation. Later, when stone crushers were available, several were set up in a wadi about 10 feet from the line. Over the hoppers a platform was erected onto which motor-trucks carted stone from the beach. Labourers pushed boulders into the hoppers, a bulldozer pushed the ballast clear of the crushers towards the railway and a dragline shovel loaded the ballast into waiting railway trucks.

The last gap in the rails was closed on 17th December 1942 near the heavy rock excavation at Maameltein headland. The ballasting of this section was quickly completed and three days later the railway was officially opened by General Alexander, Commander-in-Chief Middle East. After inspecting a guard of honour of sappers of the group, General Alexander drove the last spike at the Nahr el Kelb, selected for the opening ceremony because of its historic associations. Here is a band of hard rock with a vertical face on which are many commemorative inscriptions. The earliest celebrates the conquest of the country by Pharaoh Rameses II, Asarhaddon of Assyria, Nebuchadnezzar and the Greeks. Later ones include the French in 1860, Sultan Barquq, and the Australians in 1918. A carving had also been made in the rock commemorating the opening of the railway by General Alexander. The Commander-in-Chief and special guests boarded a full-sized passenger train drawn by a large Baldwin locomotive decorated with Australian and Lebanese flags and travelled the remaining length of the line to Bahsas, passing groups of sappers, Basutos and Swazis drawn up on their respective lengths.

Job 901—the official designation of the Beirut-Tripoli connection—was done, which completed the London to Cairo railway link. Next day, 21st December, the line was put to use, when all concerned were thrilled to see a train-load of tanks travelling north, and at night to hear four wheat trains going south.

A total length of 176 miles had been finished in a year, six months ahead of the schedule laid down by the British War Office. This rapid railway construction through semi-mountainous country ranks among the more remarkable engineering feats of the war.

Principal Quantities

Excavation, earth and sand	630,000 cu. yds.
Excavation, rock	343,000 cu. yds.
Pipe culverts	11,050 lin. ft.
Arch culverts, up to 6-ft. diameter	135
Flat slab, reinforced concrete	30 openings
Sea and retaining walls	4,500 lin. ft.
Bridging, major	1,833 lin. ft.
Masonry in walls	20,900 sq. yds.
Concrete in bridges, culverts and walls	39,990 cu. yds.
Riveted shellwork in bridges	950 tons
Rivets	56,700
Unit steel trestling (temporary)	250 tons
Track-work	66.2 miles
Ballast	140,000 cu. yds.
Explosives	357,662 lbs.
Detonators	176,648
Cement	12,103 tons

APPENDIX 3

ABBREVIATIONS

A—*Acting, Assistant*
AA—*Anti-Aircraft*
AAMC—*Australian Army Medical Corps*
AANS—*Australian Army Nursing Service*
AASC—*Australian Army Service Corps*
Admin—*Administration, Administering*
Adv—*Advanced*
AFA—*Australian Field Artillery*
AFV—*Armoured Fighting Vehicle*
AGH—*Australian General Hospital*
AIF—*Australian Imperial Force*
ALFSEA—*Allied Land Forces, South-East Asia*
Amb—*Ambulance*
AMF—*Australian Military Forces*
Amn—*Ammunition*
Appts—*Appointments*
Armd—*Armoured*
Arty—*Artillery*
A-Tk—*Anti-Tank*

Bde—*Brigade*
Bdr—*Bombardier*
BEF—*British Expeditionary Force*
BGS—*Brigadier, General Staff*
BM—*Brigade Major*
Bn—*Battalion*
Brig—*Brigadier*
Bty—*Battery*

Capt—*Captain*
Cav—*Cavalry*
CBO—*Counter-Battery Officer*
CCRA—*Commander, Corps Royal Artillery*
Cdo—*Commando*
CE—*Chief Engineer*
CI—*Chief Instructor*
CIGS—*Chief of the Imperial General Staff*
C-in-C—*Commander-in-Chief*
Cmdre—*Commodore*
CO—*Commanding Officer*
Col—*Colonel*
Comd—*Command, Commander, Commanded*
Comdt—*Commandant*
Coy—*Company*
Cpl—*Corporal*
CRA—*Commander, Royal Artillery*

CRE—*Commander, Royal Engineers (of a division)*

DAAG—*Deputy Assistant Adjutant-General*
DADMS—*Deputy Assistant Director of Medical Services*
DAG—*Deputy Adjutant-General*
DAQMG—*Deputy Assistant Quartermaster-General*
DCE—*Deputy Chief Engineer*
DCGS—*Deputy Chief of the General Staff*
DDMS—*Deputy Director of Medical Services*
DGMS—*Director-General of Medical Services*
Dir—*Director*
Div—*Division*
DMS—*Director of Medical Services*
Dvr—*Driver*

Ech—*Echelon*
Engrs—*Engineers*

FA—*Field Artillery*
Fd—*Field*
FELO—*Far Eastern Liaison Office*

Gen—*General*
GHQ—*General Headquarters*
Gnr—*Gunner*
GOC—*General Officer Commanding*
Gp—*Group*
GSO1—*General Staff Officer, Grade 1*

HQ—*Headquarters*

ICRC—*International Committee of the Red Cross*
Inf—*Infantry*
Int—*Intelligence*

KDG—*1st King's Dragoon Guards*
KRRC—*The King's Royal Rifle Corps*

L-Bdr—*Lance-Bombardier*
L-Cpl—*Lance-Corporal*
LH—*Light Horse*
LHQ—*Allied Land Forces Headquarters*
LMG—*Light Machine-Gun*

ABBREVIATIONS

LO—*Liaison Officer*
L of C—*Lines of Communication*
LRDG—*Long Range Desert Group*
Lt—*Lieutenant, Light*
L-Sgt—*Lance-Sergeant*
LTD—*Leave and Transit Depot*

Maj—*Major*
ME—*Middle East*
MEF—*Middle East Forces*
MG—*Machine Gun*
Mil—*Military*
Movt—*Movement*

NGF—*New Guinea Force*
NTF—*Northern Territory Force*

OC—*Officer Commanding*
OCTU—*Officer Cadet Training Unit*
Ops—*Operations*
OR—*Other Rank*

Para—*Parachute*
Pk—*Park*
Pnr—*Pioneer*
Pte—*Private*
PW—*Prisoner of War*

QMG—*Quartermaster-General*

RA—*Royal Artillery*
RAA—*Royal Australian Artillery*
RAAF—*Royal Australian Air Force*
RAE—*Royal Australian Engineers*
RAF—*Royal Air Force*

RAR—*Royal Australian Regiment*
RE—*Royal Engineers*
Regt—*Regiment*
RFC—*Royal Flying Corps*
Rft—*Reinforcement*
RHA—*Royal Horse Artillery*
RMC—*Royal Military College*
RMO—*Regimental Medical Officer*
RN—*Royal Navy*
RNF—*The Royal Northumberland Fusiliers*
RNR—*Royal Naval Reserve*
RTR—*Royal Tank Regiment*

SASO—*Senior Air Staff Officer*
Sgt—*Sergeant*
SHAEF—*Supreme Headquarters, Allied Expeditionary Force*
SLO—*Senior Liaison Officer*
SMO—*Senior Medical Officer*
SORE—*Staff Officer, Royal Engineers*
Spr—*Sapper*
Sqn—*Squadron*
S-Sgt—*Staff-Sergeant*
SWPA—*South-West Pacific Area*

Tk—*Tank*
Tpr—*Trooper*
Tpt—*Transport*
TSMG—*Thompson Sub-Machine-Gun*

VAD—*Voluntary Aid Detachment*

WO1—*Warrant-Officer, Class 1*

INDEX

ABADAN OILFIELDS, 600, 605
Abdiel, British minelayer, 343, 415
ABIAR, EL (Sketches pp. 25, 83), 31, 41, 58, 63-4, 66-8, 76, 78, 80, 87, 90
ABYSSINIA, 39, 143, 166, 244
ACHDAR, JEBEL, *see* JEBEL ACHDAR
ACROMA (Sketches pp. 25, 83), 87, 101, 108-9, 119, 121-2, 165, 172, 178, 188, 191, 196, 199, 209-11, 278, 280, 458, 491, 510-12, 535
ACROMA ROAD, 191, 197, 204, 206, 217-21, 318, 333
ACWORTH, Capt G. W., 53
ADAMS, L-Sgt A., 96n
ADANA (Sketch p. 517), 518
ADDU ATOLL, 753-4
ADELBODEN (Map p. 758), 770
ADEM, EL (Map p. 13; Sketch p. 83), 15, 24-5, 32, 47, 49, 53, 59, 63, 76-7, 87, 94, 100n, 101, 103, 107-8, 119, 124-5, 128, 132, 134, 136-7, 246, 254, 275, 277n, 278, 329, 427, 431, 438, 459, 462, 479, 483, 491, 495-7, 500-1, 503-4, 506-12, 535
ADMIRALTY HOUSE (Map p. 220), 188, 397-8
ADNAMS, Capt W. T., 620
AFRINE (Sketches pp. 517, 520), 516, 521
AGAR-HAMILTON, J. A. I. and TURNER, L. C. F., 429n, 433n, 437n, 482n, 485n, 500n, 547n
AGEDABIA (Map p. 13; Sketch p. 83), 14, 18, 25, 27-9, 32-3, 37, 42, 48, 51-2, 54-5, 60, 65, 81, 87, 118, 123, 511, 533
AGHEILA, EL (Map p. 13; Sketches pp. 16, 31), 15, 17-18, 21-31, 35-40, 46-9, 53, 753, 756; occupied by enemy, 38
A.I.F. News, 638
AIN MARA (Sketch p. 83), 93-4
AIRCRAFT, strength and dispositions in Middle East in March 1941, 33; dispatched to Far East in April 1942, 533; *Enemy*, destroyed at Tobruk, 413
AIRENTE, FORT (Map p. 220; Sketch p. 126), 140, 253, 256, 399, 418-19, 536
AIR RAIDS, on Tobruk, 192-3, 198, 211, 214, 240, 273, 292-3, 337-8, 353, 368-9, 410-13, 415
AIR RECONNAISSANCE, at Tobruk, 317, 338-9
AIR SUPPLY, of Axis armies in Africa, 623
AIR SUPPORT, at Tobruk, 184-5, 338-9; at Alamein, 555, 679
AITKEN, Lt-Col E. F., 755n
Ajax, British cruiser, 376, 398
AKTERIN (Sketch p. 520), 521
ALAM BAOSHAZA (Sketch p. 553), 554
ALAM BARGHUT (Sketch p. 361), 359
ALAMEIN, EL (Maps pp. 13, 668; Sketches pp. 543, 618), 24, 357, 424, 536-7, 544-5, 558, 561, 563, 566, 571, 574n, 588, 596, 599, 603-4, 613, 617, 623, 629, 634-6, 638, 752, 763-4; defence of, 542-3, 597, 624; disposition of forces at, 543; Auchinleck's plans in event of loss, 546-7; Rommel's attack on, 547-9, plans renewed offensive, 624; living conditions at, 616; enemy dispositions, 625, 655; Alexander and Montgomery fix date of offensive, 640-1; British deception arrangements, 648-9; Battle of, 663-742, casualties, 742, examination of 742-5; Rommel orders withdrawal from, 719, 738-41
ALAMEIN BOX, 542-3, 548, 558, 562, 564-5, 570, 603, 617, 621, 625
ALAM EL DAB (Sketch p. 135), 187
ALAM EL DIHMANIYA (Sketch p. 568), 568
ALAM EL HALFA (Sketches pp. 543, 628), 611, 625; Battle of, 624, 627-8, 636, 640, 642, 656, 658, British and enemy losses, 629-30, post-mortem on, 634-5
ALAM EL HAMAM (Sketch p. 361), 363
ALAM EL KIDAD (Sketch p. 361), 362
ALAM HAMZA, 511-12
ALAM NAYIL (Sketch p. 543), 550, 557, 624-5, 627
ALANBROOKE, Field Marshal Viscount, 286, 605, 613, 640; visits Washington, June 1942, 603-4; proposes Montgomery as commander of Eighth Army, 605; offered Middle East command by Churchill, 606; appraisal of Alexander and Montgomery, 607-8; chooses senior commanders in Middle East, 615; defends Montgomery against Churchill's criticism, 706
ALBRECHT, Cpl K. G., 689

ALEPPO (Sketch p. 517), 516, 517n, 520, 521, 524, 526, 529, 823, 828
ALEXANDER, Field Marshal Rt Hon Earl (Plate p. 604), 609, 611-12, 614-15, 624, 639, 699, 749, 753; becomes C-in-C ME, and career of, 606-8; on appointments to higher command, 613; issues written directive to Montgomery, 621; on importance of Battle of Alam el Halfa, 635; fixes date for Alamein offensive, 640-1; unable to release 9 Div from Alamein battle, 695-6; visits Montgomery with R. G. Casey, 706; achievements compared with Auchinleck's, 744; visits Morshead to express appreciation of 9 Div, 745; takes salute at 9 Div parade at Gaza, 751-2; farewell signal to Morshead, 754; opens Beirut-Tripoli railway, 829
ALEXANDRIA (Map p. 13), 24, 29, 113, 142, 173, 180, 243, 271, 335, 343, 356, 368, 375-6, 398-9, 414, 416 513-14, 537, 541-2, 544-5, 547, 550-2, 555, 557, 580, 608, 622n, 648
ALEY, 517
ALGIERS (Sketch p. 2), 772
ALLAN, Col H. T., 121, 385, 399
ALLAN, Lt R. T., 734-5
ALLEN, Capt J. L., 370, 594
ALLEN, Capt K. F., 714-15
ALLEYNE, Sgt F. O., 227, 713
ALLIED WAR CRIMES TRIBUNAL, 767
ALMA, 529n
ALMAZA, 368
ALOUITES, THE, 529
ALTENGRABOW (Map p. 758), 814
AMERICA, UNITED STATES OF, 341, 624; opposed to return of 9 Aust Div to Australia, 748-9; exchanges prisoners with Germany, 801
AMERICAN AIR FORCE: *No. 12 Medium Bombardment Gp*, at Alamein, 640
AMERICAN ARMY, 367; additional division proposed for Australia, 528, 537; adopts common vocabulary for US and British forces, 637-8;
—ARMIES: First, 814; Third, 814
—DIVISIONS: 7th, 814; 24th, 749n; 25th, 749n; 27th, 749n; 40th, 749n; 1st Armd, 639n
AMERICAN GOVERNMENT, proposes dispatch of additional divisions to Pacific, 537-8
—JOINT CHIEFS OF STAFF, 527-8, 603, 750
Amin, schooner, 376
AMIRIYA, EL (Map p. 5; Sketch p. 546), 111, 116, 135, 375, 514, 540, 545-6, 552, 574n
AMMUNITION, at Tobruk, 293-4, 300, 368, 377-8, 413, 451; at Alamein, 647-8, expended in battle, 743; *Italian*, at Tobruk, 240, 300, 368
ANATOLIA (Sketch p. 517), 276, 519
ANDERSEN, Capt L. E., 78
ANDERSON, Maj E., 104-5, 107
ANDERSON, Cpl F. E., 800n
ANDERSON, Capt G. G., 259, 564-5
ANDERSON, Cpl J. H., 713
ANDERSON, L-Cpl K. C., 321
ANDREW, Brig L. W., 498-9
ANDREWS, Pte R. C. S., 71
ANDREWS, Pte W., 71
ANGLO-EGYPTIAN TREATY, 523-4
ANGUS, Capt W., 618, 632-3
ANKARA (Map p. 5), 518
ANNEAR, Sgt G. M. P., 581
ANTELAT (Map p. 13; Sketch p. 25), 25-7, 29, 34-5, 40, 48, 51-4, 56, 59-60, 81
Antiklia, storeship, 293, 414
AOSTA, DUKE OF, 166, 256
Aphis, British gunboat, 145, 187, 369
APOLLONIA (Sketch p. 25), 26, 94
APPLETON, Lt F. C., 626
AQQAQIR RIDGE, 732, 737
Aquitania, British troopship, 753
ARAB EL MOULK (Sketch p. 517), 531
ARABS, THE, 42-3, 344, 529, 532, 626
ARBE (Sketch p. 522), 521
ARCO DEI FILENI, 22; *see also* MARBLE ARCH
ARDERNE, Brig E. A., 136
ARGENT, Col J. N. L., 135-6, 172, 187, 245, 254, 284, 358
Ark Royal, British aircraft carrier, 431
ARMITAGE, Captain, 247, 440, 475

834 INDEX

ARNOLD, Lt-Col A. S. W., 245
AROSA (Map p. 758), 770
ARTILLERY, strength in March 1941, 15; equipment compared with German, 20; "bush artillery", 112-13, 127-8, 134, 239-40, 262, 294, 298, 316, 336; command organisation, 120; at Tobruk, 122, 161, 171, 181-2, 185-6, 199, 201, 210-11, 265-6, 268, 293-5, 299-300, 316, 320, 337-8, 368-9, 385, 409-13; strength in Crusader, 429; at Alamein, 544, 646, 660-1, 665-6, 668, 698, strength, 639, 655; in Supercharge, 729-30; ammunition expended in Battle of El Alamein, 743. *Enemy*, use 88-mm guns, 20, 150-1, 154, 258, 278, 281, 284, 429, 446, 449, 502, 745; at Tobruk, 181-2, 294, 299, 336-7, 353, 422, strength, 385, 395; use 210-mm guns, 460, 471, 493; at Ed Duda, 503; number of guns opposing XXX Corps at Alamein, 666*n*
ASHBY, Sgt H. H., 584
ASTON, Cpl F. C., 207
ATHENS (Map p. 5), 65, 755*n*, 775
Atid, Palestinian ship, 415
ATKINS, Gnr R., 153
ATLANTIC CONFERENCE, 313, 342
AUCHINLECK, Field Marshal Sir Claude (Plate p. 589), 118, 310-11, 331, 343, 353, 382, 417, 427*n*, 491-2, 495, 499, 500*n*, 507, 509-10, 519, 526-7, 530, 544, 553-6, 564-6, 569, 571, 574, 577, 578*n*, 588-9, 597-8, 600*n*, 603, 608, 622, 624-5, 641; and Churchill, 244, 312, 341-2, 534-5, 604-5; becomes C-in-C Middle East, 285, 296-7; career of, 286; and relief of 9 Aust Div, 313, 332, 334, 345-52, 380-1; on achievements of Tobruk garrison, 400-1; and Crusader operation, 425, 428, 432*n*, 433, 451-2, 454, 487, 533; appoints Ritchie to replace Cunningham, 455; on value of "Jock columns", 501; "plan of deception" in Syria, 529; takes over command of Eighth Army from Ritchie, 536; plans for stand at Alamein, 546-7; orders counter-attack by XIII Corps, 549; orders Eighth Army to "attack and destroy", 550-1; and Morshead, 552, 579, 614; orders capture of Tel el Eisa and Tel el Makh Khad, 557; plans attack in Ruweisat Ridge area, 576; issues Special Order of the Day, 25 Jul 1942, 590; on failure of Ruin Ridge attack, 595*n*; on need to build up greater strength before renewing attack at Alamein, 596; appoints Brig de Guingand BGS, Eighth Army, 597; policy at Alamein, 603; replaced by Alexander, 606-7; achievements compared with Alexander's and Montgomery's, 744-5
Auckland, New Zealand sloop, 414
AUDA, WADI (Map p. 220; Sketch p. 126), 111, 139, 299, 337, 420
AUGILA (Map p. 13), 53
Aurora, British cruiser, 431
AUSTIN, Capt A. G., 581
AUSTIN, Maj G., 581
AUSTRALIAN AIR FORCE, 511*n*, 820
—No. 3 Sqn, 68-9, 97; No. 451 Sqn, 531, 533
AUSTRALIAN ARMY, 4, 318, 515, 538, 755-6, 765, 794; reorganised in Middle East, 6, 9; relations with British and other troops, 121, 141, 353, 525; strength, in Tobruk, 159, in Middle East, 304, 527, 600, at Alamein, 661; German estimates of, 210, 267-8; conditions of service, 306; dispositions in Middle East and proposed concentration, 256, 309-11, 348, 351, 367, 382; trains men at OCTU, 522-3; behaviour of troops in Syria, 525-6; reinforcement of, 555, 600, 695; appointments to higher command, 612
—AHQ Melbourne, 600-1
—HQ AIF Middle East, 29, 424. *Base Area*, 308, 514. *Rear Echelon*, 10
—I AUST CORPS, 7, 28, 295, 366, 444, 515, 517, 519, 546, 772; leaves Cyrenaica, 8-9; renamed Anzac Corps, 367; embarks for Far East, 527
—ANZAC CORPS, 367; proposed formation of, 307, 309, 380*n*
—AUSTRALIAN CORPS, 310, 313; proposed formation of, 307, 380*n*
—DIVISIONS: 1st Armd, 8*n*. 6th Inf, 3, 6-8, 10-11, 26-7, 111, 160, 303, 306-7, 310, 312, 334, 533, 767; relieved in Cyrenaica by 9 Div, 9, 14, 16-17; strength of, 527; return to Australia sought, 527-8; in Ceylon, 537-8; losses in Greece, 775. 7th Inf, 3, 6, 7, 32, 110, 113-14, 116-17, 157, 162, 256, 307, 310, 312, 332, 334, 533; composition, 9-10; in defence of Cyrenaica, 64-5, 115, 118, 124, 129,

AUSTRALIAN ARMY—*continued*
138-9, 141-2, 143, 306; moves to Syria, 515-16; return to Australia sought, 527-8. 8th Inf, 6, 533, 9th Inf, 307, 366, 747-8, 755; in Palestine, 3, 514; role in Middle East, 6, 8; formation of, 6-7, 10; composition, 8*n*, 9; training of, 10-11, 258, 747; in Cyrenaica, 12, 17, 24, 31-2, 34-5, 41-2, 52, 56, 58-9, 63, 67, 78, 82, 86-90, 92, 94*n*, 100-1, 109, 111, 114-15, 118, 140; relieves 6 Div, 14, 16; equipment of, 28-9, 43, 64, 75; discipline, 43-5, 525-6, 748; at Tobruk, 119-25, 129, 190, 192-3, 227, 264, 271, 288*n*, 296, 375, 385, 421, relief of, 305-6, 310-11, 313, 334-5, 344-52, 359, 378, 381, 383, 395, 399-400, 417, 421, 423; German estimate of, 267-8; role in Battleaxe, 256, 278-80; Morshead on decorations for, 353; casualties at Tobruk, 401*n*; General Scobie's tribute to, 510-11; in Syria, 515-17, 521, 525-6, 530-3; proposed recall to Australia, 527, 537-9, 600-2, 694-6, 746, 748-50; reactions to loss of Tobruk, 537; moves to Egypt, 540-1, 543-5; at Alamein, 551-2, 555, 557-8, 562, 564-5, 569, 571-2, 574, 576, 578-9, 588, 590, 593, 598-600, 603, 605, 610-12, 614-15, 617, 621-2, 625, 630, 634-5, 637-8, 642, 644-8, 650-61, 664, in Battle of El Alamein, 672-5, 676*n*, 678-9, 680*n*, 683, 685-7, 692-4, 698-700, 702, 705-8, 716, 719, 723, 732, 735, 739-40, 742, achievements at, 575, 728, 743, 745-6, casualties, 601, 742; affiliates with 51 Highland Div, 636; issued with T colour patch, 750; parades at Gaza, 751-2; embarks, 753-4; affection for GOC, 746, 754
—ARMOUR: 6 Div Cav Regt, 42, 334, 756. 7 Div Cav Regt, 306, 308, 310, 312, 334. 9 Div Cav Regt, 515, 520, 531, 541, equipment of, 544, 622; at Alamein, 558, 561, 572-3, 579, 616, 620, 630, 632, in battle of, 659, 736, 739, 740
—ARTILLERY: RAA 9 Div, proposed dispatch to Tobruk, 344, 346-7; in Egypt, 356, 359; in Tobruk, 401*n*; in Syria, 531; at Alamein, 563, 572, 708, achievements, 571, 743. *Anti-Aircraft*, 2/3rd Regt, 36; 2/4th Regt, 515, 653. 8th Lt Bty, 96. *Anti-Tank*, 2/1st Regt, 8*n*. 2/2nd Regt, 135, 137, 142, 171-2, 186-7, 254. 2/3rd Regt, 358, 514, 526, 757; allotted to 9 Div, 7, 8*n*, 9; in Cyrenaica, 54, 103; at Mechili, 77, 84, 102, 105-7; at Tobruk, 119-20, 151-2, 153-4, 340, 359-60, 375, casualties, 401*n*; on Egyptian frontier, 135-7, 172, 186-7, 245, 254, 284; absorbs 20 and 24 A-Tk Coys, 515; at Tel el Eisa and Ruin Ridge, 560-1, 563, 566, 594; equipped with 6 pdrs, 622, 661; in Battle of El Alamein, 686, 703, 704, 717, 722, 724, 726-7; number taken prisoner, 755. 16th Coy, 16-17, 38, 48. 20th Coy, 70, 389; absorbed by 2/3 A-Tk Regt, 515. 24th Coy, in Cyrenaica, 43, 64, 75; at Tobruk, 132, 202, 207, 340; absorbed by 2/3 A-Tk Regt, 515. 26th Coy, at Tobruk, 201*n*, 209, 228-9; absorbed by 4 LAA Regt, 515. *Field*, 2/2nd Regt, 15*n*, 571. 2/3rd Regt, 8*n*. 2/7th Regt, 8*n*, 368, 515, 517; allotted to 9 Div 9; on Egyptian frontier, 356-7, 358-60, 362-7; at Alamein, 563, 588, 592, 627, 634, 686, 693, 703. 2/8th Regt, 8*n*, 356, 367, 515; allotted to 9 Div, 9; on Egyptian frontier, 358-9, 363, 365-6; at Tel el Eisa, 564. 2/9th Regt, 520. 2/12th Regt, 8*n*, 514; allotted to 9 Div, 9; at Tobruk, 257, 265, 267-8, 298-9, 300, 320, 356-7, 359, 369, 374, relieved, 375; at Alamein, 727
—ENGINEERS: 9 Div, 32, 42, 515, 531; at Tobruk, 272, 300, casualties, 401*n*; at Alamein, 649, 652, 669, casualties, 742*n*. *Field Companies*: 2/3rd, 8*n*, 755; in Cyrenaica, 27, 32, 58-9, 66, 92-3; at Tobruk, 127, 138, 190, 338, relieved, 396; at Alamein, 661, 672, 699, 708, 740. 2/4th, 32; in Cyrenaica, 8, 16; at Tobruk, 111, 113, 160, 190, 303-4, 327, relieved, 334. 2/7th, 8*n*, 515; in Cyrenaica, 32, 41, 59, 92-4; at Tobruk, 181, 371, relieved, 375; at Alamein, 575, 580, 587*n*, 661, 699. 2/13th, in Cyrenaica, 32, 41, 59, 78-9, 94; at Tobruk, 131, 168, 185, 192, 199, 321, 327, 334, 384; at Alamein, 617, 631-2, 634, 652, 661, 668, 670, 699, 740. 2/24th Field Park 529*n*. *Railway Units*: HQ Rlwy Construction and Maintenance Group, 751, 823*n*. 1st Rlwy Construction Coy, 823*n*, 824. 2nd Rlwy Construction Coy, 823*n*, 824. 3rd Rlwy Construction Coy, 823*n*, 824, 828. 1st Rlwy Svy Coy, 823-4. 2nd Rlwy Svy Coy, 823*n*. 3rd Rlwy Svy Coy, 823*n*
—INFANTRY: *Brigades*, 16th, 559. 17th, 14-15, 23. 18th, 6, 8, 10, 32, 79, 157, 190, 516, 602; allotted to

AUSTRALIAN ARMY—continued
  9 Div, 7; switched to 7 Div, 9; captures Giarabub, 31; at Tobruk, 101, 113-14, 115-16, 118-19, 124, 139, 141, 160, 201, 211, 227, 230-5, 236, 241, 242, 246, 266-7, 270-1, 279-80, 293, 297-8, 310, 314, 327, relief of, 312, 331-4, 343, 345, 347-8, 375, casualties, 401n. 20th, 514-15, 746; transferred to 9 Div, 9-10; formation and training, 10-11; in Cyrenaica, 12, 14-15, 17, 23, 25, 30-2, 41, 44, 64, 68, 79, 96, 101, 119; at Tobruk, 121, 126, 128, 131-2, 139, 144, 160-1, 163-4, 178, 190-1, 221, 230, 236, 247, 266, 270-1, 273, 279-80, 288, 297-8, 314, 336, 340, 375, 385-6, 389-92, 394, 420-1, relief of, 397, 399, casualties, 401n; in Syria, 516, 519-20, 521, 524-6, 529-31, 533; moves to Egypt, 541, 552; at Alamein, 555, 565, 569, 579, 590, 603, 610, 616, 622n, 626, 630, 635-6, 653-4, 659, 661, 667, 670, 680, 685, 688, 693-4, 698-700, 702-3, 705, 708, 729, 733, 740, casualties, 742n. 21st, 516. 24th, 8, 369, 514, 555, 755; allotted to 9 Div, 7, 9, formation and training, 10-11; at Tobruk, 32, 43, 101, 112-13, 119, 126, 132, 138-9, 141, 144, 160-1, 170, 190, 193, 201, 252, 270, 279-80, 297, 301, 313, 316, 327, 333, 370; relieved, 375, casualties, 401n; in Syria, 516-17, 521, 525, 532-3; moves to Egypt, 540, 545-6; at Alamein, 551-2, 553-4, 556, 564, 571-2, 574, 578-9, 585-6, 589, 592-3, 598, 603, 610, 627, 635, 637, 654, 658n, 659, 662, 666, 671-2, 675, 688, 699, 708-9, 720, 723, 727-8, 733-4, 736, 739, casualties, 742n. 25th, 6-7, 8n, 9, 516. 26th, 12n, 514, 555; allotted to 9 Div, 9-10; formation and training, 10-11; in Cyrenaica, 32, 41, 43, 57, 59, 62, 64, 79, 95-6, 101, 112, 119, 121-2; at Tobruk, 126, 137, 160-1, 189-91, 193-5, 200, 202, 206, 241, 252, 270, 279-80, 298, 301, 333, 336, 386, 392, 397, relieved, 396; casualties, 401n; in Syria, 516-17, 521-2, 526, 531-3; moves to Egypt. 540-1, 545-6; at Alamein, 555, 558, 563, 565, 569, 574, 578, 580, 603, 606, 649, 653-4, 659-61, 669, 674-5, 679, 687-8, 692, 699-700, 702, 705, 708-9, 711, 719, 723, 739, casualties, 742n.
  Battalions: LOB component at El Alamein, 555; restoration of MMG platoons to, 622. 2/1st, 756. 2/2nd, 160. 2/5th, 15, 755-6. 2/7th, 15-16, 756. 2/9th, 8n, 516; at Tobruk, 217, 230, 233-4, 235-7, 241, 246, 248-52, 266-7, 271, 280, 303, 327, 339, 467, relief of, 335, casualties, 401n. 2/10th, 8n, 516; at Tobruk, 190, 215, 217-18, 221, 227-33, 236, 241, 245-6, 248-52, 258, 261, 263, 266, 280, 327, 333, 405, casualties, 401n. 2/11th, 756. 2/12th, 8n, 516; at Tobruk, 170, 230-2, 235, 241, 247-8, 250, 252-3, 257, 266, 280, 298, 302, 327, 405-6, casualties, 401n. 2/13th, 515, 516, 519n, 747, 755; in Cyrenaica, 12, 14, 16, 32, 41, 79-80, 85, 88, 90, 92, 95-6, 100-1, 123; at Er Regima, 43, 60, 62, 67-8, 70-2, 73-6, 78; at Tobruk, 127-8, 132-4, 150, 164, 181, 205, 207, 241-2, 249, 266-7, 270-3, 288-9, 290, 292n, 338-9, 341, 386, 392, 397, 399, 404, 417-24, 434, 514, casualties, 401n; in Crusader, 435-6, 438, 451, 463-4, 466, 469-72, 475-81, 483, 487, 492-7, 502-3, 508-10; leaves Tobruk, 511; in Syria, 521, 525; at Alamein, 555, 579, 587, 616-20, 626, 630, 635-6, 654, 659-60, 669-71, 679-81, 683, 685-6, 691-3, 696, 698-9, 700-1, 703-5, 714n, 739, casualties, 742n; as POW, 755. 2/14th, 521. 2/15th, 369, 755; in Cyrenaica, 12, 15, 27, 41, 64, 68, 72, 79, 88, 92-3, 95-6, 101; at Tobruk, 149, 154-5, 191n, 203, 216, 238, 249, 267-8, 270-1, 273, 280, 288-92, 314, 340, 391, 397, 399, 401, 406, 418, 420, 422, casualties, 401n; in Syria, 516, 521, 541; at Alamein, 616-20, 635, 667-8, 699, 701, 703-5, 709, 711, 717, 719-20, 722, 724, 727-8, 733, 735-6, 739-40; in Bulimba operation, 630-4, 687; casualties at Alamein, 742n. 2/17th, 421; in Cyrenaica, 12, 15-16, 29, 41, 64, 67-8, 78-9, 91, 95-6, 101, 121; at Tobruk, 127, 133-4, 137, 139-41, 164, 174, 178, 203, 246, 270n, 271, 273, 286n, 288, 290, 293n, 317n, 338, 340, 385-94, 467; in Easter Battle, 145, 147-51, 153-4; relief of, 397; casualties in Tobruk, 401n; in Syria, 515-16, 519n, 520, 529; at Alamein, 616, 619-20, 626, 635, 659, 663-4, 667-8, 671, 680-1, 683, 685-6, 688, 690-1, 697, 699-700, 704-5, 727, 736, casualties, 742n. 2/23rd, 755, 759; in Cyrenaica, 32, 41, 79; at Tobruk, 29n, 32, 112, 126, 165, 170, 174, 176-8, 182-4, 189, 192, 194-5, 197, 202, 205-7, 213, 217-18, 221, 224, 237-8, 241, 252-3, 257-65, 268, 287n,

AUSTRALIAN ARMY—continued
  303, 315, 319, 330-1, 334, 392, 409, relief of, 396, casualties, 401n; in Syria, 522; at Alamein, 563, 659, 687, 699, 702-3, 705, 708; at Tel el Eisa, 563-5, 570-1, 574, 580-4, 585; casualties at Alamein, 742n. 2/24th, in Cyrenaica, 32, 41-2, 57, 67, 69, 78-80, 85, 91, 95-6, 101, 126, 128, 163-5, 170, 189-90, 191-6, 199-200, 202-10, 212-16, 220-1, 223-4, 227, 238, 245-6, 249, 251-2, 301-4, 327, 333-4, 384, 392, 396, 401, 408-9, losses in evacuation from, 398, casualties, 401n; in Syria, 522, 532, at Tel el Eisa, 558, 560-1, 563-4, 565-6, 569, 580-1, 583, 585; at Alamein, 667-8, 669, 687-8, 690-1, 693, 697, 699-703, 708-12, 715-17, 719-20, 723-4, casualties, 742n; as POW, 755, 759. 2/25th, 8n, 9, 190. 2/28th, 8n, 596; at Tobruk, 112-13, 127-9, 132, 163, 238-9, 298, 313-16, 318, 320-1; 323-7, 369-70, 372-3, 403, 407, casualties, 401n; in Syria, 521, 533; at Alamein, 551-2, 555, 636-7, 672, 723-8, 734-5, 739-40; at Ruin Ridge, 575-6, 579-80, 586-96, 599, 755; casualties at Alamein, 728, 742n. 2/31st, 8n. 2/32nd, 8n; at Tobruk, 190, 237, 302, 314-17, 320, 322, 324-7, 370, 372, 404, 408, casualties, 401n; in Syria, 522, 552; at Alamein, 553, 555, 635, 636-7, 708-11, 716-17, 719-20, 722, 724-5, 728, 734, 736, 740, at Ruin Ridge, 572-5, 576n, 585-6, 588; casualties at Alamein, 742n. 2/33rd, 8n, 755n. 2/43rd, 8n; at Tobruk, 112, 127-8, 132, 140, 147, 164, 170, 201, 238-9, 314-19, 324-5, 369-70, 375, 386, 391, 396, 404, 407-8, 514n, casualties, 401n; in Syria, 521; at Alamein, 552-3, 556, 572-4, 576n, 579, 585-6, 589, 591-4, 617-18, 620-1, 627, 636, 671-2, 723-8, 734-6, 739-40, casualties, 742n. 2/48th, in Cyrenaica, 32, 43, 57, 64, 79, 88-9, 93-4, 96, 100-1, 121; at Tobruk, 122, 127, 129, 141, 145, 162-5, 167-9, 171, 174-6, 178, 188-90, 199-200, 202, 204, 211, 214-15, 217-20, 221, 224-7, 236, 238, 241, 279, 293n, 297-8, 301, 304, 313-14, 316, 319, 321, 327, 333, 384, 397, 402, 404, casualties, 401n; in Syria, 522; in defence of Alexandria, 546; at Tel el Eisa, 558-63, 566, 569, 576, 579-80, 582-5; at Alamein, 661n, 668-70, 678-9, 685, 687-90, 693, 696, 699-700, 703, 708-17, 719-24, casualties, 742n.
  —MACHINE GUN BATTALION: 2/2nd, 8n, 572; at Mersa Matruh, 356; at Tel el Eisa, 562-3, 565, 571; in Ruin Ridge operations, 572-3, 585-6; at Alamein, 659, 727
  —PIONEER BATTALIONS: 2/1st, 514; in Cyrenaica, 16, 79, 98, 119, 167, 178, 211, 216, 228-9, 236, 241, 270-1, 297-8, 303, 330-4, 375, 386, 402-3, casualties, 401n. 2/2nd, 755n. 2/3rd, 375; at Alamein, 555, 605-6, 620, 636, 652, 661, 669, 708-10, 717-24, 728, casualties, 742n.
  —CANTEEN SERVICES, 821
  —ENTERTAINMENT UNIT, 530
  —GENERAL BASE DEPOT, 559
  —MEDICAL UNITS, 748. 2/1 Fd Amb, 808n; 2/3 Fd Amb, 8n; 2/5 Fd Amb, 113-14; 2/8 Fd Amb, 8n, 755-6, 761; 2/11 Fd Amb, 8n, 396, 710. 2/4 Fd Hyg Sec, 8n. 2/4 AGH, 64; 2/5 AGH, 755, 789; 2/6 AGH, 748, 751
  —NURSING SERVICE, 753n
  —PROVOST; 9 Div Pro Coy, 91, 525
  —RECEPTION GROUP UK, 807, 820-1
  —ROYAL MILITARY COLLEGE, DUNTROON, 160
  —SERVICE CORPS, 111-12, 170, 193, 201, 238-9, 300, 332, 409, 536, 755
  —SIGNALS: 9 Div Sigs, 28-9, 246
AUSTRALIAN COMFORTS FUND, 287, 316, 514, 532, 753
AUSTRALIAN GOVERNMENT, 18, 256, 296, 343, 399, 424, 552n, 602; and dispatch of 18 Bde to Tobruk, 114; relief of 9 Div at Tobruk, 305-6, 310-11, 334, 344, 347-8, 350-2, 378-81, 383, 400; formation of Anzac Corps, 307; policy that AIF units should serve with own formations, 308; agrees to dispatch of two divisions from Middle East to Far East, 516; seeks return of forces to Australia, 527-9, 537-9, 600-1, 695, 746, 749-50; nominates General MacArthur as Supreme Commander in SWPA, 538; presses claims of Morshead for appointment to higher command, 613-14; and defence of Australia, 694; protests about treatment of Australian prisoners in Germany, 793, 795-6
  —ADVISORY WAR COUNCIL, 540, 601, 695
  —CHIEFS OF STAFF, 538, 694
  —INFORMATION DEPARTMENT, 530

836 INDEX

AUSTRALIAN GOVERNMENT—continued
—WAR CABINET, 8n, 313, 528, 540, 601; decides to form 9 Div, 6; and relief of 9 Div at Tobruk, 381; return of 9 Div, 694, 696
AUSTRALIAN NAVY, 343, 417, 513
AUSTRIA (Map p. 758), 755n, 767, 774, 777-8, 805, 812, 818
AVERY, Sig J. L., 779
AVON, Lord; see EDEN, Rt Hon Sir Anthony
AYOUN, EL (Sketch p. 522), 522
AZAZ (Sketch p. 520), 519-20
AZGE (Sketch p. 522), 522
AZ ZIB (Sketch p. 517), 823

BAB EL HAOUA (Sketch, p. 520), 521
BAB EL QATTARA, see QATTARA, BAB EL
BADSULZA (Sketch p. 809), 793
BAGHDAD, 244, 520-1
BAHSAS (Sketch p. 825), 828-9
BAILEY, WO2 L. K., 690
BAILLIEU, Maj E., 303, 581
BAILLIEU'S BLUFF (Map p. 668; Sketch p. 580), 578, 616
BAKEWELL, Capt L. N., 620-1
BALBO, Marshal, 22
BALFE, Lt-Col J. W., 133-4, 139, 141, 146-7, 149-51, 153-4, 709-11; commands 2/32 Bn, 635
BALLERSTEDT, Major, 267-8
BAMBLING, Cpl R. H., 631
BAMFORD, Pte G. H., 755n
BAMGARTEN, Maj A. E., 27, 127
Bantria, British ship, 415
BARACCA (Sketch p. 83), 41, 57, 64, 78-9
BARBARA CREEK (Sketch p. 825), 827
BARCE (Map p. 13; Sketch p. 83), 9, 14, 16, 30-1, 32n, 33, 35, 40-2, 44-5, 47, 53, 57, 63-4, 67-8, 72, 75-9, 82, 85, 88, 93
BARCELONA, 801, 805
BARDIA (Map p. 13; Sketch p. 442), 24, 112, 137-8, 172, 179, 188, 243, 245, 254, 256, 283, 299, 417, 427-8, 450, 453, 457, 464, 491-3, 497-9, 500n, 501, 505, 507, 511, 534, 655; Germans occupy, 141, 143; bombarded by RN, 164, 398
"BARDIA BILL", 299, 337, 508
BARDIA ROAD, 132, 135-6, 138-40, 144, 151, 191, 214, 217, 237-8, 269-70, 279, 301, 330, 369, 374, 385, 387, 409, 422, 431, 463-4, 467-8, 472, 504, 507
BARE KNOLL (Sketch p. 320), 320, 322
Barham, British battleship, 431
BARHAM, Brig Rev R. J., 64, 82, 91
BARLOW, Brig J. M., 77, 102-4, 108, 176, 401
BARLOW, Capt L., 98-9, 104, 119
BARNES, Lt-Col E., 407
BARNES, Lt G., 672, 713n
BARNETT, Corelli, 432n, 578n, 579n, 600n
BARREL HILL (Map p. 668; Sketches pp. 712, 725), 708, 711, 717-20, 722-8, 734-5, 739; see also POINT 11
BARREL TRACK (Sketch p. 543), 542, 721
BARRETT, Lt F. A., 778-9
BARRETT, Capt R. J., 701
BARROWCLOUGH, Maj-Gen H. E., 483-4, 487-9; commands 6 NZ Bde, 461
BARTON, Lt-Col C. N., 96
BASH OUTPOST (Sketches pp. 302, 371), 369, 408
BASTICO, General Ettore, 329, 433, 497, 505, 511-12
BASTIN, Lt-Col H. E., 561
BATTEN, Maj R. L., 95
BATTLEAXE, 243n, 286, 293, 295-6, 301, 327, 329, 346, 355, 357, 414, 422, 429, 435, 437, 457, 479; planning of, 275-9; operations, 280-5; lessons from, 354
BATTY, Sgt L. W. C., 175-6
BATY, Pte E. L., 804-5
BAXTER, Capt R. R., 795n
BAYERLEIN, Lt-Gen Fritz, 432n, 627
BAYLIS, Maj C. F. W., 821n
BAYONETS, used at Tobruk, 73-4, 106n, 148-9, 153, 156, 163, 175, 177, 220, 232-3, 271, 406, 440, at Ed Duda, 462, 477-8, at El Alamein, 550, 560, 582, 591, 620, 631, 670, 689, 714-15, 734
BEAMES, Maj W. B., 232-3
BEAN, Dr C. E. W., estimate of General Morshead, 11
BECH MEZZINE (Sketch p. 522), 531
BEDA FOMM (Map p. 13; Sketch p. 16), 14-16, 30, 39, 48, 55
BEDA LITTORIA, 419

BEDRIYE (Sketch p. 520), 521
BEER, Lt H. R., 301, 327, 402-3
BEHREND, Lieutenant, 85, 122
BEIRUT (Sketch p. 517), 530-2
BEIRUT-TRIPOLI RAILWAY, 529, 751, 823-9
BEIT ED DINE (Sketch p. 517), 532
BEIT GHANEIN BARRACKS, 522
BELGASSEM, WADI (Map p. 220; Sketch p. 409), 147, 238, 409
BELHAMED (Sketches pp. 449, 456), 446-9, 456, 458n 459-60, 462, 467-9, 472n, 473-5, 481, 483, 485-6 488, 490-4, 498, 502, 506; captured, 461; loss of, 487
BELL, Lt H. E. Y., 561
BELL, Sgt J. W., 570
BENGHAZI (Map p. 13; Sketch p. 83), 3-4, 14-18, 25-6, 28-32, 34-5, 37, 40, 43-7, 51, 55-8, 60, 66, 68-70, 80-1, 112, 129, 169, 190, 243, 343, 425, 511, 533, 599, 623, 641, 662, 665, 747, 756, 760-1, 763-4; defence of, 41-2; evacuation of, 52, 58-9; occupied by enemy, 65, 67
BENINA (Sketch p. 83), 68n, 69-70
BENNETT, Lt A. M., 585
BENNETT, Sgt L., 331
BENSON, Cpl F. A., 139
BENTLEY, Lt A. R., 686
BERESFORD-PEIRSE, Lt-Gen Sir Noel, 185, 241, 244-5, 253, 255-6, 283-4; commands Western Desert Force, 157-8
BERRY, Sgt A., 804-5
BERRY, Sgt G. T., 690
BETTSWORTH, Sergeant, 167
BHARUCHA, P. C., 738n
BIANCA (Map p. 220; Sketches pp. 218, 228), 212, 218, 221-6, 228-9, 231-2, 236-7, 249, 267, 271
BIANCO, Captain, 419
BIBERACH (Map p. 758), 779, 788
BICYCLE, 363, 365
BIDSTRUP, Capt M. L., 232
BIGGS, Cpl J. W., 209
BILSTON, S-Sgt R., 208
BINGHAM, WO2 F. P., 138, 672
BINNS, Lt-Col R. T., 760
BIR BELHAMED (Sketch p. 484), 467, 481, 487, 493-4, 496, 502
BIR BEN GANIA (Sketches pp. 25, 83), 47, 65, 76, 81, 83
BIR BERRANEB (Sketch p. 465), 490, 500-2
BIR BU CREIMISA (Sketches pp. 474, 484), 474, 479, 483, 505
BIRD, Maj A. C. B., 190, 198-200, 203-6, 212, 214-16
BIR DUEDAR, 500
BIR EL AZAZI (Map p. 220; Sketch p. 302), 302, 369, 387-94, 422, 438, 495, 503-4, 508-9
BIR EL CARMUSA (Map p. 220; Sketch p. 405), 391, 404-5, 510
BIR EL CHLETA (Sketch p. 465), 457, 466, 490
BIR EL ELEBA, 512
BIR EL GINN (Map p. 13; Sketch p. 16), 36
BIR EL GUBI (Sketches pp. 443, 454), 436, 442, 444, 446, 453, 462, 479, 500-2, 505-7
BIR EL KHIREIGAT (Sketch p. 361), 360
BIR EL MELEZZ (Sketch p. 83), 53, 76, 78
BIR EL MERDUMA (Map p. 5), 38
BIR EL TOMBIA (Map p. 13; Sketch p. 16), 16, 52
BIR EN NAGHIA, 512
BIR ES SULTAN, 43
BIR GHERSA (Map p. 220; Sketch p. 371), 280, 331, 370
BIR GIBNI (Sketch p. 443), 285, 444, 490
BIR HACHEIM (Sketch p. 83), 534-5
BIRKS, Maj-Gen H. L., 171, 204, 241
BIR SALEM, 474, 483, 506
BIR SCIAFSCIUF (Sketch p. 484), 466, 482
BIR SCIUERAT (Sketch p. 446), 490
BIR SHEFERZEN (Sketch p. 361), 367
BIR SUESI (Map p. 220; Sketch p. 302), 374, 395
BIR SULTAN OMAR, 705
BIR TAIEB EL ESEM (Sketch p. 445), 436
BIR TENGEDER (Sketch p. 25), 25, 47, 83-4, 512
BIR WAIR (Sketch p. 282), 278
BISHOP, Capt K. E., 727
Bismarck, German battleship, 274
BISMARCK, General von, 628
BISMARCK, FORT, 768, 771
BISSAKER, Lt F. S., 671
BIZERTA (Map p. 5), 599, 742
BLACKBURN, Lt-Cdr J. F., 240
BLAMEY, Lady, 527

BLAMEY, Field Marshal Sir Thomas, 14, 18, 26, 44n, 45, 116, 118, 190, 235, 241, 256, 275-6, 315, 317, 349, 360, 400, 466, 525, 551-2, 554, 622n, 694, 745, 749-50; reorganises AIF in ME, 6, 9; on formation and command of 9 Div, 7-8; on employment of 7 Div, 114-15, 124, 515-16; criticises GHQ ME decisions, 136; defence of Tobruk, 138-9, 143, 295-7; command of Western Desert Force, 157; seeks relief of 9 Div at Tobruk, 305, 310-13, 316, 332, 334-5, 343-8, 350-2, 380-2; seeks concentration of Aust forces, 306, 308-9; recommends formation of Australian and Anzac Corps, 307; returns to Australia, 424, 527; critical of Ninth Army defence plans, 519; appointed C-in-C Aust Army and Allied Land Forces SWPA, 538; seeks return of 9 Div to Australia, 538-40; reinforcement of 9 Div, 600-2; presses claims for Morshead for appointment to higher command, 612-15; on British order regarding manacling of prisoners, 794
BLUE LINE (Sketch p. 126), 158, 160, 170, 181, 183, 188-9, 211, 217, 221, 301, 314, 385-6
BOAT TRACK (Sketch p. 657), 649, 673, 681-2
BOB OUTPOST (Sketch p. 302), 331, 369, 407
BODDINGTON, Col N., 93, 99n
BODE, Capt F. L., 406-7, 630-1, 633
BOEKEMAN, Lt R., 734
BOETTCHER, Maj-Gen Karl, 468, 479
BOLDING, Lt G., 795n
BOLOGNA (Map p. 758), 766-7, 771
BOLZANO (Map p. 758), 757
BOMB ALLEY, 28
BOMBS, STICKY, 562
BONDI OUTPOST (Sketch p. 302), 302, 369, 386-9, 391, 394, 407, 504, 509
BOOBY-TRAPS, at Tobruk, 272, 289-90
BOOKER, Pte G. T., 405
BOOMERANG TRACK, 650, 679
BOON, Capt W. J., 778
BOOTH, Cpl F. O., 403, 734-5
BOREHAM, Sgt F. J., 74
BOTTLE TRACK (Sketch p. 657), 649, 673, 682-3
BOUAR (Sketch p. 825), 826
BOWDEN, Lt J. N., 221, 259
BRADY, Sgt H. M., 153
BRAUCHITSCH, Field Marshal Walther von, 19, 21, 37, 328
BREVITY OPERATION, 242-5, 253-6, 274
BREWER, Capt F. N. T., 776
BRIDGES, Sgt E. L. R., 207
BRIEN, Maj L. C., 668
BRIGGS, Lt-Gen Sir Harold, 612
BRIGGS, Maj-Gen R., 655, 732
BRILL, Gnr J. L., 760n, 813n
BRINK, Maj-Gen G. L., 356-7, 433, 437, 446
BRITISH AIR FORCE, 17, 38-9, 50, 60-1, 80-1, 85, 87, 94, 117, 145, 159, 161, 188, 244, 256, 270, 275, 297, 460, 466, 481, 520, 534, 552, 611, 642, 741, 762; strength, in Cyrenaica, 33, at Alamein, 639; at Tobruk, 129, 141, 152-4, 188, 338, 344-6, 350, 367-9, 377-9, 382, 413; in Battleaxe, 281; in Crusader, 345-6; attacks Tiberio, 416-17; and proposal to send squadrons to Turkey, 519; in Battle of Alam el Halfa, 635; in Supercharge, 730
—DESERT AIR FORCE, 611, 626-7; organisation of, 640; at Alamein, 679, 728, 736-7, 744
—GROUPS, No. 211, 640; No. 212, 640
—WINGS: No. 204 Fighter, 184-5, 317; No. 232, 640; No. 285, 640
—SQUADRONS: No. 6, 27, 140, 241; No. 73, 33, 97, 140, 181; No. 274, 181
BRITISH ARMY, 4, 11, 53, 113, 118, 203, 274, 311, 523, 525, 533, 725, 761, 763-4, 765n, 793-4; in Cyrenaica, 19, 26, 109-11; relations with Dominion troops, 121, 141, 353; appointment of Dominion generals to higher command, 157-8, 614; strength of forces in Tobruk, 159; in Crusader, 424-5, 429
—BRITISH EXPEDITIONARY FORCE, 9, 286, 410
—COMMANDS: British Troops, Egypt, 9, 142-3, 544. Cyrenaica, 8, 14, 17, 32, 53-4, 56-7, 60-4, 67-8, 80, 82, 86-7, 88-90, 93-4, 96, 102, 120, 158; takes over from I Aust Corps, 9; defence plans, 26-7, 29-30, 42, 46-7, 58-9, 117-119; discipline of Australian troops, 44; O'Connor appointed to command, 58; orders withdrawal from Mechili, 103; Lavarack appointed to command, 109; merged into Western Desert Force, 129, 142-3, 156-7. South-Eastern, 608. Southern, 286, 608

BRITISH ARMY—continued
—ARMIES: Eighth, 378, 417, 432, 547, 601, 604-5, 611, 616, 622, 644-5, 753; HQ formed from Western Army HQ, 425; in Crusader, 433-7, 440, 442, 444, 447-8, 452, 454-5, 457, 464-5, 472-3, 483, 485, 488, 491, 495, 498-9, 501; in Cyrenaica, 532-3, 534-6; strength and dispositions, 515, 542-3, 639, 655; at Alamein. 548-51, 554, 558-9, 564, 569, 577-8, 580, 588, 590, 597, 641, 643; state of, 596-8, 608, 647; tactics and training, 598-9, 621, 656; ambivalent planning of, 603; Churchill's visit to, 606; Montgomery takes command, 608, his influence on, 609, 614, 663, 744; German estimate of, 623; losses in Battle of Alam el Halfa, 630; adopts common vocabulary for British and US forces, 637-8; reinforcement and equipment of, 639, 647-8; in Battle of El Alamein, 665-6, 669, 675-7, 682-4, 686-7, 692, 697, 717, 719, 728, 731-3, 737-8, 741, 743-4, casualties, 693, 742. Ninth, 514-17, 524, 525n, 531-2, 541; plans defence of Suez Canal, 519. Twenty-First, 614n
—CORPS: IV, 286. V, 286. X, 515, 536-7, 657; at Alamein, 544, 548, 551, 612; in Battle of El Alamein, 648-50, 658, 673, 675; composition, 655; role in B. of El Alamein, 643, 645, 656-7, 700, 729; tank strength compared with Axis strength, 685. XIII, 608; formation of, 425; in Crusader, 426, 429-30, 447, 449, 450, 457, 459, 464, 467-8, 482, 484-5, 493, 495, 504, 512; in Cyrenaica, 536-7; at Alamein, 543, 548-51, 553, 557, 566-8, 576-80, 603, 609, 626, 629; Horrocks appointed to command, 612-13; in Battle of El Alamein, 674-5, 678, 684, 686, 694, 717, 729; arty support in, 666n, role in, 643, 645, 656, 658, 699, composition, 655. XXX, 579, 588, 616, 747, 753; formation, 425; in Crusader, 426, 428-9, 430, 434, 436-7, 441-2, 446, 452, 454, 457, 464, 468, 473, 478, 485, 491-2, 495, 503-4, 506-7, 509, 512; at Alamein, 536, 547-50, 552-5, 562, 564, 566-7, 576, 578, 589, 596, 598, 603, 649; command of, 606, 609, 612-13, 615, 637; role in Battle of El Alamein, 644-6, 650, 656-7, 699-700, 729; in B. of El Alamein, 658, 667-8, 672-3, 675-8, 683, 686-7, 693, 698, 719; artillery support, 666; ammunition expenditure, 743
—FORCES: Delta Force, 544-5. Western Desert Force, 9, 184, 255, 270, 297, 357; reconstituted, 142-3; absorbs Cyrenaica Command, 156-7; in Battleaxe, 275, 286; in Summer Night's Dream operation, 361, 364; goes out of existence, 425
—DIVISIONS, ARMOURED, planned employment in Crusader, 427-8. 1st, 426, 533-4, 536; at Alamein, 542-3, 548-50, 553, 567, 646, 655, 664; in Miteiriya Ridge attack, 589, 595, 598; tank strength, 577, 684, 730; in B. of El Alamein, 673, 678-9, 681, 686-7, 691-2, 694, 697-8, 707, 729, 731-3, 738. 2nd, 3; strength and condition, 4, 19, 99; in Cyrenaica, 14, 30-1, 34-5, 40, 43, 45, 48, 168; in withdrawal, 52, 55-6, 58-63, 66-7, 76, 78, 80, 84-7, 89, 94-5, 100, 103-4, 113; at Tobruk, 119-20, 159. 7th, 3, 442, 535, 536, 730; role in defence of Tobruk, 118; in Battleaxe, 256, 277-8, 281-4; on Egyptian frontier, 358, 360, 365; in Crusader, 426, 429, 430, 441, 450, 452-3, 455, 466, 468, 473, 479-80, 482, 485, 495, 500, 511-12; at Alamein, 542-3, 576, 597, 625-7; in B. of El Alamein, 643, 655, 658, 664, 675, 678, 684, 732, 737-8, 740; tank strength, 684, 730. 8th, 639, 649, 655. 10th, at Alamein, 625, 628; in B. of El Alamein, 664, 673, 677-8, 681-2, 685, 694, 698, 738; tank strength, 684. 15th, 678.
—DIVISIONS, INFANTRY: 1st, 607-8. 6th, 3, 65, 115, 121, 142; proposed as relief for 9 Div in Tobruk, 313, 334, 344, 350; arrives Tobruk, 378. 44th, at Alamein, 611, 625, 627, 639; in B. of El Alamein, 655, 658, 664, 674, 678. 50th, 312, 536-7, 555, 589, 612n; at Alamein, 542-3, 548, 553; in B. of El Alamein, 655, 658, 664, 707, 732. 51st, 791; at Alamein, 611, 639, 654-5; relations with Australians, 636-7, 747; in B. of El Alamein, 645, 656-7, 658n, 664, 672-5, 678-9, 680n, 681, 683-4, 692-4, 697-8, 707, 729, 732, 738, 740. 70th, in Crusader, 437, 440, 446, 458, 462n, 470, 485, 493, 495, 503, 504n, 507-8, 510-11; earmarked for India-Burma theatre, 528. 11th and 12th African, 3
—BRIGADES, ARMOURED: 2nd, 608; at Alamein, 567-8, 578; at Ruin Ridge, 589, 592-5; in B. of El Alamein, 657, 673n, 681, 684, 692n, 707, 729,

BRITISH ARMY—*continued*
731-2, 741; 3rd, in Cyrenaica, 15-16, 26, 34-5, 48, 51, 54-5, 58-9, 61, 63, 67, 76, 78, 80, 82, 86-7, 89-90, 94, 98-9, 103, 118; in Tobruk, 119-20, 137, 202, 246, 292, 376; in Battleaxe, 279-80, in Battleaxe, 278, 283-4; in Crusader, 429-30, 436, 440, 443-5, 447-9, 466, 489-91, 499-502, 506-7, 512; defeat of, 535; at Alamein, 550. **4th Light**, at Alamein, 589, 625; in Battle of, 645, 647, 730, 738. **4th/22nd**, 482. 7th, 366; in Battleaxe, 283-4; in Crusader, 436, 440, 443-4, 446-50. **8th**, at Alamein, 625-7; in Battle of, 673, 677, 679, 681-4, 687, 707, 729, 733, 738, 741. **9th**, in B. of El Alamein, 657, 673, 678-80, 682, 684-5, 687, 707, 729, 731-2; tank states, 684, 730. **22nd**, in Crusader, 429, 436, 440, 442, 444, 447-50, 462, 466; at Alamein, 551, 567, 625-6, 684, 741. **23rd**, 660n; arrives ME, 577; at Alamein, 578, 626, 628; in B. of El Alamein, 645, 650, 655, 657, 698, 702-3, 738; tank states, 684, 730. **24th**, in B. of El Alamein, 683-4, 686. **2nd Armd Div Sup Gp**, in Cyrenaica, 9, 15, 31-2, 46, 48-52, 54-5, 58, 60-3, 67, 78, 80, 86-7, 90, 95, 97; in Tobruk, 101, 119-20. **7th Armd Div Sup Gp**, 9, 42, 63, 79, 447-8, 466, 512; in defence of Tobruk, 118, 120, 125, 128-9; on Egyptian frontier, 132, 136, 142, 144, 171, 187, 358, 360; in Brevity operation, 245, 254; in Battleaxe, 278, 283-4; in Crusader, 440, 444, 446, 449-50, 492, 499, 507. **1st Army Tank**, 496, 588; in Crusader, 426, 430, 455, 464; at Alamein, 542, 566, 577-8, 593, 650; Australians praise, 599. **32nd Army Tank**, at Tobruk, 376, 391, 397; in Crusader, 441, 450, 457, 464, 470, 486, 496, 502, 509, 512; at Alamein, 542
—BRIGADES, INFANTRY: **14th Inf**, relieves 20 Brigade at Tobruk, 397; in Crusader, 496, 503. **16th Inf**, 141; at Tobruk, 375, 378, 385-6, 395, 397; in Crusader, 469, 496, 503, 508. **22nd Guards**, 116, 121, 533: on Egyptian frontier, 135-6, 141, 172, 179, 358, 364; in Brevity, 254-5; in Battleaxe, 281; in Crusader, 426, 430, 453, 492, 506. **23rd Inf**, at Tobruk, 397; in Crusader, 438, 496, 504, 509. **32nd Inf**, 508. **69th Inf**, in Ruin Ridge attack, 589, 592-5. **132nd Inf**, at Alamein, 625, 629. **133rd Inf**, at Alamein, 678, 697, 732. **150th Inf**, 546. **151st Inf**, at Alamein, 707, 729-30, 732, 740. **152nd Inf**, at Alamein, 699, 707, 729-30. **153rd Inf**, 732. **2nd Motor**, 657. **7th Motor**, at Alamein, 625, 693, 696, 707, 729, 732-3
—REGIMENTS, ARMOURED: **3 Hussars**, 15, 32-3, 48, 52, 54-6, 61-2, 76, 90, 98; at Tobruk, 120, 132n, 170-1, 211, 280, 334-5; at Alamein, 731. **5 Hussars**, at Tobruk, 170. **7 Hussars**, 121, 134. **8 Hussars**, 816; in Crusader, 443, 449, 487. **11 Hussars**, 59, 79, 100n, 108, 113, 119, 132; on Egyptian frontier, 142, 144, 179; in Crusader, 507. **1 King's Dragoon Guards**, 15; on Cyrenaican frontier, 17, 20, 27-8, 33, 35-6, 38-9, 47-9; in Cyrenaican withdrawal, 50, 52, 54, 56, 60-3, 66, 80, 82, 85, 90, 95, 97-8, 121; in Tobruk, 119-20, 125, 127, 137, 271, 334-5, 402; in Battleaxe, 280; in Crusader, 440, 443, 462n, 466, 500, 507. **The Queen's Bays**, at Alamein, 673, 683-4. **The Royal Dragoons**, at Alamein, 731, 733, 738. **1 RTR**, 79, 113; in Tobruk, 119-20, 129, 133-4, 151-2, 168, 171, 211-12, 214, 331; in Battleaxe, 280; in Crusader, 460, 469. **2 RTR**, 254. **3 RTR**, in Crusader, 443-4; at Alamein, 681. **4 RTR**, at Tobruk, 122, 170, 376, 392-4; in Brevity, 254, 256n; on Egyptian frontier, 274-5; in Battleaxe, 281; in Crusader, 439-40, 459-60, 467, 469-70, 474, 476, 492, 502. **5 RTR**, in Cyrenaica, 15, 32, 47-9, 52, 54-6, 58, 60-2, 76, 86, 87n, 89n, 90, 95, 96n, 99; in Tobruk, 120, 137; in Crusader, 443-4, 487. **6 RTR**, in Cyrenaica, 15, 33, 48, 52, 54-5, 58-62, 67, 76, 86, 90-1, 99n, 100; in Tobruk, 137; in Crusader, 446; at Alamein, 563. **7 RTR**, in Tobruk, 167, 170-1, 174-5, 211, 214-16, 394; in Battleaxe, 280-1, 283; in Crusader, 438, 440, 458-9, 469. **8 RTR**, in Crusader, 455, 457, 468, 488, 490; at Tel el Eisa, 570; in B. of El Alamein, 730. **40 RTR**, in Bulimba operation, 630, 632-3; in B. of El Alamein, 658-60, 670, 680-1, 703, 708, 721-2, 736. **42 RTR**, 457. **44 RTR**, in Crusader, 457, 461, 462n, 463, 468, 476, 488, 490; at Tel el Eisa, 557, 563, 569-70; in Ruin Ridge attack, 572-3. **46 RTR**, in B. of El Alamein, 699, 702-3. **50 RTR**, in Ruin Ridge attack, 578-9, 586-9, 593-4, 596; placed under command 9 Div, 603; in B. of El Alamein, 730, 732. **Royal Wiltshire**

BRITISH ARMY—*continued*
Yeo, 731. **Staffordshire Yeo**, 682-3. **Warwickshire Yeo**, 731
—REGIMENTS, ARTILLERY, part played in defence of Tobruk, 400; strength in Crusader, 429. **4 AA Bde**, at Tobruk, 397, 409-10. **14 Lt AA Regt**, 113, 273n, 37 Lt AA Regt, 36. **40 Lt AA Bty**, 411. **102 Anti-Tk Regt**, 366. **149 Anti-Tk Regt**, 375. **1 Fd Regt**, 368. **8 Fd Regt**, 134, 187, 357. **25 Fd Regt**, 357. **31 Fd Regt**, 499. **51 Fd Regt**, in Cyrenaica, 15, 31-2, 41, 78-9, 95, 101, 109; at Er Regima, 69-71, 74, 76; in Tobruk, 119, 122, 127, 161-2, 165, 168-9, 175, 199-200, 202-5, 207-8, 210, 213-14, 229, 250, 252, 261, 265, 267, 294, 320, 334, 340. **107 Fd Regt**, 388. **149 Fd Regt**, 375. **7 Medium Regt**, in Crusader, 429; at Tel el Eisa, 558, 563; in Bulimba, 630; in B. of El Alamein, 658, 678. **64 Medium Regt**, 658. **1 RHA**, in Cyrenaica, 15, 31, 38, 48, 52, 55, 60-1, 62n, 67, 75n, 78, 87, 95, 97, 109, 119, 122; in Tobruk, 126, 128, 132-3, 140-1, 146, 149-53, 156, 161, 178, 181, 191, 207-8, 210-12, 214, 229-31, 239, 246-7, 249, 273n, 279, 294-5, 298, 320, 337, 339, 392, 405, 422, 434; in Crusader, 439-40, 450, 460, 467, 469-70, 474-6, 480-2, 486-7, 492, 496, 512; evacuates Tobruk, 513; at Alamein, 664. **3 RHA**, 98; in Cyrenaica, 15, 17, 49-50, 67, 84, 100-1, 113; at Mechili, 77, 80, 102-3, 107; in Tobruk, 119-20, 132, 139, 151, 153, 167, 174-5, 201n, 208-9, 230, 375; at Alamein, 554. **4 RHA**, 113; in Tobruk, 119, 128. **104 RHA**, in Cyrenaica, 15, 31-2, 48-50, 56, 67, 79, 97, 101; at Mechili, 84, 102-3; in Tobruk, 119, 120n, 132, 151n, 161, 201, 229, 303, 330-1, 368-9, 374, 385, 388; in Crusader, 436, 440, 480n, 482, 496, 504; at Alamein, 664. **107 RHA**, 79, 113; in Tobruk, 119, 122, 126, 128, 146, 149, 151n, 161, 208, 210, 212, 214, 298, 300, 316, 320, 388, 392; in Crusader, 482. **289 Bty**, at Alamein, 717, 721-2, 724, 726. **66 Mortar Coy**, 658
—ENGINEERS, in Cyrenaica, 42; in Tobruk, 300. **42 Fd Coy**, 520, 295. **Fd Coy**, 59, 93, 669. **552 Fd Coy**, 93
—INFANTRY: **7/A & SH**, 738. **1/Bedfs & Herts**, in Tobruk, 396-7; in Crusader, 440, 481, 493-4. **2/Black Watch**, in Tobruk, 378, 397; in Crusader, 438-41, 447. **7/Black Watch**, at Alamein, 636, 681. **2/Border Regt**, 396-7. **4/Border**, in Crusader, 495-7, 502-3, 505, 509. **1/Buffs**, 512. **1/Camerons**, 281, 500, 700. **Coldstream Guards**, 544; **2/Coldstream**, 187; **3/Coldstream**, 134, 142, 144, 171-2, 186, 274-5, 366, **1/Durham L.I.**, 135-7, 142, 144, 171, 186-7, 254; in Tobruk, 378, 396, 418, 422; in Crusader, 495-7, 503-4, 509. **6/Durham L.I.**, 592. **E. York R.**, 592. **Essex R.**, in Crusader, 462n, 467. **1/Essex**, in Tobruk, 397, 421; in Crusader, 457, 460, 469, 474-5, 477, 480-1, 492, 496, 502. **2/Essex**, 396. **1/Gordons**, at Alamein, 670, 680-1. **5/Gordons**, at Alamein, 670, 738. **1/King's Own Y.L.I.**, 499. **2/King's Own** 386, 395, 438-9. **1/KRRC**, in Cyrenaica, 63-4, 79, 82, 87-8, 93-5, 97-9, 101, 120; on Egyptian frontier, 135, 142; in Crusader, 446. **2/Leicester**, at Tobruk, 386-7; in Crusader, 459, 510. **2/Queens**, at Tobruk, 386-91, 395, 422; in Crusader, 438, 440, 464, 467, 469, 509. **2/Rifle Bde**, 254, 284, 446, 697. **7/Rifle Bde**, 680-1. **1/RNF**, in Cyrenaica, 15, 43, 47, 51n, 59, 64, 88, 95-6, 101, 119, 121; at Er Regima, 69, 75; at Tobruk, 187, 212, 228-9, 231, 257, 320, 397, 405; at Alamein, 546. **Scots Guards**, 554. **2/Scots Guards**, 186-7, 254, 283, 362-5. **2/Seaforth Highlanders**, 732. **1/Sherwood Foresters**, 626. **Sherwood Rangers**, 113, 681-2. **2/Sussex**, 730. **5/Sussex**, 730. **1/Tower Hamlets Rifles**, in Cyrenaica 9, 15, 32, 36, 38, 44, 54, 56, 58, 61, 63, 80, 87, 94, 97-8, 99n, 118; at Marsa Brega, 47-51; on Egyptian frontier, 120, 142. **2/Yorks & Lancs**, at Tobruk, 378, 397, 418; in Crusader, 450, 459.
—ARMY AIR PHOTOGRAPH INTERPRETATION UNIT, 643
—ARMY AIR SUPPORT CONTROL, 555
—ARMY ORDNANCE CORPS, 29
—MIDDLE EAST OCTU, 522-3, 544
—SECURITY SERVICE, *255 FSS Sec*, 526
—SERVICE CORPS, *14 RASC Coy*, 64
—SPECIAL SERVICE BRIGADE (COMMANDO), in Battleaxe, 279; at Tobruk, 298, 315-16, 332, raid Twin Pimples, 402
—SURVEY REGIMENTS, *4 Durham*, 295

BRITISH BROADCASTING CORPORATION, 100n, 111, 286, 445, 766, 801
"BRITISH FREE CORPS", 806
BRITISH GOVERNMENT, 1-2, 6, 109, 256, 286-7, 307, 352, 379n, 399, 510, 518, 544, 600, 614; and relief of 9 Div at Tobruk, 305-6, 310, 345, 347, 378-9, 381, 383, 400; proposes dispatch of two Aust divisions from ME to Far East, 516; relations with Egyptian Government, 523-4; and Australian Government's request for return of forces, 527, 539; future employment of 9 Aust Div, 537-8, 748-9; reinforces ME, 639; and prisoners of war, 770-3, 801
—CHIEFS OF STAFF, 17, 31, 57, 116, 124, 173, 180, 243-4, 275, 286, 295, 309, 341, 352, 399, 527, 534, 601, 605, 706; supply of Tobruk, 297; concentration of AIF in ME, 311; and Auchinleck, 312, 534; relief of 9 Aust Div, 345, 351, 378; proposed employment of Australian forces in Burma, 528; recall of 9 Aust Div, 600, 695
—DEFENCE COMMITTEE, 244, 352, 534
—DOMINIONS OFFICE, 307
—WAR CABINET, 3-4, 162, 345, 352, 528, 534, 604, 606
—WAR OFFICE, 157, 342, 532, 766-7, 771, 794, 820, 829
BRITISH NAVY, 39, 146, 159, 161, 163, 274, 277, 296, 330, 513, 639, 762; at Tobruk, 376-7, 398, 411, 416
—ADMIRALTY, 173
—FLEET AIR ARM, 367, 417
—FLEETS: Eastern Fleet, 754; Mediterranean Fleet, 187
—FLOTILLAS: 10th Destroyer, 414, 417; Western Desert Schooner, 415
—FORCES: Force K, 431-2
—SQUADRONS: 7th Cruiser, 376; Inshore, 161-2, 164, 369, 377, 409, 413-14, 417
BROMLEY, Maj L. F., 294
BROOKE, General, see ALANBROOKE, Field Marshal Viscount
BROOMHEAD, Chaplain Rev E. N., 761n, 763n, 772n
BROUGH, Sgt E. J., 804-5
BROUMANE (Sketch p. 517), 515, 517
BROWN, Lt-Col A., 236, 331; commands 2/1 Pnr Bn, 228
BROWN, Lt C. S., 776
BROWN, Lt D. McD., 273
BROWN, Capt J. F. S., 740
BROWN, AVM Sir Leslie, 33-4, 117
BROWN, Maj W. F., 238, 247
BROWN, WO1 W. R., 784
BROWNE, Maj D. S., 105, 107-8
BROWNING, Maj H. G. M., 103
BROWNLESS, Lt P. P. S., 475n
BROWNRIGG, Lt C., 315
BRUCE, Rt Hon Lord, 695, 749
BRUDENELL-WOODS, Pte B., 804
BRUER, Lt-Col G., 246, 262
BRYANT, Sir Arthur, 605n, 606n, 608n, 615n, 706n
BRYANT, Lt-Col D., 220, 238, 559, 561, 669, 688-90, 714-15
BU AMUD (Map p. 5), 33, 507
BUCKINGHAM, Pte E. L., 565
BUCKLEY, Lt J. A. R., 384
BUCKNELL, Capt E. R., 266-7, 338, 404
BUDDEN, Lt-Col T. R., 49
BUDGE, Maj W. F., 190, 563-4, 566
BU DUEISA, WADI (Sketch p. 402), 420
BULIMBA OPERATION, 626, 630-4, 643, 687
BUNTINE, Lt-Col M. A., 403
BUQ BUQ (Map p. 13; Sketches pp. 135, 361), 12, 142, 179, 187, 244-5, 358, 363-4
BURG EL ARAB, 611
BURGESS, Cpl J. A., 696
BURMA, 381, 528, 608
BURRELL, Maj J. R., 71, 73, 288, 701
BURROWS, Brig F. A., (Plate p. 364) 68-9, 73-5, 82, 90, 100-1, 242, 266-7, 271-3, 288, 291, 338, 386, 418-19, 421, 423, 424n, 434, 464, 469-71, 475-7, 480-1, 483, 492-4, 519n; commands 2/13 Bn, 16; career of, 71-2
BURSTON, Maj-Gen Sir Samuel, 309
BUTCH OUTPOST (Sketches pp. 302, 439), 374, 386, 438-9, 459, 486
BUTLER, L-Bdr B. McD., 265
BUTLER, Lt G. J., 714
BUWEIBAT EL RAML, 576

CAHILL, Maj N. M., 326
CAIRN (Sketches pp. 517, 618), 579, 618, 620
CAIRO (Map p. 13), 7-8, 14, 28, 30, 40, 47, 59, 61, 64-5, 85, 109, 113, 115-17, 129, 164, 244, 275, 295-7, 309, 316, 331-3, 342, 345, 368, 377, 424, 455, 495, 501, 514-15, 517, 523, 527, 540, 542, 544, 547, 550, 557, 562, 597, 603-4, 606, 608, 648, 751, 753; Morshead attends conferences in Sep 1941, 348-9; "Cairo flap", 545; Churchill and Brooke visit Aug 1942, 605; behaviour of Aust leave troops in, 748
CALCATERRA, Colonel, 759-60, 766-7
CAMERON, WO2 F. M., 690-1, 713
CAMERON, Lt-Col R. W., 572, 585
CAMOUFLAGE, at Tobruk, 186
CAMPBELL, Maj-Gen J. C., VC, 129, 135, 142, 144, 447, 507
CAMPBELL, Gnr M. J. A., 106
CAMPBELL, Sgt N. L., 359
CAMPBELL, Maj W. H., 710, 717
CAMPO 5 (Map p. 758), 771
CAMPO 19 (Map p. 758), 766
CAMPO 52 (Map p. 758), 763
CAMPO 57 (Map p. 758), 759-60, 765, 767
CAMPO 59, 761-2
CAMPO 75 (Map p. 758), 764
CAMPO 78 (Map p. 758), 757, 764-5
CAMPO 106 (Map p. 758), 769
CAMPO PRATO, 757
CANTY, Capt L. G., 190, 194, 197-200, 202-8, 210, 213
CAPLE, Lt S. S., 714
CAPUA (Map p. 758), 756
CAPUZZO, FORT (Map p. 13; Sketches pp. 135, 282), 24, 135-7, 144, 179, 186, 188, 245, 254-5, 278, 280-4, 450, 453, 455, 457, 465, 500n, 501; loss of, 144
CAPUZZO, TRIGH (Sketches pp. 443, 454), 132, 135-6, 279, 301, 441, 445-8, 450, 452, 455-6, 461, 464, 466-8, 473, 482-3, 488-9, 498-9, 504
CARLETON, Sgt F. L., 262
CARLEY, Sergeant, 208
CARLTON, Capt W. A., 591
CARMUSET BELUDEAH, 459n
CARO OUTPOST (Sketch p. 302), 303
CARRIER HILL (Sketches pp. 175, 192), 144, 183, 198, 225, 249; raid on, 174-6
CARSON, Lt A. B., 670
CARTER, Maj A. A. C., 727
CARTLEDGE, Maj D. J., 387-8,
CARVOSSO, Pte R. W., 221
CASEY, Lady, 751
CASEY, Rt Hon Lord, 544, 545n, 605-6, 706
CASUALTIES, Australian, at Mechili, 108; at Tobruk, 235, 401n; at Alamein, 601, 693n, 728; British, at Mechili, 108; in Battle of Alam el Halfa, 630; at Alamein, 693, 742. German, at Tobruk, 235; in Battle of Alam el Halfa, 629; at Alamein, 705. Italian, at Tobruk, 235; in Battle of Alam el Halfa, 630; at Alamein, 705. New Zealand, at Alamein, 693n
CATHERALL, Capt J. McP., 207
CAUCASUS, THE, 19, 328, 518, 600, 635
CAVALLERO, General Count Ugo, 328, 512, 557
CAWTHORNE, Lt C. H., 315
CEMETERY HILL (Sketches pp. 16, 31), 39, 48-50
CEYLON, 528, 537-8
Chakdina, British armed merchant cruiser, 513
Chakla, British ship, 190-1
CHAMP, Lt J. W. K., 795n
Chantala, British armed merchant cruiser, 513
CHARLTON, Sgt T., 325
CHARRUBA (Sketch p. 83), 78, 80
CHEETAH OUTPOSTS (Sketch p. 402), 419-20
CHEETHAM, Capt R. T., 136, 187, 284
CHEKKA (Sketch p. 522), 526, 823-4, 828
CHENEY, Pte L., 236
CHERRINGTON-HUNTER, Lt B., 371-2
CHIAVARI (Map p. 758), 763
CHILTON, Lt-Col H. H. M., 68, 272
CHINCHEN, Sqn-Ldr G. T., 771n
CHRISTIE, Capt J. S., 213, 221
CHRISTSEN, WO2 J. W., 229
CHRYSTALL, Maj-Gen J. I., 748
CHURCHILL, Maj R. F. E. S., 279
CHURCHILL, Rt Hon Sir Winston (Plate p. 588) 16, 18, 31n, 40, 100, 109, 125, 242-3, 253, 256, 311, 313, 330n, 342-3, 355, 360, 425, 433, 491, 518, 598, 602, 612, 639n, 640, 695; on withdrawal in Cyrenaica, 57-8, 64-5, 116; message to Wavell on Easter

CHURCHILL—*continued*
Battle, 162; convoy of tanks to be sent to Wavell, 173; message to Morshead, 235; defence of Crete, 243; and Wavell, 244; on future operations in ME, 275; appoints Auchinleck to replace Wavell, 285; on German invasion of Russia, 287; relief of 9 Div at Tobruk, 305-6, 345, 347-9, 351-2, 378, 380-2, 400; return of 9 Div to Australia, 537-9, 600-1, 749-50; and Auchinleck, 312, 341, 534-5; seeks employment of 7 Aust Div in Burma, 528; visits Washington, 603; at Cairo Conference, 604-5; visits 9 Div, 606; reorganisation of ME Command, 606; Alexander to replace Auchinleck, 607-8; on claims of Morshead for higher command, 613; cables Mr Curtin on part played by 9 Div at Alamein, 696; on Montgomery's achievements at Alamein, 706
CLAPHAM, Capt A. D., 203-4, 210
CLARK, L-Cpl H. P., 262-3
CLARKE, Maj K. C., 583-4
CLARKE, Lt-Col T.C.A., 702
CLARKSON, Pte C. W., 769n
CLIFTON, Brig G. H., 577
CLOVERLEAF (Map p. 668; Sketches pp. 618, 739), 620, 666, 708, 739
COBB, Capt W. W., 616-17, 668
COCOA OUTPOSTS (Sketch p. 402), 402, 419-20
COLDITZ (Map p. 758), 795, 816
COLEMAN, Col S. T. G., 332
COLLINS, Maj-Gen R. J., 124n
COLOUR PATCHES, Morshead on origin of T-shaped patch, 750-1
COLVIN, Lt-Col G. E., 419, 480, 493-4, 496, 504, 686, 701, 703, 747; commands 2/13 Bn, 680
COMBE, Capt G. D., 556
COMBE, Maj-Gen J. F. B., 59, 92, 116
CONINGHAM, Air Marshal Sir Arthur, 611, 639
CONNELL, J., 455n, 495n, 500n, 501n, 596n, 598n, 606n
CONNOR, Maj G. B., 755n
CONROY, Lt-Col T. M. (Plate p. 365), 270; commands 2/32 Bn, 314-15
CONVOYS: "Tiger", 173, 180, 256; to Malta, 534
CONWAY, Capt R. A. E., 317, 320-3, 326-7
COOK, Col F. W., 232
COOK, Lt J. T., 593
COOK, Col T. P., 111-13, 121
COOMA OUTPOST (Sketch p. 302), 391, 393-4, 421
COOPER, Lt-Col G. D. T., 249-50, 252
COOPER, Cpl H., 789n
COOPER, Cpl R. C., 616-17
COPE, Maj J. F., 36, 38
COPELAND, Maj G. F., 717, 722, 726-7
COPPOCK, Gnr C. G. A., 106
COPPOCK, Capt H. T., 320-2, 326
CORBETT, Lt-Gen T. W., 547, 606
CORINTH (Map p. 758), 755n, 764, 773-4, 777
CORTIS, Lt J. F., 680-1
COTMAN, WO1 A. A. S., 759
COUSINS, Sgt H. S., 153
COWELL, WO1 C. M., 102
COX, Col J. P., 302, 575, 586-8
CRANBORNE, Rt Hon Viscount, 313, 334, 345
CRAWFORD, Capt A. D., 795n
CRAWFORD, Brig J. W. (Plates pp. 156, 364), 82, 91, 132-3, 141, 147, 149, 153, 288, 340, 385, 387-90, 392-4, 519n; commands 2/17 Bn, 15; career of, 145-6
CREAGH, Maj-Gen Sir Michael, 57, 281, 284
CRELLIN, Col W. W. (Plate p. 365), 238, 240, 314, 317-20; commands 2/43 Bn, 128
CRETE (Maps pp. 5, 13), 31, 37, 39, 188, 256, 277, 287, 306, 310, 348, 382, 385, 414, 617, 639, 755-6, 773-5, 779, 787-8; defence of, 243-4; German invasion of, 274-5
CRIBB, Maj B. G., 670-1
CROKER, Cpl M. O., 248
CROMIE, Capt R. C., 570, 583-4
CRONK, Maj R. G., 371-2
CROUCHER, Dvr C. W., 808n
CRUEWELL, General Ludwig, 449, 464, 466, 472-4, 483, 490, 497-8, 506; commands *Africa Corps*, 443
CRUMMEY, L-Cpl W., 177
CRUSADER OPERATION, 277, 352, 357, 378, 380-1, 383, 417, 423, 432-3, 533, 542, 559, 732; plans for, 279, 345, 347, 349, 364, 425; opens, 382, 435; the Tobruk garrison's sortie, 437-41; Eighth Army operations, 441-510

CUB (Sketch p. 439), 438
CUFF, WADI (Sketch p. 83), 16, 42, 67, 79-80, 85, 94
CULTIVATE OPERATION, 417
CUNNINGHAM, Admiral of the Fleet Viscount, 39, 161, 274-6, 297, 313, 332, 414-15, 417; estimate of Wavell, 57; and relief of 9 Div at Tobruk, 345, 352, 399-400
CUNNINGHAM, General Sir Alan, 347n, 349, 432n, 437, 444, 447-8, 450-4, 744; GOC, East Africa Forces, 39; appointed GOC Eighth Army, 342-3; plans for Crusader operation, 425-9, 433, 437, 442; replaced by General Ritchie, 455
CURREN, Sgt W. B., 556
CURTIN, Rt Hon John, 612, 696; requests relief of 9 Div at Tobruk, 380-1, 400; seeks return of 9 Div to Australia, 528, 537-9, 695, 746, 748-50; agrees to temporary retention of 9 Div in ME, 600-2; presses claims of General Morshead for higher command, 613-15
CYPRUS (Map p. 5), 306, 308, 310, 312, 334, 352, 518n
CYRENAICA (Map p. 13; Sketches pp. 25, 83), 8-10, 12, 16-17, 19, 24, 31, 60, 66, 68, 113-18, 120, 140, 157, 172, 195, 275, 312, 346, 356, 428, 430-1, 452, 455, 502, 518, 534, 623, 755; plans for defence of, 3-4, 6, 26, 29-30, 34-5, 40, 42, 48, 112; strength and disposition of British forces in, 14-15, 27-8; Rommel proposes to re-occupy, 23, 37-8; terrain described, 25-6; shortage of tanks and aircraft in, 32-3; discipline of Australian soldiers in, 44-5; British withdrawal in, 57-60, 85, 87-8, 111; German thrust into, 80-1, 123; British tank losses in, 100; Axis plans for defence of, 511-12
CYRENE (Map p. 5), 91, 94
CZECHOSLOVAKIA (Map p. 758), 801, 804, 810-12, 814
CZECHOSLOVAKIAN BATTALION, 396, 419-20, 495, 546

DABA, EL (Map p. 13; Sketch p. 543), 552, 557-8, 576, 579, 595, 645, 647, 655, 698, 736, 738, 740-1
DAINTREE, Lt-Col C. M., 272, 420, 480, 494, 703
DALBY SQUARE (Sketch p. 371), 408, 474; raid on, 370-1; captured, 450; loss of, 496
DALEY, Sgt D. A., 575
DALY, Lt-Gen T. J., 317-18, 332-3
DAMASCUS (Sketch p. 517), 532, 824
DANIELS, Sgt R. G., 165, 176
DARWIN, 9, 525, 538, 621
DAVIDSON, L-Cpl A. MacK., 288
DAVIDSON, Maj J. J. G., 585
DAWES, Spr L. J., 101
DEAN, Cpl R. R., 573
DEANE, Gunner, 208
DECORATIONS, 149n; for garrison at Tobruk, 352-3
Decoy, British destroyer, 237
DEERING, Lt R. T., 210
Defender, British destroyer, 237, 414
DE GUINGAND, Maj-Gen Sir Francis, 109n, 115-16, 545, 598, 608-9, 614n, 640, 678, 682, 686, 707; on role of R. G. Casey in Middle East, 544; appointed BGS, Eighth Army, 597
DEIR EL ABYAD (Sketch p. 543), 547-8, 576
DEIR EL AGRAM, 635
DEIR EL DHIB (Sketches, pp. 553, 664), 589, 596
DEIR EL HAMRA (Sketch p. 361), 245, 274
DEIR EL HARRA (Sketch p. 543), 736-7
DEIR EL MUNASSIB (Sketch p. 543), 656
DEIR EL MURRA (Sketch p. 543), 736-7
DEIR EL QATANI (Sketch p. 628), 656, 736
DEIR EL SHEIN (Sketches pp. 543, 568), 543, 548-9, 553, 557, 567-8, 576-8, 625, 644
DELFS, Sig W. G., 321, 323, 326
DEMOLITIONS, 58-9, 61, 66, 79, 93-4, 100, 300
DENNIS, Maj W. J., 366
DENTZ, General Henri, 243
DERNA (Map p. 13; Sketch p. 83), 8-9, 14, 16, 25-6, 29, 32, 34-5, 41, 44, 54, 57, 63, 77, 79, 85-6, 88-94, 96-100, 111, 118, 120-1, 123, 126, 138n, 145-6, 275, 512, 756, 761
DERNA, WADI, 42, 63, 82, 86
DERNA ROAD (Map p. 220; Sketch p. 176), 96, 112, 125, 127-8, 131, 137, 140, 144, 170, 174, 177, 181-3, 189, 241, 246-7, 250, 269, 271, 280, 297-8, 314, 369, 403, 458, 510
DERRICK, Lt T. C., VC, 562, 714-15
DE SALIS, Lt-Col S. C. F., 97
DIAMOND TRACK, 650, 679
DIARBEKIR (Sketch p. 517), 518

DIEPPE, Maj C. I. C., 795n
DIGBY, WO2 K. N. W., 566
DILL, Field Marshal Sir John, 8, 18, 115-16, 173, 306, 341; and plans for defence of Cyrenaica, 30-1; on appointment of Auchinleck, 285
DINGWALL, Lt L. J., 713
DINNING, Maj J. H., 704
DISCIPLINE, of 9 Div in Cyrenaica, 43-5, in Syria, 525-6, in Cairo, 748
DJEDEIDE (Sketch p. 517), 519, 529
DJERABLOUS (Sketch p. 517), 520
DOC, 474, 496; *see also* DALBY SQUARE
DODDS, Lt-Col N. G., 64, 91, 399
DODECANESE ISLANDS (Map p. 5), 3-4, 113, 755n
DONALDSON, Cpl G. A., 208
DONNAN, Lt R. S., 768n
DOPEY, 486; *see also* BUTCH
DORA, 826
DORMAN, Capt E. A. J. R., 53-4, 105, 107
DORMAN-SMITH, Maj-Gen E. E., 579, 596-7, 606, 610, 624
DOUBLE BAR TRACK, 650, 679
DOUGHAN, Lt C. A., 690
DOUGLAS, Maj J. A., 257
DOUGLAS, Lt-Col J. S., 168
DRAPER, Lt J. W., 595
DREW, Brig H. D., 56, 94, 98-100, 120, 171, 246, 487
DRUMMOND, Air Marshal Sir Peter, 297
DRYVYNSYDE, W. B. S., *see* ANDREWS, Pte W.
DUDERSTADT (Map p. 758), 812-14
DUFF, Lt-Cdr D. V., 99n, 111, 415-16
DULAG KRETA, 775
DUNBAR, Lt A. E., 141
DUNKIRK, 53, 159, 607-8, 612n
DUNN, Cpl E., 92
DUNN, Capt R. L., 720
DWYER, Pte A. J., 566
DYER, Lt J., 778

EACOTT, Maj D. F., 709, 722
EAGLE CORNER, *see* AIRENTE, FORT
EAKINS, Maj D. H., 824n
EAST AFRICA, 3-4, 244, 256, 342
EASTBOURNE, 808, 820
EASTER, WO2 R. K., 73, 670, 680
EASTICK, Brig T. C., 358, 360, 362, 364, 366-7; commands 2/7 Fd Regt, 356
ED DUDA (Map p. 13; Sketches pp. 474, 484), 24, 254-5, 279-80, 283, 303, 430, 436-8, 441, 445-8, 450-2, 455-6, 481-3, 485-8, 490, 501-7, 519n; operations at, 457-63, 466-80
EDEN, Rt Hon Sir Anthony, 8, 18, 65, 115, 118
EDEN, Col R. A., 84, 102-3, 107-8, 119
EDMONDS, Cpl F. E., 207-8
EDMONDSON, Cpl J. H., VC, 148-9
EDMUNDS, Maj G. S., 668-9, 690, 714-15
EDMUNDS, Lt I. G., 620
EGG FEATURE, 708
EGGLESTON, F-Lt, F. F. H., 768n
EGYPT (Map p. 13; Sketch p. 135), 1, 6, 9, 22-5, 40, 52, 77, 114-18, 121, 124, 137, 139, 144, 146, 156, 158, 169, 172, 186, 235, 244-5, 253, 256, 276, 287, 296, 305-6, 333, 345-6, 353-5, 359, 362, 375, 413, 422, 425, 430, 445, 453, 483, 490, 505, 510, 512, 516, 532, 534-5, 557, 604, 606, 608, 612, 624, 737, 753, 755, 772, 823-4; strength of British Forces in, 3; defence of, 141, 159, 180, 356-8, 605; Axis plans for offensive in, 328-9; relations with Britain, 523-4; 9 Aust Div moves to, 540-1; strength of Axis forces in, 655
EICHSTATT (Map p. 758), 792-4, 802, 808, 817
EL ADEM ROAD (Map p. 220; Sketch p. 126), 127-8, 132, 134, 139-41, 144, 146, 148-52, 181, 191, 205, 209, 214, 217, 237, 247, 269, 301-2, 330, 338, 369, 387-8, 394, 405, 421-2, 431, 496, 510-11
ELAND, Pte S., 73
ELLENBY, Lt M. R., 405
ELLIOT, Lt T. W., 768n
ELLIS, Capt C. C., 767
ELLIS, Capt H. L., 330
ELSE, S-Sgt A., 616-17
Encounter, British destroyer, 399
Endeavour, British destroyer, 397
ENFEH (Sketch p. 825), 828
ENGERT, C. van, 530
EN NOFILIA (Map p. 5), 22, 46, 753

EQUIPMENT, in Cyrenaica, 28-9, 43, 195-6, 534; in Syria, 525; of 9 Div at Alamein, 622, *Enemy*, in North Africa, 21, 29; in Crusader, 497
ERITREA, 3-4, 39
ER REGIMA (Sketches pp. 25, 69), 41-2, 44, 52, 59, 61-4, 67, 76-8, 80-1, 123, 756; loss of, 68-75
ERSKINE, Maj-Gen Hon I. D., 135-6
ESC SCELEIDIMA (Sketches pp. 25, 83), 25, 27, 55, 58-63, 66, 68n, 77, 81
ETCHES, Capt G. C., 481
EUPHRATES RIVER (Sketch p. 517), 519-20
EVANS, Pte A. G., 626
EVANS, Brig Sir Bernard, (Plate p. 621), 176, 183-4, 203-6, 217, 253, 256-65, 303, 319, 571, 583-4, 702-3, 733-4; commands 2/23 Bn, 163, 24 Bde, 727; career of, 252
EVANS, Maj G. D., 423n
EVANS, Pte G. D., 403
EVANS, Sgt L. R., 220
EVANS-PRITCHARD, E. E., 43n
EVATT, Rt Hon H. V., 538-9
EVETTS, Lt-Gen J. F., 142-4, 158, 164
EXTON, Lt R. D., 632

FADAOUS (Sketch p. 825), 824
FADDEN, Rt Hon Sir Arthur, 305, 307, 351, 380; becomes Prime Minister, 346-7
FAHEY, Capt J. P., 302
FAINE, Capt C. R., 93
FAIRBAIRN, Capt M. T., 635
FAIRLEY, Brig Sir Neil, 309
FALLINGBOSTEL (Sketch p. 809), 805, 808, 813-14, 816
FALLON, Pte M., 405
FANSHAWE, Col G. H., 67, 76, 89, 95
FAR EAST, 431, 510, 516-17, 519, 527, 533
FAREGH, WADI (Sketch p. 16), 39, 48, 50
FAROUK, King, 523
FARRELL, Lt G. J., 219-20
FATMA, 761-3
FEITEL, Maj M., 265, 294-5, 299, 369, 374
Feldpost 12545, 761-3
FELL, Maj L. A., 91-2, 190-1, 193-4, 197-200, 202-7, 209, 224n
FERGUSSON, Sir Bernard, 439n
FERGUSSON, Brig M. A., 519n
FERRES, Cpl H., 478
FIDLER, Lt T., 327
FIELD, Sgt A. E., 752n, 755
FIELD, Brig J., 231-2, 246-7, 250-2, 280, 298, 302; commands 2/12 Bn, 230
FIELDING, Capt A. W., 357, 592, 594
FIG ORCHARD (Map p. 668; Sketch p. 704), 687-8, 690, 701, 721
FIG TREE ROAD (Sketch p. 231), 231
FINIGAN, Lt-Col J. L. T., 721
FINLAY, Capt J. T., 409
FISHER, Maj-Gen A. F., 595, 732
FITZGERALD, Pte J., 769n
Flamingo, British sloop, 414
FLEMING, Lt-Col E. W., 233
FLORINA (Map p. 758), 773
FORBES, Maj W., 174-5, 190, 220-1
FORBES' MOUND (Map p. 220; Sketches pp. 192, 231), 190, 196, 207, 218, 227, 238, 248-50, 252, 271-2, 291, 319, 333, 404
FORWOOD, Capt K. B., 572
FOURGLOSS (Sketch p. 517), 532
FRANCE (Map p. 758), 1, 9, 17, 20, 53, 91, 172, 267, 286, 603-4
FRANCE, Sgt W. L., 373-4, 403
FRANCO, General, 2, 641
FRANKFURT-ON-MAIN (Map p. 758), 783
FRANKLIN, Cpl D., 556
FRASER, Lt-Col K. A., 823
FRASER, Capt T. K., 69, 72, 74-5
FREDDIE OUTPOST, 468-9, 504, 506-7
FRENCH ARMY, 23, 60, 520, 525, 764, 765n; 1st Free French Bde, 535, 658, 664, 674; 2nd Free French Bde, 536; 1st Free French Motor Bn, 15, 47-8, 53, 61, 67, 97, 101, 120, 134, 136, 187
FRENCH FOREIGN LEGION, 354
FRENCH GOVERNMENT, 339
FRENCH NORTH AFRICA, 606, 640-1
FREYBERG, Lady, 527
FREYBERG, Lt-Gen Lord, VC, 365, 444, 449-50, 456, 458-9, 465, 468, 473, 479-81, 484-7, 489, 498, 500, 512, 515, 527, 578, 610, 629, 655, 663, 693, 700,

842 INDEX

FREYBERG—continued
753; appointed to command forces in Crete, 244; proposed as commander of Anzac Corps, 307; in Ed Duda operations, 461-3; seeks return of 5 NZ Bde, 467; temporarily commands XIII Corps, 609, 613; experience compared with other British North African commanders, 612n; qualifications for higher command, 614; in Battle of El Alamein, 677-8, 686; placed in command of infantry breakout in Supercharge operation, 707, 729
FRICKER, Lt D. C., 233
FUEL, shortages, 67, 80, 270-1, 377; *Enemy*, 624, 629, 719
FUKA (Map p. 13), 542, 576, 719, 736-8; enemy withdrawal to, 740-1
FYFFE, Capt H. G., 573

GABR SALEH (Sketches pp. 443, 465), 427, 440, 443, 446, 453, 457, 500n
GABR TAIEB EL ESEM (Sketches pp. 443, 445), 436, 440
GADD EL AHMAR (Sketch p. 83), 77, 89, 102, 245
GAHAN, Capt S. M., 259-60
GAIRDNER, General Sir Charles, 655
GALAL (Map p. 13), 741
Galatea, British cruiser, 398
GALLASCH, Col A. V., 717, 721; commands 2/3 Pnr Bn, 710
GALVIN, Gnr C. J., 105
GAMBIER-PARRY, Maj-Gen M. D., 35-6, 48, 50, 52, 55-60, 62, 67, 80, 85-7, 95, 99n, 103, 106; commands 2 Armd Div, 31; takes command of Mechili garrison, 101-2; captured, 107-8, 117
GAMBUT (Sketches pp. 442, 456), 278, 281, 432, 448, 457, 462-3, 466, 507-8
GARAET EN NBEIDAT (Sketch p. 456), 452
GARDINER, Lt G., 184, 259-61
GARGARESC (Map p. 5), 756
GARIBOLDI, Marshal Italo, 54, 59, 65-6, 80, 328; appointed C-in-C N. Africa, 20; replaced by General Bastico, 329
GASR EL ARID (Sketch p. 456), 466, 499
GATEHOUSE, Maj-Gen A. H., 449, 479-80, 482, 485, 487-90, 512, 682-4; commands 4 Armd Bde, 444, 10 Armd Div, 655
GATTARA, WADI (Sketches pp. 63, 69), 35, 41, 59-62, 67
GAUSE, Maj-Gen Alfred, 328, 355
GAVI (Map p. 758), 771
GAZA (Map p. 5), 514, 516, 540, 748; 9 Div parade at, 751-2
GAZALA (Map p. 13; Sketches pp. 25, 83), 14, 24, 29, 32, 41, 43, 57, 75, 77, 86-7, 94, 96, 101, 115, 121, 245, 277n, 278, 430, 464, 507, 509, 511-12, 532-3, 542, 547, 624, 634; loss of, 534-5
GAZZARD, Cpl L. H., 212
GEALE, Capt F. B., 690
GEBHARDT, Maj P., 190, 200-1, 204-9, 218, 224, 303; takes command of 2/24 Bn, 176, 720
GEHRMANN, Lt-Col A. S., 78-9, 93-4, 99, 670, commands 2/13 Fd Coy, 634
GEIKIE, Capt W. B. A., 147, 151
GEISSLER, Lieut-Colonel, 498-9
GEMMELL-SMITH, Maj G. A., 96
GENERAL HEADQUARTERS, MIDDLE EAST, 27, 34, 44, 58, 79, 138, 145, 164, 180, 241, 244, 286, 295-6, 304, 312, 339, 343, 351, 423-4, 544-5, 547, 597, 609, 640; short of aircraft, 33; estimate of German forces in Libya, 47; policy on Tobruk, 115; and dispersion of AIF, 136, 308; reconstitutes Western Desert Force HQ, 142-3; Brevity operation, 242; Battleaxe operation, 276; and decorations for Tobruk garrison, 353; attitude to training requirements, 357; restricts use of tanks at Tobruk, 376; proposal to move 7 Aust Div to Egypt, 515-16; reorganisation of, 606; instructions to Aust war correspondents, 621n
GENEVA CONVENTION, 325, 771, 781, 790, 793
GEORGE VI, KING, 425, 604
GERALD, Lt-Col J., 530
GERIULA, WADI, 240
GERMAN AIR FORCE, 17, 39, 60, 80, 97, 140, 379-80, 383, 431, 496, 560, 624; strength in North Africa, 33-4, 639; attacks Tobruk, 154, 181, 185-6, 189, 337-8, 410-13; in Crete, 274; in Battleaxe operation, 281; attacks hospital ship, 325; strength in Cyrenaica, 346; at Alamein, 552, 626, 725, 736
—FLIEGERKORPS: II, 513; X, 22, 66, 354-5

GERMAN ARMY, 2, 53-4, 55-8, 116, 256, 274, 309, 328, 353, 527, 533, 607, 700, 736-7; plans participation in North African campaign, 1, 3, 19-21, British estimate of strength and intentions in, 6, 16, 18, 47, 116; first contacts with British in North Africa, 17, 36, 40; reinforces North African theatre, 22, 27, 35; invades Greece, 85; at Tobruk, 133, 145, 148, 171, 174, 269, 433, compared with Australians at, 267-8; relations with Italians, 166, 328; strength in North Africa, 169, 655; in Brevity operation, 254; defeats Battleaxe operation, 278; armoured tactics, 354, 429; strength and dispositions at Alamein, 547, 590, 623, 625, losses at, 742; chivalrous treatment of wounded, 722-7
—HIGH COMMAND (OKH), 1, 2, 17, 23, 169, 179-80, 245, 526n, 623, 809, 814; plans participation in North Africa, 18-19, 37, 46; and Rommel, 21, 222, 327-9, 355, 547; issues directive on North African planning and strategy, 65-6, 329-30; seeks achievement of Axis supremacy in Mediterranean, 431; orders manacling of British PW, 793
—ARMOURED ARMY OF AFRICA, 563n, 564, 574, 588, 706; armoured successes at Alamein, 599; supply and equipment of, 623-4; assumes defensive at Alamein, 629, 641; composition, 655; prepares to meet Eighth Army assault, 656; tank strength and losses at Alamein, 685, 730, 732
—ARMOURED GROUP AFRICA, 355, 440n,; formed, 329
—ARMIES, Sixth, 179
—CORPS: Africa Corps (D.A.K.), 37, 53, 248, 429; Rommel appointed to command, 22; naming of, 22; tasks listed by German High Command, 65-6; in Cyrenaica, 83, 85, 87, 109, 140; in operations on Egyptian frontier, 143, 186, withdrawn from, 506; in May battle at Tobruk, 222; in Battleaxe operation, 278; proposed increase in strength of, 329; in Summer Night's Dream operation, 360; in Crusader, 443, 450, 453, 455, 466, 472, 474, 476, 478, 480, 482-3, 487-8, 490, 498, 507, 512; captures Tobruk, 535; at Alamein, 547-8, 551, 553, 557, 559, 563-4, 567, 571, 577, 596, 625, 627, 706, 723, 730, 736, withdrawal from, 740-1; tank strength at Alamein, 549-50, 624, 737; short of fuel, 624; in Battle of Alam el Halfa, 628, 635, losses in, 629-30; composition of, 655; placed under command of General von Thoma, 656. XX Corps, 553
—DIVISIONS: 426-7, 430. 3rd Armd, 18, 20. 7th Armd, 20. 15th Armd, 23, 37, 66, 123, 137, 163, 169, 172, 174, 243, 329, 537; at Tobruk, 178, 180, 183, 187, 222-4, 278, 281-4, 431, casualties, 235; in Crusader, 444, 448-9, 453, 464, 466, 468, 473-4, 479-80, 482-3, 489-90, 499; at Alamein, 551, 556-7, 562, 567, 576, 624-5, 627, 655, 679, 698, strength, 623, 685, 705, 730; in Battle of Alam el Halfa, 628-9. 21st Armd, in Summer Night's Dream operation, 360; at Tobruk, 422, 432; in Crusader, 443-4, 447-8, 453, 464, 468, 473-4, 479, 483, 488-90, 498-9, 506; at Mersa Matruh, 537; at Alamein, 556-7, 564-5, 567, 571, 588, 624-5, 627, 655, 675, 698, 719, 725, 728, 731, strength, 576, 623, 685, 705, 730; in Battle of Alam el Halfa, 628. Afrika zbV, 328; at Tobruk, 384, 431, 440, 445; becomes 90th Light Division, 466. 5th Lt Motorised, 22-3, 172, 329; formation of, 18; composition and strength, 19-20; in Cyrenaica, 46, 55, 66, 76, 80-1, 103, 122-3; at Tobruk, 128n, 144, 155-6, 180, 222, 269, 278, 280-5. 90th Lt, 328, 431; formation of, 466; in Crusader, 469, 483, 489-90, 494, 498-9, 505-6, 511; at Mersa Matruh, 537; at Alamein, 547-9, 553, 557, 571, 574, 576-7, 587-8, 596, 624-5, 655, 675, 698, 705, 707, 719, 723, 725, 728-9, 738-40, strength, 623, 730, in retreat from, 741. 164th Inf, 623; at Alamein, 562, 571, 617, 625, 655, 698, 706, 719, 738-9, losses, 705, strength, 730, in retreat from, 741
—BRIGADES: Ramcke Parachute, 623; at Alamein, 625, 630, 655, in retreat from, 736
—FORCES AND GROUPS: *Geissler Force*, 499. *Baade Gp*, 567-8, 574. *Bach Gp*, 274. *Boettcher Gp*, 481. *Briehl Gp*, 571, 574, 588, 590, 595-6. *Cramer Gp*, 274-5. *Herff Gp*, 186, 245, 254, 274. *Kiehl Gp*, 562, 590, 674, 679. *Kirchheim Gp*, 222-4. *Knabe Gp*, 143-4, 164, 274-5, 448-9, 499. *Mickl Gp*, 481, 483, 489, 505. *Olbrich Gp*, 123. *Pfeiffer Gp*, 723. *Prittwitz Gp*, 123-4. *Reconnaissance Gp*, 625. *Schwerin Gp*, 81, 83-4, 122-3, 137, 144. *Streich Gp*, 103, 123. *Wechmar*

INDEX

GERMAN ARMY—*continued*
Gp, 274-5. 155th Battle Gp, 698. 159th Battle Gp, 698. 200th Battle Gp, 698, 705. 361st Battle Gp, 698
—ARMOURED REGIMENTS: at Tobruk, 207-16. **5th**, 37, 46, 56, 81; at Tobruk, 137, 149-52, 154*n*, 155, 166, 223-4, 245, 254; in Crusader, 443, 448, 453; at Alamein, 557, 569-71, 574. **8th**, at Tobruk, 223, 254, 283; in Crusader, 464, 474, 477, 489-90; at Alamein, 567. **15th**, 675. **Panzer Grenadier Regt**, 741. **125th Panzer Grenadier Regt**, 675
—ARTILLERY, 449; Artillery Comd 104 (ARKO), 468. **18th AA Regt**, 146*n*, 269. **75th Regt**, 46
—INFANTRY REGIMENTS: **104th Lorried**, at Tobruk, 224, 269, 317; at Alamein, 565, 569-71, 574. **115th Lorried**, at Tobruk, 267, 269, 317; in Crusader, 474, 489-90; at Alamein, 596, 675, 705. **125th**, at Alamein, 617-18, 625, 627, 688, 692, 702*n*, 705, 719, 723, 728-9, 736. **155th**, in Crusader, 445, 448, 456; at Alamein, 551, 586, 588, 705. **200th**, in Crusader, 474, 489-90, 596, 719. **258th**, 384. **361st**, 354; in Crusader, 445, 448, 452, 455; at Alamein, 574, 588, 590, 596, 625, 698, 710, 719, 723. **382nd**, at Alamein, 562, 571, 590, 625, 627, 633, 672, 675, 705. **433rd**, 625
—UNITS AND BATTALIONS: **33rd Engineer Bn**, 251, 269, 464-5. **200th Engineer Bn**, 224, 505. **900th Engineer Bn**, 269, 505. **2nd MG Bn**, 46, 81-2; at Tobruk, 223-5, 269; in Crusader, 490. **8th MG Bn**, 46, 50, 85, 124; at Tobruk, 146-7, 149, 155, 223, 269; in Crusader, 499, 505. **15th Motor Cycle Bn**, 187; in Crusader, 490, 498-9. **3rd Recce Unit**, 38; in Cyrenaica, 46, 55, 65, 80-1, 123-4, 137, 143; at Tobruk, 128; on Egyptian frontier, 164, 187; in Summer Night's Dream operation, 360; in Crusader, 443, 446, 483; at Alamein, 557, 567, 574, 596, 625, 629. **33rd Recce Unit**, 245, 498; at Alamein, 557, 567, 571, 574, 590, 596, 625, 629, 655. **580th Recce Unit**, 723. **588th Recce Unit**, 655. **Kolbeck Bn**, 494
GERMAN NAVY, 398, 431
GERMANY (Map p. 758), 1-3, 66, 109, 309, 339, 378, 433, 771-4, 777, 795, 814; declares war against Russia, 287; and Turkey, 518-19, 526; exchanges prisoners with the Allies, 801, 805-8
GHAZAL (Sketch p. 543), 698, 728, 730, 733, 740
GHEDIR ESC SCIOMAR (Sketch p. 83), 78
GHEMINES (Sketch p. 25), 30
GIAIDA, *see* BIANCA
GIALO (Map p. 13), 24, 46-7, 81, 87, 455
GIARABUB (Map p. 13), 8, 24, 31, 37, 43, 47, 53*n*, 160, 455, 756
GIBRALTAR, 1-2, 173, 328, 605
GILL, Lt W. G., 105
GILLAM, Lt W. J. F., 245
GILLAN, Maj H. G., 266, 494, 654*n*, 692*n*, 701, 703-4
GILSON, Spr J. F., 580
GIOVANNI BERTA (Sketches pp. 25, 83), 25, 41, 88, 90-1, 93-5, 96*n*, 98, 100
GLENN, J. G., 559*n*, 696
GLOVER, Lt-Col H. J. H., 84, 102
Gnat, British gunboat, 226, 369, 398, 417
GODDEN, Pte E., 398
GODFREY, Brig A. H. L. (Plates pp. 365, 605), 101, 111-13, 193, 201, 238-9, 270, 280, 297, 301, 313, 315-16, 319-20, 322-4, 326, 370, 546, 552, 554, 574-5, 585-6, 588, 592-5, 621, 659, 723-5, 727; commands 24 Bde, 32; career of, 160
GODWIN-AUSTEN, General Sir Reade, 429, 444, 447, 449-50, 452, 456, 458-63, 468, 472-3, 479-80, 482, 484-6, 492-3, 495, 498, 500, 507-8, 512; commands XIII Corps, 426; and General Scobie, 457; issues order of the day to Tobruk defenders, 502-3
GOODE, Maj P. C. R., 494, 683
GOODFELLOW, Pte J. T. R., 236
GOODHART, D., 357*n*, 362*n*, 364*n*, 545*n*, 634*n*
GOODWIN, Brig S. T. W., 294, 300, 320, 340; commands 2/12 Fd Regt, 265
GORDON, Lt-Col J. D., 573
GORLITZ (Map p. 758), 767, 799-801, 808, 811, 812
GORMAN, Brig Sir Eugene, 820
GOSCHEN, Maj G. W., 133, 150, 152-4, 178, 210, 440, 475, 486, 513
GOTT, Lt-Gen W. H. E., 119-20, 125, 128-9, 131-2, 136-8, 142-4, 157, 179, 186, 243, 253-6, 443, 446, 448, 454, 466, 473, 476, 478-80, 482, 487-9, 500-2, 506-7, 535, 537, 547, 551, 568, 608, 613; commands 7 Armd Div Support Gp, 79, 118; 7 Armd Div,

GOTT—*continued*
442; temporarily commands XXX Corps, 485; and Godwin-Austen, 512; commands XIII Corps, 536; proposed by Churchill as commander of Eighth Army, 605-7
GOULD, Capt N. S., 703
GOWRIE, Earl, VC, 271*n*, 745, 806
GRACE, Col C. H., 146*n*, 632-3; commands 2/15 Bn, 631, 727
Gradisca, Italian hospital ship, 776, 789
GRAHAM, Lt-Col G. J., 236
GRAHAM, Capt H. T., 420, 434, 475, 478, 480, 482, 492
GRAHAM, Maj-Gen Miles, 614*n*
GRANT, Maj E. C., 556
GRATWICK, Pte P. E., VC, 689
GRAUDENZ (Sketch p. 809), 809
GRAY, Brig J. R., 550
GRAY, Lt R. J., 215
GRAZIANI, Marshal, 20, 36
GREASLEY, WO2 C. A., 93-4
GREATOREX, Capt A. G. W., 667, 690
GREECE (Map p. 5), 1-4, 6, 8-9, 14, 17-18, 28, 37, 40, 48, 64, 109-10, 113-16, 124, 138, 141-3, 157, 256, 274, 306-8, 310, 312, 339, 348, 382, 526, 740, 755, 764, 779; German invasion, 39, 85; evacuation of British forces, 173, 180, 187-8, 243; Aust POW escapes, 771-3
GREEK BRIGADE, at Alamein, 664
GREEN LINE (Sketch p. 126), 183, 317
GREEN MOUNTAIN, *see* JEBEL ACHDAR
GRETTON, Capt R. J., 266, 401
GRICE, Maj K. J., 710, 717
Griffin, British destroyer, 398
GRIFFIN, Dvr K. H., 808*n*
Gripsholm, Swedish ship, 805
GROGAN, Lt B. B., 768*n*
GROS, Gnr A. F., 105
GRUMPY, 459*n*, 472
GRUPPENSTEIN, 783
GRUPPIGNANO (Map p. 758), 759-60, 763, 765-8
GTAFIA, EL (Sketch p. 16), 52, 55
GUBBI, EL (Map p. 220; Sketch p. 126), 186, 297, 472
GUEST, Lt J. C., 766*n*
GURNEY, Pte A. S., VC, 582

HABATA (Sketch p. 361), 256
HABBANIYA, 244, 256
HACKETT, L-Sgt C. G., 251
HADAMAR (Map p. 758), 768, 814
HAFID RIDGE (Sketch p. 282), 278, 281-3
HAGAMUSH NULLAH, 141
HAGART, Sgt P. C., 373
HAGFET EN NEZHA, 502
HAIFA (Map p. 5; Sketch p. 517), 514, 531, 541, 748, 751
HAIFA-BEIRUT-TRIPOLI RAILWAY, 823-9
HAIG, Field Marshal Earl, 285-6
HAILE SELASSIE, Emperor, 244
HALDER, Colonel-General Franz, 37, 179, 328-9, 355, 432
HALFAYA PASS (Sketches pp. 282, 361), 24, 134, 136-7, 142, 164, 171-2, 179, 245, 254, 278, 280, 354-5, 357-8, 362, 364, 395, 453, 500*n*; operations at, 186-7, 254-6, 274-5, 281-4, 534
HALL, Maj R. J., 403
HAMER, Lt-Col Hon R. J., 635
HAMILTON, Lt B. Y., 714
HAMILTON, Maj H. P., 265
HAMMAM, EL (Sketch p. 543), 520, 597
HAMMELBURG (Map p. 758), 783, 795, 805, 808, 811, 814
HAMMER, Maj-Gen H. H., 560, 562, 582-4, 661*n*, 668-70, 679, 687-9, 710-11, 715-16, 721; commands 2/48 Bn, and career of, 558-9
"HAMRA SCURRY", 363
HANDLEY, Maj E. A., 68, 71-3, 266, 289-90, 420, 670
HANNAFORD, Lt R. A., 668
HANNAH, Capt J. F., 403
HAPPY, *see* JACK OUTPOST
HARAR, 39
HARDING, Field Marshal Sir John, 82, 94, 101, 116-17, 121, 737; commands 7 Armd Div, 655
HARDING, Capt W. C., 565, 583-4
HARE, Capt A. I., 573, 621, 726
HARIM (Sketch p. 520), 521
HARLAND, Lt-Col L. S., 86, 90
HARLAND, Maj M., 249, 289, 401

844 INDEX

HARMAN, Corporal, 51n
HARRIS, L-Sgt E., 668
HARRISON, Corporal, 51n
HARRISON, Lt A. J., 372
HARROD, Lt E. C., 593-4, 767
HARTY, Capt E. P., 667, 669, 690-1, 712, 716
HASBAYA, 532
HASLUCK, Rt Hon P., 305n, 352n
HATCH, Maj C. G., 153, 208
HAT TRACK (Sketch p. 657), 649, 673, 681
HAUPT, Maj F. K., 247-8, 250, 405
HAY, Captain, 211, 487
HAYES, L-Sgt C. B., 331
HAYES, Lt E. D. P., 734
HAYMAN, Capt P. S., 409
HAYNES, Sgt R. N., 561
HEAD, Capt J. M., 321-2, 592
HEALTH, of Tobruk garrison, 292, 309-10, 313, 347-50, 515
HEATLEY, Capt W. C., 632
Helka, British ship, 270
HELOUE (Sketch p. 825), 823
HERFF, Colonel von, 164, 179, 187, 255
HERI (Sketch p. 825), 824
HERINGTON, J., 511n
Hero, British destroyer, 399-400, 417
HESLOP, Capt R. W., 635
HETHERINGTON, J., 309n
HEWITT, Sgt G. V., 205, 207, 209
HICKEY, Lt M. A., 370
HIGH POSITION, 363-4
HILL, Maj A. J., 68, 73-5, 272-3
HILL, Cpl J. D., 632
HILL 26, 558
HILL 28, see TRIG 29
HILL 33, 564
HILL 69, 367, 511
HILL 187, 166; see also POINT 187
HILL 209, 293; see also RAS EL MEDAUUAR
Hilmi, schooner, 376-7
HIMEIMAT, see QARET EL HIMEIMAT
HINDS, Sgt D., 152
HINSON, Cpl J., 559
HITLER, Adolf, 19, 65, 169, 274, 287, 309, 509, 623, 738, 801; plans in 1941, 1-2, 37; and Rommel, 20, 692, 737, 740-1; issues directive on "Plan Orient", 328; transfers submarines from Atlantic to Mediterranean, 354, 398; naval and air reinforcement of Mediterranean theatre, 431, 506
Hobart, Australian cruiser, 376, 398, 513
HOBSON, Lt R. W., 234
HOCKING, Sgt I. D., 284
HODGMAN, Lt-Col S. T., 390
HOGAN, Pte J. S., 583
HOHENFELS (Map p. 758), 790n, 793, 796-7, 800, 803, 808, 816-17
HOHMANN, German officer, 245, 254
HOLDING, WO2 F. W., 595
HOLLYWOOD OPERATION, 747
HOLMES, Lt-Col D. L., 265
HOLMES, Lt E. L., 372
HOLMES, Lt-Gen Sir William, 536, 544-5
HOMS (Sketch p. 517), 532, 540, 823
Hood, British battle cruiser, 274
HOOK, Lt P. R., 260
HOPKINS, Harry L., 604
HORE-RUTHVEN, Capt Hon A. H. P., 61
HORNSBY, Capt D. F., 82
HORROCKS, Lt-Gen Sir Brian, 614n, 615, 626, 629, 639n, 643, 655; commands XIII Corps, 612-13; on 9 Div at Alamein, 746n
Hotspur, British destroyer, 399
HOWARD, Capt H. R., 17
HOWARD, Lt M. A., 795n
HOWE, Gnr E., 105
HUGGETT, Maj G. R., 358, 364, 367
HUGHES, Maj-Gen I. T. P., 655
HUGHES, Sgt W. T., 581
HUITFELDT, Maj H., 709
HULSE, Lt T., 755n
HUMPHRIES, Gnr H. S., 102
HUMPHRIES, Cpl W., 620
HUNGERFORD, Pte F. S. G., 769n
HUNT, L-Sgt J. G., 272
HUNTER, Lt A., 771
HUTCHINGS, B. L. B., 60n
HUTCHINSON, Maj J. A., 177-8

HUTCHISON, Lt-Gen Sir Balfour, 349

IDLIB (Sketch p. 517), 516, 521
IKINGI MARYUT (Map p. 13), 8
Ile de France, troopship, 753
IMAYID, EL (Sketch p. 628), 555
INDIA, 286, 537, 607, 639
INDIAN ARMY, 4, 6, 39, 243, 278, 286, 318, 350, 352, 453, 535, 760; strength in Tobruk, 159; cooperation with British and Australian troops, 353
—DIVISIONS: 4th, 9, 121, 141, 358, 365; in Eritrea, 3, 295; in Battleaxe, 278, 281, 283; in Crusader, 426, 430, 491-2, 498-9, 501, 504-5, 510-12; at Alamein, 655, 664, 694, 699, 732. 5th, 3; at Alamein, 542-3, 548-9, 569, 603; in B. of Alam el Halfa, 624. 10th, 536; at Mersa Matruh, 537; at Alamein, 542, 548, 554
—BRIGADES: 5th, 664n; in Crusader, 498-9, 512; at Alamein, 567, 738. 7th, in Crusader, 450, 457, 510, 512. 9th, 366; at Alamein, 543; in B. of Alam el Halfa, 630. 11th, 364; in Battleaxe, 283; in Crusader, 500-1, 506; at Alamein, 542. 17th, 541; in Crusader, 512. 18th, at Alamein, 543, 548-9. 3rd Motor, 6, 34, 47, 53-4, 103, 105, 118, 334; at Mechili, 59, 63, 76-7, 83, 87, 102, 119. 7th Motor, 543. 161st Motor, 577
—CAVALRY: 2nd Royal Lancers, 63; at Mechili, 76-7, 84, 89, 102-8. 11th (PAVO) Cavalry, at Mechili, 76-7, 84, 89, 103-5. 18th Cavalry, 54, 87; at Mechili, 76-7, 102-4; at El Adem, 119-20; in Tobruk, 125, 128, 131, 170, 176, 178, 183-4, 189, 238, 247-8, 250, 266, 280, 298, 332, 401, 419, relief of, 334-5, 340; commended by Morshead, 335. Central India Horse, 499
—ENGINEERS AND PIONEERS: Pioneer Coys at Tobruk, 119, 300; 4 Fd Sqn, 108
—INFANTRY: 2/7 Gurkha, 536. 2/5 Mahratta, 500
INDIAN OCEAN, 528, 600, 754
INGLEDEW, Major, 79
INGLIS, Maj-Gen L. M., 467, 568, 578; commands 4 NZ Bde, 461
INTELLIGENCE, British, 17, 21, 47, 172, 183, 454; of Italian and German dispositions at Alamein, 25 Jul, 590; of enemy defences at Alamein, 643-4. German, 432-3; and plans for Battleaxe, 278; at Alamein, 548
IRAQ, 243-4, 256, 274, 350, 518-19, 543, 577, 600n, 606
IRVINE, Pte W. R., 804
ISAACS, Cpl R. A. N., 407
ISAKSSON, Col O. H., 165, 219, 688
ISMAY, General Rt Hon Lord, 173
ITALIAN AIR FORCE, 34, 346, 639
ITALIAN ARMY, 1-2, 16-17, 31, 40, 66, 161, 419, 533, 736, 765; strength and aims in Tripolitania, 18-19; relations with Rommel, 21-2, 81, 174; at Tobruk, 130-1, 171, 422, 433; relations with German Army, 166, 328; training and equipment, 169; tank strength at Alamein, 577, 639, 685, 705, 730, 732, strength and dispositions at, 590, 625, 655; losses in B. of Alam el Halfa, 630; withdraws from Alamein, 737, losses, 742
—HIGH COMMAND (COMMANDO SUPREMO), 66, 433; on advance into Egypt, 169; and supplies for North Africa, 505; and defence of Cyrenaica, 511
—CORPS: X Corps, at Alamein, 549, 553, 557, 574, 655, withdraws, 736, surrenders, 741. XX Corps, at Alamein, 548-9, 625, 655, 737-8, tank strength, 624. XXI Corps, composition and strength, 329; at Tobruk, 431-2; in Crusader, 498; at Alamein, 553, 557, 574, 655, 706, withdraws, 736-7, 740. Mobile Armd Corps, 506
—DIVISIONS: 7th (Toscana), 740; 16th (Pistoia), 623, 655. 17th (Pavia), 22; at Tobruk, 269, 278, 301, 329, 394; in Crusader, 509; at Alamein, 568, 576, 623, 655, surrenders, 741. 25th (Bologna), 22, 623; at Tobruk, 329, 336, 373, 394; in Crusader, 440, 446, 496, 506; at Alamein, 625, 655, 740. 27th (Brescia), 22, 80-1, 122-3, 124; at Tobruk, 128, 137, 144, 183, 222-3, 224, 248, 269, 329; in Crusader, 511; at Alamein, 548, 550, 568, 576, 625, 655; surrenders, 741. 55th (Savona), 22, 329. 60th (Sabratha), 557; at Tel el Eisa, 562, 571; rendered ineffective, 576, 623. 101st (Trieste) Motorised, 329, 354; in Crusader, 498, 506; at Alamein, 564, 574, 576, 590, 625, 655, 719, 732, 737; tank strengths, 685, 730. 102nd (Trento) Motorised, 19, 66, 123, 172, 186, 188, 245; at

INDEX

ITALIAN ARMY—continued
Tobruk, 144, 163, 165, 178, 180, 183, 269, 301, 329, 336; in Crusader, 496, 509, 511; at Alamein, 548-9, 557, 590, 625, 655, 692, 706-7, 730, 740; in B. of Alam el Halfa, 630; at Ruin Ridge, 574, 587. 132nd (Ariete), 19, 22-3, 65, 81, 103, 122-3, 188, 278, 329; at Tobruk, 144, 155-6, 162-3, 166, 168, 180, 222-5, 235, 269, 301; in Battleaxe, 281, 283; in Crusader, 442-3, 446, 453, 474, 482-3, 489, 498-9, 506; at Alamein, 550, 625, 655, 698, 733, 736-8, 740; tank states, 685, 730. 133rd (Littorio) at Alamein, 554, 557, 625, 655, 675, 679, 692, 705, 736-7; tank states, 685, 730. 185th (Folgore), 623; at Alamein, 625, 655; surrenders, 741. Young Fascists Div, 655
—REGIMENTS: Bersaglieri, at Tobruk, 238, 301; at Tel el Eisa, 564; at Alamein, 692; 7th Regt, at Alamein, 549, 559, 574. 19th Regt, 183. 20th Regt, 183. 61st Regt, 625. 62nd Regt, 165; at Alamein, 625, 670n, 672, 675. 132nd Regt, 269. 16th Arty Regt, 269. 46th Arty Regt, 269. 357th Lt AA Regt, 719
—UNITS: X Bersaglieri Bn, 728. XI Bersaglieri Bn, 702n, 705. Fabris Bn, 81, 89, 137; at Tobruk, 176, 178, 183. Fascist Youth Bn, 500, 506. Montemurro Unit, 137, 164, 188
ITALIAN NAVY, 39, 163, 513
ITALY (Map p. 758), 1-2, 66, 506, 526, 639, 753, 756, 799; exchanges prisoners with Britain and Australia, 772

JACKA, Sgt C. R., 576
JACKMAN, Maj J. J. B., VC, 127
JACK OUTPOST (Sketches pp. 302, 372), 303, 369, 373-4, 384, 387, 394, 438, 440, 446, 473, 492; see also NORMIE and TRIG 146
JACKSON, Brig D. R., 575, 727
JACKSON, G. J., see FARRELL, Lt G. J.
JACKSON, WO1 J. W., 213, 217
JACOBY, Capt P. R., 709
JAGOE, Pte C. H., 757n
JAMES, Lt R. W., 177
JAMISON, Pte E. E., 403
JAPAN, 382, 513, 525, 527, 533, 540, 600; attacks Pearl Harbour, 510; lands forces in Thailand and Malaya, 515-16.
JAVA, 527-8
JEANES, Lt-Col M. R., 238-9, 556
JEBEL ACHDAR (Map p. 13; Sketch p. 25), 24-6, 34, 37, 63, 76, 80-1, 111, 123
JEBEL BEIN GABIR (Sketch p. 553), 565
Jebel Kebir, ship, 415
JEBEL TOURBOL (Sketch p. 522), 521-2, 529n
JED OUTPOST (Sketch p. 302), 303, 369
JENKINS, Pte P. H., 75
JENKINS, Lt W. C., 163, 175
JERUSALEM (Map p. 5), 514, 531, 748
JESS, Lt. C. McG., 259
JEZZINE (Sketch p. 517), 532
JILL OUTPOST (Sketches pp. 302, 439), 303, 374, 386, 438-9, 492
JIM OUTPOST (Sketch p. 302), 331
JOCK COLUMNS, 129, 454, 466, 473, 492, 499, 505, 507, 598, 608; Auchinleck on, 501; Montgomery discontinues, 610-11
JODL, Field Marshal, 433
JOHNSTON, Lt-Col R. L., 358-9
JOHNSTONE, Maj J. A., 372-3
JONES, Captain, 440
JONES, Maj. A. G., 362, 686, 703
JONES, Cpl K. S., 212, 214, 216
JONES, Pte M.E., 233
JONES, Lt R. H., 768n
JONES, Sqn-Ldr R. S., 768n
JOSHUA, Lt-Col R., 370-2, 408, 709; commands 2/32 Bn, 711
JOUNIE (Sketch p. 825), 823
JOY, Lt F. N., 164, 726
JOYCE, Lt K. D., 702
JUBB, Capt W. H. V., 701
JULIS (Map p. 5), 7-8, 514

KAFR AYA (Sketch p. 522), 521-2
KALMOUN (Sketch p. 825), 828
Karapara, British hospital ship, 240
KARLSBAD (Sketch p. 809), 812
KASSAB (Sketch p. 520), 521
KATMA (Sketch p. 520), 521

KEARNEY, Lt. E. A. J., 713, 716
KEITEL, Field Marshal Wilhelm, 65-6, 328
KELLY, Lt-Col J. L. A., 90, 703-4
KELLY, Lt. M. J., 210
KELLY, Sgt. R. L. F., 105-6
KENNEDY, Maj-Gen Sir John, 285, 341n
KENNEDY, Sgt M. J., 36
KENNEDY, Cpl R. F., 689
KENNEL, 365
KEREN, 3, 39, 295
KERKENNAH ISLANDS (Map p. 5), 163
KESSELL, Capt J. S., 717, 722, 726
KESSELRING, Field Marshal Albert, 506, 512, 642, 740; appointed C-in-C South, 431
KEYS, Capt J. T., 155
Khaid el Dine, schooner, 376
KHAMSINS, in Cyrenaica, 39; in Tobruk, 125, 129, 185, 188
KHLAISSE (Sketch p. 522), 522
KIBBY, Sgt. W. H., VC, 669, 715, 728n
KIDNEY RIDGE (Map p. 668; Sketch p. 674), 680n, 683, 692-3, 696-8, 730, 732
KILBY, WO2 H. E., 778
KILLIS (Sketch p. 520), 521
KILO 6 (Sketch p. 618), 618
KILO 8 (Sketch p. 587), 588, 591, 637
KILO 9 (Sketch p. 587), 588, 591
KILO 10 (Sketch p. 581), 591
KILO 89, 12, 514
KILO 109 (Sketch p. 580), 580-1, 583, 699, 708
KILO 110 (Map p. 668), 672
KILO 113 (Map p. 668), 699
KILO 166.7, 824
KILO 840, 52
KIMBER, Capt D. G., 175, 182, 238, 582
KIM OUTPOST (Sketch p. 126), 386
KINDER, Sgt A. G., 74
KING, Fleet Admiral Ernest J., 604
KING'S CROSS, 330, 464, 536
KINNANE, Lt J., 136-7
Kipling, British destroyer, 349
KIPPENBERGER, Maj-Gen Sir Howard, 547, 550, 568
KIRBY, Pte M. N., 421n
KIRCHHEIM, Maj-Gen Heinrich, 123, 210, 222, 224
Kirkland, British ship, 415
KISCH, Brig F. H., 58, 88, 93, 100n, 650
KLEIN, Brig. B. E., 295, 299
KLOPPER, Maj-Gen H. B., 535
KNABE, Lieut-Colonel, 137, 164, 172, 179, 498-9
KNAYE (Sketch p. 520), 521
KNIGHT, WO2 A. H., 152
KNIGHT, WO1 V. H., 565
KNIGHTSBRIDGE (Sketch p. 25), 24, 511, 535
KOKKINIA, 775, 789
KOPANSKI, Maj-Gen Stanislaw, 340, 419-20, 434; commands Polish Carpathian Bde, 339
Kos XXI, British trawler, 376-7
KREMS (Sketch p. 809), 812
KRIGE, Uys, 767n
KROGER, Maj H. J., 768n, 771
KUFRA, 23-4, 641

Ladybird, British ship, 240
LAING, Sub-Lt I. H., 415
LALLY, Sgt. D. A., 373-4
LAMB, Maj L., 326
LAMPSON, Rt Hon Sir Miles, 523-4
LAMSDORF (Map p. 758), 788-9, 793, 795-6, 799-800, 802-4, 808, 811-12, 814
Lance, British destroyer, 431
LANDING GROUND 105, 740
LANDSHUT (Sketch p. 809), 810, 818
LANE, Bombardier, 167, 208
LANG, Gnr D., 785-7
LARKINS, Maj G. D., 220
LASSACH, 783
LATAKIA (Sketch p. 520), 516, 521, 529, 531, 541
LATHAM, Brig H. B., 50-1, 60, 67, 78, 87, 97; commands 2 Armd Div Support Gp, 48
Latona, British minelayer, 343, 399-400, 415, 417
LAUD, WO1 H., 249
LAVARACK, Lt-Gen Sir John, 113-14, 132, 136, 142-5, 151, 160, 307-8; commands 7 Div, 11; appointed to Cyrenaica Command, 109, 115-17; and defence of Tobruk, 118-19, 121-2, 124-5, 129, 138-41; resumes command of 7 Div, and career of, 156-8; commands I Aust Corps, 515; flies to Java, 517, 527

846 INDEX

LAWRENCE, Lt C. H., 460
LAZER, Lt B. L. B., 182
LEACH, Sgt G. L., 73
LEACH, Maj S. R., 680
LEAFLETS, at Tobruk, 145, 166, 287-8; at Alamein, 621
LEAKEY, Lt-Col A. R., 331
LEAVE, in Palestine, 514; in Syria, 532; before Alamein, 648
LEBANON, THE, 516, 519, 530, 532, 823, 826
LECLERC, General Jacques, 23
LEDINGHAM, L-Bdr L. G., 105
LEESE, Lt-Gen Sir Oliver, 614-16, 643, 655, 663, 677, 686, 693-5, 699-700, 745-7, 753; experience compared with Morshead's, 612n; commands XXX Corps, 613, 637
LEESON, Sgt H. T., 404, 574
LEGG, Lt F. H., 220, 715
LESAR, S-Sgt. H., 778
Lesbos, British merchant ship, 416
LEVINGS, Capt E. W., 760
LEWIN, Maj L. H., 201n
LEWIN, Capt R. W., 668
LEWIS, WO2 K. T., 713
LIBYA (Map p. 13), 19-20, 24, 47, 53, 93, 114, 145, 276, 285, 306, 310-11, 328, 434, 526, 608, 623-4
LIBYAN OMAR (Sketch p. 454), 450
LIBYAN REFUGEE BATTALIONS, in Tobruk, 119, 159
LIDDELL HART, Sir Basil, 22n, 256n, 277n, 281n, 502n, 588n
LIDDINGTON OPERATION, 753
LIGERTWOOD, Capt W. L., 588
LIGHTFOOT OPERATION, 733; plans and preparations, 644-63; the battle, 665-700
LINDSAY, Lt-Col M. J., 28, 36
LINDSEY, Cpl B. W. A., 689
LINES, Capt E. H. D., 232
LION OUTPOST (Sketch p. 439), 438, 440, 450
Lively, British destroyer, 431
LLEWELLEN PALMER, Lt-Col A. W. A., 271, 402
LLOYD, Maj-Gen C. E. M., 10, 14, 28-9, 32, 43, 63, 82, 160, 193, 195, 200-2, 204, 221, 241, 252, 257, 295-6, 308, 316, 331-3, 544; appointed GSO1 9 Div, 7; career of, 12
LLOYD, Brig J. E. (Plate p. 365), 313-15, 317, 319-20, 322-7, 374; commands 2/28 Bn, 127; career of, 318
LODER-SYMONDS, Brig B. G., 97, 141, 486, 507
LOMAX, Maj-Gen C. E. N., 386, 469; commands 16 British Bde, 375
LONDON, 30, 57, 109, 117, 125, 146, 172-3, 243-4, 275, 277, 295, 306, 312, 334, 342, 399, 539, 596, 603-6, 640, 695-6, 706, 746
LONG, G., 3n, 17n, 18n, 31n, 44n, 114n, 306n, 307n, 516n, 519n, 755n, 756n, 771n, 773n, 782n
LONGHURST, Lt A. W., 562
LONG RANGE DESERT GROUP, 47, 53, 61, 76, 81, 84, 358
LOOTING, 44
LOUGHREY, Lt-Col J., 95, 182, 218-20, 225, 596n, 723-4
LOVE, Pte P. L., 73
LOVEGROVE, Capt E. A., 127
LOVETT, Lt-Col B. M., 234
LOXTON, Maj F. E. C., 233
LUBECK (Sketch p. 809), 777, 780
LUCK, L-Cpl H. J., 207
LUCKENWALDE (Sketch p. 809), 814
LUMBY, Capt J. L., 632
LUMSDEN, Lt-Gen H., 551, 567, 643, 655, 677-8, 678, 682, 693, 700, 732; commands 1 Armd Div, 548, XIII Corps, 608, X Corps, 612
LYALL, WO2, W. K. McK., 323, 594

MAAMELTEIN (Sketch p. 825), 823-4, 826, 828
MAATEN BAGUSH, 117, 142, 241
MAATEN BELCLEIBAT (Sketch p. 31), 39
MAATEN EL BAGHLIA (Sketch p. 16), 52
MAATEN GHEIZEL (Map p. 13; Sketch p. 31), 30, 39, 48
MAATEN GIOFER (Map p. 13), 36, 49
MACADAM, Lt J. A., 229
MACARTHUR, General of the Army Douglas, 540, 695, 749; arrives in Australia and appointed Supreme Commander SWPA, 538; seeks return of 9 Aust Div, 539, 694, 746, 750
MACARTHUR-ONSLOW, Lt-Col E., 669, 688, 699, 727; commands 2/2 MG Bn and composite force, 659
McCARTER, Lt-Col L., 316, 324-5, 592-5; commands 2/28 Bn, 591

McCLUSKEY, Cpl J., 583
McCORQUODALE, Col D., 15, 60n, 121
McCRAITH, Capt P. J. D., 53
McCREERY, General Sir Richard, 597-8, 615, 706-7; appointed Chief of Staff, ME Comd, 608
McCULLOCH, Maj E. M., 681
McDERMOTT, Capt D. H., 265, 294, 300
MACDONALD, Brig A. L., 27
MACDONALD, Capt D. A., 768n
McELROY, Lt R. McL., 153
MACFARLANE, Maj A., 227
McHENRY, Lt S. C., 320-3, 326
McHENRY, WO2 W. R., 616-17
MACHINE-GUNS, 622, 661
MACHRHARA (Sketch p. 517), 532
McILRICK, WO2 A. A., 594
McINTOSH, Bdr R. H., 106
McINTYRE, Lt-Col A. E., 630
MACKAY, Lt-Gen Sir Iven, 14, 17, 26-7, 44, 308
MACKAY, Maj-Gen K., 363-4
McKEE, Pte E., 139
MACKELL, Lt-Col F. A., 148-50
McKELLAR, Sgt R. V., 481, 701
MACKENZIE, Capt I. S., 690, 713
McKIBBIN, M. N., 798n, 799n
McKOY, Lt A. N., 583
McLACHLAN, Sgt H. F., 631
MACLARN, Maj L. C., 246, 389-90, 407
McLAUGHLIN, Sgt R. B., 70
McLEOD, Lt E., 713
McMAHON, Bdr J. T., 561
McMASTER, Capt I. F., 389, 727
McNALLY, Lt J. S., 153
McNAMARA, Capt J. F., 560, 667
McRAE, Maj E. H., 583
MADDALENA (Sketch p. 25), 32, 41, 64, 79, 189, 425
MADDEN, Lt J. E., 635
MADJLAYA (Sketch p. 522), 516-17, 522
MAGNO, Lt-Col C. K. M., 635, 667, 701
MAGRUN (Sketches pp. 25, 83), 34, 42, 58-9, 65
MAGRUN, WADI, 420
MAIR, Lt J. L., 205-6, 210, 212, 768n
MALATYA (Sketch p. 517), 518
MALAYA, 515-16
MALLOCH, Lt-Col G. I., 205-7, 221, 237, 257-60, 264
MALTA (Map p. 5), 1, 163, 330, 431, 533-4, 640
MANN, Brig J., 93, 94n, 99, 138n, 146
MANNING, L-Sgt A. R., 592
MARADA (Map p. 13), 18, 22-3, 27, 36, 39, 47, 53
MARAS (Sketch p. 517), 518
MARAUA (Sketches pp. 25, 83), 33, 63-4, 68, 76, 80, 82, 86-7, 89-92, 94, 100n
MARBLE ARCH (Map p. 5), 22, 753
MARBURG (Map p. 758), 773, 780-1, 795-6, 805
MARDIN (Sketch p. 517), 518
Maria Giovanni, schooner, 376-7, 415-16, 451
MARIENBURG (Sketch p. 809), 809
MARKT PONGAU (Sketch p. 809), 799, 818
MARLAN, Col R. F., 15, 93, 95-6
MARSA BREGA (Map p. 13; Sketch p. 16), 14-16, 23, 25-7, 29-30, 32, 34-9, 46-8, 52-3, 109, 118; German attack on, 49-51
MARSHALL, General of the Army George C., 604
MARTIN, Brig E. O., 96, 397, 437, 463
MARTIN, Maj G. G. F., 249
MARTIN, Capt J. B., 338, 511
MARTIN, Brig J. E. G., 113, 231, 236-7, 267, 280; commands 2/9 Bn, 230
MARTIN, T. A., 460n, 475n
MARTUBA (Sketches pp. 25, 83), 34, 41, 88, 90-4, 96, 100
MARYUT, LAKE (Sketch p. 546), 546
MASAB MOUNTAINS, 518
MASEL, Brig P., 128n, 238, 374, 407, 576n, 579n, 591, 595n, 724n
MASON, Maj G. H., 97-8, 120
MASON, W. Wynne, 781n, 789n
MATTHEW, Lt-Col A. G. (Plate p. 365), 203, 374, 385
MATTHEWS, Cpl A. E., 817n
MAUGHAN, Lt-Col D. W. B., 471, 493, 703
MAXWELL, Brig A. H., 352
MAY, Captain, 210
MECHILI (Map p. 13; Sketches pp. 25, 83), 25, 34, 47, 59, 63, 67, 80-1, 83, 109, 115-16, 118-24, 128, 135, 137, 145, 176, 275, 401n, 512-13, 756; importance of, 76; area described, 77; operations at, 84-108

INDEX

MEDITERRANEAN SEA (Map p. 5), 1-2, 24, 173, 180, 188, 274, 277, 287, 350, 354, 398, 417, 431, 513
Medway, British submarine depot ship, 416
MEGGITT, Lt N. P., 300
MEIDAN EKBES (Sketch p. 520), 520-1
MEIGHAN, Lt R. D., 191
MELLENTHIN, General F. W. von, 550, 562 , 623, 628n 630
MENASTIR, 464, 507
MENZIES, Rt Hon Sir Robert, 235, 312, 346-7; seeks concentration of AIF in ME, 306, 308, 311; proposes formation of Anzac Corps, 307; requests relief of 9 Div, 313, 345
MENZIES, Lt R. W. J., 693
MERDJAYOUN (Sketch p. 517), 532
MERSA EL MAGRUN (Sketch p. 402), 420
MERSA MATRUH (Map p. 13; Sketch p. 135), 12, 24, 29, 32, 100n, 115-16, 120-1, 125, 134-5, 141-3, 158, 164, 171-2, 190, 237, 271, 306, 343, 358-9, 365, 375-6, 414, 416, 536-7, 548, 571, 580, 655, 735n, 741-2, 747; strength and disposition of British forces at, 356; defences, 357
MERSA PESCARA (Sketch p. 402), 420
MESSERVY, General Sir Frank, 283-4, 359, 498, 500-1; commands 4 Indian Div, 281
MIDDLE EAST, 1-4, 19, 100, 115, 157, 163, 173, 188, 222, 275, 286, 307, 328, 343, 364, 375, 381, 431, 433, 455, 516, 518, 529-30, 532, 537-40, 544, 601, 604, 612, 641, 665, 695-6, 753; reorganisation of AIF in, 6, 9; concentration of Australian forces in, 256, 306-11; strength of AIF in, 527, 600; American supplies for, 342; reinforcement of, 352, 639; forces sent to Far Eastern theatre, 533; British strategy in, 605; appointment to higher command, 613, 615; Aust Govt seeks return of 9 Div from, 749-50
MIDDLE EAST SUPPLY CENTRE, 544
MILES, Maj C. G., 275
MILES, Brig R., 484-6
MILLETT, Lt J. R., 795n
MINA, EL (Sketch p. 825), 824, 828
MINES, at Tobruk, 137, 168, 180-1, 185, 189, 208, 211-12, 224, 227-8, 231, 272, 303-4, 338, 386; at Alamein, 575, 599, 642-4, 652-6, 2, 661, 666-70, 673
MINOCKS, Capt J. W. N., 627, 734
MINQAR QAIM (Map p. 13), 537, 547
Miranda, storeship, 293, 414
MISURATA (Map p. 5), 21, 756
MITEIRIYA RIDGE (Sketches pp. 543, 587), 542, 558, 563, 566, 578, 604, 624, 644-5, 699; operations at, 586-90, 673, 675, 677-8, 680-4
MITFORD, Col E. C., 47, 53, 81, 84
MOLLARD, Maj K. F., 565, 581-2, 667, 690, 715
MONAGHAN, Brig R. F., 171
MONAGHAN, Cpl S. C. H., 619
MONK, L-Cpl R. J., 315
MONOTTI, Capt F. R., 563
MONSON, Ronald, 638
MONTEZEMOLO, Lt-Col Guiseppe, 505
MONTGOMERY, Field Marshal Viscount (Plate p. 604), 11, 286, 357, 544, 551, 605, 615-16, 624, 626, 628, 641, 650, 660, 677, 684-7, 694-5, 697, 700, 732-3, 737-8; appointed to command Eighth Army, and career of, 606-7; Brooke's appraisal of, 607-8; assumes command of Eighth Army, 609; visits 9 Aust Div, 610-11, 693, 745; experience compared to Morshead's, 612n; views on appointment of Dominion officers to higher command, 613-14; on need for CO's to regularly assemble units, 621-2; policy at Alamein, 625; Rommel's impression of, 629; conduct of Alam el Halfa Battle examined, 634-5; appoints Leese to command XXX Corps, 637; wins confidence of Eighth Army, 638; agrees to Alexander's choice of date for Alamein offensive, 640; plans for battle, 642-7, 656, 676, 698-700; orders training to begin, 653; briefs Eighth Army commanders, 662-3; orders for 25th October, 678; clashes with Gatehouse, 682-3; criticised by Churchill, 706; plans new break-out thrust, 707; orders for Supercharge operation, 729; achievements compared with Auchinleck's, 744-5
MOODIE, Maj R. O. K. T., 99
MOON TRACK (Sketch p. 657), 649, 673
MOORE, Lt G. McI., 672
MOOSBURG (Map p. 758), 768, 785, 795, 799, 811-12, 814, 816-18
MORALE, of Tobruk garrison, 111, 171, 286, 292, 316, 350; of 9 Div in Syria, 530

MORISH, Lt J. C., 768n
MORLEY, Pte E. A. W., 769n
MORPHETT, Maj H. C., 219
MORRICE, Pte A. O., 73
MORRIS, Lt F. W., 635
MORRIS, L-Cpl J. A., 617
MORRISON, Capt W. G., 259-64, 315
MORSHEAD, Lt-Gen Sir Leslie (Plates pp. 108, 396, 588, 604), 14, 16-17, 59, 77, 82, 91-3, 109, 111-12, 117, 124, 127, 129, 132, 136-7, 143, 145, 162, 179, 190, 192-3, 200-2, 204-5, 240, 253, 261-3, 272, 277n, 288, 295-6, 308, 335, 338, 376, 389-90, 399, 409-10, 419, 424, 437, 515, 517, 532, 545-6, 554, 557, 586-7, 589, 593-5, 602, 615, 617, 622n, 625, 633, 636, 655, 661, 680, 682, 687, 693-6, 699-700, 703, 708, 720, 723, 725, 733-4, 736, 747-8; appointed GOC 9 Div, 8, 10; career of, 11-12; in defence of Cyrenaica, 27-32, 35, 41-2, 63-4, 67-8, 72, 79-80, 85-90, 94-5, 101; and conduct of Aust troops in Cyrenaica, 43-5; appointed fortress commander at Tobruk, 119, 142, 146, 157-8; orders attempt to rescue Neame and O'Connor, 121; in defence of Tobruk, 122, 150-1, 159-60, 164, 166-7, 170-1, 174, 180-1, 183, 188, 191n, 195, 211, 214, 217-18, 220-1, 226-7, 230, 234-5, 237, 401, tactics, 536; protests at withdrawal of air support at Tobruk, 184-5, 241; policy of aggressive patrolling, 237-8, 242, 298; and Brevity operation, 245, 248; on defence of perimeter posts, 251-2; on fuel shortage, 270-1; and plans for Battleaxe operation, 279; directly responsible to GHQ, ME, 286; seeks reinforcements, 297; on health of Tobruk garrison, 309; plans operations in Salient, 313-17, 331-3; orders analysis of enemy shelling, 336; and Polish Bde, 340; attends Cairo conferences, 348-9, 377; relief of 9 Div, 351, 359; decorations for Tobruk garrison, 352-3; use of tanks at Tobruk, 376; orders recapture of Bir el Azazi (Plonk), 391; farewell visits to non-Australian units, 396-7; leaves Tobruk, 397; decorated by Polish Govt, 514; on need for training in Syria, 524-5, 530; appointed GOC AIF (ME), 527; allotted task of defending Cairo sector of Nile Delta, 544; objects to piecemeal employment of 9 Div, 551-2; on appointment of Ramsden to command XXX Corps, 555-6; issues orders for capture of Tel el Eisa, 558; protests to Auchinleck about employment of 20 Bde, 569; critical of tasks allotted to 9 Div for Ruin Ridge-Tel el Eisa attacks, 579; on development of divisional "battle cunning", 590; on state of mind of HQ Eighth Army, 598; seeks reinforcement of 9 Div, 600-1; visited by Churchill at Alamein, 606; expresses regret at Auchinleck's removal from command, 607; temporarily commands XXX Corps, 609. 637; on Montgomery, 610; claims for appointment to higher command, 612-16; complains to Alexander regarding attempts to suppress publicity about 9 Div, 621n; confidence and affection of 9 Div, 638, 746; expounds plan to CO's, 662; opposes Leese's wish to advance zero hour, 663; letter to his wife on eve of battle, 665; his plan of attack for 27 Oct examined, 698-9; orders for 30-31 Oct attack, 708-9; visited by Alexander and Montgomery, 745; cables Aust Govt that 9 Div would return to Aust, 749; on T colour patch, 750-1; at 9 Div parade at Gaza, 752; visits Eighth Army, 753; death, 754
MOULDS, Maj W. J., 92
MREIR, EL (Sketch p. 568), 550, 577
MSUS (Sketches pp. 25, 83), 25-6, 34, 42, 48, 53-4, 60-3, 65-6, 76-8, 80-2, 85-7, 103, 123
MUBARIK TOMB (Sketch p. 553), 569
Mud and Blood, 287
MUFFETT, Sgt A. J., 566
MULGRUE, Lt G. E., 84, 563
MULLER, Lt-Col D. O., 138n
MUNASSIB DEPRESSION (Sketch p. 628), 658, 684
MUNCKTON, Pte M. L., 616-17
MUNDAY, William, 638
MUNICH (Map p. 758), 778, 786-7
MUNRO, Lt-Col E. E., 76, 83, 102-4, 106, 757; commands 2/3 A-Tk Regt, 54
MUNRO, Maj N. J., 366
MURPHY, Sgt J. T., 817
MURPHY, W. E., 452n, 459n, 462n 488n, 489n, 497n
MURRAY, Maj E. D., 575

MURRAY, Maj-Gen J. J. (Plates pp. 108, 364), 11-12, 14-15, 17, 23, 30, 41, 68, 72, 121, 133, 149, 205, 211, 217, 221, 228, 236, 241, 266, 270-3, 288, 297-8, 314, 375, 385-6, 388, 390, 392-4, 397, 399, 418, 422, 424n, 514, 519n; commands 20 Bde, 10; career of, 160
MUSAID (Sketches pp. 135, 282), 135, 142, 144, 187 255, 278, 283, 450, 453
MUSSOLINI, Benito, 19, 557, 737, 741

NAHAS PASHA, 523-4
NAHR ANTELIAS (Sketch p. 825), 826
NAHR BARID (Sketch p. 522), 521
NAHR EL ASFOUR (Sketch p. 825), 827
NAHR EL DJOUZ (Sketch p. 825), 827
NAHR EL FGAL (Sketch p. 825), 827
NAHR EL FIDAR (Sketch p. 825), 827
NAHR EL KALTA (Sketch p. 825), 827
NAHR EL KELB (Sketch p. 825), 826, 829
NAHR EL MOTT (Sketch p. 825), 826
NAHR IBRAHIM (Sketch p. 825), 827
NAHR NACCACHE (Sketch p. 825), 826
NAHR SENE, 531
Napier, Australian destroyer, 417
NAQB ABU DWEIS (Sketch p. 543), 542-3, 549, 566
NATRUN, WADI, 368
NEAME, Lt-Gen Sir Philip, VC, 14, 30-1, 35, 37, 49, 57, 113, 115, 118; takes over Cyrenaica Command, and career of, 9; in defence of Cyrenaica, 34, 40, 42, 46-7, 51-2, 55, 62, 67-8, 76-82, 85-7, 90, 112; on behaviour of Australian troops, 43-5; O'Connor nominated to succeed, 58-9; captured, 92, 94, 116-17
NEHL, Maj W. B., 77, 104
NEHRING, Lieut-General, 564, 567-9, 574, 627
NELSON, Lt F. R., 713
NELSON, Pte J. C., 769n
Neptune, British cruiser, 376
NEUENDORF, Capt K. O., 259n, 570
NEUENDORF, Capt T. O., 259, 570n
NEUMANN-SILKOW, Maj-Gen Walther, 466, 473, 483, 490, 498-9, 501, 504, 506-7; commands *15 Armd Div*, 281-2
NEWBERY, Brig J. C., 726
NEWCOMB, Maj S. P., 290
NEW GUINEA, 601-2, 695
NEWTON, Lt R., 620
NEW ZEALAND, 399; American proposal to send another division to, 537
NEW ZEALAND ARMY, 4, 523, 760
—DIVISIONS: 1st, 543n. 2nd, 311, 365, 426, 451, 494, 498, 536, 651; in Egypt, 3; in Anzac Corps, 307; in Crusader operation, 429-30, 444, 450, 452-6, 458-64, 466-74, 478-91, 497, achievements in, 499; in Syria, 515, 529; at Minqar Qaim, 537, 547; renamed, 543; at Alamein, 548-50, 554, 557, 567, 577, 603, 609, 612n, 614, 653; losses at Ruweisat, 568, 578; in Battle of Alam el Halfa, 624-6, 628-9; in Battle of El Alamein, 645, 655-7, 664, 673, 675, 679, 682-3, 686, 693, 697-700, 707, 729, 731-2, 737-8, losses, 693. 3rd, 543n. 4th, 543n. 6th, 543n
—CAVALRY REGIMENT, 678, 683-4
—ARTILLERY: in Crusader, 493. 6th Fd Regt, in Crusader, 486, 490
—INFANTRY: *Brigades*: 4th, in Crusader, 456-7, 460-1, 467; at Alamein, 550, 554, 567, 568. 5th, 455; in Crusader, 457, 464, 467, 498-9, 506, 510, 512; at Alamein, 550, 567, 625; in Battle of Alam el Halfa, 629, 657. 6th, in Crusader, 449-50, 452, 455-7, 459, 461, 483, 487-9; in Syria, 526n; at Alamein, 543, 577, 657; in Battle of Alam el Halfa, 629
Battalions: 18th, in Crusader, 468, 486-7, 490, 493, 496, 502-3. 19th, in Crusader, 461, 462n, 463, 467, 469-70, 472, 478, 480-3, 488, 492; at Alamein, 550. 20th, in Crusader, 490. 21st, in Crusader, 461. 22nd, in Crusader, 464, 498; at Alamein, 567. 23rd, in Crusader, 453, 465. 24th, in Crusader, 452, 455, 461, 468, 483. 25th, in Crusader, 452, 455, 461, 483, 488. 26th, in Crusader, 452, 461, 468, 483. 28th (Maori), in Crusader, 453, 512; at Alamein, 729-30, 736
NEW ZEALAND GOVERNMENT, formation of Anzac Corps, 307; protests at repeated supersession of Freyberg, 614; and prisoners of war in Germany, 793

NICHOLLS, Maj H. W., 402-3
NICHOLS, Maj-Gen J. S., 480, 492-3, 501; commands 50 Brit Div, 655
Nieuw Amsterdam, troopship, 753-4
NILE DELTA (Map p. 13), 115, 295, 514-15, 542, 545-6, 554, 557, 596, 641; defence of, 544
NILE RIVER (Map p. 13), 142, 546, 623
Nino Bixio, Italian freighter, 763-4
NIXON-SMITH, Lt A. F., 237n
NIXON'S POST (Sketches pp. 273, 290), 237, 249, 272-3, 288, 291
Nizam, Australian destroyer, 343, 398, 417
NOBLE, WO2 E. A., 168, 220-1
NORMAN, Brig C. H. B., 202, 204, 207, 596n
NORMIE OUTPOST (Sketch p. 302), 303, 330, 369; see also JACK OUTPOST and TRIG 146
NORRIE, Lt-Gen Lord, 428, 430, 433, 442, 447, 448, 450, 453-4, 473, 479-80, 482, 484, 489-91, 499-502, 505, 507-8, 511-12, 536, 554-5, 552; commands XXX Corps, 426; views on outcome of Alamein, 547
NORRIE, Lt E. F. G., 671
NORTH, Maj S. C. F., 701
NORTH AFRICA (Map p. 13), 1-3, 16-17, 22, 109, 114, 125, 150, 161, 188, 378, 382, 455, 494, 506, 510, 516, 540, 603, 609, 662-3, 706, 742, 756; German reinforcement of, 18-21; terrain described, 24-5; German directive on strategy in, 65-6; strength of German forces, 169; German and British tank strengths, 172-3; Rommel reports to German High Command on situation, 179; reorganisation of Axis command structure, 328-9; Axis supply and reinforcement, 354-5, 431; Allied decision to mount invasion, 604; opposing air force strengths at Alamein, 639; strength of Axis forces, 655
NORTHCOTT, General Sir John, 8n
NORTH POINT (Sketch p. 361), 355, 358, 361, 365-6
NORTON, Capt E. O., 619
NORTON-KNIGHT, Sgt G. O., 764n
NORTON-KNIGHT, Bdr M. O., 764n
NORTON-KNIGHT, Gnr O. P., 764n
NOYES, Capt W. H., 233-4
NUREMBERG (Map p. 758), 810-11, 814-15

OAKLEY, Maj A. W., 190
O'BRIEN, Pte J. P., 716
O'CARROLL, Brig W. C. L., 460, 474, 492, 501
O'CONNOR, Lt C. A., 671
O'CONNOR, General Sir Richard, 57, 61-2, 67-8, 76, 79, 81, 86-7, 89, 94; on discipline of Australian soldiers, 44; appointed to Cyrenaica Command, 58-9; captured, 92, 116-18
O'DEA, Lt L. H., 134
OFLAGS (Map p. 758): IVC, 795, 816. VA, 768, 802, 816. VB, 779-80. VIB, 790-2, 804. VIIB, 792-5, 808, 817. IXA/H, 791-2, 815. IXA/Z, 792, 815. XC, 780. XIIB, 768, 814. XXIB, 792. 79, 802
OGILVIE, L-Cpl K. R., 93n
OGLE, Lt-Col R. W. G. (Plate p. 364), 112, 268, 289, 291, 314, 406, 541, 616, 630-2; commands 2/15 Bn, 288
OLBRICH, Lt-Col Dr Friedrich, 81, 83, 103, 137, 155-6
O'MARA, Capt M. J., 585
OMARS, THE (Sketch p. 454), 453, 491, 493; see also SIDI OMAR, LIBYAN OMAR
Oranje, Australian hospital ship, 801
OSBORN, Maj G. S., 229-30
OVERALL, Lt-Col J. W., 99, 146, 320, 632
OWENS, Maj G., 718, 720-1
OXALIC LINE, 656, 675, 677-81, 683-4, 692, 697, 746
OXLEY-BOYLE, Brig R. F. C., 504, 508

PACIFIC THEATRE, 537, 540, 601
PACIFIC WAR COUNCIL, 528
PAGE, Rt Hon Sir Earle, 528
PALESTINE (Map p. 5), 6-10, 16, 28, 32, 111, 113-14, 116, 120, 135, 190, 244, 292, 308, 311, 339, 346, 366-8, 511, 515-16, 518-19, 532, 600n, 606, 751, 823-4; 9 Aust Div arrives in, 514
PALMER, Lt A. B., 415
PARKER, Lt J. A., 786
Parramatta, Australian sloop, 414, 417, 513
Pass of Balmaha, British ship, 271, 377, 413-17
Pasteur, French ship, 791
PATERSON, Lt H. B., 421n
PATERSON, L-Cpl J. L., 764n
PATON, Gnr R., 769n

INDEX 849

PAT OUTPOST (Sketch p. 302), 303
PATRICK, Sgt R. A., 406
PATROLS, at Tobruk, 137-8, 147, 183-4, 237-8, 267, 288, 298-9, 301, 303, 314-15, 338-9, 370, 387, 391, 401; at Alamein, 617-21, 635-6, 734-5. *German*, at Tobruk, 384; at Alamein, 636
PAUL, Lt E. A., 768n
PAULUS, Field Marshal Friedrich von, 179, 222, 224, 245, 327
PAYNE, Lt L. J., 327
PEARL HARBOUR, 510, 513, 515, 639n
PECK, Lt J. D., 769
PEEK, Maj A. E. de L., 88, 149, 154, 249
Penelope, British cruiser, 431
PERKINS, Lt S. A., 734
PERRY, Maj W. H., 257, 259-62, 264
PERSIA, 518-19, 606
PETAIN, Marshal, 339
PETER, King, of Yugoslavia, 39
PETERSON, Capt H. A., 72, 74-5, 768n, 771
PETHERICK, Lt-Col W. G., 98
PFEIFFER, Major, 723
PHILLIPS, C. E. Lucas, 685n, 694n
PHILLIPSON, Maj E. C., 362
Phoebe, British cruiser, 343
PICKUP, Pte V. G., 617
PIENAAR, Maj-Gen D. H., 479, 482, 484, 558, 655, 663; commands 1 South African Bde, 453, 1 South African Div, 547
PIERSON BOUND, 656, 678, 682-4
PILASTRINO, FORT (Map p. 220; Sketches pp. 126, 147), 122, 127, 140, 148, 151, 161, 192, 202, 212, 214-15, 217, 222, 236, 246, 269, 337, 399, 418, 420, 423-4, 431, 451, 463
PINKNEY, Lt E. M., 703
PIRIE STREET, 219
PITMAN, Maj C. G., 147
PLAN ORIENT, 328
PLANT, Maj-Gen E. C. P., 10, 32
PLATT, General Sir William, 39
PLAYFAIR, Maj-Gen I. S. O., 255n, 256n, 277n, 352n, 623n
PLAYGROUND (Sketch p. 361), 358, 361, 365-6
PLAYOUST, Capt R. A., 777, 784
PLONK, *see* BIR EL AZAZI
POIDEVIN, Sgt G. G., 212
POINT 5, 626
POINT 11, *see* BARREL HILL
POINT 17, 618, 637
POINT 19 (Sketch p. 361), 362
POINT 20 (Sketch p. 361), 362
POINT 21, 564, 579
POINT 22 (Tobruk; Sketch p. 402), 395
POINT 22 (Tel el Eisa; Sketch p. 691), 691
POINT 23 (Tel el Eisa; Map p. 668, Sketch p. 560), 558-9, 577
POINT 23 (Makh Khad Ridge; Map p. 668, Sketches pp. 618, 631), 620, 626, 630-3, 636-7, 644, 658, 687
POINT 24 (Map p. 668; Sketches pp. 570, 580), 558, 561, 563-6, 570-1, 576, 578, 580, 582-6, 610, 669, 679
POINT 25 (Map p. 668; Sketch p. 580), 616-17; *see also* RING CONTOUR 25 and BAILLIEU'S BLUFF
POINT 26 (Map p. 668; Sketch p. 560), 558-60, 566, 603
POINT 27 (Map p. 668; Sketch p. 691), 589
POINT 29 (Sketch p. 691), 683
POINT 30 (Sketch p. 587), 594
POINT 32 (Tobruk; Sketch p. 402), 395
POINT 32 (Alamein; Map p. 668), 680, 729
POINT 46, 729
POINT 71 (Sketch p. 553), 556
POINT 132 (Sketch p. 628), 629
POINT 144 (Sketch p. 407), 407
POINT 156, 510
POINT 157, 509
POINT 162 (Ed Duda), 462
POINT 162 (Bir el Azazi), 509
POINT 171 (Sketch p. 218), 212
POINT 175 (Sketches pp. 445, 484), 445, 448, 452, 455, 457, 473, 479-86, 498, 507
POINT 178, 213
POINT 179 (Sketch p. 218), 213
POINT 180 (Sketch p. 218), 224
POINT 182 (Sketch p. 218), 224
POINT 187 (Sketch p. 218), 209, 213, 224
POINT 206 (Sketch p. 282), 245, 278, 281-2
POINT 207, 367

POINT 208 (Sketch p. 282), 278, 282
POINT 209 (Sketch p. 175), 203, 209, 219
POLAND (Map p. 758), 20, 53, 792, 796, 805, 809-10, 814, 819
POLAND, Vice-Admiral Sir Albert, 117, 413
POLISH ARMY, 3, 110, 141, 161n, 419
—CAVALRY REGIMENT, 332, 340, 386, 395, 418-19, 510
—1st CARPATHIAN BRIGADE, at Tobruk, 312-13, 332, 334, 341, 345, 348, 386, 397, 418, 421-2, 435-6, 438, 451, 458-9, 495-6, 512, 546; history of, 339-40
—POLISH OFFICERS' LEGION, 339, 418-19, 423-4
—BATTALIONS: 1st, 335, 341, 438; 2nd, 340; 3rd, 340, 438
POLISH GOVERNMENT, 312, 339, 514
POLLOK, Lt-Col J. A., 325
PONATH, Lieut-Colonel, 85, 91, 95, 122-4, 127, 146
POPE, Maj H. W., 671, 696, 714n
POPE, Lt-Gen V. V., 342, 426
PORT MORESBY, 601-2
POSTS, at Tobruk (Map p. 220; Sketches pp. 126, 147, 192), 130-1, 210, 251. K62, 511; R, 210; R1, 198, 209-10, 224, 230, 233; R2, 167, 204, 210, 212, 233, 319; R3, 182, 201, 210, 212, 225, 233; R4, 205, 210, 212, 216, 233, 319; R5, 182, 199-201, 212, 214-15, 217, 224-5, 233-4, 316, 318-19; R6, 208, 212, 214-16, 225-6, 233-4, 316, 318-19; R7, 212, 214, 216, 225-6, 229, 233-4, 316-19, 324-5; R8, 208, 214-16, 225, 229, 233-4, 249, 291; R9, 203, 205, 214-16, 229, 319; R10, 214, 216, 228-30; R11, 148, 215-16; R12, 215, 228; R14, 211, 215-16, 225, 228, 231, 234, 236; R17, 510; R19, 112; R21, 148, 405; R23, 405; R27, 148, 405; R29, 148, 405; R30, 146; R31, 132; R32, 133, 141, 148, 150, 205; R33, 133, 141, 147-9; R34, 496; R35, 139, 141, 146, 496; R37, 497; R39, 246; R40, 510; R41, 149-50, 405-6; R43, 246, 405, 407; R47, 421; R51, 421; R52, 301; R53, 301-2, 407, 422; R55, 301; R57, 301; R59, 132, 497; R63, 132, 407, 422; R65, 408, 422; R67, 408; R69, 371, 408, 469; R71, 407; S1, 182, 209-10; S2, 209-10, 224n; S3, 182, 201, 209-10, 218, 223; S4, 199, 210, 224, 257, 259-62, 264, 319; S5, 198, 201, 209-10, 231, 257, 261; S6, 204, 210, 217, 231-2, 252, 257, 259-64, 315-19, 321, 326-7, 333; S7, 198, 209-10, 213, 217-18, 223, 225, 231-2, 249-50, 251n, 252, 257, 259-64, 315-16, 318-20, 322-3, 325-7, 331-3, 419, 759n; S8, 208, 213-14, 221, 226, 237, 248, 250-3, 256-7, 262-4, 266, 271-3, 291, 319, 321, 326; S9, 208, 213-14, 221, 237, 248, 251-2, 256-8, 262-4, 319, 322-3; S10, 213-14, 217, 219, 221, 248-52, 262, 264, 271-3, 322-3; S11, 189, 213-14, 221, 250-1, 259-60, 403; S11A, 213-14, 251; S12, 322; S13, 213, 238, 250-1, 322; S14, 213; S15, 247, 250, 403; S17, 127; S19, 247, 403; S21, 271, 402; S27, 271; S33, 420; Z80, 201; Z101, 409
POTTER, WO2 A. K., 372-3
POTTER, Maj J. D., 689-90
POUND, Admiral of the Fleet Sir Dudley, 173
PRATT, Lt L. J., 238-9
PRESS, THE, 621n
PRIDDIS, Capt K. W., 592
PRISONERS OF WAR, *Allied*, taken in capture of Tobruk, 535; exchange of, 805-8. *Australian*, in Battle of El Alamein, 742; losses in ME, Greece and Crete campaigns, 755-6; experiences of, 755-822. *Enemy*, at Tobruk, 159, 296, evacuated from, 344; in Crusader operation, 441, 469; captured at Ed Duda, 478; taken by 9 Div at Alamein, 742n
PRITCHETT, Maj T. K. D., 49
PRITTWITZ UND GAFFRON, Maj-Gen Heinrich von 123-4, 127-8, 137
PROPAGANDA, German, 740, 806-7
PROVAN, Capt W. R., 216
PRYOR, Capt W. E., 582, 584

QALALA (Sketch p. 282), 278
QARAOUN (Sketch p. 517), 532
QARET EL ABD (Sketch p. 664), 562, 736
QARET EL HIMEIMAT (Sketches pp. 628, 664), 625, 629, 643-5, 648, 656, 658, 674
QARET EL RETEIM (Sketch p. 282), 245
QASSASIN (Map p. 13), 753
QASTINA (Map p. 5), 748
QATTARA, BAB EL (Sketches pp. 543, 553), 542-3, 548-9, 737

INDEX

QATTARA BOX (Sketch p. 543), 542, 548, 550, 554, 557
QATTARA DEPRESSION (Map p. 13), 24, 542, 624
QATTARA TRACK (Sketch p. 587), 571n, 573-5, 590, 618, 636-7
Queen Elizabeth, British battleship, 513
Queen Mary, British troopship, 538, 753-4
Queen of Bermuda, British armed merchant cruiser, 753
QUEEN OUTPOST, 504, 509
QUINN, Lt R. B., 324-5

RAEDER, Grand Admiral Erich, 1, 354
RAHMAN TRACK (Sketch p. 733), 731-2, 736, 738
RAILWAYS, construction in Syria, 823-9
RAINIER, Maj P. W., 648n
RAJENDRASINHJI, General Maharaj Shri, 63, 77, 103, 104n, 105, 107-8
RAJU (Sketch p. 520), 520, 529
RALPH, Maj. M. R., 358-9, 362-3, 365
RAML RIDGE, 24
RAMSAY, Maj-Gen Sir Alan, (Plate p. 621), 357-60, 558, 708, 751; CRA 9 Div, 356; career of, 571; proposed by Morshead as his successor, 615
RAMSDEN, Lt-Gen W. H. C. (Plate p. 589), 557-8, 586, 589, 598, 605, 612n, 637; appointed to command XXX Corps, 555, 612; relations with Morshead, 556, 579, 614; replaced as GOC XXX Corps, 606, 613; temporarily commands Eighth Army, 609
RANFORD, Sgt R. F. G., 714
RAS ABU EL GURUF (Sketch p. 664), 645
RAS BAYADA (Sketch p. 517), 823
RAS EL MEDAUUAR (Map p. 220; Sketches pp. 218, 291), 125, 127, 129, 144, 162-3, 165, 167-9, 174, 178, 181-3, 185, 189, 191-2, 194-5, 198-9, 201-2, 206-8, 211-15, 217-19, 222, 228-30, 248-9, 257-8, 264, 274, 280, 291, 316-18, 333, 409, 421, 755; area described, 196-7; loss of, 209-10, 223-6; recaptured, 510
RASHID ALI, 243-4, 274
RAS NAQOURA (Sketch p. 517), 823
RATIONS, at Tobruk, 237, 377-8; in German POW camps, 774, 776-7, 779-80, 785, 796
RATTRAY, Maj R., 79, 176-8
RAVENSTEIN, Maj-Gen Johann von, 364, 453, 473, 479, 513; commands *21 Armd Div*, 443
RAWARD, Cpl L. V., 403
RAYAK (Sketch p. 517), 540, 823
RAYNER, Bdr V. A., 84, 105
REARDON, Sgt J. D., 371-2
RED CROSS, 240, 266, 323, 529, 757, 760, 765, 766n, 774, 776-82, 784, 786, 788-9, 790n, 791-2, 794-7, 800-1, 803-4, 807, 810-16, 818-19, 821-2
—INTERNATIONAL COMMITTEE OF, 763, 771, 772n, 774, 781-2, 784-5, 787, 791, 793-4, 796, 803, 808, 811, 813, 817
RED LINE (Tobruk; Sketch p. 126), 121, 181, 183
RED LINE (Alamein), 658
REID, Lt A. L., 257, 298, 405-6
REID, Capt G. T., 390, 392-3
REID, Capt W. R., 715
REINFORCEMENTS, 639. *Australian*, at Tobruk, 304; for 9 Div at Alamein, 600-1, 661-2
RENNISON, Maj A. C., 136, 187, 254n, 284-5
RHODES (Map p. 5), 65, 115, 769
RHODESIAN BATTERY, *see* 289 Bty RA
Rhodi, ship 415
RICHARDS, Lt E. J., 302, 734
RICHARDS, Maj-Gen G. W., 599, 702; commands 1 Tk Bde, 588, 23 Armd Bde, 650, 655
RIEBELING, Cpl E. C., 321
RIGEL RIDGE, 24
RIGG, Capt C. G., 260n
RIMINGTON, Brig R. G. W., 48, 52, 60, 62-3, 66-7, 86-7, 94-5, 98-9; commands 3 Armd Bde, 15
RING CONTOUR 25 (Map p. 668; Sketch p. 580), 578, 580-1, 583, 728n, 729; *see also* POINT 25 and BAILLIEU'S BLUFF
RING CONTOUR 45, 732
RINTELEN, General Enno von, 21, 624
RISSON, Maj-Gen R. J. H., 92, 138n, 727
RITCHIE, General Sir Neil, 349, 467, 472-3, 478-80, 493, 495, 498-501, 505, 507, 534-5, 744; relations with Morshead, 352; appointed GOC Eighth Army, 455; plans for Crusader operation, 491-2; relieved of command, 536
ROACH, Maj W. G., 93

ROBBINS, Sgt L. S., 74
ROBBINS, Capt P., 219-21, 668-9, 688-9, 714-15
ROBERTS, Maj T. L., 359
ROBINSON, Maj C. H., 460
ROBINSON, WO2 D. S., 73
ROBINSON, Lt K. E., 154
ROCKNEST, 91
RODRIGUEZ, Lt-Col T. A., 686
ROFFEY, Lt G. C. de F., 785, 801n, 817
ROGERS, Maj A. L., 360, 366
ROME (Map p. 758), 21, 65-6, 433, 497, 512
ROMMEL, Field Marshal Erwin (Plate p. 109), 25, 45, 47, 50, 54, 59, 83-4, 101, 117, 134, 137, 141, 148, 164, 166, 168-9, 178, 181, 187, 212, 216, 221, 235, 245, 255, 269-70, 277, 288, 301, 303, 335, 357, 369, 374, 413, 426-8, 440, 443, 446-7, 457, 464-6, 472, 474, 478-80, 483, 488, 490-1, 493-4, 499-502, 504, 507, 536-7, 540, 542, 545, 547, 549-50, 552-3, 556-7, 562, 564, 566-9, 571, 574, 577, 578n, 600n, 605, 607-9, 611, 616, 626-7, 640-3, 646, 663, 670n, 697-8, 702n, 705-6, 710, 725, 728, 732, 744, 749, 754; appointed to command German forces in North Africa, 18-19; career of, 20-1; plans offensive defence, 22-3; plans operations in Cyrenaica, 37-8, 80-1; plans capture of Marsa Brega, 46, El Agheila, 55, Mechili, 85, 89, 102-4; relations with General Gariboldi, 65-6; on rules of desert warfare, 108; tactics in Cyrenaica, 110; reorganises German and Italian forces, 122-3; orders encirclement of Tobruk, 124, plans for capture, 143, 162-3, 174, 222, 329-30, 382, 430-3, 442, 444-5; comments on Easter battle, 155-6; Egyptian frontier operations, 172, 186, 453; seeks reinforcements, 179-80; on Australian soldiers at Tobruk, 210; in May 1941 battle, 223-5; his estimate of Wavell, 243; on British tanks, 253; on Brevity operation, 256; in Battleaxe operation, 283-4; and Axis High Command, 328, 355; Summer Night's Dream operation, 353-4, 360-2, 364; orders attack on Sidi Rezegh airfield, 448-9; tactics in Crusader, 454-5; and General Bastico, 497, 511-12; plans eastward advance, 498; decides to withdraw from Tobruk and Egyptian frontier, 505-6; launches counter-attack in Cyrenaica, 534-5; orders attack at Alamein, 547-8, on 9 Div at Tel el Eisa, 565; on failure of XXX Corps attack, 596; plans renewed offensive, 622-5; his estimate of Montgomery, 629; hands over command to Stumme, 656; returns to Africa to take command at El Alamein, 692; orders attack on 9 Aust Div sector 30-31 Oct, 719, 723; decides to withdraw from Alamein, 736, 738; Hitler's "victory or death" message, 737; orders general withdrawal to Fuka, 740-1
ROOSEVELT, President Franklin D., 528, 602-4, 639, 694-5, 745; and Churchill, 313, 341-2; employment of 9 Aust Div, 537-8, 749-50
ROSE, Capt G. H., 251
ROSEL, Capt J. S., 203-4, 213-14, 217
ROSEVEAR, Maj H. G. M., 718, 720-2
ROSS, L-Sgt N. D., 321, 323
ROTENBURG (Sketch p. 809), 792, 815
ROWLEY, Lt T., 17, 756
RUDD, Bdr G. T., 153, 208
RUIN RIDGE (Sketch p. 587), 321n, 572-3, 579, 599, 618, 634, 636n, 723, 755, 764n; attacks on, 586-94; casualties, 595; Morshead's views on factors contributing to failure, 598; *see also* MITEIRIYA RIDGE
RULE, Capt E. D., 127, 407, 592
RUNDLE, Pte H. R., 236
RUSES, in Cyrenaica, 37; at Alamein, 648-9, 671
RUSSELL, Capt N. H., 298, 405
RUSSIA, 1-2, 19, 37, 274, 309, 312, 328, 340, 346, 378, 381, 506, 510, 518, 527, 605, 788, 790n, 819; Germany declares war on, 287; Churchill visits, 612
RUWEISAT RIDGE (Sketches pp. 553, 568), 542-3, 548, 550-1, 553-5, 557, 564-5, 603, 624, 626-7, 630, 656; operations at, 566-8, 571, 576-8
RYAN, Spr C., 93

SAGAN (Map p. 758), 800, 803, 812
SALIENT (Sketch p. 290), 230-1, 238, 246, 248-50, 255, 263-7, 273-4, 278, 288, 291, 301, 313, 323, 332-4, 338, 384, 386, 400, 403-4, 422, 435; reliefs in, 236-7, 270-1, 290, 297-8, 327; Morshead plans offensive action, 241-2; strength and disposition of

SALIENT—*continued*
  enemy forces in, 269; health and living conditions of units, 292; enemy lays mines, 303; Australian patrols, 314-15; attacks on posts, 316-17, 320, 324-5; plans to strengthen defences, 418-19
SALMOND, J. B., 637n
SALONIKA (Maps pp. 5, 758), 755n, 773-81, 783-4, 788-9
SALT, Maj D. C. M., 246, 474-5
SALUM (Map p. 13; Sketches pp. 135, 282), 24, 31, 98n, 117, 120-1, 134-7, 142, 145, 163, 166, 172, 179, 187-8, 242-3, 245, 254-6, 275-6, 278, 283, 312, 424n, 426-8, 453, 457, 491, 493, 497, 626, 761; occupied by enemy, 144, 164; naval bombardment of, 398-9; captured, 534
SALUM FORT, 137
SALUM PASS (Sketch p. 135), 135-7, 256
SALVATION ARMY, 287
Salvia, British corvette, 513
SALZBURG (Sketch p. 809), 778, 781, 818-19
Samos, British merchant ship, 417
SANDERSON, Capt R. G., 627, 670-1
SANDYS, Rt Hon Duncan, 804
SANJU (Sketch p. 520), 520
SAUCER, 711, 716-18, 721-5, 727, 733, 736, 739, 746
SAVIGE, Lt-Gen Sir Stanley, 14-15, 23
SAYERS, Sgt W. F. R., 778
SCANLON, Lt J. O., 186-7, 254, 284
SCHMIDT, H. W., 144n, 148n, 178n
SCHMUNDT, Col I. G., 19
SCHOLFIELD, Gnr J. W., 152
SCHORM, Lieutenant, 154n
SCHRADER, Capt C. L., 359
SCHUBIN (Map p. 758), 792
SCHULZ, Lieutenant, 84
SCHWEBEL, Gnr A. H., 722
SCHWERIN, Lt-Col Graf von, 81, 83-4, 137
SCIAFSCIUF (Sketch p. 484), 479
SCOBIE, Lt-Gen Sir Ronald (Plate p. 396), 418-19, 424, 437, 441, 444-5, 447-8, 450-1, 456, 460-1, 464-5, 468-70, 472-3, 479-82, 485-7, 491, 493, 495, 501-2, 504, 506-7, 510-11; takes command of Tobruk fortress, 397; plans for attack on Ed Duda, 457-9; and Freyberg, 462-3
SCOGGINS, Capt D. W. R., 249
SCORPION OPERATION, 274
SCOTT, Lt A. R., 262
SCOTT, Brig T. H., 202
SCOULLAR, J. L., 515n, 526n, 550n, 551n, 567n, 578n
SCRIMGEOUR, Lt D. W., 295
SEARLE, Pte H. S., 95-6
SEARLE, Capt J. E., 478
SEAVIEW OUTPOST, 391
SEEKAMP, Lt A. H., 405
SEHEL, WADI (Map p. 220; Sketches pp. 126, 402), 111, 126, 129, 146, 170, 184, 189, 238, 247, 297-8, 369, 386, 395, 402, 418-19, 435, 451
SENUSSI, THE, 43, 47, 61, 75, 146, 296, 344
SERLE, Maj R. P., 41, 197, 203-5, 663n, 667
SGHIFET EL ADEM, 407
SHANAHAN, Capt M. S., 135-7
SHARP, Capt F., 104, 768n
SHARP, Gnr K. W., 768n
SHATT, EL, 753
SHAVE, Lt-Col L. K., 92
SHEEHAN, Maj W. J., 228
SHEFERZEN, 457
SHELDRICK, Lt G. A., 259-62, 264
SHELTON, Lt J. T., 199, 206-7
SHILLAKER, Capt R. S., 562, 584, 669, 688-90, 714-15
SHIPPING, 140, 276, 431, 539n; Axis, 431, 623
SHIPTON, Col E. A., 49
Shunten, merchant ship, 513
SICILY (Map p. 5), 1, 22, 34, 753, 763
SIDI ABD EL RAHMAN (Sketch p. 543), 561, 626, 630, 696, 698, 700, 705, 707, 719, 723, 725, 728-30, 736-7, 740, 746
SIDI AZEIZ (Sketch p. 135), 179, 254-5, 453, 464, 499-500
SIDI BARRANI (Map p. 13; Sketch p. 135), 135, 144, 172, 179, 187, 245, 297, 355-6, 362-5, 414
SIDI BELGASSEM (Map p. 220), 238
SIDI BISHR (Map p. 13), 545
SIDI BRAHIM (Sketch p. 83), 59-61
SIDI BU AMUD, 464, 466
SIDI HANEISH (Map p. 13), 747
SIDI MAHMUD (Sketch p. 126), 161

SIDI OMAR (Sketches pp. 135, 454), 187, 283, 285, 354-5, 367, 426-7, 444, 455, 499, 500n, 505; captured, 450
SIDI REZEGH (Map p. 13; Sketches pp. 443, 446, 449), 24, 427, 490-1, 498-500, 505; operations at, 430, 436, 441-50, 452-3, 456-63, 466-74, 479, 482-5, 487-8
SIDI SULEIMAN (Sketches pp. 135, 282), 187, 245, 274, 284-5
SIEKMANN, Capt D. C., 315, 324-5
SIKORSKI, General Wladyslaw, 312, 423, 514
SILESIA, 788, 799-800, 803, 809, 812
SIMMONS, Sgt R. E., 70-1, 73
SIMNER, Brig K. N., 823-4
SIMPSON, Capt A. M., 36, 38
SIMPSON, Maj B., 591
SIMPSON, Maj-Gen C. H., 28
SIMPSON, Maj-Gen N. W., 667, 680, 704; commands 2/17 Bn, 519n, 616
SIRRY PASHA, 523
SIRTE (Map p. 5), 21-3
SIRTE, GULF OF (Map p. 13), 25
SIWA OASIS, 24, 358, 364, 655
SKENE, Sgt W. P., 797n
SKIPWORTH, Pte G. S., 323n
Skudd 3, Norwegian whaler, 337
SLATER, Maj-Gen J. N. (Plate p. 108), 161, 181, 185-6, 409-11
SLAUGHTER, Capt S. R., 635
SLESSOR, Kenneth, 638
SLINN, Capt G. J. S., 210
SLONTA (Sketch p. 83), 79-80, 85, 94-5, 96n
SMITH, Lt-Gen Sir Arthur, 34, 138, 143-4, 167, 308, 331, 455, 495, 500n, 501, 507
SMITH, Capt F. M., 161, 188
SMITH, Lt-Col J. S., 820n
SMITH, Lt-Col J. W., 99, 146
SMUTS, Field Marshal Rt Hon J. C., 604-6, 706
SNELL, Maj H. W., 561, 563
SNELL, Maj L., 631-3
SNEEZY, 459n, 470
SNIPE, 693, 697, 732
SNOWWHITE, 495n, 508
SOFAFI (Sketches pp. 135, 361), 142, 172, 179, 245, 358, 361, 363, 365
SOLARO, FORT, (Map p. 220) 399, 431
SOLUCH (Sketch p. 25), 30, 39, 59, 81
Sophie, ship, 415
SOUTH AFRICA, 4, 415, 527, 639; historians' comments on British tactics in Crusader, 429
SOUTH AFRICAN AIR FORCE, 414; No. 3 Wing, 640
SOUTH AFRICAN ARMY, 4, 311, 523, 535, 547
  —DIVISIONS: 1st, 3, 356-7; in Crusader, 426, 429-30, 433, 436-7, 441, 444, 446; at Alamein, 536, 542, 547-50, 557-8, 562-3, 565, 572, 577-8, 589, 593, 595n, 603, 612, 636-7, 645, 653-8, 664, 673, 675, 687, 694, 697, 699, 732. 2nd, in Crusader, 492, 499, 505, 507; at Alamein, 542-3.
  —ARMOUR: 4 Armd Car Regt, 358, 361. 4th/6th Regt, 733, 738
  —ARTILLERY: 4 Fd Regt, 358
  —ENGINEERS: in Syria, 823-4, 828
  —INFANTRY: *Brigades*: 1st, in Crusader, 467-8, 472-3, 479-86, 488, 490, 492, 500; in Battle of Alam el Halfa, 630. 2nd, 628. 3rd, at Alamein, 543, 548. 5th, in Crusader, 446, 448-50, 452-3, 455-6, 458, 496
SOUTH-WEST PACIFIC AREA, 527, 538, 540, 601-2, 749
SPANGENBERG (Map p. 758), 791-2, 815
SPAVIN, Pte J. L., 176
SPEARS' MISSION, 526, 531
SPENDER, Hon Sir Percy, 8n, 114, 306, 308-9, 334, 345n, 348
SPIER, Maj P. E., 32, 41, 79, 182, 197, 260-1
SPITTAL (Map p. 758), 767, 781, 796, 799, 804-5
SPOONER, Pte A. D., 74
SPOWERS, Col A., 190, 196-206, 209, 214-15, 217, 227, 301-4, 560-1, 563; commands 2/24 Bn, and career of, 189
SPROULE, Pte I. H. St. G., 769n
SQUARE TRACK, 650, 679
SQUIRES, Lt-Gen E. K., 157
SRAR (Sketch p. 522), 521
STALAGS (Map p. 758; Sketch p. 809): IIIA, 814; VIIA, 768, 785-8, 790, 795, 799, 814, 816-18; VIIIA, 767, 799-801, 808; VIIIB, 788-9, 793, 795, 799-800, 802-3, 808, 812; VIIIC, 800, 803, 812; IXC, 793; XIA, 814; XIB, 816; XIC, 813; XIIIC,

STALAGS—continued
777n, 784, 795, 805, 808, 811, 814; XIIID, 814-15; XVIIB, 812; XVIIIA, 763, 781, 795-6, 782-3, 807-8, 818; XVIIIA/Z, 767, 781, 796, 799, 804-5; XVIIIB, 781, 796; XVIIIC, 799, 818; XVIIID, 773, 780, 795; XXA, 789-90, 796, 809; XXB, 809; 344, 802, 806, 808, 811-12; 357, 805, 808, 816; 383, 790n, 793, 796-9, 801, 803-4, 808, 816; Frontstalag 183, 774, 788
STALIN, Marshal, 604
Stand-To, 751n, 760n, 768n, 808n
STAR TRACK (Sketch p. 657), 649, 673
STEDDY, Lt E. M. C., 252, 298
STEILBERG, Spr W. H. C., 805
STENHOUSE, Maj T. R., 591
STEPHENSON, Pte H., 757n
STEVENS, Maj F. D., 365
STEVENS, Maj-Gen Sir Jack, 615
STEVENS, Maj J. W. C., 718, 720-1
STEVENSON, WO2 E. F., 782
STEWART, WO2 D. P. S., 95
STIRK, Pte F. A., 409
Stoke, British minesweeper, 240
STRANGE, Maj B. D., 289-90, 701
STRASBOURG (Sketch p. 809), 768, 771
STREICH, Major-General, 46, 144, 155, 222
STRETCHER BEARERS, at Alamein, 716-17
Stuart, Australian destroyer, 414
STUMME, General, 656, 674-5
STURDEE, Lt-Gen Sir Vernon, 8n, 114, 116, 527-8, 750
SUBMARINES, 431; German, in Mediterranean, 354, 431, 513
SUDAN, 6, 121, 141
SUDELEY, Major Lord, 279
SUDHOLZ, Capt R. F., 238, 407, 585
SUEMMERMANN, Maj-Gen Max, 445, 466
SUEZ CANAL (Map p. 5), 1-2, 7, 12, 23, 124, 222, 519, 540, 546-7, 557, 753
SULEIMAN MURSHED, 529
SULMONA (Map p. 758), 757, 764-5
SUMMER NIGHT'S DREAM OPERATION, 354, 360, 364, 430
SUMMERTON, Lt-Col J., 228-9, 711
SUMMONS, Lt W. I., 755n
SUNTER, Maj J. S., 147
SUN TRACK (Sketch p. 657), 649, 673
SUPERCHARGE OPERATION, 746; planning of, 707, 729, 743-4; the battle, 727-37
SUPPLY, in Cyrenaica, 28, 35, 431; of Tobruk, 111, 161-2, 270-1, 276, 293, 296-7, 343-4, 377-9, 415-16; of Malta, 534; of Eighth Army for Battle of El Alamein, 647. Enemy, of forces in North Africa, 169, 179, 330, 354, 431-2, 505, 510, 623; shortages in Crusader, 497, at Alamein, 547
SUPREME HEADQUARTERS ALLIED EXPEDITIONARY FORCE (SHAEF), 819-20
SUTHERS, Lt-Col R. A., 620, 632-3
SUTHERS' HILL (Sketch p. 618), 620
SWITZERLAND (Map p. 758), 768-71, 786, 800, 802-3, 818
SYME, Capt D. M., 251
SYMONS, Cpl E. W., 759n
SYRIA (Sketches pp. 517, 520, 825), 1, 19, 243, 256, 287, 308-11, 334, 339, 342, 348, 382, 385, 514-18, 528, 606, 751, 755n; defence of, 519-20; behaviour of Australian troops, 525-6; food shortage, 529; morale of Australian troops, 530; 9 Div training, 531; leave camps, 532; departure of 9 Div, 540-1; railway construction, 823-9

TABARJA (Sketch p. 825), 826
TACTICS: use of Jock columns, 144, 164, 548, 554, 610; in Easter Battle, 156; with armour at Tobruk, 253-4; in Crusader operation, 428-9; at Alamein, 598-9, 624. Enemy, in desert warfare, 108; at Tobruk, 156; in armoured warfare, 354; in Crusader, 429
TAGGART, Lt C. E., 689
TAIEB EL ESEM (Sketch p. 445), 490
TANKS: American, 342, 604, 639. British, 3-4; in Cyrenaica, 15, 32-3, 37, 40, 47-8, 57, losses, 100, 534; at Tobruk, 119-20, 143, 211, 247, 253, 258, 260-1, 265, 375-7; in North Africa, 243, 276; in Battleaxe, 277, 280, 283, losses, 285; in Crusader, 425-6, 429, losses, 443, 447, 451-2; at Alamein, 549, 577, 582-3, 639, 652, 655, 730; losses in Battle of Alam el Halfa, 630; in Bulimba operation, 634;

TANKS—continued
number sent to Middle East in 1942, 639. Enemy, 4; Italian tanks used by British in Cyrenaica, 15, 28, 33, 48, 56, 60, 167-8; at Tobruk, 212, 225, 261, 269, 277, losses, 168; in North Africa, 172-3, 180, 655; captured tanks taken to England for examination, 191; in Battleaxe, 277, 280, losses, 285; in Crusader, 427, 429, losses, 443, 445, 450-2, 454; at Alamein, 547, 549-50, 557, 564, 576-7, 705, 730, losses, 742; Mark IV Specials, 624, 639; in Battle of Alam el Halfa, 630; in Supercharge operation, 730
TAPP, Lt R. P., 324
TAQA, EL (Sketch p. 543), 641, 736-7
TASKER, Lt-Col H. McK., 32, 78-9, 91, 163, 532
TAURUS MOUNTAINS (Sketch p. 517), 518
TAYLOR, Lt A. J., 232
TAYLOR, Maj A. L. F., 315, 326-7, 726
TAYLOR, Maj C. F. S., 39
TAYLOR, Pte J. D., 686
TBEREGH, WADI, 421
TECASIS (Sketch p. 83), 87, 90
TECNIS (Sketches pp. 25, 83), 32, 34, 42, 53, 78, 80, 82, 85, 89, 99n
TEDDER, Lady, 751
TEDDER, Marshal of the R.A.F. Lord, 276, 297, 313, 345-6, 378-80, 605
TEL AVIV (Map p. 5), 514-15, 748
TEL EL AQQAQIR (Sketches pp. 664, 733), 656, 698, 729-30, 732, 736-8
TEL EL EISA (Map p. 668; Sketches pp. 560, 570, 580), 557-8, 590, 599, 617, 619, 621n, 624, 650, 718, 729, 746, 752; operations at, 559-64, 566, 569-71, 574, 576, 578, 580-5
TEL EL MAKH KHAD (Sketches pp. 575, 587), 557, 603, 617-18, 625, 637, 654; operations at, 562, 572, 574-6, 578
TEL EL SHAMMAMA (Sketch p. 543), 552
TEL KALLIAKH (Sketch p. 517), 531
TEMPLEMAN, Sgt B. A., 187
TEREZIN, FORT (Map p. 758), 805
TESCHEN (Sketch p. 809), 800, 802-3, 808, 812
TEWFIK, PORT, 753
The Camp, 806, 807n
THERON, Maj-Gen F. H., 547n
THOMA, General Ritter von, 650n, 656, 692, 719, 738, 744
THOMAS, Lt E., 636
THOMAS, Lt-Col K. B., 247
THOMAS, Lt L. H., 672
THOMAS, Maj V. C., 186
THOMPSON, Corporal, 477n
THOMPSON, Pte H., 73
THOMPSON, Capt J. K., 619
THOMPSON, Brig L. F. (Plate p. 108), 120, 160-61, 339, 374
THOMPSON'S POST (Map p. 668; Sketches pp. 691, 704), 619, 687, 690-1, 699, 701, 705, 708-9, 713-14, 716, 721, 726, 728n, 736, 739
THOMSON, Cpl A., 210
THORN (Map p. 758), 789, 796, 805, 809
THURMAN, Maj E. B., 216
TIBERIAS, 540-1
TIBERIAS, LAKE (Sketch p. 517), 517
Tiberio, British schooner, 415-17
TIGER CONVOY, 243, 253
TIGER OUTPOST (Sketch p. 439), 438-40, 446-7, 450-1, 459n, 470, 476, 486
TILLY, Maj-Gen J. C., 3
TINSLEY, Brig W. N., 356, 359, 365-6
TIVEY, Maj E. P., 564
TMIMI (Sketches pp. 25, 83), 16, 76-7, 81, 83, 88, 91, 93-6, 100-1, 120, 491
TOBRUK (Map p. 220; Sketches pp. 126, 442), 8-9, 12, 14-16, 24, 26, 28, 32-5, 37, 41, 43-4, 51, 66, 75, 81, 87, 99, 101, 103, 107, 110, 114, 122, 507-8, 510-12, 514-15, 524, 532-5, 544, 546, 552, 576, 580, 590, 599, 602, 607, 623, 626, 638, 639n, 664, 742, 747, 750, 752, 754-6, 760-1; equipment shortages at, 29; British plans for defence of, 85, 109, 112-13, 115-22, 124, 126-7, 129; terrain and defences, 111, 125-6, 129-31, 301, 419, 522; Rommel plans attacks on, 123-4, 163, 174, 179, 329-30, 382; siege of, 132-505; patrols at, 137-8, 160, 238, 298-9, 338-9, 370, 401; leaflets dropped on garrison, 145, 166, 287-8; the Easter Battle, 146-56, 162, 164; composition and strength of garrison, 159, 211, 237,

TOBRUK—continued
296; artillery strength and deployment, 161; British tank strength at, 172; air support withdrawn, 184, 241; supply of, 191, 293, 297, 343, 379, 398, 413-15; ships sunk on run to, 513; air attacks on, 192-3, 198, 211, 214, 240, 273, 292-3, 337-8, 353, 368-9, 410-13, 415; the May battle, 195-211, 215-35; health and morale of garrison, 241, 287, 292, 316, 350; and operation Brevity, 242-3, 244-5, 253-6; artillery (including "bush" arty) employment, 257, 262, 265, 294-5, 336, 356n, 409-13; infantry-tank cooperation at, 265; German infantry compared to Australian, 267-8; Axis strength and dispositions, 269; fuel shortages at, 270-1; booby-traps, 272; and operation Battleaxe, 275-6, 277, 279, 281, 283, 285-6, 288; outposts at, 301-3; enemy minefields, 303; relief of 9 Div, 305-6, 309-13, 331-5, 344-8, 350-1, 375-8, 380, 395, 399-400, 416-17, 423, 458; decorations for members of garrison, 352-3; enemy shelling of, 398; unofficial truce, 385; achievements of garrison, 400-1; casualties, 401n; in Crusader operation, 428, 430-33, 436-8, 441-2, 446-8, 456, 458, 460, 462, 495-6, 509; siege lifted, 505, 509, 514; Germans capture, 535-7, 604, 624; British attempt raid on, 641
TOBRUK HARBOUR (Map p. 220; Sketch p. 126), 85, 190, 293, 343, 376
Tobruk Truth, 111-12, 287
TOCRA (Map p. 13; Sketch p. 83), 14, 35, 41-2, 57, 67, 78, 94
TODHUNTER, Lt-Col E. J., 120n
TOLMETA (Sketch p. 83), 41-2, 57
TONKIN, Sgt L. K., 220
Totensonntag, 450, 452-3, 480, 487
TOVELL, Brig Hon R. W. (Plates pp. 108, 621), 32, 41, 79, 96, 163, 167, 170, 189, 198-9, 201, 204-5, 215, 217, 220-1, 227, 241, 270, 280, 298, 301, 392, 517, 521, 545-6, 581, 615; commands 26 Bde, 10-11; career of, 160
TRACEY-PATTE, Sgt J. J., 127
TRAINING, 304, 357; given low priority in ME, 433; of 9 Div in Syria, 515, 524-6, 531-3, for Lightfoot operation, 653-4, after Alamein, 747; of Eighth Army for Alamein battle, 647, 650, 744
TRANSJORDAN (Map p. 5), 9, 824
TRANSPORT, for 9 Div in Cyrenaica, 43, 64, 67, 75; for Eighth Army, 639
TRAVERS, Capt W. H., 793n
TREACLE OPERATION, 343, 416
TRENWITH, Maj R. G., 727
TREWEEKE, Lt F. S., 671, 691
TRIG 22 (Map p. 668; Sketches pp. 572, 587), operations at, 572-5, 579-80, 585-6, 588, 617-18, 620
TRIG 29 (Map p. 668; Sketches pp. 712, 725), 679; operations at, 687-93, 696, 698-701, 704-5, 710, 720, 729-30, 743
TRIG 30 (Sketch p. 587), 579, 589
TRIG 33 (Tel el Eisa area; Map p. 668; Sketches pp. 560, 618), 558-9, 561, 564-5, 569, 578, 584, 603, 617, 620, 626-7, 672
TRIG 33 (Kidney Ridge area; Map p. 668), 658, 660, 678, 680n, 683, 693
TRIG 63 (Sketch p. 568), 566-8, 577
TRIG 87, 626
TRIG 93 (Sketch p. 553), 553
TRIG 96 (Sketch p. 553), 553
TRIG 146 (Map p. 220; Sketches pp. 372, 407), 303, 330, 373, 407; *see also* JACK and NORMIE OUTPOSTS
TRIG 157, 487
TRIG 178 (Sketch p. 449), 448, 456
TRIGH CAPUZZO, *see* CAPUZZO, TRIGH
TRIGH EL ABD (Map p. 13; Sketches pp. 25, 83), 25, 35, 47, 52, 65, 76-7, 81, 83, 85, 123, 285, 427, 468, 491, 495, 499, 505-6
TRIPOLI (North Africa; Map p. 5), 3, 6, 17, 19, 21-4, 27, 52n, 66, 169, 183, 222, 243, 328, 417, 452, 513, 532-4, 580, 599, 623, 742, 756, 760-3
TRIPOLI (Syria; Map p. 5; Sketches pp. 522, 825), 516-17, 519-22, 524, 529-31, 540-1; behaviour of Australian troops in, 525-6; railway to Haifa, 823-9
TRIPOLITANIA (Map p. 5), 3, 16-19, 23-4, 27, 30, 38, 53n, 430-1, 511, 559
TRUCES, at Tobruk, 323, 325, 384
TUCKER, Lt-Col F. A. G., 167, 219-21, 562, 669, 689
TUGUN OUTPOST (Sketches pp. 302, 439), 369, 386, 391, 438, 440, 451, 473

TUIT, Sgt W. J., 325
TUKER, Lt-Gen Sir Francis, 655
TUNISIA (Map p. 5), 1, 22, 24, 753
TURKEY (Map p. 5; Sketch p. 520), 65, 287, 328, 516, 526, 755, 772, 776, 823; in British defence plans, 518-21; in Auchinleck's "plan of deception", 529
TURKISH ARMY, 518-19, 525-6
TURKISH GOVERNMENT, relations with Britain and Germany, 518
TURNER, L. C. F., 429n, 433n, 437n, 482n, 485n, 500n, 547n
TURNER, Lt-Col R. W. N., 72, 74, 146n, 424n, 670-1, 680; commands 2/13 Bn, 519n, 616
TURNER, Lt-Col V. B., VC, 697n
TUTTON, Maj J. K., 300
TWIN PIMPLES (Map p. 220; Sketch p. 402), 402, 438, 459
TWIN POLES, 510
TYRE (Sketch p. 517), 532
TYSON, Sgt J. B., 362

U.79, German submarine, 398
URQUHART, Maj G. F., 583

VAERST, General von, 627-8
VAL-D'ISERE (Map p. 758), 769
Valiant, British battleship, 513
Vampire, Australian destroyer, 257, 414
VAUGHAN, Brig E. W. D., 76-7, 83-4, 89, 102-8; commands 3 Indian Motor Bde, 54
Vendetta, Australian destroyer, 414
VERCELLI (Map p. 758), 760, 765, 768-9
VERRIER, Col A. D., 221, 226-8, 236, 266; commands 2/10 Bn, 215
VIA BALBIA (Sketches pp. 14, 443), 14, 22, 85, 463n, 498
VICTORIA CROSS, awarded to Cpl J. H. Edmondson, 2/17 Bn, 149; Pte A. S. Gurney, 2/48 Bn, 582; Pte P. E. Gratwick, 2/48 Bn, 689; Lt-Col V. B. Turner, 2/Rifle Bde, 697n; Sgt W. H. Kibby, 2/48 Bn, 715
VICTORY ROAD (Sketch p. 361), 358, 363
VIGAR, Pte R. L., 769n
VINCENT, Capt M. D., 394, 701
VINCENT, Maj T. H., 250-1
Volo, British ship, 415, 513
Voyager, Australian destroyer, 414

WAIN, Col W. J., 573-4, 723, 727, 740; commands 2/43 Bn, 556
WAINEWRIGHT, Pte H. G. L., 769n
WALKER, Cpl A. M., 817
WALKER, A. S., 293n, 648n, 760n, 789n
WALKER, Lt L. C., 209
WALLDER, Lt A. F., 686, 726
WALLED VILLAGE (Sketch p. 302), 302, 331, 407
WALLER, Brig R. P., 553-4
WALLIS, Capt D. N., 402
WALSH, Maj-Gen G. P., 551
WALSH, WO K. W., 756
WALSH, Lt S. R., 632-3
WALSOE, Maj O. M., 74, 338, 420, 475, 477-8, 480-2, 492, 626
WALTER OUTPOST, 468, 504, 506-7
Wanganella, Australian hospital ship, 801
WARBURG (Map p. 758), 780, 790-2, 796
WAR CORRESPONDENTS, relations with GHQ ME, 621n
WARDLE, Capt A., 165, 175
WARING, Capt E., 326
WARREN, Lt R., 128
Warszawa, merchant ship, 513
WASHINGTON, 341, 603-4, 746, 750
WATCH, Lt-Col J. R., 72-4
Waterhen, Australian destroyer, 414-15
WATER SUPPLY, in Cyrenaica, 46, 76; in Tobruk, 419; in Syria, 533; at Alamein, 648
WATER TOWER (Sketches pp. 218, 263), 213, 218-19, 232, 260-1, 263-4, 315, 319, 321-2, 327
WAVELL, Field Marshal Rt Hon Earl, 2, 9, 19-20, 23, 26-7, 34, 45, 55, 59, 61-3, 79, 100, 119, 121, 129, 161-3, 190, 191n, 274, 308, 341, 352-3, 385, 598, 604, 607, 614; tasks in Feb 1941, 3; disposes forces, 4, 6, 8; estimates of enemy strength and intentions, 16-18, 21; in defence of Cyrenaica, 30-1, 35, 40, 46-7, 51, 64-5, 109-10, 113-14, 134; and Churchill, 57, 116, 244; appoints General

WAVELL—continued
O'Connor to Cyrenaica Command, 58; decision to hold Tobruk, 85, 109, 113, 116-17, 124-5; orders 18 Aust Bde to Tobruk, 114-15, 118; visits Blamey in Greece, 138; in defence of Egypt, 141; reorganises command in Western Desert, 142-3; on importance of holding Tobruk, 146, 159; and Lavarack, 156-7; congratulates Morshead, 166, 235; seeks increase in tank strength, 172-3; decides to evacuate British forces from Greece, 173; reports to British Chiefs of Staff on enemy strength in Cyrenaica, 180; and Brevity operation, 242-5, 253, 256; Rommel's estimate of, 243; and Battleaxe operation, 275-7, 279, 284; replaced by Auchinleck, 285-6, 296-7, 312; and formation of Anzac Corps, 307; attends Cairo conference, 604-5; on generalship, 609
WEAVER, Lt M. H., 36
WEDDAN, WADI (Sketch p. 409), 201, 409
WEINSBERG (Map p. 758), 768, 802, 816
WEIR, Lt-Col C. G., (Plate p. 621), 581, 667, 691, 710-11, 713-16; commands 2/24 Bn, 580
WEIR, Capt J. H., 48
WEIRS, Gnr P. A., 104
WEISSMANN, L-Cpl F. B., 71, 73
WELLS, Lt-Gen Sir Henry, 546, 551-2, 586, 598-9; GSO1 9 Div, 544
WESTERN DESERT, 65, 114, 256, 274-5, 286-7, 295, 297, 307, 385, 600, 605, 638, 755; strength of British forces in, 3; Wavell's plans for defence of, 115; reorganisation of command in, 142-3, 146; plans for offensive in, 244, 350; discussions on appointment of commander in, 342
WESTON, Sgt. J. K., 404
WESTPHAL, Lt-Gen Siegfried, 454
WHEATLEY, Maj M. I., 563, 766n
WHETHERLY, Maj R. E., 38, 49
WHITE, General Sir Brudenell, 382
WHITE, Sig L. L., 321, 323, 326
WHITE, Brig T. W., 95, 201
WHITE CAIRN (Sketch p. 372), 370, 372-3
WHITEHALL, 286, 378, 381, 534
WHITEHEAD, Brig D. A. (Plate p. 621), 573-4, 585, 659, 679, 687-8, 702-3, 708-9, 720, 723, 734; commands 2/2 MG Bn, 356, 2/32 Bn, 572, 26 Bde, 615
WHITE HOUSE (Acroma), 101, 108, 233
WHITE KNOLL (Tobruk area; Sketches pp. 247, 403), 247-8, 391, 403
WHITE KNOLL (Alamein; Map p. 668; Sketch p. 560), 560
WHITELEY, General Sir John, 296, 597
WHITE POST, 407
WILLIAMS, Lt-Col B., 722
WILLIAMS, Capt C. F., 559, 561-2, 582
WILLIAMS, Maj C. G., 330
WILLIAMS, Maj E. C., 727
WILLIAMS, S-Sgt E. M., 681
WILLIAMS, Brig E. T., 17, 38, 614n, 655, 707
WILLIAMS, Brig S., 338-9, 476

WILLIAMS, Capt W. H., 111-12
WILLIAMSON, Maj H. J., 740
WILLISON, Brig A. C., 393, 441, 457, 460, 462n, 469-70, 472, 475-7, 481, 487, 492; commands 32 Army Tank Bde, 376
WILMOT, R. W. W. (Chester), 12, 21n, 92n, 114n, 133n, 149n, 154n, 165n, 240, 260n, 406
WILSON, Field Marshal Lord, 26, 35, 124, 244, 342, 525-7, 530, 607, 614; appointed to command expedition to Greece, 9
WILSON, Brig C. H., 142, 172, 187
WILSON, Capt C. H., 147, 154
WILSON, Capt K. C., 71, 670-1
WIMBERLEY, Maj-Gen D. N., 636, 655, 663, 693, 747; commands 51 Highland Div, 611
WINDEYER, Capt H. F., 389-90
WINDEYER, Maj-Gen Rt Hon Sir Victor (Plate p. 604), 96, 100-1, 146, 163, 165, 168, 171, 174, 183, 202, 214-15, 217-21, 226, 236, 301, 313-14, 322, 569, 610, 616, 633-4, 699, 703, 705, 722, 733; commands 2/48 Bn, 88, 20 Bde, 519; career of, 162
WISHKA, EL (Sketches pp. 553, 664), 589-90, 683-4
Wolborough, British trawler, 368, 416
WOLF OUTPOST (Sketch p. 439), 459
WOLFSBERG (Map p. 758), 763, 780-1, 783, 795-6, 799, 807-8, 818
WOODCOCK, 693, 730
WOODS, Capt H. A., 218-20, 224
WOODS, Cpl W. A., 617
WOOTTEN, Maj-Gen Sir George (Plate p. 108), 31, 101, 113, 121, 139-40, 201, 211, 230-2, 234-5, 237, 241-2, 246, 251-3, 257, 261-3, 265, 267, 270-1, 280, 297-8, 317, 332-3, 437; commands 18 Bde, 8; career of, 160
WOOZLEY, Maj. A. D., 60n
WRAY, Lt G. R., 680
WRIGLEY, Brig H., 555, 659, 671, 680
WYKEHAM-BARNES, AVM P. G., 140
WYNTER, Lt-Gen H. D., 7-8

Yarra, Australian sloop, 140
YARROW, WO2 W. H. T., 632
YATES, Capt R. A., 154-5, 735
YENDALL, Sgt G. L., 573
YENDALL, Cpl O. R., 573n
YOUNG, Lt-Col G. E., 99, 192
YOUNG, Maj V. L., 294
YOUNGHUSBAND, Col G. E., 87
YOUNG MEN'S CHRISTIAN ASSOCIATION, 771, 789, 802
YUGOSLAVIA (Map p. 5), 39, 755n, 773-4, 778, 785, 804-5

ZAAFRAN (Sketch p. 456), 456, 468, 473-4, 488-90
ZAREMBA, Lieut-Colonel, 434
ZEITUN, WADI Es (Sketch p. 409), 129, 170, 193, 201, 238, 301, 369, 409, 536
ZIESING, WO2 F. G., 321-2
Zingarella, British ship, 415
ZUETINA, EZ, 55

www.ingramcontent.com/pod-product-compliance
Lightning Source LLC
Chambersburg PA
CBHW070752300426
44111CB00014B/2377